Railroad Bridge – Swan Creek, Illinois – 1890/1900.

William T. McBride – August 1, 1919 – approximately 1 mile north of Little York, Illinois.

Warren County, Illinois

Warren County, Illinois

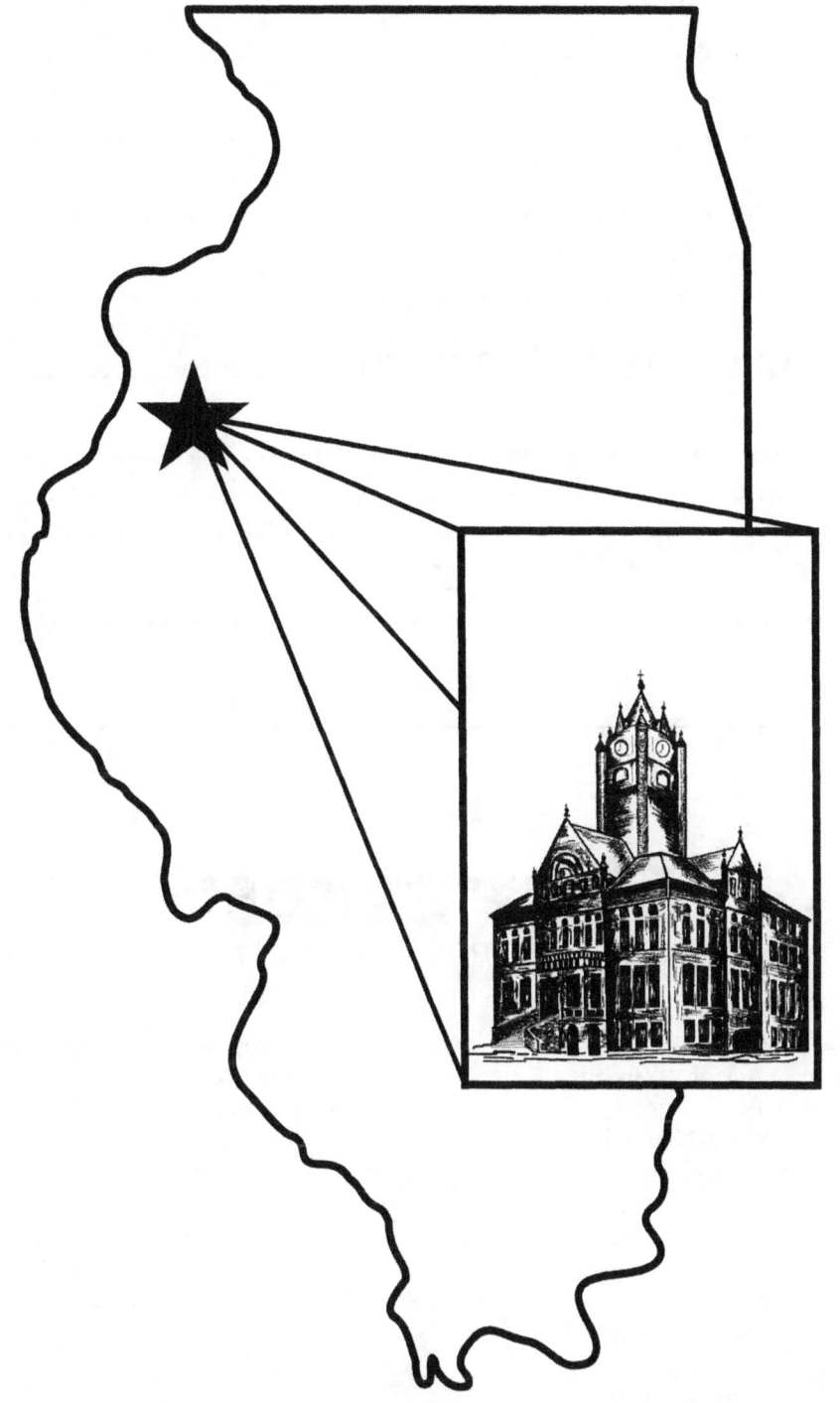

History and Families

Contents

Acknowledgements 3
Preface 4
History 5
Churches 25
Schools 47
Clubs, Organizations & Memorial 57
Businesses 67
Families 87
Index 289

Turner Publishing Company
Publishers of America's History
P.O. Box 3101
Paducah, Kentucky 42002-3101
270-443-0121

Graphic Designer: John L. Mathias

Copyright © 2003
Warren County Genealogical Society

This book or any part thereof may not be reproduced without the written consent of the Warren County Genealogical Society History Book Committee and the Publisher.

The materials were compiled and produced using available information; Turner Publishing Company and the Warren County History Book Committee regret they cannot assume liability for errors or omissions.

Library of Congress
Control Number: 2003103263
ISBN 978-1-63026-952-4

Limited Edition of 1000 copies of which this book is number _____

Acknowledgements

The publication of the Warren County History and Families has been over a year-long project for the Warren County Illinois Genealogical Society. 36,000 brochures were sent out in the "Penny Saver", delivered countywide. A special thanks to all the banks for mailing brochures with their statements, asking for participation, WRAM Radio for providing air time to promote our book and to Iva Kay Homer for getting the word out in the *Review Atlas*. Brochures were placed in displays at the Library; Zimmer's and Axline Pharmacies; YMCA; Strom Center; Soda Works; Farm Bureau; Meling's and Cottage Corner Restaurants, Kirkwood Senior Center; Elsie's Cafe (Smithshire); Roseville, Security and Community Banks and Chamber of Commerce Office.

Examples of the book were on display at the Genealogy Room and at group meetings of organizations, promoting our project. Every effort was made to give everyone the opportunity to participate and to the ones that did we are grateful for their support. The book would not have been possible without the contributions of histories, patron support pages and book orders.

Special thanks to: Dorothy Casteel, Ruth Kinney and Ethel Trego for checking and logging biographies. To Lois Strickler, Kate Grant, Gertrude Davis, Jim and Loma Atkisson, Lois Schmalshof, Judith Jones, Wayne Rader, Frances Conway, Gladys Olson, Marjorie and Rolland Stone, Barbara Herron, Vern Hill, Mary Lou and Harold Parsons, Ruth Kinney, Joyce and Tim Denison, Ethel Trego, Dorothy Casteel, Carol Carlberg, Lucille and Dale Morling for writing "updates" on individual townships. To "Bud" Barnes for writing the older history and Jeff Rankin for editing. To Lillian Vice, Dean and Carolyn Sandstrom, Mabel Westerfield and David Reid Clark for writing special history sections. The society is grateful to Keister's Tire Service for a monetary donation and to Everett Hardin, Gracie Peterson and Joyce and Tim Denison for allowing their biographies to be used as examples in the brochures.

Little York Illinois - Hotel Amy - Early 1900's - George Washington Young in buggy

Preface

Warren County is located in the Military Tract, a territory created by Congress to reward soldiers who fought in the War of 1812. The first 30 or 40 settlers to inhabit Warren, Henderson and Mercer counties were taxed in Peoria County, but since their region was not seeing any of the tax money, they petitioned for a county of their own. By the spring of 1830, the required number was reached and the request was granted, with Monmouth officially becoming a village on November 29, 1836 Several excellent histories have been written about the county, which include : The Past and Present of Warren County, Illinois-1877- by H. F. Kett & Co. Portrait and Biographical Album of Warren County, Illinois-1886- Published by Chapman Brothers; Historical Encyclopedia of Illinois & History of Warren County--1903- (2 Vol.) --Hugh R. Moffet & Thomas H. Rogers--by Munsell Pub. Co.; Historical & Biographical Record of Monmouth & Warren County, Illinois - 1927--(2 Vol.) - Luther E. Robinson--by Munsell Pub. Co. Born of the Prairie, Monmouth, Illinois, the First 150 Years--- 1831-1981 --Jeff Rankin--by Kellogg Printing Co. Anyone interested in finding early information about the county will find these books located in the Genealogical Section of the Warren County Public Library.

On June 26, 2001, the Warren Co, Il. Genealogical Society voted to publish the Warren Co.,IL. Family History Book., in cooperation with the Turner Publishing Co. 36,000 brochures were inserted in the "Penny Saver", delivered countywide, brochures were mailed to businesses and organizations, churches and schools soliciting a free 500 word family history with picture.

The published material is printed as submitted except where length required. No attempt was made to verify submitted information or to correct small grammatical errors. Each family history was scanned and an optical text recognition program was used to convert the image to text and then re-read and corrected if obvious errors were found.

Part of 3M Plant

Warren County History

Sumner	Spring Grove	Kelly
Little York	Gerlaw	
Hale	Monmouth	Coldbrook
	Monmouth	Coldbrook
Tompkins	Lenox	Floyd
Kirkwood	Larchland	Cameron
Ellison	Roseville	Berwick
Smithshire	Roseville	Berwick
Point Pleasant	Swan	Greenbush
	Swan Creek	Greenbush

Prime Beef Festival Parade. Marshall Gracie Peterson with Roy Ewalt driving - September 2002

Monmouth Square 1860

Warren County, Illinois

Warren County, Illinois is divided into 15 Townships containing 540 square miles. Originally its terrain was mostly covered with prairie grass which grew to 6 feet high and timber along the many water courses. Coal deposits of superior quality were discovered in 1871. Even more valuable was a vein of clay found beneath the coal. One of the county's first industries (the Monmouth Mining and Manufacturing Company) was formed to produce pipes of all sizes from sewer pipes for cities to field pipes to drain sloughs. The clay eventually led to an extensive pottery industry.

In the winter of 1822 and 1823, the Legislature of the State of Illinois laid out into counties, the "Military Tract" (land situated between the Illinois and Mississippi Rivers that had been set aside as payment for War of 1812 veterans). Warren County was named in honor of General Joseph Warren of Bunker Hill and Revolutionary War fame. It originally included all of what is now Henderson County, but the area became two counties in 1841.

Railroads

The coming of the railroads made all the difference in the growth of the county. The main line of the CB&Q and the Iowa Central (M&ST L) both ran through the county. Abner Harding and Ivory Quinby brought in the CB&Q and Delos Phelps and William Hanna, the Iowa Central. Monmouth has always enjoyed a good relationship with the railroads. The CB&Q came to Monmouth in 1855 and is on the main line to Chicago and parts west. At the present time the Western Stoneware (pottery), and Lovdahl Grain and Dryer are served by the now Burlington Northern Santa Fe with switching off the main line, performed by Galesburg area. then Monmouth Twp., then south of Coldbrook Twp., through Cameron before entering Knox Co.

A north-south branch of CB&Q entered Warren Co, from the north Aug. 22, 1870 at the village of Alexis in Spring Grove Twp., continued south to Gerlaw, proceeded into Monmouth, continued south into Lenox Twp., with a flag stop at Larchland and a full stop at Roseville. It then continued south to Swan Twp. and Youngstown, Walnut Grove and terminated at St Louis.

The first train into Roseville was in July 1870. By 1958 the rails had been taken up, the depot deserted and the window office closed.

This railroad went east and west through Tompkins Township and served Kirkwood,

The stretch from Alexis to Monmouth was taken out, leaving only a spur to serve the Wilson Packing Plant, Gamble-Skogmo Warehouse and Huskee-Bilt Co. These tracks were removed June 18, 1998,

Passenger service was taken over by Amtrak May 1, 1971, At this time the passenger train maintained a flag-stop at Monmouth. In 1983 Amtrak discontinued service at Monmouth. The Monmouth Depot was razed July 18, 1984; but Amtrak passenger service is available at Galesburg No stops are made in Monmouth It still runs through Warren County, but the name has been changed to BNSF (Burlington Northern Santa Fe)

Another railroad line going across Warren County was the M&St L The Minneapolis and St Louis Railroad entered the county from the northwest in Mercer County into Little York, a small village located on Cedar Creek, continuing on south-easterly through Sumner and Hale Townships into Monmouth. A large roundhouse was built and in 1898 a pond formed to supply the engines with water. A depot was built November 5, 1899. The railroad continued in a south-easterly direction through Phelps in Lenox Township and the village of Berwick in Berwick Township. From there it went to Abingdon in Knox County and terminated in Peoria. Passenger service was almost non-existent on this line as it was mostly a freight hauler. On November 1, 1960 the Chicago and North Western R.R. purchased the M&St L. The last regular trip to Little York was made December 13, 1974, to pick up an empty box car. In 1975 the line was abandoned.

The A T S Fe. entered Warren County through Ellison Twp., going through Smithshire to Ponemah in Tompkins Twp., Ormonde in Lenox Twp, the north part of Floyd Twp. and Cameron and the south part of Coldbrook Twp.. In an attempt to obtain a line to Chicago, the Santa Fe was constructed across the prairie and was running in Warren county in the summer of 1888. Freight stops were made at Ponemah and Ormonde, mostly for cattle.

The Rock Island Southern was developed as an Inter-Urban and trolley system for Monmouth and Galesburg in 1906. Passenger service and light freight service was conducted by electricity through Monmouth Twp.., Coldbrook Twp. into Knox Co. and Galesburg. The Rock Island Southern then completed the north line on June 7, 1910, extending itself north in Monmouth Twp., through Spring Grove Twp into Mercer and Rock Island Counties.

As roads were developing around 1923, the passenger service plummeted and the trolleys in the city were discontinued. The Inter-Urban remained, carrying passengers and a few freight cars for light switching duty in Galesburg, Monmouth, Aledo and Rock Island. The loss of the Pope Creek bridge by fire, severed Rock Island from Monmouth and any passenger service to the north. The line continued to function by steam engines north of the bridge, and the electrical system handled the Galesburg-Monmouth route. Much switching to various lumber yards and oil companies were handled by the "Rocky-Doodle" until its demise in 1952. It had a depot at 510 South Main Street, but it has been gone for a number of years.

Roads and Bridges

Over the years, many improvements have been made to all the roads and bridges in the county. Instead of the dirt roads and narrow concrete highways of the early '30's, Warren County now has gravel roads and blacktopped or concrete highways in most of the area. Highway Route 34 from Burlington to Galesburg has been widened and plans are underway for it to become a four lane from Burlington to Monmouth. It now bypasses the town and continues on to Galesburg as a four lane and connects to I-74. Highway Route 67 is now four lane between Macomb and Monmouth, except for the by-pass around Roseville, which is to be completed in late 2002. Plans are being considered for it to continue as four lane (at a future time) to the Quad-Cities, but has been widened and blacktopped again from Monmouth to Route 135 in mid 2002. State Route 135 was also resurfaced at the same time. State Route 164 between Oquawka and Galesburg also passes through Monmouth. County bridges have been widened and replaced at various places as the need arose. Bus service has been available periodically at various points in the county.

SCHOOLS IN WARREN COUNTY ILLINOIS

Kelly Township
District No.
1 Union
2 Shanghai
3 Republican
4 Science Hall
5 Tylerville
6 Locust
7 Forest Flower
8 Starr

Lenox Township
District No.
56 Hillis
57 Center Fairview
58 Enterprise
59 South Henderson
60 Phelps
61 Ridge
62 West Prairie
63 Larchland
132 Brannon

Spring Grove Township
9 Alexis
10 Ritchey
11 Mohler
12 Lone Star
13 Union
14 Foster
15 Center
16 Indian Grove
17 Gerlaw
18 Ralston
215 Alexis High School

Tompkins Township
64 Center Grove-Pape
65 Coonville
66 Moore
67 Kirkwood
68 Columbia
71 Tubbs
72 Hickory Point
73 Liberty
74 Nichol
150 Kirkwood High

Sumner Township
19 Brownlee
20 Cedar Creek
21 McGaw
22 Little York

133 Little York High
23 Denny
24 Iveydor

Ellison Township
76 Smithshire
77 Meridian
78 Empire
79 Ward
80 Center
81 Ellison
82 Jackson Corners
83 Salem
84 Rayburn

Hale Township
25 Junkin
26 Hale-Sugar Tree
27 McKelvey
28 Center
29 Barr
30 Hoornbeek
31 Farmers Academy
70 Pleasant Green

Roseville Township
85 Picayune
86 Pleasant Hill
87 Union
88 Carr
89 Center
90 McCurdy
91 Roseville
92 Stem
93 Taylor
94 Pierce
200 Roseville

Monmouth Township
32 Cedar Hill
33 Hazel Dell
34 Chapman
35 Frymire
36 Washington
37 Law
38 Monmouth
39 Grier
40 Hickory College

Greenbush Township
102 Holeman
103 Greenbush
104 Starr

105 Sailer
108 Sloey
110 Taft
111 Hall
208 Olive
210 Greenleaf

Coldbrook Township
41 Scotchtown
42 Lucas
43 Barnett
44 Atchison
45 Conard
46 Hedgepeth
47 Coldbrook
48 Cameron

Swan Township
112 Downey
113 Sugar Loaf
114 Adkisson
115 Swan Creek
118 Holsington
119 Crawford
121 Sisson
131 Youngstown

Floyd Township
49 Kenon
50 Stringtown
51 Means
52 Shortsvilie
53 Cherry Park
54 Ritchie
55 Muddy Corners

PointPleasant Township
122 Boyd
123 Chattanooga
124 Pleasant View - Allard
125 Piper
126 Center
127 Booth
128 Parker
129 Colfax
130 Wagggy

Berwick Township
95 Berwick
96 Brick
97 Center - Cottington
98 Miller
100 Nance-Lincoln
136 Pretty Prairie

Berwick Township

Berwick Township was one of the first townships settled in Warren County. The settlers were Solomon Kaisey and Solomon Perkins (brothers-in-law) who located here in 1829. Samuel G. Morse was also among the early settlers.

The village of Berwick was first called Bowling Green and was platted by surveyor Peter Butler on July 9, 1836. Owners of the site were Samuel G. Morse and Thomas Pearce. The town consisted of a public square and sixteen blocks.

The first schoolhouse was built near the village and was taught by Miss Jane Allen, who later married Judge Ivory Quinby, also an early resident of Berwick. Later schools were about 2 or 3 miles apart and the children walked or rode horses to school.

The postman and doctors also drove a horse and buggy, and doctors made house calls. Smallpox broke out in January 1863 with sixteen fatal cases.

Reverend Barton Randall was an early Methodist circuit rider and a few Methodists met in homes until 1837, when a permanent meeting place was found. They erected their first church in 1852 and a second one in 1868, but it did not survive. In 1901, Reverend D.E. Hughes of Monmouth held revival services in the old Methodist building and organized a Christian Church, with forty members. A group of Baptists congregated in the home of John Smith and on July 28, 1833, Reverends John Clark and John Logan organized a church, which is still active. The Christian Church at Meridian, 1 1/2 miles east of Berwick was organized on April 28, 1839, which included several members from the old Coldbrook church. It was remodeled in 1899 but no longer exists. Meridian Cemetery is beside where the church was located. The Berwick Cemetery was laid out in 1840.

Berwick became a station on the Iowa Central Railroad (later M & ST L) and was a thriving trading post The Berwick Bank was organized in August 1899 as a private institution, but was reorganized in 1900 as the State Bank of Berwick. It no longer exists. Berwick Lodge No. 765 I.O.O.F. was instituted on June 25, 1889; the Rebecca Degree Lodge on April 11, 1901; Berwick Camp No. 4717 on May 20, 1897 and a Reading Club of Berwick on August 17, 1900.

The town had a slaughter house, mitten factory, lumber yard, barbershop, three grocery stores, post office; a depot (where it cost 35 cents to ride from Berwick to Abingdon), a bank, Woodman's Lodge where dances were held on Saturday nights, and two churches (Baptist and Christian). Later there was a gas station, grain elevator and fire station. All that remains today is the fire department, post office and the Baptist Church.

In the late 1800's and early 1900's the main occupation was farming, 160 acres being considered a large farm, where horses and very small farm equipment was used. A farm consisted of hogs, cattle, horses, sheep, chickens, ducks, geese, turkeys and milk cows. Around 1925 the six-horse hitch was introduced, being used to pull plows and other equipment. Corn was planted with a 2-row planter and cultivated with a 2-row cultivator. Discs and harrows were about five feet wide and pulled by three or four horses, small grains were sown with a little seeder that fit in the back of a wagon with one person riding in the wagon to scoop the grain into the seeder. Small grains were cut in July with a binder that tied bundles and dumped them onto the ground. Several bundles would then be formed into "shocks" and left in the field until August when the grain had dried. Then a steam engine with a separator and about 25 neighbors would come to the farm and thresh the grain. The separator would separate the grain into wagons and blow the straw back onto the ground, where the men stacked it for use as bedding for animals in the winter. The neighbor women helped cook and the men were given dinner and supper.

In the fall, the best ears of corn were picked and stored to dry. In January it was hand shelled and stored in cloth bags until planting season in May. The rest of the corn was picked by hand or shocked, brought in and scooped into large bins, to be fed later to the livestock.

Coldbrook Township

Coldbrook Township was organized April 4, 1854. It is a broad prairie watered by Talbot and Cedar Creeks and their branches. In 1828 Peter Peckenpaugh came from Indiana and staked out the first claim. Solomon Perkins, Peter Butler, William Whitman, John Haley, the Murphy family, Thomas C. Wallace, Richard Ragland, Andrew and George Claycomb, and George Bruington were also early settlers.

Forty members organized the Talbot Creek Christian Church in the home of William Hopper, splitting off from the original church at Savannah (Coldbrook) because of the flooding at Talbot Creek. Savannah was a settlement larger than Monmouth at that time. The stage line of "Brinker and Walker" stopped there each trip for meals and lodging at the Butler home, changed teams and continued the next morning to Monmouth, ending at Oquawka (Yellow Banks).

In its early years, Cameron was located about the middle of section 29, Coldbrook Township. When the CB&Q Railroad was built, the Christian Church moved there--the town was half in Coldbrook and half in Floyd Township. Ivory Quinby and John B. Warren owned land on the north side of the track where the school was built. Robert Cameron, for whom the town was named, owned the south side where the church and bank were located. Jacob Meloan dedicated the town on June 9, 1895.

After 1900 there were two grocery stores on Railroad (Main) Street. One was operated by Earl Yard and wife Maud; the post office was located in this store. Harry Haley had a barber shop where the present post office is now located. The other grocery store, two doors west of Yard's, was operated by the Millward family. The Odd Fellows Lodge was between the two grocery stores. The Morling family operated a blacksmith shop and a Chevrolet garage as well as a feed mill and corn shelling business. There were two stockyards, one on the CB&Q and one on the Santa Fe. There were two passenger stations in Cameron, one on each railroad, as well as the "Doodle-Bug" which carried passengers to Galesburg and Monmouth. Each railway had a wooden grain elevator which closed many years ago. There was a lumber yard, Warfield's, run by Warren Yarde.

There were three churches in Cameron: the Cameron Christian Church, which is still there, and the Methodist and Baptist churches which have both been closed for many years. The Dollinger family operated a pool hall on Main Street which closed in 1973. The Cameron telephone exchange was located in a home south of the pool hall.

Cameron had one school, it being a two story building with 1st through 4th grades downstairs and 5th through 8th grades upstairs. It was consolidated with others when Warren School District 222 was created. The State Bank of Cameron was open for several years but closed during the Depression.

Surrey was located in the SW 1/4 of section 28. There was a stockyard and a blacksmith shop.

Old Route 34 (now Route 164) had two gas stations, one run by Harry Gardner, located on the SW corner of the SE 1/4 of section 10. The other was run by Harry Terpening, located on the NW corner of the NE 1/4 of section 15. Pro Flo was later located on the SW corner of the SE 1/4 of section 10. The new Coldbrook School was just north of the station at Pro Flo. Midwest Canvas Products is now where Pro Flo was and is run by Mike Rahn. The Thompson

Grain Company is on the NW corner of section 13 and east of it is the Heat and Control Company. The Cardinal Machinery Products is located in the Coldbrook School building on the SW corner of the SE 1/4 of section 10.

Coal mining brought the Scots and Welsh to this area. Thomas Welch was one of the first settlers.

The Coldbrook Township schools were: Scotchtown District 41--located on the north side of section 30; Lucas District 42--located on the north side of section 18; Barnett District 43--located on the east side of section 15; Atchison District 44-- located on the SW corner of section I; Conard District 45-- located on the SE corner of section 14; Hedgepeth District 46--located on the SE corner of section 27; Coldbrook District 47--located on the NE corner of section 11; and Cameron District 48-- located on the south side of section 31 in Cameron. All schools have now been consolidated into larger districts.

Ellison Township

Ellison Township, one of the southwestern townships of the county, is bordered on the west by Henderson County. It was first called New Lancaster, but soon changed to Ellison. The soil is rich and fertile, principally prairie, but somewhat broken and timbered in the southwestern part. Ellison Creek, its branches and some of the tributaries of Nigger Creek furnish an ample water supply. Agriculture is the leading industry and the farms are well improved. Field Jarvis settled there in 1829, followed by Benjamin Tompkins, Jr.; Morgan Dewey; John Brakeman; Jesse Coleman; George S. Pearce; James Hanan; Robert Moore; William Galbreath; John M. and Lambert Hopper; Matthew Cox; and David Robinson ; and Rodney Crozier, all arriving prior to 1835. Issac Watson and William P. Thompson came in 1835 and Kenner Brent (a veteran of the War of 1812) in 1836. Seneca S. Salisbury and his family came in 1836; Decatur Lofftus in 1837; John Birdsell in 1838; Andrew Meacham and Horace Sexton and wife in 1840 were also among the pioneers.

The village of Ellison was laid out on May 10, 1836, on land owned by Joseph DeHague, and contained eighteen blocks. On May 10, 1858, a severe tornado struck without warning, killing fifteen people and disabling many for life. The whole town was demolished and never rebuilt.

New Lancaster was platted May 31, 1836 on property owned by John M. Hopper. As early as 1850 a post office was established, but when the CB&Q Railroad was built through Roseville Township and Roseville was established, the New Lancaster office was merged with that of the new village. New Lancaster no longer exists.

Smithshire was platted on June 22, 1888, by C. A. Slas on land owned by E.B. Purcell, and it contained twenty blocks. The post office was established in March 31, 1888, with William J. Deator as postmaster. It was settled because of its proximity to the Atchison, Topeka & Santa Fe Railroad (1887). Other postmasters: Charles Barnett; Henry Brown; James Sawvell, Jennie C. Brent, Elizabeth E. Corzatt; Charles J. Passage; Orilla Anderson, Carl E. Cassiday; Gertrude Davis and Carol Olson. The post office is now located in the former State Bank building. There is one rural route with Media being an intermediate office served by the carrier.

A bank was established in 1894 with Dr L.L. Tensman as president. Two insurance lodges were active as was the Women's Christian Temperance Union.

Population has declined in the township. Many houses are gone as well as all school buildings. In 1927 nine schools were listed. The Smithshire School was the last to close in 1967. The school districts in the township are Southern (with buildings in Media and Stronghurst) Yorkwood (located between Kirkwood and Little York) and Roseville. Even these larger districts are not large enough now and consolidation plans are being considered in all districts at this time.

The Smithshire United Methodist Church (org. 1888) is still active. When the Liberty Chapel Methodist Protestant Church (near Ponemah) closed, the Methodist Annual Conference gave the building to Smithshire. It was moved in 1950 and placed beside the church, remodeled and renamed Liberty Hall.

The first township officials were elected April 4, 1854. Since 1924 the following have served as township supervisors: Emil C. Anderson; Glen M. Davis; Kenneth E. Davis; Constance Davis; James Oliver, Jr; George C. Crookham; and Karen Jack. Present township officers are: Supervisor -Karen Jack; Town Clerk- Donna Hilten; Road Commissioner- Dennis Gibb; Trustees- Michael Brent, Russell Jensen, Douglas Smith, Paul Hennefent; Multi-Twp Assessor- Jack Winebright.

Township cemeteries are: Ellison - Section 17; Salem- Section 33; and Asbury- Section 34. Cemetery trustees are ; Edward G. Thomas, Julie McLaughlin, and Marcia Meachum.

In 1945, Victor Twomey purchased a small wood frame elevator from Davis Grain Company. In 1956 the elevator and office were destroyed by fire and were replaced by a large concrete elevator holding 180,000 bushels. Business flourished and after Victor's death the business was taken over by his five children. Their first venture outside Smithshire was the construction of the Larchland facility in 1967. In 1972, a facility was built at Gladstone on the Mississippi River. An elevator was constructed between Kirkwood and Little York in 1976, followed by the Galdstone Bluff facility in 1980. They have a storage capacity company-wide of 50 million bushels, and are rated the twentieth largest multiple grain storage business in North America. The main office remains in Smithshire.

The Roseville, Swan, Point Pleasant, and Ellison Fire Protection District was formed in the 1940's. Volunteer firemen make up the force. The fire station in Smithshire also serves as the Polling Place for the township. John Lafary serves as the fire chief for Ellison, The RSPE District consists of four trustees with John S. Kane representing Ellison.

Floyd Township

Floyd Township was organized on April 4, 1854. It has rolling prairie land, a portion of which is under laid with a surface vein of bituminous coal, and mines operated there for years. A portion of the north drains into Cedar Creek, then into Henderson Creek and the Mississippi River. Southeast it runs into Slug Run, then into Cedar Fork in Berwick Township and the Spoon River and the Illinois River. Early settlers were : Jonathan Tipton; J. A. Reynolds; the Vertrees brothers; Elijah Davidson and Benjamin F. Allen. Originally known as Cameronville, the village of Cameron is situated within Floyd and Coldbrook Townships. Cameron was platted in 1854 and is located just south of the CB&Q Railroad line that was constructed in 1855.

The Christian Church of Cameron is the oldest organization of that denomination in the Military Tract. It was organized April 30, 1831. From this church came the Talbot Creek , Monmouth and Meridian Christian Churches in Warren County. The new Cameron Christian Church was built in the same location as the old church. The parsonage next to the old church was torn down and a new parsonage was built on a new location at the edge of town on Shelton Street, known as Berwick Road. In the 1930's, the Methodist and Baptist churches closed.

The Town Hall in the center of town was moved to a new township building built in the early 1970's on the east edge of town behind the post office.

The new post office was built in 1965, in the same location as the old building. A mail carrier does the rural delivery--everyone in town picks up mail at the post office. Small individual family farms in Floyd Township have decreased by approximately 50% since the 1930's. Many of the farm homes have been torn down to make way for more farm ground now owned and operated by multi-family large farms.

The Silent Home cemetery, located 3 miles south of Cameron, was added to in 2001 by the estate of Clarence and Althea Giddings. At one time there were several small family cemeteries.

The two-story Cameron School located north of the tracks in Coldbrook Township was closed in 1948 and the students were transferred to the Galesburg District. Junior and Senior High students attended Galesburg schools. A new building was erected on the south end of town near the Abingdon blacktop for grades 1-6. Cameron students were changed to Warren District #222

in 1961 with grades 1-6 still in the Cameron building. This building has since been closed, and is now a day care center.

Cameron Odd Fellows Lodge was closed in 1961. Those members who wished, transferred their membership to the Monmouth Lodge #61. The building was torn down and is now the site of the new Central Warren Fire District, Cameron Station.

A gas station was built by Willard Malone in 1960 at the intersection coming into town from the north. west and south. Different people operated the station until it was sold in 1980. It is now a small manufacturing plant opened in 2000. Also used for this plant is the building across the street operated for many years by Dewey Morling for his corn shelling and milling business, which closed in 1962.

Most of the businesses in Cameron have been closed. These include the grocery store (1960's); feed store (1950's); bank (1929); pool hall and gas station (1971); Ed Younquist garage (1969): and stockyards (1929). The CB&Q train depot was closed in the mid 1950's. The blacksmith shop was closed in the 1950's, and the building was then used by Riley and Olson earth movers. Now the building is privately owned.

The 2000 census of Floyd Township was 514,

Greenbush Township

Greenbush is in the southeast corner of Warren County bordering on McDonough Co on the south and Fulton Co on the east. Nigger Creek enters at the northwest corner and is joined by Little Swan Creek. Roland Simmons settled there in 1830. Major Bond came in 1832 and was prominent in the pioneer history of the township.

Greenfield was platted April 29, 1836. The name was later changed to Greenbush. An outbreak of cholera in 1851 resulted in 12 deaths within a week or ten days. A tornado caused a great deal of damage to the township in 1873.

The New Hope Church of the Old Predestination Baptist denomination was organized at the home of Caleb Hodges in July 1836. The Methodist Church organized in 1838 and held services in the Academy after it was erected. The Olive Christian Church was erected 2 1/2 miles northwest of Avon in the Greenleaf schoolhouse February 12, 1859, with 23 charter members. Later they had a membership of 125. They merged with the Congregational Church. It was torn down in 1996

There were several stores and businesses. In 1853, a two-story building was erected for a high school, called Greenbush Academy, with one room to be used by different denominations for religious purposes when school was not in session. At one time there were 100 students in attendance. The school, finally abandoned, was so well built that it had to be taken apart piece by piece when it was demolished in the 1900's.

In 1917 a Community Hall was erected. In the 1940's the Hall was used for first aid classes, school graduations, movies at 10 cents, bridal showers and Saturday night dances where many of the local young people learned to dance. Later it was sold for taxes, moved to the west edge of town and used as a hay barn. The school was finally abandoned and later was owned by the New Hope Baptist church

The Long Private Air Strip, three miles west of Avon was licensed by the State of IL (on air charts for navigation as Long Private) It had a licensed instructor, Frannie Enlow. At one time it had three hangers, and fifteen planes were based there. At the start of the Stearman Fly-in, they hosted, on Labor Day or the Monday of celebration, whatever planes were in. At one time they handled 25 planes from all over the US and hosted a hamburger sandwich lunch. Some Swan Lake Veterans helped park the planes. Three generations of Greenbush families flew off the air strip at Long's. The Strip is not registered now as the planes were sold in 2000.

There was a historic covered bridge, built about 1888 over Swan Creek that was destroyed by arsonists on July 3, 1973. It was later replaced by a cement bridge.

Greenbush School 1938-1939
Back Row: Bill Vandeveer, Daniel Whisler, Audrey Mitchell, Miss Burkholder Teacher and Jane Hunt music Teacher. Middle Row: Charles Cannon, Norma Canes, Eugene Blunt, Ernest Canes, Shirley Ragon, Martha Ragon. Front Row: Ernest Blunt, Marjorice Whisler, Lois Simmons, Francis Cable, Donald Canes

Greenbush Christian Church, built in 1870 (as Methodist Episcopal) closed in 1986, because of declining membership. Contents were auctioned off and the building was dismantled and ground returned to original state as designated in the by-laws of the original church.

Little Swan Lake

Little Swan Lake was formed by damming Swan Creek about four miles west of Avon, covering about 250 acres, with about 10 miles of shoreline for residential building in 1967. It was a cooperative project shared by eight farmers with no government aid involved. A Supper Club called "The Driftwood" was erected and sold in late 1970's to Mr. and Mrs. Ivan Ray of Avon. In 1970 a 9-hole golf course was built by Jim Owens, 1/2 in Greenbush and 1/2 in Swan township. Kent and Ellen Westfall now own it and plan to add an additional 9-holes in the near future. There are over 200 homes at present and a new water tower was built recently.

Saunders Hospital in Warren County on the west edge of Avon was built in 1930 on the Saunders farm. In 1957 a new wing was opened. It was a fully licensed hospital and operated until September 1987. A clinic was opened next door in 1974-75 by the Hospital Board and is still in operation.

Cemeteries in Greenbush Township are: Bond; Holeman (Olive); Greenbush; McMahill and (Old) Prairie City.

Township census in 2000 was 569.

Hale Township

Hale Township was first called Sugar Grove, then Westfield and finally named Hale. It is watered by Cedar Creek and its tributaries. The Iowa Central (M&ST L) and CB&Q Railroads passed through the southeast corner but have been discontinued. and the tracks have been removed. There are no towns or villages, trading being done in Monmouth, Kirkwood and Little York.

Early residents were: Adam Ritchie, and part of his family, coming here in 1828, having wintered in Fulton County. Their son, Henderson Richie, was the first white child born in Warren County. John B. Talbot, Thomas Paxton, W. S. Weir and R.S. Joss were other early settlers here.

There was a church at Pleasant Green, but it is now located in Henderson County. The first religious society organized in Warren County was the old Seceeder Church at Sugar Tree Grove, which was called the Henderson United Presbyterian Church, but is now the Sugar Tree Grove Presbyterian Church. Here David S. Wallace performed his duties as pastor as well as that of President of Monmouth College until 1876. The cemetery at this church is the oldest in the county, with the first burial being that of William Turnbull in 1834.

Hale Township is primarily farming country, and has continued as such, with changes being the small farms combined into larger ones with some becoming large hog confinement operations.

Kelly Township

Kelly Township is located in the northeast corner of Warren County. It was first called Milton, then changed to Warren and finally named Kelly after Captain John Kelly. Little Henderson Creek and its branches water the township. With much of its land being broad level prairies, it has always been primarily a farming area.

James B. Atwood was a first settler, arriving in 1828, he claimed to have broken the first ground and planted the first crop of corn in Warren County. Andrew Robison and his six children came from Indiana in 1829, and finding the land where he had located was already taken, he moved to another location, later called "Robison's Corners", located where four townships meet --- Kelly, Spring Grove, Monmouth and Coldbrook. His daughter, the first white girl born in Warren County, later married James Gardner. John Miles came from Harrison County, Indiana in 1830, and having been admitted to the bar there, was the first resident lawyer in the county. Another early settler was Benjamin Gardner, lovingly called "Uncle Ben", who came in 1835, after spending a short time in Monmouth. He opened up one of the first coal mines in the county, finding a superior quality of coal that was a good source for blacksmiths. Chester Potter built a grist mill in 1833 and operated it until 1846. When the water was low he used horsepower. He had come from Sumner Township and made the millstones himself out of boulder granite. His daughter, Mrs Helen Ingersoll of Alexis, for many years kept as a relic, the "niggerheads" which were 12 1/2 inches in diameter and the nether millstone. Potter had quite a flour trade extending north to Rock Island and westward into Iowa.

The famous corn planter was invented and patented by George W. Brown in Kelly Township, It was a great novelty then, but it did excellent work. It was made in Galesburg.

In 1858, Shanghai City was platted and laid out, but on May 3, 1868, a tornado destroyed all but a few homes. About 200 people were assembled in the Advent Church, where Elder George W. Hurd was preaching. This and the Methodist Church, the school house and several residences were destroyed. The track of the storm was about 1/2 mile wide---fifteen people were killed or severely injured. A school was later erected there.

Utah was established in 1872. A church was built and it was thought to have been of Methodist faith. In 1964, Albert Britt wrote a book; "An American that Was". He wrote : "I was born in a town that didn't exist . It was called Utah, Illinois, but it will not be found on highway maps." He was born in 1874 and died in 1968. He graduated from Knox College, continued his education elsewhere, and was President of Knox College 1925-1936. He was the son of Edward and Sarah (Foster) Britt. His father, an Englishman, came to the United States in 1852 with $100.00 in his pocket, rented a farm owned by Captain Kelly, late of Her Majesty's Merchant Marines, and where the name of "Kelly" came from for the Township.

The first school in Kelly Township was taught by Peter Terpening in 1837, in a log school house in section 28 in the Tylerville (Utah) neighborhood. There were 8 schools established --- Union, Shanghai, Republican, Science Hall, Tylerville, Locust, Forrest Flower, and Starr. All schools have been closed with Union being owned by the Grange; Science Hall and Starr were converted to homes.

There are 6 cemeteries--- Hope, Terpening, Potter, Tylerville, Miles-Bullman and a private cemetery of the Adcock family.

The 2000 census population was 398.

Lenox Township

Lenox Township was first called Ripley, but when the townships were permanently organized in 1853, the name was changed to Lenox. It is the center township in Warren County. The land was mostly prairie. The Henderson Branch and Cedar Creek water it with their tributaries. Lenox was not settled as early or thickly as other townships, since the land was rather low and badly drained for the most part.

One of the first settlers was Sheldon Lockwood, who had preempted a claim at Roseville in 1828, but sold out there and located in Lenox where he lived until his death. In 1837 Porter Phelps, Garland Ray, Jesse Riggs and Matthias Armsby were also among the early settlers. James Dixson and one of his sons owned the Larchland town site. Asa Ogden, Henry Howard and Jacob Jewell later moved into the township. At one time the township was crossed by the CB&Q mainline, Quincy division, running south; Iowa Central running diagonally northeast and southwest; and Atchison, Topeka & Santa Fe through the center.

Larchland was platted on January 10, 1870 on land originally owned by C.C. Dixson, who located here in 1834 when there was only one house between him and Monmouth. First called Lenox, then Canes Run, back to Lenox, it finally became Larchland because of a grove of Larch trees where the William & Marion Gillen farm is now located.

The first post office was established there in 1856, the first postmaster being John O. Sherwin. Larchland was the first station on the St Louis Division of the CB&Q railroad, At one time there was a doctor's office and residence-, church,- two blacksmith shops-, school-, grocery with the Woodman's Hall above it; ice house; grain elevator-, stockyards-, depot and 12 houses. Two freight and four passenger trains ran each day.

The general store was in the east part of town near the railroad tracks with the Woodman's Hall above and the post office in the southeast corner of the store. Merchandise consisted of everything from kerosene lanterns, hammers, nails and tobacco to patent medicines, dress materials and sun bonnets, with vinegar and kerosene in barrels where customers had their jugs filled. Box socials and other community events were held in the Woodman's Hall.

In the early 1930's George Rader ran the gas station and lived in the north part of the building. The truck taking the Review Atlas to Roseville dropped off the papers for the community. The Davis family built a new grocery store across the highway from the station. John and Vic Twomey bought several acres of land and built a large storage building and grain drying apparatus to take care of the community's grain harvest, their main office being in Smithshire. The dirt roads were dragged and oiled. In 1924 a two lane cement road was built from St Louis to the quad-cities, going through Larchland. Larchland had once been a stage stop and was known as "The half-way Place" between Monmouth and Roseville.

There was a Presbyterian church and a Methodist Church, known as Grace Chapel., in Larchland. The early telephone switchboard was in a corner of the living room of Mr. Waugh's home, and, as with all areas in the 1920's and '30's, was a party line where everyone listened to conversations to find out what was going on.. Emergencies were a series of short rings to alert everyone.

Fairview Center United Brethren Church later merged with the Methodist and is still very active. Phelps, a small settlement. named after the Honorable Delos P. Phelps, was on the Iowa Central and was quite a shipping point. Nemo and Ormonde on the Santa Fe were shipping points in the community, Nemo being a pumping station on the Oil Pipeline. Phelps and Nemo were never platted.

Warren County Home

The Warren County Home was purchased by the County in 1857 and the buildings were erected that year to house the sick and disabled as well as some who needed extra care during the winters. At one time many children were housed there and later it became a home for destitute older people as well. A big herd of cows was kept there and those who were able helped milk and care for them and for the hogs and chickens used for produce. There was a large vegetable garden. An addition was added on the east side, second story with three sides being windows. These rooms were used for TB patients for bed rest and special care. The Home was closed in 1970 and people were moved to other facilities. The buildings were torn down but the county retained the land and rents it to farmers. An attempt was made at one time to build an Ethanol plant there but it was unsuccessful. A building was erected and ceramic coasters are manufactured there now.

In 1991, when Rt 67 was widened to a four lane highway, the County Farm graveyard was moved to Lenox-Union Cemetery. The bodies were placed in new caskets, the 100 bodies being placed in rows of 10 with headstones. There is a plaque placed by the State marking the location of the former cemetery and showing where the graves were.

Monsanto

The Monsanto site covers 480 acres of farmland about 2 miles south of Monmouth. Originally purchased in 1984, it included a small farm house, barn, and feed lot. The first Monsanto building was constructed in 1986 and by 1989 a new office building had been added. As Monsanto progressed, a new research and training facility replaced the old. In 1998 the new facility was completed and now houses corn breeding programs, improving the genetics of Asgrow and DeKalb brand seeds. It is a research farm where trials are studied for carryover, longevity, volatility and yield check.. They employ 50 full time workers with interns and part time help needed in the summer. At the farm is a learning center, complete with labs for the scientists, where guests can come visit and then tour field plots.

Monmouth Township

Monmouth Township, located in the north central part of Warren County, is watered by Cedar and Talbot Creeks, with Markham Creek flowing through the center of Monmouth. Markham, in the early years, was the cause of a great deal of flooding at times, however it is controlled now by sewer systems. There is good farming land outside the city of Monmouth.

Monmouth, the county seat, is the only town in the township, and was settled in 1831. Daniel McNeil was an early settler, holding many offices. He purchased most of the lots that didn't sell in the northeast section and donated the land for the first cemetery, which still exists at Sixth Street and Archer. Other early settlers included Hezekiah Davidson; Marsham Lucas (who assisted in laying out the roads in the city and township); and William Turnbull, who later moved to Hale Township. His son Alexander resided in Monmouth and served as county commissioner from 1836-38. Jacob Wright ran a small distillery, the first in the county.

The Courthouse

The first Warren County Courthouse, built of logs, was erected in 1831. Located on the northeast corner of North Main and Archer Avenue. A second courthouse was built on the same lot in 1835, but being unable to obtain the proper kind of lumber it was never completed but used in an unfinished condition until a third one was built, near the current courthouse site on the

Monmouth Square early 1900's - National Bank Building on right. Other stores in background - Millinery is currently Kellogg Printing

Public Square in 1841.

In June 1893, the county commissioners asked for a new and stable structure for a courthouse. It was completed in the early part of 1895, and accepted in March of that year. It was constructed of red Portage sandstone, fireproof, commodious and convenient. The courthouse furniture and records were transferred to the new courthouse and the old structure was razed. A large statue of Justice, surmounted on the south gable, blew down in a heavy windstorm on July 7, 1895. In 1907 a weathervane, made by Pattee Plow Company, was placed on the peak of the tower. In 1970, the top portion of the tower, including the four clocks, was taken off for safety reasons. Later thermal glass windows were installed, making the building more heat efficient. The former City Hall building, at 112 North Main Street, was recently renovated to house some of the county offices. (City Hall offices weere moved to the former National Bank building at 100 East Broadway in 2000.)

Civil War Monument

In 1905, John W. Lusk, then commander of McClanahan Post, G.A.R., conceived the idea of erecting a monument in memory of the men from Warren County who enlisted in the Union Army during the Civil War. This finally resulted in placing a substantial memorial in the courthouse grounds that will remain intact for generations. The monument was dedicated June 14, 1909. A practically complete roster of all those who enlisted during the years 1861-1865, inclusive, had been compiled and their names inscribed on the tablets of the memorial. The statue on top of the pedestal depicts a young volunteer soldier of, under light marching orders, headed southward. The bronze tablets contain the names of more then 2,200 soldier who enlisted from Warren County, alphabetically arranged by regiment and company. Sixty-one parts of regiments are represented, and in addition there are 49 names of unassigned recruits on the north tablet.

In 1998, the Civil War monument was cleaned and restored.

Warren County War Memorial

The Warren County War Memorial was dedicated on May 25, 1998, in loving memory of those who made the supreme sacrifice and in honor of those who so honorably served and continue to serve in the armed forces of our country in war and in peace. The memorial is a testament to those sacrifices of American citizens which will forever symbolize the American commitment to fight for freedom.

Sculpted by Greg Todd of Greeley, Colorado, the bronze statue depicts forward-surging American infantryman in his early 20's, the victorious soldier of the Twentieth Century. It represents the county's finest soldiers, sailors, airmen, and marines, their resolute and determined defense, their swift and sure attack, their indomitable purpose, and their complete and decisive victory.

The committee chose to commemorate the actions of two Warren County heroes on the memorial, which it believed best exemplified conspicuous gallantry and intrepidity at the risk of their own lives above and beyond the call of duty. Both were chosen by their peers and superior officers, and recognized by the Congress of the United States of America to receive the highest award the country bestows for military action: the Congressional Medal of Honor.

The first is George H. Palmer, a bugler with Company G, 1st Illinois Cavalry, during the Civil War who fought at Lexington, Missouri, in September 1861. Musician Palmer volunteered to fight in the trenches and lead a charge which recaptured a Union hospital filled with wounded soldiers. Although the Confederate forces recaptured the building the next day, Palmer's gallantry was not forgotten, and he was awarded the Medal of Honor in 1896.

The second is Captain Robert Hugo Dunlap. As Commanding Officer of Company C, 1st Battalion, 26th Marines, 5th Marine Division, on February 20-21, 1945 on Iwo Jima. Disregarding his own safety, Dunlap placed himself in an exposed vantage point to direct more accurately the American supporting artillery and naval gunfire and, working without respite for two days and two nights under constant enemy machine-gun, sniper and mortar fire, skillfully directed a smashing bombardment against the almost impregnable Japanese positions.

Despite numerous obstacles and heavy Marine casualties, Dunlap, inspired his men to heroic efforts during their critical phase of the battle. He was awarded the Medal of Honor by President Truman later that year.

Behind the major monument rest two large granite stones topped with bronze American eagles inscribed with the names of more than 875 veterans whose families, friends and brother and sister warriors gave on their behalf to memorialize their sacrifice and military service. These 875 represent the more then 10,000 Warren County residents who have served since 1865.

The committee for the Warren County War Memorial was : David Reid Clark, chairman; David D. Fleming, David A. Rutledge, Buster L. Kellogg, Jr., Edward A. Skinner, Daniel W. Merry, John E. Twomey, George W. Pape, Ralph E. Whiteman, and Pauline Lantz Winbigler.

The monument was designed by Roy E. Dixon and built by Leyda, Burrus and Metz Monument of Bullington, Iowa.

Medal Of Honor Presented To Marine Captain Robert Hugo Dunlap, USMCR Citation

"For conspicuous gallantry and intrepidity at the risk of his life above and beyond the call of duty as Commanding Officer of Company C, First Battalion, Twenty-sixth Marines, Fifth Marine Division, in action against the enemy Japanese forces during the seizure of Iwo Jima in the Volcano Islands, on February 20 and 21, 1945, defying uninterrupted blasts of Japanese Artillery, mortar, rifle and machine-gunfire, Captain Dunlap led his troops in a determined advance from low ground uphill toward the steep cliffs from which the enemy poured a devastating rain of shrapnel and bullets, steadily inching forward until the tremendous volume of enemy fire from the eaves located high to his front temporarily halted his progress. Determined not to yield, he crawled alone approximately 200 yards forward of his front lines, took observation at the base of the cliff fifty yards from Japanese lines, located the enemy gun positions and returned to his own lines where he relayed the vital information to supporting artillery and naval gunfire units. Persistently disregarding his own personal safety. He then placed himself in an exposed vantage point to direct more accurately the supporting fire and, working without respite for two days and two nights under constant enemy fire, skillfully directed a smashing bombardment against the almost impregnable Japanese positions despite numerous obstacles and heavy Marine casualties. A brilliant leader, Captain Dunlap inspired his men to heroic efforts during this critical phase of the Battle and by his cool decision, indomitable fighting spirit and daring tactics in the face of fanatic opposition, greatly accelerated the final decisive defeat of Japanese countermeasures in his sector and materially furthered the continued advance of his company. His great personal valor and gallant spirit of self-sacrifice throughout the bitter hostilities reflect the highest credit upon Captain Dunlap and the United States Naval Service."

Medal Of Honor Presented To George H. Palmer 1st Illinois Cavalry Citation:

" For conspicuous gallantry and intrepidity at the risk of his life above and beyond the call of duty as a musician in the 1st Illinois Cavalry, in action against Confederate forces at Lexington, Missouri, on 20 September 1861. Musician Palmer volunteered to fight in the trenches and also led a charge which resulted in the recapture of a Union hospital, together with Confederate sharpshooters then occupying the same."

Monmouth

With the coming of the railroad in the 1850s, Monmouth flourished as an industrial town. Early on, the city was a center for the manufacture of agricultural implements, first with the Weir Plow Company in the 1860s, and followed by the Pattee and Monmouth plow companies. The latter became a national mail order retailer, changing its name to Brown Lynch Scott Company. Monmouth's first large-scale industry, Monmouth Mining and Manufacturing Company, made use of the excellent native clay to produce sewer tiles for many of the country's major cities. The Monmouth and Weir potteries soon followed, manufacturing storage and canning jars, and in 1905 they were consolidated into Western Stoneware Company, which survives to this day, making decorative and utilitarian stoneware. Other early export industries included the Maple City Soap Works (later sold to Procter and Gamble); the Maple City and Monmouth cigar companies; the Milne Manufacturing Company, which made stump pullers; Maple City Manufacturing Company, which made oil cans; and Boss Manufacturing, which made mittens.

The advent of the Civil Conservation Corps and Works Progress Administration projects gave employment to some. When World War 11 started on December 7, 1941, many young men and a few women from the area entered the service. Many others worked in defense jobs. People shared "Victory Gardens." The war ended September 2, 1945, but it was a while before all were back home, trying to return to normal. living. There was a lack of work opportunities for most.

Formfit

Negotiated by Algot Bowman, chairman of the Chamber of Commerce Industrial Committee in mid-1940s, the Formfit garment factory located in Monmouth in February 1946. Formfit took over the third floor of the Colwell Annex at 200 South A St.. The bowling alley on the first floor closed and was taken over by the company. The second floor was finally obtained when Colwell's beauty parlor closed there. In a few years, Formfit officials were debating whether to take over the fourth floor, close the plant or build a new facility. A building site became available from Howard Bryant of Kirkwood, who offered a location at 1201 N. Main St. Under the direction of Thomas E. Moore, manager for more than 20 years, the building was completed in 1955 and operated there until 1969. More than 300 people were employed there. Average starting wage for machine operators was 75 cents per hour, with an eight-hour day, five-day week. Potential wages could be almost doubled, if earned, by piece work. Women's foundation garments were made there. It was a division of Genesco, Inc., world's largest apparel organization. Formfit closed operations here in 1969 and the plant was taken over by Smoler Fashion in 1970 for manufacturing dresses, coats, etc. This company operated in Monmouth until 1980. Average wage at closing was $5.25 an hour. The property is now occupied by the Pottery Barn, an outlet of Western Stoneware.

Wells Pet Foods

Algot Bowman was also the key man in getting the dog food plant after WWII, when the Chicago Tribune told of a fire wiping out the Vitality plant near Aurora. He contacted officials and worked out a complicated plan under which DeKalb, then located in the old Pattee Plow Co plant, would build a new warehouse and the Pattee plant would be turned over to Vitality, which eventually became Wells Pet Food ,and DeKalb became a large seed corn company here. In 1998, DeKalb Genetics was acquired by Monsanto, which today operates a major agronomy center on the south edge of Monmouth.

These plants were followed by Rochelle Manufacturing locating on West 9th Avenue, Monmouth. Materials on South 2nd Street-, and Monmouth Grain and Dryer on West Broadway.

Gamble-Skogmo

Several communities were working on the project to bring the large company of Garnble-Skogmo to their area, with Burlington, Iowa, and Galesburg, Illinois, being in the competition, but through the efforts of the Monmouth Chamber of Commerce and particularly Algot J. Bowman, the company decided to locate here. (Helping the deal was the fact that the site was offered free.) An option was taken on the land just north of Monmouth for $10,000 for 10 acres, with a sewer connection from the city to the plant. Distribution of its goods was made possible by the locations of junctions of routes 67 and 34. A railroad spur connecting to the CB&Q railroad was built and the building elevated enough to allow easy access for boxcar unloading..

Gamble-Skogmo's roots and main offices were in Minneapolis, Minnesota. A warehouse there served stores in Minnesota, North Dakota, Wisconsin and Michigan. Other warehouses were located at Denver, Colorado, and Coldwater, Michigan. The firm had more than 2,500 retail outlets, mostly in the midwest. At the beginning, the stores carried mostly hardware, competing with the local Western Auto firm, selling items like tires, batteries, tools, paints and some building goods. Additional items were added and by the mid-1950s almost everything was available : refrigerators and freezers, fishing equipment, wagons and bicycles, tools, furniture; TVs and carpeting.

Monmouth Gamble-Skogmo was a great employment opportunity for the community. Built in 1951, it suffered a disastrous fire , but reopened 1953. It]eased a large fleet of trucks through Hoj Trucking Co. and later through the Jensen firm on East Jackson Street. Truck drivers, office personnel, order fillers. warehousemen (to unload freight cars) stockmen, and dock workers to load semi-trailers were employed. The building covered 153,000 square feet and it was all used. The Monmouth warehouse served 420 stores in the Midwest, reaching Arkansas, Kentucky, Missouri, Wisconsin, Indiana, Iowa and Kansas.

The Gamble store in Monmouth was located at 84 Public Square with Clem O'Brien as manager. Later managers were Howard Musgrove, Phil Nelson and Glen Holler.

During the recession of 1980s, the Monmouth Warehouse closed, as did the uptown store.

Munson Transportation

In 1980, Courtney and Robert Munson opened a business under the name of Munson Transportation on North Sixth Street. The company expanded to a fleet of about 1,000 trucks and 1,600 trailers. They did commercial hauling nationwide and employed 1,300 people. They had refrigerated trailers and one of their biggest customers was General Mills. In 1994 they sold the business to Heartland Corp. This company operated for a few years before discontinuing business here, with Chandler Trucking taking over part of the business.

Pork Packing Plants

On December 7, 1963, Agar announced its decision to open a $ 1.5 million plant in Monmouth that would employ 300 workers. A tract of land was purchased on North Sixth Street Road and building was started August 4, 1964. The Agar Plant opened on April 15, 1966 and killing operations started with a staff of 75. At first carcasses were shipped to Chicago for cutting. By the end of June, cutting operations had begun locally, and employment reached 215.

On June 6, 1968, Agar announced it would sell the plant to Wilson & Company. Ownership changed in July and Wilson expanded plant wise and product wise. During Wilson's stay in Monmouth the company name was Wilson-Sinclair; Wilson & Company and finally Wilson Foods, Corp.

In October 1986, it was announced that the Wilson Plant was being sold to Illinois Pork. The property was bought on February 5, 1987, by three partners: Chuck Merrick, Oklahoma City, Oklahoma; Carl Ohlemeyer, Mountain Lake, New Jersey; and Sash Spencer, Key Biscayne, Florida. Plans to renew operations were set for April 1, 1987.

Illinois Pork began operations by concentrating on hog slaughtering, selling fresh pork to other processors, and eventually restarted the processing line. It was out of business by1989.

Purina Mills purchased Illinois Pork on October 3, 1989. Purina Mills, the parent company of Mariah Packing, expected to reopen the plant in October 1989. By July 27, 1992, Tyson Foods was considering buying Mariah Packing but the plans did not materialize. By February 2, 1993, Mariah Packing had been sold to the fifth owner, Farmland Foods, which took over on February 15.

As of 1993, there were 558 employees and the plant was processing 5,800 hogs per day, based on a five day work week. In 2002, Farmland is still in operation in Monmouth.

Western Stoneware Company

By the late nineteenth century, there were several potteries within 100 miles of Monmouth, which was then known as "The Maple City." In 1905, these potteries were brought together to form the Western Stoneware Company and the "maple leaf," which remains the company trademark, identifies the location. The heritage of the Weir Pottery, one of those that merged to become Western Stoneware, brought to the company the now famous Sleepy Eye pieces. These have become treasured collector's items. The pieces were originally made as premiums for the Sleepy Eye Milling Company, Sleepy Eye, Minnesota, and show the profile of Old Sleepy Eye, a Sioux Indian Chief. Most of the pieces were in cobalt blue on white. Other colors are more rare as fewer pieces were produced. The company is still in operation, despite several fires. The Pottery Barn is a factory outlet.

Library Services

The Warren County Library opened as a reading room in 1868, with only newspapers and periodicals available for the first two years. In 1870, William P. Pressley provided funds for additional reading materials and erected a building deeded in trust to the Warren County Library and Reading Room Association. A white marble plaque is still located on that building, now occupied by the Buchanan Center for the Arts, which states that this is the first building in the State of Illinois given for a people's library. In 1907, Pressley erected another building adjacent to the former quarters, which is still the main part of the library building. In 1921, twelve branches were established. Because of personnel shortages, three branches are now in operation. They are in Alexis, Kirkwood and Roseville. Julian Bruening is head librarian, Genie Doty, children's librarian and Betty Loomis is acquisitions librarian. Special services available include video and audio tape rental, faxing, copying, online card catalogue system and interlibrary system loan through Alliance Library system in Pekin.

Department Stores

Among the department stores that have served Monmouth have been: Colwell; Bowman-Colwell, John C. Allen; Mayfred's; J.C. Penney's; Spurgeon's; P.N. Hirsch and Brown Lynch Scott, (which opened as a farm implement store, later adding appliances and women's and men's clothing. When the farm implement part was discontinued it became a women's clothing store called Martha Brown Ltd.). Some other stores have been Murdock and Bowman Shoes Stores; Bowman-Switzer Shoes, Hall's Shoes, Wirtz Book Company, Norris Office Equipment (succeeded by Office Specialists), Parolee's, Phone Set, Mode O'Day, J.T.'s Men's and Boys' Wear, Knepp's Shop, The Glendora Shop, F.W. Woolworth and Kimble 5&10; The Model; Pillsbury's, Western Auto, and Max's Auto Supply.

Wirtz Book Company - 200 East Broadway Monmouth Ill.

Colwells Department Store

In 1895, Edward B. Colwell started a department store in Monmouth. By 1904, the business had grown to the extent that he erected a new five-story building in the 200 block on South Main Street. It came to be known as the most complete department store in Western Illinois and the largest of its kind in the world for a town the size of Monmouth. It contained 50 departments and had a clerical force of 75. By 1951 the store was managed by his son, Edmund B. Colwell. It later was known as Bowman-Colwell and continued under this name for a number of years before discontinuing business. It then operated for a time as Bowman Furniture Co.

Grocery Stores

Grocery stores changed along with everything else. In 1927 there were thirty-seven stores throughout Monmouth, along with six meat markets and five fruit and produce stores. Most of these were the small neighborhood kind. By 1952, the small stores were losing ground to the larger stores like Kroger, Benner Food, Barnes Brothers, C.W. Woods, etc., which yielded to the super-markets. In 2002 there are four such stores and two Mexican groceries.

Furniture Stores

Furniture stores in Monmouth since 1928 have been: Anderson Furniture; J. C. Allen; E.B. Colwell; Hogue furniture-, J.J. Welty (new & used) and Frank Whiteleather, Anderson and Hogue were strictly furniture. Later the Hogue store was sold and became White Furniture. C.O.V. Larson was associated with the Hogue Company and later had his own store. His store burned in 1975 and he opened at a different location and about 1979 sold the business, which was then called Larson Furniture Mart, Inc. By 1986 they were out of business. In 2002 there are two furniture stores: Vickroy's and Term City (a rent-to-own store.). During this time there were other stores that dealt in a small assortment of furniture, including Gamble's.

Hospitals

Monmouth hospital was located on East Euclid Avenue for many years, and in early years had a school for nurse's training. A new hospital was built in 1968 on West Harlem Avenue and is now called Community Medical Center and Clinics. The old hospital building operated as Pinewood Nursing Home until 2002. Monmouth Nursing Home is located on South I Street.

Post Office

The post office was located on South Main Street for many years. On November 30, 1959, the Monmouth Hotel at South First Street and East Second Avenue was torn down and the new post office was erected there. The Farm Credit Services offices now occupy the former post office building which was extensively remodeled. Other changes that have taken place include : the Colonial Hotel was razed in 1970 for the National Bank Drive-In, expanded in 2000 to the current Midwest Bank; Security Savings Bank is now located on East Broadway; City Hall is now in the former Midwest Bank building and that building will soon be the Courthouse Annex, occupied by the county clerk, treasurer and assessor's offices. Supersweet elevator on South Main has been razed and has been replaced by a Dollar Store, Nichol's Hatchery, Hamilton Feed and Produce, Sandstrom Produce, Azdell Creamery and Pearson's Harness Shop have closed. Theaters that have operated here have included the Rivoli, Bijou and Ada. The last to leave was the Rivoli and Monmouth is now without a theater.

Other former industries included Bersted's Hobby Craft, Glastex Boats and the Forman Company.

Government housing, mainly for senior citizens, has been built : Oak Terrace and Costello Towers, on East Harlem Avenue. There have been several apartment complexes built. Monmouth currently has three motels: Meling's Motel and Restaurant and Super 8 Motel in the north part of town and Hawthorne Motel and Suites on the west side. The Highland Courts Motel, just north of Monmouth, was razed in the 1990s.

There are two printing businesses in Monmouth: Seybold's and Kellogg's, both in the downtown area

Fraternal organizations include the American Legion, VFW; Knights of Columbus; Odd Fellows and Rebecca's; Mason and Eastern Star and Eagle's Club.

Businesses now located on the outskirts of Monmouth include: Farm King, (a general farm supply and clothing store for men & women); Mayrath; Bums Auction ; Mutual Wheel ; Keister's Tire Supply Store (which started in 1950s as a service station and has grown to a large tire company and repair store, moving to larger accommodations during the last year); Bruce Foote Chevrolet and Storage; Cavanaughs' Motors, City Ford, ShopKo discount store; Dollar General; Monmouth Implement Company; Monmouth Grain & Dryer; Pottery Barn, Cavanaugh Bus Company, Painter Farm Equipment, Envision Boats; Kistler & Co.; D.J's Brake and Alignment and numerous other small businesses.

Monmouth Township

Former dealerships have included: E & A Motors; Gaskill Motors-, Elmer's Repair" Martin Motors-, LT. Hall Ford; Barrows & Addleman Chevrolet-, Thompson Motor Sales, Prince Motors and Russ Motors.

Cemeteries

There are several cemeteries in Monmouth Township: Pioneer, Cemetery, Monmouth Cemetery (includes what was once Glendale) St. Mary's (Catholic) Cemetery , all within the city limits, Warren County Memorial Park Cemetery and Mosher outside the city limits.

Public Safety

The Monmouth Fire Department currently has 13 paid firemen, 14 volunteers, 14 qualified EMT's--three pumpers, one aerial ladder truck, one ambulance and three motor vehicles. The Monmouth Police Department has 18 officers, 10 dispatchers, 14 active & trained (auxiliary) volunteers, nine pieces of motorized equipment, and one mobile unit for civil defense and auxiliary, one van truck for animal control and one K-9 unit, it also has a 911 system for emergencies.

Prime Beef Festival

In the early 1920s Monmouth started celebrating every fall with a "Fall Festival." This consisted of vendors, concession stands and various shows and demonstrations, with one main show at night. One of the best remembered was Oscar Babcock with his "Loop-the-Loop" show on a bicycle. Starting from a high platform, he rode his bicycle down a ramp, looped the loop and jumped a gap to another platform.

The celebration was held in the downtown area in and around Central Park. Eventually it was moved to Monmouth Park and was set for the first Wednesday after Labor Day through the following Saturday. Later , Monmouth became known as the "Prime Beef Capital" and beginning in 1947 the celebration was called the Prime Beef Festival, with a princess contest held each year. Starting with a parade through downtown and ending at the park, led by a parade marshal with school bands, floats, marching units, farm equipment and saddle horses, competing for prizes for first and second place in each category, and shows and carnivals at the fairgrounds, including stock car races, demolition derbies, or tractor pulls.

The parade marshal for the year 2002 was 100-year-old Gracie Peterson, long-time music teacher and musician in Monmouth.

Parks And Recreation

Monmouth has seven neighborhood parks in addition to Monmouth Park and Citizens Lake. Monmouth Park has five shelter houses, three restroom buildings, one baseball diamond and concession stand, six tennis courts, horseshoe pits, a basketball court, an ice-skating rink, playground equipment, forest trails and the Myron Mikita Outdoor Theater.

Buster White Park has a softball diamond, tennis courts, playground equipment and restroom facilities. Harmon

101 Ranch Show on the Square Monmouth

Park has a shelter house, playground equipment, a baseball diamond and restroom facilities. North Park has a shelter house, a "tot lot" playground area and baseball backstop Warfield Park has a baseball diamond and playground equipment. West Park features a fitness fun center sponsored by local businesses, and a baseball backstop and will soon have a round-court basketball. Garfield Park has a basketball court.

The YMCA has a variety of services and facilities available.

Gibson Woods Golf Course is a 130-acre facility, opened in 1966, and features an 18-hole par 71 course, a practice putting green and driving range, and a snack bar that is open to the public.

Monmouth Country Club has a nine-hole golf course. The 55-acre site was opened in 1901.

The Rainbow Roller Rink features the second oldest maple floor in the United States. The floor was originally used as a portable rink but was permanently installed at the Monmouth site in 1939. It was operated for many years by George Schweigert and, since 2000, by Randy Davis.

The Monmouth Bowling Lanes are operated by Neal and Shelly Ault. The alley used pinboys to set the pins when it opened but now has automatic pinsetters and automatic scoring on eight lanes with numerous leagues.

Citizens Lake

Citizens Lake, located on the west edge of Monmouth, has its origin with the Iowa Central Railway Company. In 1883, the company completed the track segment from Monmouth to Keithsburg and in 1898 made Monmouth a division point on the line, During the spring and summer of 1898, a roundhouse, rail yards and reservoir were constructed. The earthen dam for the reservoir was located across a shallow valley in the headwaters of a small prairie creek. Local residents started calling the reservoir the M.&St. L. Pond about 1910, when the Iowa Central Railway Company was consolidated with the Minneapolis and St. Paul Railroad Company. During the 1955 through 1969 period, the M.&St. L. Pond was]eased by a group from Monmouth area citizens for use as a public swimming and fishing site. The group was called the Citizens Lake Committee and the reservoir became known as Citizens Lake in 1960. In 1970 the railroad company terminated its lease with the Citizens Lake Committee.

In late 1970 and early 1971, the Illinois Department of Transportation (IDOT) purchased the Citizens Lake site from the Chicago and Northwestern Railway Company and the "Q" Pond from the Burlington Northern, Inc. These lands were used in 1974 as earth borrow areas in the construction of the bypass (U.S. 34 & 67) around Monmouth. Under the agreement, the City of Monmouth was to maintain the new recreation area. and it was opened to public fishing in April 1979.

During the September 1991 through July 1992 period, the lakes were enlarged and combined to form a 26.5-acre lake. The original 1898 earthen dam was re-conditioned. In August 1992 the historic 1895 "Campbell Bridge" near Little York was salvaged and moved to a permanent location on the old Iowa Central right of way over a narrow channel of the new Citizens Lake.

The Monmouth Municipal Pool at Citizens Lake has been in operation for 24 years. There is a maximum capacity of 800 swimmers, with a maximum of five lifeguards on duty at one time., depending on the population at the pool.

Citizens Lake, on the far west end of Monmouth, is open from May through October for camping, fishing and picnicking. There is a small play area for children and a new baseball area.

Strom Center

A number of senior citizen services, ranging from meals to blood pressure checks to information and referral services are available at Strom Center, 211 South A Street. Services at the center include: congregate and home-delivered meals and frozen meals that can be stored in home freezers. Activities available at the center include bingo, canasta, bridge, crafts, sewing, card playing, movies and pool. In addition to scheduled blood pressure checks, hospital equipment loans are also available free of charge, including crutches, wheelchairs, and commodes. Medicare logging is also available. Escorts are available to take seniors to grocery stores, hospitals, doctor's offices, beauty parlors and other locations. The transportation services are available through Warren Achievement. There is also a thrift shop open on Tuesdays and Thursdays.

Jamieson Community Center

Jamieson Community Center was established in 1963 as a private nonprofit comprehensive human service agency serving Monmouth and Warren County. The target clientele are the underpriveledged socio-economically handicapped, educationally deprived and minority persons. Services offered by Jamieson Center include free income tax preparation, a thrift shop, emergency food pantry, government surplus commodities, and neighborhood recreation programs.

Warren Achievement Center, Inc.

Warren Achievement Center, Inc. is a not-for-profit corporation providing services for adults and children with developmental disabilities. The corporation is governed by a 12-member board consisting of men and women from the community.

In 1961, Warren Achievement School was founded as a day care center for children with developmental disabilities. The school opened with a total of four children. With the growth of the population and programs to encompass more than just an education program, the name was changed to Warren Achievement Center, Inc. Services are available to children and adults. In the year 2000, services were provided to more than 600 different individuals. Programs include case management, parent-infant education, educational services for people ages 3 to 21, residential facilities for children and adults, vocational training, living skills training, adult day training and transportation for senior citizens and people with disabilities.

Radio Station

WMOI-FM and WRAM- AM on the Public Square are both owned by WPW Broadcasting. WMOI features adult contemporary music, while WRAM features country music. News , sports broadcasts, and other items round out the broadcasts of both stations.

Monmouth College

Monmouth Academy, founded in 1853 became Monmouth College in 1856 and was chartered by the State of Illinois on February 16, 1857. The first permanent building of the college was erected on North A Street. The present campus was at the edge of town when the college moved from North A Street in 1862.

Holt House is the birthplace of Pi Beta Phi, which was the first National Fraternity for women and was established in 1867, (402 East first Avenue). Stewart House is where Kappa Kappa Gamma National Fraternity for Women was organized in 1870. (1015 East Euclid Avenue)

Monmouth College was founded as an academy of the Associate Reformed Presbyterian Church in 1853 Situated on more than 70 acres of land, the college today has an enrollment which has nearly doubled in the past decade. Today's student body totals 1,087 from 19 states and 24 foreign countries, and there are 82 full-time faculty members. The college recently built a baseball/soccer complex and a biological field stateion on North Eleventh Street, and is constructinga $22 million athletic center on campus. Monmouth College is seeking to ensure that it remains a key player among undergraduate liberal arts institutions in the United States.

Monmouth College is one of the founding members of the Associated Colleges of the Midwest, a consortium of 12 colleges organized to support quality liberal arts education and to provide a broad range of exciting off-campus opportunities to undergraduate students. Monmouth is fully accredited by the North Central Association of Colleges and Schools.

Sombrero Club

Following a challenge in 1942 by high school student Robert Grimsley, to create a recreational facility for high school students, for dancing, games, talking and food, a group met at the YMCA to formulate plans. Student representatives were Robert Grimsley, Jane Walker, Joan Hutchison, and Loren Henderson. Y board members met with them and a few parents and representatives from civic organizations. At first dancing was allowed in the gym with nickelodeon music and parental supervision, but that interfered with sport schedules and was damaging the gym floor. Also students wanted a place of their own. In 1944, Robert Grimsley, Martha Lee Bailey and June Ericson spent the summer scrubbing and cleaning the downstairs rooms of the YMCA.

"El Sombrero" was chosen as the name for the club by Mary Jane Carson, in a contest by the students. Grimsley decorated the walls with a Mexican mural showing a Spanish dancer and a small boy with a burro. Mrs. Parolee Ericson found material with a Mexican design for drapes and Mrs. Clarence Bailey made drapes for the windows. Furniture was donated and by fall the Sombrero Club was opened. Adult supervision was by board members. Jean Ellsworth was chaperone the first few years and Mrs. LeRoy Hook gave much time and effort along with many other adult helpers. The Club continued at least until 1967. The club was open on Tuesday, Friday and Saturday evenings

A spin-off was Teepee Town for Central Junior High students, open on Friday afternoons. The name came from the name for junior high athletic teams called the Central Indians.

Monmouth Municipal Airport

Billed as the oldest continually operating airport in Illinois, this is where some of the earliest barnstormers got their wings and took to the skies. Jonathan Livingston buzzed the barns around Monmouth and it is said that Charles A. Lindbergh made US mail stops here many years ago. The 2,900 foot runway can easily accommodate single and twin-engine airplanes and an occasional corporate jet. An airport attendant is on the radio 8 A.M. to 5 P.M. every day except Monday for airport advisory information.

For many years the Monmouth Flying Club has sponsored an annual July 4th drive-in, fly-in breakfast, and it also farms the city's land, and donates its earnings to the city so that the airport here has been able to continue without a special airport tax being levied.

Illinois Bankers Life Assurance Company

Founded at Monmouth in 1897, the Illinois Bankers Life Association was located for many years in the building at the comer of South A Street and West First Avenue. Incorporated by W.A. Sawyer, J.R. Ebersole, G.C. Rankin, D. Turnbull, C.G. McPherron, J.R. Hickman and I.A. Ewing, its name was changed in 1929 to Illinois Bankers Life Assurance Company. In 1951 the company was consolidated with Central Standard Life Insurance Company of Chicago, and the Monmouth office was eventually closed. At the time of the consolidation, the assets had grown to $32 million and insurance in force was more than $133 million. The work force while in Monmouth numbered between 250 and 350 employees.

Wyatt Earp Birthplace

Wyatt Earp, frontier lawman and American legend, is Monmouth's most famous native son, born March 19, 1848. Wyatt's grandfather, Walter, served as justice of the peace in Monmouth. Earp lived in Monmouth during his early childhood before moving on to Iowa, Missouri, Kansas, Arizona, Colorado, California, Alaska, and Idaho. His birthplace home at 406 South Third Street has been restored and furnished with late- 1800s period furniture and memorabilia. The home is open on Sundays during the summer and by appointment.

Famous Monmouth Residents

Ralph Greenleaf born in Burlington, Iowa, but raised in Monmouth, was the first full- time, professional billiards player in this country. He learned the game at the age of eight. in his father's restaurant and billiard hall on South Main Street. He was the Illinois Champion at the age of 12 and the national champion at nineteen. From 1919 to 1926, he won successive national titles, and in 1929 won his eighth title, 125-0, sinking 126 balls without a miss in 50 minutes.

Charles and Will Nichol made Monmouth a well-known name among magicians and students of illusions because they used this city as a retreat for rest and to prepare their difficult illusions. Charles performed under the name of "Von Arx" and Will performed under the stage name of "the Great Nicola." During World War II, both men toured with the USO at their own expense to entertain the troops.

President Ronald Reagan attended second grade during the year that his family lived in Monmouth (1917-18). The family home still stands at 218 South Seventh Street.

Market Alley

A street, one-half block long running from the southeast comer of the Public Square to South first Street, has always been known as "Market Alley." Headed by John Kesinger, a businessman, a group was successful when they petitioned the city to close Market Alley to vehicle traffic , restored the original brick surface , installing antique street clocks and fountain and outdoor tables and chairs. Market Alley has now become a center of community events, such as National Night Out, book fairs, ice cream socials, and summertime weekly MuFoFu (Music-Food-Fun) on Wednesdays at noon, when different groups and organizations furnish entertainment, music and lunch at a nominal price.

Numerous unusual area shops now located on Market Alley include Monmouth Soda Works, The Salon Company, A Touch of Country; Memory Lane; The Bath House (on the square),- and on South First Street such shops as Dawg Patch Diner restaurant; La Pequenita (Mexican Grocery and Restaurant); O' Fleeting Time and Bev's Flowers R Us florists.

"The Model," located on East Broadway at South first Street, operated for over 100 years as a men's clothing store, but has gone out of business. In 1994, John and Diane Kesinger opened the Maple City Candy Company at that location This is an old-fashioned candy store with a soda bar, hand-dipped ice cream and over 300 types of bulk candy. It has expanded, weaving through five buildings and 30 rooms, with items from home decor to giftware, and a recently-opened restaurant called " Coconuts."

Monmouth's Sesquicentennial

In 1981 the Monmouth Area Sesquicentennial , Inc. was formed to plan a celebration of the Sesquicentennial. Ross Williams was general chairman of the executive committee to plan the event. The headquarters were opened on April 27, 1981, with much fanfare. Monmouth men were prohibited from shaving until the sesquicentennial ended or were subject to fines. People dressed in old-time clothes, promenades and kangaroo courts were held with Keystone Cops.

On Friday, June 19, 1981, the celebration started with different activities each day which included: Boardwalk Days, celebration of Ralph Eckley's 80th birthday, Faith Day, Brother's Day, Belle's Day, Youths Day, Agriculture Day, Industrial Day, Pioneer Day and Faith in the Future Day. A stage show, "Born of the Prairie," was presented and a "bank robbery: was staged at the National Bank, along with many other special events for a memorable celebration

The Fountain

At a meeting of the city council in August 1890, it was voted to appropriate $350 for the erection of a fountain in the square. A contract was given to J.L. Mott Iron Company of New York City and the fountain was received and installed in October that yea. It was made of iron, 18 feet high and stood in a pool 20 feet in diameter. Atop the Renaissance style fountain was the figure of a boy (possibly Cupid) holding a short staff. The fountain was removed during the mayoralty of John Hanley because it was too great a drain on the city's water supply. The upper basin was used for a while as a flower planter in front of the "Hairdresser" salon on North 11th street and other parts have disappeared. A replica has been constructed and is now placed in the center of the square by the Downtown Business Council and the patronage of several Monmouth businesses and individuals. The Fountain was formally dedicated to the city on 21 October 2002.

There are also nearly fifty antique street lights and nine historical markers and park benches that been placed about the downtown area.

Restaurants And Fast Foods

Monmouth has had many excellent restaurants over the years, Hawcock's Cafe was among the first, starting in the 1920s. It became a renowned eating place, well known over the entire area as a fine place to eat, with customers coming long distances to enjoy the food and atmosphere. The facility hosted many banquets and served many organizations., but was out of business by the 1950s. Beginning around 1958, Hubert "Hubie" Hedrick had many restaurants in various locations in Monmouth. One was the Sunset Drive in which opened about 1962. It later became the Barnstormer in1978 and Cerar's Barnstormer by1989. The decorating theme is the old barnstorming era with early plane models being used. Hedrick also operated the "Filling Station III", which opened about 1977 in an old service station and used that as its theme. Clarence Meling opened an ice cream shop on North Main, which developed into a sandwich shop and later became Meting's Restaurant and Motel, which is still operating under the same name but under different management. Harper's Restaurant was located in the east part of town, opening about 1984. The Prime Beef Room in the Colonial Hotel was quite popular for fine dining.

Maxey's Drive-In, complete with "car-hops" was located on West Broadway, starting about 1948, and was a very popular place, especially well-known for their tenderloins. It operated for many years, was closed for several years and opened again as Patti's Place in 1989, was under several managers, and has operated for a number of years as Cottage Comer. Among other small, popular eating places have been: Cub Café, Country Kitchen-, Gibbi's, Staley's, A&W, Little Chef-, Mr. Quick, Dairy Queen; Tastee-Freez, Happy Joe's, Higgins Dairy and Maid-Rite, which became Park-N-Eat, and now is Maple City Restaurant. Recently opened businesses are: "Coconuts" and "Sharkey's" in the downtown area and "Generations" in the Country Club, which is open to the public.

Italian Village opened a pizza house in 1958, and is still in business, along with Alfano's and Breadeaux Pizza. Pizza Hut was opened in 1974, enlarged and still operating. Other fast food facilities include: Hardee's-1977 ; McDonald's -1991 (replaced "Dog' n 'Suds"); Subway and Burger King-1996; Kentucky Fried Chicken has been here a number of years.

Statistics Comparisons

(taken from Monmouth City Directories)

1943

Population (1940 census: 9,096 ; area: 2.58 square miles five parks ; 18 churches (14 denominations) three banks; one newspaper and one college , three hotels (150 rooms); one hospital (75 beds); Education--Monmouth College, four public schools including one senior & one junior high; one parochial school --(public school pupils-- 1,653 and 58 teachers) one hospital one municipal airport.

Transportation: Railroads --Burlington, Minneapolis & St. Louis, Rock Island Southern; U.S. Highways 34 & 67 intersect; and Burlington Trailways & Illinois Transit lines operate buses in all directions.

Fire department: six regular men and 75 volunteers, three pieces of motor equipment; police department: seven men, one station, two pieces of motor equipment; chief industries, city and surrounding territory: agriculture and manufacturing; principal manufacturing; pottery, farm equipment, furnaces, sheet metal products, and poultry equipment.

2000

Population (1996 census) Monmouth : 9,200.) Area: three square miles; five banks, 24 churches(14 denominations) ; 48 civic organizations; 10 parks; one daily newspaper, two radio stations: WRAM-AM & WMOI-FM : 3 motels: Hawthorne Inn & Suites, Meling's Motel & Restaurant, Super-8 Motel.

Transportation: municipal airport; Highways U.S. 34 & 67 and State highway 164 (16 miles to 1-74) ; hospital: Community Medical Center-(68 beds 24-hour physician coverage with 14 physicians on staff).

Principal manufactured products; Pottery, dried animal feeds, boats, sheet metal products, soybean processing and hog packing.

Education: four elementary schools-(790 students); one junior high school (235 students); -one high school (472 students); and one parochial school (125 students).

Farmland Foods-- largest employer with 1,040 employees; Warren Achievement Center – 285 employees; Monmouth Public School District-230 employee; - Monmouth College- 204 employees; Community Medical Center-200 employees.

Monmouth Firsts

The Pioneer Cemetery is the oldest free public burying ground in Warren County. It was founded in 1833 and used until 1861. It is the final resting place for relatives of Wyatt Earp and several soldiers who fought in the War of 1812, Blackhawk War (1832) and the Civil War. (A list of names (as complete as possible) can be found in the Genealogy Department of the Public Library.)

The oldest commercial building is occupied by Frank Romano Agency at 72 Public Square and West Broadway. The building was built in 1846. There was once an apple orchard between the building and where the Warren County Public Library is located.

Warren County Public Library was established in 1870 and was the first free public library given in Illinois.

Monmouth Municipal Airport is the oldest continually operating airport in the State of Illinois. The airport is dates back to 1921 as a "flying field" where planes landed to load passengers for rides for $5.

Point Pleasant Township

Point Pleasant Township, in the very southwest comer of Warren County, was the last section of Warren county to be settled, perhaps because of the absence of timber. Timber land was, in those days, far more valuable than prairie since lumber was in great demand. Timber land was worth $15 per acre, compared to $1.25 per acre for prairie. This was a rolling prairie, somewhat broken, with rich soil. Drained by the middle branches of Nigger Creek which empties into the Illinois River, and Honey Creek that empties into the Mississippi. There were no railroads, villages or trading posts.

In 1849 a school was built in the area, but the township was not organized until 1854-- and at that time there were few settlers and only 50 votes were cast at the first election, The name Point Pleasant aptly describes the township. It is a fertile stretch of land, a part of the larger section often called "The Garden Spot of the World".

In 1864, ten years after the organization of the township, a post office was established at a spot called Colfax. Just what Colfax was is not told in the earlier books of Warren County apparently just the school and post office were there. The post office was served by an extension of a route from Monmouth. It was asked by some: "Just where is Colfax?" In answer a correspondent for the newspaper "Review" replied : "It is about five miles southwest of the beautiful little

19

village of Swan Creek." Perhaps Colfax was named for Schuyler Colfax, who had two speaking engagements in Monmouth and became Vice President under Grant.

In 1853, a Methodist Society was organized- Just 28 years from the time the Indians had roamed the area. There were circuit preachers and the services were held in the school house. In 1864, Reverend William McCamy organized the Cumberland Presbyterian Church. A new church was built in 1867, shared jointly by the Methodists and Presbyterians. In 1875 it was sold to the Presbyterians and a new church was built for $1700. At this time the Methodists from Swan Creek and others formed the Colfax Methodist Church near the center of the township, with services every two weeks.

The news in those early years was full of feuds, murders, fires and various forms of "skullduggery"

In 1906, the ladies of the Colfax community met for the purpose of organizing the Ladies' Aid Society. There were 15 members present and eventually 60 ladies belonged to this Society during the 18 1/2 years of activity. The society disbanded in 1924 when the church closed. The building was moved one mile north of it's former site, and became the Township Hall. The Society then became known as the Colfax Community Club and today it still exists with eleven members remaining.

Today many of the old familiar homes and places are gone, as well as the hedge fences and one room school houses. "Back Then " there were nine schools in the township., which have been consolidated with the village of Roseville. There are no churches remaining in the township, but the Point Pleasant Cemetery is located in Section 14. It is improved and maintained by the Point Pleasant Cemetery Association.

According to the plat book of 1872, some of the early residents were: Strong, Lofftus, Moore, Dixon, Boyd, Pendarvis, Livermore, Strickler, Clark, Stice, Green and McCleary families. In 1912 the names of Watson, Davis, Bacon, Pinney, Tubbs, Ross, Kritzer, Kirkpatrick, Tucker, Thompson, Bycroft, Brainer, Hall, Cochran, Lee and Monroe are included.

Roseville Township

Roseville Township was originally called Hat Grove, and is watered by Nigger and Cedar Creeks. Early settlers were Sheldon Lockwood; Caleb Hedges; Truman Eldridge - the Lofftus family and Henry Staat. Truman Eldridge owned the land where Roseville now stands. The town was laid out on May 25, 1870. The first railroad entered Roseville in 1870 and most of the town of New Lancaster (Ellison Township) moved to Roseville.

Coal was mined in different places in the township. The late Burl Ives once owned a farm near Roseville and Don Knotts often visited his father-in-law, a local pastor. Roseville is the only town in the township. Train service has ceased to exist and the depot has been torn down.

Township census, 2000 was 1,341.

According to the U.S. Post Office Historian, the first postmaster at Hat Grove, was Truman Eldridge who was appointed on January 4, 1843. The name was changed to Roseville on June 23, 1852 when Benjamin Morford was appointed. Since then these have served as postmaster: Ezra P. Emans; Amos Pierce; William T. Gossett; William H. Buckley: Charles A. Hebbard; Samuel W. Taliaferro: William T. Gossett;: James W. Prouty-, Melville S. Yoho; Homer F. Kelly; Glenn G. Watson; J. Wesley Young; Charles C. Paul], 1977 Officer in Charge, Avis M. Mason; 1978 Officer in Charge, Ruby 1. May; 1978-92: Edward Lee Leary,- 1992 Officer in Charge, Mary B. Farrenkopf; Current Postmaster, Donnie L. Tafflinger, was appointed Officer in Charge on March 10, 1993, and ten days later was appointed Postmaster.

Today there are five churches in the township, all located in Roseville; Roseville United Methodist Church-, First Baptist Church, Roseville Christian Church; Church of the Nazarene; and Living Light Tabernacle.

Two highways run through the township, intersecting in Roseville. State Highway 116, a 2-Lane road runs east and west. U. S. Highway 67 runs north and south, and there will be four lanes from Monmouth to Macomb when the new by-pass around Roseville (west side) is completed in late 2002.

A volunteer fire department has served the village since 1895, when the horse drawn equipment was used. The first motorized truck was purchased in 1923, with Will H. Taylor as first chief, followed by Elgie Atchison, Earl Stice and C. M. Scott. The Roseville, Point Pleasant, Swan and Ellison (R.S.P.&E.) Fire Protection District was formed, providing protection for the village and surrounding countryside. Fire trucks were housed at the Village Hall garage until 1968 when the fire station moved to the "old high school" building on East Penn Avenue. A Fire Marshall oversees the entire district which includes the fire stations at Roseville, Smithshire, and Swan Creek. Serving in this position have been Wayne Green, Everett Brooks, A.J. Blevins, Rolland E. Swanson, Donald Triplett, Gary Johnson, Gary Green, Todd Adkisson; and David Hayes, 1995 to present. Current Fire Chiefs at the three departments are: John Adkisson, Roseville, Steve Davis, Smithshire, and Randy Winbigler, Swan. Present equipment at Roseville includes: 2 pumpers, a brush truck-, a tanker truck; a rescue van; and a Fire Marshall's van, at Smithshire: 2 pumpers ; at Swan Creek: 2 pumpers, and a brush truck.

E. Lynn Hill was appointed Superintendent of the newly formed Roseville Unit School District for the 1948-49 school year and held that position until 1968. Since then Edward Siltman, William Hughes, Marilyn Yokel, William Hughes, John Mowery, Dr. Donald Frailey and currently F. Michael "Mike" Kirby have served. The current elementary school was built in two phases. The wings on the east and west, the front offices and gym were dedicated on April 24, 1955. The old two story elementary building which stood in the middle was torn down and the middle wing was built in 1969-70. The Class of 1965 was the last to graduate from the "old high school". A new high school was built three blocks south and was first occupied on January 3, 1966.

Today the "old high school" houses the Warren County Historical Society, the Roseville Fire Department (main station for R.S.P. & E Fire Protection District), the Roseville Ambulance Service (started in 1972), the Friendship Center for senior citizens which began in 1974, and the old gymnasium is used for many community functions as well as for public auctions.

Warren County Museum

The Warren County Museum is housed in the "old High School" in Roseville. It is managed by the Warren County Historical Society on a volunteer basis. The Museum's memorabilia, dating from the War of 1812, includes everything from fancy period clothing and Victorian artifacts to a Pattee Plow, invented in Monmouth in 1873. There are pieces of old farm equipment, train memorabilia and the old Little York Jail. Separate rooms display old stores, doctor's and dentist offices, living quarters in homes and an old one room school. Historical Records include the Declaration of Loyalty cards of Warren County for World War I and military uniforms. Records of many of the county schools are in separate rooms. There are many other interesting items, making it a well rounded Museum. It is open from Memorial Day to Labor Day on Sundays and holidays, and other times by appointment.

In 1875, Roseville was incorporated as a village, and at that time it had a population of 500. The first officials were: J.C. Turnbull, Ezra P. Emans, John A. Gordon, James S. Reed, JT. Lathrop, trustees, of whom Mr. Emans was chosen president. Other known presidents are: D.A. Woodward- 1908; Robert Gray- 1909; D.A. Woodward1911, -1 W.B. Ditch- 1917-1 John Conlon1919, -1 M.P. Wilkins- 1922, Dick Manuel-, Herman Kington; Robert L. Wood1959-1 J.C. Bagley- Oct. 1960, and the current president: F. Michael "Mike" Kirby who was first elected in April 1993. Other current officials are Carla Oliver- clerk; Ramona Allen- Treasurer-, and Trustees William H. Cook, Marlin W. Perrine, Bill Wainman, Melinda Green, Gene Larkin and Dale Lybarger.

Township Supervisors have been: Lee Johnson, Frank C. Kirkpatrick, J.J. Marrah, Everett L. Brooks, Donald Leighty, Marvin Hawk, Norman Watson, and Edwin D. Anderson is the present Supervisor.. Other present township officials are: Sheila Livermore, Clerk; James Anderson, Highway Commissioner-, and Trustees-, Jeff Corzatt, David Hollenberg, Rodney Huston and Greg Livermore.

Construction of the LaMoine Christian Nursing Home, located at 145 S. Chamberlin Street in Roseville, was started in 1970, and the 62-bed facility opened on June 2, 1971 with James M. Oliver as administrator, a position he held until October 3, 1997. It was increased to 99 beds when additions were built in 1974-75. Following Oliver's retirement, the position was filled by Jamie Bray, then Terry Thompson and currently by Sherry Guttermuth who took over the administrator's duties on August 16, 2002. Rudy Corman, a businessman in Roseville was very influential in starting the Nursing Home, which is part of Christian Homes, Inc., Lincoln, IL.

Roseville Township

A landmark in every small village is its water tower and Roseville is no exception. The first water system was built around 1897 using a straight standpipe as a holding tank. In 1934, a 60,000 gallon capacity tower was built which served for 66 years. It was silver in color with "Roseville" painted in black letters. In 2000, a new 250.000 gallon capacity, 129 1/2 " tower was erected with a modern 43 1/2' round shaped bowl and painted a brilliant white. In April 2001, following a fund-raising project led by Helen Perrine, red roses, which Mrs. Perrine had designed were painted on the tower's east and west sides, along with "Roseville"

Spring Grove Township

Spring Grove Township is mostly a farming community, watered by Middle Henderson and Cedar Creeks. Within the last fifty years the creeks have been straightened and farming can be done much closer to the creeks. Much woodland is gone and farms have been enlarged with many houses and outbuildings being razed.

Among the first settlers in the township were: John Humphreys (being one of two commissioners selected to locate the road from Monmouth to Rock Island (Rock Island Road) Colonel Robert Gilmore; William Hanna-, Captain Peter Mauk (settled in a grove that has since born his name.)

Alexis and Gerlaw are the two towns in the township. Alexis was incorporated on March 31,1870. and was first named Alexandria, but the name was later changed to Alexis. It is unique, being located in two counties: Warren and Mercer and four townships -1 Spring Grove and Kelly in Warren and Suez and North Henderson in Mercer. The Rock Island and St Louis Division of the CB&Q Railroad entered the township at Alexis in the northeast comer. It closed by 1920's, but did not completely leave Spring Grove Township until 1955, when the rails and ties were removed. The Rock Island Southern bridge across Henderson Creek burned in 1946.

The United Presbyterian, Presbyterian, United Brethren Christian, Baptist and Methodist churches have all been represented here, as well as several Fraternal Lodges. The last services of the Alexis Methodist Church were held in August 1994. In 1995 an organization was formed and the church building became the Alexis Museum in 1996 and houses a number of fascinating displays reminiscent of the community's early history.

By 1951 Alexis High School started using school busses and by the middle '50's the country schools were being closed due to lowered enrollment.. Alexis has its own school with a total elementary through high school enrollment of about 400 students. Like all school systems, at this time consolidation is being considered.

Alexis has a volunteer fire department, a police department and an emergency 911 system.

The Alexis Fire Equipment Company was established in 1945 and now employs about 50 people. Their distribution area in the U.S. is mainly in the central area, however they have sold fire trucks as far away as Brazil and Greece. The fire trucks are custom made to each purchaser's specifications, tested and delivered.

A newspaper," The Alexis Journal" was started in February 1874, changing publishers and names several times : "The Alexis Index" "Alexis Argus" -"The Warren Mercer Visitor" and "The Alexis Visitor". being some of the names.

Robert Gerlaw laid out Gerlaw City on April 19, 1871. Elder L. S. Wallace had organized the Christian Church on June 20, 1859 at Mauk's Grove with 29 members. The building was moved nearly three miles to Gerlaw, repaired and served the congregation until 1894, when the present building was erected.. The name was changed to Gerlaw Christian Church. The United Presbyterian merged with the North Henderson Presbyterian Church to make the Spring Grove Presbyterian Church, which moved to Norwood.

The Gerlaw post office closed December 30, 1990. The town has deminished in size, but has a church and a very well kept cemetery at the edge of town. Railroad service to Gerlaw and Alexis was discontinued in the 1970's.

At the junction of Routes 67 and 135, a gas station stood for many years, and at one time there were small sleeping cabins available., but by 1940's the cabins were no longer in use. The small station was later owned and operated by the Vilets, closing in the early '60's.

The High Point Gun Club opened in 1970, started by Bob Mckelvie and Tom Holloway on the Tom Holloway farm. It was operated by Donald Smith 1972-1988 and by Jack and Danny Foster for two years, then by Dan Porter for four years. The last trap shoot was held in 1998. Many special shoots were held for Admiral-Maytag employees for Thanksgiving turkeys and other prizes. Other groups also had special shoots. The Alexis FFA sponsored safe gun handling classes there, which were well attended.

Lake Warren

In 1949, R. Taylor Mitchell, Henry A. Geers, G. Olen Keister and Richard Strand sought a charter to form a lake for recreational purposes. A charter was

Old & New Water Towers at Roseville

issued by the Illinois Secretary of State on October 24, 1949 for the parent organization, The Lake Warren Club. In December 1950, the main tract for the lake was purchased from Theodore Larson and wife. The Lake Warren Club conveyed the land to the Hickory Grove Corporation on October 11, 1951 The two dams that made the lake possible were completed in 1953. The water drains from approximately 1700 acres east and north of the lake, entering through two creeks, and is also spring fed.

Hickory Grove Lake Company, commonly called Lake Warren, is located six miles north of Monmouth in Section 29 of Spring Grove Township. The Lake consists of 52 acres, with 225 leased lots surrounding part of the shoreline. Most of the lots have seasonal or year round dwellings. The Lake is operated by a board of directors elected by the shareholders. There is a beach for swimming, as well as boating, fishing, and water skiing on the lake. There is a shelter house with picnic facilities, bathhouse with showers, a boat launch, a permanent campground and overnight campground for members.

Sumner Township

Originally called Martinsville, Sumner Township was organized on April 4, 1854. The Middle Henderson and Cedar Creeks water it. Among the first settlers were the Richeys from Indiana. There were several families and they settled in the southern part of Sumner and the northern part of Hale in 1828. Adam Richey built a blockhouse in the area, and sold land to Lovett P. Rockwell in 1832. Rockwell and Jonathon Buffum built a small saw mill on Cedar Creek The next spring they brought their families to Sumner and built another blockhouse and stockade. The famous Rockwell Mill was erected in 1836. Other early settlers were Hugh Martin, Sr, Hamilton and David Brownlee, David H. McCrery, J.F. Arthurs and Charles H. Paine.

Little York was the twelfth town platted in Warren County. It was on the Iowa Central (later M&ST L) Railroad which entered the township on its northwest comer, ran almost due south a couple miles and then crossed in a southeasterly direction. There were two stations, Little York and Eleanor. In 1833, John Kendall opened the first store in the township in the blockhouse not far from the present site of Little York. It was part of the old Monmouth-Aledo- Muscatine (M.A.M.) Stage Line. The towns of Eleanor and Denny have both disappeared

Little York has had a bank since 1890, operating under different names. For most of its history it was located on the comer of Broadway and Main Street, a familiar landmark to several generations. In 1971, the First State Bank of Little York moved across the street into a new building. In 1984 it became a part of the Monmouth Trust and Savings Bank. When that became the Marquette Bank, the hours at Little York were reduced and when Marquette was taken over by Wells Fargo in July 2002, the Little York facility was closed.

The only newspaper in the village was the "Little York Ensign" started by R.S. Hook in 1885, and had a number of publishers in it's short history.

The Little York Methodist church was dedicated August 16, 1891 by Reverend A.P. Beal but it has been discontinued. The Little Cedar United Presbyterian Church represents the union of the Cedar Creek and Little York United Presbyterian Churches which took place in July 1961. In 1976 the church was raised and a basement added.

In 1937 a gymnasium was added to the Little York school building to serve both the grade and high schools which were in the adjoining brick structure. In 1938, the Little York Community High School became a four year institution. In 1941-42, a new high school was built and occupied in February 1942. In 1960, the Little York and Kirkwood schools were combined into the Yorkwood School District. The new Yorkwood Junior-Senior High School opened in the fall of 1969; In the fall of 1979, grades K-6 moved onto the new Yorkwood Elementary School built to the west of the High School. The former school building has been transformed into an apartment building. The first school in the township had been built in 1837.

Little York has had some type of fire protection with a volunteer force since 1886. A fire protection district was formed in August 1963 and in October a new fire truck was ordered from the Alexis Fire Equipment Company which was delivered the following April. In November 1968 a new fire station was completed on Main Street which houses the fire equipment and also serves as a community center for all types of occasions.

In the early 1930's the Gene-Bar Coffee Shop was built by Bud and Genevieve Bar-rows on Broadway south of the main business block. Its dining room and bar attracted customers for miles around, but after Bud's death in 1944, it became a private residence. Ed Stotts built a brick restaurant in 1930's and later sold it to Hylma Anderson, becoming known as Anderson's Cafe. until her retirement in 1949. It is now housing Gary's Plumbing, Heating and Electrical. A succession of restaurants on Broadway have been called the York Cafe. It closed around 2000. The Sweetwater Tavern, is now located there. The old bank building became the Sweetpea Cafe but is now known as Beany's Cafe.

A post office was first established on February 15, 1840, and has had many different locations. On November 30, 1976, it moved into a new building at the comer of Spruce and Walnut Streets and has remained there. Postmasters have been: George F. Dickson 1929-34; Mary 1. Brown 1934-59; Donald Adair 1959-61 -1 Martha G. Krusmark 1961-95 ; Perry Jackson 1995-96 -1 Lori Davis 1996-98 - Lucille Biddle 1998--- In 2002 , Linda Shimmin is substitute clerk; Rural carriers are Troy Raymond- Route I and Dean McCaw- Route 2.

The Little York Lion's Club was organized in March 1973, and has been an organization that has provided many services to the community such as helping families in need, purchasing the Little York Ball Park and putting up street signs. The current president is Tom Bertelson. In the 1940's, Little York had three grocery stores : Addleman's, Stott's and Fox's. Addleman's and Fox's closed, but Stotts continued for several years, succeeded by stores run by Kathleen Leary-, Hillmans; Neals; Bill's Super Value and others, but there has been no grocery store for the past five years,

Swan Township

Swan Township is in the southern tier of townships in Warren County. The Nigger and Swan Creeks flow through the northeastern part. The township was officially organized on April 4, 1854. Probably the first settlers were Peter Scott, Donald Perkins, Elijah Hanen and Abijah Roberts who came in 1832- 1833; Larned Kidder came in 1837. H. V. Simmons opened the first store in Youngstown, and Adam Futhey built the first house in that village.

The St. Louis Division of the CB&Q Railroad entered the township in the northeast quarter and passed nearly south to Swan Creek, then to Youngstown, where both villages had railway stations. The railroad remained in service until 1980 when it was disbanded and the tracks were removed in 1982.

Youngstown was the first town, located south of the center of the township. Coal mines in the hills and draws north of Youngstown attracted a large population at one time. After the railroad station was built, the town prospered and supported two churches the Baptist (an offshoot of the New Hope Church established in 1836). moved to Youngstown in 1862. Reverend W.U. Bybee of Cuba, Illinois, organized the Christian Church of Youngstown on January 6, 1890. It remained active until the early 1950s.

Several fraternal organizations existed as well as several stores and businesses. A

Broadway - Swan Creek, Illinois

grocery store was operated by Calvie Hayes family in the 1950s, then Jessie and Earl Demoss had a small grocery store in their home. It closed December 31, 1972.

A two story brick high school existed for a number of years in Youngstown as well as six one room school districts and a two room school in Swan Creek. The school districts were consolidated in 1948 and students bussed to Roseville and the first through sixth grades were held in Youngstown. Swan Creek school closed in 1958 and Youngstown closed in 1960. The eight school districts were : Downey #112; Sugar Loaf #113; Adkisson #114; Swan Creek #115; Hoisington #118; Sisson #121 and Youngstown #131.

Swan Creek was laid out and surveyed in 1871. A railroad station was built after residents raised $1000 to persuade the railroad to agree. Then the post office was moved from a home north of town into the new village. The Ratekin addition was added on the northwest side of town - a small unkempt cemetery still exists in that addition.

The Methodist Episcopal Church was organized in 1872. The present day building was built in 1874-1875. Now known as the United Methodist Church, it celebrated 125 years in 1999. They have shared a minister with Roseville United Methodist Church since 1949.

The schoolhouse was built in 1876 for approximately 50 students, and it served the community for 82 years. The school closed in 1958 and was vacant for a few years before being made into a home. Since 1990 the building has housed the Bible Way Fellowship Church. Other churches that have come and gone are: Christian Science; Universalist Church; and Swan Creek Gospel Center. The bell from the Gospel Center now stands in the Bible Way yard.

Of the many Fraternal organizations, one is still in existence. Mutual Benefit Club (MBC), a woman's club, was organized by Mrs Clara (Bedford) Ray in 1923 when she invited the ladies of the community for an afternoon. The club has had over 150 members and still meets once a month.

Frank Wise family moved to Swan Creek in 1969 and served as manager for Bader's Elevator. In 1970-1971 the Baders took over the Sands elevator and the Wise family remained as managers. In 1994-1995 Continental Grain took over Baders and the elevator is now owned by Western Illinois Grain of Macomb with the Wise daughter as manager.

The telephone company was operated out of the home of George Braselton and the last operators were Mick and Maysil McDonald in the 1950s, when the McDonough Telephone Coop was established. The most modern telephone service is serving the rural community with continually updated equipment.

Swan Township formed a volunteer rural fire district, in 1946. The first fire truck was delivered in late 1947. At first a cement block building was used to house the truck and fire meetings and became a meeting room for the township and the polling place. Swan is part of the Roseville, Swan, Point Pleasant and Ellison Fire Protection District. Herman Kington- Roseville, Dale Sands-Swan Creek and Glen Homey- Smithshire were the first charter directors. This was the first volunteer rural fire district in Illinois. It has continued to upgrade their equipment and fireman's training. A new modem fire station was erected in 1996, east of the intersection in Swan Creek, that is also used for township meetings and a polling place. Swan received one of two new fire trucks in the spring of 2002.

Little Swan Lake Association was formed in 1966, the dam being in Greenbush Township with the west end of the lake in Swan Township. Homes have been built around the lake and a nine hole golf course lies in Swan Township. In 1970, the "Driftwood Supper Club" was constructed and has gone by several names over the years which include: Swan Hills Supper Club; The Edgewater; Little Swan Lake Supper Club and The Catfish Place. The Association dissolved in 1976, but the Little Swan Lake Board continues to oversee the management of the lake.

There are several cemeteries in the township, but only one is maintained. The Stice cemetery lies on the Stice homestead southwest of Youngstown. The township took over the upkeep in the 1980s. Other small family plots are known to exist.

Township officers continue with a Supervisor, Town Clerk, Highway Commissioner and four trustees. Early records were destroyed by the great tornado of 1872. A township hall, located in Youngstown, was also used as the voting place and a library. This was torn down in the 1950s. A township garage was built in Youngstown, after much discussion.

Swan Creek supported two banks in the early 1900s - Swan Creek State Bank and The Farmers and Merchants Bank. Both banks closed on the bank holiday in March 1933 and neither one ever reopened. During 1900-1920s there were also a number of businesses, like a barber, blacksmith, lumber yard, several stores, grain and stock buyer, a hotel, doctor, telephone office, meat market, garage, stockyard and livery stable, and a gambling hall. As late as the 1940s there was a post office, Willis's Grocery, two elevators and Hardy Mitchell's Tavern. The last grocery store was run by Myra Quigley along with a home cooking restaurant, which was known for her chicken and noodles and her pies.

Several families have farmed the same land for two generations. A sign of the times is larger farms and fewer farm families and with that fewer farm houses, people and children. At this time the school district is looking toward consolidating. again. Things from telephones to farming are run by computers now and time will tell what the next generation will see.

Tompkins Township

Tompkins (first called Center Grove and later changed to Tompkins) was organized in 1854. It is well adapted for stock raising and farming, with South Henderson Creek and Tom Creek running through it into Henderson Creek. John Quinn was the first to build a house, but left a short time later. Other early settlers were: Hanna, Kendal, Gibson, and Creswell, coming in 1830. Most land was purchased for $1.25 an acre.

Lyndon was listed as a post office in 1856, but the village was platted as Young America on September 19, 1854 and incorporated in 1865. The name was changed to Kirkwood in 1874 and was the trading center and second in size in the county. After the railroad was completed in 1855, the town really thrived. The CB&Q (later Burlington Northern) and the Atchison, Topeka and Santa Fe (later the Santa Fe), cross Tompkins Township, with the CB&Q going through Kirkwood.

The town had newspapers, 1867-1933, under various owners, the longest being published by O.H. Akin, 1911- 1933.

23

Mineral Springs Northwest of Kirkwood Illinois

Mineral Springs

A flowing spring was discovered in 1875, one mile NW of Kirkwood by coal miners, while digging a coal shaft. It was found to have medicinal properties, and a few weeks later Kirkwood Mineral Springs Company was formed with 50 stockholders. A resort was developed with a hotel, cottages, restaurant, bowling alley, dance hall, and a small lake, plus other facilities. It was quite popular for a number of years with many people coming from long distances to drink the water which was also sold in town and shipped over the country as far as New York. People enjoyed the outdoors with as many as 1000 attending the Old Settlers' reunions. The resort was closed by 1910 and everything was gone but the pagoda, the hotel was moved to Kirkwood and the cottages were moved to serve as homes in the area.

Center Grove Cemetery was established in 1855 about 1/2 mile NW of Kirkwood and is still in use today having been enlarged and is well maintained. There was a Ladies Cemetery Association for years which raised money and saw that the cemetery was well maintained. It no longer exists and the work is done by the Town Board. A cannon, used in the defense of Ft. Donelson during the Civil War, was captured by Union Forces. It was shipped to the home of Lt. Cyrus Bute as a memento for the town, was donated to the GAR and is now on the mound at Center Grove cemetery. Memorial Day Services are conducted there every year. Hickory Point Cemetery, SE of Kirkwood, was established in 1858 and is no longer used for burials.

The first school in the township was erected NW of Kirkwood by Mr Hanna on his property, called Center Grove, and taught by Squire James H. Martin. Later there were eight rural one room grade schools: Center Grove, Coonville, Moore, Columbia, Tubbs, Liberty, Nichol, Maple Grove, and a grade and high school in Kirkwood. Most rural schools closed between 1956-1961, the last being Liberty. The high school was changed to Kirkwood Township High in 1937, with the last class graduating in 1960. The school then consolidated with Little York to form Yorkwood School, half way between the towns. Grade school remained the same until a new elementary school was built. The high school was demolished, the gym bought by the Kirkwood Park District and is used by the community for various activities. The first Kirkwood School was built in 1861, later used as a gymnasium and agricultural shop, but burned in July 1975. The stone grade school was demolished, the metal building sold to be used as storage for farm implements.

There were many grist mills in the township and a steam mill built in 1867. A new burr mill built in 1886, as a flour mill, was idle several years, then was opened in 1927 as a grain mill with Howard Bryant as manager and called Central Feed and Produce. It was known locally as "The Mill." The building burned in 1930 and was rebuilt of brick. Later a store opened on Kirk Street, selling paints, hardware and appliances. Dri-gas was added in 1931 and it was managed by James Lauver until closing in 1996.

In 1976 there were 32 businesses in Kirkwood, There were many businesses and two doctors for several years, but there are no doctors now and the businesses have slowly closed. At the present time there are the following: U.S. Post office, Public Library, Midwest branch Bank, T&L Grocery, Billington's gifts, Bi-County Veterinarians, Total Input and FS Fertilizer, Rosemary's Beauty Shop, Darnell's Beekeeper Honey, William Gullberg, Attorney, the Village Center and the Volunteer Central Fire District. Police protection is provided through the Warren County Sheriff's Department.

Through the years there were as many as eight church denominations, but today only two remain. The United Presbyterian and Presbyterian joined in 1958 to form the present Westminster Presbyterian Church. The Methodists, organized in 1850 are now the United Methodist Church, whose present church was erected in 1912. Liberty Church near Ponemah was organized and built in 1863 and closed in 1947. The building was moved to Smithshire and used by the M.E. Church as a hall called Liberty Hall.

Once there were 25 fraternal or community organizations, some have closed and some have relocated to join with members in various towns. Today these exist: Senior Citizens, Kirkwood Community Club, a Home Extension Unit, a Boy Scout Troop, Kirkwood Alumni Association, and Mason's Lodge.

Ponemah, a station on the Santa Fe Railroad, was never incorporated, but had a post office - 1881-1920s. There was a pumping station for a pipeline, and at one time a grain elevator. There are a few houses there now.

In 1950 came TV and in 1952 dial phones were installed, so the "Hello Girl" was no longer needed. Now in the "computer age" of the twenty first century there are many changes, and most homes and businesses are equipped with computers.

Young's Lake

The Warren County Soil and Water Conservation District was organized in 1942 under the jurisdiction of the U.S. Department of Agriculture. Raymond Johnson of Kirkwood and Woodrow Salter of Biggsville got the idea for the watershed in 1948, the year after Old Tom Creek overflowed its banks blocking all traffic on U.S. 34 near Biggsville.

Old Tom Creek watershed encompasses an area stretching from three miles west of Monmouth, running southwest to where it empties into South Henderson Creek near Biggsville. Covering 18 square miles, it involves about 1,000 acres and 34 farms. There are 10 flood water structures, one located on Clyde Young's property northwest of Kirkwood, replaces a bridge that was washed out. This formed the largest body of water in the watershed.

The Prime Beef Chapter of the Isaac Walton League was organized on May 16, 1949. When the watershed formed a twenty acre lake on the Young property in 1957, they met with Mr. Young about the possibility of leasing the lake area.. The lease was signed on May 24, 1957. and the area was converted to a beautiful conservation and recreation area named "Young's Lake" in honor of Mr. Young. Picnicking, boating, fishing, swimming, camping and just enjoying nature was available. The lake has a swimming raft, shelter house, shower house, and toilet facilities, and many picnic tables and a utility shed. The lake grounds were purchased by the members from Andrew Young about 1987. In August 2000, the membership voted to disjoin from the Isaac Walton League and is now owned by the membership.

Many descendants of the original settlers still live in the village and Township. Some of the farms are still operated by descendants of the original owners, but most of the small farms have been bought out to make larger farms.

Warren County Churches

Sumner Little York	Spring Grove Gerlaw	Kelly
Hale	Monmouth Monmouth	Coldbrook Coldbrook
Tompkins Kirkwood	Lenox Larchland	Floyd Cameron
Ellison Smithshire	Roseville Roseville	Berwick Berwick
Point Pleasant	Swan Swan Creek	Greenbush Greenbush

Roseville Baptist Church 1893

Berwick Baptist Church

Berwick Baptist Church - present.

On July 28, 1833 seven people gathered at the log cabin home of Mr. And Mrs. John Smith one mile west of Berwick. In addition to the Smiths, Mrs. Elizabeth Hanon, Mr. and Mrs. Sheldon Lockwood, the Reverend John Logan and the Reverend John Clark were in attendance. The day was spent in deep thought, prayer, praise and discussion. These seven people had met for the expressed purpose of founding a church. The church they charted was named the Cedar Fork Baptist Church. This church was renamed eight years later in 1841, when it became the Berwick Baptist Church. It has retained its name and identity ever since. The Berwick Baptist Church has served the township as a center of Christian faith and of healthy activity throughout the years.

At the time of the founding of the Baptist Church, the first settlers had been in the township for several years, although the actual town of Berwick was not platted until 1836. Berwick is located seven miles west of Abingdon and twelve miles southeast of Monmouth. As early as 1831 the community was extensive and need for spiritual life in the area was apparent. At the time the first meeting house was built in about 1835, it stood only two doors north of the site of the present structure. Many people assisted in the building of the present building, including the pastor who is said to have made some of the shingles.

To varying degree, the Berwick Baptists played an active role in the formation of several other churches in the area, namely, Abingdon, Cameron, Greenbush, Monmouth, Roseville and Union.

The Reverend Gardner Bartlett was the first pastor of the congregation. Rev. R.M. Wilbur whose term as pastor was one of the longest and was highlighted by the building of the first church structure succeeded him.

Berwick Baptist Church was the first Baptist meeting-house between Burlington, Iowa and Peoria, Illinois. The present church structure was built in 1857. Many additions have been made since, only slightly altering the appearance of the church.

One addition that has beautified the church is the stained glass windows on the west side of the sanctuary. These windows were dedicated in memory of Deacon B.P. Matteson, who passed away shortly before the church's 80th anniversary. Benjamin Matteson was a descendant of one of the early pastors, a member of the church for 54 years and Deacon for 36 years.

Reverend John Spillman was pastor in 1956. At this time the congregation was busy with a major building project. The Sunday school had grown to the point of needing new classrooms. A building committee consisting of Ernest Johnson, Norris Meachum, Harold Koch, Arnold Pratt, Lloyd Massingill, Dale Smith, Max Harris, Carl Berg and James Conway undertook the work and completed the addition to the north side of the church. Restrooms were included in the project also. Countless hours of volunteer labor went into this new addition.

In 1963, while Reverend L.L. Newell was pastor, the congregation worked to remodel the dining room. In 1966, the sanctuary was carpeted for the first time.

On May 4, 1975, groundbreaking ceremonies were held for the construction of the church office and the pastor's study. At this time, new Sunday School classrooms were completed. In addition to the construction, the church also had new siding applied and the sanctuary underwent extensive refurbishing.

After Reverend Robert Beard became pastor in 1979, the church held its ceremonial mortgage burning service. This was a rare occasion for the Berwick Baptist Church; it was practically unheard of to borrow money in order to undertake building projects. However, this event marked the end of indebtedness.

In 1982, the carpet in the church was replaced and new pews were purchased. At the same time, ceiling fans were installed in the sanctuary. In recent years, the church kitchen has undergone remodeling to make it more spacious and efficient. There has also been work done to the foundation and roof

The Berwick Baptist Church is strong in the faith and ever loyal to its Covenant and Articles of Faith. It has come far from the log cabin of its origin, but has lost nothing of the hardy pioneer survival instinct or of the trust and obedience prompted by true faith in Christ, It is a church proving its ability to weather change.

The church still maintains an active Sunday School, Sunday Worship Services, Woman's Fellowship Society and Baptist Youth Fellowship. Annual events held at the church include Vacation Bible School, Harvest Festival, Easter Sunrise Services, Mother-Daughter Banquet and Father-Son Banquet. Reverend Julian Cowell is the present pastor at the church.

The Berwick Baptist Church has withstood wars, economic hard times and the test of time. The spirit of the living Christ abides at the center of this church.

Berwick Baptist Church remodeled in 1909 and 1919.

Coldbrook Christian Church
(Disciples Of Christ)

The first church of the Christian denomination in Warren County was organized at the little settlement of Savannah with records going back to 1831. This site was one mile north and one half mile west of the present village of Cameron. The name was later changed to Coldbrook because of a near by cold stream. The members met at homes until 1838 when the first church building was erected. In the spring of 1839, forty-three persons who lived on the north side of Cedar Creek asked to be released from the Savannah church because of difficulty crossing the creek during flood times. Permission being granted, the group of forty-three left to form a new church. After the railroad went through, the remaining members of the Savannah church moved to Cameron and became the Cameron Christian Church.

The new Talbot Creek Church was organized at the home of William Hopper on March 3, 1839, Early meetings were held at a schoolhouse in Section 12 of Monmouth Township and at Morrow's Meeting House. In 1845, a church was built by David Morrow on land about one half mile west of the Mosher Cemetery. This building was used until 1859 when it was decided to move further east to the present location of the Coldbrook Church, The new church was built for $1000 and stood just a few feet west of where the present building stands. About this same time, a group of members, by mutual agreement, left Talbot Creek Church to form Mauck's Grove Christian Church, now Gerlaw Christian Church.

In 1895, a much larger and more modern church building costing about $4,000 was built at the same location. The auditorium, which seated two hundred fifty, was handsomely decorated, the carpeted floor was laid on an incline and the ceiling had a large circular dome from which hung a chandelier. In that same year, the Christian Women's Missionary Society and the Christian Endeavor Young People's Group were organized. In the early 1900s, Sunday School Classes were started for the "Loyal Men and Women", the "Loyal Daughters" and the "Loyal Sons". In 1921, the Just-A-Mere Sunday School Class was organized. A memorial table and benches sit outside the west entrance to the present church to honor the fifty-five years of service the Just-A-Mere Class gave to the church and community. During the period from 1904 to 1916, the church changed its name five times, switching from Talbot Creek to Cold Brook to Talbots Creek Christian to Coldbrook Christian and back again to Talbot Creek Christian Church. The adoption of the constitution on February 18, 1940 made Coldbrook Christian Church the official name.

Coldbrook Church (Second building on this site) Burned February 12, 1939 R. E. Mangers - Pastor

In October of 1925, the Coldbrook Women's Club was organized. This organization not only provided social life for the women of the church, but it also raised many dollars for repairs, remodeling and extras needed at the church and parsonage. A new class for young married couples, the Twentieth Century Class, was organized in 1932. During these same years the church opened a new parking lot, wired for electricity, redecorated the church interior and in 1938 installed a new furnace with a blower.

On February 12, 1939, just three weeks before the church would celebrate its one hundredth anniversary, the building caught fire and burned to the ground. Almost immediately it was decided to rebuild. Services were held in Lucas School and in the church parsonage while construction was in progress. On February 11, 1940, just one year after the old church burned, the new red brick church was dedicated. In 1946, the Whatsoever Sunday School Class was organized and in 1947 an electric organ was installed as a memorial to the 46 men and women of the community who had served their country. A new parsonage was constructed in 1954 and the Pairs and Spares Sunday School Class was organized in 1959. In 1964, the church not only celebrated its one hundred twenty-fifth anniversary, but also dedicated a new education wing. In 1976, another new class, the Good News Sunday School Class was organized. In 1978, a major change was made in the way the church operated. The church board was changed to a rotating board and for the first time, women could be elected to the board. In 1989, a sesquicentennial celebration was held. Many of the participants were descendants of the original forty-three church members. In 1992, the newest class, the Genesis Sunday School Class was organized. A new sound system was installed in 1998 and in 2001, a handicapped accessible addition containing an elevator was erected on the north side of the church building. Also in 2001, the church hired its first woman minister. Forty-eight ministers have served the Coldbrook Christian Church as pastors or interims in its 163 years of existence.

Present Coldbrook Christian Church

Countryside Bible Church

On the first Sunday of January 1979, a group of families started an independent bible church. The founding families include: Robert Jr. and Bonnie Cozadd, Carl and Harriet Ewing, Gary and Sherry Fernald, Ronald and Carol LeGate, David and Janet Meling, John and Wanda Ryner, Richard and Irene Stevenson, Janet Talley, Kent and Katherine Willis and Lyle and Kathleen Worthington. Inspired by the expository teachings of Larry Moyer, an Evantell evangelist, their mission became to provide their community "the Bible as it is, for people as they are."

From humble beginnings of meeting in a family's garage, to holding services in a room at Meling's Restaurant and Motel, as well as the National Bank's Colonial Room, Countryside Bible Church eventually found its home on the corner of U.S. Hwy. 67 and Gerlaw Road in Monmouth, IL. In the fall of 1979, the families of Countryside proudly completed hours of hard labor on their new church. A Huskee-Bilt prefabricated structure, erected almost entirely by the Countryside families, accommodated the ever-growing congregation. The very first church service with a modest 37 people, back in January 1979, had grown to over three times that number when they completed their building that fall. Equipped with pews purchased from Colonial Baptist Church in Galesburg, and a donated electric organ and piano, Countryside has had to make few changes to the building over the years.

The inspiration of Larry Moyer continued as the search for a pastor began. A student of Dallas Theological Seminary was recommended to visit Countryside and later became its first pastor from 1979 until 1986. Roger Coulter, a native of Peoria, IL cultivated the basic beliefs originally inspired by Moyer within the congregation. Countryside, formed as a fellowship of believers in the Lordship of Jesus Christ, founded their belief in the deity of Jesus Christ, salvation solely through faith in Jesus Christ and the Bible as the inerrant word of God.

Following Roger Coulter, Richard Shaw became Countryside's interim pastor from 1986 until 1988. Pastor Shaw, from Burlington, IA, continued the church's mission and traditions. Countryside continued to uphold the mission to serve Christ. Countryside's Sunday morning Bible School for all ages, and church services that reach families of the greater Monmouth area, still continue today. The church family consists of believers from such neighboring communities as Alexis, Galesburg, Gerlaw, Kirkwood, Little York, Monmouth, Roseville and Swan Creek.

Currently, Pastor Kenneth A. Muck, also a graduate of Dallas Theological Seminary, has been Countryside's pastor since 1988. Originally from Erie, PA, Pastor Muck has spent the last 14 years with Countryside. He has seen the church support six missionaries annually including, Christian Friendliness, a Christian youth center in Moline, IL; Ben Long, a Navigators missionary; Larry Moyer, an Evantell evangelist; John Stark, a Seminary School student; Starting Point, a Christian habilitation home in Monmouth, IL and Harry Walker, an Unevangalized Field Missionary.

Pastor Muck has been a witness as the founding Countryside family's second generation, along with others, continues what their parents began in 1979. As their commitment to knowing Christ and making Him known to their community only strengthens through the years, so does their desire to relate the bible as the true word of God.

The year 2002 sees Countryside in the same building with many of the same faces in its pews plus many more. In 2004, Countryside will celebrate its 25th Anniversary. Larry Moyer, who has remained a spiritual guidance to Countryside's families since its very beginnings, will be attending this special celebration, as well as many families that have been a part of Countryside's history.

Countryside Bible Church with congregation

Fairview Center United Methodist Church

Brothers, Henry and Jacob Miller were members of the United Brethren Church in Lewis County, West Virginia. Henry and Mary Miller and family first came to Knox County, Illinois in 1856. After one year they moved to a farm near Berwick in Warren County. Six years later they came to the Ormonde area. This would have been about 1862. These are the dates recorded in the obituary of Henry's son, John, an active member of the church from its beginning until his death in 1916.

For the Jacob Miller family, the exact date of their arrival to Warren County from West Virginia is unknown. Jacob was married to Mariah Efaw.

According to the 1903 Warren County History, Jonas Holgate arrived in New York in May of 1857 from Yorkshire, England, where he was born in 1835. one month later, he, with a brother, Thomas, began farming near Larchland. He married Mary Smith, who was from Virginia.

The three families, the Henry and Jacob Millers and the Jonas Holgates, are the known charter members of the United Brethren Class that was organized around 1862 and later met in the Center School house.

According to the 1931 history of Fairview Center by pastor W. H. Arbogast, "In 1870 the two brothers, Henry and Jacob Miller, largely through their own efforts, erected the church building known as the Larchland United Brethren Church," located on the northwest corner one mile south and one mile west of the present church.

Several descendants of Henry and Jacob Miller remain as members today.

There are no descendants of the Holgates in the present church. Gracie Peterson is a descendant as is the family of Frank Long, who always attend church when in the area.

The earliest membership book dates from 1872 when the church with 58 members was a part of the Ellison Circuit and in 1893 a part of the Roseville Mission Circuit. In 1904 it was known as Larchland Station.

In the center of Lenox township, which is also the center of Warren County, "in 1910 a new location for the church was secured and a new building was erected, and renamed Fairview Center United Brethren Church and dedicated October 23, 1910 by Rev. J. M. Phillipi. In 1916 the parsonage location was secured and the parsonage erected. Cost $3000," (quoting Dr. Arbogast). The cost of the church was approximately $6000. Mr. William Rinker and his two sons, Oscar and John from Monmouth were contracted to do the work. Oscar's wife cooked their meals and they all lived in a temporary cabin on the site. The Center school children across the road, north would watch all the activity at recesses.

In 1953 the steeple was removed, the sanctuary enlarged, and the Fairview Center Church building changed from frame to brick. The Sunday School addition and new parsonage were built with the dedication in 1980. one acre of ground to the east was added for a playground in 1941 and another acre in 1960 for a ball diamond.

In 1947 with a denominational merger, Fairview Center became Evangelical United Brethren and in 1968, United Methodist. In 140 years under three denominational banners, 54 pastors have served. The present church membership is 279 with an average attendance of 99.

Fairview Center Evangelical United Brethern

Faith United Presbyterian Church

Faith United Presbyterian Church

Faith United Presbyterian Church resulted from the merger of four separate but similar congregations whose individual roots are more than 160 years deep in Monmouth's spiritual history.

At simultaneous meetings on Nov. 17, 1963, the former First, Second, Grace and Ninth Avenue United Presbyterian churches voted to join in the union that created Faith Church. West Side United Presbyterian chose to remain independent.

The Rev. L.B. Bell, a Presbyterian circuit-riding minister., established the first organized church in Monmouth with 16 members. The First Presbyterian Church held its first service in 1837, only six years after Monmouth original town plat was surveyed and two years before another denomination organized the village's second church.

Until 1839, when the Rev. Samuel Wilson was installed as the church's first resident pastor, Rev. Bell and four other itinerant preachers alternated as "supply pastors" of the small parish.

Before 1842, when a small frame church was built on South 1st St., Sunday worship was conducted in various locations, including a dry goods store and the American hotel. But as Monmouth's population grew so did church membership and a larger sanctuary was built in 1851. That structure was replaced in 1882 by a large Gothic building with manse attached on East 1st Ave. between South 2nd and 3rd Streets.

Following the national merger uniting the Presbyterian and United Presbyterian denominations in 1958, First Presbyterian became Grace United Presbyterian.

Monmouth already had a First United U. P. church established in 1853 with 21 charter members. Separation of church and state was not yet an issue and the new church held Sunday worship in the county court house until 1856, when a new sanctuary was built on W. Broadway at N. B St. In 1890 it was replaced by a sandstone building with imposing tower on E. Broadway at N. 2nd Street.

Dr. David A. Wallace, first president of Monmouth College, was chairman of a committee that organized Second United Presbyterian Church in 1862, a decade after the college received its charter. Establishing a close relationship between college and church, Dr. Wallace also became the new parish's co-pastor.

After meeting in the college chapel and at the homes of various parishioners, the congregation moved into a building of its own in 1867, replacing it in 1879 with the graceful building of colonial architecture on E. 1st Ave. at S. 8th St. that now is a part of Faith Church.

Ninth Avenue U. P. Church started as an outreach mission that grew out of the Christian education program at Second Church, with H. P. Espy, assistant pastor, as its administrator. In 1895, the mission was reorganized as Ninth Avenue Church, with Rev. J. F. Jamieson, its first pastor, serving the congregation until he retired in 1909. His successor was Rev. F. S. McBride, who later became national president of the Anti-Saloon League.

When the members of four congregations with the same religious beliefs but different social and spiritual backgrounds voted to join as one they did so because they had faith that God would guide them into a stronger and more relevant church at a time in history when much of the world was in idealistic turmoil.

For each disagreement that arose a satisfactory solution followed, including a decision on which of the existing buildings was to become a part of the new Faith Church. While the choice was being debated, Sunday worship rotated among the churches, with administrative offices and Sunday School located in the former Second Church.

The choice of a permanent location was between Grace and Second, the two largest churches both in available space and membership. Each was well maintained and, in its own way, a distinctive structure with unique advantages over the other.

Second Church had recently completed a new church school addition and was generally considered the most architecturally appealing, but Grace Church had a more beautiful and convenient sanctuary, recently remodeled.

What could have become crippling rift was settled amicably when the Grace Church chancel, focal point of an elegant sanctuary, was dismantled, panel-by-panel, and restored exactly as before in the new Faith Church sanctuary built south of the former Second Church. The compromise incorporated the most beloved features of both churches without dividing the members.

Ninth Avenue Church has continued to serve as a community center named in honor of Rev. Jamieson, its first pastor. The former First U.P. Church was purchased by the West Side congregation and became Heritage United Presbyterian Church. The Masonic Hall now occupies the West Side building.

Church services at Faith are committed to spreading the word of Christ through spoken words in a strong ministry, and in song, thanks to a choir of talented musicians.

Christian education is stressed both on Sundays and through a midweek youth program. A wide variety of adult activities and social organizations fill its calendar, and Faith Church's mission outreach serves the spiritual and personal needs of a less fortunate constituency both in Monmouth and as far away as India.

The church was responsible for starting and continues to support Jamieson Center, and its members also have been generous in helping maintain such agencies as Starting Point, a shelter for indigents in search of new beginnings; Achievement Industries, a workshop facility for the handicapped, and many other worthwhile charities.

One of the most notable accomplishments of Faith is Kandathankulum, a village in southern India, where the generosity of members has served an entire community by providing food and clothing, building a new school, digging a water well, and most recently, raising and donating money to build a health clinic and establishing an endowment to pay a doctor and nurse to attend to the medical needs of the village.

The Rev. William Myers, current pastor of Faith Church, is a native of Moline and 1985 graduate of Monmouth College with a Master of Divinity degree from Princeton Theological Seminary.

First Christian Church of Monmouth

First Christian Church, Monmouth 1893-1953

On March 31, 1839 the First Christian Church originated in Monmouth when 22 persons received letters of transfer from the First Church Of Christ in Warren County at Savannah (later Coldbrook) located 6 miles east of Monmouth, which in 1873 moved to Cameron. This church was formed in 1831 after Alexander Campbell's example in Virginia-being "Christians Only" with no creed but the Bible and following the pattern of the New Testament church. Originally from Bourbon County, Kentucky, pioneer charter members meeting at Peter Butler's home were William C. Whitman, Henry C. Haley, Elijah Davidson, Henry Meadows, John C. Haley, Stephen Howard, Josiah Whitman and their wives. They relied on themselves for leadership and trained others to establish more congregations, which was done at Talbot Creek (now Coldbrook), Hendersonville (Schuyler County), Meridian, Jacksonville, and Monmouth. William C. Whitman and Alexander Reynolds were early ministers. Some members went on a wagon train, 1853, to Oregon helping to establish Monmouth, Oregon along with a Christian Church and a college.

To Monmouth were sent three organizing elders - Pliny Hatchitt, Livy Hatchitt, and James R. Ross with 19 charter members - Hezekiah (elder) and Eleanor Davidson, Alexander (elder) and Rachael Davidson, Elijah (clerk) and Mary Davidson, William and Rebecca Butler, William C. and Ann Hall, Jacob L. and Nancy Buzan, James Hodgen, Amelia Ann Davidson, Solomon Davidson, Thomas Davidson, William Davidson, Elizabeth Davidson and Nancy Davidson.

In 163 years the congregation has constructed four church buildings. After having meetings in the courthouse, school houses and a second floor hall on the north east corner of the public square, in 1841 they built the first church building in Monmouth for $800 at the southwest corner of North 2nd Street and East Archer Avenue, the lot deeded to them by Elijah Davidson January 16, 1841. Also used as a schoolhouse Monmouth College had classes there in 1853. N.A. Rankin gave them the first church bell in Monmouth. With remodeling and additions it was used in later years by various motor companies and recently torn down for Security Savings Bank's parking lot-may have been the oldest building in town.

With 327 members in 1858 a larger church was needed. November 16, 1859 Alonzo W. Dewey issued a warranty deed for $750 to Josiah Whitman, Nathaniel A. Rankin and Lawrence Douglas, trustees, for a lot at the southeast corner of South First Street and East Second Ave. In 1860 contractor R. A. Davies erected a frame building 40 x 65 ft. for $4700. Isaac Errett, founder and for years editor of The Christian Standard in Cincinnati gave the sermon at dedication March 10, 1861. In 1871 T. V. Berry, minister, did much repair.

On same site, dedication of third building occurred Dec. 31, 1893. It was of brick and stone, 63 x 90 ft. cost $13000, O.A. Bartholomew, architect, E. L. Gibbler, contractor. At the entrance a square tower topped with an open observatory with 10 ft. columns supported a pinnacled roof and ornamental apex about 70 ft. from the ground. In 1910 the spire was lowered to tower brick walls and in 1938 the tower completely removed with new entrance and vestibule constructed. During these years, in 1908 600 members and in 1922 had one of finest bible schools in U. S. - 400 members.

Due to deterioration, in 1942 plans began to build again on the same site. On May 3, 1953 the last service was held in the old building. It was soon razed and the new limestone was constructed by architect C.R. Miller & Sons, Decatur IL. various contractors and much volunteer labor-cost $120,000. First service was held Nov. 21, 1954 and dedication March 20, 1955. During construction the congregation met in the Monmouth College Chapel - 100 years earlier the college had used the church building for classes. In 1971 an education wing was added and later a parking lot. A parsonage at 223 South 2nd Street was purchased in 1928 and sold in 1939 when one bought at 229 East 2nd Avenue. In 1964 a new parsonage was built at that site and in 1967 a 2nd parsonage bought at 312 South 2nd Street.

Since 1839, 27 ministers have served the congregation-James E. Gaston, J.W.Matlock, J.W. Butler, L.S. Wallace (1965), John Errett, A J. Aten, Frances M. Bruner, John LaGrange, Thomas V. Berry '75, J.M. Williams, A.J. Cane, Lansence S. Wallace, N.E. Corley, John W. Kelsey, A.W. Kidd, Marion Stevenson '88, W.A. Meloan '91, C.S. Stearns '99, Delaney E. Hughes '99-'14, Guy V. Ferguson '14-'22, Ivan W. Agee, John Givens, C.P. Snyder '28-'31, Frank W. Leonard '31-'46, Orville L. Wright '46-'56, Ellis B. Beeman '57-'89, and James C. Epperson-present time. Since 1961 there have been 17 youth and/or associate ministers-presently Lewis Smith, associate and Nathan Cooper, youth.

With a membership of 400 having three worship services each Sunday and activities for all ages, the church hopes to construct a new building in the near future at 516 North Sunny Lane continuing to reach out to the community and world with the Gospel of Jesus Christ.

First Christian Church, Monmouth, 1954-Present

First Lutheran Church

In 1853 a group of Swedish immigrants gathered to worship, at the courthouse in Monmouth, under the pastoral leadership of The Rev. T.N. Hasselquist. Dr. Hasselquist served First Lutheran Church in Galesburg. In 1859 a congregation was organized and duly recorded. For four years the small congregation (13 communicants) kept its doors open. However, those were hard times and when Pastor Hasselquist left Galesburg for Paxton, the efforts halted. However, the dream lived on.

A new beginning began February 2, 1868. Fifteen communicants signed their names to the charter roll of the Swedish Evangelical Lutheran congregation in Monmouth of Warren County, Illinois. They had a baptized membership of 40. John Beck, Olof Nelson, Oscar Nelson and N. Holm were elected deacons. Peter Ringdahl, Gustaf Weddelin and Johannes Jacobson were chosen trustees.

There was no resident pastor during the first eight years. Assistance was obtained from neighboring clergy, including Pastor H. Olson of New Sweden, Iowa. However, the members were very faithful. A frame structure, 34 feet in width, 50 feet long and 18 feet high was erected in 1870. Its cost, $886.80, was fully subscribed by the members and the lot was donated. Located in a hollow just a short walk from town, its address in Monmouth today would be 200 South "E" Street. That structure, with enlargements and remodeling, served the congregation until 1914.

The first resident ordained pastor was Rev. Elias Peterson, 1877-1878. After a six year vacancy, Rev. J.E. Floren was pastor for two years. Then, on March 13, 1887, a Call was sent to Rev, August Johnson who was serving at Andover, IL.. He accepted and began his ministry the first Sunday in September 1887. He served until 1907. Subsequent pastors include T.A. Conrad, Oscar Purn, A.T. Lorimer, C.R.E Friedstrom, H.R. Ekerberg, Gerald K. Johnson, Raymond Swanson, Gerald Youngquist and David Johnson. Rev. Frank Moyer served as interim beginning in June 2001.

In the early 1900s, church members became divided over the need to erect a new structure. The Rock Island Southern line tracks were just west of the church and frequent trains interrupted services. In 1909 Mr. A.L. Martin said at a Men's Society meeting: "I think, too, that within a year from now we will have another track outside here, and if they are going to have a ball park on this new railroad, and Sunday games and Company H is going to have a shooting gallery out this way, too, it will make more noise and travel ... and will be most unpleasant. I think it would be the wisest plan to move away from it, and do it just as soon as we can."

A lot, at the corner of West First Avenue and South B Street was purchased in 1912 for $4,700. The foundation was laid in the fall of 1912 and dedication of the new church was February 8, 1914. The total cost, including the land, was $52,504.26.

The architecture of the new structure is Gothic. The main structure is 104 feet long and 64 feet wide. It has two towers; the highest is 132 feet and the other is 106 feet. The walls are of Bedford, IN. stone and Danville, IL. brick and the inside is oak. It has three large stained glass windows, with emblems representing the Holy Trinity; and it has several smaller stained glass windows with "Christ Knocking", "Christ in Gethsemane", "The Good Shepherd", "Saint Paul", "Saint John", and a large flower window above the balcony. The majestic altar, with a full statue of Christ and the Lord's Supper in relief, serve as the focal point of worship.

The inscription on the cornerstone includes the words: "Sola fide". Latin for "faith only", it served as the major principle for Martin Luther and the Reformation. As one former pastor stated, these words are of timeless value to those seeking salvation.

The congregation was the only foreign language church in town for many years. The Swedish language was used in services until the 1920s. As was true for many others, the church doors were closed for several weeks in November-December 1918 due to the influenza epidemic.

In 1957 the congregation voted to build an educational wing, located immediately to the north of the church. This building has also housed the Lutheran Day Care and PreSchool, which was begun in 1974.

Music always holds an important place for Lutherans in worship. In the early 1900s, First Lutheran installed a $9,000 pipe organ in the first structure and later moved it to the current facility. After more than eight decades of use, a new pipe organ was installed in 1989. In addition to fine organ music, the congregation enjoys a choir, a bell choir, and annually hosts several local choral ensembles.

As First Lutheran Church enters the 21st century, she faces new challenges and opportunities. Monmouth and Warren County are different than they were in the 1860s. Today's immigrants are usually not from Sweden; large farms have replaced the small acreages which supported so many of the early members; and, multiple other voices compete for the attention of her residents. Yet, sola fide still serves as the cornerstone for her ministries. The message of Christ is still the foundation for hope as we meet these tasks.

First Lutheran Church, Monmouth.

Foursquare Gospel Church

Foursquare Gospel Church - Monmouth

In May of 1942, on the corner of 8th Avenue and South Main Street, a gospel tent was erected. This revival laid the groundwork for what today is called the Foursquare Gospel Church. The evangelists were Rev. and Mrs. Carl Folk, Rev. and Mrs. Fred Steinman, and Rev. and Mrs. Harold Morgan. Changed lives and a hunger for more of God punctuated this outreach.

In the fall of 1942, Kelly's Garage just off South 1st Street behind the Christy Hotel was acquired, and Miss Velma Egley assisted the Rev. and Mrs Folk at the "Gospel Center." In the early part of 1944 a move was made to the Johnson Building, 221 South First Street.

New pastors Rev. and Mrs. W. J. Stevens, helped the congregation change its name "to "Christian Tabernacle." 1944-49 saw several pastoral changes with Rev. and Mrs Bruce Sholes, Rev. and Mrs Joe Watkins, Rev. and Mrs Roth, Rev. and Mrs Archie Wilson.

In 1947-48 the congregation of the Christian Tabernacle looked into joining a denomination. In late 1948 after corresponding with various groups, the Great Lakes District of Foursquare Churches was approached. An agreement was reached for the organization to purchase all equipment and property from Rev. Stevens. The church became part of the International Church of the Foursquare Gospel.

In January of 1949 Rev and Mrs William Schafer were appointed as pastors of the church. The name was changed to the "Foursquare Christian Tabernacle," later the "Foursquare Tabernacle," and now the "Foursquare Gospel Church."

In May of 1949 a lot at 416 West Fourth Avenue was purchased, leaving $23.00 in the treasury. By faith the work of construction began. Volunteer labor with a tractor and blade, donated by the Galusha family, dug the basement. On May 21, 1949 the footings were poured.

This Foursquare Family worked side by side with help from area congregations throughout the hot summer and fall. Most men worked full time jobs, and the evening work often lasted another 6-7 hours. Despite the limited time there was NEVER work on Sunday! Their vision and dream was beginning to take shape. The building was erected with a total investment of $13,000.00. It could not have been done on a contract basis for under $30,000.00.

On November 20, 1949, those taking part in the dedication service were Rev. and Mrs. Wm. Schafer, church pastor; Rev. James Skinner, Pastor Oquawka Christian Tabernacle; Rev. John Vail, Pastor Ninth Avenue U. P. Church; Rev. John Kern, Pastor First Baptist Church; Rev. C. K. Sparks, Pastor Church of the Nazarene; Mr. Ralph Wells, Mayor of Monmouth; and Mr Charles Nichols of Kirkwood.

Pastoral Assignments:

January 1949 - June 1951, Rev. and Mrs William Schafer - Building erected.

June of 1951 - November 1954, Rev. and Mrs Leroy Bussinger. - An attendance of 225 on Easter of 1953.

November 1954 - June 1958, Rev. and Mrs. Herman Rosenberger - Steady growth and maturity of the body continued through their ministry.

June 1958 - July 1962, Rev. and Mrs. Dan Howse. A new record of 303 in attendance was set on Easter Sunday 1962. Home purchased on Pine Park. The Howse family left to become missionaries in the Phillipines.

July 1962 - November 1963, Rev. and Mrs. Otis Ewbank continued solid teaching and preaching.

November 1963 - 1968, Rev and Mrs. Delmar Walker. Previous remodeling was completed. The home of Miss Wilma Walker was donated in 1966, and the parsonage was sold completely dissolving the church indebtedness.

1968 - November 1972, Rev. and Mrs. Stanley Rogers. New seating paneling, pulpit, and Communion Table, purchased.

August 1971 Rev and Mrs Marlow began assisting.

January 1973 - November 1974 Rev. and Mrs. Harry Poling arrived, and many more improvements, including a paved parking lot, glass front doors, and complete basement remodeling were done.

November 1974 - Summer 1984, Rev. and Mrs. Tom Smith. An adjoining property owned by the Greenlief family was purchased. In 1977, the church body became involved in a food tent at Fall Festival which led to great times of fellowship and memorable experiences.

October 1982 saw the church begin broadcasting on WMOI live every Sunday morning (moved to WRAM in 2001).

November 1982 brought the "Community Thanksgiving Dinner." Richard and Joan McVey began the event with church support, and that of many other Monmouth residents. It remains a vital ministry and, a true community project. In March of 1983 the Foursquare Soup Kitchen was established and still operates.

Summer 1984 - September of 1989 Rev. and Mrs. Paul Griffis became pastors and saw much spiritual growth take place.

September 1989 - August of 1996 Rev. and Mrs. Chandler West as pastors. During their tenure, a Good News Bears program was established to begin reaching out to age 4 years to 6th grade children of the community.

August 1996 - Present, Rev. and Mrs. Gerald Marlow, The church body initiated several outreaches, resulting in lives of many youth being touched for eternity.

Gerlaw Christian Church
Disciples of Christ
Gerlaw, Illinois

Gerlaw Christian Church

The first church in the area was the Church of Christ, which was organized in April, 1831. Meetings were held in the homes of the early settlers, in groves and in school houses, as they were built. In February of 1838 the congregation met in Savannah and decided to build a chapel there. Savannah was located north and west of Cameron, along what is now known as Cedar Creek. In March of 1839 a group asked permission to be released from the Church of Christ, in order to build a church on the north side of Cedar Creek. This church was known as the Talbot Creek Church. In the spring of 1859 this church ,"mothered" the Mauck's Grove Church, now known as the Gerlaw Christian Church.

The new congregation consisted of 29 charter members, representing 12 families, who had been members of the Christian Church in other states and were attending church at Savanna, decided to build at Mauck's Grove. Now Mauck's Grove was about 1 1/2 miles East and North 1 1/2 miles of the village of Gerlaw, in Spring Grove Township. The Grove was named after a well liked gentleman by the name of Captain Peter Mauck. He had owned the 80 acres until 1855, but in 1859 the Grove was owned by Robert Lair, one of the charter members of the church.

The first service in the new building was June 20, 1859 with 29 members. Thirty five more joined the following Sunday. By the year 1871, the Rockford, Rock Island railroad had built a line through the community, and the village of Gerlaw was laid out and declared a town site, on May 2, 1871.

By the year 1873, many of the elder members had passed away, and many of the younger people joined a wagon train, heading West, and settled in Monmouth, Oregon. The remaining members of Mauck's Grove Church agreed they should move the church building into town. Robert Gerlaw and his wife, each gave a lot on which to put the church. The move into town was in September of 1873. The building was repaired and some improvements made and the congregation re-organized, with 29 members, the same number that started at Mauck's Grove. It is possible at this time the name was changed from Mauck's Grove to Christian Church of Gerlaw.

In 1876 the first Sunday School was organized, meeting on Sunday afternoons, with John Newton Carson as its superintendent. The work of the church was of vital interest to him, and he also served long as an elder. To this day, his great grandson, Marvin Lee Carson of Gerlaw, is an elder emeritus, and a great-great grandson, Robert Lee Carson of Gerlaw, is an elder. Both are faithful members of the Gerlaw Christian Church.

In 1880 the Women's Missionary Society was organized. This society is now called Christian Women's Fellowship. In 1887, over a 3 week period, meetings were held and there were 25 additions to the congregation. In 1890 the first organ was purchased. In 1894 more meeting were held. This time 60 members were added to the membership.

By the summer of 1894 the congregation felt the need for a larger and more convenient house of worship. A contract was let to John Foust. John was a carpenter from Gerlaw and a member of the Gerlaw Christian Church. Some of his tools have been given to the church and are on display for interested persons to look at. Mr. Foust received $2028.00. The masonry and foundation cost $225.00, windows $307.57, seats and pulpit were $321.40, furnace $200.00, carpet and draperies $156.20 and paint $175.00. Total cost of the new, larger, and improved building being $3630.00. On the eve before the dedication $250.00 was still owed. The women donated $100.00 and the building committee paid the rest. The church was dedicated debt free.

During the First World War, 18 young men from this small church served their country.

In 1904 Gerlaw's only missionary, Rollin McCoy, was ordained, and he and his wife, left for Japan, remaining there 38 years. Upon returning to the Gerlaw area, they immediately renewed their ties with the church. Both served as teachers and Rollin served as an elder.

Again, during World War II, several young men left to serve their country and all returned home safely.

The church building has seen many changes through the years. We have replaced the "2 holer" with modern plumbing; gone from coal to central air; replaced the cement baptistery, dynamite was used to break it into smaller pieces, with a fiberglass one; several new roofs; new siding; new lighting; a sound system. The church has been served by 55 ministers since L. S. Wallace served at Mauck's Grove. The church has been served by single men, married men, women, husband/wife, student ministers and several interim ministers.

What makes the Gerlaw Christian Church special? The Gerlaw Christian Church is a loving and caring family congregation. Sunday School and worship are the primary ministries of the congregation, providing excellent and inspiring opportunities to learn about Jesus Christ, to praise God, and to grow in our faith.

As we look back, we can clearly see ours is a rich heritage, given to us by those who have so faithfully carried on the work of this church. May those who follow in their footsteps, be loyal to the Word of God, so the light of the Gospel may ever shine steadfastly in the community.

You are invited to be a part of this church no matter where you may be, on your faith journey. *Submitted by Pat Carson Church Historian*

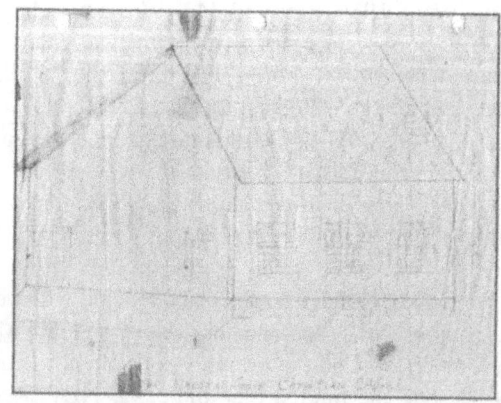
Pencil drawing Mauk's Grove Christian Church

Immaculate Conception Roman Catholic Church
Monmouth, Il

Immaculate Conception Catholic Church, Monmouth 1920.

The first Catholic Church in Monmouth, known then as the Church of the Epiphany, was built at Boston Avenue and C Street in 1864. This simple frame structure served the needs of the Catholics of the area, who had, up to this time, been attended by priests from St. Louis, Chicago, and later, Galesburg.

The first recorded priest to visit Monmouth was Father O'Neil of Galesburg, who came in 1857 and offered Mass in various homes until construction of the church in 1864. The first resident pastor of Epiphany Parish was Father Joseph D. Bowles who came in 1869 and remained until 1872.

Father Michael Luby, who served until 1873 when Father James Halpin succeeded him, succeeded Fr. Bowles, Father Halpin organized St. Patrick's in Raritan during his pastorate at Epiphany.

In 1876 Father Thomas O'Farrell succeeded Father Halpin and served to 1878 when Fathers Michael Weldon and Will Murphy were appointed. Father O'Farrell organized St. Theresa's Parish in Alexis during his pastorate at Epiphany.

After Father F. C. Duffy was assigned to Monmouth in 1882, he directed the construction of a new church on West Broadway. Bishop John L. Spalding dedicated the building in 1884.

Father Martin Kelly served the parish from 1887 to 1892. During this time Fr. Kelly purchased land for St. Mary Cemetery.

For many years the rectory was located three blocks from the new church. In the pastorate of Father P.P. Owens, who served the renamed Immaculate Conception Parish from 1893 to 1927, a brick rectory was built next to the church in 1908.

In September, 1914, the parish school was opened. A private residence was used until a school building could be built.

An overheated furnace in the church basement caused a fire that ruined the church in January of 1918. In a few months the church was rebuilt and blessed.

The cornerstone for the first school building was laid in 1919 and by 1920 it was ready for classes. Until 1926 high school courses were offered.

Msgr. W. J. Drummy became the pastor in June of 1927. Msgr. Edward S. Dunn was appointed to the pastorate in February of 1940 and he served until his death in 1955. Father Thomas P. Kelly who served until 1957 when Father Martin J. Spalding was appointed to succeed him.

In June of 1960 Father Harold Prendergast was appointed. In September of that year tuckpointing of the church was begun and a new entrance was built. In October of 1961 a new garage was added to rear of the rectory. Soon after the garage was built work began on the new Immaculate Conception School and gym.

In 1964 the old school was torn down and a blacktop playground was made and 10 acres of cemetery property was cleared and prepared for crop production. In June of that year two rooms were added to the rectory over the garage and in December the old convent on South B Street was sold. A breezeway was constructed between the school and the convent in 1969 and the convent also received a new chapel. Two classrooms and a library were added to the school in 1966. In October of 1970 Bishop John B. Franz invested Father Prendergast as a Monsignor. He served the parish until his retirement in 1980.

At that time Father John Podlashes was appointed administrator of Immaculate Conception Parish. Two years later he was named pastor. He continued to serve the parish until his death in January of 1991.

In May of 1991 Father Thomas Mack was appointed pastor. The church was renovated in 1995. In November of 1997 Father Ronald Enderlin was appointed pastor and continues in that role.

Immaculate Conception Catholic Church, Monmouth 2002.

Kirkwood United Methodist Church

Old M. E. Church, Kirkwood

The first meeting of the Methodists in the Young America area, later to be called Kirkwood, was on the 11th of February 1850. It was held at the White's School House. The school stood some two and a half miles east of where the village now stands. Settlers gathered under a grove of trees and a worship service was conducted by the Rev. O. Swartz,

During the next few years meetings were conducted irregularly and at various sites by "circuit riders" or itenerant pastors who would gather a group of worshippers together at various homesteads in the area. Young America became a part of the "Ellison Circuit." In fair weather the meeting place of choice was in a grove of trees on the Lemuel Tubbs property. He was the father of the Rev. James Tubbs, the first pastor of the church.

Rev. L. Kerns was named the first pastor of the Ellison Circuit. He was followed in 1857 by the Rev. W. J. Beck and then by the Rev. A. C. Higgins and then Rev. W. B. Morse. The Ellison community was almost totally destroyed in 1858 by a tornado. The Reverend Beck's wife was killed during the storm.

Young America soon became a thriving community and a need was felt to organize the church into a congregation. A "Class" (the people who wished to form a congregation) was soon organized. The people met in several locations in the area.

The Presbyterian Congregation erected a house of worship on Harding Street. For a time the Methodist and the Presbyterian congregations met in the same building on alternate Sundays.

In 1860 the "Class" felt that they had enough members to organize a separate congregation. The organization consisted of thirteen members. These "charter members" organized what is now the present congregation. These members were: John and Elizabeth Ramsdell, Mary E. Yeoman, Daniel and Martha Tinker, Oliver, Henry and Emily Fall, William and Margaret Roberts, Ira Barnum and Merritt and Lavinia Paddock. Lavinia, known as "Aunt Polly" Paddock was the only charter member still living when the present church building was dedicated in 1912.

The church was still without a parsonage in 1865. The devoted early church members prayed that their dream of a home for a pastor might become a reality. The congregation voted on March 20, 1865 to start construction of a parsonage. A building committee was established and plans were formulated for the building. A site was secured and most important, funds were raised for the project. The committee also became the first trustees of the new congregation. Thus the prayers of the new congregation were answered.

At this time the salary of Pastor Tubbs was $450.00 a year. The search for a suitable site for the parsonage and a church was located at the corner of Kellogg and Locust. The cost of this site was $300.00. The contract for the church building was signed with G. G. Balcon of Galesburg for $5,600.00. Many forms of money raising were used and in February 1866 the new church was dedicated free of debt, to the Glory of God.

This church building was used for 42 years and in 1908 a decision was made to build the present church. The congregation met for the next year and a half in the Gamble Hall. S R. Badgley, an architect from Cleveland, Ohio designed the new building. On August 1, 1911 the general contract was placed with Apsey and Fusch, contractors from Monmouth, Illinois. The cornerstone was laid November 11, 1911. The formal dedication took place on December 1, 1912. The cost of the building was $35,000.00

After many years of planning, a new parsonage was constructed in July of 1955. Many members of the church assisted in the construction. It was dedicated on March 11, 1956. A new organ was dedicated in the church on June 30, 1951.

In the summer of 1984, the congregation observed the special 200th celebration of Methodism in America. The special service was held in the grove of the home of Mrs Glenn Smith, the site of the first "Camp Meetings". The church still has several 5th and 6th generation children of the early charter members. It has had over 46 different pastors.

The congregation from Kirkwood joined the Smithshire Methodist church in 1960 to become one charge. In 1999 the Little York Methodist Church was added to this charge also. The congregation is small but it is involved with prayer and Bible studies. With God's help it is still growing as there is much work left to be done in order to be ready for the return of Jesus Christ.

Present United Methodist Church, Kirkwood

Little Cedar Presbyterian Church Little York, Illinois

Little Cedar Presbyterian Church was created from the union of Little York and Cedar Creek United Presbyterian Churches on August 6, 1961. The name was chosen by using the name of Little from the Little York Church and Cedar from Cedar Creek, thus at least part of each church was retained. To better understand the present church, it is important to know some of the history of the two churches from which Little Cedar was formed. Cedar Creek was founded July 4, 1835 as a part of "The Associated Reformed Church of Warren and Mercer Counties in Illinois". The first services were conducted in a log cabin owned by John Ritchie. In the spring of 1837, the congregation divided forming Cedar Creek and South Henderson congregations. Cedar Creek continued to meet in the Ritchie cabin until a new building was erected north of the Cedar Creek Cemetery, which was also the site of a third church building. In 1866 a fourth church was built one mile east of the cemetery at a cost of $4000. The first regular pastor of Cedar Creek was Reverend James A. Porter, who, along with Reverend Robert Ross the pastor of South Henderson, was responsible for the original suggestion that a college be established in the area. They worked together for this cause differing only in their opinions as to where the location of the college should be. Reverend Porter wanted the college to be built in Monmouth and Reverend Ross in Sparta. On the way to the decision making meeting, Reverend Porter, with the help of John McCreary, had the foresight to gather $1100 in subscriptions for a building if it were erected in Monmouth. After presenting his case in favor of Monmouth and having the money to start a building, he won the dispute and Monmouth College was established in 1853. Among other accomplishments worth noting, Cedar Creek had the distinction of having 18 of its members who dedicated themselves to full time Christian ministry, a rather remarkable record for one small country church.

On April 28, 1863, Reverend Marion Morrison (actor John Wayne's grandfather) assisted by Reverend John Scott was appointed to organize Little York United Presbyterian Church. The presbytery governing this action was the Rock Island Presbytery and coincidently, met on the occasion of this motion in the Cedar Creek Church. Since records are incomplete, some perhaps lost, it cannot be determined when the present church building was erected. In 1926, a yoke was established to share a minister with the Sugar Tree Grove Church. In 1931 records mention meeting with the Henderson session and in 1943 a yoke was formed with Cedar Creek to share a minister jointly. Reverend F. R. McLean was the first minister in this yoke, with succeeding ministers serving both churches until the merger in 1961. Reverend Edward Wilcox would have been the last minister to serve both the Little York and Cedar Creek congregations and in fact, was the first minister to serve the merged church, known as Little Cedar United Presbyterian Church.

As a merged congregation, Little Cedar decided that the Little York building would be used as a place of worship. Neither church had an adequate parsonage. Since Cedar Creek had a relatively new Christian Education Unit, it was converted into a manse and was ready for occupancy in the fall of 1963. Points of interest: the original roll of members listed 130 communicant members as of August 6, 1961; the sanctuary and Sunday school rooms were completely redecorated in 1970; a project to enlarge the kitchen snowballed into a new foundation and basement in 1975. Projects used to help finance this work were food tents at the Monmouth Prime Beef Festival, ice cream socials, lunch stands at farm sales, sweet corn suppers, Fall bazaars and breakfasts put on by the women's groups, bake sales and suppers. These were times of hard work, but they were also times of good fellowship and getting to know our church family better. In 1968, a yoke was established with Sugar Tree Grove, which continued until 1994. Over the years, our congregation has provided a meaningful worship, a good Christian Education program, and has been dedicated to service in the Little York community. We have enjoyed working with the other churches in our community in many areas-worship services, service and youth programs of the past and present such as Junior Missionary, Youth Group, LOGOS, and Bible School. We have tried to do our share in the World-Wide Mission of our denomination as well as in helping support local mission projects such as Jamieson Center and Starting Point. Although our numbers are small, Little Cedar continues with the enormously joyful task of spreading God's Word.

Little Cedar Presbyterian Church - Little York

Little York United Methodist Church

Original Church Building 1891 razed 1913-1914

The first regular services of the Methodist Episcopal Church in Little York were held in a building, which was part of the Oscar Pardue livery barn and feed stable. Pastoral duties were probably taken care of by circuit riders and supply pastors.

Rev. R. A. Brown of Sunbeam (1881-84) held services 'in the school house at Little York on Sunday afternoons. An oyster stew was held at Schuchman's blacksmith shop to raise money to pay Rev. Brown.

Sunbeam's pastors continued serving this community on Sunday afternoons until 1890. Union revival services were held at the United Presbyterian Church, with Rev. N. W. Deveneau as evangelist. Following these meetings, the Methodists met at the old Opera House during the winter, and after some months decided to build a new church.

The lots where the church and parsonage now stand were purchased on March 4, 1891, from C. D. Thieme, parents of the late A. L. Thieme and Mrs. John Riley for $160. The contract for building the church was let on March 6, 1891, to Applegate Brothers. The church was dedicated on Sunday, August 16, 1891, at 10:30 a.m. Rev. T. A. Beal and Dr. Evans of Hedding College conducted the dedication ceremony. Dr. Evans informed the congregation that over $500 was needed to clear the indebtedness. Nearly $700 was subscribed in a short time.

A partial list of charter members follows: Mrs. Bell Appellate, Nancy Schuchman,, Albert Walker, Mrs. Lon Hays, Mary and Alice Hays, Frank Kitzmiller, Addison Trostle, Grace Fink, W. H. Walters, Salinda Smith McCoy, and Mary A. Smith Heasley.

The small room on the west was added during the pastorate of Rev. N. D. Hanes (1904-06). It was used as a kitchen for a number of years. In 1916 the church was raised and the basement excavated. This was during the pastorate of Rev. H. T. Russell (1915- 16).

The Little York church was in the Sunbeam charge until 1922. At that time, Little York and Fall Creek were brought together. The Livingstone House was used as a home for the pastor until 1923 when the parsonage was built. Hardwood floors were laid in the church at the same time. In 1927, the Belmont church was added to the Little York charge, making it a threepoint circuit.

During the pastorate of E. E. Mehl (1936-38), the old Bald Bluff church was torn down, and a large part of the lumber was used to make the garage. On April 19, 1941, a windstorm did considerable damage to the church. Five windows were replaced, a part of the roof was reshingled, the seats were refinished, the woodwork was varnished, and a new carpet was laid on the rostrum.

The church and parsonage were roofed in the summer of 1955. The first week in March, 1979, the old pews were removed and sold for $15 each. The floor was sanded, varnished, and waxed. On March 28, 1979, the new padded pews were installed at a cost of $4,327.

The church woodwork was redone by Dick and Jay Ballard. Following water damage in 1993, the kitchen was redone by Jay Ballard. In 2001, the church was reroofed by Jim Ballard and a ramp on the east side of the building was added to make the sanctuary handicapped accessible.

In 1995, the Belmont church was closed. In 1998, the Fall Creek church was closed. Following the closing of these two United Methodist Churches, the Little York church was joined with the Kirkwood-Smithshire Charge and again became part of a three-point circuit. Compiled for the 50th anniversary August 17, 1941 Updated 1979 and 2002

Pastors Of The Little York Methodist Church	
1890-91	T. A. Beal
1892-93	R. T. Ballew
1894-96	G. W. Periogy
1897-99	C. F. Crane
1900	J. P. McCormick
1901	Henry Brink
1902-03	G. H. McClung
1904-06	N. D. Hanes
1907-09	H. T. Jackson
1910-14	Abraham Jaggers
1915-16	H. T. Russell
1917-20	A. C. Wood
1921-22	G. L. McDonald
1922-23	Edward Jones
1924-26	W. H. Gillis
1927-28	R. A. Reeves
1929-30	C. W. Leonard
1931-35	Ross W. Bracewell
1936-38	E. E. Mehl
1939-43	Donald R. Lemkau
1943-45	A. C. A. Lee
1946-49	Paul E. Low
1950-53	Duane Heap
1953-54	Miss Harriett Gitterman
1955-56	Warren Christian
1957-59	Donald Mann
1960	Ralph Waldo Johnson
1961-68	Stanley Rapp
1969-70	William Dunker
1971-73	Kenneth Taylor
1974-76	Dallas S. Lankford
1976-84	Wayne Nordstrom
1984-89	Betty Coffey
1989-92	J. Steven Smith
1992-96	Dianne Duncan
1996-98	Brian Culver
1998-2001	William Renner
2001-	H. Suzanne Geer

Roseville Baptist Church

First Baptist Church - Roseville 1893

The Roseville Baptist Church was organized February 18, 1852, following evangelistic meetings in Hat Grove, IL. Twenty-five persons from the Berwick and Roseville areas were charter members. Eventually this became 253 members, 158 active and 88 non-resident members.

When organized in 1852 it was called the Baptist Church of Hat Grove, later changed to the Baptist Church of Roseville, when they moved into their first building east of the 'future' railroad tracks. James Tucker was elected temporary chairman, and Eliphalet Mitchell temporary clerk. The organization was under Rev. George Minor, who organized the First Baptist Church in Monmouth in 1841. Tucker was elected clerk, and Birdsey Smith and Mitchell were deacons. Truman Eldridge and Tucker were appointed to secure a pastor; on March 20, 1852, Rev. Joseph Elliott was called to be the first pastor of the Hat Grove Baptist Church, and the church joined the Salem Baptist Association.

Before building their first church there was no baptistry available as they worshipped in schoolhouses. No river was close enough when the first converts were baptized. Members of the church built a mud-and-wooden dam in Nigger Creek on the property of Truman Eldridge. This lake was used for baptismal purposes until a baptistry was built in the new church in 1893. In the fall and winter the deacons broke the ice with their canes before the converts could be immersed.

When a new school was built in the village near the present library, Baptist members used it for worship until 1864. On July 18, 1863, the church voted to erect its own building. Tucker and Mitchell were appointed to the building committee; on February 27, 1864, Dedication was held. The simple white twenty by forty feet church was located near the cemetery, and west of Forrest Crookham's home. It had no steeple or vestibule, but a wooden platform at the front door kept out the mud and dirt. This church was used for twenty-nine years, the first service led by Rev. P. Shirley. The United Brethren Church, organized in 1841, disbanded sometime after 1876; that congregation joined the Roseville Baptist Church.

They voted to build a parsonage in July, 1864; Deacon Mitchell contracted for a one-acre lot and construction of a house. The large parsonage had a parlor, bedroom, and a kitchen-dining room. Two more bedrooms and a study were upstairs. Years later a new kitchen and bathroom were added. The parsonage was used by all the Baptist ministers until 1991, when the present parsonage at 490 North Chamberlain was purchased. The old property was sold to the Lamoine Christian Nursing Home.

Forty-seven pastors have served the church since its founding (1852). Thirty of these served after the red brick church was erected in 1893. Rev. Robert Church was, appropriately enough, pastor when it was built. The present pastor is Betty Weaver, who came in April, 2001. In 1892, the little white building was no longer sufficient for the growing congregation. They purchased a large lot near the center of town from Pratt and Pratt for $750. The cornerstone was laid in February, 1893; a Dedication service was celebrated October 29, 1893. The impressive brick building, built to the Glory of God, has beautiful stained glass windows on three sides, given as memorials by church members. The final cost of the building was around $10,000. In 1924 fire gutted much of the interior, destroying part of the large north window. Members met for a time in the Congregational Church.

125th Anniversary - 1977. Serving at reception - Avis Lawhorn Hutchins, Evelyn Chewning, Liberta Taylor, and Irene Johnson

A major project during the pastorate of the Rev. Thomas Walsch (1945-51) was the building of an adequate basement, with a large kitchen, furnace room, restroom, classroom, and fellowship hall. Much sanctuary improvement was included, all at a cost of $40,000. Raymond Hutchins and Avis Lawhorn were married on June 13, 1948, while this remodeling was in progress - a real challenge to have the wedding and reception there!

By 1982 it was apparent that major repairs were needed if the familiar landmark would survive. The congregation voted: PRESERVE. Work began July 5, 1984, under Rev. Paul Holder. The Rededication Service was May 5, 1985. The extensive work included releading the huge windows, plastering and painting the sanctuary, adding Christian symbols, refinishing woodwork, adding two furnaces and air-conditioners, and more. The cost: $88,200. Decorator Paul Schaumbacher, Springfield, and Thorson Construction, Quad Cities, handled the project. Later, stained-glass door panels were commissioned by Helen Perrine in memory of Flossie Ewing and Paul Perrine. Later improvements have included basement insulation and paneling, nursery renovation, a new ramp, two restrooms, and storage space.

The "Big Red Church on South Main Street" stands ready to serve God for another 150 years, God willing!

Roseville Christian Church

Roseville Christian Church, circa 2000

The Roseville Christian Church was organized at the Downey schoolhouse in Swan Township about 1845 and had a charter membership of thirty. John E. Murphy, Milton Dodge, John Reynolds and Smith Wallace were among the early pastors. The group moved to Taylor schoolhouse in Roseville Township, east of Roseville beginning about 1867. In 1871 another move was made, this time to the Village of Roseville, the membership augmented by eight names from Ellison, northwest of Roseville. Services were held for a time in the Methodist Church on South Main Street under the pastoral care of C.E. Aids. Later the congregation was reorganized at a meeting held in the two story frame schoolhouse on West Penn Avenue. The date of the reorganization was May, 1871 and at that time twenty-eight members were on the roll. J.F. Leck held a series of meetings which added 30 members to the membership. Mr. Leck remained for two years as pastor. During these early years Mr. Matthew Jones pastored the congregation, held a revival and the church grew to 100 members.

The original building was erected in 1871 at a total cost of $1,500. It was built on the present site, 215 West Broadway which was purchased at a public sale of John Reeves Estate on February 15, 1871 for $159. A parsonage was built about 1877. The original church building was enlarged from time to time and a major improvement was the addition of a basement equipped for social gatherings. A dedication of the remodeled building was held August 12, 1894.

The congregation membership had growth to 173 during the early 1900s. Pastor Clifton Butler served the congregation during 1940's and 1950's, followed by pastors William Griffin, Richard Hurley. O.S. Lincoln and Paul Rast. The first phase of a new building program was the construction of the two story brick educational building. This unit was first used for Vacation Bible School in 1957 and was formally dedicated on February 16, 1958. At a special meeting of the congregation on January 17, 1965, the church voted to begin construction of the second phase of the building program. This portion was under the direction of Goodman Church Builders, Joplin, Missouri and supervised by Mr. Grady Smith.

The final services in the old church building were held Easter Sunday, April 18, 1965 with 301 in attendance. Early the following Monday morning the folk of the congregation met and moved the furnishings out to prepare for the razing of the building. During the construction of the new building, which was begun about July 1, the congregation met in the American Legion Hall in Roseville. James Oliver was leading the congregation as pastor during this period, serving from 1964-1970. The first official services were held in the new sanctuary on February 6, 1966 with 296 in attendance. The final work on the building was completed about February 20, 1966 and the Dedication Services were held on March 13, 1966. At the Dedication Services there were 595 people present.

Various programs have been added to the church the past 35 years. A Faith Promise Rally for missions was begun in November 1967 with a $11,260 goal. The Rally has grown to over $70,000 support for missions. One living link missionary has grown to include several supported missions. A youth minister, Lynn Ragsdale, was added in 1973, followed by several youth ministers. Active youth groups after school and in evenings are part of the program of the church. Ministers serving the congregation in recent years were Robert Bryan, Fred Keim, David Winner and Robert Brunk. In 1989, dual services were begun while Tom Mehaffy was minister. He served the congregation from 1981-1998.

Roseville Christian Church, circa 1870

Several properties adjacent to the church have been purchased for church growth. An office complex was constructed in 1995. Tim Randall has been serving as minister since March, 2001. Ideas and plans are currently being considered for a multi-purpose building with additional classrooms. The congregation now looks forward to the future with anticipation of greater service to the Lord.

Roseville Church of the Nazarene

In August 1954, while Rev. Lyle Eckley was serving as District Superintendent of the Northwest Illinois District, it was felt that a Church of the Nazarene should be organized in Roseville, Illinois. Rev. Cainan Dale held a tent meeting at the site of the present church, after which a new church was organized. Money for land was borrowed from an uncle of Rev. Willard Teel, the first pastor and the one who oversaw the erection of the first church building.

Most of the early pastors lived elsewhere and commuted to the church for preaching: Rev. James Hayes, (1957), Rev. Gaylord Houseman (1958-1959), layman Marvin Jones from Macomb, (1959-1961), Rev. E. L. Bowlyou (1962-1963), Rev. Everett M. Trimble (1963-1964), layman Fred Kelly from Rock Island (1964), Rev. Florence Poole (1964-1966), Rev. Marion Dodson from Burlington, Iowa (1966-1968), Mrs. Mildred Gilliam from Galesburg (1968-1974).

By 1974, the church had reached a low ebb. Finances and membership were down. Some of the church members lived out of town, making it impossible for them to attend all the services. This made it necessary for some of the services to be cancelled. In 1974 three couples who lived in the Roseville community but who attended the Monmouth Church of the Nazarene felt they should be working to revive and save the church at Roseville. Following another tent revival Rev. Floyd Pounds, the District Superintendent, reorganized the church with new members being added from the Monmouth congregation. Rev. Jack Price (who had been the evangelist for the tent revival) felt led to move from full-time evangelism to pastor the church at Roseville (1974-1977).

During that time the house directly east of the church was purchased for a parsonage (1974), and a new church building was built primarily with volunteer labor. The first service in the new building was December 19, 1976.

After completion of the church building, Rev. Price Felt called back into the Evangelistic field. The next pastors were Rev. Keith Ross (1977-1978) during whose ministry the Sunday School rooms were completed and the church dedicated, Rev. Willard Hollis (interim), Rev. Sherman Hunter (1979-1983) during whose ministry air conditioning was installed and many improvements were made, Rev. Willard Hollis (interim), Rev. James Thompson (1983-1986), supply pastors (1986), Rev. Steve Sears (1986-1989), layman Greg Hall (a local carpenter who was preparing for the ministry), Rev. Brian Martin (1989-1992), Rev. John Trotter (1989-1995) during whose ministry a new parsonage was purchased on Railroad Street (1994) so that the previous parsonage could be converted into a fellowship hall and office, supply pastors (1995), Rev. Sam Stone (1995-1996), and a series of supply pastors (1996-1997).

After much prayer, Tom Smith, a member who was also preparing for the ministry, volunteered to pastor the church without salary to provide consistency and a local spiritual leader. In 1997 Rev. Smith was officially appointed to pastor the church. Under his leadership the parsonage was refurbished and the fellowship hall completed.

The Church of the Nazarene is a strongly Bible based church with a doctrine that stresses salvation and a total commitment to God. Church members and friends enjoy active Sunday School classes for all ages, Sunday morning worship services, Sunday evening services, missionary emphasis and support, and a Wednesday evening Bible study and church growth class. All are welcome.

Church of the Nazarene, Roseville

Smithshire United Methodist Church

The Smithshire Methodist Episcopal Church was organized in 1888 when the Meridian Methodist Episcopal Church reorganized, moved into Smithshire, and changed their name. They first worshiped in a school house, then in the Christian Church which had been moved into Smithshire from its location two and one-half miles east of town. In 1895 the Methodists built the first unit of their present church building. The Santa Fe Railroad donated the ground for the church site.

Other Methodist Churches are part of our history. The Ellison Methodist Episcopal Church closed in 1908 and members of this church joined with Smithshire. The Ellison Methodist Episcopal Church was the oldest in the township, being organized in 1833. They worshiped in a log school house until their church was built in 1844. They were on the circuit with Berwick, Roseville, Swan Creek, and. twenty other preaching places and was comprised of all territory west of these places to the Mississippi River. A tornado on May 30, 1858 destroyed the church and its records, killed 15, and demolished all the houses in the village. The church was rebuilt but the town never recovered and businesses moved to Smithshire when the Santa Fe Railroad was built in 1888. The village site was surveyed by the county surveyor, C. A. Sias in June 30, 1888.

Salters Grove Methodist Episcopal Church (northwest of Smithshire) closed and several families from that church joined Smithshire. Material from Salters Grove was used to build an addition to the north of the existing building. After this remodeling, the church was rededicated September 1, 1912 by Dr. Joe Bell, the District Superintendent, assisted by Dr. W. D. Agnes, president of Hedding College. Rev. F. N. Wright was the minister. The original building had a steeple that was struck by lightning twice and was not replaced after the second time.

The former Liberty Chapel Methodist Protestant Church building near Ponemah was given to our church by the Methodist Annual Conference. It was moved and located near the present church on September 29, 1950. The church was given the name Liberty Chapel because it was dedicated debt free. The new building had a kitchen and dining room and was used for Sunday School classes. It was renamed Liberty Hall. The Daily Vacation Church School was the first to use it in 1953.

Smithshire Methodist Church - Present

After the three Methodist divisions (The Methodist Episcopal Church, The Methodist Episcopal Church South, and the Protestant Methodist Church) combined our church changed its corporate name to The Methodist Church of Smithshire on September 9, 1943. In 1968 there was a merger with the Evangelical United Brethren and The Methodist Church resulting in the name being changed to The United Methodist Church.

The church was completely redecorated in 1957. New pews, a pulpit, lectern, an altar and other wood furnishings were purchased for $2995. The sanctuary was changed completely facing west instead of south. Rev. Harold Bodeen was the minister at this time. A Consecration Service was held July 21, 1957 with Dr. Eugene Stauffer, Galesburg District Superintendent, giving the sermon.

A fire on Memorial Sunday afternoon in 1988 resulted in more repairs. All the furnishings were carried out so everything was saved. Three weeks later on June 18 and 19 a Centennial Celebration was held for the church and for the town. Rev. Bruce Bolin Ghitalla was the host minister for the Sunday services with former ministers, Rev. Howard Fisher, Rev. Harold Bodeen, and Rev. George Terry participating. Repairs were made and the Dedication Service was held October 8, 1989 with Dr. Gary Bass, District Superintendent, giving the sermon.

Smithshire Methodist Church - 1888

There were 12 charter members of the Smithshire Methodist Church. Miss Dora Yoho (McElhinney), Mr. and Mrs. James Watson, Mrs. Mary Yoho, Mr. and Mrs. William Edwards and daughter Grace, and Mrs. Ed Patch were among the twelve. Today there are 87 members. Mildred Tinsman Dowell was honored with an Open House in April, 1993 for being the church pianist for over fifty years.

This church became a two-point charge with the United Methodist Church of Kirkwood in 1963. Little York United Methodist Church became a part of the charge in 1998. It is in the Spoon River District (formerly Galesburg District) and the Illinois Great Rivers Conference. The pastor is Suzanne Geer and Peggy Kulczewski is the lay pastor.

St. James African Methodist Episcopal Church

Charles and Daisy W. Brooks
"Remembering Our Roots and Honoring Our Parents"

The St. James African Methodist Episcopal Church was organized in 1868 in a hall on South Main Street with the following members: Mr. and Mrs. David Crutchville, Mr. and Mrs. Zachariah Price, Mrs. Blair, Mary Bright, Mr. and Mrs. Baber and son Lewis, Charles Knight, A. H. Knight and Harriet Lee.

In 1869 they purchased a lot from N. A. Harding on South Second Street between Eighth and Ninth Avenues and built their house of worship there, 22 by 30 feet. W. M. Smiley was the contractor.

On May 23, 1890 the congregation sold this lot and bought one on South Third Street and Seventh. They moved their building to that place. It was remodeled in 1896 and dedicated by Presiding Elder F. J. Peterson of Chicago. Later the M & St. L railroad was built along Seventh Avenue and the church decided to move its location.

On July 22, 1912, the present lot was purchased and the foundation laid during the pastorate of Rev. W. A. Searcy. In 1917 this church was erected and dedicated with Bishop L. J. Coppins preaching the dedicatory sermon. The Rev. Eugene Thompson was the pastor.

In 1963, Rev. Joseph Evans initiated the Herculean task of building a new church. The side walls and beams were erected.

In September, 1963 the Rev. Robert Cox was sent to St. James. Under his administration the church paid over two thousand dollars in back debts and over twenty-five hundred dollars was raised for the building fund. The roof for the church arrived in August making it possible for the members to worship in the church by winter. This was made possible with help of the business community of Monmouth. The new edifice was dedicated in 1964.

In 1968, the Rev. Anne Barton was appointed to serve as pastor. This was a milestone in the Church. Pastor Barton was the first woman minister to be appointed a church in the Illinois Conference.

In March 1973, the mortgage was liquidated and on July 22, 1973 the mortgage-burning took place under the administration of Rev. Fred M. Starling.

Rev. Thomas D. Elmore. Under his administration the parsonage was completely renovated.

The pastor was Rev. Berry (1997-2000) M. Cooke. Under her supervision the church has undergone many physical changes and the membership is flourishing. The present pastor is Rev. Cynthia Newman, who was first appointed to St. James in August/September 2000.

The Church History was submitted by Ira Brooks Walsh in honor of her parents Charles and Daisy Brooks.

Early Building St. James African Methodist Eposcopal Church - Monmouth

Sugar Tree Grove Presbyterian Church

Sugar Tree Grove Presbyterian Church

A few members of the Associate Church had settled in the vicinity of Sugar Tree Grove as early as 1828 coming from Ohio. The Associate Church was known as "Seceders" having seceded from the Church of Scotland.

The dwelling of John Caldwell, Sr. was the place of organization in 1830. He and Adam Richey were chosen as elders. Twenty-nine members were enrolled: 2 Kendalls, 3 Gibsons, 5 Junkins, 3 Caldwells, 2 Findleys, 2 Maleys, 12 Richeys and 1 Campbell.

This was the first church in Warren County, which was a log cabin 30 x 36 feet. It was completed in the Fall of 1833 and was called the Henderson Church. Rev. James Bruce was installed as pastor. The congregation became too large and in 1837 a brick structure was built. It was 54 x 60 foot with walls of hard burned bricks, which were made near the site.

These churches were formed along a stream known as David's Creek. David's Creek flowed into Cedar Creek, which emptied into Henderson, thus the name Henderson Church.

The Sugar Tree Grove Cemetery was established on the ground near the first church. It was used as a graveyard in the spring of 1834 and the first burial was William Turnbull. There is an American Indian buried there and a black woman who worked for the Rodgers family. With the closing of the angling trails and the fencing in farms the location became difficult to access. It was voted to purchase a site on the main road. The present church was built and occupied in 1874 and the cupola was added on in 1895 when remodeling was done. Remodeling was done in 1917 to its present external appearance. Various changes were made to the interior.

During the next years. attendance grew. People came from Little York, Sunbeam, North Henderson, Viola, Spring Grove, Center Grove and Pleasant Grove: each locality being represented by members who were regular in attendance except those in Viola-some twenty-five miles away. They never failed to be present during the service of Communion, which was celebrated twice a year. When the Viola people came for that service they were absent from home about four to six days. They would travel in the box of a lumber wagon to come to church to be seated on hickory bark bottomed chairs with straight backs.

In the new church the pulpit box was 12 feet from the floor to the top of the minister's head. Only 24 inches of the minister could be seen from the pews.

There were two long services on the Sabbath. Sabbath School began at nine and was followed by preaching, which lasted until twelve. Then came intermission and a frugal lunch after which the congregation returned for another long worship service.

Dr. D.A. Wallace, later president of Monmouth College was pastor in 1874 when the present church was built. Although the official name was Henderson it was always referred to as the Sugar Tree Grove Church, but in 1941 the congregation voted to make it official.

The early church banned tunes and choirs. A presenter who "lined out" the Psalm two lines at a time led the singing. The whole congregation became the choir. The Henderson United Presbyterian Church celebrated its Centennial Celebration on October 3-5, 1930 with the history given by Mrs. W.F. Schweitzer. Rev. J.W. McClenahan was pastor. The elders were D.R. Acheson, J.H. Shaw, R.H. McClenahan, R.M. Ray, W.H. Turnbull and J. Edgar Robeson. Officers of the congregation were: Chairman, A.E. Graham; Secretary, Mrs. Willard Seldon; Treasurer, H.L. Schweitzer.

On July 9, 1979 the Illinois State Organization National Society of the DAR placed a plaque of dedication honoring the oldest church in Warren County.

In 1980 the church celebrated the 150th year. The pastors were Forrest and Sue Krummel. The elders were: Terry Moore, Fred J. Hall, Larry Michael, Gene Moore, Bob Garth and David Moore.

In 1982 the first two women were nominated to the board: Eleanor Schweitzer and Mrs. Robert Johnston. The church was now yoked with Little Cedar United Presbyterian Church.

There have been many pastors and the present one is Rev. William A. Shumate and the elders are: Charles Michael, Mrs. Gary Cooper, Maxine Giddings, Jerry Dutton Jr., Helen Hartzell and Myra Bell. The church is now yoked with Westminster United Presbyterian Church in Kirkwood.

The Turnbull family has had the longest connection with the church and the session of any in the congregation.

Sugar Tree Grove is about six miles northwest of Monmouth, Illinois on the M.A.M Trail.

While Jim Ballard was working on the church in fall of 2001 he found the following message in an old bottle:

Monmouth ILL. Oct. 23 1895

This building was put up by T. O. Hamsher Contractor during the summer of 1874 assisted by R. Y. Frew, James Shoemaker, James Neis, Jacob Deberry and remodeled by James S. Applegate Contractor Oct 1895 assisted by his brothers Frank & Hall Applegate, Fred Braselton, Chas. Johnson & Jacob H. Foust.

The old paper said it was very dry & looked like rain. It is very dry now also, but instead of looking like rain it is pretty cold to work on a tower after standing so long without one. J. H. F.

Sugar Tree Grove Presbyterian Church near Monmouth - "The Old Brick Church."

Cameron Christian Church

Serving the Community since 1831

Church of Christ on the Cedar Fork of Henderson's River in Warren County ... "On the 30th day of April 1831, this church was constituted upon the belief that the scriptures of the Old and New Testament are the only rule of faith and practice, and sufficient for the government of the church." Seventeen charter members signed this covenant. They were: William M. Davidson, Elizabeth Davidson, Elijah Davidson, Sr., Margaret Davidson, Sr., Elijah Davidson, Jr., Margaret Davidson, Jr., Henry E. Haley, Elizabeth Haley, John G. Haley, John E. Murphy, Frances Murphy, Richard Ragland, Nancy Ragland, William Whitman, Sarah Whitman, Josiah Whitman, Julia Whitman.

Thus, begins the first record of the Cameron Christian Church, only the second church organized in Warren County. They hold the distinction of being the oldest continuously operating congregation of the Christian Church (Disciples of Christ) in Illinois.

In its first ten years more than 200 joined its membership, making a meeting house necessary. On the last Sunday in January 1837 plans for such a house were approved. The village of Savannah flourished at the site of this meeting house, but it was soon discovered that another town of Illinois had claimed the name. Coldbrook was chosen instead.

Also during its first ten years three new congregations sprang from the "mother" church. The first, Talbot Creek Church, began meeting in the northeast corner of Monmouth Township at the home of William Hopper, March 3, 1839. Of forty-three charter members, most were of the "mother" congregation. In 1859 a number of the Talbot Creek Church members organized at Mauck's Grove a few miles farther north. When the town of Gerlaw sprang up they moved to that location to become the Gerlaw Christian Church. Remaining members of Talbot Creek Church resurrected the Coldbrook name and in 1860 built two miles east and a mile south of their first site; the Coldbrook Christian Church of today.

In April 1839 twenty-two persons of the "mother" church formed the nucleus of Monmouth Christian Church. Three months later, the third new congregation, Meridian Christian Church, organized in Berwick township.

In 1855 the Chicago, Burlington and Quincy Railroad laid track and built Cameron station. One mile away, Savannah/Coldbrook began to dwindle. In five years the congregation moved to Cameron and changed its name again. The new meeting house was constructed on the southeast corner of Church and Care streets. Music was vocal until a Sunday evening in 1892 when no strong voice was present to lead. An ice cream social netted sufficient funds to buy an organ. In 1900 a new house of worship was built at the southwest corner of Church and Depot streets. In 1971 accessibility issues were resolved when the current building was constructed on the south part of the same lot.

In the last ten years pastors of the congregation have been; Robert and Linda Kempt-Baird - 1991-1995, who also served Gerlaw Christian Church, and Dennis E. Knotts - 1997-2001. Since August 2001 Steve Bridwell serves as interim pastor.

Immanuel Baptist Church

Present Immanuel Baptist Church - Monmouth

On August 13, 1852 Gustav Palmquist baptized three persons in the Mississippi River, and the first Swedish Baptist Church in the U.S.A. was founded in Rock Island, IL.

The church known today as the Immanuel Baptist Church had its beginning on September 13, 1888 when a group of Scandinavian people, sixteen in number, united together to form a visible church known as the First Swedish Baptist Church of Monmouth, Illinois.

For a time they met in a rented hall on South Main Street, but a church building was erected at West Archer Avenue and North E Street at a cost of $2,000.00. This building was dedicated September 14, 1890.

In 1910 a lot was purchased at 409 South First Street. The building erected there was dedicated April 14, 1912. The name of the church was changed to Immanuel Baptist on May 4, 1924.

In the early 1930's we experienced a season of revival while holding services in a large tent which was erected in the rear of the church building. In 1932 it became necessary to enlarge the building. The front porch was removed, the front wall was moved out to the sidewalk, and the building was enlarged. A balcony was one of the additions.

In October of 1959 the church looking to the future purchased 4.7 acres of ground along the West side of North Sunny Lane in the 100 and 200 blocks. In the following years many tent revival meeting were held at this location.

Needing a larger facility we broke ground at this location in May of 1966, which became known as 206 North Sunny Lane. The first service in the building was March 26, 1967 Easter Sunrise Service in the Fellowship Hall. The first services using the entire unit were held May 21, 1967. The building was dedicated on January 21, 1968.

Our parsonage was built at 120 North Sunny Lane, in 1970.

The Lord blessed us with rapid growth in our Sunday School, creating a need for the south wing to be added to the church building in 1973.

We continue to serve our community by following the Lord's guidance whether it be through home or foreign missions. For however long the Lord allows, we will continue to "Press Forward With Our Eyes On Jesus," as we have the previous 114 years.

The Living Light Tabernacle
275 South Meadow Roseville, Illinois 61473

Living Light Tabernacle - Roseville

In September of 1982, several Roseville community members met at Gerald and Bonnie Huston's home south of Roseville with Rev. Clayton J. Bowman, from Burlington, Iowa. It was decided to have a tent revival and see what the interest would be in starting a full gospel church in the community. A big red tent was set up on the north side of Bonnie and Gerald's home at 468 65th Street, Roseville, Illinois and revival services were held. We had about thirty-five people in attendance.

After the revival it was then decided to start a church, titled The Living Light Tabernacle with its Founder, Rev. Clayton J. Bowman. Founding members were Norma Bowman, Tim Bowman, Dave and Carol Stinemates, Lois Sims, Wayne and Barb Rankin, Gerald and Bonnie Huston, Gene and Martha Dakin, Rodney and Sandy Huston, Cheryl Britt, Elaine Churchill and Earlene Finch. We continued in the red tent until colder weather and then we went to the home of Gene and Martha Dakin and had church services in the basement of their home. We met there for several weeks and then Marion Lewis let us rent his store on North Main Street, Roseville. We met there for 2 1/2 years while we started construction of a new church building on South Meadow in Roseville. We moved in the upstairs of the new building in January of 1985 and continued to finish the building. It was finished by November of 1985.

We had a Christian Academy with approximately thirty students for several years. Because of low attendance we closed the school in the mid 90's. Several of our students attended and graduated from Western Illinois University in Macomb, Illinois.

Rev. Clayton J. Bowman, Founder, along with his son, Tim J. Bowman, pastored the church for almost eighteen years. Rev. Bowman retired from pastoring in 2000 and his son, Tim, had already gone to found Calvary Church of the Quad Cities in Moline, Illinois.

In May of 2000 Pastor Orval "Butch" Black came to be our new pastor. The church is growing and reaching out to not only the Roseville community but other surrounding communities.

Westminster United Presbyterian Church

115 people met at Center Grove School. They organized the United Presbyterian Church of Young America. In 1894 this church had 180 members. A sanctuary was built in 1896 at a cost of $6,500. This building was used until 1949.

In 1856 a group of men met to discuss a church for Young America. On June 26 the South Henderson Presbyterian Church was organized. with 26 members. The first building was built on the corners of Harding and Chestnut Street in Young America.

In 1896 the congregation built a new building and moved to the south side of town. The total cost was $10,700. This amount was pledged, and the building was paid for.

In 1874 Young America became Kirkwood. The church's name was changed to the First Presbyterian Church of Kirkwood. The Universalist Church closed its doors and the building became an opera house. The Presbyterians bought the building in 1906. They moved their church to Chestnut and Harding and attached it to the opera house. The church was dedicated on December 16, 1906, with 250 members.

In 1948 the two churches met to consider uniting. On April 9, 1949, the first joint service was held, and the Rev. John Acheson was chosen as a Supply Pastor.

In May 1950 the Rev. Eugene Clements became the first pastor of the Federated Presbyterian Church. In 1958 Ester Simmons became the first woman elder of the Federated Church.

Westminster United Presbyterian Church, Kirkwood

Warren County Schools

Sumner	Spring Grove	Kelly
Little York	Gerlaw	
Hale	Monmouth	Coldbrook
	Monmouth	Coldbrook
Tompkins	Lenox	Floyd
Kirkwood	Larchland	Cameron
Ellison	Roseville	Berwick
Smithshire	Roseville	Berwick
Point Pleasant	Swan	Greenbush
	Swan Creek	Greenbush

Monmouth Central School

Warren County Public Library

Front of Library

Several early attempts were made to establish a library in Warren county. The first attempt occurred in 1836, less than nine years after the first settler came to the county, and only 4 1/2 years after the first log courthouse was built. Over a period of several years, a small collection of books was maintained, but no financial support was provided and no property was acquired.

Other attempts were made in the years 1856, 1859, 1864, and 1867.

On June 1, 1868, the Monmouth Reading Room and Library was opened. Twenty-five persons collected and paid a total of $2,500 to meet the estimated expenses for two years. They formed themselves into an association of directors. A room provided free of charge, and during the first two years only newspapers and magazines were available.

One of the 25 directors, Mr William Pressley, who had established a prosperous dry goods store in Monmouth, was distressed by the lack of books. In 1870, he provided funds for additional reading materials, including books. And having noted the success of the library during its first two years, he wanted to see the library become a permanent landmark. In 1870 he erected a 2-story brick building in the southwest corner of the public square to be used as a permanent home for the library. A white marble plaque is still located on the building, which reads: "This is the first building in the State of Illinois given for a People's Library". (Mr Pressley was an unusual individual. He subscribed to the philosophy that $10,000 in assets was sufficient to provide for his needs; whenever his assets exceeded this amount, he would give the overage to charity, primarily the new library, Monmouth College and a girl's school in Egypt.)

It was Mr. Pressley's wish that library privileges be extended to people living in the county, since they contributed financially to the business community. In keeping with Mr Pressley's wish, the constitution and by-laws of the Monmouth Reading Room and Library were altered by a special charter issued by the state on March 25, 1870, and the Association was legally incorporated as the Warren County Library and Reading Room Association.

The Association was comprised of 25 directors, constituting a trust corporation to hold property and manage the institution. The governing corporation subsequently consisted of 15 members, whose places, when vacant, were filled by the Association itself.

In 1893 the Warren County Library was placed on a select list of the best American libraries. It was notified of this honor by Melville Dewey.

The use of the reading room and library was not free. A nominal yearly membership fee was required to cover such expenses as salaries and fuel, although the building and books were provided without expense to the reader. Perpetual tickets also were sold (for $3/year) which allowed families continual use of the library. (This method of financing was discontinued in 1920.)

A remodeling program begun in 1962 ended with the construction of an addition to the main library in 1966. This addition houses the Administrative Offices, Conference Room, Periodicals Department and Local History and Genealogy Room.

The bookmobile has been discontinued. The four branches operating currently are located in Alexis, Kirkwood and Roseville.

In 1976 the Warren County Library was the recipient of a $500 grant from the Illinois Bicentennial Commission for an oral history of Warren County project. The Library Board of Trustees contributed matching funds. In addition to an oral history project, the Board has funded the production of slides of historic Monmouth.

Library service in Warren County changed dramatically on January 22, 1990. The Warren County Library and Reading Room Association gave up the operation of the library to the Warren County Public Library District. This meant the library operation converted from a not-for-profit corporation to a public library administered by an elected board. What makes this elected board different from all other district library boards is that it is made up of fifteen trustees rather than the normal seven. The Illinois law especially designed for the Warren County Public Library District, responsible for providing library service to an area of approximately 540 square miles, allows for no more than ten trustees from any one township. This precaution was made for fear that the district might be controlled by Monmouth township, which has the majority of the population. It is interesting to note that the present number of representatives from Monmouth Township is nine.

The second most striking difference between the management under the Reading Room Association and the new district library was that while the County Board could only tax .08 cents/$100 equalized assessed valuation (EAV), the new library district could tax at .15 cents/$100 EAV under the district law.

The Warren County Public Library District immediately increased its basic tax rate to .15 cents/$100 EAV under the provisions of the district library law and also levied history project, the Board has funded the productions of slides of historic Monmouth, additional taxes for special items for insurance, audit, etc. In the 1993-1994 district year it was decided for the first time to tax for a working cash fund (.05 cents) and a building maintenance tax (.02 cents). Where the old Reading Room Association had a taxable income of $117,965 in its last year of existence (1989), the new district library had a projected income of $369,871 from all sources for fiscal year 1993-1994. The projected income from all sources for fiscal year 2001-2002 is $532,326.

Today the main library's floor space is 12,814 square feet (10,188 sq. ft. of handicapped-accessible first floor space; 2,626 of second floor space, which is not handicapped-accessible). The book collection consists of 24,607 children's volumes and 47,066 adult volumes for a total of 71,673 volumes, of which approximately 10,000 volumes (3,400 juvenile volumes, 6,000 adult volumes) are shelved in the branches. The periodical subscriptions currently received total 185 (with back issues of all titles held seven years.) The main library currently has 599 juvenile videos and 2,274 adult videos, 76 adult DVDs, and 1,589 adult books on audiocassette (mostly unabridged) and adult books on CD.

In the last calendar year, approximately 2,000 volumes were weeded from the collection to make room for new purchases and to remove outdated material.

A remodeling of the main adult area was undertaken in 1989. The ceilings were lowered four feet, new light fixtures were installed and double in number, windows were reworked, new lounge furniture was purchased, the circulation desk was refurbished, and the area was freshly painted and newly carpeted.

In 1992 the children's area was expanded by 589 square feet. This space fronted on the public square and had been used by a dentist. The area received a new ceiling, walls, lighting, carpeting and solid oak shelves. The shelves were of such fine craftsmanship that additional units were purchased from the same source for the entire children's library. New windows were installed which provided visibility from the public square for the first time in 90 years, and a new large sign was installed identifying the library.

A major room configuration and expansion of the two-story library was completed in 1996. An additional 3,664 sq. ft. (of primarily first floor space) was wrapped around the existing building, and all public spaces (including the Board Room/Public Meeting Room) and all staff offices are now located in handicapped-accessible first floor space. The library received a $250,000 grant from the Illinois State Library to make this project feasible. The reconfiguration/expansion literally transformed the earlier library, both functionally and aesthetically, Bridget Lamont, the Directive Illinois state Library, who had previously been the consultant to the Western Illinois Library System (of which the Warren County Public Library District is a member) on viewing the finished product, exclaimed she had never seen such a spectacular change in any library.

The library continues to plan for the future. The library continues to weed on a periodic basis and now has an up-to-date well organized collection ready for expansion.

The library automated its circulation procedures and catalog in the main library in 1994-1995. The branches will eventually be tied into the main library's automated system via Internet.

The main library now has six staff computers that provide circulation and OPAC access, of which two also provide Internet access. It also has a staff computer that provides access to software applications. It has six patron OPACs and five patron computers that provide access to software applications, one of which also provides Internet access.

In 1991, what the library believes to be one of the better sheet music collections in the state was given to the Warren County Library. The library currently estimates that there are 4,000 to 5,000 sheets of music plus numerous volumes of materials. Gracie Peterson, the donor of this collection has also arranged for approximately a dozen collectors around the state to donate their sheet music collections in the future. One person has already done so. The library is presently placing the items in these collections on its computer by title, composer, artist and type of material. The library will be storing these collections in the remodeled portion of the library.

One of the library's long-time board members, Ralph Whiteman, has donated his Lincoln Collection to the Library along with substantial funds to up-date and maintain the collection. He has made arrangements for the past three years to sponsor a Lincoln speaker; several hundred people have attended this program each year.

Mrs Grace Buchanan, in her will, left over a million dollars in assets to the Warren County Library and Reading Room Association to establish a cultural center for Warren County. She thought the Association board represented well what she wanted in a managing team for her center. When the Warren County Library and Reading Room Association gave up its management of the library, the Association did not go out of existence. The Association still operates the Buchanan Center for the Arts.

On July 1, 2001, the Library purchased the building east of the main library. The building was remodeled as a Genealogy room and an addition to the children's room.

Library Interior

Kirkwood and Little York Schools & Creation of Yorkwood

Shortly after the creation of Warren County, during the 1824-1825 Legislature of the State of Illinois session, schools were also created. Each township was divided into school districts, which were referred to by both name and district number. As the communities grew there was a need for larger, more modem schools until we have come to the creation of Yorkwood, CUSD # 225, as we know it today.

Kirkwood Schools

Shortly after Young America, later named Kirkwood in 1874, was platted on September 1874 the first schools were budt. The first subscription school in this neighborhood was built northwest of Kirkwood, on what was known as Mineral Springs ground or the "hooking quarter". Another school for younger students of Kirkwood was later built. The first public school was located in Ray's Hall in a warehouse owned by Knowles, Ray and Chapin. In 1861, Kirkwood built its first public school north of the tracks. Another school was also in existence at the same time on the south side of town in a room over the previous storeroom of J.H. Gilmore. In October 1867 a new schoolhouse north of the railroad was opened. at a cost of $3,000. On December 6, 1898, Professor Wettengel discovered and reported a fire at the North School. Believed to have started from a faulty stovepipe, the fire completely destroyed the school. Student education continued elsewhere and a new brick building was constructed, costing $9,000. Both elementary and high school students attended there. By 1902 Kirkwood's school population was 225 with five teachers. In May 1912, Kirkwood citizens petitioned for a new high school and on June 1, 1912 a contract for approximately $ 15,000 was signed and the High School opened in September 1913. In 1937, Kirkwood High School became Kirkwood Township High School to include rural schools of Center Grove, Coonville, Moore, Columbia, Tubbs, Liberty, Nichol, and Maple Grove in Tompkins township and later parts of Hale and Ellison townships. Kirkwood consolidated with Little York in 1960. The High School Gym is now a community Center with many activities for the young people to enjoy.

Among many Kirwood dedicated citizens contributing to successful schools, early ones were Squire James H. Martin, teacher of Kirkwood's first subscription school; W.C. Tubbs-- board president when new brick school was built after 1898 fire; W.W. Pease--teacher at school built especially for younger children; David Abbey--teacher at first public school. More recently, Verne Conway of Kirkwood became Warren County's Superintendent of Schools; Marion Johnson, last school board president of Kirkwood schools before consolidation; and Tom Avery, a graduate of the school system, later taught at Yorkwood and is currently superintendent for Yorkwood CUSD 4 225.

Little York Schools

March 5, 1832, Hugh Martin, Anthony Cannon and James G. Barton were appointed trustees for school lands in what is now Sumner Township The first school opened in 1834 and included Little York. After several changes in township boundaries, schools in Hale and Sumner townships included Barr, Brownlee, Cedar Creek, Denny, Hale, Iveydore, Junkin, and Pleasant Green.

A brick building built in 1903-1904 in Little York probably served as both elementary and high school Little York High School served as a two year school in 1904, a three year school in 1905, a four year school in 1906 to 1920. Eight elementary and four high school grades were in this four room building, three for elementary. In 1921 the high school reverted to a three year school with some finishing fourth year at Monmouth. In 1923 it was a two year and then a three year school again. In 1938 it became a four year school again, There was an addition to the school in 1927 with a second addition in 1930's including a gymnasium. Little York Community High School # 133 was built in 1941-42 for estimated $85,000, opening in February 1942, classes being held six days a week in second semester due to WWII and manpower shortage. The former brick building became the elementary school with both schools being maintained until consolidation with Kirkwood in 1960.

Among those contributing to successful schools here were : Miss Betsy Hopper teaching the first school in Sumner Township in 1834; Peter Terpening teaching first school in Little York in 1837 Cecil Waugh first board president of Little York High School # 133 and C.S. Bilderback first principal. There were five high school and three elementary board members, later consolidated into one board for both schools.

Creation Of Yorkwood

Times changed and consolidation of Kirkwood and Little York was considered. Little York High School enrollment in 1950's was 75 and Kirkwood was 96. Additional curriculum and finances were

great concerns. Other issues were: new district boundaries; incorporating grades one through eight; location for schools and use of existing buildings. After careful consideration, a petition was submitted to Verne Conway, Warren County Superintendent, asking for an election for the purpose of consolidation, stating this new district would maintain grades one through twelve and retain most of the present Little York and Kirkwood High School Districts. In November 1959, both communities voted to create Yorkwood CUSD #225 beginning July 1, 1960. Both towns would maintain their K-6 elementary buildings, Kirkwood High School would become Yorkwood's 7th-9th Junior High and Little York High School building would house Yorkwood's 10th-12th High School. By mid-1960's a new Jr/Sr building was needed and on September 30, 1967 a bond issue was voted for construction of a new building located between the two towns on land previously owned by E.T. Gillen Construction of the $1,012,899.93 building began May 1, 1968 and the first day of school took place September 2, 1969. Yorkwood reorganized their buildings with fifth and sixth in Little York High School building; Little York Elementary building was Little York Kindergarten and grades 2-4; Kirkwood Grade School was Kirkwood Kindergarten and first grades. A bond issue passed August 27, 1977 and construction on the $1,758,866.67 building for a new elementary school began March 1, 1978 with school opening on August 21, 1979. Upon consolidation, Bob Armstrong served as board president-, Paul Luckenbill--high school principal-, Leon Clements--junior high principal-, Mary Johnson--principal of Kirkwood Grade School and Elizabeth Waugh --principal of Little York Grade School. In 1969, the first year of the new high school building- Keith Erlandson--president of board-, Louis Wallace --superintendent; Roy Asplund-high school principal. In 1980, first year of new elementary building, John Moberg-president of board; James Cox-- superintendent and Richard Lee-- elementary principal. Since 1992, Kindergarten is an all day program; Pre-K program was added in 1998. Enrollment in 2001-2002 was 394 students in grades K-12--a small school which ranks high in State and National standings. At this writing, Wendell Shauman is board president; Tom Avery--superintendent; Kristen Nelson-- high school principal- and Sue McKee--- elementary principal

Thank you to Mrs Rita Williams and 1900-200 Social Studies Class for initiating the "Our Town" project including local schools-, Kirkwood and Little York residents who compiled information for sesquicentennial books; 2001-2002 administration and board and many community members for sharing their memories.

Kirkwood High School

Kirkwood Township High School in Kirkwood

The first school in the village of Young America, renamed Kirkwood in 1872, was taught by David Abbey. According to old settlers, it was in a room over the elevator.

The property for the first school building of the district was donated by David Irvine and A. G. Kirkpatrick. This gift is presumed to have occurred soon after the CB&Q railroad reached here in 1855 and after the prairie was surveyed for a village. This wooden building was later referred to as South School. It was last used as the farm mechanics classroom of Kirkwood Township High School.

A new school north of the railroad tracks was built in 1867 for three thousand dollars. The North and South Schools housed all grades. No part of it was a high school until 1889 when the principal added enough subjects to formally graduate a class of 1890 with one member receiving a diploma. The North School burned in 1898 and was replaced in 1899 with a new tan brick building for use as both grade and high school.

By September 1913 a new red brick high school building was ready for classes. This building cost about fifteen thousand dollars and was on the same property and located just east of the South School. Then in 1927 voters approved the building of a new gymnasium on the site of the high school grounds at a cost of eighteen thousand dollars. At that time Kirkwood High School had a star basketball team which defeated many of the larger schools in the area including Monmouth, Galesburg, Macomb and even Canton once. Canton then defeated KHS team and went on to become state champions that year.

In 1930 two courses, Agriculture and Home Economics were placed under Smith Hughes state supervision. Being no longer needed as a gymnasium, the little old south schoolhouse was remodeled and equipped as a farm mechanics building used by the classes in agriculture. During the years many more classes were added to the curriculum along with an improved library, physical education, music, band, drivers education and School bus transportation.

Commercial courses were added to the curriculum in 1937. Typing, shorthand and bookkeeping proved very popular with the students. With the addition of this course the faculty was increased to six members.

The Board of Directors brought before the voters the need of high school district in the township. This was decided on favorably in an election in April 1937. When school opened in September 1937, it opened as Kirkwood Township High School.

Through the years the school maintained a high standard of education due to the interest and cooperation of teachers, students, board of education and parents.

In 1960 Kirkwood Township High School and Little York High School consolidated to become the Yorkwood School District. Existing buildings were used until new ones were constructed. A new junior-senior high school was built. The first class to graduate from the new school was the Class of 1970. A few years later the new Yorkwood Elementary School was built west of the high school. The schools are centrally located between Kirkwood and Little York.

A unique event in Kirkwood High School history is the Annual Kirkwood High School Alumni Association Banquet. The first banquet was held in 1902, and in May 2002 this organization held its Centennial Celebration with 251 in attendance. Those who attended KHS, loyal alumni, former teachers, friends and spouses gather each May to greet former classmates and friends.

The secretary's record books from the past are interesting reading. In 1917 the decorations for the banquet were in a patriotic theme appropriate for the times. Stars and Stripes, small tents, soldier dolls in khaki and nurse dolls in Red Cross uniforms adorned the tables. In 1944 Mrs. Bert Thompson read the Honor Roll of all the Kirkwood High School alumni in the Armed forces of our country. There were 84 in service at that time. In 1959 there were 172 who attended the banquet which was the largest number ever at that time.

In 1961 after the Kirkwood and Little York consolidation, at the annual banquet the association voted to retain the name Kirkwood High School Alumni Association and ask Yorkwood seniors to be their guests if they cared to come. it was a standing vote and passed by a large majority.

All the banquets close with standing and singing with nostalgic fervor the Kirkwood High School Loyalty song.

High School was held in tan brick new North School 1899

Monmouth College

Monmouth College's "Old Main" Built 1863 - Burned 1907

Acknowledged as one of America's distinguished liberal arts colleges, Monmouth College ushered in the new millennium anticipating its sesquicentennial celebration in 2003. Founded as a Presbyterian academy on April 18, 1853, Monmouth was elevated to a college by an act of the Illinois Legislature, receiving its charter in 1857.

Monmouth's first president, the Rev. David Alexander Wallace of Boston, ushered the fledgling college through its most financially difficult years, including the Civil War, when more than 230 Monmouth students, faculty and trustees enlisted in the Union Army. Wallace was succeeded by Jackson B. McMichael, less charismatic than Wallace, but a strong administrator who helped shape a modern curriculum.

Jackson McMichael's son, Thomas Hanna McMichael, was inaugurated as Monmouth's fourth president in 1903. An alumnus who had become pastor of a large Presbyterian church in Cleveland, the younger McMichael would become the college's longest tenured president, serving 33 years. During his administration, most of the modern campus was built, and Monmouth began to acquire a strong academic reputation throughout the country.

James Harper Grier, pastor of Second United Presbyterian Church in Monmouth, assumed the presidency in 1936. Within five years, the country was on the verge of war, and virtually all male students prepared to leave campus. Responding to the potential crisis, Grier traveled to Washington with his business manager, where he secured a contract with the Department of the Navy to train future aviators at Monmouth College. Over the next three years, more than 3,500 cadets trained on the college campus and were taught such subjects as navigation by Monmouth College faculty.

A string of capable administrators succeeded Grier-- Robert Gibson, Duncan Wimpress, Richard Stine, DeBow Freed, Bruce Haywood, Sue Huseman and Richard Giese. Wimpress presided over a period of expansion in the 1960s when enrollment reached a high-water mark of 1,350. Freed successfully steered the college through a prolonged recession in the 1970s, and Haywood brought a new focus to the liberal arts curriculum during his 14-year tenure. Huseman, the first woman to be elected president, is remembered for the sense of community she helped establish among students, faculty, alumni and townspeople.

Today, under President Richard Giese, Monmouth College is home to 1,100 students from 18 states and 22 foreign nations. New facilities include Bowers Hall, a contemporary suite-style residence opened in 2001, and Huff Athletic Center, featuring a gymnasium, natatorium and fieldhouse, scheduled to open in 2003. In recent years, the former Carnegie Library was transformed into an elegant student services building named Poling Hall, while a former fraternity house was remade into the Mellinger Teaching and Learning Center.

Most of the college buildings are located on the rolling, tree-crowned campus on the east side of Monmouth. Peacock Memorial Athletic Park, a state-of-the-art soccer and baseball complex, was recently constructed along U.S. Route 34, just blocks from campus. Adjoining the park is LeSuer Nature Preserve, which serves as a biology field station and features a public nature trail. The college also maintains a valuable freshwater biology research station on the Mississippi River near Keithsburg.

Currently under construction, the 155,000-square-foot Huff Athletic Center will be the largest structure on campus, extending the 1925 gymnasium and the current Glennie Gymnasium more than half a block to the west. It is part of an extensive campus-wide improvement program that includes major renovations to Hewes Library, classroom facilities, Stockdale Student Center and the historic Dahl Chapel and Auditorium, Monmouth's oldest academic building.

Solidly financed with a growing endowment of $50 million, today's Monmouth College is able to keep pace with rapidly changing technology while offering generous financial assistance to its students. For a majority, the cost of attending this nationally ranked private liberal arts college is comparable to that of most state universities.

Two of the first national women's fraternities, Pi Beta Phi and Kappa Kappa Gamma, were founded at Monmouth and still have active chapters here, along with another fraternity for women, Alpha Xi Delta. National men's fraternities on campus are Alpha Tau Omega, Sigma Phi Epsilon and Zeta Beta Tau.

Monmouth offers students opportunities to develop leadership, teamwork skills and a sense of responsibility in a wide variety of interests. Campus service organizations play an important role as students reach out to the community. During spring break, Monmouth students have traveled to Indian reservations, Appalachia, and the inner city, volunteering to help those in need.

Proud of its Scottish heritage, Monmouth has an official registered tartan, sports teams are named the Fighting Scots and each spring traditional Highland games are played during the Ceilidh festival. The famed Monmouth College Pipe Band is featured at sporting events, in parades, and other public venues.

While some colleges seek to become universities, Monmouth is committed to remaining a teaching institution. For a century and a half, it has prided itself on the quality of its graduates, many of whom did not realize their full potential until they were inspired by the Monmouth faculty. It also remains committed to the local community, with nearly one in five of its students a resident of western Illinois.

The Campus Today

Monmouth Unit District #38 Schools

Although earliest residents of Illinois did not make a commitment to public schools, the early residents of Monmouth were more determined to support education. Limited to revenues from the sale of the 16th section of land from each township (providing $850 for Monmouth) and the three percent fund from the sale of federal lands, "subscription schools" were the rule where tuition was paid by the term. The first school, taught by Robert Black in the summer of 1832, had 44 pupils meeting in the first court house. Black, Virginian recently from Ohio and a church elder, used rote learning as students "blabbed" the three R's, math facts, and Bible verses. Similar schools, of various qualities, sprang up as Monmouth District #1 was organized (1834), for 50 children ages 5-21. One such school, opened in 1835, was said to have been led by a "Wild Irishman named McElory who was equally proficient in penmanship, prayer meeting and whiskey drinking." (1) The first district building (1835) was a 16 by 16 ft. frame school at the site of the old YMCA. Until 1863, the city council acted as the school board, although each principal and teachers were responsible for their classrooms.

With the population growth of the 1840-50s, almost 40 private schools met in churches, store fronts, homes, and a local tavern. Anna Watson from Galesburg, for example, offered Reading, Writing, and Geography for $2 a term of 3 months. For students wanting subjects like Latin and Algebra, "select schools" were available. W.B. Jenks, teaching at the Presbyterian church, provided an institute for training and examining future teachers. The need for additional buildings was addressed by purchasing land; however, not until 1848, with over 300 children in the district, was $800 raised to erect a 26 x 36 ft. structure.

The first tax supported and unified school, a two story and six room "Union East Ward School," was completed (1856) on an assessment of 60 cts for every $100. With A.H. Tracy as principal and instructor, who visited schools from across the Midwest to adopt the best practices, this school stood on the site of the present junior high. With more classrooms needed, churches and businesses rented property to the first superintendent, C.V. Brooks, until the "Union School-West Ward," was finished (1859) on the site of the current high school, featuring the first blackboards and factory purchased furniture.

Economic difficulties during the Civil War led to the school year shortened to six months and school suspended during the winter of 1861-62. By 1863, the city council absolved itself of school responsibilities, providing for the creation of District #38. By 1865, peace and financial stability returned-- yet, the panic of 1873 was more costly causing high school and vocal music to be eliminated Another victim of finances was the Berwick School on South 6th St. Started for black children in 1869 when voters rejected allowing black students in the ward schools, this school was integrated by 1871 but then soon closed. Residents remained unwilling for 15 years to resume programs, leaving teachers to accept pay cuts while often teaching in their homes and churches.

By the late 19th and early 20th century, elementary grade schools were constructed in the wards starting with Central (1888) for $52,000. Meant for grades four and higher, Central's arrival was part of the mission of leaders to improve the city's infrastructure with paved and lighted streets and proper sewer and water systems. Harding School came next (1899), named for school board director Harry Harding, remembered for assisting in fighting the use of tobacco and alcohol by students. Garfield (1902) honored president James Garfield, who visited Monmouth in the 1860s. Willits School (1906) honored local judge and school board leader Elias Willits. The first high school met in the old north ward school from 1870-73, when the prepatory school at Monmouth College filled that void. In 1888, with 50 students, high school returned to Central. By 1900, with enrollment near 400, the current high school building was erected (1909) for $151,000. A diversified curriculum was created for students bound for college, industry, home and child care, and classrooms as teachers. The gym (1939), library and AP rooms (1971) were later added.

During World War I, schools taught how to sacrifice and learn military procedures, with high school boys purchasing uniforms, staging marches, and accepting the decision to drop German as a foreign language,

After the World War II baby boom, citizens replaced the original ward schools and erected Lincoln, 1951, with additions in 1961 and 1971; Harding, 1954, additions 1971; Willits, 1954, additions 1974; and Garfield, 1974. Central School's days were also numbered, replaced by Central Junior High (1959) for $557,000, with additions made in 1971.

In the last two decades, new construction has featured improvements to the track and training and locker room facilities at Sunny Lane field. In 2001, the district, facing a dwindling population and financial base, underwent a reorganization which converted Harding and Willits Schools to attendance centers for K-3 students, Lincoln into an intermediate school for all district 4th-6th graders, and converted Garfield School to the Early Childhood Center.

(1) Newton Bateman and Paul Selby, Historical Encyclopedia of Illinois and History of Warren County, Chicago: Munsell Publishing Co., 1903, p. 752.

Monmouth High School

Warren Consolidated Unit School District #222

Warren School District #222

In the fall of 1999, the Fourth Grade Class at Warren Elementary School, and their teacher, Mrs. Debbie Burke, created a project titled Progress on the Prairie: The History of the Warren School District #222". The quotes in the following article were taken from The Daily Review Atlas, Monmouth, IL, Friday, March 20, 1959. The complete project is found at the Internet address: http://warriors.warren.k12.il.us (Warren School History)

Following the School Survey Act of 1945, a committee was chosen by county school board members to study, survey, and recommend changes. The study brought about interest in school improvement. In 1948, the schools of Hillis, Center, Enterprise, South Henderson, Phelps, West Prairie, Larchland, and Brannon were part of the Lenox Consolidated School. In 1950, these schools were added: Chapman, Ralston, Gerlaw, and later Hazel Dell.

Between 1948 and 1950, many small schools consolidated. "On November 29, 1955, a petition was presented requesting an election be called to give the voters of Law, Coldbrook, Muddy Corners, Lenox Consolidated, Foster-McGaw Consolidated and the Gerlaw Consolidated an opportunity to approve or disapprove the organization of a community unit district. This approval came on April 14, 1956 with the creation of the new district."

Monmouth (Dist. 38) loaned the territory around Monmouth so that District 222 could be formed. Two meetings were held on June 30, 1955 to decide what to do with the non-high territory. "...on July 21, 1955, a petition was filed asking for the creation of a community unit school district taking in Lenox, Gerlaw, Frymire, Coldbrook and ... a portion of the Galesburg community unit school district 205 in the area just to the east of Monmouth. 1,326 signatures were presented to Verne Conway, the Warren County Superintendent of Schools."

In August, the Galesburg territory was dropped. The district was legally created and voted upon on April 24, 1956 -. The new district to take over on July 1, 1956. An election was held on July 21, 1956 to settle the matter of money to build a new school.

The farmers first considered having attendance centers at Gerlaw, Law, and Fairview Center, with a high school campus east of Monmouth. "Sam Phelps is credited with suggesting the idea of a campus type school, with the high school and elementary school using the same site and the same building."

"After casting about for locations, the board picked a 30 acre tract on the Kettering farm as a suitable site and paid $24,000 to buy it."

From 1956-1958 the older pupils attended Monmouth High School on a tuition basis ... and the younger pupils went to Gerlaw, Law, Fairview Center, Frymire, Larchland, Muddy Corners, Phelps, Enterprise and Coldbrook 47." Law School was kept open but the other nine schools were sold by the Warren County Board of Trustees and the money went to District 222.

"For all practical purposes the district's history began in late June, 1955, after proposals to form a dual district with Monmouth had been rejected by the voters of District No. 38. By the following summer, the architectural firm represented by Cletus R. Foley, former Monmouth resident, had completed some sketches that pleased the new board of education.

"On June 21, 1957, at Law School bids were opened and proposals were submitted by about six firms for the general contract. "One year's time was required to plan the project and work out the details and more than one year was required to construct the project.

Warren School District #222 was formally dedicated on Sunday, March 22, 1959.

When Warren School began, Clinton Hagemann was the superintendent and Donald Gibb was the elementary principal. The board of education members were: Lee A. Rogers, President, Sam Phelps, Secretary, Jerry Hanson, Paul Lee, A. Lewis Long, Earl Lyons, Hugh McConnell. Faculty members included: Eldon R. Aupperle, Aaron Downey, Vada Forbes, Rodney Galusha, Mildred Geisz, Leland Gleasman, Eunice Heston, Maybelle Hurka, Shirley Jones, Phyllis Kettering, Ethel Kniss, Barbara Lair, Nancy Lupton, Edna Malley, C.P. Patterson, Beulah Patterson, Laurellen Porter, Betty Seward, Marilyn Yarde, Robert Yarde.

Fairview Center Schhol *Coldbrook School* *Enterprise School* *Frymire School* *Muddy Corners School*

Larchland School *Law School* *Phelps School* *Gerlaw School*

Foster School Fall 1922
Esther Brownlee - Teacher
Back Row: Unknown, Unknown, Unknown, Elleworth DeJanes, Unknown. Front Lines: Unknown, Randolph Liggett, Edith Livington, Bernice Albert, Lucille Shunick, Alberta Albert. On the Ground: Unknown, Bill Livington
* Pearson boys in school - some of the blank names

Frymire School

Warren County Memorial & Clubs, Organizations

Sumner	Spring Grove	Kelly
Little York	Gerlaw	
Hale	Monmouth	Coldbrook
	Monmouth	Coldbrook
Tompkins	Lenox	Floyd
Kirkwood	Larchland	Cameron
Ellison	Roseville	Berwick
Smithshire	Roseville	Berwick
Point Pleasant	Swan	Greenbush
	Swan Creek	Greenbush

1906 Roseville High School Baseball Team
Top Row: Davenport-first base, Harrington-pitcher, Downs-left field, Pittman-2nd & catcher. 2nd Row: Prouty-r.f. & pitcher, Prof. Booz-2nd & MGR., R. Watson-pitcher & s.s., Ockert-centerfield. 3rd Row: Fisher-3rd base, Kiddler-catcher

MEMORIAL

Alta R. Grimsley

Alta Grimsley before polio.

Alta was born on June 16, 1922 at McLeansboro, Illinois, to Guy and Edna Mullen Grimsley. When Alta was ten months old, the Grimsley family moved to Ponemah, Warren County, Illinois. Alta attended Liberty School, until 1933, then the family moved to Monmouth. Here she attended Central grade and Junior High School and graduated from Monmouth High School in 1942. During her high school years she earned several awards for athletic accomplishments in volleyball, tennis, and basketball. She also loved fishing, baseball and bowling.

Following high school Alta worked at the Rock Island Arsenal. For about five years she was owner and operator of Grimsleys' Cafe. She later worked at the Park N' Eat Restaurant in Monmouth and then at Gale Products in Galesburg.

During this period in time Alta's life changed dramatically. On September 14, 1959, Alta was mowing her lawn when she felt something was not quite right. Even though she was only thirty-seven at the time, she attributed the feeling to "old age." A week later, after fishing with her sister and her sister's two children, she developed severe pain in her back and stomach. At first she was diagnosed as having the flu, but later in the week, another doctor broke the news that she had polio. She was admitted to St. Francis Hospital in Peoria on September 21, 1959. This was the beginning of a long and painful sixteen months.

Polio hit Alta hard... she was placed in an iron lung, laying in one position, and not being able to move on her own was a horrible ordeal. There was not even a radio to listen to, just iron lungs lined up side by side with patients enduring very long days. There was no dignified way of eating, brushing teeth, having hair shampooed, and etc. She was completely dependent on others.

Then came the day that Alta had yearned for. While still in the lung she recovered movement in her index finger on the right hand. She thought she was on the road to complete recovery and let out a scream of joy. Unfortunately, movement to other parts of her body were either very slow to return or were to never return. When she was able to be out of the lung for short periods of time she was started on long sessions of therapy. During the course of her hospital stay she had many setbacks, including pneumonia. Not only did she have to learn to breathe again, but because her muscles were no longer working in many parts of her body, she could not sit up or walk. Walking was something she never succeeded in doing.

She had an inner strength to be admired and envied. After returning to the home she shared with her mother, she set goals one by one and met them. Both she and her mother decided a house would be better than their mobile home. They bought and moved into a one-story house in 1962. As Alta found there were still a lot of things she was not able to do, she set her mind to work, inventing ways to do what used to be simple tasks. She dug a garden with a hoe while sitting in her wheelchair, planted the seed with a can attached to a long pole. She also canned her vegetables while sitting in her wheelchair. If she couldn't physically accomplish a task she merely invented methods, tools, or ways she could accomplish the task. Later on, she was able to get a motorized cart, which made her outdoor work much easier. After her mother died in 1983, Alta lived by herself. She was able to do this with electric lifts, electric bed, and much later a threewheeler. She was quite dependent on electricity and quite nervous when storms were brewing, not knowing if she could get in or out of bed.

One could accurately call Alta a competitive person. In 1964 she saw an ad in the paper wanting an Avon Products salesperson. After convincing the manager she could indeed handle the job, she took on the challenge and became one of the top salespersons in her district. She was also quite a bridge player. Her brother introduced her to the game and later she took advantage of the instructional classes held at the high school. She then played regularly in her home and at Strom Center until she met with a severe accident on June 29, 1998. After that her health began to fail. Soon she was being cared for twenty-four hours a day, in her home, and died there on December 29, 2001. With the cards of life she was dealt, she played the game the best she could. *Submitted by Mabel Westerfield and Janis Erickson*

Alta Grimsley after contacting polio.

American Legion

By an act of congress, the American Legion organization was incorporated on September 16, 1919, as a nonpolitical organization.

The Marion B. Fletcher Post #136 was organized in Monmouth in 1919 also. Their first forming meeting was held in the Odd Fellows Hall with 100 men attending. They received their charter that same year, but didn't get under way until March 17, 1920. Dell B. Hardin was elected their first commander, with Larry Byrne serving as commander now. A committee suggested the name of Marion B. Fletcher as the post name, which was accepted. He had left high school to go with company H, 6th. Illinois Infantry, in 1917 and was killed in France in 1918. He is buried in Ellison Cemetery. Every memorial day, the Legion members pay tribute to him at his grave.

In 1926, they formed a Drum & Bugle corps and a ritual team, the first ones in the district. They have had a firing squad for many years. November 2, 1933, they leased the second floor of the Holliday Building, on the southwest corner of east First Avenue and south First Street. In 1939, they purchased the whole building, holding formal dedication services on April 2, 1940. Mr. O.E. Sterett was commander then. The Ladies Auxiliary were to hold their meetings there also.

The Legion Post can be very proud of their past sponsorships. Junior Legion baseball teams, Legion rifle & pistol club, junior American Legion, Boy Scout troops, Cub Scout packs, an Explorer Post, Sea Scout ship and a Rover crew. They had a fund to aid veterans and their families, a food basket and toy distribution for needy families in Monmouth and aided veteran's hospitals. They were instrumental in getting an Auxiliary Police Corps formed here, after the Elks Club burned down. Many Legionnaires helped out that night.

The Ladies Auxiliary was chartered on February 18, 1923, with 58 members listed. Mrs. Alida Buckley was their first president, with Mrs. Judy Potter serving as president now.

They kept busy, holding dances, teas, and card parties, to raise money. A sewing club made comfort items for the veteran's hospitals. They had their own drill team and award winning glee club. Mrs. Gracie Peterson was their musician and also led the singers. She is still a member, at the age of 100. They still do a lot for our veterans in local nursing homes and other hospitals, as well as the residents in the home at Quincy, Illinois. They contribute to many worthwhile projects, (too numerous to list), and cater parties at the post home.

They have been very actively involved in the poppy program, for disabled veterans, since it first began and have promoted educational programs since the early 40's. They send cards to service personnel and are conducting a coupon campaign to seven military bases overseas. After the September 11th attack on the Pentagon, they spearheaded a fund drive and collected $3,375.00, which was sent to them.

The 40 & 8 voiture, was chartered on June 13, 1932. You must be a Legion member to belong. Veterans talked about riding in boxcars across France that would carry 40 men or 8 horses, hence the name. It originated because of a shortage of nurses. They held fund raisers, in order to award nursing scholarships. This is on going, with their famous spaghetti suppers. They also support child welfare, youth activities, and Legion projects. The first Chef de Gares of record were, Dr. Firth and Stanley Merion, with Fred Burgland serving in this office now.

They are most famous for their locomotive, boxcar, and eventually, old fire truck. The original engine was a 1936 Cadillac chassis, with a Dodge flat head engine. The boxcar was patterned after the French ones and bore the M&ST, L railroad insignia. The fire truck was purchased from the Monmouth Fire Department in the 1950's, for $1.00, with the stipulation that it would never be sold or given away. Both can still be seen in parades today.

In 1967, construction began on a building at the corner of North Eleventh Street and the by-pass road. It was the "permanent home" for the Legion family. Ten men had put up $5,000.00 apiece, to make this long time dream a reality. Mike Romano was commander then. The auxiliary held their first meeting there in June and Gerry Harvey Erwin was their president. The building was formally dedicated on July 6, 1968 with appropriate ceremonies and a dance.

The sons of the American Legion were restarted in 1996, and John Morrison was their commander. It had run from 1933 until 1940, when it is presumed the "sons" went off to world war II. When they returned, they were eligible to join the Legion. Bill Waller has been commander for the past three years. They now have 54 members and generously donate to the Legion projects and veteran organizations. You must be a male descendant of an American Legion member to join.

The Junior Auxiliary is for girls under the age of eighteen, who are descendants of ex-service men. The first recorded president was Linda Law, for the Monmouth unit, in 1952, and they were active for many years. Interest dwindled until 2001, when Cher Young "jump started" them again. They held fund raisers to provide comfort items for veterans. In 2002, Judy Potter and Barb Byrne took over as their leaders. They have 35 members and continue to raise funds by making craft items for sale. They have gone to the veteran's home at Quincy twice, and presented them with the funds they have made for their personal use.

The "Legion Family" is, "all for one and one for all" - for the good of the post and our veterans.

American Legion Hall

Kirkwood Senior Citizens

In August of 1969, a group of older Kirkwood residents who had been meeting on a weekly basis to play cards in the Park District Gym organized the Kirkwood Senior Citizens. They elected Golden Dobey President, Mildred Rowley Vice President, Edna Hancock Secretary, and Rev. Roy Hofstetter Treasurer and decided to meet the third Wednesday of each month for a noon meal and program. They met in the shelter house at Young's Lake in summer and in the Methodist and Presbyterian churches and, occasionally, the Community Club room and the Masonic hall the rest of the time. They enjoyed good fellowship and took up collections to do their part for the community when needs arose.

In a few years, members decided they needed a permanent meeting place and approached the Park District board about repairing and remodeling the old Ag building by the gym. They were well along in this when the building burned. In November of 1990, a committee met with the town board about buying the empty Community Club building and adjoining barbershop and renting them to the Senior Citizens who would clean up and renovate them. The Community Club gave the board $1,000 to apply against the cost. The purchase was made and a lease signed for $1.00 a year.

The Senior citizens had raised about $10,000 and received a grant of $5,000 from the *Len Everet Endowment Fund* administered by the Warren County United Way. This plus hundreds of hours of donated labor, both by members and by the community, removed the dividing wall, roofed, wired, plumbed, heated, carpeted, painted, and airconditioned it. They named it *The Village Center* to indicate that, as the community had shared in the work, they should share in its use. From the start of the program the Senior Citizens had taken responsibility for delivering "meals on wheels" in the Kirkwood area and, in October of 1991, the Bi-County Nutrition Project selected the Center as a site for serving congregate meals for those sixty and older.

Volunteers open the Center at 8 AM on weekdays, make coffee and bring refreshments. Members and non-members come in to drink coffee, visit and play cards. Hot meals are served at 11:30 and, on the third Wednesday, between thirty and forty members and guests hold a business meeting and enjoy a program after the meal. The Center is also used for family reunions, class reunions, and other meetings on a first come-first served basis. A free-will contribution is usually given for use of the building.

Kirkwood Senior Center

The expenses of utilities, cleaning, and repairs required much more income so the Senior Citizens have raised money with fried chicken feeds, ice-cream socials, sausage and biscuits breakfasts, etc. We are also a United Way agency and receive monthly payments. Our stated purpose is, "to be of service to people in general, to the Senior Citizens in particular, and to help in community affairs where it is possible".

We feel we are doing this by providing a safe, clean, comfortable building with handicapped accessible rest rooms and by holding meetings and parties where newcomers can get acquainted and all can escape the isolation and loneliness that so often go with aging. We have taken responsibility for the United way campaign in Kirkwood and give over $500 a year in donations to the Kirkwood churches, the Jamieson Center, United Way, Starting Point, Kirkwood Fire Department, the Salvation Army, Boy and Girl Scouts and other needs as they are presented. Members have gone to Yorkwood Grade School to listen to first, second and third graders read and help them with arithmetic for about five years as well as being pro-tem grandmothers when needed,

Our present officers are Randell Lovell President, Archie McIntosh Vice President, Dick Speer Secretary, Martha Murphy Treasurer, and Gerri Smith Corresponding Secretary. In our thirty-two years, we have had twenty-two presidents: Golden Dobey, Mildred Rowley, Rev. Roy Hofstetter, Tom Snodgrass, Verne Conway, George Baxter, Robert Work, Florence Higgins, Park Byers, Hazel Frank, Ruth Lewis, Ed Frank, Arlene Rhinehart, Bob Snodgrass, Myrtle Sullivan, Jo Paris, Glenn Sanberg, Martha Murphy, Dick Speer, Archie McIntosh, Ada Galbreath, and Randell Lovell. Verne Conway, Mary Alice Hall, Wm. McLaughlin, Lucille Poling, Mildred Warner, Martha Murphy, Arlene Rhinehart, and Glenn Sanberg have been recognized as *ageless achievers* by the Western Illinois Agency on Aging. Jo Paris served on that board.

Our goals are to continue providing a clean, comfortable place for the community to meet, for old friends to make new friends, and to help bind a town into a community.

Kirkwood Senior Citizens

Kiwanis Club

In the autumn of 1923, two representatives from the Galesburg Kiwanis Club came to Monmouth and interviewed C. M. Huey regarding the organization of a Kiwanis in Monmouth. Mr. Huey and W. W. Brent, the first president, talked with several professional and businessmen. A club was organized with the charter being presented by the Illinois Kiwanis Governor, Dan Wentworth, on November 12, 1923.

In December of 1923 the club voted to award cups to the fraternity at Monmouth College securing the highest grades. It was later done on the same basis to the sorority and both of these are still being done today.

During the 1920s our club helped families in need at the County Home, furnished milk to needy babies, furnished glasses to children recommended by the school nurse, took about 100 children on a trip to New Salem, presented portraits of Abraham Lincoln to rooms of fourth grade classes whose pupils wrote the best essay on the Springfield Trip, and took first prize to the best float in the District Convention Parade at Peoria. The big highlight during this era was the building of the Shelter House at Monmouth Park in 1926. In 1929 our club sponsored a picnic at Monmouth Park at which International Secretary Parker, various District Officers and the Governor of the state of Illinois were present. About 3,000 people attended this event.

Even with the Depression in the early 1930s our club was able to continue its function of service to youth and this community. The club sponsored Boy Scout paper drives, 4-H events, sent a boy to Boy's state each year, band concerts at the Warren County Home, and helped maintain a Community Social Center. The club also helped pay for remodeling the Black Masonic Hall.

In 1936, the club sponsored the erection of the Band Shell in Monmouth Park. About this time the club began to hold Farmers' Nights at which members entertained farmers at a meeting. This is still being done today.

The District Convention Parade was held in Burlington, Iowa in 1936 and our club took the Monmouth High School band over there to participate in the event. We performed numerous minstrel shows for the benefit of youth. Another major project was started in 1947 - the organization of Lake Youngquist Camp for Youth. The entire club became active in this endeavor. This activity continued for many years.

The keys for the Gibson Woods Starter House at the new Gibson Woods golf course were presented by our club in 1966. In the spring of 1973 major improvements were made to the bleachers and playground equipment at South Park by our club.

We did much cleaning in 1975 on the Strom Senior Citizens Center when they moved into the building on South A street. In 1989, boat docks were built at Citizens Lake, a good place for fishing. In 1982 the club helped set-up the bleachers, etc., in the new YMCA. Costing $15,000, in 1984, we rebuilt our Myron Mikita Community Theater in the same location where we had earlier constructed a covered Band Shell in 1936.

In 1987 the Club, through the help of Joel Anderson, Chairman of the Spiritual Aims Committee, started having a prayer breakfast during National Prayer Week. It was held in the First Christian Church. The second was held in 1988, a memorial for Joel Anderson, who had passed away. Dr. Stafford Weeks, Rev. Jerry Hazen, Rev. Dale Catlin, Rev. John Irwin, and Steve Siemens have addressed these groups.

In 1991 the Club furnished the labor to build a shelter house at Pinewood Nursing Home. Mel Siverly, Division 19 Lt. Gov., wife Joyce, and Charlie and Marie Courtney drove to Abingdon for its 50th anniversary.

Pancake Day in 1992 - It was reported that according to past records we had our greatest profits in the amount of $4,172.14 - Charlie Courtney sold 791 tickets. Members again helped with various Red Cross bloodmobiles.

The Kiwanis Club of Yucca Valley, CA., told they would be honoring Dr. Russell Jensen with his 50- year Legion of Honor Golden Pin and certificate. Russ joined our club in 1945 and was president in 1947.

In 1997-98, Don Perrin was elected to serve as Lt. Gov. of our Division 19 and we celebrated the 81st birthday of our piano accompanist, Ruth Finch. We purchased a new banner from Lee Merrill's memorial fund. We also started placing our monthly Kiwanis magazine in the offices of Drs. Arora, Johnson, Sexton, Guerrero and the Warren County Public Library.

A Circle K club at Monmouth College was organized. The Monmouth city car sticker features our Kiwanis Club 75th anniversary.

On January 20th, we displayed our flags representing the countries where Kiwanis Clubs are located - given in memory of Beverly Davis. Noted that our local hospital was the first one in state of Illinois to meet criteria for EMSC - a Kiwanis project. Club participated in Summerfest on city square. Purchased new aprons for Peanut Day. Our first woman farmer of the year (Marcia Morgan) was honored.

Kiwanis Logo

Knights Of Columbus
Monmouth, Illinois

The Order of the Knights of Columbus is a Catholic Fraternal Order, was founded in 1882 in New Haven, Connecticut, by Father Michael J. McGivney, a parish priest, from a small group of Catholic laymen. They sought strength, and security through unity of purpose and devotion to a holy cause: they vowed to be defenders of their country and their families and their Faith. These men were bound together by the ideal of Christopher Columbus, the discoverer of the Americans, the one whose hand brought the Holy Faith to this New World. From the beginning Knights of Columbus has grown from several members in one council to more than 12,000 councils and over 1.6 million members throughout the United States, Canada, the Philippines, Mexico, the Dominican Republic, Puerto Rico, Panama, the Bahamas, the Virgin Islands, Guatemala, Guam, and Saipan.

Monmouth Third Degree Council #1496 was charted July 3, 1910 and is located at 200 South Sunny Lane. The Charter Membership list: Rev. P.P. Owens, Rev. P.V. Egan, Rev. J.J. Lyons, D. O'Connor, J.D. Toal, J.A. Callow, R.J. Fraser, J.D. Lynch, T.E. Shunick, W.T. Fitzpatrick, W.E. Morris, J. Lee, M.D. Shunick, J. O'Dowd, A.L. Bobb, M.J. Graham, W. Burns, J. Collins, G.L. Clayton, M.W. Costello, M. Costello, F.H. Cavanaugh, H. Huston, J.G. Leins, M.C. Lee, C.J. Leary, A. McCleary, W.J. Reedy, W.C. Spiegel, G. Slater, M.E. Shunick Jr., J. Smith, J.P. Shunick, F.C. Shunick, E.J. Shunick, F.X. Weklenbauger, W.W. Brady, D.P. Barry, J. Brannan, J. Costello, J. Callow, C. Callow, W.E. Flannigan, H. Landuyt, J.G. Laughlin, J. Laughlin, J.S. Mason, M. Murphy, H.P. McLaughlin, F. Patterson, T.A. Roche, J.K. Sullivan, T. St. Ledger, A. St. Ledger, J. St. Ledger, D. Shunick, J.M. Sullivan, J. Slater, R. Shunick.

On June 24, 1952 Fourth Degree assembly #0230 Monmouth Assembly was charted. The charter members were: Faithful Navigator Carl Schreiber, Faithful Friar Rev. Dean E.S. Dunn, Faithful Captain Albert D. Fayette, Faithful Admiral Lawrence C. Towney, Faithful Joe McCleary, Faithful Leo Leary, Faithful Pilot Michael E. Tabone, Faithful Inside Sentential J. Henry Gordon, Rev. Father Arthur Bray, Rev. Father Edmund Blough, Donald Brannon, Les Enderlin, C. L. Gavin, Dr. S.R. Gottler, Emory V. Hawcock, Lambert Healy, Frank Horn, John L. Kinney, Michael Lee, Joseph A. Letchfield, John D. Lynch Jr., J. L. Lynch, W.B. Lynch, Charles Lo Preste, William McCann, William A. Moran, Clement J. O'Brien, D.W. O'Connor, Clarence O'donnell, Robert C. Read, Arthur Roche, Ed J. Shunick, John Shunick, Robert E. Shunick, George Slater, John Slusser, Joseph D. Toal, Joseph E. Toal, Dr. F.C. Winters, Dr. Harold F. Wimp.

The Knights of Columbus hall was built in 1972 at 200 South Sunny Lane with many volunteer helpers. Prior to this they met on the second floor of 200 South Main next to WRAM radio studio. Before this they met on the second floor on the west side of the square. Above the Koke-Sparrow or Romano Insurance.

In 1985 the council celebrated its 75th Anniversary. Many council charitable activities are run to support church, school and community. One is the Newman Fund for students at state colleges, a disaster fund run by Illinois State KC Council, supporting vocations of young men studying for the priest hood, and the best known "Tootsie Roll Drive" for the mentally handicapped. Approximately $2000.00 is raised annualy for distribution of 90 percent locally to Warren Achievement and Special Olympics. The other 10 percent goes to the Illinois State Council for a statewide distribution for special mentally handicapped programs.

Current Council 1496 officers are Steve Bohn Grand Night, Tim Denison Deputy Grand Knight, David Driscoll Financial Secretary, Gary Dulin Recorder, Claire Driscoll Chancellor, Ray Cavanaugh Advocate, Joe McClery Treasurer, Trafford Anderson Warden, Jim Schreck Inside Guard, David Noel Outside Guard, Trustees are Chuck Dixon, Don VonKannon, and Ed Skinner.

Assembly 0230 officers are Tim Denison Faithful Navigator, Chuck Dixon Faithful Captian, David Driscoll Faithful Admiral, Ed Skinner Faithful Comptroller, Robert Roche Faithful Scribe, Dutch Saettler Faithful Pusar, Raymond Gillen Faithftil Pilot, Donald Vonkannon Inner Sentinel, Stephen Bohn Outer Sentinel, Trustees: Don Barannan, Victor Cokel, and Gerald Schisler.

Knights of Columbus Hall - Monmouth

Warren County Masonic Lodges

On, Dec. 14, 1843, I.W.F. Edmundson, Benjamin Hibbard, John Miles, George Lanphere, Samuel Webster, John Young, Daniel McNeil, Simeon Scripture, David Cohen, Henry McCartney, and Daniel Markham received a dispensation from the newly formed Grand Lodge of Illinois to form Monmouth Lodge #37. They were chartered October 6, 1846. After renting a few years, they erected a third story on what became the Trust and Savings Bank building. After about fifty years, they bought the Brererton mansion on South Main in 1917 and remodeled it into a Masonic temple. About fifty years later, they rented the second floor above the "Candy Kitchen" on S. Main Street, then bought and remodeled the old West Side church forty years ago. The lodge supports Masonic charities and grants annual college scholarships. Prominent Masons include Daniel McNeil who held appointed and elected offices in the Grand Lodge and Clifford Shafer, 33, who served many years as DDGM and as Junior and Senior Grand Deacon of the Grand Lodge. Others serving as DDGM were A.B. Holliday, D.D. Dunkle, James R. Dick, and Eldridge Sloan. Principal officers are Wm. Ischer, Rod Collins, Francis Pearsall, Carol Heflin, and Verne Barnes.

Eighteen Masons in Young America, (later renamed Kirkwood), received a dispensation in 1866 and a charter Oct. 1, 1867 to form A. Lincoln lodge #518. First officers were Nathan Pierpoint, B.C. Davis, L.M. Mitchell, J.B. Gregory, S.A. Elliott, Cyrus Bute, and D. E. Perkins. They rented the second or third floors of five business buildings on Kirk Street before buying the present lodge hall in 1981. Fred Edgerton, Ralph Tinkham, and Richard Speer have served the Grand Lodge as DDGM. Principal officers are Wendell Brooks, Phillip J. Brooks, Dan Hahn, Dennis Edwin, and Will Brooks. The lodge sponsors the Kirkwood softball league and grants college scholarships.

Seventeen Masons of Roseville received a dispensation in 1866 and a charter on Oct. 1, 1867 from the Grand Lodge of Illinois to form Roseville Lodge #519. The first officers were D. Adams, W. Clayton, J.B. Wilsey, B. Ragon, D.M. Taliaferro, J. Bradley, Wm. Stanfield, and Israel Jared. They meet in the building they have owned for many years at the intersection of Rts. 67 and 116. Howard Bradley served as DDGM. Raritan Lodge #727 merged with Roseville in 1970 and Good Hope Lodge #617 in 1996. Lester Levengood, 33, of Good Hope Lodge served many years as DDGM and on Grand Lodge committees. Present officers are John Brewer, John House, Rudy Corman, Harold Anderson, and Jim Anderson. The lodge honors outstanding members and community builders at an annual ice cream social.

In 1856, nine Master Masons in Warren County chartered Warren Chapter #30 Royal Arch Masons, meeting in Monmouth with David B. Rice, Wm. A. Seaton, and Samuel Stanley as the three dais officers. The chapter was a central meeting place for leading masons from ten lodges, Monmouth and Trinity of Monmouth, Roseville, Youngstown, Berwick, A. Lincoln of Kirkwood, Fortitude of Gladstone, Raritan, Alexis and Oquawka. Four of these lodges remain. The Chapter owned a three-eighths interest in the Monmouth Masonic Temples where they met for the first one hundred years. They then gave their interest to Monmouth Lodge and rented from them, presently at 200 S E Street. Verne E. Barnes, Verne F. Barnes, Theo. Clarke, Richard Speer, Howard Butler and Don Bulen have served as DDGHP and in other appointive Grand Chapter offices. Principal officers are Don Bulen, Art Hammon, Alan Lester, Cliff Shafer, Wm. Schlobohm, and Michael McDorman.

Monmouth Chapter 227 Order of the Eastern Star received a dispensation on Aug. 8, 1894 and a charter on Oct. 4, 1894 to form a chapter with Mary Miles, D.D. Dunkle, and Effa Shoemaker as principal officers. In 1920, they helped form and install officers in Roseville Chapter #836 and Mary Lincoln Chapter #837 of Kirkwood. Mary Lincoln Chapter merged with Monmouth in 1982, as did Roseville Chapter in 1988, Oquawka Chapter #165 was chartered in 1897 and merged with Monmouth Chapter in 1981. The Illinois Grand Chapter has honored Elizabeth Hickman, Dorothy Clarke, Vera Trimble, Letha Palmer, Susanna Webb, Roger and Jane Smith, Francis Nott, and Doris Nipper with appointments as Grand Lecturers, Grand Board members, Grand Representatives and Grand Officers. Present officers are Fran Nott, Dick Speer, Tony and Darlene Spiker, Marge Schaumleffel, Maxine Giddings, Rose and Bob Trimble, Howard and Luanne Butler, Virginia and Bob Cornell, Louise and Jim Fair, Beth Alumbaugh, Martha Murphy, and Don Bulen. Over the years, Monmouth Chapter has contributed thousands of dollars to state and local charities including music scholarships.

Galesburg Commandery #8 KT first met in 1859 and was chartered in Galesburg Oct. 26, 1860. First officers were J.A. Thompson, Caleb Finch, J.W. Spalding, H.M, Hale, J.H. Marshall, Geo. C. Lanphere, Sidney Myers, A.C. Dannaken, S.H. Mathews, and E.L. Ives. They met in four Masonic Temples in Galesburg before moving to Monmouth in 1885. George C. Lanphere and Charles H. Toothe served as Grand Commanders of Illinois. Past Commanders Chester Allen served as Grand Master of Illinois, Ben Need as Grand High Priest of Illinois Royal Arch Masons and Grand Master of Illinois Cryptic Masons and Glyn Stewart as Grand Master of Illinois Cryptic Masons. Don Bulen, Howard Butler and Dick Speer served as Aides to the Inspecting Officer, Principal officers are Michael McDorman, Arthur Hammon, Harry Hopping, Joe Halford, and Willard Staggs.

Masonic Emblem

Warren County, Illinois Genealogical Society

Starting with shared interests in genealogy in chance conversations in the Post Office in early 1981, a meeting was soon called to assess local interest in forming a genealogical society. A meeting was held in the community room of the Community National Bank, and the Warren County, IL. Genealogical Society came into being and was organized in April 1981. We were instituted by the Knox County, IL Genealogical Society. Officers elected were: Tim Denison, President; Barbara Klein, 1st vice-president; Richard Koehn, 2nd Vice-president; Don Perrin, Treasurer; Ethel Trego, Recording Secretary; Sharon Todd, Corresponding Secretary, Directors: Harriett Reynolds and Betty Kinkaid. By-laws and guidelines were adopted with Board meetings on 2nd Thursday and regular meetings on 4th Thursday each month.

Our first money-making project was publication and sale of combined 1872 and 1893 Warren county Atlas. The next major project was walking and cataloging all existing cemeteries in Warren county.

Our purpose being to encourage and help others gather information of genealogical and historical value for educational purposes. Many students have used our materials for school work. We have answered queries from numerous States also from Canada, England, Australia, Hawaii and Greece.

Publications for sale and public use include: Courthouse records copied (as allowed by State law) such as birth, death& marriage indexes naturalization records, will indexes; funeral home records; many church records; all existing cemetery inscriptions; census records; local DAR applications and MANY obituaries. Our holdings have expanded to a full room and still growing. Located at 56 Public Square, we are proud to be known as one of the finest genealogical libraries in the State, having, also materials from other counties and States. We have over 300 publications for sale and many more for use in the Library.

We are a non-profit organization and welcome the loan or donation of old records, family histories and Bible records, which can be copied and returned unharmed to the donor.

Volunteers are usually at the Library each afternoon to help visitors find information of interest to them. We gladly help people get started on and continue their own research to the best of our ability. Memberships are always welcome and include a quarterly newsletter with items of local and genealogical interest.

We have two certificates available: The Early Pioneer Recognition Certificate for those whose ancestors lived here in 1850 or earlier and the Early Resident Certificate for those whose ancestors resided here in 1885 or earlier. Information is available from the Society.

Charter members: Tim and Joyce Denison, Barbara Klein, Betty Kinkaid, Ethel Trego, Donald Perrin, Sharon Todd, Harriett and Marshall Reynolds, Larry and Diane Bogart, Robert Acheson, Tom and Donna Archer, Durwood Allaman, Lois Bishop, Gregory Bogart, Velma Bosworth, George Baxter, Thomas Beardsley, Alva Barta, Phyllis Carter, Patricia Carter, Karen Condreay, Kenneth Cox, Verlee Dauma, Samuel Dicks, James and Debbie Darrah, Date and Louise Dawson, Anna Davidson, Lynne Devlin, Gail Edmison, Alice Edwards, Mrs Duane England, Jane Evans, Linda Fredrickson, Esther Fick, Streeter Flynn Jr, Jean Forbes, Evelyn Garrett, C. C. Gossett, Maralee Guiher, Wanda Grabowski, M/M Charles Green, Doris Haynes, Lucille Hall, Margaret Hamilton, Marjorie Hamilton, Dr & Mrs Michael Henry, Rosetta Henson, Gloria Holverson, Bertha Hooks, Anne Houlihan, M/M Bob Inman, M/M James Ishmael, Bonna Jean Johnson, M/M Richard Koehn, Raymond Kelly Jr., Ruth Kinney, Mary Lozier, Dorothy Mitchell, Shirley Melin, James and Martha Mattoon, Eva Mounce, Glenn and Elwilda Osborn, Sarabelle O'Daniel, Joyce Parrish, Anna Petrick, John and Barbara Pierce, Ray and Nellie Pine, Leonard Porter, Camille Radmacker, Dr and Mrs Wendell Roller, Rita Souther, Martha Strong, Dean and Carolyn Sandstrom, Joseph Stevenson, Lois Schmalshof, Russell and Donna Sheese, Merle and Amy Sanford, M/M Jeff Simmons, Mrs Edward Stephenson, Harry Stokes, Charles and Linda Talley, Barbara Thompson, Rosa VandeVoort, Jean Weir, Mabel Westerfield, Daniel Whisler, Susie Wallace, Thomas and Zelma Wallace, Louise Weston, Lee Zuker.

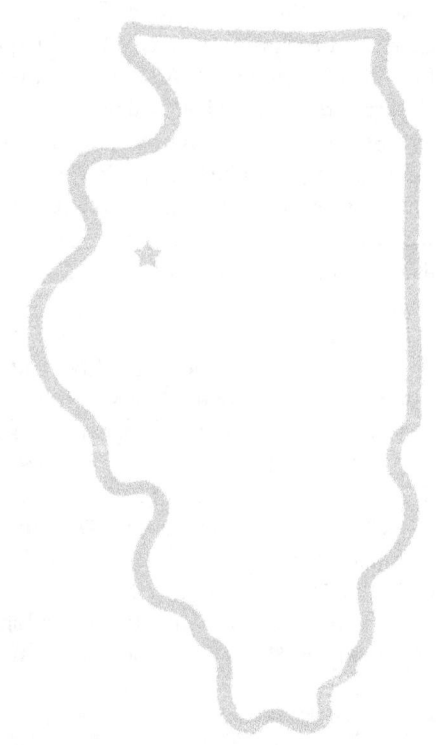

Warren County Illinois Genealogical Society Logo

Monmouth YMCA to Warren County YMCA

Present YMCA

The Monmouth YMCA was formed on February 18, 1882. In that first year, the members of the Monmouth YMCA worked hard to establish their place in the community and spread Christianity. Having no facility of their own to use, the YMCA used rooms at the Crusade Temperance Union until they were able to generate enough income to rent and furnish rooms of their own.

YMCA leaders worked with inmates teaching them the Word of God until their release, established a YLCA auxiliary for the young ladies of the community, and formed a library that housed a growing collection of books, daily and weekly papers.

The early YMCA strove to bring Christianity into the lives of all young men. This was achieved through Bible studies, prayer meetings, Gospel meetings and fellowship.

In a letter written by W.T. Wiley, the first General Secretary of the Monmouth YMCA, dated February 20, 1883, he explained the membership structure of the YMCA and associated fees per year. However, as in the YMCA mission, only young men who were of good moral character and seeking a Christian life were considered for membership.

Now, 120 years later, the Warren County YMCA still focuses on Christianity and spiritual wellness, but also physical and mental wellness.

The YMCA now offers programs ranging from swimming lessons to fitness classes to parent/child outreach to youth sports. In all YMCA programs and member services, basic core values of caring, honesty, respect and responsibility are practiced by staff and required by YMCA participants.

As in the beginning, there is no person turned away from YMCA services because of inability to pay, race, faith, and mental or physical wellness.

The National YMCA recently celebrated its 150th anniversary in 2001 in North America. In June 2001, 8,000 YMCA staff and volunteers from YMCA's all around the world gathered in New Orleans to celebrate the anniversary. More importantly, however, they came to enjoy Christian fellowship.

Early YMCA

Warren County Illinois Chapter DAR

The National Board of Management of NSDAR authorized "Mildred Warner Washington" and "Puritan and Cavalier" chapters to merge into a new chapter named "Warren County" on April 15, 2000.

Mildred Warner Washington "Hearts of Oak" of Monmouth, Illinois was organized April 2, 1902 from Warren Chapter which was organized April 7, 1897 with Mrs. Susanna I. (Nye) Webster (Mrs. John R.) with fifteen charter members.

Puritan and Cavalier Chapter of Monmouth, Illinois was organized April 26, 1902 with Mrs. Sarah (Bond) Hanley (Mrs. John F.) as organizing regent with eighteen charter members.

The Purpose of NSDAR is: To perpetuate the memory and the spirit of the men and women who achieved America's independence; to promote the development of an enlightened public opinion, to foster patriotic citizenship. National DAR motto is "God, Home and Country".

The chapter regularly contributes to state and national DAR projects, Bible records and cemetery records.

Some DAR projects: Remodeling DAR headquarters in Washington DC; supporting the following DAR schools: Bacone College, Berry College, Chemawa, Kate Duncan Smith, Tamassee, Crossnore, Hillside, and Hindman schools.

Several members have served District, State and National offices and committees including State Regents: Mrs. John (Sarah Bond) Hanley 1918-1920, Mrs. Ralph (Frances Brent) Killey 1963-1965 and Mrs. Victor (Jane Gregg) Lucas 1979-1981.

Genealogical Records Committee is charged with the responsibility of preserving valuable unpublished records of a genealogical nature. This committee copies, prepares in proper form, and places in the DAR Library annually many volumes of otherwise inaccessible data.

The Chapters have marked the following historical markers: The sites Where Abraham Lincoln spoke on October 11, 1858 about a senatorial contest at the Northeast corner of the Square and the corner of South First Street and Fourth Avenue in Monmouth. These sites were marked in 1909.

Other markings are: The Sugar Tree Grove Church in Warren County, Pope Creek Church in Mercer County, and The Lincoln/Indian Trail on the Cabeen Farm near Pope Creek Church in Mercer County.

First train to Rock Island R.I.S. on Cedar Creek Bridge May 30th 1910

Warren County Businesses

Sumner	Spring Grove	Kelly
Little York	Gerlaw	
Hale	Monmouth	Coldbrook
	Monmouth	Coldbrook
Tompkins	Lenox	Floyd
Kirkwood	Larchland	Cameron
Ellison	Roseville	Berwick
Smithshire	Roseville	Berwick
Point Pleasant	Swan	Greenbush
	Swan Creek	Greenbush

Bowman-Colwell Building 200 Block South Main

Barnes Bros. Groceries and Meats

From Hermon, Knox County, Illinois, the Barnes Brothers, Verne Franklin and Renalt John started their Groceteria in Monmouth, Warren County, Illinois after buying the stock and fixtures of the William Johnson Grocery. This was in July 1922. The store located at 216 East Broadway. It was a brick building that stood just east of the new Colonial Hotel operated by Ralph Fraser (torn down recently, for the new Midwest Bank building). In 1927 the Barnes Brothers moved two doors west sharing the Robert E. White building with the Scott Brothers Cardinal Grocery store. They merged in 1927 when the Scott brothers retired - tearing down the wall separating the two stores. They remodeled bringing George Shaw to run the butcher shop when they purchased his new marble fixtures - also adding home made ice cream, three delivery trucks, and two wholesale meat trucks that covered the three adjoining counties. Archie Stewart, Leroy Dew, and Harry Ray were the primary drivers. They renamed the business Barnes Bros. Grocery and Meats and operated there for the next 15 years. In 1942 when World War II was in its beginning they retired. Verne moved to Vallejo, California and worked at the U.S. Naval Yard on Mare Island. "Rennie" moved to Biloxi, Mississippi where he bought a tungnut tree farm.

When a local grocer, Harold Murk, was drafted in 1944, he asked Verne, who had returned to Monmouth and bought a farm, "Would you buy my grocery store?" Verne replied, "I will call my brother." He did and he said, "I'll be there tomorrow." They were told they had to move from the Murk location, and bought the old Star Livery barn building at 200 North Main from Mabel Gray Schell for $10,000. It had been built by the widow of Samuel Douglas, Monmouth's mayor when it was voted dry. It was remodeled each year until it became the areas first SUPER MARKET. By this time Robert Rawson and Verne "Bud" Barnes had joined the firm. Both were returning in 1946 from military service. In 1949 it had one of the first complete self service meat markets in the mid-west. In 1952 the stock and fixtures of Hawcock's Delicatessen and Bakery were purchased and Emory Hawcock came with it. Two years later at noon, July 21, 1955 the store was extensively damaged by fire. It was completely remodeled before reopening for business September 26, 1955. Since then the parking area was expanded when they leased and eventually bought the Charles Turner property north of the store. Hamilton Produce Company leased the Turner garage building before it was turned into a laundry in 1960. It now holds "The Bottlery" and "The Bread Dough Pizza" establishments. They became the largest food business in Monmouth. They added stores in Bettendorf, Iowa, Rushville and Mt. Sterling, Illinois. Verne and Rennie passed away after long and successful lives. Bob and Bud retired in 1983 after selling their business' and later the building at 200 North Main to a nice young couple, William and Kathryn Grupy, who changed the name from "Barnes Super Valu" to "Bill's Save-a-Lot". Bob passed away shortly after retiring leaving his wife Cleone (Barnes) Rawson and their two married daughters. He was very intelligent and a hard worker. He was Monmouth's "Man of the Year" being president of the Chamber of Commerce, appointed to the Hospital board, and a Police Commissioner.

Bill and Kathy Grupy came to Monmouth in 1983 after purchasing the business Barnes Super Valu. Originally they are both from Fort Madison, IA. Bill started in the grocery business at 15 working for Hy Vee. After high school he started working for A&P Tea Company in Ft. Madison. And then transferred to Moline with A&P as a Produce Manager. He also worked in the Rock Island A&P as Produce Manager and while there was offered the chance to go through A&P managers training school in Chicago. After completing that he was sent to Toulon, IL to manage the A&P there. They were in Toulon for two years when he was transferred to a larger A&P in Pontiac, IL. This is when Kathy started working in the store with Bill when their two children ((Christine and Craig) started school. They were in Pontiac for eleven years until A&P closed their Chicago Division . They then moved back to Burlington , IA. Where they managed a Super Valu supermarket for two years, while there they were offered a partnership in a I.G.A. store in Rochelle, IL. where they lived for almost two years. Wanting to get back closer to home they had the chance to buy the Barnes Super Valu in Monmouth so they sold their share of the Rochelle store and moved to Monmouth. They changed the store's name from Barnes Super Valu to Bill's Super Valu. In the 19 years they have lived here, they have went thru several remodelings and owned the Little York store for 5 years. In 1989 they purchased into the franchise of Save A Lot. That proved to be a good business move and they have prospered since then. In 1998 they remodeled and enlarged the store to the size it is now. At the present time they are planning a minor store upgrade on the inside and outside to Save A Lot latest franchise guidelines. This past year marked 80 years in the food business for Kathy and Bill combined.

Bruce Foote Chev Olds Cad, Inc. Monmouth Storage, L.L.C.

Bruce Foote came to Monmouth in 1981, from Louis Lakis Ford in Galesburg, Illinois, when he acquired the Chevrolet, Oldsmobile, and Cadillac dealership then owned by Jack O'Brien.

Bruce married Denise Lakis and they have two daughters. Christy is a student at the University of Iowa, and Amy is a student at Purdue University. Bruce attributes his continued growth and business success to having a fine group of people working with him. Many of them have been with him since his arrival in Monmouth in 1981.

In addition to owning and operating a respected car dealership Bruce is also the owner of Monmouth Storage, a self-storage facility. With a portion of the farmland acquired with the purchase of the dealership he built the first building in 1991 and the 6th building was completed in 1999.

CURRENT STAFF
Jerry Yocum - Sales
Willard Tinkham - Sales
Charles Thomas - Sales
Terri Boock - Office Manager
Chris Wright - Office Staff
Lyn Hardesty - Office Staff
Steve Pearson - Service Manager
Robert Eldridge - Service Advisor
Dale Mowen - Service Technician
Gaylord Robbins - Service Technician
Scott Bushong - Service Technician
Paul Nelson - Service Technician
Dennis Bethell - Parts Manager
Carl McLaughlin - Body Shop Manager
Steve Smith - Body Shop Technician
Chad Cordell - Body Shop Technician
Kevin Cunningham - Detail Department
Bob Hardesty - Detail Department
John Moore - Janitor

Bruce Foote, Oldsmobile, Cadillac Inc. Monmouth Storage, L.L.C.

Cavanaughs' Motors Inc.

Cavanaugh Motors

Cavanaughs' Motors history actually begins five years before their franchise agreement. Robert J. (Bob) Cavanaugh had started in business July 29, 1939 in a small service station on West Broadway, just west of the tracks, and then had a station on North Eleventh Street at East Boston.

His brother Richard worked with him until he was inducted into military service. Brother William D. (Don) Cavanaugh attended business college and was inducted into the military in 1942. They acquired the Chrysler-Plymouth franchise in October of 1944, although it would be over a year before there would be any new cars to sell. The first location was at 918 South Main Street, however, misfortune struck on February 17, 1945, when that location was destroyed by fire. All three brothers had intended to go into business together, unfortunately Dick was killed in the Philippines March 14, 1945. After operating from temporary quarters for a year, a new building was opened in 1946 at 104 North 2nd Street, (now the location of Security Savings Bank).

Over the next 27 years, many family members participated in the work and growth of the business, including work at the DX (later Sunoco) station they owned, that was located on the corner adjacent to the dealership. This is where Mike and Dennis Cavanaugh (sons of Bob and Don) got their start, first doing service work, and eventually auto sales.

Growth over these years was good, but created the problem of too little space, so in 1972 it was decided to make another move. The move this time was to an area that was in its infancy for growth, the route 34 bypass at North 6th Street. The plot of ground they chose had once been the south end of the runway for Monmouth Airport, but now offered good visibility from the new four lane highway. They moved into their new facility on February 6, 1973, and held a grand opening on May 19 and 20th.

Over the years more franchises were added; Dodge truck in 1976, Dodge car in 1981, and Jeep in 1992. In 1976 Dennis Cavanaugh, a graduate of Northwood University, left a management position with Goodyear Tire & Rubber Co. and returned to fill a sales position. For some years to come, with Bob, Don, Mike, and Dennis, working fulltime, and other sons, daughters, and spouses helping parttime, it was a true family business. Unfortunately in the late 1980s, Bobs health failed and necessitated his sellout to Don in 1988. Robert J. Cavanaugh passed on in March of 1989.

After purchasing Bobs share of the business, Don decided to incorporate and bring Dennis and John Cavanaugh in as partners- John had been working parttime at the business for several years and had recently graduated from Western Illinois University. The three of them enjoyed successful years through the 1990s, which was evident by their loyal customer base and their consistently earning Chryslers Five Star Award for Excellence.

October 20, 1998, brought the unexpected death of Don Cavanaugh. Dennis and John decided to buy Dons share and continue in the business that was now 54 years old. They were to see the final days of the Plymouth name, other franchises that came and went at Cavanaughs were International, Imperial, Eagle, Simca, and Cricket.

Cavanaughs' Motors for 58 years has strived to offer a quality service and sales experience, and be a friendly and generous supporter of the community. It is our goal that this tradition continue for years to come.

Cavanaugh Motors - Present

Cavanaugh Motors North 2nd Street

Cavanaugh Motors after the fire

Community Medical Center of Western Illinois, Inc.,

Community Medical Center of Western Illinois, Inc., is a private, not-for-profit organization for Monmouth and it's surrounding communities with a primary role of inpatient, outpatient, and long-term care.

Community Medical Center of Western Illinois, Inc.'s roots are from Monmouth Hospital, founded in 1897. In a pioneering venture, the hospital, through a fundraising campaign and Monmouth's "Street Fair," raised $7,000 to build a new hospital that opened for service in April 1904. Dr. J.R. Webster, the oldest practicing physician of the city, was named to direct the operations of the hospital. The hospital was popular and, after several years, a larger hospital was needed with additions being added in 1910, 1939, and 1957.

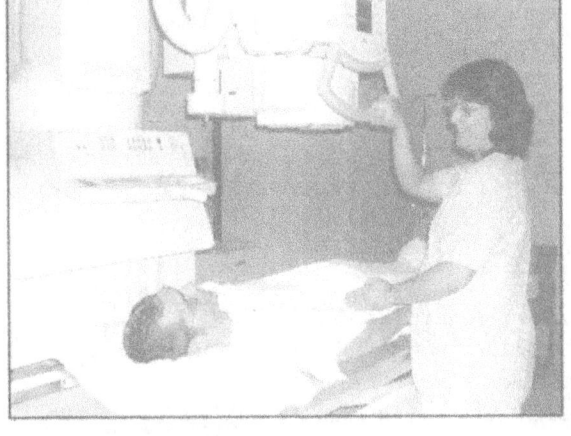

Not only did Monmouth have a new hospital in the early 1900's, but it also had a two-year training school for nurses and later a three-year training program. The first nursing class of four graduated in 1906 and 117 graduated before the school closed in 1936.

The hospital continued to grow until the decision was made in 1963 to build a new hospital that became known as Community Memorial Hospital. The funding for the new hospital was a unique combination of a government grant, a federal loan, and local subscriptions with one million dollars being raised from citizens of the community. The occupancy of the acute care area and the long-term care unit began in August 1968.

Community Memorial Hospital's name was changed to Community Medical Center of Western Illinois, Inc. Today, Community Medical Center is a private, not-for-profit hospital that continues to care for patients in acute care and skilled nursing beds and has also expanded its outpatient services to include a 24-hour clinic. The CMC Clinics opened in 1999 and provide primary medical care for patients of all ages. Examples of the services the Clinics provide are: treatment and diagnosis of medical illnesses and injuries; annual physicals; well-patient visits; workman's compensation exams; employment exams; school physicals; sports physicals; and immunizations. The CMC Clinics are staffed by several physicians, a physician assistant, and a team of nurses and support staff.

Hospital services include acute and skilled nursing care beds, a full range of diagnostic and therapeutic services, including nuclear scanning, computed tomography (CT) scanning, stress testing, magnetic resonance imaging (MRI), bone densitometry, and ultrasound, as well as patient and community education programs.

At Community Medical Center, we continually strive to meet the health care needs of our communities and to provide new and appropriate services through patient surveys, focus groups, continuous quality improvement studies, and through the Patient Advocacy Program. The CMC Patient Advocacy Program provides a liaison between patients and the hospital staff and assists patients in interpreting the hospital's policies and procedures. The Patient Advocate visits with our patients to ensure that their hospital stay is as pleasant as possible. Serving as a representative through whom patients may voice their problems and concerns, the Patient Advocate assists the staff to gain awareness of patients' perceptions of their hospital experience.

More than 200 volunteers provide a variety of support services, donating nearly 15,000 hours each year. These services include escort, mail sorting and delivery, secretarial aid, skilled nursing activity aid, gift shop, reception hosting, Medicare counseling, and yard services.

Chaplain services are provided voluntarily by area clergy. They minister to the spiritual needs of the hospitalized patients and their families as well as to the hospital staff, and are on-call 24 hours a day.

The mission of Community Medical Center of Western Illinois, Inc. is to provide a broad range of high quality primary medical services and long-term care, and to coordinate the availability of other medical services to area residents. This has been the hospital's commitment to area residents for more than 100 years and will continue as the hospital heads into its second century of operation in Warren County.

Community National Bank Monmouth

In January 1964 following the decision of the shareholders to voluntarily liquidate the Second National Bank of Monmouth, a group of local business men and women, headed by Robert Howard and Arthur Padella of the law firm of Howard and Padella, investigated the possibility of obtaining a charter to organize a new national bank in Monmouth. Several meetings were conducted and at one held in the offices of Bowman Shoe Company a non-binding poll was taken to determine how much money could be raised to purchase capital stock for a new bank. It was quickly determined that the necessary funds could be obtained.

An application was prepared and submitted to the Comptroller of the Currency of the United States. The application included a projection of operating results for the first three years of the bank. Everitt Hardin, former president of the Second National Bank, who would be retained to head the new bank, prepared the projection. The Comptroller determined that initial capital of the bank should be $450,000. The organizers of the bank who signed and submitted the application were:

> Robert Cavanaugh - Franchised Chrysler auto dealer
> David Edwards - Partner & Manager of fertilizer plant
> Robert Moore - Farmer
> Thomas Moore - Plant Manager, Formfit Company
> Arthur Padella - Lawyer
> Wendell Roller - Physician and Surgeon
> David Turnbull - Funeral Director

In late July permission to organize was received from the Comptroller. The stock was offered, purchased and money paid in a little over two weeks. Twenty thousand shares were sold to 447 shareholders from this community for $22.50 per share. On August 7, 1964 the first meeting of shareholders was held in the Monmouth High School auditorium. The above named organizers as well as Everitt Hardin and Walter Enfield were elected to the Board of Directors. The following day the Directors met and elected the officers who then made arrangements to get the bank open for business.

The charter was granted on September 8th and the bank opened for business on September 10, 1964. The bank occupied a vacant storefront formerly housing Higgins Dairy on the west side of the Square. It remained in this location for the next 22 months until the new building in the 300 block of North Main Street was completed. The move north took place over the July 4th holiday of 1966.

The bank became profitable only about a year after opening and declared its first dividend to shareholders in 1968. Extended hours were first offered shortly after opening so that customers could get to the bank on the way home from work and utilize all of the bank's services. Additional land was obtained in the same block and in 1978 a new five-lane drive-up facility was constructed on the east side of the bank with exits on North First Street. Some years later one of the lanes was equipped with a drive-up automatic teller machine in order to provide service to customers and others 24 hours a day.

The bank retained a portion of its profits and added them to its capital funds. This strengthened the bank and permitted it to better serve its customers. As the bank grew, the value of its shares increased. By 1981 the book value of the shares was about $78. In order to keep the value of the shares at a lower figure and to enable shares to transfer more easily, a 3-for-1 stock split took place.

Today, 38 years later, the bank has a broad local customer base. There are 25 officers and employees. The officers are Douglas D. Hardin, President; Jon R. Edwards, Vice President and Cashier; J. Frank Doyle, Vice President; and Trina L. Lybarger, Assistant Cashier. Capital funds exceed 10 times the beginning capital and dividends have been paid every year since 1968. It proudly serves customers in a three county area and is firmly established in the surrounding community. Ownership continues to be broadly based as there are now in excess of 300 shareholders.

Community National Bank Drive-In

Community National Bank

David Reid Clark Law Office

The law office of David Reid Clark was established on 1 June 1976 at 109 North Main, Suite Four, Second Floor, above Dayton Fresh Realty, in Monmouth. By the summer of 1979, David's offices occupied the entire second floor and he purchased Sickmon Cigar Store at 93 Public Square, remodeled, and moved in August of 1979. In the late 1980s, David purchased the building immediately west of 93 Public Square and opened his annex, providing additional office space for his paralegal, Michelle Sperry, and a large conference room.

The building at 93 Public Square, Northeast Quadrant, has had an extensive number of owners since its erection in 1871. It has served as a dry goods store, law office, paint and wallpaper store, saloon, cigar store, and pool hall. The decorating scheme of the Clark Law Office reflects the colorful history of the building with an 1880s motif.

Subsequent to receiving his law degree form the University of Iowa in 1975, David served as a Criminal Justice Professor at Western Illinois University in the Department of Law Enforcement Administration until June 1976. On 1 June 1976, he became the Warren County Public Defender, a part-time job he held for fifteen years, and started his own private practice. David was also the Henderson County Public Defender from 1978 to 1990. Experience in these positions allowed him to develop trial experience which enabled his private practice to expand. His primary interest has always been criminal defense, but he has also practiced family law, personal injury, and civil litigation. In his career, he has defended thirteen murder cases, none resulting in the death penalty. David has served as the President of the Warren County Bar Association and is a member of the Illinois State and American Bar Associations, the Illinois Trial Lawyers Association, the Association of Trial Lawyers of America and the Capital Litigation Trial Bar (Death Penalty Defense).

David has been associated in the private practice of law from time to time, with Christopher W. Kanthak, Charles Graham Webb, Pamela S. Connell, John C. Redington, Douglas C. Clark, R. Philip Steele, Maureen A. Mahoney, and John J. O'Gara, Jr. Present members of the staff at Clark Law Office are Michelle Sperry, paralegal, and Regina A. Mangieri, secretary. Though the names and staff have changed through the years, the caring and professional service, first provided by David Reid Clark over twenty-five years ago, has remained constant. A motto adopted by Mr. Clark, "Defending the Citizen Accused," continues to be the theme of the Law Office of David Reid Clark.

David Reid Clark

Hoover-Hall Memorial Chapel

Hoover-Hall Memorial Chapel

On February 20, 1894, R. E. White of Davenport, Iowa, announced the opening of an undertaking parlor at 61 Public Square in Monmouth (later the site of Wiley Light Jewelers and currently A Touch of Country). Later he was at 209 South Main St. as White Furniture and Undertaking, and in June 1899, he moved his establishment to the south rooms of the fine new livery stable just erected by Mrs. Louisa Douglass on North Main (later Barnes Super Valu and currently Save-a-Lot Grocery). There he opened a large undertaking parlor and display room, with his hearses stored on the second floor and lowered by elevator.

Shortly thereafter, White erected his own funeral parlor across the street at 207 North Main (now Buff's Photography), which he ran alone until 1920, at which time he formed a partnership with John Lugg. In 1923 Lugg purchased the entire business. Sometime between 1923 and 1928 Lugg demolished a house and built a chapel (now known as Standard Law Office). Five years later he formed a partnership with Mitchell E. Holliday under the name of Lugg & Holliday.

William C. Hoover of Alexis came to work for the firm on January 1, 1947, and after the death of Lugg and Holliday he assumed operation along with Mrs. Holliday, and her sons, William and John. Mrs. Holliday sold her interest to her sons in 1956. William Holliday left the business in January 1963, and his brother left in August 1965, leaving Hoover as sole owner.

In 1965 Hoover changed the name to Hoover Memorial Chapel and continued to operate the business alone. In 1974, Hoover erected a new funeral home at 900 North Main St. and held an open house in June of that year. He opened and operated a funeral chapel in Oquawka from 1977 until the end of 1993. In December 1978 he purchased the McKnight Funeral Home in Alexis, now known as Hoover-Hall Memorial Chapel.

Stephen S. Hall, originally of Kirkwood, began working for his father-in-law, William Hoover on September 11, 1974 and purchased the business, now known as Hoover-Hall Memorial Chapel, on January 1, 1993, when Wm C. Hoover retired, but continues to assist in the conduction of funerals.

Aloysius J. McGuire of Hanover Park, IL joined the firm as an employee on November 11, 1991 and continues to this date to assist in the operation of the business.

Hoover-Hall Memorial Chapel, it's predecessors and successors have served the Monmouth and Alexis areas for over one hundred years.

Lugg Memorial Chapel

Koke & Sparrow TV & Appliance

1930

Koke and Sparrow TV and Appliance located at #70 Public Sq. has roots in Monmouth Business going back to 1921. Ernest L. Crow, son of George Crow, long-time superintendent of the Monmouth Water Department, worked 48 years uptown, starting with the E.B. Colwell Department Store, Dunbar Drug Store, Zimmer Drug Store, and later for Augie and Frank Johnson Drug Stores. Just after WWI around 1921, Augie Johnson went into the music business, the Brunswick Shop, handling phonographs, records and sheet music and Mr. Crow managed the store. He also did piano tuning, when the radio came out on the market, he became interested in selling and repairing them. He started his own business above Johnson's Drug Store, located at the S.E. corner of E. Broadway and South 1st Street. In 1932, he moved to the corner of Market Alley and South 1st Street above the Hensieigh, Dugan, and Pierce Barber Shop. In the 1940s he moved across the street for a few years around 1945-1950, moved back above the barber shop. Then he purchased the building at 108 South 1st Street and Market Alley, tore it down and replaced it with the building where Dr. Stuart Walker D.S. is currently located. In 1952 Delbert H. Koke, became a partner with Mr. Crow and at this time became exclusive RCA delears. In 1959 Delbert purchased the business and became sole owner of Crow and Koke, at this time he changed the name to Koke TV & Radio and later moved his business to 213 South Main. Gene Sparrow was hired by Delbert in 1964 as his television technician. Gene became a full partner with Delbert in 1972. At this time the business name was changed to Koke and Sparrow TV. In 1980 they took on Whirlpool appliance's, they were exclusive dealers for RCA, and added appliance's to their logo and became Koke and Sparrow TV and Appliance. In 1982 Delbert retired and Gene Sparrow became sole owner. In 1986 the building at 213 S. Main was destroyed by a fire. Gene moved his business to #70 Public Square where he has remained since. His product line today consist of RCA, Zenith, Phillips, Corsley and Whirlpool.

1969

1950

2002

Maple City Steel Supply Co.

L. to R: James O'Daniel (1906-1999), John W. O'Daniel, John Andrew O'Daniel, James and Charles O'Daniel, circa 1986

The present site of the Maple City firm was first used just after the Civil War by the Roberts, Dunn & Co. which had a sash and blind factory there, acquiring the property July 12, 1865. However, the plant burned in September 1869. They did not rebuild and the tract was sold to David R. Stevens in 1870. Then it was acquired by Torrance and Hamilton and William Hamilton sold it to Levi Roadhouse in 1886 and the McIntosh ownership began in 1894, although the elder McIntosh may have been there longer. The "foundry" located on the east side of South Main Street (603 S. Main) just south of the "Q" Railroad. It took its name from Arthur D. McIntosh who came to Monmouth from Massachusetts in 1877 to work at his trade of machinist. He later went into the foundry business with John Torrance under the name of McIntosh Ornamental and Structural Iron Works. In 1898 Arthur C. McIntosh, son of the founder, bought Mr. Torrance's interest and the McIntosh Foundry and Machine Co Inc. was formed. They operated it until 1912 when the business was sold to William C. Talbott who had come here two years earlier. Furnace production had been started about 1906 by the pioneer firm and furnaces bearing the name "Maple City" were shipped from there. Around Monmouth many years later there still could be found various iron castings in store fronts and in hundreds of homes in Monmouth area and in distant places, Maple City Furnaces, made in the Monmouth plant between 1906 and later, still operating, some coal fired and others converted to oil or gas. Native of Lumpkin, Georgia, William Cole Talbot attended College at Valpraiso, Indiana and later went to Indian Territory (now Oklahoma) where he ran a music store and peddled musical instruments from a wagon, including pianos for which he found a market among even the Indians (sometimes the piano was the only piece of "real" furniture around the place.) Later he was a railroad Mail Clerk, running on the "Katy" Railroad from Dinison, Texas to Kansas City, Missouri. It was there in 1907 that he met his future wife, Miss Belle Firoved, who had been visiting her aunt and uncle Mr. and Mrs. Isaac Woods in that city. They lived in Kansas City for three years while he continued his mail run and then came to Monmouth in 1910. Presently he bought out the McIntosh Foundry and continued it until his death in 1936, making Maple City Furnaces there throughout the years he ran the foundry. Sometime after his death the foundry was discontinued, but production of furnaces did not end for a good many years through use of castings made from the firms molds at other founderies.

James O'Daniel, his son-in-law (married Sarabelle Talbot) had no previous background in the furnace business when he began to look after the Maple City Furnace Co. in 1936 after Mr Talbot's death. He came out to this county as an engineer in the late 1920s when the "humps" or switching yards of the CB&Q Railroad were being built. The project wasn't finished when the depression came along and Mr. O'Daniel shifted to work with the U.S. Coast and Geodetic Survey.

As the weather conditioning began to develop however, he used his engineering training, augmented by further instruction at the University of Illinois to design the installations that now warm homes, offices and factories in the winter and cool them in the summer.

The old building of the McIntosh firm, much remodeled and expanded, is still in use by the present firm under the management of James O'Daniel's son, John.

Sarabelle T. and James O. O'Daniel
1980s

Marquette Bank

The Monmouth Trust and Savings Bank was organized April 29, 1905, with a capital $125,000.00. It began business May 1, 1905. The organizers were John D. Lynch; L. B. Cowick; John K. Teare; W. S. Holliday; J. Ralph Firoved; W. H. Woods; F. M. Hallam; W. A. Sawyer and C. E. Duke.

Presidents of the Bank have been: 1905-1932 John D. Lynch Sr.; 1932-1956 Dr. F. C. Winters; 1957-1960 Harold U. Scott; 1961-1980 Merton H. Bowden; 1980-1986 Mark D. Pingrey; 1986-1995 David S. Burrell; 1995-1998 William R. Kahler; 1998-1999 Tom Johnson; 1999-current John D. Winston.

The year of 1979 was a progressive year for the Trust Bank opening the North Main Drive in facility in May and moving into the current building located at 100 South Main Street in July.

The First State Bank of Little York merged with Monmouth Trust and Savings Bank in December of 1984.

The Bank has always been a leader in the community through the years with the introduction of new services. The bank was a pioneer in western Illinois in the practice of opening for business on certain evenings of the week (Tuesday and Saturdays) when the downtown merchants were open on Saturday nights. The Bank in 1961 opened the first installment loan department in Monmouth. In 1967 the Trust Bank was the first bank to process its checking accounts by computer. Several other firsts for the bank are; offering Farm Record Keeping services; ATM off premises located at Econo Food Store; Debit Cards; Free Checking Accounts; in addition to Online Banking. In October of 1996 we opened the grocery store branch located at Econo Food store.

On June 1, 1999 Monmouth Trust and Savings Bank changed its name to be Marquette Bank Monmouth. Ownership remained the same as during the past 30 years. On February 1, 2002 we merged with Wells Fargo Bank. This merger has brought many new product offerings to the Monmouth area.

The original Monmouth Trust and Savings Bank (left) was constructed in 1865, and served until 1979 when it was replaced by the beautiful new bank building pictured below.

Midwest Bank Then and Now

National Bank of Monmouth

The National Bank of Monmouth, originally known as the Monmouth National Bank, was chartered on September 9, 1870, under the provisions established by the banking act of the Lincoln administration. The Monmouth National Bank could have qualified for a charter with only $50,000 but the bank directors put up twice this amount.

The original stockholders in the bank were General Abner Clark Harding, Claudius Jones, Chauncey Hardin, H.G. Harding and W. F. Wiley. The General and Jones held the most shares. The General was made the first president serving from 1870 to 1874.

Abner Clark Harding was born in East Hampton, Connecticut in 1807. He became a lawyer and moved to Monmouth in 1838. By 1870, he was considered one of the richest men in Western Illinois, with a fortune of $2,000,000. General Harding was very generous and became one of the earliest benefactors of Monmouth College.

The Monmouth National Bank was barely established when a deep depression started from the tremendous losses of the great Chicago fire in 1871. The bank survived these disturbing times and emerged as one of the strongest banks in the Midwest. The National Bank of Monmouth, now directed by President Henry Tubbs, actually expanded its interest during that period. Tubbs was president from 1884 to 1899.

W.H. Frantz was president from 1900 to 1902. During his term the national banking system was becoming obsolete, but the legislation to correct the situation was not enacted until many years later. G. S. Tubbs followed Frantz as president from 1902 to 1907. Finally, during the presidency of Willard Tubbs (1907-1921), the Federal Reserve System was established on December 23, 1913. Twenty-two days later, President Tubbs authorized the bank's cashier to join the new organization.

D. E. Gayer, who was president from 1921 to 1927, had a relatively quiet and successful term. When J. Arthur Tubbs became the president in 1927, the Wall Street bull market was in full swing. The Wall Street crash came in October of 1929, but there was never any question about the solvency of the bank. The National Bank of Monmouth conducted business as usual.

Arthur Tubbs' twenty-three year rein came to an end in 1950 when John E. Zimmer was elected president. Zimmer had an unusual career, starting out as an errand boy on January 10, 1906 when he was only 15. Zimmer retired in 1956 but served as Chairman of the Board until 1968.

Chalmer P. Spiker picked up the reins in 1957. During the Spiker years assets increased from over $8,000,000 to $17,000,000. The bank received extensive remodeling under the Spiker administration. The first drive-in service in the community was introduced in 1963. Electronic bookkeeping equipment was installed and a trust department was established in 1964.

Jack D. Lemmerman became president in 1966 after serving the bank in various capacities for nineteen years. During his term, a computer system was established in 1969 that brought greater efficiency to the bank's operations. The bank installed its first automated teller machine in 1976. In 1982, the bank opened The Village Banking Center in Kirkwood, Illinois, near the family home of Dr. Henry Tubbs.

Recent presidents who succeeded Lemmerman include Howard E. Gladfelter from 1979 to 1988, Douglas S. Heaton from 1988 to 1993 and Roger C. Davis from 1994 to 1998. During Davis' term, the board of directors made a decision to transfer ownership of the bank to a holding company located in Melrose Park Illinois. On January 3, 1993, The National Bank of Monmouth became a subsidiary of First Midwest Corporation of Delaware, now Midwest Bank Holdings, Inc.

The bank has expanded to neighboring counties since becoming part of the Midwest family. Midwest Bank of Oquawka was purchased in September of 1994 and is now the Oquawka Banking Center and the Galesburg Banking Center was built in August of 1996.

Christopher J. Gavin became the seventeenth president of the bank in 1998. Under his leadership, the bank converted to a state banking charter to purchase Porter Insurance Agency. In October of 1998 the name of the bank was changed to Midwest Bank of Western Illinois to more accurately identify its market area. The following year Associated Bank in Aledo was purchased and became the Mercer County Banking Center. Internet Banking was introduced in 1999, allowing customers to bank from their home of office.

A beautiful colonial style building became the new home of Midwest Bank on January 10, 2000. At this time the bank formed a partnership with Raymond James Investments. They now offer both insurance and investment services. Another chapter in banking began when the first supermarket branch was opened at County Market on January 4, 2001.

Midwest Bank of Western Illinois currently offers six banking locations and nine ATMS located in four counties. They are proud of their long history of serving the residents of Warren County and the surrounding area. *Submitted by Terri Ryner, V.P. & Cashier*

Midwest Bank of Western Illinois

Monmouth Soda Works
112 South 1st Street
Monmouth, Illinois 61462

A turn of the century ice cream parlor, lunches, unique gift shop and museum

Back in 1874 this building housed Armsby's Pork Packing plant and at one time was a carriage repository. In 1902 it became Clarke and Company grocers and later a clothing store and millinery owned by a Jewish man named Nick Thabit. Billiard halls were also on the second floor. During World War II sewing machines were busy manufacturing clothing. In the 1930s and 1940s a dance studio was upstairs with individual music rooms on the east side and a stage on the west side. In the 1940's Martin Motors purchased this building for their showroom and displayed DeSotos and Plymouths. Martin poured a terrazzo floor over the top of the original pine floor to prevent a fire hazard created by oil leakage. The cement has been popped off and the original pine floor has been restored. Martins garage was located south of Soda Works with their offices built in between, which now is the courtyard. The cars would be brought up to the second floor of the garage by an elevator and driven across the brick ramp and parked on the second floor of this building. Take the original stairway, which has been moved, up to our kitchen pantry. The tin ceiling is the original tin that was on the first floor and the pine wood wall was originally the second floor sub-floor. Visit upstairs and stroll along the garden path that leads you to the one- room schoolhouse and takes you back in time.

Monmouth Soda Works

The place for lunch, relaxation and reminising

Security Savings Bank

The Monmouth Homestead and Loan Association was established as the result of a petition directed to the authorities of the State of Illinois dated May 23, 1882. The petition recited that the purpose was to form a body corporate to enable an association of persons to raise funds to be loaned only among the membership of such association. The capital of the corporation was proposed as $1,000,000.00 and the location as Monmouth, Illinois.

At the outset, the only form of investment offered was by monthly payment of "dues" on the purchase of a certificate, calling for the number of shares desired by the customer and on which the monthly payments were fifty cents a share. Payments were due on the first day of each month with a penalty of five cents per share for each month the payments were delinquent. The certificate "matured" when the dues paid by the member plus the earnings apportioned to the account each six months totaled $100.00 per share.

During its existence, there have been but six managing officers, four having been father and son succession. Lyman W. Case was the first secretary and he served until 1884. Judge T. G. Peacock was elected in 1884 and served until 1921 to be succeeded by his son C. Shellar Peacock who served as managing officer until 1943. Wendell F. Whiteman became managing officer in 1943 and was succeeded in 1966 by his son, Ralph, who served until 1990. Stanley D. Jenks has been managing officer since 1990.

The first location of the Association was nothing more than a desk drawer in the law firm of Lyman W. Case, the first secretary. When T. G. Peacock assumed responsibility, the office was located on the second floor of the three-story Woods office building. Judge Peacock later moved to the first floor quarters in the southwest corner of the public square in a building owned by the Warren County Library Association. In 1938 the former People's National Bank Building located in the southeast area of the public square was purchased and occupied. During 1958 the office was remodeled and the name changed to Monmouth Savings and Loan Association. That structure was destroyed by fire in 1974 and temporary office quarters were established in the 300 block of North Main Street.

A new building at 220 East Broadway was completed in December, 1974. Expansion took place in 1977 when offices were constructed in the basement to match the main floor and became the home of the loan department and the accounting department. Another expansion occurred in 1980 when additional office space and a safe deposit vault were added on the main floor.

In 1972, the Stronghurst Building and Loan Association merged with Monmouth Savings and Loan Association and the name of Security Savings and Loan Association was adopted. A branch office continued in Stronghurst and a new office building was erected and occupied there in 1978.

In 1994, Security Savings changed its charter issued under the Illinois Savings and Loan Act. The new savings bank charter was adopted under the Savings Bank Act that had been enacted by the Illinois legislature in 1990. So, the organization that was once known in succession as Monmouth Homestead and Loan Association, Monmouth Building and Loan Association, Monmouth Savings and Loan Association, and Security Savings and Loan Association, became Security Savings Bank on July 1, 1994.

A new addition, built in 1999, nearly doubled the building size of the Stronghurst branch office. The existing building interior was completely renovated to match the new addition. The additional space provided larger offices and meeting rooms to better accommodate expanded securities and agribusiness services and a growing customer base in Henderson County.

In 2000, the Monmouth main bank building was also extensively enlarged and renovated with a twostory building addition that nearly tripled the space. Included were exterior changes to the grounds that changed the traffic flow and parking areas. The additional space allowed for all banking services to be placed on the main level, convenient to all bank customers, with more customer privacy provided by enclosed private offices. A community room, available to families and non-profit community groups, was included in the lower level of the new addition.

Also in 2000, Security Savings Bank expanded its financial services through the acquisition of the accounting firm, Lovdahl & Shimmin, Inc. The firm relocated to the lower level of the main bank building, providing new and existing bank customers with bookkeeping, payroll and tax preparation services.

Security Savings has seen many changes over the years since its meager beginnings in 1882. However, the underlying purpose for its existence remains to provide a means to the goal of financial security through savings and homeownership for residents of the communities it serves.

Security Savings & Loan on southeast side of Square in the late 1950s.

Turnbull Funeral Homes
Monmouth, Illinois

Blackburn & Turnbull with caskets

During the late 1800s, families were moving from the East to the West in the United States to find new land and new opportunities. "Blackburn and Turnbull, Undertakers and Liverymen." was established by David Turnbull and Charles E. Blackburn, who purchased the undertaking business of Joseph Espy in Monmouth, on January 24, 1884.

David Turnbull and Charles E. Blackburn, opened the livery stables on the Northwest corner of South Main Street and West Third Avenue. They offered livery of all types to families moving into Monmouth. Many persons arrived on the train with all their possessions, and Blackburn and Turnbull supplied carriages and wagons to move them into their new homes. Other transportation needs, such as hacks, surreys, and buck boards were offered along with a Hearse, black in color for Men, and one in White for Ladies and Children.

In those days, when a family member passed away funerals were performed in the family home, and the job of the Undertaker was to come to the home and "undertake" all the chores and responsibilities for the family during their time of mourning. These duties included preparing the deceased in the home, repositioning furniture to accommodate friends and neighbors and performing the usual chores of every day living for the family. Essentially, the Undertaker was responsible for facilitating everything about the "wake" and funeral.

At the turn of the century, attitudes were changing regarding having funerals in the home and the subsequent disruption of family life. The preference became to have such events elsewhere or in a church. In 1905 David and Ada Turnbull built a large home to accommodate funerals. It was constructed on the south east corner of South Main Street at East Second Avenue. Thus, the term "Funeral Home" became the definition of a residence to accommodate a family's funeral needs. David and Ada resided there until he passed away in 1915. Ada, also a licensed funeral director, continued the operation and living with the business. After David's death, Will Loftus, who began his career with the Turnbulls eventually became a partner with Ada, forming "Turnbull & Loftus."

In 1928 a major renovation of the original funeral home/residence was completed. Almost half of the funeral home structure was razed, to make way for the new structure designed just to function as a funeral facility.

John Maxwell Turnbull, known as "Max" was the second son of Ada and David Turnbull and was born in Monmouth, IL. He began his career as an Osteopathic Physician, attending the Osteopathic School in Kirksville, Missouri. It was there that he met and married Marie Guiltner from Ottumwa, Iowa, and after completing their training, returned to open a husband and wife practice in the former Commercial Arts building in Monmouth, IL After Will Loftus passed away, Ada needed Max's help in running the funeral business. Max left his osteopathy business, and joined his mother in the funeral business. Ada was actively involved in funeral service from 1884 until 1950. She passed away in 1952.

Max and Marie Turnbull, had two children, Maxine and David. David graduated from the University of Illinois in 1937 and then received training as a funeral director at Worsham College of Embalming, graduating in 1939. Serving in the National Guard 133rd Field Artillery in Monmouth, his unit was activated in 1941 taking him to service in the Philippines and New Guinea. David returned home in 1945 to join his father at the firm. Eventually, David became partners with his father in the operation of Turnbull Funeral Home. Max Turnbull passed away in 1952 and David continued the firm in the Monmouth area.

David married Ruth Buchholz in 1938 and they had three children, the youngest of which was John. John was reared and educated in Monmouth attending two years of college at Iowa Wesleyan College and finishing in his funeral training at the University of Minnesota in 1972. He returned to Monmouth, where he joined his father at the funeral home as an apprentice. In 1974, a friend and colleague of David Turnbull, Arthur Sederwall passed away and David purchased Sederwall Chapel in Biggsville, Illinois. He hired Arthur's widow, Avis Sederwall, as an employee. John eventually joined in partnership with his father and after David's retirement came into ownership of the firm in 1981 with facilities in Monmouth and Biggsville, Illinois

David passed away in 1989. In 1991, John fulfilled a dream of his father's by building and establishing a firm in Oquawka, Illinois. This not only fulfilled his father's dream, but afforded the town of Oquawka a modern facility for funeral service. In 2001, the three facilities were named Turnbull Funeral Homes in Monmouth, Oquawka, and Biggsville, Illinois.

Many changes in funeral customs, as well as the public's personal preferences, have molded the funeral business into what it is today. The primary purpose of the profession is to provide a meaningful rite of passage honoring the memory and life of a loved one lost. Turnbull Funeral Homes continues to strive to do this by providing everything necessary for a family and community to address their grief and proceed through the days to come.

Blackburn & Turnbull
Undertakers & Liverymen with hearses.

Vaughn Jewelers

Vaughn Jewelers was originally started in 1932 by Merlin M. Vaughn at 113 South Main Street as M. M. Vaughn Watch Repair. Merlin had learned his trade at Swazy School of Watch Repair in Chicago, Illinois. He had taught at the school and worked for the Ball Company of Chicago, IL. as watch inspector on the inter urban trains in the Chicago area before coming home to Monmouth, IL. to open his shop at 113 South Main Street. In 1962, Merlin moved to 221 South Main St. and changed the name to Vaughn Jewelers, at which time his son, Sid Vaughn became associated with the business as watch and jewelry repairman. Sid had learned his trade at Bradley University School of Horology and had worked for Peoria Jewelry Company and Zale's Jewelers in Colorado. In 1972, Sid became a partner in the business, and in 1975 became owner of the business. In 1982 Sid moved to 223 South Main St. and to the present location of 200 South Main St. in 1988, each time expanding and adding more employees.

Previous occupants of the different locations were: 113 South Main St. --Toddy Allen and Charles T. Menely had Tailor shops at that location; 221 South Main St --it was Mitten's Caramel Corn and then Dr. Jon Talbott, Optometrist; 223 South Main Street was Hewitt's Flowers; 200 South Main St. it was Peter's Jewelry Co. and then Wiley Light Jeweler.

In 1999, two street lights were put up on the north side of the building at 200 South Main St., and a clock was installed in front of the building which is owned by David and Virgene Winkler. In 2000 a mural was painted on the north side of the building through the joint efforts of the city, Chamber of Commerce, State, landlord and tenant.

Vaughn's Jewelers

Vickroy's

In 1956 Clarence and Marietta Vickroy moved to Monmouth where he opened the doors of Vickroy's, a "complete home furnishing store." The community welcomed him with open arms and has supported the fine furniture store ever since.

Prior to moving to Monmouth, Clarence was employed by a furniture store in Geneseo for eight years where he gained valuable experience for what was to come.

Located at 120 East Archer Avenue, Vickroy's Furniture opened with only 6,000 square feet of display floor and another 6,000 square feet of warehouse space. In 2002, the store features 15,000 square feet of each, and there is a plan to add 1,000 square feet to its current display area.

Starting from scratch, Clarence worked day and night for the first few years to establish his business and to win the confidence of the customers. An independent retailer, Clarence operates the store with the assistance of his wife of 52 years, Marietta, and children, Dawn and Rick. At one time or another all five Vickroy children have helped in the store.

In addition to carrying name-brand furniture, the store features well-known lines of mattresses and floor covering. However, the merchant prefers that Vickroys be thought of as the brand and believes that more and more people are beginning to realize it.

The various styles of furniture are arranged in room-like settings and features both the upholstered and wood pieces.

Enhancing the display of fine furniture are the lighting and decorative items which are found throughout the store. Attractive mirrors, lamps of all styles, and beautiful items of glass and ceramics are appealing to the customer who wants to add a personal touch to the home or is looking for a gift for a special occasion.

As one of the few remaining family-owned furniture stores in the area, it is always looking for growth. Toward that end it is reaching out all the time to the surrounding towns in the area believing that provides growth potential.

One of the goals of the Monmouth furniture store is to offer true savings to their customers. The owner believes that the prices should compare favorably with anything found elsewhere.

As Vickroy's Furniture carries an estimated $650,00 or better in retail inventory, the merchant knows what it takes to move his stock. He believes that the secret is to have what people want. To be able to turn stock, it has to be kept fresh and new which is difficult because there are so many colors and styles from which to choose.

To keep current on the newest trends and styles in furniture, the Vickroys attend the National Furniture Market in High Point, North Carolina, that is held every six months. This market is a must for all enterprising retailers.

One inducement to shop at Vickroy's is it still offers free delivery. One Monmouth customer remembers when she had purchased a sofa from Vickroy's and the delivery truck reached her house before she did.

This fine furniture store is one of the very few of the smaller, family owned furniture stores that continues to offer financing for the customers. There's no interest for a year, no hidden charges and no small disclaimers.

Because of the participation of the family, the locally owned furniture store is one of the very few in the area that still survives. Currently Dawn handles sales, buying and merchandising and Rick serves in all capacities including sales, managing deliveries and floor displays. It could be said that it is also because of the hard work and dedication put forth by Vickroy and his family that Vickroy's Furniture continues to provide the services that have area residents returning for their furniture needs.

In 2000 Vickroy's Furniture was named "Retailer of the 20th Century" by the Illinois Retail Merchants Association joining "more than 100 other Illinois retailers whose companies have played an important part in the history of Illinois retailing in the last century and who continue to play a vital role in the communities and the industry."

Vickroy's of Monmouth

Warren County Courthouse

Present courthouse with WWII Memorial

Jill Morris was appointed Circuit Clerk Pro-tem in November 1997, official appointment being made in December 1997. She started with Warren County as a young student in 1975 The responsibilities of her office are numerous, dealing with criminal and domestic court cases being a few of her duties. Anything concerning the court must go through her office, ranging from probate, wills, to murder cases- scheduling when the judge might perform a wedding, to closed juvenile cases and divorces.

Nancy Clayton, Treasurer and Collector was elected and took office in December 1994. She had worked in the Circuit Clerk's office since May 1967, deciding she needed a change she ran for office. She is in charge of all the bank accounts and investing the County's money. Besides overseeing the accounts her office collects property tax money. After collection is made, the tax money is distributed to all of the taxing bodies. They also sell and keep track of the dog tags for Warren County.

Albert "Chip" Algren started working in the States Attorney's Office in June 1989 under the leadership of Greg McClintock. Greg was chosen to be a judge in Fall 1995, therefore "Chip" was appointed States Attorney September 1, 1995. This office prosecutes all the criminals that appear in front of the judges in the County Courthouse- any case that charges are filed against. Besides prosecuting the criminal element, he is also the legal council for the county. He is involved in any legal cases (or questions) involving the county.

Richard "Floaty" Hart took office as Sheriff in December 1994. He had been a deputy sheriff since January 1973 until his election. Duties of the Sheriffs office varies from serving papers in court to arresting violators of the law, and patrolling the County.

Janet Hammond took office as County Clerk and Recorder in December 1986, having worked there since October 1978. Duties of this office are numerous, a few being Secretary of the County Board, keeper of all records pertaining to the County's everyday operations like bids and contracts, conducting all elections in the County. All land records and anything pertaining to filing ownership of property, issuing marriage licenses and keeping all birth, death and marriage licenses occurring in the County. Property taxes are actually figured by the County Clerk's office, and any taxes sold at tax sales are collected in the Clerk's office.

Janice Hamberg was hired as a deputy clerk in the Assessor's office in November 1979. On December 1, 1982, she was appointed Supervisor of Assessments -Duties entail determining the market value of all taxable property, other than farmland and farm buildings, assessing that property at 1/3 its market value. The purpose of the assessed value is to proportion the tax burden, as established by the taxing bodies, over all property in a fair and equitable manner based on the value of the real estate. Other duties include homestead exemptions, clerk of the Board of Review, maintaining ownership records, dividing property for taxation and maintaining mailing addresses.

Raymond Miller started as Veteran's Aid Officer in June 1998, Duties include helping veterans who are in need of some assistance in their everyday lives, such as rent or food., and various questions that arise concerning other benefits.

Emergency Services and Disaster Administrator (ESDA)--Gary Kitchin started with the County as Civil Defense Coordinator over 25 years ago. With changing times, so does the job title and responsibilities. He is in charge of disaster planning and coordination, and observing weather changes, such as tornadoes.

The County has always had a full time County Engineer until this year (2002) when they hired a part-time engineer. Jimmy Justus is a retired State employee and along with the years of knowledge from Gene Larkin, the assistant engineer, the county roads and bridges are well taken care of. With 170 miles of County roads and 23 bridges, the Highway Department crew are kept busy year round.

Tuberculosis "TB" Nurse has cut back considerably on the duties over the years. Christine Ayers has been able to work full time at the local hospital, keep active with her busy family and still take on the work of the TB Nurse, checking and testing the few patients that Warren County might have.

James Gaskill has been County Animal Control Officer since December 1984. Duties are primarily making sure the ordinances pertaining to dogs , that the County Board has passed, are being abided by - such as licensing dogs and not running loose - besides wild animal experiences.

Early courthouse with clock tower and Civil War Memorial

John C. Dunbar Drug Co., DBA Zimmers Apothecary

Present day Zimmers Apothecary began in November 1835 when William F. Smith opened a general merchandise business on the NE Corner of the Square with a $1000 investment. This business was merged with a drug store; and in 1843 Mr. Smith erected a building on the SW Corner of the Square. In 1869 William B. Smith, his son, and John C. Dunbar, his son-in-law, became associated with the elder Mr. Smith. In 1875 the drug store, now known as Smith and Dunbar Drug Store, moved to 105 South Main Street.

John C. Dunbar purchased Mr. Smith's portion of the business in 1895, and named the business the John C. Dunbar Drug Store. In 1904, Mr. Dunbar acquired a Rexall Agency, one of the first druggists to do so. In 1910 the business was incorporated as John C. Dunbar Drug Co. Inc.

In 1916 Arthur P. Zimmer and E. 0. Nussle formed a partnership and purchased the business from the Dunbar estate and named the business Nussle and Zimmer Drug Store. This partnership lasted for ten years until Mr. Nussle retired. At this time Mr. Zimmer named the business Zimmers Drug store and relocated to 220 South Main Street. In 1937 Mr. Zimmer remodeled the business. The innovative design of the remodeling was awarded with two full pages of articles in the Rexall Ad-Vantages, a national pharmacy magazine.

Edmond W. Kelly was a Zimmers employee prior to WWII, and rejoined Zimmers as a pharmacist in December 1949 after attending Butler University Pharmacy School. In 1968, Mr. Kelly and James L. Vugteveen formed a partnership to purchase the business. Jim was a 1960 graduate of the University of Iowa and had worked in Macomb and Astoria. This partnership lasted until May 1, 1977, when Mr. Kelly retired and Jim and Betty Vugteveen became owners.

Zimmers has been fortunate to have many valuable employees that helped them to be successful. Such employees as Chris Almaguer, Kenny Applegate, Annetta Chase, John Cooper, Pat Evans, Randy Goodwin, Ron Hallbick, Connie Haptonstall, Karen Hayes, Irene Hill, Jo Holmberg, Carl Jobusch, Chuck Lange, Robb Miller, Jim Nichols, Kenny Noel, Doug Ray, Mitchell Ray, Marcella Ray, Jim Root, Dixie Reimolds, Larry Sharpe, Randy Sheese, David St. Ledger, Roy Schwass, Dyke Wells, Randy Wells, and Bud Zimmer.

Most of its owners have worked into their 70's. Mr. Smith was involved in the business for over 50 years. Art Zimmer was over 80 years old when he retired, and had owned the business for 42 years. Ed Kelly was involved in the business for 31 years. Jim Vugteveen has owned the business for 34 years.

On July 17, 1977, the business moved to 401 North Main Street and was named Zimmers Apothecary. At this time the pharmacy changed from a traditional drug store to a prescription only oriented pharmacy.

Zimmers has been fortunate to have many loyal customers, some for many years. Zimmers has enjoyed the loyalties of many families, some for 3 and 4 generations. *Submitted by Jim Vugteveen*

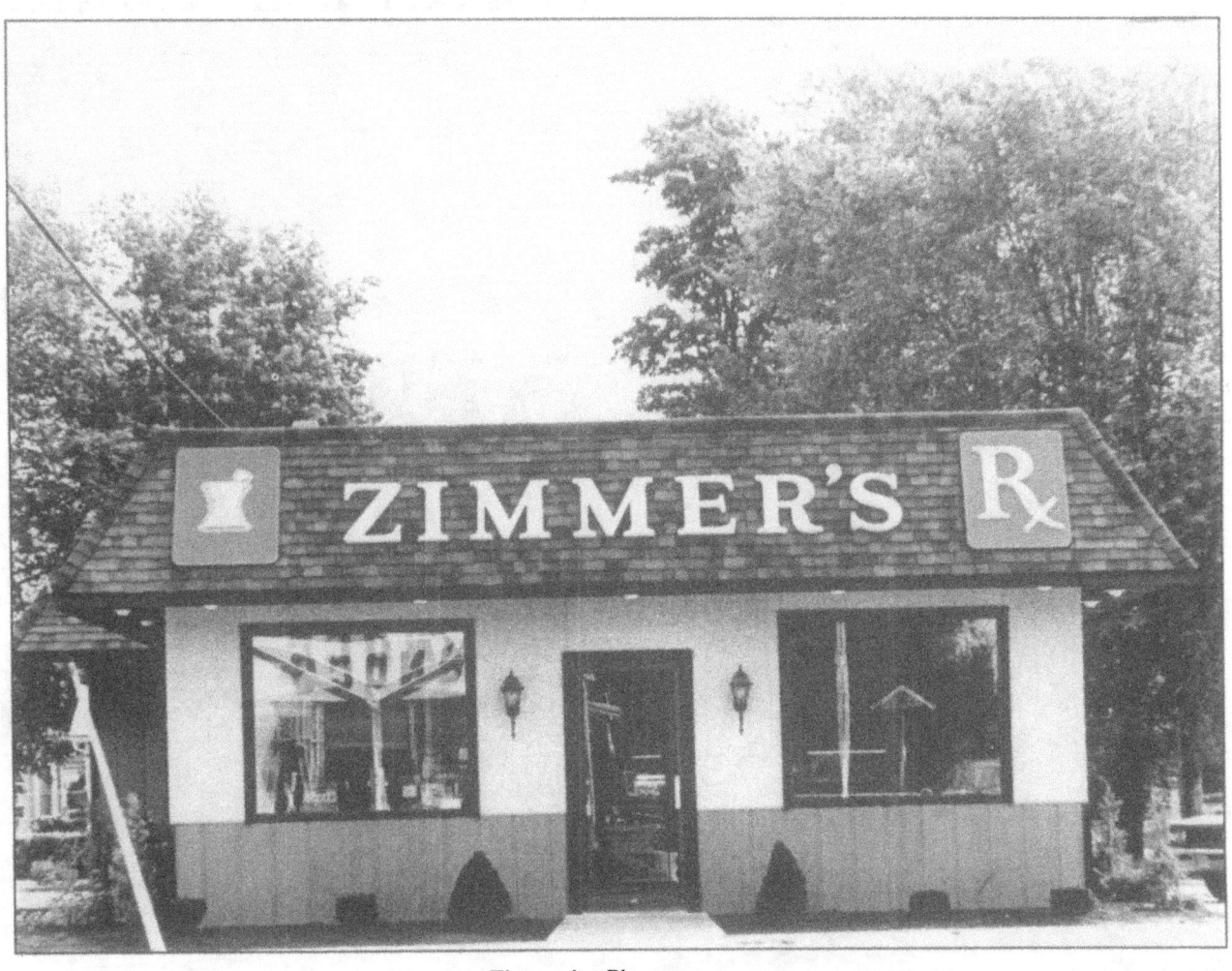

Zimmer's Pharmacy

Review Atlas

Since 1846, residents of Warren County and the City of Monmouth have gained from the services of a newspaper.

From the early days of tin-type to the high technology printing created in using a Web printing press today, the Daily Review has come a long way in its 156 years of existence.

In one form or another, the Monmouth Daily Review Atlas has been keeping the area informed for the past 156 years beginning as the Monmouth Atlas on October 30, 1846. In 1855, Alexander Hamilton Swain founded the Review, which he sold in November of 1886 to J.D. Diffenbaugh and Hugh R. Moffet, who had worked as a reporter for the paper since1884.

Purchased by a local company in 1892, the Atlas then became the Republican Atlas Advance. Through a couple more sales, the Review and the Atlas united as one to form the Review Atlas in 1924, with Moffet serving as publisher.

The local newspaper retained the same ownership until 1976 when it was purchased by Windsor Newspapers, Inc. Ten years later in 1986, the daily newspaper became the property of American Publishing Company. In January of 1998, the Daily Review Atlas was purchased by Liberty Group Publishing of Northbrook, IL.

In addition to printing the daily edition of the Daily Review Atlas, newsprint rolls through the press printing two daily newspapers, two weekly newspapers and six shoppers. Products printed each week at the local press plant include the McDonough County Shopper, Fulton County Shopper, Penny Saver, The Paper (formerly the Penny Saver Press), Oquawka Current, Aledo Times Record, Aledo Town Crier, Kewanee Star Courier, Macomb Journal, Geneseo Republic, Western Illinois University's Western Courier, Monmouth College's Courier, as well as the Review Atlas.

With the purchase of the McDonough County and Fulton County Shoppers, along with the Geneseo Republic in recent years, along with the increased production, the decision was made to acquire an inserting machine now manned by two shifts of employees. Because of the vast amount of printing taking place in Monmouth, a second printing and a plant superintendent were added to the press department.

Liberty Group Publishing operates approximately 330 newspapers in 17 states, most of which are small-town publications.

Submitted by Iva Kay Horner, Managing Editor

OFFICE SPECIALISTS, INC.

143 E. FERRIS ST.	87 N. SIDE SQUARE	212 N. TREMONT ST.
GALESBURG, IL 61401	MONMOUTH, IL 61462	KEWANEE, IL 61443
PHONE 309/342-7711	PHONE 309/734-8441	PHONE 309/853-1202
FAX 309/342-0700	FAX 309/734-7404	FAX 309/853-1382
1-800-747-0071	1-800-374-6175	1-866-853-1202

"Your Office is Our Business"

**OFFICE FURNITURE • INTERIOR DESIGN • SPACE PLANNING
OFFICE & COMPUTER SUPPLIES • OFFICE MACHINES**

SHARP. AUTHORIZED DEALER

Warren County Families

Sumner	Spring Grove	Kelly
Little York	Gerlaw	
Hale	Monmouth	Coldbrook
	Monmouth	Coldbrook
Tompkins	Lenox	Floyd
Kirkwood	Larchland	Cameron
Ellison	Roseville	Berwick
Smithshire	Roseville	Berwick
Point Pleasant	Swan	Greenbush
	Swan Creek	Greenbush

L: to R: Karl Gullberg, Karlene Gullberg, Susan Gullberg, Bill Gullberg, Bill Allen - Purina Feed Salesman. Taken in 1937-1938

GEORGE ADAMS - George Adams was born on September 1, 1849 at Over Cambridgeshire, England, the son of James and Sarah Day Adams. At the age of 20 he came to the U.S.A. and traveled to Chicago by train, then to Warren County by covered wagon. On February 18, 1875, he married Tempe Lavona Hively and they moved into Spring Grove Township where he raised fruits, berries, and his prize seed corn, all of which he sold in Monmouth. He must have made a lot of friends that way for his granddaughter, Rosie, remembers that when she went "up town" on Saturday night as everyone did, people would ask her mother how Mr. Adams was. Whenever he did go to town he always ate lunch at Foster Bros. Cafe which was located on the north side of the square, a very popular meeting and eating place.

Back L: to R: Henry Adams, Frank Adams, Front: Dorothy (Adams) Kersey, George Adams, John Q Adams

George and Tempe were the parents of eight children before Tempe passed away on October 12, 1890. Five years later, on April 24, 1895, George married Sarah Lucinda Kinkaid who was born in Spring Grove Township on June 19, 1869, the daughter of James Nathaniel and Anna Elizabeth (Patterson) Kinkaid. Her father had been the Spring Grove postmaster until it became the Gerlaw Post Office. The Kinkaid home was also the stagecoach stop between Monmouth and Rock Island.

George & Sarah Lucinda (Kinkaid) Adams 24 April 1895.   *George Adams 1920.*

George and Sarah were the parents of four children: Henry, Frank, John and Dorathy (Rosie's mother). Sarah passed away on July 10, 1905 when her daughter was thirteen months old. The funeral was held at the family home, and as the family and mourners left to accompany the casket to the Monmouth Cemetery, the bridge on Highway 67 gave way due to a rise in waters from recent storms, and caused one buggy to be thrown in the creek. Mrs. Elizabeth Day was rescued from the creek, but the remaining buggies had to turn back and return to the family home.

As a small child Rosie recalls that one of greatest treats was getting to go to Grandpa Adams' house. Then it seemed to be way out in the country when actually it was only a short distance north of Monmouth on Route 67 to the Gerlaw corner. When she could see the Ralston School which her mother had attended, she knew that a left turn and then a right turn would take her to Grandpa's. Although she and her sister were anxious to go out to play, first they had to go in to see Grandpa and give him the chocolate creams or stars that they had brought him. Secretly they hoped he would share with them before going outside to play. Rosie was especially eager to get on his pedal grindstone and pedal as fast as she could. Now she has her own pedal grindstone.

Grandpa Adams lived till he was 98 and passed away on February 8, 1947. His funeral was held at Lugg's Funeral Home and his good friend, James Harper Grier, president of Monmouth College, conducted the service. Through the years the Adams and Kinkaids attended the Gerlaw Christian Church, and today there are still a number of great grandchildren and great great grandchildren that still attend.

NOTLEY THOMAS ADCOCK - Notley Thomas, third child of Robert Hillock and Mary (Robertson) Adcock, was born November 24, 1863, Kelly Township, Warren County, Illinois. He was a farmer and breeder of registered Scotch Shorthorn cattle and thoroughbred race horses. At the time of his death on August 4, 1911, he owned 60 horses, many descended from the famous Godolphin Arabian stud.

Notley Thomas Adcock Circa 1880

Notley married October 6, 1890, Warren County, Illinois, Mary Drusilla Adcock (born November 19, 1864, died October 19, 1924), daughter of Joseph Washington and Mary Elizabeth (McMurtry) Adcock. Notley and Mary Drusilla are buried in Hope Cemetery, Kelly Township, Warren County, Illinois. Both Notley and Mary Drusilla died on the farm where Mary was born and which had been owned by her grandfather, Edmund Adcock who had moved from Virginia to Kelly Township, Warren County, Illinois about 1833. Notley and Mary Drusilla were each descendants, but through different sons' lines (Notley through Henry Adcock and Mary Drusilla through Edmund Adcock), of Joseph Adcock who served in the American Revolution. Joseph Adcock's father John Adcock, of Scotch-Irish descent, settled in Buckingham County, Virginia in the early 1700's.

Notley and Mary Drusilla Adcock were the parents of 8 children, 5 of whom survived to adulthood.

Laura Adcock, born September 8, 1896, Kelly Township, Warren County, Illinois (died February 10, 1980, Aledo, Illinois), married February 19, 1924, Walter Earl Price, eldest son of Frederick Franklin and Emma Matilda (Strand) Price. Laura had a B.A., magna cum laude, Phi Beta Kappa, Knox College, Galesburg, Illinois, class of 1920. Laura and Walter lived and farmed for nearly 5 decades in Coldbrook and Kelly Townships, Warren County, Illinois. Laura's special interests were family, literary pursuits and horticulture. They were the parents of 4 children: Mary Emma Aubertin, Alice Lucille Hare, Charles Francis Price, and Esther Anne Patrick, and grandparents of 15 grandchildren.

Florence Adcock, born April 24, 1899, Kelly Township, Warren County, Illinois (died December 13, 1976, Rockford, Illinois), married February 22, 1935, Washington Franklin Schott (born January 6, 1893, Burlington, IA, died June 2, 1966). Florence had a B.A. from Knox College, Galesburg, Illinois, an M.A. from the University of Michigan, and later attended the University of Chicago. She taught biology at Illinois Woman's College (now MacMurray), Jacksonville, Illinois, and at Sweet Briar College in Virginia. After their marriage, Florence and Frank Schott farmed near Cameron, Illinois. They were the parents of 2 sons: Joseph Washington Schott, and Edmund Adcock Schott and grandparents of 9 grandchildren.

Blanche Adcock, born February 15, 1901, Kelly Township, Warren County, Illinois (died October 20, 1988, Quincy, Illinois), married November 9, 1933, John Quincy (J.Q.) Lawless 11 (born February 7, 1901, died July 25, 1984), Decatur, Illinois. Blanche attended Knox College; Western Illinois University at Macomb, and received a B.A. in education at University of Michigan in 1930. She taught elementary and high school students for many years. Her avocation was the breeding of Persian cats. J.Q. was an attorney and judge Brown County, Illinois for 5 decades. Their daughter Carolyn Elizabeth Lawless manages the farms of her parents in Brown, Adams and Warren counties.

Frances Adcock, born November 28, 1902, Kelly Township, Warren County, Illinois (died June 30, 1998, Kingsport, Tennessee), married June 16, 1928, Aubrey Ernest Broderick, Kelly Township, Warren County, Illinois. Frances, a graduate of Western Illinois University Academy, Macomb, Illinois, attended Knox College, Galesburg, Illinois, and earned a B.A. in Spanish from the University of Wisconsin. Aubrey (born April 13, 1901, died May 12, 1970) had a B.S., University of Illinois; M.S. and Ph.D. in chemistry, University of Wisconsin. Aubrey and Frances were the parents of 2 daughters: Marjorie Elizabeth Griffith and Patricia Ann Ausdenmoore, and grandparents of 8 grandchildren.

Robert Adcock, born May 7, 1904, Kelly Township, Warren County, Illinois (died April 26, 1965), married May 18, 1929, Mary Irene Montgomery (daughter of Edmund Max and Mary Nida (Hope) Montgomery), born October 29, 1907, died January 22, 1980, Galesburg, Warren County, Illinois. Robert attended Galesburg High School, was a prosperous farmer and civic leader in his community. Mary Irene attended Western Illinois University and Monmouth College, taught at Tylerville School, Kelly Township, Warren County, Illinois and taught accordion lessons in Galesburg, Illinois. Robert and Mary Irene were the parents of 3 children: Robert Notley Adcock, Edward Montgomery Adcock, and Elizabeth Hope Adcock (deceased), and grandparents of 4 grandchildren. Edward Montgomery Adcock and his son Robert Thomas Adcock farm the farm settled by their ancestors in the early 1830s.

ROBERT AND IRMA ADKISSON - Robert Allen Adkisson was born November 5, 1927 to Joe T. and Martha Moore Adkisson in Point Pleasant Township, Warren County, Illinois. His grandparents were Allen and Emma Davis Adkisson, and William V.D. and Mattie Strong Moore, all of Roseville. Robert attended Chattanooga country school, Roseville High School, and the University of Illinois where he earned a degree in electrical engineering in 1949.

Robert and Irma Adkisson

Irma White was born November 11, 1926 to George and Maude Taylor White in Roseville Township, Warren County. Her grandparents were Thomas and Mary Earp White of Monmouth, and Rufus and Mary Kirkpatrick Taylor of Roseville. Irma attended Pleasant Hill country school, Roseville High School, and Monmouth College where she earned her degree in 1948. Next she completed a one year course at Northwestern University Medical School in Chicago which prepared her to become a registered medical technologist.

Robert and Irma were married September 17, 1949 in Roseville. Following their marriage they lived in Grand Rapids, Michigan until 1951, and in Jackson, Michigan until 1955. During these six years in Michigan, Robert worked for Consumers Power Company. In Grand Rapids, Irma was a medical technologist at Butterworth Hospital.

In 1955, Robert and Irma moved home to Illinois. Robert became a farmer on his family's home place in Section 10 of Point Pleasant Township. Robert is the fourth generation of his family on this land. The home eighty acres was purchased in 1876 by Robert's great grandfather, Francis Marion Moore, a native of New Jersey.

Besides being a mother and active farm wife through the years, Irma worked at McDonough District Hospital in Macomb, Illinois from 1972 to 1991 as a medical technologist.

Robert and Irma are the parents of a son Stanley, born February 1, 1952, and a daughter Robyn, born June 4, 1955. Stanley married Aleta Mahon December 15, 1984. They have two children, Nathan George and Lauren Elizabeth. They live in Cedaredge Colorado. Robyn lives in Iowa City, Iowa.

ORVILLE AND ALICE DAVIS AGAN - Orville Agan was born in Orange Co., IN on March 23, 1906 and Alice Davis Agan was born in Orange Co., IN on August 20, 1909. They grew up on neighboring farms and attended the same one room school. In the early 1920's two of Alice's brothers, Lawrence and Clarence Davis, moved to farms in Warren and Mercer Counties. Orville's sister Ella was married to Alice's brother, Clarence. In the mid to late 1920's, Orville moved to Illinois from New Albany, Indiana with his father, two brothers, and a sister.

In 1930, Orville married Stella Damewood from Kirkwood, IL. To this marriage were born John Milton in 1931 and Betty Ann (Beeson) in 1933. Orville and Stella divorced in 1935. During the thirties Orville farmed, drove trucks and helped build US highway 94.

Alice visited her brothers in Illinois several times and became reacquainted with Orville, her former neighbor and schoolmate in Indiana. On October 10, 1942 they were married in the Norwood parsonage. They farmed a few years and then moved to Alexis in 1946. To this marriage were born James Maurice in 1943, Janet Mae (Shauman) in 1945, Judy Marie (Malcolm) in 1947, and Dennis Ray in 1948.

During the time he lived in Alexis, Orville worked for the John Deere planter works and Service Rubber Company in the Quad Cities. He was a custodian at Alexis High School for several years where he was very popular with the students. He also worked on highway maintenance on US 67 in Warren and Mercer counties. Orville was very active in the Evangelical United Brethren Church in Alexis where he served as a deacon and taught Sunday school. He was active in the community with the fall festival and the centennial in 1970. Alice spent most of her time raising her family, but she did work a few years in a nursing home in Alexis. Later she stayed nights with older people and helped them in their homes, performing a service much like home health care. She baby-sat families of children in their homes. She also was active in her church with women's groups, Sunday school and playing the piano and was a member of War Mothers.

Orville died on November 10, 1972 and Alice died November 5, 1988.

MARGARET MARIE (COURSEY) ALDRIDGE - Marie was born in Point Pleasant Township, Warren County, Illinois on March 15, 1906, Her parents were Thomas Marion Coursey (1874-1967) and Lettie Jane Aulgur (1878-1967). She attended various rural Elementary Schools and Roseville High School, She married Charles Melvin Aldridge Jr. on December 18, 1926 at Monmouth, Warren County, Illinois.

Charles was born April 29, 1906 at Sullivan, Moultrie County, Illinois, his parents were Charles Melvin Aldridge (1883-1966) and Edith Peterson (1884-1956).

They started their life together working farming for Earl Duke near Rozetta, Henderson County, Illinois.

They also farmed for George Filker, north of Roseville, Illinois, George Okert and Glen Davis, both southeast of Smithshire, Illinois. Glen was the last farmer they worked for prior to moving to Monmouth in about 1942. Charles worked for Butler Mfg. in Galesburg, Illinois until his retirement about 1971. Marie worked for Western Stoneware in Monmouth, Illinois for several years.

They had 2 children: Martha Fern born February 18, 1928 and died March 31, 1994. She is buried in Memorial Park Cemetery at Monmouth, Illinois and Thomas Melvin born March 21, 1929 he lives at Monmouth, Illinois. They raised Joanne Coursey from the time her mother died until her marriage in 1950.

Charles and Marie Aldridge, 50th Anniversary, 1976.

Richard W. Coursey also lived with them from September 1940 until finishing the first grade at Ellison School 1 and 3/4 miles southeast of Smithshire, Warren County, Illinois.

There are a lot of fond memories crowded into that 8 month span in 1940, although in reality times were hard and togetherness was about the only thing they could afford. Living in the farming industry they had plenty to eat, although the gardening, butchering, canning and preserving process was hard, it was a labor of love and a necessity to survive. The farmhouse was hot in the summer and cold and drafty in the winter, it would have been wonderful to have had that cold breeze blowing through the windows and the siding during the hot months.

Marie remembers everyone going to the movies at the Old Opera House in Greenbush, Illinois on Sundays. When the movie was over they all tried to be the first on the road, as the dust could be 3 inches deep, and none of them wanted to drive in that dust cloud back to Roseville. She also remembers her first and only sleigh ride. In late February 1909 her uncle Vete Aulgur worked for Johnnie Larkin, he borrowed Larkin's sleigh and took Glenn, Harold and Marie for a sleigh ride. Everyone had bells on the harness and you could hear the bells everywhere, as most of the neighbors were out sleigh riding. Her mother Lettie wouldn't go because she was very close to delivery for her son John.

Charles died February 13, 1983 and is buried in Memorial Park Cemetery at Monmouth, Illinois.

JOSEPH BYNOM ALEXANDER - Alexander Joseph Bynom had his beginnings in Asheville, North Carolina in 1871, the son of Philetas Benson and Amanda Rebecca (Smith) Alexander. They moved to Colwich, Kansas. History records Philetas delivered U.S. Mail to a nearby town twenty miles distant on horseback, never missing a day for thirty years. He also rang the Methodist Church bell every Sunday morning. "Byn," as he was called, married Lenora M. Levis, the daughter of Joseph Brinton and Amanda Kathryn (Smith) Levis on the 16 September 1891 at their homestead in Colby, Frontier County, Nebraska. She was almost 16 and he 20 years old. While living there, three daughters were born: Sara Ellen 1892, Ednah Lavine 1893, and Donnie Kathryn 1895. The family moved to homestead a farm near Byron and Cherokee, Oklahoma, near the northern border and the Salt River. While here stillborn twin boys were born and three more girls

: Amanda Rebecca 1902, Viola May 1904, and Minnie Belle 1905. Poor crops caused them to send the three older girls to live with his parents at Colwich until better times, which never came. Lenora passed away after five years 26 May 1910. The other girls were also sent to his parents while he returned to Wichita looking for work. A friend owned a house that he had moved to Maize, Kansas and allowed Byn the use of it. He called for his girls. Two, Sara Ellen and Donnie Kathryn had married, leaving seventeen year old Ednah to be the mother and manage the cook shack Byn was operating during harvest. It was here she met her future husband, Verne Franklin Barnes. He had come to attend Maize high school for two years. His brother Renalt came for one year. On 15 February 1917 Verne called from his home in Hermon, Knox County, Illinois and asked her to meet him in Kansas City, Kansas, where they were married. When she left the three younger girls were now older and boarded with towns folk. The newly marrieds moved to Hermon, where he was in business with his father, Oliver Milton Barnes. They ran a general store.

Joseph Bynom Alexander

When his brother Renalt John, who had married Myra Bowton and had a baby girl, Allena Cleone, was drafted for military service, Verne stayed at home since only one son could be drafted for service. Myra and Cleone stayed with his parents. On his return from France the brothers looked for a grocery business and purchased one from William Johnson in Monmouth, Warren County, Illinois. They opened their "Groceteria" the 1 July 1922. Two months later Verne and Ednah had a son, Elwyn Verne, called "Buddy." This expanded their family to a girl, Elynore Lavern and a son.

Byn remarried in 1920 to Amanda Higgs, who had two sons and a daughter. Together they raised both families. On her death Byn moved lock-stock-and model T Ford to Monmouth to live with his daughter. Byn was a huge man, always seen smoking his corn cob pipe unless working in the Super Market in the produce or meat department. He was a Republican and elected Road Commissioner of Sedgwick County, Kansas, retiring after 30 years. He joined Valley Center Masonic Lodge, the Wichita Consistory, and Royal Arch Masons in Monmouth. He was also active in the Odd-Fellows Lodge being Past Noble Grand in Maize. He left 35 grandchildren and 58 great grandchildren at death the 17 November 1960 - 89 years old. He is buried next to his daughter in Monmouth's Memorial Park Cemetery.

DENNIS BRUCE ALLAMAN - Dennis Bruce, the son of Bruce Caldwell Allaman and Maxine (James) Allaman, was born in Macomb on Sept 21 1946. He had a sister Carolyn (Allaman) Bowman and a brother Lonnie Allaman. Dennis grew up on the farm and showed Angus cattle and played football. He was a member of the Sciota Christian Church, 4-H, and FFA. He graduated from Northwestern High School. Dennis married Sarah (Hanna) Allaman in the Kirkwood UP church on Sept 29, 1965. They moved to the Charles Rhinehart family farm in Hale Township, Warren County in January of 1966 where they have farmed and raised Angus Cattle and horses. Sarah, the daughter of Ross E. Hanna and Ellen (Rhinehart) Hanna, was born in Monmouth on March 26, 1947 and also grew up on the farm. She was a member of the Fall Creek Methodist Church, MYF, 4-H, and FHA. She also showed Angus Cattle and horses. She attended Pleasant Green, a one-room country school and graduated from Yorkwood High School.

Dennis and Sarah were blessed with four sons. Chad Harrison was born Aug 7, 1966. Craig Charles was born Feb 12, 1968. Clinton Bruce was born Mar 28, 1975. Carlton Ross was born May 10, 1978. The boys were all active in 4-H, FFA, church, and sports. They showed Angus cattle. The younger boys showed horses. Carlton competed in high school and college rodeo in the events of calf roping and team roping. The boys all graduated from Yorkwood High School. Chad and Craig were on the Class I A State Football Championship team. Craig and Clint were both quarterbacks and Chad was a receiver. Chad, Craig, and Clint graduated from Western IL University where they were very active in student activities and leadership. Chad married Laura Whitsitt July 9, 1994. Their daughter, Grace Anne was born May 28, 1999 at Canton, IL. They now live in Mason City, IL, where Chad is the elementary principal. Laura, a Biology major and schoolteacher is enjoying being an "at home Mother". Craig married Heidi Wray Hollar August 28, 1993. Their sons, Andrew Maurice was born June 12, 1997, and Ian James was born May 26,1999 at Galesburg, IL. Craig and Heidi live on a farm on the Warren-Henderson county line. Craig works for Twomey Co. and farms in his spare time. Heidi is a Mary Kay Consultant and also an "at home mother". The boys attend MELC preschool in Monmouth and Drew will start Kindergarten at Yorkwood. Clint married Chelsey Lee Ratermann Feb 26, 2000. They live in Andover, IL Clint is a sales rep for Syngenta Seeds. Chelsey works for John Deere. Carty is working on his degree at UTM at Martin, Tennessee.

Dennis has served as a board member for Hale Township, Lamoine Valley and Illinois Angus Associations. Sarah has been a 4-H leader, Sunday School teacher, Good News Club and Awana leader. She has been active in Home Extension, Angus Auxiliaries, PEO, and church groups. They attend the Faith Bible Church in Oquawka.

ELIZABETH LAW ALLEN (ZACHARIAH ALLEN) FAMILY - Elizabeth Law Allen was born March, 1782 in Kentucky. She married Zachariah Allen December 11, 1804 in Davidson County, Tennessee. Zachariah Allen died July 24, 1839 Greene County, Illinois. Three of the children of Zachariah and Elizabeth Allen arrived in early Warren County. Thomas Allen came from Greene County, IL. in the 30's and settled on a farm in the east part of Hale Twp. Two brothers of his, David and Isaac Newton Edney Allen came at the same time.

In 1839 Elizabeth Law Allen joined the Sugar Tree Grove Presbyterian Church. Also listed among church members were ten of her children.

1. Sarah "Sally" Allen, born Feb. 28, 1799 North Carolina. Married June 28, 1831 Fayette Co. Il. to Hiram Wood, and to Grieves Walker. She died Oct. 25, 1883 Gray Summit, Franklin Co., MO.

2. Hardy Allen b. abt. 1807 Davidson Co. TN. m. Jane Monteath April 20, 1837 Greene Co.

3. Jesse Allen b. June 9, 1808 Davidson Co. d. April 5, 1874 Greene Co. IL. m. Mary Bell/Boyd March 24,1831.

4. Thomas Smith Allen b. January 1810 Davidson Co. TN., d. September 22, 1845 Monmouth. He married Jane Gibson, April 9,1835 Warren Co.

5. Margaret Allen born 1812/1814 Nashville, Davidson Co. TN. She married June 12, 1832 Greene Co. IL, to Rev. James Clark Bruce.

6. Joseph Allen was born about 1815 Davidson Co. TN and married May 19,1836 Monmouth, to Rachel Bruce, sister of Rev. James C. Bruce. After Rachel's death, He married Elizabeth C. Brownlee Feb. 27, 1840 Warren Co. Jospeh died after April 1842 in Warren Co.

7. David Allen was born about 1817 Davidson Co. TN and married Elizabeth Hanna March 14, 1844 in Warren Co. He died 1851 in Oregon.

8. Jonathon Lindley Allen was born January 30, 1819 Madison Co. IL and married July 6, 1843 Warren Co. to Martha McCallon.

9. Mary Jean Allen was born about 1821 Greene Co. IL and married April 19, 1844, Warren Co. to Thomas "Jackson" Caldwell. She died July 29, 1868 Warren Co.

10. Isaac Newton Edney Allen was born July 1822 Greene Co. IL and married December 25, 1845 Warren Co. IL to Anna Maria "Aleri" Rodgers. He died Nov. 9, 1863 Warren Co.

11. Andrew Allen was born about 1825 Greene Co. IL.

12. Henry Allen was born June 9,1828 Greene Co. IL and married January 27, 1848 Warren Co. to Mary McKissick. He died February 13,1907 Albia, Iowa.

Elizabeth Law Allen died May 12,1842 in Hale Twp., Warren Co.

Zachariah Allen was born January 8,1760 in Rowan Co., North Carolina. He and his first wife (maybe Sarah?) had at least seven children, and in 1804, Elizabeth Law Allen became mother to these Allen children:

1. Elizabeth (Boyd) b. aft. 1780; William, b. abt. 1785 (Sally Gaskins); John, b. 1791 (Martha "Patsy" Burrow); James Martin, b. 1794 (Elizabeth Ann Morrow); Zachariah Jr. abt. 1797 (Elizabeth Stubblefield); Samuel, b. 1798 (Anna Clark); George Washington, b. 1801, (Caroline Henderson).

Submitted by Carol L. Burris Garafola, fourth great-grand daughter of Zachariah and Elizabeth Law Allen.

JOSEPH AND RACHEL N. (BRUCE) ALLEN - Rachel N. Bruce (Robert 1) was born about 1816 in Ohio. She cared for her aged father, then married Joseph Allen May 19, 1836 Monmouth. Joseph Allen had been married previously, and had children by this marriage. Rachel and Joseph had a son named Bryson Allen, who died February 11, 1863 at Fort Donelson TN, during the Civil War. It has been reported that Rachel and Joseph lost five sons in the civil war.

Nancy Bruce (Robert 1) was born 1824 Ohio. She married Andrew Gibson April 30,

1835, Monmouth. He is the son of Thomas Gibson and Martha Hogue Gibson of Monmouth. Andrew Gibson and Nancy Bruce Gibson had three children: Sarah Gibson b. 1836 and died young. Julia Ann Gibson b. 1838 and married Charles L. Pate October 10, 1865. She died Oct. 2, 1866 at age 28. Buried Sugar Tree Grove Cemetery. The third child was William Gibson b. 1840 and died Aug. 16, 1866, Warren Co. IL. Robert Gibson b. April 12, 1843 and died February 6, 1900. Martha Gibson born 1844.

Andrew Gibson died April 16, 1845/46 Kirksville, Adair Co., Mo. Nancy Bruce Gibson remarried to David D. Lozier. Their children were James, born 1857 IL, Joseph born 1860 IL and Nancy M. W. Lozier who married Joseph White Gibson, September 30, 1869. Their children: Effie Gibson, b. Sept. 1870; Graffe R. Gibson b. Oct 1872; and Jessie Gibson who died young. The elder two moved to Denver, Colorado.

Addendum on Joseph Allen. After Rachel Bruce Allen died, he married Elizabeth C. Brownlee. Shortly thereafter, he died. His widow married June 26,1849 Henderson Co. IL. to Thomas Gibson. Living in the household at that tine were Gibson children and Joseph S. Allen, born 1842, David B. Allen born 1844 and Henry Allen born 1846.

Elizabeth C. Brownlee Allen Gibson and Thomas Gibson were the parents of Robert Gibson born about 1850 Henderson Co. IL. And died July 1892 in Wellington, Kansas. He married Emma McCurdy about 1870 in Henderson Co IL.

This information is submitted by Carol L. Burris Garafola. Fourth great-granddaughter of Rev. James Clark Bruce, and John Kendall. And, fifth great-grand-daughter of Thomas Gibson and Martha Hogue Gibson.

DAVID CAROTHERS ALLISON AND JOYCE KEATING ALLISON - David was born to Frederick Avery Allison and Dorothy Rankin Allison February 25, 1931. Joyce was born to William Arnot Keating and Marjorie Root Keating December 23, 1931. David had two brothers: Stuart Rankin Allison born September 16, 1925 - killed in action, WWII, August 11, 1944, and Richard Gordon Allison born February 3, 1927 - died January 1969. Joyce has two sisters: Gewndolyn Keating Lowe born June 30, 1928, and Linda Carol Keating born September 5, 1943, and a brother William Blake Keating born May 22, 1930. Joyce and David were married June 16, 1954 and have three children: Stuart Keating Allison born October 10, 1958, William Frederick Allison born December 21, 1960, and Marjorie Carol Allison born February 4, 1963. Joyce and David, at the time of this writing, have two granddaughters: Gillian Christine Allison was born to Stuart and Holly Whiffet-Allison November 6, 1998. Clara Marie Barclay was born to Marjorie Allison Barclay and Daniel Barclay January 9, 2001.

Joyce attended Monmouth College and graduated from Milikin University in 1953 with a BA in Elementary Education. She taught grades 2 and 3 in two school districts in Illinois and one in Pennsylvania. David attended Monmouth College and earned BS and MS degrees in 1956 and 1957 in Agronomy from the University of Illinois. In 1960 he earned a Ph.D. degree from Pennsylvania State University in Genetics and Breeding. David was employed by the University of Arizona from January 1961 to August 1962 as a cotton geneticist at the Assistant Professor rank. He joined the faculty of Monmouth College in 1962 as an Assistant Professor of Biology and retired from Monmouth College following the 1995-96 academic year as Professor Emeritus of Biology. He served as the chair of the Biology Department for 15 years. From May 1951 to May 1954 David served as an enlisted man on a U.S. Coast Guard Weather Vessel, earning the Korean Medal with extensive service in the Pacific area and off shore from Korea.

Joyce is active in the Presbyterian Church USA having served as an Elder in Faith U.P. Church three different times. She was elected to the Monmouth School Board, District Number 38, serving for 12 years. She held the office of Secretary and President during her tenure on the board. She has been active as a Volunteer in the Auxiliary of Community Medical Center in Monmouth for 27 years. Joyce has also been a member and officer of the Illinois-Alpha Chapter of Pi Beta Phi for 35 years and is a 50-year member of Pi Phi. Joyce has been a member of Illinois LE of PEO since 1969, serving as President and other offices during this period. For 15 years Joyce was active in the American Red Cross Blood Bank at the local level. Joyce was selected as "Woman of the Year" in Monmouth by the Altrusa organization in 1992.

David has also been active in the Presbyterian Church. He was elected an Elder in the Second United Presbyterian Church and then for two different periods in Faith U.P. Church where he also has served as a trustee for two different terms. David served on the Board of Directors of Warren Achievement School, which became Warren Achievement Center, from 1969-1975 serving as Chair of the Board for two years. David was elected to the Board of Directors of the National Bank of Monmouth in March of 1975, remaining on the board when the National Bank was acquired by the Midwest Bank Holding Inc. He is currently the Corporate Secretary of the Midwest Bank of Western Illinois. He has served on the Alumni Board of Monmouth College and was a member of the Zoning Appeals Board of the City of Monmouth in the 1970's. He is currently a member of the board of directors of the United Presbyterian Home in Washington, Iowa and is also a current member of the board of the Addleman Foundation in Monmouth.

ELIZABETH ANN ALUMBAUGH - Elizabeth Ann Lubben was born 1-4-1924 at Stone Lake, WI to Herman Fred and S. Harriett Zoliver Lubben. She and her brother Henry skied to the country school in the winter. She graduated from Spooner, WI High School and went to Racine, WI to Business School. She then worked at Great Lakes Naval Hospital from 1941 to 1946.

She married William Jefferson Alumbaugh 5-17-1946 in Waukegan, IL. They moved to the Peoria, IL area where Bill attended Bradley University. Beth worked for Standard Oil in Peoria.

While living in the Peoria area, two of their children were born: Marion Jean 9-25-1947 and Randy Jo 3-1-1950. Susan Kathleen was born 7-20-1952 while the family lived in the Bloomington-Normal area.

After moving to 227 South B Street, Monmouth, IL in early 1955, she went to work for Illinois Power Company and retired in July 1989.

The family has been active in the First Lutheran Church, where she has actively participated in the life of the congregation by serving as Sunday School teacher, on committees, delegate and on the Church Council. She has been active in the community - in the BPW Club, Woman's Club, Travel Club, President of School PTA, helping at Starting Point, committee of Habitat for Humanity, and the Red Cross. She is still actively involved in CMC Auxiliary and Order of Eastern Star.

Susan, Randy, Jean, William J., and Elizabeth Alumbaugh, January 1972.

While the family was in schools in Monmouth, Beth enjoyed taking them to all the school activities of music, sports and other school events. In addition she was active with the Rainbow Girls Assembly.

Jean graduated from Illinois State University with a degree in Special Education. She married Fred Wildermuth, Jr 7-5-1969 in Monmouth. They moved to the Chicago area to make their home. Their children, Amy Joelle, born 9-6-1972 and Todd Andrew born 4-6-1975 have graduated from college. Amy has advanced degrees in Law and Environmental Engineering. Todd is still studying for his Ph.D. in Environmental Engineering. Todd married Sanne Knudsen 8-18-200 1. Jean earned her master's degree and is a school administrator in the Crete-Monee, IL area.

While attending Monmouth High School, Randy was active in sports and was inducted into the Hall of Fame. He graduated from Eastern University, Charleston, IL in 1972 with a degree in Business. He worked as an accountant in Houston, TX for a year and relocated back to Monmouth where he worked in the family food business and as manager of the Far & Near Travel Agency. While living in Monmouth he was very dedicated to the Special Olympics program, and was Field and Track Director of field events, He was also active in coaching youth and church activities. He remained in the food business after leaving Monmouth in 1982. He married Stephanie L. Scharf in Hudson, IL 12-20-1986. Their sons, Zachary Jon born 11-21-1987 and Karl Jacob born 4-20-1991, are attending schools in the Champaign area; after moving from Bloomington, IL where they were born.

After graduating from Monmouth High School in 1970, Susan attended University of Northern Colorado at Greeley graduating in 1974. She taught in the Arvada High School for three years before moving to Columbus, OH where she earned her master's degree in Journalism Communications at Ohio State University. She married Charles I. Henderson in Springfield, OH 9-6-1981. After working as a newspaper reporter, she joined the Miller Brewing Company in various areas of Public Relations for 20 years. She is now Vice-President of the Kohl Department Stores and lives in the Milwaukee, WI area with her husband and two sons. Charles Alexander was born 6-2-1987 and Samuel Cornell was born 2-6-1993 in Milwaukee.

Beth has really enjoyed family gatherings and participating in all possible events with her six grandchildren.

WILLIAM J. ALUMBAUGH - William Jefferson Alumbaugh was born February 15, 1923 in Sullivan, IL. He served in the U. S. Navy as a Pharmacist Mate (attached to the U. S. Marine Corps) in the Pacific Theater, serving on Okinawa and Pelilieu.

After returning from service he married Elizabeth Ann Lubben on May 17, 1946 in Waukegan, IL. They moved to the Peoria area where Bill graduated from Bradley University in May 1949 with a Bachelors Degree in Business.

The family relocated from the Bloomington-Normal, IL area in early 1955. They lived at 227 South B Street, Monmouth, IL.

Their family consisted of Marion Jean, born September 25, 1947 at Peoria. IL, and Susan Kathleen born July 20, 1952 in Bloomington.

After graduation he was associated with the Jones-Weiskopf Insurance Agency, and later sold farm equipment to dealers in Illinois and Iowa. He was associated with McBride Ford Equipment Company. During the years his business activities included the reconstruction and rebuilding of the 300 block of North Main Street, acquiring Mr. Quick, Inc; construction of the A R T Professional Building; and the formation of Far & Near Travel Agency. He especially enjoyed his activities with the Masonic Lodge.

They were divorced September 27, 1976. He remarried and moved from the area to Normal, IL. He died in Normal on September 3, 2000.

KENNETH EUGENE AMBROSE - Kenneth Eugene was born in Mahomet, Illinois on Nov. 14, 1925 to Curtis Emory Ambrose and Lela Julia (Rickwood) Ambrose who had one child Marjorie, age 2, 18 months later a second girl: Dorothy was born, also, in Mahomet. Shortly thereafter, the family moved to Bloomington, Indiana, where Curtis earned an MA degree. They moved to Oblong, Illinois where Curtis was the high school principal for 23 years. The children attended grade and high school, in Oblong where Kenneth graduated in 1943, and was sent July 1 of that year to the Navy College Training Program at Duke University in North Carolina where he remained until graduation with an M.D. degree, in 1949. He interned at the Wayne County General Hospital, in Michigan. He then started a residency in General Practice at the University of Iowa Hospitals, which was cut short in 1951 when he joined the US Public Health Service. He was stationed in Washington, D.C. but mostly traveling with survey teams in various Cities in the U.S., six months in Mexico and approximately a year on the San Carlos Apache Indian Reservation, in Arizona. He next did a year of solo private practice in Rockport, Indiana during which he met his future wife, Genevieve Goldsmith, a nurse/teacher in the Evansville, Ind. School system, who is the daughter of Clarence and Flora (Mollenkamp) Goldsmith and a Registered Nurse and Indiana University graduate with a degree in education. On Jan. 1, 1956, Ken, who had remained in the USPHS Reserve was recalled to active duty, assigned to the USPHS Hospital (Now called the Gillis P. Long Memorial Institute for Hansen's Disease [formerly known as "Leprosy"] Research) at Carville, La.

In June 1956, Ken and Genevieve were married in Evansville, Indiana. In July of 1957, their first child, Susanna arrived. In May 1958, a second daughter: Rebecca was born.

In January 1959, the family moved to Monmouth, where Ken joined Dr. Chamberlin in the practice of family medicine. A third daughter, Carol Marie was born, in Monmouth in Dec. 1960.

The partnership with Dr. Chamberlin lasted till Dr. Chamberlin retired in July, 1990. Dr. Ambrose continued in solo practice for six months longer, before retiring.

The family has been active in the First Methodist church where Ken and Genevieve have served in various capacities (including "Charge Lay Leader", member of the Administrative Board and Board of Trustees(which Ken has served as chairperson) Lay Delegates to the Central Illinois Annual Conference, Presidents of the local church Women's and Men's organizations. Genevieve has also held offices at the District and Annual Conference level. In the community, Genevieve was on the committee that organized the Strom Center and the Hot Meals Delivery program. Ken has served on the Carl Sandberg College Foundation Board, the YMCA Board and the Wesley Village Board (Macomb). Ken's professional activities have included memberships in the AMA, Ill. State and Co. Medical Societies, Monmouth Medical Club, American Association of Family Physicians, The Civil Aviation and Aerospace Medical Associations. He has been certified by the "National Board of Medical Examiners" and the "American Board of Family Practice". He served 29 years as an Aviation Medical Examiner and was "Regional Representative for the Admissions Committee of the Duke University School of Medicine. He was on the "Courtesy" Staff, of Burlington and Galesburg Hospitals and the "Active Staff"of the Monmouth Hospital, holding offices, including president, of the later.

Since retirement, Genny and Ken have served on Mission trips to Bolivia (with daughter Carol), Jamaica, Mexico and Alaska, in National Health Service Corps Clinics in Idaho, Oregon, North Carolina and Illinois and Public Health Service/Indian Health Service Hospitals in Arizona, Nebraska, South Dakota and Minnesota.

ALFRED JONAS ANDERSON - Alfred Anderson the son of Andrew and Grunella Abrahamson was born in Kronberg Sweden in 1867. When he was about 15 years old, he came to America on a cattle boat, and became a citizen when he was 21. Taking his naturalization oath in Warren Co. Prior to this, by 1880 his brothers John, Peter Augusta, Charles and a sister Betty had already arrived and were farming in Lenox Twp. Alfred also became a farmer. Alfred married in 1895 to Mary Jane Humes daughter of Charles and Lucinda Clatterbaugh Humes of Rockingham Co. Va.

To them were born 7 children. Effie May (1896-1984) married Saylor Conard. Charles Trafferd (1898-1974) married Josephine Frank Lawrence Everett (1899-1976) married Betty Conard Edmond (Andy) (1901-1975) married Maxine Snape Robert Marion (1903-1984) married Dorothy Bennett Ferndell (1905-1905) Leonard Frank (1906-1989) married Jaunita Bostic

The first Mrs. Anderson died in 1915 when the boys were quite young, Mr.Anderson married a second time in 1923 to Mary Clary (1883-1936) of Eldorado, IL She was the daughter of Hugh and Cora Clary.

Alfred Jonas Anderson and wife, Mary Jane Humes Anderson.

Alfred and his new wife lived on a farm near Larchland for a couple of years then moving to Monmouth in 1925 where they resided at 745 E. Tenth Ave. Alfred became a janitor in the Monmouth Schools. Mrs. Anderson died in 1936 and Alfred in 1942. Except for one son (Edmond), all are buried in Monmouth Cemeterys.

MAX AND JOYCE ANDERSON - Max and Joyce Anderson and their four children moved to Monmouth in June, 1966. Max was the head hog buyer for the newly opened Agar Packing Co. They purchased the former Leary Dairy Farm, later owned by Ralph Painter. The home is located at 2012 62nd Street on the northwest edge of Monmouth.

Max and Joyce Anderson family

Max Anderson was born March 2, 1926 and raised on the family farm near Princeton, IL in Bureau County to Frank and Jenny Anderson, the youngest of six brothers and two sisters. He attended a one room grade school and graduated from Wyanet High School, participating in all sports. Max was active in 4-H, FAA, and the Bureau County Rural Youth, a farm organization for young adults. At one of these events in Whiteside County, he met Joyce Franks of Erie, IL. They were married on May 23, 1948 at the Congregational Church in Prophetstown, IL.

Joyce Franks was born in Whiteside County on April 16, 1925 to William and Hazel (Upton) Franks, the sixth child of nine daughters and two sons. She graduated from Erie High School and attended Augustana College. She taught at Portland School, where her mother and grandmother had attended. Her grandparents, Harrison and Esther Upton homesteaded in Portland Township, where a family member still lives.

Max, Joyce, and their four children made their home on the family farm west of Princeton. Max farmed for eighteen years. He was a 4-H leader, Superintendent of Swine for the Bureau County Fair, and served on the Wyanet School Board for nine years. Max and Joyce were active members of the Mission Covenant Church in Princeton.

Max and Joyce had a farm closing sale in December, 1965 before moving their family to Monmouth for Agar Packing. In March 1970, Max became an area feed salesman for Moorman Manufacturing Feed Company (Quincy, IL). He retired in March, 1990. Joyce worked for 21 years at Community Memorial Hospital as a unit secretary. They are active members of the First United Methodist Church, both serving as past trustees. Max was beef chairman for the Prime Beef Festival. Max became involved with cornhusking in 1989, continuing today. He won the state title in 1997 and picked at three National contests.

Their four children graduated from Warren High School.

Rick attended Carl Sandburg Junior College, served in the Army Reserves, and works for Burlington Northern/Santa Fe Railroad. He is married to the former Deborah Olson, who works for Midwest Bank of Western Illinois. They live in Monmouth and have grown sons, Craig and Christopher.

Cindy is married to Ralph Schoen and they live in Peoria, IL with their daughters, Ann and Maureen. Cindy graduated from Western Illinois University and works part- time for Bradley University in the Health Center. Ralph is the Director of Training and Development for AFFINA Corporation in Peoria.

Jill is married to Oscar Krieger and lives in Mokena, IL with their daughters, Rachel and Claire. Jill graduated from Western Illinois University with a Bachelor and Masters degree. She teaches computer technology at Oak Forest High School in Oak Forest, IL. Oscar is employed at Aurora University as Program Director for Athletic Training

Tamara is married to Harry Einfeldt and lives in Barstow, IL with their children, Audrey and Jared. She graduated from Patricia Stevens School in Milwaukee, WI and works as dairy manager for Jewel. Harry is owner of Quad City Acoustical Ceilings. Tamara has been competing in cornhusking at the state level for ten years and has qualified for national competition all ten years. Tammy has won the National Cornhusking title twice.

MARTHA MARIE ARMSTRONG - Martha Marie (Johnson) (Martin) Armstrong was born in Warren County, Illinois, February 18, 1926. She was the first of nine children born to Harlan E. and Clytie (Logsdon) Johnson. Martha attended Monmouth schools. She began working at the age of fourteen at the Candy Company in Monmouth, where she earned three dollars a week. Later she worked at the Monmouth Maid-Rite making six dollars a week. On September 20, 1941 Martha married Robert E. Martin and later divorced. She had one child from this marriage, Karen Marie (Martin) Bruce. Martha also worked at Western Stoneware in Monmouth, she was employed there on and off for fifteen years. Then Martha went to work at the Maid, Rite in Viola, Illinois as a grill cook. In 1978 she began working at Smolers in Monmouth as Supervisor. Later, Martha began as floor girl at Formfit in Monmouth, she worked her way up to Supervisor there also. In December of 1967 Martha married J. Leroy Armstrong. In April of 1984 she purchased Martha's Family Restaurant and Maid-Rite in Viola, Illinois. Martha owned and operated her business for fourteen years. In January of 1998 she sold her restaurant and has since retired. Martha is the great great grand-

Martha Marie Armstrong

daughter of the early Warren County pioneer, John C. Bond. He was one of the Commissioners of Warren County in 1839. In 1853 John C. Bond along with Samuel Hallam and Robert Gilmore were appointed to divide Warren County into Townships, which still exist today. Martha is also the descendant of other early pioneers who settled in Warren County, including Walter Johnson and John Wingate. When they came to Warren County all three men, John C. Bond, Walter Johnson and John Wingate all settled around Little Swan Lake. As of Today, if you travel to Little Swan Lake you will see that Wingate Drive still exists. Today Martha lives in Viola, Illinois with her daughter Karen. She is the grandmother of four, great-grandmother of thirteen and great-great grandmother of one.

RALPH AND DOROTHY (SCHWEITZER) AULT - Ralph Frederick Ault was born (and raised) in rural Newberry, IN. on November 26, 1917. His parents were Fred and Ellen (Reed) Ault. As a teenager his hunt for work during the later years of the Depression led him to Warren County. Three other boys and he traveled to Illinois on the advice of the brother of one who was working in Monmouth. A week after his arrival he began temporary work on Russell White's farm East of Monmouth for $30 a month and board. A few months later he went to work on Max Montgomery's Dairy Farm, which was located directly West of present day Warren School.

Ralph and Dorothy Ault

While working on a tractor in the field he met his future bride over the fence that ran between the White's farm and Schweitzer's farm. Dorothy Schweitzer was born on October 31, 1918 to Harry and Ruth (Lucas) Schweitzer at home because of a flu epidemic at Monmouth Hospital. Dorothy and her parents made their home on the family farm in Hale Township. In 1929 the Schweitzer's moved to another family farm in Monmouth Township, East of present day Gibson Woods Golf Course. She and Ralph eloped on June 24, 1939. Upon their marriage Ralph began farming with Harry Schweitzer and they moved into the Monmouth Township farm with Dorothy's parents. Ralph and Dorothy had five children; Wayne Hilbert (4-7-40), William Albert (11-22-42), Ruth Ellen (10-7-47), Margaret Jean (12-17-48), and Richard Neal (10-15-59). 1962 found the Ault family building a new home on the Southwest portion of the family farm. The family attended Sugar Tree Grove Presbyterian Church located in Hale Township.

In addition to farming Ralph worked over 50 years at Western Stoneware Pottery. He began working for the pottery when a hailstorm wiped out his entire crop in order to pay off his debt to the bank for seed, equipment, and livestock. Hard work and helping people were his favorite pastime. He considered his fellow workers as family and did various things to help out any who were going through tough times; putting some through school, buying medicine, paying for car repairs, etc. He was honored for his contributions to the community and inducted into the Western Illinois Area Agency on Aging's Gallery of Ageless Achievers. Dorothy was a homemaker most of her life. She drove a small school bus for Grier School, which was a one-room schoolhouse, located just East of Monmouth. Later she worked in food service at Monmouth College and Warren School. Dorothy Ault died on August 3, 1999.

WILLIAM AND CAROLINE (JENKS) AULT - On November 22, 1942, William Albert was born in Monmouth, IL, Warren County, to Ralph Frederick and Dorothy Jean (Schweitzer) Ault. His wife, Caroline Faye, was born in Monmouth, IL to Kenneth Blaine and Elsie Mae (Smith) Jenks on June 25, 1945. Bill and Caroline were married August 2, 1963, at Westminister U.P. Church in Kirkwood, Illinois. They have 3 daughters; Sherri Dawn born July 29, 1964 in Monmouth, Kathy Marie born November 2, 1966 in Monmouth, Kimberly Ruth born June 19, 1970 in Monmouth. Bill was in the 2nd graduating class of Warren High School, graduating in 1960. He worked at Western Stoneware for a year, then went to Sterling College in Sterling, Kansas for 1 year. He then transferred to Tarkio College in Tarkio, Missouri, graduating in 1965. He taught and coached at Yorkwood Junior High for 2 years; Alexis for 4 years; and 23 years at ROWVA in Oneida, IL-also served as administrator in the elementary. Bill received his Masters Degree in 1975 from Bradley University, Peoria, IL. He retired in 1995, worked for Warren Achievement for 6 1/2 years. He loves to hunt, farm, and work with wood. He resides on the family farm just east of Monmouth.

Ault Family Back: Bill, Caroline, and Kathy. Front: Kim and Sherry.

Caroline was a homemaker until the girls were in school. She worked at Fidelity Federal Savings and Loan Association for 3 1/2 years. During this time, they moved back to the Ault family farm, in the summer of 1977. In 1979 she went to work at Warren School as district bookkeeper and secretary to the Board of Education. She continues to work there, this being her 23rd year. In 2001 their daughter Kathy, moved back to Monmouth from Florida, and she and Caroline opened Memory Lane Scrapbook Store in Monmouth.

Bill and Caroline are members of Fairview Center United Methodist Church; Bill has served as Sunday School teacher, Chairman of the Trustees, and as leader of the youth leading them on several summer work trips. Caroline is a member of the United Methodist Women, currently serving as President, has been Sunday School teacher and Bible School director. Bill is a member of the Monmouth Rotary Club. He and Caroline have served as host parents to students from Sweden, Japan, Poland, and Denmark. In 1990, Bill and Caroline built a log home on the Ault family farm, east of Monmouth where they currently reside. They both enjoy the history of the Monmouth area, and continuing on with the collections of Caroline's parents, Kenneth and Elsie Jenks. After finding an original Pattee Tongueless One-Row Horse-Drawn Plow in their barn rafters, Bill began to purchase and restore antique farm equipment. Further research has shown that Ithmar Pillsbury, Treasurer for the Pattee Plow Company and brother-in-law of the Pattee Brothers, owned the farm prior to the Schweitzer/Ault family.

ELDON R. "BUD" AUPPERLE - He was born 9 Sep 1932 and raised on a livestock and grain farm near Fairbury, Livingston County, Illinois. After graduating from a one-room country school, he next experienced Fairbury Township High School [Class of 1950]. Being the youngest of a family of five,, three brothers and one sister,, he was the first to venture off to college. He attended Illinois State Normal University [ISNU] with a major in agriculture education. Aupperle wanted others to have a similar opportunity as he did in receiving the chapter's National Gold Emblem plaque on stage at the National FFA Convention in Kansas City, MO. After two years at ISNU, Aupperle transferred to the University of Illinois, Champaign, so he could qualify to teach vocational agriculture, graduating with a BS degree in 1954 and a MS Degree in 1960, later completing additional course work.

One of Aupperle's most valuable experiences was his selection to participate on the International farm Youth Exchange [IFYE] program as a delegate to Chile, South America in 1954. While serving as National IFYE Alumni Treasurer, he met his wife-to- be, Virginia Edgington [IFYE from Ohio to Australia in 1959], who was Ohio's state treasurer. They were married August 11, 1968. Trips have been made to visit host families in Australia and Chile after 17 and 25 years.

Aupperle began his teaching career at Buckley-Loda High School, Buckley, IL. He was drafted on December 5, 1955 and served in the U.S. Army in Fort Leonard Wood, MO; Fort Carson, CO; Fort Lee, VA; Fort Sheridan, IL.; Fort Dix, NJ; plus a one-year stint in Ulm, West Germany.

Aupperle's first contract with the Board of Education of District No. 222, County of Warren, State of Illinois was for eleven months during the school year beginning July 1, 1958 and ending June 30, 1959, for the school term beginning September 1, 1958, or as soon as building was ready, for the annual salary of $5,000.00, plus 7 cents per mile for necessary travel connected with teaching vocational agriculture. Mr. Lee A. Rodgers, President, and S. M. Phelps, Secretary, signed the contract on 26 April 1958. On 10 June 1958, Mr. Clinton Hageman, Superintendent, sent a corrected contract conforming to State requirements stating 12 months employment with a month vacation. Employment at Warren School as the teacher of vocational agriculture and adviser of the Warren FFA Chapter was from 1958-64. Starting a vo-ag program in a newly formed school district was a tremendous opportunity - a chance of a lifetime. In six short years the most memorable moments would be the many individual accomplishments by students in numerous FFA award areas and national recognition of the Warren FFA Chapter.

Eldon R. "Bud" and Virginia E. Aupperle at Aupperle's retirement from Black Hawk College February 4, 1989.

Pines Miniature Golf became a reality in 1964 at 1300 N. Main in August of 1963. W. R. Grace & Co. employed him as a Sales Promotion and Personnel Development Specialist to introduce a newly developed form of fertilizer ["Slurry Mix"]. W. R. Grace & Co. built a manufacturing plant in Monmouth retailing through Monmouth Grain & Dryer, Duane Huston Farms,, Roseville,, etc. He was called to Decatur where his territory enlarged to five states - Illinois, Indiana, Iowa, Kentucky, and Missouri.

Since Aupperle's time in Monmouth and Warren County, he and his wife, Virginia acquired additional acreage at 1226 N. Main. Numerous trips to Monmouth have allowed them to keep in contact with former students' many successful accomplishments since leaving the halls of Warren High.

For the past several years Uncle Bud's Apple Cider Slush concession, sponsored by the Warren County Genealogical Society, has been at the Warren County Prime Beef Festival.

Aupperle began his community college experience in 1966-67 at Wabash Valley College, Mt. Carmel, IL. Next he initiated the nationally recognized agriculture program at Black Hawk College from which he retired after 21 years, having spent 38 years in education. For 34 years he and Virginia have resided on two and one-half acres three miles east of the college in Henry County.

OSCAR V. BABCOCK - Born in New York City July 30, 1875 he was the son of Oscar Y. Babcock, a native of West Point, and Hattie Crofton Babcock, who was from England.

Mr. Babcock attended grammar school and high school in New York. For a time he was employed with the Wall Street News for $3.00 per week, which was a goodly wage at this time period.

He was always interested in bicycles, in 1890 he worked for the first bicycle academy in New York, where road racing was becoming popular. He began to race as an amateur in 1892. His first race was at Manhattan field (polo grounds); his next race was at the Armory (the 12th Regiment Armory) where he finished second. He entered six-day bike racing; the first time teams were ever used. He continued his career with bikes the rest of his life.

In 1907, he won the championship of Greater New York, and turned professional. He rode in several six-day bike races and finally went into vaudeville, where he became interested in doing the loopty-loop. Although many previous riders had been injured in this feat, he perfected the spring mechanism on the loop and became an instant success and secured many bookings.

From 1903 on, he toured every state in the union and many foreign countries. His act was presented at the Panama-Pacific Exposition in San Francisco, Denver Exposition, Insular Exposition in Puerto Rico, Insular Exposition in Manila, and the Peace Exposition in Japan in 1922; going on to Hong Kong and Shanghai.

He first appeared in Monmouth on Sept. 22, 1921, during the Fall Festival and returned to the Philippines and Japan in 1922.

Appearing in 1923 for another performance in Monmouth. Mr. Babcock met his wife-to-be at that time. She was Emergene Johnston. The Babcock's were married the following year, June 7, 1924.

After their marriage he considered Mrs. Babcock's family home at 1224 East Broadway his permanent residence, although the Babcock's were still on tour for a good many years.

His last bicycle ride was made in 1943, but he continued to instruct others in the sport until 1956.

Mrs. Emergene Babcock was employed, (when home), by Colwell's Dept. Store, as a clerk and bookkeeper. She passed away June 4, 1953.

Mr. Babcock passed away Easter Sunday April 23, 1957. He was a regular member of the First Methodist Church where the funeral was held April 25, 1957.

ERNEST C. BACON - Ernest C. (1895-1971) born May 8, 1895 and died November 14, 1971, was the son of Charles Albert (1867-1923) and

Ernest and Alberta Bacon

Susie Tate Bacon (1867-1947). He was born in Point Pleasant Township, Warren county, and lived there all of his life. He was the oldest son of four living children, Ernest, Howard, Channing and Marie. He graduated from Roseville High School. In 1920 he married Hazel Marie Reed, daughter of George (1857-1936) and Mattie Greenley (1865-1918) Reed. Hazel was born in Indianola, Iowa on Jan 23, 1896 and died Oct 30, 1938. She attended Western Illinois State Teachers College, Macomb and taught at Salem Grade School in Point Pleasant Township, Warren County. To this union were born two children, Eugene Roger and Dorothy Frances. He married Alberto Slusher Braun (born Oct 2,1913-1992) in 1942. She was the daughter of Benjimin F. (1885-1978) and Vylotte A. Nordstrom Slusher (1892-1964). Mr. Bacon served as Supervisor of Point Pleasant Township for 28 years where he farmed for 51 years.

FANNIE GENEVIEVE (BRADFORD) BAILEY - Fannie Genevieve Bradford Bailey was born January 22, 1882, in Belleville, Kansas, the second child of John Hall and Carrie Capron (Holt) Bradford. Part of her childhood was spent in Coffeyville, Mississippi. She moved with her family to Monmouth in 1895 and was graduated from Monmouth High School in 1901. After one year of college she taught five years in the rural schools of Warren County before going to Egypt as a missionary for the United Presbyterian Church. At Khartoum North in the Egyptian Sudan she helped found a girls' boarding school for the training of Sudanese teachers. After four years there she returned home and finished her college work at Monmouth College where she graduated cum laude in 1923.

Fannie G. Bradford Bailey

She then began teaching Civics, History and Social Science at Monmouth High School where she taught twenty-seven years. She was the adult sponsor for the Girl Reserves. At times she had students memorize poetry. If she didn't know the parents of her students, she would visit their homes in order to meet the parents.

On Nov. 22, 1950, she married John W. Bailey, a retired farmer of Coal Valley. After Mr. Bailey's death she remained on the farm until 1963 when she went to Frenchburg, Kentucky, to a retired missionaries home. She renewed her teacher's certificate and on a volunteer basis helped the adult handicapped in their homes. After suffering a broken hip she went to Urbana in October 1965 to be with her niece, Virginia Bradford, where she resided until 1966. She then went to Shamel Manor in Normal, Illinois and died in Brokaw hospital in Bloomington on August 19, 1965.

Mrs. Bailey's mother, Carrie Holt Bradford lived in the Holt House in Monmouth for a time. Mrs. Bailey's grandparents' portraits are hung in Holt House, now owned by the Pi Phi sorority of Monmouth College.

DAVID AND MARY BAKER - David Eugene Baker was born May 2, 1928 in Macomb, IL and raised in Good Hope, IL. Mary Elizabeth Pease was born March 5, 1933 in Monmouth, IL and raised on the family farm near Norwood in Mercer County. As Good Hope is south of Monmouth and Norwood is North, it was not surprising for them to have met in Monmouth at a Rural Youth Square Dance. David and Mary were married Dec. 6, 1953 at Norwood Presbyterian Church and settled in Monmouth. They are the parents of three children: Daniel Eugene B: 9-11-55 of Morton, IL, a CPA employed as Corporate Chief Financial Officer for OSF Healthcare System. Dan and his wife Patricia Susan (Farrell) are the parents of six children; Steven, Sarah, Joseph, Mark, Rachel and Maria. Linda Gayle B: 8-12-56 of Monmouth is Controller for IMI Cornelius Equipco, a remanufacturer of Coca Cola soft drink dispensers. Linda's daughter, Samara was born in Moscow, Russia where Linda worked for three years. Carol Lynn B: 9-24-61 of Elgin, IL and her husband, Michael McKellar are the parents of three children, Kathryn and twins Kristen and Matthew. Carol works as Youth Director of their church and with the children's activities.

David is the oldest of five in his family with three brothers: Kenneth, Jim, George Wayne, and sister, Janice. David's parents were George Henry Baker B: 3-15-95 in St. Patrick, Clark County, MO. and Carrie Eva Rozena Arntzen B: 1-28-1896 in Adams County, IL. David's grandparents were Leopold Fredrick Arntzen B: 2-15-1866 and Marie Catherine(Disseler) B: 10-24-1866; Henry Bevington Baker B: 7-20-1832 or 36 in Ohio and Sarah Ellen (Ball).

Mary has one older brother, Leonard Pease, Jr. and his wife, Marie (Pheiffer) who live on the family farm near Norwood. Her parents were George Leonard Pease, Sr. B: 10-6-1891 in Mercer county and Ada Amelia (Meals) B: 10-7-1894 in Riverton, New Jersey. Her grandparents were Harvey Leon Meals B: 12-25-1868 and Mary Rebecca (Swiger) B: 1-14-1872 in Cumberland, Penn.; George William Pease B: 6-19-1869 and Nellie W. (Hill) B: 1869.

David was an electrician and after working for other firms for several years, he formed his own electrical business. One of his customers was Monmouth Hospital and when they decided to build a new building, they asked David to head up their maintenance department. Twelve years later, while at work at the hospital, he suffered a cerebral hemorrhage for which he required surgery and a seven week stay in Moline Public Hospital. Upon returning home, he was unable to return to work, so in time he began doing volunteer work, including working with a reading program for children and various odd jobs at Strom Senior Center. Previously, he had been a volunteer fireman for approximately twenty years while he was able. In the meantime, Mary searched for information about brain injury and helped form the Illinois Brain Injury Assoc. for which she served as a board member for several years.

EVERETT G. AND NANNIE BELLE (KETCHUM) BALDWIN - Everett G. Baldwin was born in Mercer County, IL on June 29, 19121 the son of James B. and Hilda A. (Salmons) Baldwin. He was the middle child of five. His brothers and sisters were Otis, Florence (Humphrey), Orville, Marcella (Lutz). He spent his early life in Henderson and Mercer Counties. He also spent some time in Colorado.

Nannie Belle Ketchum was born in the state of Virginia August 18, 1916. She moved to Illinois at a young age, and to Warren County in 1924. She attended Center Grove grade school, graduating from Kirkwood High School.

Everett and Nannie Belle were married on November 3, 1934 in Henderson County. Everett worked on farms in the area; also was Road Commissioner in Rozetta Township. At that time he lost four fingers on his left hand in an accident at the rock crusher. Nannie Belle was a homemaker until after their children were born.

They had two sons, Glenn R. born Jan 31, 1936; David A. born June 4, 1942, and one daughter Margaret L. born June 19, 1938.

They moved to Monmouth in 1947, Everett worked for Brown Lynch Scott as a dock worker and truck driver. Nannie Belle worked as a waitress for a while and then went to work at Formfit.

They both loved to golf. Everett worked at area golf courses for a few years. They also bowled for many years in Monmouth. Nannie Belle did a lot of sewing for other people as well as for her grandchildren. They liked to visit with family and friends.

Glenn married Loretta Ripple on March 15, 1958. They had two children: Jeff born September, 2 1958, and Jeri born October 13, 1960.

Margaret married Henry Myers on March 3, 1957. They had four children: Debbie, born November 26, 1957 married Roger Conard August 27, 1977. Kary born November 29, 1958 married Judi Robinson December 18, 1982. Douglas born January 12, 1962 married Sandy Frakes, (divorced),- married 2 Helen Mettler in January 1993. Lisa was born January 26, 1965.

David married Sandra Henry June 1962, two children, Toni and Duane (divorced); married 2 Vada (Payne) Pettett and had son Brian.

BLAKE EVERS BARNES - Blake Evers, is the son of Estelle (Evers) and Bud (Verne Elwyn) Barnes. He was born June 4, 1954 and attended local schools in Monmouth, Illinois (Warren County). An excellent student, he was valedictorian and president of his senior class of 1972. Their senior basketball team was superior and written up for the grade point average of the whole team. Blake graduated from Cornell College in Mount Vernon, Iowa in 1976 with a Bachelor of Special Studies with emphasis in biology. Blake began dental school at the University of Iowa in the Fall of 1976 and graduated in 1980. On July 1, 1978, Blake married Nancy Ann Currie, daughter of Richard and Helen (Avelchas) Currie of Mason City, Iowa who graduated from Cornell College in 1978 with a double major in Spanish and Sociology.

On July 7, 1980, Blake opened his dental practice in Mason City, Iowa where he practices general dentistry. In 1991, Blake bought a dental practice in Rockwell, Iowa. In 1996, Mike Louscher became Blake's dental partner. They employ nine women in their practice.

Blake and Nancy have three children, Cory Alexander (April 16, 1982), Melissa Ann (May 19, 1984) and Eric Currie (August 12, 1987). Cory currently attends Minnesota Life College in Richfield, Minnesota. Melissa will be in the freshman class at Cornell College in the fall of 2002. Eric is completing his 8th grade year in May 2002. Nancy uses her Spanish major as a substitute teacher in the schools and an adjunct instructor at the local community college. Nancy is also involved as a volunteer in many local and school groups. Blake is a member and Past President of Noon Lions Club and the Vice-President of the Mason City Country Club where he also practices his golf game.

The family resides in a home situated between a spring fed lake and a river. Blake's father's love of birds has inspired the family to be birdwatchers and nature lovers. At this time their family also includes two perky mixed breed dogs and several fish. Summers are spent in their Clear Lake, Iowa home on North Shore Drive.

ESTELLE BARNES - Estelle Evers was born in Stanwood, Iowa, Cedar County, August 16, 1923 to Bertha (Bixler) Evers and Otto Evers. She was the youngest of five children. Her oldest sister, Caryl, married Edward Chorlian of Egypt and Long Island. Her brother Lorance was an Ear, Eye, Nose, Throat specialist. He married Kathryn (Field), and moved to Bend, Oregon, to join a Medical Clinic. Doris married Howard Werner,then Burney Dusch, a Naval Warrant Officer. They moved to San Diego to be near her younger sister Bethany, then married to John Mickey , later to William Engel, a retired Lt. Colonel. Both girls became retired business women. Estelle's father when but twenty, served as president of the Citizens Bank before merging with the Union Trust & Savings Bank. He became executive vice-president of both when they merged a few years later as The Union Trust and Savings Bank, eventually with a branch bank in nearby Olin.

Estelle Barnes

Estelle attended Elementary, Junior High, and High School in Stanwood. She ,graduated valedictorian of her class when but sixteen. Her family attended the United Presbyterian Church. This was why the children all attended Monmouth College, Illinois. Estelle enjoyed college very much, having for her roommate Evelyn Myers from Lisbon, Iowa. It was here she met Bud Barnes, her future husband.

After two years, in the midst of World War II, she transferred to Iowa State College, Ames, Iowa, and graduated with a BS degree in Home Economics. This was a pleasant experience, Doris Hanson was her roommate for the remainder of her college life, graduating from ISU in March of 1945. Her first teaching experience was teaching home economics and science in West Branch, Iowa, high school. Instead of continuing her teaching career, Estelle left for California to live with her sister, Bethany, and took a position to teach home economics at Memorial Junior High School in San Diego, where the students represented several multi-cultural backgrounds.

Marriage to Verne (Bud) Barnes, who had been honorably discharged from military service, took place September 18, 1946 in Stanwood. Bud was in the food business with Bob Rawson, his father, Verne Franklin, and his uncle "Rennie". They moved into an apartment at 412 North B Street for a year then moved to a larger apartment at 322 North Main. When a newly built house became available at 502 College Manor in 1948, they bought it for their family home and lived there over 50 years.

Children born to the couple were: Jennifer 1947, Mark 1950, Blake 1954, Lance 1957, and Heidi 1960. They are all living and married. All were excellent students, reaching Bachelor and extended degrees. The three boys were valedictorians, Mark, Phi Betta Kappa, also obtained the "Order of the Coif" from his University of Illinois Law School, Jennifer received her Masters degree from University of Arizona, Doctor Blake graduated from Dental School from the University of Iowa, Lance received his Masters degree in business at the University of Indiana, and Heidi has added teaching experience and hours to her teaching degree.

When Heidi was in the 4th grade, Estelle accepted a Title I teaching, position with Monmouth's School District #38. The main thrust was solving reading problems. She took classes at Western Illinois University and attained her Masters Degree in reading as well as a Learning Disabilities Degree. She retired in 1987 and until the year 2000 substituted in elementary schools.

A special interest was in the American Association of University Women Art Presenter Program. She served as presenter 5 years, then became coordinator for 6 years. The "Hall of Achievement" Award was presented to Estelle in 1999, for her volunteer work with children. For many years Estelle taught kindergarten classes at the First Christian Church, helped with Bible School, and served 5 terms as deaconess.

Other organizations to which Estelle gave her time include: A.A.U.W., P.E.O.. Delta Kappa Gamma - a teachers honorary, Kappa Kappa Gamma National Fraternity, served on the "Stewart House Foundation Board" which included purchase, restoration, and placing the home on the National Register of Historic Places. At Monmouth College she participated in Crimson Clan and served on the Alumni Board for six years.

Her children, their spouses, 13 grandchildren and great grandchildren are the treasures of Estelle's life.

LANCE AND REBECCA BARNES - Verne Lance, son of Estelle and Bud Barnes was born January 12, 1957. He had an older sister, Jennifer, two older brothers, Mark and Blake, and a younger sister, Heidi. He attended Garfield School, Central Jr. High and Monmouth High School. He was given the "Jim Olson" Award in Jr. High and the "Chuck Petersen" award at High School graduation as well as "Hall of Fame" recognition and other athletic awards. He was valedictorian of his graduating class.

Lance and Rebecca (Ambrose) Barnes, also raised in Monmouth and the daughter of Dr. Kenneth and Genevieve Ambrose, were married in 1980. Both graduated from De Pauw University Cum Laude. "Becky had a four year scholarship as she was an accomplished oboe player. She was a member of Kappa Alpha Theta sorority and Lance joined Phi Kappa Psi, both living in their various Greek houses. After marriage they moved to Bloomington, Indiana, where Lance obtained his MBA degree. Emily, their first child, was born there in 1981. She became valedictorian of her high school, Clarion-Goldfield, before attending Central College, Pella, Iowa and will marry Erik Fisher in 2003. Lance and Becky's next move was to Galesburg, Illinois, where he worked for Admiral Corporation. Stephen, their second child, was born in Monmouth in 1983. He graduated from Clarion-Goldfield High School, valedictorian and will attend Central College, Pella, Iowa. Blake Andrew, 3rd child, was born in 1987 in Carterville, Illinois. He was named for his Uncle Blake, a dentist in Mason City, Iowa.

Rebecca and Lance Barnes

As finance officer Lance moved his family to several locations: Fairfield, Iowa and the Rockwell Corporation, to Carterville, Illinois and Sheller-Globe Company, to Fairmont, Minnesota and the Weightronix Company for seven years, to Clarion, Iowa, and the Hagie Corporation and is now employed by CHART Industries at La Cross, Wisconsin.

Becky has participated in many community activities and made new friends as they moved. She has worked for schools, in churches, at insurance offices, and most recently with Wright County Family Environment Team as program coordinator. Lance and Becky follow the many athletic pursuits and other activities of their children, supporting them in every way. With her beautiful voice she has enjoyed performing with "THE CHORALAIRES" by singing and playing her oboe.

MARK ALEXANDER BARNES - Mark Alexander, son of Verne "Bud" and Estelle Barnes was born 10 December 1950. He graduated from Monmouth High School as Co-valedictorian and earned varsity letters in Football, Track, and Swimming. When in Central Jr. High he received the prestigious "Jim Olson Award" as the top student athlete. Mark chose to attend De Pauw University in Greencastle, Indiana. He graduated Phi Beta Kappa. While on a semester abroad from De Pauw at the same time Rebecca Beal attended the University of Illinois, Mark presented her with an engagement ring at Bristol, England. They were married in December of his senior year and lived in Greencastle. Mark chose to attend the Law School at Illinois where they purchased a mobile home and he worked as the janitor of TLC Day Care and painted for Kraft Foods. While there they had a daughter, Sarah Caryl. Mark graduated in the top ten percent of his class and received 'The Order of the Coif'. On the bulletin board he noticed John Deere Plow Company was hiring lawyers for their industrial relations department. Thanks to a recommendation from then States Attorney Fred Odendahl, who he worked as an intern one summer, who knew the director, he was hired immediately. He has remained in that department and is now the director.

Mark Alexander and Rebecca Barnes

Rebecca Beal attended grade and high school in Monmouth and received a four year scholarship at the University. After Mark graduated they moved into a farm home near Lynn Center, Illinois. Thinking to rough it out there, because of poor insulation, smelly cattle, and mice, they moved after a year to nearby Orion, just twenty minutes from John Deere Headquarters. and Quad City airport.

By now they have added two boys - Nathan and John and a girl Jane. All have graduated from the University of Illinois. Jane just recently gave birth to a baby boy, Oliver Marion. She married and graduated with Ryan Jones and live in Michigan. Jane graduated number one in her class. Nathan graduated as Agricultural Engineer and was immediately hired by Caterpillar Tractor Company. After a brief indoctrination at the Peoria Plant he has been sent to Decatur, Illinois on another learning experience.. He married Victoria Poblanz, his high school sweetheart. They have produced a baby boy, Carter Michael. John is unmarried and jobless, but is very interested in his high school sweetheart. Older daughter Sarah married Ben Tellefson and are buying a new home in Washington, Illinois. They have a young son, Max Alexander and a dog. Ben is a Civil Engineer with the city of Peoria.

The Barnes clan is very close and for the last twelve years have met in South Haven, Michigan at "Casa Galla", near where Jane and Ryan were married on the beach.

MARK AND REBECCA (BEAL) BARNES - Rebecca (Beal) was born on April 10, 1961 at Monmouth Hospital, the second child of Marion Lee and Dorothy (Small) Beal. Her father grew up on a farm west of Monmouth in Henderson County, attended the University of Illinois, and practiced law in Monmouth. Her mother grew up in Southern Illinois, and graduated from the University of Illinois. She had two brothers, Richard Lee, and Ronald Lynn. "Becky", her nickname, attended Willits and Garfield Grade Schools, Central Junior High, and Monmouth High School. She attended the University of Illinois, studying Early Childhood Education. On December 30, 1972, she married Mark Alexander Barnes, son of Verne Elwyn (Bud) and Estelle (Evers) Barnes. Mark graduated from the University of Illinois in 1973 and its Law School in 1976. Their first two children Sarah Caryl (November 29, 1974) and Nathan Beal (April 16, 1976) were born in Champaign while Mark was attending law school. Mark accepted a job in Labor Relations with John Deere in Moline, Illinois in June of 1976. They rented a farm home in Lynn Center, Illinois, where their third child, Jane Anne, (September 18, 1977) was born. In 1978 they purchased their first home in Orion, Illinois. Their fourth child, John Mark (August 13, 1979) completed their family. In 1993, "Becky" was employed by TLC Pre-School as a teacher and later became director. Mark is currently Director of Industrial Relations at John Deere in Moline.

All four children attended and graduated from the University of Illinois. The oldest three are married. Mark and "Becky" are grandparents to three boys: Max Alexander Tellefson, Carter Michael Barnes, and Oliver Marion Jones. Sarah married Benjamin Tellefson, a Civil Engineer, and have just purchased their new home in Washington, Illinois. Nathan married Victoria (Poblanz), he graduated as an Agricultural Engineer and works presently at Caterpillar Tractor Company's plant in Decatur, Illinois. After graduating the top of her class in 2001, Jane married Ryan Jones - they live in Linden, Michigan.

VERNE E. "BUD" BARNES - Bud (Verne Elwyn) Barnes of the grocery firm of Barnes Brothers was born September 16, 1922. It was two months after his father, Verne Franklin, and his uncle, Renalt John, bought the grocery business at 216 East Broadway from William Johnson. His mother, Ednah Lavine (Alexander) and his father lived in the apartment above the store. After two years his parents purchased their family home at 519 North A from Verne's mother, Emma Allena (Smith). She purchased it as an investment after the death of her husband, Oliver Milton Barnes. A burst appendix was the cause of his death, which occurred in December 1924 in Hermon, Knox County, Illinois. He owned a general store there where both boys worked. It was called Barnes & sons.

Verne Elwyn "Bud" Barnes

Allena Barnes decided to complete her college education in order to teach in a missionary school for blacks in Mississippi. It was after World War I, when Corporal Rennie returned, that the brothers decided to join in a business enterprise in Monmouth. The entire family belonged to the Christian Church.

As Bud grew up he attended Garfield School. Central Jr. High, and Monmouth High School. "Junie" Ramback and Glenn Smith were his neighborhood pals. Bud was inducted in the high school's "Hall of Fame", receiving letters in football, basketball, and track.

World War II began while Bud was in Monmouth College. He was not drafted until December of 1942. He had finished 2 1/2 years of college, two at Monmouth and a half year of credit at the University of Illinois. The army placed him in the Medical Department when they noticed he was preparing for a degree in medicine. After medical basic training and a month of preparation for officers candidate school, he was chosen to attend O.C.S., graduating as a second lieutenant July 21, 1943, a "ninety-day-wonder" and just twenty years old. He was placed for assignment at Fort Douglas, Utah, at Salt Lake City, then sent to Fort Lewis as a medical supply officer.

From Fort Lewis Bud joined M.A.C. Captain Lawrence C. Austin in driving his Buick Century to Laguna Beach, where he visited his sister, Elynore King and her baby girl. Her husband Lloyd Vincent, a Marine, had just returned from Guadacanal. Bud joined Captain Austin when reporting to their new assignment at Camp Bouse, twenty miles into the Arizona desert. The 150th Station Hospital there had recently reorganized, it called for two more Medical Administrative Corps officers. It was serving a tank Battalion with a Company of Armed Infantry designed to night fight in the hedge rows of France. We were sent overseas on the cruise ship SS Argentina that joined the largest convoy to cross to cross the Atlantic. It departed three days after D-Day, June 6, zigzagging across the ocean for 14 days. It was at Fishguard, South Wales that they set up their hospital, but were soon sent to London to a hospital vacated by another hospital moving to Paris. Ours was the only American hospital in London and took care of the staffs of the American Embassy, the Red Cross, and visiting dignitaries as well as American soldiers on leave. All officers had rooms on the top floor of the hospital, but were required to rent a room on the outside, thus Bud stayed at 56 Warwick Square with Mrs. Wilkie - an English lady. He returned to the United States on the Queen Mary in four days. A week later the Japanese surrendered after two atomic bombs were dropped on them.

On returning home Bud joined Robert Rawson in buying into Barnes Brothers (now a Super Market). Robert had married Cleone, Uncle Rennie and Aunt Myra's daughter. On September 18, 1946 Bud married Estelle Evers, daughter of Bertha (Bixler) and Otto Evers, executive vice-president of the Union Trust & Savings Bank, in Stanwood, Iowa. They had met at Monmouth College but chose not to marry during the war. Their first home at 412 North B was next door to that of H.T. Jackson, a favorite teacher of Bud's. They were in Kiwanis and Masonry, which were important in the life of each. Bud is now a 50 year member of each.

In 1983 Bud Barnes and Robert Rawson retired from the grocery business after owning three super markets. They sold to Bill and Kathy Grupy.

Estelle and Bud had five children: Jennifer, Mark, Blake, Lance, and Heidi. In 1948 a ranch style house was purchased at 502 College Manor. It was enlarged in 1957 by a design of Philip Welch, architect.

DOROTHY LOU (SMALL) BEAL - Dorothy Lou, called "Dottie", the daughter of Dee and Bertha (Fox) Small of Marion, Illinois. She attended school there and graduated from Marion High School in 1944. She attended the University of Illinois majoring in Child Development. Her sister Betty living in Reston, Virginia, married David Jackson and was called from teaching in Chicago to Washington D.C. to serve the Department of Education. Her brother "Bob" graduated from Purdue University in the School of Engineering. He married Jane Turner from Marion.

The Small family moved to Greenville, Illinois where he was Farm Advisor for Bond County. Dottie's mother passed away in 1975 and her father in 1989.

"Dottie" Beal

Dottie married Marion Beal at Wesley Foundation in Urbana with Reverend Paul Burt presiding. After returning to Monmouth - Marion joined the law firm of Love & Ranney. Their first home in Monmouth was in Pine Park. It was built by James Fusch. Here they had three children and a dog "Jill". Their oldest son, Richard, loved sports - played football and swam on the record setting relay team. He is in the "Hall of Fame" at Monmouth High School, also played in the band in high school and the University of Illinois marching band. He graduated in business and is now a Corporate Banker for State Farm Insurance.

Rebecca, the daughter, played baritone in her high school band and attended the University of Illinois. She married her high school sweetheart, Mark Barnes. After Mark graduated from the University Law School he became an attorney for John Deere Plow Company. They live in Orion, Illinois. "Becky" has just retired from teaching pre-school. They have four children.

Ron, the youngest, attended St. Olaf College in Minnesota. He enjoyed sports - both football and wrestling. He played trombone in the high school band. He was selected captain of the All State Football Team as a middle linebacker. He earned a law degree from William Mitchell Law School and practiced in Minneapolis three years. He then went to Temple University in Philadelphia earning a Master's Degree in Jurisprudence. He now is a Professor in Baylor University in Waco, Texas.

Dottie and Marion purchased the Bowman home on North B Street after the children were born. Their last move was in 1962 to 830 North 11th, where Walter McVey built them a new home.

Dottie was a charter member of "Four Seasons Garden Club" that tried to beautify Monmouth. She served twelve years as Secretary of the School Board and volunteered as a teacher at the first Warren Achievement School. She is also very active in the Methodist Church and has for years been active on the Cancer Board.

Her pride and joy are her children - seven grandchildren - and will soon have three great grandchildren.

MARION LEE BEAL - Marion Lee, son of Perry Lee and Mabel (Allaman) Beal, whose parents came from Ohio in 1835 and settled in Warren County. They chose land in Warren County before it was divided into another county called Henderson. 320 acres made up their farm.

Perry and Mabel raised four children - two boys and two girls. They all attended the Rozetta Baptist Church along with other relatives. A country school called Cedar Ridge was built on the main road between Monmouth and Oquawka. The neighbor across the road, Florence Gordon, was the teacher. The farm was located equal distance from four towns: Monmouth, Kirkwood, Biggsville, and Oquawka. They had their choice of high schools, but all chose Monmouth.

Marion Lee Beal

Marion was the complete student, excelling on the French Horn, winning all kinds of medals while playing in the high school band. He joined with "Hack" Shaw to be Monmouth's first tennis team to go to State. He loved to play golf, racketball, handball, volleyball, softball, and bridge, and was an avid fan rooting for the Chicago Cubs and Bears as well as the Illini.

He was chosen to give the graduation address for his class. In college he played in the marching band and sang in the glee club. He was President of the university YMCA and Wesley Foundation.

World War II emerged after 2 1/2 years and all eligible men students were drafted into service. His father was losing his eyesight, so Marion quit school to help on the farm, since older brother, Perry, was in the service. He was called into service in 1943 and became a Navigator in the Army AirForce. While there he received notice that he had been selected for Phi Beta Kappa and had the highest honors in Political Science. The Law Degree came later when his service was completed. On graduation he received the "Order of the Coif" being in the top 10% of his class.

When returning to the university after military service he met and married Dorothy Small. She served on the Wesley Foundation Board with him. They were married between semesters on 8 February 1948.

His father passed away and he again returned home to help his brother "put in the crops." He then left the farm and joined the law firm of Love & Ranney. Their offices were above Hartman's 5 & 10 cent store on South Main. Later Conn Whiteman joined the staff while Ed Love was President of the Illinois State Bar in Chicago. In 1958 Channing and Jane Pratt joined the firm. Murdock's Shoe Store was purchased and remodeled at this time for easier access to their office. Marion passed away at the age of 77 in 1999. He had practiced law in Warren County for fifty-one years. He was the Elder Statesman of the Kiwanis Club as well as Past President and fifty year member. He enjoyed playing bridge and was a charter member of the Kiwanis Bridge Club. We all miss his calm understanding manner.

MARY JOSEPHINE (GORANSON) BECKER - Mary Josephine (Goranson) Becker, the oldest child of Johan (John) Gotthild Goranson and Ida Elda. (Hull) Goranson, was born in Monmouth on March 24, 1917. She had two brothers, John Frederick Goranson born January 18, 1921 in Monmouth and William Earl Goranson born September 2, 1927 in Monmouth. They attended Monmouth Public Schools. They resided at 122 W. 8th Ave., which was an exhibit house at the 1904 World's Fair in St. Louis. After WWII, John married Hilda Elaine Howes on June 19, 1945 in Hagerstown, MD. They had 2 daughters and 1 son and resided in Camp Spring, MD. William (BI) married Barbara Ann (Beam) Carter on November 1, 1962 in Monmouth. He adopted her son and they resided in Monmouth.

Harry and Mary Becker - 1983

After graduation, Mary went to work at the telephone company. She married Harry Samuel Becker, the only child of Samuel Dom Becker born in Philadelphia, PA and Matilda Josefina Sundin born June 26, 1886 in Karlskoga, Sweden, on September 5, 1945. Harry was born August 13, 1915 in Moline and died July 25, 1996 in Peoria. He attended Henry Co. Public Schools. In 1938, he enlisted in the 14th Cavalry of the U.S. Army and was honorably discharged in 1940. After their marriage, Harry and Mary farmed in Lynn Center. In 1956, they moved to Dumas, TX where Harry worked as a truck driver for Frontier Chemical Co. In 1967, they moved back to Monmouth and in 1968 to Eleanor, where Mary now resides. Harry worked and retired from Gambles Warehouse; Mary was a homemaker.

Mary had 6 children. John Dom Becker was born September 26, 1949 and died November 21, 1949 in Monmouth. Susan Elizabeth (Becker) Welty was born January 8, 1951 in Monmouth. She married Alan Welty on September 12, 1970 in Monmouth and had 2 daughters. Mark Darren Becker was born October 31, 1952 in Monmouth. He married Catherine Howard on July 15, 1972 in Galesburg and they had a daughter. They divorced in 1974. Mark married Patti Lee Ashby on June 14, 1975 in Monmouth and had 3 daughters. Alice Agneta Becker was born December 6, 1953 in Monmouth. Harry Kevin Becker was born November 24, 1954 in Monmouth. Idalu Josephine (Becker) Turnquist was born September 16, 1957 in Dumas, TX. She married Ronald Dean Turnquist on May 28, 1977 in Monmouth and had 3 daughters. Mary had 3 great granddaughters and 3 great grandsons.

Johan (John) Gotthild Goranson was the son of John Peter Goransson born May 3, 1852 in Sweden and died January 26, 1935 in Monmouth and Agneta Josefina Carlsdotter born June 17, 185 8 in Sweden and died September 11, 1900 in Monmouth. Ida Elda (Hull) Goranson was the daughter of Alvey Pierce Hull born April 17, 1852 in Maryland and died June 12, 1932 in Davenport, IA and Susanna Elizabeth (Roop) Hull born May 11, 1848 in Ashland Co., OH and died June

12, 1923 in Monmouth. John and Ida were married September 5, 1914 and resided in Monmouth. John was employed at the Monmouth Pottery and Ida was a homemaker.

MADELINE KAY (CLAYTON) BEHRENS - Madeline Kay - the youngest daughter of Clifford O. and Eunice B. (Andrews) Clayton was born in Monmouth, Illinois on August 2, 1946. She has six brothers and two sisters. They are: Arnold, Charles, Richard, Melvin, Bonnie, Maurine, Carl Dean, and James. She spent her childhood in Monmouth and attended Harding Grade School, Central junior High and graduated in 1964 from Monmouth High School.

Madeline Kay (Clayton) Behrens and daughter Brooke Elizabeth Behrens

During high school she was employed by F. W. Woolworth and was a member of Rainbow Girls. She was a member of the Ninth Avenue Presbyterian Church.

Upon graduation, she moved to Davenport, Iowa to attend American Institute of Commerce. In 1966, she started her working career at Nichols Homeshield as an aluminum products production manager.

In fall 1968 she went to work for WOC Broadcasting Company (Davenport) as a Traffic Manager for the radio station division. In spring 1969, she enrolled at Palmer Junior College and earned an Associate Degree in Communications.

In 1971 she left the broadcast industry to become the Media Buyer for Advertising Communications, Inc. (Davenport, IA).

In fall 1975, she began her shopping center career with General Growth Companies (a Des Moines based shopping center developer) at Duck Creek Plaza (Bettendorf, Iowa) as Marketing Director.

In fall 1977, she additionally became the Marketing Director of Northpark Mall (Davenport, IA). In spring 1981 she was promoted to Assistant Manager of Northpark Mall and in summer 1982 she returned Duck Creek Plaza as General Manager.

Spring of 1983 took her to Des Moines, IA corporate office, as a Regional Marketing Director.

She headed west to Woodland Hills, California - as General Manager of Fallbrook Mall, April 1986.

In fall 1989, she returned to the Midwest as General Manager of SouthPark Mall (Moline, Illinois) to head up the renovation/expansion. In spring 1990 she was promoted to the position of Group Manager of four properties (Moline, IL/ Bettendorf, IA/Davenport IA /Cedar Rapids, IA.)

In fall 1992, she relocated to Minneapolis, Minneapolis corporate office as Senior Vice-President of Marketing Services. Tiring of the Minnesota snow, she was off to sunny Florida to open West Oaks Mall, Ocoee, FL (Orlando) in May 1996.

During her shopping center career she earned the designations of CMD (Certified Marketing Director) and CSM (Certified Shopping Manager).

November 9, 1972, she married Rodney Erwin Behrens, from Bennett, Iowa. She and Rodney had one daughter, Brooke Elizabeth Behrens, born June 5, 1977. She and Rodney were divorced May 10, 1979.

Brooke enjoyed her many relocations with her mom and attended schools in Bettendorf, IA, Des Moines, IA, Los Angeles, CA, Pleasant Valley, IA and graduated in 1995 from Minnetonka High School, Minnetonka, MN. Brooke works for AT&T Wireless and resides in Eden Prairie, Minnesota

Kay was engaged to Bill Shell (from Pontiac, MI) in fall of 1992. Bill is a retired Detroit Police Officer and is employed by the State of Florida - Juvenile Justice Department and Phoenix University.

Kay is active in many community and professional organizations. She served as the PR Director for the Miss Iowa Pageant and Quad City St. Patrick's Society.

In Florida, she is an active Rotarian, West Orange Chamber of Commerce Member (Chairman of the Board 2001), Boys and Girls Club Board Member, Committee of 101 Board Member, WOPA Board Member and the Health Central Hospital Foundation Board.

WILLIAM RAY BELLIS - William Ray, was born 27 October 1915 in Abingdon, Illinois. His parents were John and Edna (Gettemey) Bellis. He had two brothers, Ernest and Joe; and a sister, Margaret (Ohraelt). They moved to Monmouth from Abingdon in June 1918. Ray attended Monmouth public schools and graduated from high school in 1934. On 27 October 1939 he married Mary Louise Chenowith and they had two children, a son Richard L. and a daughter Carol Ann. Carol married Robert Sierbenski and they had two sons, Mark and Kieth.

On 20 April 1933 Ray joined the 123rd Field Artillery Regiment of the Illinois National Guard. He was employed as a Federal Caretaker stationed in Monmouth. In 1937 he was transferred to Moline, Illinois, as Federal Caretaker of Battery B 123rd Field Artillery. After his marriage he and Mary lived in Moline until 1939. On 5 March 1941 the Illinois National Guard was called to active duty in World War II and he served four years in the European Theater. Ray was awarded the Bronze Star for meritorious service and five campaign medals. Upon return to the United States in 1945 he was released from service and employed at 2nd National Bank in Monmouth until the bank was liquidated in 1964. He immediately was hired by Monmouth Trust & Savings Bank and retired as Vice President and Cashier in 1981. After his release from active duty he resumed his service in the National Guard and again was called to active duty in the Korean War in 1951 and served two years. He was awarded the Commendation Medal for meritorious service when he retired in 1955 as a Chief Warrant Officer - Grade 4 - after 22 years.

He was active in community serving as campaign chairman in Warren County fund drives. Over the years he was treasurer of School Districts 37 & 38 & 205, First United Methodist Church, where he sang in its choir 30 years. In 1932 the Monmouth JC's elected him "Man of the Year" and in 1954 the Monmouth Chamber of Commerce elected him "Man of the Year."

He was widowed in 1999 when his wife of 59 years 11 months passed away. In 1961 he and his friend Ralph Carwile were the driving force in the building of Gibson Woods Golf Course. He along with many others volunteered and worked endless hours over a five year period cleaning rough areas, building bridges, and storage buildings to make it the beautiful golf course it is today. He is a Past President and 50 year member of the Monmouth Kiwanis Club and a charter member of its Bridge Club. He still attends the couples dinner club each month. Ray is proud to be an American and call Monmouth his home.

FRANK CLIFFORD BENNETT - Frank Clifford, son of John C. and Mary (Scott) Bennett was born 28 March 1888 in Monmouth. He attended local schools and married Vera Smiley. They were the parents of two boys, Frank Jr. who died in 1919 and John William "Jack" who married a Craig sister. They had a son and two daughters. Nora Peck was Vera's sister. Vera was a beautiful young lady with dark eyes, jet black hair, and a pleasant smile. They bought a home in the southeast section of town intending to modernize it, but eventually rented a duplex just a block north of Barnes Bros. Grocery at 200 North Main. The life of Frank Bennett is the story of Barnes Bros. He looked like a Barnes and many customers thought he was. He was so entwined we forget standing on the only heat register - a large one - that provided heat for the East Broadway store. Frank's heat, no one was cold, we wore heavy sweaters with long sleeves - some had leather sewed on the elbow area. This was credit and delivery, most city customers called in their orders. Our feet didn't suffer for we were always moving. Frank always opened the store each morning, swept the floor, and fired the furnace. He did this by arriving around five each morning and had everything ready for business by the time the rest of the employees arrived at seven, except three meat cutters getting orders ready for the wholesale trucks.

Frank first worked for Vogt Grocery until he became the first conductor on the new electric street car of the Rock Island Southern Railroad. It traveled several time-each day to Galesburg and back. He quit the rails in 1925 and went to work for the Barnes Bros. Grocery. When they retired with a big sale in 1942, Frank was hired by Frank Chapin's Grocery on South Main. When Harold Murk was drafted in 1944, he enticed the Barnes Bros. to buy his grocery business. They did and with Frank aboard remodeled widow Douglas's livery stable on North Main into a modern Super Market. Verne and Rennie valued Frank so much they put him in business running Bennett's Grocery on the Southside of the 200 block on East Broadway. It was short lived and he returned to the main store across the street.

An illness that began at least eleven months ago and kept him under treatment in Monmouth Hospital for the past four months brought death by heart failure at 2:30 Wednesday afternoon 6 November 1950 - 62 years old. Vera, several years younger than Frank, and Maud Brownlee, who rented the other half of the duplex, continued working at Barnes Bros. until they retired.

PERCY BENJAMIN BENNETT - Was born in Knoxville, IL to Frank G. Bennett and Pheobe Permellia Cheesman. The year was 1884 he was not one year old when his father died, in 1885. His mother married a second time in 1890 to Acklinwood Lawson (1850-1924) of Knox Co. moving to Monmouth in 1894. There Had been seven children in the Bennett Family and there were four surviving, Elizabeth 1879 Harvey Leroy (1880-1937) Percy Benjamin (1884-1943) Willis Edward (1886

Percy Benjamin Bennett and Jessie May (Sage) Bennett

In Pheobe's second marriage there were three children Mable G. (1890-1979) Acklinwood Jr. (1894-) Helen Doris (1901-) Percy Bennett married Jessie May Sage Sept. 12 1901 in Galesburg, IL. She was the daughter of George Sage and Sarah Harriett Streeter born May 19, 1884 in Henderson Co. IL. Died October 7, 1950 in Monmouth, IL.

To this marriage was born 13 children with 11 surviving. Arthur Leroy born 8-14-1902 died 1958 married Lillian Carstensen. Clifford Edward born 12-13-1903 died 3-17-1987 married Blanche Cole.

Frank William born 6-24-1910 died 3-10-1996 married Marjorie who died young, married Evelyn Parrish.

Dorothy May born 12-10-12 died May 21-2000 married Robert Anderson. James Harley born 3-11-1915 died 7-6-1995 married twice Francis ? Marceline Edwards. Alice Lorraine born 8-17-1917 died 7-8-1937 married Clarence Gibson. Jessie Mae born 11-3-1919 married three times King , Sullivan, Leslie Lindburg. Ethel Louise born 10-20-1921 died 1-30-2000 married Ernest Barry. Mable Irene born 5-30-1923 died 1-9-1993 married Francis Martin. Howard Joseph born 11-20-1924 died 3-25-2001 married Norma Needham. Charles Robert born 11-13-1926 died 9-10-1997 married Mary Kennett. Mable Lawson born 9-20-1891 died 10-31-1979 married a Cunningham and Fred Zuber. Acklinwood Jr. Lawson born 1894- Helen Doris Lawson born 1901 married a Showalter.

Percy Bennett worked most of his life in the Monmouth Pottery, He died quite suddenly on 3 20 1942. Mrs Jessie Bennett lived among her children until 10-7-1950. They are both buried in Memorial Park Cemetery Monmouth, IL.

THOMAS BEST - Thomas Martin Best was born in Fort Smith, Arkansas on October 17, 1957. He has two brothers, Jeffrey Max Best and Dr. Bradley Jay Best. Thomas has two sons, James Paul Best (b. 8-14-81), and William Riley Best (b. 7-17-97). He married Candace Kay Smith in 1979, but has since divorced in 2000.

Thomas Best

Best grew up in Marshalltown, Iowa and graduated from Marshalltown High School in 1976. While attending Marshalltown schools he participated in athletics, speech competitions, wrote for the school newspaper, and worked for the YMCA. He attended Marshalltown Community College (1976-77). He transferred to the University of Northern Iowa in Cedar Falls, studying history, political science, and coaching. He was president of UNI chapter of Phi Alpha Theta, and graduated in 1981, as the "Most Promising Future Educator and Outstanding Graduate in the Department of History." His masters degree in history is from Western Illinois University (1991).

He first taught in Bayard, Iowa (1981-1982) and Marshalltown (1982-1983) in junior and senior high school studies, coached football, baseball, and basketball, and worked as a substitute teacher.

He was employed by Monmouth District #38 Schools in 1983 to teach 7th grade social studies and coach at Central Junior High (football, track, and basketball). He is also an instructor in both departments of education and history at Monmouth College teaching secondary social studies methods, the Civil War, and various courses in their "College for Kids" Program.

During his time in Monmouth, Best developed the gifted curriculum for Monmouth's elementary students; started the CJHS history club; created much of the school, district, and regional geography bee for Henderson, Mercer, and Warren Counties; administered the Warren County Lincoln Essay Contest; assisted in the restoration of the Pioneer Cemetery; and worked on many ISBE committees developing state standards and assessments. Numerous national, state, and local workshops and lectures have featured his research on subjects ranging from primary sources to the Oregon and Santa Fe Trails. His publications in historical and educational journals varying from cemeteries to Lonesome Charley Reynolds, George Custer's chief civilian scout.

Professional groups and associations of which Best has been affiliated and worked for are the National and Illinois Council for Social Studies, Illinois Historical Society, Illinois Preservation Agency, Little Big Horn Associates, Civil War Trust, and the Warren County Genealogical and Historical Societies.

Among his awards are recognition as a Western Illinois master teacher (1991), a finalist for the teacher of the year from the ISBE and their Award of Excellence Program (1995-1996), and distinguished alumni award from Western Illinois University in 1997.

MICHAEL AND KAYLENE (TREGO) BLANCHARD - Kaylene Louise Trego was welcomed into this world in Monmouth on 7 January 1946 by her parents: Gerald and Ethel (Ketchum) Trego and an older brother Carroll. A few years later she was blessed by a younger brother, Claude "Butch."

Kaylene was raised in Monmouth and attended Garfield school. her first two years, then the boundary lines changed and she was transferred to Willitts. She attended Central Junior High in the old school for her 7th grade and 8th grade in the new building. She graduated from Monmouth High in 1964.

Mike and Kaylene Blanchard

Part-time jobs during High school were: babysitting, cooking at Meling's sandwich shop (which later became Meling's Restaurant and Motel) and cashier at Barnes Grocery. Throughout her life she has done many types of work: office work at Gamble's Warehouse,; Inspector at IAAP in Burlington, IA; shipping department at Smoler Fashions; bartender; janitor; cashier; cosmetologist and electrologist in Galesburg and Burlington. She did front desk and office work at Ramada Inn in Burlington and clerical work at Southeastern College when she attended there.

Kaylene graduated from the Institute of Cosmetolgy Arts in Burlington, IA and from Southeastern Community College in West Burlington, IA with an Associate and Applied Sciences Degree in Microcomputers.

Unpleasant experiences during, her working years have been working at Ramada Inn with a shattered ankle she suffered in a fall on some steel steps while going to work. Another unforgettable experience was being held up at knife-point when working at night in a convenience store.

Kaylene is the mother of a daughter, Jennifer Lynn and step-mother of 2 step-sons and 5 step- daughters the proud grandmother of 7 grandchildren (soon to be 8)

Kaylene met her husband, Mike Blanchard over the internet in 1997, and they were married 15 July 2000

Michael Blanchard was born 28 August 1949 in Houma, LA to Stanley and Edna (LeBoeuf) Blanchard. He was raised in Houma and has worked as a salesperson, tour guide; radio announcer; and musician. He is presently employed as a salesperson for the radio station KTIB in Thibodaux, LA, and Kaylene is office manager at Louis Infant Center in Houma.

Kaylene and Mike reside in Houma, LA – pure Cajun country!

GILBERT AND KATHARINE (PHELPS) BOONE - Gilbert Boone, born June 25, 1905, at Fulton, Maine, was the son of William M. and Emma Currie Boone. He grew up in Maine and Canada; attending public schools in Holton, Maine. He attended Northeastern University at Boston, the Naval Intelligence Course, and the

Strategic Intelligence Course at Washington, D.C. He practiced architecture in Falmouth, Massachusetts until entering Navy Service in 1940, serving in Japan three years, 1956 to 1959; retiring in 1960.

Boone House

Katharine Phelps, born October 08, 1908 in Greeley, Colorado, was the daughter of Charles E. and Bertha McKinnie Phelps. She was reared and educated in the Fairview Center area in Warren County, Illinois. High School was at Westminister Junior College, Salt Lake City, Utah. She graduated from Monmouth College in 1930, and received her master's degree from Penn State University. She worked several years for National Security Agency, Washington D.C. After their marriage, March 12, 1955, at Washington D.C. they obtained a large collection of oriental art. After building their home at 750 North Ninth Street, Monmouth, Illinois; they taught Oriental Art for Monmouth College for 12 years. They transferred their collection to the Field Museum, Chicago, at the end of their teaching career; and were named benefactors of the Field Museum, Chicago. They were members of the Japan-America Society, Chicago; International House of Japan. He was veteran of World War II, Korean Conflict; where he was commander in United States Navy ONI. He was a member of the Retired Officaers Association. She was member Phi Kappa Phi; Sigma Omicron Mu; Pi Beta Phi Sorority. In Japan she became chhairperson of Red Cross Gray Ladies at Navy Hospital, Yokosufa, Japan.

Katharine and Gilbert teaching college students

Mr. Boone died February 26, 1985; Mrs. Boone died July 18, 1998. Both are buried in National Cemetery at Rock Island Arsenal.

Boone House, 750 North 9th Street, Monmouth, Illinois.Is nestled in the woods just two blocks north of campus and is one of the strangest and loveliest houses in Western Illinois. Designed as their retirement home by the Boones; it was built in 1961. Commander Boone took his inspiration for the design from their love for early American craftsmanship and their devotion of Oriental Art. The courtyard and entrance have a Japanese flavor, while the five fireplaces reflect 18th-century English Mediterranean design. A central gallery with display cases runs the length and width of the building.

Boone House came to the college as a gift of Mrs. Boone's nephew, Dr. Hugh M. Phelps, graduate of 1963, and his wife Norma. The house is being used as a new retreat center and Meditation room. It also houses the Harlow Blum Gallery.

DAYTON A. BOOSTROM - Dayton A., next to the youngest of Ben and Louessa McCaw Boostrom's nine children, was born on September 16, 1918, in Mercer Co. near Viola. He attended schools in Alexis and Viola, graduating from Viola High School. While in junior high school he became a boy scout and at one time saved his scout master from drowning in the Mississippi River. While in high school he was already interested in mechanics and worked part time in a garage. After graduating, he worked for John Deere Harvester and the Rock Island Railroad.

Dayton Boostrom

He married Ethel Burrill in Viola, September 1, 1940. She was born June 19, 1921, also in Mercer County and graduated from Viola High School. After attending Monmouth College she and Dayton were married and moved to Monmouth in Warren County where he went to work for the Illinois State Highway Garage. They were parents of three children. Sue, born in 1942, became a nurse, then an elementary teacher. She married Wayne Ault, a high school commercial teacher. They both retired from the Sherrard School District. Second was Debby, born in 1947, a swimming teacher at Schaumberg High School, also taught night communication classes on the college level. and did camera work at Willow Creek Community Church at South Barrington. She married Rod Fuess, a computer consultant in the Chicago area. The youngest, Rusty, born in 1955, taught Science at Central Jr. High School, in Monmouth for 25 years, also coaching football, basketball, and track. He married Joy Malone, the band instructor at Central.

In September of 1943 Dayton enlisted in the US Air Corps. and after spending a year at air fields and tech schools in the States, he spent two years in England as a Crew Chief and mechanic on B-24 Bombers. After discharge in 1945, back to Monmouth and to the State garage. Later he worked at Hall's Ford Garage for a few years, before moving to the Gerlaw area and farmed with his brother Bert for ten years. Then, with the help of his friend and co-worker, Lawrence Fusch, he built a house on the south side of Lake Warren. The Boostrom family became one of the first families at the lake. During those first few years he farmed their 100 acres and worked in town for Frank McBride Farm Service, then Frank Cavanaugh's which became Jerry Painter's Farm Service, until his health forced him to retire. During those years the children went to Warren School and Ethel worked at Warren School, Monmouth Hospital, Formfit and the last 15 years as a deputy at the Warren County Clerk and Recorders Office, retiring in 1982.

Dayton and Ethel have four grand-children and 3 great-grand-children. They were members of the Gerlaw Christian Church. He was a member of the 446th Bomb Group Association, Inc., a life member of the American Legion and a 50 year member of Viola Masonic Lodge, taking his first work in England. Dayton passed away August 28, 2000.

Ethel still lives at the Lake and Rusty and Joy live out there now too.

RICHARD AND ETHEL BOOZAN - Ethel Mary Boozan, who died January 5, 2002, at Heritage Manor Nursing Home in Springfield, was a life-long resident of Warren County. She was born May 15, 1910 in Gerlaw, the daughter of Harry Lee and Anna (Meleney) Greenstreet. She had a halfbrother, Leonard, who died in 1971; a brother, Willard, who died in 1987; and a sister, Lois Louise, who died in 1916.

Mary, Ethel, and Helen Boozan, October 1989

Ethel married Richard William Boozan on December 20, 1930, and he preceded her in death on May 13, 1981. Ethel and Dick had two daughters, Mary Louise and Helen Marie.

Mary was born in Monmouth on June 24, 1931 and graduated from Monmouth High School in 1950 and began working in the law office of Henry D. Lewis. She also worked for Martin Motor Sales and spent 8 years as secretary to the State's Attorney, Bufford W. Hottle, Jr. Mary moved to Springfield in 1961 where she was employed in the offices of first the Secretary of State and then Superintendent of Public Instruction. She moved to Chicago in 1968 working first in the office of the Chancellor at the University of Illinois-Chicago Circle, and then as administrative secretary to the executive director of the Illinois Board of Higher Education. She spent the last six months of 1973 working for the Lily Endowment in Indianapolis, Indiana. Mary was very active in Republican politics. She was a member of the Young Republicans for 15 years, holding county, state and national offices over the years. She also worked full-time in two campaigns for the Superintendent of Public Instruction.

In 1974, she married Harry A. "Bud" Stivers and moved to Las Vegas, Nevada where she worked for 18 years for Catholic Charities of Southern Nevada retiring in 1995. She now serves as secretary-treasurer of five senior housing corporations sponsored by Catholic Charities. Mary and Bud also own their own business, Western States Petroleum Company.

Helen was born in Monmouth on December 20, 1933, the third anniversary of the marriage of her parents. She graduated from Monmouth High School in 1952. She first started working at Barnes Brothers Super Market and then worked for Community Motors for seven years. Helen moved to Springfield in 1966 and started working with the Bunn-O-Matic Corporation and later with the Franklin Life Insurance Company. She worked part-time at Sears Department Store for 11 years while also working with the office of the Secretary of State where she has been employed for the past 31 and a half years.

ORVILLE, ALLEN, AND ALGOT BOWMAN

Bowman Brothers, three nephews Orville, Allen, and Algot, all natives of Sweden came to Monmouth, Illinois and bought the shoe business of their uncle, Eric G. Bowman, who started a shoe store in Monmouth in the year 1900. Algot came to America in 1913 at the age of 16. His brothers arrived a few years earlier. In the year 1920 the three brothers bought the shoe store with a capital, around $24,000. It was raised by borrowing one-half at the Monmouth Trust and Savings Bank and the other $12,000 they had in cash.

They paid full price for the shoes and started a clearance sale immediately, in order to liquidate all the old shoes, most of which were poorly made and of poor quality due to the war period just ended. The tremendous success of this sale enabled them to make a complete turnover of the stock: then restocked with better made shoes at the new and lower prices. The initial operation was so successful that they recouped the entire cost of investment in about two years. They paid off the Monmouth Trust and Savings Bank, thus their credit was firmly established.

This initial operation in Monmouth, almost doubled the sales of their uncle's operation. It confirmed they had hit on the idea of selling shoes that was entirely new in small towns and decided to carry it further.

In 1922 they purchased the old Dobbin Shoe Store at Kewanee, Illinois, which was on the brink of bankruptcy. They paid $5,000 for the store which included a lease calling for a complete new heating unit for the building to be installed by the tenant. They again started with borrowed capital and some personnel who had been trained in their Monmouth store. With this the three brothers and their wives, working at 35c an hour established another successful unit. On opening day, 16 September 1922 their sales were $1718.07, which was a record up to that time. Their salaries were $30 per week.

The uncle Eric G. was the sole proprietor of the original store at 101 Market Place. He was recognized as one of the leading businessmen of Warren County and one of its leading citizens. He was born in Sweden 27 October 1850 and was one of seven children of Gumme O. and Kerstin (Swanson) Bowman, both natives of Sweden. He was a cabinet maker and came to America in 1869. He worked at his trade with the Weir Plow Company before embarking on the shoe business. He married Sarah Nelson and they had one daughter, Mabel, the widow of George M. Hallam. The Hallam's had a daughter, Dorothy, wife of Glenn C. Shaver. The Bowman's beautiful home is at 202 North Third Street. He was a Democrat, and a member of the Elk's Club. Eric died 28 September 1924.

RICHARD AND JOYCE (MCCULLOUGH) BOWMAN

Joyce Lee (McCullough) Bowman, daughter of Richard Lee McCullough and Nell Lucille (Wallace) McCullough, was born March 7, 1939 in Monmouth, Illinois. She has two sisters, Shirley Jean (McCullough) Camp of Chicago Hts., Illinois, and Carol Joan (McCullough) Conn of Monmouth, Illinois (deceased). Joyce attended Willits grade school, Central Jr. High, and Monmouth High School graduating with the class of 1957. While in high school, Joyce worked at the old F.W. Woolworth store as did many girls her age. Going wage at that time was 60 cents an hour. After graduation from MHS, Joyce went to work for Bowman Shoe Co., 59 Public Square in Monmouth. At that time, Bowmans had around 22 retail shoe stores and their main office was in Monmouth,

In 1966, Joyce married Richard Algot Bowman, son of Algot Johnson Bowman and Maxine Mae (Kobler) Bowman, in Hales Corner, WI. The Reverend Lloyd E. Haney married them and Virginia Haney was maid of honor. The Haneys had served at the West Side Presbyterian Church years before and Joyce used to baby-sit for them.

August 24, 1967, Pamela Jo Bowman was born in Monmouth to Richard and Joyce. Pam attended Monmouth public schools, graduated from Monmouth High School in 1985, and from Monmouth College in 1989. Pam has taught children with learning disabilities in Annawan, Illinois, at Warren School in Monmouth, and is currently teaching at Hedding Grade School in Abingdon, Illinois. Pam married Larry Ide on June 11, 1994. She and Larry have two children: Heather Christine born March 25, 1996 and Jacob Dean born May 7, 1999.

May 11, 1969, William Algot Bowman was born in Monmouth to Richard and Joyce.

Bill also attended Monmouth public schools, graduating from Monmouth High in 1987. He graduated from Illinois State University in Normal, Illinois in 1991 with a degree in Communications and is currently employed at Human Kinetics in Champaign, Illinois. Bill married Liezl Orobia on September 16, 1995 in Chicago, Illinois. They have a son, Dylan Christopher, born January 20, 2002. Richard and Joyce closed the last of the Bowman stores in 1995 and are enjoying retirement. They reside at 1245 East Boston Avenue, Monmouth, Illinois.

BRAGD-STARK

Karl Albin Johannesson, only son of Johannes Johannesson Bragd and Helena Christina Svensson, was born May 6, 1876 in Olmstad, Sweden. His father was born Dec. 15, 1843 in Olmstad and his mother Nov. 20, 1841 in Hasselakra. His parents were married Feb. 2, 1867. He had three sisters, Helga, Mina, and Hanna and two step-sisters, Elsa and Ester. He emmigrated to the United States in 1902 on the vessel "Invernia." He met his sponsor in New York City, then traveled by train to Rock Island, Illinois. As no transportation was available, he walked to Monmouth.

Edith Louise was born June 21, 1885 in Monmouth, Illinois. She had four sisters, Emma, Swea, Hattie, and Mary and two brothers, Frank and John. Her father, Gustaf Johanasson, was born Dec. 12, 1836 in Saby, Sweden. Her mother, Anna Christina Johnson, was born June 15, 1843 in Marbach. In 1869, her parents emmigrated from Saby. They were married Oct. 19, 1869 in Illinois.

Now in America, Karl changed his name to Charles, and he and Edith were married May 6, 1908 in Monmouth. He was a carpenter by trade and she was a homemaker. They were members of the Lutheran church. On May 5, 1913, he became a naturalized citizen of the United States of America. He always believed it was a great privilege to five in this country and appreciated his right to vote. Edith passed away at her home on West Clinton Ave. on Jan. 18, 1956 and Charles died five years later on Aug. 9, 1961. They had three sons. Leonard, Melvin, and Kenneth, and one daughter, Frances.

Charles Bragd and Edith Stark

Oscar Leonard was born Oct. 2, 1911. He married Evelyn Mae Anderson on March 28, 1941. She was born in Macomb, Illinois on Nov. 11, 1921. They had three sons, Charles, James, and Robert. Leonard worked for the Maple City Dairy, retiring in the 1980's. On July 11, 1987, he passed away from cancer. His wife died on April 2, 1998.

Albert Melvin was born June 12, 1916. He worked as a carpenter for John Erickson before being drafted into the army. He served in the South Pacific during World War II. On returning home, he was employed by Axel Allstrand as a carpenter. A few years. later, he became self-employed, building homes in the Monmouth area. His hobbies have been fishing, gardening, furniture making and handcrafting musical instruments. He lives on a farm northwest of Monmouth.

Kenneth Carl was born Jan. 26, 1924. He was drafted into the army in Jan. 1943 and was wounded in action July 15, 1944 in France. He spent eighteen months at Wakeman General Hospital in Indiana recuperating from a spinal cord injury. Upon discharge, he returned to Monmouth to live with his parents. He married Dolores M. Owens on Dec. 7, 1951 in the Luthern church. They are the parents of two children, Stephen Wayne and Kendolyn Mae. In 1956, they moved to Idaho and are currently residing in Meridian. His hobbies include genealogy and music. He worked for the Idaho Office on Aging for seventeen years as an accountant, retiring in 1986.

Frances Louise was born Dec. 2, 1925. After graduating from high school, she worked for Illinois Banker's Life, When the company moved to Chicago, she transferred with them to continue her employment. She met Edgar Allen Potratz and they were married in Chicago on Nov. 6, 1954. They had one son, Gregory Scott. Her husband passed away Sept. 4, 1965 in Michigan where they were living at the time. Her life interests have been in her family, friends, and church.

She has made her home with her brother, Melvin, on his farm near Monmouth. *Submitted by Kenneth C. Bragd*

ROBERT BRENT - Robert Eugene Brent was born in Ellison Township, Smithshire, IL, on March 27, 1921, the son of Glenn and Opal (Galbreath) Brent, and grandson of Schuyler and Elizabeth (Ochert) Brent. He had one sister, Alice (Frazier), who was born June 8, 1925, and passed away May 5, 1981. He was raised and educated in Smithshire and Roseville. He and his father farmed together, until Glenn's declining health and death in 1965. His mother passed away in 1985.

Robert was inducted into the Army on September 4, 1942, Anti-Tank Co., 21st Inf., 24th Div. at Scott Field, IL. Having served in the South Pacific, he was discharged a Sargent on December 5, 1945, at Camp Grant, IL. He was a member of the VFW Post #2301, American Legion Post #136, Monmouth Masonic Lodge #37 AF & AM, Mohammed Shrine at Peoria, and the First United Methodist Church.

One June 4, 1947, Robert married Martha Mumey from Oquawka, IL (Henderson County). She worked as a bookkeeper at Monmouth College for eight years, and at Gamble-Skogmo Warehouse for three. She has since been employed as a baliff for the Ninth Judicial District of Warren County. In recent years she also has been an election judge in Warren County Precincts.

Robert and Martha had their first child, Linda, on August 1, 1953. She graduated from Midstate College in Peoria in 1972 and is employed as a secretary/bookkeeper at Achievement Industries in Monmouth. Michael Glenn was born September 27, 1956. He took over the farming operations in 1986 due to his father's failing health (and death on July 30, 1991). Michael married Laura DeVitalis on June 8, 1988, whose profession is a registered nurse. To that union one son, John Robert, was born on June 25, 1993.

WILLIAM E. AND CECELIA (STEEPLETON) BRIGGS - William E. Briggs was born July 9, 1889 in Henry County. He was the son of Ransome S. Briggs and Margaret Susan Shaklee. Ransome was born on August 25, 1843 and died in 1905. He was buried in Oxford, Illinois. Margaret was born on May 27, 1847 and died in 1922 in Oxford, Illinois, which is part of Henry County. William and Celia were married and later moved to Monmouth, Illinois in 1926.

*Edd and Cecelia Briggs
August 1937*

Celia Belle Steepleton Briggs was born in Mercer County on March 4, 1895 and died in 1986. Celia was the daughter of Woodford Steepleton and Sofia Meeker. William and Celia had five children: Cleo G. (1912-1993), Bonito B. (1916), William E. (1920-1980), Betty June (1922-1927), and Jackie Lee (1930-1930).

Cleo was married to Iliene Saloway and Juanita White. He had one step daughter, Donna Hefner. Cleo was a foreman at both the Monmouth Pottery and the Abington Pottery.

Bonita was married to Russell Waddell (1938-1952). They had two children. Dennis D. (1943) and C. Lynne (1948). Dennis has a real estate business in Rock Island, Illinois. Lynne has been a first grade teacher in Wilton, Iowa for 31 years. Bonita married Everette S. Belt in 1967. He had three daughters: Mary Ann Ward, Marcia Cooper, and Myra Bell. Everette died in 1997. Bonita worked for Ralph Wells for many years, Russell Waddell owned and operated a service station and wrecker service, and Everette was a farmer west of Monmouth for most of his life.

William Jr. was married to Betty Betson and they had three sons: James R., William E. III, and Michael. William Jr. made a career of the army.

James R. is married to Sara Hutchin. They have one son, Rick. James is a barber in Monmouth.

William E. III is married to Gwen Cobb. William has two daughters, Tracey Owens and Shaila Hart. William Jr. was a maintenance worker in the Maytag Corporation in Galesburg.

Michael is married to Susan Appleby. They have two sons., Michael Jr. and Randy. Michael also works at the Maytag Corporation in Galesburg.

Those men who served in the armed services are: Cleo Briggs, World War II veteran, William Briggs Jr., World War II veteran in Army Air Force, Russell Waddell, World War II veteran in Army Air Force, Everette Bell, World War II veteran, James Briggs, served in the Marine Corps

GOLDIE BRINTON - Goldie, living in Vermont, Illinois, Fulton County was born 27 March 1888 in Astoria, Illinois. She, the daughter of Eli and Mary (Rauch) Stremmel, married Harvey Brinton - he died 30 October 1930. They lived in Monmouth, Warren County from 1912 to 1924. He was a contractor.

They had four daughters: Hilda who married Monmouth Heating and Air Conditioning Contractor Don Miller, two sisters Fay Gore and Eunice Horwedel living in Vermont, and Opel Shook living in Rozetta, all in Illinois. Three sons: William Brinton of Cameron, Roy Brinton of Vermont, and Dale Brinton of Horn, Tennessee. Goldie passed away at 97 years leaving 20 grandchildren, 52 great grandchildren and 26 great great grandchildren.

She was preceded in death by two sisters, one brother, two sons, two granddaughters and two great grandsons. She is buried in the Vermont cemetery. One son, Roy Brinton, was 83 on 6 July, 1994, when he drowned in a pond three miles north of Astoria. He married Frances E. Parrish 23 January 1932 in Rushville. He was a coal miner for 30 years retiring in 1972, a member of United Mine Workers of America. In Vermont mining coal was a major industry with many strip mines nearby. He left all memorials to his Methodist Church and the Vermont Rescue Squad.

LINDA JEWELL (MILLER) BRISTOW - Linda Jewell, daughter of Lawrence A. and Edith Kyle Miller, was born January 22, 1938 at Monmouth, Illinois. She and her three brothers, Lawrence Jr. (Larry), Thomas, and Stephen, grew up in the Fairview Center community. Linda attended Fairview Center School for six years and Phelps School for two years before going to Monmouth High School. She participated in numerous school activities during those years, including serving on the school paper and yearbook staffs. She was also in the Honor Society. Following her graduation in 1955 she went to Western Illinois University where she graduated in 1959 with a degree in Education. In later years, Linda did post graduate work at Pacific Lutheran University in Tacoma, Washington. Following her childhood dream, Linda became a teacher, spending thirty-two years in the field of education. She taught kindergarten at Harding Elementary School in Monmouth, first grade in Casa Grande, Arizona, and ended her career as an elementary librarian in Puyallup, Washington.

Linda and Terry Bristow 1997

Linda married Terry Bristow on November 25, 1959 at the Fairview Center Church. They have four children: Brenda (Michael Hall), Stephen (Barbara Manuel), Ann (Samuel Allegro) and Susan (Kent Hernandez) and have nine grandchildren. All are presently living in the state of Washington.

Linda and her family left Monmouth in 1963, settling in Casa Grande, Arizona, where both she and Terry taught for five years. In 1968 they moved to Puyallup, Washington where Linda taught in the Puyallup School District and Terry was an administrator in the Tacoma School District. Terry retired in 1990 after thirty-nine years as a teacher, coach and administrator, teaching in Biggsville, Little York, and Monmouth, Illinois, Casa Grande, Arizona and Tacoma, Washington. Linda retired in 1993 from the Puyallup School District, Puyallup, Washington. Terry H. Bristow was born July 14, 1929 in Ottumwa, Iowa to Leonard W. and Madaline Bristow, both deceased. He has three sisters, Elsie Vanderpol, Iris Vanderpol and Joan Brodsky. Terry attended school in Ottumwa, Iowa, graduating from Ottumwa High School in 1947. While in high school Terry played Junior Legion baseball. After high school, Terry went to Iowa Wesleyan College in Mount Pleasant, Iowa, graduating in 1951. He later earned his Master's Degree in Education from the University of Arizona in 1967. Since retirement, Linda and Terry have pursued their hobbies; traveling, golfing, fishing, genealogy, various crafts and reading. They presently divide their time living in Arizona during the winter months and spending the rest of the year in Washington state. They frequently visit relatives and friends in the Monmouth area.

BROOKS - The story begins with the family of Thomas Brooks who was born in Missouri in

1845 and later moved to Lebanon, Illinois sometime before the 1880 census. He was widowed and remarried three times and was the parent of ten children - Charles, Anna, William, Bertha, Fred, Mamie, Nellie, Emma, Mabel, Herbert – one of whom, Charles (b. 1874, d. 1927) and his wife Laura Nichols (b. 1882, d. 1933), moved to Monmouth in 1914. One of their first acts was to affiliate with the Calvary Baptist church, an affiliation that was to carry on through future generations of Brooks. This was to be the path that subsequent generations took – service to their community be it military service, service to their church or to the greater community. Additionally, the family were often pioneer-like as they crossed social frontiers: Paul the first black referee in the QuadCities, Charles one of the first black interstate semi-truck drivers in the state, Walter one of the first two blacks to participate on the Western Illinois Football team and Marjorie the first black cheerleader at Monmouth High School. Of the ten children, four remained in Monmouth for the rest of their lives – Ralph, Charles, Clyde, and Leland – and were well known for their contributions to the life of the community.

Brooks family Leland, Charlie, Ivan, Fred, Clyde, Walt, Thelma, Ralph, and Ruth.

Ralph Brooks (b. 1900, d. 1983), his wife Gertrude White (b. 1901, d. 1996), and their daughter Maxine (b. 1932, d. 1983) continued the family tradition of membership in Calvary Baptist where they all played an active part in church affairs. Ralph served as chairman of the Deacon Board, Gertrude was a member of the church auxiliary, while Maxine served as Church Clerk, taught Sunday School, and sang in the choir.

Clyde Brooks (b. 1910, d. 1993) and his wife Mary Wallace (b. 1923, d. 1992) continued the family affiliation with Calvary Baptist where Clyde was Deacon and Treasurer. He was a World War II veteran having served with the 837th Aviation Engineers, a past president of the Monmouth Lions Club, a member of the Stronghurst American Legion Post 765, a member of the Macomb VFW Post 1921. While he was not a graduate of Monmouth College, he was none the less inducted into the M Club Hall of Fame in 1989 in recognition of his contributions both as a track official and a most loyal fan. Mary was a member of the Mary Bethune Club and the Bi-county Legion.

Leland Brooks (b. 1913, d. 1996) and his wife Eliza Mitchell (b. 1911, d. 1967) continued the affiliation with Calvary Baptist where Leland was a Deacon and a member of the choir. He was also a World War II Navy veteran, a member of the American Legion, co-founder of the former Sam Skinner American Legion Post, and a member of the Masonic Lodge. They had seven children – George, Leland, Teresita, Cecil, Duwayne, Denise, and Dennis.

Charles Brooks (b. 1902, d. 1992) and his wife Daisy Williams (b. 1905) acquired property at 1128 south 11th Street shortly after they were married. This became the family homestead where two of Charles' and Daisy's sons still reside. It is also at the homestead where every August the family gathers for a reunion on their mother's birthday. Very early in their married life, Charles and his wife affiliated their family with St. James AME church where Daisy's father the Reverend C.Z. Williams was the preacher. In keeping with the family tradition of service, Charles became a Trustee at St. James. He was one of the first black interstate semi-truck drivers in the state. Later he worked at Monmouth College, Head Start, and Jamieson Center. It was here in Monmouth that they raised their nine children - Charles, Paul, Donald, Raymond, Marjorie, Ira, Ada, Glenn, and Chris. With the exception of Charles who died in infancy, all the other children attended Monmouth College. Sons Raymond and Glenn were inducted into the Monmouth College Athletic Hall of Fame in recognition of their contributions to the college via sports. Raymond and his sister Ira were inducted into the Harding School Wall of Fame in recognition of their scholarly and professional accomplishments. Daughters Ada and Ira were voted outstanding senior athletes at Monmouth College. Ira also received education's most prestigious award, a lifetime appointment as a Danforth Fellow as an outstanding college teacher. She has made further contributions through her professional papers, articles and book chapters. The most recent paper, which she coauthored with her daughter Suzanne and her husband Anthony, was presented at Oxford University, England. Son Donald was inducted into the Monmouth High School Athletic Hall of Fame. Son Paul was a World War II veteran of the Marines and was later the first black football and basketball referee in the Quad-Cities. Two of the children - Glenn and Chris - still reside at the homestead and play an active role in the affairs of St. James AME church and the community as did their parents before them. Glenn is the Coordinator for the Even Start Program while Chris is an adjunct faculty member with the Monmouth College Music Department. Additionally, Ada, Marjorie, cousins Leland and Duwayne and numerous relatives all contribute their talents to the religious services at St. James whenever they visit Monmouth.

This theme of service is still being carried on by the descendants of Thomas Brooks in many fields such as law, politics, religion, education, and various civic organizations. Whatever they did or do, the Brooks family has brought honor not only to themselves but also to the task at hand.

WENDELL AND JANET BROOKS - Wendell Lawrence Brooks, son of George Leland and Mae (Snell) Brooks was born December 30, 1934, at home in Roseville Township, Roseville, Illinois. He has two older brothers: George Leland Brooks Jr. who was born in 1929, and Robert Thompson Brooks who was born in 1933.

He attended Pleasant Hill Country Grade School and graduated from Roseville High School in 1954. As a boy he helped his father and brothers with the planting and other farm chores. In high school his FFA project was raising Hampshire hogs which he continued to do until his marriage.

In 1959 he and Janet moved to Dayton, Ohio, where he worked in his uncle's business and in a local camera store.

Later they returned to Monmouth where he worked first at the John Deere Implement Dealership, and later at the C and E Motor Supply Store.

In 1963 they moved to Kirkwood when he went to work for the Central Gas Company in that village. Wendell started Brooks Heating and Cooling Company in 1993 which he operated until retirement in 1996.

He is a member of the Westminster United Presbyterian Church where he is an elder and a former Sunday School Superintendent. In addition he is an active member of the A. Lincoln Lodge having been a member 45 years.

Janet Elaine Williams, daughter of Howard E. and Elizabeth Mae (Hall) Williams, was born January 1, 1937, in Oquawka, Illinois. She had two brothers and one sister: Ross Williams, John E. Williams (who died in 1987), and Wilma J. Williams Weidler. Two other sisters died in infancy.

During World War II her family moved from Rozetta Township, Henderson County, Illinois, to Omaha, Nebraska where her father helped to build B-29 airplanes. In 1945, the family moved to Monmouth where Janet entered third grade at Central Grade School. She graduated from Monmouth High School in 1955.

Wendell and Janet were married on November 25, 1956, at the West Side United Presbyterian Church in Monmouth, IL. They are the parents of six children: William Thomas born in 1957 in Dayton, Ohio; Linda Mae born in 1958, Lawrence Alan born in 1959; Jane Elizabeth born in 1961; John Robert born in 1962; and Phillip Jay born in 1965. With the exception of William Thomas, all the children were born in Monmouth.

Janet worked at the Warren County Clerk's Office from 1955 until they moved to Dayton, Ohio, in 1957. After their children were in school, she worked for Dr. Joseph D. Simmons in his Kirkwood office until he retired in 1982.

Since that time Janet has been a volunteer at the Monmouth Community Medical Center. An active member of the Westminster United Presbyterian Church in Kirkwood, she has served as an elder and clerk of the Session. Janet is very active in the Oquawka Rebekah Lodge and serves in several state appointee offices in the Rebekahs.

BROWN-RANDALL-LIVINGSTON-MCCOY-SANNER - Samantha Ruth Brown came to Warren County from Butler County, Pennsylvania as a teenager with her father, Robert, and step-mother, Mary (nee Lane). Robert purchased 80 acres in Section 13 of Tompkins Township which, as Samantha related to her grandchildren, "was just prairie grass." She said they planted anything that would grow. Robert built a house on the land, according to Cliff Sanner, without a level or square. The house has been added onto and modernized and still stands today. Those 80 acres along with 80 additional acres acquired by Samantha's husband, Walter Randall, raised Samantha, her children and one family of her grandchildren, the Will Livingstons. Later it supported her grand-daugther, Margaret McCoy Sanner and husband, Clifford, for 40 years. The quarter section remains under the ownership of direct descendants, Dean and Russell Stewart.

Samantha and Walter were married in 1865. Walter had come to Warren County from Portage County, Ohio by horseback. He helped haul ties for the CB & Q railroad when it was built in Warren County. After Robert Brown's death in 1867, Walter and Samantha farmed the land mentioned above and raised their family there. They had two daughters, Mary Florence and Lulu. Samantha's stepmother lived with the Randalls during her last years for which a room was added to the house. She died in 1895. The 1880 agricultural census shows that the Randalls had cattle, swine, and poultry. Crops included corn, oats, potatoes and apples.

Randall family home built by Robert Brown circa 1860, taken circa 1895. Still standing 2002

The Randalls moved to a home on South Main just outside the city limits of Monmouth in 1904. Walter died in 1915. Samatha died in 1939 at Lula McCoy's home where she lived her last years. The farm was operated by William Livingston to whom Mary Florence was married in 1897. The Livingstons interacted frequently with Ralph and Lulu McCoy's family (see McCoy, Thomson). They traded farm work and enjoyed family visits and picnics. Will and Florence had three children: Grace, Nellie and Howard. Grace married Tom Duncan, Nellie did not marry and Howard married Bernice Killey. Howard and Bernice farmed and fed cattle in Floyd township. They had three daughters: Alice, Lorraine and Jean. Alice married Charles Allaman who farm in Henderson County. Lorraine married Bruce Greene. Jean married Warren Sanders. Howard died at age 55 from injuries suffered from a fall while hauling hay from his barn.

After Will Livingston's health failed, the Randall farm was farmed by Ralph McCoy. In the 1940's, the farming was assumed by Cliff Sanner. Cliff was from Michigan and married Margaret McCoy there when she was teaching elementary school in Harbor Beach. Previously Margaret had taught school at the Coonville school. When Lulu McCoy died in 1955, Cliff and Margaret moved to the Randall place and lived there the rest of their life. Margaret died in 1995 and Cliff died in 1997.

CHARLES L. BROWN - Charles L. was born in Warren County June 5, 1932, the son of Harry E. and Grace Clute Brown. He had one brother, Everett H. Brown, who died in 2001 and one sister, Louise Elaine Brown Hogan.

Mr. Brown is a descendent of one of the first settlers of Knox County, Harmon G. Brown, whose son, John Hobbs Brown, moved to Warren County after serving in the Civil War. Charles Brown's father, Harry, and grandfather, Fred J. Brown, lived all their lives in Kelly Township, Warren County. Charles Brown's mother, Grace Clute, also lived all her life in Warren County. The Clute's originally settled on Clute Hill on the Angling Road in Kelly Township.

Charles L. Brown

Charles Brown was raised on top of Wildcat Hill on what is now 170th Street in Kelly Township. He has lived on 155th Street, Kelly Township for 46 years and will soon move into a new home on Wildcat Hill.

Mr. Brown attended Forest Flower Grade School, which was located 7/8 of a mile north of his home. He graduated from Galesburg High School and Western Illinois University. While in high school, he was treasurer and president of the Galesburg FFA. He received the Dekalb Agricultural Award and a State Farmer degree.

He married Lois Nelson in 1952; they have 5 children: Sandra Sherman, a lawyer in Morristown, NJ, Linda Tammen, a teacher and farm wife at Thawville, IL, John L. Brown, a lawyer for John Deere Credit, James C. Brown, who works for Maytag, and Joseph T. Brown, a bridge engineer for New York State.

Lois and Charles were divorced in 1974. He married M. Joan Harris in 1975. She is the mother of Robert C. Nelson, a semi driver for Farmland Foods, David K. Nelson, an LP Plant Manager, Donna Sue Nelson Benedict, a musician and teacher, and Nancy J. Nelson, a student at Carl Sandburg College and a waitress. Joan Brown was a registered nurse employed by St. Mary Medical Center. She died in 1994 after a long suffering from cancer.

Charles Brown served as president of Henderson Grove Grange and an officer in the Illinois State Grange. He served on the committee to establish the Alexis/North Henderson Ambulance District and served as one of the original trustees. He served as Kelly Township Supervisor and a member of the Warren County Board of Supervisors. He also served as township trustee. In 1966, he received the outstanding Young Farmer award for Warren County. He was a Republican Precinct committeeman and a director of the Monmouth Motel Insurance Co.

In 1995, Charles Brown and Catharine Baker were married. Her former husband also died of cancer. She and Joseph Baker had been married 41 years. She is the mother of John and Paul Baker, who are farmers in Union County, Iowa, Annette Baker Rice, Hospice volunteer coordinator at Greater Community Hospital in Creston; and Alicia Baker Hamze, a marketing manager for National Food Services in Omaha, NE. Their second oldest daughter, Mary Joan Baker, died in a car accident at age 17.

Before her marriage to Joseph Baker, Catharine had been a Catholic nun and teacher. After leaving the convent, she was employed by J. C. Penney Co. Later on, she worked at Crossroads Mental Health Center.

Charles Brown has been a carpenter-building contractor and farmer all his adult life. He and Catharine still farm in Kelly Township, where they raise cattle and sheep.

MERLE AND PATRICIA BROWN - Patricia Mahaffey Brown was born August 10, 1924, the daughter of Floyd James and Sadye Alphansine Mahaffey. She was blessed with a sister, Grace Ding, and a brother, Forrest.

She grew up in the Alexis area, attending Lone Star School. After graduating from Alexis High School, she attended and graduated from the American Institute of Commerce in Davenport, Iowa.

Merle and Patricia Brown

She married Merle Brown at the Treasure Island Chapel, San Francisco, California in 1943. They are the parents of four sons: James (1944), Tary (1949), Dennis (1952), and Kriss (1956). All four sons were born and raised in Monmouth, Illinois. Merle and Patricia Brown have lived at same address of 120 North C Street in Monmouth all of their married life.

For a number of years, Pat and her mother did commercial entertaining in their home at 120 North C Street in Monmouth, Illinois. She also was a licensed beautician and worked out of her shop in her home for 30 years.

One of her real thrills was being honored as the First Lady of Monmouth's Sesquicentennial in 1981.

Both Merle and Pat have been involved in school and community activities, with Pat serving on the school board for four years. Merle served as a Deacon and Trustee of Faith United Presbyterian Church, with Pat also serving as an Ordained Elder and Deacon. Community support continued to be evidenced by their membership on the CMC Hospital Auxiliary, Chamber of Commerce, Tourism Committee and the Strom Center Board. Merle was named Citizen of the Year in 2000. He is a member of the Marion B. Fletcher Post 136 of the American Legion, with Pat a member of the Legion Auxiliary.

Merle Wayne Brown was born December 30, 1923 in Mercer County, Aledo, Illinois. He was the youngest child of Oliver Leslie Brown and Myra Etha Park. He had three brothers and three sisters: Dallas, Lyle, Clair, Opal, Inez and Lela.

Merle attended Dunlap and Kimel elementary schools in Mercer County near Aledo, graduating from Aledo High School on May 26, 1941.

After a brief period of employment at the L and G Grocery Store in Aledo, he worked at John Deere Spreader Works in East Moline, Illinois.

In February of 1943, he enlisted in the United States Navy and then received basic training at the Great Lakes Naval Training Station. He was then sent to Treasure Island, California where he was assigned to a destroyer, the USS Owens. For 30 months, he served as a sonar technician in the Pacific battles of World War II.

After being discharged from the Navy, he joined his wife and son in Monmouth, Illinois, where he was employed by Illinois Power Company for 35 years, retiring in 1985.

Merle has been recognized as the City Santa for 28 years – the jolly man in the bright red suit who brought special joy to children of all ages, young and old alike.

JAMES STEVENSON AND MARGARET (STRUTHERS) BROWNLEE

James Stevenson Brownlee, (b. June 22, 1824 Claysville, Washington Co., PA, d. April 18, 1891 Monmouth, Warren Co., IL)was the son of David and Ann (Stevenson) Brownlee. He married Feb. 12, 1855, Warren Co., IL Margaret Struthers (b. Feb. 2, 1830 near Xenia, Greene Co., OH, d. Dec. 16, 1915 Momnouth, Warren Co., IL). Margaret was the daughter of William Struthers and his first wife Martha Saville.

James S. and Margaret (Struthers) Brownlee

James moved from Pennsylvania to Illinois in the early 1830's with his parents and they lived on a farm in Sumner Township near Little York. James' father met an unfortunate death in April of 1838 and his mother, Ann Brownlee, was able to raise her family thanks to the efforts of James Struthers (an uncle of Margaret Struthers, the future Mrs. James Stevenson Brownlee); Elijah Davidson, and James G. Barton.

Margaret moved from Ohio with her father and stepmother Elizabeth (Alexander) in 1854 and they settled on a farm north of Monmouth.

Margaret and James both came from families who were willing to answer the call to protect our country. James' grandfather, General James Stevenson, fought with the Pennsylvania Militia in the American Revolutionary War; and Margaret's father was in the Virginia Militia in the War of 1812.

James Brownlee was a farmer on the family homestead and was known as "Big Steve" in part because of the large cattle that he raised. In 1882, James and Margaret moved to Monmouth and resided at 129 S. 8th Street. Margaret sustained a broken hip in 1903 and lived the remaining days of her life with their daughter Lillie (Mrs. Samuel Leigh Hamilton) at 323 S. 8th Street, Monmouth, IL.

James and Margaret were members of the Presbyterian Church. They are buried in Monmouth Cemetery, Monmouth, Warren Co., IL. Their children are: Calvin, Ann, Lillie, Frank, Nettie and Carrie.

JAMES BROWNLEE, JR.

James Brownlee, Jr, living in Taylorstown, a spot in the road near Washington, PA was a Justice-of-the- Peace. In late 1700's and early 1800's it meant serving in a quasi-legal manner. He is also reputed to run a hostelry, a stopping point on the National or Cumberland Road (1805).

It was very common for church congregations to settle in one place, moving westward as a group. Pioneers seemed to go to church communities where they knew people. In time, James Jr. followed his daughters, Jane and Abraham Ritner, Ann and Abraham McKinney to Monmouth, IL area. He settled with Eleanor and his new family just across the Warren County line in Mercer County, near Aledo, Illinois. Here in the County Courthouse in Box 27 are his estate papers. In Aledo he again works as a Justice-of-the-Peace and at his death people owed him $2,223 - a great deal of money in 1850! Ironically he died intestate. By December 13, 1850, his death date, both daughters Jane and Ann were dead. In the weeds of the abandoned Brownlee Cemetery on a country road, a stone was found lying on the ground with the name broken off, but with death date December 13, 1850. At the time of his death he was living with his four younger children (1850 census), but there was no mention of Eleanor. No record has been found of her death or burial. Supposedly the young family moved to Shelby, Illinois.

James, Jr. had a brother Thomas, and a sister Elizabeth living near him in Mercer County. They both had families, so there was a transfer of the "clan" from Washington, PA to Illinois. Many Presbyterian ministers came from the Brownlee "clan" in Pennsylvania and Illinois. The Brownlees, as a group, were intelligent, well-respected, successful, and often wealthy.

How did I find Ann Brownlee McKinney when she was not listed on any Brownlee record? Looking through many wills in the Courthouse in Washington, PA, I found, in James Jr.'s older brother John's will, dated August 4, 1854, a bequest to the children of his deceased niece, Ann C. McKinney. Does the "C" stand for Clark, James Jr. s first wife, Ann Clark? John also left money to the children of deceased Ann Ritner. Elisha Jolley, in his will dated December 24, 1836, left money to the children of his deceased daughter, Mary "Polly" Jolley Brownlee, Ann Brownlee McKinney inherits from his bequest, also. A mystery! Who was the mother of Ann Brownlee? Was it Ann Clark or Polly Jolley? Ann Brownlee named her first daughter Mary Jane. Her third daughter is Sarah Ann, nd her fifth daughter is Adaline Clark. We need the Clark family tree!

James Brownlee Jr. (child No 3), born 27 Sept 1780 Washington County, PA married (1) Ann Clark; (2) Mary "Polly" Jolley; (3) Eleanor "Phemican"? Children Ann, Archibald, Elisha, Jane, James, John. Children of Eleanor: Jackson, Mary, Margaret, Harrison (order of birth uncertain). Ann (Anna) Brownlee born circa 1810 (mother Ann Clark or "Polly Jolley") married circa 1826/27, died circa 1845.

JOHN W. AND MAY (ARMSTRONG) BROWNLEE

John Wilbur Brownlee was born November 6, 1863 on the family farm in Sumner Township of Warren County, one and a half miles north of Little York. He was one of the eleven children born to John and Nancy Ann Barr Brownlee. He attended the Brownlee School which was nearby. In 1886 he went west and homesteaded in Cheyenne County, Kansas where he also drove a stagecoach. He told about rattlesnakes being in the ruts in the road and of looking for them in his bunk before going to bed.

Returning to Illinois he and his brother Bob farmed one of his father's farm three miles north and one-half mile west of Little York. His father had bought the 160 acre farm on October 15, 1865, from a William Hawthorne for $4,200.00.

John W. Brownlee and Nellie May Brownlee Feb. 5, 1896

Prior to his marriage, a house was built on that farm with a part of the lumber coming from the old schoolhouse which had been across the road. On February 5, 1896, he married Nellie May Armstrong in her family's home in the Cedar Creek neighborhood. They moved to this farm where their new home had two bedrooms, a living room, a kitchen and pantry on one floor. One bedroom was unheated, but there was a "pull-down" bed in the living room which was hidden by a curtain when it was against the wall and not in use.

In the living room was a "straw carpet," a carpet stretched over straw and tacked down. Once a year the carpet was taken up and hung on the clothesline. Nellie May's mother and sisters would come to help beat the carpet and gather up the old straw to be burned. New straw was put down and the "clean" carpet put down over it.

Each bed had a straw "tick" and a feather "tick" mattress. When it was carpet cleaning time, the old straw was taken from the straw ticks and burned; then the mattress covers were washed and dried before new straw was inserted. In the summer time the straw tick was on top of the feather tick since it was cooler; these were reversed in the winter so the sleeper could benefit from the warmth of the feather tick.

A black hard coal stove with isinglass "windows" heated the living room and the adjoining bedroom. In the kitchen was a black iron range with a flat top and a reservoir to keep water, and it was used for cooking and heating.

As a wedding present the couple received two sows from the bride's sister and her husband, Fannie ad Len McCrery. Later John said this gave him his start in hogs.

The groom's parents' gift was $1,000. After his father's death, his share was less than that of some of the other heirs and when questioned, he said he got his when he needed it.

On February 14, 1901, they purchased the farm from his parents for $11,200.00. On June 25, on that year their daughter, Esther Katheryn, was born. Prior to her birth they had a stillborn son.

On August 31, 1903, a second daughter was born and named Mary Jane.

Six years later on September 6, 1909, a son was born, Orrie W. Brownlee.

Following two years of suffering from terrible headaches, May Brownlee died on January 18, 1911. Although several specialists in Chicago had been consulted, none had been able to help her.

Around 1912 the family moved to a nearby farm on Henderson Creek which John W. had bought while retaining ownership of the home place. Both girls attended Little York High School, but graduated from Monmouth High School as did their brother Orrie.

In 1920 the Browlees moved to a home at 728 E. Second Avenue in Monmouth, Illinois.

Esther taught school until her marriage to Frank E. Kinney on February 12, 1923. Mary kept house for her family and after high school she worked at McQuiston's Book Store on the square.

John W. Brownlee died on May 28, 1927, after an attach of apoplexy. On January 25, 1927, Mary married Francis Gavin.

After high school Orrie attended Monmouth College where he was a member of the TKE fraternity. Then he worked for the Illinois Bankers Life Assurance Company. He worked there until his sudden death caused by a heart attack on December 23, 1938.

Mary and Francis had three daughters: Marjorie, Martha, and Lucille. Mary died on May 23, 1965. Francis died October 10, 1981.

Esther and Frank had six children: Ruth, Gerald, Marian, Howard, Harold, and Melba. Esther died January 13, 1996. Frank preceded her in death on February 26, 1976.

JAMES C. BRUCE JR. (REV. JAMES CLARK BRUCE 1) - James C. Bruce, Jr. was born June 12,1836 in Monmouth. He married Sarah Kendall, daughter of John and Elizabeth Gibson Kendall, December 6, 1855, in Monmouth. James and Sarah Bruce had six children in six years, and that included two sets of twins. They had a two year old daughter, Emma Josephine (born October 8, 1856), when twin sons, John Kendall Bruce and James C. Bruce, were born April 16, 1858. Emma died June 26,1858. Margaret Elizabeth "Maggie" Bruce, was born March 31,1860 and died November 9, 1905 Moody County, South Dakota. She married David Burris in Wisconsin. They had five children, two died in infancy. With four year old twin sons, and a two year old daughter, Sarah again gave birth April 16, 1862, to twin daughters Ella and Eva Bruce. Mother Sarah Kendall Bruce died April 20,1862 and is buried in Monmouth. Ella died at 10 days old, and Eva died at 24 days.

James followed his parents to Wisconsin, and certainly grandmother Margaret Bruce played a role in raising his children. He remarried to Minerva Allen, May 19, 1864, West Salem, Lacrosse County, Wisconsin.

James and Minerva Allen Bruce had two children. George Thaddeus Bruce who was born January 29, 1865 West Salem, Wisconsin. He died April 16,1913 Wisconsin. Bertha May "Birdie" Bruce born November 20, 1873 and died January 28, 1907 Chicago, IL. March 1, 1871, twin son, James C. Bruce, died. (son of Sarah Kendall Bruce).

James C. Bruce Jr. died May 19, 1888 in Yankton, Yankton County, South Dakota. It is unknown when and where Minerva Allen Bruce died.

REVEREND JAMES CLARK BRUCE - James Clark Bruce was born October 8, 1800 York, York Co. Pennsylvania to Robert and Ann Crosby Bruce. Shortly thereafter, his parents moved to Youngstown, Ohio, and then to Athens, Ohio. He, like his parents belonged to the Associate Presbyterian Church. He was ordained in 1831, at Cadiz, Ohio, to preach. He was a missionary for the first year, very likely serving the Henderson congregation, and was then unanimously called to return as a resident pastor. In June 1832, he married Margaret Allen in Xenia, Ohio. She was the daughter of Zachariah and Elizabeth Law Allen. In October of that same year, he moved to Warren County. He was installed as pastor of the Henderson United Presbyterian Church in 1832. This was the first religious organization in Warren County. The first church was a 24 by 30 foot log structure.

Rev. James Clark Bruce was born October 8, 1800 in Pennsylvania and died April 26, 1857 in Wisconsin.

In June 1847, he left the Associate Church, and connected himself with the Associate Church of North America. (also designated as the Bullions Church). Many of the congregation joined his church, and he continued to preach until 1852. This same year he resigned his charge and became a member of the Associate Reformed Presbyterian Church. Then, during the summer of 1853, he accepted a call to preach in Wisconsin, and moved to Wyoming, Iowa County, Wisconsin in 1854.

While residing in Monmouth, Rev. James Clark and Margaret Allen Bruce had seven children.

Their first son was William G. Bruce, born 1833. He married twice, first to Margaret Ann Allen, and secondly, to Margaret Freand. The second marriage took place in Wisconsin. When a young man, he was crippled with rheumatism, and did not walk for 42 years. He drove a wagon, and sold notions. In later years, he lived in Oklahoma, and visited his sister, Mrs. Jackson Caldwell (in Monmouth), in 1898.

James C. Bruce, Jr. (see article on him)

Mary Ann Bruce, born 1838, died 1911, Cedar Rapids, Linn Co., Iowa. She married Jeremiah Sturgeon McDaniel in Wisconsin. Their children were: Alice M. McDaniel, Mary Elsie McDaniel, Clara Belle McDaniel, and Edwin Bruce McDaniel. Matilda Jane "Jennie" Bruce, daughter of Rev. James and Margaret Bruce, was born 1841, and married Thomas "Jackson" Caldwell. They had two children: Sherman E. Caldwell, born 1864, and Beulah Caldwell, born 1871 in Monmouth. Beulah married Ira Azdell. Albert C. Bruce, born 1843, and likely died in his teens.

Robert A. Bruce, was born in 1845 and died in 1917 Iowa County, Wisconsin. He married Annie Lucas, 1882 in Wisconsin. They had two children: Adrien Bruce and Luella Bruce. Sarah A. Bruce, daughter of Rev. James, was born about 1847 and married a Foster. They resided in Cedar Rapids, Iowa, and had two children, Della Foster and Charles Foster.

ROBERT BRUCE - Robert Bruce, father of Rev. James Clark Bruce, was born in Morebattle, Roxburyshire, Scotland. Apparently Robert came to the USA with his three brothers, James C., Andrew, and William, soon after the Revolutionary War. Maybe there was a sister, who married a Culberson. All four brothers settled initially in York Co. PA, near the old Seceder Church of Quinston. Then James C. settled in Indiana Co., PA, Andrew in Washington Co. PA, and William in Lawrence Co., PA. They were all shoemakers. Robert Bruce married Anne Crosby of York Co. PA. Robert moved from York Co. PA to Youngstown, OH. Afterwards, he moved to New Athens, OH. Robert and his family moved to Warren Co., IL in 1834 where his eldest son, Rev. James Clark Bruce was located. He died at his daughter Rachel's house, sometime after July 1835.

Robert and Anne Crosby Bruce had seven children, and all but one of them resided in Warren County, Illinois.

Andrew Crosby Bruce, born May 28,1804 York, PA. He left his home in New Athens, OH in 1828 to study medicine in Beaver Co., PA. He married Mary Graham on November 4, 1829. Her parents were James and Sarah Boise Grimes of Washington Co. PA.

Andrew and Mary had seven children:

James Bruce, born May 15,1831 Hillsville, Lawrence Co., PA. Became a Presbyterian pastor.

David Graham Bruce born July 13, 1833 Amsterdam, Jefferson Co. OH. Robert Bruce, born February 28, 1836 Minerva, Stark Co., OH.

Sarah Jane Bruce, born May 12, 1839 Fairview, Beaver Co. PA. Bryson Bruce, born February 22, 1842, Gibson Co. IN. Elizabeth Ann, born December 18, 1844 Gibson Co. IN. Mary Emeline Bruce born August 13, 1847, Princeton, Gibson Co. IN.

Andrew's wife Mary, died October 2, 1860 in Beaver Co. PA. and Andrew died January 14, 1876 in Cannonsburg, PA. (source: Thelma Bruce Connor 2001)

Hugh "Bryson" Bruce (Robert 1) was born 1839, and married Cynthia Ann McCracken 1842 in Warren Co. IL. He was a doctor. He died before August 1842. Cynthia Bruce remarried William M. Robinson and moved to Ohio.

Sarah Jane "Sally" Bruce (Robert 1) married William Johnston/Johnson. She resided in Ohio. Her death was April 1857. They had three children - Juliann, James Barrick born 1834, and Armas Bruce Johnston born Oct. 3, 1838. Rev. William Bruce (Robert 1), was born June 2, 1812 Youngstown, Ohio. He was a Presbyterian minister. His first pastorship was the Bethel Congregation in Eden, Illinois 1837-1847. He also served in Adamsville and Conneautville, PA 1853-60; and Ryegate, VT 1868-70. He married Margaret Brownlee September 5, 1838 in Monmouth. His second wife was Mary (probably Brownlee, also). He died at Low Point, IL Aug. 26, 1881, where he had served as pastor from 1872-74. Seven children are known: Rachel J. Bruce born 1839 IL. Maria Bruce born 1840 IL; David C. Bruce, born 1842 IL; Matthew Bruce born 1845 Monmouth, Nancy Ann Bruce born 1849 PA. twins Laura and William Bruce, born 1860 PA.

GRACE BUCHANAN - Grace Elizabeth Stephenson was born in Wyoming, IL, in 1894, only child of Fred Stephenson and Nellie Black. The family moved a number of times during her childhood to locations where her father operated lumber yards. They lived in West Virginia for a few years. They lived in St. Joseph, MO, when Grace met Matt Gross, a young man who worked at the post office. They were married in 1917.

Matt had a dream of farming. In 1921, the two couples, Matt and Grace and Grace's parents, moved to Warren Co. where Fred's sister Lizzy (John) McCulloch lived. They bought a farm east of Monmouth, which they called Highlawn Farm. Making the dream a reality was not easy. All four worked hard on the new venture. They had a herd of dairy cows. Grace milked the cows and delivered milk to customers in the area.

Matt was an out-going person with a wonderful sense of humor. In addition to farming, he had an interest in politics. The Young Republicans backed Matt with the slogan, "Vote for Our Milkman!" He served as a State Representative for one term. Despite popular support, he declined to run again.

In the fall of 1940, Grace's father died. It was the beginning of many changes. In August of 1942 a devastating hailstorm totally wiped out the crops. They were simply gone. The buildings were damaged; windows in the house were blown in. Glass lay on the beds where they were sleeping. They made repairs and persevered.

In 1943 Matt had a massive stroke and died a few days later, at age 53. Later that year Grace's mother died. In three years, everyone was gone. Grace was alone.

A good friend, Agnes Lamberson, came to live with Grace. Agnes had been a housemother at one of the fraternities where Grace delivered milk. In time, she introduced Grace to her cousin, Charles Buchanan.

Grace and Charlie married in 1947 in Chicago. He was a widower with two adult children. Charlie was in management with Maytag. He was also active in Rotary. They traveled extensively, including a trip to Japan. Grace brought home many artifacts from their travels. Charlie enjoyed decorating outdoors at Christmas. He built animated, lighted reindeer for their front yard. Hundreds of people drove by to see the display.

Charlie Buchanan died in 1965. Grace continued to care for Aggie until her death.

Grace enjoyed painting. She and several other women met at the Coldbrook Christian Church to paint together. They called their group The Dab and Daub Club.

Grace wanted to create a place where young people could take art lessons. She envisioned her home with her collections of art and Japanese items as a cultural center. She designated funds for the creation of a center that would encourage the arts. She would be very pleased with the scope and success of the Buchanan Center for the Arts.

Grace suffered from macular degeneration as her mother had. Though her sight was failing, she continued to attend community events and she enjoyed being included in family functions of her many friends.

Grace died in 1985 at her home. She was aptly named. Whatever befell her, good fortune or hardships, she appreciated what she had. She valued friendships more than any possession. She was a gracious lady.

RUSSELL O. BURKITT - Russell O. son of Ralph and Vaida (Kremer) Burkitt was born 20 October 1911. He was reared and educated in West Chicago. He came to Monmouth in 1930. His father passed away shortly afterwards, whence his mother ran a restaurant in the basement below Pearson's Harness Shop on North Main and the Square. She featured veal cutlets. He married Helen Gardner 29 November 1934 at the Little Brown Church in Nashua, Iowa. He was working at Barnes Bros. Grocery at the time. He later went to work for Nicol's Hatchery sorting baby chicks. They were very busy mailing chicks all over the country. He moved to the furthest small home across from Monmouth airport that had a small acreage. He decided on a new concept at the time. He would raise young pullets to about three pounds, frying chicken size, sell them to Barnes Bros. meat department for a gigantic chicken sale. His wife was to dress them - picking and gutting. He had forgotten they all arrived at that weight about the same time. Not only that, but thousands of wild rabbits had dug holes around the yard pump and were enjoying a free meal. They did this only one year.

Russell then became a self employed painter and interior decorator. When Monmouth College approached him to join their staff as a painter, he accepted and worked there 12 years, Their family grew with three sons and two daughters; William of Monmouth, David of Decatur, Georgia, and Danny of Sterling, Illinois; the girls were Donna married to Robert Objartel and Karen married James Hull, both of Monmouth. Altogether there are 11 grandchildren. He has a brother Donald of Seattle, Washington and a sister Letha Nelson of Cary.

When moving back into town to 830 North 6th Street he purchased from Monmouth College two old army barracks that he placed side by side, living in one until the other was insulated and ready. They had a small pasture for a pony and the children loved this. They were Methodists. Russell died at his home 23 April 1979.

ALBERT DELL BURNS - Albert Dell Burns was born in Spring Grove Township, Warren County on Aug 12, 1904. They called him Dell. He was the son of a farmer Albert Burns (b. 1855 and d. 1918 in Warren County) and Sarah Hill Johnson Burns (b. 1862 in Randalstown, Antrim County, Ireland d. 1948 in Warren County).

His grandfather was Edward Burns b. about 1835 in Ireland d. 1892 in Warren County and he was married to Adaline Bunker b. 1835 in Michigan d. 1916. They farmed in Warren and Henderson County.

On Jan 12, 1932 Dell married Caroline Amelia Scott, born Apr 17, 1908 in Monmouth Township the daughter of John Peter Scott and Carrie Isaacs Scott both immigrants of Denmark who met in Warren County. Prior to his marriage Dell attended Union Grammar and Monmouth High School. Caroline was a housewife. They farmed all their working life and raised their children in Warren County at Monmouth, Little York and Alexis. Their first son Leonard Dell b. Aug 13, 1932 passed away on Jan 4, 1933. They were also parents of Edward Scott, Ruth Carolyn, Dorothy Leona and Vera Iliene.

They were very active in Cedar Creek Church, Duck Creek and Little York Schools and community affairs. After moving to the Alexis community they became members of the Henderson Grove Grange and the Gerlaw Christian Church. In 1958 they bought a farm in Monmouth Township on which his son, Edward, resides. In 1963 they bought a farm in Spring Grove Township where he fanned until retiring in 1980. They moved to Lake Warren and then to Monmouth in 1986.

Dell died Nov. 1991. Caroline continues to live at home with assisted care.

Edward born Aug 8, 1933 married Sarah Melton and is an auctioneer and owner of Burns Trailer Sales in Monmouth Township. They have five children Connie, Charles, D. Herb, Sarah and Scott.

Ruth born Dec. 27, 1935 married Paul Fredrickson a farmer in Henderson County. They are parents of Diane (deceased) Will, Chris and Todd. Dorothy born Dec 06, 1939 married Clyde Goff and they had 3 daughters, Jeanne, Barbara and Susan. She later married Lynn Long and they reside in Monmouth. V. Iliene married Brent Ogilvie, a farmer, and they live on Dell's farm in Spring Grove Township. They are the parents of Timothy (deceased), Russell, currently Mayor of Alexis, and Dustin.

EDWARD SCOTT BURNS - Edward Scott Burns is the son of Albert Dell Burns and Caroline Scott Burns born in Sumner Township August 08,1933. He attended Cedar Creek and Duck Creek grade schools, and Little York High School. On Dec. 24, 1950 he married Sarah Arlene Melton, youngest daughter of Ora Melton and Minnie Bryant Melton. She was born in Sumner Township, attended Duck Creek grade school, Little York High School and Western Illinois State College.

They started farming on the Cook place in Sumner Township and then moved to the Reasoner Farm in Spring Grove Township. Here Edward, an avid auction-goer, decided to become an auctioneer. He graduated from Repperts School of Auctioneering in Decatur, IN.: in 1957 and received his Real Estate License in 1958. They moved to a farm in Monmouth Township in 1958 where they still reside. It was on this farm they raised their five children Connie Jean, Charles Edward, Dell Herbert, Sarah Kathryn, and Scott E. all born at Monmouth Hospital. They all attended Warren School. The children and their friends enjoyed many hours of horseback riding, fishing, hunting, camping and sledding on this farm

Edward raised livestock along with his auction and real estate business. Sarah was executive secretary at Monmouth College from 1963 to 1976. In. 1976 Sarah became a licensed Real Estate Broker and joined Edward in opening Burns Real Estate and Edward S. Burns & Sons Trailer Sales, a retail store selling trailers and supplies on Route 67 north of Monmouth.

Connie born June 19, 1951 married Jerry Cokel Mar 28, 1970. They are parents of Amy Christine b. Oct. 25, 1970; Alexander J. stillborn Dec 19, 1972 ; Melinda Jean b. Feb 04, 1975. Connie later married Robert Loving on Mar. 31, 1979, a USDA meat inspector, and they had one son Austin Levi born Mar 18, 1981 at Community Memorial Hospital. Connie a graduate of Carl Sandburg College works as a Technician in the Dialysis Unit Cottage Hospital, Galesburg. They live in Kirkwood, IL.

Amy, a graduate of Western Illinois University is presently working in Peoria IL in National/Regional Sales for AAA Entertainment Radio Groups. Melinda spent four years in the United States Navy and married Derek Wade Perry still of the United States Navy, in Kirkwood, IL May 31, 1997 They have two children Alexandra Jean b. Jan 04, 1999 and Bergen Wade b. Dec. 26, 1999. Melinda is currently a student in the RN program at Carl Sandburg College. Austin, who suffered kidney failure at the age of 10, has had two kidney transplants and is still living at home.

Charles born June 19, 1953, graduated from Illinois State University. He married Sheree Sorrels Adams on April 07, 1979. They are both realtors and live on a farm in Suez Twshp., Alexis. They are parents of Chandler Dell b. Mar 21, 1981 currently a student at University of Illinois and Chase Mylon b. June 11, 1983 currently a student at Southern Illinois University.

Dell Herbert known as Herb born May 26, 1955, a graduate of Reppert School of Auctioneering is an Auctioneer/Realtor. He married Jennifer Vincent November 25, 1978; and they reside in Cameron, IL Jennifer is employed in Sales Administration at Monmouth Pottery. They are parents of Blake Edward b. Apr. 14, 1981 currently a student at Illinois State University and Carrie Dee, b. Sept 08, 1982 currently a student at Western Illinois University.

Sarah Kathryn (Sally) born Sept. 21, 1956 a graduate of Carl Sandburg College married Gregory Shields May 5, 1978 and later married Donald Crose on May 30. 1987, a Plumbing Inspector for the City of Galesburg. Sarah is a Lincare Medical Regional Manager. Their two sons, Warren Michael b. July 02. 1988 and Cameron Keith b. May 01, 1990 are both students at Churchill Jr. High, Galesburg.

Scott E. born Feb. 18, 1958 a graduate of Reppert School of Auctioneering married Michelle Miller on Oct. 7, 1988. Scott is an Auctioneer/ Realtor and Michelle is an Office Manager for XPedx. in Springfield, MO. They are parents of Sarah Cheyenne b. Oct 13, 1992, Bailey Kathryn b. Apr 20, 1994 and Shelby Caroline, b. Apr. 24, 1996 currently students at Strafford MO elementary school.

ARTHUR HOWARD BUTLER - Arthur Howard, is the great great grandson of Peter Butler, one of the first settlers of Warren County. Peter came with his family and friends to settle east of Monmouth near Savannah Creek in Coldbrook Township. They were seeking land in the newly opened Military Tract, set aside for pay to the veterans of the Revolutionary and War of 1812. After helping each other build their homes, they built the Christian Church out of nearby hardwood. This was called Butler country since the Stagecoach line from Springfield to Oquawka stopped at the Butler home to change horses and buy a meal.

Arthur Howard Butler

Peter, being the only surveyor in the area was called upon to do this in the new town of Monmouth. When lots were put up for sale, many of the members of the Christian Church purchased them. The community was larger than Monmouth. Later, Peter Butler took a group on the Oregon Trail to the west and settled, built their church and a college that is still in existence. They left behind John M. Butler (1850), the grandfather of Arthur Howard Butler, called Howard, whose father Arthur Hanson Butler and mother Lela May (Allaman) who lived at 1810 110th Street in Monmouth. The farm was left to Howard born 14 July 1932 in Monmouth Hospital. Howard married Luan Doll of Bushnell 1 October 1961. They are the parents of Beverly Tolliver of Highland Village, Texas and Linda Butler of Springfield. They have two granddaughters in Texas. Howard is also a relative of Alexander Tracey, one of the first public school teachers of Monmouth.

Howard attended grade school at Hornbeck District and attended high school at both Kirkwood and Monmouth, graduating in the class of 1950. He is a veteran of the Korean conflict and a member of the American Legion Post. He attends and is active in the First Methodist Church of Monmouth, having served on many committees. He has been a member of the Warren County Farm Bureau and served on its board of Directors as well as Stockland FS (now Riverland). He was elected to the board of directors of McDonough Power Cooperative in 1979 and still serving.

Howard has served as Master of all the Masonic Bodies of the York Rite and was initiated into the "York Cross of Honor", the highest degree administered. He is still serving as Chaplain of his Blue Lodge.

Luan and Howard have now retired and are enjoying their motor home, being able to travel south to Texas to be with their daughters family each winter.

SQUIRE JENKINS BUZAN - S. J. Buzan was born in La Rue County, Kentucky, September 21,1829. La Rue County was named after Jacob La Rue, who was a grandfather of S.J. Buzan.

Mr. Buzan, came with his parents to Monmouth, Illinois in 1831. In 1843, he went to Macomb,

Illinois, where he was engaged as clerk or salesman in the store of N. P. Tinsley until the fall of 1849, when he came to Greenbush and commenced business for himself, running a general store the most of the time up to 1866.

He was married to Mary E. Walker, August 4, 1854. She was born September 25, 1834, and was a daughter of Abner and Jane (Damron) Walker who kept a hotel in Greenbush for many years. To Mr. Buzan and wife the following-named children were born:

Fannie, 1855 died young.

Harry Arthur, born September 4,1856; died February 27, 1879. Carre, 1858 died young. Eva, born March 10, 1860; married Galen B. Anderson, November 12, 1884. She died February 12. 1885. Chauncey, born June 27, 1862. Nellie, born September 1, 1866; married Charles Spooner, October 8, 1902. Frank, born October 6,1870. Pearl, born October 11, 1873; married Frederic W. Kaster, October 10, 1894.

In 1857 Squire and Mary Buzan, became legal guardians for three younger siblings, due to the deaths of Mary's parents; Abner and Jane Walker.

The younger siblings were: Joseph Gilmer Walker, served in Co. E 33rd Illinois Infantry and died in the Civil War. Joseph Kelso Walker, served in Co. H 83rd Illinois Infantry. Mildred Walker, married R.R. Fouke a Civil War Veteran, December 24,1870 in Hiawatha, Kansas.

Squire Buzan operated a General Store in Greenbush until after the Civil War when they moved West. They first settled in Iowa, then Kansas and purchased land in Missouri where they lived out their lives.

Squire J. Buzan, became a prominent businessman and agriculturist in Forrest City, Missouri.

In politics Squire was a Republican; his faith was Presbyterian.

He died at St. Joseph, Missouri, June 30, 1893.

CHARLES AND JOYCE CANNON- Charles and Joyce Cannon with their three children moved to the family farm west of Greenbush in April 1977. They had lived in Greenbush since their marriage August 21, 1965.

Charles Cannon family with Joyce's parents. 24 Nov. 2001

The Cannon farm was the site of the first barn built in Greenbush township and was owned by Wm. Trailor who was the subject of a murder which brought Abraham Lincoln to town to question area residents. Amos Seigler, Charles's great grandfather then purchased the farm and it has been in the Cannon family for over 100 years. The farm then went to John and Laura Seigler Cannon and Charles inherited the farm from his father and mother, William Cleo and Harriet Cannon. Cleo was the only child of John and Laura.

In addition to farming, Charles drove a school bus for several years. He served on the Warren County Farm Bureau Board from 1982 through 1988. He retired from crop fanning in 1986 but has retained his herd of cattle. Joyce taught home economics at Avon High School for several years then served as editor of the Avon Sentinel for 20 years also working 14 years for Acklin Newspaper Group in Abingdon. She retired in 1997.

In 1987 they purchased Herb's Trophies in Abingdon and moved the business to their home. They continue to operate the business today.

Twins, John Glen and Jerry Earl were born January 16, 1968. John holds a B.A. in Agriculture and a Master's Degree in Education from the University of Illinois and presently teaches agriculture at Nauvoo-Colusa High School. Jerry holds a BA and Masters Degree in Meat Sciences from the University of Illinois and Doctorate in Meat Sciences from Colorado State University. He and his wife, Macey, are employed by Hormel in Austin, MN. Karen was born June 23, 1971, and graduated with BS in Hospitality from Western Illinois University. She is married to Jon Johnson and they have two children, Eric, age 6 and Rebecca, age 4. They reside in Canton where Jon is Supervisor of Parks and Karen manages Amerihost Inn in Macomb.

The Cannons are active in the Berwick Baptist Church, Illinois IFYE Alumni Association and have hosted numerous foreign exchange students through the International 4-H Programs. Joyce serves as president of the Warren-Henderson Association of Family and Consumer Sciences along with President of the Berwick Baptist Women's Fellowship and is a past president of Warren County HEA.

ASA CAPPS - Asa Capps was born on 1819 at Warren County (now Edmonson County), KY, sixth of nine children of Lancaster Capps and Nancy Catherine Cox. Lancaster Capps was the descendant of pre-Mayflower settlers of Tidewater Virginia where Capps descendants still live. Lancaster died in 1826 in Kentucky and Nancy Capps remarried first in 1839 to David Cutlip, and after his death in 1844 to Rev. Jesse Moon. The Capps family belonged to Beaverdam Baptist Church, north of Brownsville, and most of Asa's brothers and sisters married there.

1895 Portrait of Asa Capps' children. Front row: Thomas Lancaster Capps b. 1843, Orville Capps b. 1858, Lewis Marion Capps b. 1853, Nancy Capps Perrine b. 1845. Back row: Sarah Jane Capps Ingram b. 1849, John L. Capps b. 1847, Edwin Ruthven Capps b. 1859, Lucy Caroline Capps Jenks b. 1855

In 1840 Asa and his younger brother Jesse traveled to Warren County, IL, on horseback, settling first at Roseville Township. On 30 Dec 1841, Asa married Mary Ann Brooks, daughter of Thomas Brooks and Elizabeth Lee, natives of Kentucky. In 1846, Asa began purchasing land in Lenox Township, eventually amassing 640 acres. Asa also bought land in Iowa. In 1849, Asa's sister Sarah and her husband Rev. John Ray moved to Swan Township, Warren County; in 1874 his brother John S. Capps moved to Roseville but left for Iowa in 1871; and his brother William H. Capps moved to Knox County before 1850 and then to Warren County before 1880.

Asa and Mary Ann Capps had nine children; a daughter Mary E. died in 1866. The other children grew to adulthood and married in Warren County. Thomas Lancaster Capps b. 1843 married Mary Jewell, daughter of Reuben and Elizabeth Johnson Jewell and lived in Lenox Township; Nancy E. Capps b. 1845 married John L. Perrine, son of D.H. and Dorcas Perrine, and moved to Guthrie County, Iowa; John L. Capps b. 1847 married Frances McLaughlin who died young and then to Clarinda Ingram, daughter of George and Lydia Ingram and settled in Guthrie County, Iowa; Sarah Jane Capps b. 1849 married Lorenzo Ingram, son of George and Lydia Ingram, and moved to Madison County, Iowa; Lewis Marion Capps b. 1853 married Ella Eaton and moved to Guthrie County and then Des Moines, Iowa; Lucy Caroline Capps b. 1855 married Warren B. Jenks, son of Erastus and Polly Wilbur Jenks, and lived in Lenox Township; Orville Capps b. 1858 married Minerva Ray, daughter of John and Elizabeth Landis Ray, and lived in Lenox Township, retiring to Dallas, Texas, and Edwin Ruthven Capps b. 1859 married Emma in Iowa, and moved to Kansas and then to Anaconda, Montana.

In 1872 Asa became a member of the Warren County Old Settlers Society. Asa died on 14 December 1877 and was buried at Lenox Union Cemetery. Mary Ann Brooks Capps lived the rest of her life with her son Thomas Lancaster Capps on the home farm. She died 21 January 1895 and all her children returned to Warren County for her funeral. Her obituary writer noted that the average weight of her children was 199 2/3 pounds.

ORTON ALESTE CAPPS - Orton Aleste (O.A.) Capps was born on 08 July 1878 at Lenox Township, Warren County, IL, last child and only son of T.L. Capps and Mary Jewell. O.A. worked the Capps farm with his father, and attended high school and Brown's Business School in Galesburg. He was a fine singer and young man about town.

On 11 January 1905 O.A. Capps married Mary Adaline Ogden, daughter of F.D. Ogden and Harriet Lewis. The Ogdens discouraged the match, going so far as to send Mary to relatives in California, but finally relented, hosting a large wedding at their home in Floyd Township.

O.A. and Mary Capps lived on the Capps farm, where their older children had an idyllic childhood. Like his father, O.A. was an excellent and progressive farmer. His traveling steam tractor "Old Betsey" and equipment was used on neighboring farms. He was said to have inherited the mechanical aptitude of his Jewell relations.

O.A. Capps and Mary (Ogden) Capps

When his father died in 1920, the Capps farm was valued at $650 an acre. O.A. could not afford to purchase enough improved land in Warren County, so he found 800 unimproved acres near Mayville North Dakota and moved his pregnant wife and six children in May of 1920. He had broadcast oats in the snow the previous fall and planted a section of potatoes and 250 evergreens. That fall, he harvested two carloads of Idaho potatoes that he shipped back to Illinois. He was a large, powerful man; his children remember him throwing the 200-pound sacks of potatoes into the boxcars. But in November 1920, he died suddenly of peritonitis. Mary Ogden Capps' brother and sister Asa and Evelyn Ogden came to help operate the farm.

O.A. and Mary Ogden Capps had seven children, the last born after O.A.'s death. Ernest Asa Capps b. 1906, Harold Ogden Capps b. 1907, Mary Elizabeth Capps b. 1908, Evelyn Jeanette Capps b. 1910, Thomas Lewis Capps b. 1913, Caroline Capps b. 1918 and Harriet Ann Capps b. 1920. After the death of their father, the oldest children had to quit school to run the farm. After six years, the boys had had enough and the family sold up, moving to Beloit, Wisconsin, where they found a small farm and the younger children could attend school.

Most of the children remained in Beloit. Ernest married Fae Taylor and worked as a machinist, Harold married Marie Bourne, and moved to Houston, Texas where he had his own machine shop, Elizabeth married Robert MacMaster and was active in the Baptist Church and Beloit College activities, Evelyn married Richard Krull, Thomas married Mary Parrinello then Lavina Jordan and served as a police officer, Caroline married Robert Florey and was active in the Baptist Church and civic affairs, and Harriet married Lloyd Monroe and moved to Hollywood, California.

O.A. and Mary Ogden Capps are buried at Berwick Cemetery, with grave markers designed and cast by their son Harold. Mary is the only Ogden descendant at Berwick not buried in the Ogden plot.

THOMAS LANCASTER CAPPS - Thomas Lancaster Capps was born on 06 June 1843 at Roseville Township, Warren County IL, the oldest of eight children of Asa Capps and Marianne Brooks. T.L. Capps worked the Capps farm in Lenox Township with his father, and attended Abingdon College. After his father's death, the land was divided among the surviving Capps children and T.L. took over the original Capps farmstead. He added to that acreage until he had amassed a farm of 240 acres of prime land.

Thomas Lancaster Capps and Mary Jewell Capps

On 16 September 1866 T.L. Capps married Mary Jewell, daughter of Reuben Jewell and Elizabeth Johnson, at Lenox Union. Reuben Jewell was born in New York, son of Nathaniel Jewell and Elizabeth Crane, a descendant of a long line of pioneers. Mary Jewell was the second of 11 children and was raised in Berwick Township.

T.L. Capps was a splendid farmer, known locally as "Squire Capps." He competed to have the first crops in and the first harvested, and was among the first to employ mechanical farm equipment, including an entire suite of steam-powered machines. Not content to improve the farm operation, he improved the farmhouse; it had a hot air furnace and hot and cold running water in 1903. His son, O.A., installed an acetylene lighting system just a few years later. T.L. served as town supervisor, school director, trustee and tax collector over the years. He was a member of the Odd Fellows.

T.L. and Mary Capps had four children; Minnie Jennie Capps b. 1868 married Milton DeWitt Sprout, son of William Sprout and Catherine Hempt, lived in Packwood, Iowa, and then returned to Monmouth, where they operated an egg farm; Nettle B. Capps b. 1870, died age 17 of consumption, and was buried with her Capps relatives in Lenox Union Cemetery: Ada Caroline Capps b. 1873 m. George 0. Killey, son of William and Isabella Killey, and lived in Monmouth, Orton Aleste Capps b. 1878 married Mary Adaline Ogden, daughter of F.D. and Harriet Lewis Ogden, and worked the home farm until the death of his father.

In 1905, T.L. Capps gave over the operation of the farm to his son O.A. and moved in retirement into Monmouth. He spent much of his retirement on the farm, assisting O.A. He was distressed over the division between his son and daughters and would bring the Capps children to visit their Killey and Sprout cousins while O.A. was working the fields. T.L. died 19 Jan 1919 and was buried at Berwick Cemetery. Mary Jewell Capps lived with her daughter Jennie Sprout in Monmouth until her death in 1922.

JOHN CARLSON - "Happy Birthday, March 17, 1908. I'm healthy and everything is well. Wish you and your family the same." The words carefully inscribed in Swedish, filled the available space of a postcard addressed to "Mr. John Carlson, Mommouth, Ills, Warren Co, RFD 4." The card depicted an impressive mansion in Halmstad, Sweden and the spartan message was from his mother, whom he hadn't seen in 25 years.

John and Hilma Carlson and their children, circa 1900. (L: to R:) Raymond, Arthur, Mande, Harry, Elizabeth, Bessie, Clyde, and Chester.

Born in 1860, in Tronninge parish, in southwestern Sweden's province called Halland, "Jons Peter" was the son of Carl Pearrson and Svenborg Persdotter. He was born at the farm "Paarp number 1 " where his parents were employed as laborers. Five years later John's sister Jenny was born there also. By 1870 John's widowed mother and Jenny were on their own, while 10-year-old John, employed as a farm hand, boarded with his employer.

At age twenty, John was faced with mandatory military service if he remained in Sweden. Opportunities available in America compelled him to emigrate instead. He arrived in Illinois in 1881 and immediately found employment farming in Warren County. Soon he was a self- employed tenant farmer. Eventually he owned and operated his own large, successful farm in Coldbrook township.

John met his wife in Kirkwood. Hilma Johnson, was from Monsteras, Kalmar Lan, in southeastern Sweden's province of Smaland. She was the fifth of seven children born to John Peter Goransson (changed to Johnson when they immigrated in July 1876) and Sarah Lena Nilsdotter. Hilma and John married February 24,1887 at the Lutheran Church in Monmouth. Nine children were born to the couple: Bessie (December 1887); Arthur (December 1888); Elizabeth "Lizzie" (April 1890); Chester "Chet" (June 1891); Harry (September 1893); Raymond (November 1895); Mamie (February 1898), Clyde (May 1900), and Nina (August 1907).

From 1900-1904, the Carlsons were homesteaders engaged in farming outside McCool Junction, York County, Nebraska. This venture was carefully planned and eagerly anticipated. All their worldly possessions, including farm implements, accompanied them as they traveled by train to Nebraska. Although the four-year-endeavor proved successful, John was persuaded by Hilma's urgent desire to return to Illinois.

Back in Warren County the Carlson's farmed near Coldbrook for almost 15 years. Hilma's health deteriorated and she died in 1913 at age 44. Harry succumbed to tuberculosis in August of 1917. Ray was killed in action, September 1918, while serving in France during WWI. Shortly thereafter, John Carlson retired, sold his farm, and moved the girls to a house in Monmouth. Two daughters, Bessie and Nina, remained sngle and cared for their father until his death in 1933.

After serving in WW I, Art married and farmed in Knox County. Clyde made his home in Henderson County. Mamie resided in Roseville with husband Enas Talley and their daughter. Elizabeth married Robert Venard, lived in Monmouth, and was the mother of five children. Chet and wife, Mae Miller, farmed in Warren County and had eight children.

JAMES ARTHUR CARR - James Arthur Carr was born in Warren Co., Ilinois, on 14 Mar 1867. He was a son of James Otho Carr and Martha Pearl Warner, daughter of Daniel H. Warner. He was the ninth of their twelve children. James Arthur Carr's grandparents were Absolom Carr (Jr.) and Sarah (Sally) Claycomb, daughter of Baltzer Claycomb and Catherine Rice. Absolom was an original settler of Warren Co., who came from Breckenridge and Mende Cos., Kentucky and Perry Co., Indiana.

James Arthur Carr

James Arthur Carr married Blanche Emily McGinnis, daughter of William McGinnis and Margaret Hempt, on 18 August 1890 in Holdrege, Phelps Co., Nebraska. Their first child was Boyd Harrison Carr, who was born "on a ranch 4 miles north of Stockville near Curtis", Frontier Co., Nebraska, 15 May 1891. James was a cow rancher and purchased land in Frontier Co. in 1893. James Arthur moved his family to Greeley, Weld Co., Colorado. Boyd had two younger brothers, James Arthur, Jr., born about 1906, and Lloyd Warren, born 23 Apr 1909. James Arthur and Blanche had a grocery store with living accommodations near Estes Park, Colorado, in Rocky Mountain State Park. Backpackers and mountaineers would come to the store to purchase provisions and hear the latest news. They also had several mountain cabins, which they rented out to vacationers.

Their son, Boyd, married Viola Lillian Merrell, daughter of Timothy Marcellus Merrell and Mary Catherine Harrison, 21 Aug 1918, at Norfolk, Virginia. Their children: Blanche Mary, Boyd Harrison, Jr., Helen Lucille, James Marcellus, and Marlin Dwight. Blanche married Joe Brown and had Joe Dansfield Brown. Helen married Arthur Jolley. Helen is a member of the DAR and much of the information about James Arthur Carr came from her; some from her brother, James; and some from their father, Boyd. James Marcellus married twice: first to Esther Helgerson, they had Bonnie Lee and second to Theodora Gleason, they had James, Tanya, Victoria, and Alexander. Theodora married first to Herbert Phiffer had Stella Phiffer. Marlin married Diana Joan Brandy, daughter of Robert John Henry Brandy and Marguerite Joan Stanton. Marguerite married second, Walter Thomas Kelly, Jr. Marlin and Diana have two sons, Christopher and Nicholas.

James Arthur's grandchildren, Helen and James, children of Boyd Carr, remember visiting their grandparents and staying at the store. They remember one incident in which a boulder rolled down the side of the mountain and smashing through the roof of the store. James Arthur and Boyd helped fight a serious forest fire there that threatened many homes. It was about a mile away from the grocery store.

James Arthur Carr died on 15 Oct 1946, in Greeley, Weld Co., Colorado. His wife, Blanche, died in Greeley, at the Greeley Hospital, on 26 April 1936.

CARSON - Come here, Baylee Nichole McKeown, sit on your great Grandpa Carson's lap. I want to tell you about some of your ancestors. This is the year 2002 and you are just two years old. Long, long ago, in the year 1792 a little baby boy was born in North Carolina and was named Andrew Robison. His parents were Robert and Mary (Park) Robison.When he was four years old, his family started moving west. Their first stop was near Dayton, Ohio. Andrew's father fought in the War of 1812. Years later your great great grandpa fought in the First World War and I served in the Second World War. While living in Ohio, Andrew married Nancy Stitt on May 30, 1815. They all moved on west in 1822 and lived in Parke, Indiana. But in 1829 all headed west again by ox team and settled at what came to be known as "Robison's Corner." "Robison's Corner" is three miles east and one-half mile south of the village of Gerlaw, Illinois in Warren County.

Andrew and Nancy were the parents of nine children, the youngest being Milton Columbus Lafayette. We call him Uncle Clum. Andrew and Nancy died at Robison's Corner, Andrew in 1849 and Nancy in 1876. Both are buried in Terpening

Cemetery. After they died Uncle Clum continued to live at the same location. Uncle Clum married a girl, Druzilla, on February, 20, 1860, but on March 1, 1861 both his wife and month old baby, Nancy, died. Now Uncle Clum didn't die till in 1920. All are buried in Terpening Cemetery. A great great great grandson of Andrew and Nancy's, Robert Lee Carson and his family now reside at that location.

Margaret Ann (Robinson) Gardner circa 1880.

Now, Baylee, Andrew and Nancy had a daughter they named Margaret Ann. She is pretty important to the ancestors, as she was the first white girl born in Warren County. She was your great great great great grandma. Her parents, Andrew and Nancy, would have five greats in front of "grandparents."

On May 10, 1853 Margaret Ann married James Gardner and lived her entire life of 88 years within 1 1/2 miles of her birthplace. To this couple were born eight children, including Milton Elvin, who married Laura Ann Ryner. They had a son, Lee, and a daughter, Edith. My Uncle Lee married Anna Mae Anderson and they had a son, Cousin Lowell. Lowell married Marian Jensen and they have three daughters and one son, David. David and his wife, Jean, farm in Kelly Township. Elvin and Laura's daughter, Edith, married Paul Bryan Carson, and they had one son, me, your great grandpa. On Christmas Day 1950, I married Patsy Page. We have three daughters, your Aunt Beverly, Aunt Janice, your grandma Nancy and one son, Uncle Bob. Now, Baylee, this is where you come into the picture. Your grandma Nancy has two daughters and one son. One daughter is Jenny Lee, your Mom.

The Carson name will continue down through the years as your Mom's Uncle Bob and Aunt Susie, have two sons, Gary Lee and Christopher Bryan Carson.

Baylee, as far as we can tell, we have always been farmers. It is a good life.

Andrew, Nancy, Uncle Clum, Druzilla, baby Nancy, Margaret Ann and James are buried in Terpening Cemetery. Milton, Laura, Lee, Anna Mae, Paul and Edith are buried in the Gerlaw Cemetery. *Submitted by Marvin and Patsy Carson*

ADEL BINGHAM CARSON - Adel Bingham Carson was born March 28, 1870 on a farm, SE 1/4 of Section 6, Hale Township, Warren County, to John Newton Carson an Lovina Johnson Carson, both natives of Ohio. They migrated to Warren County in early 1860s and settled in Hale Township. John Newton Carson later purchased another farm in Monmouth Township, NW 1/4 of Section 3, one mile south of Gerlaw and moved his family to this farm in early 1870s.

Adel B. Carson Homestead, Monmouth Township, one mile south of Gerlaw.

Adel Carson was the sixth of seven children and grew up as a young farmer. It was while attending Oskaloosa College, in Oskaloosa, Iowa he met his future wife, Tennie Chaffin Bryan. They were married at the home of her brother, W.H. Bryan in Prairie City, Iowa at noon Christmas day, December 25, 1894. Tennie Bryan was born February 6, 1870 in Marion County, Iowa, to George Theodore Bryan and Jane Hopkins Barger Bryan. The newly married couple returned to Warren County and resided with Mr. Carson's father until their home was completed on an adjoining farm, one mile south of Gerlaw.

Adel and Tennie Carson were parents of seven children all born at their farm home.

The first child, Paul Bryan Carson was born March 15, 1896; followed by George Dale Carson on August 1, 1898; Doris Ellen on July 13, 1901; June Claire on January 15, 1903, died nine months later; Veda Beth February 20, 1904; Leland Keith Carson on May 4, 1908; Adel Bertram Carson Jr. on September 1, 1913.

The Carson family were active, long-time members of Gerlaw Christian Church, Mr. Carson's father was one of the charter members of this church. Adel served many years as an elder and his wife Tennie was a charter member of the missionary society.

Mr. & Mrs. Carson retired from the farm in 1939 to make their home in the village of Gerlaw their remaining lives. Mr. Carson passed away January 19, 1950 and Mrs. Carson passed away November 29, 1953.

Paul Bryan Carson married Edith Coy Gardner October 16, 1922 in Galesburg and resided on a farm east of Gerlaw. They were parents of one son, Marvin Lee Carson born November 6, 1923.

George Dale Carson married Alta Blankenship July 20, 1929 in Detroit, Michigan and made their home there several years before last settling in Mexico, MO. They were parents of four children, George Dale Jr. born March 4, 1930; Phillip Dean born February 21, 1933; Alta Jane born October 16, 1938; Gene Edward born March 16, 1941. Doris Ellen Carson married George Thatcher Haynes May 25, 1921 at the farm home of her parents, and made their home on a farm southwest of Alexis. They were parents of two children, Mary Beth born April 1, 1930 and James Thatcher born August 30, 1932 Veda Beth Carson married Ben Bert Boostrom September 20, 1933 at Nickolasville, KY and first made their home at North Henderson, later settling on her parents farm. No children were born to this union. Leland Keith Carson married Winifred Walters April 12, 1945 in Chicago, after serving many years in the U.S. Army, the Carsons resided in Little York. They had no children.

Adel Bertram Carson Jr. first married Cleo Downer in 1936 in Monmouth and were parents of one son, Willard Neal Carson July 3, 1937. Adel Jr. later married Mary Jane Deschene in 1943 in Chicago. They were parents of four children, Derick Myron born July 31, 1944; Phyllis Rae born April 28, 1950; John Bryan born April 26, 1951 and Tennie Marie born June 10, 1959. Adel Jr. served in the U.S. Army during World War II, upon return resided in Rock Island.

DAVID CUMMINGS AND DOROTHY (KETCHUM) CASTEEL - David (Dave) Cummings Casteel born May 6, 1919 Abingdon, Washington County, Virginia; father David Cummings Casteel born April 27, 1897; died April 19, 1963; adopted son of John and Mary (Litton) Casteel; mother Virginia Alexander (Campbell) Casteel born February 14, 1900; died August 20, 1982;1 daughter of Joseph Trigg and Elizabeth (Snavely) Campbell; came to Warren County about 1921 to a farm southeast of Smithshire. Siblings: Dorothy, Joseph, Mary, Robert, Leroy, Patricia.

Dave and Dorothy Caster, September 1, 1995.

Attended Meridian grade school, graduated Kirkwood High School 1937; farmed with father. Enlisted US Air Force February 12, 1942 serving at Sheppard Field, Texas; Chanute Field, Illinois; Groton, Connecticut; departed overseas August 6, 1942 serving in England, North Africa and Italy, airplane maintenance technician and line chief 301st Bomb Group, 352nd Bomb Squadron, 8th Air Force; returned US March 12, 1945; sent Kirtland Field, New Mexico; discharged June 5, 1945.

The "Dottie Mae" B-17 WWII Italy. M/Sgt. Dave Casteel on ladder.

Dorothy Mae Ketchum born October 23, 1922 Henderson County near Kirkwood; father Frank Martin Ketchum born January 20, 1887; died June 27, 1966; mother Mary Margaret (Swarts) Ketchum born February 12, 1887, died September 22, 1969. (See Ketchum/Swarts)

Moved early 1923 to small farm northwest of Kirkwood. Siblings: Clarence, Lucille, Roy, Hazel, Nannie Belle, Ethel, Robert, Grace, William.

Attended Center Grove grade school, graduated Kirkwood High School 1940; attended Peoria Institute of Business. Worked Muller Insurance-, secretary to Rationing Chief OPA (which set prices and rationed gas, tires, meat, sugar, shoes during WWII), secretary Vice-President Hiram Walkers all Peoria.

They met in high school, began dating 1939. She was honored, having B-17 bomber in his squadron carry her likeness and name "Dottie Mae," flying many missions while the squadron was in Foggia, Italy. Married September 1, 1945, St. Mary's Cathedral, Peoria; resided Peoria, Dave doing wheel alignment J. T. Bower Motors; Dorothy home caring for family. Children:

Thomas Alan born February 22, 1947, married Margaret Mary Gillen January 25, 1969

Sue Christine born August 12, 195 1, married John Charles Chrisman May 12, 1973.

Richard Eugee born October 8, 1952, married Kathleen Ann Fogarty October 19, 1974.

Kathleen Ann born April 7, 1955, married Gary Dean Hoffman May 4, 1974.

Frederick Paul born/died November 9, 1957

Harriet Louise born April 25, 1960.

Moved Des Moines, Iowa 1956; Dave salesman for Sun Electric, later carpenter-, Dorothy waitress various restaurants. Returned Warren county 1961 rural Gerlaw, Monmouth and Coldbrook township. Children attended Des Moines, Warren and Galesburg schools. Dave carpenter for Harry Foust, Carl Nelson; construction superintendent Galesburg and Lundeen Construction companies on commercial buildings in area, including Oak Terrace, DeKalb dryer, WIU dormitories, Galesburg Clinic, Security Savings; raised pheasants. Dorothy gardening, canning, sewing, 4-H leader five years and County Council, worked JoAnn Fabrics.

Retired 1981, full-time RVing, caretakers three summers Young's Lake; worked campgrounds TX, MO, FL, AZ five years. Traveled several years, settled in Florida 1995. Dorothy does oil painting saws, canvas, exhibited Knox Scenic Drive ten years. Dave keeps busy during retirement. Their motto "Keep your hands and your mind busy."

TOM AND PEGGY (GILLEN) CASTEEL - Thomas Alan, son of David Cummings Casteel Jr. and Dorothy Mae (Ketchum) Casteel was born on Februay 22, 1947 in Peoria, Illinois. He is the oldest of five children, with his siblings being Sue Christine, Richard Eugene, Kathleen Ann and Harriet Louise. He attended schools in Des Moines, Iowa; Peoria, Illinois, and Monmouth, Illinois, graduating from Warren High School in 1965. Upon graduation from high school he attended Illinois State University and graduated in 1973 with a Bachelors of Science Degree in Education. Tom was employed as an insurance agent with Country Companies for 18 years, was self-employed in the advertising specialty business for 6 years, and has been employed as a physical education teacher and coach since 1994. He is currently teaching and coaching at Alwood Middle School in Woodhull, Illinois. On January 25, 1969, he married Margaret Mary (Peggy) Gillen at the Immaculate Conception Church in Monmouth. Peggy was born September 15, 1949, the daughter of William E. Gillen and Marian Jean (Engdahl) Gillen. Peggy was the second oldest of six children, her siblings being John Edward, Katherine Rose, William George, Edgar Francis, and Jean Ann. She attended schools in Monmouth, graduating from Warren High School in 1967. She attended Illinois State University for one year. She spent 12 years as a homemaker and stay at home Mom while working some parttime jobs, including typing at home for college students. In 1980 she became employed as a legal secretary and remained in that position for 17 years, having worked for the law firms of Standard and Tenold, Ronald Stombaugh, and James Standard, all located in Monmouth. In 1997 she accepted a position with Community Memorial Hospital, now known as Community Medical Center in Monmouth and has been employed since then as Administrative Assistant to the CEO and Medical Staff Coordinator. Tom and Peggy are the parents of three children: Jeffrey Thomas, born November 14, 1969; Julie Anne, born August 5, 1974; and James Michael born August 18, 1976. Jeffrey married Hollie Hippen on May 6, 2000 and they reside in Monmouth. Jeffrey graduated from Western Illinois University and Hollie graduated from Illinois State University. Julie married Mitchell Russell on June 20, 1998 and they reside in Monmouth. Julie and Mitchell both graduated from Monmouth College. Julie and Mitchell are the parents of Chloe Casteel Russell, born March 17, 2000 and Carter William Russell, born June 21, 2002. James is engaged to be married to Marissa Lozier on August 2, 2003. James graduated from Western Illinois University and his fiance, Marissa Lozier graduated from Monmouth College. Tom and Peggy currently reside at 1126 Kimberly Drive in Monmouth, Illinois

JAMES HUGH CAVANAUGH - Francis J. Cavanaugh came from Ireland, probably during or shortly after the Potato Famine. He had one son, James Hugh Cavanaugh, by his first marriage. James Hugh's mother, Catherine Mills, passed away when he was about a year old. He and his father came west to Warren County when he was quite young. In the 1870 County Census, he was 16, his father was 50 and remarried to a 27-year-old woman, also Catherine. Francis moved to Lenox, Iowa and left his son here with some friends of his. Even though they were of the Protestant faith, they made sure that he got to the Catholic church for services every Sunday.

L: to R: Back row: James Cavanaugh, Margaret Kinney Flanagan, Michael Flanagan, William Gavin, Kathryn Gavin Kinney. Front row: Rose Kinney Cavanaugh, Jane Kinney Stokes, Kathryn Kinney Gavin, Terrence James Kinney

James H. married Roseanna Kinney. Her father and mother were also natives of Ireland, Terrance Kinney and Rose Lenahan, who farmed west of Monmouth. James H. bought a farm in Hale Township on what is now Highway 164, two and a half miles west of Monmouth. They raised eleven children-nine girls and two boys. The two sons, Frank H. and Terrance James, both farmed west of Monmouth.

Frank H. had seven children - Frank M. who founded Cavanaugh Trucking and Bus Service; Bob and Don, who founded Cavanaugh Motors; Dick, who was originally supposed to be one of the founders of Cavanaugh Motors, but was killed during World War II on Luzon, in the Phillipines; George, who is the only one still living, is a retired civil engineer and now lives in Arizona; Rose Marie, who married John Jebb; and Ruth who married Russ Manuel. They are also both deceased.

Terrance James purchased his father's farm west of Monmouth. He married Helen Lee. They had six children - five girls and one boy. Roberta married John O'Brien. Maryrose is married to Bill Sullivan. Delores is married to Joe McCleary. Betty married Dick Shea and Kathleen is married to Richard Rowley.

James Michael Cavanaugh married Rosalie Schmit whose parents were both born in Europe and who both came to the United States after World War 1. After serving in the Army in Southeast Asia, he has been in agriculture equipment sales. He travels in Illinois and Wisconsin as a factory representative, selling grain bins and grain handling equipment. Rosalie is parish secretary at Immaculate Conception Church. They have five children.

Kevin James is married to Michelle Burke and they have three children. Kevin works for the Federal Government and resides with his family in Cedar Rapids, IA. Steven Michael is married to Sandra Ray and they have four children. Steve is the owner of Shamrock Sales and does Ag construction. Raymond Arthur is married to Kathy Guanzon and they have five children. Ray is currently the Warren County Assistant States Attorney. Mary Karen teaches Spanish at Marquette Catholic High School in West Point, IA. Diane Lee is married to Kevin Kavanaugh (spelled with a K) and they have four children. Kevin is an electrician in the Quad City area. Diane is a Registered Nurse and works at Genesis West Hospital in Davenport, IA.

The Cavanaughs came from Ireland. Since most of the C/Kavanaughs came from Southeast, Ireland, it is assumed that this is the area from which Francis J. came. Another note of interest is that in Ireland, almost all the C/Kavanaugh's names were spelled without the "u" - both the "C" Cavanaughs and the "K" Kavanaughs. As many of the Irish immigrants didn't know how to read or write, nobody knows what the true spelling should be. All that is known is that they are all from the same clan.

Apologies are made to the female members of the Cavanaugh family; however, the writer is trying to write solely about the history of the Cavanaughs.

As a footnote to this history, James Hugh married a Kinney and therefore, became a part of the Kinney, Gavin, Gillen, Flanagan and Thompson connection. Old Terrance and Rose Lenahan couldn't have had any ideawhat they started would be a great part of Warren County. (The picture explains this connection.) Submitted by James M. Cavanaugh

GLENN W. AND PATRICIA S. CHAMBERLIN - The Chamberlin family is descended from New England Puritans who moved west on the frontier arriving in Ogle County, Illinois in 1835.

Dr. and Mrs. Glenn Chamberlin family

Glenn W. Chamberlin, born May 26, 1925 in Des Moines, Iowa is a member of the fourth generation in Illinois and is the second of four children born to Glenn Williams Chamberlin and Ethel (Hartsook) Chamberlin. He spent his childhood in Oregon, Illinois and served in the U.S. Army during World War II in the battle of Okinawa, Pacific Theatre, and Korea 1943-1946. He completed pre-medical studies and enrolled at the University of Illinois College of Medicine in Chicago and received a Doctor of Medicine degree in 1952 followed by a Rotating Internship at the University of Indiana General Hospital in Indianapolis, Indiana. He successfully passed the examination for Board Certification in Family Practice and became a Diplomate of the American Board of Family Practice in ceremonies held in New York City in 1970.

He married Patricia Stafford, August 6, 1950, in the Methodist Church in Wedron, Illinois (LaSalle County).

Patricia Stafford was born in Ottawa, Illinois to Roland Walter Stafford and Clotilde (Waltz) Stafford and, is descended from an early Virginia family that moved west, settling in Indiana and finally, in Ottawa, Illinois (LaSalle County). Her great grandfather, John M. Groninger of Camden, Indiana was wounded in the battle of Gettysburg. He survived and lived to age 97.

Patricia studied dancing and performed in musicals and reviews with many of the Big Bands of the era before joining the U.S.O. entertaining U.S. troops in France, Germany, Austria, Pacific Islands, the Philippines, Japan, China and Korea. She was captain of the dancers in the musical "Irene," and in a Variety Unit 1945-1947. She graduated from Northern Illinois University and earned a M.S.Ed. degree from Western Illinois University. She was a member of the Illinois State Medical Society Auxiliary, the Warren County Medical Society Auxiliary, and the First United Methodist Church.

The Chamberlins moved to Monmouth July 5, 1955 (in 105° F. heat) along with children Barbara, three years old, and Cynthia, 10 months. Dr. Chamberlin began his practice of medicine in the Medical Arts Building on South Main Street.

Kenneth E. Ambrose, M.D. joined Dr. Chamberlin in January 1959. They practiced. Family, Medicine in partnership in their new medical office at 219 E. Euclid Avenue for thirty-one years.

Dr. Chamberlin served as Secretary of the Warren County Medical Society from 1957-1991. He was a member of the American, Medical Association and the Illinois State Medical Society as well as the American Academy of Family Practice. He was chief of the Monmoutht Hospital Medical Staff for six years and a member of the Monmouth Medical Club. He was one of the founders of Warren Achievement School and President of the Board of Directors. He also served as a member of the Board of Directors of Monmouth Hospital Home Health Care and was a member of the United Methodist Church, the Veteran of Foreign Wars and the American Legion.

All three Chamberlin children attended Monmouth Schools and were graduates of Drake University in DesMoines, Iowa where their great-great grandfather, Benjamin F. Prunty, was an early member of the Drake University Board of Trustees and President of the University State Bank.

Barbara, born December 28, 1951 in Chicago (Cook County), was one of six women admitted to the first class of Mayo Medical School in 1972. She received a Doctor of Medicine degree in 1976, and married classmate David R. Daugherty of Rochester, Minnesota on April 17, 1976. After completion of a four year residency in Psychiatry at Mayo Clinic and Board Certification, she established the Chamberlin Clinic for Adult Psychiatry in Memphis,, Tennessee. She was a faculty member of the University of Tennessee Medical School Department of Psychiatry before her appointment to Mayo Clinic Department of Psychiatry. She resides in Rochester, Minnesota with her physician husband and their three children, Alicia, Reams and Molly.

Cynthia, born September 4, 1954 in Ottawa, Illinois, (LaSalle County), received Certification from the Katharine Gibbs Secretarial School in Boston, Massachusetts. She was Secretary to the Chancellor of the University of Colorado before her marriage to Scott K. Irish, D.D.S, of Golden, Colorado on August 9. 1980. After earning a Juris Doctorate degree from the University of Denver College of Law in 1983, she was appointed Program Director at the Colorado Department of Banking in Denver, Colorado. She and her husband live in Parker, Colorado with their son, Byron.

John Byron was born August 22, 1958 in the old Monmouth Hospital on East Euclid Avenue. He received a Doctor of Medicine degree from the University of Illinois College of Medicine in 1983. He completed a four year residency in Internal Medicine, and was the head resident at the University of Missouri Medical School Consortium of Hospitals in Kansas City, Missouri. He was Board Certified in Internal Medicine and an Assistant Professor in the Department of Internal Medicine, University of Missouri, Truman Medical Center, Kansas City, Missouri, before joining Midwest Hospital Specialists.

He married Debra Suits, surgical technician, on October 8. 1989. They are the parents of a daughter, Gabrielle, and live near Parkville, a suburb of Kansas City, Missouri.

The Glenn Chamberlin family home in Monmouth was located at 803 East Broadway and was sold to Monmouth College in 1994. Dr. and Mrs. Chamberlin purchased a home at 1110 E. Boston Avenue for their residence in retirement.

DENNIS CHANDLER - Dennis Lee, the third son of Loren William Chandler and Marie Jane (Brownlee) Chandler, was born May 23, 1946 at Monmouth Hospital. They returned home to R.R. Smithshire IL., where his family resided and his father was engaged in farming. Dennis was the third of four boys. Richard and Marshall who were older and a younger brother James. He attended Smithshire school from grade I through 4. The family in 1956 moved to the Berwick IL., area where his father continued farming. Dennis attended Avon Schools grades 5 through 12, where he graduated in 1964. He furthered his education at Browns Business College where he Graduated in 1966. Dennis enlisted in the U.S, Army in 1966 but was honorably discharged for medical reasons. He took flight instruction at Galesburg airport and received his pilots license in 1967.

Dennis Chandler family

Dennis began farming in 1966 with his father and brother Marshall until the death of his father in 1977, he then continued farming with his brother Marshall. As their fanning operations and families grew they decided in 1996 to split up their partnership to farm separately. Marshall now farms with his sons and Dennis farms with his son-in-law.

In 1968 Dennis met Connie Lynn Olson. Connie was born at Monmouth Hospital on August 29, 1948 to the parents of Donald R. Olson and Betty J. (Stotts) Olson. Connie was the 2nd of two children. Her brother Dennis R. Olson (Denny) was two years older. They resided in RR Biggsville IL. Denny and Connie attended Biggsville schools. In 1956 their family moved to Monmouth IL. They then attended Monmouth Schools, where Denny graduated in 1964, and Connie Graduated in 1966. Denny went on to enroll in the Navy Reserves. He was married to Judy Holmberg in 1965 and they had two children daughter Becky and son Chad. Later he became a Firefighter. He served 23 years with the Monmouth Fire department until he died in the line of Duty on March 6, 1993. Connie was employed at Farm King in 1967 until 1968. She then was employed at Montgomery Wards from 1968 to 1973. At which time she became a fulltime mother and assisted her husband in the farming operation.

Dennis and Connie were married on June 18, 1971. They had three children. One son, Jason Dee Chandler, born July 11, 1973, and Twin daughters, Amanda June and Julie Marie Chandler born July 2, 1975. Their son Jason died on July 2, 1983 when he was involved in a tractor accident. Amanda and Julie attended Avon Schools from Kindergarten through 12th grade. They graduated in 1993. Amanda and Julie both attended Western Illinois University. Julie graduated in December 1996 with a major in Ag Business and a minor in Finance and Management. Amanda Graduated in May of 1997 with a major in Finance. On January 11, 1997 Julie married Jeff Emerick of Abingdon IL, and resides outside Abingdon. They have two sons Trenton Dee, born July 27, 1999 and Schuyler Robert, born

September 5, 2001. (For her biography see Emerick) On June 28, 1997 Amanda married Kevin Ross of Kohoka, Missouri and resides outside of Kahoka where Kevin farms with his father and Amanda works part-time at eoples bank. They have two daughters Karlee Marie born April 8, 1999 and Jade Nicole, born July 31, 2001.

Dennis and Connie are members of the Berwick Baptist Church, where Dennis has -served as a Trustee. He was also a Trustee of the Berwick Township. Dennis and Connie reside in R.R. Berwick where Dennis grew up. They both are still actively involved in the farming operation.

LOREN CHANDLER - Loren Chandler was born in Crookston, Minnesota on June 2, 1914 to George Robert Chandler and Kathryn (Bost) Chandler. Marie Jane Brownlee was born in Warren County on June 2, 1916 to Brice Brownlee and Lena (Jones) Brownlee. Loren was one of six children, four boys and two girls. Marie was one of five children, three boys and two girls. Loren and Marie were married on January 30, 1941 in Burlington, Iowa and had four sons.

Chandler family: Jim, Richard, Marie, Loren, Marshall, Dee

Loren and Marie's first son, Richard, was born on April 26, 1942. Richard is a welder and farmer living northwest of Monmouth. He married Susan Hall on November 1, 1964 and they have two children. Peggy was born on May 29, 1968 and married John Perrin of Little York on October 17, 1992. John and Peggy live in Monmouth and have two children, Bradley born on August 12, 1993 and Katie born on February 2, 1995. Richard and Susan's second child, John, was born on November 1, 1974. John married Jodi Sprout on April 13, 1996 and they live in Monmouth with their son Brenton, born on March 21, 2000. Richard and Susan were divorced on June 3, 1978. Richard later married Mildred (Lewis) Feehan on May 13, 1989.

Marshall, Loren and Marie's second son, was born on December 17, 1944. He is a fanner southeast of Berwick. Marshall married Brenda Steele on July 25, 1965 and they have two sons, Courtney and Stacy. Courtney was born on April 28, 1966 and is a farmer. Courtney married Ann Gilfillan of Greenbush on July 8, 1989 and they live south of Roseville with their four children; Augusta born on November 14, 1992, Shelby on December 15, 1993, Wyatt on December 29, 1997 and Ashton on November 8, 1999. Marshall and Brenda's second son, Stacy, was born on September 13, 1967 and also farms. On March 11, 1995, Stacy married Jennifer Moore of Donnellson, Iowa and they live in rural Avon. Marshall and Brenda divorced on March 18, 1974.

Dennis, Loren and Marie's third son, was born on May 23, 1946 and farms southeast of Berwick. Dennis married Connie Olson on June 21, 1971 and they had three children, one boy and twin girls. Their son, Jason, was born on July 11, 1973 and was tragically killed in a tractor accident on July 2, 1983. Twin daughters Amanda and Julie were born on July 2, 1975. Amanda married Kevin Ross from Kahoka, Missouri on June 28, 1997. They live in rural Kahoka with their two daughters, Karlee born on April 8, 1999 and Jade on July 31, 2001. Julie married Jeff Emerick of Abingdon on January 11, 1997 and they live in rural Abingdon with their two sons, Trenton born on July 27, 1999 and Schuyler born on September 5, 2001.

James, Loren and Marie's fourth son, was born on April 23, 1950. He married Doris Downs on August 25, 1969 and they divorced on February 6, 1971. He later married Brenda (Steele) Chandler. Jim and Brenda own a trucking company in Monmouth. Jim never had any children.

Loren Chandler passed away on June 29, 1977. Marie later married Harry Tenhaaf on December 9, 1979. All four of Loren and Mari's sons ere born in and still currently reside in Warren County, Illinois.

REV CHESTER AND EMMA CHANDLER - Emma L. (Peterson) Chandler and the late Rev. Dr. Chester E. Chandler became permanent residents of Monmouth on their retirement in 1976. But their ties to Monmouth and Warren County began long before that as residents of neighboring Mercr County.

Emma was born on Reynolds, Illinois in December 1913 to Effie J. (Baker) and Charles G. Peterson. She is the second generation of this Peterson family to be born in America, her grandmother Peterson having immigrated from Sweden in 1880. Several years after the untimely death of Emma's mother in 1914, Emma moved to the home of her grandmother Emma Peterson in Seaton. She graduated from Seaton High School in 1931.

Chester E. Chandler was born on a farm, between Seaton and Aledo, to Nellie (Johnson) and George G. Chandler in May 1912. Chester was one of the eleventh generation of direct decendants to John Alden, Priscilla Mullins, and Miles Standish of the Mayflower. (In 1953 after years of research, Chester published a book of this genealogy.)

Chester lived on the farm outside of Seaton until graduating from Aledo High School and leaving to attend Monmouth College. He graduated from Monmouth College with an A. B. Degree. He attended McCormick Seminary in Chicago to become a Presbyterian minister, receiving B. D. and Master of Divinity Degrees in 1937. In 1964 he received an honorary Doctorate Degree from Parson's College in Fairfield, Iowa.

Emma and Chester were married in May 1937 with Chester holding a yoked pastorate in the Joy and Millersburg churches. In 1941 they moved to Kirkwood to serve that church. The Chandler's also served the Presbyterian churches in Winfield, Iowa 1947-1966, and Gibson City, Illinois 1966-1976. He worked with scouting and received the Silver Beaver Award in 1950s. After their move to Monmouth in 1976, Chester continued to temporarily fill pulpits in the Monmouth area until his death in 1992. He is buried at Rock Island National Cemetery.

During WWII, Chester served as chaplain in the Army/Air Force in the Burma/China Campaign. He returned in 1946 and continued in the Air Force reserves. He was recalled into active service during the Korean Conflict. He retired a Lt. Col. from the Air Force reserves in 1972.

The Chandlers had two children, both born in Monmouth, George Bernard, born in 1941, and Connie Lea, born in 1947. George Bernard attended Monmouth College for one year before enlisting in the Air Force. He resides in Tigard, Oregon. Connie lives in Creve Coeur, Illinois.

Emma and Chester were always very active in church and community organizations. In Monmouth they belonged to the Heritage Presbyterian Church where Emma is still active. Chester belonged to the Monmouth Lion's Club, the Masonic Lodge, and the Warren County Historical Society. Emma continues to be actively involved in her church choir, the quilting group, and women's circle. She is also active in the United Presbyterian Women's group, the P.E.O. Sisterhood, New Century, and the Warren County Historical Society. She can occasionally be seen as hostess at the Warren County Museum in Roseville. She sees the benefit of preserving the history of Warren County and wishes more of the younger generation would take an interest to show off and preserve this heritage.

CHAPMAN - Samuel and Mary Chapman

Chapman family history in Warren County begins about 1860 when Samuel and Mary (Jones) Chapman moved their family from Licking County, Ohio to Roseville, Warren County, Illinois. Their family consisted of the following children in early 1860:

Melinda, age 22 (married Richard M. Johnson 1860, married Wm. W Harkins 1866, 4 children; Melinda died 1919);

James, age 20 (married Massie Elizabeth Parish 1864 Warren Co IL, married Charlotte Janette Carothers Clark 1885 Monmouth, Warren Co IL, 15-17 childrn; James died 1898);

Dennis, age 17, no further information;

George D., age 16 (married Margaret H. Terry, 1 child [Mary Harriet "Hattie"], married Lucy Edmondson McCormick 1882, 6 children, George D. died 1898);

William, age 14 (died April 1860);

Andrew Spitzer, age 10 (married Alice Scott 1878 Ottumwa IA, 10 children, Andrew Spitzer died 1936);

Anna/Nancy, age 9 (married Fred Beckert 1885, married Frank Godfrey 1923, 2 children, Anna/Nancy died 1935); and

Mary, age 3 (married Charles Hough 1878 Ottumwa IA, married Joseph A. Malin 1911, 1 known child, Mary died 1934).

Two other children were born later: Marion (born about 1860) and Joseph S. (born Sep. 1865 at Swan Creek, married Cora A. Roberts 1888, 10 children, Joseph S. died 1956).

Samuel gave his birthplace as Hampshire, Virginia (later West Virginia). He was born there between 1808-1815. His early life and date of marriage to Mary Jones (born Ohio) are unknown.

He and Mary lived in Licking County OH from before 1840 to 1857/60, when they moved to Warren County IL.

Samuel and his sons James and George D., and possibly Dennis, all fought in the Civil War.

Afer the Civil War, Samuel and Mary lived in Raritan, Henderson Co. IL. They are buried beside each other in the Raritan Cemetery, grave 1, lot 318. Mary died in 1874 and Samuel died 1896; he has a government (Civil War) headstone.

JAMES CHAPMAN - James, Samuel and Mary's eldest son, enlisted in the Civil War in 1861. He was wounded in his first skirmish at Cape Girardeau, MO, when a minie ball entered his face on one side and exited on the other. He was left for dead but survived, and went on to marry twice and father 15-17 children.

James married Massie Elizabeth Parish in 1864. Massie was the daughter of Edward Parish and Massie (Edgington) Parish of Warren County IL (the Parishes were from Youngstown Ohio). Her siblings were: Joshua, Nathan, Mollie, William, and Scott:

Joshua married Sarah Gordon; their children: Edward, Robert, Rachel, Gordon, and Esther (married William Bennett);

Nathan married Hannah Best; their children: Mary Ella (married James Fitzgerald), Andrew (married Rose Huston), Edward, and Wylie;

Mollie married James Huston of Swan Creek.

About 1880, James and Massie Chapman and their young family (Joseph, b. 1868, Rosa b. 1872, Keziah/Kate b. 1873, Esther b. 1876, and Charles b. 1878) left Warren Co. and moved west via wagon to Pottawattamie County, Iowa where they lived with James and Mollie (Parish) Huston of Warren Co IL. Later they continued west to Walla Walla, Washington Territory (somewhere on the journey, an infant son died) and in 1882, James' wife Massie and daughter Rosa died. Disheartened, James brought the remaining four children back to Warren and Henderson counties. In 1885 James married again to Charlotte Janette Carothers Clark and they had 4 children:

Laurel Eva (b. 1885, married John Cyrene 1912, married Charles Norris 1919, 2 children); [Laurel Chapman Norris wrote reminiscences of her early years in Roseville in the early 1900s. These were published in the "Roseville Independent" in 1958. Some of those articles are held by family members and are available upon request.]

Benjamin Harrison "Harry" (b. 1888);

Georga Anna/Mary Georgiana (b. 1889, married Harry Stough 1917, 3 children);

Edward Arlington "Ted", (b. 1896, married Esthol Mae Green, 1 child Martha Carol married Horst Marschall - no further information).

James Chapman, in addition to his war wounds, had tuberculosis (consumption) after the war. He is listed as "farm worker" and "laborer" in the censuses. James died in 1898. He left his wife "Nettie" and their 4 young children, plus the 4 older children of his and Massie's. He is buried in the Roseville cemetery, with a government (Civil War) headstone.

JOSEPH A. CHAPMAN - James and Massie Elizabeth Parish Chapman's first surviving son Joseph Alvero was born in Raritan IL in 1868, baptized in the Methodist- Episcopal church in Raritan by Elder Richard Haney, and graduated from Roseville High School in 1886, Monmouth Collee in 1892 and Garret Biblical Institute in 1895. The first member of his family to go to college, he became a Methodist-Episcopal minister.

In June 1896 Joseph Chapman married Mabel Locke Harrington, eldest daughter of Dr. Henry L. Harrington and Martha Louise Taylor of Little York. Dr. Harrington practiced medicine in Monmouth for many years. He also had tuberculosis, and during one attack was stricken with hemorrhages so severe that he feared he would not survive the night. He called the young couple in and had them married at his bedside. He died two months later and is buried in Monmouth. Dr. Harrington left his wife Martha Louise and four children: Mabel, Grace (married John S. Patton), Paul (married Nellie Johnston), and Marion.

Mabel Locke Harrington Chapman and Rev. Joseph Alvero Chapman, 45th Anniversary in 1941.

Joseph and Mabel Chapman had four children: Joseph Harrington (b. 1897, married Lela B. Bastian); Margaret Louise (b. 1899, married Elmer L. Courtney, married Herbert A. Disney); Theodore (b. 1901, married Delores F. Harlan, married Martha Jean Scott); Grace Elizabeth (b. 1908, married Theodore H. Hoffmann).

Rev. Chapman had pastorates in: Morton and Groveland IL 1895-96, Peoria IL 1897-1900, Pekin IL 1901-02, Ketchikan Alaska 1903-08, Newport KY 1908-09, Herkimer NY 1910-13, Fairbury IL 1914-16, Dwight IL 1917-19, Rock Island IL 1920-28, Quincy IL 1929-34, Winchester IL 1935-37, and Reynolds IL 1938.

Rev. Chapman died in 1942 and is buried in the old Monmouth cemetery beside his wife of 46 years, Mabel Locke Harrington Chapman.

James and Massie Chapman's other children who survived to adulthood and lived in the Monmouth area were Keziah/Kate and Esther:

Kate married Albert ("Little") Gilbert and W.E. Stevens. Kate had at least 3 sons: Roy Gilbert, Donald Montross Gilbert (married Elmyra Morrell), and Robert Scott Gilbert; and one daughter Mildred (married Stanley G. Alcock) who was raised by her sister Esther. Kate is buried in the Roseville cemetery.

Esther Sarah Chapman married Rev. George Wallace Scott, a minister from Morton IL, in 1898. They raised Mildred and Martha Jean, adopted. They later settled in Van Nuys, California.

SUE CHRISTINE (CASTEEL) AND JOHN CHARLES CHRISMAN - Sue Christine (Casteel) Chrisman born August 12,1951 St. Francis Hospital, Peoria, Illinois.

Parents: David Cummings and Dorothy (Ketchum) Casteel.

Siblings: Thomas, Richard, Kathleen, Frederick and Harriet.

Schools: Pope Pius X, Des Moines, Iowa 1957-1961 (1st-4th grade) Warren School, Monmouth, Illinois 1961-1966 (4th-9th grade) Galesburg High School, Galesburg, Illinois 1966-1969 (Graduated) Illinois State University, Normal, Illinois 1969-1973 (B.S. in Education) Rollins College, Winter Park, Florida 1982-1984 (MBA studies) NOVA Southeastern University, Winter Park, Florida 2002 (MBA studies)

Met John Charles Chrisman of Aurora, Illinois at Illinois State University in November 1969. Married May 12, 1973 Immaculate Conception Church, Monmouth, Illinois. Honeymooned at Caneel Bay Plantation, St. John, V.I.

John and Sue first livedin Aurora, Illinois. John worked for General Mills, Inc. in West Chicago. Sue was a substitute teacher. In February 1974, they moved to Minneapolis, Minnesota. John worked in the General Mills home office. Sue worked for Nationwide Trucking Company. In July 1974, they purchased first home in Maple Plain, Minnesota. Sue began employment in the General Mills Corporate Accounting Department in 1977.

In December 1977, they transferred to Orlando, Florida. John worked in the Quality Assurance Department for Red Lobster (General Mills subsidiary). Sue joined CNA Insurance Company in September 1978 as an accounting clerk. She began their Claim Adjuster Trainee program in 1979 progressing through the ranks to Claim Specialist by 1984.

John and Sue Chrisman

In 1984, they transferred to St. Louis, Missouri then Columbus, Ohio returning to Orlando in July 1985. During this period, Sue did not work. John worked for various General Mills Restaurant Subsidiaries.

Sue returned to CNA Insurance in July 1985. Sue has managed increasingly complex claim system projects since 1986. In 1998 and 1999, she was temporarily assigned to the CNA Insurance home offices in Chicago, Illinois to manage a major Y2K project.

In February 2001, John transferred to Singapore on a one-year assignment to manage the seafood quality program in Asia. He traveled extensively throughout Asia during this year.

John celebrated 30 years with General Mills/Darden Restaurants in 2001. Upon his return from Singapore, he was named Director International Seafood Quality. Sue has been employed by CNA Insurance Company for 20+ years. She is now the Manager of Claim Systems for the CNA Group Operations Division in Maitland, Florida.

John and Sue became interested in Figure Skating in 1992. They try to attend a major competition every year. They also enjoy collecting antiques, particularly Tea Leaf Ironstone. They are members of the Tea Leaf Club International and have attended every National Convention since 1989. John is currently the club Vice President.

John and Sue have traveled extensively. They particularly enjoyed their Australia/New Zealand Millennium Cruise. They make it a point to return to Caneel Bay Plantation every 5 years. They own a timeshare at South Seas Plantation, Captiva Island, Florida where they have vacationed almost every September since 1980. In 1999, they began another vacation tradition when they purchased a cabin at Lake Warren.

CHARLES E. AND JENNIFER J. (WELTY) CLARK - Jennifer Jean (Welty) Clark, daughter of Allen Melvin Welty and Betty Jean (Lusk) Welty was born June 3, 1950 in Monmouth Hospital at 515 East Euclid Ave. Monmouth, IL. Jennifer married Charles Edward Clark born June 22, 1945 the son of Lyle Simpson Clark and Helen Leola (Lenz) Clark. Jennifer and Charles were married April 13, 1969 at the United Presbyterian Church at 302 East Broadway Monmouth, Illinois.

Charles E. and Jennifer J. Clark 1997

They have four children; Marla Jean Clark married Rob Parker from San Antonio, Texas. They have together five sons; Wade; Austin; Jared; Noah and Luke.

Kaila Jo Clark has a daughter Margaret Mae Daley. Marla and Kaila's families now live in Alaska.

Twins sons; Seth Edward and Jonathan Alan Clark still live in the area.

Charles has worked for the BNSF Railroad for 34 years. Jennifer has worked for Butler Manufacturing Company for 10 years. Together they live on a small acreage south of Galesburg, Illinois where they raise Angus cattle and play with quarter horses, cats, dogs, rabbits and an emu, a perfect place for grand kids. As retirement grows near, they hope to have more time for their hobbies of gardening, auctions and remodeling houses and always making plans for visits from grandchildren.

DAVID REID AND BARBARA (BOULTON) CLARK - Clark, David Reid, son of Dr. Marvin E. and Dorothy (Reid) Clark, was born in Urbana, Illinois, on 26 June 1946, the oldest of six children. The Clark family arrived in Warren County in 1948, when his father became he Assistant Farm Advisor for Warren County. The family left in 1949 for Ames, Iowa, where David's father earned his degree in Veterinary Medicine at Iowa State University and returned to Monmouth in 1952 to start his practice. Along with his five siblings, Howard, Dennis, Gregory, Michael and Marlene, David attended Warren High School and graduated in 1964.

In April of 1966, David enlisted in the United States Marine Corps and served in the Eleventh Marine Regiment, First Marine Division, in the Republic of Vietnam from October 1966 to November 1967. He was promoted meritoriously three times and attained the rank of Corporal. He served in the Chu Lai and DaNang areas in the artillery. He was awarded the First Marine Division Commander General's Certificate of Commendation for outstanding performance of duty while serving with his regiment and the First Marine Division was awarded the Presidential Unit Citation for extraordinary heroism and outstanding performance of duty in action against enemy forces. He was honorably discharged in 1972.

David Reid Clark Family

David majored in Sociology and graduated with honors from Southern Illinois University in 1971, received his Master of Science in Administration of Justice from SIU with high honors in 1972, and earned his Juris Doctorate from the University of Iowa in 1975.

The year of 1975 proved to be an important one in David's life; not only did he receive his law degree that year, but he was also married on the 27th of December to Barbara June Boulton. On 18 May 1978, David and Barbara's first child, Adrienne Renee, was born. Their only son, Morgan Reid, was born on 20 April 1980. Three years later, on 4 July 1983, their third child, Meredith Anne, was born.

David's interests are not limited only to the field of law; he is a sports enthusiast and, along with his wife, Barbara, is highly involved in the Monmouth community. In 1993, David founded the Monmouth Shooting Stars girls basketball program, of which he is the Director and has served as a coach. Meredith's varsity team finished in the Sweet Sixteen in 2000 and Elite Eight in 2001. He is also active in the Veterans of Foreign Wars, American Legion, and the First Christian Church. David has received the Monmouth Community Service Award (1995), and is a frequent speaker at Memorial Day and Veteran's Day ceremonies. He served as the President of the Warren County War Memorial Foundation, which was responsible for the creation of the Warren County War Memorial at the Warren County Courthouse dedicated on 25 May 1998. In 1999, David was presented with the Dad of the Year award by the University of Iowa.

Barbara June Boulton Clark was born in Fayette, Iowa, and graduated from the University of Iowa (B.S.) in 1973 and University of Iowa College of Medicine Physician Assistant Program in 1975. In the first group of Physician Assistants licensed in the State of Illinois in 1976, she has worked in Family Practice and Obstetrics/Gynecology. She is currently in practice with Daniel K. Piper, M.D. and Jeffrey C. Koszczuk, D.O., with offices in Monmouth and Galesburg. She has served as President of the Illinois Academy of Physician Assistants and on the first Governor's PA Advisory Committee to the State Medical Licensing Board. She also served as the President of the Association of PA's in OB/GYN and the American Academy of Physician Assistants Liaison to American College of Obstetrician/Gynecologists. She was also the first PA to be elected to the National Association of Reproductive Health Professionals Board of Directors in 2001.

Barbara served on District 38 Board of Education and was elected President in 2001. She also served on the Maple City Community Concert Series Board and is a member of AAUW, PEO (Chapter E), Ecumenical Singers and the First Christian Church. Their three children, Adrienne Renee ('96), Morgan Reid ('98) and Meredith Anne ('01) all attended Monmouth High School and all three served as Student Body Presidents. Adrienne and Meredith were both Homecoming Queens. Adrienne graduated from the University of Iowa ('00) and serves on staff with Campus Crusade for Christ Ministries at the University of Minnesota. Morgan attends Harrington Institute of Design, Chicago, and Meredith attends the University of Illinois, Champaign/Urbana.

In addition to raising their own three children, the Clarks have also been a host family for four Youth For Understanding High School Exchange Students: Eric Mulder (Holland), Amanda Gebauere (Latvia), Benjamin Greifenberg (Germany), and Amanda's brother, Rolands Gebauere (Latvia).

Since October, 1977, the Clark family has resided at 400 East Broadway, Monmouth, a Queen Anne-Tudor style home built in 1894 by William S. Weir, Jr., a wealthy industrialist. In August of 1992, the home was placed on the National Register of Historic Places.

GERALD L. AND BEVERLY (SPROUT) CLARK - Clark, Gerald L, oldest son of James W. and Ada Snyder Clark, was born, March 13, 1933 in Monmouth, Ill. Gerald and his younger brother, Dean, now live in the Rozetta area. Gerald attended Hazel Dell grade school and Bggsville high school. Gerald has been engaged in farming since 8th grade, renting land from a neighbor. In May 6, 1956, Gerald married Beverly D. Sprout, daughter of Orrin E. and Leona Peterson Sprout, at the Fairview Center E.U.B. Church in Rural Monmouth. Beverly, attended Warren County grade schools, graduating from Monmouth High School in 1955. She worked at the National Bank of Monmouth in the bookkeeping department, for a year and a half. August of 1956, Gerald was drafted into the U.S. Army. He spent one and a half years in Ludwigsburg, Germany. Beverly joined him for fourteen months. Traveling to 10 different countries while being stationed there.

Beverly and Gerald Clark December 1999

After returning home from Germany in August of 1958, Gerald and Beverly, resumed farming the same farm, they had been farming for several years. Their first born son Bradley D. Clark was born October 17, 1958, graduated from Union HS, attended Carl Sandburg in Galesburg. Married Nancy Kruse, in August 5, 1981, parents of Christopher, attending, Stanford University, in California. Megan, freshman at Union HS. Son, Brian L. Clark, born November 15, 1961, graduated from Union HS. attended Kirkwood Jr. College in Cedar Rapids, Iowa. Married Melinda Stoutt, on August 8, 1987, parents of Miranda a 6th grader and Jared, a 4th grader at Union grade school. Daughter, Brenda K. born, October 24, 1964. Graduated from Bradley University in Peoria, with a BSN. Going to Baylor Medical Center in Dallas, TX, as a orthopedic nurse. She now is in Sales for Abbott Laboratories in Dallas area. Youngest son, Brandon J. born January 20, 1975 married Mindy Brinton, June 2000. Parents of Payton Danielle born New Years Eve 2000. Brandon works for Hend-Co Hogs.

Gerald has farmed all his life in the Rozetta area. His sons are now in partnership with him. Raising hogs for many years, farrow to finish. Gerald has been a member of the Rozetta Baptist church for 52 years. Serving as trustee, and several other boards. A member of the Warren-Henderson Farm Bureau, serving as board member. Helped organize the Henderson County Pork Producers.

Beverly is a member of the Rozetta Baptist Church, teaching Sunday School for 24 years. Involved in the Sunday School programs for many of those years. Is one of two ladies who now cook for the Senior Citizens group at the church, "Shining Stars". She enjoys her grandchildren, growing flowers, feeding birds, and genealogy. Is a member or the Warren Co. Genealogical Society, has served as Pres., secretary and editor of their quarterly.

In 1964 they bought the farm that they had started up farming, living there for 39 years. In January of 1995 bought a home on Route 94, 10 miles west of Monmouth., where they are now residing. Son, Bradley, lives on the family farm.

ARNOLD AND RUTH CLAYTON - Arnold Eugene - the oldest son of Clifford O. and Eunice B. (Andrews) was born in Cameron, Illinois on December 18, 1926. He has five brothers and three sisters. They are Charles, Richard, Melvin, Bonnie, Maurine, Carl Dean, James and Madelyn. He spent his childhood in Cameron attending Cameron Grade School. He graduated from Galesburg High School with the Class of '44. Arnold joined the U.S. Navy in March of 1944 and was discharged in June of 1946. Arnold later attended Browns Business College and studied business and accounting.

Arnold and Ruth Clayton

Summers he worked on the Youngquist Farms and during the school year at Strand Bakeries and Butler Manufacturing Company. After his discharge he worked as a baker at the Scandia Bakery in Galesburg. For a short time he worked as a mechanic at Burlington Truck Lines. In September of 1947, he was employed as a truck driver for Willis Steel Corporation. They were wholesale distributors of building materials, wire products, and furnaces and heating equipment. After graduation from Browns Business College, Arnold became assistant to the sales manager at Willis Steel. Beginning in 1950 he became a territory salesman selling their products to lumberyards, hardware stores, and heating and sheet metal contractors. Early in 1955 he was given the opportunity to specialize in the sales of heating and air conditioning for residential and small commercial systems. At this time he attended the Milwaukee School of Engineering to study refrigeration and air conditioning systems. His customers were to be limited to heating, air conditioning and sheet metal contractors. In 1959 he accepted the position of manager of the warm air heating and air conditioning department at May Company in Galesburg. They were distributors of plumbing equipment and industrial supplies with a branch warehouse in Moline, Illinois. In 1968 the May Company built a new branch warehouse in Princeton, Illinois and Arnold was appointed to be its manager. In 1974 he was promoted to vice-president of marketing and was responsible for all three branch operations. In 1980 Arnold purchased the Princeton branch warehouse from the May Company. The Princeton warehouse was operated as the A/C Plumbing and Heating Supply until the beginning of 1987. Arnold was then employed by Faber Motors as rental and leasing manager, as well as used -car manager. At the end of 1900, Arnold retired from Faber Motors.

At the time of Arnold's retirement, he had been elected to serve on the Bureau County Board. During his term, from 1990 to 1995, he served as County Board Chairman for two years. In 1995 Arnold was elected to a four-year term as Mayor of the City of Princeton.

Arnold married J. Irene Wenstrom in May of 1947. Two children were born to them: Karen S. and Barry E. In 1982 Arnold married Ruth Eckard who had two children, G. Whitney and Quinta. Ruth was employed by the LCN Division of Ingersoll-Rand Company in Princeton as an executive assistant to the president and general manager.

During his years of residence in Princeton, he has been active in St. Matthews Lutheran Church, the Elks Lodge, Industrial Golf League, Princeton Business Boosters Club, Woodcrafters Club, and Senior Golf League. His past years of retirement have been devoted to his hobbies of golf, woodworking and antique cars.

CARL DEAN CLAYTON - Carl Dean Clayton was born the seventh child of Clifford Orville and Eunice Bernice (Andrews) Clayton Cameron, Warren County Illinois on July 22, 1938. His family moved to Monmouth, Warren County, Illinois in the summer of 1943. He attended Central grade school, Central Junior High School and Monmouth High School, graduating in 1956.

He worked at the Monmouth Country Club from 1951 through 1956. In October 1956, he enlisted in the Air Force. After basic training at Lackland AFB and technical school at March AFB in Riverside, California, where he was trained as a Radio Intercept Analyst.

After graduating from technical school, he was assigned duties at the following locations: Templehof AB, Berlin,Germany, Darmstadt, Germany, Lakenheath AB, England, Sumter, S.C. , Hampton, Va., Taipei, Taiwon, NORAD, Colorado Springs, Co., Tan Sohn Nhut AB, Vietnam, Zweibrucken AB, Germany, and Luke AFB, Glendale, AZ. He retired as a Msgt. on April 1, 1977.

After attending college, he was employed by the Arizona Department of Revenue. He started as a payroll clerk and progressed to bingo enforcement Auditor, supervisor of bingo licensing and enforcement, Sales tax auditor I, II, III and a short stint as temporary Sales Tax Audit Supervisor. In January 1994, he retired again and is now living the life of a country squire.

He married Gisela Eva Baumann of Darmstadt, Germany. They have a daughter Corinna Angela and a son Jeffrey Dean and they have given them six grandchildren. He spends his time gardening, watching TV and working on this #$%^ computer. " What has my heart is volunteering for the local Salvation Army Corps, helping the less fortunate in our local communities."

JAMES CLIFFORD CLAYTON - James Clifford, the eighth child of Clifford Orville Clayton and Eunice Bernice (Andrews) Clayton. His grandparents were Orville Owen Clayton and Lynda Landon Clayton of Warren County. Great-Grandson of Wiley Clayton and Artamisha (Ray) Clayton of Edmonson County, Kentucky.

Jim and Bev Clayton 1987 in Tennessee

Jim was first child of his family to be born in a hospital at Cottage Hospital, Galesburg, Illinois, on February 28, 1941. He lived in Cameron, Illinois until the age of three. Moved to Monmouth, Illinois in 1944.

Jim worked at Western Illinois Ice Company, Standard Oil Gas Station on South Main Street while attending Monmouth High School. Butler Manufacturing in Galesburg, Illinois before joining the military service.

Entered the Army on November 2, 1959, took basic training at Ft. Leonard Wood, Missouri. Second eight weeks training was at Headquarters Battery 2nd GM, BN , Ft. Bliss, TX, February 26, 1960. Ordered for overseas movement April 25, 1961. Depart Ft. Dix, New Jersey, July 14, 1961 on USNS Patch destination Bremerhaven, Germany. Final destination Co B, 2nd BG, 38th US. Inf., 3rd Inf. Div. Schweinft, Germany. Discharged November 4, 1962 at Ft. Hamilton, New York.

Gained employment as a switchman on December 22, 1962 with Chicago, Burlington & Quincy Railroad (merged Burlington Northern Railroad June 1970-merged again Burlington Northern Santa Fe Railroad September 1995). Promoted to Yardmaster October of 1968 to April 1977. Promoted to Conductor June 3 of 1989. Was selected by Galesburg Terminal employees as "Employee of the Month (April-June) 1997". Retired January 31, 2002 after 39 years of service.

Met Beverly Ann Swartz on September 17, 1959, daughter of Allan Clifford Swartz and Kathryn Joy (Kenan) Swartz. Beverly was born May 2, 1941 at the Cottage Hospital, Galesburg, Illinois. Jim and Bev were married March 17, 1963 in Galesburg, Illinois at the First Lutheran Church. To the union was born a daughter, Jamie Ann and a son, James Clifford.

After their marriage, they lived in Galesburg, Illinois until 1973. At that time they moved into their new home in Knoxville, Illinois. Then in 1976 they constructed another new home, in the same area, doing much of the work themselves, at which time they still reside.

ORVILLE O. CLAYTON - Orville O. was born in Berwick Township, Warren County, Illinois, on April 12, 1857. He was the son of Wiley and Artamisha (Ray) Clayton and the great-grandson of Augustine Clayton.

Laura May Clayton Carl, Lydia Ann Laudon Clayton, Lissie June Clayton Howard, Clifford Orville Clayton, Orville Owen Clayton, and Wylie Melvin Clayton.

He married Lydia Landon on February 2, 1892 in Warren County, Illinois. They had three sons, Wylie, Clifford, and Wilmer; two daughters, Laura and Lissie.

Following their marriage they lived in Berwick, later moving to Coldbrook Township, Warren County, Illinois. In 1919 they moved to Caeron, Illinois to make their home until their deaths. Lydia died March 3, 1934 and Orville died July 23, 1935. They are buried in the Berwick Cemetery, Berwick, Illinois.

Most of Orville's active life was spent on the farm. He had a great love for horses and was respected for his knowledge of horses.

RICHARD LEE CLAYTON - Richard Lee was born April 4, 1930. He was the third child, out of nine children of Clifford and Eunice Clayton. He grew up in Cameron and attended school there through the eighth grade. As a young boy, he had a paper route with about 12 subscribers (Chicago Daily News) and when he was 10 years old, he would work in the summer time on a hay bailer, balling hay, for about four summers.

In the summer of 1944, they moved to Monmouth, Illinois because of a job change of his father, who worked for the CB&Q railroad. He attended Monmouth High School for two years and worked part time at Woolworth's Dime Store and later for the Review Atlas paper.

The summer of 1947, he started working full time on the M&STL railroad and in the fall of that year was laid off for the winter. He then went to work at the Chevrolet Garage until March 1948, at which time he went back to work on the railroad. He didn't stay there long, because on April 7, 1948 he joined the Air Force.

Richard Lee Clayton

In September 1951, while stationed at Carswell AFB in Fort Worth, Texas, he married Eleanor S. Hillis, she was his mate and best friend for 42 years. She passed away on December 9, 1993. They had three children, the oldest, Cathy Horton of Arlington, Texas, Nancy Vanderwall of Jenison, Michigan, and Richard Jr. of Pierpont, Ohio. Of the three, only Richard gave them three beautiful granddaughters. They are his pride and joy.

He made a career in the Air Force, on June 30, 1970, he retired from the Air Force with over 22 years of service. They made their home in Fort Worth, Texas. He went to work for the Post Office in February 1973 as a clerk at the Main Mail Processing Center. After working for over 22 years, he retired from the Post Office in November 1995. He has over 45 years of Government service, he is now what you would call a triple dipper.

"Life is one's own makin, looking back over mine, I've had a good life, family and friends and I wouldn't change any part of it."

WILLIAM AND NANCY (McINTYRE) CLAYTON - William Leroy (Bill) Clayton and Nancy Ann McIntyre began their life together on September 2, 1966, in Monmouth, IL. Bill is the son of Harold Leroy and Minnie Marguarette (Ortery) Clayton. He was born on September 5, 1943, in Monmouth. Nancy is the daughter of John Edward and Phyllis Katherine (Stromire) McIntrye. She was born July 6, 1947, in Monmouth. Bill and Nancy have lived at 404 South 6th Street, Monmouth, since May, 1969. They are parents of two sons. Todd Alan, born August 9, 1968. Todd married Rebecca S. (Toops) June 9, 1990, in Monmouth. They have three children: John Lucas born February 18, 1992; Hannah Marie born October 30, 1995; and Sarah Elizabeth born December 7, 1997. They reside in Galesburg, IL. Their second son, Chad Michael Clayton was born February 20, 1972, in Monmouth. Chad married Angela D. Brand, November 24, 2001, and have a daughter Cassandra D. Ellison, born May 26, 1995, in Kahoka, Missouri, and are expecting their first child together this summer.

Bill's mother (Minnie) was born October 20, 1912, in Drake, North Dakota, and raised in Monmouth. Minnie was one of thirteen children. She will be ninety years old this October and lives in her home at 1015 West 4th Avenue, Monmouth. Bill's Father was Harold L. (Olie) Clayton and was born July 7,1905, in Clearfield, Iowa, and was one of four children. He later moved to Monmouth and operated a corn shelling business. Phyllis Katherine Stromire was born August 28, 1921, in Little York, IL. The daughter of Amzie Ray and Maude (Kishline) Stromire. Phyllis was the first of two daughters born to the Stromires. John Edward McIntyre was the only child born to Arch and Tillie (Foreman) McIntyre on December 10, 1918, in Monmouth. John and Phyllis lived in Peoria, IL, until 1945 then moved to Monmouth and built their home where they raised their two daughters. Phyllis currently lives at 603 North G Street, Monmouth. Nancy graduated from Warren High School then attended Brown's Business School and Carl Sandburg College. Nancy worked one year at Warren County Service Company, then accepted a deputy clerk position for Warren County Circuit clerk, Roger Johnson and later Beverly Davis for a total of twenty eight years. In 1994 Nancy was Republican Candidate for Warren County Treasurer. She took office as Treasurer and Collector December 1, 1994, and is serving her third term.

William and Nancy Clayton

Bill graduated from Monmouth High School. In 1962 he became employed at Admiral in Galesburg, during which time he served six years in the National Guard. He worked as a truck driver for Miller Trucking, then accepted a position with Mayrath Industries for twelve years. In 1990 Bill started work at Well's Pet Food in Monmouth, where he is presently employed.

Bill and Nancy are doing some traveling on vacations and playing golf. They enjoy having their mothers living in Monmouth and having their children and grandchildren close.

DON AND MARILYN (HENNENFENT) CLUTE - Don Clute was born March 6, 1932 in a country home in Mercer County near Alexis, Illinois, and Marilyn Hennenfent was born December 12, 1931, married in 1957, at the Norwood Presbyterian Church. Their only child is Patricia Jane, who married Tony Helms, June 15, 1991 and lives at Greer, South Carolina, with her husband and daughter, Tiffany Erin. Janie is a nurse that is employed by the state of South Carolina.

Don's parents were Lee Clute (1898-1970) and Ruth (Donaldson) Clute (1905-1983), married in 1928 and both were from the Alexis area. Don was the only child born to Lee and Ruth. His maternal grandparents are Eli and Susan Emma (Cater) Donaldson. His paternal grandparents are James and Lucy Belle (Landon) Clute. He attended Star and Union Grade School, Alexis High School, and graduated from Western Illinois University. For 34 years Don taught in the Aledo School District, retiring in 1994.

Marilyn was the first child born to Charles (Chick) (1903-1979) and Hazel (Simpson) Hennenfent (1905-1979), married in 1928 at

Norwood. Her maternal grandparents are Charles and Margaret (Bennett) Simpson. Margaret Bennett came from Ohio to work for the Miller family, near Alexis. This is where she met Charles Simpson and they were married. Their only child was Hazel, who married "the boy next door" that had come to work on the farm for a family friend. Marilyn's paternal grandparents were Barney and Svena Hennenfent from Monmouth. Barney came from France/Germany to this country, met Svena Frank and they were married. Charles was one of nine children born to this union. Those children were a deceased baby, Kathryn (Arthur) Martin, Margaret (Arthur) Johnson, Florence (Rex) Simpson, Anna (Luther) Haines, Frank (Gladys) Hennenfent, William (Mabel) Hennenfent (Charles twin), and John (Dorothy) Hennenfent.

Marilyn and Don Clute

Dean Hennenfent is Marilyn's only sibling. He is a farmer, who lives next to her. Dean has two daughters-Kerry, a marine biologist who lives in St. Petersburg, Florida and Cristin, who is an accountant in Naperville.

Marilyn's schooling included Lone Star Grade School, Alexis High School, Western Illinois University and University of Illinois. She taught school for over 40 years starting at Duck Creek's one room school, at ROWVA, at Winola, at Rock Island, and finishing her career at Sherrard in 1994.

Since retiring from teaching Marilyn and Don have renovated and sold seven older homes.

In 1960 the Clutes built their home and now spend time trying to "keep up" with the grass and weeds in the back yard around the lake that was built in 1995.

CLARENCE WILBERT (BILL) COCHRAN

- Clarence Wilbert (Bill) Cochran was born in June 1923, the only child of James Wilbert Cochran and Naomi Godfrey Cochran, Bill attended Kirkwood Grade School and Kirkwood High School. In 1942, he was attending Bradley Polytechnic Institute in Peoria, Illinois when he enlisted in the U.S. Army during World War II. He served in the Finance Section in New Guinea until 1946 at which time he returned to Bradley University, graduating in 1948 with a Bachelor of Science.

In August of 1946 Bill Cochran and Jane Menely were married in the First Methodist Church in Monmouth. From this marriage came three daughters; Jan Marie Johnson born in 1948, Cathy Ann Daily in 1951, and Karen Sue Logan born in 1952. All three were born in Peoria, Illinois, but the Cochrans moved to Kirkwood in 1956 where all three girls graduated from Yorkwood High School, Jan graduated from Western Illinois University, Cathy from Iowa Wesleyan College and Karen from Illinois State. They all three became teachers.

Bill Cochran and his dad.

Bill spent the rest of his life as an accountant in the Warren County area. He also served as Tompkins Township Supervisor and Treasurer and Board Member of the Kirkwood United Methodist Church.

In 1963 Bill and a friend, Maurice Lee, made the walnut, lighted cross that hangs in the front of the Kirkwood Methodist Church sanctuary.

CHARLES AND MARIELLA (BRIDE) COLCLASURE

- Charles A. Colclasure was born April 11, 1927 in Monmouth, Illinois. His parents were Charles J. and Estellene (McClellan) Colclasure and they resided in Mercer County. The senior Charles Colclasure came from Xenia, Illinois to Mercer County and married Estellene McClellan in October, 1913 at Sunbeam, near Aledo. Charles A. Colclasure attended various grade schools throughout Illinois as his father was employed by the State Highway Department installing guard rails along Illinois highways. Later the family returned to the Monmouth area where they farmed in Lenox Township. Charles graduated from Monmouth High School in 1945. He served in the U.S. Coast Guard from 1946- 1949, and upon his return to Monmouth he farmed with his father in Lenox Township until the time of his fathers death in January of 1959. He moved to the family farm in 1963 where he continued to farm until his own death on October 1, 1995. Charles also worked as a union carpenter for most of that period. He married Mariella Bride on October 26, 1950 in Monmouth.

Mariella Bride was born on September 20, 1928 to James and Helen (O'Brien) Bride of Cork Street in Kelly Township near Alexis. Mariella's descendants of the Bride family immigrated from County Cork, Ireland in the 1840s to Connecticut and her greatgrandfather came to Warren County and purchased land on Cork Street in Kelly Township where the family farmed until 1936. Some of this same land is still owned and operated by family members. Mariella's parents moved to the Monmouth area in 1936, later to the Roseville area in 1938. Mariella attended country grade schools, Picayune and South Henderson. She attended Roseville High School and graduated from St. Mary's Academy in Nauvoo in 1946. She and Charles A. Colclasure were the parents of five children all born at Monmouth Hospital.

Thomas E. Colclasure was born January 16, 1952. Tom married Yolette Louquet in Maryland on December 7, 1996 where they reside. Tom is retired from World Bank of Washington, D.C.

J.C. Colclasure was born January 14, 1953 and lives on and operates the family farm in Lenox Township. He is employed at Twomey Company in Smithshire, Illinois. J.C. also farms in several other locations in Warren County and has a cow and calf herd.

Charlene Colclasure was born on November 11, 1955. Charlene married Lucian Burt of Denver, Colorado on September 26, 1987 in Monmouth. They reside in Wheat Ridge, Colorado with their two children, Connor (May 19, 1990) and Cori (August 9, 1994). Charlene is employed at Lutheran Medical Center as a Physical Therapy Assistant.

Mark V. Colclasure was born on December 1, 1957. Mark married Joni Twomey at St. Patrick's Church in Raritan on April 30, 1983. He is a Country Companies insurance agent in Monmouth. They reside in rural Roseville with their three children, Alexandra (October 6, 1984), Emily (October 16, 1986), and Joseph (May 8, 1995).

Tad J. Colclasure was born on September 8, 1961 and died September 10, 1961.

Mariella worked as a bookkeeper for many years at Monmouth Hospital, Jerden Plumbing & Heating, and finally Maple City Steel Supply. She is now retired and moved to Monmouth from the farm in 1998.

MICHAEL AND MARY ELIZABETH MCANALLY COLLINS

- In 1855 the Collins family, emigrants of Counties Donegal and Antrim, Ireland, settled in Roseville Township on the 160 acres granted to Patrick Herring for service in the War of 1812. The land grant was signed by President James Monroe in 1817. This deed was purchased by Patrick Collins of New York City for $75.00 who subsequently gave it to his brother Michael, then living in Nova Scotia. Michael (born 1799 - died 26 March 1874) and Mary Elizabeth (born 12 May 1797 - died 16 January 1868) were parents of John and Mary.

John and Rose McFarland Collins Family L: to R: Back row: Mary Collins Henderson, Ellen Collins Barry, and Josephine Collins Tierney. Middle row: Anna Collins Crowe, John Collins, Rose McFarland Collins, and Elizabeth Philomena Collins Hanlin. Front row: Agnes Collins Huston, John Peter Collins, and Teresa Gertrude Collins Costello.

Their first home was a log cabin. They farmed with oxen and later with teams of horses. Homesteading in Illinois was difficult work for Michael because in his native country he was a weaver of paisley shawls. After a few years, Michael moved his family into a house he had built which had one large room and two bedrooms.

John Collins married Rose Anna McFarland at St. Augustine Catholic Church on 3 June 1866.

Rose Anna's parents were John (born February 1794 - died 5 July 1865) and Rose Anna Rice McFarland (died 15 August 1845 in County Louth, Ireland). After the death of his wife, John McFarland and children sailed to North America when Rose Anna was nearly three, landing at Boston in 1847. Their next move was to Pittsburgh. When relocating to a farm in Illinois, they traveled on the Ohio, Mississippi, and Illinois Rivers to Coopers Landing near Peoria. Their long journey ended with a stage coach ride to St. Augustine. Rose Anna attended Lincoln school in Berwick Township, and a Catholic school in Morris, Illinois.

John (born 24 December 1825 - died 11 July 1909) and Rose Anna McFarland Collins (born 15 August 1845 - died 26 May 1921) were parents of nine children: Rose Anna (Crow), Elizabeth (Hanlin), Mary (Henderson), Michael William, Ellen (Barry), Josephine (Tierney), Agnes (Huston), Teresa Gertrude (Costello), and John Peter.

Everyone assisted with the farm work, growing corn, small grains and hay, raising poultry, and gardening. Their livestock consisted of horses, hogs, sheep, and milk cows.

In 1890 their home was enlarged by building a two-story addition with a living room and bedroom downstairs and three bedrooms upstairs. The children attended Center School in Roseville Township. After that, the eldest daughter, Anna attended St. Joseph's Boarding School, Evansville, Indiana, but she became very homesick and did not enroll again.

Gertrude Collins Costello recalled traveling to Monmouth in a wagon pulled by a team of horses. In the spring of the year the dirt roads were muddy and deeply rutted. She said they felt sorry for the farmers living along Highway 67, south of Monmouth, because the land was wet and difficult to farm. After tiling, these farms proved very productive.

Over the years the Collins family prospered and owned eight farms, five in Roseville Township and three in the Russell and Abilene, Kansas areas. The Collins burial plot is in St. Augustine Catholic Cemetery.

CHESTER ELLISON CONNER - Chester Ellison, born at Phillipstown, White County, Illinois on November 15, 1877, son of George H. and Sytha (Graham) Conner. 3 October, 1900 he was married at Coldbrook to Lena May Young. They had a foster daughter Dorothy Elkipton of Del Paso Heights, California. He had three brothers, Oscar, Owen, and George, and one sister Clarissa. Chester attended high school at Carmi and was ordained to the Christian ministry there 11 July 1897.

His first pastorate was at Coldbrook Christian Church when he first came to Warren County at 19. He later graduated from Drake University Law School at Des Moines, Iowa. His admittance to practice law in Iowa took place 1900, six years later in Illinois. He was a member of the Warren County Bar Association and the Monmouth Ministerial Association.

He held pastorates a period of years in a number of churches in both states. In later years he devoted his time to lecturing schools, service clubs, and other groups. While serving with the YMCA overseas following World War I he took many historic pictures, which were a source of pleasure to him in later. His lectures dealt principally with Lincoln and Washington.

Reverend Chester and Sytha established their first home at Sheridan, Iowa, for five years before they moved to Galesburg for fifteen years before coming to Monmouth in 1920. They resided in their present home at 311 East 2nd Avenue until Chester passed away from a stroke April 23, 1949. He had been in failing health for four years. He was buried in Mosher cemetery. His wife survived him many years.

In later years he became a collector of unpaid bills to increase his income. His cheerfulness at all times was an inspiration to all who knew him.

LYLE AND FRANCES CONWAY FAMILY - Dorothy Frances Smith was born at home in Lenox Township, Warren County to David R. and Sena Elizabeth Ray Smith on June 21, 1915. Both of her parents were natives of Lenox Township, Warren County. Sena was the daughter of Hiram Edward Ray and Delia Jane Eaton Ray. Only three years old during World War 1, she would put a dish towel over her head and say "I'm a Cross Red nurse." On October 14, 1918, her twin brothers were born, David Clete and Ray Edward. Frances attended Windy Ridge School, only 40 rods from her home.

In the spring and summer her father taught Frances how to farm with horses and to do other chores.

Frances Conway

On April 5, 1930, Frances was baptized at the Berwick Baptist Church which had been built by some of her ancestors. The very cold water in the baptistery was blamed for the pneumonia and pleurisy that she developed and which required round-the-clock nursing by Vada Brooks and house calls by Dr. Ralph Graham.

Upon entering Monmouth High School she rented a room in town during the week, returning to her home on weekends. She graduated in 1934.

The following September she entered nurses' training at the Methodist Hospital in Peoria. The following March, she had to leave because of illness. She returned the next fall, but after two months the doctor said she would have to quit.

After a recuperation period, she was able to work at Ford Hopkins Drug Store in Monmouth for $8.00 a week - her room rent was $4.00 a week. Several nights she went to bed hungry.

Later she worked for Illinois Bankers Insurance Company at $65.00 a month.

Frances met Lyle Conway when her father hired him to help with the farm work. She was immediately smitten with him. After nine years of dating they were married in Clinton, Iowa on December 25, 1937. The marriage was kept secret during the Depression married women were not allowed to work. The following September 16, her mother invited all the family to

their home and introduced them as "Mr. and Mrs. Lyle Conway." After a dinner was served at the Hawcock Restaurant in Monmouth, the guests visited the new home on the John Gibson farm a quarter mile south of Nemo, IL.

James Douglas was born to this union on April 6, 1943. That same spring the couple bought a farm in Roseville Township and moved there. Gary Morse was born April 25, 1946. The boys attended a rural school until the schools were consolidated. Then they attended Roseville schools until graduation from Roseville High School.

After her marriage Frances was active in school and community affairs. She was Sunday School Superintendent for the Berwick Baptist Church for sixteen years, taught Bible School for seventeen years, and now is serving as a deacon.

For 63 years she has belonged to the Home and Community Education Organization.

She worked at the original Monmouth Hospital for one and a half years, and later worked for Dr. Mannon for twelve years.

In 1996 she became a volunteer for the Community Medical Center in Monmouth.

Lyle died on April 25, 1998. The next spring Frances moved to 1455 East Broadway in Monmouth where she enjoys her hobbies of sewing, china painting, knitting, piecing quilts, and making and dressing porcelain dolls.

James was first married to Mary Kay Goettsch in August 1977 in Davenport, Iowa. Later he married Barbara J. Clark in San Ramon, CA.

Gary married Lynn Alice Liebenthal on December 30, 1967, in La Grange, IL.

HAROLD "BINGO" COOK - Cook, Harold "Bingo," son of Ernie from the Gladstone area, where Bingo was born. Ernie managed lumber companies in Aledo and Warfield's in Monmouth, while his mother was a valued employee in the laundry of Monmouth City Hospital. His sister Shirley moved to Kewanee.

Bingo worked for Rankin & Shaub Grocery all during high school - butchering and grinding meat. Drew Rankin, being an ex-football player saw to it that he had time off to anchor the line as a tackle on Monmouth's championship team. He married Mary Anne Massey. They had two boys, John and Douglas. He was called back to serve in the Korean Conflict, returning to Rankin & Shaub before they closed. Drew recommended him to Bud Barnes and Bob Rawson of Barnes Super Valu, where he worked as manager and trainer of personnel for twenty years. His hobby was buying rundown homes and remodeling them. He sold them all at high market price. He told Bud he wanted two requests during his lifetime; one beautiful wife, the other to retire at forty. At 45 he retired to Sarasota, Florida in 1976 where he had two more sons, Aaron and Brian, both living in Sarasota and losing John, his eldest by suicide. Douglas married with two children living in Chattanooga, Tennessee. While in Florida, Bingo kept busy working as janitor at McDonalds and helping his neighbor, who was hired by "Sunbirds" to ready their homes for winter. Anne took the reality board and began selling homes.

Bingo was a Kiwanian and forty year member of the American Legion. Bingo represented Barnes Bros. by working full time on Kiwanis Pancake Day, taking care they had meat, groceries, utensils and plates. and whatever else they needed, while Bud worked in his place at the store. He owned a restored red Volkswagon that he drove to work. He also used it for errands around town gathering the needed materials for his rental properties. He did this after his eight hour day, when he jumped into his working clothes - usually wearing a pair of shorts. He joined a Volkswagon club that met as a group to visit towns here and there.

Anne became obcessed with antiques and they enjoyed going to auctions. They were buying so many antiques that Bingo built a red barn next to the boys playhouse to store it. He later became the supply person for the McBride's Antique House north of Monmouth. He was a master at selling junk for big money.

At work he set his own hours and was told he was to always receive the highest wages of any meat cutter in town. He attended and was welcome at any policy meeting in town. He retired at 45, when his oldest son, John, got in trouble with the police about something. At Sarasota, Florida, John got mad at someone and took a maul to his car - shortly afterwards we heard he had committed suicide.

He and Anne rode donkeys down the Grand Canyon one vacation. He relatives were at New Orleans where a sister lived. Her husband was the National Commander of the VFW one year, another sister married Dan Hayes, who moved to Monmouth and ran a cleaners. He and Bingo bought a trailer camp in Oquawka for pennies - fixed it up - and sold it for dollars. He joined Monmouth Masons Lodge #37 and Royal Arch #30, keeping his membership active. In Florida he joined the Shrine. He was the best friend I ever had. He left this world at the age of 66 on the 8 March 1996.

THEODORE AND JEAN COOPER - Theodore E. Cooper was born in Bald Bluff Township, Henderson County, IL on January 27, 1925, the youngest child of Lenard E. and Gertrude (Waugh) Cooper. Ted has two sisters, Frances A. Cooper Oaks and Ruby J. Cooper Garland. Grandparents were John C. and Anna (Thieme) Cooper and Orvill K. and Lula (Moore) Waugh. Ted attended Bald Bluff Grade School and graduated from Little York High School in May, 1943.

M. Jean Cooper was born July 18, 1926 in Ohio Grove Township, Mercer County, IL the second child of three born to John Leo and Theo (Darrah) Perrin. Grandparents were Arthur D. and Carrie (Stevens) Perrin and William W. and Sarah (Fair) Darrah. Jean has a sister, Marian L. Kneen and a brother John L. Perrin. Jean attended Duck Creek Grade School and graduated from Little York High School in May, 1944.

Ted and Jean were married September 22, 1946 in the Fall Creek United Methodist Church, Henderson County, IL. They are the parents of three children. Phillip K. Cooper, residing in Little York, IL, Mark D. Cooper, residing in Phoenix, AZ, and Terri Lynn Cooper, residing in Glendale, AZ.

Ted farmed with his father after finishing High School and until his marriage. For four years, he worked for other farmers in Warren County, returning again to farm for his father for one year. He farmed for himself until 1973. He worked for Central Feed and Produce for nearly five years, and then attained work with the State of Illinois as a Highway Maintainer. He retired from this work in December 1991

After graduating from High School, Jean worked for the Kissinger Insurance Agency and later in the office of Veternarian Dr. Roy B. Price. After raising their family, she worked part time in the ASCS Office in Aledo, IL and later became employed at the First State Bank of Little York, IL where she worked for nearly twenty years, retiring in December, 1991.

Ted and Jean joined the Cedar Creek Presbyterian Church in 1955. That Church later merged with Little York Presbyterian Church becoming known as Little Cedar Presbyterian Church where the couple are still active members. Ted has served as Trustee and as an Ordained Elder. Jean served as Church Organist for twenty years, and is still serving as Substitute Organist. She has also served as an Ordained Elder and Clerk of the Session.

In 1977 the Coopers purchased a home on West Harlem Ave. Extended, now known as 200th Ave., Monmouth, IL, where they still reside. After retiring both became active Volunteers for Community Medical Center.

CORNELIUS ELWOOD CORZATT - Cornelius Elwood was the forth child of five born to Samuel Elwood, born August 21, 1855 and died June 16, 1922 and Mary Gertrude Brokaw born January 19, 1860 and died August 21, 1937. They lived one-half mile North of Raritan, Illinois Henderson County. They went to School and the Reformed Church in Raritan. Cornelius was born June 16, 1896 and died September 15, 1987, and Married November 3, 1925 to Hazel Maurine Lofftus born September 15, 1903, and died October 14, 1991.

Cornelius and Hazel Corzatt

They bought a farm four mile Northeast of Roseville, where they called home and raised their family. "Neal" was his nick-name, made a lot of improvements on the farm. Building all new farm buildings as well as a house. He always had more work lined up to do than he could get done. He feed cattle out, raised hogs, and always milked several cows, had a flock of chickens, and sheep. Samuel Elwoods father was John Corzatt born January 16, 1812, and died July 5, 1877 and Mother Elizabeth Bogard born May 16, 1814 and died May 28, 1893, they married January 14, 1833 and came from Hunterton County, New Jersey. Settled near Canton Illinois, Fulton County. They moved their family to the Raritan community and soon were leaders in the community, Two sons Peter T. and Manning Force Corzatt died in the civil war, Manning is buried near Canton. Mary was a seamstress and Elwood raised French Coach Horses, swine and crops. They are buried in Raritan Cemetery Henderson County, Illinois. Neal and Hazel have four children Evelyn born June 3, 1927, married Cecil Shimmin and they had five children, Lynn, Randal, Bruce, Celia and Ann. Carol born December 21, 1928 and died October 29, 1990. She married Clyde Kneen, and they have four children, Lila, Krista, Sharla and Karita. Max born June, 21, 1930, married Erva Mohr, and they have Jeffrey and Bradley. Marie born December 18, 1933 and married Richard Walker and they have Tina Lou and Roger Lee.

HAZEL (LOFFTUS) CORZATT - Hazel Lofftus Corzatt born September 15, 1903, the daughter of Kenton Azro Lofftus born October 23, 1873 and died January 26, 1953, and Bertha Ann Torrance, born August 26, 1874 and died November 3, 1952. Kenton and James Lofftus lived in the same house in Point Pleasant Township, and they married Torrance sisters Bertha and Laura. and lived together their entire life. When the banks closed in the 1920s they were instrumental in keeping the Raritan State Bank open, and used some of their own resources to do so. They feed cattle and raised hogs and corn and beans, oats and clover. They had horses, a flock of chickens, and milk cows. They were spoken of highly and were officers in the county and township. Kentons father was Andrew Jackson Lofftus born January 16, 1815 and died September 19, 1878 and Lavina Meacham born in Christian County, Kentucky, February 26, 1822 died March 8, 1894. Bertha's father was Charles Torrance eighth child of sixteen, born November 17, 1834. He came to Warren County in 1858 married Margaret Hindman born January 18, 1844 in Green County Indiana, and died November 13, 1895, and they had five children, one died as a infant. Charles set out with others for Pike's Peak, making the trip with ox-teams. But being disappointed in finding riches they returned to the rich farm land. His parents Riley born May 13, 1801 at Bennington Vt. and Lydia born February 5, 1804 at Plattsburg, New York. They came to live out their lives with Charles. Lydia died, October 27, 1873, and Riley died May 28, 1874, and they are buried in the Raritan Cemetery, Henderson County Illinois. After Margaret's death Charles married Mary Watson, after a time they went to live in California. they had a son Charles Jr. when he was around eight he got scraped up from falling off a grape cart and the wounds became infected and Charles and son Charles Jr. are buried in the same grave in Fresno, California.

JOHN MYLES AND VERA CARMEN COSTELLO - John Myles Costello, son of Miles 'Ted' and Teresa Gertrude Collins Costello, was born in Monmouth on 29 April 1907. He attended Immaculate Conception Catholic School in Monmouth and Carr School in Roseville Township. Myles and Vera Carmen Johnson were married on 14 August 1934 in St. Augustine. They farmed the Collins land in Roseville Township until 1951 when they purchased a farm formerly owned by Lester and Vesper Crane in Section 35, Lenox Township. Myles died 25 March 1957.

Carmen was born 18 April 1908 in Swan Township. Her parents were Orion Leon and Alezanna White Johnson. She attended Downey School and graduated from Roseville High School. Graduating from Knox College in June 1930, her first teaching position was in the Avon High School where she taught Latin and English. In the following twenty-five years she taught in various elementary schools including Stem School, Roseville Township; Alexis School; Enterprise and Windy Ridge Schools, Lenox Township. She was Principal of and teacher in the Berwick School. Following that she taught in the

Schaumburg School District, Schaumburg, Illinois, and in the Immaculate Conception Catholic School, Monmouth.

John Myles Costello 1955 *Vera Carmen Johnson Costello 1955*

After her retirement she was active in the Warren County Historical Society, assisting in establishing the Warren County Historical Museum in the former Roseville High School. She was a member of the Illinois State Teachers' Association and the Mutual Benefit Club, a neighborhood club of which her mother was a lifetime member. Carmen was named Woman of the Year in Warren County in 1980. She died 20 July 1997. The Costello burial plot is in St. Augustine Cemetery.

Myles and Carmen were active members of St. Augustine Catholic Church. Their two daughters are Mary Ruth and Carmen Anne.

After graduating from Monmouth High School, Mary Ruth attended Marycrest College, Davenport. In 1955 she married George Raphael Starr in St. Augustine Catholic Church. Their daughter Catherine Marie married John Young. Catherine earned an M.S. in Library Science and is employed as a Computer Librarian.

Mary Ruth earned a degree in Business and Social Sciences and also a Doctor of Jurisprudence Degree. She is owner/broker of Pear Land Properties, Inc. and serves as Director in the Texas Association of Realtors. She is active in the Women's League of Voters.

Anne attended the University of Illinois, and in 1961 married William Ray Martin in St. Augustine Catholic Church. Bill graduated from the Oklahoma State University, Stillwater, Oklahoma. He is president of the Perry State Banks in Northeast Missouri. Their three sons are Gregory Kent, William Ray and Michael John Martin.

Gregory graduated from the University of Missouri. He married Janice Marie Tepen in 1984, and they are parents of Tyler Patrick and Kathryn Anne.

After graduating from the Oklahoma State University, William 'Bill' married Stephanie Kim Long in 1986. Their three children are Travis Alan, Julia Anne, and Jenifer Leigh.

Michael attended the University of Missouri, Columbia, Missouri. He and Mary Ann Edwards were married in 1988, and they are parents of twin girls, Claire Amarilla and Laine Colette.

MILES ARNOLD AND BRIDGET BURNS FOLEY COSTELLO - Miles and Bridget, early residents of Monmouth, were parents of one son Miles 'Ted', and two daughters, Margaret Costello Chapin and Nelle Costello. Miles Arnold was born in 1846 in Lancaster, England of Irish parents. Working as a cabin boy on a ship, he eventually emigrated to the United States. He enlisted in and served in the Union Navy 24 February 1863 to 31 March 1864 on the U. S. S. Western World and the U. S. S. Coeur De Lion. These ships were on blockade duty in Chesapeake Bay during the Civil War. After being honorably discharged from service, Miles moved to Monmouth to join his older brother, Thomas. Their parents were James and Margaret Blake Costello of County Mayo, Ireland. Miles Arnold died 17 May 1912. He and Bridget (born 1844-died 6 July 1884) are buried in the Monmouth City Cemetery.

After the death of Bridget, Miles Arnold married Alice Day. Four sons were born to this union: George Arnold, James, Fred, and Ralph Eugene Costello.

Miles Arnold Costello born 1846 Lancaster, England, Irish descent U. S. Navy Civil War died May 17, 1912.

Miles was employed as a stationary engineer at the Three M Tile Works, later known as Maple City Pottery and then Western Stoneware. For his midday lunch, he would take along a piece of beef steak and cook it on the furnace at the plant. His half-brother Christopher Foley was merchant policeman in Monmouth for twenty-two years. Chris carried a loaded gun in a holster and his trained dog walked with him. He, along with others, helped save the lives of fifteen men who were trapped in a burning mine at the Three M plant in 1890.

Miles 'Ted' was born 6 October 1879 - died 20 February 1943. He served in the U.S. Army in Cuba in 1898 with the Illinois Volunteer Infantry, Sixth Regiment, Company H, during the Spanish-American War. He was an Alderman for the city of Monmouth and married Teresa Gertrude Collins of Roseville Township on 24 July 1906 at St. Augustine Catholic Church. Their attendants were John Collins and Nellie Kane. The couple resided in Monmouth where Miles was an employee of the Maple City Pottery. For a number of years, he along with his brother-in-law, Guy Chapin operated 'The Cuban', a cigar store and billiard room. They also sold candy and ice cream and as one old-timer recalled, "It was a good place to go for an ice cream cone on a hot day." Miles and Gertrude were parents of John Myles, Elizabeth Rosemary (Paulson), Joseph Collins, Gertrude Alanna, and Paul Michael. They were members of Immaculate Conception Catholic Church.

In 1919 the family moved to the Collins farm in Roseville Township where they farmed 320 acres. While living here they were members of St. Augustine Catholic Church. The children attended Carr School, St. Mary's Academy and St. Ambrose.

In 1928 the parents and four children relocated to Fort Madison, Iowa where Miles was employed as a Guard First Class at the Iowa State Penitentiary. Three of the children were employees of W. A. Sheaffer Pen Co. The oldest son, John Myles married Vera Carmen Johnson and farmed in Warren County until his death 25 March 1957. They were the parents of two daughters, Mary Ruth Costello Starr and Carmen Anne Costello Martin.

PAUL MICHAEL AND JEANETTE M. COSTELLO - Paul and Jeanette have resided in Warren County since 1946. Mike's parents were Miles 'Ted' and Teresa Gertrude Collins Costello. His paternal grandparents were Miles Arnold and Bridget Burns Foley Costello; paternal great grandparents were James and Margaret Blake Costello. Maternal grandparents were John and Rose Anna McFarland Collins, and maternal great grandparents were John and Rose Anna Rice McFarland. Except for his parents, all were emigrants from Ireland.

Patrick, Charlyn, Mark, Kathleen, Daniel. Parents: Jeanette M. Costello and Paul Michael Costello.

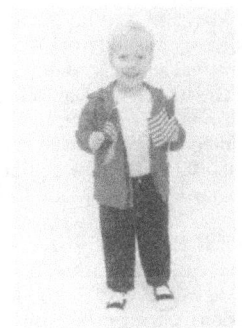

Joseph Miles Costello - three years old youngest grandson of Mr. and Mrs. Paul Michael Costello

Mike was born in Monmouth, IL, 11 October 1918. He graduated from St. Joseph's Catholic School in Fort Madison, Iowa and was employed in the War Department in Washington, D.C. In January 1942 he enlisted in the Naval Reserves, serving in WWII until September 1945. An Aviation Radioman and Gunner in Squadron VS 58, he spent twenty months in the New Hebrides Islands. In 1945 he married Jeanette Martha Boeding of West Point, Iowa and began farming the Collins land in Roseville Township. Now retired from farming and from Gates Rubber Company, he is a fifty-six year member of Roseville's American Legion, and Monmouth's Knights of Columbus. The Costellos are one of six generations who have been members of St.

Augustine Catholic Church. Mike and Jeanette have lived on farms in Roseville and Lenox Townships since 1953 and are parents of five children who attended Berwick, Roseville, and Warren schools.

Jeanette's parents were Herman Edward and Mary Adelaide Holtkamp Boeding. Paternal grandparents were Johann Heinrich and Elizabeth Boecker Boeding; paternal great grandfather Franz Xavier Boeding emigrated from Neuenkirchen, Germany. Maternal grandparents were John and Mary Adelaide Ostdiek Holtkamp. Maternal great grandparents Heinrich and Mary Sand Holtkamp and Ferdinand and Anna Catherina Schnitker Ostdiek emigrated from Westphalia, Germany.

Mark Joseph graduated from the U.S. Coast Guard Academy in 1968 and served twenty-two years in the Coast Guard. He commanded a LORAN Station in Thailand during the Vietnam War. Mark holds an Unlimited Master's License in the U.S. Merchant Marines. He married Rita May Olin in 1989.

Charlyn Mary graduated from Western Illinois University in 1969 and received an M.S. from the University of Illinois in 1970. She married Dean Stanley Canada in 1979. Their daughter Collins Mary attends Williams College. Charlyn is director of the Eagle Valley Library District in Colorado.

Agnes Kathleen graduated from Western Illinois University in 1973 and received an M.S. from the University of Illinois in 1974. She married John Michael Chandler in 1985. Their daughters are Vashti Madeline, Eleanor Marie, and Rosemary Celeste. Kathleen is director of the Pitkin County Library, Aspen, Colorado.

Daniel John graduated from the U.S. Naval Academy in 1978. He served until 1984 flying an A-7E Corsair II from the U.S. S. Eisenhower. Dan married Kimberley Renee Hartley in 1990 and is currently a Captain with Southwest Airlines. Their children are Michael William, Alanna Nell, Emily Margaret, and Joseph Miles.

Patrick Lee graduated from Western Illinois University in 1980 and was commissioned as an Ensign in the U. S. Naval Reserves. An Anti-Submarine Warfare pilot, Pat flew the P-3 Orion and served in the Persian Gulf War in 1991. He retired in 1997 and is now a pilot for United Airlines. He married Debra Marie Roob in 1988.

GLENN WESLEY COURSEY - Glenn was born in Point Pleasant Township, Warren County, Illinois on August 25, 1901. His parents were Thomas Marion Coursey (1874-1967) and Lettie Jane Aulgur (1878-1967).

Glenn Wesley Coursey 90th birthday - Mr. Odd Fellow

He attended various rural Elementary Schools, Roseville High School and Gem City Business College at Quincy, Illinois.

He married Bertha A. "DeWitt" Thompson on October 30, 1932, Bertha was born on December 6, 1897, her parents were P. H. DeWitt and Anna Thompson. She was adopted by Oliver and Eliza Thompson, I am not sure but I believe they were her aunt and uncle. They moved to Macomb, McDonough County, Illinois in 1933 and lived there the remainder of their lives. They had no children.

Glenn joined the Postal Service and later became a railroad mail clerk and retired from that profession. Glenn joined the Odd Fellows Lodge 537 at Roseville in 1925 and transferred his membership to the Macomb Lodge in 1933. He was dedicated to the organization in that he held most if not all of the local and state offices over the years. He was a member of the Grand Lodge and was appointed district deputy grand master of District 50 in 1953. He served on the Grand Lodge Endowment Fund Committee since 1966 and was treasurer of the Grand Lodge of Illinois from 1971 to 1987. He was a member of the International Order of Odd Fellows Housing Inc. and served on the Odd Fellows Children's Home Board for five years.

He was a member of Rebekah Lodge 342, He served on the resident council of the Macomb Nursing and Rehabilitation Center and the resident advisory board of the Everly House in Macomb. He was awarded the Meritorious Service Jewel and was named honorary past grand master and grand treasurer emeritus.

Bertha died on August 20, 1984 and Glenn on February 19, 1992. They are both buried in Oakwood Cemetery in Macomb, Illinois. Submitted by Richard W. Coursey Feb. 26, 2002.

HAROLD FAYE COURSEY - Harold was born in Point Pleasant Township, Warren County, Illinois on February 5, 1904. His parents were Thomas Marion Coursey (1874-1967) and Lettie Jane Aulgur (1878-1967). He attended various rural Elementary Schools and Roseville High School.

Harold Faye Coursey High School Graduation 1922.

He married Erma Grace Hendrix April 19, 1930. Erma was born May 8, 1909 at Industry, McDonough County, Illinois, her parents were James Richard "Tine" Hendrix (1873-1961) and Anna May McMillan (1878-1957). Harold and Erma were married at Detroit, Wayne County, Michigan, where he was working at the time. They returned to Monmouth, Illinois where he worked for the Illinois Highway Dept. Maintenance Garage. They then lived at Camp Point, Adams County, Illinois, a short time where they ran a grocery store. They then lived in Browning, Schuyler County, Illinois where Erma died on August 15, 1940.

They had 3 children: Joanne born July 23, 1931 at Monmouth, Warren County, Illinois, and died April 20, 1960 at Monticello, Piatt County, Illinois, where she was involved in a car train accident. She is buried in Memorial Park Cemetery at Monmouth, Illinois; Richard Wayne born February 23, 1934 at Monmouth, Illinois and presently resides in the Fort Madison Iowa area; Larry Thomas born August 10, 1935 at Browning, Illinois and presently resides in the Biggsville, Henderson County, Illinois area. Harold married Snoda Mae "Bence" Gulick June 22,1943 at Wayland, Clark County, Missouri. She was born October 25, 1902 in Iowa. They had one child Gloria Ann Coursey born July 12, 1945 at Burlington, Des Moines County, Iowa, and presently resides at Macomb, Illinois. Harold and Snoda divorced February 26, 1969. Harold died February 23, 1970 and Snoda August 1982.

Harold learned the meat cutting trade and worked at it from time to time, but basically worked as a carpenter the majority of his life. He moved around a lot with his second family until 1947 when they bought a house in Kirkwood, Warren County, Illinois, where their children attended schools and they lived until their divorce.

Harold and Erma are buried in the Roseville Cemetery at Roseville, Illinois.

Snoda is buried in Aspen Grove Cemetery in Burlington, Iowa. Submitted by Richard W. Coursey.

THOMAS MARION COURSEY - Thomas was born March 11, 1874 in Brooklyn Twp., Schuyler County, Illinois, he died February 9, 1967 at Monmouth, Warren County, Illinois. His parents were John William Coursey (1843-1931) and Sarah Jane Allen (1852-1937).

Thomas and Lettie Cousey 50th Anniversary

He married Lettie Jane Aulgur August 29, 1898 at Littleton, Schuyler County, Illinois she was born November 24, 1878 at Littleton, Illinois, and died February 3, 1967 at Monmouth, Illinois. Her parents were John Wesley Aulgur (1857-1925) and Margaret "Maggie" Cox (1859-1934).

Thomas and Lettie had five children as follows: 1) a daughter (1899-1899), she lived 2 days, and is buried in White Oak Cemetery, Brooklyn Twp., Schuyler County, Illinois; 2) Glenn Wesley (1901-1992); 3) Harold Faye (1904-1970); 4) Margaret Marie (1906) she lives at Monmouth, Illinois; 5) John William (1909-1994).

Thomas and Lettie Coursey and John and Margaret Aulgur are buried in the Roseville Cemetery at Roseville, Warren County, Illinois. John and Sarah Coursey are buried in Ellison Cemetery, near Smithshire, Warren County, Illinois.

Thomas' grandparents were John Louis Coursey (1812-1869) and Mary Edwards (1807-1883), they are buried near White Hall, Greene County, Illinois. Lettie's grandparents were John Milton Aulgur (1828-1902) and Letta Jane Hawkins (1837-1904), they are buried in White Oak Cemetery, Schuyler County, Illinois.

Thomas' father was a farmer and he attended rural schools in Brooklyn Twp., but as he grew older, only when he wasn't needed to help with the farming. There were 11 children in the family and only two were boys, born eight years apart, Thomas being the oldest. He first came to Warren County in the mid 1890s and returned to Schuyler County to marry Lettie. They remained there until 1900 when they moved back to Warren County to farm. Their first farm was a Frank Birdsell farm about 3/4 mile north of Smithshire, Illinois (1900-1901). They moved to an unnamed farm near Colfax in Point Pleasant Twp. (1901-1903), Glenn was born there. They moved to a Charles Livermore farm (1903-1905), Harold was born there. They moved to a Derek Livermore farm (1905-1910), Marie and John were born there. They then moved to Earle R. Pinney's farm for a while and later to an Andy Livermore farm. The last 5 farms were southwest of Roseville in Point Pleasant Twp. (The dates are estimates based on their children's birth years.)

In 1922 they bought a farm 2 1/4 miles north of Roseville on Route 67, which they owned at the time of their death. It then became an estate in equal shares to their 4 surviving children. When Erma Coursey died in 1940 they took Richard and Tommy to live with them. The boys attended McCurdy School 2 1/2 miles northeast of Roseville, Illinois 1941 and 1942. Thomas and Lettie prospered as farmers and I never heard either of them say they wished they had done something else. Lettie was a very religious lady, a member of and deeply committed to the Roseville Methodist Church. Submitted by Richard W. Coursey Feb.26,2002

GEORGE W. COX - George Wells Cox was born to Tilden and Ruth (Wells) Cox on February 24, 1932, on a farm east of Blandinsville, Illinois. George had an older brother, Duane Cox, who was born in Macomb, Illinois on May 26, 1930. The family moved to a farm two miles east of Larchland and then moved west of Prairie City 'in 1938. The family purchased a farm east and south of Roseville in 1939, which is where George has resided since 1960. George attended school at the Hoisington School and then graduated from Roseville High School in 1950. George joined the Naval Reserves in 1951 and then went on active duty on May 14, 1952. George went to the Great Lakes boot camp and after a leave he left for Korea by the way of Panama, San Diego, Pearl Harbor, Hawaii, Sasebo, Japan and then to Korea. He was discharged in March 1954. He graduated from Western Illinois University, Macomb, in 1958. He married Janelle Galloway in Perry, Missouri, on November 26, 1959. They lived in Burlington, Iowa for three months where George was employed as a technical writer for J. I. Case Company. George returned to the farm in 1960 and continues to live there.

George and Janelle have two children, both born in Macomb, Illinois, Aaron, who was born on November 23, 1961, and Angela, who was born on November 7, 1967. Aaron graduated from Roseville High School in 1980 and Western Illinois University in 1985. Aaron married Pamela Duke October 19, 1991. Aaron has two daughters, Courtney born June 29, 1993 and Megan born on July 8, 1995. Aaron and his family live in Chatham, Illinois and Aaron works in Springfield as a computer consultant for LRS, Inc. Angela graduated from Roseville High School in 1986 and Western Illinois University in 1990. Angela married Andrew Stodolkiewicz May 30, 1992. Angela has a son, Casimir, born November 14, 1997 and a daughter, Magdalena, born March 19, 2001. Angela and her family live in rural Roseville. Angela is employed by ARAMARK as the catering manager at Monmouth College.

George W. Cox

George farmed the family farm as well as worked for King Seeley Thermos Co. in Macomb for eleven years and for Achievement Industries in Monmouth for thirteen years before retiring in 1997. His wife, Janelle, is an Avon Representative and is a Roseville community correspondent for the Review Atlas. George and Janelle enjoy their retirement by traveling and growing a large garden each summer. They are also active in their church, the First Baptist Church of Roseville.

KENNETH AND BERNICE CRITSER - Kenneth and Bernice Critser moved to Monmouth in 1957 following Ken's graduation from the University of Illinois Law School. He came to work for John J. Kritzer and later they became partners. It amused and confused many that the two lawyers names were spelled differently but pronounced the same way. Later he and Ted Stansell became partners and still later Richard Whitman became a partner.

Critser family ca. 1976 Kenneth, Bernice, Jim, and John (front).

Ken and Bernice met at Knox College and married in 1951. After spending two years in the army during the Korean War, Ken entered the University of Illinois Law School. Bernice taught school in California and Champaign, Ill. and later did tutoring and substitute teaching. Their sons John and Jim were born in 1953 and 1957 respectively and went to Monmouth schools. Later John attended Ripon College and University of Wisconsin. Jim went on to Danville Jr. college.

Ken was active in the community serving on Monmouth College Senate and Trustees Chairman of the hospital board, Grace Church trustee, Warren Achievement board, National Bank Board, Library Board. He also worked promotion Harness Racing in Illinois. He loved harness horse racing and he and Bernice had brood mare operation near Monmouth. He enjoyed training horses and was qualified for county fair racing He died in 1983.

Bernice served on Dist.# 38 School Board and later the Dist. #38 Foundation Habitat for Humanity, Warren Co. Library Board, Buchanan Center for the Arts. She is a member of Faith Presbyterian Church and has served as elder and trustee, is a member of PEO and volunteers at Community Memorial Center.

The Critsers have always been very happy that they chose Warren County as their home. It is a great community. Jim and his wife Diana and children Dirk and Jessie live near Monmouth, John and his wife and children Paul and Rebecca live in Columbia, MO and enjoy "coming home" when it is possible.

HAZEL CURTIS - Hazel Elizabeth Manlove was born 9 October 1915 on a farm near Birmingham, Schuyler County, IL. She had 6 brothers and I younger sister. When she and her younger sister couldn't get along she would climb up a tree to get away from her.

Hazel and Robert Curtis 40th Anniversary

When she was four or five years old, their house burned down. Her father hired a carpenter to build a big ten room house with full attic. The carpenter's wife and 2 children lived across the field from them. When the carpenter and his helper were putting the frame up, she would climb up to help them. The higher they got, the better she liked it. His wife, saw her up there. Little girls wore plaid ribbons in their hair, she told Hazel if she would stay down from the roof, she would buy her a ribbon. She never did get that hair ribbon.

When Hazel was eight years old, her folks sold out and moved to Quincy, IL. and she found city schools were quite different from country schools. Hazel liked school and was an average student. When she was about 15 years old and had her first boy friend, she thought she was in love so they ran off and got married. She didn't tell her mother for several months. She had a baby boy who was her pride and joy. Hazel and her husband divorced when they had been married four years. She remarried when her son was 9 years old. and as her husband was a farmer they moved to her parents 345 acre farm at Brooklyn, IL. Hazel's mother had taught her to cook, bake sew, and do housework so she enjoyed farm life. She made lots of mistakes and furnished her neighbors with lots of laughs and she laughed with them.

Later they moved to Coal Valley, IL. and then to Monmouth. Hazel worked at Monmouth Hospital in the purchasing department 14 years, then retired. They then lived at Lake Warren near Monmouth. After retirement they spent 6 months at Lake Warren and 6 months at Payson, AZ. When in Payson she and her husband took classes at the Pueblo Junior College in oil painting. "I'll never be a famous painter but I enjoyed it."

During their 50 years of marriage they traveled a lot, seeing 49 of the 50 states, and Canada from east to west, Mexico, and a trip to Germany to see their grandson who was in the Air Force in Germany. In their 3 weeks tour they also saw Ireland, Luxemburg, Belgium, Switzerland and Austria.

In 1991 they came home to Lake Warren and celebrated their 50th anniversary. Her husband passed away in July from cancer. "My husband of 50 years was my friend, buddy, and sweetheart and I have wonderful memories."

Hazel married Stanley Hemm-1931; divorced-married Robert E. Curtis-1941. Son: Vern Lee Hemm born 1932 - married Phyllis Rupp-1984.

JAMES AND LUCILLE (KETCHUM) DAMEWOOD - James Anderson Damewood was born 6 January 1900 at Eagle Rock, Virginia. He was the son of John Anderson and Emma McHenry (Martin) Damewood. He came to Illinois with the family in 1915 His siblings were: twin girls – John Emmett; Eva Lake; Pearl M.; George William; Arthur Watt, Carl M.; Talmage; Mary, Roy Raymond and Stella. During WWI he served in France in the Marines from 27 September 1917 to 14 March 1919. He served in. the Meuse, Argonne offensive. He was also in the Marines from 3 September 1920 to 28 August 1922 serving as a private. He served in the Army from September 1924 to September 1927. He was a Corporal in Battery "H" 13th Coast Artillery in Fort Crockett, Texas. He was discharged on 10 September 1927, serving a total of 6 years, 5 months and 5 days.

Lucille and Jim Damewood

He was married 12 March 1932 in Galesburg, Knox County, IL to Lucille Ketchum.

Lucille Virginia Ketchum was born 11 December 1910 near Abingdon, Virginia to Frank Martin and Mary Margaret (Swarts) Ketchum and came to Illinois in 1919 with the family. Siblings were: Clarence; Roy; Hazel; Nannie Belle; Ethel; Robert, Dorothy; Grace and William. She attended public schools, graduating from Kirkwood High School in 1929. She attended Monmouth College and received a teaching certificate 22 July 1930, teaching for one year at Coonville School near Kirkwood before their marriage.

The couple worked on farms in Warren and Henderson counties, among them being Halsey Jewell, Engdahl, Harry Jewell, Graham, Turnbull, Stratton and Theime.

Their children were: Mary Ruth born 21 October 1934 (Jim Johnson – 27 February 1955), no children; Doris Marie born 4 August 1936 (Ernest Grabowski – 29 December 1955) 2 children; William Arthur born 23 March 1938 (Jeanne Foster – 20 June 1964 – divorced) 2 children; James Franklin born 7 October 1939 (Ruth Stevens – 14 June 1959 – deceased) (Edith Stevens) 5 children.

James died 6 February 1974. Lucille lived in Kirkwood for several years and then in Lamoine Nursing Home, Roseville. Lucille died 28 January 1994. Both buried Memorial Park Cemetery, Monmouth, Illinois.

JOHN A. AND EMMA (MARTIN) DAMEWOOD - John Anderson Damewood was born 20 August 1853, Botetourt Co., Va, the son of Erastus and Sarah "Sally" (Abbott) Damewood. He married Emma (McHenry) Martin on 31 January 1883 in Botetourt County. She was born 11 November 1857, Craig Co., Va., daughter of Thomas and Elizabeth (Looney) Martin. In 1900 they lived in Eagle Rock District, Botetourt County. While living there John and sons worked in coal mines and timber cutting. They came to Illinois prior 1910. They were farmers, he retired to Kirkwood about 1926. John died 17 January 1944, Emma died 26 January 1944. Both buried Cedar Creek cemetery. They had 15 children:

Twin girls born 1882 – both died about age 6 months.

John Damewood with grandchildren Carl and Mary Ruth and Emma Damewood with grandson Johnnie.

John Emmett, born January 1866 – died 1931, buried Center Grove cemetery. He married Maggie V. Gallaghan. They came to Little York area about 1911. She died and he returned to Virginia and married Mattie J. Broughman, coming back to Warren County. Emmett and Maggie had four children: Cecil, Gertrude, Lillian and Ralph. Emmett was a farmer.

Eva Lake, born March 1888 – died 1949/50.

Pearl M., born 1892 – died 1912 – measles.

George William , born May 1894 – died 26 August 1969.Retired US Navy Marines. Married (2) Thelma Welch 20 February 1953.

John Damewood, late 1930s.

Arthur Watt, born 1 February 1896 – died 24 March 1927. Married Florence Jeanne McKee 26 August 1927. 4 children.: Rebecca Jean, Rocelia Lee, Elizabeth Ann and Donald Claire. Arthur was a truck-driver.

Carl M., born 1898 – died about 1904.

James Anderson, born 6 January 1900 – died 6 February 1974. He married Lucille Ketchum 12 March 1932. They had four children: Mary Ruth, Doris Marie, William Arthur, James Franklin. He was a farmer.

Talmage, born 1902 – died 1912 – measles.

Mary, born1904 –died 1907.

Roy Raymond, born 16 December 1907– died 18 February 1974. He married Hazel Ketchum 31 July 1933. They had six children: Carl Talmage, Robert Leroy, John Howard, Harold McHenry, Sarah Lou, George Raymond. Roy was a farmer and truck-driver for Gamble's.

Stella, born 24 May 1910 – died 18 August 1969. Married Orville Agan – 2 children John and Betty Agan. She married (2) Arthur Bramstadt.

Infant – deceased.

JOHN HOWARD DAMEWOOD - John was born on January 2, 1939, to Roy and Hazel (Ketchum) Damewood. He was the third of six children, Carl, Bob, John, Harold, Sara and George. He attended elementary school in Warren and Henderson counties. He graduated from high school in 1956 from Monmouth High

John and Martha Damewood

School. After high school, he worked for Dick and George Gillen and then for Bill Gillen. He joined the Illinois National Guard for several years. He married Martha Larkin on February 6, 1960. They lived at Route 4, Monmouth until 1965, when they moved to Ponemah (southeast of Kirkwood) and John went to work for Clarence Neff Implement. Their son Steve was born in July of 1966. John went to work for General Telephone in 1970. John and Martha bought a house in Kirkwood in 1975 (Martha still lives there). John and Martha bought John's Grandparent's (Frank and Mary (Swarts) Ketchum) farm from their son Robert Ketchum in 1986. John retired from GTE on December 1, 1995, and passed away on December 9, 1995, from cancer. He thoroughly enjoyed his family and his farming hobby.

Martha (Larkin) Damewood was born in July of 1940, to Leroy and Cecilia (Woerly) Larkin. She was the oldest of four children, Martha, Margaret, Bill and Tom. Martha attended elementary school in Warren County and graduated from Monmouth High School in 1958. She worked at Gambles Warehouse in Monmouth and then at Benner Foods, which later became Giant Foods, then Easter Foods and now Econo Foods, where she still works. Son Steve attended Kirkwood and Little York elementary schools and graduated in 1984 from Yorkwood High School. He married Marnie Fleming in 1988. Steve and Marnie have two daughters, Andrea Krystynne and Stephanie Lou. Steve works as a guard at Hill Correctional Center in Galesburg and Marnie works at Midwest Bank in Monmouth. The girls attend Yorkwood School. In 1997, Steve and Marnie built a new house at the family farm.

ROY RAYMOND AND HAZEL (KETCHUM) DAMEWOOD - Roy Raymond Damewood was born 16 December 1907, Eagle Rock, Botetourt County, VA to John Anderson and Emma (Martin) Damewood. He came to Warren County, IL with the family in 1915. Siblings: twin girls, John Emmett, Eva Lake, Pearl M., George William, Arthur Watt, James Anderson, Carl M., Talmage, Mary, Stella, infant. He attended area schools. He served in the Army in the Philippines during 1920s.

Hazel and Roy Damewood

Roy married Hazel Ketchum 31 July 1933, Warren County, IL He worked on farms in Warren and Henderson counties. He later moved the family to Monmouth where he was a truck driver for Gamble-Skogmo Co. Later he had his own truck, doing hauling for others. Roy loved flying and was co-owner of a small plane with his son John, and Joe Danforth. He also enjoyed duck hunting.

Hazel Arizona Ketchum was born 14 October 1914, Bristol, SuIllivan County, TN to Frank and Maty (Swarts) Ketchum. Siblings: Clarence Preston, Lucille Virginia, Ernest Roy, Nannie Belle, Ethel Lorraine, Robert Lee, Dorothy Mae, Grace Marie, William Eldon. The family moved to Warren County, IL in 1919. She attended Hazel Dell school, Henderson County, and Center Grove, Warren county; graduating from Kirkwood High School. She did housework for different families before her marriage. After moving to Monmouth she worked several years at Formfit Co. Later she was an expert at cake decorating and handicrafts. She was baptized in Kirkwood Methodist church. Children: all born in Warren County, IL.

1. Carl Talmage Born 10 October 1934, Married Mary Frances Ray, 2 daughters: Pamela Sue and Rebecca Lynn.
2. Robert Leroy Born 5 June 1936, Married (1) Gwen Hughes, step-daughter Cindy Norville; adopted daughter Kim Dawson, Gwen's daughters by previous marriages; and one son Jason Robert; Divorced; Married (2) Mary C. (Ross) Rakoczy, divorced.
3. John Howard Born 2 January 1939, Died 9 December 1995; Married Martha Larkin, 1 son, Steve.
4. Harold McHenry Born 9 September 1940, Married Mary Ann (Hanson) Modglin, daughter Diane Modglin, Mary Ann's daughter by a previous marriage; Cheryl Renee and Carolyn Kay.
5. Sarah Lou Born 15 February 1942, Died 9 October 1991, Married Lorin Dean Schaeffer, 2 daughters Nicole Suzanne and Amanda Collette.
6. George Raymond Born 4 January 1944; Married Janice Hickerson, 2 sons, Anthony Miguel and Brett Raymond, divorced.

Roy died 18 February 1974 and Hazel died 14 April 1984. Both are buried at Memorial Park Cemetery, Monmouth, IL.

KENNETH EUGENE AND BEULAH GERTRUDE DAVIS - Kenneth Eugene and Beulah Gertrude Davis have been residents of Warren County nearly all their lives. Kenneth was born in Monmouth February 26, 1928, the son of Harry and Anna Johnson Davis. His father was born near Camden, IL while his mother was born in Sweden arriving in this country in 1910 with her parents Otto and Augusta Johnson and her two brothers and three sisters. Kenneth has two brothers, William L. and Otto Leonard and two sisters Ruby and Betty Jean. He attended Smithshire Grade School and graduated from Media High School in Henderson County. He operated a grocery store in Smithshire after graduation and started farming. He married Beulah Gertrude Davis August 13, 1950 in the Kirkwood Methodist Church. He served in the Army from 1951-1953. All two years were at Ft. Leonard Wood, Missouri. He became an Amy cook. After leaving the service he returned to farming. He served as Ellison Township Supervisor from 1968-1981 and serving on the Warren County Board of Supervisors which later became the Warren County Board.

Gertrude and Kenneth Davis

Beulah Gertrude Davis was born April 14, 1928 in Monmouth Hospital, the only child of Glen Milton and Helen Brent Davis. The family lived in the Coldbrook area of Warren County where her father had always lived. His parents were Ellsworth and Jessie Bruington Davis. When she was three years old they moved to Ellison Township near the Ellison Cemetery. Her father farmed land owned by her grandfather, Schuyler Brent, in the area where they lived. She graduated from Roseville Township High School and Brown's Business College in Galesburg. She started working at the Smithshire Post Office as a part time flexible clerk in 1965 and was appointed Postmaster in 1985 retiring in Oct. 1992.

Their first son, Steven Eugene Davis, was born May 25, 1952 in Monmouth Hospital. He married Nancy Horney (whose parents and grandparents lived in this county). They have two sons, Erik Glen and Alex Eugene.

Their second son, Alan Richard Davis was born August 19, 1953 in Monmouth Hospital. He married Lisa Garrison Schisler and they have two sons Bradley and Andrew.

They have lived in the Smithshire area where they farmed and owned land. They are members of the Smithshire United Methodist Church and reside in the unincorporated village of Smithshire.

LEROY W. & MARGARET MARIE (ROBERTS) DAVIS - LeRoy Walter Davis born June 3, 1915 in Mount Hamil, Lee Co., Iowa. He was the third of eight children born to Walter L. Davis of Scotland Co., Missouri and Dora G. Herrmuth of Lee Co., Iowa.

Mary Lou (Davis), Rowena Y. and Harold S. Parsons, 1998.

Margaret M. Roberts was born Jan. 27, 1904 the eldest daughter of nine children of Richard Rueben Roberts and Katie Isabelle Cotton, both born in Clark County, Missouri.

Isabelle was a descendant of George Soule of the Mayflower.

LeRoy married Margaret Marie Roberts Jan. 15, 1936 in Kahoka, Missouri. They moved to the Little York, Illinois area where they worked for Doug Armstrong and others.

They later moved to Monmouth, where LeRoy worked at the Vac and Keister's. On May 3, 1941, a daughter, Mary Lou, was born in Monmouth. In the spring of 1942, they moved to the Fall Creek area where LeRoy went to work for Jack Jones.

Mary Lou attended Pleasant Green Grade School and graduated from Little York High School 1959. She married Harold Slyvester Parsons April 1, 1961 at the home of her parents. They have three children, Sylvia Lou Renee, July 25, 1963; Rowena Yvonne, February 4, 1966, and Harold Sylvester Jr., May 15, 1968; all born in Monmouth, Ill.

LeRoy passed away March 31, 1967, in Monmouth, at the age of 52. Margaret passed away August 13, 1999, in Galesburg at the age of 95. Both are buried in the Little York Cemetery. They had many, many friends over the years.

"There are many good memories we have of our Grandparents LeRoy and Margaret, including their collie dog, Ringo, who loved to retrieve corncobs from the pond. The first time that we fed lambs with a pop bottle and nipple. Coloring Easter Eggs for Grandpa's hunting buddies. Helping out with the farm chores. Finding out where real Christmas Trees came from. Pretty green Christmas Tree lights are hot when turned on. Just because the iron is sitting up doesn't mean it's cooled down. Our kitties were different. Cats like milk directly from the cow. Making cookies and pies. Our favorite memory is the little box Grandpa made for us to stand on to reach the sink and wash our hands. We still have our little box.

LeRoy and Margaret were a big part of our childhood and we shall never forget them."

THOMAS AND SUSAN (HENDEL) DEAN - Susan Marie, daughter of James R. and Clarice (Watson) Hendel of Roseville, Illinois, was born October 8, 1956, in Saunders Hospital, Avon, Illinois. She has two brothers, Jerry Robert Hendel and Michael Duane Hendel. She attended the Roseville Public Schools, graduating in 1974. She then went to Iowa Wesleyan College in Mount Pleasant, Iowa, and earned a Bachelor of Science in Nursing, in 1978. Since that time she has been employed by the University of Iowa Hospitals & Clinics in Iowa City, Iowa, as an Assistant Nurse Manager in the Department of Orthopedics and Urology.

On September 5, 1981, she married Thomas Richard Dean of West Branch, Iowa, in the Roseville United Methodist Church. He is the son of Edward Lawrence and Donna (Clemmensen) Dean of West Branch, Iowa, and was born August 12, 1954, in Iowa City, Iowa. He received his education in the West Branch Public Schools, graduating in 1972. Tom has a Bachelors Degree from the University of Oklahoma. He is a Physician's Assistant at Mercy Hospital in Iowa City, Iowa. Tom has been a member of the Iowa Army National Guard since 1973, and is currently a Major and Commander in the 109th Medical Battalion in Iowa City, Iowa.

They are the parents of three children. Benjamin Patrick Dean was born February 20, 1983, in Iowa City, Iowa. He attended Mark Twain Grade School, Iowa City, Iowa, through the 6th grade, then the family moved to West Branch, where he graduated from West Branch High School in 2001. He received a congressional appointment to the United States Air Force Academy in Colorado Springs, Colorado, and is currently finishing his first year. Abby Elizabeth Dean was born January 17, 1986, in Iowa City, Iowa. She attended Mark Twain Grade School in Iowa City, Iowa, through the 3rd grade and is currently a sophomore at West Branch High School. Tyler Jay Dean was born August 23, 1990, in Iowa City, Iowa, and is a 5th grader at West Branch Grade School.

Susan was always active in church and 4-H activities while home and liked to play girls softball during the summer. Moving from Iowa City, in January 1996, she and her family live in West Branch, Iowa.

STEVEN DECOUNTER FAMILY - Steven L. DeCounter, son; of Vaughn and Irene DeCounter, was born on August 22, 1942 in Macomb. He is the youngest of three children. Betty J. (Hillyer) DeCounter, daughter of Eugene and Betty Hillyer of Macomb was born October 9, 1943. She is one of five children, three sisters and one brother (deceased).

Steven DeCounter family, December 24, 2001.

They were married May 11, 1963 at Sciota Illinois Christian Church. They were in the fertilizer business in Roseville from 1963 to 1976. From 1976 to 1987, Steve was in the trucking business. He then started his present business, Appearance Reconditioning Company in 1989.

Steve served on the Roseville Village Board for ten years, Roseville Ambulance ten years, Lions Club Past President and member for 35 years and is a member of the Roseville Christian Church.

Betty was a Girl Scout Leader and Den Mother for several years. She was on the committee for Warren-Henderson Town and Country Art Show for twenty years, past member of WSCS Club, LCNH Auxiliary, Roseville Chamber of Commerce, Roseville Woman's Club Past President and current member of 35 years, and active volunteer at Community Medical Center, Monmouth. She is a member of Roseville Christian Church. She has sold advertising specialties to area businesses for the past 34 years.

They have three children. daughter Jamie (DeCounter) Becker is employed as a behavioral health specialist at Community Mental Health Center, Macomb. She was born in Monmouth June 10, 1965 and is married to Brad Becker. They have one daughter, Carly Jo born August 5, 1996.

Darin, born October 3,1967 in Monmouth, is employed by the Las Vegas Review Journal and lives in Henderson, Nevada.

Kevin, born May 19, 1970 lives in Henderson, Nevada and is employed by MGM Grand Hotel, Las Vegas.

DANIEL R. DEFENBAUGH - Defenbaugh, Daniel R., was born in Warren County and is the oldest son of Raymond E. and Alice J. Defenbaugh. He is married to Johanna Adair. Daniel and Johanna farm in Tompkins Township-Warren County and Biggsville Township-Henderson County. They are general grain and livestock farmers and partners in Beulah Land Farms, living on the Edgewood Farm at the south edge of Kirkwood. They are engaged in custom trucking, subsurface drainage, and backhoe work. There is a large shop located on Daniel and Johanna's Edgewood farm used for maintenance and repairs. Daniel graduated from Southeastern Community College with a degree in Agriculture and is active in community affairs.

Daniel and Johanna have two children, Nathaniel J. born March 18, 1998, and Ella Marie born June 10, 2002. Johanna is the daughter of John and Joyce (Dixon) Adair of rural Kirkwood who are also general livestock and grain farmers.

Defenbaugh reunion, August 16, 1925

Daniel and Johanna are members of the Warren County Farm Bureau and Big River Resources Cooperative. They are quite active in value-added agriculture.

Nathaniel John and Ella Marie Defenbaugh

The first Defenbaugh ancestors came to America in June, 1710, for three reasons 1) escape the destruction of Centuries of Wars, especially that of fanatical religious extermination of the French armies led be Louis XIV, 2) 1709 "ein erschrecklick grausame Kalte" (a frightfully dreadful gruesome cold) in which even the birds died on the wing and men and cattle froze to death 3) invite of William Penn and Queene Anne of England offering large farm lands, laws of their own making, religious toleration to all Christians, and pursuit of peace.

The Defenbaugh family has their family cemetery in Reading Township, Livingston County, as well as a large family museum open to the public by appointment. It includes a top hat worn by a Defenbaugh to Lincoln's inauguration. There also remains the first Defenbaugh home of 1851.

Daniel owns the Edgewood farm and has farmed on a commercial basis since a freshman in high school and helping on the farm before that time. His earliest endeavors were raising cattle, hogs, and grain. It is anticipated that Nathaniel J. and Ella A will also want to farm as they mature and realize the merits of that endeavor.

DEBORAH J. DEFENBAUGH - Defenbaugh, Deborah J., born in Warren County is the fourth child of Raymond E. and Alice J. Defenbaugh. She lives on the Hermitage, west of Kirkwood, Illinois and notes her family is sesquicentennial farmers in Illinois with the celebration occurring in 2001. She is employed in the Real Estate Loan Department of the Midwest Bank of Western Illinois, Monmouth, Illinois. She graduated Suma cum Laud and Department Scholar from the School of Agriculture at Western Illinois University. She is also computer programmer, bookkeeper helper, and farm Management advisor to Beulah Land Farms. Additionally, she is co-manager and computer programmer for Beulah Land Grain, the families storage and drying facility in Kirkwood, Illinois, which is utilized for the family farms grain and value added operation.

Deborah J. Defenbaugh

Deborah is an accomplished pianist-organist and has played for various churches and weddings throughout the community. Her Defenbaugh ancestors were early organ builders in America with the first being built in 1777. Many are yet in existence and one can be found in the Berks County historical Society Museum in Pennsylvania. Her interest is in Banking, Agriculture, and her family.

JENNIFER M. DEFENBAUGH - Defenbaugh, Jennifer M., born in Warren County is the third child of Raymond E. and Alice J. Defenbaugh. She lives in Kirkwood, Illinois, adjacent to the Edgewood farm to the North. Along with helping her family on Beulah Land Farms, is employed full-time at Great River Medical Center, a hospital in Burlington, Iowa. She is also attending Southeastern Community College, in a cooperative effort with Carl Sanburg Community College, to complete her Registered Nurse degree. She previously was employed as an insurance claims adjuster for a few years out of high school.

Defenbaugh family organ, 1777

She enjoys fellowship with and working together with her family and especially her niece and nephew, Nathaniel and Ella Defenbaugh. She attends the large gathering of Defenbaughs annually and learning of their history. She notes that her earliest ancestor in America was James Chilton, who died on the Mayflower in harbor on December 8, 1620. He, being the oldest Mayflower passenger, was one of the first to die after reaching the New World. On board with him was his wife, who died the first winter, and daughter Mary, age 13. Popular legend gives her the distinction of being the first female to step ashore at Plymouth.

Jennifer's family includes the Mortlands, Hooblers, Armstrongs, Pickerall, Gillman, Kuns, Leonard, Chandler, Chilton, Remmington, Mason, Lundy, Norris, and Koltveit. Also that her family were early staunch abolitionists and actively participated in the underground railroad to free slaves in Amity township, Livingston county. Her grandfather Leonard, fourth removed, served under General Sherman in Co. A. 129th I.V.I. from August 2, 1862 through June 8, 1865. He participated in the campaign against Atlanta and was present at the capture of that place; was also with General Sherman during his March to the Sea and the capture of Savannah and the campaign through North and South Carolina. On the night of March 13, 1915 Mr. Leonard called his living relatives to his bedside, one by one, and expressed his farewells and expectations of them to remain strong in the Christian faith, treat all individuals equally, and love as Christ taught. The folowing morning March 14, 1915, he passed peacefully away at 79 years old, setting a firm pace for succeeding ancestors to follow even to this day.

MATTHEW J. DEFENBAUGH - Defenbaugh., Matthew J. born in Warren county, is the second son of Raymond E. and Alice J. Defenbaugh and is married to Tony M. Peel, daughter of Ralph Peel. They are general grain and livestock farmers and partners in Beulah Land Farms. They live on the Golden Pond farm, sec. 24, Biggsville Township, Henderson County.

L: to R: Mark Kineer; Jennifer, Tonya, Matthew, Johanna, Daniel, Deborah Defenbaugh; John Green; Nathaniel, Alice, Raymond Defenbaugh.

Matthew and Tonya have a strong attachment to the soil and exemplify it, as taught by prior generations of Defenbaugh's, through soil stewardship and an attitude of preserving the land for future generations.

Matthew has farmed since early High School days and owns the Timber Creek and Drawback farms. Matthew and Tonya are members of the Warren County Farm Bureau and Big River Resources Cooperative. They are quite active in value added agriculture.

Matthew flies a para-plane and Gyro Kopter, experimental flying machines, which are utilized for crop scouting and photography. He and Tonya have an extensive collection of fowl and all types of animals.

Tonya works at Midwest Bank of Western Illinois and helps her husband on the farm She enjoys all activities associated with her immediate and extended family and is particularly fond of caring for animals.

As historical note the Defenbaugh's have provided relatives in US service thirteen times 1) French and Indian Wars 2) Yankee-Pennanits War 3) American Revolution 4) War of 1812 5) Mexican War-1846 6) Civil War 7) Spanish American War 8) World War I 9) World War II 10) Korean Police Action 11) Vietnam 12) Desert Storm 13) AfghanistanWar on Terrorism. The total number in service for World War II totaled 335 with 13 gold stars and 3 silver stars. They were referred to in 1944 as a "Fighting Family" and the Heroism of Major Lyle J. Defenbaugh, under heavy machine gun fire helped sell war bonds for the US Treasury Department in 1943. A member of the Defenbaugh Family, Johan Friedrich, born February 1, 1792, is considered the Father of Plastic Surgery, as he developed a method for correction cross-eyes.

The Defenbaughs' hold a large family reunion every year the third week in August and have since before 1914. Careful records have been maintained in a book of the family since before arriving in America and provided the information for this biography.

RAYMOND E. DEFENBAUGH - Defenbaugh, Raymond E., the second child of Charles M. Defenbaugh and Esther M. Koltveit Defenbaugh, was born in Livingston County, Illinois on the families' general livestock farm near Manville, Illinois. He and brothers John Dennis (Sandy), Leslie Charles, Dale Lee (Ann), Brian (Cathy) and sister Kathie Marie (Ralph Gebrig) are the fifth generation of Defenbaugh families to farm on Illinois soil and the tenth successive generation of Defenbaugh families to farm in America. All brothers are farming yet in 2002 with the exception of Dale Lee who died of Blackmall melanoma cancer in 1996 at the age of 40. Sister Kathie M. lives in Wheaton, Illinois where she is an educator and her husband is a supervisor in the Tower at O'Hara Airport.

Raymond E. Defenbaugh

Raymond E. Defenbaugh is married to Alice J. Norris, daughter of John H. and Ardith Armstrong Norris. He a retired dairy farmer and she a retired elementary teacher having taught in one-room rural schools. Alice J. has one brother, Richard A. Norris a lifetime farmer. Raymond and Alice have four children. Daniel R. Defenbaugh (Johanna Adair), Matthew J. Defenbaugh (Tonya M Peel), Jennifer M. Defenbaugh, and Deborah J. Defenbaugh.

Raymond E. and Alice are general livestock farmers. Having livestock (cattle, Percheron and standard bred horses) they engage in trucking, subsurface tiling, and backhoe work with their sons. Owning farmland in Warren, Henderson and

Livingston counties, they are heavily involved in value-added agriculture projects. Raymond earned a MS graduate degree in Economics and holds a current Illinois teaching certificate. He has taught Vocational Agriculture in Illinois and business-banking-coop development in the countries of Moldova and Russia. He is chairman of the Board of Directors at Midwest Bank of Western Illinois, Co-chairman and Co-General Manager of the Board of Directors of Big River Resources Cooperative (Ethanol), and serves on the Board of Directors at Riverland Farm Service Company. Additionally, he has served with community projects and organizations including Treasurer of the Warren County Prime Beef Festival, Chairman of the Warren Co. Cancer Crusade, Chairman of Henderson County Soil and Water Conservation Board, Kirkwood and Biggsville Lions, Treasurer of Prime Beef Chapter Isaac Walton League, Monmouth Kiwanis Club, Charter member National Cattleman's Association, Area Vocational Center Advisory council Chairman, Farm Bureau, Warren-Henderson-Mercer Counties Administrative Aide Supervisory Council, Warren-Henderson County Livestock Producers Association, Warren County Ag Extension Council, Henderson County 4-H Council, Kirkwood bicentennial Council, Volunteer Fireman (chief engineer, trustee, assistant fire chief, EMT).

Along with Farming, Alice J. Defenbaugh is a housewife, bookkeeper for Beulah Land Farms, has served as a 4-H leader, PEO, and engages in all facets of farm life. She earned an Associate Degree as Medical Secretary and has worked in the Medical Center at SIU, and Chamber of Commerce office in Pontiac, Illinois. She owns farmland in Warren and Henderson counties and her family has farmed in America for 10 successive generations. Alice and Raymond were raised in the same local community, educated together from one room grade school through college, and have been friends since pre-elementary school days. Their ancestral families came to Illinois together in 1851 and were together in Ohio and Pennsylvania since 1710. They were married on June 10, 1967. They own and operate the following farms: Seldom Seen, Eastwood, Golden Pond, Hermitage, Cribshed and the Triple Creek in Warren-Henderson counties and Karr and Gilman farms in Livingston County.

CHARLES DOUGLAS (DOUG) AND MARY (HULTZ) DENISON - Charles Douglas (Doug) Denison was born April 16, 1927, Denison Ferry, Kentucky; died Feb. 10, 1985, Monmouth, IL.

Mary Elizabeth (Hultz) Denison was born Sept. 24, 1933, Troy, IL.

Doug and his older brother William (Leon) and sister Brownie (Louise) moved to Monmouth in 1929 with their parents Eddie Lee and Mallie Buckingham Denison. It was a growing family, with a total of nine. They moved several times as the family grew; Doug went to several schools. He enlisted in the Army first, then went to the Air Force – 20 years total. Growing up he always loved to hunt and fish. One year he got a pair of skates for his birthday and was told not to skate in the street. Of course, he did, and got hit by a car and had a broken leg! In the hospital it itched a lot. His father brought him a pen knife to peel oranges with. Well, he almost "Peeled" his cast off. There were lots of things for boys to do then: sell newspapers, scrap iron and metal, and work on farms during the summer.

After many moves in the Air Force and meeting and marrying Mary, their family started growing; Cathy and Charlie born in Louisiana; David in Georgia; Chris in Illinois; Cindy in Brazil and Denny in California. A two year tour in Alaska was an adventure with forest fires, earthquakes and floods; also some very good hunting, a moose was enjoyed by all; and fishing, everyone liked salmon too.

Doug and Mary Denison

After retirement the family settled in Chula Vista, CA where the children finished growing and considered California their home. Doug worked at a Stationers and ocean fished and golfed. Mary was first a homemaker, then a C.N.A. at a nursing home. In December 1982, Doug had a heart attack. It was decided that Mary and Doug move to Monmouth; so the parents left home! It was a good move! Doug was reunited with his mother, brothers and sisters; and Mary got a new family and many friends. Mary still enjoyed working with "special" people and worked for Warren Achievement at the school and in respite care.

Mary had grown up in Troy, IL. Her mother, Helen (Mueller) Hultz died with Mary was three. Her father, Louie raised her, he didn't see any problem in raising a girl. With help from Mary's Aunts Fanny and Lizzie, and Grandma Mueller, Mary enjoyed a happy childhood, loved music, sang in the Glee Club and played in the school band. She loved the bus trips! After graduation she worked at the Ralston Purina Company, St. Louis, MO. She met and even ate Christmas dinner at the company party with founder William Danforth!

Meeting and marrying Doug began her travels and wonders of life. After Doug's death, Mary joined the First Christian Church and was a Deaconess for several years and was active in many church events. She learned to cross stitch, which is still a favorite thing to do. She also joined the hospital volunteers. She likes collecting bears, clowns, angels and Hummels, taking trips to visit all the children and grandchildren; and now a great grandchild is a fun and great thing to do also.

DONALD LEE AND NELLIE ELIZABETH (LENZ) DENISON - Don's parents were Eddie Lee born 1-8-1898 in Munfordville, Ky; died 6-7-66 in Monmouth, Il and Mallie (Buckingham) born 4-2-05 in Norhttown, Ky; died 2-2-85 in Monmouth, Il.

Nellie's parents were Nettie Ethal Virginia (Ghrist) born 4-17-18 in Gallipolis, Ohio; died 10-27-92 Kirkwood, Illinois and David John Lenz born 12-24-18 in Burlington, Ia.

Don was born in Monmouth 2-11-34. He had 4 brothers and 4 sisters. He grew up in Monmouth, attended Harding grade school and Monmouth High School, graduated in June, 1953. He worked 3 years at the Y.M.C.A. while attending high school teaching Swimming classes. During the summer he was a sound man for the Little League Baseball Teams and umpire. He was a die-hard Cub fan and took trips to Chicago to see them win.

Donald Denison family

He took vacation time in September every year for squirrel hunting. Don joined the U.S.A.F. in 1953 and served for 4 years, was stationed in Tripoli, Libya. In 1955 Don flew 7,000 miles home to join his family for Christmas. Don, his 4 brothers and father served over 91 years in the military. After getting out of the A.F. he worked as a Loan Officer for State Loan Co. of Galesburg, later was transferred to Monmouth. Later he worked in the Loan Department of the National Bank and worked his way up to Assistant Vice President where he was appreciated greatly.

Nellie was born June 15, 1941 in Oquawka, Illinois. She has 2 brothers and 3 sisters. Her father farmed in the Baldbluff area and mother helped with the crop planting, there were pigs to feed and cows to milk and chickens to feed. Nellie helped her mother with picking and canning fruits and vegetables in season. The children had many chores, Nellie's favorite was churning the butter as whoever shook the jar got to drink the buttermilk! Nellie started School at Baldbluff, a country one-room school house with 8 grades, she went to high school at Little York and Kirkwood, graduated in 1959. She worked as a waitress at The Park-N-Eat, she also worked at Bersted Hobby Craft, Bowman's Shoe Store and First Street Fashions, she is well known for her friendly smile!

Don and Nellie were married Jan. 30,1960 at the Methodist Church, Kirkwood. They lived in Galesburg for 2 years then moved to Monmouth and later to Lake Warren. They enjoyed many happy times at the lake, fishing and water sports.

Their son, Richard Wayne was born March 7,1961, their pride and Joy! Richard has 2 children, Dru Richard born 5-5-83 and Mallory Page Buckingham born 9-29-84. Richard is now living in Springfield, Ill. and is correspondent for Metro Link News at the Capitol. Now Nellie is waiting for a new grandchild! She is a member of First Christian Church, is a volunteer at the hospital and a member of the Loyal Order of Moose Lodge Women, Burlington, Iowa. She enjoys painting very much, doing crafts and fishing. At present Nellie is a caregiver for the home bound.

HUBERT AND CHRISTINA DENISON - Hubert Denison was born in Milton Illinois, Pike County, son of John Otis Denison and Virginia

Madden French. Hubert did not finish high school having to drop out to help his father on the farm during the great depression. The farm was northeast of Milton where Hubert grew up with a brother Melvin and three sisters Hilda, Norma and Margaret. When WW II broke out Hubert was drafted into the Army Air Force. He was sent to New England Aircraft School to learn to work on B-17 bombers. After school he was sent to Knettishall England as part of 388th Bomb Group. During this time on leave he meet Nora Christina Hanafni, who was from Ireland and working in England building airplanes. As the war was coming to an end he married Chris and she came to America with many other war brides.

Hubert O. Denison and Nora Christina Hanafin (taken in London, England during WWII)

On returning to the U.S. and being discharged he and Chris began a farming career. After working for himself and others he migrated to Monmouth in 1961 and worked for Carol Walters. After a period of time he got a job at Monmouth College and gave up the farm life and purchased a house in Monmouth in 1964. Later his brother Melvin and Mother purchased a home and moved to Monmouth after the passing of John Otis Denison.

Hubert and Chris had three children Timothy (Joyce Reynolds), Mary (Ray Carlstedt) and Maurice (Lynn Jenks). After retiring Hubert & Chris built a new house in rural Little York Illinois. Several years later they decided to move to Zapata, Texas. Where they enjoyed their retirement with out snow. Chris passed away April 18, 1993 and Hubert followed February 17, 1994 and are both buried in the Catholic Cemetery in Zapata, Texas.

MICHAEL KENNETH AND CHRISTINA LOUISE (WILEY) DENISON - Michael K. Denison was born July 29, 1972 in Monmouth, Il to Joyce E. (Reynolds) Denison and Timothy O. Denison, with one younger sister Maura E. (Denison) Miller. Christina L. Denison was born June 5 1973 to Barbara L. (Kemplin) Wiley and Gary L. Wiley, with two younger siblings, a brother Nash Russell Wiley and a sister Jamie Jeanine (Wiley) Atwell. Michael's grandparents were Hubert Otis Denison and Nora Christina (Hanafin) Denison on his side. On his Mother's side Kenneth Glenn Reynolds and Dora (Rose)(Munson) Reynolds. Christina's Grandparents were Donna Dean (Anderson) Murphy and Russell J. Wiley on her father's side. On her mothers side Carol Ann (Main) Vance and Arthur Bernan Kemplin. They met in the year of 1992 started dating, two years later in 1994 they purchased a piece of property from his grandparents, Kenneth and Rose 656 – 275th Avenue, Little

Mike, Chris and Johnathon

York, IL They also purchased a mobile home for temporary living. In 1996 they purchased three cows and calf pairs, built a pole building and began farming with the hope to purchase more ground later. Michael works for Painter Farm Equipment as a farm mechanic. He enjoys his job very much and has been working there for 7 years, Working weekends running his own business D.J.'ing wedding and class reunions takes up the rest of his free time. Christina works as a manager at the Subway of Monmouth for the last 8 years, 2 years as the manager. December 7th 1996 they were married in Sugar Tree Grove United Presbyterian church in a beautiful ceremony preformed by Rev. Maura Mcgrath Nagel. March 2nd 2001 they announced the birth of their first child, a son Johnathon Michael Denison, weighing 5 pounds 12oz. Later that spring they started digging a basement for a house they plan to build. The house will be slow going, for they will be building it themselves. So far with the help of Michael's father Timothy, uncle Karl and many others they have finished a basement. Michael has also built a sawmill to saw his beams for the timber frame they plan to erect as a house in 2002.

TIMOTHY AND JOYCE DENISON - Timothy O. Denison was born June 9, 1946 in Pittsfield, IL and Joyce E. Reynolds was born April 16, 1946 in Monmouth, IL. They were married on July 1, 1970 at Immaculate Conception Church in Monmouth. They have two children Michael K. Denison who married Christina Wiley and they have a son Johnathan. Maura E. Denison is married to Craig Miller and they have two daughters Lindsay and Hana (Hanafin).

Joyce and Timothy Denison

Tim's parents were Hubert O. Denison and Christina Nora Hanafin of Pittsfield then Monmouth. Chris was born in Ireland and married Hubert in England during WW II. His grandparents were John O. Denison and Virginia Madden French of Milton, IL. and great grandparents were James Denison and Emily Stemp(Stamp) of Montezuma, IL and originally from England near Liverpool.

Joyce is second of four children of Kenneth G. Reynolds and Rose Munson of Monmouth, IL. Her grandfather was Arthur Glenn Reynolds and Dora Rule, great grandparents were James Walker Reynolds and Mary Eva Liggett, great great grandparents were John Wilson Reynolds and Jane Campbell all of Warren County. The oldest relative that settled in the county was her great great great grandfather John G. Reynolds who came here in 1833. Joyce has worked at Save-A-Lot in Monmouth for about 10 years.

Tim worked for Kroger grocery while in high school and when he returned from the service. He serviced in the United States Marine Corps for 3 1/2 years and is a Vietnam Veteran and is a member of the Knights of Columbus and Immaculate Conception Catholic Church. After becoming interested in helping Joyce research the Reynolds family, genealogy got in their blood, and they index the 1886 Portrait and Biography Album of Warren County. He also was one of four persons, Richard Kane, Barbara Kline and Sharon Todd, who started the Warren County Illinois Genealogical Society and was elected first president in April 1981. In October of 1970 the US Postal Service hired him where he is employed today.

In 1976 they built a new home one-mile west of Monmouth. They did much of the work themselves; Tim did the wiring, put up dry wall and siding. Joyce taped, strip, mudded and sanded all the drywall, while watching two kids less than 5 years old. They both laid the hardwood and vinyl floor and painted the interior and exterior.

ROBERT DENNIS - Robert Dennis was born in 1816 in Washington Co, PA. His mother was a Bedillion who died at his birth and his father two months previous. Robert married Elizabeth Ryan on 13 Feb 1840, she was born 2 Sep 1820 in Washington Co, PA. They moved with their family to Tompkins Twp, Warren Co, IL sometime after 1850 and before 1856.

During the Civil War Robert was a Captain in Company I 91st Regiment IL Infantry from 1862 to 1865 enlisting at White Hall. He was captured at Elizabethtown, KY 27 Dec 1862 and confined at Richmond by General Morgan till 10 Jan 1863.

Robert and Elizabeth had six children: Joseph Ryan Dennis born 25 Nov 1840; Mary Dennis born 28 Sep 1842 and died 2 Mar 1843; Elizabeth Jane Dennis born. 6 Mar 1845 married Nels Peterson 7 Nov 1869 in Young America, Warren Co, IL and died 1908 in Russell Co, KS; John M. Dennis born 1847 married Nancy Ann McCormick 12 Jun 1871 in Warren Co, IL and died 2 May 1889 in Monmouth, Warren Co, IL; Robert Wiley Dennis born 10 Jun 1849 married Lizzie Moody 7 Aug 1894 in Warren Co, IL and died 1913 in Burlughs, KS; Mary Elizabeth Dennis born 1856 Monmouth, Warren Co, IL married Frank Vosburg 28 Aug 1873 in Warren Co, IL and died about 1920 in Bedford, Taylor Co, Iowa.

Robert Dennis died 15 Jul 1875 in Tompkins Twp, Warren Co, IL, and his wife Elizabeth died 29 Mar 1900 in Cameron, Warren Co, IL. They are both buried in Center Grove Cemetery, Tompkins Twp (alias Kirkwood), IL.

DEUGER-MCKELVIE - McKelvie, Joan Lucille was born on May 16, 1932 in Alexis, Illinois, Warren County, to parents Arch Logan

(1889-1959) and Fern (Mills) McKelvie (1891-1986). She had two brothers- Clyde Raymond (1912-1988) m. Metta McKay McNeil, Archie Lee (1925) m. Betty Fergueson, and one sister Mary Jane (1916-1974) m. Albert Pempek.

Joan and Don Deuger

Joan resided in Alexis until graduation from Alexis High School in 1950, then moved to Monmouth where she received a BA degree in mathematics from Monmouth College in 1953. During this time she worked at the Rivoli Theater and as a nurses aide at Monmouth Hospital. She taught a year at Arlington Heights High School then returned to Monmouth and married Donald Robert Deuger on July 17, 1954. After Joan taught a year at Central Jr. High and Garfield schools they started a family of five children: Mark Steven b. 1955 m. Jodi Lee Dufva; Jayme Lynn b. 1957; Donna Jolene b. 1961 m. Per Christian Guldbeck; Roberta Jane b. 1962 m. Willard Eugene Goforth; Gary Frederick b. 1965 m. 1st Angela Huber m. 2nd Terri Emily Varner (3 sons and 2 daughters). There are presently 13 grandchildren: Drew Donald Deuger; Ashley Nicole, Amanda Marie, Christen Joy, Cassandra Faith and Alexander Christian Guldbeck; Trevor Lucas and Emily Kate Goforth; Brandon Donald Detmer, Shannan Nicole, Jonathan Alexander, Michael Andrew, and Sean Jacob Deuger.

Joan later attended Western Illinois University, taught at Achievement Industries, did some substitute teaching for awhile, worked at Far and Near Travel Agency for a time after which she did alterations for the Model Clothing store and for many years did clothing alterations in her home.

Deuger, Donald Robert was born April 4, 1931 in Minneapolis, Minnesota, Hennipin County, son of Frederick (1895-1965) and Johanna Mabel (Rogers) Deuger (1902-1935). His father was originally from East Peoria, son of Fred and Lena (Linde) Deuger, and his mother from Minnesota) daughter of John and Julia (Fairbanks) Rogers.

Don grew up in Brainerd, Minnesota, served in the Army Air Corp, and U.S. Air Force 1947-1950, attended Chicago College of Laboratory Technique graduating in May 1952. He then became employed as lab and x-ray technician at Monmouth Hospital until 1963 when he went to work at Wells Pet Food Company in quality control until retirement in 1996.

Being active members of the Monmouth First Christian Church Don has served as deacon, trustee, and elder for many years. Joan has been church treasurer for 16 years, sang in the choir for 50 years among other areas of service. She is also active in DAR, Warren County Genealogical Society, CMC Auxiliary and Crimson Clan.

Don's maternal ancestry included John Fairbanks whose home in Dedham, Massachusetts, built 1636, is oldest frame house in U.S., preserved by the Fairbanks Family in America. Donald is also a member of the Minnesota Chippewa Indian Tribe, a descendant of "White Raven" a chief of the Wisconsin Chippewas.

Joan's maternal ancestry includes early pioneers to Cameron, IL. Warren County in 1830s: great-great-grandparents Christopher and Martha (Lucas) Whitman and David R. and Patsey (Haley) Shelton-descendants of people who came to America in early 1600s. David's father, Samuel Waddy Shelton served in the War of the Revolution, as well as Joan's great-great-grandfather James Mills. Her paternal great grandparents, Thomas and Janette (Muir) McKelvie came from Scotland in 1850 via Maryland to Knox County and then Spring Grove, Warren County about 1860. Her grandfather Michael McKelvie served in the army at Ft. Donalson during the Civil War. He then married Marian Peacock from Knox County and had a family of 11 children, most of whom lived out their lives in Warren County.

MARIE (DOWNES) DILTS - Marie Elizabeth Downes was born on April 2, 1946, to Grace (Ketchum) and Roger Downes of 833 N. Main St., Monmouth. She was their first child. At the age of two, her parents moved to 700 N. First St.; in 1952 she moved to Henderson County, when her parents took over the farm of her grandparents, Maurice and Florence Downes of Monmouth. She attended Rozetta Grade School from grades one through six. At the age of twelve she joined the Rozetta Baptist Church; she was a member of the Rozetta Lucky Four's 4-H Club for eight years. She went to Biggsville Junior High and was member of the first graduating class of Union High School, Biggsville, IL, graduating in 1964.

Marie Elizabeth Dilts

She then moved to Burlington, IA, where she attended Burlington Business College. After graduation from BBC, she worked at a variety of office jobs, prior to her marriage to John Richard Anderson of Burlington on May 12, 1972. Their daughter, Stephanie Michelle Anderson, was born January 21, 1974. Marie was divorced from John Anderson in 1977.

Marie married John Strauss of Burlington in 1980; he died in 1981, and she married Richard Eugene Dilts, retired, on June 4, 1994.

Marie's daughter Stephanie has given her three grandchildren: Jasmine Sue Marie Crowe, born July 27, 1993, Jordan Scott Crowe, born April 9, 1995, and Jamie Grace Carlisle, born July 18, 2000.

Marie and Richard Dilts moved back to Burlington in 2001 and currently reside at 1428 S. 5th St. Marie stays active doing crafts, volunteering at her church, and playing with her grandchildren.

DOTY - In the fall of 1921, Hubert Frank Doty arrived in Monmouth to attend Monmouth College. He was born on Nov. 1, 1898 in Custer Park, IL. and resided with his family in Stuttgart, Arkansas for most of his boyhood. The Doty family got their start in America with the arrival of Edward Doty in 1620 at Plymouth, MA aboard the good ship Mayflower. Hubert graduated from Stuttgart High where he was an outstanding athlete. He was followed to Monmouth by three younger brothers, Carl Babcock Doty, Warner Woodworth Doty, and John Roy Doty. All four were graduates of Monmouth College.

Cynthia Merrill Woodworth, wife of Eli Hunter Doty, circa 1852-55.   *Alma and Hubert Doty 1925*

Hubert was a star athlete at Monmouth College. He played football under the tutelage of Glenn Smith who produced winning football teams at Monmouth during the early 1920s. He was selected by Midwestern sportswriters as first string left tackle on the all Midwestern team in 1924. Hubert and his brothers worked at Hawcocks restaurant and he worked summers on a farm in Rushville, IL.

His great-grandfather, Lysander (Justus) Woodworth was a pioneer resident of Warren County in the latter half of the 1830s. Lysander was a builder and a preacher who founded the Methodist Church in Monmouth. After his death during an epidemic, in 1841, his family returned to Ohio where his daughter, Cynthia Merrill Woodworth met and married Eli Hunter Doty. Lysander is buried in the pioneer cemetery in Monmouth.

Hubert met his future wife, Alma Lottie Feighner, in Parkville, MO. in 1918. She was born on August 14, 1898 in a log cabin outside the tiny village of Fontana, KS. The Feiahners were of German descent. Christoffel Feighner (aka Feichtner) arrived on the ship Neptune at Philadelphia, PA on Oct. 4, 1752. He was a Mennonite farmer and is referenced in a publication, *Pennsylvania German Pioneers*. Following a long distance courtship Alma and Hubert were married in Leavenworth, KS on Aug. 31, 1924.

Following graduation from Monmouth College, Hubert attended the Rush Presbyterian Medical School in Chicago for one year leaving due to illness. He returned to Monmouth and accepted the position of general science teacher at Central Jr. High. He held this position until his death on April 9, 1953.

Hubert and Alma had two children born in Monmouth. William Hubert was born on July 8, 1933 and Alma Genevieve was born on Feb. 8,

1935. Both children attended Monmouth public schools and were graduates of Monmouth High School and Monmouth College. Hubert was a devout Christian and a faithful member of the Second United Presbyterian Church which he served as treasurer and ruling elder. During WWII he taught at the Naval Flight Preparatory school based at Monmouth College, was a member of the militia, and worked at the Galesburg Butler plant in support of the war effort. All of this in addition to his regular teaching duties at Central Jr. High. In the early 1950s he was instrumental in founding the Warren County Teachers Credit Union.

His wife Alma was active in church women's groups, worked at the Warren County Public Library, and was a volunteer librarian at the Harding School learning center for many years. She was active until her death on October 22, 1984.

His daughter, Genevieve, became an elementary school teacher at the fourth grade level at Harding school. She later became the learning center director for Harding and subsequently for the school district. After her retirement from teaching she became children's librarian for the Warren County Public Library. In 2000, Genevieve was awarded the prestigious Studs Terkel award by the Illinois Humanities Council for her outstanding work in promoting children's literacy in Warren County.

His son, William, after graduating from Monmouth College in 1957, studied biochemistry at St. Louis University and then joined the Ralston Purina Co. in St. Louis. He was director of the research libraries and later served as marketing director of the Raltech Division. In retirement, he resides in St. Louis and has two children. Catherine Janine is a pediatrician with St. Louis Children's Hospital and William Hunter is a business computer networking consultant with Charter Communications. He has four granddaughters: Katie 19, Amber 17, Sarah 5 and Jaden, one month.

Hubert and Alma Doty could never imagine living anywhere else but in Warren County. They refused many other job offers over the years in order to continue their long-term relationship with the community they loved.

BONNIE CAROLE DOWNES - Bonnie Carole Downes was born on October 27, 1948, to Grace (Ketchum) and Roger Downes of 700 N. First St, Monmouth, IL. She was their third daughter. In 1952 she moved to Henderson County, when her parents took over the farm of her grandparents, Maurice and Florence Downes of Monmouth. She attended Rozetta Grade School from grades one through six. At the age of ten, she joined the Rozetta Baptist Church and was a member of the Rozetta Lucky Four's 4-H Club for nine years. She went to Biggsville Junior High and Union High School, from which she graduated as valedictorian in 1966.

She enrolled at College of the Ozarks, Clarksville, AR, in 1966, majoring in English and speech. In 1968 she was chosen at the first C of O student to participate in the Junior Year Abroad program, and spent 1968-69 at Beirut College for Women, Beirut, Lebanon. While the Middle East, she traveled widely, visiting countries such as Egypt, Iran, Turkey, Israel, Greece, and Italy. She returned to C of O for her senior year, where she was selected for *Who's Who Among American College Students*, was a member of Delta PSI Omega dramatic fraternity and Alpha Chi Omega honor fraternity, and graduated magna cum laude with a B.A. in 1970.

In 1970 she moved to Mazon, IL, where she began teaching English at Mazon Township High School; the school later became Mazon-Verona-Kinsman High School. In addition to her assigned teaching duties, she developed the speech classes and a humanities class for the school; she directed the school plays; started the drama club, and sponsored the yearbook and National Honor Society. She served five years on the state committee for the Illinois High School Theatre Festival. She was active in the MVK Education Association and was chair of the committee that negotiated the first master contract at MVK.

Bonnie Carole Downes

In 1973 she moved to Dwight IL. In 1975 she obtained an M.A. in literature from Governors' State University. In 1985 she obtained an M.S. in theatre arts from Illinois State University and moved to Morris, IL, as she became more involved with the Morris Theatre Guild community theatre. She has since directed and appeared in numerous plays for the guild, has held every office in the guild, has won several Outstanding Actress and Director Awards, and has served on the board of directors since 1986.

In 1987, while at MVK, she began teaching part-time in the speech department at Joliet Junior College. She continued this until 1990, when MVK High School merged with Seneca High School, Seneca, IL, and Bonnie began teaching at SHS, where she began a new drama club and continued to direct plays. In 1996 she became chair of the English Department at SHS. She has been named to *Who's Who Among American Teachers* eleven times, has received Most Inspirational Teacher Awards from Western Illinois University and Illinois Valley Community College, and the Seneca High School Excellence in Education Award.

In 1997 she purchased a house at 1611 Schubert Dr. in Morris, where she currently lives. She plans to take early retirement in 2004.

MAURICE AND FLORENCE (CHEWNING) DOWNES - Maurice Emil Downes was born in 1902 to John Finley and Jennie Day Downes of Smithshire, Warren County, Illinois. He attended local grade schools until he dropped out to go to work, working as a day laborer for local farmers. He married Letha Florence Chewning (Florence) in 1924. They had three children during the 1920s: Maurice Roger (Roger), retired, and now of rural Abingdon, IL. Herville Finley (Finley), retired, and now of Strongville, Ohio. Elizabeth Ann (Betty), retired, and now of Marshfield, WI.

After their marriage they farmed one year at Smithshire. In 1925 they moved to Rozetta Township where he was a tenant farmer for four years. In 1929 they moved two miles East of Monmouth. In 1930 the family moved to a rented farm near Roseville where they lived for several years. In 1947 Mr. and Mrs. Downes purchased a farm in Henderson County, northwest of Kirkwood, where they lived until 1952.

In 1952, due to a degenerative eye disease, Mr. Downes turned day-to-day farming operations over to his oldest son Roger, who had married Grace Marie Ketchum of Kirkwood in 1945. Maurice purchased a house at 412 E. Archer Avenue, Monmouth, and they moved there. Maurice became an active member of the First Baptist Church of Monmouth and was a member of the Odd Fellows in Monmouth.

Maurice Emil Downes died in 1982, following a series of strokes. Florence Chewning Downes died in 1987. They are buried in Monmouth Cemetery.

They were survived by their three children, one daughter-in-law, Grace Downes (now deceased); seven grandchildren, Marie Elizabeth (Richard) Dilts and Jane Irene (Jerry) Hummell of Iowa; Bonnie Carole Downes of Illinois; Letha Ann (Tom) Dernlan and Lester Lee (Judy) Wood of Wisconsin; Pamela Lois (Jim) West of Ohio; and Richard Finley (Theresa) Downes of Texas and nine great-grandchildren.

ROGER & GRACE (KETCHUM) DOWNES - Maurice Roger Downes, was born 17 January 1925, Monmouth, Warren County, IL, son of Maurice Emil and Letha Florence (Chewning) Downes. Siblings: Herville Finley, Elizabeth Ann. Roger attended local schools, graduating from Roseville High School.

Grace and Roger Downes

Grace Marie Ketchum, was born 8 January 1926, Kirkwood, Warren County, IL, daughter of Frank and Mary (Swarts) Ketchum. Siblings: Clarence Preston, Lucille Virginia, Ernest Roy, Hazel Arizona, Nannie Belle, Ethel Lorraine, Robert Lee, Dorothy Mae, William Eldon. Grace attended Center Grove school, graduating from Kirkwood High. Before marriage she did office work.

Roger and Grace were married 9 September 1945, at Berwick Baptist Church, Warren County. They lived in Monmouth for a few years. Roger worked for the M and ST L railroad as a brakeman.

In 1952 they moved to his father's farm northwest of Kirkwood where they farmed until the farm was sold. They had a large garden and Grace did much canning and freezing of foods for the family. In 1974 they purchased a home northwest of Abingdon. Roger worked for Abingdon (Briggs) Pottery until retirement in

1990. Grace worked as a meat cutter at Crystal Lakes Packing Co, Galesburg. She later worked in nursing homes in Knoxville and Abingdon. Grace also enjoyed making jellies, pickles, relishes, breads and rolls for a booth they had for several years at Knoxville during the Knox County Scenic Drive.

Grace and Roger were members of the Baptist faith.

Roger is a member of IOOF, Monmouth; Eagles and Moose Lodge #880 Galesburg, where he is very active. He has held many offices there, including Governor, Trustee, Prelate, Treasurer, and has the Fellowship degree.

Grace was a member of Rebekah Lodge #22, Monmouth, where she served as Noble Grand, L.E.A., L.A.P.M; Women of the Moose #115, Galesburg where she served as Senior Regent; and former Eagle's Auxiliary, #518, Galesburg.

Children, all born in Warren County are: 1.) Marie Elizabeth born 2 April 1946, m. 1 Douglas W. Aldridge, divorced. m. 2 John Richard Anderson, divorced. One child, Stephanie Michelle, born 21 January 1974. m. 3 John Edward Straus, deceased. m. 4 Richard Dilts. 2.) Jane Irene born 2 April 1947, married Jerry Gordon Hummell. One child, Jason Gordon. 3.) Bonnie Carole born 27 October 1948. 4.) Elaine June born 7 June 1950, died 17 January 1952.

Grace died 14 October 1992. She and daughter Elaine are buried at Monmouth Cemetery.

DRIFFILL - Joseph Driffill was born October 6, 1811 in Laxton, Yorkshire, England and died August 29, 1874 in Ionia, IL. He married Mary Catherine Messenger October 20, 1840 in Brooklyn, NY. Mary was born March 15, 1812 in NY, and died February 06, 1907 in Alexis, IL.

By 1856, the family had moved from Clifton Park, NY and were living in Iona (later known as Shanghai) where Joseph had a blacksmith shop.

Joseph enlisted in the army on August 1, 1862 in Henderson, IL and was mustered in on Sept 2, 1862 in Knoxville by Lieut Knox. Joseph was a private with Co F 102nd Reg Ill Vol Inf and served as the regiment blacksmith. He was discharged from service on June 12, 1865 and returned to his blacksmith shop in Iona.

On Sunday May 3, 1868 a tornado tore through Ionia and destroyed the town, leaving a few buildings. Joseph's blacksmith shop was destroyed.

The children of Joseph and Mary Driffill are:
Jane, b. October 28, 1841 m. James Jones September 16, 1863, Warren Co, IL.

William was born July 1, 1843 married (1) Sarah E. Churchill December 13, 1868 in Iona, IL, daughter of Carmi Churchill and Alivra Conant. She was born February 27, 1852 in Henderson, IL. He married (2) Isabell J. Fell October 12, 1904 in Warren Co, daughter of Daniel McKenion and Sarah Hughes.

Ann, b. October 23, 1847 in Schenectady, NY married John Leland Salts August 18, 1868 in Warren Co. He was born March 24, 1821 in Jonesboro, TN;

Joseph, Jr, b. July 25, 1850, m. Melissa Jane Brown, April 29, 1880, Warren Co.

John Henry, b. July 1, 1851 in Schnectedy, NY married (1) Josephine A. Churchill October 9, 1876 in Monmouth, daughter of Benjamin Churchill and Sarah Rowland. She was born May 26, 1850 in Alexis, IL. John married (2) Emma Johnson October 23, 1901 in Monmouth, daughter of William Chicken and Sarah Scott. He married (3) Ruth A. Witte.

Daniel was born March 10, 1856 in Warren Co and died January 17, 1912 in Shanghai, (Ionia) Warren Co. He married Matilda Ann Reed January 14, 1878 in Monmouth, daughter of James Reed and Fanny Collins. She was born April 3, 1853 in New Albany, IN, and died January 7,1915 in Alexis.

Etta Mary was born June 7, 1865 in Warren Co and died September 8, 1909 in Alexis, IL. She married John W. Reed December 11, 1879 in Ionia, IL, son of James Reed and Fanny Collins. He was born January 1848 in New Albany, IN, and died August 14, 1902 in Alexis.

Harriet, b. March 21, 1866, married John Brown.

CLAIRE AND MARTHA DRISCOLL - W. Claire Driscoll, the son of W. Alfred and Helen (Marston) Driscoll was born October 11, 1932 in North Henderson, IL. He had two brothers Dan and David, and one sister Delores. He attended grade school in the Warren County area. He attended high school for 3 years at Roseville High School and the 4th year at Monmouth High School from which he graduated in 1950.

Front row: Susan Byers, Claire Driscoll, Mary Louck. Back row: Rosemary Kesinger, Martha Driscoll, Margaret McCreight.

On May 27, 1953 Claire married Martha J. Thompson at the Immaculate Conception Church in Monmouth, IL. Martha was the youngest of nine children born to Roy and Rose (Gavin) Thompson on Feb. 1, 1933. She had four brothers: Bill, Lawrence, Harold, and Bob. Her four sisters are: Helen, Margaret, Florence, and Grace. Martha, and all her brothers and sisters, attended Farmers Academy Grade School in Hale Township. She attended Monmouth High School, and she also graduated with the Class of 1950.

In 1953 Claire served in the U.S. Army with part of the time served in Korea. While he was in the Army, Martha worked as office secretary at DeKalb Ag. Ass'n in Monmouth. When Claire returned from service in Korea, he worked at DeKalb Ag. as a plant employee.

In 1957 they moved to Marshall, Mo. where Claire was employed as a plant inspector. Later they moved to Grinnell, Iowa where he was plant inspector at the Grinnell plant. In 1962 they returned to Monmouth, and in 1964 Claire left the DeKalb Co. to begin a farming career which was something he had always wanted to do.

By then the family consisted of four daughters: Peggy and Mary who had been born in Monmouth; Susan who was born in Marshall, Mo.; and Rosie born in Grinnell, Iowa. They moved to the Harry Lafferty farm south of Aledo where they started their farming career. They attended St. Catherine's Church in Atedo where Claire served as a trustee. The girls attended grade school at Ohio Grove and Seaton. They attended and graduated from Aledo. High School. While living south of Atedo, the Driscolls also farmed land in Warren and Henderson counties.

After living on the farm south of Aledo for 28 years, Claire and Martha moved to 804 N. 9 1/2 St. in. Monmouth. They now attend Immaculate Conception Church. Through the years, Claire has been active with the Knights of Columbus. He is also a member of the American Legion and the VFW. He has served on the Board of Directors of the F & M Bank in Galesburg and the Trust and Savings Bank and Marquette Bank in Monmouth.

The family now consists of their 4 daughters, 4 sons-in-law, 8 grandsons, 1 granddaughter, and 1 great-granddaughter.

DUNGAN AND WELLS - David Melburn Dungan was born in 1833 in Ohio. He married Elizabeth Ann Failor in 1854. The Dungans moved to Warren County and lived at 429 North First Street in Monmouth. David was a Civil War Veteran, serving in the 17th Illinois Infantry in Company C from April 1861 to May 1862. He was a cabinetmaker and an undertaker in Dungan and Krollman Undertakers located in Monmouth. David and Elizabeth had seven children, including George W. Dungan who was born in 1879.

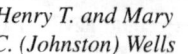

Henry T. and Mary C. (Johnston) Wells   *Elizabeth Ann Failor Dungan*

George married Luella Wells in 1899. George was a master plumber in Monmouth. George and Luella had four children, Earl Lucian, Mary Elizabeth, Martha Lucille, and Junelyn. Earl married Theresa May Reeves and had three daughters, Mary Louise, Elizabeth, and Lois Estelle Dungan, and one son, George Clinton Dungan. Martha married William Lovell and had three sons, James, Thomas, and John Lovell. Elizabeth married William Berner and had one daughter Carol Ann Berner. Junelyn married Lloyd Blanchard and had one daughter, Diane Lee Blanchard and later married Spurgeon John Widener and had two daughters, Mary Ellen and Amy Lou Widener. Spurgeon came from Meadow View, Virginia at a very young age and was a farmer all of his life. Junelyn was a nurse and worked at the Monmouth Hospital.

Carol Ann Berner; great-granddaughter of David Melburn Dungan, married Ralph Eugene Davis and had two children William Lee and Laura Beth Davis.

George Clinton Dungan; great grandson of David Melburn Dungan, married Esther Maureen Powers and they have five children, George Clinton II, Kurt Joseph, Kathleen Marie, Mark David, and Michael John Dungan. George H married Sharron Lauthridge and had two children, Theresa Maureen and George Clinton

Dungan III. He later married Josephina Piccolo. Kurt married Andrea Balasic and had one son Joesph Patrick Dungan. He later married Patti Powell. Mark married Diane Scymanski and have three children, Sarah Elizabeth, Shane David, and Michaela Elizabeth Dungan. Mark married Marianne McKenna and have two children, Katelyn McKenna Dungan and Sean Michael Dungan.

Diane Lee Blanchard; great granddaughter of David Melburn Dungan married F.W. Snell and had one son David Michael Snell. David Michael married Margarita Francine Esquibel and have two children, Vanessa Kerrin and Michael Elijah Snell.

Mary Ellen Widener, great-granddaughter of David Melburn Dungan, married Jerry Stokes and had one son Jeremy Allen Stokes. She later married Jerry Dale Lefler and they have two sons, Christopher John Ross Lefler and Tyler Dale Lefler. Jeremy married Jennifer Rogers and they had two sons, Cody Allen and Cory Ryan Stokes.

Amy Lou Widener, great-granddaughter of David Melburn Dungan, married James L. Lox and they have one daughter, Amanda June Lox. James works as an arborist in a family business.

Luella (Wells) Dungan was one of nine children born to Henry Thomas and Mary Cassendanie (Johnston) Wells. Henry Thomas Wells served in the Civil War in the 64th Ill. Infantry – Company D and also worked as a Stonemason during the construction of the Immaculate Conception Catholic Church. One of Luella's brothers, Billie, was a vaudeville entertainer and traveled with the Great Nicola.

DAVID A. DUTTON AND LINDA L. (HALL) DUTTON - David Allen Dutton was born in Monmouth on September 1, 1947, the fifth child of Eldon and Garnet (Husted) Dutton, originally of the Summum, IL area. He attended Little York Grade School and after graduation from Yorkwood High School in 1965, joined his father's farming operation. On August 20, 1967, he married Linda Louise Hall at Sugar Tree Grove Church. Linda (born on March 25, 1949, in Monmouth) is the third of four children, born to Fred D. and Grace E. (Higbee) Hall, of rural Monmouth. Linda attended Hale school for her first five grades and after its closure, continued in the Yorkwood district, graduating in 1967.

Linda and David Dutton

David and Linda have three children, Melissa Bennett of Fairmont, MN; Kimberly of Amsterdam, NY; and Matthew of Alexis, IL. Melissa and Jim Bennett (son of Mazy and the late Chuck Bennett) are both Monmouth College graduates. Melissa taught at Monmouth High School until their move to Minnesota in 1998, where Jim became the news director for KJLY Christian radio station. They have six children, Kayla and Lyndsay of Santee, CA. and Krystal, Grace, Jamie, and Hannah of Fairmont.

Kimberly Dutton received her B.A. at MacMurray College in Jacksonville, IL. She then attended Miami University in Oxford, OH receiving her M.A. in 1998. She served as Director of Students at Rochester Institute of Technology, Rochester, NY for two years and is currently Student Activities Director at Fulton-Montgomery Junior College near Amsterdam, NY.

Matthew received his B.A. in Business and Finance from Augustana College in 1996 and became a partner in Dutton Farms. On June 21, 1997, he married Kristin Adamson, of Rockford, IL also an Augustana graduate). Kristin received her Masters in Physical Therapy from Hahneman University, Philadelphia, PA. and is a physical therapist at Monmouth Medical Center. They have one son, David Jonathan, born on September 29, 2001.

David and Linda spent their first 9 years of marriage in Spring Grove Township, and in 1977, moved to the "home place" in Sumner township when his parents built a home in Monmouth. In 1983, they started construction on a new home which was completed in spring of 1984.

David and Linda are members of the Norwood Presbyterian Church. In 1978, they both received their private pilot licenses. David has been active on numerous agricultural committees, including Warren County Soil & Water, Farm Bureau, and Riverland F.S. In 1996, he completed a two-year course of study to become a Presbyterian lay pastor. In November of that year, he was commissioned to the Little Cedar Presbyterian Church in Little York.

Linda was a leader of the Alexis All Star 4-H club for ten years and became the Area Representative for the Aledo Christian Women's Club in 1994. She is an inspirational speaker for Stonecroft Ministries. David and Linda enjoy spending time with their family and traveling.

FRANCIS LOUIS "JUG" EARP - Jug Earp was a second cousin, once removed, of Monmouth's most famous citizen, Wyatt Earp. He came to Monmouth College in 1918, and in his sophomore season was the center on the football team. Earp, who also played baseball and basketball at Monmouth, was the captain and fullback on the 1921 Scots during his senior season. "He was one of the greatest players I have ever seen," recalled Jud Jones, MC graduate and long-time sports editor at the *Review Atlas*. The *Ravelings*, MC yearbook, said "Earp, the center, did more damage than any other lineman."

Earp was also the pitcher on the baseball team for the Conference Champion Scots.

In his senior year, he moved off the line to fullback position and in their opening game against Hedding College Earp scored the first two touchdowns and kicked the extra points in a 48-17 triumph. He missed two games from an injury, then the rest of the season played brilliantly. He was the backer and passer, and much of the defensive strength of the line was due to Jug's ferocious boding up.

Earp graduated from Monmouth College in 1921 and began his pro career with the Rock Island Independents. While at Rock Island he played alongside one of the greatest athletes of his time, Jim Thorpe. He played there one year before Coach Curly Lambeau wired him an offer to play for Green Bay. In his eleven years with the Packers, they never had a losing season and won three league championships.

In his first year with the Packers, Earp played center on offense and tackle on defense as Green Bay went 7-2-1. He played those two positions throughout his career with Green Bay. In 1929 Green Bay went undefeated on the way to their league championship. With Earp anchoring a defense that allowed only 24 points (an average of less than two per game) while the Green Bay offense put 212 points on the board.

While playing in the NFL Earp was credited with being the first to make the one hand snap from center to the quarterback. When going to the Packers he had to argue three days to get $100 per game.

Jug Earp played one year of professional baseball with the New York Yankees in 1927.

After his retirement, Earp later returned to the Packers as Public Relations Director from 1950-1954. In 1970 he was inducted into the Green Bay Hall of Fame.

When the Scots were looking for a new football coach in 1938, he influenced Monmouth College to hire Ivan Calhoun, a former pro-rank teammate. The college thought he over-emphasized athletics and complained about the amount of work required of the players and replaced him with Monmouth legend, Bobby Woll.

In 1942 he joined the Office of Price Administration and in 1946 he took over the direction of the Wisconsin O.P.A. Before his death he was a salesman for a corrugated box company. He died at the age of 71.

WALTER EARP - Walter Earp was born in Montgomery County, Maryland, in 1787. Sometime after Walter's birth, his parents moved to Pittsylvania County, Virginia, to occupy land earned through his father's Revolutionary War service.

Walter Earp

Walter met Martha Early in Virginia and married her in Pittsylvania County, Virginia, in 1809. Martha Early was born August 28, 1790, in Avery County, North Carolina.

Walter Earp's ancestry dates back to Thomas Earp during the reign of Charles I of England (1625-1649). Thomas Jr. was born in 1665 in England and died in 1720 in Maryland. His son, John Earp, married Rebecca (?) in Fairfax County, Virginia. Joseph, one of their sons, was born in Maryland and died in 1750. Joseph's wife, Ruth Tates Earp, was born in 1700.

One of their sons, Joshua, wed Mary Budd. Their son William was born in 1729 in Maryland. He married Priscilla Nicholas in Montgomery County in 1752.

Their son Phillip was born in Montgomery County, Maryland, in 1755 and was the father of

Walter Earp. Walter and Martha Earp moved to Lincoln County, North Carolina, where their first child, Lorenzo Dow, was born December 18, 1809. They were to have two more children there: Elizabeth in 1811, and Nicholas Porter on September 6, 1813. In the fall of 1813 they migrated with their three small children. It was a perilous, treacherous and difficult journey. They stopped along the way in Tennessee and spent two or three years near the Cumberland River, then settled in Logan County, Russelville, Kentucky. He taught school there and in Morgantown, Kentucky. He was a licensed preacher in the Methodist E. Church. Next, they moved to Ohio County, Kentucky, where they improved a farm and lived there 20 years.

Walter, Martha, sons and daughters and families moved from Kentucky to Illinois settling in Warren County, Monmouth, Illinois, November 9, 1846. In addition to the three children mentioned above there were six more: Josiah J., born October 16, 1816; James O. K. was born in 1818; Francis A. was born June 11, 1821; twins – Walter C. and Jonathan D., born April 28, 1824; and Sarah born March 2, 1827.

Walter Earp was three times commissioned Justice of the Peace in Monmouth. He lived seven years in Monmouth until his death January 30, 1853, at age 66. He is buried in Pioneer Cemetery in Monmouth. He preceded his wife in death by 28 years. Martha Earp lived ninety-one years, dying September 24, 1881, and is buried in Pioneer Cemetery also. At the time of her death she had eight children, eighty-five grandchildren, 130 great grandchildren and 13 great-great-grandchildren, totaling 236 living descendants.

Walter and Martha were the progenitors of the Earps in this area. One of their sons, Nicholas, married Abigail Storm, and they had two children: Newton and Mariah. She passed away after three years of marriage, and Nicholas married Virginia Cooksey. Their children were James, Virgil, Martha, Wyatt, Morgan, B. Warren, Virginia A. and Adelia D. Wyatt, whose full name was Wyatt Berry Stapp Earp, is the famed frontier marshall, who with some of his brothers, figured in Western history. Their best known episode is the historical OK Corral shootout.

(Submitted by Clyde Kneen.)

WYATT BERRY STAPP EARP - Wyatt Berry Stapp Earp, the world famous Old West lawman, Deputy U.S. Marshall was born on March 19, 1848, in his Aunt Elizebeth Earp Ezell's home at 406 South 3rd Street in Monmouth. His parents were Nicolas Porter and Virginia Cooksey Earp who owned a home at 125 North 1st Street, 1845-49, and the eastside of the 200 block of North 1st Street. They also lived in Wyatt's birthplace home, 1849-50.

The family went west for the Gold Rush, got as far a Pella, Iowa, 1850-56, and returned to Monmouth, 1856-59, where they bought a home at 409 South B Street, owned lots for farming at 300 South A Street, and owned the westside of North 5th Street, where they lived. The family moved to their farm in Pella, farmed in California, 1864-68, and in Lamar, Missouri, 1869.

Other siblings were Newton and Mariah, born to Nicolas's first wife, Abigail Storm, who died, and James, Virgil, Martha, Morgan, Warren, Virginia and Adelia.

Wyatt's grandparents, Justice of the Peace Walter and Martha Early Earp, and six other children settled in Monmouth later. His grandfather had been a Methodist preacher, teacher and farmer in Kentucky. The Earp ancestors originated in England, moved to Ireland, and then emigrated to the United States before 1776.

Wyatt became a constable in Missouri 1869, married Urilla Sutherland 1870. After her sudden death that year, he became a buffalo hunter with a Government Surveying Party. Earp became a city policeman in Wichita and Dodge City, Kansas before going to Tombstone, Arizona 1879, where he became a county sheriff. His second wife, Celia Ann Blaylock from Iowa, was with him. She died 1888.

Wyatt Earp

On October 26, 1881, the Earp lawmen, Wyatt, Virgil, Morgan, along with "Doc" Holliday, were arresting cowboy rustlers, which erupted into the now famous "Gunfight at the O.K. Corral." The judge ruled in favor of the lawmen.

Wyatt was mainly a businessman – a cooper, a prospector, realtor, saloon owner, movie consultant, prizefight referee, Wells Fargo detective, a constable, alderman, and provost Marshall in Iowa, and a Justice of the Peace in Missouri. He was a lawman for about five of his eighty years. Wyatt died January 13, 1929, in Los Angeles and is buried in Coloma, California, in Eternity Hills, next to his third wife, Sara Marcus Earp, who died in 1944. Wyatt Earp's "Life and Legend" lives on in many books and films.

In 1956 the State of Illinois presented a bronze plaque honoring Wyatt Earp and his birthplace at 406 South 3rd Street. The plaque was placed on an immense granite stone donated by M.&St.L. Railroad in Monmouth Park.

In 1974 the Illinois State Historical Society and the Wyatt Earp Birthplace, Inc., in conjunction with the Illinois Department of Transportation donated a cast marker highlighting Earp's birthplace and life. It is also on the National Register of Historical Places.

FORREST AND MARY GALBREATH EASUM - Forrest G. Easum was born 10-30-1922, in Clayton, Illinois, Adams County, the only child of Elmer and Blanche Rampy Easum. The family moved to rural Roseville, Warren County, Illinois, in 1930. He attended Picayune Country school and Roseville High School. Forrest farmed with his father from 1940 to 1968.

Mary L. Galbreath was born 1-18-1922, Monmouth, Illinois, Warren County, to Ivan Galbreath and Mabel Jones Galbreath. She has one sibling, Geraldine Galbreath Smith, in Kirkwood, Illinois. Mary attended Hornback, Kirkwood and Coonville grade schools, Warren County, and graduated from Kirkwood High School in 1940. After attending the Peoria Institute of Business School, Peoria, Illinois, she was employed with Illinois Department of Public Aid in June 1941.

Mary, Nancy and Forrest Easum

Forrest and Mary were married in Kirkwood, Illinois, at her sister's home, August 8, 1943. Two daughters were born to this union: Vicky A., born 7-7-1946, deceased 9-20-1960, and Nancy G., born 9-1-1956. Nancy attended Roseville and Warren Grade schools, graduating from Warren High School. She graduated from Illinois Wesleyan University and Valparaiso, Indiana, Law School and is currently living in Springfield, Illinois, employed as Special Counsel to the Director of the Illinois State Police.

After farming with his father for over 25 years in the Larchland and Roseville area, Forrest and Mary moved to Monmouth in December 1968. Forrest was employed with Stockland F S for 17 years and retired 1-1-1985. Forrest has a love for cars and has worked part-time at Tatman I Auto Sales. Both Forrest and Mary are members of the First United Methodist Church of Monmouth.

Mary returned to work at the Illinois Department of Public Aid in May 1968, retiring 2-1-1984. She is active in Altrusa International Inc. of Monmouth, Illinois, enjoys reading to K-2nd graders after school, is a Daughter of Warren County Chapter of NSDAR; CMC Hospital Auxiliary Volunteer and enjoys the Ruth Circle at church.

For the past 11 years, they spend the winter months at their condo in Naples, Florida, returning to their home at 521 North 10th Street, Monmouth, Illinois.

EATON - Walter Earl Eaton, the second child of James Washington Eaton and Mary Eliza Eaton, was born in Berwick, Illinois, July 23, 1896. His father was a carpenter and had a big apple orchard and sold several different kind of apples. He had two brothers, Leslie Howard, born 1895, and Lonnie Melvin, born 1902. He married Mildred Ardis Clendenen in West Union, Iowa, November 15, 1922. Two children were born to this union in Iowa. He moved to Berwick in Warren County Illinois in 1925, where he lived the remainder of his life. Eight more children joined this family including a set of twin girls. He was a farmer, machinist, road commissioner and rural substitute mail carrier. He hauled a lot of coal, going to the coal mine and staying all night to get loaded early in the morning in order to get back and unload by hand. In his later years he purchased a farm and continued to farm as long as he was able.

My mother, Mildred was a piano player and played at church. We went to different country schools to entertain as well as singing for many church programs.

Mom and dad, Mildred and Walter Eaton

Eaton, Vance Duane was born June 28, 1922, Fayette, Iowa. He attended Berwick Grade School, served in World War II. After returning from service he was a machinist in his garage in Berwick and restored antique Model A cars. His family included two boys and three girls and they attended the Berwick Church.

NEED CAPTION !!!

Merrill Kenneth Eaton was born April 8, 1924, in Fayette, Iowa, died May 27, 1924.

Ardis Earlene Eaton was born January 31, 1926, in Berwick, Illinois, attended Berwick Grade School and Avon High School and was an in-home music teacher. Her family consisted of a boy and girl.

Evelyn June Eaton was born June 28, 1927, in Berwick, Illinois, attended Berwick Grade School and Avon High School. Her family consisted of two boys and two girls.

Shirley Jean Eaton was born July 4, 1928, in Berwick, Illinois, attended Berwick Grade School and Avon High School. Her family consisted of two girls and a boy.

Deloris Vivian Eaton was born November 9, 1929, in Berwick, Illinois, attended Berwick Grade School and Avon High School. Her family consisted of two girls and a boy.

Kenneth Clendenen Eaton was born May 13, 1938, in Berwick, Illinois, attended Berwick Grade School and Roseville High School. His family consisted of three girls and a boy.

Margaret Ilene Eaton was born July 28, 1943, in Monmouth, Illinois, attended Berwick Grade School and Roseville High School. Her family consisted of two boys and a girl.

Marion Elaine Eaton was born July 28, 1943, in Monmouth, Illinois, attended Berwick Grade School and Roseville High School. Her family consisted of two boys and a girl.

Janeth Kay Eaton was born August 21, 1945, in Monmouth Illinois, attended Berwick Grade School and Roseville High School. She went through Practical Nurse training. Her family consisted of two boys and a girl.

ECKLEY - The Eckley family arrived in Warren County in 1887. Dr. George C. Eckley and Rose (Barnes) moved from Stark County to 513 North Fifth Street. An 1892 graduate of Chicago Veterinary College, he set up his practice in Monmouth. Rose attended Knox College and taught in a rural school. They later moved to a farm west of Monmouth. They enjoyed spending time at their cottage in Oquawka. Their children were Isal Bernice Eckley Garrett Shrode and Ralph Barnes Eckley.

Dr. George and Rose Eckley wedding.

Isal taught Latin at MHS and was an active leader of the Queen Esther's in the Methodist Church, where the entire family attended. While attending Monmouth College, her daughter, Grace Rose Garrett, died in 1941.

Ralph worked for *Monmouth Review Atlas* until his death. He became well known for his historical articles about Warren County. The Monmouth Airport and flying were of special interest. He was inducted into the Illinois Aviation Hall of Fame. He also taught classes at Monmouth College for the Naval School, including journalism. He married a "Georgia peach," Marcia, who was the hospital dietitian. She later taught fourth grade at Lincoln Elementary. Their two children were John Fanning and Marcia Anne.

John married Peggy Keller and they are the parents of five children. John David married Toni Clark, parents of John William and Kathryn Ann (Clinton, Illinois). George Keller married Tina Anderson, parents of Tracey, Andrew and Aaron (Mooresville, North Carolina). Steven Thomas married Deborah Tee (Oquawka). Robert Ralph married Deborah Schoener, parents of Elias and Richard (Cordova, Alaska). Patricia Ann married Terry Cook, parents of Adam and Robert (Biggsville). After graduating from Monmouth College, John had a career in education. Now retired, he and his wife reside in Oquawka and Sarasota, Florida.

Anne worked at Wirtz Book Store while in MHS and Monmouth College. She married James Thatcher Haynes of Alexis. They lived in Alaska and Texas before settling in Bushnell, Illinois. Both taught school. After retirement they bought a winter home in Green Valley, Arizona. Parents of Emily Sue who married Ronald Nelson of Kirkwood. She teaches at Central Junior High in Monmouth. He is a Financial Planner. They are parents of Emily Sue and Abbey Leigh, currently attending Yorkwood High School. George Thatcher was married to Lynn Armstrong of Monmouth. They are parents of Jason Thatcher and Rachel Lynn. He lives on a farm west of Monmouth, he works for Pharmacia Corporation. Mary Anne married Robert Schwartz from Minnesota. They reside in Galesburg. They are parents of Allison Marie and Michael James. Both are involved in law enforcement. Sarah Beth married Dirk Benn of Kansas. They are residents of Adel, Iowa. They are parents of Dylan Jack and Carson Wyatt. Sarah is a sales representative for Russell Stover Candies. Dirk works for a grain cooperative.

PRAIRIE GROVE FARM – ROBERT A. ELLIOTT - Robert A. Elliott, farmer and livestock raiser in Lenox Township, is a representative of an old English family which has a most interesting history. His grandparents in the paternal line were Thomas and Mary (Holden) Elliott. Their son, Thomas H. Elliott, was born at Stonehouse, England, on October 14, 1797. He married Amelia Helvestine, a native of Winchester, Virginia. Thomas H. Elliott came from England to Virginia in 1817 and was a merchant there until 1823 when he moved to Ohio, settling in Madison County. In 1828 he went to Jackson County, where he later died and where his son, Robert A. Elliott, was born on January 8, 1849. Mary A. Holden, grandmother, was a descendant of Elizabeth and a daughter of Sir Thomas Clifford of Frithem Lodge near the River Severn in Frampton, England, and a sister of "Fair Rosemond," mistress of Henry II, who was poisoned by Henry's Queen Eleanor while the King was in Flanders subduing a rebellion led by his two sons.

Robert A. Elliott was one of a family of 12 children. Robert A. Elliott and Sarah Elizabeth Shirley were married on March 14, 1869, and were then parents of ten children, eight daughters and two sons. They had 54 grandchildren, many great grandchildren and great-great-grandchildren, as well as great great-great-grandchildren. Robert A. was a leader in the Democratic party in Warren County for the Thirty-second Senatorial District in the Forty-eighth and Forty-ninth General Assemblies. He was a member of the Union Baptist Church. In addition to his farming and legislative career, he was long interested in the banking business as a Director of the Monmouth Trust and Savings Bank.

Mr. Elliott was not only a widely-read man but also a traveler in foreign lands, visiting England, Holland, Belgium, Luxemburg, Switzerland, Austria and Italy, returning home by way of Paris and London.

Mr. Elliott, until 1865, lived with his parents, but that year he came to Warren County and worked by the month, then rented land to farm for himself.

In 1871, he bought 80 acres of unimproved land in Lenox Township, where he erected all of the buildings and in 1874 built a large frame house. He added to his land until he owned more than 600 acres.

Mr. Elliott died at the age of 87 and is buried in the Union Cemetery in Lenox Township.

JEFFREY AND JULIE EMERICK - Jeffrey Robert Emerick was born on December 10, 1973, in Englewood, Colorado, to the parents of John Robert Emerick and Carol Sue (Johnson) Emerick. Jeff has two other siblings, Michelle Doreen (Emerick) Lehmann and John Rolland Emerick. In 1975 they moved back to the area to reside in Abingdon, Illinois. Jeff attended Abingdon Schools from kindergarten through 12th grade. He graduated in 1992. He then attended Western Illinois University and Illinois Central College. In 1991 Jeff met Julie Chandler. In 1995 he started farming with his future father-in-law full-time.

Emerick family

Julie (Chandler) Emerick was born to Dennis Lee Chandler and Connie Lynn (Olson) Chandler, on July 2, 1975. She had two siblings, one brother, Jason Dee Chandler (deceased) and a twin sister, Amanda June (Chandler) Ross. Julie attended Avon School from kindergarten through 12th grade. She graduated in 1993. She attended Western Illinois University and graduated in December 1996 with a major in Ag Business and a double minor in Finance and Management. She was employed by Monmouth Trust and Savings Bank in January of 1997 until July 1997. She then became a consumer loan officer at Citizens National Bank of Macomb until July of 1999. In July of 1999 she became a stay-at-home mother.

Jeff and Julie were married on January 11, 1997. They have two boys, Trenton Dee Emerick, born July 27, 1999, and Schuyler Robert Emerick, born September 5, 2001. They currently reside outside Abingdon in Warren County. Jeff is currently a trustee in Berwick Township and they both belong to the Abingdon Methodist Church. They are also members of the Warren-Henderson Farm Bureau Young Farmers Committee. Julie continues to be a stay-at-home mother and Jeff continues to farm.

LARRY AND ALICE ENDERLIN - Robert Lawrence (Larry) Enderlin was born in Warren County on April 24, 1938. He was the second son of Lawrence and Verna (Noonan) Enderlin. He married Alice Gavin on November 26, 1960 at Immaculate Conception Church in Monmouth. Larry attended grade school at McGaw and Foster Schools and graduated from Monmouth High School in 1957.

Alice was the youngest of three children born of George and Rose Hennenfent Gavin on September 12, 1937. She went to Farmers Academy and Immaculate Conception School and graduated from St. Mary Academy at Nauvoo in 1955. She received a BS in Nursing from Saint Ambrose University and a Master Degree in Nursing Administration from Bradley University.

Larry was a farmer. He started his career northwest of Monmouth in 1958 with a neighbor, Roy Winbigler, and purchased the Don and Jim Gabby farm in 1963 where Larry and Alice lived for 32 years.

Other land purchased during those years had been owned by Jim Shunick and Harty McConnell.

Alice was the Director of Nursing Service at Community Memorial Hospital before accepting a position as a nursing instructor at Carl Sandburg College in 1973. She taught at Sandburg for 27 years.

Larry and Alice have three children: Kevin Joseph, Mary Jane and George Gavin.

Kevin, born October 29, 1961, graduated from Carl Sandburg College and Western Illinois University. He received his Masters and Doctorate Degree in Education from the University of Illinois. He is an Agriculture instructor at Normal Unit 5 High School. He married Melissa Moorhead and they have a daughter Rebecca and a son Gavin.

Mary Jane was born July 18, 1963. She is a graduate of Carl Sandburg College and received a Baccalaureate Degree in Nursing from the University of Illinois. She is a Certified School Nurse for School District #38. She married John Tucker and they have two children, Logan and Caitlin.

George was born February 7, 1965. He attended Carl Sandburg College. He is the Director of Safety at Farmland Foods. He married Colleen Johnson. They have twin sons, Ethan and Drew, and two daughters, Sidney and Hanna.

In 1982 the Enderlins moved to 1403 East 2nd Avenue in Monmouth.

PAULINE EPLEY - Pauline Lawton Epley was born January 29, 1919 in Tilden, Illinois, the daughter of Thomas and Elizabeth Baxendale Lawton of Bolton, Lancashire, England. At one year of age, they moved to Canton, Ohio, where she was raised and educated.

Pauline and Dean Epley, New York City, 1948.

She married Dean G. Epley on May 2, 1941 in Canton, Ohio. Dr. Dean Epley was the former chairman of the Sociology Department at Monmouth College, coming here in 1970. He preceded Pauline in death in 1977.

Pauline and her family have lived on many college and university campuses where her husband taught including, Kent State University, Ohio; Michigan State University, Michigan; Memphis State University, Tennessee; University of Miami, Florida; Concord College, West Virginia; Bradley University, Illinois; Mara Institute of Technology, Petaling Jaya, Malaysia; and the University of Nijmegen, Netherlands.

She is a member of the First United Methodist Church, Monmouth, Illinois and has supported their activities in various ways. She was a member and past president of the Faculty Wives of Monmouth College. Pauline was also a member and past president of The Fortnightly Club, as well as a member of the New Century and Zetetic Book Club. She was a member of the local YMCA and an avid supporter of their exercise programs for senior citizens. A number of people may also know her for her participation in the Odd Jobs Group.

Pauline has two daughters: Deanna Epley of Tallahassee, Florida and Laura Selken of Fort Madison, Iowa. She has five sons: Paul of Peoria, Illinois; David of Atlanta, Georgia; Thomas of Albuquerque, New Mexico; Bryan of Monmouth, Illinois; and John of Galesburg, Illinois (and Thailand). She has six grandchildren: Jennifer, Sarah, Bradley, Andrew, Lauren, and Heather.

Preceding Pauline in death were her parents, three sisters, and one brother.

Pauline's hobbies include reading, writing, knitting, traveling, and socializing. She is known for many things: her wonderful smile, caring attitude, lasting friendships, patience, being a good listener, charity, Christmas cookies, and her red hair. Pauline's honesty and grace have touched all those who have had the honor of being a part of her life's journey.

CRAIG AND JANIS (WESTERFIELD) ERICKSON - Craig R. Erickson was born May 22, 1950, in Burlington, Ia. and Janis E. Westerfield was born December 1, 1949, in Monmouth, Il. They were married on August 28, 1971, at the First Lutheran Church in Monmouth. Their parents are John and Weona Erickson, and Howard and Mabel Westerfield, residents of Monmouth. They are parents of two children Bryan Scott born December 3, 1977 and Erin Elizabeth born February 22, 1982. Both born at St. Francis Hospital in La Crosse, Wi.

Erin, Craig, Janis, Byron Erickson

He attended both grade school and high school in Monmouth and then went on to study drafting at the Institute of Drafting and Technology of Morrison, Il. He graduated February 7, 1970 with a degree in engineering. He then moved to La Crosse where he was hired as a draftsmen for Trane Heating and Air conditioning. After moving from La Crosse he was in the back-hoe business for himself and also working for the state as Fish Technician.

Janis's schooling started with Jane Smith's Pre-school and a year at Garfield, before moving west of Monmouth. She then attended grade school at Rozetta and Biggsville. She attended two years at Union High School, west of Biggsville, before the family moved back to Monmouth. Here she graduated in 1967. She attended one year at Robert Morris College at Carthage, Il. She then went on to complete her education at Augustana College in Rock Island. She received her B.A. degree in 1971. As she had wanted to be a Medical Technologist she took her internship at St. Francis Hospital in La Crosse and earned her B.S. degree in 1972. She has been employed at the same place for thirty years, but recently the name changed to Franciscan Skemp Healthcare.

As they are out-doors people, they finally decided to move and enjoy the country life. They bought a house between Chaseburg and Coon Valley and they are still living here. Their two children attended grade school at Chaseburg and graduated from high school at Westby. Bryan thought he wanted to be a surveyor, but after one year of college at Rochester, Mn. he decided to go to work. Now he is furthering his education after he decided to enter the field of radiography. Erin is in her third year, studying Art Therapy at Edgewood College in Madison, Wi.

Even though their children are now in their 20's they still enjoy vacationing with Mom and Pop. They all love to ski, scuba dive, swim and go birding. They always attended all the children's school activities, of which there were many. They wore out their camcorder taking pictures in sports, plays, musicals and such. A few years from now people will probably say, what is a camcorder? Technology marches on.

For Erin's Girl Scout gold award he helped her on her pond project and she named it Erin's Golden Pond.

(Submitted by Craig Erickson)

JOHN ERIC ERICKSON - Erickson, John Eric, son of Otto E. and Hazel (Emery) Erickson was born February 22, 1927 in, Burlington, Iowa, the sixth of nine, namely: Thelma Iola, William Emery, Dana Lester, Vivian Ceola, Otto Immanuel Jr., Robert Lee, Roberta Lou and Clinton Earl. John attended school in Burlington.

Weona and John Erickson, December 24, 2001.

In 1943-1946, while working for the C B & O Railroad as a callboy, he was injured when he fell into an unmarked ditch. This accident would change his life forever. While in the hospital, John met Weona Mae Shoemate, who was studying nursing. They were married September 22, 1946 at the Messiah Lutheran Church in Burlington. Weona is the daughter of Arval and Susiemae Shoemate of Terre Haute, Illinois. 1947-1948, John worked at the Dahlin & Davis Brothers Furniture Mfg. Their lives changed again when John Eric Erickson, Jr. was born June 5, 1947. 1948-1950, he worked for John Witte Paint and Drug Corp. as a factory worker. Craig Randall was born May 22, 1950. During 1950-1953, John worked as a route man for the Burlington Clean Towel Service. In 1953, the family moved to Monmouth, Illinois where John became branch manager for the Clean Towel Service. Bradley David was born here, July 1, 1955. 1956, John became route manager for the Maple City Dairy. Their only daughter, Julie Michele, was born on June 3, 1959. In 1967, John bought the Sealtest Dairy distributorship in Monmouth. The entire family worked hard at this endeavor, until 1979.

John, then attended the Police Training Institute in Champaign, Il., and began working for the Warren County Sheriff's Department in Warren County. As a deputy, he put all of his people skills and knowledge of the area to good use. In 1984, through dedication and lots of hard work, he was promoted to detective, and lieutenant in 1989. After thirteen years of service he retired in August of 1992.

Weona worked as hard and long as her husband. In July of 1988, after 25 years of service, she retired from the Warren County Assessor's Office and Election Registration Department. As she raised their children she helped her husband with their business.

John Jr. married Joyce Reese, of Galesburg, Il., November 2,1968. John served as a nurse in the Viet-Nam conflict. They lived for many years in Monmouth. Their three children, Dana Douglas, born November 27, 1971, Nathan Michael, July 9, 1974 and Joshua Ryan, December 14, 1977. The family moved to Coon Valley, Wisconsin in 1998. John is a nurse anesthetist at the Gunderson Lutheran Hospital in LaCrosse.

Craig and Janis Elaine Westerfield, married August 28, 1971, in Monmouth. Janis graduated from Augustana College May 1971. From LaCrosse, they moved to Chaseburg in 1974. Janis is a Medical Technologist at the Franciscan Skemp Hospital in LaCrosse. Craig works for the state of Wisconsin as a Fisheries Technician. Their children are: Bryan Scott, born December 3, 1977 and Erin Elizabeth, February 22, 1982.

Bradley and Kris Janssen married, July 17, 1976, in Monmouth and moved to Chaseburg in 1978. Brad is a Master Welder at Trane Company of LaCrosse. Kris graduated from Illinois State University In 1976, and is now a secretary in the Westby School system. Their children are: Megan Caroline, born September 4, 1980; Tyler David, February 9, 1984, and Amanda Mae, October 1, 1985. Brad and family now reside in Westby, Wisconsin.

Julie Michele Erickson graduated from Augustana College in 1981. She became a state trooper with the Illinois State Police in 1985. She now resides in Petersburg, Illinois, and holds the rank of lieutenant, following in her father John's footsteps. He retired in law enforcement as Detective Lieutenant.

To John Erickson, Sr. "Leader of the Band" Thank you! From all your family.

He earned his love through discipline, thundering velvet hand his gentle means of sculpting souls took me years to understand The leader of the band is tired and his eyes are growing old but his blood runs through my instrument and his song is in my soul My life has been a poor attempt to imitate the man I'm just a living legacy to the leader of the band I thank you for the music and the stories of the road I thank you for the freedom when it came my time to go.

I thank you for the kindness and the times when you got tough and father, I don't think I said "I love you" near enough I am the living legacy to the leader of the band. "The leader of the Band," by Dan Fogelburg3

KEITH AND MARY RUTH (PERRINE) ERLANDSON - Charles Keith Erlandson born. Aug. 22, 1925, Monmouth, Ill., married April 2, 1947 to Mary Ruth Perrine born Feb. 25, 1927, died Aug. 30, 1994, Monmouth, Ill. They lived all their lives in Tompkins Township, Warren County, where they farmed.

Keith attended Liberty school, graduated Kirkwood High School 1943. Member and President of Yorkwood District School Board. Sister: Irma Jean Duncan.

Mary Ruth attended Roseville schools, graduated Kirkwood High School 1945. Sisters: Carol Douglas and Joan Smith.

Charles Stephen - see Steve & Karen (Johnson) Erlandson.

David Keith, born 4/25/1949, married 6/26/1971 to Kathleen Jean Smith born 12/13/1948. Children: Ann Marie born 6/1/1974, Michael David born 3/14/1977, Kelly Jean born 3/28/1980.

Mary Lou born 9/7/1950 died 12/7/1963.

Gerald Lee born 11/28/1951, married 6/11/1983 to Mary Elizabeth Hammond born 2/2/1951. Children: Erin Elizabeth born 5/11/1987, Leigh Ellen 12/11/1988, Amy Ruth born 2/11/1991, Alex Keith born 9/24/1993.

Joseph Dean born 9/7/1959, married 6/4/1995 to Nancy Jean Wheeler born 8/20/1958.

James Wayne born 5/22/1961, married 9/13/1986 to Kimberly Denise Penn born 10/13/1960. Children: Jeffery Scott born 12/28/1987, Jennifer Nicole born 7/1/1991.

Keith and Mary Ruth's four sons all graduated from college. Steve, Dave, Joe, and Jim from the University of Illinois and Jerry from Western Illinois University.

Keith and Mary Ruth members of the First Lutheran Church, Monmouth, Ill .

Keith died August 5, 2002.

STEPHEN & KAREN (JOHNSON) ERLANDSON - Charles Stephen Erlandson born Jan. 8, 1948, Monmouth, Ill., son of Keith and Mary Ruth (Perrine) Erlandson. Married July 12, 1970, Kirkwood, Ill. to Karen Ann Johnson born Aug. 2, 1948, Monmouth, Ill., daughter of Marion and Winnifred (Downes) Johnson. Brother; James.

Steve attended Smithshire school, Yorkwood Jr./Sr. High, graduating in 1966. Graduated University of Illinois 1970, B.S. General Agriculture. Member of Nabor House. After graduation started farming southeast of Kirkwood. Member Warren County Board. Siblings: Dave, Mary Lou. Jerry, Joe and Jim.

Karen attended Kirkwood Grade School, Yorkwood Jr./Sr. High, graduating 1966. Worked at the Trust Bank and National Bank.

Paula Ann born Oct. 26, 1972 Monmouth, Ill. Attended Yorkwood schools, graduating 1990. Attended Carl Sandburg College graduating 1992 with an Associates degree in Science. Graduated Augustana College 1994, B.S. in Accounting. Worked at the National Bank and is Assistant Financial Aid Director at Monmouth College. Married Sept. 16, 1995, Monmouth, Ill. to Mark Edward Nuckles, born July 29, 1970, Monmouth, Ill. Mark graduated Monmouth High School 1988. Then went to the Marines. Works for the Ill. State Highway Dept. Children: Rachael Ann born April 20, 1997 and Emma Katherine Sophia born Dec. 28, 1999.

Sara Kay born Jan. 19. 1975, Monmouth, Ill. Attended Yorkwood schools, graduating 1993. Graduated Monmouth College 1997, B.A. in Physical Education. Teaches at Illini Central. Mason City, Ill. Coaches volleyball.

Wendy Lou born June 11, 1978, Monmouth, Ill. Attended Yorkwood schools. Graduating 1996. Was a member of the National Honor Society. Graduated Monmouth College, Magna Cum Laude, 2000, B.A. in Elementary Education & Middle School Endorsement. Teaches in Mt. Pulaski, Ill. Coaches volleyball.

Cynthia Sue born June 11, 1978, Monmouth, Ill. Attended Yorkwood schools, graduating 1996. Was a member of the National Honor Society. Graduated Monmouth College, Cum Laude, 2000, B.A. in Elementary Education and Middle School Endorsement. Teaches at Chester East, Lincoln, Ill. Coaches volleyball and track.

Steve, Karen, Paula, Sara, Wendy and Cindy are all members of the 1st Lutheran Church, Monmouth, Ill.

ROY L. AND MARY L. EWALT - Roy L. Ewalt was born in Knox County, Missouri, November 13, 1934 and Mary Lois Wolter was born November 1, 1935, in Albia, Ia. They were married on December 22, 1956 at the Colony Methodist Church in Colony, Missouri. They have four children, Johan Christian Ewalt, Franz Frederick Ewalt, who married Kathi Sells, and they have a daughter, Caitlin, and two son's Rodney Wade, and Mike. They have a daughter Golda Ellen who married Robert Strietmatter, and a son, George Turner who married Mistie Hagar and they have a daughter, Isabella, and a son, Chad.

Mary and Roy Ewarlt

Roy's parents were Fred and Rae House Ewalt, born in Knox County, Missouri. Fred Ewalt is a direct descendent of Henry Ewalt, born in Palatine, Germany in 1754. He was a soldier serving in the Continental Line commissioned an Ensign 6th Co. lst. Bat. Penn. Militia 1777. Appointed Captain 13th Reg. Ky. Militia, 1796. The home he built in Bourbon County, Ky. is standing in good repair as a National Historic Home. He also developed the Ewalt apple. Mary's parents were George Herbert Wolter and Lois Ellen Burkhart Wolter, born in Knox County Missouri. In 1934 they moved to Albia, Iowa where they operated a nation wide truck line, P & W, hauling steel out of Chicago areas in Illinois and Iowa. They hauled hogs and cattle from the local sale barns back to Chicago during the war years. Roy is one of ten living children. Mary is an only child.

Roy graduated with a Master's Degree in Ag. Econ. And a Batchelor's degree in Voc. Ag. From the U. of Mo. at Columbia, Mo. He taught Agriculture at Jamestown, Mo., Hamilton, IL. and joined Illinois Farm Business Farm Management in Pontiac, Il. In 1967. He retired from Western Farm Business Farm Management in Monmouth, IL. in 1999.

Mary received a Bachelor of Science degree in Dietetics from St. Mary of the Wood's College in Terre Haute, In. and a Master's Degree in Health Care Administration from the U. of St. Francis, Joliet, IL. She continues to be a Registered Dietitian and Consultant. She retired from OSF St. Mary Medical Center at Galesburg, IL. in 1999.

They purchased the Lynch House in Monmouth in 1976. The home is Queen Elizabeth In style and was built from 1900 to 1904. They are members of the Coldbrook Christian Church, Disciples of Christ, Cameron, Il. Both are elders with Mary being the first woman Board Chairperson, 1988-89. They are Members of the Mason's, Easter Star, at the Colony Missouri Chapter's. He is a member Of the American Legion, and she a member of the Auxiliary at the Knox City, Mo. Unit. Hobbies include their Registered Quarter Horses, gardening, family, and travel.

BEN AND NELLIE SWANSON FARLUND - Bernhard L. Fahlund and Nellie Swanson were married on February 27, 1901 in Biggsville, Illinois. They moved to Monmouth in 1902 and were the parents of Lillian Brown Brinton of Peoria, Bartonville, and Orlando, Florida; Vera Adeline Johnson (Mrs. Roy A.) and Eunice Rosalie Larson (Mrs. C.O.Virgil) of Monmouth, and grandparents of Edwin Brown of Crawfordsville, Indiana; Melba Larson Matson, Monmouth; Dr. Alan Larson, Dunwoody, Georgia; Delbert Johnson, Oakland, California, deceased; and Theodore Johnson, Chicago. The Fahlunds were members of the Lutheran Church in Monmouth.

Bernhard (Ben) Leonard Fahlund was born

Nellie and Ben Fahlund

on February 23, 1870 in Galesburg, Illinois, to Benjamin Fahlund (Bengt Johan Bjorenson in Sweden) and Ida Catherine Peterson Fahlund (Ida Katrina Leonilda in Sweden). His father iirnmigrated to America in August of 1868 from Gothenburg to Galesburg, Illinois, arriving on September 28 with twenty-five cents in his pocket. His father wasan early pioneer, was naturalized in 1869, moved his family to Nebraska and became a lay minister in the Fridhem Lutheran Church in Phelps County. In 1905 the family moved back to Galesburg. His father died in 1920 and was buried in Linwood Cemetery. His mother died in 1923 in Cadillac, Michigan. Ben's youngest siblings were Jennie Almida of Galesburg, Dr. George Alvin of Detroit, Arthur Emanuel of DeKalb, Axel Frederick of Knoxville, and Walter John. Bernhard (Ben) Fahlund worked for Western Stoneware, Central School, was elected constable of Monmouth Township, and served as sergeant in the Monmouth Police Department. Ben Fahlund died on December 30, 1950 at the age of eighty in Monmouth.

Nellie Swanson (Pernilla Svensson in Sweden) was born on October 1, 1868 in Vestana, Nasum, Kristianstads Lan, Skane, Sweden, on a farm her family (named Stenkil after King Stenkil) farmed for 250 years. She immigrated in 1891 at the age of twenty-three years and moved to Monmouth in 1892. Her parents were Swan and Inga (Olson) Swanson of Sweden. Her oldest siblings were John Swanson (b. 1854), living in Sweden; Swan Swanson (b. 1856), Monmouth; Anna Person (b. 1858), Sweden; Bettie Johnson (b. 1860), Prophetsown; Ola Swanson (b. 1862), Sweden; and Elsa Swanson (b. 1864), Monmouth. Her niece was Ida Peterson (Mrs. Verner) of Kirkwood and Monmouth. Nellie Swanson Fahlund died on August 11, 1940 in Monmout at the age of seventy-one.

EDWARD FAIR - Fair, Edward, son of William and Jane (Welsh) Fairs was born April 14, 1836 in Fedden County Fermangh, Ireland - He was 14 years old when he came to America with his father.

Edward married Mary Elizabeth Williams, February 17, 1875 who was born July 27, 1845 in Williamson County Tennessee, to John Williams and Elizabeth Younger. Elizabeth Younger was a sister to "Cole" Younger who rode with the outlaw Jesse James.

Edward Fair was raised a farmer and bought an 80 acre farm in Bald Bluff township. He later bought a farm in section 12 Rozetta, Township from John Williams, his father in law. He also owned land in Hale Township. He was well educated, a staunch republican and a lay preacher of Methodist faith who died March 17, 1899. His wife died, May 14, 1922. They are buried in Fall Creek Cemetery, Little York, Illinois.

Their children were John William born March 17,1876. He was married to Geneva Louck and then to Florence Hoy. His daughter was Verna.

Ross Edward was born July 29, 1879. He married his first wife, Minnie Myrtle Russell, February 12, 1902, the daughter of William Russell and Ann Hartley, who was born July 27, 1882 in Bald Bluff Township. Their only child, Lucy Maud, was born. November 23, 1902 in Hale Township Warren County, Illinois. Minnie died in 1907 and is buried in Fall Creek Cemetery.

Lucy Maud married William Henry Thieme, October 20,1925 in Aledo, Illinois. Bill Thieme, born July 22, 1901 in Warren County, Illinois was the son of Charles J. Thieme and Anna Gallaugher. Lucy died January 16, 1996 and Bill died October 5, 1970. Their children are Marjorie Lucille who married Edward Smith; Dorothy Ann Fair, born December 17, 1934 who married John Raymond Spence March 1, 1952 at Fall Creek Church; and Charles Ross, born. January 1947 in Monmouth, Illinois, married Delores Ann Davis January 5, 1974 at First Church Nazarene, Rock Island, Illinois.

Ross's second wife was Evelyn (EVA) Armenta Harvey who was born. September 28, 1890 in Keithsburg, Illinois. Her parents were George Harvey and Evelyn Thomas. She had one daughter Ruth, when she entered the marriage. Ruth married Dewey Mudd from Biggsville, Illinois. They ran the Mudd funeral home in Biggsville. She died August 26,1940.

Josephine B. Sabrina was born to Ross Fair and Eva Harvey April 14, 1915 in Warren County, Illinois. She married Edward T. Flack, February 27, 1937 and died December 5, 1991.

The third son, Elmer Leon was born October 9, 1885 in Rozetta Township, Henderson County. He was married in May 1907 to Fannie May Campbell. He died December 1960.

Their children were Ethel Lorena, born February 29, 1908, married Elmer Sedwick April 3, 1928. They had one daughter JoAnne.

Ruth Edna, born August 19, 1909, married Kenneth Roundtree May 3, 1941 and died February 2, 1999.

Cora May, born May 8, 1911, married Glenn Little, September 6, 1931.

The Fair, Welsh, and Campbell families left County Fermangh, Ireland from Warren's Point, went to Liverpool, England and spent 4 months at sea. A storm came up and they had to throw freight overboard to lighten the load. Among the things lost, was the family bible. They landed at

New Orleans and took a boat up the Mississippi River. The Fair family settled in Rozetta but later bought a farm near Oquawka, Illinois.

William Fair was very active in the Fall Creek Church. In 1984 the first annual reunion of the three families who came from Ireland was held at Fall Creek Church. About 75 descendents attended.

WENDELL AFTON FAUDREE - Wendell Afton Faudree, the only child of Christopher and Florence Wykoff Faudree, was born in Macon, Missouri, December 13, 1925. He married Violet Gilbert in Hannibal, Missouri, August 3, 1947. Violet was born February 3, 1924 to Roy and Blanche Hayes Gilbert.

The children of Wendell and Violet are Roy, born April 20, 1948 in Quincy Illinois. Renee, born December 14, 1951 in Fort Madison, Iowa. Blaine, born June 15, 1955 in Newton, Iowa. Sally, born May 29, 1957 in Burlington, Iowa.

When Dad was 17 years old, he enlisted in the Navy. He was stationed aboard the destroyer, The USS Patterson, during WWII. While on board the ship, the baker was killed and a new one was needed. They asked if anyone had baking experience and my father mentioned that his father was a baker. Dad's commanding officer said, "Congratulations son, you are one of our new bakers."

This profession served my father well and led our family to Warren County in Illinois in 1958, where we moved from Burlington, Iowa. Dad was employed as the Bakery Manager at Barnes Super Value in Monmouth., Illinois. We lived at 214 North 1st St. Roy and Renee attended the old Garfield School.

We moved to the country in 1960 to a farmhouse belonging to Frank Cavanaugh. At that time, the farm was farmed by Kenny Jenks. Our address was Route 3 Monmouth, Ill. We now attended Yorkwood Grade School in Little York, Illinois and got to ride a school bus everyday. Living in the country was an interesting time for all of us. The worst of which were the muddy roads. Dad was always getting stuck on his way to work in Monmouth. While living here, we attended Sugar Tree Grove Church.

Our next move was to Kirkwood, Illinois. We still attended Yorkwood School but now the classes were in Kirkwood and we could walk to school.

A few years later, Mom and Dad were able to buy a house in Kirkwood from Orville and Mabel Keener on West Plum Street. Dad still lives there today.

Dad was still baking at Barnes Super Value, and Renee and Sally were also working in the bakery. In 1969, Renee was hired as a cake decorator and baker's helper. Sally was a wrapper and bakery helper.

Roy married Kathy Mattson and later Cynthia Chapman. He has two sons, Christopher and Matthew. Renee married Gary Spence and has two children, Tracy and Bryan. Tracy married Alexander (Andy) Engstrom. Bryan married Jaclyn Johnson. Blaine married Jean McBride and has two stepdaughters and seven grandchildren. Sally married Barry Bishop and has two children, Mandy and Craig. Mandy married Chris Hughes and has one child Nathaniel.

GARY & SHERRY FERNALD - In the year 2002, Gary Lee and Sherry Lynn (Stevenson) Fernald lived at 416 East Broadway Avenue in Monmouth, Ill. Gary was working with Case-New Holland Company in East Moline, Ill. Sherry was working with Community Medical Center as a registered nurse. Their children were: Terry Lee (Mrs. Larry Dean), Kimberly Dawn, (Mrs. Bryon Robbins) and Jennifer Liberty, (Mrs. Jason Robbins).

Sherry and Gary Fernald

Gary was of French extraction. His family were Heugenots who had come to America with hopes of religious freedom. His father, Leon Eugene, had been an engineer for the Chicago North Western and M & St. L. Railroad. His mother Lonetta Iola (Schisler) a homemaker.

Sherry was of Swedish, English extraction, whose family had come to America from England aboard the Mayflower. Her parents were Richard Doyle Stevenson and Irene Lucille Vance.

Gary and Sherry were born and raised in Monmouth and met at Monmouth High School as classmates.

JOHN CUDBETH FERRIS - John Cudbeth Ferris was born about 1787 in NY and died 1865 in Galesburg, Illinois. He married (1) Bullock 1808 and (2) Eliza Kattell 1820 born about 1803 in Vermont. Around 1858 the family moved to Illinois.

The children of John and Bullock were Elias (married Watterman), George, Albert, Sally (married Smeed), Thomas (two daughters: Julia married Burlingame and Phoebe; his son Theodore was killed during the Civil War), and Elisha H.

Elisha H. Ferris was born March 2 8, 1817, Ballston Spa, NY and died March 27, 1869, Galesburg, Illinois. He married Harriett Banta born about 1824 NY.

The 1860 Coldbrook Township, Warren County, Illinois Federal Census, Dwellings #2271-2, Families #2784-5 shows John and Elisha as farmers. Elisha's family is in the 1870 Coldbrook Township, Warren County, Illinois, Federal Census, Dwelling #198, Family # 188.

The 1860 Plat of Coldbrook Township, Warren County, Illinois, shows Elisha owned the following land: N 1/2NW 1/4 Section 10, Range 1, Township 17 (house located here) and E1/2SW1/4 Section 3, Range 1, Township 17. By the 1870 Plat of Coldbrook Township, Warren County, Illinois, we know Elisha owned the N 1/2NW 1/4 Section 10, Range 1, Township 17.

Since Hope Cemetery [SW corner NW1/4 section 36 Kelly Township] is located about 2 miles from the farm of Elisha Ferris, we do believe he and his father & their spouses are buried there. Land was deeded to Hope Cemetery Association in 1873, but was used for burials before that time. In 1998 we visited the cemetery caretaker, but there was no record of burials for Elisha, John C., or wives on the cemetery plat. However, he told us there was a burial of an infant, which we located on the east side. In our 2001 visit to the cemetery, we noted these infant burials on one small tombstone: Grant Ferris 1917 infant son; 1920 infant girl.

The children of Elisha and Harriett include: Mary E. (born about 1848 NY), George Henry (born October 5, 1851 NY; died November 27, 1921, Merrick County, NE), Harriett (born about 1856 NY), Henrietta (born about 1856 NY), Albert (born about 1858 IL), Martha (born about 1860 IL), and Lilly (born about 1867 IL).

My great grandfather, George Henry Ferris, married Mary Johnston December 27, 1876 in Knox County, Illinois. They both died in Merrick County, Nebraska. Their children include Maude (bom December 2, 1878; died May 26, 1950); Ora (born February 12, 1882; died January 10, 1957); Mamie (born June 15, 1885); Lee Johnston, my grandfather (born April 3, 1889; died April 21, 1953); and Lisle W. (born October 10, 1894).

The children of John's second marriage to Eliza Kattell were Ben, John, Solomon (born about 1841, NY), Mary (born about 1841, NY), Henry and Henrietta. Solomon was a Nurseryman at Hamburg, Iowa and his child, Earl, was head of nationally known Earl Ferris nurseries at Hamburg.

GARALD AND GWENDOLYN FISHER - Garald Fisher was born on December 14, 1918, In Mercer County near Viola, IL. He was one of the nine children born to John R. and Nell Brown Fisher. The Fisher family had its roots in Baden, Germany where Garald's great-grandfather Jacob Jr. was born before immigrating with his parents to the United States at age eleven in 1834.

Mildred Gwendolyn McGaughey as born January 11, 1921, on a neighboring farm. The second child in a family of five, her parents were James T. and Mildred Corsepius McGaughey. Gwen's Corseplus greatgrandparents came from Berlin, Germany in 1869, and the McGaugheys were of Scotch-Irish descent.

Garold and Gwen Fisher, 50th Anniversary, 1986.

When they married on October 8, 1938, Garald was working for International Harvester in East Moline; to supplement this income he rented a small farm near Aledo where Cheryl Gwendolyn was born on April 16, 1939. Colleen Yvonne, their second child, was born on November 29, 1940.

In a very few years they were able to purchase an eighty acre farm where they were living when he was drafted at the age of 24 and entered the Marine Corps in January, 1944. On Okinawa he suffered a head wound on April 15, 1945. After a long hospitalization and rehabilitation, he returned to his family In November 1945.

The family lived on a farm east of Aledo, and the girls went to a one-room school called Goodwell. While living there, Gwen and Garald had a son born on March 18,1949, whom they named William.

Shortly after his birth the family moved into Aledo so the girls finished grade school there and later graduated from Aledo High School. It was in Aledo that Bill started to school.

In 1952, Garald purchased the Warren County Livestock Barn just north of Monmouth and held his first sale on October 2, of that year.

They moved into a new house they had built in Monmouth around 1959, so Bill went to high school there.

Garald owned and operated the Livestock Barn for 24 years, at the same time he was raising livestock and purchasing more farmland. At present he owns 1700 acres.

Garald and Gwen have nine grandchildren. Howard and Cheryl Kinney's children are Kimberley, John, and Jeffrey. Harold and Colleen Kinney have Tracey, H.T. and Julie. Bill and Kathy Fisher have Jessica, Allison, and Rebecca.

MICHAEL AND MARGARET FLANAGAN - Michael Joseph and Margaret Kinney Flanagan were the children of Irish emigrants. Michael was the second of five children born to James and Johanna O'Brien Flanagan who came to the United States from Ireland in 1861 and were married in Monmouth October 20, 1869. Michael was born on October 17, 1875.

Margaret and Michael Flanagan, circa 1935.

Margaret was the youngest of seven children born to Terrence and Rose Lenihan Kinney who emigrated from Ireland and were married in New York City. They came to Warren County in 1863 with their four children. Three children including Margaret, the youngest, were born in Warren County. Margaret's birthdate was June 10, 1876.

Michael's mother, Johanna Flanagan, died on May 13, 1905 at 600 West Broadway, Monmouth where the couple lived after leaving their farm in 1904. James Flanagan died May 27, 1927. Of the 28 grandchildren five are still living: James and Harriet's daughter, Patricia; Theresa Vaughn Shunick of Arizona; Genevieve Shunick Woods of California; and Rose and Helen Flanagan.

Margaret's father, Terrence Kinney, died May 16, 1892. Her mother, Rose Lenihan Kinney, died January 12, 1898. Terrence Kinney had acquired two 80 acre farms in Section 22 and Section 35 in Hale Township after coming to Warren County. Of the 53 grandchildren only three are living. They are Helen and Rose Flanagan and Gertrude Kinney.

Michael Flanagan and Margaret Kinney were married at Immaculate Conception Church on February 9, 1904. They lived on Michael's father's farm for two years. On February 26, 1906 they purchased the 80 acres in Section 35 in Hale Township for $12,000 from her sister Rose Cavanaugh and her husband who had purchased it from the Terrence Kinney heirs in 1899. At the same time they sold 40 acres in Section 22 for $5600 to Margaret's sister Kate Gavin and her husband with whom she had lived after her mother's death until her marriage.

Michael and Margaret lived on this farm for 32 years raising their seven children there. In April, 1938 they moved to 309 West Third Ave., Monmouth to the house which Margaret had owned since her mother's death and which had been renovated. Michael died there on January 1, 1939. Margaret died April 5, 1952. The farm in Section 35 along with 80 acres to the east, later acquired, were sold after her death.

Three of the Flanagan sons were married at St. Patrick's Church in Raritan. Terrence James, born November 11, 1904, married Monica Mills on April 3, 1937. They had four children: Terry, Stephen, John and Marie, five grandchildren, and four great-grandchildren. James died on July 11, 1972. Monica's death was August 30, 1994. Two sons are deceased: Terry at age 59 in 1997, and Stephen on January 11, 2002 at age 62. A grandson, John Kevin Flanagan, died in May 2001 at age 31.

William Flanagan who was born August 30, 1906 married Mary Mills on April 18, 1938. William died on October 18, 1968. Mary Mills Flanagan is still living. They had five children: Michael, William, Eileen, David and Jean, and seven grandchildren.

Michael Leroy was born on April 23, 1908 and died after an appendectomy on April 11, 1923.

Leo Flanagan, born on March 23, 1909, married Eileen Barry on February 24, 1936. Leo died at age 85 on May 19, 1994 survived by his wife, Eileen who now lives with her daughter in Florida. They had three daughters: Margaret, Elizabeth and Barbara, 12 grandchildren and 13 great-grandchildren.

Mary, born April 3, 1914, married Robert Sullivan at Immaculate Conception Church on October 4, 1938. They had five children: Kathleen, John, Robert, Marcia and Jane, seven grandchildren and three great-grandchildren. Their son, Robert, and grandchild, Erin, are deceased. Mary Sullivan died on September 12, 1979 and Robert Sullivan died January 13, 1996.

Rose Johanna Flanagan, born May 18, 1910, taught at McGaw Corners rural school four years and five years at Hoornbeek. During this period she took courses at Monmouth College and Western Illinois University and through extension courses. After being a caseworker at the Department of Public Aid from 1940 to 1951 she became its county superintendent, a position she held until her retirement in 1973.

Helen Cathryn Flanagan, born September 1, 1912, began her career as a legal secretary at the firm of Bardens and Melburg, later at Love and Beal.

After caring for her mother for five years, she became secretary to Thomas O'Neill at Central Standard Insurance Co. When the company moved to Chicago she worked at Illinois Power Company until she retired in 1977. After selling their home at 309 West Third Ave., Monmouth in December, 1977 Rose and Helen moved in February, 1978 to their present home which they had built at 700 North I St., Monmouth.

DAVID D. & MARY H. FLEMING - Though neither was born in Warren County, David and Mary Fleming have been residents of the county for much of their lives. David (born 10-12-23) grew up on a farm near Ipava, Illinois and Mary (born 9-17-24) was reared in Glen Ellyn, Illinois, a Chicago suburb. David came here as a student at Monmouth College in 1940 and Mary arrived in 1946 as a newly appointed instructor of women's physical education at Monmouth College. The couple met in 1946 and were married on June 7, 1947. They have been residents of Warren County ever since and have lived in the same house since 1949.

Their three sons all grew up in Monmouth and attended Monmouth schools. Michael (born 12-5-49) is now an attorney in Peoria. He and his wife Lynne have three daughters, Lauren, Eryn, and Morgan. David (born 10-28-51) was in the U.S. Air Force during the Viet Nam War and then lived in Alaska for 15 years. He is now a cabinet maker in Scottsdale AZ and he and his wife Marcia have two sons, Kevin and Eric. After 11 years in the U.S. Air Force Joel (born 10-15-58) returned to Monmouth to work for Munson Trucking and later became a member of the maintenance staff at Monmouth College. He and his wife Violet have a daughter and a son, Dawn and Michael.

After two years of college David entered military service during World War II and served in the Army Air Corps as a navigator including duty with the Eighth Air Force based in England. He returned here after the war, graduated from Monmouth College in 1946 and began work in the college administrative offices. He was a staff member until 1972 (except for 18 months back in military service during the Korean War), serving in admissions, public relations and development. He was named Assistant to the President in 1966. In 1972 he became Vice President for Development at Cottage Hospital in Galesburg serving there until he retired in 1985. Since then he has been president of the Mellinger Educational Foundation in Monmouth. From 1966 until 1995 he was on the board of directors of the National Bank of Monmouth, serving as chairman 1970-1980 and 1983-1995.

Mary taught physical education at Monmouth College prior to the birth of her children and then again in later years, retiring finally in 1973. Altogether she taught at the College for almost twenty years.

Throughout their lives both David and Mary have been actively involved as volunteers in many community organizations, including the YMCA, United Way, Girl Scouts and Boy Scouts, Community Medical Center, Maple Leaf Community Concert Series, Junior Achievement, Rotary Club, PEO, and others. Both were honored by the Chamber of Commerce as Citizens of the Year, Mary in 1983 and David in 1993.

SARAH ELIZABETH FORESMAN - Sarah Elizabeth Foresman (1855-1936), the fourth child of ten children born to John Piati Foresman (1826-1891) and Anna Filbert (1828-1907), born 21 March 1855 in Lycoming County, PA. She moved with her parents to Illinois in 1856. On 23 July 1877 she married Simon Martin Raymond (1836-1909), his second wife, in a ceremony performed by S. P. James at the Pleasant Mound Church situated one mile north of Walnut Grove, IL. She spent her entire life near and in Walnut Grove, IL. She was an active and faithful member of the Methodist Church of Walnut Grove and was especially active in the Ladies' Aid Society and was one of the leaders of her Busy Bee Sunday School Class. Sajah hand made a pieced quilt for each of her grandchildren which were distributed following her death. Sarah died 28 November 1936 and is buried in the Prairie City Cemetery, Prairie City, Illinois.

Simon M. Raymond and Sarah Elizabeth Foresman wedding 23 July 1877.

Sarah and Simon were parents of eleven children: James Edward (1878-1938), 1m 1898 Blanche Larkins (1880-1912), Issue: Max, Albert, Mildred and Maxine. 2m 1931 Auddie Albina, Smith (1891-1959), Issue: step-son, Alf.

Cordia, Kaiser (1879-1953) Married 1902, Samuel Irwin (1875-1956), Issue: Paul, Robert, Clarence, Leona. Ernest born 13 March 1881, died 25 Feb 1883 of pneumonia. Anna Louesa born 16 Feb 1883, died 13 March 1903 of measles & pneumonia. Robert "Elmer" b 8 March 1885, died 26 July 1898, killed by C.B.&Q Railroad. "Killed by the Cars" Above three children all buried McMahidl Cemetery. Harvey "Samuel" (1887-1952), married Mayme Euphemie Bagley (1888-1951), Issue: Harry, Naomi. Laura "Beatrice" (1888-1958), married 1908 Ernest "Victor" Freburg (1882-1941), Issue: Charles, Bernice, Elmer, Ernest, Kenneth. Charles Vilasco (1890-1964), married 1919 Ruby May Thomson (1894-1978), Issue: Martin, R. Lyle, D. Keith, Reta, Roland, Sarah. Ruth Regina (1896-1968) married 1926 George William Williams (1898-1975) Issue: Gail, Martha, Leo. John Guy (1899-1986) 1m 1918 Elizabeth Fern Ernest (1901-1995), Issue: Harold, John Jr, Merlin. 2m 1946 Mrs. Clarice Rich Beard (1918-1980), Issue: Larry. Naomi Edna (1902- 1977) 1m 1931 Jesse William Aber (1908-1931), Issue: Lois. 2m 1942 Dennis Patrick Reardon (1899-1984), Issue: 0.

Foresman ancestors: John Piatt Foresman, son of John Foresman (1800-1877) first marriage 1822 to Mary Piatt. Second marriage to Marie B. Follmer, (Sister of Judge Piatt). Son of Robert Foresman, Jr. (1761-1829) married 1785 to Catherine Jacoby (1769-1831). Son of Robert Foresman, Sr. (1725 Ireland - 1806, PA) married 1748 Ireland Jane All (1728 Ireland - 1810 PA), Daughter of Samuel All. Son of Hugh Foresman born late 1600 century Ireland.

According to Henry S. Jacoby Lineage Books, Robert Sr. Foresman's ancestors came from Scotland and settled in Ulster Province, Ireland, for 119 years before he came to America in 1765.

HERBERT FOREMAN - Foreman, Herbert, called "Herbie" was born 19 September 1906 at Monmouth. He the son of John W. and Ida (Jones) Foreman. His father was a railroad engineer, while his mother was raising three girls; Nita, wife of Glenn Stewart of Wataga, Florence, wife of Donald Bolender of Princeton, and Hazel of Monmouth. She was to marry Chad Lusk but death befell him just prior to the marriage. Later she was happily married to Jimmy Davisson, who shortly afterwards passed away. Hazel clerked in Axline Drug Store until she retired. The elder Forman's lost an infant son and a sister died earlier.

"Herbie" was reared and educated at Monmouth, where he met and married Lois Wong 25 November 1926. She was a beautiful brunette slightly taller than her husband. They lived a short while on East Euclid, next to the McDill Grocery - across from Garfield School. Later as his family increased, moved to a. home oil North 3th Street 300 block in back of Walter Tomlin, where falling from a small tree his oldest son of four broke his arm. They raised four sons and two daughters; Jack of Plano, Illinois, David of Kirkwood, and Jim and Paul living in Monmouth; Diane married James Kane and Carole married Donald Millard of Oquawka.

"Herbie" was red headed, short, but very quick - able to outwork his fellow workers. He first clerked at Barnes Bros, Grocery from 1923 to the early thirties. He was responsible for delivering groceries to the. North section of town five times daily and the afternoons sacked powdered, light brown and dark brown and granulated Sugar along with rice daily as well as sacking potatoes in the basement. His passion was buying baseball tickets betting on various Professional baseball teams - spending large sums at that time which he couldn't afford. He took up meat cutting at Youngs Grocery located at the far end, east side of South Main Street. It. was from here Rennie Barnes of Barnes Bros. sought to rehire him, but he had just accepted an offer to work for the R&V Grocery. When they closed he worked five years on the Illinois Highway Department and lastly for seven years operated a pool room at Kirkwood. Everyone liked "Herbie" in spite of many setbacks he came out smiling. He never tired of conversing about his amusing exploits, keeping everyone laughing. He was a member of the Christian Church, but we seldom saw him there.

It is his son David we note is active in Kirkwood's Abe Lincoln Masonic Lodge and performs regularly in the Galesburg Commandery located in the Masonic Temple ill Monmouth. We count 38 years that he worked in the grocery business. He was 70 when he passed away in 1976, leaving 19 grandchildren and four great grandchildren.

JAMES CROSBY FOSTER - James Crosby Foster was born January 8, 1892, Kirkwood, IL., youngest of three children of Samuel C. and Ella Foster. His father was a pharmacist, but had eye trouble and became blind.

Jim was four when the family moved to Monmouth, living with Jim's uncle, William P. McClung, 216 South 5th. His mother was housekeeper for brother William, who ran a grocery store with brothers Charles and James.

Jim attended old Central and Monmouth High schools. October 1909, Jim was employed by George O. Wirtz, clerking at the bookstore Wirtz opened the previous August. Store's original daybook records Jim's salary—six dollars a week; a handsome salary for a seventeen year old in 1909. Jim later became manager and finally owner.

Jim attended Monmouth College, class of 1914, didn't graduate, but maintained a lifetime interest in the college and students.

Wirtz purchased Marshall Book Store, Chicago 1916. Jim was sent to help operate that store. He worked there till 1918, when called to the Army, World War I. Basic training near Mobile, Alabama, went to France, Battery A, 3rd Battalion, Anti-Aircraft Artillery. Discharged in 1919, he returned to Wirtz Book Store, Monmouth. 1921, purchased a house at 118 South 7th, his home until his death.

James Crosby Foster

1923, married Hannah M. Hillen, daughter of Henry and Emma Hillen, a double wedding with his friend James Burkholder and Esther Gillander. Bold newspaper headline, "Double Wedding This Morning Big Surprise, James C. Foster and James Burkholder Desert Single Life Today." Parents of the two couples were the only attendants at a simple ceremony at First Presbyterian Church. Planned a Breguet airplane flight to Chicago, bad weather made rail transportation necessary.

1925 Jim became an equal partner in Wirtz Bookstore, in 1942 he became sole owner. Original site of Wirtz, 213 E. Broadway, 1944 the store moved to 200 E. Broadway. 1972 Phillip Wheeler bought the business and operated under Wirtz name, closed the business in 1982.

The downtown store sold college books until Scot Supply was established on campus. Jim made friends with generations of college students, some found college-days employment at Wirtz. Many graduates never returned to Monmouth without stopping at Wirtz Comer to see Jim. For years he wrote newspaper advertisement column including news of people stopping at the store. Graduates and former Monmouth people wrote from around the world requesting books or items they could not find.

Scot Student Supply opened on campus about 1960. Jim sold the downtown business 1972, then worked at Scot Supply daily, maintaining active contact with students until his death in December 1978.

Although working long hours in his business, Jim found time for community activities. He was a Presbyterian elder; taught high school Sunday school class for several years; was Monmouth Rotary Club secretary for 25 years; also a Rotary Paul Harris Fellow; Security Savings and Loan director 34 years; maintained American Legion and Masonic Lodge memberships for over 50 years.

For recreation, Jim enjoyed "going to the river". His Mississippi River cottage north of Oquawka was called " Windblown" because a storm blew the roof off shortly after construction. On Sunday afternoons the family would often be found "at the river."

The Fosters had two sons; Robert, chemist for Sinclair Oil and successor Atlantic Richfield; Richard, civil engineer Bechtel Corporation, with overseas career in pipeline construction. Hannah worked with Jim at Wirtz when the boys were older. She continued living in the family home until her death in September 1984.

SAMUEL FOSTER - Samuel Foster was born about 1784 in Abbeville District South Carolina the son of James Couples Foster Jr. born 1753 in Ireland died September 19, 1837 and buried in Spring Hill, Decatur County Indiana and Jane Morrow born about 1757 in Maryland and died December 3, 1823 and buried in Cedar Springs Cemetery, South Carolina. James Couples Foster fought in the Battle of Cowpens January 17, 1781 serving with the 6th So. Regiment. James served under Capt. Samuel Morrow of 96th Dist of South Carolina. In 1780 James Couples Foster married Capt. Samuel and Elilzabeth Carmical Morrow's daughter Jane. Samuel came to Warren County about 1835 and settled in Spring Grove Township on a farm he received from the government for serving in the War of 1812. Seven of his children came to Warren County namely: Jane Foster that married John C. McCrery in South Carolina; Margaret "Peggy" married Hamilton Hill in South Carolina; James Foster married Susan Giles in Warren County IL; William A. Foster married Jane McDill; John A. Foster married Martha J. Struthers and Mrs. Rachel W. Mitchell in Warren County IL; Martha L. Foster married Jonathan Mulnix 4/11/1839 in Warren County, Martha died 2/25/1849 Jonathan Mulnix married Mrs. Mary Graham 2/28/1850 in Warren County IL and later moved to Iowa; and Samuel Hamilton Foster, a dwarf, never married, born August 16, 1827 in South Carolina died September 25, 1877 and buried in Cedar Creek Cemetery, Warren County Illinois and was a carpenter and had a tailor shop in his father's home. Samuel married Margaret B. Lusk 10/4/1839 Warren County Illinois. Margaret died 3/7/1841 at age 42 years; Samuel married Eleanor Pollock 4/17/1845 Warren County Illinois. Samuel died 8/13/1845 and is buried in Cedar Creek Cemetery, Sumner Township, Warren County Illinois. Nothing is known about Nancy, Samuel's first wife and mother of his children. The family belonged to the "Associate Reformed Church," which later became the strict United Presbyterian Church.

DONALD E. FREDRICKSON - Donald E. Fredrickson and Judith Squire Fredrickson moved to rural Seaton in August of 1999, back to the homestead where Donald was born and raised. A new home was erected at that time. Bertha Ranney Fredrickson was still living on the original homestead.

Donald graduated from Little York High School and works at General Electric in West Burlington, Iowa at an assembly job and also has farmed the existing homestead since 1976.

Judith graduated from Galesburg High School and works at Great River Medical Center in West Burlington, Iowa. They had three children:

D. Lane Fredrickson was born in 1967 and works as a manufacturing engineer. He married Karen Earp and they have two sons, Brandon Lane and Cole Axel. This family is now the 5th and 6th generation to live on the homestead in the old family home.

J. Lynette Fredrickson was born in 1968 and is a speech pathologist.

Shawnna Fredrickson Roberts was born in 1970 and is a computer support specialist. She has a daughter, Kaytlyn Reann Roberts.

The original owners of the homestead were: 1st generation: Nathan C. Ranney (1842-1906) and Emily C. Ranney (1848-191). 2nd generation: William C. anney (1871-1945) and Hilma V. Ranney (1876-1935). 3rd Generation: Everett A. Fredrickson (1910-1997) and Bertha Ranney Fredrickson (1914-2000). 4th generation: Donald E. Fredrickson (1941-) and Judith K. Fredrickson (1944-). 5th generation: Donald Lane Fredrickson (1967-) and Karen J. Fredrickson (1965-). 6th generation: Brandon Lane Fredrickson (1995-) and Cole Axel Fredrickson (1998-).

EVERETT AXEL FREDRICKSON - Everett Axel Fredrickson and Bertha Ranney Fredrickson were the 3rd generation to live on the farm and homestead of Nathan C. Ranney. Bertha was the organist of Belmont Church for over 50 years and taught music in her home. They lived all their married life on the homestead.

They had 3 children, LaJune, Paul and Donald.

Everett & Bertha Fredrickson

The original owners of the homestead were: 1st generation: Nathan C. Ranney (1842-1906) and Emily C. Ranney (1848-1912). 2nd generation: William C. Ranney (1871-1945) and Hilma V. Ranney (1876-1935). 3rd Generation: Everett A. Fredrickson (1910-1997) and Bertha Ranney Fredrickson (1914-2000). 4th generation: Donald E. Fredrickson (1941-) and Judith K. Fredrickson (1944-). 5th generation: Donald Lane Fredrickson (1967-) and Karen J. Fredrickson (1965-). 6th generation: Brandon Lane Fredrickson (1995-) and Cole Axel Fredrickson (1998-).

LANE AND KAREN EARP FREDRICKSON - Lane and Karen Earp Fredrickson moved to rural Seaton, Illinois in March of 2001. They reside in the homestead originally established by: 1st generation: Nathan C. Ranney (1842-1906) and Emily C. Ranney (1848-1912). 2nd generation: William C. Ranney (1871-1945) and Hilma V. Ranney (1876-1935). 3rd Generation: Everett Axel Fredrickson (1910-1997) and Bertha Ranney Fredrickson (1914-2000). 4th generation: Donald E. Fredrickson (1941-) and Judith K. Fredrickson (1944-). 5th generation: Donald Lane Fredrickson (1967-) and Karen J. Fredrickson (1965-). 6th generation: Brandon Lane Fredrickson (1995-) and Cole Axel Fredrickson (1998-).

Lane Fredrickson Family

Lane grew up in Biggsville, Illinois and graduated from Union High School. He works as a manufacturing engineer. Karen grew up in Kirkwood, Illinois and graduated from Yorkwood High School. She works as an administrative assistant. They have two children, Brandon, 7 and Cole, 4.

LAWRENCE E. FREDRICKSON - Lawrence(Larry) Edward Fredrickson born December 13,1938 in Monmouth, Il., son of Mr. And Mrs. Pete Fredrickson. Larry attended Belmont Elementary school and graduated 1956 from Little York High School. Graduated Bailey Trade School in St. Louis, Mo. 1957. He farmed in Henderson County until 1971,when he moved to Monmouth, Il. where he currently resides. He was employed at various locations including Alcoa, Admiral, Wilson Packing, Caterpillar and Butler Mfg. of Galesburg, Il. Retiring 2001.

Lawrence Fredrickson family.

He is the father of three sons Timothy Edward born November 6,1959,married Wendy Edwards, their children are Timothy, Sarah and Carol. They reside in Galva, IL. Daniel Wade born December 10, 1962, married Kelly Kinney, their children are Tabitha, Conner and Chase. They reside in Towanda, Il. Matthew Blake born December 30,1964, married Christina Overstreet, their children are Anthony, Kailiand Heath. They reside in Alexis, Il.

PETER EDWARD FREDRICKSON - Peter Edward Fredrickson born March 18, 1913 died Sept. 2, 2000. Son of Axel Albert Fredrickson born 8-24-1885 died 5-23-1971 and wife Beda Osterberg born May 27, 1884 died Aug 9, 1949, from Finspang, Sweden to Illinois Feb. 1910. He married Mae Betty Ranney Dec. 22, 1937 in Burlington, Iowa. Taken from Prairie Farmers Reliable Directory of Warren and Henderson counties.

Pete and Mae Fredrickson

Father Ranney, Willian C. (Hilma Johnson) Children: Clyde born May 31, 1896 and died May 14, 1913, killed by lighting. Bertha Clara born April 15, 1914 died June 1, 2000. Bernice Emily born October 7, 1915. Mae Betty Born July 21, 1917 died May 22, 2000.

They retired from fanning in the Belmont area in Henderson County, in 1969 to 501 North Sunny Lane, Monmouth, Ill. They were the parents of three sons Larry of Monmouth, Il., John (Marilou) Fredrickson of RR Seaton, Il., Michael (Pat) Fredrickson of RR Seaton, Il., and one daughter Darlene Jo (Hugh) Forbes of Media, Il. 10 grandchildren and 18 great-grand children.

DR. WILLIAM ARTHUR FRYMIRE, M.D. - Dr. William Arthur Frymire was born September 12, 1883 in Monmouth Twp., Warren County, IL. His great grandparents, William and Polly "Bruner" Frymire had migrated to Illinois with their 6 children from Breckenridge County, KY by covered wagon in 1839. His father, Arthur was born in New York in 1855 to William W. and Mary Lydia "Barnum" Frymire. His father married Melvina"Forbes" rymire August 2, 1880 in Warren County.

Lulu Josephine and Dr. William A. Frymire with children James and Irma, 1922, Belgian Congo, Africa.

Dr. Frymire's formal education began at Galesburg High School after which he began premed studies at Eureka College. He attended the American Medical Missionary College of Battle Creek, Michigan in 1909 and received his doctorate degree from the University of Illinois College of Medicine in 1913.

Dr. Frymire immediately began his career as a medical missionary to the Belgian Congo, Africa in 1913. He returned to the United States in 1918 and interned at the Charity Hospital in New Orleans, Louisiana.

In 1919, Dr. Frymire taught courses in "Tropical Medicine" and "Hygiene, Sanitation" at the College of Missions in Indianapolis, Indiana. That same year, he returned to the Belgian Congo as a missionary for the United Christian Missionary Society of Indianapolis and was in charge of the sleeping sickness program for the Belgian Government in the Momboyo River District until August 1922. Upon returning to the United States in 1923, he opened a private medical practice in Decatur, Illinois.

Dr. Frymire returned to the Congo in late 1923 for a third time to continue his medical missionary work. He was given an honorary degree from King Leopold of Belgium for his work with sleeping sickness. During WWI, he enlisted for the service in the Belgium Expeditionary Forces.

During Dr. Frymire's first term in the Congo, he met Charles Hedges who was an engineer/minister, and his wife Lilly who was a schoolteacher in a neighboring village some 100 miles away. He began corresponding with Lilly's sister Lula. Josephine Boyer, and met her during his first furlough to the United States. At the time, Josephine was completing her RN degree at the "Kellog Sanitarium," Battle Creek, Michigan.

Dr. and Mrs. Frymire were married in Bement, Piatt Co., Illinois on February 1, 1919. Their children Irma J. Frymire MacDonald, James A. Frymire, Robert M. Frymire and Kirby L. Frymire were born in the Congo except for Robert, who was born in Decatur, Illinois in 1923.

In 1928, Dr. Frymire and family returned to the U.S. permanently, where he was named chief of staff at Monmouth Hospital, Monmouth, Illinois. Later, he became part of the staff advisory committee and was named chairman of that group. He also taught at Monmouth Hospital School of Nursing for several years. In 1937, he was engaged in post-graduate work at the St. Louis Clinic in Missouri.

Dr. Frymire co-authored a book entitled *Spying Out Congo Land* in 1914.

HENRY FRYMIRE - Henry Frymire(1869-1934), was one of 11 children born to Hardin Davis Frymire (1842-1903) buried in Kansas (m1864) to Elizabeth Cannon(1847-1886) buried at Mosier Cemetery, the daughter of John Cannon(1808-1887) and Mary Spangler Cannon, who was the daughter of Private Henry Spangler (1750-1791), and Maria Hoke Spangler. Elizabeth Ann was sister to John, Levi, Denver and Mary. Henry Frymire's grandparents were William Frymire (1806-1882) buried at Coldbrook Cemetery, and Mary "Polly" Bruner (1808-1882) born in Breckenridge, KY. She was daughter of Henry Bruner and Eve Frymire (1786-1837) buried Monmouth. The Frymires' came to Warren Co. in 1837, along with other siblings.

Hardin Davis Frymire, Ida, Henry, Hardin Jr, Pearl, Harry, Maude, Ray, Margarette and Lydia.

The first Frymires' landed in New York in 1710. Some traveled west through Pennsylvania, Ohio, Kentucky, and settling in Illinois. They were very successful farmers, active in the community and the church, and donated property for the Frymire School.

Henry Frymire (m) Emma Goyer on the 29th of March, 1892, in Warren Co., IL. Their children were (1) Harden H. (1896-?) (m) Lillian Fisher, one daughter, Adele. (2) Alden (1898-?) (m) Mary Alice, had 4 children; Jack (m) Marilyn, Jill (m) James, Richard (m) Ann, Joyce (m) Harland.

LEWIS SR. AND ETHEL (COOK) FRYMIRE - Lewis L. Frymire Sr. (1900-1968), buried in Galesburg, IL, Lived in Warren Co. as a child with his parents, Henry Frymire (1868-1934), and Emma Goyer (1867-1929), both buried at Silent Home Cemetaryin Warren Co. Lewis Sr. married Ethel Cook, born in Harvy Il. In 1902, her father, William Delos Cook built the Gale automobile, named after the founder of Galesburg. Her mother was Etta May Cook, of Cook Co. Lewis and Ethels' children were; (1) Janet (m) Michael Addis Arnold, their son Greg and wife Annie had 2 sons.

Ethel (Cook) and Lewis Frymire.

Lewis L. Frymire Sr., Lewis "Lee" Frymire Jr., Lewis "Lee" Frymire III, December 27, 1963, San Francisco, California.

Daughter Ann and Bob Burbridge had daughter Britt, sons Michael and Mark. (2) Jean (m) Rick Fendler, they had 2 sons, Daniel and Matthew who had 2 sons. One daughter Lynn and husband had daughter Azure and son Kepper. (3) Jacquelin – died at age 18, buried in Galesburg. She attended Galesburg High School. (4) Lewis Lee Frymire Jr. (1928-1991), buried at Silent Home Cemetery in Cameron. He married "Pat" Marie Cadena. He worked as an electronic tech. for FAA., after he retired from 22 years of military service. His son Lewis L. Frymire III (1956-2001), buried at Silent Home Cemetary. No children, worked as a computer programmer/analyst. Daughter Gayle Susan (1957) (m) Charles E. Hoots who has AAA Electric & Engineering in Galesburg. They have 2 children together (1) Natomi Leana (1978) attending college in Milwaukee, WI and (2) Destan Lukas (1980) working with his father as electrician/welder and 1 step daughter Amy Christine Graves (1974) (m) Joe Carl Reeves, they have 4 children; Christina Nicole, age 5, Ashten Marie 4, Joseph Cleve (died at 1 1/2), Joe Carl Jr. age 10 mos. Amy's mother is Elaine Graves. (3) Teresa Jane (1961) (m) William Andrew Bartlett Jr. They had 5 children. (1) Olivia Constance (1981) working in payroll management and attending college part time. (2) William Andrew III (1984) graduating 2002 and will be attending college. (3) Stuart Michael (1989) (4&5) twins Ava Louise and Grace Marie (1994). The fifth child of Lewis and Ethel was Henry Delos, twin to Lewis, Jr., died at 11 days old, buried with grandmother Etta Cook. (6) William Edward (1931), (m) Margaret Northam. They had 3 children. (1) David Lewis (1958), (m) Margot, they have son Daniel and daughter Malena. (2) Eric (1960), (m) Erma, they have one daughter Emelda, and are expecting a child in the fall of 2002. (3) Diane, born (1962) works as a teacher in California.

LESTER R. GALE - Lester R. Gale was born 1 March 1909, in Galesburg. His early life and schooling were in Galesburg. He graduated from high school there. His marriage to Theresa H. (Spisak) took place 13 September 1932, in Joliet, Illinois.

He worked for Rankin and Shaub during the war years and until they closed. Les was then employed 21 years at Barnes Bros. Grocery as produce manager. He was there during the fire and when it became the first Super Valu Store in Illinois.

He was a member of the Immaculate Conception Church. His hobby was hunting and fishing. He had been semi-retired for six years.

His widow survives as well as three sons, Robert L. of Westminister, California, Richard D. of Macomb, Illinois, and Ray E. of Galesburg; six grandchildren; a sister, Mrs. Robert (Betty) Herman of Arvada, Colorado; and a brother, Harold Gale of Hawaii. Another brother was Edward, who died earlier.

Les was always "neat as a pin", methodical in his work, and dependable. He loved his family and they were very close. He shared a duplex on South 8th Street across from the 2nd UP Church with Rennie and Myra Barnes. It was from here he was hired to work for Barnes Bros. as they became a Super Market after the fire in 1955 and joined Super Valu stores incorporated. He passed away 29 January 1974, from lung cancer living at 416 West 1st Avenue.

GALLAUGHER - William Gallaugher was born January 27, 1824, in Scotland. He came to America when he was 31 years old. His wife was Margaret Muir. For 45 years, William was a resident of Warren County. He died August 9, 1900, at his home nine miles north of Monmouth, Illinois. He was 76 years old. Margaret was born May 1, 1825, and died April 1, 1902. Together, they raised ten children.

The oldest was Margaret (Maggie), born January 19, 1850. She married Robert Henderson.

Nettie was born November 22, 1851. She married Frank Hogue. Charles Gallaugher was born October 7, 1852. Agnes (Aggie) was born April 26, 1855 and died in 1925. She married Stewart Ellis Leonard. Michael R. was born May 8, 1857. He farmed east of Monmouth, Illinois. He married Minnie Thompson on March 12, 1884. Michael died August 14, 1946. Their children were

Merle May, born in 1885, and Elizabeth Chloe, born March 12, 1890. Mary Jane was born January 12, 1859. She married Carl L. Harper. They ran a photography studio. Many of the Gallaugher family pictures were taken by him.

Belle Gallaugher was born November 18, 1862, and married Emerson Woods. William E. was born January 31, 1863. His wife was named Myrtle. He died in 1937. James L. was born November 11, 1867. He was a bachelor and lived in California.

Anna Gallaugher was born January 11, 1868, in Mercer County, Illinois. She married Charles J. Thieme, son of Henry and Lena Jacob Thieme, November 28, 1894, in Gerlaw, Illinois. She died July 25, 1957. Anna and Charles Thieme are buried in Little York, Illinois. On her tombstone, the spelling of Gallaugher has been changed to Gallaher.

GARLAND-PETERSON - Ida and John Peterson came from Sweden and settled in Henderson County, Illinois. Roy Clayborn Peterson, one of seven children, was born in 1901. In 1927 Roy married Lucille Maude Stripe, the daughter of Arthur and Dollie Stripe. Roy passed away in 1959 and Lucille passed away in 1975. They had four children: Mary Roylene Peterson, born in 1928 and passed away in 1994; Doris Jean, born in 1929; Everett Ray, born in 1931, and just recently passed away in 2002; Patricia Ann, born in 1933 and was deceased in 1989.

Doris Jean Peterson married James (Jack) Lewis Garland in the year of 1948. Jack was the eldest of three born to Joe and Jennie (Craig) Garland. Joe came from North Carolina at the age of 18, served in his country's army at 19 in WWI and was stationed in France. Joe was a farmer in Henderson County until 1920, moving to Warren County, Illinois, in Sumner Township in 1940. Joe and Jennie had two other children, they are Robert Garland, born December 7, 1928, and Joan, born October 14, 1933.

Jack and Doris have two children: Jean Kay Garland, born in 1952, and Jacklyn Jeannette, born in 1956.

Jean Kay married Robert Dennis Jacobs in 1972. Their children are Robert Jacobs, born 1977, and Emily Kay Jacobs, born in 1981. Robert Jacobs and Jennifer Housh have a son, Chase Robert Jacobs, born in 2001.

Jacklyn Jeannette Garland married Mark Palmer in 1998.

Roy Clayton Peterson was a lifetime farmer, who lived most of his life in Warren County, Illinois, with all of his children graduating from Little York High School.

Doris and Jack Garland are now living on the Peterson Family Farm.

JANET GASKILL-OLIPHANT - George and Betty Gaskill- George was born to George and Gladys Short Gaskill on 7-10-1926, and Betty was born to Roy and Mabel Isaacson Nelson on 12-12-1926. They had three children, Sharon, born 1-20-1948, Janet, born 8-28-1950, and Gary, born 9-1-1952.

Janet married Dennis Oliphant on 3-14-1977, and they had three children, Ginger, born 7-5- 1981, Scott, born 1-19-1984, and Kent, born 12-18-1986. Ginger attends Western Illinois University in Macomb, Illinois. Scott attends Carl Sandburg College in Galesburg, Illinois, and Kent is a sophomore at Yorkwood High School, Little York, Illinois.

Janet Gaskill and family

Janet lives on a family farm and has for 25 years. She's been involved with her children's activities, is a musician, singer and song writer and is a choir director at the First Lutheran Church in Monmouth. She owns and operates Monmouth Soda Works in Monmouth.

DONALD AND BENITA BRIDE GAVIN - Donald Eugene Gavin was born at home on October 19, 1927, in Monmouth, Illinois. He is the son of George Gavin (5/9/1899-3/5/1965) and Rose Hennenfent Gavin (4/24/1902-6/06/2001). Donald grew up on the Smith Farm west of Monmouth and attended Farmer's Academy School. He graduated from Monmouth High School in 1945. He served in the Korean War from 1951 to 1953 and then returned to Monmouth to farm.

Donald Gavin Family

Benita is the daughter of James Bride (10/26/1898) and Helen O'Brien Bride (9/8/1900). Benita was born on June 21, 1930, at St. Mary's Hospital in Galesburg, Illinois. Until the age of 6, she lived on Cork Street in Alexis, Illinois. Her family then moved to a farm south of Monmouth where she attended South Henderson School. In about 1939, they moved to a farm south of Larchland where Benita finished grade school at Picayune School. She attended Roseville High School in Roseville, Illinois, and St. Mary's Academy in Nauvoo, Illinois, graduating from St. Mary's in 1948. Prior to marriage she worked in the office at Strands Bakery in Monmouth.

Donald and Benita were married on June 27, 1953, at St. Patrick's Catholic Church in Raritan, Illinois. They started their married life on an 80-acre farm in Hale Township in Warren County that was initially purchased in 1887 by Donald's great-grandparents, Terrence Kinney and Rose Lenehan Kinney. In 1960 they moved to the Hardin farm on the west edge of Monmouth where they currently reside. Donald has enjoyed collecting antique farm equipment and has hosted threshings on his farm several times. He has been seen in Prime Beef Festival Parades and other events, driving his team of Belgian draft horses. Donald and Benita had five children.

Teresa Marie Gavin (b. 4/3/1954) is a Clinical Nurse Specialist in Waterloo, Iowa.

Gary Eugene Gavin (b. 7/31/1955) married Sandra Kay Horton (b. 12/4/1958) at Immaculate Conception Church in Monmouth, Illinois, on December 16, 1978. They farm in Warren County and Sandra is a certified public accountant. They have five children: Matthew Eugene (b. 6/22/1979), Amanda Kay (b. 10/8/1980), Paul Joseph (b. 4/3/1982), Andrew Michael (b. 7/8/1983) and Melissa Ann (b. 7/18/1984). Matthew continues the farming tradition with his father.

Gloria Ann Gavin Geer (b. 11/26/1956) married Charles Geer (b. 2/10/1954) at Immaculate Conception Church on July 2, 1977. Gloria is a surgical technician at St. Mary's Hospital in Galesburg and a real estate agent. Charlie is a conductor for Amtrak and farms. They have three children: Adam Joseph (b. 5/25/1981), Maggie Marie (b. 6/13/1985) and Lucas Gavin (b. 4/1/1989).

Stanley Joseph Gavin (b. 3/19/1959) died of leukemia on January 26, 1986.

Christopher Jon (b. 5/14/1961) married Lisa Louise Spray (b. 4/7/1962) at St. Patrick's Catholic Church in Andalusia, Illinois, on October 19, 1985. Chris is president of Midwest Bank of Western Illinois in Monmouth and Lisa does bookkeeping from their home. They have five children: Aaron Joseph (b. 10/9/1987), Patrick Christopher (b. 2/18/1989), Alex Michael (b. 6/21/1992), Jacob Phillip (b. 5/19/1994) and Madeline Lee (b. 2/26/1999).

FRANCIS AND MARY GAVIN - Francis Edward Gavin was born in Hale Township on December 11, 1901. His parents, born of Irish immigrants, were William and Kathryn Kinney Gavin, natives of Warren County. Bill was probably born in Monmouth Township, but Kate was born in Hale Township. Francis married Mary Jane Brownlee in Monmouth, Illinois, on January 25, 1927.

Mary and Francis Gavin

Mary was born in Sumner Township on August 31, 1903, the daughter of John W. and Nellie May Armstrong Brownlee. Both parents were natives of Sumner Township with faily roots in Washington County, Pennsylvania.

Francis attended the rural school near their home. Mary attended Duck Creek ad Brownlee schools. She attended Little York High School and graduated from Monmouth High School in 1922 after her family moved to Monmouth in 1920. Following graduation she kept house for her family, and later worked in McQuiston's Book Store in Monmouth.

Francis was a farmer and, after their marriage, they started farming on the Brannon farm in Lenox Township. After a short time they moved to the Martin farm in Sumner Township in Section 6. Later they were able to purchase a farm from Fred and Margaret Severs in the northwest quarter of Section 17 in Sumner Township. It was there that they lived until Francis left farming because of his health. They moved to a home in Little York, and Francis became a John Deere salesman for the Thede Company in Aledo. It was at that home that Mary died suddenly on May 23, 1965.

Francis died at Community Memorial Hospital on October 10, 1981. Both Mary and Francis are buried at St. Mary's Cemetery in Monmouth.

Their first child was Marjorie Jean, who was born February 13, 1928. On her parents' anniversary, January 25, Marge became the bride of Robert Eugene Mills in 1952, at the home of her parents in Little York. Robert's birthday is October 28, 1923. Robert is a farmer and for some years raised hogs on a rather large scale. Marge has been an excellent homemaker for her extended family.

Martha Ann was their second child, who was born on November 7, 1935. In the 1960s she became the postmistress at Little York, Illinois. On April 25, 1970, she married Carl Robert Krusmark in Aledo, Illinois. Bob's birthday is July 15, 1940. Martha died of breast cancer on September 21, 1995, and is buried at Cedar Creek Cemetery near Little York.

Their third daughter was Margaret Lucille, who was born on March 27, 1937. She married William Jesse Biddle in Aledo on June 5, 1954. Her husband was born on January 30, 1936. For several years she served as her sister's assistant at the post office. Later, she became the postmistress at Seaton, Illinois. Now, she is the postmistress at Little York. Bill has combined farming with other jobs, such as at a pork plant and at an army munitions plant, from which he has retired after many years of employment.

WILLIAM AND KATHRYN KINNEY GAVIN - William Gavin was born April 23, 1866, probably in Monmouth Township, the son of Patrick and Mary Heffernan, both Irish immigrants. He married Kathryn Kinney at the Immaculate Conception Church on February 9, 1892.

Kathryn was born on January 20, 1866, in Hale Township. She was the child of Terrence Kinney and Rose Lenahan, also Irish immigrants.

William and Kathryn began farming on a farm in Hale Township where Kathryn had grown up. It was here that Bill and Kate raised their family.

There were eleven children born of this union. Rose Mary Gavin was born January 30, 1893. She married L. Roy Thompson and they lived just west of hergirlhood home. He was a farmer and the township road commissioner. They had nine children: William, Lawrence, Harold, Robert, Helen, Margaret, Florence, Grace and Martha.

Kathryn was born February 26, 1894. She was wed to Edward Gillen, and they also lived just west of the homestead across the road from her sister Rose. Their children were Katherine, Margaret, Mary, Lucille, William, Leroy, Frances, Richard, Betty and George.

Terrance William (Will) was born September 15, 1895. He married Frances Burns. He was a farmer and livestock breeder. They had five children: William, Mary, Lucille, Helen and Jean.

Kate Gavin and family, 1966. (l. to r.) Front: John, Francis, Kathryn, Will and Roy. Back: Kate Gillen, Ellen, George, Margaret and Rose Thompson.

Will and Kate Gavin, 1956

Margaret was born January 20, 1898. She never married and worked as a sales clerk.

George was born May 9, 1899. He married Rose Hennenfent, and they farmed the Kinney-Gavin home place in Section 22 of Hale Township. They had three children: Robert, Donald and Alice. Donald and his sons still own and farm the home place.

Ellen was born October 24, 1900. Ellen never married, but helped her parents at home. She and her sister Margaret took care of them until their death.

Francis was born December 11, 1901. He married Mary Brownlee. Francis was a farmer and a John Deere implement dealer. They had three daughters: Marjorie, Martha and Lucille.

The ninth child, Mary, was born June 18, 1903, and died August 30, 1903. A son, Charles Leroy, born June 27, 1904, died on April 3, 1906.

Another son, born Mary 14, 1906, was also named Leroy. He married Verna Brooks. Roy was an automobile salesman. Their children were James and Donna.

William and Kathryn and all of their children are buried at St. Mary's Cemetery in Monmoth. *Submitted by Alice Enderlin.*

DONALD AND PATRICIA GIBB - In the summer of 1958, the Donald Gibb family moved to Monmouth and resided at 403 North B Street. At this time, Donald and Patricia comprised the family. On February 1, 1959, Gregory Donald was born at Monmouth hospital. On July 15, 1960, the three of them moved to 620 East Second Avenue, where they purchased their first home. Douglas Alan became a member of the family on January 8, 1963. He also was born in the old Monmouth hospital located at 515 East Euclid Avenue.

Donald and Pat, Mother's Day, May 12, 2002, Galesburg

Donald was born August 20, 1923, in Biggsville. He was the youngest member of the John and Erma (Burrell) Gibb family. His siblings were Gertrude, Marguerite and Jack.

His wife, Patricia Joan Williams, was one of five children born to Walter and Verla (Baker) Williams in Concord, Illinois, on April 20, 1932. Her siblings were Mary, Jane, Willard and Richard.

Donald and Patricia were married in Concord, Illinois, on June 9, 1957. They had met in the spring of 1956 while both were chaperoning a group of junior high school students at a dance in Farmington. Donald was then a teacher-principal of Hanna City and Patricia was elementary-junior high vocal instructor in the Farmington school system. They had their first date that summer while both were doing graduate work at the University of Colorado in Boulder.

The couple moved to Monmouth when Donald accepted the position as elementary principal of Warren School when it opened in the fall of 1958. He remained in that position for 13 years before coming to Willits School in Monmouth for 8 years. This was followed by eight years as the first regional superintendent of schools in the Henderson-Mercer-Warren Counties, due to reorganization.

He served his community by being involved in many activities, such as a member and president of Warren County YMCA, same for United Way Board, Warren Achievement Board, Maple Leaf Community Concert Series, Warren County Retired Teachers Association and Teachers Credit Union of Warren County. He was an active member of First Christian Church and Kiwanis Club.

Patricia started as a housewife and then became involved with some substitute teaching, piano teacher, taught at Warren Achievement Center, and GED instructor at Farmland Foods. She was an active member of the First Christian Church and PEO.

Both sons were educated in the Monmouth public school system. Gregory furthered his education at the University of Illinois, Illinois Wesleyan, Western Illinois University and received a Ph.D. in Microbiology from Ohio State. Doug received his bachelor's from Monmouth College and his master's from Western Illinois University. Greg is in industry and Doug in the education field.

Greg married Scheralyn Knickerbocker in Fairview on August 13, 1983. Children born to this union were Lucas Gregory and Kayla Michelle.

Doug married Julie Swan in Galesburg on July 22, 1989. Children born to this union were Zachary Pierce and Jordan Douglas.

GIBSON - There is so much information available on the Gibson family of Hale Township near Monmouth, Illinois, that it is not necessary to record it all here. There is a book written by Sarah Davidge Gibson, circa 1910, in Monmouth about her family. She was very detailed and very accurate in recording her family history.

The Gibson family were members of a church split off of the Presbyterian Church in Scotland. A group calling itself Associate Presbyterian Church, or Seceder Church, was established. The Gibsons were followers of this church from Pennsylvania and into Blount County, Tennessee, into Green County, Ohio, near Xenia and finally into Warren County.

In 1831 Thomas Gibson and his wife, Martha (maiden name Hogg), left their farmstead of 25 years in Massies Creek, two miles east of the current town of Xenia, Ohio. They had a large farm on the main road from Columbus to Cincinnati, Ohio. Thomas' father, John Gibson, lived next door on one side and the Hogg relatives lived on the other. They all cleared this land of timber when they moved there in 1807 to establish their homes in the Ohio Territory. My wife and children and I found this land in the 180s and found it still farmland with richblack dirt and open spaces. It's hard to imagine someone leaving this beautiful place to go westward, but that's what they did. This Gibson family and my Allen ancestors were moving westward looking for a better life. They moved in large groups by church and family. In 1830-31 twenty five Gibson family members moved from Green County, Ohio, en masse to settle where some had earlier gone into Monmouth. When Thomas and Martha arrived in Hale Township, they would have had no time to put a crop in the ground, so food had to be a priority.

The first ancestors of Thomas Gibson came from Stewarts Town in Northern Ireland prior to 1730 because they owned land here in Pennsylvania at that time. Their children included Robert Gibson, born about 1700 in Ireland and died in Lancaster, Pennsylvania in 1754. He married Mary McClellen, also of Ulster Province, Ireland. She was murdered by Indians in Pennsylvania in 1756. Their children were Robert, born about 1722 in Ireland; Andrew, born 1724 in Ireland (Thomas Gibson of Monmouth is from this line.); John, born 1726, and died in 1761 in Lancaster, Pennsylvania; Israel, born 1728; Hugh, born 1730; and Mary, born 1732.

Andrew Gibson was born in 1724, was married to Elizabeth Karns/Carnes, and died in 1783 in Franklin County, Pennsylvania. Andrew was a frontier fighter during the Revolutionary War. Their children were Margaret, born 1750; Thomas, born 1752; John, born 1754; Jean, born 1756; and Elizabeth, born 1758. John was married to Martha Hogg; he died at Massies Creek, near Xenia, Green County, Ohio. Both are buried at Massies Creek Cemetery in Green County, Ohio. They were the parents of Thomas Gibson, first patriarch of the Gibson family in Warren County. John served as a private in Captain Poe's Command during the Revolutionary War.

Thomas Gibson was born in Pennsylvania and married Martha Hogg near Lexington, Virginia. Some of Martha's family members also moved into Warren County, Illinois. They also left Pennsylvania and settled in Blount County, Tennessee. They left here to go settle as a group near Green County, Ohio, in 1807, then on to Warren County, Illinois, in 1830-31. Thomas Gibson and some of his sons were drafted the same day to serve during the War of 1812. He had to leave his wife and youngest children. As was common in those times, if you could find a replacement for yourself, you could return home. Thomas found someone who needed the money and they exchanged places and Thomas came home.

The children born to Thomas and Martha (Hogg) Gibson in Blount County, Tennessee were Margaret, born 1793; John, born 1794; Elizabeth, born 1796; Esther, born 1798; James, born 1800; William, born 1802; Samuel, born 1804; and Thomas, born 1806. Children born at Massies Creek, Xenia, Green County, Ohio, were Martha, born 1809; Andrew, born 1811; George, born 1913; Robert Armstrong, born 1815; Jane, born 1818; and Mary (Polly), born 1819, died 1822, buried at Massies Creek Cemetery next to her grandparents, John and Martha (Parks) Gibson. They had moved from Prebble County, Ohio, to Green County to stay with Thomas and Martha in 1825.

Martha Gibson died in 1828 at 75 years old; John died in 1830 at 76 years of age. Thomas had uncles in Baltimore, Maryland, and had spent time there in his younger years where he learned the skills of brick masonry and put them to use in making chimneys for homes and churches and would help anyone who asked his help. Many times he filled in for ministers because he knew his Bible so well and had studied it fervently in his lifetime.

In 1830 the Seceder Church was organized at Sugar Tree Grove, Warren County, Illinois. This was to become the Sugar Tree Grove Presbyterian Church. Twenty-five settlers gathered together to organize this church, the first pastor was James Bruce, who married an Allen girl. Most of the Gibsons and early Allens are buried in the Sugar Tree Grove Cemetery in Warren County.

Jane Gibson was born in 1818 in Green County, Ohio, to Thomas and Martha Gibson. This is my personal Gibson line. She married Thomas Smith Allen on April 9, 1835, in Warren County. He moved here as a young man as Warren County was growing. He was born in Greene County, Illinois, in 1809 to Zachariah Allen and his second wife, Elizabeth (Law) Allen. Old Zachariah Allen had 25 children, 17 by his first wife and 8 by Elizabeth Law. Zachariah was born in 1760 in Rowan County, North Carolina. He is buried in the Belltown Cemetery in Greene County, Illinois. Elizabeth Law was much younger than her husband and moved into WarrenCounty as well. She lived out the rest of her life there until 1842 when she died. She is buried in the Sugar Tree Grove Cemetery.

Thomas Smith Allen died September 22, 1845, leaving Jane Gibson Allen a young widow with six young children. Jane's mother died in 1844. Thomas Gibson offered to help his youngest daughter raise her children and keep her farm going. He stayed with them for about 15 years until her oldest boys were able to run the farm. When Jane was older, she moved to Garrison, Kansas, in Pottawattamie County to live with her second son, Robert Gibson Allen, who had 15 children with two wives. She stayed a member of the United Presbyterian Church in Kansas and was very active until shortly before she passed away on March 22, 1908. She was buried in the Garrison Cemetery. Garrison, Kansas, was in a valley which had flooded many times over the years. In 1957 the U.S. Army Corps of Engineers moved any building people wanted moved and any graves that people wanted moved to higher ground. There is no record of Jane Gibson Allen being moved from the cemetery, so she is now in the bottom of the water reservoir. Evidently there was no family left in 1957 to have cared, or her marker was removed or so worn with age that her name could not be read. She raised her children without a husband just as my mother Catherine Allen Cover did when she was also widowed young at 39 years old. Jane Gibson and Thomas Smith Allen's children were James Bruce, born 1836 in Hale Township, Warren County, Illinois; Margaret Ann, born1838 in Hale Township; Robert Gibson, born 1839 in Hale Township; John Law, born 1841 in Hale Township; Martha White, born 1843 in Hale Township; and Henry Thomas, born 1845 in Hale Township.

James Bruce Allen married Theresa Daggett in Douglas County, Nebraska, in 1860 who had moved to Warren Count about 1850. She was born in Pennsylvania. Family tradition has it that James Allen was a pony express rider in 1859, the only year the Pony Express operated before telegraph lines were located all over the country. After this was over, they came back home to Warren County and farmed. When they were older they moved to Ellston, Iowa, along with their daughter, Carrie, who married John Maxwell, and they operated the lumber yard there. A son, Frank, never married and farmed in Ellston, Iowa. All three are buried in the Ellston, Iowa, cemetery. Their children were Charles Augustus, born in 1859 in Warren County, Illinois; Frank R., born in 1860 in Warren County; Ralph, born in 1863 in Warren County; Carrie May, born in 1865 in Warren County; and Stella, born in 1867 in Warren County, and died the same year.

Charles A. Allen moved to Scotia, Greeley County, Nebraska, as a young man and became a barber. He died in 1923 in Bridgeport, Merrill County, Nebraska. In 1887 he married Isabelle Currie, who was born in 1867 in Woburn, Massachusetts, a daughter of John Currie and Eliza Saddler/Foy. She died in 1945 in Casper, Wyoming, and is buried there. John Currie was a land investor and came to the Leo Valley in Nebraska. The children of Charles and Isabelle were Charles Clifford, born 1889, Scotia, Greeley County, Nebraska; Foye Vincent, born 1890, Scotia, Nebraska; Grace, born in Scotia, Nebraska; Margaret, born in Scotia, Nebraska; Myrtle, born 1892, Scotia, Nebraska; Lee, born 1894, Scotia, Nebraska; Mary, born 1896, Scotia, Nebraska; Frank, born 1898, Scotia, Nebraska; James, born in Scotia, Nebraska; and Raymond, born in Scotia, Nebraska.

Charles Clifford Allen farmed all his adult life in Greeley Township, Greeley County, Nebraska. He married Jennie Berryman in 1911. They both were born in 1889, he in Scotia, Nebraska, and she in Rockwell City, Iowa. They both passed away in 1969. They were members of Sacred Heart Catholic Church in Greeley and are buried in the Greeley Cemetery. Their children were Margaret, born 1912 on the family farm in Greeley, Greeley County, Nebraska; James, born 1915 on the family farm in Greeley, Nebraska; Elizabeth Rosella, born 1918 on the family farm in Greeley, Nebraska; and Catherine Leone, born 1926 on the family farm in Greeley, Nebraska.

Margaret Allen died at birth. James Allen served in the U.S. Army in WWII in Patton's Third Army, and married Lucille Armatus in Greeley, Nebraska, in 1953. They had eight children. Elizabeth Allen married Charles Wilson of Cleveland, Ohio, in 1944. They had six children and lived in Cleveland, Ohio. He died in 1968 and she in 1991.

Catherine Allen married Robert Eugene Cover at St. Mary Catholic Church in Berea, Ohio, a suburb of Cleveland, on May 28, 1949. Robert died January 16, 1966, at Harper Hospital in Detroit, Michigan. He was an engineer/supervisor at General Motors Technical Center in Warren, Michigan. Their children are Thomas A. Cover, born 1951 in Cleveland, Ohio, married Julie Anna Zivanov in 1974; Robert C. Cover, born 1953 in Cleveland, Ohio, married Cheryl Cromwell in 1978; Gregory P. Cover, born 1956 in Detroit, Michigan; and Karen M. Cover, born 1958 in Detroit, Michigan. *Submitted by Robert C. Cover.*

CHARLES MEEK GIBSON - Charles (Charlie) Gibson was born February 4, 1875, in a log cabin at Fall Branch, Tennessee. He was the son of William and Martha Galloway Gibson, and had seven brothers and sisters. His parents were tobacco and vegetable farmers.

Charles Gibson, Irene, Verna

Charlie moved to Illinois in the early 1900s, where his brother, George had moved to Smithshire to run a general store. Later, their sister, Ida, moved there also and later lived in Larchland.

He found work with Cameron Joyce & Co., of Keokuk, Iowa. They were rebuilding the dirt roads for the construction of cement pavement. Charlie was responsible for the hiring of his crew, many from St. Louis and Cairo, to drive wooden dump wagons that were pulled by mules. The wagons picked up the dirt removed by a road grader and moved by a conveyor belt into the wagon. He was well respected by his workers and also respected them.

He had married Verna Blevins of Smithshire on April 1, 1918, and they had a daughter, M. Irene Gibson. His work required him and his family to live in house wagons and camp near his work. He worked from Chicago to the Peoria area. He also worked at Lake Bracken, the Hennepen Canal, and constructed the Springfield racetrack at the fairgrounds.

The Gibsons bought a Sears Roebuck kit home and built it in Roseville. Charley continued the road construction by commuting and returning home on weekends. Irene attended grade school and high school in Roseville.

The Caterpillar Co. of Peoria began the manufacturing of heavy equipment that replaced the mule driven wagons and Charley decided to retire. He bought a restaurant and later a tavern in Roseville.

Irene later married Gerald McKee and they moved to Monmouth. They had two children, Gerald McKee (Jerry), Jr. and Jo Anne McKee.

Charlie's greatest enjoyment was his grandchildren and his many friends. On October 1, 1949, he passed away at his home in Roseville.

Irene McKee still resides in Monmouth. Verna, Gerald McKee, Sr. and Gerald McKee, Jr. are deceased. JoAnne resides in Florida.

JOHN (HOOT) AND MARY GIBSON - John Wilfred (Hoot) Gibson, the son of John Wilfred (Will) Gibson and Vera Gilmore, was born February 11, 1923, near Alexis. John has six sisters, Lois, Irene, Bernice, Thelma, Annabelle and Willadean. He was reared in Kelly Township and then Warren County, where he attended

John (Hoot) and Mary Gibson

Larchland School and graduated from Monmouth High School in 1941. He married Mary A. McConnell, daughter of Harry C. McConnell and Chloe (Gallaugher) McConnell on October 7, 1943. They were married at Mary's parents' home in Spring Grove Township. John served in the United States Army from January 1943 to January 1946. He was a Tech. Sergeant with the 725th Railroad Battalion in India for two years. After returning from service, he farmed for several years and then drove a semi truck for Eagle Foods for 23 years, retiring in January 1985. Mary was a homemaker and in later years drove a school bus for several years and then was a Deputy Clerk in the Circuit Clerk's Office for 20 years, retiring in November 1984. They had four children, Mrs. John (Ann) Gillen, John Michael Gibson, Scott William Gibson and Mrs. Michael (Jane) Newberry. The Gibsons are members of Faith Presbyterian Church. John was a member of the Church Board and the Gerlaw School Board. The Gibsons and their four children are all living. There are nine (9) grandchildren and one grandchild deceased. There are three great grandchildren.

JOHN WILFRED (WILL) AND VERA (GILMORE) GIBSON - John Wilfred (Will) Gibson, the son of John and Bell Gibson, was born in Sumner Township, Warren County, on October 20, 1879. He had one brother, Edward Gibson. He married Vera Gilmore, daughter of George Washington Gilmore and Mary Angeline (McKelvey) Gilmore. Will Gibson was a farmer by occupation and Vera was a homemaker. The Gibsons had seven children, Mrs. Lawrence (Lois) Gardner, Mrs. Ivan (Irene) Frakes, Mrs.

Robert (Bernice) O'Brien, Mrs. Harold (Thelma) Noonan, Mrs. Pul (Annabelle) Lee, Mrs. Charles (Willadean) Allen and John Wilfred (Hoot) Gibson. The Gibsons lived in Kelly Township, Warren County, before moving to Warren County where the Gibsons were Superintendent of the Warren County Home Farm from 1929-1944, and then resided. in Monmouth. Will was an Elder of the Alexis U.P. Church for many years.

John (Will) and Vera Gibson

Will died in 1960 and Vera in 1966 in Warren County. All the children were living at the time of their parents death.

THOMAS GIBSON - Thomas Gibson was born July 31, 1774, in Chambersburg Franklin County, Pennsylvania, and died July 28, 1860, in Sumner Township, Warren County, Illinois. Thomas Gibson and Martha Hogue were married near Natural Bridge, Lexington, Virginia (while on the way to Tennessee.) She was the daughter of James Hogg/Hogue and Margaret Parks. Thomas and Martha were the parents of 15 children, these of my family tree: Elizabeth Gibson, born October 13, 1796, in Blount County, Tennessee, married John Kendall on December 28, 1819, in Xenia, Ohio. "Elizabeth was always lively and entertaining, and both young and old enjoyed visiting at their home, for they always made all welcome." She died of "old age" August 15, 1882, and is buried in Sugar Tree Grove cemetery beside her husband. John Kendall was born January 2, 1795, near Big Cove, Bedford County, Pennsylvania, the son of Frances and Jane Gibson Kendall. John and Elizabeth had seven children: Jane, born 1820 and died at age two; Martha Anne, born 1823 and died 1907 in Monmouth; Mary Isabel, born 1825, died 1837 in Monmouth; Margaret, born 1829, died 1842 in Monmouth (see article on her); Sarah, born 1835, died 1862 in Monmouth (see article on her); Thomas B., born 1837, died after 1850 in Monmouth; Francis Beveridge, born 1838, died 1908 in Monmouth (see article on him). The first four children were born in Xenia, Ohio, the last three in Monmouth, Illinois.

Andrew Gibson was born January 6, 1811, Xenia, Greene County, Ohio, died April 16, 1845, Kirksville, Missouri, married Nancy Bruce (see data on her).

Jane Gibson was born January 23, 1818, Xenia, Greene County, Ohio, died March 12, 1908, in Garrison, Kansas, married Thomas Smith Allen on April 9, 1835, in Warren County, Illinois, son of Zachariah and Elizabeth (Law) Allen. They had six children: James Bruce, born May 27, 1836, Warren County, died September 16, 1913, Ellston, Ringgold County, Iowa; Margaret Ann, born January 14, 1838, Warren County, Illinois, died March 1, 1864, Warren County, Illinois, married William G. Bruce on September 18, 1862; Robert Gibson, born September 3, 1839, Warren County, Illinois, died Riley, Kansas; John Law, born May 12, 1841, Warren County, Illinois, died in Big Timber, Riley County, Kansas, married Laura Eberhart and then Artilla Striffler on September 1, 1873; Martha White, born March 12, 1843, Warren County, Illinois, married Obediah Findley on November 29, 1860, Warren County, Illinois; Henry Thomas, born March 10, Warren County, Illinois, died in Princeton Mercer County, Missouri, married Lavinia Bird, February 26, 1874, Henderson, Illinois. *Source: Gibson Genealogy by Marie Gibson Davidge.*

EDWARD AND KATHRYN GAVIN GILLEN - Kathryn Elizabeth Gavin was the second child of Bill and Kate Kinney Gavin and was born on February 26, 1894. She married Edward Thomas Gillen on February 25, 1916. He had been born in Mercer County on February 28, 1890, the son of William Henry and Nora Shunick Gillen.

After their marriage, they moved to a farm in Hale Township a few miles west of her parents' farm. It was there that they lived and brought up their family until they moved to Monmouth in 1961 into a new house. Kate died on January 27, 1965. Ed followed her in death on November 23, 1967. Both of them are buried in St. Mary's Cemetery in Monmouth.

Edward and Kathryn Gavin Gillen Family, 1941. L: to R: Back: Leroy, Mary, Ed, Kate, Frances and Bill. Front: Lucille, Margaret, Betty, George, Katherine and Dick.

Blessed with ten children, the couple's first four were daughters: Katherine, Margaret, Mary and Lucille. These were followed by two sons: William and Leroy. From then on they alternated between the sexes. Frances was followed by Richard; then Elizabeth was followed by George.

Katherine Nora was born April 9, 1917. Her marriage to Stephen Arthur Mills took place on October 6, 1942. Steve, a farmer and a teacher, was born June 20, 1910. He died March 13, 1984.

Margaret Rose Gillen was born August 15, 1918. She married John Francis Sullivan on November 21, 1944. John, a farmer in the Galesburg area, was born April 28, 1911.

Mary Theresa was born April 21, 1921. She married Keith Webber, but she died at the age of forty-two on December 31, 1963.

Helen Lucille Gillen was born August 23, 1922, and lived with her parents until their deaths. She held several positions in Monmouth but worked the longest for the Stanton Insurance Agency.

William Edward was born June 7, 1924. He married Marian Engdahl on September 17, 1945. Marian was born December 21, 1923. He farmed south of Monmouth for many years until retirement when they moved to Monmouth. Bill died on October 24, 2000.

Leroy Frederick Gillen was born February 25, 1926. On January 25, 1951, he married Helen Marie Hennenfent whose birth date was November 23, 1930. Leroy also became a farmer.

Frances Jane was born on December 18, 1927. On February 9, 1948, she married Ralph Franklin Elliot and added another farmer to the family. Ralph's birthdate is August 5, 1922.

John Richard was born on May 13, 1929. Dick married Karen Ann O'Connor on January 13, 1962. Karen was born September 19, 1938. He farmed for many years before becoming a real estate agent in Monmouth. Karen is an administrative assistant at the Buchanan Center of the Arts.

Elizabeth Joan was born May 31, 1931. On April 9, 1953, Betty married another farmer, Michael Richard Hennenfent who was born December 16. 1928.

George Edward was born April 28, 1933. On June 20, 1959, George married Mary Larita Olin; her birthdate is January 5, 1938. He also chose farming as his career. Mary has worked in the Yorkwood Schools for several years.

CHARLES ELLIOTT GILLETTE - Charles Elliott Gillette, my great grandfather, was born in Warren County in 1872. He married Jessie Crosier in 1895. Her parents were Henry and Melissa (Webb) Crosier. Henry was the son of Rodney Crosier and came to Warren County in a covered wagon. The first night they camped at Olmstead Mill so they could water their cattle. They then settled a mile south and a mile west of Roseville. Rodney was 94 years old when he passed away in 1904 and still lived on the same land. He and Melissa had six children, Bernard, Charles, Max, Halbert and a boy and girl who died in infancy.

Charles Elliott and Jessie Gillette

Bernard, my grandfather, was born near Biggsville in 1896. In 1919, he married Cecil Hanna Orndoff. She was born in 1903 in Washington, Iowa, to William and Carrie (Sheare) Orndoff. Bernard worked for the city of Monmouth tiling the sewers. Eventually, he started his own tiling business. Most of the tile laid in Monmouth was done by him. Five children were born to Bernard and Cecil. Charles, who married Kathryn (Howell) Gillette. They had four children: Larry, Barbara, Patricia and Carla. Shirley Brown Barron Gillette was married to Walter Brown and had two children, Phyllis and Wayne. In 1957 she married Martin Barron and they had three children, Dixie, who resides in the home Bernard built, Roger and James. Betty Gillette married Harold Chick in 1943. They had six children: Howard, Gloria (Ann), Ethel, Harold Jr., Jeffrey and Nancy Jane who died in 1945 after being hit by car at age four. George Arnold

Gillette died at age 21 in 1944 in Lorraine, France. He was a Private in the Army and was single with no children. Raymond Oliver Gillette was my father. He married Frances Arlene (Spicer) in Monmouth on April 5, 1945. He worked with his father in his tiling business, later going to Kistler Construction Company until he retired. He and a son, Danny, owned and operated the Trading Post north of Monmouth for a few years. For the remainder of his life he did lawn care for Monmouth, Roseville, Little York and surrounding areas. He and Frances had six children. Carol Arlene Gillette married Donald Darnell and had three children. Leslie married Anthony Woerly, and they have three children, Adam, Michelle and Bruce. Michael married Lisa and had two children, Matthew and Megan. Later, he married Sharla and has three stepchildren, Crystal, Bethany and Mariah, and one granddaughter, Chelsea Lynn. Lonnie married Lynn and has two children, Shane and Tara. Misty Starr Darnell has three sons, Salvador (Cruz), Marco and Antonio. Carol then married John Charles Holter II and had one son, John Charles Holter III. He married Sandra (Young) and they had six children: Alexander Bree, Amanda Lynn (deceased), Zachary Arron (deceased), Rachael Mary Marie, Brooklyn Carol (deceased) and Jacob John. As of today, Michael has another grandchild, Austin Michael.

Michael Gillette married Brenda Raymond and had three children: Reginia, Cara Sue and Amy. Later he married Corlias Barnes and he has two stepsons, Ty and Todd Barnes.

George Gillette married Molly Barron and he has two stepsons, Roger and Billy Barron.

Daniel Gillette arried Marlene Bloomfield and they had two girls, Angela and Tammy. Later he married Brandy.

Mary Gillette married Don Zellmer and they have six children: Jennifer, Jaylene, Jon, Justin, Joshua and Jasmine.

Kathy Gillette married Gene Smith and had three children, Niki, Chris and Tarah. Later, she married Mike Malone.

MACK A. AND SARAH E. GLASS - Mack Glass's great great grandfather, Calvin Glass, platted the town f Henderson, Illinois, and built the first grist and sawmill in Illinois on Henderson Creek. Mack's great grandfather and grandfather farmed in Kelly Township. Mack's parents, Mary Allen and Tanner Glass, farmed in Canada in 1918. In 1920 Mack was born and they lived in Canada until he was five. The family returned to Kelly Township and farmed land where Mary was born.

The great grandfather of Sarah E. Wallace Glass came to Illinois in 1833 from Warren County, Kentucky. He purchased land from the government in Section 16 in Coldbrook Township. Sarah's grandfather and family have farmed the land since then. Sarah's parents were Grace Fleharty and H. Chris Wallace. Sarah was born in 1924 and a brother, John Chris, was born in 1922 and died in 1975. Mack and Sarah were married in 1944 at the Coldbrook Christian Church. They have three daughters: Rhonda married Don LeFebvre; Beverly married John Stamp; Lisa married Jim McKenzie and they have two children, Daniel (8 years) and Sarah (4 years). Mack attended the University of Illinois Agriculture School and served four years in the Army during World War II. He taught Agriculture at Kirkwood High School. He was with Smith-Douglass and Borden Company for

Mack and Sarah E. Glass

twenty-two years in fertilizer and chemical, sales and management. They lived in Illinois, Iowa, Minnesota, Ohio and Virginia. In 1970 they returned to Illinois and Mack was with 1st National Bank of Galesburg. They built a home on an acreage they had purchased in 1966. At one time some of the farm was owned by Mack's grandfather Allen. Mack grazes cattle and has had buffalo, deer, peacocks, etc. They have shared their farm with hundreds of groups at cookouts for U. of I., Kiwanis, 1st Presbyterian, P.E.O. and Pi Beta Phi.

HELEN L. YOUNG GLENN - Helen Young Glenn was born October 29, 1927, at Good Hope, Illinois, the fourth of seven children to Orville and Mabel Beal Geltmacher. She graduated from Good Hope High School in 1945 and continued working as cashier at BLS Store in Macomb, later transferring to the Monmouth office. She married George K. Young on October 26, 1947, and they made their home in Monmouth. She worked at the Second National Bank for 15 years.

Cousin Doris Lusk and Helen Glenn

Debra Kay and Rodney Lee were adopted on May 5, 1955. They graduated from Monmouth High School in 1971. Debra graduated from CSC with an Associate Degree in Child Development. She moved to Peoria in 1986 and has been plagued with serious health problems.

Rodney was in the Army three years, and came back to Monmouth and has remained here, except for one year as a Supervisor of Cooking at the Federal Prison in Chicago. He married Charlotte Mills of Alsip, who had attended Monmouth College, on October 25, 1975. Michael Todd was born May 3, 1977, and Brian Lee on August 1, 1980. Rodney has also been plagued with serious health problems, but their family has been busy volunteers as volunteer fireman, weather watchers, Scouting, and with the Red Cross.

Helen was Welcome Wagon hostess for five years, and later owned and operated Young's Addressing Service for 12 years. During these years, their home was a haven for many people, including foster children. This was a very busy time of large gardens, canning and a very busy schedule. One of the family's favorite activities was the starting of Golden Friendship at the Methodist Church. Up to 45 people had monthly meetings and potlucks at their home or church, sight seeing trips and lots of food, fun and fellowship. She still visits the few remaining members.

After many years of illness, George died on October 7, 1975. She then began working on her hobby of redoing houses, trying to give something back to Monmouth and making affordable housing for those not able to have regular houses.

For the past 25 years, she has been receptionist at the Galesburg Post Office. She married retired carpenter, Lawrence Paul Glenn of Plymouth, George's army buddy, on October 7, 1989. He died in November 1991. She has been a care giver all her life to many people, including her 90-year-old Aunt Eva, who lived with her for three years. She has volunteered many years at the Orpheum Theater, served on Habitat for Humanity and, has been very active in the Methodist Church.

Being able to share with Debra and Rodney's birth mother, Betty, before her death, was a happy goal. Brother Jim, and sisters, Lori and Shlly and their families, are a vital part of the Young's extended family. The latest addition is Alex, adopted from Russia, by Carl and Shelly Roy.

Surrounded by a family with many health problems, she thanks God for the good health she has had, and says she has "Rolled with the Punches."

GOODE, PALMER AND MOREY FAMILIES - Josephine Frances Goode was born in Kentucky on March 14, 1821. She moved from Kentucky to Henderson County, Illinois, in 1841. Josephine married Alfred Palmer (1816-1857) in Henderson County on November 22, 1841. The 1850 Henderson County census shows them living in Biggsville Township. In 1853 they moved to Cameron (Coldbrook Township) Warren County, Illinois, and Josephine united with the Methodist Episcopal Church. Josephine and Alfred Palmer had six children, three daughters and three sons. Their oldest child, a daughter named Elizabeth, was born in 1842. In 1891 Josephine, now a widow, moved to Iowa where she lived until her death on July 17, 1901 in Humeston, Wayne County, Iowa. Josephine, her husband, two young daughters, and a granddaughter, Phebe Morey, are buried in the Berwick cemetery, Warren County, Illinois.

Elizabeth Palmer (1842-1932) married Charles F. Morey on July 4, 1861 in Warren County, Illinois. Charles (1841-1909) was six months old when he migrated from Erie County, Pennsylvania to near Cameron, Warren County, Illinois, with his parents, Charles and Polly Blair Morey. To Elizabeth and Charles' marriage, eight children were born, seven daughters and one son. Their youngest, a girl named Josephine Florence, was born in 1880. In 1874, with five of their children, Elizabeth and Charles moved to near Humeston, Wayne County, Iowa. They moved to Garber, Garfield County, Oklahoma, about 1900-1901.

Other Palmer-Morey family members were also married in Warren county, Illinois. In 1850 Charles Morey's sister, Iantha Morey, married Joseph Cramer. They moved to Taylor County, Iowa; and then Iantha and her sons moved to Garber, Oklahoma. In 1874 Elizabeth (Palmer)

Morey's brother, Alfred Harrison Palmer, married Mary Alice Giddings, the daughter of Charles Morey's sister, Phebe (Morey) Giddings. They settled and raised their family in Humeston, Iowa.

Josephine Florence Morey (1880-1944) and Harley Herman Dodd (1877-1928) were married in 1900 in Iowa and settled near Garber, Oklahoma, the next year. In 1929 their daughter Elizabeth "Maxine" (1909-2000) married Joe Wesley Stewart (1905-1985), in Enid, Garfield County, Oklahoma. They had one child, Harland G. Stewart (1930-1976).

Josie and Harley's second daughter, Minnie "Berdine" (1912-1934), was married to Ernest Worth. Sadly, both she and her baby died in childbirth.

Harland G. Stewart and Marlene Hume were married in 1951 at Enid, Oklahoma. In 1954 they moved from Garber to Ponca City, Kay County, Oklahoma. They raised three children, Karen, Laurie and Mike. *Submitted by Karen L. Stewart.*

WILLIAM C. GOSSETT - William C. Gossett, the son of Carlton Carr Gossett and Mary Robson Gossett, was born in Monmouth, Illinois, May 12, 1934. He has a sister, Elizabeth Kalb (Ted), of Lebanon, Pennsylvania, born December 11, 1936, and a brother, George Gosett, born March 19, 1947, living in Monmouth, Illinois.

William and Nancy Gossett

William began his school days at Stem Country School 1 1/2 miles east of Roseville. Junior High schooling was at Roseville Elementary School and he graduated from Roseville High School, 1952. He received BS and MS degrees in Agriculture Economics at the University of Illinois and was commissioned a Second Lieutenant in United States Air Force.

Nancy (Monroe) Gossett, daughter of Harlan and Goldie (Heap) Monroe was born June 30, 1934, in Raritan, Illinois. She has one sister, Kay Ault (Scott), of rural Good Hope, Illinois, and two brothers, Harlan (Butch) Monroe of Rock Springs, Wyoming, and Terry Monroe of rural Roseville, Illinois. Nancy attended rural Roseville schools and graduated from Roseville High School, 1952. She received a BS Home Economics Education degree from the University of Illinois.

William and Nancy were married in Roseville, Illinois, January 30, 1955. Following William's University of Illinois graduation, they were stationed with the Air Force at Lackland Air Base, San Antonio, Texas, and 3902 Air Base Wing, Offutt Air Force Base, Omaha, Nebraska. An overseas assignment with 3926th Combat Support Group sent them to Ben Querir Air Base, Morocco, North Africa, where William served in the Strategic Air Command (SAC).

Both of their children were born while in the Air Force. Their first child, Ann Kaylene, was born at Bellevue, Nebraska, January 12, 1959. A son, Mark Carlton, was born May 9, 1961, at Casablanca, Morocco. Daughter Ann Willis resides in Morresville, North Carolina, and son Mark and family live in London, England, where Mark is employed in the International office of Northern Trust Bank. Their children are Sarah Willis, Carlton and Emily Gossett.

The Gossetts returned to the Gossett Family farm (homesteaded by George Gossett, 1853) in Swan Township in 1961 to partnership farm with Carlton (Tony) and Mary Gossett and continue to reside on the farm. They are both active in the farming operation. William and Nancy retired from winter employment with University of Illinois Western Farm Business Farm Management after more than 25 years. William serves as a director of Citizens National Bank, Macomb, and served several years as a trustee and supervisor of Swan Township. Nancy serves as a trustee of the Warren County Public Library District. They are active members of the Roseville Christian Church and community activities.

ERNEST AND DORIS (DAMEWOOD) GRABOWSKI - Ernest J. Grabowski was born 10 February 1930, in Chicago, Illinois, the son of Ernest S. and Jane L. (Rorabaugh) Grabowski of Scotland County, Missouri. His parents farmed in Illinois and Missouri. Ernest was educated in the Warren County public schools, graduating from Little York High School in 1948. He joined the U.S. Air Force in 1953.

Ernest and Doris Grabowski

Doris Marie Damewood was born 4 August 1936, in Kirkwood, Illinois. She is the second of four children of James and Lucille (Ketchum) Damewood of Little York, Illinois. Her brothers and sister are Mary Ruth, William Arthur and James Franklin. Doris was educated in Warren County, graduating from Little York High School in 1955.

Ernest and Doris were married 29 December 1955, at the First Christian Church in Monmouth, Illinois. They have two children: Vada L. married David Stone (divorced). They have three children, Jennifer, James (deceased) and William. Brenda married Jeffrey Reinhold. They have twin girls Sara and Megan.

Ernest and Doris moved around to different parts of the world while he served in the Air Force, from New York to Japan and Germany. He retired from the Air Force in 1973, went to work for the Department of Defense, Civil Service, at Chanute Air Force Base, Rantoul, Illinois, retiring in 1993. They have resided in Fisher, Illinois, since 1974.

DON AND VIRGINIA (SMITH) GREINER - Virginia Gertrude Smith was born 2-12-1940, to Clete and Gertrude (Tierney) Smith. Her siblings are Irene F. (Smith) Johnson, Winfield, Iowa, David R. Smith, Monmouth, Illinois, Earl L. Smith, Kirkwood, Illinois, and Allen Clete Smith, deceased in infancy.

Don and Virginia Greiner

Virginia attended Immaculate Conception Catholic Grade School and Monmouth High graduating in 1957. She worked part time at Spurgeons while in high school and whenever home from MaryCrest College, Davenport, Iowa. On November 21, 1959, Virginia married Donald J. Greiner (Don deceased 12-4-1998) and moved to the Greiner home farm in Washington, Iowa. In March 1962 they moved to a farm north of Mt. Pleasant, Iowa. In 1968 they bought a farm 5 1/2 miles northeast of Fairfield, Iowa, where Virginia still lives. They raised cattle, hogs, sheep and grai.

The Greiner's have six children. Mark (1960) and ife Karen of Fairfield, Iowa, have three daughters, Alisha, Sabrina and Samantha. Cindy (1961) and husband Curtis Bunker of Cedar Rapids, Iowa, have two foster sons, Stephen and Michael Taylor. Jeff (1962) and Lori of Lockridge, Iowa, have children Jacob, Hanna and Allen Jeffrey (A.J.). Sally (1965) lives in Ottumwa, Iowa. Phil (1968) died at age 18 in a tractor accident on their farm. Chris (1970) and Kristin of Runnells, Iowa, have a son, Luke, and are expecting their second child in May 2002. *See also articles on Marshall B. Ray; Tierney; David and Pearl Smith; Earl and Phillis Smith; and Irene Johnson.*

WILLIAM ELMER AND MATTIE EDNA GRIFFITH - William Elmer Griffith was born 18 January 1864, in Galesburg Township of Knox County, Illinois, to Morris and Elizabeth Harmony Griffith. He was known as Elmer. Mattie Edna Brooks was born 3 March 1869, in Hermon, Knox, Illinois, to Landrine E. and Rachel E. McGrew Brooks. Mattie and Elmer were married 27 January 1882, in Knoxville, Illinois.

Elmer and his brother, Arthur Addison Griffith (born 22 January 1866), matured on the Griffith family farm in Knox County and came to Coldbrook Township of Warren County as young men, purchasing 80 acres each and building houses within a mile and one half of each other. Arthur purchased 80 acres in Setion 2 while Elmer purchased 80 acres in section 12.

Elmer and Mattie had seven children within 13 years, all born on the farm: Florence E., born 21 July 1893; Chester E., born 9 April 1895; Elsie R., born 7 April 1897; Edith B., born 7 August 1899; Doris M., born 23 February 1902 (died 7 May, 1903); Ross W., born 15 July 1904; and

Ethel L., born 12 July 1906. All the children attended and graduated from Atchison School District 44 in Section 1, except Doris who died as a toddler. The children also attended and graduated from Galesburg High School, many boarding in Galesburg during some of the school year.

Elmer and Mattie farmed their 80 acres in a traditional method, with chickens, hogs, horses, dairy cows, fruit orchard, a large vegetable garden and raised corn, oats, popcorn and hay. The trees on the property consisted of Boxelders, American Elms and Silver Maples. A tree was planted in the yard upon the birth of each child. The grove which was planted as a wind break of Silver Maples were originally seedlings dug from the Spoon River area.

Elmer Griffith family, 1912-13

The property was completely fenced. Pasture was always in short supply and the family even used the road in front of their home, which is the county line, as pasture for the livestock.

Elmer purchased an additional 80 acres, the Atchison home place in Section 1 to fulfill his desire to provide a farm for each son. However, the house Elmer and Mattie first lived in burnt in 1917 or 1918 while the sons were at the Atchison place farming. Upon seeing the smoke, Chet the oldest son jumped on the faster horses and hightailed it home. Smoke was visible to many, and many neighbors came to help fight the fire. Two men carried out the upright piano, and it later took six to pick it up and carry it into the building the family lived in while they built the new house.

The new house was the final home for Elmer and Mattie. They died in 1943, within two months of each other. In 1943, Ross and his wife, A. Maude Cunningham Griffith, and their two daughters, R. Jeannine and R. Jolene Griffith, purchased the siblings' shares of the property and remained on the 80 acres. Ross and Maude were married 4 September 1927, in Galesburg, and purchased and built a Sears home on the property in 1930. Ross and Maude established a Jersey Dairy herd, which existed until 1971. They had a retail dairy route in Galesburg for many years. Ross and Maude also raised Morgan horses.

R. Jeannine Griffith married Ronald L. Dyer on 20 November 1948, in Galesburg, Illinois, and in 2002 moved to the Griffith family home. Ron and Jeannine continue to raise Morgan horses on the property.

CHARLES LEWIS GRIMSLEY - In 1876, at the age of sixteen, Charles moved to Warren County, Illinois, from Culpeper County, Virginia, where he was born December 27, 1860. He followed an older sister, Sarah, who with her husband, Erasmus Spicer, had settled on a five-acre homesite in Tompkins Township in 1872.

Charles Lewis Grimsley taken about 1910

Despite a humble beginning as a farm laborer, Charles soon bought a farm in Point Pleasant Township, eventually giving it up to become a merchant and grain dealer in Swan Creek. After a time he sold the store to his partner, Harry Simmons. He continued the elevator business until his death at the age of fifty-four.

The youngest of ten children, Charles was the son of John Samuel and Lucy Ann (Freeman) Grimsley. Children born to them were William, Amanda, Roberta, George, Mary, Sarah, Lucy, John, Silas and Charles. Their mother died in 1863. His father then married Mary Ellen Stringfellow, July 7, 1864.

The Grimsley line has been traced back to Thomas, born in 1585 in Leicestershire, England.

When Charles was only seven months old, his oldest brother, William, was killed in the first Battle of Bull Run, July 21, 1861. He served as Private with the Confederate Army, Co. B, 2nd Reg. of the Virginia Infantry. His brother, George, was a Private in the Union Army, Co. A, 9th New Jersey Infantry.

After arriving in Warren County, Charles worked on the farm of the John W. Watson family of Point Pleasant and the James C. Morris family of Ellison Township. He married Effie Pinney, in Missouri, on April 14, 1881. Her parents were Ethan Orson and Sarah Jane (Eldridge) Pinney of the Roseville community and she was born August 26, 1864 in Warren County.

Their three children are Clarence Vincent, born November 27, 1882. He first married Ruth Hayden, July 5, 1905; she died in 1910. He then married Edna F. Mullen, May 15, 1911, in Knox County, Illinois. Avis Janette was born September 15, 1886. She married Sidney Brazelton in Warren County, January 1, 1907. He died May 7, 1927. She later married Howard Liggett. Avis died August 18, 1947, in Monmouth. Guy Ereld was born January 29, 1889, in Warren County. He first married Lottie Smith, June 10, 1909. They were divorced in September 1915. His second marriage was to his brother's widow, Edna F. (Mullen) Grimsley. They were married July 12, 1919, in Warren County. Guy died in Knox County, May 21, 1967. C. Vincent died, October 16, 1918, during the flue epidemic, while his brother, Guy was serving his country In France.

Effie died December 19, 1903, at an early age. Her husband died July 16, 1914 Point Pleasant Township. They both were faithful members of the Methodist Church of Swan Creek, and are buried in the Roseville Cemetery. Her twin sister died at an early age, they had a brother, Norman Eldridge Pinney, of Roseville.

Effie was vice president of the Women's Christian Temperance Union, third vice president of the Epworth League, recorder of the Royal Neighbors, and secretary-treasurer of the Rebekah Society.

Charles was a Mason and member of the Independent Order of Odd Fellows and Modern Woodman of America.

GULLBERG - The Karl Arthur and Susie Cornelia (Brown) Gullberg family of Warren County were well known, long time residents. Susie spent much of her growing-up years in Monmouth and attended Monmouth High School. Both Karl and Susie are buried in the Monmouth Memorial Garden Cemetery. They started housekeeping and farming on the Kelly farm at Coldbrook. From there they moved to the Statt farm at Youngstown and then to the Lamphere-Paschal farm north of Ponemah. When Ponemah lost its post office their address became "Rural Route", Kirkwood.

Bill Gullberg, Sr. Nov. 2001

Karl was born October 5, 1889, at Gullabo, Sweden, thence the name "Gullberg". He came to America in 1910 and watched Halley's Comet from the ocean. He came with Uncle Nels Benson and family, a brother to Gus Benson, whose place was located east of Kirkwood, now on route 34. In 1925 Karl and Susie, with son Bill, born December 18, 1925, moved to the Ponemah farm. This farm was purchased in 1888 by Lamphere-Paschal from the Butlers who left for Monmouth, Oregon. In the early 1890s the Gus Benson family rented the farm. When Nels Benson died, Karl Gullberg started renting it. Today grandsons and great grandsons of Karl and Susie still rent this farm from the same family that bought it in 1888 and who still own it, a period lasting well over a hundred years. Grandsons Bill Jr., Kimmer and Jon have each lived in the house. The house was originally a private schoolhouse located on the corner west and when public schools came, it was moved to its present location and used as the core to the present house. The farm family name had gone from Lamphere-Paschal, Lockridge, Olson and now to their daughter. Bill Gullberg Sr. started a turkey farm there in 1939. What started out as a 4-H project lasted for 24 years and during that time the farm became known as the "Gullberg Turkey Farm". Their holiday ads can be found in contemporary copies of the Monmouth Review Atlas Society Page.

Susie had a good singing voice and was engaged several times a month to sing at local PTA meetings, at church functions and funerals in homes, sometimes without a piano. She had sung and entertained in most rural schools in Warren and Henderson Counties. Because her children were non-singers, she involved them in poetry recitations and piano solos. Reports of those entertainments are often found in the Monmouth Review Atlas.

Two more children were born to Karl and Susie: Susan, May 6, 1930, and Karlene, January 22, 1934. Susan graduated from Monmouth College and received her Master of Arts degree from the University of Iowa, retiring as a college professor. She married Edwin Pfuehler, Fail River, Wisconsin, and their son Erich is an Administrative Assistant to David Bonior, the Minority Whip in the U.S. House of Representatives. He has traveled the world as a member of numerous delegations sent to learn on-site and is particularly involved with environmental issues.

Karlene graduated from Western Illinois University and got her Masters at Carbondale. She taught Home Economics and is retired although she remains active with her "Susie Brown Antiques" business.

Bill Sr. and his sisters attended Liberty Grade School and graduated from Kirkwood High, Bill Sr. in just 3 1/2 years. As soon as he graduated he signed up to serve his country in the Air Force during WW II but was rejected for reasons of health – a result of having barely survived a childhood bout with pneumonia. He started farming with his wife Shirley and raising their family of three sons on the Reid Everett Farm at Stronghurst in 1949 and while continuing his interest in farming he started a real estate business, Stronghurst Reality, in 1980. His son Bill Jr. lives in Kirkwood, Kimmer in Stronghurst. Jon resides in Media and continues with the real estate business.

On October 19, 1781, British General Charles Lord Cornwallis surrendered at Yorktown, Virginia, bringing an end to the last major battle of the Revolutionary war. George Washington had achieved the inconceivable. With victory at Yorktown he had won independence from one of the most powerful nations on earth.

Andrew Brown, great great grandfather of Bill Gullberg Sr., served under Cornwallis and surrendered at Yorktown, Virginia. He was witness to Washington's receiving the British Sword, a symbol of surrender, and the birth of a new nation. (See 1881 and 1911 historic books on Henderson County under T.J. Fort.) Instead of going back to Scotland, he stayed in America, joined the American Army and was paid with a land grant in Kentucky. He married a Scottish lassie, Jane Smith. Their boy, named Smith Brown, came to Warren County and bought 480 acres in Section 32 and 33 in Tompkins Township. His wife died in 1849 and is buried at Ellison Cemetery. He sold his land, log cabin and timber lot at Ellison for $10,000. Today this property would be worth more than 1 1/2 million dollars. Andrew Brown's daughter, Sarah, married T. J. Fort and her brother Joseph married a Westfal of Carman. They came together from Kentucky to Henderson County in 1833. Joseph hauled stone for the new courthouse in Oquawka in the 1840s. Andrew was a smart man not to go back to Scotland. His life touched many families including the Brown, Burrell, Fort, Dowell, Lant, Kemp, Westfal, Hicks, Huss. Coffman, Marsden, Barnett and many others include Native Americans. Bill Gullberg. Sr. and sisters are 1/16 Native American, and proud of it. Their maternal grandmother was a Burrell. It was her family that left New York after having established the Burrell Woolen Mills and came to Illinois bringing the eastern Native American blood line with them.

Today William Karl Gullberg resides just outside of Stronghurst and remains active in the real estate business as well as involved in local and national issues. He is presently an active member on the Hawkeye Readers Advisory Council and over the years has served his community in various capacities. Bill is a twenty-first century sort of Will Rogers. He has a keen intellect and remains the eyes and ears for the little guy, speaking out for him and writing articles on issues close to their hearts. Some of his most gratifying moments come when a stranger approaches to thank him for speaking out on a matter they could not find the words for or did not feel they had the nerve to say or probably wouldn't be heard even if they did. It is their appreciation and respect that makes him keep on listening and providing them with a voice. Bill says, half joking, his life expectancy is not based on his health, just how long it will be before someone takes his commentary too personally.

WILLIAM K. GULLBERG, JR. AND CHRISTINE L. GULLBERG - William Karl Gullberg, Jr. was born in Monmouth on August 5, 1952, to William K. Gullberg and Shirley Marie (Reitman) Gullberg. He is the oldest of three children. His siblings are Kim Reitman Gullberg and Jonathan Arthur Gullberg. William is the third generation to live in Warren County. He follows to this county his grandparents Karl Arthur Gullberg and Susie Cornelia (Brown) Gullberg. Karl emigrated from Sweden in May, 1910, arriving at Ellis Island aboard the Helig Olav. He came to Warren County shortly thereafter, where he married and raised his family. William was raised on a farm near Stronghurst, Henderson County, Illinois.

William K. and Christine L. Gullberg Jr.

He attended grade and high school in Stronghurst, graduating in 1970. William attended Carl Sandburg Junior College in Galesburg, Illinois, followed by attendance at Western Illinois Univeristy graduating with a Bachelor of Arts in Political Science and Bachelor of Business in Accounting in 1976. He then furthered his education at the University of Illinois Law School graduating with a Juris Doctor degree in 1979. William spent a number of years practiing law in Chicago, ending up owning his own practice. In 1990 William purchased an historic home in Kirkwood, Warren County, Illinois, known as the Davidson House. A few years later, William transferred his law practice to Kirkwood where he practices today. William is also an avid woodworker specializing in chairmaking. He is the proprietor of a small business called the Chairwright that makes reproduction Windsor chairs using the tools and methods of the 18th century.

On April 1, 1972, William married Christine Lea Shambaugh at the Lutheran Church Chapel in Monmouth, Illinois. Christine is the daughter of Delbert Neil Shambaugh and JoAnn (Wilson) (Shambaugh) Skubic. She was born in Warrensburg, Missouri, on January 21, 1953, near the Sedalia Air Force Base where her father was stationed in the Air Force. After her father's discharge from the service, Christine's family moved to Knoxville, Knox County, Illinois, where she attended school, graduating in 1971. Christine attended Carl Sandburg Junior College in Galesburg, Illinois, where she met William. Furthering her education, Christine graduated from the University of Illinois in 1980 with a Bachelor of Science degree in Ceramic Engineering. She spent a number of years working for the A.P. Green Refractories Company outside of Morris, Illinois, as a Ceramic Engineer focusing on the needs of the steel industry located near Chicago.

In 1982 Christine began working with William in his law practice as a paralegal. She continues to hold this position. Christine is also involved with her husband's woodworking business and helps with the finishing. She also has designed and maintains the business' webpage.

ELVIN GUSTAFSON - Elvin R. Gustafson was born in Monmouth, Illinois, on March 11, 1930. Elvin's father, Joseph, immigrated from Sweden to the United States via Ellis Island (New York) on October 11, 1911. After returning to Sweden in the early 1920s, Joseph came back to the United States with Elvin's mother, Elin, in October 1922. Joseph and Elin were the parents of five children, Willard, Elvin, Helen, Elsie and Mary Jane (Lenz).

L: to R: Back: Darci Glisan, Mike Gustafson, Camee Compton, Marc Gustafson, Elvin Gustafson, Martin Gustafson and Joe Gustafson. Front: Coty Gustafson, Maxine Heck (Fay's mother), Fay Gustafson and Sarah and Heather Gustafson.

Elvin was drafted into the U.S. Army in 1952 and attended basic training at Ft. Gordon, Georgia. He was assigned to the U.S Army Signal Corps and was stationed in Salzburg, Austria. During that time, Elvin and his cousin, Emery Johnson (also in the U.S. Army and also born in Monmouth), visited relatives in Sweden. Over time, Emery traced their family genealogy in Sweden back to November 1788. After his discharge from the Army in 1953, Elvin returned to Monmouth and began farming with his brother, Willard.

On January 7, 1956, Elvin married Fay Heck from Aledo, Illinois. Fay, the daughter of Donnie and Maxine Heck, was born on October 14, 1936. She was raised on a farm near Aledo, Illinois, and graduated from Aledo High School. She worked at Hank's Auction Service in Monmouth and at Monmouth College prior to joining the Community National Bank in Monmouth, Illinois, as a bookkeeper in 1979. Elvin and Fay have three sons; Martin (Springfield, Illinois), Marc (Madison, Wisconsin) and Michael (Monmouth, Illinois). All three sons graduated from Warren High School. After graduation, Martin attended Augustana College (Rock Island, Illinois), Marc attended Monmouth College, and Michael attended Carl Sandburg College (Galesburg, Illinois). Elvin and Fay are the grandparents of Joseph, Heather and Sarah Gustafson (Abingdon, Illinois) and Coty Gustafson (North Henderson, Illinois).

Elvin has lived on the family farm (two miles north of Berwick) since the age of six. Elvin and Fay raised cattle and hogs and farmed for 40 years before retiring from farming. The farm is now cash rented. During the years spent farming, the Gustafson family showed many steers at the annual Prime Beef Festival in Monmouth.

In addition to farming, Elvin and Fay restored antique furniture which Fay sold in an antique business called Red Pump Antiques. Fay and her friend, Pat Carson (Gerlaw, Illinois), sold antiques from the Red Pump Antique store at the Carson family farm and at various antique shows for a number of years. In addition, Fay collected Sleepy Eye Pottery and remains a member of the Sleepy Eye Club. Over the years, Elvin and Fay have collected many Monmouth Pottery (Western Stoneware) and Abingdon Pottery pieces. In addition to restoring antiques, Elvin and Fay were members of many bowling leagues in Abingdon and Monmouth. Fay bowled at the Monmouth Bowling Lanes for almost 30 years.

Elvin and Fay continue to live on the farm raising one lonesome pony (for the grandchildren). Both continue "farming" on a much smaller scale annually planting a large garden and many flowerbeds.

JOHN HABEN - John Henry Haben and Patty Woolley were married June 20, 1942, while he was in the service during World War II. He was stationed at Scott Field near Belleville, Illinois. After teaching in country schools for five years, Patty got another school near Belleville where they lived for eleven months before John was sent overseas to India. While he was there, Patty taught at the Pleasant Green School near Little York, Illinois, for two years. When John was discharged from the service, he and Patty bought the Cold Storage Locker from his mother, Nellie, and her husband, Ed Stotts.

Patty and John Haben

John and Patty had two children – Nancy, born December 9, 1946, and Dale, born May 17, 1949. They both graduated from Yorkwood, in 1957 and 1962. Nancy was married to Stephen Altenbern at the United Methodist Church in Little York on August 20, 1967. Dale was married to Alice Hasten at the Immanuel Baptist Church in Monmouth, Illinois, on August 30, 1969.

John was born August 1, 1916, in Seaton to Helen (Nellie) and Henry Haben. John's sister, Mary Hanna, was born November 9, 1917, in Seaton. His parents, Henry Carl August Haben and Helen Kathryn (Nellie) Flatley were married on June 22, 1915, in Little York. Henry had been born in Holloway, Minnesota, on March 21, 1892. He worked at the M.&ST.L. Railroad Station in Seaton. About 1920 this family moved to Stronghurst, Illinois. John was in the first grade when the schoolhouse burned down. He was very upset because he lost his pencil box. John died at St. John's Hospital in Springfield, Illinois, on August 12, 1992. Henry was injured when a big door came down on his back. The family then moved to Des Moines, Iowa. It was there that Henry died of cancer on October 19, 1926.

Nellie was born August 14, 1896, in Little York to Mary and John Flatley Sr. Nellie was the youngest, with seven older brothers. She was a very good pianist and played for the silent movies in the Opera House in Little York. It was where the bank is now.

After Henry died, Nellie and her two children moved back to Little York. She worked as a telephone operator there until she married Ed Stotts. They then ran a grocery store in Little York for many years. Nellie died September 25, 1964.

Nellie's father, John Henry Flatley Sr., was born in Middletown, New Jersey, in 1850. He worked as a Section Foreman for the M.&ST.L. Railroad from the station in Little York. He died in Little York in 1941.

Nellie's mother, Mary Agnes Concannon, was born in 1857 in County Cork, Ireland. She died in 1926 in Little York.

DR. WILLIAM S. HALDEMAN - Dr. William S. Haldeman, emeritus professor of chemistry at Monmouth College, became a legend in his own time. A bachelor until retirement, he was married to one of his students, Ruth Bishop, in 1958. Despite the fact that he didn't have time to get a high school diploma, he received national recognition in 1950 when he was honored as head of a chemistry department which sent a higher percentage of chemistry students on for their Ph.D. than any other college or university in the nation. He was presented the American Chemical Society's Midwest Award.

His award read, "Partly through his zeal, Professor Haldeman has succeeded in raising the standards of chemical training there to a point where the college turns out more candidates for the doctoral degree in chemistry than many a large university." The citation noted he had loaned thousands of dollars of his own money to his students in order that they could continue graduate study. He often borrowed money himself to loan it to students at a lower rate of interest than he was paying. It was a matter of pride with him that not one of his student borrowers failed to repay him.

Born 25 April 1881, on a farm near Pine Grove, Pennsylvania, Professor Haldeman was the youngest in a family of eleven children. Because his family was poor, the youth had to conclude his education with grammar school. After several years of work at their barren small farm, he was able to enter Pennsylvania State Normal School through a series of proficiency tests after a period of arduous self-study. He received a teaching certificate in 1904 and immediately began his teaching career, which was to end 48 years later when he retired from the chemistry department at Monmouth College. While teaching at a small high school near Philadelphia, he continued to pursue his first goal: a B.A. degree. Each day he commuted to Philadelphia for a day of classes at the University of Pennsylvania. This continued for about ten years plus three summer terms and a year of residence. In 1914 when he was 33, he received his long-sought B. A. degree.

Immediately he began studying for his Masters degree at Harvard University under Dr. James Conant. He earned it in 1920, two years after he joined he joined the Monmouth College faculty. During the first few years, he taught all the chemistry courses offered. He took graduate courses at the University of Illinois, selecting courses that he thought would help him in presenting chemistry to his students. The department graduated 343 chemistry majors and inspired and qualified 86 or 25% to go on to doctorate. Monmouth was the 6th in the nation in the number of graduates who earned the Ph.D. and first in the nation in the percentage of chemistry graduates who earned the Ph.D.

Among "Haldy's Boys" are the men who were instrumental in developing methods of producing penicillin in commercial quantities. Others are in atomic research and hold key posts in the chemical industry. He refused several honorary degrees lest they dim the luster of the earned degrees by his students. In 1952 he accepted an honorary Doctor of Science from Monmouth College.

FREDERICK D. AND GRACE E. HALL - Frederick D. Hall was born in Kirkwood on November 29, 1915, the son of Claude J. and Sarah Hamberg Hall. He was the youngest of seven children, having a brother, Thomas, and five sisters, Josephine, Cora, Merle, Emma and Lois.

Fred D. and Grace E. Hall

When he was four or five, the family moved south of Kirkwood three miles to land in the estate of his grandfather, Eldad Hall. He attended Nichols School and graduated from Kirkwood High School in 1933.

He married Grace E. Higbee on October 5, 1940, in Burlington, Iowa. She was the daughter of Virgil and Mary Edith Van Cleave Higbee. Grace attended Kirkwood Grade School, Liberty School, graduating from Kirkwood High School in 1936. The year 1936 stands out in memory due to the deep snowdrifts in winter and the dry hot summer.

Fred worked at the Ralph Wells Elevator and farmed. Following the severe hailstorm in 1943 that destroyed crops, he worked at the International Harvestor Plant and Rock Island Arsenal until the spring of 1944 when they moved to a purchased farm in Hale Township.

They are the parents of four children, Grace Ann, Frederick Jesse, Linda Louise, Terry Thomas.

Fred served on the Hale School and Yorkwood School boards and the Farm Bureau and Extension boards. They are members of the Kirkwood United Methodist Church and former members of Sugar Tree Grove Presbyterian Church.

ISAAC K. HALL - Isaac K. Hall, second oldest of five children of Alvin and Polly Ann Hall, was born in Tippecanoe County, Indiana, on March 26, 1837. His parents were from New York State. Isaac came to Illinois in 1863, and in 1864 married Eliza Jane Stone in Henry, County, Illinois. They had nine children: Alvin Richard, 1865-1920; Sarah Hall, 1867-1867; Charles Isaac "Charley," 1868-1925; Elva and Alva, 1871-1935/1953, respectively; Ida Hall, 1873-1952; Daisy, 1876-1942; Lora Eugene, 1878- 1956; and Sherman Wilbur, 1880-1972.

Isaac K. Hall, 1890   *Sherman William Hall, 2000 (Isaac's youngest son)*

Isaac and Eliza first lived in Section 6 in the northeast corner of Sciota Township about three miles north and one and a half miles west of the present town of Sciota. On October 29, 1889, Isaac K. purchased land from John Van Kirk. He purchased 105 acres for $5,200 in Section 34 of Point Pleasant Township of Warren County, Illinois, recorded as No. 98965 in Book 79, page 442 at the Monmouth, Illinois, courthouse. The abstract for Isaac's farm indicates that a William Burtiss first acquired this land from the government as Military Bounty Land on January 14, 1819. Probably Burtiss was a veteran of the War of 1812. The U.S. Congress had set a large area in west central Illinois aside as bounty land for veterans of the War of 1812 with England.

Isaac's farm was in the area of southern Warren County, which was usually referred to as "Colfax". There had been a post office and also a Colfax church.

Isaac K. Hall died in Warren County, Point Pleasant Township, on February 13, 1903. He died of paralysis after an illness of 16 days. He was first buried in Hillsborough Cemetery and a few months later, his body was moved to Good Hope Cemetery. Quoted from his obituary, "Mr. Hall had been a hard worker all his life and was one of the most successful farmers in the community. Mr. Hall was willing to sacrifice himself for his country and offered to enlist in the civil war, but was rejected on account of physical disabilities."

Isaac's youngest child, Sherman Wilbur Hall, married Jessie Van Alstine, 1890-1952, on January 4, 1905, and had three children: Glenn Sherman, 1905-1989; Freeman Francis, 1980 and Delia Helen Hall, 1913-1991. Glenn married Lucille Snyder in 1946. They had two children: Alice Jean, b.1948, married 1993 to Owen Jury; and Steven Glenn, b. 1952, married 1979 to Nancy Pirtle, they had one son, Brent Steven, born 1984.

Sherman purchased Isaac's farm from the other heirs, after Elva's death in 1935, who had a lifetime quit claim to the farm.

Isaac's great-grandson, Steven Glenn Hall, is presently farming the old homestead. It is interesting to note that the farm has now been in the hands of the Hall family for four generations and 2001 marks one hundred and twelve years of continuous ownership by members of the Hall family. The present farmhouse is the same one in which Isaac resided.

DAVID MILTON HALLAM - The roots of the Hallam family run deep in the history of Monmouth, Illinois, and surrounding Warren County. Family, education, farming and cattle breeding, Christian leadership and community involvement are heritages that dominate the lives of David Milton Hallam, his brother, Charles Edwin Hallam, their ancestors, and descendants.

Family: David Milton was born March 16, 1922, in Monmouth to George Milton and Anna Eloise (Robb) Hallam. His brother, Charles Edwin, was born in Monmouth as well on December 31, 1924. Their father, George, was born on October 22, 1877, in Monmouth, son of David Milton and Cordelia (Murphy) Hallam. Their mother, Anna, was born on February 21, 1893, in Vernon, Van Buren County, Iowa, daughter of Harvey and Cecelia (Fitzgerald) Robb.

David Milton Hallam

George died at age 86 in Monmouth on March 29, 1964, resulting from a stroke. Anna died just over a year after her husband at age 72 in Monmouth on July 27, 1965. She died peacefully while resting due to heart failure.

David's pioneer Hallam ancestors came to this country from England before the Revolutionary War, possibly as early as 1701. In 1781, their great-great-grandfather, Thomas Hallam, served with a rank of private in the First Battalion, Third Company under Captain Evan Cessna (Cesna) in the Bedford County Militia of Pennsylvania in the capacity of Ranger On The Frontier. His great-great grandmother, Sarah (Sally) Vorys (Van Voorhees) is of Dutch extraction, her ancestors having originally settled on Long Island in 1660 when it was yet the Dutch colony of New Netherlands.

David's great-grandfather, Samuel Hallam, was born in Washington County, Pennsylvania, and went to Clinton County, Ohio, with his father in 1829 at age 21 where he eventually cleared 400 acres of timberland through purchases and trades. In spring of 1850, Samuel and his wife, Mary Ann (Polly) Mills, brought nine of their ten living children to Warren County by wagon train when David's grandfather and namesake, David Milton, was 13 years old. While their oldest daughter, Elizabeth Jane, had married Dr. Isaac Chrisman in 1849, she initially stayed in Ohio but eventually came to Warren County where she died. Samuel and Mary Ann's youngest child, Samuel Thomas Hallam was born in Monmouth Township, Warren County on October 22, 1853, three years after the family's arrival in Illinois.

On June 18, 1949, David married Elizabeth (Betty) Jane Caldwell. She was the daughter of George Graham and Arminta (Cowden) Caldwell, born April 30, 1927, in Monmouth. They had four sons, all born in Monmouth, Illinois, and all graduated from its high school.

David Mark Hallam, born August 2, 1952, graduated from North Central College in Naperville with a major in business. He is Vice President for Harris Bank of Naperville. He never married.

John Robb Hallam, born January 12, 1954, graduated from the University of Illinois at Champaign and with advanced degrees at University of Florida in Gainesville, Florida. He specializes in hospital administration, consulting and mergers, having led the merger of Barnes, Jewish, and Children's Memorial Hospitals in St. Louis, Missouri. On July 6, 1984, he married Laura Ann Terry, born March 19, 1955, at Jacksonville, Florida, daughter of James and Dorothy (Terry) Terry. James Terry was from the "Georgia Terrys" and Dorothy was from the "Florida Terrys". John and Laura have two children: Erika Lee, born August 18, 1985, and Sean Caldwell, born October 26, 1986, both born in Gainesville, Florida. They were divorced in 1999 at Orlando, Florida.

Charles Timothy (Tim) Hallam, born January 6, 1963, graduated from Monmouth College with studies in computer science. He works as computer software specialists in Las Vegas, Nevada. On January 25, 1986, he married Cynthia Lea Fillman, born June 29, 1965 at Milwaukee, Wisconsin, daughter of William Audley Fillman and Martha Marie Kersey. Her mother, Martha, and her stepfather, William Killey, raised her. Cynthia and Tim have five children: Allyson Sarah, born November 1, 1986; David William, born February 21, 1988; and Nicholas Patrick, born June 5, 1990, all three born in Monmouth; Tyler Charles, born December 14, 1993, and Flannery Elizabeth Marie, born September 16, 1995, both born in Dubuque, Iowa.

Peter Graham Hallam, born March 19, 1965, graduated from North Central College at Naperville. While there, his recognition and honors included president of student body for two years, Most Outstanding Man and Citizens awards, graduation with honors and students' commencement speaker. He is an equity partner in the law firm of Seidler and McErlean in Chicago, specializing in commercial trial law. On October 14, 1989, he married Suzanne Marie Erzinger, born April 18, 1965, at Matteson, Illinois, daughter of Kenneth Leonard and Mary Anne (Bisluk) Erzinger. Sons, Jack Andrew, born May 26, 1996, and Philip Robb, born April 27, 2000, were both born in Flossmoor, Illinois.

On February 25, 1950, David's brother, Charles Edwin, married Martha Smith, born July 21, 1921, at Monmouth, daughter of Lester and

Eunice (Vantine) Smith. Martha had two children, William, born July 24, 1943, and Jeffrey McMaster, born April 17, 1946, both in Monmouth. Charles and Martha have grandchildren Kristin and Kimberly Hallam and Patrick McMaster.

Betty died quite unexpectedly on February 20, 1991, due to a massive heart attack, in her home after dinner with friends.

On February 14, 1999, David married Deava Leininger in Peoria where they now reside. Deava's daughter, Temica, a teenager, resides with them.

Education: Beginning with his great-great-grandmother, all of David's ancestors could read and write. Sarah learned as a grown woman; Samuel was educated in the early 1800s in Pennsylvania. David's grandfather and namesake, David Milton, was educated at an early age in Ohio and Illinois; he began the tradition of attending Monmouth College that has continued through four generations. At age 18, David Milton, began teaching one year before graduation and continued for eighteen winters in the schools of Warren and Knox Counties. David's father, George Milton, was educated in the Warren county schools and attended Monmouth College before taking over the family farm at a young age.

Between 1928 to 1934, David attended a one-room schoolhouse known as Hickory College, District 40, one mile southeast of the family farm. His teachers included Miss Loso, Mrs. McConnell and Miss Bertha Carter. After a long weekend in the dead of winter, they often huddled by the huge furnace register while the inkwells thawed. In 1935, he transferred to Grier School – slightly over one mile west of the family farm and one mile east of Monmouth.

Prior to entering Monmouth High School, rural students took two days of entrance examinations to prove they were capable which applied to David Hallam. After school, David would walk to McQuiston's Bookstore (located on the square in Monmouth at the site of the current Warren County Genealogical Library) where his father would pick him up and return to their farm home. While there, he excelled in studies and was elected to National Honor Society. As a member of Debate Team, they were in the Northwest Conference and co-champions with one of the Quad-Cities schools, probably Moline. He won 3rd place in state competition for his original oratory of "Ice Ahead" in which he likened our nation's moral problems to an "unsinkable Titanic". The content of his speech was so impressive, "School Tracks" newspaper published it.

David enrolled at Monmouth College in 1940. The College required each student to take a physical education course. David chose to take either golf or swimming. His father asked, "How much would each cost?" David said, "Golf, $29.00 and swimming, nothing." His father said, "Take swimming!"

David graduated Cum Laude from Monmouth College in 1944 with a major in Psychology and Philosophy with a minor in Political Science. He attempted to enlist in the Army but was "turned down" due to a heart murmur. He then attended law school for one year at Northwestern University at its downtown Chicago campus.

Likewise, David's wife, Elizabeth, was educated in Monmouth schools and graduated from Monmouth College in 1949 with a major in English. Beginning when their youngest son was three, Elizabeth taught English and Journalism for 22 years at Monmouth Warren High School. Prior to their marriage, she taught swimming at the YMCA and was Society Editor for the Review Atlas. All of their children are college graduates. Timothy graduated from Monmouth College.

David's brother, Charles, attended the same rural schools and high school. Then he attended the University of Illinois at Champaign with a major in political science.

Farming and Cattle Breeding: David and his brother, Charles, continue to own the family farm three miles east of Monmouth, part of which their great-grandfather purchased in 1850. Its size expanded and contracted over the years. His grandfather, David Milton, purchased the farm from his father when Samuel retired. Now, the farm is in two different tracts, all in Monmouth Township.

David's great-grandfather was an early agricultural leader in the county. Samuel was one of the organizers of the Warren County Agricultural Society, only two short years after arriving in Illinois. He was their first President. Under his leadership, the first annual Warren County fair was held at the courthouse on October 15 of that same year.

David's father, George Milton Hallam, was widely known as a breeder of purebred Angus cattle. At age of thirteen, David read a book on the Angus breed and insisted they purchase a heifer. The family breed started at that time. While in high school, he regularly attended Angus sales with restrained approval from Mr. G. Ray Imbody, principal. George was a director of the Warren County Farm Bureau. Similarly, David was active in the Illinois Angus Breeders Association, serving on its Board of Directors in the mid 1960s. His interest in farming and breeding continues today, though in 1999 he retired from this pursuit. Still, he returns at least weekly to the community he loves, meeting with brother, Charles, and friends.

David's brother, Charles, has been the long-time Farm Editor with Rock Island Argus since 1952. Even though the brothers are renting their farm, they continue to be active in the agriculture industry.

Occupations: After college, David held various jobs before settling into real estate and appraising. These included clerk for the Burlington Truck Line, registrar for the Poland China Hog Breeders Association and reporter for the Rock Island Argus (1948 to 1952). David's brother, Charles, then became the manager of the Monmouth office of the Argus.

In 1960, David established the David Hallam Agency that sold real estate and auto and life insurance. In 1969, David was appointed Assistant Supervisor of Assessments for Warren County and Monmouth Township Assessor, becoming Supervisor of Assessments in 1973. In 1978, he joined the Security Savings and Loan (later Security Savings Bank) of Monmouth as its Chief Appraisal Officer where he worked for 21 years. He retired in 1999 and moved to Peoria.

Christian Leadership and Community Involvement: David, his family and ancestors have a tradition of giving back to the community. It began with his great-grandfather, Samuel, influenced the succeeding generations, and continues even today. A few are already documented above.

In 1853, Samuel was one of three men named to a committee to divide Monmouth County into townships and name the townships. In 1855 he became the Monmouth Township Supervisor and again from 1860 to 1863.

Samuel was active in the Christian Church of Monmouth. David's grandfather, David Milton Hallam, was a deacon of the same Christian Church for many years and was Superintendent of its Sunday school for 20 years. David's father, George Milton, was a trustee of Grace United Presbyterian of Monmouth that later became the Faith United Presbyterian Church.

When David was but 31 years of age, he was ordained an elder in the First Presbyterian Church of Monmouth; he served its Session for six, three-year terms. When the First Presbyterian Church joined with three United Presbyterian churches to form Faith Presbyterian Church, David was the first clerk of its Session. After moving to Peoria in 1999, he was elected to the Session of the First Presbyterian Church of Peoria.

In 1954, David joined the Monmouth Rotary Club, served as president from 1966 to 1967, received the Paul Harris Fellowship Award and continued his membership until his retirement. From 1955 to 1999, he served on the City of Monmouth Planning Commission and was its chairman for 12 years. From 1970 to 1972, David was president of the Monmouth Area Chamber of Commerce and served several terms as a director.

In 1978, David and his wife, Betty, were recipients of the Monmouth College Certificate of Service Award for dedicated service to the community. From 1980 to 1999, the stockholders of the Industrial Development Corporation elected David a director. From 1982 to 1999, he served on the Economic Development Committee and was its Vice-chairman. From 1985 to 1988, David was on the Monmouth College Alumni Board of Directors. Later, he became a member of the McMichael Heritage Society. Additionally, David served as chairman of the Warren County unit of the Salvation Army and on the board of directors for the local United Way.

Similarly, David's brother, Charles, was a member of the First Presbyterian Church before the formation of Faith Presbyterian Church. He wrote the history of the union of the four churches in Monmouth. Charles is a devoted servant to his church and is an active elder in its Session. Charles was a member of the Kiwanis Club of Monmouth. Both he and David have been life-long supporters of the Republican Party.

David's son, Timothy, continues the tradition of active leadership and involvement in church activities. Timothy and his wife, Cynthia, are both ordained elders in the Presbyterian Church, having served in the communities of Dubuque, Iowa, and Las Vegas, Nevada.

David and his wife, Betty, enjoyed collecting Old Sleepy Eye pottery for many years. They were among the organizers of the Old Sleepy Eye Collectors Club. Betty was their secretary-treasurer until her sudden death in 1991. David then became the Club's secretary-treasurer.

The roots of the Hallam family run deep in the Monmouth, Illinois, area. The above biography is only a partial story of the history, traditions and giving-back that characterizes the Hallam family of Monmouth.

SAMUEL LEIGH AND LILLIE MARTHA (BROWNLEE) HAMILTON - Samuel Leigh Hamilton (b. September 15, 1860, in Cedarville, Ohio, d. December 16, 1935, in Tulsa, Ohio) was the son of Samuel Robert and Hadassah (Orr) Hamilton. He married, May 3, 1887, in Monmouth, Illinois, Lillie Martha Brownlee (b. June 9, 1862, Little York, Illinois, d. December 8, 1933, Rock Island, Illinois). Lillie was the daughter of James Stevenson and Margaret (Struthers) Brownlee.

Leigh was educated in Cedarville, Ohio, and

Samuel Robert Hamilton home at 903 East 2nd Avenue, Monmouth, Illinois. His store at right on South 8th Street. Hadassah and a daughter, lower left-hand, and Samuel Robert, near store.

Princeton, Indiana. Lillie was educated in the Little York, Illinois, area. In 1882, while living in Princeton, Indiana, Leigh took an embalming course in Cincinnati, Ohio, and then helped his father in the undertaking business before going to work for "The Clarion" newspaper in Princeton, Indiana.

L: to R: Front: Samuel Robert, Mary "Mame" Lillian, Hadassah Orr and Jeanette McMillan. Back: John Orr, Charles Stuart and Samuel Leigh.

Their wedding was on a Tuesday at 8 p.m., and it took place at her father's home located at 129 S. 8th St., Monmouth, Illinois (in 1887 it was known as the corner of Garden and College Streets). Following the wedding, the Monmouth Marine Band assembled outside the home to perform some music. Leigh played the tuba in the band. He was a 2nd Lt. of Co. H, 6th Illinois Infantry, I.N.G. A week after the wedding they returned to Ness City, Kansas, where Leigh had been engaged in the grocery business, to establish their new home.

After two years they moved to Blair, Nebraska, where he owned a newspaper. Later he worked in newspaper offices in Omaha, Nebraska, and Chicago, Illinois, before they returned to Monmouth, Illinois. They bought from the college the Hogue property at 323 S. 8th Street, Monmouth. Leigh's hobby was raising poultry and they were judged with high ratings. Leigh became the Head of Job Department at the

Monmouth Review Atlas circa 1905. Later he took a medical leave for about five years from the paper and was a conductor on the Galesburg to Monmouth Interurban Trolley. Leigh returned to the paper from which he retired about five years before his death. They are buried in Monmouth Cemetery, Monmouth, Warren County, Illinois, in the North Hill Section. Their children are Guy, Cliff, Harry, Ethel, Esther and Helen.

SAMUEL ROBERT HAMILTON - Samuel Robert Hamilton, b.September 8, 1835, Clifton, Ohio, d.December 19, 1923, Monmouth, Illinois, son of Samuel and Nancy Stuart Hamilton, married October 26, 1859 in Cedarville, Ohio, Hadassah Orr (b.April 21, 1837, Cedarville, Ohio, d.April 3, 1913, Monmouth, Illinois), the daughter of John and Jeanette (nee McMillan) Orr. Both were educated in the Cedarville, Ohio area.

Samuel and Hadassah Hamilton

On September 17, 1861, "SR" enlisted in the 44th Ohio Infantry Regiment and his rank was Musicial 1st class (Rank Band Sergt). He fought in a number of Civil War battles, was wounded in 1862 during a skirmish at or near Charleston, West Virginia, and soon was discharged. They lived in Cedarville, Ohio, from 1862 to 1864, Washington County, Iowa, 1864 to 1865, and Princeton, Indiana, from 1865 to 1883 where Samuel was in the furniture and undertaker business. In April 1883 they moved to Monmouth, Illinois, and he entered the furniture business in a building on the north side of the city's square. Later he became a co-partner in the Page and Pinkerton furniture store and undertaker business before he operated a grocery store behind his home at 903 E. 2nd Avenue on South 8th Street. Samuel Robert Hamilton was one of the first grocery men in Monmouth. His store was a success, but on March 18, 191-, the store was destroyed by fire. His hobbies were knitting and writing poems. SR and Hadassah are buried in Monmouth Cemetery, Monmouth, Illinois. His grave has been marked by a special military headstone noting his service in the 44th Ohio Infantry Band. Their children are Samuel, Jeannette, John, Charles, and Mary (known as Mame) who married Fred A. Martin.

JAMES RILEY HANLEY - James Riley Hanley was born January 16, 1843, in Ohio, and died November 27, 1929, in Little York, Illinois. He provided for his family as a farmer. He married (1) Harriett (Hattie) Snodgrass, March 13, 1879, in Henderson County, Illinois, daughter of Daniel Snodgrass and Mary Wimmer. She was born in 1864 in Bald Bluff, Henderson County, Illinois, and died before 1900 in Warren County, Illinois. After her death he was unable to care for his sons. They were placed in the Illinois Soldiers and Sailors Orphans' Home. He traveled out of state to find employment, and met and married Emma Jane Hammock Morris in 1905 in Williamsburg, Kansas, daughter of Asa Hammock and Ruth Sutes. She was born January 11, 1871, in Missouri, and died May 4, 1929, in Warren County, Illinois. Emma was a widow with three children. They returned to Warren County in 1905 and re-established a home for their children.

James Hanley   Harriet (Snodgrass) Hanley

James Hanley listed residence as Orange, Illinois, when he enlisted as a Private with Company D, Seventh Calvary Regiment at the age of 19. He was mustered into the unit on December 30, 1863, by Captain Allen in Peoria. (Family stories report that due to his small stature and agility, he was utilized to carry the colors of the unit into battle. This is unverified information.) He was mustered out of the army on November 4, 1865, by Captain Chickering in Nashville, Tennessee. *Information from military retirement record, Illinois State Archives Office, Office of Secretary of State, Springfield Illinois.*

The children of James Hanley and Harriet Snodgrass are George Hanley, b. Little York, Illinois; Dan Hanley, b. Little York, Illinois; Perry Hanley, b. Little York, Illinois; and William Franklin Hanley, b.April 28,1882, Little York, Illinois, d.March 28,1951, Monmouth, Illinois, m. Mary Elizabeth Morris, b.March 4, 1890, Choctaw Nation, Oklahoma, d. March 25, 1957, Monmouth, Illinois.

The children of James Hanley and Emma Hammock are Cleda Helen Hanley and Violetta Maudina Hanley.

CLYDE AND ADA (CAMPBELL) HANNA - Clyde Lloyd Hanna was born in 1870 on the Hanna Family farm in Sumner Township, Warren County, Illinois. His father, Oren Lafayette, was also born on the family farm on March 14, 1842. His father, John Hanna (1799-1862), first settled on the farm and married Sarah (Crawford) from New York in 1821. O.L. Hanna married Sarah Jane (Curtis) September 26, 1867. They had three children, Fara, Lillian and Clyde. Clyde married Ada May (Campbell) November 15, 1905. Ada grew up in Hale Township, the daughter of James Campbell Jr. and Nancy Ella (Williams) who farmed also. Clyde and Ada had one son, Ross Edgar Hanna, born September 10, 1906. The Hanna family donated the property for the Pleasant Green schoolhouse, which still stands today. Through the years the Hanna men served on the school board. The Hannas attended the Fall Creek Methodist Church. Ross graduated from Monmouth College with a degree in

Chemistry and returned to the family farm to raise purebred Angus cattle, Poland China hogs and Rhode Island Red chickens. Ross also did custom baling, ran a sawmill and trapped. Ross married Mary Ellen Rhinehart on September 4, 1943. They were both very active in the community serving as officers in church, Farm and Home Bureau, extension, school boards, Angus cattle associations and 4-H leader. They had two children, Ross Edgar Hanna Jr. born July 11, 1945, and Sarah Mae, born March 26, 1947. They were both active in 4-H and school and church activities. Edgar served in the military in Vietnam. He was a radio announcer, jet pilot and is now a computer specialist. Ed and his wife, Nancy, live in Rock Island. He has three married daughters, Becky Zug, Jenni Guidry and Merry Linnenkemp. Becky and Jay have three children, Jamie, Sea Jay and Michael. Merry and Matt have two daughters, Maddelyn and Mattie. Sarah married Dennis Bruce Allaman from McDonough County August 26, 1965. They have also been active in the community and livestock organizations. They live on the Rhinehart family farm and also farm the Hanna family farm. They raise purebred Angus cattle. Their four sons are Chad, Craig, Clint and Carlton. Chad and Laurie have a daughter, Grace. Craig and Heidi have two sons, Drew and Ian.

Ross lost his life while bulldozing in his timber in 1969. His mother Ada had passed away the year before at the age of 90. Ellen continued on with the farm and her many church and Home Extension duties. She traveled all over the USA while serving on the Council of Finance and Administration of the National United Methodist Church for eight years. She toured the Holy Land and returned home to give programs. She presided at many United Methodist Women meetings and served as Dean of School of Christian Missions. In October 2001 she enjoyed a 90th birthday party at the Kirkwood Senior Center.

HENRY HANSON AND FAY FISHER - Henry Hanson was born to Swen Hanson and Bengta "Bertha" Ericksdotter in Monmouth, Warren County, Illinois, on October 14, 1893. He lived all of his life in Monmouth and attended Monmouth schools, starting in the Lutheran Swedish school. He died October 4, 1969, and was buried in Monmouth Cemetery. He married Martha Elizabeth Fay Fisher on November 6, 1915. Fay was born February 13, 1895, to Isaac Benjamin Fisher and Susan Emily Mulhatten in Avon, Illinois. Fay was named after her two grandmothers, Martha Hall Fisher and Elizabeth O'Neil Mulhatten. Fay graduated from Avon schools and attended Hedding College in Avon. They moved to Monmouth, residing at 115 West 8th Avenue. Her father worked at McCullough Lumber Yard and the Icehouse. Fay had one sister, Leah Fisher Alhstrand, and two brothers, Oliver and Roy, who died in infancy. Fay died June 7, 1988. Henry was employed by the railroad at the roundhouse, as a painter, at Miller's Manufacturing, and retired from Monmouth Pottery. From this union there were six children, all born in Monmouth and at home.

Jennie Frances was born December 13, 1917. She married Maxin Eugene Caldwell on June 12, 1938, in Mt Pleasant, Iowa. They had two children, Roger Eugene and Vicki Elaine Modrena. Jennie was co-owner of Caldwell's Dry Cleaners, a tailor for McVey's Model. She moved to Galesburg's High Rise in 1980 and died February 18, 2001.

Henry and Fay Hanson and family: Louise, Jennie, Dick, Art, Henry Jr., Jeanne, Henry Sr. and Fay.

Martha Louise was born March 2, 1920. She married Cecil Ion Law on August 20, 1940, in Clinton, Iowa. Cecil was in the Navy Air Force during WWII. They had two children, Linda Louise White and Larry Kenneth Law. She worked at the Formfit and did babysitting in her home. Cecil was employed at Maple City Dairy, and then the U.S. Post Office until retirement. Linda died January 1988.

Henry Alden "Bud" was born July 2, 1922. He married Eula Jean Newberry September 20, 1941, in Monmouth. Bud worked for Young's grocery store, Monmouth Pottery as Kilnman and Illinois Power. Upon moving to Bettendorf, Iowa, he worked at Alcoa till retirement. He was in WWII on a Navy Tanker. Eula worked at Benner's grocery store, babysat in her home and retired from Walgreen's Drugs in Bettendorf. They have three children, Rev. Robert Lee, pastor of Presbyterian Church in Greenview, Illinois, and Carolyn Jean Bell, a teacher in Holton, Kansas. Carolyn was Teacher of the Year for her district. Glenna Fay, born February 9, 1949, and died March 22, 1949.

Arthur Darrell was born June 10, 1924, and married Ellen Jean Hanson on August 5, 1944, in Bastrop, Texas, while Art was in the WWII Army as a cook with Patton. They had two sons, James and John. Art was employed by Staley's restaurant, Barnes Grocery Store, and for Metlife until he retired. Ellen died March 16, 1999.

Richard Lloyd was born December 13, 1929, and married Mary Kathryn Bonawitz on June 9, 1957, in Sellinsgrove, Pennsylvania. Dick was employed by Staley's, YMCA, Pottery and, after graduating from University of Illinois as a Mechanical Engineer, he worked for Bettendorf's Alcoa until retirement. He was in the Army during the Korean conflict. Dick was inducted into the 1999 Hall of Achievement. Mary was a schoolteacher in Little York, Illinois, and substitute teacher at several Quad Cities schools. They had three daughters, Mia Kay Dobkins, Nancy Ann Williams and Susan Kay. Susan died at birth April 14, 1961.

Lenore Jean was born November 5, 1934, and married Chuck Merrill Orwig in Biloxi, Mississippi, on September 12, 1953. (See related biography.)

SVEN AND BENGTA ERICKSDOTTER HANSON - Sven Hansson was born November 17, 1848, in Slatten, Jamhog Parish, Bleking County, Sweden. He died in Peoria, Illinois, at his son Olaf's home, January 20, 1911. Sven was the son of Hans Hansson and Majia Stina Sonesdotter. Sven Americanized his name to Swan.

Sven was married to Bengta Ericksdotter on May 10, 1881, in Kyrkhult, Sweden. Bengta was born March 27, 1857, in Gylsbode, Sweden. She is the daughter of Erick Johnsson and Elna Jonsdotter.

Bengta was the second child of seven children, all born in Sweden. Bengta (Americanized Bertha) died in Monmouth April 14, 1935. They are both buried in the Monmouth Cemetery.

Swan came to Monmouth about 1882. His earliest wage stub was dated October 19, 1883, and signed by John Turnbull. Swan denounced the King Oscar on October 8, 1888, under the name of Swan Celin. His family is "Resident of Warren County, Illinois" for over 100 years.

Bengta and Sven Hanson

Swan and Bertha's first child Olaf was born in Kyrkhult, Blekinge, Sweden, July 2, 1882. Bertha and Olaf came to USA in about 1888. They had 6 children:

1. Olaf married Mayme Rossman. He was employed at Avery's in Peoria, where he lived most of his adult life. They had two children, Raymond and Madeline.

2. Emmiley "Emma" was born December 7, 1891, and married James Clarence Switzer August 6, 1912. Emma died in Monmouth June 17, 1969, and Clarence August 6, 1974. There were four children born to this union: Fredrick, Edward, Sarah and Emiley.

3. Emma was a twin and the twin was stillborn.

4. Henry was born October 14, 1893, and he lived all of his life in Monmouth. He married Fay Fisher November 6, 1915. Henry died October 4, 1969. Fay died June 7, 1988. There were six children born to this union: Jennie Caldwell; Louise Law; Henry Jr. (Bud); Arthur; Richard and Jeanne Orwig.

5. Minnie was born October 15, 1893, a twin to Henry. She died February 18, 1894.

6. Esther was born December 15, 1899, and she died March 3, 1970. She married Daniel Thompson and Arthur Boyer. From the union of Esther and Daniel there were three children: Jeralds, Alta Kersey and her twin Alvin.

DELEVAN BALDWIN HARDIN - Delevan Baldwin Hardin, who was president of the Second National Bank in Monmouth until his retirement in 1963, was born in Monmouth, Illinois, on October 4, 1895, the son of Everitt C. and Caroline (Baldwin) Hardin. He had two sisters, Mrs. Clara (Clark) Warfield and Mrs. Jane (Robert) Brainard. The Hardin family dates from 1840 in Warren County, and Dell was the fourth generation of the family to head the bank and to be associated with the financial affairs of Warren County.

Delevan B. Hardin was educated in the public schools of Monmouth and attended Monmouth College. He married Bessie Fee on

May 11, 1918, in Clarksburg, Decatur County, Indiana, at the home of her father who was a prominent farmer and livestock producer. Bessie Fee was the daughter of Edwin S. and Enrie (Hamilton) Fee and the granddaughter of John G. Fee, an abolitionist preacher who was a founder of Berea College in Madison County, Kentucky, an institution that survives prominently today.

Dell B. Hardin

Dell Hardin served in France in World War I in the 22nd Aero Squadron rising to the rank of Captain. After the war he was instrumental in the organization of the 123rd Field Artillery Battalion of the Illinois National Guard while continuing the family banking tradition with the Second National Bank of Monmouth, an institution organized by his great grandfather in 1874. As the storm clouds of World War II gathered in the late 1930s, the 123rd Field Artillery was expanded to become a regiment with units located in a number of communities in western Illinois. Dell commanded the regiment as a Colonel.

In March 1941 the 123rd was activated into federal service at Camp Forrest, Tennessee. Subsequently the regiment was divided into separate battalions. Following training in military government at the University of Virginia, Col. Hardin was assigned in 1943 to the General Staff of the VIIth Corps U.S. Army in England as G5. On June 6, 1944, the Allied invasion of Europe began. Col. Hardin landed on a Normandy beach on D-Day after wading ashore when the landing craft in which he crossed the English Channel sank.

Following World War II Dell B. Hardin returned to the Second National Bank as its president and also assisted in the reorganization of the Illinois National Guard. He retired from the military with the rank of Brigadier General. Mr. Hardin was elected president of the Second National Bank in January 1942, following the death of his father Everitt C. Hardin. He headed the bank until 1963 when he was elected Chairman and his son, Everitt F. Hardin, was elected as President.

Delevan Baldwin Hardin died in Monmouth on October 5, 1976, survived by his widow Bess and two children Everitt Fee Hardin and Mary Ann Hardin Miller. Following World War I he participated in the organization of the Marion B. Fletcher Pot 136 of the American Legion in Monmouth and served as its first commander and as a member until his death. He was also active in the Republican Party in Warren County. He held membership in the J.W. Clendenin Post Veterans of Foreign Wars, the Monmouth Rotary Club and Benevolent and Protective Order of Elks.

DOUGLAS DELEVAN HARDIN - Douglas Delevan Hardin is president of Community National Bank in Monmouth. He was born in Munich, Germany, May 4, 1950, the son of Everitt F. Hardin and Jane (Bruington) Walker Hardin. At that time his father was stationed in Augsburg, Germany, with the United Sttes Army of Occupation. In 1956 his father resigned from the army and the family moved to Monmouth where his father joined the Second National Bank in Monmouth, a bank founded and operated by the Hardin family since 1874.

Douglas D. Hardin

Douglas Delevan Hardin attended Monmouth Public Schools, Oregon State University and Monmouth College, from which he graduated in 1972. He held several positions over the next several years, but in 1975 he began employment at Community National Bank in Monmouth, making the sixth generation of the Hardin family to be in the banking business in Monmouth. In order to become better qualified, he attended and graduated from the Graduate School of Banking at the University of Wisconsin and the Commercial Lending School at the University of Oklahoma.

In September 1976 he married Constance Brownlee Hutchinson in Valley Forge, Pennsylvania. They had met as students at Monmouth College. Her father was raised on a farm near Biggsville but sought his fortune in the East after graduating from Monmouth College. Doug brought Connie back to Monmouth and she has devoted much time over a number of years in chairing the Red Cross Blood Bank visits to our community. In April 1981 a son, Alexander Chauncey Hardin, was born to this union. He attended Monmouth Public Schools and is currently a student at Arizona State University in Tempe, Arizona.

In March 1993, Doug was elected President of the bank to succeed his father. The bank has continued to grow and prosper under his leadership. It is the only locally owned bank remaining in Warren County and competes successfully with other larger banks owned outside this area and this state.

A competitive swimmer in both high school and college, Doug has been an Illinois High School Association swimming official for a number of years, officiating swimming meets at a number of high schools in western Illinois. He is a member of the School District 38 Board of Education, a member of the Monmouth Rotary Club and the City of Monmouth Zoning Board of Appeals. One of the achievements to which he points with pride is that he has given 17 gallons of blood to the Red Cross Blood Bank. Doug has been a Monmouth High School Sports Booster and has contributed much time to further that

organization's activities. He enjoys sailing a catamaran on the Mississippi River.

EVERITT FEE HARDIN - Everitt Fee Hardin, the oldest child of Delevan Baldwin Hardin and Bessie

Everitt Fee Hardin

Fee Hardin, was born in Monmouth n May 11, 1925, the seventh anniversary of the marriage of his parents. He and a sister Mary Ann Hardin, six years his junior, were the fifth generation of the Hardin family in Monmouth. Both attended Monmouth Public Schools. Mary Ann then matriculated at DePauw University in Greencastle, Indiana. She married Major Clarence Benjamin Miller Jr., a fighter pilot in the United States Marine Corps. She has three children and resides in California.

Everitt F. Hardin received an appointment to the United States Military Academy at West Point, New York, entering the Academy on July 1, 1943. He completed the war-shortened course of instruction there, receiving a B.S. degree, and was commissioned a Second Lieutenant, Cavalry, United States Army, on June 4, 1946. He then served on various assignments in Germany and the United States until the end of February 1956, when he resigned to return to Monmouth and continue family participation in the Second National Bank in Monmouth.

While stationed in Germany with the Army of Occupation, he married Jane Bruington Walker of Monmouth, in Augsburg, Germany, on July 29, 1949, where Everitt was stationed with the 2nd Armored Cavalry. Jane was the daughter of Donald Buckmaster and Ila Bruington Walker, from the Alexis line of Bruingtons. Their first born, Douglas Delevan Hardin, was born in Munich, Germany, on May 4, 1950. Their second child, Susan Elizabeth Hardin, was born at Fort Knox, Hardin County, Kentucky, on May 24, 1952, while her father was a student in the Advanced Armor Course. Three more children were born to this marriage, all after the return to Monmouth, Caroline Walker Hardin in 1959, Margaret Ann Hardin in 1961 and Sarah Jane Hardin in 1963.

At the Second National Bank, Everitt worked in various positions learning the business. He attended the Graduate School of Banking at the University of Wisconsin, graduating in 1959. In January 1963 he was elected the seventh President of the bank, replacing his father Dell B. Hardin who became Chairman. Principal ownership of the bank was in the Hardin and Pattee families. In January 1964 at the Annual Meeting of the bank, it was proposed to voluntarily liquidate the bank. Although the vote was not unanimous, the necessary two thirds of the shares were voted in favor of the proposal.

As the Second National Bank of Monmouth wound up its affairs, a group of Monmouth businesspersons decided to investigate the possibility of obtaining a charter to establish a new bank to replace the Second National. After months of preparation, Community National Bank in Monmouth opened for business with capital of $450,000 on September 10, 1964. Everitt F. Hardin was its first president. The bank had more than 400 shareowners at its opening.

Mr. Hardin served as president of the bank until succeeded by his son Douglas in 1993, and was a Director of the bank until 1996. The bank grew steadily over the years, with capital increasing to $3,665,000 after paying cash dividends to its shareowners over those years of $1,464,000.

During the administration of Mayor Donovan Vance, Everitt was appointed to the City Plan Commission and has continued to serve on that body. He is a Trustee of the Warren County Library and Reading Room Association and an initial Trustee of the Warren County Public District Library. An active member of Faith United Presbyterian Church, Mr. Hardin has served as a Trustee and as an Ordained Elder. He is a life member of Marion B. Fletcher Post 136 of the American Legion. Jane W. Hardin, in partnership with her brother Dr. F. Stuart Walker, owns and manages farmland in Mercer County. She is a former member of the Board of Education of School District 38 in Monmouth. Jane has been a member of Trinity Episcopal Church in Monmouth.

LOUIS LEROY HART - Louis LeRoy Hart (1888-1969) was born on January 18, 1888, at Hale, Iowa. His father was Peter Hart Jr. (1835-1910); his mother was Anna McHale (1844-1888). Roy's parents were Irish immigrants. Peter came from Sligo County to Canada in 1841. Anna's genealogy is unknown, but she worked in the Phelps household in Oquawka, Illinois, as a bondservant and married Peter in 1862. Moving to Jones County, Iowa, they had 13 children.

Frank J., Louis L., Richard L., Mary E., Martha J., Mary A. and Charles E.

On January 18, 1915, Roy married Mary Ester Creger (1890-1958) at Lost Nation, Iowa. Mary was of German ancestry. Her father was John Henry Creger (1863-1938) and her mother was Anna Herkelman (1870-1932). Mary was a graduate of Our Lady of Angels Seminary, Lyons, Iowa, (1908) and a teacher.

The couple established their household in Menlo, Iowa, where Roy farmed. A son, Richard LeRoy Hart, was born on January 12, 1916. By 1917 Roy was a Rural Route Mail Carrier working out of Stuart, Iowa. On March 21, 1918, a second son, Francis Joseph Hart, was born. Roy joined the Railway Mail Service in 1919 and, after training in Chicago, he moved to Monmouth, Illinois, in 1920.

A daughter, Mary Ann Hart, was born on December 14, 1920. 308 S. E Street, 512 S. C Street and 510 E. Archer were Hart addresses before they permanently settled at 525 S. 11th Street. A second daughter, Martha Jane Hart, was born on August 25, 1926, and with the arrival of Charles Edward Hart on August 13, 1932, the family was complete.

The family's life in Monmouth during the 1920s and 30s was fairly humdrum. Healthy parents saw healthy children pass through the local parochial school and graduate from Monmouth High. There was one exception, Martha Jane attended high school at St. Mary's Academy, Nauvoo, Illinois.

Mary Ester was active in the Catholic Church lay activities, but Roy, whose job kept him away from home frequently, was content to pay his taxes and leave public affairs to others. The war years were different, very stressful, as the family had two sons and a son-in-law in the war. Mary Ann had married Elmer B. Scovill in 1942, and as a combat engineer officer he fought his way through France and Germany. Dick, called up with the local guard unit in 1941, served as an officer in the 94th Infantry Division Artillery, seeing action in France and Germany. Frank, enlisting in the Army Air Corps in March 1942, was flying European B-24D bombing missions as an aerial gunner by November 1942.

Following the war, Elmer Scovill pursued a military career with Mary at his side. They traveled extensively while raising six children – sons John, Tom and Mark and daughters Sally, Mary and Nancy.

Dick worked as a feed salesman/executive and farm owner operator and, with Mary Jane Martin Hart, raised three children in Warren County – sons David and Joe and daughter Mary Lynn.

Frank graduated from Monmouth College in 1949 (chemistry) and made a career in pharmaceuticals and, with Geraldine Keefer Hart, raised three children in Kankakee, Illinois, – sons Allen and John and daughter Janice.

Martha Hart loved aviation and after high school (1945) learned to fly. Continuing, she graduated from Marycrest College and pursued a career in education, a flight instructor and co-owner of an air charter service. She made her home in the Rockford, Illinois, area. There was no time for marriage for her.

Charles Edward graduated from MHS (1950) just in time for the Korean War. After a short career handling the mail in Davenport, Iowa, Charles enlisted in the USAF in January 1952. He trained as a radio operator and saw service in Morocco, Florida, the British West Indies and the Baffin Island. He entered Western Illinois University and graduated in 1960 (physics). A career in naval weapons research and development followed and, with Joanne Arrant Hart, he raised two children in King George, Virginia – daughter Denise and son Stewart.

From their 11th Street home, Roy and Mary Ester would watch their extended family grow and prosper. Then in 1957 Mary suffered a heart attack. She died on January 19, 1958. Roy would pass the 1960s in declining health and pass away on February 5, 1969. In closing, it is most appropriate to salute this couple and say the following . . . "many thanks for your love, guidance and a job well done. The journey is ended; you were successful; rest in peace – we love you" . . . Dick, Frank, Mary, Martha and Charles.

EMORY HAWCOCK - Emory Hawcock, son of Ernest and Jennie (Atkins) Hawcock, was born 27 June 1896. Emory was linked with Hawcock's Cafe, Monmouth's premier restaurant. He married Jane Hart in Burlington, Iowa, 16 June 1938, when he was 43. The restaurant began when his grandmoter, Mary Atkins, and his mother, Jennie, ran a boarding house at 217 East First Avenue. They rented the building on the southside of the 100 block just a block west of the boarding house. His father, called "Ernie", a cigar maker by trade, joined them as front-end manager. Once in operation, they never closed its doors. It expanded rapidly, taking in several rooms on the second floor as well as renting the store to its west for a delicatessen. Emory was associated as a chef with the business since graduating from Monmouth High School. On the death of his mother and father, he sold the restaurant, keeping the delicatessen. He was a lifetime member of the National Rifle Association and enjoyed as a hobby using the Monmouth College rifle range with Dr. Thiesen and M.L. Kobler – all excellent shooters. He was a member of St. Anthony's parish in Bartonville. He served in the Cavalry in World War I and was a member of the American Legion. When his friend Dr. Garrett Thiesen urged him to complete his education in chemistry at Monmouth College, he sold his business to Barnes Super Valu and ran it for them while in college. He then entered Iowa University and received a degree in dietetics. Then he and Mary moved to Route 3 Hilton Lane in Peoria, where he worked until retirement at Methodist Hospital. He was the last survivor in his family, passing away 3 October 1974.

DENNIS PATRICK AND BETTY LOU HAWKINS - The Hawkinses were new to Monmouth in 2002, arriving from San Antonio, Texas. Dennis took the job of Vice President of Finance at Community Medical Center. Both Dennis and Betty were raised in Shoals, Indiana (Martin County). Dennis was born on March 25, 1945, to Samuel Raymond and Thelma Marinda (Cessna). Betty was born January 4, 1946, to Edward and Harriett Jane (Williams) Allen. They were married at Washington, Indiana, on October 18, 1963. They have a son, Patrick Alan, who married Julie (Liu) and they have a son, Pascal. They have a daughter, Miranda Jane Rock, who is married to Jamie and has three sons: J.T., Jared and Jacob.

Dennis and Betty Lou Hawkins

During their married life, the Hawkinses have been travelers in employment and for recreation. Between 1967 and 1985, Dennis worked in the finance arena of Sears, Roebuck and Co. and was transferred frequently in Ohio and Indiana. In 1985 Dennis took the first of a series of employments in the healthcare finance industry with Community Hospital in Indianapolis. From there he took positions in Crawfordsville, Indiana; Lihue, Kauai; Liberal, Kansas; Topeka, Kansas; Kokomo, Indiana; and San Antonio, Texas, before accepting employment in Monmouth. Betty was a great wife who accompanied and held a number of positions in the banking and healthcare industries in the communities Dennis' jobs took them to. Dennis was an active member of the Healthcare Financial Management Association and held a variety of leadership positions in the organization. He was on the Kansas Board of Directors and the National Advisory Board for Patient Financial Services.

In addition to the areas where employment took them, the Hawkinses vacationed and traveled extensively throughout the United States, Mexico, Canada and the Caribbean. Dennis has been active with the Boy Scouts for over 30 years and camped, biked, hiked, canoed, hang-glided, caved, skied and rock climbed with various Troops in dozens of states, many times accompanied by Betty. In addition to Scouting, Dennis has held a number of volunteer positions, from the Hawaii Governor's Task Force on Juvenile Delinquency and Gangs to Board Member of a humane society and an art museum. Dennis was a member of the advisory committee for the Brown v. Board of Education National Historic Site in Topeka, Kansas. Both Dennis and Betty have held a variety of positions within the churches where they have had membership and with civic organizations in their various cities of residence. They joined the First United Methodist Church in Monmouth where Dennis works with Boy Scout Troop 355.

The Hawkinses collect antiques and have an eclectic variety of furniture and other collectibles in their home. Betty collects teddy bears, glassware and old toys. Dennis collects and wears cuff links and has a number of Southwest items displayed in their home.

Dennis completed his BS in Human Resources Management at Friends University in Wichita, Kansas, and his JD at Washburn Law School in Topeka, Kansas.

DAVID D. HAYNES - David Deyarmon Haynes was born on May 25, 1864, in Jefferson County, Ohio, to George and Mary Jane (Deyarmon) Haynes. George Haynes had migrated from England with his father, William Haynes, in 1840.

David Haynes was the fifth child in a family of nine children and, at the suggestion of his brother William, migrated to Warren County in 1886. His brother had preceded him two years before and had settled in Gerlaw.

David Haynes worked as a farm laborer in the Gerlaw area and on January 23, 1888, was married to Ada Porter at the bride's farm home. Ada Porter was the daughter of Joshua Thatcher Porter and Kate (McCoy) Porter who resided at their farm home in Section 26 of Spring Grove Township. The newly married couple returned to Jefferson County, Ohio, where their first child, Ward Porter, was born there on June 4, 1889. The couple returned a year and a half later and settled on a farm located in the Southwest Quarter of Section 9 of Spring Grove Township. The couple prospered and lived their remaining lives on this farm. In addition to Ward, twins, Margaret Dorothy and George Thatcher were born on April 14, 1895, an unnamed stillborn son in 1898, and Roger Alvin on January 22, 1903.

All of the children attended Lone Star School that was but a mile north of their home. The one exception was in 1901, when the school burned down and the children temporarily attended Mohler School located 1 1/2 miles to the east.

The David D. Haynes home shortly after completion in 1907.

When Roger Alvin was born the house became crowded with the family of six. In 1906, construction was started on a new farmstead approximately 200 yards to the south, placing it directly next to a county road. By the end of 1907, the house and outbuildings were completed and the family moved into the spacious eight-room home.

David and (unknown) Haynes

Ward Haynes engaged himself in farming and was united in marriage to Muriel Young on January 24, 1917. The couple took up residence on a farm near Smithshire.

The David Haynes family was an active member of the Gerlaw Christian Church and it was there that George Thatcher and Doris Ellen Carson met and were united in marriage on May 25, 1921, at the bride's home. They moved into the farm home that had been purchased by David Haynes a few years earlier and was located in the Northwest Quarter of Section 21 of Spring Grove Township.

Margaret Dorothy Haynes was united in marriage to Josiah Smith on July 18, 1918, in Mercer County. Smith was in the U.S. Army at the time and, when WW I ended, the couple engaged in farming.

Roger Haynes was first married to Ona Eldridge, then to Gladys Daves and finally to Mabel Swanson. He engaged in a career as an accountant for Illinois Bankers Life Assurance Company in Monmouth.

The grandchildren of David and Ada Haynes consisted of Dorothy Violet (McWhorter), born July 23, 1925, to Ward Porter and Muriel Mary Haynes; Violet (1920-1922), Ada Margaret (Sickmon), born August 20, 1921, and Richard Lee, born February 14, 1932, to Margaret Dorothy Haynes (Smith); Mary Beth (Watson), born April 1, 1930, and James Thatcher, born August 30, 1932, to George Thatcher Haynes; and Roger Alvin Jr., born January 28, 1922, John David, born May 21, 1930, and Nancy Fae (Horschler), born October 15, 1936, to Roger Alvin Haynes.

JAMES ROYAL HENDEL - James (Jim) Royal Hendel, son of Jay Robert and Sadie Kreps Hendel, was born December 21, 1931, in Greenbush Township. He has one sister, Leitha Fay Lock, and two brothers, Larry Kreps Hendel and Joseph Jay Hendel. Two sisters are deceased. His father was born August 1, 1899, in Linwood, Kansas, and came to Illinois in 1918 with his mother and two sisters. His mother purchased a farm in Greenbush Township, Sec. 28 and he farmed and lived there the rest of his life. Today, the farm is owned by his son James. Jay died January 13, 1977, in Avon. He married Sadie Kreps, who was born February 28, 1904, in Fulton County. She died May 5, 1983 in Galesburg.

James and Clarice Hendel

James attended Taft grade school and Avon High School. On August 11, 1951, he married Clarice Juanita Watson in Avon. She was born July 17, 1932, near Roseville, the daughter of LeMoine Earl and Norma (Suter) Watson. Clarice has one brother, Larry Alan Watson. She received her education in rural schools in Warren County and Avon High School, where she and James met. She was employed at Formfit Co. before her marriage. She then stayed home to raise their family and help her husband farm.

As a member of the Illinois National Guard, James was called into active duty in 1952 during the Korean Conflict. After he returned from Korea, he moved his family to the Stem farm northwest of Roseville. He worked for Mr. Stem during the farming season and was employed at the Pottery or Wells Co. in Monmouth during the winter months. In 1957 Mr. Stem quit farming and rented the farm to James, which he continues to farm today. In 1976 they moved to 696 60th Avenue to a farm they had purchased earlier.

James and Clarice have three children. Jerry Robert Hendel was born in 1951. He is a self-employed Electronics Technician in Monmouth. Michael Duane Hendel was born in 1954. He farms and lives on his grandfather's farm in Greenbush Township.

Susan Marie Hendel (Dean) was born in 1956. She is a registered nurse at the University Hospital in Iowa City, Iowa. She lives in West Branch, Iowa.

James believes in being a good steward of the land and has tried to keep informed with the latest farming information. He was a director of the Farmers Grain Co. for 22 years, which also included being Chairman of the Board. James and Clarice have both been active in the Methodist Church and served on the Agriculture and Youth Extension Councils. She was a 4-H leader and HEA member for 30 years. They enjoy their families and six grandchildren and like to help where they are needed.

JAY AND SADIE HENDEL - Jay Robert Hendel was born August 1, 1899, in Linwood, Kansas, son of James Hamilton and Susan Ellen Higgins Hendel. In February 1918, after his father's death, Jay and his mother moved to a farm in Section 28, Greenbush Township, Warren County, Illinois. They became members of the Avon Methodist Church where Jay met his wife to be, Sadie Kreps. They were married March 15, 1923, by Rev. L.J. Sailer in the church. Sadie was the youngest daughter of William and Lillious Mitchell Kreps. She was born and raised in Lee Township, Fulton County, Illinois.

Jay and Sadie Hendel, 40th Wedding Anniversary

After marriage, Jay and Sadie continued to live on the farm in Greenbush Township where they raised their family. They were the parents of three sons: James Royal, born December 21, 1931; Larry Kreps, born August 7, 1937; and Joseph Jay, born August 7, 1940; and three daughters: Marion Lois, born January 13, 1924, died February 27, 1924; Leitha Faye, born August 13, 1926; and Delana Dale, born January 26, 1929.

Jay's mother, Susan Ellen Higgins Hendel, spent much time in the home and passed away there in June 1934. She is buried at Mount Vernon Cemetery near North Henderson, Illinois.

All the Hendel children attended the Taft country grade school, then rode a school bus to the Avon High School, where all graduated from high school. Leitha married Dean Lock in May 1945, and continued to live in the area. Dale married Ernest Lynn in August 1947, and lived in the area awhile, later moving to Florida. Ernest died in December 1995. In March of 1998, Dale married Robert O. Dilkes. Dale passed away in July 2000. Both Dale and Ernest are buried in Florida National Cemetery, Bushnell, Florida. James (Jim) married Clarice Watson in August 1951. After Jim served in the Korean Conflict, they farmed in the Greenbush and Roseville area. Larry joined the U.S. Air Force and served twenty-two years. He married Karen Potter in January 1957. After he retired from the service, they settled in San Angelo, Texas. Joseph (Joe) served four years in the U. S. Air Force. He married Markay Simmons in February 1961. They live in Avon. He had worked at Briggs in Abingdon for many years until it closed. He also had a public address system business, "Hendel's Sound", providing sound for many fairs, homecomings and public events around the area.

Jay and Sadie were both active church workers. Both had been 4-H club leaders for the community young people. Jay was active in local politics, having been elected justice of peace and road commissioner for several terms in Greenbush Township. He drove a school bus a number of years for the Avon Unit Schools. After the children were grown, Sadie worked at Saunders Hospital and Avon Nursing Home, which were both in Greenbush Township west of Avon. Jay passed away January 12, 1977, in Avon Nursing Home. Sadie stayed on the farm for awhile then moved to Avon. She passed away May 8, 1983, in St. Marys Hospital in Galesburg, Illinois. Both are buried in the Avon Cemetery.

JERRY ROBERT HENDEL - Jerry Robert Hendel, son of James R. and Clarice (Watson) Hendel, was born October 12, 1951, in Saunders Hospital, Avon, Illinois. He has one brother, Michael Duane Hendel, and one sister, Susan Marie (Hendel) Dean. Jerry received his education in the Roseville Schools, graduating from high school in 1969. He then went to United Electronics Institute in Louisville, Kentucky, graduating in 1971. He enlisted in the United States Air Force and served four years as a Communications Technician, stationed at Scott Air Force Base at Belleville, Illinois. On October 30, 1971, he married Kristine L. Strickler, daughter of Edwin and Lois (Anderson) Strickler. They were married in the Roseville United Methodist Church. They were the parents of two children. Brian Kurt Hendel was born September 26, 1974, at Scott Air Force Base, Belleville, Illinois. Brian died September 19, 1991, in Monmouth hospital as a result of Muscular Dystrophy. He was a senior at Monmouth High School. They adopted a daughter, Lauren Kathryn Hendel, who was born June 6, 1986. She is a student at Monmouth High School. Jerry and Kris were divorced in 1995. On April 19, 1997, Jerry married Anne Elizabeth Carman in Galesburg, Illinois, at the home of her parents. Anne was born January 15, 1957, in Galesburg, Illinois, to Charles and Elizabeth (Chatters) Carman. She is an art teacher in the Galesburg schools. After his discharge from the Air Force, Jerry worked for Carterfone Communications as a Service Representative and then for Techtron Business Machines in Monmouth. In 1994 he started his own Independent Computer sales and service business in Monmouth. He was a partner in Colonel Mustard Antiques Shop from 1989 to 1993. Jerry was very active in 4-H and church activities while growing up and has continued to take part in community activities. He has been a member of the Monmouth Municipal Band and Leo Ramer's Ecumenical Singers for a number of years. Both he and his wife, Anne, participate in some of the Prairie Players Civic theater productions in Galesburg, Illinois.

MICHAEL DUANE HENDEL - Michael Duane Hendel, son of James R. and Clarice (Watson) Hendel of Roseville, Illinois, was born December 27, 1954, in Saunders Hospital, Avon, Illinois. He has one brother, Jerry Robert Hendel, and one sister, Susan Marie (Hendel) Dean. Michael attended the Roseville schools, graduating from high school in 1973. He married Sue Ann Lock of Avon on February 2, 1973, in the Prairie City Presbyterian Church. She was the daughter of Ray and Margaret (Pickard) Lock of Avon. They were the parents of two sons. Shawn Travis Hendel was born May 21, 1973, in Galesburg, Illinois. He attended Bushnell Prairie City schools and WIU. He lives in Greenbush Township, Warren County, and works at John Deere Co. in Macomb, Illinois. Brandon Paul Hendel was born November 7, 1976, in Galesburg, Illinois. He also attended Bushnell Prairie City schools and WIU. He lives in Hartsburg, Illinois, and works as parts manager for Central Illinois Ag, Inc. at Pekin, Illinois. Michael started farming north of Bushnell, Illinois, and farmed till he and Sue were divorced in 1986. He then worked various places in the area: The Prairie City Elevator, Riden's Farm Service at Walnut Grove and Briggs Pottery in Abington, Illinois. In 1997 he furthered his education and graduated from Carl Sandburg College in 2000 with an Associate Degree as a Microcomputer Technical Specialist. He also returned to farming. He lives in Greenbush Township on the farm his great grandmother Hendel brought her family to when she came to Illinois from Kansas in 1918. While growing up, Michael was active in 4-H and church activities and during his school years was a participant in all the school sports.

DORIS RILEY HENRICHS - Doris Riley was born on May 18, 1920, in Hancock County. She was the daughter of Victor and Inez Riley, who were natives of that county. After graduating from Colusa High School, she attended Western Illinois University for two years before she began her teaching career.

Doris Henrichs

Doris taught at Bross School, her home school, for four years before she returned to Western to get her degree in 1943. The next year she taught at Golden High School in Adams County.

On July 30, 1944, she married Leonard Henrichs, and they moved to Tucson, Arizona. It was in Tucson that their first daughter, Judy, was born on March 30, 1945. The following year they moved to Ajo, Arizona, where their daughter, Connie, was born on April 20, 1946. Judy died at the age of 37 years.

In the late 1940s, the family returned to Monmouth where Leonard entered the insurance business. Doris taught one year at Lincoln School before job transfers took them to Freeport where Doris found a teaching job. Their next move was to Woodstock, and she taught in Crystal Lake. Upon moving to Macomb, Doris found employment in the elementary schools there. When they moved back to Monmouth she taught at Harding for one year before she transferred to Garfield, where she spent many years before her retirement in 1985.

Shortly after retirement, Doris and four other women were instrumental in founding Starting Point, a residential facility for people who need a new start in life, those fighting to overcome an addiction or those who need to find safe harbor from abusive or dysfunctional homes.

For many years she was very active in this work and still serves on the Board for the organization, which is very important to her.

Connie Henrichs first married Robert Bartlett and they had two sons: Robert Leonard and David Edward. Later she married Jim Stewart and they moved to Hawaii where they lived for twenty years before returning to the mainland. Presently they live at Lake Calhoun, near Galva, Illinois.

Doris is enjoying apartment living in the Birchwood Apartments in Monmouth.

JAMES WARREN HILL - James Warren Hill was born September 30, 1839, in South Carolina. His father was Hamilton Hill who owned a plantation, but died at an early age in 1839. His mother was Margaret (Peggy) Foster Hill. She took six-months old James to Warren County, Illinois, by covered wagon in 1840.

Hill-Herron, early 1900s.

James Warren Hill married Martha A. McGregor in 1858. They lived on a farm nine miles north of Monmouth, Illinois, which is now on Highway 67. They had five children. One of them was Thomas who married Elizabeth Maude Simpson of Norwood, Illinois. Both of them had been members of Norwood Presbyterian Church. Thomas and Lizzy lived on the home place where he had been born. Their three children were Olive Fern, Robert Cleo and Richard Leon.

When Cleo married Edith Leone Earp in 1923, a second house on the farm was remodeled for their use, and Cleo farmed the home place where he had been raised.

Cleo and Edith's two children were Cleo Verne and Barbara Leone. In time Verne took over farming the home place.

Barbara married Richard Lloyd Herron in 1956. Their three children were Richard (Rick) Lloyd Jr., Vicky Leone and Dicksy Lea. This family lived in the larger house on the same farm.

Their daughter Vicky married Ed Tye in 1985, and they lived in Kewanee, Illinois. She passed away in 1996, leaving her husband and two sons, Andrew (Drew) Jacob Edwin and Eric Christopher.

Dicksy married Dan Colwell in 1987. They live in Abingdon, Illinois, with their sons, Bryan Andrew and Scott Daniel.

Rick married Teresa Marie Wood Ashby in 1982. They live on the home farm, and Rick helps with the farming. Their two sons are Stephen Dean Ashby and Bradley James Herron.

Stephen has married Tiffany Lawson. They live in Galesburg, Illinois, with their son, Payton Adam.

Brad is the sixth generation to live and work on the same farm.

JAMES WARREN HILL - James Warren Hill was born September 30, 1839, in Abbeville District, South Carolina, son of Margaret Foster and Hamilton Hill. Hamilton Hill died in May 1839

Emma Green, 1860-1920; Joseph Pressly, 1863-1940; Nellie W., 1869-1942; John Thomas Hill, 1872-1933; and Mary Leona, 1874-1938, children of James Warren Hill, 1839-1897, and Martha A. McGregor, 1839-1894. Twin Margaret "Maggie" L. Hill (born 1874) died September 9, 1878, at age 4 years, 3 months and 14 days.

in South Carolina and was a plantation owner there. John C. McCrery and wife, Jane Foster McCrery, went to South Carolina in the spring of 1840 and brought Margaret and James to Warren County by horse and wagon. James Warren Hill married Martha A. McGregor July 18, 1858, in Warren County, Illinois. Martha was born June 17, 1839, in Washington, Ohio, and died March 10, 1894. James died December 21, 1897. Both are buried in Spring Grove Cemetery in Warren County, Illinois, with their daughter, Margaret L. Hill, a twin, born 1874 and died September 9, 1878. Their other children include: Emma Green(e), 10/27/1860-5/28/1920, married Alexander Cunningham Simpson March 7, 1888, all in Warren County, Illinois; Joseph Pressly Hill, 12/29/1863- 11/24/1940, married Cora May Lightner; Nellie W., 11/21/1869-5/27/1942, married George W. Pease, May 7, 1890, in Warren County, Illinois; John Thomas Hill, 10/18/1872-6/15/1933, married January 16, 1894, to Elizabeth Maud Simpson (12/3/1873-6/29/1958); Mary Leona Hill, a twin (1874-1938), married January 30, 1895, to William Jasper Sharer in Warren County, Illinois; and Margaret L., a twin, 1874-9/9/1878 (4 years, 3 months, 14 days). James and Martha Hill owned and lived on a farm in Spring Grove Township, Warren County. Their son, Thomas, became the owner of this farm and reared his family there. Thomas and Elizabeth's son, Robert Cleo, took over the farm later. The family were members of the Presbyterian Church.

CURTIS ALDWIN AND ALICE DERA (RISK) HINTON - Curtis Aldwin Hinton was born October 2, 1913, at La Belle, Missouri, to Herbert Aldwin and Nancy Susanna (Biles) Hinton. He grew up being a farmer and was one all of his life. He died April 17, 1990. He moved in 1940 to Plainville, Illinois, first and than to rural Kirkwood to work for Clare Smith in 1942. Clare had a farm at Biggsville, Illinois, so Curtis moved his family there. Then, in November 1945, the family moved just south of Kirkwood, Illinois, to work for Reid L. Everett. He lived there until retiring in 1985 and moving into Kirkwood at 235 E. Walnut Street.

Curtis and Alice Hinton's 50th Anniversary, August 1, 1985. Sue, Leroy, Luchien, George, Joan, Fay, Curtis, Alice, Becky and Geneva.

He was very active in the WUP Church from the time of joining. He taught Sunday school for many years. He served as Deacon and Elder a number of times. He read the Bible through once a year.

He married Alice Dera Risk, January 26, 1935, in Williamstown, Missouri. Alice was born March 4, 1916, in Stecker, Oklahoma, to Lucien Edwin and Cora Avis (Flanagan) Risk. She was a homemaker caring for her family and friends. They had nine children.

1. Alice Joan was born January 20, 1936, in rural Canton, Missouri, and was married June 12, 1955, to Paul Emerson Williams. They have five children and nine grandchildren.

2. Avis Sue was born February 13, 1939, at Canton, Missouri. She married James Peterson May 6, 1958. They are divorced. She has two children, three grandchildren and four great grandchildren.

3. Redmond Aldwin was born December 20, 1940, at Plainville, Illinois. He died October 17, 1957, at Kirkwood.

4. Herbert Luchien was born April 22, 1942, at Monmouth Hospital. He married Donna Marie Emory, August 3, 1968. She was born December 12, 1946, to Marshall and Geraldine (Thurman) Emery. They have five sons and six grandchildren.

5. Geneva Jane was born October 1, 1943, at Monmouth Hospital. She lived at Biggsville, Illinois, and was married February 16, 1965, to Ronald Marcase, born January 1, 1941, to Howard and Mary (Duffner) Marcase. They have three children and nine grandchildren.

6. George Edward was born December 8, 1945, at Monmouth Hospital. He lived at Kirkwood, Illinois, and was married March 6, 1971, to Sally Marie Olson. She was born June 7, 1949, to Einer and Ruth (Anderson) Olson. They have three sons.

7. Fay was born July 9, 1947, at Monmouth Hospital and was married January 30, 1970, to Karl Roger Fowler. Karl was born May 18, 1939, to William and Gracia (Allen) Fowler. They have two sons and Karl had two sons (four total). They have nine grandchildren.

8. Ivan Leroy was born December 29, 1948, at Monmouth Hospital and was married November 6, 1973, to Beverly Joyce Jones. BJ was born November 5, 1949, to Clyde and Rhonda (Barnes) Jones. She had two sons. They have four grandchildren.

9. Rebecca Dera was born December 1, 1958, at Monmouth Hospital and was married May 21, 1994, to John Edward Paternoster. John was born April 24, 1964, at Jos, Nigeria, to Ivan and Junita (Kaiser) Paternoster. They have twin daughters and one son.

GEORGE AND SALLY (OLSON) HINTON - George Edward Hinton was born December 8, 1945, to Curtis and Alice (Risk) Hinton in Monmouth Hospital, Monmouth, Illinois, about two weeks after his parents moved. George graduated from Yorkwood High School, Monmouth, Illinois, in 1964. He enlisted in the Army. After basic training, he went to Glenhousen, Germany. While there he worked on the vehicles. He was discharged in 1968.

George and Sally Hinton, Dustin, Brett and Drew, September 5, 1999.

After coming home, he got a job in 1969 working for Martin and Clark Motors in Monmouth, Illinois. In 1972 he worked for Cavanugh Motors in Monmouth, Illinois. In 1975 he started working with his father and brother on Reid Everett Farms until 1989. He is presently working at Farmland Foods in Monmouth, Illinois.

He married Sally Marie Olson on March 6, 1971, in Aledo, Illinois. Sally was born June 7, 1949, at Aledo, Illinois, to Einar and Ruth (Anderson) Olson, who were living on a farm in the Alexis area. She graduated in May 1968 from the Alexis High School, Alexis, Illinois. She graduated from the Burlington School of Cosmetology at Burlington, Iowa, in 1968.

She started working at Stepp's Beauty Solon in Monmouth, Illinois. She also worked at Hair Happening on the square in Monmouth, Illinois. When their building was sold, her and friend Connie Larimer opened their own shop on Broadway Avenue. It is called Broadway Salon.

They bought a home at 345 W. Walnut Street in Kirkwood, Illinois, in 1975. They belong to the WUP Church in Kirkwood, Illinois. Sally has served as deacon and elder and on the Board. They have been the custodians for several years now.

They have three sons.

1. Bret Allen was born March 15, 1974, at Monmouth, Illinois. He graduated in 1992 from Yorkwood High School, Monmouth, Illinois. He is employed at Shop-Ko in Monmouth, Illinois. He lives at home.

2. Dustin Craig was born November 9, 1976, at Monmouth, Illinois, while living at Kirkwood, Illinois. He graduated in 1994 from Yorkwood High School, Monmouth, Illinois. He worked at Jack's in Monmouth, Illinois, and went to school for two years at Carl Sandburg at Galesburg, Illinois and for two years at WIU in Macomb, Illinois. In 2002 he started working for Spacemark Buildings, headquartered at Decatur, Illinois. He drives from Kirkwood, Illinois, everyday.

3. Drew Edward was born October 28, 1981, in Monmouth, Illinois, while living in Kirkwood, Illinois. He graduated from Yorkwood High School, Monmouth, Illinois, in 2000. He is going to college at Southern Illinois in Carbondale. He works at Shop-Ko in Monmouth, Illinois, when he is on break from school.

ROBERT HODGE - The Hodge farm, five miles west of Monmouth, in Hale Township, has been in the Hodge family since 1868. On May 9, 1848, Robert Hodge, 30, wife Margaret, 30, and infant Martha, left Belfast, Ireland, for the United States. They had come originally from Derry, a county in the west of Ireland. They went at first to (West) Virginia, then to Pennsylvania, and from there in 1868 to Warren County, Illinois. It is not certain when Robert's two brothers, Alexander and James, had come to the United States, though it is possible they had come earlier. (They were not on the ship *Wolfsville* with Robert.) Alexander stayed behind in Pittsburgh. (He was a jeweler.) The other brother, James, is supposed to have gone to Canada, but the family lost track of him.

Hodge homestead, five miles west of Monmouth. Margaret Hodge and mother, Anna Clark Hodge.

Alex Hodge

Robert farmed 160 acres in Hale Township, five miles west of Monmouth; he rented it from its owner, Hill, (one of the owners of the Pittsburgh jewelry store, Hodge and Goddard), who had bought 320 acres in Warren County. When Hill decided to return to Pennsylvania, Robert's children, who were still living at home, persuaded Robert to buy the 160 acres. They, the three girls and two boys, would all work together to help pay for it. Eventually (after some difficulties), the farm was paid for. It was never again mortgaged! Evidently the original effort to clear it had made an impression on the children.

The next owner was Alexander, the oldest son of Robert (one of the boys had died). Alexander married Anna Belle Clark, of Aledo; they had twin boys and one girl.

One of the twin sons of Alexander, Edward Clark Hodge, born 1898, graduated from Monmouth College and received his Master's degree from the University of Chicago. He became a teacher, and eventually a school superintendent. The other, Robert Alexander, did not marry, and stayed home to take care of the farm. The daughter, Margaret, born 1903, married Percy Roney, owner of a farm about two miles west of the Hodge farm.

The three children of Alexander and Anna were the last to live on the home farm. Robert died in 1973. Edward, his twin brother, was superintendent of the Kirkwood school for twelve years. Married to Catherine Dunn of Keithsburg, he had three children, Jeanne, Thomas Robert, and Edward Dunn. He died in 1978. Margaret, whose husband had died at age 102, died January 7, 2002.

The farm now belongs to the three children of Edward Clark Hodge. Thomas, who is a professor at Franklin College, Franklin, Indiana, has bought part of the Hodge farm. Edward, who lives in Mexico, Missouri, was an attorney, and later a judge; he has recently retired from the judgeship. Jeanne, the oldest of the three, taught high school English, and married Warren Spring, teacher and, later, businessman. They live in Milledgeville, Illinois.

The west 80 acres had been split off (belonging at times to the descendants of Martha Hodge (Miller), to Edward Hodge, and to Margaret and Percy Roney) – at present the entire 160 acres belong to the three children of Edward Clark Hodge: Thomas Hodge, who had, for some time owned part of it, Edward Dunn Hodge, and Jeanne Hodge Spring.

The 160-acre Hodge farm is thus, in 2002, still in the ownership of the Hodge family; it is a treasured part of the past, and of Warren County.

GARY DEAN AND KATHLEEN ANN (CASTEEL) HOFFMAN - Gary Dean Hoffman was born May 24, 1953, Galesburg, Knox County, Illinois. His father, Theodore Earl Hoffman, was born November 3, 1922 and died November 22, 1999. He was the son of Theodore and Pearl (Terpening) Hoffman. Gary's mother, Frances Lorraine (Blodgett) Hoffman, was born May 27, 1929; she was the daughter of William John and Mabel Jean (Wright) Blodgett. Gary's siblings are Theodore, Steve, Edward Joe and Lisa.

Gary attended Galesburg schools, graduating in 1971. He was a varsity letter winner in wrestling. He then attended Carl Sandburg College. He worked for United Facilities, Bailey Excavating and in various retail sales positions, including Kinney and Bloomquist Shoes, Klines Department Store and Gale Ward Athletics. He owned and operated Hoffies Imprinted Sportswear from 1986 to 1996 in Abingdon, Illinois. He went back to Carl Sandburg College in 1993, and graduated with an Associates Degree in 1997. He transferred to Monmouth College and received a Bachelor's degree in Secondary Education/History major at age 46 in 1999. He is currently teaching at Knox County Academy. He has coached Junior High and Senior High volleyball for several years and is currently coaching Junior High wrestling.

Jennifer, Kathy, Gary and April Hoffman, 1995.

Kathleen Ann Casteel was born April 7, 1955, in Peoria, Illinois. Her father, David Cummings Casteel, was born May 6, 1919; her mother, Dorothy Mae (Ketchum) Casteel, was born October 23, 1922 (see Ketchum/Casteel). Her siblings are Thomas, Sue, Richard and Harriet.

Kathy moved to Des Moines, Iowa, in 1956. She attended kindergarten 1960-61, in 1961 moved to Warren County in 1961 – rural Gerlaw, then rural Monmouth. She attended Warren School first through fifth grade. She moved to rural Galesburg, Coldbrook Township, in 1966 and attended Coldbrook School for the 6th grade, and then Galesburg Schools, graduating in 1973. She was active in Warren County 4-H (1964-1973) and attended State Fair 4-H events several years for flower arranging and sewing. She graduated from Carl Sandburg College with an Associates in Applied Science in Accounting in 1976. She worked for Monmouth and Knox Colleges, Soangetaha Country Club (1978-1988), was a partner in Hoffies Imprinted Sportswear (1986-1996), and Blucker, Kneer & Associates, Ltd. Accounting Firm (1993-present).

They met in high school in 1971, began dating in 1973, and married on May 4, 1974 at Bethel Baptist Church, Galesburg, Illinois. They resided in an apartment in Galesburg for a few months, then rural Galesburg, Coldbrook Township for two years. They moved to their present home in Abingdon in December 1976. Both have been active at Bethel Baptist Church: Kathy with Wednesday night youth programs and as Co-Director of the Easter Production; Gary playing guitar with the Worship Team and as Assistant Director for the Western Illinois Baptist Camping. Both have been youth sponsors at various times. Kathy's current hobbies include flower gardening, scrapbooking and crafts. Gary also enjoys landscaping and continues to sing and play guitar. They also enjoy "antiquing" and working on their 100-year-old home.

Children: Jennifer Colleen was born August 31, 1977, attended Abingdon Schools, graduated in 1995, received a Cosmetology Certificate in 1996 and an Associates in Marketing and Mid-Management in 1998. She married Thomas Lee Wolford June 19, 1999, in a backyard garden ceremony. Their son, Austin Lee, was born October 29, 2000.

Christine Ann was born April 6, 1982, and died November 29, 1985 (brain tumor).

April Suzanne was born June 10, 1987, attends Abingdon Schools and will graduate in 2005. She is active in choir and band, plays volleyball and enjoys learning to cook.

HOLLOWAY-STRICKLER - Thomas (Tom) Diven Holloway was born July 17, 1915, in Mercer County, Illinois, where he grew up, the son of William Tompkins Holloway and Bonnie (Diven) Holloway. William was the son of Colonel Holloway, who was one of the founders of Alexis, Illinois, and a breeder of Clydesdale horses in the late 1800s.

Tom Holloway married Eva Pauline Strickler January 6, 1941. Eva was the third child of Harry Alexander and Inez Olive (Trone) Strickler. Harry was born in Illinois, the youngest child of Alexander Hamilton Strickler of Fayette County, Pennsylvania, and Sarah Angeline Van Gilder, born in Knox County, Illinois.

Tom and Eva lived near Keithsburg, Illinois, after they were married, later moving to Keithsburg, where they resided for many years. They had three children: Richard (Dick), born January 4, 1942; Robert (Bob), born December 29, 1942, died February 20, 1966 in the South China Sea during the Vietnam War; and William (Bugs), born August 26, 1946.

In 1970 Tom and Eva moved to rural Alexis where he farmed 80 acres and worked in a machine shop in the Quad Cities. They also ran the High Point Gun Club for quite a few years.

Tom died July 30, 1999, and is buried in the Green Mound Cemetery, Keithsburg, Illinois.

HOLT - Jacob Holt was born in Plattsburg, New York, on December 3, 1803. He set out at age 14 to make his fortune. He wandered as far west as Kansas City and as far south as New Orleans – as a peddler, steamboat crewman, shopkeeper, school teacher and cargo trader. Finally, he returned to New York with a small fortune.

Holt House (birthplace of Pi Beta Phi).

He became a law student, then the Purveyor of Cadet Commons and hotelkeeper for West Point.

In 1847, President Polk appointed him Customs Collector, and in 1850 he was elected to the New York legislature.

He owned land in Illinois, Missouri and Arkansas, and came west to look over his properties. He decided he liked Warren County, Illinois, the best and settled here in 1855 (the year the "Q" was completed).

Coming with him were his wife, Sarah, their son, Alexander, and five daughters: Josephine (1841-1915), Adeline (1844-1910), Margaret (1847- 1915), Frances (1849-1915) and Carrie. Their sixth daughter, Susan, was born in Monmouth in 1858 and died in 1944.

In 1856, Jacob bought a home at 402 East First Avenue from William Rogers who had built it in the late 1840s.

He ran a store on the corner of First Street and East Broadway. In 1858 he was elected Mayor of Monmouth and served one term. In 1874 he was elected again and served three consecutive terms.

While he was mayor a fire company was formed to operate the chemical engine at Engine House #2 (near South Third Street), and it was given the name of Major Holt Engine Company. "Major" was an honorary title given to Jacob.

In October 1859 his wife Sarah died at 39 of typhoid fever. During the Civil War, he donated money and horses to equip a Union regiment. Alexander enlisted and served in three different outfits, rising to the rank of Lt. Colonel.

Alexander married Kate Babcock (1837-1908), the youngest of the Draper Babcock family. Born near Wales, Massachusetts, she came to Monmouth with her parents in 1842. The Alexander Holts had three children: two daughters, Sarah and Mary, who died in infancy, and a son Frank, who died at 7 years. For a number of years Alexander and Kate lived in Washington, D.C., where he worked for the IRS. After his death, Kate returned to Monmouth in 1893.

Margaret and Carrie were schoolteachers. Carrie married a Bradford and moved to the Little York area. She had four children: John, Abner, Margaret and Frances.

John Bradford married Anna, a librarian at Monmouth College. They had three daughters: Margo, Mary Louise and Virginia.

Abner moved to Turner, Oregon. Margaret married James Swanson and moved to Canton, Illinois. Frances married a Bailey and remained in Monmouth.

Jacob, Sarah and five of their daughters (Josephine, Adeline, Margaret, Frances and Susan) are buried in the Holt plot in Monmouth Cemetery.

Also buried there are Kate, their daughter-in-law, and her three children, as well as their granddaughter, Fannie Bradford Bailey, and Anna Bradford, their granddaughter-in-law.

DELL JOSEPH HOUSE - Dell was the son of Edward and Minnie (Boozan) House. He was born December 1903, in Kelly Township. He had two sisters, Lorretta (House) Hennenfent of Roseville and Violet House of Galesburg.

He attended Science Hall School and then later attended Alexis High School. He farmed with his father and mined coal in the Alexis area. In September of 1933 he married Winifred Gilmore and they had three children: Shirley Elaine (House) Flanagan of Kingsland, Texas; Edward of Monmouth; and John of Roseville.

He moved his family to Gerlaw, Illinois, in 1937. He later became Road Commisnier of Spring Grove Township and retired after thirty-eight years of dedicated service. Dell taught his grandson, Douglas House, son of Edward, how to run a road grader and how to maintain the roads. Douglas has followed in his grandfather's footsteps and has been Road Commissioner of Black Hawk Township in Milan, Illinois, for the past eighteen years.

Dell and his wife Winnie had eight grandchildren and twelve great grandchildren. Dell and Winifred lived in Gerlaw, Illinois, until their passing. Dell died in June 1994 and Winifred in January of 1999. They were of the Catholic Faith.

EDWARD EUGENE HOUSE - Edward was the son of Dell Joseph and Winifred (Gilmore) House. He was born June 18, 1937, in Monmouth, Illinois. He has one sister, Shirley Elaine Flanagan, born in 1935, and a brother, John House, born in 1942.

Edward attended Gerlaw School for his first eight grades. He then went to Monmouth High School, graduating in 1955. Ed worked during high school at Earl Ryner's Garage in Gerlaw, Illinois. After graduating from high school, he worked for the Ford Garage in Monmouth for two years and then went to work for the Warren County Highway Department in 1956. In June of 1959, Ed married Tjodie (Hughes) in the Little York Methodist Church. Tjodie is the daughter of William and Melba Hughes.

Ed and Tjodie had three children, Douglas, Brenda and William. Douglas and his wife, Kimberly, of Rock Island, Illinois, have three children: Thomas, 15; Hamah, 2; and Spencer, 8 months. Brenda (Nimrick) and her husband, Jeff, of Wilton, Iowa, have two sons: Tyler, 17, and Ryan, 14. William and his wife, Renee, of Aledo, Illinois, have two children: Evan, 10, and Alyssa, 7.

Ed went to work at John Deere Planter Works in Moline, Illinois, in February of 1964 as a welder and then later received an apprenticeship as a Millright Machinist. Ed attended Black Hawk College for two years. He retired from John Deere after thirty years in June of 1994.

After retiring, Ed and Tjodie moved to Texas for four years and then moved back to Warren County, living out at Lake Warren in Monmouth, Illinois, where they can enjoy spending time with their children and grandchildren.

Ed and his wife always loved cars. Before his retirement, they loved racing and showing Corvettes. They received many awards over the years.

Ed and Tjodie are members of The First Christian Church of Monmouth.

WILLIAM AND MELBA (STEWART) HUGHES - William Hughes and Melba Stewart were married October 11, 1932, in Carthage, Illinois. They resided in Carthage for five years before moving to Little York. June 8, 1937, was the year in which Bill and Melba Hughes claimed Little York as their home.

William Hughes Family

The couple started a produce business, which bought from farmers and Bill transported and sold the goods, primarily eggs and chickens, to the Chicago area. The business ran for approximately 35 years, until farmers no longer had the ability to sell goods to local merchants. After the close, Bill was employed by Boyston Lumber Company. Bill worked for Boyston for 11 years, while also sitting on the city board. He is recognized as the individual who got Little York roads graveled and paved. Melba held the position of City Clerk and ran the York Cafe for eight years. In November Bill died of pneumonia. Melba remained in Little York until moving to Monmouth in the mid-70s. She continues to live in Monmouth.

Bill and Melba had eight children: seven daughters and one son. All children attended Little York public schools, until the inception of the Yorkwood School District. Their seven daughters include Gwen Farm of Alexis; Joyce Lantz of Monmouth; Paula Endicott of Monmouth; Tjodie House of Lake Warren; Mary Lee of Monmouth; Kay Todd of Monmouth; and Angie Fullerton of Orlando, Florida. Bill, their only son, is the only deceased. He departed in September of 1999. Bill resided in Roseville where he held the position of Superintendent of Schools.

HULL-TATMAN - George W. Hull, a Kirkwood native, married Flora B. Berry on July 18, 1898. They had eight children: Vearl Dean, Lawrence Glenn, Dale, Howard Mack, Ruth (Burgland), Lois (Olson), Harold and Lenora May. George died July 13, 1955, and Flora died March 3, 1934.

Howard Mack Hull married Erma F. Tatman in Kirkwood. Erma F. was the daughter of James Tatman and Madge Ostrom of Monmouth.

Erma's parents, James and Madge, were married March 28, 1914. They had 12 children: Erma F., Charles, Leona May, Harold (Red), Raymond, Lena (Renwick), Melvin (Pete), Melva (Melvin's twin) died at birth, Howard (Shorty), Don, Robert and Richard. James died November 5, 1947, and Madge died September 26, 1974.

Howard M. and Erma F. had three children. Donna M. was born January 13, 1934, in their Kirkwood home, married Charles Reyburn and currently lives in Galesburg. Betty J. was born July 17, 1937, married Eugene Lind and also resides in Galesburg. Larry L. was born in the old Monmouth Hospital December 6, 1939.

Larry graduated in 1958 from the Monmouth High School. He joined the United States Air Force, January 1963-1966, thereafter serving two years in the Air Force Reserves with the Rank E6, Sergeant. Larry traveled to numerous military bases throughout the world before being discharged in 1968. Larry is extremely proud of being a Vietnam Veteran while serving our country in a time of great distress. Larry continues to reside in Monmouth.

JERRY G. AND JANE I. (DOWNES) HUMMELL - Jane Irene Downes was born on April 2, 1947, to Grace and Roger Downes of 833 N. Main Street, Monmouth. She was their second daughter. While she was a baby, her parents moved to 700 N. First Street; in 1952, she moved to Henderson County when her parents took over the farm of her grandparents, Maurice and Florence Downes of Monmouth. She attended Rozetta Grade School from grades one through six. At the age of eleven she joined the Rozetta Baptist Church; she was a member of Rozetta Lucky Fours 4-H Club for six years. She went to Biggsville Junior High and Union High School, from which she graduated in 1965.

She then moved to Burlington, Iowa, where she attended Burlington Business College, graduating in 1966. She worked for Benner Tea Co. while attending college and continued working there until 1967 when she began working for J. I. Case Company.

In 1967 she met Jerry Gordon Hummell, son of Don and Mary Hummell of Burlington, Iowa; Jerry Hummell was born August 30, 1942, attended and graduated from Burlington Schools, served in the army, stationed in Korea, from 1960-63, and was working at the Burlington ordinance plant when Jane met him. They were married August 18, 1968, and set up housekeeping at 801 South 7th Street, Burlington, Iowa, a house they later bought and where they still reside today.

Jane, Jerry and Jason Hummell, 1996

On October 6, 1978, their only child, Jason Gordon Hummell was born. Jason graduated from Burlington High School in 1997 and served in the military from 1998-1999, where he was a member of the Army band.

In 1971 Jane began working for National Research Bureau; she remained there until 1974 when she began working at Chittenden and Eastman; she worked there until 1986. In 1987 she left the field of office work and began employment with the Burlington Community School District as a teacher's associate, working with severe and profoundly handicapped children, a job she still holds to this day.

Jerry Hummell is also employed by the Burlington Community School District as a full-time school bus driver. Jason Hummell is currently employed by Pro-Lube in Burlington, Iowa, and is a member of the Army Reserve.

The entire family are active members of the Oak Street Baptist Church in Burlington, where Janes teaches Sunday School, oversees the nursery and works with the Awana program.

DR. AND MRS. WILLIAM R. HUNTER - Dr. William R. Hunter purchased the farm home at 2939 U.S. Hwy. 67 in 1963. He was born in 1923 on the family farm in Johnson County, Iowa, where his father, George McCrory Hunter, had been born. His great grandfather was Adam Hunter, immigrant from Ireland in 1815. His mother was Minnie Belle Buck of Welsh and German ancestry. Dr. Hunter was educated in Iowa City schools and received his degree in Veterinary Medicine from Iowa State University in 1949. The veterinary practice in Alexis was begun in 1950 and he continued until retirement in 1988. He also farmed, maintained a partnership in swine production for over 40 years with Gene Fell, and bred Angus cattle and Standardbred horses. Dr. Hunter helped establish the Illinois State Veterinary Medicine Association's Hog Cholera Eradication Committee and served as its chairman. In 1970 he received the Goodyear Award for outstanding achievement in soil conservation in Warren County. Dr. Hunter was an active member of the Alexis United Presbyterian Church and was a charter member of the Alexis Lions Club.

Doc Hunter was a student of genetics and animal breeding. He bred, raised and raced top Standardbred horses in Illinois and maintained a top broodmare herd while also building an outstanding herd of Angus cattle. He died 11 May 2001, and his grandson, David Shike, manages the herds of Angus Cattle and Standardbred horses.

Dr. and Mrs. (Janet Stewart) Hunter raised six children. Their daughter Jane married Daryl Shike and they farmed east of Alexis. Jane taught school in the Yorkwood District before her untimely death at 51 years. They were the parents of David, Daniel and Ellen. Betsy married Tom Bradley, a National Park Ranger serving as superintendent of several National Parks. Their children were Anne and Ben. Betsy earned a doctorate degree in historic architecture and worked in this field. Tom married Susan Tonnemaker. His business career was mainly with Pillsbury/General Mills. They were the parents of Ross, Emily and Mitchell. Laura was a family physician and married businessman Hank Kuhlman. Their two daughters were Caroline and Margaret. Carrie taught junior high students with learning disabilities before earning a master of divinity and marriage and family counseling degrees from Louisville Seminary and working at a family crisis center. Martha married businessman Jim West. Their children were James and Maren. Martha volunteered at her children's schools and was involved with Bible Study Groups.

Janet's parents were C. Ross Gale Stewart and Ellen Carrie Jensen. Both were born in Iowa. Ellen Jensen's parents emigrated from Denmark as children. Mr. Stewart's father was born in Ontario of parents who emigrated from Ireland. His mother's line can be traced back to Richard Warren, who came to this country on the Mayflower, through her parents, Moses Ingersoll and Susan Decker.

The original patent for the land was received from President James K. Polk. The Robert T. Shaw family built the house in the 1920s. Hunters acquired the farm from Guy and Stella Boggs.

JOHN C. AND ETHEL JACKSON HUSTON - John C., son of Ira and Naomi Cochran Huston, was born in Warren County on May 15, 1921. He attended Sisson and Parker grade schools in Point Pleasant Township. Graduating from Roseville High School in 1939, he attended Iowa State University for two years. In 1942 he joined the Navy and served on a sub-chaser that was attached to the Hawaiian Sea Frontier for two and a half years.

After the war he joined his father in farming. In 1954 he married his high school classmate, Ethel Jackson, the daughter of Earl and Blanche Schoonover Jackson. During the war she had worked with the Rationing Board. Afterwards, she became the office assistant of Dr. Russell Jensen in Monmouth where she acquired some basic medical skills and thoroughly enjoyed working with the patients.

They were blesse with four children: David, Susan, Michael and Linda. David has become a veterinarian with a practice in Bushnell. He married Suzanne Drexel, and their son is named Mark.

Susan married Rick McWhorter and works for State Farm Insurance in Bloomington, Illinois. Rick is a representative for self-guided laser systems. They have a son, Joshua, and a daughter, Christina.

Michael Lee, a psychologist, has his own private psychiatric clinic and lives in New Windsor, Iowa. Deborah Hutchins, his wife, is a school social worker. Their children are Brad, Tina and Emma.

Linda, married to Michael McConnaughay, works as a research associate with marketing the health program for Governor State University. Michael works for the Federal Reserve in Chicago. Their children are Ryan and Melissa.

GEORGE AND LENA HUTCHINS - William Lewis Hutchins and Lillie Boozel lived near Bushnell, Illinois, when their son, George Lewis, was born 11-8-185. His great-great grandfather was George Washington Boozel from Pennsylvania. Their three other children were Glen (Grace), Bushnell; Elizabeth (William Worthington), Bushnell; and Cleo (Edgar Forrester), Memphis, Missouri. They remembered fox-hunting in Missouri with Edgar's hounds.

Lena (Moore) Hutchins and George Lewis Hutchins, 1975.

George and Lena were married 65 years. He died 10-5-1983; she died 5-18-1990; both are buried in Roseville Memorial Cemetery. Lena Flo Moore was born 3-17-1898; her parents were Paxton Moore and Fannie Richard. Twelve girls and one boy were in the family: Louetta, Maggie, Lewis, Nellie, Nora, Daisy, Annie, Lottie, Ruby, Lucy, Lena, Eunice and Isabel. Lena was appointed the "ironer" for the family. She was also known for her canning, culinary skills, sewing and knitting. She made many quilts and handwork items now treasured by her family. Their five children were Harry, Vera Harriet, Raymond Ray, Max J. and Inez Lenore. Harry died in 1938.

The family farmed near Bushnell until 1929. They moved to Warren County and operated the Ellison Township farm of C.F. Godfrey, three miles northwest of Roseville. When George retired, he worked as a carpenter with Francis Perdue. He enjoyed fishing, card-playing with Clifford A., Clifford H., and Murphy Ross, barn dances and practical jokes (on himself and others). He was a well-respected farmer. It was a challenge for him to invent small useful items. He rebuilt an old elevator so ear corn could be lifted into cribs.

Lena was a hardworking wife and mother. Home-butchered meat was processed and cured to hang in the smoke room. Gallons of pickles, kraut, vegetables and fruits were preserved. Chickens were sent in crates by train to Chicago. Eggs and cream were sold locally. She was a cook for many years in the Roseville National Cafe. She enjoyed her friends in the Ellison Sewing Circle and loved flowers. They were members of the Roseville Christian Church. Family reunions were special days. After retiring, she did ceramic painting.

Their children attended Rayburn School with the Mills, Norvilles, Markleys, Yocums, Howells and Pearl and Henry Schisler families.

Their "tormented" teachers were Sarah Graham, Bruce Leaverton, Kyle Milligan and Fern Romine.

In 2002 Raymond (wife Avis Lawhorn) lived in Roseville, Illinois; Vera (deceased husbands Ernie Crummer and Henry Utescher) lived in Carthage, Tennessee; Max (wife Mildred Tribble; first wife was Ruth Reed) lived in Sterling, Illinois; and Inez (husband Harold Kline deceased 1990) lived in Macomb, Illinois. The fifteen grandchildren were William, John and Kathryn Hutchins; Sharron, Arthur, Samuel, Richard, Jerry and George Crummer; Charles, Ellen and Nancy Hutchins; and Cynthia, James and Ronald Kline.

Ancestors of the Hutchins-Moore families originally emigrated from Germany, Austria, Holland, England, Ireland and Scotland. They represented many families and vocations. The Biebers from Germany changed the name to Beaver in Pennsylvania. Phoebe Beaver died in Pennsylvania when 104 years old. The families gradually moved overland and by rivers to Ohio, Kentucky, Tennessee, Indiana, Illinois and westward. They had strong, honest work ethics. They were fiercely loyal to one another and to their Haven of Opportunity – AMERICA. *Submitted by Avis L. Hutchins.*

JOHN H. AND JOYCE HUTCHINS - It was a snowy morning when Raymond and Avis Hutchins drove twelve treacherous miles to Monmouth for the birth of their scond son, John Howard, on 12-14-51. Impatient then as now, he barely waited for Dr. Icenogle. He was twenty-eight when he fell hard for Joyce Ann Cook. They were married in the Bishop Hill Old Colony Church 7-19-1980. He graduated- from Roseville High School in 1968; she graduated from Avon High school, 1969, and Illinois Wesleyan College, Bloomington, Illinois. Everett and Bertha (Hart) Cook had five children: Richard, Jeanne (Morrison), Julia (Williamson), Joyce (Hutchins) and David Cook.

John and Joyce Hutchins, Jon Kenton and Erin Elizabeth, May 1987.

John and his brother custom-farmed ten years. Bill was married, with three children, so John sold his business share to him. He decided there was money and excitement on the river towboats! He and his best friend, Leo Ramer, a fantastically gifted musician, did "house-sitting" for vacationing older friends. John bought a house in Monmouth, Illinois, where they and Leo's mother lived.

His initial towboat experience was in April 1979. A small boat, the *Tennessee*, was headed for St. Paul on the flooding Mississippi River and needed another deckhand immediately. What an initiation for that young man who, as a child, was afraid of the water! Over the years he traveled the Illinois, Ohio, Tennessee and Mississippi Rivers. After his marriage, he transferred to the lower Mississippi River route for year-round work (no winter ice there). They bought Dr. Bagge's house in Avon, Illinois, in 1987. As their children grew, they accepted the celebrations of birthdays and holidays "when Daddy was home." Those first few years were difficult for everyone. John's schedule was usually four weeks away and four weeks home; usually something broke or someone was injured the day after he left!

Joyce came from a very musical family and taught music privately and in schools. Their red-haired children were Jon Kenton, born 9-12-81, and Erin Elizabeth, 6-11-83, both in Galesburg, Illinois. All used their talents for school, church and community and were active members of the Avon Methodist Church. Jon was a pianist, organist and drummer; he graduated from Avon High School in 1999. He enlisted in the Army for two years, then remained in the National Guard while working with construction crews. Erin never met an instrument she didn't like, but excelled in piano, oboe, bassoon and organ. She graduated from Warren High School in 2001. She attended Carl Sandburg College, working part-time giving music lessons and was organist for area churches. She did beautiful craftwork.

John worked for several barge lines over the years. One of his happiest moments was to be appointed captain of AEP-MEMCO's newest eight-million-dollar towboat, the *Joy Anne Keller*, in 1999. The one favor he asked of the company's president was permission for his parents to take a one-week cruise from St. Louis to Baton Rouge. What a wonderful adventure they had as they rode the river together!

John and Joyce taught their children the pleasures of family togetherness, hunting, music and reading. They all discovered that "absence does make the heart grow fonder," but it took a loving, cooperative family to prove it. *Submitted by Avis Hutchins.*

RAYMOND R. AND AVIS HUTCHINS - The essay in the hometown paper brought wistful memories to the lonesome sailor stationed in Hawaii. There were memories of crisp days trapping along the creek in Ellison Township. He could visualize again those cold mornings running his traplines. How could a girl know so much about those things? He vaguely knew the brothers of the young high school girl who had written the story. He sat down and began a short letter.

Hutchins family, September 2, 1968: John, 16 years, 9 months; Bill, 19 years, 2 months; Avis, 41 years, 3 months; Kathy, 9 years, 10 months; Raymond, 46 years, 11 1/2 months. They resided at R#2 Roseville, Illinois, on the Fred M. Johnson farm.

Raymond Ray Hutchins, born 9-16-1921, New Philadelphia, Illinois, was the son of George Lewis and Lena (Moore) Hutchins. His parents and five youngsters moved to the C.F. Godfrey farm in Ellison Township, Warren County, in 1929. The children were Harry, Vera, Raymond, Max and Inez. They walked each day to Rayburn School, 1 1/2 miles. Chores had to be completed before and after school, despite the weather. He was a Metalsmith in the U.S. Navy from 1942-1946, repairing damaged airplanes brought to their base in Hawaii. He returned home and farmed with his father.

Avis Amner Lawhorn was the only daughter of Albert and Alma (Lewallen) Lawhorn. She was born 5-9-1927, at Glen Mary, Tennessee. Dohy and Roger, older brothers, avoided her as a "tattle-tale." The younger ones, Buck and Odell, avoided her so she couldn't "boss them." However, their ties of love were never broken until death slipped in. The family had moved to Illinois in 1930 – THE GREAT DEPRESSION. Thoughts of the past made them realize that what they did without wasn't as important as their togetherness. They all attended Taylor School. Lena Belle Brewer was her favorite teacher; Mildred Tinsman encouraged her love of music. She was a 4-H member, winning many ribbons and was a State Fair delegate. How excited she and Louise Beachler were! The family had an antique pump organ, and she played it. Unable to reach the pedals and keys at the same time, her younger brothers were 'encouraged' (bribed was more like it!) to pump while she happily played.

Their wedding, 6-13-1948, was the culmination of that high school essay! The wedding and reception were in the historic Roseville Baptist Church, with her best friend, Evelyn Corzatt (Shimmin) as bridesmaid, and Max Hutchins as best man.

The newlyweds moved in January to the Roseville Township farm of Fred and Ethel Johnson and lived there thirty-eight years. In 1976 they purchased 80 rolling acres nearby. Raymond immediately hand-set 500 black walnut seedlings and established two bird sanctuaries. Their squirrels were the fattest in the county!

They were the proud parents of William Ray, born 6-28-49, during hay season; John Howard, born on a snowy day, 12-14-1951; David Lee, stillborn 11-30-53; and their adopted daughter, Kathryn Jean, born 10-31-58. She was welcomed into their home 6-19-61, an anniversary gift.

Their pleasures in life included their church, Historical Society, Eldridge Park, Farm Bureau, Home Extension, Garden club, their friends and gardening. They loved their three children and four exceptional grandchildren. Their home was shared with others: a niece one year, two foster sons another year, and "fresh-air" children from Chicago two years. They called their beautiful yard of flowers, trees and birds their "therapy." Many visitors stopped for a look.

They purchased a home in Roseville in 1986 and completely remodelled it. They retired from the farm and moved to Roseville in February 1987.

Their motto was: "DON'T COUNT YOUR YEARS; MAKE YOUR YEARS COUNT!" They always felt truly blessed. *Submitted by Avis L. Hutchins.*

REV. KATHRYN J. HUTCHINS - Her brothers thought of her as the Halloween pumpkin, or the wicked witch, because she was born on Halloween, 10-31-58, in Kewanee, Illinois. The whole family - mother, father, two brothers – lovingly welcomed this two-and-one-half year-old adopted daughter into their circle of love. As a blue-eyed, blonde, she fit perfectly into their family. They had waited ten years for this event!

Kathryn Joan Hutchins, December 1991

Kathy attended Roseville Elementary School and High School, graduating in 1976. She worked at various summer jobs, including Happy Joe's Pizza, Formfit, detasseling corn and walking beans, to earn spending money.

She attended Augustana College, Rock Island, Illinois, and graduated with a B.A. degree in Education. She taught Junior High sciences and coached basketball for a year. She assisted with youth at Galesburg's First Baptist Church and led the Worship service. They traveled to the Baptist World Youth Conference in Providence, Rhode Island. Later that summer she went home to inform her parents that she finally knew what she was to do, and arranged to attend Northern Baptist Theological Seminary in Lombard, Illinois. Her parents thought, "We've just got college paid off – now we're looking at another three years?" But they recognized the call to His service.

She received her Master of Divinity Degree in 1985, worked in the Batavia Baptist Church and awaited a call. She had always vowed not to live in a small town because of 'nosey neighbors,' lack of shopping and entertainment, boredom. So, where did God send her? To Thomson, Illinois, half the size of her hometown of Roseville!

What a blessing she became to those welcoming people. An elderly gentleman in her church admitted he was not in favor of a "woman – an unmarried one, at that, as their new pastor." But he came to love her as a daughter of God. The first crises came when a jealous teen bludgeoned his girlfriend to death. The young people crowded to her home for hours, for days, because she listened and comforted them. In a few years came a teen car-train collision – an accident? Again the young people looked to her for solace, as did other townspeople.

Soon she was asked to serve on the School Board, to be a substitute teacher in area schools and to build up the music department activities. The Cub Scouts needed a leader; she was in Rotary and the Women's Club, and worked on Thomson's famous Watermelon Days.

She was assistant manager and senior high counselor for the northern Illinois American Baptist Camp. She was on many church boards at the Springfield, Illinois, office of the Great Rivers Region Churches.

She was on the last S.C.A.T. team sponsored by NOVA to work at Ground Zero in New York City. As she brought home her hard-hat, she said it was a life-changing experience to give crises intervention help with the many firemen and construction workers still at the site. The few citizens who still came sought solace for their grief. Her words were "You just can't imagine how lucky you are here in the Midwest. God is good!"

Yes, God is good! He was especially good to let us share our lives with this young person. We, too, learned much from her. *Submitted by Avis L. Hutchins.*

WILLIAM R. AND SAUNDRA HUTCHINS - William Ray Hutchins was the oldest son of Raymond and Avis Hutchins. He was born 6-28-49, at Monmouth, Illinois. He married Saundra Lyn Griswold 7-25-71, in the Roseville Methodist Church. She was born 6-1-49, a daughter of Clark and Dorothy (Trummel) Griswold. They attended Roseville and Berwick area schools and Roseville High School. His siblings were John Howard, 12-14-51, and their adopted sister, Kathryn Jean, 10-31-58. The boys adored – and teased – their new two-year-old sister. For some reason she was frightened when their car crossed the old iron bridge into town. They finally lured her onto the bridge, tossing handsful of pebbles into the creek. That was fun! In a few moments her fears were forgotten. Saundra's family included Linda, Michael, Saundra, Marna and Melanie.

Hutchins family: Bill (32), Sandy (32), Steven Ray (3 1/2), Laura Jean (3 months) and Janet Lyn (4 1/2), September 1981.

Bill and John custom-farmed for area farmers for ten years. Bill went to Southern Illinois University at Carbondale for a computer course. He secured work with TSC, a new East Peoria company, and he became skilled at designing, installing and maintaining complex systems for large companies and factories.

Sandy was a computer programmer. After marriage, she became a full-time mother. They home-schooled their children through high school. Janet Lyn was born 3-15-1977, and died of a rare genetic disease – Hallervoorden-Spaatz – on 8-17-84. She was a bright and beautiful child. Stephen Ray was born 12-21-1978, and Laura Jean arrived 6-24-1981. All were born at Monmouth, Illinois.

Sandy became an accomplished long-distance runner and ran the Quad-Cities Bix Race. She became an excellent swimmer, and she, Steve and Laura earned Red Cross Lifesaving certificates. She taught many swim classes and coached several winning teams in Decatur, Springfield and Danville.

Both Bill and Sandy were active in the Riverside Baptist Church in Decatur, Illinois, where they lived. An excellent singer, he participated in many church services and programs. He also attended Judson College and the University of Illinois for a time.

He was a ham-radio operator. All computers were a challenge to him and his family. He had an extensive stamp collection. They collected, and used, castiron cookware, especially Griswold (what else!). As a boy, he trapped mink and muskrat in nearby Negro Creek. One especially fine mink was purchased from him by his Dad; it was sent to Paris, Illinois, and fashioned into a beautiful collar for his mother.

When he entered fifth grade he joined the school band. His mother decided she could now enjoy some long-coveted piano lessons. After her first lesson, Bill came home and started playing from her lesson book. He asked to play the piano rather than the baritone horn. Mother's first lesson was her last! He enjoyed the piano long after his eight years of lessons.

Steve and Laura tried part-time jobs and college. They eventually found their callings. They were a family that enjoyed being together, especially after the death of Janet. *Submitted by Avis L. Hutchins.*

JULIA ANN (YOUNG) HYNEK - Julia Ann (Young) Hynek, the only child of Otto Lee (1892-1981) and Lulu (Bond) (1893-1975) Young, was born September 9, 1927, in Macomb, Illinois. Her parents lived on a farm in Section 13 of Swan Townshipwhich they purchased after their marriage which took place in Knox County, January 14, 1914.

Julia Hynek, 2001

Julia attended Hoisington School all eight years of elementary school. She graduated from Prairie City High School in 1945. She also attended Western (WIU) in Macomb.

She married John F. Gunther in 1946, and to that union two children were born. Katrina Elaine was born in Warren County October 13, 1954. She married Jerry Brown and they live in San Francisco. Frederick Lee was born in Phoenix, Arizona, August 13, 1959. He married Marian Lynne Curtis. They have two daughters, Britney, born October 21, 1982, and Brooke, born September 19, 1987. They live in North Little Rock, Arkansas.

Julia worked in department and grocery stores. In 1966 she went to work for the Census Bureau as an interviewer, collecting statistical information for many branches of the government. She retired in 1989.

In 1990 she married Emil Hynek of Schuyler County, Illinois. He was a widower whose wife was Mary Jane Stevens. Her parents were Arthur and Minta (Simmons) Stevens. Emil was born in Saunders County, Nebraska, March 26, 1927, to Joseph and Antonio (Kalina) Hynek. He served in Koea with the 7th Calvary in 1951, where he was wounded. He has three children, David, Cynthia and Terry.

Julia is descended from two early Warren County families. Her Young family settled in Roseville Township on Section 36 in 1837. John Young (1811-1908), the immigrant, arrived in 1830 from Germany. He became a citizen while still in New York and he married CatherineEhrhardt there in 1835. Their children were John (died at 4 months), Mary, Julia, John F., Sally, Emily and George.

John F. (1842-1919) first married Caroline Simmons (1845-1876); their children were George, Lewis, Allen and Catherine. His second wife was Emma Drake (1858-1927). Their children were Anna (Kington and Mulberry), Pheobe (Kington), Frank, Ilena (Singleton), Charles and Otto.

Julia's Bond family came to Greenbush Township in the early 1830s. Jesse Walton (1774-1840) and Susannah (Crane) (1777-1859) Bond settled on Section 18. They previously lived in Tennessee and Alabama. They had seven children: John Crane (1799-1882), Benjamin (1802-1843), Joel C. (c. 1805-?), Ruby (Looney) (1808-1900), William Bamett (1810-1885), Jesse Walter (1814-1847) and Nathan Walker (1816-1889), all of which spent some time in Warren County. Ruby and Nathan moved to Oregon and William B. to Kansas. Benjamin, Joel and Jesse died fairly young, all leaving families. Julia is descended from Maj. John C. and his first wife, Mary "Polly" Grimsley. Their children were Susannah (Johnson) (1819-1902), Anna (?), William G. (1823-1892) and Jesse W. (1825-1905).

Susannah married Walter Johnson (1805-1876) and their daughter Catherine married John C. Bond Jr., whose parents were Jesse W. (brother of Susannah) and Sarah Ellen Terry (1832-1853), making Julia's grandparents first cousins. Their children were Arvie (1874-1948), Clarence (1877-1942), Jesse (1881-1971), Randall (1884-1944), Xanna (1887-1889), Fielding (1889-1931), Hanley (1891-1898) and Lulu.

HARLAN AND BARBARA (ADKISSON) JACOBSON - Barbara A. Jacobson, only daughter of Frank E. and Viola M. (Pinney) Adkisson, was born August 14, 1928, in Monmouth, Illinois. She attended rural Booth School and graduated from Roseville Township High School in 1946. Following two and one half years at Iowa State College, Ames, Iowa, she worked at E.B. Colwells for several years. In 1949 she married D.W. Mills. In 1976 she married Harlan E. Jacobson, born in Uehling, Nebraska, in 1929. He graduated from the Uehling Schools in 1946. Harlan served his country from 1951 to 1953 in the Army Seventh Division in Korea, serving on the front at the "Iron Triangle" and the historic "Pork Chop Hill". The majority of his Company was either wounded or killed in action. Following his honorable discharge, he attended school in Pueblo, Colorado, and subsequently became telegraph-teletype operator for the Illinois Central Railroad in Freeport, Illinois. In 1961 he became a Supervisor-Auditor for the Selective Service System until its demise in 1976. He then took over the family farm and later they purchased the adjoining Lloyd Adkisson farm, where he still actively farms.

Barbara has been a homemaker-chauffeur during her children's years in the Roseville school system. All five children graduated from

Roseville High School and either Western Illinois University, Southern Illinois University, Illinois State University or Eastern Illinois University.

Harlan (Jake) and Barbara (Adkisson) Jacobson

The children are Denise S. Mumma, teacher, Plymouth, Minnesota; Douglas Mills, agronimist, Avondale, Pennsylvania; Marriane M. Mills, supervisor, National Park Service, Interior, South Dakota; Jonathan W. Jacobson, supervisor, Caterpillar, Inc, Joliet, Illinois; and Matthew S. Jacobson, program specialist, University of Illinois, Champaign, Illinois. Among them are five masters degrees and one doctorate.

There are five grandchildren: Nicole Mumma, Emily Mumma, Ian Mills, Ryne Jacobson and Brooke Jacobson. All are attending schools in their respective states.

The Jacobsons belong to Roseville garden club, Telegraph association, Warren County Farm Bureau, Galesburg American Legion and the Macomb Veterans of Foreign Wars as well as the Wesley United Methodist Church in Macomb, Illinois.

WILLIAM JAMES - William James born 7 February 1913, married 4 December 1945 Mildred Sloss, two children: William inducted 1942 Scott Field, IL. Overseas January 1944, served England, Belgium, France and Germany, wounded in action in France, back to States at Fort Riley, Kansas, discharged 5 October 1945. Lives on own farm northwest of Monmouth.

Herman, born 11 March 1915, married 8 September 1937 to Lucille Hawk. 5 children. He died 6 April 1996. Farmer and cemetery sexton.

Egbert Edward, born 1 September 1917, married Catherine Coogan July 1943. She died October 1943. Married 6 October 1947 Ruby Smith. Inducted 5 March 1941 Camp Forrest, Tennessee, cook until May 1945 overseas February 1944 served Ireland, England,France, Grmany. Austria, Scotland, Wales, Belgium discharged 9 November 1945 Camp McCoy, Wisconsin. Died 24 April 1957.

Helen Arizona, born 2 November 1919, married 18 February 1942 Howard Hardin. 2 Children. She died 22 July 1985.

Gilmer, born 17 April 1922. (Separate biography) Laura Virginia, born 12 September 1924, married 3 July 1950 LaVerne McFate, 1 son. Died 21 November 1985.

Katherine Lee, born 30 July 1927, married 22 October 1949 Don Waterson. 2 children. Died 27 February 1994.

Last 5 children born Warren County, IL.

KENNETH JENKS - Kenneth Blaine Jenks was the oldest son in a family of seven boys and one girl of John Clifford and Ruth (Bruyn) Jenks. Upon his January 7, 1914, birth on the Lenox Township, Section 17, family farm, Ruth called her Hale Township friend, Emma J. Smith, to announce the arrival of her little boy. A few weeks later Ruth received a call from Emma stating she had a girl, Elsie Mae Smith, on January 28, 1914. Little did the two friends know their offspring would become high- school sweethearts and later marry!

Kenneth and Elsie Jenks

Kenneth and Elsie both attended Monmouth High School. After graduation Kenneth worked on the Santa Fe Railroad pipeline from Ft. Madison to Chicago while Elsie went on to Monmouth College's Teachers school. After their wedding of November 28, 1935, they moved into a small house in Section 8 owned by relatives just North of the Jenks family farm. About eight years later they set up house on the Smith homestead in Section 21, Hale Township with Elsie's parents, Fred Brown and Emma J. (Drake) Smith, where Kenneth began farming. Elsie began her teaching with a two-year certificate in a one-room schoolhouse located in Henderson County and then Hale Center School. She stopped teaching to raise a family. Three additions were added to the Jenks family: Frederick Clifford, November 1, 1941; Caroline Faye, June 25, 1945, who married William Ault; and Lynne Marie, December 16, 1947, who married Maurice Denison. The family was very active members of Fairview Center EUB Church and later at the Kirkwood Westminster United Presbyterian Church. 4-H was another activity that the Jenks family was involved with. Kenneth had been a member around six years of age in the first 4-H Club in Warren County that began about 1920. Mr. Jenks led the Hale Boosters 4-H Club for 17 years, while Elsie led the girls counterpart, the KB 4-H Club.

Kenneth was Hale Township Road Commissioner from 1963 to 1977. In 1971 the town hall caught on fire which contained a newly purchased $25,000 Caterpillar maintainer. Firemen decided the building was beyond saving and turned their attention to helping Mr. Jenks, who drove the maintainer out of the burning building. The only damage to the maintainer was to the windows which shattered from the extreme heat. Kenneth Jenks received burns to his hands from the steering wheel. This was not the first time the gentleman had exhibited such bravery. One Sunday while driving his family to church he noticed an orange glow in the distance and upon investigation found a house in full blaze. He charged into the burning house and pulled the male owner out who had been overcome by smoke.

After her children were born. Elsie returned to teaching for the Yorkwood District and attending Monmouth College as Illinois had passed a law that teachers must have a four-year degree. She graduated again from Monmouth College in 1972. She taught in the classroom until she was given the opportunity to utilize her artistic talent as an art teacher until her retirement. When the elementary art program was going to be cut, she offered to keep the program going and return as a full-time volunteer teacher. Elsie also worked with the Monmouth District's Young Authors program. In 1989 she received the Phi Delta Kappa WIU Chapter Excellence in Education Award for her commitment to providing youths with a fine arts education. She held offices in Warren County Retired Teachers, Monmouth College Crimson Clan and Warren County Republican Women of which she was awarded 1994 Woman of the Year.

Mr. and Mrs. Jenks, with three other couples, founded the Old Sleepy Eye Collectors Club of America, Incorporated in 1976. They acquired quite a collection as Kenneth enjoyed following leads that resulted in the addition of many rare pieces to his pottery collection. Spending time with family and traveling were other favorite pastimes of the couple. Because of Kenneth's health, they moved to town, 101 North Sunnylane, in December of 1994. Kenneth died on November 21, 1998. Elsie died on November 18, 2000.

HANS AND CHRISTINA JENSEN - Hans and Christina Jensen married in 1919 and lived long lives and raised a family on a farm three miles north of Gerlaw.

Hans and Christina Jensen, married April 4, 1919.

Although they met in Warren County, they actually began their lives only a few miles apart on the Jutland Peninsula of Denmark.

Christina was the daughter of Jens and Gundar Jensen of Bredebro, a small village about 15 miles south of Ribe, Denmark. Hans was the son of Metla Marie and Christian Jensen and was born in Gredstedbro, only a few miles north of Ribe.

They both made the long and, no doubt, frightening journey to America. Christina traveled with her entire family - parents, sister Ingeborg and brothers Paul and Tommy - and arrived at Ellis Island in New York on March 8, 1912.

It is worth mentioning that the family nearly did not make it to the shores of America. Jens Jensen, who became known as John in America, purchased tickets for the family journey on the S.S. *Titanic*, due to sail in April 1912. As winter waned, however, the family grew impatient and decided to leave earlier. They exchanged the tickets for steerage passage on the S.S. *Mauritania*, due to sail from Liverpool, England. That impatience saved them from the passage aboard the ill- fated "unsinkable" Titanic.

Hans arrived at Ellis Island on February 28, 1913, also on the *Mauritania*. Unlike Christina, he left his entire family, including four sisters, behind in Denmark.

Christina's family settled in the Berwick area where other family members had already settled. Hans worked for an uncle who had immigrated earlier and owned the farm where Hans and Christina would eventually live.

The two raised four children on their farm. Raymond, Paul, Lorence and Marion (now Mrs. Lowell Gardner) – all attended school at Alexis and raised children themselves who also graduated from the Alexis High School.

Raymond and Kathryn Jensen raised three children: Greg, Ron and Susan. Paul and Florence Jensen raised Gary, Paula and Angela.

Lorence and Shirley Jensen had two children, Gail and Larry and Marion and Lowell Gardner raised Diane, David, Kristine and Kendra.

Hans Jensen passed away in 1981 following an accident on the farm. He was 86. Christina died in 1996, at the age of 98.

Raymond and Kathryn retired from farming and moved to Galesburg five years ago. The other children of Hans and Christina still reside in Warren County, as do some of the grandchildren.

Ron Jensen completed a circle in 1989 when he visited Denmark and met offspring of the sisters Hans had left behind when he moved to America.

In 1994, Raymond and Kathryn, too, visited Denmark, meeting cousins and visiting the boyhood home of Hans and the site of Christina's girlhood home. The original house had been torn down, but another had been built on the site.

In 1997, Hans Kristensen, a nephew of Hans Jensen, visited Illinois with his wife, Else. They met their American cousins and visited the family's homestead near Gerlaw.

It is also worth noting that the landscape of Warren County is very similar to that of the Denmark left behind by Hans and Christina Jensen nearly 100 years ago.

JACOB JEWELL - Jacob Jewell, b. 11-9-1814, d. 10-25-1898, was married 4-10-1843, to a widow, Julia Ann Brooks Harrison, b. 8-12-1814, d. 8-7-1906. Both are buried in Berwick. Jacob was born in Rome, New York, came to Warren County in 1839, and farmed in Lenox Township. He was the first of six generations to do so. He and Julia had six children who grew up: William Hardin, Charles, Henry Lemuel, Olive, Dudley and Emily. In 1858 or '59, Jacob built a new house which neighbors called "Jake Jewell's big house" because, at the time, it was the largest one between Berwick and Monmouth. In 1867 Jacob moved to Monmouth and the farming was carried on by his sons, particularly Charles and Henry Lemuel.

Charles Jewell, b. 12-17-1845, d. 4-1-1882, in an accident, was married 6-26-1871, to Hannah M. Townsend. They had five children: Olive, Merritt Schofield, Halsey Townsend, Frances and Emmet. Halsey married Frances Pinkerton. Teir only child, Martha, married John Hillen, who died in 1949; they had four daughters: Virginia, Hannah Jewell, Genevieve and Martha Joan. Martha then married James Strong. Part of the original home farm plus Jacob's "Big House," now remodeled, passed down through Martha to her daughters.

Henry L. and Lydia Crandall Jewell and family, September 21, 1921. L: to R: Back: Gertrude H. and Henry R. (Harry) Jewell, Harriet Jewell, Irma and Clyde Johnson, Olive Huey (family friend), Jewell Bake, Louis and Orpha Bake, Ivory Quinby III, and Margaret Quinby. Middle: Ralph D. Kyle Sr., Edith J. Kyle, Merle J. Kyle holding Robert (Bob) Kyle, Helen Jewell, Lydia A. C. and Henry L. Jewell, Inez J. and Ivory Quinby II. Front: William C. (Bill) and Ralph D. Kyle Jr., Richard H. (Dick) and Louis C. Jewell.

HenryLemuel (H.L.) Jewell, b. 5-19-1847, d. 2-23-1932, was married 9-14-1871, to Lydia Ann Crandall (b. 5-20-1854, d. 11-17-1933); both are buried in Berwick, Illinois. They had five children who grew up and married: Inez, Orpha, Irma, Henry Richard (Harry) and Edith Merle. A prosperous farmer and cattle feeder, he was also active in the public life of the county and served in the Illinois Legislature in 1907 and 1909, the 45th and 46th sessions. In 1907 he moved to Monmouth and his son, Harry, managed the farm. His youngest daughter, Merle, married Ralph D. Kyle and they farmed near by. Her oldest daughter, Edith Jewell, married Lawrence A. Miller and they too farmed in the county, as did their oldest son, Lawrence (Larry) A. Miller, Jr. (see below).

Henry Richard (Harry) Jewell, b. 5-31-1879, d. 8-21-1969, was married 8-14-1907, to Gertrude Dixon Henderson, b. 12-1-1880, d. 5-16-1962; both are buried in Berwick, Illinois. They had five children: Harriet Lee, Helen Gertrude, Richard Henry, Louis Charles and Paul Duncan. He farmed the Jewell place until 1953 when he moved to Monmouth and his son Louis took over the farm. Harry was active in many activities including being director of the local school board, a director of the National Bank of Monmouth, president of the Warren County Farm Bureau and president and manager of the Bi-County oil company.

Louis Charles Jewell, b. 3-16-1917, Warren County, Illinois, was married 12-9-1942, to Helen Ilene Stevens, b. 9-10-1920; they had two children and then divorced in May 1972. He then was married on 8-21-1972, to Jane Pearson Objartel. The farm was sold and they left Warren County. His children are Harry Richard and Janis Ilene. He operated the Jewell farm after his father moved to Monmouth. During WWII he was a 1st Lieutenant in the U.S. Army and served in the Pacific Theater.

Jacob Jewell has many living descendents, but most do not live in the county. His original "big house" and the farm on which it stands are presently owned by the daughters of Martha Jewell Hillen Strong. For many years it was operated by a great-great grandson of Jacob Jewell, Lawrence (Larry) A. Miller, Jr., b. 3-71935, d. 7-15-2001, married b-2-1958, to Judith Ann (Judy) Glenn, b. 4-23-1938. Larry specialized in raising sheep and hogs. He was president of the Warren County Pork Producers, president of the Illinois Lamb and Wool Producers, a board member of the National Sheep Producers Council, a member of the National Meat Board and was elected to the Agricultural Hall of Fame at Western Illinois University. The farm is presently operated by their second son, Craig L. Miller (adopted), b. 4-16-1974, married 5-1-1999 to Maura Denison, b. 3-18- 1975. Submitted by Lee Kyle.

JACOB JEWELL FARM - Jacob Jewell, then age 25 and a native of Rome, New York, came to Warren County Illinois, in 1839. He had bought land in the Militar Tract from a War of 1812 veteran who did not wish to be a pioneer. Eventually, his parents, Lemuel and Jane (Cole) Jewell, his five brothers and one sister all came to this area.

The Jewell Farm

In 1843 Jacob married Julia Ann Harrison, widowed daughter of Thomas and Betsy (Lee) Brooks who had brought their family from Kentucky a few years earlier. Besies Julia, there were Emily (m. Willis Riggs), William . (did not marry), Thompson (m. Harriett Ray), Mary Ann (m. Asa Capps), and Asenath (m. Andrew Simmons).

By 1860 Jacob and Julia had moved from their original cabin to a new large house nearby (now 1182-140th Avenue) with their children William (16), Charles (15), Henry (13), Olive (11), Emily (7) and two farm hands. Olive later married Charles Blackburn of Blackburn and Turnbull's Livery and Funeral business. Emily married Dr. W.S. Holliday. After her death in 1890, he remarried, and Mitchell Holliday, longtime mortician in Monmouth, was one of the "second family".

In 1880 Charles was living in the house with his wife Hannah, daughter of Aaron and Frances (Schofield) Townsend, natives of Putnam County, New York. The children were Olive Emily (8), Merritt Schofield (7), Halsey Townsend (5), Mary Frances (Fannie) (3) and Emmet Charles (2). Charles, the inventor of the knotting device used for a time on McCormick reapers, died in 1882. Then Jacob gave Hannah 80 acres of land for his grandchildren and she bought 80 more, so their farm was the E 1/2 of the W 1/2 of Section 24 in Lenox Township.

By 1910 Halsey lived there with his wife Frances, daughter of William M. and Martha

(Finley) Pinkerton, and their daughter Martha (7). Halsey bought out the shares of his brothers and sisters.

In 1930 Martha lived there with her husband John Hillen and their daughters, Virginia (4), Hannah Jewell (2 1/2) and Genevieve (less than a year old). They moved into Monmouth that fall, and Martha Joan was born the following year. John Hillen died in 1949. Several years later, Martha married James K. Strong of Keithsburg. She died in 1985.

Halsey had built a smaller house on the site of Jacob's original cabin and the large house was occupied by various families until after his death in 1958. Frances died in 1960, Larry and Judy (Glenn) Miller operated the farm for Martha. Larry, great grandson of Charles' brother Henry, remained there until his death in 2001. It is now occupied by Larry and Judy's younger son Craig, his wife Maura (Denison) and their two little girls Lindsay and Hana, and owned by Martha's surviving daughters Virginia (Mrs. Dean Carlson, Galesburg), Genevieve (Mrs. H.E. Hiett, Clinton, Iowa) and Joan (Mrs. George Beasley, Quincy).

Seven generations are reprsented in the Berwick Cemetery: Lemuel and Jane, Jacob and Julia, Charles and Hannah, and Halsey and Frances Jewell; Martha and John Hillen, Jewell Hillen Borstel, and Amy Eileen Hiett.

DR. MERRITT SCHOFIELD JEWELL - Dr. Merritt Schofield Jewell, optometrist, was named after his father, a medical doctor practicing in Little York who was the second son of Charles and Hannah Townsend Jewell. They had four children: Olive, Merritt, Halsey, Fannie and Emmet, all living near Little York. The Doctor loved to hunt and fish - thus, Little York. Merritt and Minnie had three sons: Blake, Merritt and Melville. He was probably born at Denny rather than the family farm at Berwick in October 1873. He graduated from the University of Louisville Medical School 1898. Minnie, a schoolteacher, met him practicing in Olena. She came from Burlington, Iowa. Jewell bought the medical practice of Dr. Browning in Little York.

Our subject graduated from Monmouth College, laying out a year as meat cutter at the local A&P. He was there during the "Big Depression", after which he entered military service. He was in the Military Police during WWII, serving in Europe. After his discharge, he entered Optometry School in Chicago. His first wife divorced him, and he had trouble getting a practice started, so returned to Monmouth as Meat Manager for Barnes Bros. Super Market. He became a Kiwanian and Mason (Monmouth Lodge #37) later, after returning to Optometry, when he married Louise, daughter of a family friend. He was rewarded with an excellent practice and eventually retired when Dr. Gary Distin bought his practice. He was an Elder in the United Presbyterian Church.

Brother Blake worked in New York City buying blood for local hospitals and living into his nineties. Brother Melville joined the Red Cross after graduating from Monmouth College, went Alaskan brown bear hunting in Alaska with Verne Barnes, and later married an Asian girl while working there. Cliff and Margaret Shafer, Masonic friends, looked after them when Louise lost her hearing and Merritt his eyesight.

Merritt was a self-made man very deserving of his reward. The American Legion and VFW colorguard fired bullets over his casket.

FRANK A. JOHNSON - Frank August Johnson was born May 15, 1869, in Odenski, Sweden. He arrived in the United States with his brother, Alfred, in the spring of 1890. His destination was Sioux City, Iowa, where he worked for the railroad. Later he moved to the Biggsville and Kirkwood areas. On February 24, 1897, Pastor August Johnson of the First Lutheran Church in Monmouth married Frank and Tekla Carolina Carlson. They remained members of the church and played an active role in the building of the present church.

Frank August Johnson family of Monmouth, early 1900s. (l. to r.) Frank, Elmer, Mildred, Bert and Tekla.

Frank and Tekla started farming on their own farm south of Biggsville, later moving on to a farm at Gladstone. They had three children: Bert Marcus, born April 25,1898; Elmer August, born December 7, 1902; and Mildred Christina, born July 7, 1905. In the spring of 1908 they purchased a farm southwest of Monmouth where they raised their family. All of the children attended schools in Monmouth, graduating from Monmouth High School. In 1936 Frank and Tekla moved to a forty-acre farm northwest of Monmouth. Their east orchard was home to numerous beehives and Frank became a honey farmer.

Bert M. Johnson graduated from Augustana College. Following ten years in the banking business in Kirkwood, he founded the Johnson Insurance Agency in Monmouth in 1931. Bert married Ida Swanson of Stronghurst in 1922. They had four children, Vincent, Kenneth, Carolyn (Sherman), and Wendell, seven grandchildren and eight great grandchildren. Kenneth, still residing in Monmouth, joined his father in the business after World War II and remained active in the insurance business and Monmouth community for over forty years.

Elmer married Gertrude Hull. Elmer attended barbering school and operated his own barbershop in Monmouth for forty years. They had one daughter, Marlene (Moulden), two grandchildren and two great grandchildren, all of whom continue to reside in Warren County.

Mildred attended business school in Peoria where she met and married Charles Geiger. They remained in the Peoria area until retiring to Tyler, Texas. At the age of 96, Mildred resides in the Monmouth nursing home.

Several of Frank and Tekla's descendants have graduated from Monmouth College with the promise of others to follow.

FRED AND BONNA JOHNSON - John Frederick Johnson and Bonna Jean Parrish were married on February 19, 1950, at First Lutheran Church in Monmouth by Rev. Gerald K. Johnson. Fred has farmed all his life, of which 38 years were spent southwest of Little York, Illinois. Born of this marriage were three children, Janice Marie (3-10-1952), Ronald Lynn (1-11-1955) and Larry Walter (7-26-1956). Janice has worked 22 years for Warren County. Ronald works for Gates Rubber Company in Eldon, Missouri. Larry and son reside in Little York. Our granddaughter, DeAnna is married to Mark McCurdy. Amber Goodwin, another granddaughter, is the 2001 Miss Warren County and was the 1999 Prime Beef Festival Princess.

Einar Johnson (1-26-1892) and his brother, Algot Johnson, left Norby, Sweden in 1911 on a ship to the United States. The trip took 30 days. Their uncle brought them to Galesburg, where they worked at the brickyard. Einar married Hilda Fredrickson (also from Sweden in 1913) on December 29, 1916, at First Lutheran Church. Both became U. S. citizens. Algot Johnson returned to Sweden (in 1917) and died two years later. Einar and Hilda had three children, Annie (1915, died 1927), Violet Evelyn (1917) and Frederick (1923). They lived in Eleanor, Illinois, on the Peterson, I.K. Bell and Sam Smith farms. Hilda died of a stroke in 1944. In 1952 Einar bought the Spence farm. Einar lived 10 years with Fred and Bonna, then in Monmouth for 10 years, and finally 7 1/2 in a nursing home. He died in 1973 at the age of 92. His daughter, Evelyn, died in Idaho in 1983. She was married to Rev. Karl Ladwig who had preceded her in death. Fred never knew his grandparents from Sweden.

Fred and Bonna Johnson

Bonna Jean Parrish was born August 7, 1928, to Jess Clarence and Marjorie Adeline (Smith) Parrish in Oquawka, Illinois, in her grandparents home.

On the Smith side, (George) Walter Smith and Myrtle Huss were married in 1908. Myrtle Huss had brothers Jim, Bill and Irey, all fishermen of Oquawka. Her father was John Huss who had served in the military. Walter had a steam engine and a sawmill in Oquawka. Six children were born to their marriage: Wilbur, Marjorie (3-15-1910), Freda, Ruth, Don and George. At age 10, Marjorie drove their car to school with five brothers and sisters in it. If they got stuck in the mud, they would leave the car and walk to school. After school her Dad, Walt, would bring the horse and pull the car out and on home they went. Walt's father, George Smith of England, farmed east of Oquawka. On his death in 1928 at age 82, his farm sold for $36.00 an acre.

On the Parrish side, Jess C. "Doc" Parrish was born 3-25-1907, in Gorin, Missouri. His mother died when he was 18 months old, leaving his father, Jess Lorenza Parrish, with five children. He received a job in Illinois working for a farmer who gave him a house, milk, eggs and a garden spot to raise food. Hazel, the oldest, cooked and washed for the family. All the children attended school.

Jess C. "Doc" Parrish married Marjorie Adeline Smith on September 20, 1926, in Burlington, Iowa. They resided in Oquawka with daughters Bonna Jean (8-7-1928) and Wynona Mae (4-11-1931). In the 21 years Bonna lived with her parents, they moved 18 times from places like Savanah, Illinois, to Burlington, Iowa, and finally to Monmouth (where they lived north of town on a fruit farm). Jess's brother, Lloyd Parrish, owned a 360-acre farm, which Doc inherited and farmed for five years. Due to health reasons the farm was sold in 1960. In later years Doc Parrish helped build the Scholtzhauer Home and ran the Oquawka Hotel for two years until making it into a home for 17 mentally handicapped women for 14 years. His wife, Marjorie, has been a lifelong caregiver to multiple people in her family. She also sewed quilts for over 100 people. Marjorie is 92 years old and still living in Oquawka.

JAMES AND SANDRA (NELSON) JOHNSON

James Joseph was born September 27, 1942, Monmouth, Illinois, the son of Marion and Winnifred (Downes) Johnson. His sister was Karen (Erlandson). He was married June 28, 1964,

Monmouth, Illinois, to Sandra Louise Nelson, born July 14, 1944, Galesburg, Illinois, daughter of Vail and Louise (Rask) Nelson. Her siblings were Judith, Ronald and Douglas.

Jim attended Tubbs, Coonville and Kirkwood schools, graduating in 1960. He graduated from Western Illinois University in 1964 with a B.S. in Education. He was a charter member of Alpha Gamma Rho fraternity. After graduation he began farming south of Kirkwood with his father. Jim's graduating high school class was the last to graduate from Kirkwood High School.

Sandy attended Maple Grove, Kirkwood, Roseville and Yorkwood schools, graduating in 1962. She attended Western Illinois University for two years.

Kristin Louise was born July 9, 1966, Monmouth, Illinois, and graduated from Yorkwood High School in 1984 where she was a cheerleader for the 1983 State Champion football team and a member of the National Honor Society. She attended Carl Sandburg College, Galesburg, Illinois. Kris is Unit Secretary for the Yorkwood School District and coaches cheerleading. She was married April 20, 1985, Kirkwood, Illinois, to Patrick Scott Repp, born May 14, 1963, Avon, Illinois, son of Richard and Shirley (Vernoy) Repp. Pat graduated from Avon High School in 1981, attended Carl Sandburg College and is owner of Pat Repp Attractions, L.L.C. and coaches basketball. Their children are Matthew Scott, born October 5, 1985, Monmouth, Illinois, and Adam Joseph, born August 25, 1988, Monmouth, Illinois.

Jeffery James was born June 26, 1969, Monmouth, Illinois, and graduated from Yorkwood High School in 1987 where he was a member of the 1983 State Champion (class 1A) football team. He graduated with an Associate Degree in Agriculture from Southeastern Junior College, Burlington, Iowa. He was married December 2, 1989, Kirkwood, Illinois, to Jill Marie Fredrickson, born January 12, 1969, Fort Polk, Louisiana, daughter of Mike and Pat (Madigan) Fredrickson. Jill graduated from Yorkwood High School in 1987 and from Robert Morris College, Carthage, Illinois, with an Associate Degree in Business. She worked for Modern Woodmen of America, Rock Island, Illinois, and now works at the Soda Works, Monmouth. Jeff farms with his dad and coaches basketball. Their children are Ryan Jeffery, born November 2, 1994, Galesburg, Illinois, and Natalie Louise Marie, born March 31, 1998, Galesburg, Illinois.

Jim and Sandy are both members of the Presbyterian Church, Kirkwood, Illinois. Matt, Adam, Ryan and Natalie are the sixth generation to be baptized in the Presbyterian Church of Kirkwood.

JIMMY ROGER AND MARY RUTH (DAMEWOOD) JOHNSON

Mary Ruth Damewood was born October 21, 1934, at Kirkwood, Illinois. She is the daughter of James Anderson and Lucille Virginia (Ketchum) Damewood. Her siblings are Doris Marie, William Arthur and James Franklin. She attended public schools in Warren County, graduating from Little York High School in 1953.

She married Jimmy Roger Johnson on 27 February 1955, in Roseville, Illinois. They have no children.

Mary Ruth and Jim Johnson

Jimmy Roger Johnson was born 25 February 1936, in Cave City, Kentucky. He is the son of Harry Ray and Annie Irene (Norman) Johnson. At the age of five he came to Illinois with his family, living in the Roseville, Illinois, area. His siblings are Delores (Johnson) Randolph (deceased), Gerald, Thomas, Riley and Joann (Johnson) Brown. He attended public schools in Warren County, graduating from Roseville High School in 1953.

They lived in Monmouth four years, Mary Ruth working at Gamble Skogmo and Jimmy working at Benner Tea Company. In February 1959 Jimmy was drafted by the U.S. Army, taking his basic training at Fort Leonard, Missouri, and serving the remaining time at Fort Campbell, Kentucky, and they lived at Clarksville, Tennessee. He was discharged in 1961, and they returned to Monmouth, living there until February 1962 when they moved to Dixon, Illinois. While living there, Jimmy worked at Borg Warner Automotive and Mary Ruth at City National Bank. In 1980 Jimmy was transferred by Borg Warner Automotive to Blytheville, Arkansas. He assumed the responsibility of Purchasing Supervisor and Production Control Manager. Mary Ruth worked at First National Bank and Presbyterian Christian Academy. In 1985 Jimmy was transferred to Borg Warner Automotive at Cary, North Carolina, as Manufacturing Manager. Mary Ruth worked at Austin Quality Foods as Payroll Clerk. They lived there until they retired in 1998. At that time they moved to Fairfield Glade (Crossville), Tennessee. They are currently living there and enjoying their retirement.

MARION AND WINNIFRED (DOWNES) JOHNSON

Marion Paul Johnson was born September 16, 1915, Kirkwood, Illinois, the son of Paul and Daisy (Ryner) Johnson. He had a brother, Kenneth (1922-1948). He was married at the home of her parents near Biggsville, Illinois, January 18, 1940, to Winnifred Irma Downes, born December 13, 1916, died November 29, 1987, Monmouth, Illinois, daughter of Loren and Eva (Jones) Downes. Her siblings were Thelma, Eugene, Eloise, Lorena and Marcia.

The Johnson home near Kirkwood.

Marion attended Columbia school and Kirkwood High School, graduating in 1933. He attended Western Illinois University. He started farming north of Galesburg in 1940, then moved southeast of Kirkwood in 1941 and, after his father's retirement, moved southwest of Kirkwood. This farm became a centennial farm in 1992, first being purchased by his grandfather J.O.F. Johnson. Marion was Farm Manager for the Palmer-Ricketts farms from 1967 to 1998. He started farming with horses at a cost of $100 a horse and $65 for a planter, and lived to the era of $275,000 for a combine.

Winnie attended Roseville, Crystal Lake, Grove Hill and graduated from Biggsville High School in 1934. She worked for the A.S.C. office in Stronghurst before she was married, and later was secretary of the Westminster United Presbyterian Church in Kirkwood. She loved playing golf and bowling.

Marion and Winnie were members of the United Presbyterian Church in Kirkwood, Illinois. Their children are James Joseph (see James and Sandra (Nelson) Johnson) and Karen Ann (see Stephen and Karen (Johnson) Erlandson).

RICHARD AND IRENE FRANCES (SMITH) JOHNSON

Irene Frances (Smith) Johnson, daughter of David (Clete) and Alice (Gertrude) Tierney Smith of Monmouth, Illinois, was born October 9, 1941, at St. Mary's Hospital in Galesburg, Illinois. Her siblings are Virginia G. (Smith) Greiner, Fairfield, Iowa, and three brothers, David R. Smith, Monmouth, Illinois, Earl L. Smith, Kirkwood, Illinois, and Allen Clete Smith, deceased at age of three months. She lived on a farm at the north end of G Street, and was a member of Immaculate Conception Catholic Church, where she attended Immaculate Conception, grades 1-3 and 5-8. Fourth grade the family moved to Wesleco, Texas, for the year, and then came back to Monmouth and lived on a farm northeast of Monmouth Park. Irene attended Monmouth High School for three years and graduated in the first class of Warren High School in 1959. She was Warren County's Prime Beef Festival Queen in 1959. She attended Western University in Macomb, Illinois, for three years and graduated in 1963 with a business degree from Marycrest College, Davenport, Iowa. On August 17, 1963, she married Richard L. Johnson, a farmer from Washington, Iowa. From this union there were three children. Richard Clete Johnson was born 7-10-1965, and married Toby Brummer from Council Bluffs, Iowa, 10-12-90. Their children are Bailey Nichole, b. 12-1-1993, Savana Elizabeth, b. 9-8-1997, and Nolan Porter, b. 3-17-2000). They reside in Ankeny, Iowa, where Rick is a computer system analyst for Principle Financial Group. Toby is a gymnastics teacher.

Michael Shane Johnson was born 10-25-1966, and married Jennifer Jo Davis from Clear Lake, Iowa, 5-4-1996. Their children are identical twin girls, Arin Morgan and Amy Jo, b. 6-8-2000. They reside in Clive, Iowa, where Michael is a Senior Consultant for America Media Corporation. Jennifer is a registered surgical nurse at Mercy Hospital in Des Moines, Iowa.

Jacqueline Jo Johnson married Shannon Messer of Fairfield, Iowa, 9-9-1989. Their children are Alexandrea Ray, b. 10-09-1991, and Abigail Renee, b. 8-3- 1994. Jacqueline later married Donald A. Kaska of Fairfield, Iowa, 8-19-2000. They reside in Fairfield, Iowa, where Jacqueline is Production and Key Account Manager at Frontline Graphics and Don is a crop and livestock farmer.

Irene and husband Richard moved to Winfield, Iowa, in 1971. Richard had both kidneys removed and was on a kidney machine at home for nine months. He received a kidney transplant in December 1972, and died on January 22, 1973. Irene went to work after her husband's death at Peoples State Bank in Winfield and has been there for 29 years. She lives at 104 Golf Circle, Winfield, Iowa.

ROGER H. JOHNSON - Roger was born December 4, 1930, in Monmouth, Illinois. He passed away February 7, 2000. His parents were Leslie C. and Hazel A. Palmburg Johnson. He had one brother, Herbert G. Johnson.

All his grandparents came from Sweden. His Grandma Hannah (Peterson) Palmburg came from Halmstad in Halland, Sweden, at the age of sixteen.

He attended Monmouth public grade schools, and Monmouth High School in Monmouth, Illinois, and Brown's Business College, Galesburg, Illinois.

He worked for Benner's and Kroger's grocery stores while in high school and worked for Dave McCrery in his drug store as soda jerk in the soda fountain.

Roger H. Johnson

He married Dolores L. Davis on June 11, 1950, at the Coldbrook Christian Church, Cameron, Illinois, by Rev. Charles Willey from Coldbrook and Pastor Gerald Johnson, First Lutheran Church, Monmouth, Illinois. They lived in Monmouth most of their married life.

They have two children, Linda (Todd) Hammond and James Johnson, and six grandchildren, Tracie and Lena Johnson and Mia, Nils, Emma and Elsa Hammond. Roger's great granddaughter, Keirstyn Johnson, was born after his death.

Roger served in the United States Army, 1951-1953, and in Korea with Second Battalion, Ninth Regiment, Second Infantry Division. He was awarded Korean Service Ribbons, with battle stars, Presidential Citation Ribbon, Combat Infantryman's Badge and Good Conduct Medal.

After serving in the army, he worked for the title company which later became the Bi-County Title Company, as Abstractor for Real Estate Titles.

In 1958 he was appointed Clerk of the Circuit Court and County Recorder. He then served as Clerk of the Circuit Court of Warren County for 32 years.

He graduated from the Institute for Court Management based in Denver, Colorado, and served as delegate at the ninth Judicial Circuit Convention.

He was in Illinois Association of Circuit Clerks and Recorders, Legislative Committee, Circuit Clerk Advisor, and Executive Committee of the Chief Judges Association on Judicial Reform.

In 1988 he was appointed as the Clerk of the Third District Appellate Court of Ottawa where he retired in 1992.

A member of the First Lutheran Church, Monmouth, Illinois, he sang in the Choir, was President of the Lutheran Churchmen, Congregational Secretary, Congregational Treasurer, a member of Church Council, Secretary of Church Council, Delegate to three Conference Conventions, Delegate to Constitutional Convention (Synod) and Chairman, Fiance Committee.

He was 5th Precinct Committeeman, a member of Warren County Republican Central Committee, President of Warren County Young Republican Club, and Vice President of Young Republican Organization State of Illinois. He was named outstanding Young Republican Club President of the State of Illinois.

He was a member of the Rotary Club of Monmouth for over 32 years, including many committee assignments as well as President during 1983-84. He was named a Paul Harris Fellow on May 3, 1997.

He played the bass drum in the Monmouth Municipal Band, was the Exchange Club Secretary in 1958, Chairman of the Warren County Red Cross Fund Drive, Campaign Chairman for the Warren County United Way, on the Publicity Committee for the Warren County YMCA Fund Drive, a member of the Monmouth Chamber of Commerce, a canvass worker for various charitable fund drives, and a member of the local American Legion Post.

His hobbies were woodworking and music, especially listening to organ and band music. He enjoyed being with his family.

He loved to watch the Chicago Cubs baseball games on TV and go see them at Wrigley Field. He was also a Chicago Bears football fan.

ROBERT LAVERNE AND ALICE LOUISE (HANNA) JOHNSTON - Alice Louise (Hanna) Johnston was the youngest child of Howard Landon Hanna and Elsie Evelyn (Armstrong) Hanna, farmers. She was born in the Gerlaw neighborhood on November 3, 1925.

Her brother Harold Raymond Hanna was born July 20, 1922.

Howard, Crystal, Alice and Robert

They attended Indian Grove Country School in Warren County and the Alexis Community High School. Harold graduated from Brown's Business School and Alice graduated from Monmouth College.

She married Robert Laverne Johnston October 2, 1948, who was a farmer and a Seabee in the Navy during World War II. He was the son of Bruce and Hazel (Witt) Johnston. His family lived near Burgess in Mercer County. To them six children were born: Irene, Ilene, Theodore, Maribel, Albert and Robert. When they attended school they moved to Alexis and later moved back to Burgess.

Alice taught Indian Grove School for three years. She taught rural music in twenty schools in Warren County and six in Mercer County. She ended her teaching career at the Yorkwood High School teaching English, speech and directing plays for 16 years.

To Robert and Alice was born Howard Floyd Johnston on February 24, 1951, and Crystal Ilene Johnston on December 26, 1953. Howard graduated from Illinois College in Jacksonville, Illinois. Crystal graduated from University of Nebraska School of Technical Agriculture. Howard is employed at Dick Blick's in Galesburg and Crystal is an employee of John Deere in Moline.

This family has lived on a farm at 353 210th Avenue for 53 years and is now at Sunset Road in Monmouth. Their church affiliation is with Sugar Tree Grove United Presbyterian, the oldest church in Warren County.

LOUISE PIERCE JONAS - Louise Pierce Jonas was born on September 20, 1920, at the Monmouth hospital to Jesse Carl Pierce and

Isabel Baldwin Pierce who resided at the Pierce farm in Roseville. She is a third generation Pierce in Warren County. The first was Amos Pierce, of New York, who moved to Warren County in 1834, establishing the Pierce farm one mile south of Greenbush. He built a sawmill; used as a station for the Underground Railroad during the Civil War, it was a refuge for the slaves on their way to Canada for freedom.

Louise Pierce Jonas and Paul Jonas family. Front: granddaughter Laura Bowers, grandson Westley Jonas, Louise Pierce Jonas, Paul Jonas and grandson Timothy Bowers. Back: daughter-in-law Kathy Jonas, daughter Pamela Jonas, son Michael Jonas, daughter Karen Jonas Bowers and son-in-law Stephen Bowers.

Louise's sister, Eunice Aline (1914-60) and brother, George Carlton (1909-1919), were born in Warren County and both attended the Pierce School. Aline also attended Roseville Elementary School. The family belonged to the Roseville Methodist Church. At age 6, her family moved from Roseville to Macomb, where she and Aline attended Western Illinois College Training School. Louise graduated from Macomb High School and was the first female student to receive an Illinois State Grant to attend Knox College in Galesburg, where she earned her Bachelor's degree in Art and Biology in 1944. After college she worked at Eli Lilly Research Institute in Indianapolis, Indiana, as a hematologist/medical research assistant. During the war, she worked in the Photography Department at the USO, teaching the soldiers to develop their film. In 1947, Louise returned to Macomb and worked at Standard Clinic as a medical technologist. She met Paul Jonas Jr., from St. Louis, Missouri, a medical technologist at St. Francis Hospital. They were married, December 30, 1948. After the birth of their first son, Paul David (1949-51), they moved to Scottsdale, Arizona, where Louise bore and raised three more children, Karen Yvonne (1951-), Pamela Louise (1954-) and Carl Michael (1955-). In addition to her responsibilities as wife and mother, she built a career as a medical technologist and was the head of the Urinalysis Department at St. Joseph's Hospital in Phoenix, Arizona, for 22 years, retiring in 1981. She and her family were members of the Scottsdale United Methodist Church, where both Louise and Paul served on various boards and committees. Louise's daughter, Karen, married Stephen Bowers in 1973, and they lived in Boulder, Colorado, for 12 years where they began their family, Timothy Paul (1979-) and Laura Diane (1981-), both students at the University of Arizona in Tucson. Karen and Stephen live in Chandler, Arizona. Her daughter, Pamela, lived in Texas and California, and now resides in Chandler. Michael married Kathy Rowe in 1983; they moved to St. Louis in 1989 and have a son, Westley Carl (1993-). After serving two years for the U.S. government in Germany, they now reside in St. Louis, Missouri. Louise's husband, Paul, passed away in 1998. She lives near her two daughters in Chandler, Arizona, remaining active in the UMW group at Dayspring United Methodist Church in Tempe, Arizona and with her music sorority Sigma Alpha Iota.

MARTHA A. KENDALL JONES - After having been a resident in Warren County for seventy-seven years, having come here in 1830, Mrs. Martha A. Jones died the evening of August 24, 1907, at her home, 222 North C Street. She had been failing rapidly for the preceding year, and the end was probably hastened by a fall about two months before when she dislocated a hip. She had lived in Warren County ever since the erection of the very first log cabins, and in Monmouth ever since there had been such a city. Her parents came here from Xenia, Ohio, on October 22, 1830, her father, John Kendall , settling in the vicinity of Sugar Tree Grove. She was born in Ohio on May 22, 1823, so was about 84 years old at the time of her passing.

Martha Kendall married Edward Jones April 27, 1848, in Monmouth. They had six children: Francis Edward Jones, born April 4, 1849, died December 7, 1877; John Jones, born August 12, 1852, died young; Edward Sumner Jones, born December 21, 1854, died September 24, 1877; Mary Carlene Jones, born September 23, 1856, died November 9, 1874; Christopher Young Jones, born July 13, 1859, single and living with his parents in 1900; and William Kendall Jones, born October 8, 1861, died young. *From Moffitt Book Volume 9 page 72.*

FRANCIS B. AND FLORENCE KANE - Francis B. Kane, the oldest child of Edmond and Alice Kane, was born in Monmouth, Illinois. His parents moved to the farm where Francis now lives in 1928; it was then owned by Eli Dixon. It was later owned by Dr. and Mrs. F.C. Winters.

Francis & Florence Kane

Francis attended Piper School and Roseville High School. His father passed away in 1949 and Francis took over the farming operation. He served in the U.S. Army and spent 18 months in Germany. His mother passed away in 1980.

After returning from service, he married Florence Thompson on February 23, 1957, at the Immaculate Conception Church in Monmouth, Illinois. Florence is the daughter of Rose and Roy Thompson and was one of nine children. Her parents have both passed away, Roy in 1974 and Rose in 1981. Florence attended Farmers Academy Grade School and Monmouth High School.

Francis and Florence live in Point Pleasant Township on the same farm as his parents did. They purchased the farm in 1975. This place has been farmed by three generations of Kanes for 70 years. Francis is a member of the Warren County Farm Bureau, St. Patrick's Catholic Church and the American Legion. Florence is a member of St. Patrick's Catholic Church, St. Patrick's Altar and Rosary Society and the Colfax Club. They are the parents of four children. Ed, who married Kelly Wagy, lives near Raritan. They have four children, Lindsey, a second-year student at Southeastern College in Burlington, Iowa; Kourtney, a junior at Southern High School; Matt, a sophomore at Southern High School; and Luke, a sixth grader at Southern school.

Mary married Stan Day and they live near Macomb. They have three children, twins Ryan and Brittany, are in sixth grade at St. Paul's School in Macomb, and Ashton, a fourth grader in the same school.

Bill married Jeanie Markham and they live southwest of Roseville. They are the parents of four sons, Nolan, a third grader; Jackson, a second grader; and Drew, kindergarten, all at Roseville Grade School. Reese was born February 13, 2002.

Connie married Rick Elting and they live at Little Swan Lake. They are the parents of four children and three of them attend Avon Grade School. Mitchell is in fifth grade; Hannah is in fourth grade; and, Nathan is in the second grade. Nicholas is 3 years old.

KELLY-BROWN - John Kelly, son of Owen and Jane (Gibb) Kelly, born in Ireland, came to the U.S. and worked on a farm, then was a bridge carpenter. He was killed in Kirkwood by railroad cars. He married Agnes Gibb.

Nancy Agnes Gibb was born in County Antrim, Ireland. A daughter of John and Hannah (Rea) Gibb and a granddaughter of James and Jane (Agnew) Rea. She and her sister Mary came to America and lived near Biggsville, Illinois.

John and Agnes Kelly lived in Gladstone and other small towns, then moved to Kirkwood, Illinois, where their younger children were born and raised. They had eleven children. Both John and Agnes are buried in the Center Grove Cemetery at Kirkwood. Hannah Rea Kelly was born May 1884, in Gladstone, Illinois. A graduate of Kirkwood High School, she taught school until she married Ralph Brown.

Ralph Morrison Brown was born July 1880, at Sugartree Grove near Monmouth, Illinois. He was the son of James and Rebecca (Morrison) Brown. He farmed near Kirkwood.

James Brown, 1825-1911, son of John and Ellen (Greenlee) Brown, was born in Ireland. He moved to America and served in Civil War. A member of the 83rd Illinois Regiment, B Company, he attended many of their reunions. He was married twice. After his first wife died in Ireland and after the war, he married Mrs. Rebecca Moore.

Rebecca Ewing (Morrison) Moore was the daughter of James and Rebecca (Ewing) Morrison. James Morrison was born in Ohio, son of Robert and Mary (Mitchell) Morrison and a grandson of John and Nancy (DeScregges) Morrison. Mary Mitchell was the daughter of Gavin and Sarah (Matthews) Mitchell.

Ralph and Hannah (Kelly) Brown are buried at Fairfield, Iowa. They had nine children; six are still living.

OSCAR NEWTON KENAN - On March 27, 1843, Sandusky County, Ohio, welcomed the newest member to their community with the birth of Oscar Newton Kenan, son of Silas Kenan and Barbara Overmyer and next to the youngest of their eleven children.

Oscar N. Kenan and his wife, Margaret Ickes Kenan

Oscar Kenan spent the first 20 years of his life in Ohio until July 23, 1863, when he moved to Illinois and worked for the first three years as a farm laborer. Around 1867 the young man purchased his first team of horses, and began his own private farming career. Young Oscar made his residence during this time with his uncle, until December 23, 1869, when he married Margaret Ickes, the twenty-one year old daughter of Michael and Hannah Ickes of Bedford County, Pennsylvania.

The young couple took up housekeeping and raising their family in Warren County before purchasing their farm in the Floyd Township. Oscar and Margaret quickly started their family life together with the births of their five children: Eugene Chesney born February 9, 1872, Elba Corene born February 20, 1876, Royal Ickes born February 27, 1879, Dennis Ward born September 16, 1883, and Walter Ross born April 29, 1886.

The Kenan family remained in the Floyd community until the spring of 1913, when they decided to retire from an active social and business life and moved to Cameron. During his life in Cameron, Oscar was very active in his community ñ he was one of the directors and founders of the Cameron State Bank, and served as one of the trustees of the Silent Home Cemetery for many years. Though considered as an outstanding citizen in his community, and known for his honesty and high integrity, Oscar never sought public office ñ not as a private citizen nor as a Republican.

Throughout his life, Oscar Kenan continued to show his knowledge and appreciation of fertile farming property, and at the time of his death was the property owner of 300 acres of some of the most prime farming property in the Cameron region.

Surrounded by his family and loved ones, on a Saturday afternoon, January 8, 1918, at 4:20 p.m., Oscar Kenan passed away after a long illness. His health had been failing during the past six years, and finally forced him to his bed during his last five weeks of life. Leaving his devoted and beloved wife of nearly 50 years, his five grown children, seven grandchildren, and two sisters, Mrs. Mahala Eldridge residing in Kendallville, Indiana, and Mrs. Minerva Jackson residing in Fremont, Ohio, Oscar was laid to rest in Silent Home Cemetery in Cameron, Warren County, Illinois.

Almost 17 years to the date of his death, Margaret Kenan joined her husband upon her death on January 9, 1935, and was buried beside Oscar in Silent Home Cemetery.

Oscar Newton Kenan will be remembered by his descendents as a loyal and loving husband and father, as well as a man of high morale character to his friends and people in his community.

FRANCIS BEVERIDGE KENDALL - Francis B. Kendall, son of John and Elizabeth Gibson Kendall, was a farmer. He was born in Warren County, Illinois, October 6, 1838. He owned 150 acres of land, in section 16, was a democrat, and belonged to the United Presbyterian Church. He married Sarah J. Gardner in 1858. She was born in Kentucky, and died November 6, 1875. They had five children: John Thomas, Clark, Roland Augustus, Alice Alure and Clara Mabel.

His second wife was Agnes Patterson, who he married March 8, 1877. They had two children: Francis Beveridge Kendall, born 1787, died 1821, married Maude Hoon; and Elizabeth "Bessie" Kendall, born 1892.

From the Moffit Book 10, page 38, "Bev" Kendall Gone: Francis Beveridge Kendall, better known as "Bev," died at his home on North F Street, October 8, 1908, after a short ilness from heart failure. Mr. Kendall was born three miles northeast of Monmouth in October of 1838, so was just seventy years ofage. He had lived in Monmouth for sixteen years. In 1858 he married Sarah Gardner of Kentucky, who died in 1875, and to them were born five children, only two of whom survive him. There were Mrs. G. Hotelling of Gerlaw and John T. Kendall of Oklahoma City. He was married the second time to Agnes Patterson and she bore him two children, Mrs. Bessie Allen and Frank Kendall, both of Monmouth. Mr. Kendall had been quite prominent in this city because of his numerous inventions. Among those especially worthy of mention were a patent corn planter, a double row corn shocker and a disk harrow. His burial was in Monmouth Cemetery. The children of Francis B. Kendall were Francis Beveridge Kendall Jr., also known as "Hinckle." He married Maude Hoon, 1905. He served as a fireman in Monmouth. Elizabeth Kendall, born 1880, married 1896 to Charles Henry Allen and had children Charles Albert Allen, born 1897 and died in 1899, and Earlest Carl Allen, born 1898. Alice Alure Kendall, born 1858, Knox County, Illinois, married 1886 to Arthur G. Hotelling. The three Hotelling children were Vera May, Hazel Irene and Arnold Milton. Clara Mabel Kendall, born 1892, married Lewis E. McIntyre. She died 189. *The source for this data is the 1877 History of Warren County, IL.*

FRANK KENDALL - Frank Kendall, known to his friends as "Hinkle," died Sunday evening at his home, 232 C Street, following along period of ill health. His death was due to a general breaking down and was not unlooked for. Mr. Kendall had been at the hospital or treatment of a broken knee cap, which he suffered in a fall about a month ago, but returned home about a week before his death.

For a number of years, Mr. Kendall was a member of the fire department and after leaving the city employ, was with Martin Motor Co. In both places, he gained a wide acquaintance and his friends will join the relatives in mourning his death.

Mr. Kendall was born in this city in 1878, the son of (Francis) Beveridge Kendall. On November 16, 1905, he was united in marriage to Miss Maude Hoon, who survives him. His mother, one sister, Mrs. Harry McLoskey of Rock Island, a brother John of Wyoming and a half sister, Mrs. Arthur Hotelling of Gerlaw.

The funeral will be held at his home tomorrow afternoon, with Dr. W.H. Craine of the First Methodist Church in charge.

His sister, Elizabeth Kendall, born October 4, 1880, married Charles Henry Allen.

Alice Alura Kendall married 1886 to Arthur G. Hotelling. Their children are Verna May, born 1892, Hazel Irene, born 1895, Arnld Milton Hotelling, born 1897.

His sister, Clara Mabel Kendall, married 1892 to Lewis E. McIntyre. *Source: Gibson Genealogy.*

JOHN AND ELIZABETH (GIBSON) KENDALL - A small group of Presbyterians, which had migrated from Pennsylvania to Xenia, Ohio, located in Warren County. October 22, 1830, John and Elizabeth Gibson Kendall arrived in Monmouth. Not until 1831, was Monmouth laid out and named. The Kendall and Gibson families had the contract to build the courthouse in Monmouth. John Kendall, or his brother, Robert Kendall, built the first cabin in the Sugar Tree Grove area of Monmouth. (From family data.)

John Kendall, b. January 2, 1795, in Pennsylvania, d. April 6, 1877, in Illinois. Elizabeth Gibson Kendall, 1797-1882

The day the courthouse was raised, Ann (Kendall), Elizabeth and Mrs. John Kendall cooked the dinner at Robert Kendall's home. He had come to Monmouth earlier, and had the only cabin in that section with a fireplace, stone hearth, back walls with jam stones. Here the Kendall women cooked the dinner and carried it one mile to the workmen at the courthouse, where it was spread out on the prairie grass. The meal consisted of pork, beef, cabbage, loaves of bread, biscuits, maple syrup, honey, applebutter, pickles, custard, sugar, coffee and tea. This had all been brought by covered wagon. Reportedly, it was the first meal eaten in Monmouth.

Hardships were many that following year. The flour they brought with them was consumed long before wheat could be planted.

John Kendall was a carpenter and farmer. He bought a farm 2 1/2 miles northeast of Monmouth. Soon after, he moved to the southeast quarter of Section 16, Monmouth Township. He served in the Black Hawk War.

The Kendalls, John and Elizabeth, were among the parties who organized the Henderson Congregation, now the Sugar Tree Grove United

Presbyterian Church. It has been recorded that they also were the largest donors to Monmouth College and to the construction of churches in Monmouth.

In 1860 John and Elizabeth Kendall moved to Monmouth City to reside with their eldest daughter, Mrs. Martha Kendall Jones. John Kendall was walking in his garden when he died of a stroke on April 7, 1877. His obituary reported, "He was a man of modest and retiring disposition and did not seek, but rather shunned anything that would give him prominence in his neighborhood."

Jhn Kendall was born January 2, 1795, near Big Cove, Bedford County, Pennsylvania, to Francis and Jane Gibson Kendall. His wife, Elizabeth Gibson, was the daughter of Thomas and Martha Hogg/Hogue Gibson, who also resided in Monmouth. Elizabeth Gibson Kendall died August 15, 1882. Both are buried in Sugar Tree Grove Cemetery. John and Elizabeth Kendall had seven children: Jane, born 1820 and died 1822; Martha Anne, born 1823 and died 1907; Mary Isabel, born 1825 and died 1837; Margaret Kendall, born 1829 and died 1842; Sarah Kendall, born 1835 and died 1862; Thomas B. Kendall, born 1837 and died after 1850; and Francis Beveridge Kendall, born 1838 and died 1908 (see biography). The first four children were born in Xenia, Ohio, and the last three in Monmouth.

JOSEPH WILSON KENDALL - Joseph Wilson (Wilson) Kendall was born on January 14, 1806, in Greene County, Ohio, the fifth son of William Kendall and Janet Linn, natives of Air Township, Bedford County, Pennsylvania, who had come to Ohio in 1805 after living in Scott County, Kentucky, for a number of years. They were part of the Associate Presbyterian migration from the latter state because of their opposition to slavery. Wilson was married to Amanda Steele (daughter of James Steele and Elizabeth Peck) on September 6, 1828, in Greene County, Ohio. In 1831 Mr. Kendall, other Kendall family, his brother-in-law James Gibson, and other Gibson family all moved to Warren County, Illinois. They were among the first settlers in the county. Wilson built a sawmill on Ellison creek. He served on the first Circuit Court Grand Jury in June of 1832, along with his brother-in-law James Gibson, Samual Gibson and their father, Thomas Gibson, Sr. In 1836 the first organized church in Olena township was the Associate (Seceder) Presbyterian. Mr. Kendall was installed as a ruling elder of the congregation.

Six children were born to Wilson and Amanda Kendall in Olena township, William L., Mary A., James B., Francis S., Rachel J., and Joseph L. The last two were technically born in Henderson County with its formation in 1841. Following a short illness, Mrs. Kendall passed away in July 1849, at the age of 37. On Sept 18, 1850, Mr. Kendall married Mrs. Mary Josephine Robertson Carothers, a neighbor and widow of Andrew Carothers. She was born in Ohio in 1818, and had three young children, James, Mathew and Martha. In the spring of 1853, Wilson and Mary, with eight of their combined children, crossed the plains to Linn County, Oregon, where they took up a land claim in the new territory. The oldest son, William L., followed them the next year, taking up a claim in Linn County near his father. Once settled in Oregon, J.W. and Mary had three more children, Arora, Argyle and Josephine. Mrs. Kendall died in 1889, and Mr. Kendall in 1891, both having been true pioneers. *Prepared 19 December 2001 by great-great grandson Mike Sweeney.*

ROBERT KENDALL - Robert Kendall, brother of John Kendall, was born April 10, 1801, in Bedford County, Pennsylvania, and died January 17, 1882, in Monmouth, Illinois. His life mate was Ann R. McNair, whom he married in 1829. Their children were Clark A. Kendall, born 1824 in Pennsylvania and died February 17, 1862 at Ft. Donelson, Tennessee; David M. Kendall, born 1830 in Pennsylvania and died June 27, 1839; Francis Gibson Kendall, born 1834 in Pennsylvania; Margaret E., born 1834 in Pennsylvania, married Amos Burford and had sons Clark M., William K. and Frank A. Burford; and William E. Kendall, born 1837 in Pennsylvania and died 1858. Ann McNair Kendall died February 14, 1870, in Warren County.

Two other brothers of John and Robert Kendall resided for a time in Monmouth, Illinois. They were Francis Gibson Kendall, who married Jane E. Merrifield and moved to Iowa in 1833, and Andrew Kendall, who married Mary Jones and moved to Iowa in 1837-38.

DANIEL LYNN KEPPLE - Daniel Lynn Kepple was born 17 November 1954, in Macomb, Illinois, the second child of four of Donald Lee and Wanda LaRue Parrish Kepple. He grew up in the Greenbush, Illinois, area attending all 12 grades in Avon schools. He was active in 4-H, FFA and sports. Dan graduated from Western Illinois University and is a member of Alpha Gama Rho Fraternity. He met Linda while there.

Daniel, Linda, Matthew, Jacob and Kelly Kepple

Dan married Linda Mary Bodenbender at St. Stephens Church, Des Plaines, Illinois, 9 June1979. Linda was born 21 August 1957, in Chicago, Illinois, the older of two daughters of John Richard and Patricia Norene Brankin Bodenbender. She graduated from Main West High School in Des Plaines and Western Illinois University. She taught school and also founded, managed and taght at the Merry-Go-Round Pre-School in Avon for several years before the family moved to the Chicago area. She continued to offer day care in her home.

Kelly Patricia was born 4 November 1982, at Macomb, Illinois. Jacob Donald was born 8 April 1985, at Macomb, Illinois. Matthew John was born 2 August 1989, at Lake County, Illinois. The family was living in Lindenhurst, Illinois, when Linda passed away 17 August 1993, at her home from a malignant brain tumor. *By Kelly Kepple.*

DONALD KEPPLE - Donald Lee Kepple was born 8 October 1929, at Phelps Hospital in Macomb, Illinois, to Ghlee Walter and Dolly Kramer Kepple. Along with a twin brother, Ronald Ghlee, other children are Frederick William and Lena Geneva. He attended Holeman School until nine years of age. His parents divorced 5 May 1939. He lived with his father and attended Warren School District 112 from grades five through eight. In September 1943, he attended Avon High School and farmed with his brother.

Fiftieth wedding anniversary of Donald and Wanda Kepple, 27 November 1999. (l. to r.) Front: Daniel, Donald and Wanda Kepple; Brenda Boydstun. Middle: Jacob, Kelly, Pam and Matt Kepple; Whitney Tabb; Kara Kepple; Kristin and Teresa DeKeyrel; Amanda, Brandy and Terry Boydstun. Back: David and Brandon Kepple; Melanie and Ronald Tabb; Patrick, Danielle and Jim DeKeyrel.

Donald married Wanda La Rue Parrish 27 Nov 1949 in Adair Methodist Church. She is the oldest daughter of Marvin Oscar and Goldie Leah Hensley Parrish born 28 October 1931, in Adair. As an Air Force mechanic from 1951-1955, he was stationed in North Carolina, Massachusetts and Kansas. He spent from March 1954 to March 1955 in Korea. David Lee was born 30 April 1953, at the Otis Air Force Base, Buzzards Bay, Massachusetts, and Daniel Lynn was born 17 November 1954, in Macomb, Illinois.

Upon finishing his tour of duty, Donald and Wanda settled and farmed in the Greenbush area. Here, Brenda Lou, born 3 January 1956, in Monmouth, and Teresa Leah, born 1 August 1959, in Avon. All graduated from Avon high school.

David Lee was active in 4-H and FFA. He attended Western Illinois University and was a member of the Alpha Gamma Rho Fraternity. He married Lynn Ashley, 6 March 1976, in Abingdon.

Brandon Lee was born 17 July 1978, in Galesburg, and Kara Jennifer was born in Galesburg on 21 October 1980. David married Pamela Sue Sandberg Tabb on 28 May 1988, in Avon. She had Whitney Rebecca, born 17 May 1975, in Galesburg; Ronald Michael, born 14 September 1977, in Galesburg; and Melanie Jo, born 27 May 1981, in Galesburg. They live in Abingdon, Illinois.

Daniel was active in 4-H, FFA and sports. He graduated from Western Illinois University and was a member of Alpha Gamma Rho Fraternity. He married Linda Mary Bodenbender on 9 June 1979, in Des Plaines, Illinois. Kelly Patricia was born 4 November 1982, in Macomb; Jacob Donald was born 8 April 1985, in Macomb; and Matthew John was born 2 August 1989, in Lake County, Illinois. Linda passed away 17 August 1993, from a cancerous brain tumor. They live in Lindenhurst, Illinois.

Brenda was active in 4-H and Make It With Wool Contest, graduated from Patricia Stevens Career College in Milwaukee, Wisconsin, and Western Illinois University. She married Terry Eugene Boydstun on 5 March 1977 in Avon. Brandy Melissa was born 18 October 1981, in Galesburg and Amanda Marie was born 18 November 1984, in Mount Pleasant, Iowa. The family lives in Abingdon, Illinois.

Teresa was active in 4-H and was salutatorian of her high school class. She attended Western Illinois University where she met her husband, James Edward DeKeyrel, and was married 2 November 1980, in Avon. Patrick John was born 24 April 1981, in Dupage County; Danielle Mary was born 27 August 1986, in Dupage County; and Kristin Leah was born 27 August 1986, in Dupage County. They live in Carol Stream, Illinois.

Donald has been the Greenbush Township supervisor since 1982. He is active in Avon Harmony Lodge serving as Master and, in 1972, president of Galesburg El Bon Shrine Club. *By Wanda Kepple.*

GHLEE WALTER KEPPLE - Ghlee Walter Kepple was born December 4, 1892, in Marietta, the second of seven children of Samuel Walter and Maud Geneva Morey Kepple. He attended school in Bardolph. He was called to his country's service June 26, 1918. He was stationed initially at Camp Wheeler in Macon, Georgia. From there he served nine months at Camp Holabird, Baltimore, Maryland. On May 14, 1919, in Galesburg, Ghlee married Dolly Wilhelmina Kramer. Ghlee died on 5 June 1969, in Avon.

Aunt Manda Doll Burridge; Dolly, Ghlee, Donald, Ronald, Lena and Bill Kepple

Dolly graduated from Peoria High School and Western Illinois Normal in Macomb. She was a teacher in the public schools of Warren County before her marriage. She was born January 14, 1895, to Frederick William and Magdalena Doll Kramer in Greenbush. She lived in Monmouth 11 years, then with her daughter for two years. Dolly died June 26, 1967, in Avon.

They had four children. Frederick William was born on the 13 June 1924, in Macomb. Lena Geneva was born 26 February 1927, in Macomb. Donald Lee and Ronald Ghlee were born 8 October 1929, in Macomb. The family lived on a farm east of Greenbush for 15 years. The couple divorced 5 May 1939.

Ghlee and Donald moved to Knox County south of Galesburg. Donald attended Warren School District 112 from grade five through eight. Ghlee married Flo Babbitt Hass on the 23 December 1939. Flo died on the 22 December 1966. Ghlee married Elizabeth E. Ray June 30, 1968. Elizabeth died on the 3 June 1993.

After serving in World War II from March 1943 to December 1945, Frederick William returned to farming in Avon. He married Betty Lewis May 26, 1948, in Galesburg. They had three children. In Galesburg, Rebecca Jean was born January 21, 1951, and Debra Kay, December 16, 1952. Roger Ghlee was born on the January 3, 1954, in Avon.

Lena Geneva married Lawrence Edward Pepper on 7 July 1945, in Roseville. All five of Lena's children were born in Monmouth. Edward Allan was born on 16 April 1948. Michael Laverne was born on 1 August 1950. Sharon Marie was born on 1 December 1952. Karen Jean was born on 4 September 1954. Marvin Dale was born on 15 February 1961.

Donald Lee married Wanda La Rue Parrish on 27 November 1949, in Adair. They had four children. David Lee was born on 30 April 1953, in Cape Cod, Massachusetts. Daniel Lynn was born on 17 November 1954, in Macomb. Brenda Lou was born on 3 January 1956, in Monmouth. Teresa Leah was born on 1 August 1959, in Avon.

Ronald Ghlee married Deloris Vivian Eaton 15 October 1948, in Berwick. They have three children all born in Galesburg: Vivian Diane, February 21, 1951; Sheryl Lynn, October 19, 1952; and Ronald Dean, October 8, 1955.

All four of Ghlee and Dolly's children have celebrated their 50th wedding anniversaries together. *By Donald Kepple.*

DON AND MARCIA (SHORES) KESINGER - Don Edward Kesinger, youngest child of Ross and Lydia (Marks) Kesinger, was born December 24, 1919, in Wrights, Illinois. Don, brother Harvey (1916-2001) and sister Alma (1915-1993) were raised on a family farm in Wrights, largely by their mother Lydia (1879-1967), a German immigrant, after their father Ross died in 1932.

Harvey Earl, David Mark, John David, Janet Donna K. Warren, Don and Marcella, Susan K. Mills Margaret "Peggy" K. Salazar

Don graduated from Blackburn College, 1941, and the University of Illinois School of Agriculture, 1949, serving as Radioman in the South Pacific with the Army during World War II. He married Marcella (Marcia) Shores November 22, 1945, in Carlinville, Illinois.

In 1945 he began his career in Carthage, Illinois, later being assigned as Unit Conservationist in Warren County in 1950. He served with the U.S. Soil Conservation Service for 37 years. Retiring in 1982, he was recognized by the U.S. Secretary of Agriculture, John Block, for his long years of service. The Old Tom watershed was one of the outstanding projects of his career.

Vivian Marcella Shores was born in Salem, Missouri, November 26, 1923, to Virgil (1896-1974) and Vivian (Mayberry) Shores (1898-1945). Both parents were ordained ministers. Marcella's mother died in 1945, her father later resided and owned grocery stores in Richmond and Sacramento, California. Marcella's brother, Virgil (Ernest) resides in Phoenix, Arizona, with his two children.

While at the University of Illinois, daughter Donna was born in 1949. They moved to Monmouth in 1950 and raised six more children. They were active in church and community, Cub Scout and Girl Scout Leaders and school Band Parents.

Marcia was employed at Brown Lynch Scott and in 1960s at Colwell's Department Store. She served as election judge, Monmouth hospital auxiliary member for 40 years and as fundraiser for Monmouth swimming pool. She sewed clothes for her children and 23 grandchildren, and, with Don's help, raised and canned the family's fruit and vegetables.

Her mother's spiritual influence taught Marcia to always reach out to those needing love and support. She could be found at a local restaurant talking with friends, with never a Thanksgiving or Christmas dinner that didn't include someone else.

Don and Marcella were faithful members of the First Baptist Church where he was a Deacon and trustee and she served on many committees. The church was disbanded in 2001 and son John, Monmouth businessman and church member, bought the building, later selling it to the Maple City Baptist congregation.

Don's passion for preserving the soil and land, carried over into work with Crop World Service. For many years he marched in the Warren County CROP walk to feed the world's hungry. His SCS superiors, in early years concerned about his church work interfering with state, commended his lifework and the impact it made in awakening the public to preserve their environment.

Marcella, fifth-generation descendant of Willis Presmie Davidson, whose uncles, Elijah Barton and Hezikiah Davidson, settled in Monmouth, Illinois. Elijah, Monmouth county clerk (1838-1843) and county treasurer and assessor (1831-1836) had a grocery store in Monmouth in 1831. Elijah's daughter, Mary Ann, married Ira Butler and traveled with Elijah in the Murphy-Butler wagon train to Polk County, Oregon, where Monmouth, Oregon, was founded in the same city plan as Monmouth, Illinois. Hezikiah's son, James W., attorney/schoolteacher, and second wife Mary E. Coleman lived at 613 E. Broadway where, since 1839, the Davidson name can still be seen carved in stone on the front risers to the house.

Don and Marcella bought a home at 205 North Sunny Lane, raising their family and living there until Don's death, March 7, 1994, the yard being planted in fifth-generation peonies and tulip poplars. Their children are Donna Elaine Warren (1949), Minneapolis, Minnesota; Margaret Ellen (Peggy) Bank Salazar (1951), Monmouth; Susan Eloise Mills (1953), Little York; David Mark (1954), Warrensburg, Missouri; and John Daniel (1957), Harvey Earl (1959) and Janet Elisa Cohn (1960) all of Monmouth.

FRANK AND MARY (SWARTS) KETCHUM - Frank Martin Ketchum (born 20 January 1887, Abingdon, Virginia, to Joseph Lee and Martha Lavinia (Sanders) Ketchum) and Mary Margaret Swarts (born 12 February 1887, Abingdon, Virginia, to John Isaac and Arizona Hinda (Creger) Swarts were married 4 March 1908, Abingdon, Virginia. Frank worked in lumber camps/sawmills and as a carpenter in Virginia. Mary worked in an overall factory before marriage. In 1919 they came to Warren County, Illinois. Frank farmed by the month in Warren and Henderson counties until 1923 when they bought a small acreage northwest of Kirkwood near Mineral Springs, from where their farmhouse came. Frank gradually added 5/10-acre tracts, ending with about 70 acres. Supplemental income came from day work: stump/hedge pulling and custom sawing at his own small mill.

Frank and Mary (Swarts) Ketchum, 50th anniversary, 1958

Mary raised most of their food in a large garden, canning it; home-butchered meats; raised chickens; sewed family clothing; crocheted; and made quilts.

They were noted as honest, hard-working people. During the first Depression years, when many farms were foreclosed, Frank went to the bank expecting to lose the home. The bankers sent him home, telling him to keep working and raise his family ñ they knew they would eventually get their money.

Frank and Mary's children follow:

Clarence Preston, born 4 March 1909, died 8 January 1910, Abingdon, Virginia;

Lucille Virginia, born 11 December 1910, Abingdon, Virginia, died 28 January 1994, Roseville, married 12 March 1931, Galesburg to James Anderson Damewood four children; Ernest Roy, born 9 September 1912, Bristol, Tennessee, died 12 October 1945, Monmouth, married 18 November 1939, Kahoka, Missouri, to Nancy Rosamond Allen one child; Hazel Arizona, born 14 October 1914, Bristol, Tennessee, died 14 April 1984, Monmouth, married 31 July 1933, Monmouth to Roy Raymond Damewood six children;

Nannie Belle, born 18 August 1916, Bristol, Virginia, died 29 May 2001, Monmouth, married 3 November 1934, Rozetta, Illinois, to Everett Glenn Baldwin ñ three children;

Ethel Lorraine, born 27 July 1918, Bristol, Virginia, married 15 July 1939, Kahoka, Missouri, to Gerald Fillmore Trego, – three children; Robert Lee, born 6 April 1920, Henderson County, Illinois, died 20 April 1992, Monmouth, married 31 October 1942, Ft. Donelson, Tennessee, to Merle Marian Niles – one child; Dorothy Mae, born 23 October 1922, Henderson County, Illinois, married 1 September 1945, Peoria, Illinois, to David Cummings Casteel – six children; Grace Marie, born 8 January 1926, Kirkwood, Illinois, died 14 October 1992, Peoria, Illinois, married 9 September 1945, Berwick, Illinois, to Maurice Roger Downes – four children; and William Eldon, born 29 April 1928, Kirkwood, Illinois, died 3 August 1992, Escondido, California, married 4 June 1950, Kirkwood, Illinois, to Isabel Jane Grimm – two children.

All children attended Center Grove and graduated Kirkwood High School, walking over a mile to grade school and 2 1/4 miles to high school, carrying their lunches mostly peanut butter sandwiches, cookies and occasional fruit.

Frank died 27 June 1966; Mary died 12 September 1969. After their death, the farm has been kept in the family. It is now owned by great-grandson Steve Damewood. The original home and barn were taken down in 1997. Great-grandaughter Sherry (Trego) LeFils remembers vacation highlights were visits to the farm. *By great-granddaughter Sherry (Trego) LeFils.*

ROBERT AND MERLE (NILES) KETCHUM - Robert Lee Ketchum was born 6 April 1920, in Rozetta Township, Henderson County, Illinois, (address Kirkwood) to Frank and Mary (Swarts) Ketchum, formerly of Abingdon, Virginia. Siblings: Clarence Preston, Lucille Virginia, Ernest Roy, Hazel Arizona, Nannie Belle, Ethel Lorraine, Dorothy Mae, Grace Marie and William Eldon. Bob moved with the family to a farm they had purchased two miles northwest of Kirkwood, Warren County, in 1923. He attended Center Grove School and graduated from Kirkwood High School in 1937.

Merle and Bob Ketchum, 40th Wedding Anniversary, October 31, 1982

Bob was working at Western Stoneware Co. as a shipping packer when he entered the service during World War II at Camp Grant, Illinois, on 28 June 1942. He served in the Asiatic Pacific Theater in the Philippines, and other areas in the Pacific. He received his honorable discharge as a Supply T/Sgt. at Ft. Sheridan, Illinois, on 6 January 1946, having served with the 523rd Ordinance H.M. Co (FA) 3 years, 11 months and 9 days.

Bob and Merle Niles were married 31 October 1942, at Ft. Donnelson, Davidson County, Tennessee. Merle Marian Niles was born 25 October 1919, in Gerlaw, Illinois, the only child of Charles Robinson and Verna (Hoteling) Niles. She attended local schools, graduating from Alexis High School. She did office and some factory work and was later self-employed in the upholstery business in her own shop.

Bob and Merle lived in Gerlaw a number of years before he bought the Ketchum homeplace northwest of Kirkwood. He was self-employed as a carpenter/contractor and built a new home on the land where he grew up. In the fall of 1986 he had that house, a new three-stall garage and Merle's upholstery shop moved to a lot at W. Broadway and N. Sunny Lane in Monmouth. He sold the farm to a grandson of Frank and Mary Ketchum, John and Martha Damewood. It still remains in the family.

Bob continued to work during the summer months, spending the winters at Alamo, Texas. Bob's pastimes were bowling and cribbage.

They had a son, Donald Joseph, born 30 April 1947. Bob died 20 April 1993, and Merle died 17 February 1998. Both are buried in Mosher Cemetery.

WILLIAM AND JANE (GRIM) KETCHUM - William Eldon (Bill) Ketchum, youngest son of Frank and Mary (Swarts) Ketchum, was born 29 April 1928, in the family home northwest of Kirkwood, Warren County, Illinois. His siblings were Clarence Preston, Lucille Virginia, Ernest Roy, Hazel Arizona, Nannie Belle, Ethel Lorraine, Robert Lee, Dorothy Mae and Grace Marie. He attended Center Grove school, graduating from Kirkwood High School in 1945.

Ketchum family: Bill, Jane, Linda, Tilcia and Mike

Bill entered the Navy shortly after graduation; it was discovered shortly thereafter that he had tuberculosis. He spent a lot of time in the Naval Hospitals, and eventually the doctors removed a part of one lung. He had no further problems with the tuberculosis

On 4 June 1950, at Kirkwood, Illinois, Bill married Jane Grim, daughter of Lee Vern and Elsie Lucinda (Lemmon) Grim, born 15 Sept 1917, Steuben County, Indiana.

Bill graduated from the University of Arizona in 1956 with a B.S. degree in Mechanical Engineering. He was in the General Electric Training Program, then worked for Farnesworth in Ft. Wayne, Indiana. In July 1958, he was employed at Convair Astronautics (now General Dynamics Corporation) where he was a Proposal Development Specialist, remaining with the company until his death in 1992. They resided in Escondido, California.

Jane worked as a Lab and X-Ray Technician while Bill was in college. She is a member of Epsilon Sigma Alpha Sorority and was very active in that. She is still active in church work.

Bill and Jane's children are

Michael Lee Ketchum, born 26 August 1955, Tucson, Pima County, Arizona, married Tilcia Serrano, born 23 March 1952, Republic of Panama ñ grandchildren: Anthony Michael Ketchum, born 21 June 1983, Edwards Air Force Base, California, and Cynthia Lynn, born 9 Sept 1985, Pappillion (near AFB), Nebraska;

Linda Kay, born 22 December 1965, San Diego, San Diego County, California, came to live with Bill and Jane at 10 1/2 months on November 16, 1966, and was legally adopted June 16, 1967, in San Diego; and Bill, died 3 August 1992, Escondido, California, and is buried at Oak Hill cemetery.

Jane now resides in Arizona.

DONALD WAYNE AND PHYLLIS ANN LANPHERE KETTERING

Donald Wayne Kettering was born July 11, 1930, in Monmouth, Illinois, and Phyllis Ann Lanphere was born August 23, 1936, in Monmouth, Illinois. They were married July 29, 1956, at the Methodist Church in Monmouth. They have two daughters, Ann Louise Kettering Sincox who was born September 24, 1959, in Monmouth, Illinois, is married to David Sincox of Byron, Illinois, born February 25, 1954, and Laura Jean Kettering Everly, born April 1, 1966, in Monmouth, Illinois, is married to Thomas Everly of rural Avon, Illinois, born January 20, 1965. The Sincoxes have two children: Thaddeus Orin Sincox born June 13, 1984, and Abagail Lane Sincox born November 28, 1987. The Everlys have one child, Audrey Grace Everly, born July 11, 1993.

Donald Wayne and Phyllis A. Kettering, 2002

Don's parents were John Ray Kettering, born December 16, 1892, in Beatrice, Gage County, Nebraska, and died January 21, 1993, in Monmouth, Illinois, at the age of 100, and Florence Louise Weston, born October 12, 1895, and died September 30, 1957, in Monmouth, Illinois. They were married December 21, 1911, in Burlington, Iowa. Of this marriage, five children were born: Earl Ray Kettering, born October 21, 1912, died August 5, 1914; Wilda Marie Kettering Miller (John), born July 3, 1915, died August 9, 1996; Audrey Louise Kettering Anderson (Virgil), born April 7, 1919, died December 30, 1994; Lois Josephine Kettering Moore (Robert), born November 14, 1920, died July 17, 1995; and Donald Wayne Kettering. After Florence's death, John later married Minnie Orwig McKeown who taught music in the Monmouth Elementary Schools.

Phyllis' father was Orin Samuel Lanphere, born May 26, 1904, in Ponemah, Illinois, and died October 12, 1981, in Monmouth, Illinois. Her mother, Dorothy Sunderland Lanphere, was born March 6, 1907, and died June 18, 1999, in Monmouth, Illinois. They were married July 19, 1927, in Galva, Illinois. Of this marriage was born one daughter, Phyllis Ann.

Don worked in the administration at Monmouth College, of which he is a graduate, from 1957 to 1975, after which he was employed by Martin and Clark Co., a Case International dealership, from 1975 to 1992 when he retired. Phyllis, also a graduate of Monmouth College, taught at Warren School east of Monmouth the first year it was in existence. Later she taught at Warren Achievement Center and then at the Roseville Elementary School in Roseville, Illinois, for 17 years. Phyllis retired from teaching in 1994.

Both Don and Phyllis were reared on farms in Warren County and continue to maintain an interest in agriculture. They were both active in 4-H and the Rural Youth organization.

The original surname of Kettering was Kettenring and family members represent a branch of the descendants of the Kettenring family of Germany dating back to the 15th century. The name Kettenring means chains of links or rings. All emigrants from Germany with the name of Kettenring or Kettering who came to America have been traced to Hans Jacob Kettenring of Landstuhl, Germany.

BARBARA JOYCE KILLEY

Barbara Joyce was born on September 9, 1933, in Monmouth, Warren County, Illinois. Her father and mother were Ralph Allen Killey and Frances Ada Brent Killey. Her grandparents were P.I. Killey and Alice Maud Winebright Killey; they are buried in the Warren County Memorial Park in Monmouth. She remembers visiting at the home of her maternal grandfather Frank Brent in Ellison Township where they went on collecting trips in the timber to find hickory nuts, hazel nuts, morel mushrooms, bittersweet (foliage with red berries) and went fishing for catfish in the creek. The Brent farm was adjacent to the Ellison Cemetery. Her great grandfather Kenner Brent had originally donated the land for the cemetery and the Brent family kept up the Ellison Cemetery for many years; many of the Brent relatives are buried there. Kenner Brent and his family walked from Virginia to Warren County, Illinois, in 1836. Kenner's father was Charles Brent who fought in the War of 1812 and his grandfather was George Brent who fought in the Revolutionary War. Barbara's paternal great grandfather William Killey emigrated from the Isle of Man in 1861 and then returned to the Isle of Man in 1864 and married Isabella Kinvig. They returned to Warren County and in 1876 and in 1876 built the Killey homestead near Larchland; they are both buried in the City of Monmouth Cemetery.

Barbara Joyce Killey Hedberg and Ray A. Hedberg

She graduated from Monmouth High School and then Monmouth College in June 1955. She moved to Van Nuys, California, and taught elementary school in the Los Angeles County School System. She met Ray Hedberg in California and they married in Monmouth on October 6, 1956, and then moved to the San Francisco Bay area where she taught elementary school in the Palo Alto schools. In 1963 they moved to Los Angeles where Ray took a position with IBM. They moved to Boulder, Colorado, in 1967 where they built a house on an acre-plus lot along South Boulder Creek. She has developed her yard and garden into one of the premier perennial gardens in Boulder County; it has been on multiple garden tours over the years.

Barbara and Ray (pictured) have three children: Nicholas (1963), Stephen (1965) and Samantha (1970). Barbara is a Colorado State University Master Gardner and an advisor to the Shakespeare Garden at the University of Colorado. She has served on related State of Colorado and Colorado State University Extension Service advisory committess and boards. She is a member of the American Orchid Society, the American Gourd Society, The Boulder Garden Club, The Denver Botanical Garden, The American Horticultural Society, The Royal Horticultural Society in Great Britain and the Delphinium Society and is a member of Chapter EY of P.E.O. She is also an estate and antique appraiser for many banks and lawyers in Boulder, Colorado.

BRUCE KILLEY

Bruce Winebright Killey and Adeline Stevenson were married on January 27, 1940, at the home of her parents, James and Grace Bainter Stevenson, in Biggsville, Illinois.

Killey Family L: to R: James, Richard, Adeline, David and Bruce

After graduating from Monmouth High School, Bruce attended Iowa State University for three years, then returned to farm with his father, P.I. Killey. Adeline graduated from Biggsville High School and attended Illinois State University and earned her B.E. Degree and taught business subjects and speech in Mahomet, Illinois, and Monmouth, Illinois.

Following their marriage, they moved to a farm north of Roseville where Bruce was engaged in grain and livestock farming. In addition, he found time to serve on the Warren County Fair Board, the Roseville State Bank Board and to serve his church, Monmouth United Methodist, on various committees. Adeline became a homemaker.

They were blessed with three sons, David, Richard and James, who attended the Roseville schools and graduated from the University of Illinois College of Agriculture. They eventually returned to farm with their father. Girls were added to the family when they married: Janet Maginn (David), Mary Phebus (Richard) and Maribeth Allen (James). What a joy it was to become grandparents ñ eight times: Karen (Mike Mickle), Elizabeth (Stephen Pichaske), Kevin (DeNeene Crandall), Shannon, Stephen (Sherry Mowen), Benjamin, Seth and Sara. Now we're blessed with seven great-grandchildren: Megan Pichaske, Kolton Killey, Kyle Mickle, Sydney Killey, Katelyn Mickle, Matthew Pichaske and Koby Bruce Killey.

Two links in our family chain were sadly broken when Bruce passed away on May 17, 1997, and David on September 17, 1999.

FRANCES ADA (BRENT) KILLEY - Frances Ada was born on October 3, 1911, in Smithshire, Ellison Township, Warren County, Illinois. She was a daughter of Frank Jesse Brent and Ada Flossie Savage. She had a half-brother, Farrand Ogden Brent, and a half-sister, Carol Louella Brent (VanRiper). Frances grew up on the Brent family farm which was settled by her pioneer great-grandfather, Kenner Brent, when he came from Virginia to Illinois in 1836. The Brent family can be traced back to George Brent who fought in the Revolutionary War and to Hugh Brent in the early 1600s in Virginia. Her mother Ada Savage was descended from Leven Savage who fought in the Revolutionary War. Her mother Ada's grandmother Nancy Haney, was part Cherokee Indian. Frances went to Monmouth High School, graduating in 1928. George Brent, a brother of Frances' grandfather, David Cralle Brent, in his later years gave each of his grandnieces $2000. Frances used hers to attend her first two years at Monmouth College and to get her teacher's certificate; she then taught in a one-room schoolhouse in Ellison Township. She was married to Ralph Allen Killey on May 27, 1932, in Monmouth. Frances told the following story about the early days of her marriage:

Frances Ada Brent Killey

"Before the depression, I was teaching in a country school in Warren County; then a law was passed that stated if you were married, and a woman, you couldn't keep your job as teacher. I used to make $85 a month for eight months out of the year. Now we have moved into the tenant house at Ralph's father's farm where he earns $35 a month. We are provided with chicken feed, all the milk from one cow we could use, a little plot of land to grow food and flowers on, 1/2 a hog, and 1/4 of one of the many cattle his father owns. We only go to town once a week. So, we survive on what we can. To give you an idea of what things cost, eggs are seven cents a dozen, 25 cents for a pound of cream. Corn is so cheap we are using it for fuel in the stove. Most people don't have any kind of money to go to movies and entertainment of that sort. Mostly, we listen to the radio and play cards with our friends to keep our selves entertained. Lately, we've had quite a few bums and hoboes come around. They usually move along the railroad tracks and we just happen to live quite near them. Whenever they come begging, we usually just give them some food and a place to spend the night. We didn't have any money in the bank when they closed. We manage, I guess. We sleep outside in the summer because of the heat. Our neighbors are less fortunate though. Chinch bugs took over their fields. They have no irrigation and hardly any horses to help them. We eat well, I suppose. So, we share a lot with them. We raise cows, chickens, pigs and cattle. For clothing we use old flour sacks a lot. We only wear our good clothes to church on Sundays. If a friend needs help, we'll all pull together and help out."

Frances and Ralph had four children, Barbara Joyce Killey Hedberg (1933), Lester Brent Killey (1936-1992), Ralph William Killey (1938-1994) and Frank Phillip Killey (1945). Frances was active in many civic, historic and church organizations and in raising orchids. She did extensive genealogy research into her family history and joined the Daughters of the American Revolution. She became a state officer in the DAR and then a national officer. She was active in the Children of the American Revolution organization, the P.E.O. sisterhood, the Methodist Church and the Republican Party. She attended the 1980 Republican Convention as one of the Illinois delegates. She was Illinois Mother of the Year in 1964. She returned to Monmouth College and received a Bachelors Degree in 1967 in the same graduating class as her youngest son, Frank. She then taught at Willits Elementary School in Monmouth.

Frances Ada Brent Killey died on October 6, 1999, and is buried in the Warren County Memorial Park Cemetery in Monmouth.

RALPH ALLEN KILLEY - Ralph Allen was born on March 7, 1908, on the Killey family farm near Larchland in Warren County. It was built in 1876 by Ralph's grandparents, William Killey and Isabella Kinvig, who had both emigrated from the Isle of Man; they are both buried in the City of Monmouth Cemetery. Ralph was the son of Philip Issac Killey (P.I.) and Alice Maud Winebright; they are both buried in the Warren County Memorial Park Cemetery, Monmouth. P.I. Killey was born on the Killey farm in 1880, the sixth of eight children. Alice Maud Winebright born 1882 was the youngest of nine children of George Winebright, born in Germany in 1833 and emigrated in 1852, and Mary VanFleet, born in New York in 1843 and moved with her parents to Henderson County, Illinois, in 1846. George Winebright and his wife Mary are both buried in the Center Grove Cemetery, Kirkwood.

Ralph A. Killey

Ralph loved to play practical jokes and tell stories. One story about his childhood was how his mother made him keep his room picked up and once, when he didn't do "as he had been told," his mother nailed his overalls to the floor. He was the oldest brother of Bruce Winebright Killey, Bernice Winebright Killey (Livingston) and Lucille Isabelle Killey (McVey). Ralph went to the West Prairie one-room country schoolhouse and attended two winters at the Brown Business School in Galesburg.

He raised grain crops and fed beef cattle and pigs for many years on the family farm. He also raised popcorn that he picked, husked, dried the old fashioned ways and then donated one pound bags for many charitable purposes, or gave them away to friends and relatives. He was past Master of the Masonic Lodge #519 at Roseville and a Shriner in Monmouth. He was chairman of the Warren County Republicans for 12 years. He was President of the 1956 Prime Beef Festival, headed the fund raising and steering committees for the Methodist Church and the new Monmouth Hospital and received many honors for his community work. Ralph died in December 1999 at the home of his son, Frank P. Killey, in San Rafael, California. He is buried in the Warren County Memorial Park, Monmouth.

Ralph married Frances Ada Brent in 1932 and they had four children. Barbara Joyce Killey (Hedberg) was born September 9, 1933, in Monmouth (see separate biography).

Lester Brent Killey was born on August 2, 1936, in Monmouth. He died on April 27, 1992, in Los Angeles, California, and is buried in the Warren County Memorial Park, Monmouth. He served in the U.S. Air Force as a radar electronics specialist and then attended Bradley University for one year. He taught at DeVry Institute in Chicago, then worked for CBS Television (at the transmitter location) in Los Angeles, Lockheed Aircraft (where he was responsible for the final inspection of L 10 11 aircraft); and Rocketdyne Corp. as a robotics electronics maintenance specialist. He had strong interests in precious metal recovery. In 1960 he married Melissa Melvin and they had three children, Barbara Lee Killey (Sanchez), Adam Killey and Lynne Killey. Melissa and Lester later divorced.

Ralph William Killey was born on January 25, 1938, in Monmouth. He died on May 4, 1994, in Lancaster, California; he is buried in the Warren County Memorial Park, Monmouth. Bill attended the University of Illinois for one year, then worked for the National Bank of Monmouth, Container Corp. of America, Weyerhauser Corp. and Inland Container Corp. He then farmed in Monmouth and then worked for the Valic Corp. in Las Vegas, Nevada. In 1958 he married Marlene Tinder; they had two children: Rebecca Killey (Donegan) and Roger Killey. Bill and Marlene later divorced. In 1974 he married Martha Kersey (Fillman) and together they raised her three children: Cindy Fillman (Hallam), Lisa Fillman and Michelle Fillman.

Frank Phillip Killey was born on October 27, 1945, in Monmouth. Frank graduated from Monmouth College in 1967, then became an officer in the U.S. Navy and served on the U.S.S. Guadalcanal. After the Navy, he was a sales representative for Merck, Sharp and Dohme Pharmaceuticals, then returned to school and received his PHD in Physiology from the Medical College of Wisconsin (Marquette University). He worked for Allergan Pharmaceuticals as Director of Safety Evaluation, then Herbert Laboratories as Vice President of Research and Development, then Oclassen Pharmaceutical as Vice President of R&D. In 1967 he married Barbara Baughman; they have two children: Kristin Killey and Brent Killey. Currently, he is a consultant in Pharmaceutical development and toxicology. He and his wife reside in San Rafael, California.

RICHARD BRUCE KILLEY - Richard Bruce Killey is the son of Adeline Stevenson Killey and Bruce Winebright Killey. (Adeline is the daughter of James and Grace Bainter Stevenson. She grew up in the Biggsville area. Bruce, the son of Phillip Isaac and Alice Winebright Killey, grew up in the Larchland /Monmouth area.) Richard (Dick) graduated from Roseville High School and the University of Illinois. After graduation, Dick served in the U.S. Army for four years. Afterwards, he and his wife returned to Roseville where Dick began farming with his father and brothers, David and Jim.

L: to R: Back: Mary Killey, Richard Killey, Elizabeth Killey Pichaske, Matthew Pichaske, Sherry Mowen Killey and Sara Killey. Front: Megan Pichaske, Stephen Pichaske, Adeline Killey, Stephen Killey and Koby Killey.

His wife, Mary Frances Phebus Killey, was born and raised in Urbana, Illinois, and graduated from the University of Illinois. (Her sister, Margaret, Mrs. Larry D. Moore, and family, also live in Roseville.) Mary teaches high school Spanish and social studies. Dick and Mary have three children, Elizabeth Frances Killey Pichaske, Stephen Bruce Killey and Sara Virginia Killey. Elizabeth is married to Stephen Geoffrey Pichaske and they are the parents of two children, Megan Katherine, 4, and Matthew Richard, 2 years. Elizabeth graduated from Augustana College and Steve graduated from the U.S. Naval Academy, Annapolis. Steve will receive his Masters of Divinity from Duke University Seminary in May 2002, and they plan to return to Illinois to begin his service in the ministry. Steve is from Peoria, the son of Elaine Pichaske Solokowski and David Pichaske. Stephen Killey is married to Sherry Mowen Killey. Steve graduated from St. Ambrose University, and will finish her degree in Cosmetology at Carl Sandburg College in May. Sherry grew up in the Raritan area, daughter of Dan and Robyn Mowen, and graduated from Southern High School, Stronghurst. They have one son, Koby Bruce, 18 months. They live in Roseville, where Steve is an insurance producer for Citizens National Bank. Sara is currently in her Junior year at Illinois State University. She is majoring in Ag Business. The Killeys are active members of the Roseville United Methodist Church. They are also very active in many Roseville area clubs, activities, and projects.

FRANK E. KIMBLE - Frank E. Kimble was born in Brooklyn, New York, July 19, 1894, to Mary Ann Barber and Loren Kimble. As a young man he worked as a designer in his father's cut glass factory in Honesdale, Pennsylvania. During World War I, he joined the army and served in France.

Frank E. Kimble

After the war, Frank moved to Gary, Indiana where he was employed as an electrician. Frank suffered from an on-the-job accident and was badly burned. After returning to good health, he married Jessie Verkler, the nurse who had taken care of him during his recovery.

Jessie was born, January 26, 1897, in Buckley, Illinois, the daughter of Jacob and Lena Verkler. Their families had come to America from Switzerland and settled near Buckley. After growing up, Jacob and Lena married and had a family, which included Jessie.

Jessie and Frank lived in Gary. She worked as a nurse and Frank was store manager for the Woolworth Company. In 1922 Florence was born, and five years later, after moving to Monmouth, Illinois, Norma was born.

While Florence was a student at Central Junior High School, Frank resigned from his position at Woolworth's. He then started a store of his own, Kimble's 5¢ to $1.00 Store. It was located at 108 South Main Street, while their family home was at 1139 East Broadway.

Their daughters, Florence and Norma, attended Garfield and Central Junior High School. Florence graduated from Monmouth High School in 1940 and Norma in 1945. They both were graduates of Monmouth College.

After college, Florence was employed in Chicago for two years, while Norma moved to Denver, Colorado, to teach school.

Florence moved back to Monmouth and later married Frederick "Tom" Joyslin in 1947. Tom served in World War II, and later was employed by the First National Bank of Monmouth. Norma married Charles Coop of Denver in 1951.

Frank Kimble died in 1947, at the old Monmouth Hospital, 515 East Euclid Avenue, now Pinewood Health Care Center. His wife, Jessie, was killed in an automobile accident in 1955.

Born to Florence and her husband were twins. They were named Kimble, "Kim", and Kathy. "Kim" lives in Monmouth, while Kathy lives in Jacksonville, Florida. A third child, Martha, married to Jim Missavage, lives twelve miles southwest of Monmouth.

Norma and Charles became the parents of four children: Crystal Ann, Mahlon, Leonard and David.

Florence taught third grade at Willits School from 1965-1987, and is now retired.

Frank was a member of the American Legion and Veterans of Foreign Wars, the Clinton Lodge No. 54, A.F.A.M., the Moline Consistory, the Monmouth Low Twelve and local Elks Club. The family were members of the First Methodist church. Jessie was a member of the local Eastern Star. She had also been a nurse's assistant in the office of Dr. Wendell Roller. *By Florence Joyslin.*

LLOYD VINCENT KING - Lloyd Vincent King, son of William M. of Maysville, Kentucky, and Mildred (Carpenter) Knarr of Bellevue, Kentucky, was born 18 January 1918, in Maysville, where he was raised and educated. He attended Eastern State Teachers College at Richmond, Kentucky. He joined the Marine Corps shortly after the beginning of World War II where he became a Sergeant. His Division was the first to land at Guadalcanal in the South Pacific. When relieved, they returned to Camp Pendleton Marine Base just north of San Diego. While on furlough, he met and married Elynore LaVerne Barnes, at Maysville, Kentucky, 26 April 1943. She was the daughter of Verne Franklin and Ednah LaVine (Alexander) Barnes of Monmouth Illinois. Elynore was working at the Army Ordnance Plant in West Burlington, Iowa, as a government inspector. The young couple lived in Laguna Beach, near Oceanside, California. He became officer-in-charge of the Provost Marshall Office for the remainder of his service.

Vincent and Elynore King

Growing up in high school, "Vin", as he was called, became a window decorator and played in a small band for extra money. Many times in later life he used these talents decorating floats in the Prime Beef Festival Parade and organizing the Jazz band when president of the Western Illinois Shrine Club.

After the war and his three years of service, Vincent, Elynore, and their baby, Billee LaVerne, returned to Bellevue, and lived with his mother and stepfather, Frank Knarr. They found employment in the local Wadsworth watch factory, but their other family, the Barnes, insisted they move to Monmouth and become truck farmers. Vin took a course in agronomy in 1949 in Kentucky to learn about farming. It was very hard work, but seasonable.

Their second child, Debra Jo, was born in 1961 while they were living at the farm as was Kenneth L., born in 1966. They became involved in the new Warren School where all their children attended. Because of a heart condition, he was advised to quit farming, eventually selling the farm and moving into a new home on land he reserved for building his new home. He took on the job of tax assessor for three years for rural Monmouth Township before deciding to run as a Republican for Warren County Treasurer. He took office 1 December 1962, then after a required layover, won another term. He was in this term when on 21 October 1972, he passed away from a heart attack while pheasant hunting near Huron, South Dakota. He loved all outdoor sports ñ hunting, boating, fishing, especially his yearly elk hunt on the western slope of the Rocky Mountains near Craig, Colorado.

Vin was a member of the First Christian Church. He was active in all branches of the

Masons, serving as Past Master of the Royal Arch branch and first president of the Western Illinois Shrine Club. He helped organize the Warren-Henderson Angus Association. He was a member of the Monmouth Chamber of Commerce and worked at their Prime Beef Festival. He served two years on the Warren County Selective Service Board and was an honorary member of Rotary.

Elynore LaVerne King (born 8 February 1921) graduated from Monmouth High School and Whitworth College in Brookhaven, Mississippi, then attended Monmouth College in the class of 1943. After the sale of their farm and the children were all in school, she applied for work at Formfit-Rogers and was hired to work in the office. After ten years, Formfit closed and she became office manager of the new company of Smoler Bros. for two years. Her husband had passed away and, being an election year, she was encouraged to run for the office of County Clerk and Recorder, succeeding Dan Brown, who was retiring. The election was in her favor and she took office 1 December 1974, and retired in 1986, after three terms in office, to Sun City, Arizona.

Elynore loved to travel and took several tours to Europe and Hawaii, mostly to visit her son-in-law, Eugene Conard, and daughter, Billee, while he was stationed with the U.S. Navy in Spain, Europe and Alaska. After his service retirement from the Navy, he was hired by Booze Allen, a consulting firm. Elynore vacationed with them and arranged for her brother, Verne Elwyn "Bud" Barnes, and his wife, Estelle, to visit on their 46th anniversary when she was in Hawaii.

Their daughter, Debra, married into the Edwards farming clan by marrying Leroy. He farms northeast of Monmouth on the farm that John Talbott, the first settler in Warren County, settled. They have three, sons, all athletes at Warren High School and all college graduates. Kenneth is in nuclear maintenance and married Nanci Steele. They have two sons and a daughter and now live in Winthrop Harbor, Illinois. He works in the nuclear plant in Zion, Illinois. Eugene and Billee have two daughters, Kim and Terry, both live in Raleigh, North Carolina. Brother Bud and Grandmother Elynore were included in Terry and Jeff's wedding in Virginia Beach, Virginia.

WAYNE AND BETTY (SMITH) KINKAID - Wayne Lee Kinkaid was born April 24, 1932, in Warren County, Illinois, to Frank Allen "Dutch" and Rita Lottie (Niles) Kinkaid. Wayne's brother and sisters are Richard, Lynne Devlin and Sharon Anderson.

Wayne and Betty were married July 3, 1952, at the Fall Creek Methodist Church in Henderson County, Illinois.

Betty Joan was born to David and Alta Leone (Ryner) Smith February 19, 1934, Monmouth, Illinois.

Wayne and Betty both graduated from Little York High School, Wayne in 1951 and Betty in 1952.

Wayne was in the Army from December 1952 until November 1954. He served in Korea. He worked for Alton Box Co. in Galesburg, which later became Jefferson Smurfitt Corp. from which he retired in 1994. Betty worked as a telephone operator in Monmouth and Little York, at Banker's Life in Monmouth, Woolworth's, Pottery, Monel's, and Smoler Fashions, from which she retired in December 1979. They both enjoyed trap-shooting. Betty enjoys ceramics, crafts and genealogy and is a Charter Member of the Warren County Genealogical Society, having served on the cemetery committee.

Kinkaid Family: Carol Joan, Betty Joan, Caren Lynn, Wayne Lee and James Lee.

To this union were born four children.: Connie, Carol, Caren and James. Connie Marie was born and died in June 1953. Carol Joan was born September 1956. Carol has a daughter, Bettie Alexandra "Sandy", by her first marriage. Sandy married Thomas Bowles and they have a son, Christopher. Carol's second marriage was to Randy Lee Devlin. Randy has a daughter, Kristen Lee, by a previous marriage. She has a daughter, Taydem Lee Devlin. Carol has worked as secretary to one of the fire chiefs at the Galesburg Public Safety Building for many years.

Caren Lynne was born January 12, 1959. She has two children by her first marriage: Amy Jeannene and Derrick James. Amy is married to Ricardo Garza; they have a son, Richie, and a daughter, Madalyn. Derrick and April have a daughter, Aaron Lynne, and she also has a son, Vincent. Amy lives in Alliance, Nebraska, and Derrick lives in Middlesex, North Carolina. Caren's second marriage is to Stephen Stanley and they have three boys: Ian, and twin boys, Johnathan and Kellan. Caren works at Thiele Pharmacy and Gifts and Stephen works for the railroad. They live in Alliance, Nebraska. James Lee was born March 12, 1963. He is divorced and he and his son, Donald Wayne, live in Monmouth. He works as night supervisor for Elliot at the Moline Airport. Donald Wayne has a half-brother, Waylon Eugene Clark, who lives with his grandmother, Mary Jane Clark, in Monmouth.

Betty and Wayne have lived in Gerlaw for 43 years.

CHERYL AND HOWARD KINNEY - John Howard Kinney was born April 3, 1931, the fourth child and second son of Frank and Esther (Brownlee) Kinney's eventual six children. He grew up on the family farm 3 1/2 miles northwest of Little York, specifically the southwest quarter of Section 5 of Sumner Township. He graduated from Duck Creek Grade School and Little York High School. While in high school he participated enthusiastically in softball and basketball.

After graduation from high school, he helped on the family farm and continued to play softball and baseball on Little York and Monmouth teams. Also, he played professional baseball briefly in 1951 for the Tifton Blue Sox of the Class D Georgia-Florida League.

In February 1952 he entered active military service at Ft. Leonard Wood, Missouri. After graduation from Leadership School at Ft. Leonard Wood, he was transferred to Camp Cooke, California (now Vanderberg Air Force Base).

After training at Camp Cooke and Hunter-Liggett Military Reservation, he left San Francisco for Korea in September 1952 on the troop ship General A.W Brewster. The Brewster made stops at Guam, Ilo Ilo and Manila in the Philippines and Yokohama, Japan, before arriving at Inchon, Korea, in late October. In Korea Howard served in Battery C, 64th FA Bn of the 25th Infantry Division; the Bn saw action in the Kumwha, Chorwon and Munsan sectors. The Battery was considered "light" artillery and used 105 mm howitzers in support of infantry. At the time of the Armistice in July of 1953 he was a Chief of Howitzer Section and Color sergeant commanding the Bn Honor Guard at military functions across Korea. After the war he was returned to the U.S. on the same General A. W. Brewster to San Francisco and was discharged at Fort Carson, Colorado, September 30, 1953.

Cheryl and Howard Kinney

Following his military service, he returned to help on the farm until he enrolled at Reedley College, Reedley, California, in September 1956. While at Reedley he participated in baseball and basketball and graduated in June of 1958 with an Associate of Arts degree. Howard then enrolled at the University of Idaho in Moscow, Idaho, in September of 1958 and graduated with a B.S. in Political Science in June of 1961.

Cheryl Fisher was the first child and daughter of Garald and Gwendolyn (McGaughey) Fisher born April 16, 1939, in Mercer County. She graduated from Aledo Grade School and Aledo High School in 1957. She attended Ada Gaffney Schaft's School of Modeling in Davenport, Iowa, and worked at Peterson, Harned and Von Maur's Department Store in the same city. She also modeled for the school's agency at various functions in the Quad City area. Cheryl began schooling at Toby Coburn's School of Fashion and Design in New York City in 1959, and worked at Sak's Fifth Avenue store while there. She returned to Monmouth in 1960 where her father was a prominent land owner and owner/operator of the Warren County Livestock Auction. She managed the jewelry and leather departments at Bowman-Colwell's Department Store and worked at the Warren County Livestock Auction on sale days.

Cheryl and Howard were married November 4, 1961, at the Immaculate Conception Church in Monmouth. They were attended by Cheryl's sister Colleen as Maid of Honor and Howard's brother Harold as Best Man. They went to New Orleans for their wedding trip and returned to Monmouth and resided at a cottage at Lake Warren for two years.

They moved to 23 Lincoln Court in Monmouth in January of 1964 where they lived until they built a home at 601 N. Sunny Lane in 1965. 601 N. Sunny Lane was home for them until they moved to their current residence at 728 East Euclid Avenue in June 1974. Kimberley Yvonne Kinney was born June 26, 1963, while they lived at Lake Warren. John Francis Kinney was born November 6, 1964, during their time at 23 Lincoln Court. Jeffrey William Kinney was born September 12, 1969, while they lived in the home they built at 601 N. Sunny Lane.

Howard began working for the Warren County Agricultural Stabilization Servic (ASCS) part-time during summers while in college. In August of 1961 he began working full-time for the Mercer County ASCS Office in Aledo succeeding to County Office Manager in November of that year. He was appointed District Director for Northwestern Illinois by the Illinois ASCS State Committee in April of 1963. He continued in that position, supervising the operations of 8 to 15 county offices and their committees until retirement in October of 1996.

Cheryl worked for Paralee's Dress Shop in Monmouth and at the Warren County Livestock Auction on sale days for a few years. After the children came, she worked for Queens Way to Fashion and maintained the home and mothered the children. They began an interest in farming in 1974 which they still maintain at this writing.

FRANK AND ESTHER KINNEY - Frank Edward Kinney was born in Hale Township on September 5, 1894. His parents, born of Irish immigrants, were Terrance James and Kathryn Gavin Kinney. His father was born in New York City and came to Warren County as a child. His mother was a native of this county.

Frank and Esther Kinney family, August 3, 1963. L: to R: Ruth, Marian, Melba, Esther, Frank, Howard and Harold. (The photographer, Charles B. Merrill, is deceased and there is no longer a Merrill Studio.)

On February 12, 1923, Frank married Esther Brownlee, who had been born on June 25, 1901, in Sumner Township. She was the daughter of John W. and Nellie May Armstrong Brownlee, both natives of Sumner Township but with family roots in Washington County, Pennsylvania and Triadelphia, West Virginia.

Prior to his marriage, Frank farmed with his father. After graduation from Monmouth High School, Esther took a teacher-training course at Normal. She then taught at Foster and Phelps one-room schools. For the first two years after their marriage they lived on the McCale farm in Lenox Township east of the County Farm. The next year they moved to the Graham farm in Floyd Township south of Cameron.

In March 1926, this couple, with their first child, Margaret Ruth, moved to the Brownlee farm in Section 5 of Sumner Township, which they bought in 1937. While living there five more children were born: Gerald Edward, Frances Marian, John Howard, Harold Terrance and Melba Rose.

There they reared their six children and participated in community activities at Duck Creek and Little York. In addition to farming, Frank served as Democratic Township Committeeman for many years. He enjoyed playing baseball on the Little York teams. Esther devoted her time to her home and family, but still found time for sewing, quilting, crocheting and other needlework.

After fifty years on this farm, Frank and Esther moved to Monmouth in January 1976, where Frank died on February 26 of that year.

Esther continued to live in her Monmouth apartment until health problems caused her to move to Monmouth Nursing Home in November 1985. Although her health continued to fail, she retained her mental acuity and interest in her family and activities until her death on January 13, 1996.

Ruth, born November 10, 1924, was a teacher who eventually became a school librarian. Gerald, born November 4, 1926, helped on the farm in his early years. He died February 16, 1997. Marian, born June 23, 1928, became a nurse. She married George W. Hand, a furniture representative; they live in Columbus, Ohio. They have four children: Karen, Laura, Michael and Martha. Howard, born April 3, 1931, worked for the U. S. Department of Agriculture. He married Cheryl Fisher, who worked in retail sales, and they have three children: Kimberley, John and Jeffrey. Harold, born January 25, 1937, operates The Bottlery, a liquor store, and is a farmer. He married Colleen Fisher, a school teacher, and they have three children: Tracey, H. T. and Julie. Melba, born August 3, 1938, also became a nurse. She marred Dr. William Rogoway, an oncologist. The Rogoways have three children: Michael, Julia and Amy. They live in Portola Valley, California. Ruth, Howard and Cheryl, and Harold and Colleen live in Monmouth.

HAROLD AND COLLEEN KINNEY - Harold Terrance Kinney was born in Monmouth, Illinois, on January 25, 1937, the fifth child and third son of Frank and Esther Brownlee Kinney. He grew up on the family farm northwest of Little York, the southwest quarter of Section 5 of Sumner Township of Warren County. He graduated from Duck Creek Grade School and in 1954 he graduated from Little York High School. In high school he played softball, basketball and football.

He entered Colorado A. and M the nextfall where he majored in agriculture, played football and joined the R.O.T.C. When he graduated in 1958, he received a B.S. degree and was commissioned as a Second Lieutenant in the U. S. Army. In November he reported for duty at Fort Knox, Kentucky, where he received training.

Later he was transferred to Camp Irwin in the California desert, the U.S. Army Desert and Training Center. It was there that he was promoted to First Lieutenant, and when his two years were up he was discharged in November of 1960.

While stationed at Camp Irwin, his brother Howard was attending Reedley Junior College at Reedley, California. While visiting there, Harold met Brother John of Christian Brothers Winery. Brother John offered him a job at the winery in the business office after his discharge, which Harold accepted.

Harold and Colleen Kinney Family

In November of 1961 he went home to Little York to be the best man for Howard as he married Cheryl Fisher, whose maid of honor was her sister, Colleen. This led to a long-distance courtship which ended in their marriage on August 3, 1963.

Colleen was born in Moline, Illinois, on November 29, 1940, the second daughter of Garald and Gwendolyn Fisher. She grew up in Mercer County and graduated from Aledo Grade School and Aledo High School in 1958. The next fall she enrolled at the University of Miami in Florida, but soon transferred to Monmouth College, graduating in 1962 with a major in psychology and a minor in education.

That fall she started her teaching career at Mt. Prospect, Illinois, which was short-lived since she was married the next August and moved to Napa, California, where Harold was employed. She taught there for one semester before they moved back to Monmouth where Harold worked for her father at the Warren County Livestock Auction Barn. On June 27, 1964, Tracey Kathleen, their first child, was born in Moline, Illinois. Two years later H.T. (Harold Terrance) was born there on August 27, 1966. Julie Ann was born in Monmouth on November 28, 1968.

In May 1972, Harold opened The Bottlery at 206 North Main Street in Monmouth which sells fine wines, beer and liquor. Operating this business is combined with his farming operations.

Colleen resumed her teaching career in 1979 when she accepted a position at Immaculate Conception School in Monmouth where her children were enrolled.

Tracey has become a nurse anesthetist and is employed at St. Mary's Hospital in Madison, Wisconsin.

H.T., a quarterback in high school and college, is a football coach at Hofstra University on Long Island, New York.

Julie is a kindergarten teacher in Abingdon, Illinois. On May 8, 1999, she married Rick Vickroy who works at Vickroy's Furniture Store. They live in Monmouth with their two children: Tess, who was born on October 27, 1999, and Cullen, who was born January 27, 2002.

TERRANCE JAMES KINNEY - Terrance James Kinney was born in New York City on January 20, 1860, the son of Terrence and Rosa Lenahan Kinney, both Irish immigrants. He came to Warren County, Illinois, with his family around 1863. On October 2, 1888, he married Kathryn Gavin in Monmouth, Illinois.

His wife was born on November 14, 1869, in Warren County, the daughter of Patick and Mary Heffernan Gavin, also Irish immigrants. Both families were members of the Roman Catholic Church in Monmouth.

Terrance James Kinney Family, 1907

They began farming on the Paine place in Hale Township, and it was there that their first four children were born. Margaret Elizabeth was born July 25, 1889; George was born on December 9, 1891; Frank Edward was born September 5, 1894; and Rose May was born July 1, 1896.

Around 1897, the family moved to the Lynch farm about three miles straight west of Monmouth, also in Hale Township. It was there that their last five children were born. Terrance William ("Willie") was born November 16, 1898; John Leo was born October 2, 1900; Edna Kathryn was born August 31, 1902; Mary Alleyne was born August 14, 1906; and Helen Gertrude was born August 11, 1907. The children, with the exception of Gertrude, attended the Farmers Academy one-room school.

The Kinneys moved to the Killey farm in Lenox Township a few miles south of Monmouth around 1912. The school-age children then went to Fairview Center.

Their next move was to the Clark place just northwest of Little York where they farmed a whole section of land. By this time, Margaret had married Carl Moon and they lived across the road with Carl helping with the farm work. They had two daughters, Dorothy and Catherine.

While living there, the Kinneys lost their first son, George, who died unmarried on June 21, 1917, at the age of 25.

Around 1923, the family moved to a farm a few miles east of Monmouth where they lived until February 1927, when Ted and Kate with Rose, John and Gertrude, moved to 310 West Detroit in Monmouth.

Frank, a farmer, married Esther Brownlee; they had six children: Ruth, Gerald, Marian, Howard, Harold and Melba. Rose was a sales clerk who never married. "Willie" died at age seven. John drove a gasoline truck and married Vada Brooks, a nurse. They had a daughter, Janet. Edna became a school teacher and married Percy Goff, a farmer at Henderson, Illinois. A few years after his death she married Cecil Cofield, also a farmer in Knox County; there were no children. Alleyne was a bookkeeper who married Wallace "Pete" Ekwall, a Galesburg fireman. They had no children. Gertrude, their last child, was a bookkeeper for Martin Motor Sales for many years. Gertrude, who never married, and her sister-in-law, Vada, are the only members of the immediate family who are living in 2001.

TERRENCE AND ROSE LENIHAN KINNEY - Terrence Kinney, who was born in County Cork, Ireland, in 1830, emigrated to the United States in 1852. Rose Lenihan was born in Ireland in 1838 and came to Boston with her parents when she was four years old. The family moved to New York City where she married Terrence Kinney. Terrence and Rose came to Warren County in 1863 with their four children: Mary Jane, John Thomas, Terrence James and Roseanna. Born in Warren County were Kate, Edward and Margaret.

Mary Jane, who was born on October 12, 1855, married John Stokes on August 2, 1881. John Thomas, whose birthdate was July 12, 1857, married Nora Gavin on February 1, 1881. Terrence James, known as "Ted", was born January 20, 1860, and married Kate Gavin on October 2, 1888. Roseanna, whose birthdate was December 23, 1861, married James Hugh Cavanaugh on February 8, 1883.

Also marrying a Gavin was Kate Kinney, who was born January 20, 1866, and married William Gavin on Februay 9, 1892. Edward Kinney, born February 25, 1868, married Kate Boylen on November 27, 1895. Margaret Kinney, the youngest member of the family, born June 10, 1876, married Michael Joseph Flanagan on February 9, 1904.

On July 10, 1879, Terrence Kinney purchased a farm in Hale Township, the north half of the northwest quarter of Section 35. It was bought for the consideration of $3600 from Azro Patterson.

On June 23, 1886, Terrence Kinney purchased another 80 acres of land in Hale Township, described as the east half of the southeast quarter of Section 22, for $6,000 from William Mackey.

Terrence died on May 16, 1892. Rose and her daughter, Margaret, moved to 309 West Third Avenue in Monmouth. After her mother died on January 12, 1898, Margaret lived with her sister, Kate Gavin, and her family until she married.

On January 2, 1899, the heirs of Rose Lenihan Kinney conveyed their interest in the 80 acres in Section 22 in Hale Township for $7,600 to Maggie Kinney, who on the same date transferred 40 acres to her sister Kate Gavin and her husband for $3,800. Another transaction on that date was the transfer of the 80 acres in Section 35 from the heirs of Rose Lenihan Kinney to Rose and J. H. Cavanaugh for $7,200.

On February 26, 1906, the Flanagans purchased the 80 acres in Section 35 in Hale Township from the Cavanaughs for $12,000 and sold the 40 acres in Section 22 to the Gavins for $5,600. In April 1938 Michael and Margaret moved to 309 West Third Avenue, Monmouth, where Michael died on January 1, 1939, and Margaret on pril 5, 1952. Following Margaret's death the arm with the adjoining 80 acres to the east was sold. The real estate in Section 22 of Hale Township is still owned by Terrence Kinney's great-grandson, Donald Gavin.

Of the 53 first cousins, grandchildren of Terrence and Rose Lenihan Kinney, only three are now living. They are Rose and Helen Flanagan and Gertrude Kinney. There are many great grandchildren and great-great grandchildren living in this area and in many other states. Submitted by Rose Flanagan.

CLYDE KNEEN - Clyde Kneen was born April 2 5, 1929, on a farm 2 1/2 miles southwest of Monmouth. He attended Coonville elementary school. His first and second grade teacher was Margaret McCoy, who married Clifford Sanner. The third and fourth grade teacher was Mrs. A'Hern. His fifth, sixth, seventh and eighth grade teacher was Mrs. Martha (Francis) Thomson. He graduated from Kirkwood High School. He served in the Korean War.

Clyde married Carol Corzatt of Roseville in 1952. She attended Roseville Center elementary school and graduated from Roseville High School. Returning from Korea, he received his discharge at Camp Carson, Colorado Springs, Colorado, in October 1953. He worked on the farm as a farmhand for 14 months just west of Monmouth. Locating a farm to rent, they moved to a farm four miles northeast of Roseville, a farm known as the Proughty farm, owned by Joe and Mary Voorhees. Clyde farmed that farm for 43 years. He also farmed some other small farms.

Clyde and Carol Kneen

Clyde and Carol had four daughters. Lila was born July 12, 1954, and married Melvalee Jenkins. They live at Pittsburg, Missoui, and have seven children, Lydia, Wyatt, Rana, Tiara, Brie, Teel and Brock. They home-schooled and are home-schooling their children through grade 12.

Their second daughter, Krista, was born July 16, 1956, and married John Vanskike. They live in the country at the southeast edge of Monmouth. Their children are Johnathan and Devin.

Their third daughter, Sharla, was born September 30, 1963. She married Tandy Hawkins. They live at Bethel, Missouri, and have three children, Clayton, Daysi and Mindi.

Their fourth daughter, Karita, was born March 12, 1966. She married Mike Hines. They live northwest of Roseville and have one child, Jesse.

Clyde served on the Warren County Farm Bureau Board, being the Vice-president one term. He also served on the Ag Extension Council Board. He served on the Board and Committees at the Monmouth First Christian Church many years where the family attended. He served on the steering committee for the Lamoine Christian Nursing Home.

Carol Kneen passed away unexpectedly in November 1990.

Clyde later married Marian (Perrin) Adkins on December 3, 1998. She attended Duck Creek school and graduated from Little York High School. She had returned to this area after living about thirty years in the Phoenix, Arizona, area. Her husband died in 1994 after a very extended illnessof ALS ("Lou Gerhig Disease").

Clyde is semi-retired from farming and they live in the country on a farm 2 1/2 miles northeast of Roseville.

JOHN KNEEN - John Kneen was born in 1854 on the Isle of Man. He was a deep sea fisherman while living there. The Isle of Man is a small independent country between England and Ireland. He probably came to this area because there were other Manxmen living in this area and quite a few around Galva. A Manx reunion was held at one time in Galva.

He worked for the 3M factory (Monmouth Mining & Manufacturing Company) for a period of time. Approximately 1889, he purchased a farm 2 1/2 miles east of Monmouth, just east of the Sickman Corner. He married Celesta Ann Eby in 1889. She was born Jan 5, 1860 and went by the name of Anna. Her father was Andrew J. Eby. He served in the Civil War and received a pension from war injuries. He was a carpenter by trade. Anna's mother was Sarah Ann Earp, daughter of Walter and Martha (Early) Earp. Walter and Martha moved here from Kentucky and were the progenitors of the Earps in this area Walter and Martha had 9 children and about 85 grandchildren Anna (Eby) Kneen was a first cousin of Wyatt Earp, Frontier Marshall.

John Kneen II

The first child of John and Anna Kneen was John Andrew Kneen born July 10, 1890. He attended Washington grade school but due to helping on the farm, he did not attend high school. He married Daisy Dell Fugate from Pittsburg, Missouri. Daisy taught country school with as many as 38 students in the eight grades. She had to walk three miles to the school to teach. She later worked at the Hermitage, Missouri telephone office, then the telephone office in Kansas City, Missouri. They resided on a farm 2 1/2 miles southwest of Monmouth, known as the Zimmerman farm, whom they bought the farm from. Part of the farm was in Lenox and part in Tompkins townships, with the residence in Tompkins township. The farm burned completely to the ground, with very little saved, in November 1938. They had three children: John S., dying in infancy; Howard and Clyde. Daisy died in 1938 and John in 1974.

The second child of John and Anna Kneen was Mona, who married Hugh Weir. They farmed northeast of Roseville, then bought a farm near Old Henderson, Knox County. They had seven children: Lee, Anna Colclasure, Blanche Shafman, Hugh, Shirley Brown, John and Thomas.

The third child was Sarah, born 1895, who married Noel Gettemy. They farmed 1/2 mile north of the Coldbrook Church. Their two children were John and Marilyn Maliskis The fourth child of John and Anna Kneen was Jeanette, born in 1903, who married William Brooks. They farmed northeast of Roseville. He died at an early age and Jeanette married Charles McMaster. They farmed her homeplace east of Monmouth many years. He passed away and she married Charles Boock. They farmed a few years. He died about 1977 and she died 1993.

John and Anna Kneen moved into Monmouth upon retirement, to 511 South 6th Street. He died in 1933 and she in 1946.

FREDERICK WILLIAM KRAMER - John Philip and Helena Meusborn Kramer, Greenbush, Illinois, saw their first son Frederick William Kramer born 6 July, 1862. He married Magdalena Doll on May 23, 1893.

As a landowner Frederick is considered a pioneer farmer in Greenbush Township. He contracted blood poisoning after having two teeth extracted in 1936. He died a few days later on July 4, 1936, in Macomb, Illinois.

Frederick William Kramer and Magdalena Doll wedding, 1893

Magdalena Doll was born on July 17, 1866, in Baden, Germany, to Philip and Wilhelmina Olbert Doll. Magdalena came to America at the age of 17 months with her family. They lived on a farm two miles southwest of Bushnell. A heart attack took her January 13, 1946, in Greenbush.

Frederick and Magdalena had five children. Their first child, Eda Helene, was born January 1894 and died in July the same year. Their second daughter, Dolly Wilhelmlina, was born in Greenbush, Illinois, on January 14, 1895.

Dolly married Ghlee Walter Kepple on May 14, 1919, in Galesburg, Illinois. She lived in Avon, Illinois, until June 26, 1967. Her four children included Frederick William, Lena Geneva and the twins, Donald Lee and Ronald Ghlee.

Their third child Ruth Esther was born 6 June 1897 in Greenbush, Illinois. Ruth married Herschel Dixon in January 1920. She married Frank Cheyney Kimble on December 10, 1924, in Berwick, Illinois. She died on March 13, 1958, in Macomb, Illinois. Her children were John Kramer, Mary Ellen, Rachel Ann and Frank Cheyney Jr.

Edith Louise was the fourth Kramer child, born September 4, 1900, in Greenbush, Illinois. She married Edgar Davis on December 15, 1927, in Macomb, Illinois. On May 2, 1992, Edith passed on, leaving her children, Marjorie Louise and Dorothy Marie.

John Philip was born June 8, 1910, in Greenbush, Illinois. He married Ruth Speer on November 15, 1945. They had two children, Don William and John Philip. John Philip Sr. passed away October 13, 1994. *By John Philip Kramer.*

JOHANNES PHILIP KRAMER - Johannes Philip Kramer was born in Haden, Westphalia, Germany, December 20, 1824. He attended public school. He was confirmed in the Lutheran church. Johannes learned the tailor trade and worked at that occupation in different towns near the Rhine River.

In 1855, he and friend Louis Hollenberg started for America to meet up with Mr. Hollenberg's two brothers, Henry and George. The brothers had come to America a few years earlier.

Johannes and Louis took a sail-ship from Bremen. It was a perilous journey of eight weeks. All the passengers suffered from malnutrition. They arrived in New York City. The railroad brought them to Galesburg. While in Galesburg they were lucky to come across Amos Seigler. Amos took them with his wagonload of merchandise to Greenbush, where they found Mr. Hollenberg's two brothers.

Johannes Philip Kramer and Helen Meusborn, circa 1890

Mr. Kramer first found work at his trade in Monmouth, were he stayed about a year, and then he went back to Greenbush where he kept a tailor shop until 1866. He married Helena Meusborn, on November 1, 1858, whom he had known in Germany.

Helena was born in Vorm Wald, Westphalia, Germany, on February 13, 1839. She and her parents, Johann Adam and Marie Katharina Jung Kramer, came to America in 1858 with some friends. In 1878 with her oldest daughter, Helena visited her old German home.

Louise Katrina was born September 19, 1859, Greenbush. She married Karl Lotz on April 23, 1879. She died in Peoria on May 9, 1948.

Emma was born March 11, 1861, married Karl T. Luecke on April 23, 1890, and died August 30, 1892, in Stover, Missouri.

Frederick William was born July 6, 1863, in Greenbush, and married Magdalena (Lena) Doll May 23, 1893. She died January 13, 1946. He died July 4, 1936, in Macomb.

Bertha Marie was born August 15, 1865, in Greenbush, and married Ferdinand Schoendeider May 24, 1893. She died December 30, 1961, in Peoria, Illinois.

Wilhelmina Amelia was born June 10, 1868, in Greenbush, and married John R. Armes July 27, 1897. She died March 12, 1940.

Clara Helen was born April 9, 1872, in Greenbush, lived with her mother, who moved to Peoria in March 1903, after Mr. Kramer died on April 13, 1902.

Alvena Louisa was born April 9, 1872, in Greenbush, and married Olaf Olson March 9, 1903. She died November 1, 1977, in Milescity, Montana. By Jim DeKeyrel.

JUDSON AND BETTY KRUIDENIER - The history of the Kruidenier family in Monmouth began in early 1920s when Henrietta Kruidenier brought her family to Monmouth after her husband, Jud's grandfather, died in Egypt. Reverend Jeramiah Kruideneir was a Presbyterian missionary in Alexandria, Egypt, when he passed away. Four of their children attended Monmouth College, Margareta, John (Jud's dad), Elisabeth and Clarence.

Margareta and Elisabeth were teachers at Monmouth High School. Margareta married Bruce Buchanan and they spent their early married years in Ethiopia as missionaries for the Presbyterian church until the Italians invaded Ethiopia. They returned to Monmouth where two of their sons graduated from Monmouth College, Dr. Lee Buchanan and Robert Buchanan.

Jud and Betty Kruidenier, Kim, Kathy and Kurt

Jud's father, John, and mother, Frances Kruidenier, moved to Monmouth in 1934 where he took a job as an Assistant Secretary to Ralph Wells at the Production Credit Association. He worked there until he retired in 1968.

Jud attended Central and Willitts grade schools and attended Monmouth High School until he was drafted out of high school in 1944. He was in the Army until 1946 at Fort McCleland, Alabama. He attended Monmouth College and graduated in 1950.

Jud married Betty Liggett, a high school classmate, in 1949. Betty worked for Monmouth District #38 in the High School Library Media Center.

In 1951 he acquired a teaching and coaching position with School District #38 at Central Junior High and the elementary schools as physical education teacher. He stayed at that job for 30 years; later he coached at Monmouth College for 10 years.

In 1955 their daughter Kim was born. She attended Monmouth Public Schools and graduated from Warren High School and from Monmouth College in 1977 and is now raising Arabian horses in Hackett, Arkansas.

In 1960 Kathy was born. She attended Monmouth Public Schools, graduated from Warren High School and from Monmouth College in 1982, and is now manager of MC Sports in Flint, Michigan.

In 1964 Kurt was born. He graduated from Warren High School and attended Carl Sandburg Jr. College and now has his own boat restoration business.

RALPH DEAN KYLE - Ralph Dean Kyle, b. 1-30-1885, d. 8-2-1931, the son of Robert J. and Lura Ella Dean Kyle, was born in Darke County, Ohio. Robert was a farmer who a few years later became a United Presbyterian minister. Ralph worked his way through Monmouth College where he majored in Mathematics and was a noted athlete. Graduating in 1908, he took a position as Professor of Mathematics and Coach at the then small College of Idaho (now Albertson College of Idaho) in Caldwell. He married in Monmouth, 8-8-1911, a fellow teacher, Edith Merle Jewell. In 1912 he became Secretary of Education of the United Presbyterian Church, and moved his family from Caldwell to Monmouth, Illinois, where its home office was then located. In the fall of 1916 he and his home office were moved to Chicago. In this work he traveled a great deal and was a successful fundraiser. He was instrumental in establishing religion departments in the Presbyterian colleges. Because his eyes were bothering him, and to spend more time with his growing family, he resigned in 1919 and moved his family to a farm in Lenox Township in Warren County. The Fairview Center E.U.B. Church sits on one corner of the quarter section he owned and farmed. Besides farming he was active in the community as a 4-H club leader among the boys of the county, the livestock shipping manager for his vicinity, an active member of the local Parent-Teacher Association, and an Elder of the Second United Presbyterian Church of Monmouth In August 1931 he died in Rochester, Minnesota, following a brain tumor operation.

L: to R: Ralph D. Kyle, Sr., Ralph Galloway (his nephew) and Ralph D. Kyle, Jr., 1928

He was survived by his wife and eight children: Edith Jewell, Ralph Dean Jr., William Crandall, Robert Henry, David Cherry, Phoebe Catherine, Edwin Samuel and Herbert Lee. His wife, Merle Jewell Kyle, b. 6-13- 1888, in Warren County, d.6-7-1974, in Prescott, Arizona, was the youngest daughter of Henry L. and Lydia Crandall Jewell. She graduated from Monmouth College in 1909 and, before her marriage in 1911, taught one year each in a school at Neponset, Illinois, and at the College of Idaho. After his father's death, Ralph Jr., operated the farm through 1940 while the family slowly scattered all over the country. Merle took the younger children to Texas in 1938. In 1941 her daughter, Edith, and her husband, Lawrence A. Miller, took over the farm and Ralph Jr. also went south. Sickness forced Lawrence to stop managing the farm and Merle sold it about 1958. Lawrence died in 1961. At the time of her death Merle was living with her widowed daughter Edith in Prescott, Arizona. Both Ralph and Merle are buried in Monmouth Cemetery. Their grandson, Lawrence A. Miller Jr., b.3-7-1935, d.7-15-2001, continued to farm in Warren County for many years and his son, Craig L. Miller, b.4-16-1974, still does. *Submitted by Lee Kyle.*

SLOAN LANPHERE - Sloan Lanphere, born 1850 in Warren County, died in Monmouth 1924. Married Belle Ackerman, born at Kirkwood, 1855, died 1933. Farmed parts of Sections 2, 10 and 11 of Tompkins Township. They had five children: Willis Lanphere, born 6-3-1876, died 6-8-1932. He attended a one room school and Monmouth High School. He married Lillian McClintock. They had no children. He farmed in Sect 10 of Tompkins Township. He speculated in land in North Dakota and Illinois. His principle interest was his church, the Kirkwood United Presbyterian. Lillian was born in Mercer County, PA on 9-29-1872 to Rev. Joseph McClintock, a United Presbyterian minister. She attended Monmouth College and taught school before marriage. She died 10-20-1931.

Glen Lanphere, born 1889, married Bessie Pape. She was the daughter of Charles and Elizabeth Pape. They were childless, He also attended Coonville grade school and Monmouth High School. He farmed the home place and added land in Sect. 9, Tompkins Township. They loved fishing and spent many days at their cabin on the river north of Oquawka. Bessie was organist at the Presbyterian Church for many years. She died in 1954. He married Pearl Cummings, widow of Fred Cummings. Glen died in 1954, Pearl died in 1983.

Francis Lanphere Elder, born 1885, died 1978. She attended Coonville grade school, Monmouth High School, and Monmouth College. She married Rev. Ray Elder, a Presbyterian minister. They had four boys, James, Robert, William, and Stanley. His last pastorate was in Cincinnati and, after his retirement, they continued to live there. She died in 1978.

Hazel Lanphere Speer, born Sept. 1, 1891. She attended Coonville grade school, Monmouth High School and Monmouth College and the Oberlin College conservatory majoring in piano. She married Roscoe Speer. They had two children, Marian and Richard, She and Roscoe farmed in Sect. 2, Tompkins Township. She loved arts and crafts and taught piano. She and Roscoe were active ;in their church, First United Presbyterian of Monmouth. She died Oct. 25, 1956. Roscoe died June 21, 1966.

Fern Lanphere Jackson, born in 1894. She attended Coonville grade school, Monmouth High School and Monmouth College, always getting top grades. She taught school until she married Howard Jackson, a fellow teacher in Niles, Michigan. They lived in Michigan and Waukegan, IL. where he taught in the high schools. They had two daughters, Roberta and Joan. They moved to the Willis Lanphere farmstead after retirement. Fern died in 1992. Howard Jackson died in 1967.

EARL AND MAZIE LANTZ - Earl Warren Lantz was born 3 July 1897, the son of Odell Wherry Lantz and Laura Sigafoos. He married Mazie Lillian Black 4 June 1918. Mazie was born 5 January 1896 the daughter of James Grant Black and Ora Pence. Earl and Mazie had 8 children.

Earl and Mazie Lantz Family L: to R: Front: Mazie, David, Dorothy, Donald, Earl Back: Rex, Pauline, Chuck, Mary Jane, Robert.

Dorothy Mae, born 7 May 1920, married David Neil McCrery (5/7/1920) on 16 September 1937, in Monmouth; they farmed north of Monmouth in Spring Grove Township. They had three sons David Neil II born 1 September 1938, Dennis Lantz, born 19 December 1943, and John Douglas, born 10 August 1952.

Robert Dell, born 19 May 1921, married Pauline LaGrow (4/16/1921) on 16 July 1941 Bob served in the army 4 years and then the Reserves for 22 years retiring as a Captain. He owned his own cattle buying company for many years. They had two sons: William Eugene, born 12 December 1948, died 18 April 1992; and Samuel Edward, born 25 September 1962 died 25 September 1962. Polly died 18 December 1978. He then married Peg Taylor of Monmouth in 1993.

Rex Eugene, born 6 November 1922, married Barbara Kilgore on 26 March 1949. Rex served over 30 years in the U.S. Navy living in San Diego, CA. He retired a Lieutenant Commander. Rex and Barb had two sons, Scott Warren, born 17 January 1950 and Mark Allan, born 28 April 1956.

Mary Jane, born 25 September 1924 married Robert McMaster (4/l/1923) on 28 December 1946. Mary Jane served in the Army for 2 years and was a homemaker, Robert worked for J.I. Case Company where he was a vice president in sales. They had two children Robert Glen, born 26 December 1949, and Barbara Jo born 28 April 1953. Mary Jane died 30 April 2002.

Ora Pauline born 27 September 1926, married Donald Roberts on 12 May 1946 in Washington D.C., where Pauline was serving in the U.S. Navy during WWII. They had one son, Ronald (Ron) Greg Roberts, born 3 April 1948. They were divorced in 1950. Pauline married Lloyd Winbigler on 28 July 1951, at the Warren County Farm. Lloyd farmed with his brother north of Monmouth in Spring Grove Township. Lloyd had two children from a previous marriage: Carol June, born 23 August 1943, and Kathryn Jean, born 24 September 1947. Lloyd and Pauline had five children: Regina Kay, born 4 April 1952; Richard Alan, born 29 August 1954; Donna Ann, born 15 August 1956; Randall Kent, born 19 August 1959; and Roy Charles, born 23 August 1961. Lloyd adopted Ron in 1958.

Charles Dean born 8 October 1931, married Joyce Marie Clark (1 /22/1941) on 17 October 1964. Chuck served two years in the Army and achieved the rank of Corporal. He was a chemist and Vice-President of International sales for Pierce Chemicals and live in Rockford, IL. They had three children: Jeffery Warren, born 9 October 1965; John David, born 8 November 1965; and Kristine Mazie, born 18 September 1968.

Donald Dale, born 10 August 1937 married Alberta Cox (2/18/1944) on 9 April 1964. Don served in the reserves from 1955-1979. He was a Command Sergeant Major. He worked for the Illinois Department of Transportation and was hit and killed when directing traffic to removing snow on 10 January 1979. Don and Alberta had two children: Bradley George, born 19 March 1967; and Christine Gail, born 7 October 1969.

David Gale born 10 August 1937 married Martha Pullen (2/13 /1939) on 30 November 1956. David was superintendent of the Warren County Farm when it closed and retired from Monmouth Stone Company north of Monmouth. He serves in the Reserves from 1956-1964 retiring as a Staff Sergeant. They had five children: Cynthia Lee, born 7 July 1957; Laura Lynn, born 6 April 1959; David Gale, 1 June 1960; Christopher Earl, born 22 April 1963; and Robert Douglas, born 7 May 1966. David and Martha divorced in 1970.

Collectively, the seven brothers and sisters served their country proudly for over 80 years.

VIRGIL AND EUNICE FAHLUND LARSON - Carl Oscar Virgil Larson and Eunice Rosalie Fahlund were married in the First Lutheran Church parsonage in Monmouth on July 6, 1927, and built their home at 401 North B Street in 1928. Their children are Melba Rose Larson (Robert) Matson (b.1930) of Monmouth and Dr. Alan Virgil Larson (b.1933) of Dunwoody, Georgia.

Virgil & Eunice Larson

C.O.Virgil Larson was born in Woodhull, Illinois on April 10, 1902. His parents were Carl Oscar (1875-1901) and Josephine Adelia Carlson Larson (1880-1939). His grandparents were Charles Johan and Johanna Charlotte Nelson Carlson of New Windsor, Woodhull, and Aledo, who adopted him after his mother's second marriage. He was confirmed in the Aledo Lutheran Church and worked at Berg Shoe Company. After graduation from Aledo High School in 1920, he resumed his Larson name, attended post graduate school in Long Beach, California and Knox College in Galesburg, where he was a member of Lambda Chi Alpha. He worked in his grandfather Carlson's furniture store in New Windsor, at O.T. Johnson's furniture department in Galesburg, and became a partner in Hogue Furniture Company in Monmouth. He started his own store, Larson Furniture Mart at 209 1/2 South Main Street, and then founded Larson, Neilsen, Peterson, Inc., with his half-brother, Curtis B. Peterson, and Anton P. Neilsen, in Monmouth, Galesburg, Stronghurst and Galva. He was a Sunday School superintendent in the Lutheran Church and a member of the Gideon Society. After his wife of eighteen years died, he married Mildred Gabrielson of Galesburg, mother of Betty and Shirley, and moved to 325 North 6th Street. Virgil passed away on June 12, 1980, in Monmouth, after suffering a stroke at his Oquawka home at the age of seventy-eight.

Eunice Rosalie Fahlund Larson was born in Monmouth on October 10, 1905. She was the youngest daughter of Bernhard Leonard (1870-1950) and Nellie Swanson Fahlund (1868-1940). Her grandparents were Benjamin and Ida Peterson Fahlund of Sweden and Galesburg, who immigrated in 1868, and Swen and Inga Olson Swanson of Sweden. Her older sisters were Lillian Brown (Mrs. Joe E.) Brinton (Mrs. Albert) of Peoria, Bartonville, Orlando (widowed two times); and Vera Adeline Johnson (Mrs. Roy A.) of Monmouth. Eunice attended the local schools and graduated from Monmouth High School in 1924. She was employed as the bookkeeper at the Shunick Grocery store prior to her marriage. She was active in the Lutheran Church organizations and sang in the choir. Eunice died on March 31, 1945, at the Monmouth Hospital of cancer at the age of thirty-nine, leaving her children of twelve and fifteen years old.

ALBERT AND ALMA LAWHORN - Albert Andrew Lawhorn, born 5-17-1894, Sunbright, Tennessee, was the eldest of nine children of Frank and Eliza Amner (Buck) Lawhorn. He married Alma Lewallen (born 2-15-1903, Keota, Missouri) in Rugby, Tennessee, 3-26-1921. She was the oldest of seven children of Cicero Granville and Ollie Belle (Parker) Lewallen. As a toddler, her father showed her Haley's Comet and predicted she might live to see it again.

The Lawhorn Family, 1936. L: to R: Front: D. Odell, L. Buck and Avis A. Back: Roger V. and Dohy C.

Albert's brothers and sisters included Noah, Annie, Harry, Nelson, William, Esther, Hall, and Vernon. Alma's brothers and sisters were Olen, Mabel, Carl, Violace, Victor, and Bruno.

They had six children: a baby girl; Dohy Cicero, born 2-27-1923, died 2-03-2002; Roger Vernon, born 6-21-1925; Avis Amner (Hutchins), born 5-09-1927; Landon Buck, born 7-12-1929, died 3-06-2001; and Darl Odell, born 5-19-1931, died 10-17-1995. The family moved to Illinois in 1930.

Albert worked in lumber in Kentucky, Missouri, and Tennessee. In Illinois he was a "hired-man" for Emery Underwood, Homer Martin, and Paul Taylor. Those were the days of horse-drawn equipment, hand-shucking corn, hand-feeding cattle and hogs, caring for horses. Butchering was a fall job, and Alma made her own lye soap. A big community event was raking and burning the cornstalks; what a great smokey aroma for miles! He also worked at Monmouth Pottery. He married Bertha Cole in 1962. He died 4-12-1970, and Alma died 12-10-1983. They are buried in Roseville Memorial Park Cemetery.

After elementary school graduation, Alma was licensed to teach in Tennessee. She urged Albert to move to Illinois for educational opportunities for their children. She was a 'singing' Baptist. As a typical Depression wife, she grew and preserved hundreds of jars of fruits and vegetables, raised chickens for meat and eggs (and exchanged them for groceries), "put-down" meats, pickles, and saurkraut in great stoneware jars, sewed clothing for her family on a treadle sewing machine, and taught her children responsibility and moral values. She didn't tolerate laziness; during Depression years she could find a bite for a hungry transient who would work!

They shared the joys of the world with their children. Sunday afternoons often found them going on a picnic in their 'Model T' car. They encouraged their children to use individual abilities ñ working for neighbors, doing housework, trapping in nearby creeks. They played with the three Martin boys ñ one day as the Martins and Lawhorns splashed in the creek, Odell slipped off their homemade raft. Fourteen hands quickly grabbed him and saved him from an impromptu baptism!

The parents retold stories of early years in Tennessee: Great-Grandmother Alvatine Parker (English and Cherokee Indian) in her black silk dress with lace collar, rocking away while smoking her corncob pipe; "moonshiners" paths which were best left alone; unsuspecting travelers murdered as they slept; "Old Rugby Town" established for England's second sons. Stories of the Cecils, Parkers, Bucks, Llewellyns, and Lawhorns leaving the 'old countries ñ Ireland, Scotland, Wales, England, Germany, Holland, and France ñ to the Carolinas and Virginias, and over Cumberland and Smokey Mountains, into the forests, fields, and mines in search of better futures! Submitted by Avis Lawhorn Hutchins.

LAWRENCE AND DORIS LEE - Patrick Lawrence Lee was born on St. Patrick's Day in 1933, and Doris Arlene Shike was born on January 30, 1938. Both were born in Monmouth. On November 23, 1957, they were married at the Immaculate Conception Church and began farming in the Little York area.

P. Lawrence & Doris A. Lee

They have two children. DeAnne Lisa married Gregory Don Foley of Monmouth, and they have two daughters, Allison and Lindsey, and live in Broken Arrow, Oklahoma. Mark Lawrence married Monica Sue Welch of East Moline, IL. They have two daughters, Marissa and Morgan, and reside in Acworth, Georgia.

Lawrence's parents were Maurice B. Lee and Edna M. Doyle of Monmouth. His paternal grandparents were John M. Lee and Kathryn Hayes while his maternal grandparents were John D. Doyle and Emma F. Meleney, all of Warren County.

Doris is the daughter of C. Merlin Shike and Bernice Ranney of rural Seaton. Her paternal grandparents were Charles M. Shike and Sarah Ellen Morehead of rural Little York. Her maternal grandparents were William C. Ranney and Hilma V. Johnson of rural Seaton.

Lawrence and Doris have farmed in Warren County all their married life with the exception of two years in Henderson County. In 1971, while at Kirkwood, they purchased a farm in Warren County from Mrs. Ethel Martin of Monmouth. They rebuilt the farmhouse, doing much of the work themselves with the help of friends and family, and moved there in April of 1976.

In 1990 they purchased an adjoining farm from Murl Melton which was the original 1851 farmstead of Royal and Betsy Gates Ranney, Doris' great-great grandparents.

Lawrence has always enjoyed sports and at Little York High School played on its first football team, a six-man team. He played fast pitch softball on the Little York Aces for several years and later coached grade school and high school boys in the Warren County Junior Sherriff's League at both Kirkwood and Little York. Today he prefers golfing with friends and remains an avid Chicago Cubs and Bears fan.

With a life-long interest in music, Doris took piano lessons from Gracie Peterson for ten years. She sang in the Belmont Methodist Choir, and at Little York High School she participated in chorus, vocal ensemble and band. Later she taught piano lessons in her home.

Doris was a part of the Wesleyettes Barbershop/Gospel Quartet of Kirkwood for twenty-nine years and joined them in the heartfelt experience of making a tape called "Joy in the Journey" in 1995. She now sings with the D.J. Trio of Little York. She has been participating in the Monmouth Christian Women's Club (now the Monmouth Area After 5) since it began in 1974 and serves as an inspirational speaker for that organization, Stonecroft Ministries of Kansas City, Missouri.

Lawrence and Doris are members of the Kirkwood United Methodist Church and are now active in the Little York Methodist Church where she is a pianist.

Today they enjoy traveling with a couples' group, called the Biggsville Bunch, which has been together for over forty years, and visiting their children and grandchildren.

MORRIS AND BRIDGET LEE - Many families living in Warren County trace their origin back to Morris Lee (1835-1911) who was born in County Cork, Ireland. Residing in Warren County in 1862, he married Bridget Boozan Shunick (1836-1918), also an Irish immigrant. Widowed only the year before, she brought with her an infant son, Morris E. Shunick. The young couple purchased land in Sumner Township in 1869. The original home was located east of Little York on the present farm owned and resided on by the family of Michael W. Lee, grandson of Morris. The original 80-acre tract of land was purchased for $3600 from the descendants of John McClanahan, a 66 year-old farmer who died in the battle of Ft. Donelson, Tennessee in 1863.

Surviving aunts, Kathryn Lee (wife of Michael W. Lee) and Aileen Redington (husband Edward), pictured with grandchildren of M.R. and Nellie Doyle Lee, the fourth generation of Lees with roots in Warren County. (August 2001)

The 1870 Warren County census indicated that Morris and Bridget Lee's family included Morris Shunick (8), Margaret (7), John (5), Richard (3), and Hanora (2). Many of their descendants remain in the area.

The youngest sons, William and Michael R., born in 1872 and 1874, married two sisters, Fannie (-1957) and Nellie Doyle (1883-1944), also the children of Irish immigrants living in Warren County. Living side-by-side, these brothers farmed the gradually expanding Lee holdings near Little York. William's death in 1913 left Fannie a widow with six children: Nellie Twomey (1899-1989), Florence Stipe (1901-1985), Dennis (1903-1969), Everett (1906- 2000), Bernice Johnson (1908-1996), and Bernard (1908-1975) Lee. All three boys spent their entire lives working on their family farm. All of this family is now deceased, with descendants being the children of Nellie and Matt Twomey (Marilyn Homrich and Nancy Loduca and their families).

In 1918, Nellie Doyle Lee, having lost one infant son, Robert, in 1911, was left by the death of M.R. Lee at age 35 to raise 7 children, five of whom raised their families in and around Warren County. The eldest, Helen (1904- 1989), married T. James Cavanaugh who farmed west of Monmouth. There are many descendants of Helen and Jim who continue to live in the Monmouth area, including some of their children and their families: Roberta O'Brien, Mary Rose Sullivan, Dolores McCleary, Betty Shea/Duvall, Jim, and Kathleen Rowley.

Nellie and Michael R.'s oldest son, Harold (1905-1954), married Anastasia Pittard, raising their family in Warren County and Alexis. Their children include their eldest son, Fr. Robert E. Lee of Moline, James, Larry, Mary Alice Stewart, Carol Ann DeCosta (1941-1993), Nelle Rose Blakewell and David Lee.

Daughter Nona Lee (1908-1984) married John Rogers of Alexis. Their family consists of an infant daughter, Nell Ann, eldest son John of Godfrey, and Charles of Alexis, presently farming the land originally owned by Wm. and M.R. Lee.

Three more daughters and a son completed Michael R. and Nellie's family. Frances Lee (1912-1993) married Arthur Williams. This couple had son Michael, daughter Ruth Morgan, and infant daughter, Mary Frances. Edna Lee (1914-1982) married Gale Anderson. Their two sons are Raymond and Don. Son Michael W. (1916-1992) married Kathryn Shea. Their family, raised on the Lee farm, includes Michael R., Mark, Marian Thomas, Malia, and Matthew. M.R. and Nellie's youngest daughter, Aileen Lee (1918-), married Edward Redington of Galesburg. Their children are Patrick, Pam Curley, Peter, Philip, Paul, and an infant child.

With the younger generations now numbering over 240, the family of Morris and Bridget Lee continues to grow. Their descendants share a common Irish heritage, with immigrant roots planted in Warren County nearly 150 years ago.

ELIPHALET CROSS LEWIS - Eliphalet Cross Lewis was born on 11 May 1799, at Basking Ridge, Somerset County, NJ, son of Thomas Lewis and Susannah McCoy. He was the fifth of 11 children. In 1837, he came overland to Sangamon County, Illinois, with his brothers John and Thomas and their sister Susan Van Nostrand.

Eliphalet Lewis married Mary Ann Mills on 24 May 1823, at Basking Ridge. He was an oyster fisher near Amboy NJ. In 1837 he came overland to Illinois with his brothers John and Thomas and their sister Susan Ann Van Nostrand and their families, settling first in Springfield. In 1839 he moved to Berwick, purchasing a farm and adding to it until it totaled 750 acres. In 1839, he was baptized by the Rev. R. Wilbur at the Berwick Baptist Church.

Eliphalet remained on the farm until his death in 1869. Eliphalet and Mary Ann Lewis are buried at Berwick.

Eliphalet and Nancy Lewis had six children, five of whom survived to adulthood. Henry Mills Lewis (b.1824), Phebe Ann Lewis (b.1826), Mary Amanda Lewis (b. 1838), Susan Elizabeth Lewis (b.1841) and Thomas P. Lewis (b.1843).

Henry Mills ("Mills") Lewis, began amassing farm land in Berwick as a young man, then married Jane Carr, daughter of Absalom Carr and Sarah Claycomb, in Iowa in 1849, remaining an active citizen in Berwick his entire life; Phebe Lewis married A. Newton Baldwin and famed near Berwick until his death; Mary Amanda Lewis married DeWitt Phelps and famed in Tompkins Township until retiring into Monmouth; Susan Lewis married William R. Chaplin and moved to Missouri, and Thomas P. Lewis married Zilpha Morford and farmed in Roseville Township.

JOHN LEWIS - John Lewis was born on 24 April 1792, at Basking Ridge, Somerset County, NJ, son of Thomas Lewis and Susannah McCoy.

On 22 March 1815, John Lewis married Nancy Parrott Beach, daughter of Noah Beach and Joanna Thompson at Basking Ridge. In 1819 John prepared to move to Illinois with his uncle Jacob and brothers Joseph and Eliphalet, but his plans were changed by the serious illness of his wife and children. In 1837, 27 family members, including the families of John, Eliphalet, Thomas, and their sister Susan Ann Van Nostrand, traveled for two weeks overland to Springfield, Illinois, with one carriage, one horse and three 2-horse wagons. They joined other family members already settled in Springfield, and some of the party settled there.

Two years later, John and Eliphalet moved their families to Berwick. In 1841, John Lewis bought a farm and joined the Baptist church. He died suddenly of congestive fever on 5 October 1853. His widow then lived with her daughter Joanna Whitenack in Monmouth for twenty years. Nancy Lewis died in February 1872. John and Nancy Lewis are buried at Berwick Cemetery.

John and Nancy Lewis had seven children who survived to adulthood, another child who died in 1819 and possibly two sons named John (b.1824 and 1835) who died young. Joanna Lewis (b.1816) married Samuel Whitenack, Zephaniah Lewis (b.1818) married Eliza Ogden, Alpheus Lewis (b.1820) married Rebecca Cheney, Fanelia Beach Lewis (b.1822) married John Cox, Sarah Jane Lewis (b.1828) married John Rockwood and Aaron Thompson Lewis (b.1831) married Amy Josephine Russell.

Samuel and Joanna Lewis Whitenack farmed at Berwick, then retired to Monmouth. Zephaniah Lewis farmed at Berwick then retired to Galesburg. Alpheus Lewis farmed at Berwick and owned land in Roseville. John and Fanny Lewis Cox farmed at Roseville and Ellison Townships. John and Sarah Jane Lewis Rockwood farmed in McLean County and retired to Gibson City. Aaron Thompson Lewis farmed in Point Pleasant Township, then moved to Denver, Colorado, where he managed a department store.

THOMAS LEWIS - Thomas Lewis was born on 11 May 1765, at Basking Ridge, Somerset County, NJ, son of Zephaniah Lewis and Anna Doty, a Mayflower descendant. He lived his entire life in Basking Ridge, died there in 1831 at age 67 and is buried in the Presbyterian Churchyard Cemetery. Thomas was a great reader of the law and took an interest in politics, having been a youth during the Revolutionary War, in which his father served and died.

Thomas Lewis married Susannah McCoy, daughter of Captain Gawin McCoy and Susannah Kinnan on 10 November 1789. She died in 1821. Thomas and Susannah Lewis had 11 children.

Susannah refused to baptize any of the children until Thomas joined the Presbyterian church. He finally capitulated when their eleventh child and only daughter was born and a mass baptism of Lewises was held.

Of Thomas and Susannah Lewis' children, seven moved to Illinois, several settling at Berwick. John Lewis (b.1792) married Nancy Beach and settled in Berwick. Joseph Kinnan Lewis (b.1795) married Letitia Sutton and moved first to Springfield and then to Macon County, where he settled. David Lyon Lewis (b.1797) married Sarah Voorhees and settled in Ohio; his son John Voorhees Lewis later moved to Berwick. Eliphalet Cross Lewis (b.1799) married Mary Ann Mills and moved to Berwick with his brother John. Levi Doty Lewis (b.1801) married Eliza Sutton and died in California during the Gold Rush; two of his sons, James S. and John B. Lewis, settled in Berwick; his daughter Sarah married Reuben Coon and settled in Monmouth. Thomas Lewis (b. 808) married Margaret Ann Van Nostrand and had an illustrious career in Springfield, being sponsored by Abraham Lincoln to practice law. Susan Ann Lewis (b.1814) married Henry Van Hoff then Rev. Bergen, remaining in Springfield, Illinois.

ZEPHANIAH LEWIS - Zephaniah Lewis was born on 31 March 1818, at Basking Ridge, Somerset County, New Jersey, son of John Lewis and Nancy Parrott Beach. He attended school in New Brunswick, New York, and learned the carpenter's trade in Amboy, New Jersey. In 1835 Zephaniah Lewis came west by himself, stopping for one year in Hamilton, Butler County, OH, where other Lewis family members had settled early in the century. In 1837 Zephaniah arrived in Berwick. He worked as a carpenter for several years, helping to build the Baptist meeting house where his future wife attended school. In 1841 the Reverend R.M. Wilbur baptized him. Until his marriage, he lived with his parents who had followed him to Berwick in 1839.

Zephaniah & Eliza Ogden Lewis

On 26 October 1842, Zephaniah Lewis married Eliza Ogden, daughter of Abraham Ogden and Keziah Houghton at Berwick. For the next 27 years, they farmed 2-1/2 miles north of Berwick. During the war, Zephaniah was a member of the Union League and raised funds for the Union Army.

Children of Zephaniah & Eliza Lewis: Charles Ogden Lewis, Harriet Lewis Ogden and Adeline Lewis Egan.

Zephaniah and Eliza Ogden had four children; John Lewis (b.1854), Harriet Ann Lewis (b.1845), Adaline Lewis (b.1855) and Charles Ogden Lewis (b.1857). John Lewis died 1859 of a broken neck, Harriet married Franklin Delos Ogden and farmed in Floyd Township, Addie Lewis married John Egan but divorced after a short time and eventually moved to California, and Charles Ogden Lewis married Clara Kingsbury and moved to Galesburg.

In 1869, Zephaniah Lewis retired from farming and moved to Galesburg in retirement. He engaged in the lumber business there from 1870 to 1880, and was on the Board of Directors of the First National Bank. He joined the Galesburg Baptist Church, where he was a deacon and involved in the works of the church. He was a worker in the Reynolds Temperance Movement. Eliza Ogden Lewis died in 1886 and Zephaniah lived in the home in Galesburg until 1894. Zephaniah and Eliza are buried in Hope Cemetery, Galesurg.

ALLEN AND NELLIE LINCOLN - Allen Lincoln was born in Greenbush Township November 3, 1886. His parents were Artie and Sarah

Lewis Reunion, August 29, 1912

Belle (Woods) Lincoln. Allen's paternal grandfather, Clinton Lincoln, was from Cortland County, New York. He came to Greenbush in 1853. His paternal grandmother, Helen Stokes, was from Ohio. His maternal grandfather was E. Wilford Woods, son of Asa Woods, one of the founding fathers of Avon which was called Woodsville from 1837 to 1843. His maternal grandmother, Rhoda Butler, was the daughter of Col. John Butler of the 84th Illinois Militia.

Allen married Nellie Shinkel on January 6, 1910. They traveled by sleigh to St. Augustine, IL, and then by train to Galesburg where they were married.

Allen & Nellie (Shinkel) Lincoln's 50th Anniversary, 1960: Orville, George, Deen, Wilford, Forrest, Doris, Nellie, Allen, Louise and Maribelle.

Nellie Shinkel was born December 26, 1887. She was the daughter of George and Mary (Walker) Shinkel. Her father came from near Philadelphia, Pennsylvania, in 1869. Her mother's family were early settlers in Fulton County. Allen and Nellie married. Most of their farming years were in Greenbush and Berwick Townships. They did spend several years in the Woodhull and Herman area. In 1946 they moved to their farm near Avon in Fulton County, the former Shinkel homestead.

Nellie died March 28, 1976, and Allen on December 13, 1976. They had eight children.

Forrest, born February 16, 1911, was first a farmer and later a machinist at Caterpillar in Peoria. He married Dorothy Ruthe. They had two children: Nancy and LeRoy. Forrest died in 1992.

Wilford born October 8, 1912, was a farmer. He married Jessie Meadows. They had five children: Gary, LuAnn, Janet, Tom (deceased), and Chris.

Orville was born July 23, 1914. He was a farmer and later worked at various businesses. He was a World War II veteran. He married Rachel Jean Harris. They had three children: Karen, Sharon, and Bruce. Orville died July 31, 1992.

Deen, born August 31, 1915, was a farmer and World War 11 veteran. He married Mary Melton. They had three daughters: Sarah Jane, Virginia, and Marianne.

Louise was born September 26, 1918. She worked at factories in Avon and Galesburg and at the Burlington Ordinance Plant. She first married Joe Byerly and later Clarence Barker. Both are deceased. She had three sons: Deen, Donny and Wendel.

Doris born December 14, 1920, was a homemaker. She married Henry Marshall, a farmer and World War II veteran. They had three children: Larry, Deane, and Darla.

George was born December 2, 1927. He was a farmer and then became a fireman for the Burlington Railroad. He was a veteran of the Korean Conflict. He married Barbara Rylander. They had two daughters: Loraine and Laura. George was tragically killed on September 28, 1964, in a train collision.

Maribelle was born June 20, 1930. She was a homemaker. She married George Fitch. He worked for Burlington Northern Railroad. They had four children: Allen, Marsha, Kathy, and Evelyn.

DEEN AND MARY LINCOLN - Deen Shinkel Lincoln was born in Greenbush Township on August 31, 1915. He was the fourth of eight children born to Allen and Nellie Shinkel Lincoln. Both parents were natives of Greenbush Township.

Deen and Mary Lincoln

On August 12, 1951, he married Mary Melton of Little York. Mary was born July 7, 1924, in Sumner Township, the fourth of the seven children of Ora and Minnie Bryant Melton. Her parents came to Illinois in 1917, from Elizabeth, Harrison County, Indiana.

Deen attended Greenleaf Country School and Avon High School where he graduated in 1932. To get to high school he made a fourteen mile round trip on horseback.

Mary went to Duck Creek Grade School in Mercer County. Graduating from Little York High School in 1942, she entered Western Illinois State Teachers College in Macomb. In 1967, she received a B.S. in Education. She taught at both Sunbeam and Duck Creek Schools in Mercer County, then at the elementary schools in Roseville and Avon.

Deen farmed with his father prior to his Army service during World War II. He was stationed 31 months at Kodiak, Alaska, with the 250th Coast Artillery.

In 1945 Deen began farming at the Saunders' farm in Section 27 of Berwick Township. It was there that the couple began their married life. They moved to another farm in the same section but one mile to the east in 1965 which they purchased from Frank Clore in 1966.

In 1859 this farm had been purchased by Deen's great-uncle, Levi Lincoln. It was here that Lincoln School No. 100 was built on land donated for that purpose. The last Lincoln School building was used until 1963, and was demolished in 1999. In addition the Lincolns have acquired land in Section 25 and 26 of Berwick Township.

They are members of the Roseville United Methodist Church and life members of the Warren County Historical Society. Deen belongs to the American Legion Post 0614 in Roseville and a life-time member of J.W. Clendenin V.F.W. Post 2301 in Monmouth.

Mary and Deen have three daughters. Sarah Jane, born November 27, 1952, graduated from Barnes Hospital School of Nursing in St. Louis. She married Paul Seward of Leon, Kansas, and they have one daughter, Elizabeth Abigail (Abby).

Virginia Lea (Ginger) was born September 15, 1954. She is a graduate of Graham School of Nursing and Spoon River Valley Junior College. She has a B.S. in Nursing from Excelsior (formerly Regents) College in Albany, NY. She married David Lewis of Canton. Their three children are Jennifer, Christopher and David. Jennifer married Michael O'Riordan of Clane, County Kildare, Ireland. They have a daughter, Virginia Clare.

Marianne, born January 20, 1956, received her B.S. in Education from Western Illinois University and teaches in Monmouth. Her husband is Robert H. Peirce of Cameron. Her stepchildren are Ryan, Marc and Erin.

ROBERT L. LINMAN - Robert L. was born 18 October 1919, in Monmouth, Illinois, the son of Jalmer Nathaniel and Minnie Viola (PaImburg) Linman. He was raised on a farm with a brother, Gerald, and two sisters, Evelyn Rosander and Eleanor Braman. His mother passed away at the birth of Gerald and the boys were raised by her sister, Mildred PaImburg, living on a nearby farm. It was touch and go whether the baby would live. Charlie and Evelyn Rosander became farmers near Galva ñ in fact he farmed Rolland Swanson's land. Eleanor lives in Ft. Adkinson, Wisconsin, near where Chief Black Hawk was defeated. Gerald's first wife, Jean, passed on after their two boys, Jeffrey and Jon, completed high school, he remarried to the widow Wilma of Hampton, Illinois. Her parents own an apple orchard. Jeff shared valedictorian honors with two other boys on the basketball team. They were the first team to beat Galesburg high since 1940, Jeff made the winning basket. He went on to become a Lutheran Minister. Jon, the other son became a medical doctor with many degrees. When visiting the Rosanders at Galva on a birding jaunt, Charlie drove us to his fishing club, called "Hook and Bullet".

"Bob" married the oldest Goddard girl, Evelyn Marie. She had three sisters: Helen Rehn, Dorothy Petersen and Katie Fritz. The girls were very close, each inheriting excellent farm land from their parents, Harold and Harriet Goddard. Bob and Evelyn were married 11 August 1946, when he returned from army medical service in Italy during WWII. Evelyn had been teaching in a country school when they first met. The Goddard's bought them a farm. Bob was especially fond of the animals, especially horses. The couple adopted a boy, Donnie, who helped on the farm, and a girl, Jane, noted for her grades in Warren High School. Jane had problems in college, divorcing herself from her family until just recently, when all was forgiven. When the farm was sold, Bob and Evelyn moved to town and rented an apartment at 1238 Birchwood Drive. Donnie drove his truck for a while, then found work in El Mirage, Arizona. He offered to move Bob there.

Bob and Bud Barnes were birders and took many birding drives around the area. They drove in "the little red wagon", while watching they talked on any subject ñ always agreeing. Bob became a birder when listening to Bud make a bird talk at Rotary. He said, "I can do that." He was honored a Harris Fellow and seldom missed a meeting. While birding, they went to places that were brimming with bird songs, tramped through woods and ate goodies their wives sent along. Once in a while they got lost. Bud's Little Gray Coupe" gave up as did Bob, when he contracted diabetes, that took his right leg. He was a tall friendly strong man, but now he needed two crutches to move around ñ no more walking in the woods, only watching from the wagon. He now attended his Methodist church and joined the MARCO Sunday School Class. He was a student of the Bible, often sharing with me his thoughts. He joined "Christian Keenagers," meeting each month, where I kept busy serving in the kitchen. We grew apart. He continued attending Warren Athletic events with pain. When John Jenks, his boyhood pal passed away, he was devastated. John's son David and family saw he always had a seat with them attending games. Max Anderson was another "buddy" and they often attended State and County Fairs attending horse events. It was he that noticed Bob was having trouble walking. Bob was an avid Republican and John Deere green man.

Evelyn left us 16 January 1999, and Bob on 29 January 2002. They were buried side by side in Monmouth's Memorial Park Cemetery.

JAMES ARTHUR LIPES - James Arthur built his home at 902 South 4th Street, a brick mason and contractor for over 30 years. He was born 11 October 1903, in Monmouth, the son of Edgar and Edith (Gummerson) Lipes. He was reared and educated in Monmouth. For a number of years he was employed at the Irvine & Torrance Grocery, when they retired he and follow employee Andy Hines bought the stock and fixtures and operated it until a feed store leased the room. He then began showing motion pictures as a business to nearby smaller towns as a promotion to keep residents at home to spend their money.

He was a member of the former Ninth Avenue Church and when the Presbyterians consolidated he joined the Faith United Presbyterians. Jim taught Sunday School at the Ninth Avenue Church and at Jamieson Center as long as he was able. A member of the Kiwanis Club, he was recently honored as Bulletin Editor for 17 years of service. He was always interested in youth activities.

His marriage to Margaret L. Simpson took place 26 September 1958, at Monmouth. From an earlier marriage she had two daughters, Mrs. Harland (Hazel) Powell and Mrs. Marjorie Cavanaugh, both of Monmouth, and also two stepsons, Robert H. Simpson of Alexis and John B. "Jack" Simpson of Monmouth. There were ten grandchildren, 16 great-grandchildren, one brother, Charles Lipes of San Bernardino, California, a brother Gerald Lipes of Bloomington, California, and a sister, Mrs. Holley (Cristine) Sweeney of Monmouth. Besides his parents, he lost a brother in 1974.

When the Kiwanis club restored an old barn at Lake Youngquist, Jim donated his services in building a massive fireplace and it was used as a dining room for the YMCA Camp Youngquist. It provided reasonable facilities for the youth of the State of Illinois. It was closed when the state required them to build a swimming pool costing in the hundred thousands. The Youngquist families now use it for a picnic area.

SOPHIA LIPP - Sophia Lipp came to Warren County from Meldorf, Germany, with her son Glenn in 1909. They remained here all their lives. Sophia died in 1983. She is buried in Warren County Memorial Park Cemetery.

Sophia and Glenn each purchased land in Spring Grove Township.

Glenn graduated from Monmouth College in 1930 with a degree in Chemistry. He married Mildred Blunt in 1940. There were two children, Glenn Irvin, born 1945, married Susan Plotz and lives in Wilmington, Delaware. A daughter, born in 1942, Deanna Bulkeley, died in 1994.

Deanna and Irvin graduated from the University of Illinois. Since Irvin came home from Vietnam (1972), he has been employed by Du Pont. With Du Pont, Irvin and his wife have spent time in Singapore and India.

Deanna was employed by Bristol Meyers with Clairol Professional Products as National Director of Education. Deanna's son Michael was a policeman in Vail, Colorado. He has now decided to get a degree in computers. He married Cary Walters. Deanna's second son, Andrew, lives in East Berlin and is employed as a financial reporter.

Mildred lives in Monmouth, Illinois. Glenn died in 1997. He is buried in Warren County Memorial Park Cemetary.

HOWARD AND BERNICE LIVINGSTON - Howard Livingston and his wife, Bernice, were both born in Warren County. They spent their entire married lives in Warren County with the exception of one year in their early marriage when they lived and farmed in Henderson County. Both are buried in the Monmouth Memorial Park Cemetery in Warren County.

Howard & Bernice Livingston

Howard Randall Livingston was born July 22, 1907, in Tompkins Township in the farm home built by his maternal great-grandfather, Robert Brown, about 1860. His daughter, Samantha Ruth Brown, married Walter Randall and with their two daughters, Mary Florence and Lulu, occupied the home for many years. After Florence married William Henry "Will" Livingston in 1897, the Randalls moved to Monmouth and the Livingstons raised their family of Grace, Nellie and Howard in this farm home which was located about four miles southwest of Monmouth. Will Livingston's parents were John Henry and Esther (Perrin) Livingston. Howard attended Coonville Grade School and graduated from Monmouth High School with the class of 1925. He then began farming with his father.

Bernice Winebright Killey was born to Philip Isaac (P.I.) and Alice Maud (Winebright) Killey on February 14, 1911, in Lenox Township in the farm home built by her paternal grandfather, William Killey in 1872. Her father P.I. was also born in this house in 1880, and her mother was bornto George and Mary Van Fleet Winebright in 1882 in Kirkwood. P.I. and Alice were married January 17, 1906, and they lived on the Killey farm in Lenox Township east of Larchland until they retired and moved to Monmouth in 1948. Their oldest son, Ralph, moved onto the Killey far. with his wife Frances (Brent) and children Barbara, Lester, William and Frank.

Bernice also had a twin brother, Bruce, who with his wife Adeline (Stevenson) and sons, David, Richard, and James lived and farmed near Roseville. Her younger sister, Lucile, married Walter McVey, a carpenter, and lived in Monmouth with their son Philip. The Killeys have all been active in the Methodist Church and many community organizations. P.I. and Alice were married for sixty-three years before he died in 1969 and she in 1970.

Bernice attended West Prairie Grade School and graduated from Monmouth High School in 1929. She then chose a career in nursing and graduated from Burlington Hospital School of Nursing in 1932. She worked in that hospital for the year preceding her marriage to Howard in 1933. They began their years together on a rented farm southeast of Monmouth and lived on several farms until 1938 when they moved to a farm in Floyd Township which had been purchased by her father. Later they purchased this farm and spent the rest of their married life there.

They became the parents of three daughters - all born in Burlington, Iowa, Des Moines County. Alice Lucile was born September 13, 1935. Lorraine Grace was born June 18, 1937, and Martha Jean on October 17, 1938. All three attended nearby Muddy Comers Country School and graduated from Monmouth High School.

Alice attended Northwestern University for two years and Wesley Memorial Hospital School of Nursing for one year before her marriage to Charles Allaman on September 9, 1956. They have spent their entire married life on the Allaman family farm in Henderson County and raised four sons, William, Timothy, Daniel and Kenton.

Lorraine graduated in nursing from the University of Iowa. She married Bruce Green from Council Bluffs, Iowa, and he later became a pilot for United Air Lines. They built a home near St. Charles, Illinois, where they still reside. They have four children, Jeffrey, Jon, Kathryn and Bryn.

Martha Jean graduated in Dental Hygiene from the University of Iowa. She married Warren Sanders, a graduate of Monmouth College and a native of Earlville, Illinois. His career in business took them to several cities and states, lastly to the Minneapolis area. They will soon be retiring to a newly purchased home near Knoxville, Tennessee. They have two children Mark and Amy.

Howard Livingston died on April 16, 1963, at the age of 55 as the result of a fall from a haymow on the farm. His wife, Bernice, continued to live on the farm, and with the help of her brother, Bruce, continued to manage the farming operation. Bruce and his sons farmed in partnership with her for many years. She returned to her nursing career and worked part time at Monmouth Hospital and Community Memorial Hospital. She enjoyed needlework, travel, an active social life and especially her ten grandchildren. She suffered a fall while visiting her daughter in Minnesota and died a few days later on July 19, 1998, in the hospital there. She was eighty-seven years old. Her grandsons, Bill, Tim and Dan Allaman are currently farming the family farm and grandson,

Ken Allaman is living in the home with his wife Lori and daughter Katie.

MARY GERTRUDE LIVINGSTON - Mary G. Livingston (1844-1876) was the daughter of Giles Fonda Livingston (b.5-10-1807, d.3-7-1881), married 9-25-1834 to Elizabeth Hand (b.4-3-1812, d.11-19-1881). She was the granddaughter of Henry Hand and Sarah Davis, natives of New Jersey. Henry's ancestors were natives of Holland, and the Davis ancestors were from England and Holland. Ten children were born to Giles and Elizabeth Livingston:

Frank and Harriet Frances (Beckner) Raymond, Farragut, Iowa. 50th Anniversary, September 23, 1940.

(1) Henry Hand (b.6-24-1835, d.12-3-1896), married 6-13-1858 to Ann Allmira Long, who died 6-4-1915.

(2) Sarah Jane (b.9-19-1836), married 6-17-1854 to Lemuel Provost.

(3) Elizabeth Hand, (b.12-26-1837).

(4) Rush (b.11-14-1837).

(5) Giles Fonda (b.8-12-1842).

(6) Mary Gertrude (b. 5-12-1844, d. 4-19-1876), first wife of Simon Martin Raymond (1836-1909), married 12-1-1859.

(7) Edward (b.2-23-1847).

(8) Horatio Reed (b.1-10-1849).

(9) Alfred M. (b.2-19-1851, d. 8-23-1933).

(10) Albert Frank (b.7-28-1853).

(Source: Livingston Bible of Ruey Raymond, Farragut, Iowa, 8-19-1967).

The Hand family, Mead family and Simon Martin Raymond all came to Prairie City, Illinois, from Ohio in the 1850s.

The children born to Simon Martin Raymond and first wife, Mary Gertrude Livingston were Ralph K., died 16 June 1864 (3 years old) while his father was away serving in the Civil War; Mary Ellen, died 3-7-1879 (age 14 years) ñ buried in the Raymond lot in McMahill Cemetery; Frank Raymond, born 12-27-1866, died 12-15-1953 at Farragut, Iowa.

Frank was married 9-23-1890 in Swan Creek, Warren Co., Illinois, to Harriet Frances Beckner (b.8-17-1869, d. 8-31-1949). She was the daughter of George Washington Beckner (1825-1921) and his wife, Deborah Van Kirk, (1826-) ñ buried Bond Cemetery, Greenbush Township, Warren Co., Illinois. They had three children: Sumner, Ralph and Ruey. Frank and Hattie Raymond moved to Farragut, Iowa, where their descendants (five generations) still live today on former Livingston lands.

WILLIAM AND MARGUERITE LIVINGSTON - William Livingston was born December 15, 1916, on the family farm at Woodvale, about eight miles north of Monmouth. He was the fifth of eight children born to Asa B. and Grace Butler Livingston. At the age of 85, you will still find him living in the same house where he was born.

Bill & Marguerite Livingston 1995

William, known as Bill to family and friends, attended the Foster School. He has been a member of Farm Bureau and the Odd Fellows in Little York. Since his youth, farming was Bill's interest, and became his livelihood. He has raised corn and alfalfa as well as cattle, hogs, and sheep. He now rents the farm to his daughter and son-in-law.

Bill married E. Marguerite Waring on May 26, 1957, in the Bethel Lutheran Church in Stronghurst, which holds their membership. Marguerite is the oldest of six children born to Axel and Teckla (Johnson) Waring. She was born December 20, 1921, in Terre Haute Township in Henderson County. She graduated from Roseville High in 1940, and the Burlington School of Nursing in 1944. She then worked in obstetrics at the Monmouth Hospital until after her marriage. Marguerite's father came to the United States from Sweden at the age of 19. Her maternal grandparents were both from Sweden.

The Livingstons are the parents of one daughter, Grace. She is married to Robert McCrery of rural Monmouth, and Bill and Marguerite are grandparents to William and Sarah.

Bill is a great-great grandson of pioneers Peter and Rachel Butler, who were very prominent in early Warren County, and headed the wagon train from Monmouth's town square to Oregon territory where they were instrumental in the founding of Monmouth, Oregon. Great-grandparents were John M. and Eliza (Smith) Butler. Bill's grandparents were Ralph O. and Floy (Tracy) Butler, and John H. and Esther Ann (Perrin) Livingston, the latter couple coming to Illinois from New York.

DEAN AND LEITHA H. LOCK - Leitha Hendel Lock, the second oldest daughter of Jay R. and Sadie Kreps Hendel, was born August 13, 1926, in Greenbush Township, Warren County, Illinois. She grew up on the same farm where she was born, attended Taft School eight years and graduated from Avon High School.

On May 5, 1945, she married Dean S. Lock, son of J. Hobart and Ethel Gray Lock, in the Avon United Methodist Church by Reverend Gorden White. Dean was born October 13, 1924, in Joshua Township, Fulton County, Illinois. The Lock family moved to a farm southeast of Avon in 1938. Dean was drafted into the U. S. Army and sent to Japan.

Leitha attended Western Illinois University in Macomb, Illinois, for awhile and received an emergency certificate to teach school. She taught at the Hall School in Greenbush Township for three years, living with her parents during this time.

Dean was discharged from the service in the fall of 1946 and they lived east of Avon until March 1950, when they moved to the "Old Sailer Place" west of Avon in Section 25, Greenbush Township. A new house was built that summer.

Dean and Leitha had four children ñ Nancy Dea born December 7, 1947, Jill Diane born April 22, 1951, Jane Ann born June 28, 1952, and Richard Dean born March 7, 1958. All the children attended grade school and graduated from Avon High School.

Dean & Leitha Lock

Nancy attended a technical school in Elkhart, Indiana, and became a medical laboratory technician. She married Eldon Leighty and they had a daughter, Gretchen. Jill attended Western Illinois University and received her diploma posthumously after dying as result of injuries in a car accident. Jane graduated from Illinois State University and taught at the high school level. Jane married Guy Hood and they had two children, Lauren and David. Richard lives on and farms the farm where he grew up. He married Cynthia Jo McGrew and they had Michael, Hanna, Kevin and Matthew.

In 1964 Leitha graduated from the first class to graduate from the Practical Nurse Program in District 205, Galesburg, Illinois. She received her license and worked at the Avon Nursing Home for a number of years.

In 1980, Dean and Leitha moved to a farm they nicknamed the "white house" because it had belonged to a White family. This farm was on the Taft Road in Greenbush Township. They lived there only three years, moving back next door to Richard for a short time. Leitha's mother had passed away and they acquired her house in Avon in 1983 and live there now. Submitted by Dean Lock.

RICHARD & CYNTHIA JO LOCK - Richard Lock, son of Dean and Leitha H. Lock, was born March 7, 1958, at Saunders Hospital, Greenbush Township, Warren County, Illinois. Richard was the youngest in the family, having three older sisters. He grew up on a farm west of Avon in Section 25, Greenbush Township, Warren County, Illinois, where he still lives. He graduated from Avon High School. His first business adventure was a chicken business on the farm just east of his parents' home. He had several thousand caged hens and sold eggs. While he had the hen house before graduating from high school, he did not move to that farm until after he graduated. September 13, 1980, he married Cynthia Jo McGrew, daughter of Tom and Jane McGrew of Walnut Grove community. She had one sister and two brothers. After they were married, they moved into the house that Richard had been raised in. They still live there.

They are the parents of Michael Dean born September 1981, Hanna Marie born June 1983, Kevin Thomas born November 1996, and Matthew Richard born March 1999.

Richard liked to farm and is still farming. In the early 1980s he operated a tire repair business along with farming. He later discontinued that when he got a job at Maytag. He continues to farm and work at Maytag.

Richard and Cindy are both active members of the Walnut Grove United Methodist Church. Submitted by Richard Lock.

JAMES A. LOFFTUS - The head of the family (James A. Lofftus) was born in Warren County. His grandfather was from Virginia - his wife from Kentucky. The farm in southern Point Pleasant Township was bought by Arzo and Martha Hume Lofftus. They were the parents of seven children. The oldest son, Kenton, married Bertha A. Torrance and settled on the half section of land across the field from the homestead. His brother, James A. Lofftus, married Laura M. Torrance (a sister of Bertha) and they all lived in the same house and raised their families. My father, Everett H. Lofftus, was the son of James and Laura.

The Lofftus Family. L: to R: Front: Keith Lofftus, Marjorie Lofftus Wallace, Jean Ann Lofftus Smith. Back: Everett A. Lofftus Jr., Martha M. Lofftus Reid, James Wesley Lofftus, Irene G. Lofftus Jardine.

As an elementary school student, he attended Piper school. As things happen, this is where he met our mother who had moved from a school in Clearwater, Kansas. They were farmers until Mildred passed away in 1958. There were nine children born to this union. Only seven survived. Among the children listed in the picture are two teachers, one U.S. government agriculture worker (he also served in the National Guard and France), one policeman who had also served in the Air Force and his wife Midge passed away from cancer and he passed away from complications from a train wreck. The youngest brother drives an eighteen-wheeler (his wife passed away from cancer). One sister, Jean Ann, has worked for the government since she graduated from high school. One sister graduated from the University of Illinois in 1945. She was a registered dietician for sixteen years. Her husband had a bad heart and passed away in 1991.

Mildred M. Lofftus' parents were Lillian Ross and Fredrick Michaels. When he and Lillian were married, they moved to the Clearwater, Kansas, to farm. Because Wesley Michaels, his father, was in rather poor health, they moved back to Illinois. Their new house was built next to the original Michaels property in southwestern Point Pleasant Township. Wesley's wife, Sarah M. Piper's parents also lived in the neighborhood. She was one of six children who came from Massachusetts by way of the Erie Canal to Chicago by barge and down to Canton, Illinois, by covered wagon. They later moved to the home place near the Piper school. On January 11, 1868, she married Wesley M. Michael (a Civil War veteran). They had two children, Fredrick and Nita, and raised her niece, Mary Michaels. Wesley lived until 1912, and Sarah lived until 1937. Her Civil War widow pension was $13.00 a month!

Mildred's mother was Lillian A. Ross. Her father was Daniel Ross and her mother was Malinda Newkirk. The Ross family came from Delaware and Scotland. The Newkirk's were German.

Everett H. Lofftus' grandfather Torrance came from a large family from Jay, New York, and Connecticut. He left his family here in Illinois and traveled to Cuba, Pike's Peak and bought land. His grandmother, Margaret Hindman, came from a family who were original settlers in Indiana. They moved to Warren County where some of the family still live. Charles and Margaret had five children - three survived.

Activities of the family - we belonged to 4-H. The four oldest attended high school at Western Illinois Teacher's College. The last three attended school in Roseville, Illinois. Members of the family were active in Farm Bureau, Home Bureau, 4-H Leaders (25 years), teaching Sunday School, NSDAR and NSCAR. Irene served as Chapter Regent for five years of the Chief Shaubena Chapter in Roseville, Illinois.

CHALMER A. AND RACHAEL R. LOVDAHL - Chalmer A. Lovdahl was born on March 11, 1892 the son of John W. and Matilda Lovdahl.

Rachael R. Monticue was born on July 9, 1899 the daughter of Frank and Blanche Monticue.

They were married on February 26, 1919 after Chalmer returned from overseas duty in World War I.

Chalmer & Rachael Lovdahl

They were the parents of twelve children Blanche Lucille, January 17,1920; Bessie Darlene, February 22,1922; John William, June 4, 1923; Chalmer Creighton, September 8,1925; Robert Martin, November 7,1927; Rachael Elizabeth, May 9,1929; *Elsie Mae, March 19,1932; *Donald Francis, January 6,1934; Theodore Eugene, June 4, 1938; Harold Cecil, July 17,1939; James Murray, July 25, 1941; Rachael Rebecca, May 31, 1946 (*died in infancy).

Their oldest son, John W. (d. 3-26-92) was a painting contractor.

Creighton and Martin formed the accounting and tax business known as Lovdahl Bros. in 1948, and it continues now as Lovdahl and Shimmin Inc., a division of the Security Savings Bank.

Ted retired after several years in the data processing field.

Cecil and James purchased the Monmouth Grain and Dryer business and have greatly expanded its operation in this area.

Members of this family have served in each of our nation's conflicts from World War I to date.

While most of the family still reside in Illinois some now are in Arizona, California, Iowa, Kansas, Mississippi, Ohio, North Carolina, Utah and Texas.

JOHN WILLIAM AND JULIA (JUDY) (ICENOGLE) LOVDAHL - John William Lovdahl was born 4 June, 1923, to Chalmer August and Rachael Rebecca (Monticue) Lovdahl in Lenox Township. His siblings are Blanche, born 17 January 1920, m. Harold Icenogle (four daughters); Bessie D., born 22 February 1921, m. Ardie Snider (two daughters, one son); Chalmer Creighton, born 8 September 1925, m. Barbara Icenogle (three daughters, three sons); Robert Martin, born 7 November 1927, m. Renie Leake (one daughter, two sons); Rachel Elizabeth "Bibby," born 9 May 1929, m. Paul Bethel (one daughter, one son); Theodore "Ted" Eugene, born 4 June 1938, m. Bonnie (three daughters, three sons); Harold Cecil, born 17 July 1939, m. Kay Irey (three sons); James Murry, born 24 June 1941, m. Suzanne Todd (one daughter, one son); Becky, born 31 May 1946.

John Lovdahl, 1976, age 53

John lived with the family on a farm four miles southeast of Monmouth on the Cameron Road. He attended Fairview Center School.

John married Julia Ann (Judy) Icenogle, oldest daughter of Edgar and Edith (Murrell) Icenogle, 13 June 1944. John worked 22 years at Nichols Hatchery, 300 block N. 9th Street, where they shipped baby chickens all over the U.S. He was self-employed 20 years as a painter/ decorator operating Rite-Way Painting and Decorating.

John was proud of his family: daughters Joy Marie, born 9 November 1955, m. Roger L. Johnson (three sons ñ Craig, Luke and Andrew); and Janet Fay, born 3 November 1957, m. Don Huddlesons (three daughters Erin Lynn, Heather Ann and Samantha Dazwn).

Julia has done babysitting for many families for many years. They were both members of Foursquare Gospel Church.

John died 16 March 1992, age 69, buried Memorial Park Cemetery.

LOVERIDGE-LUCAS - Heman (pronounced Hayman) Loveridge was born July 15, 1809, in the farming village of Curry Rivel, Somerset, England. He married Mary Masters (baptized February 16, 1812, South Petherton) on February 14, 1833, in Curry Rivel. They had twelve children. From this family, two moved to Australia, five remained in England and five came to the U.S. From this five, four settled in Warren County, Illinois.

Robert Loveridge

James, born August 3, 1833, married his cousin, Harriet Hector, on August 24, 1854, in Curry Rivel. Their first child, Heman, was born December 21, 1854. In the early part of 1855, the family arrived and settled in Kelly Township, where nine more children were born. They were Elizabeth, Enza, Emma, Mary, Fannie, Samuel, Olla, Alice and Jessie. James was a hotelkeeper in his early years, but by 1880 and the 1900 census he was shown as a farmer. James died of pneumonia on May 12, 1912, and his wife, Harriet, died November 2, 1924, both in Alexis.

Thomas, born March 6, 1841, arrived later and enlisted in the Union Army on October 8, 1861, and served as a Sergeant with C Company, 11th Cavalry Regiment of Illinois. He was discharged with a disability on October 30, 1862. Enlistment details listed: 20 years, 5 feet 7 inches, light hair, hazel eyes, fair complexion, single, farmer, nativity England, residence Ionia, Warren. He married Margaret (Maggie) Waddill on September 16, 1868, and they had three children, Alina, Ray and May. In 1880 he was a hotelkeeper in Alexis. He served as county treasurer on a Republican ticket. He was an elder in the Presbyterian Church. He moved his residence to Aledo in the 1890s. Thomas Loveridge died June 21, 1908, in Hudson, Wisconsin, and was buried in Aledo. His wife, Maggie, died September 26, 1933.

A sister, Elizabeth Loveridge, born April 20, 1837, married James (Henry) Lucas in 1859/60 and had five children: Ada, Annie, William, Kate and Heman. The family came to Kelly Township, Warren County, in 1870, where another three children, Charles, Willis and Archie, were born. Henry was a farmer. He died January 31, 1890. Elizabeth remarried Aaron Yarde, a man who was 27 years her senior, on November 12, 1891. Aaron died May 30, 1898. Elizabeth died March 10, 1915.

Robert Loveridge, born December 19, 1849, was the last to arrive in the U.S. and came to Alexis on August 14, 1870. His occupation was a house painter. Robert married Berthena F. Boggs on April 20, 1876. They had three children: Bertha, Frederick and Clarence. Berthena died in 1886. He remarried Mary Bell Morgan on February 13, 1889. They had two daughters: Marye (Edith) and Bessie. In late 1925, Robert and his wife, Mary, went back to England for a visit and reunion with the surviving three members of his family. They were Eliza (Keech), his unmarried sister, Mary Ann (Polly), and brother, Frederick, visiting from Australia. The four family members had not met for 47 and 55 years. Robert was a member of the Presbyterian Church, an elder, a Mason and a Modern Woodman. Robert died of pneumonia May 6, 1931, and is wife, Mary, died in 1933.

Another brother, Samuel Loveridge, also came to the U.S.

LOVERIDGE-WILSON - Around 1890, Thomas John Squire Dare Loveridge left a quaint, rural village called Stoke St. Gregory in Somerset, England, to find his relatives, Aunt Mary and Uncle James Jeanes, in Kelly Township, Warren County, Illinois.

Thomas John Squire Dare Loveridge and Mildred Pearl Wilson, wedding, October 2, 1900.

Within three years he convinced his younger sister, Annie Selina, to come to the Jeanes home. A number of years later, their brother, Elias, joined them in Warren County.

In the late 1890s, Thomas John, a farmer, met Mildred Pearl Wilson, daughter of James John Walker Wilson and Elizabeth (Townsend) Wilson, who also lived in Kelly Township. On October 2, 1900, Thomas and Mildred Pearl were married in Galesburg, Illinois.

Living at the James Jeanes home was a young man by the name of Charles Hunt. On February 6, 1895, Annie Selina Loveridge became Mrs. Charles Frederick Hunt. Charles was the son of Alfred and Mary (Paul) Hunt. Charles was born December 27, 1871, in Illinois and died in 1922. Annie was born March 16, 1877, and died September 21, 1957, in Galesburg, Illinois. Both Charles and Annie are buried in Fuller Cemetery in Knox County, Illinois.

Charles and Annie had three sons: Arleigh Francis, Frederick Charles and Clarence John Hunt.

Now let's take a look at the ancestors of the Loveridges. Thomas, Annie and Elias' parents were John Elias Loveridge and Mary (Squire) Loveridge. John Elias was born about 1848 in Stoke St. Gregory, Somerset, England, and died around 1891 from a horse accident. He was the son of Samuel Dare Loveridge and Martha (Pipe) Loveridge. Mary Squire was born about 1847 in Stoke St. Gregory and died August 17, 1930, in England. She was the daughter of John Squire and Ann (Stacey) Squire. John and Mary had ten children.

Mildred Pearl Loveridge was one of six children of James John Walker Wilson and Elizabeth (Townsend) Wilson.

James was born in 1861 in Gerlaw, Warren County, Illinois, and died in 1927. He is buried in Hope Cemetery in Warren County. James was the son of James J. Wilson, born June 19, 1824, in Yorkshire, England, and Elizabeth (Brotton) Wilson, born March 1, 1820, in England. Both James and Elizabeth Brotton Wilson are buried in Spring Grove Cemetery in Warren County, Illinois. James and Elizabeth Brotton Wilson were the parents of three children:

William Henry, Enoch J. and James John Walker Wilson.

Elizabeth Townsend was born September 3, 1858, in Tylerville, Warren County, Illinois, and died in September 1942, in Galesburg, Illinois. Elizabeth was the daughter of Alexander Townsend and Sarah Jane (Stegall) Townsend.

Both James and Elizabeth Wilson are buried in Hope Cemetery in Warren County, Illinois. James and Elizabeth Townsend Wilson had six children: Ozro William, Mildred Pearl, James Alexander, Alvin LeRoy, Marie and Iva R. Wilson. Alexander and Sarah Jane (Stegall) Townsend were the parents of nine children: Daniel, Sarah, Charlie Wesley, Margaret, Susan, Francina, Elizabeth, Irene and Soloman E. Townsend. Written by Fran Bradburn Henley and Ron Hunt, great-grandchildren of James and Elizabeth (Townsend) Wilson.

HEIMO AND EILEEN LOYA - August of 1936, a young couple from Chicago had an interview with Dr. Thomas Hanna McMichael, retiring president of Monmouth College, and moved to Monmouth in September from Chicago to begin their life in Warren County ñ he as a violin teacher and orchestra conductor in the Music Department of the College ñ and she as a part-time secretary at the Illinois Bankers Life Assurance Company and part-time college student.

Heimo & Eileen Loya

Heimo A. (Hal) Loya was born in Rock Springs, Wyoming on September 14, 1909, the son of Ilo and Advi Loya, who came to the United States in the early 1900s from Finland. In 1934 he married Eileen Sandberg in Chicago, Illinois. She was born July 16, 1913, in Chicago, the daughter of Gunnar and Ines Sandberg, natives of Finland, who also became American citizens in the early 1900s.

Hal and Eileen raised three children: Mervyn, born Feruary 20, 1940; Karin, born November 15, 1941; and Alan, born July 17, 1944. All three benefited from a good education with excellent teachers in the local school system, and all three graduated from Monmouth College.

Hal's contribution to the community ñ in addition to heading the music department at Monmouth College for many years ñ includes directing various church choirs in Monmouth, being song leader of Rotary Club, director of the Monmouth Municipal Band, and judging many music contests in and out of state.

In 1941, when Monmouth College was designated a Naval Flight Preparatory School and sent fifteen of its faculty, including Hal, to Fulton, Missouri, for training to teach naval cadets, Hal taught navigation and mathematics to these young men. He and Jean Liedman, dean of students, spent many nights in the Loya kitchen "boning up" on the subjects they taught. In 1944 this program was replaced by the Navy Academic Refresher Unit.

In addition to raising her family, Eileen served as Administrative Assistant to four presidents of Monmouth College, first president of Garfield PTA, and leadership positions in numerous clubs and church organizations.

Mention should be made that the Loya name had its origins in Finland. In June 1999, Hal and Eileen's daughter, Karin, on a visit to Finland, brought back a book from relatives entitled, "The Vicissitudes of the Village of Loya and its People." As a result, Eileen has translated the book from Finnish to English to enable American family members to learn about their roots since none are familiar with the Finnish language. A copy is being made available to the Warren County Library.

JAMES RAYMOND LOZIER - James Raymond Lozier was born November 25,1927, to William (Edward) Lozier and Irene J. Smith Lozier in Roseville, Illinois, the only child. He was a farmer and worked at Gambles in Monmouth for 27 years as a night watchman at the warehouse. He operated Lozier Trucking till his death on September 8, 1985.

Jim married Ruth Slagle Steel March 1, 1949. They had the following children: Nora, born January 30, 1950. Nora married Michael Crandall August 19, 1967, and they had two children: Michelle, born February 10, 1968, and Eric, born November 11, 1972. Michelle married John Taylor June 8, 1991. Eric married Jennifer Mayfield August 10, 1996. Their child, Jackson (Jack), was born October 20,1999.

Wanda, the second child of Jim, was born March 24,1951, and married William Johnson July 3, 1970. Their children are Mark, born August 8, 1971, died September 3, 1971; Matthew, born August 15, 1972, married Ann Lafrey November 18, 1995 ñ one child, Parker, born June 13, 2000; and Megan, born August 1, 1975, married Jeffrey Frieden September 30, 2000 ñ one child, Jenna, born April 8, 2001.

Donna, Jim's third child, was born March 11, 1954, and married Layne (Rick) Evans July 15, 1974. Their children are: Jason, born April 28, 1975, married Susan Smith May 21, 1995, ñ three children, Kalab Smith, born August 6, 1993, Kage, born February 5, 1996, and Keirsten, born March 10, 1997; Jason, born May 21, 1978, married Bette Worley ñ two children, Rheana, born August 29, 1998, and Levi, born June 2, 2000. Donna married Edward Schroder June 5, 1981, child Joshua, born April 29, 1983. Donna married Paul Loper February 23,1981, child Cliff, born March 6,1992.

Jim's fourth child, Jim Jr., was born January 6, 1957, and married Brenda Switzer August 20, 1982. They had the following children: James, born September 27, 1984; Jesse, born October 16, 1987; and Nicole, born August 13, 1990.

Jim married Mary Conlee December 8, 1962. He thought a lot of his children and his grandchildren. Jim liked to travel and to go camping.

LUSK AND LOPTIEN - "Today I'm writing my life history...a small dot in generations of the Lusk-Loptien Family"

When Betty Lusk's parents were married, they lived north of Monmouth, Illinois, what seemed like a very small settlement, only a few houses on a county road, not far from town. She was born there July 4, 1927, soon after a terrific summer storm. A neighbor friend of her parents was a nurse named Margaret Granger who took one look at her and said "Oh, that's Betty Jean, "and so she was named. The name was so popular at that time there were five Bettys in her class at school.

Wilson & Ada (Loptien) Lusk, 1938

Less than two years later the family was living in Monmouth, across the street from 818 North D Street, her father's birth place. Her grandparents, Harvey Wilson Lusk married Mary Evaline (Estell), and raised their family at that residence. There were five children: Ethel - 1886; Gladys - 1887; Charles (Peg) - 1892; Ralph - 1895; and her father Wilson - 1898.

Ethel married Fred Palmer; their children were Nettie, who died at age 5 years; Mary (Conard) Lusk; and Lizzie.

Gladys married James W. Norman; their children were Evelyn, Alfred and Ellen.

Charles (Peg) Lusk married Jennie (Jebb); their children were Charlotte, John, Genevieve, Doris Lusk, and Chad, who was killed in Vire, France during WWII.

Ralph married Viola (Beuhl); their children were Ralph Jr., Louise and Jo-Anne.

Wilson Thomas Lusk, Betty's father, married Ada Irma (Loptien); their children were Betty Jean (Lusk) Welty; Dorothy May Lusk, who died soon after birth; Donna Ilene (Lusk), who married Clifford Lodwick ñ their children were Janice, Cary, Ada, Stanley, Linda, Greg and Jessie; Billy Wayne Lusk, who married Shirley (LeFort) ñ their children were Debra and Mark. Ada Irma (Loptien) Lusk was born September 8, 1897. Her parents were Edward Charles Loptien and Nellie Threasa (Fetterley) Loptien.

Betty started to school in the Gerlaw area during the Depression years. My first school year I walked two miles down a country road. The school was a small one-room building sitting on a knoll, and beside it, to the side rear, was a pony shed. My teacher's name was Miss Jean Lukens. I liked Miss Lukens; she let me ring the bell, calling the children in from playing at recess. They were always in a pasture, next to the school yard. They'd climb through the fence and play along a shallow creek nearby. How they would run for the school yard when I rang that bell with all my might and recess was over!

Betty attended Garfield school and graduated from Monmouth High School in 1945. Before she met and married Allen Melvin Welty, Betty painted, free-hand, cookie jars at Western Stoneware Company. Allen chose farming and during their married life they lived on a farm. Their first child was a son, Alan Welty, born May 13, 1949, then a daughter, Jennifer Jean Welty ,born June 3, 1950.

Betty's wonderful mother Ada (Loptien) Lusk passed away in June 1964, her father in 1974.

Betty and Allen's children married and had six children between them. Alan married Susan E. Becker ñ their children were Malinda Marie and Tristen Sue. Malinda married Keith Myers and they have three children: Devin, Kyle and Conard. Tristen has a daughter, Lauren.

Jennifer Jean Welty married Charles Edward Clark. They have four children: Marla Jean, Kaila Jo, Seth and Jonathan (twins), not married. Marla married Rob Parker ñ their children are Wade and Luke. Kaila Jo has a daughter, Margaret Dailey.

Marla and Kaila's families live in Fairbanks, Alaska, at the present time.

WILSON THOMAS LUSK - Wilson Thomas Lusk, son of Harvey Wilson Lusk and Mary Evaline (Estell) Lusk, was born on November 15, 1898, at 818 North D St., Monmouth, Illinois. As a young boy, Wilson attended Garfield Grammar School in Monmouth, Illinois. Wilson started his plumbing apprenticeship at 14 years of age. He later ran a plumbing business out of his 827 North D St. residence. Wilson's love of hunting was surpassed only by his love for his family.

Wilson Thomas Lusk, circa 1930s

Wilson's grandparents were Wilson Lusk and Mary Jean (McCoy) Lusk and William Estell and Rosella (Ater) Estell.

Ada Enna (Loptien) Lusk, daughter of Edward Charles Loptien and Nellie Threasa (Fetterley) Loptien, was born September 8, 1897, in Kenosha, Wisconsin.

Wilson and Ada had four children: Betty Jean Lusk, Dorthey May Lusk, Donna Ilene Lusk, and Billy Wayne Lusk.

FLOYD AND LOIS LYNCH - Floyd Eugene,was born August 16, 1927, to Lee and Ina (Cooper) Lynch of North Henderson, Illinois. Floyd has one brother, Richard, born June 19, 1938. Floyd attended Ethel Country Grade School, and graduated from Alexis High School in 1945.

Floyd was engaged in farming with his father and in October of 1949. He met Lois J. Ditmars. They were married March 5, 1950.

Floyd & Lois Lynch

Lois was the daughter of Harry A. and Mary C. (Cook-Vail) Ditmars. Lois was born July 20, 1931, at Fairview, Illinois, moving to a farm near Knoxville, Illinois, when she was eleven. She has a half-siste,r Opal P. Vail Polich, in California.

Lois graduated from Knoxville High School in 1949, and worked as a secretary for the Accounting Systems in Galesburg. Also, she worked part time at Kline's Department Store.

After their wedding and wedding trip to Kentucky, they moved to the farm in Warren County, Kelly Township, where they have lived at 1644 290th Ave., Alexis, Illinois.

On August 28, 1953, a son James "Jim" Eugene was born to them. A year later, on July 24, 1951, a son, John David, was born two months premature, living 1 1/2 days. On March 31, 1956, a daughter, Lori Ann, was born and on March 17, 1960, a son, Kevin Ray. Their children all graduated from Alexis High School.

James worked as a welder, later moving to Galveston, Texas. He had married Suzanne Wignall of Galesburg ñ a daughter, Heather, was born to them. Jim and Suzanne later divorced and Jim died of a fatal heart attack September 17, 2001, in Galveston.

Lori married Norman McKeown April 5, 1975, and two children were born to them ñ Carey Anne and a son, Cory Brandon. Carey married Nathaniel Feltmeyer April 7, 2001. She is a teacher in Galesburg, Illinois. Cory is attending college to become an attorney. Lori and Norman later divorced and she is employed by the Postal Service.

Kevin has farmed since graduating from high school and took over the family farm operation when his father retired in 1988.

Kevin met and later married Fawn McGraw on June 25, 1993. She has a son, Nathan. Fawn is employed by the Cancer Treatment Center of Western Illinois as a radiologist. They live on a farm northwest of North Henderson, on one of the farms that was originally owned by Floyd's maternal grandparents, Louis and Agnes Cooper. This land was purchased by Floyd, Lois and Kevin in 1995.

Floyd and Lois have farmed land in Warren and Mercer County since their marriage. Floyd also worked for 20 years for Galesburg Builders Supply as a mixer driver, retiring in August 1988.

Floyd passed away September 14, 2000, after being in ill health for several years. Lois still lives on the farm.

JAMES WILLIAM MARSHALL - James William Marshall, M.D., son of Bert and Genevieve Nicklin Marshall, was born in Monmouth, Illinois, on August 2, 1915. He was the oldest of three children. His sisters were Betty Jane (married to Judge Durbin Ranney for fifty-four years) and Adelaide (married to Dale Heitzman for forty-six years). Bert Marshall was Superintendent of Mail at the Monmouth Post Office for many years. Bert was born in Morning Sun, Iowa, on December 3, 1882, and died on April 20, 1941. He spent most of his life in Monmouth, where he attended Monmouth College, playing on the college's first basketball team. Genevieve Nicklin Marshall was born on August 7, 1889 in Ottumwa, Iowa. She was a graduate of Drake University, Des Moines, Iowa. They were married on October 9, 1912. Genevieve's death occurred on April 4, 1975.

James. W. Marshall, M.D.

James attended elementary school in the Central School building, graduated from Monmouth High School and went on to Monmouth College, graduating in 1936. It was at Monmouth College that he met and later married Isabel Bickett, who had come to Monmouth College from Roney's Point, West Virginia. James attended the University of Illinois Medical School in Chicago. He and Isabel were married on March 30, 1940. He then served one-year internship and two years residency at Milwaukee County Hospital, Milwaukee, Wisconsin.

James joined the United States Army in 1943 as a First Lieutenant in the Medical Corps and was stationed at Lowry Field, Denver, Colorado, where he became Chief of Medicine. He was honorably discharged on August 1, 1946

James and Isabel returned to Monmouth where he practiced medicine as an Internal Medicine Specialist. His first office was with Dr. Kampen at 106 East First Ave. on the second floor. In 1951, he and Dr. Russell Jensen built an office at 319 North Main Street, which was one of the first air-conditioned offices in Monmouth. This medical partnership continued for twenty-five years, at which time Dr. Jensen retired. Dr. James Marshall continued his practice of medicine until July 1, 1991, practicing medicine for fifty years, when he retired.

Dr. Marshall served Monmouth College as its physician for forty years. He also was a member of the college Senate for thirty years. His interest in education was evident as he also served as a member of the District 38 School Board for sixteen years.

James and Isabel had two children, John Bertis and Jane Marshall Kellogg (married to Buster L. Kellogg, Jr. of Monmouth on December 19, 1970, who had three children, Scott, Lucy Jane (married to Kent Thompson on August 11, 2001) and Ann) and raised three children of Isabel's deceased sister; Carolbel Creswell Peters, deceased, Alis Creswell Chy and John Ward Creswell.

Dr. Marshall was a member and elder of Faith United Presbyterian Church, Rotary Club, and the Warren County and Illinois State Medical Societies, as well as the American Medical Association and the Monmouth Country Club. He started the cardiac unit of Monmouth Hospital and supervised it in both the old and new Monmouth hospitals. James also served on the Board of Directors of the Illinois Heart Association.

Dr. James W. Marshall's death occurred on May 25, 1997.

CHARLES RAYMOND MARTIN - Charles Raymond Martin, was born 4 April 1972 in Cottage Hospital, Galesburg, Illinois, third son of James Edward Martin (b.1937) and Sarah Joan Raymond (b.1936), named for his grandfather, Charles Vilasco Raymond (1890-1964) and wife, Ruby May Thomson (1894-1978). He has two brothers, S. Bradley (b.1956) and Jay Edward (b. 1959). He was married in Tulsa, 3 October 1998, to Jayme Lynn Wingo, born 27 December 1975, daughter of Gary Wingo and Lynda Kennon. Jayme is a kindergarten teacher at Miss Helen's Private Academy of Tulsa. They are parents of Blake Hunter, born 22 December 1999, are expecting their second child in November, and living in Broken Arrow, OK. Charlie's first home was in Monmouth Township north of Cameron, Illinois. From birth, he was a bright and happy child, with an awareness and intimate relationship to GOD producing a charisma affecting family and all who know him. Raised in a church environment, he developed a strong positive character. His childhood was filled with action, biking, swimming and team sports sponsored by Broken Arrow Community Center. He learned to work helping his father with garden and yard upkeep. As he grew up, he had a passion for camping, fishing, hunting, and later golf.

Charles R. Martin Family
Charles, Jayme, Blake (18 months), June 2002

At age five, in a tent revival of the Four-Square Church of Monmouth, he gave his heart and life to Christ Jesus. In 1977, moved with his parents and brother, Jay, to Broken Arrow, Oklahoma. There he attended Tulsa Christian Schools and graduated from Victory Christian School in 1990. In Oak Crest Kindergarten, he played soccer, later basketball and baseball. At age 14, tragedy struck with the fracture of his right femur in spring football. Three surgeries and a miracle made possible realization his dream of playing college baseball at Evangel College in Springfield, Mo.

His career experience began as a carry-out at Skaggs Alpha Beta Grocery Store in Broken Arrow at sixteen years old. He soon was promoted to cashier because of his reliability, trustworthy and courteous manner with customers. The grocery changed owners several times but Charlie worked vacations and summers during high school and college. Faultless of cause, he suffered severe injuries resulting from car collisions but experienced remarkable and full recoveries.

Charlie has a Business Administration Associate Degree from Tulsa Community College, and Bachelor of Business Administration, May 1997, from Northeastern State University, OSU-Tulsa.

Charles' career in banking began in Tulsa with Boatman's as a Teller/Customer Service Representative, 1992-1996; September 96, accepted position of Assistant Manager/Senior Customer Service Representative at Local America Bank; November 97-present, employed by Bank of America. He has specialized in Business Loans receiving awards, "4 for 4 Goals Banking Center Manager" both in 1997 and 1998 as an Eastern Oklahoma Business Specialist; Awards candidate, January 2000; and on his thirtieth birthday, April 2002, Charles was promoted to Vice President in Business Banking. His qualifications are an exemplary career in banking, managerial style, focused and analytical, skilled communicator, computer literate, high energy level and focused on achieving goals.

HARRY BENFORD MARTIN - Martin, Harry Benford (1885-1963) was born on March 29, 1885 on the family farm 1 mile west of Gerlaw, Illinois. His father was Jon Martin (1855-1922), his mother was Anna (Anderson) Martin. (1851-1920). (Note: After immigrating from Sweden Jon's family changed the family surname from Larson to Martin.) Harry grew up on the farm with his three brothers (Albert, Charles, & Edward) and three sisters (Blanche, Selma, and Anna). Like his father, Harry became a farmer and eventually took over the family farm.

L: to R: Seated: Helen Louise Martin, Harry B. Martin, Hannah Martin, Doreen Martin. Standing: Beulah Martin, Harriett Martin, Mary Jane Martin. 1936

On Dec. 27, 1911, Harry married Hannah Marie Erlandson (1887- 1978) from Monmouth. Hannah had immigrated from Sweden 10 years earlier. She had been employed as a maid and cook for a family in Monmouth. They settled in on the family farm, where their five daughters were born and raised.

Their first daughter was Beulah Marie Martin (1912-1969) who was born on October 19, 1912. After graduating from Monmouth High School, Beulah attended Monmouth College. Later she worked at Knepps, a dress shop in Monmouth. On July 30, 1939 Beulah married John (Jack) Geers (Iowa). After Jack was discharged from the Navy in 1945, they moved to Missouri where Jack went to college and received his MD in Psychology. After graduation, they moved to Dallas, Texas where Jack became a college professor and psychologist. Beulah worked for Nieman-Marcus. Beulah died in an auto accident in 1969 at the age of 57.

Helen Louise (Em) Martin was born on October 14, 1914. After graduating from Monmouth High School, Helen trained to become a bookkeeper/stenographer, and worked for the Federal Farm Association and Production Credit.. On March 3, 1943 she married Kenneth (Olie) Freburg (Prairie City). After Olie's discharge from the Army in 1945, Helen and Olie resided in Bushnell. They moved to Arvada, Colorado in 1961 where Olie worked for the local auto dealerships. Helen worked for the State of Colorado. They raised two children, Kenny (Westminster, Co.) and Donna (Arvada, Co.)

Harriett Bernice Martin was born on August 9, 1917. After graduating from Monmouth High, Harriett went to school at Gem City Business College in Quincy. She moved to Macomb where she worked for a doctor. While in Macomb she met Perry Barclift (Quincy), who was a student at Western Illinois University. They were married on July 30, 1938, and settled in Quincy. After Perry's service in the Coast Guard during World War II he enjoyed a long career with Pepsi-Cola. Harriett worked for a medical center. They raised three daughters: Linda (Quincy), JoHannah (Downers Grove, Il) and Debra (Salt Lake City, UT.).

Mary Jane (Red) Martin was born on January 7, 1919. After graduating from Monmouth High School, Mary Jane attended the Liberty Beauty School in Peoria Illinois. Upon graduation, she worked at the Kobler Beauty Shop in Monmouth Illinois. On November 5, 1941 she married Richard (Dick) Hart (Monmouth). After Dick's discharge from the Army in 1945, they lived in Monmouth until 1959, when they moved to a farm two miles north of Gerlaw. They returned to Monmouth in 1970. Besides farming, Dick worked for Moorman's Feed and Huskee-Built Construction. They raised three children, Mary Lynn (Springdale, Ark.), David (Columbus Ga.) and Joe (Littleton, Co.).

Hannah Doreen Martin was born on February 15, 1922. After graduating from Monmouth High School, Doreen attended Augustana College and later a business school in Chicago. She eventually returned to Monmouth, where on November 17,1944 she married Jack Helm (Monmouth), who was serving in the US Marine Corps. In 1950 they moved to the family farm near Gerlaw where Doreen and her sisters had been raised. Besides farming, Jack was also the Sales Manager at Ray Green Motors Doreen had a long career at the Warren County Agricultural Stabilization and Conservation Services (ASCS). They raised two children, Steve (Scottsdale Az.) and Patti (Monmouth).

In 1950, Harry and Hannah Martin moved from the farm to Monmouth, where they resided on Euclid Ave. and enjoyed their retirement years.

HUGH T. MARTIN - The Martins of Little York have a long history in Warren County. The first Hugh Martin and his wife, Margaret, met and married in Pennsylvania, lived in Muskingum County, Ohio, for several years and came here by wagon in 1832. Their second son, William, who came ahead of the family, was killed by Indians while he was plowing just a few weeks before their arrival. Among the earliest pioneers, they built and lived in a log cabin, acquiring and clearing what eventually was 600 acres in what became Sumner Township before Mr. Martin died. In or before 1856 his son Hugh built the large brick house that still stands just east of Little York. They made the bricks, which were also used to build the old opera house, long gone now, and houses in Little York for daughters who married. Records indicate that during the Civil War the family raised mules for the Union Army and the house is said to have been a station on the underground railroad. With minor modifications, inside and out, and painted white, the house remains much as it was originally. In front of it, visible from the MAM Trail, is a plaque in memory of the young man killed by Indians, unveiled one hundred years after that tragedy.

Hugh Martin Home in Little York, Illinois

The present owner, Hugh T. Martin, and his wife, Nancy, divide their time between Little York and Chicago. Because his father, Hugh T. Martin, Sr., worked as an attorney first in Monmouth and later in Chicago, Hugh spent time as a child in both places. Though her parents were both Iowans and she grew up in China, where her father was a missionary, Nancy also has family history in this area. Her great grandfather, Abram Cain, came with his family from the Isle of Man and lived several years in Monmouth before moving on to Iowa.

Hugh is retired from a career in law and media research and Nancy from one as an industrial psychologist. Their eldest, Hugh M., works for the Gas Technology Institute and lives in Lake Forest, Illinois, with his wife Christine and daughter Meg. His sister Pamela is currently with the Peace Corps as Deputy Director for Russia, living in Moscow. Her husband, Laslo Palocz, who was born in the former Yugoslavia, interprets for U.S. Army officers with NATO in Bosnia. Another son, Jim, and his wife, Matilde, who was born in Mexico City, live in Little York with their three children: Gabriela, Adriana and Alexandro. He is engaged in research and is writing a book and she works part time at the Community Memorial Hospital in Monmouth.

JAMES EDWARD MARTIN - James Edward Martin, son of Eugene Edward Martin (1911-1993) and Nellie Gertrude Staat (1912-1996), was born July 9, 1937 in Monmouth, Illinois and grew up on the Staat-Martin Farm east of Roseville on Highway 115. He attended school at Taylor, Roseville Elementary, and graduated from Roseville High School in 1956. He married Sarah Joan Raymond, daughter of Charles V. and Ruby (Thomson) Raymond of Good Hope on 3 Sept 1955. They began farming the StaatMartin farm where they resided until Jan 1960. Living on the Mason Farm in Bald Bluff Twp. of Henderson County two years, they removed back into Warren County farming the next eleven years on the Anderson Bros Farm north of Little York. Jim was nominated several times as a candidate for Outstanding Young Farmer award being a grain and livestock operator. Jim and Sarah were 4-H Club leaders for two years. Jim helped coach the Little York Blue Baseball team in the Jr. Sheriff League when Brad and Jay played. Jim also worked for the Dept. of Transportation out of Monmouth, Illinois. Selling their farm operation in 1970, they built a home near Cameron in Monmouth Twp where they resided for seven years.

James E. Martin family group at wedding of Charles Martin and Jayme Lynn Wingo in Tulsa, Oklahoma, 1998

They are the parents of Stephen "Bradley" (b. 24 Oct. 1956), Jay Edward (b. 27 Nov. 1959) and Charles Raymond (b. 4 April 1972). In 1977, the family moved to Broken Arrow, Oklahoma where Jim and Sarah graduated in May 1979 from Rhema Bible Training Center. Jim worked two years learning to be a machinist then was employed for 18 years by the American Red Cross on Blood Drives, retiring in 2000. Jim now enjoys boating, fishing and developing a resort lot on Easy Street at Toppers on Ft. Gibson Lake, east of Wagoner, Oklahoma. Jim and Sarah live in Broken Arrow, OK.

JAY EDWARD MARTIN - Jay Edward Martin, second child born 27 November 1959 in Cottage Hospital, Galesburg, Illinois, to James Edward Martin (b.1937) and Sarah Joan (Raymond) (b. 1936), his first home east of Roseville on Hwy 115 in Roseville Twp. of Warren County. His two brothers are S. Bradley Martin (b.1956), and Charles Raymond Martin (b.1972).

Martin: Jay and Connie; Sarayah and Yisrayl 1998

Jay was a loving and active child who said Brad was his best friend. Growing up together, they attended Belmont Church, Little York Elementary School, shared pets, were in local parades, played Warren Co Junior Sheriff League Baseball, Monmouth YMCA swimming, Jay in Cub Scouts, both transferring to the Warren Unit Schools when their parents sold their farming operation in 1970. Jay and Brad helped clear timber to build the family's new home north of Cameron in Monmouth Township.

As a preteen, Jay was always active, rebuilding a go-cart and enjoyed riding a mini-bike. He used his artistic gift and eye for color in decorating his room, building a closet organizer, and a stage for rebuilt drum set. One Oklahoma University professor commented that his oil well drawings were of text-book quality. Diligent in study and work, he cut corn out of bean fields, mowed lawns, and worked as a lifeguard at Monmouth Country Club before age sixteen. Later, he worked at Tractor Supply, Inc. of Galesburg before moving with his parents to Broken Arrow, Oklahoma, in 1977.

This was a defining time in Jay's life, leaving Warren High School as a Junior playing football, basketball, snare drums in the band, leading his class scholastically, to be a Senior at Broken Arrow, Oklahoma, in a class of over nine hundred graduates.

Jay planned to be a medical physician so he entered Oral Robert's University in Tulsa where there was a Medical School. However, after one year of study, he took time-out working as a plumber's helper, attending classes at Tulsa Jr. College, then passed the State Examination to became a licensed plumber at age nineteen.

He was married 18 April 1980 in Broken Arrow Oklahoma, to Constance Marie Nolen, born 12 February 1961, daughter of Howard and Emma (Savage) Nolen. Seeking a better future, he returned to school and graduated from Oklahoma University College of Engineering with a degree in Petroleum Engineering May 1984. In summer of 1983, having worked in the oil fields of West Texas for Getty, was hired as a Field Engineer by Texaco Oil Co. that fall, to begin following spring graduation. The couple moved to Snyder, then to Sweet Water Texas. Texaco lost their court battle with Penns Oil Co, and closed their oilfields but retained Jay to sell their oil leases. Becoming involved in the House of Yahweh, Jay worked learning Civil Engineering, building an industrial size septic system, learning surveying and other contracting skills. The couple lived at rural Clyde, TX. the next ten years where their two children were born, Sarayah Chananyah Martin, born 26 September 1990 and Yisrayl Ibri Obadyah Martin born 26 August 1993.

In 1998, Jay was employed as an Engineer by the Department of Transportation of Texas, in the building of a by-pass super highway around Abilene, Texas.

NELS E. MARTIN - The Martin Family owned the property at 209 East Spring Grove Ave. in Alexis where they lived from 1907 to 1924. Some or the children had left home prior to moving to this property in 1907. Prior to moving to Alexis the Martins farmed in the Alexis, North Henderson area.

Nels Martin and wife Anna J. Steinberg Martin were both natives of Sweden. He was born near Malmar Sweden 27 July 1850 and died 16 September 1922 in Mercer County. Anna's birth place is unknown but occurred in Sweden 16 September 1849 Her death occurred 19 September 1931 in Washington, Washington County. Iowa.

He came to the U.S.A. in 1873 at age of 23, and worked as a farm hand in Mercer County upon his arrival. Anna came as a teen and it is believed she was enrolled at the Ansgari College in Knoxville, Illinois.

The couple met in Knox County Illinois and were married on December 22, 1875 in Galesburg by Rev. John Anjon who was on the faculty and a trustee of Ansgari College.

Six children were born to this union:
Arthur, born 26 September 1876, he was educated in Germany and was a Minister in Colorado churches.

Fred, born 10 January 1878 graduated from Northern Indiana Law School (a department of Valparaso College) with a Bachelor of Law Degree.

Demarius Anna (Macie A), born 25 July 1880, was a housewife and married Edwin E. Sedwick a Mercer County native. Minnie, born August 1881 was a teacher in area schools and in Chicago. Nellie, born January 1884 was also a teacher in area schools. Paul, born 10 August 1893 and at 14 was living with the family in 1907.

Submitted by Lyle D. Sedwick, Alexis, IL., Great Grandson

STEPHEN "BRADLEY" MARTIN - Stephen "Bradley" Martin, was born 24 Oct 1956 in Monmouth Hospital to James Edward Martin (b.1937) and wife, Sarah Joan Raymond (b.1936), the eldest of three sons. Growing up in Warren County, attending Little York Elementary School, Yorkwood Jr. High, graduating in 1975 from Warren High School, Brad has always been a very involved in life person with a wide range of interest and abilities.

Martin: Stephen "Bradley", Linda, Bryan, Kal: 1998

As a boy, he played Warren County Jr. Sheriff League Baseball, Monmouth Y Swimming Program, a Boy Scout and in 4-H Club. He had pet dogs, cats, raccoons and his horse "Queenie". Musically talented both instrumentally and vocally, Brad was recipient of the coveted "Arion Award" in Warren High School Band. He participated in all school activities and sports, as well as plays, and served as Senior Class President. Following graduation, his activities included Private Airplane Pilot, Slow Pitch Baseball, Photography, Motorcycle Racing, Football, Volleyball and currently an enthusiastic Golfer. He is admired and a great role model for his younger two brothers, Jay Edward (b.1959) and Charles Raymond (b.1972).

Brad was married 22 June 1984 to Linda Joan Peterson, born 10 April 1961, daughter of Everett Peterson and Shirley (Hennenfent) of Monmouth. They are parents of Bryan Jordan (b.

23 Aug 1986 in Monmouth) and Kali Lynn (b. 7 July 1992 in Waterloo, Iowa). Brad's work experience began at age sixteen, while a high school student, as a part-time teller at The Farmers and Mechanics Bank in Galesburg and Farm King. Following graduation, he chose bank employment but soon decided "to do something more physical" so began his fourteen year career in the tire/equipment industry.

Employed as a Salesman-Credit Manager by Keister's Inc. in Monmouth, then nine years as Factory Representative by Iowa Mold and Tooling Company of Clear Lake, Iowa, a truck body and crane manufacturer.

The hobby of computing became his career future. With a small Timex, application brought him success receiving IMT's Sales Achievement Award five consecutive years. Sales above One Million Dollars brought induction into IMT President's Club in 1984. Then the ultimate goal, IMT National Top Salesman of the Year in 1985. He was awarded the Outstanding Membership Development Plaque by Illinois Tire Dealers and Retreaders in 1987. IMT moved Brad and family from Monmouth to Clear Lake, Iowa, in 1990 advancing him into Market Communications. Continuing his self-education, Brad was also a Computer Consultant for MicroAge Computer Centers, Inc. Moving his family to Waterloo, Iowa, in 1992, he entered the computer revolution in the prepress and printing industry. As Department Manager with American Graphics Service in Cedar Falls, he became a featured seminar speaker regarding Desktop Publishing and how it relates to the Prepress industry.

Brad honed his ability as an innovator in computer technology. In 1993, he became the founder of self-owned "HumanWare Company" specializing in prepress and printer applications, while simultaneously contracting as a System & Workflows Consultant for Scitex America Corp. By December, he was employed as System Demonstrator/Technical Consultant for Scitex, the largest Prepress and Graphics Communications company (Chicago) in the world. As Major Accounts Systems Specialist, he moved his family to Bollingbrook, Illinois in 1995.

Recruited in May 1996 by Oce' Printing Systems, USA, as the first POD Senior Systems Engineer, Brad relocated his family to Boca Raton, Florida, in 1998. Today, as National Manager of National Systems Engineering Support for On Demand Print and Publishing, he has twelve reporting Systems Engineers Nationwide. Always interested in family, Brad volunteered as Sec-Treas. of Raymond Family Reunion in 1990's, establishing web sites on the Internet as well as publishing The Raymond Review Newsletter.

HILDING F. MATSON - Hilding F. Matson and Edna S.A. Melburg were married on July 16, 1919 in Monmouth at her parents' home, and lived in the same block at 215, 221, and 225 South D Street all their married lives. They were the parents of Howard John (1921 - 1991) m. Norma Combs, Loda, Illinois; Dorothy Jeanne Johnson (1925 - 1996) m. R. Vincent, Waukegan; and Robert Theodore (b. 1926) m. Melba Larson, Monmouth. They had ten grandchildren: Eric, Linnea, Alan, and Kris Matson; Lynette, Douglas, and Cynthia Johnson; John, Jane and Theodore Matson. They also had twenty-one great grandchildren. The Hilding Matsons attended the First Ward School, now Willitts, and graduated from Monmouth High School in 112. They were members of the First Lutheran Church.

Hilding and Edna Matson 1919

Hilding Fritiof Matson was born in Monmouth on April 10, 1893 to John Matson (Jans Mattison, Skane, Sweden), church sexton, and Bessie Nelson Matson (Bengta Nilsson, Blekinge, Sweden), who lived at 122 South E Street. His sibligs were Nels Alfred, Sven Oskar, Henning, Hilding (died as an infant), Hilma Wise, Olga Seaton, Edith Bengtson, Maywood; and Per, a half-brother in Sweden. He was drafted and sent to Duluth for Army training for World War I. He graduated from Brown's Business School in Galesburg, and became the Warren County Treasurer. He was secretary-treasurer of the Western Stoneware Company and a member of the Rotary Club. He was a choir director and a soloist at the First Lutheran Church. Hilding died on November 18, 1954.

Edna Sagred Amaia Melburg was born on April 6, 1893 to August (Gus) Teodore Melburg (Magnsson in Smaland, Sweden), a tailor, and Bessie Nelson Linman (Bengta in Blekinge, Sweden) of 221 South D Street. Her siblings were Arthur Theodore, Oquawka; Ernest Clifton, Ames, Iowa; and Leonard Wilfred, Riverside, California, a former Monmouth attorney. The Melburg family lived in the Schulz mansion on the site of the First Lutheran Church, after her father and A.L. Martin purchased the home for the new church. She enrolled in the Conservatory of Art at Monmouth College for painting classes. She was active in the church societies, Monmouth Woman's Club, New Century Club, and Kappa Kappa Gamma Mother's Club. She was known for her Swedish cooking nd was featured in the Review Atlas. She was the oldest member of the church at the time of her death on November 30, 1995 in Mason City, Iowa, where her granddaughter, Jane Matson Lee, has her home.

JOHN MATSON - John Matson (originally Jans Mattison) and Bessie (Bengta Nilsson) Nelson were married on February 14, 1880. Natives of Sweden, he immigrated in 1882 and returned for his family in 1886. They lived at 122 South E Street in Monmouth and had six children. Born in Sweden were Nels Alfred (b. 1880), Henning, (b. 1883 and died on the boat to America), S. Oscar (b. 1883), and Hilding (1883-1885). They immigrated with their mother and father in 1886. The younger children born in America were Hilma Augusta (Omie) Wise (b. 1887), Hilding Fritiof (b. 1893), Olga M. (Fred) Seaton, and Edith M. (Dr. C.O.) Bengtson (b. 1888.)

John Matson was born on May 31, 1853 in Orkened Parish, Lonsboda, Skane, Sweden. He had a son, Per, born o his first wife. His first wife died. His son Per remained in Sweden and raised a family there. His great grandson, Leif, has visited in Monmouth. John was a church sexton for the First Lutheran Church, when it was on South E Street to the south, and he did work for the railroad. John died on July 13, 1921 in Monmouth.

John and Bessie Matson, family and friends, 1914

Bessie Nelson was born July 10, 1855 at Vaghult, Jamshog, Blekinge, Sweden to Nils Nilsson (b. 7/29/1812 at Jamshog) and Hanna Andersdotter (b. /19/1818) of Gilesnas. Her sisters were Johanna (b. 6/19/1837), Elsa (Ollie) Swanson (b. 215/1843) who lived across the street on South E. Street, Inga (b. 3/3/1845), Kerstin (b. 4/7/1847), Lovisa (b. 4/12/1850), and Anna (b. 3/5/1853). Her whole family moved to Vanga on October 1, 1855. Bessie also died in 1921 in Monmouth, as did her husband.

Their grandchildren were Louise Matson (Ed) Beaty, Evelyn Matson (Clyde) Darrah; Marjorie Wise (Robert) Foster, Edith Wise (Warren) Schlaf; Howard J. Matson, Dorothy Jeanne Matson (R. Vincent) Johnson, Robert T. Matson; C. Anders Bengtson, John Bengtson, and Rev. Earl Bengtson. Of these, Marjorie Foster, Robert Matson, C. Anders and Earl Bengtson are still living.

ROBERT MATSON - Robert Matson of 221 South D Street and Melba Larson of 325 North 6th Street, third generation Monmouth natives, were married on June 22, 1950, in the First Lutheran Church of Monmouth. They built their Monmouth home at 1020 E. Detroit Avenue in 1956. Prior residences were 310 E. Detroit Ave., 117 and 200 W. Clinton Ave.

Robert and Melba Matson Family 1966

Robert Theodore Matson was born on July 15, 1926 to Hilding and Edna Melburg Matson of 215 South D Street, former treasurer of Warren County and secretary/treasurer of Western Stoneware. His older siblings were Howard and Dorothy Jeanne. His grandparents were Gus T. and Bessie Melburg and John and Bessie Matson of Monmouth, natives of Sweden. Robert attended Willitts, Central Junior High, Monmouth High School (c.1944), Monmouth College (A.B.1950), and Western Illinois University (M.S. in Ed 1970). Matson served in the U.S. Army in World War II in the Philippines and Japan. He was a school principal/junior high teacher in Little York, an elementary teacher in Lincoln School in Monmouth (1951-1991) and received the first State of Illinois Educational Excellence Award. Matson was inducted into Phi Delta Kappa, an honorary education fraternity, and was president of the Illinois Education Association for Western Illinois. He served on the Monmouth City Council (1975-1987) and as Mayor ProTem. Matson was the Warren County Bicentennial chairman and Schoolmasters' secretary, Kiwanis Club secretary, March of Dimes Chairman, Lutheran Church trustee, and a member of the ATO fraternity. He was a historical writer for the Review Atlas and a weather observer for the National Weather Service and television stations in Chicago and the Quad Cities.

Melba Rose Larson was born on January 30, 1930 to Carl Oscar Virgil and Eunice Fahlund Larson of 401 North B Street, owner of Larson Furniture Mart, and part owner of Hogue Furniture and Larson, Neilsen, Peterson, Inc., of Monmouth, Galesburg, Galva, and Stronghurst. Her younger brother is Dr. Alan V. Larson. Her grandparents were Carl Oscar and Josephine Larson of Woodhull and Bernhard and Nellie Fahlund of Monmouth. Her great grandparents from Sweden were the Charles J. Carlsons, Aledo, and the Bengt Fahlunds, early Galesburg pioneers in 1868. Melba attended school in Tucson, AZ; Palo Alto, CA; and Garfield, Junior High, Monmouth High School (c. 1948), Monmouth College (A.B. 1966), and Western Illinois University (M'S. in Ed. 1970). She attended a NDEA Reading Institute at the University of Wisconsin-Milwaukee, studied at Purdue University, and is listed in Who's Who. Melba taught in country schools in Henderson and Warren County (1950-54), Warren Achievement School, and was the first Title I-Chapter I reading teacher and special reading coordinator for the Monmouth elementary schools (1966-92). The special reading program received national recognition. She was a member of the International Reading Association and the Monmouth Civic Orchestra as a violinist. She was president of Kappa Kappa Gamma Alumnae, Garfield School PTA, Monmouth Preservationists, and the Wyatt Earp Birthplace Board of Trustees. Melba was named Woman of the Year by the VFW Auxiliary. She has authored Wyatt Earp booklets, and wrote the nomination for the National Register of Historic Places listing and the Illinois State Historical Marker for the Wyatt Earp Birthplace and Boyhood Home.

The Matsons formed the Mark and Mary (Lutheran Friends) group and were Sunday School superintendents and choir members of the Lutheran Church. They attended a teachers' seminar at London University in England. They received a Human Services Award from the Illinois Education Association for their work as chairmen for the building of the Monmouth Municipal Swimming Pool, for purchasing and establishing the Wyatt Earp Birthplace Historic House Museum, and for chartering the Monmouth Preservationists and its Decorators' Showhouse. The DAR awarded them certificates for their services to Monmouth.

The Matsons are the parents of John Robert Matson, student at Monmouth College and Carl Sandburg College (1954-1975); Jane Carol Matson Lee, a special education teacher (b. 1956, m. Dr. Phillip C.) of Mason City, Iowa; and Theodore Alan Matson, owner of a healthcare consulting business and author (b. 1958, m. Michelle Blank) of Oro Valley, Arizona. Their children chose the name for Carl Sandburg College in Galesburg. Their grandchildren are John Phillip (b. 1986), Mark Theodore (b. 1988), and Daniel James Lee (b. 1990) of Iowa; Madison Kate (b. 1998), Wyatt John and Lucy Michelle Matson, (twins b. 2001) of Arizona.

ANN OGDEN MATTESON - Ann Ogden was born on 15 April 1810 at Rome, Oneida County NY daughter of Abraham Ogden and Keziah Houghton. She grew to adulthood and in about 1830 she married Elon Matteson there. Their oldest children were born on their farm in Floyd Township, NY. In the late 1830s, the Mattesons moved to Warren County where they farmed and three more children were born. In 1845 Elon Matteson died at age 39, and his widow remained in Warren County for another five years. In 1850 she moved her family to Galesburg where they could advance their educations, and she became an active member of the First Baptist Church there.

Ann Ogden Matteson

Elon and Ann Matteson had six children. All six of the Matteson children grew to adulthood in Galesburg, all six attended Knox College and all except the youngest son were married there. Orville married Emma Hannaman, Charles married Elizabeth Ross, Asa ("Ace") married Helen ("Nellie") Gardner, Anna married Orange O. Comstock, Arthur married Helen Henshaw and Aaron married Alice Blossom.

Capt. Orville Matteson enlisted at age 30 and served in Company D, 102d Illinois Infantry during the Civil War. He died at age at age 41 in Galesburg. Capt. Charles Matteson enlisted at age 27 and served in Company G, 103d Illinois Infantry during the Civil War. He subsequently moved to Chicago where he died at age 73. Asa Matteson lived for a while in Macomb County but moved back to Galesburg where he was a bank bookkeeper and died at age 58. O.O. Comstock, husband of Anna Ogden, was an insurance agent in Galesburg. Arthur Matteson moved to Chicago after college, and died there at age 77. Aaron Matteson joined the army in 1864 and was with Sherman on his march to the sea. After the war he moved to Chicago and then Brookfield, where he was in banking. He died there at age 33 of consumption. All the Matteson children except Anna Comstock are buried at Hope Cemetery.

Ann Ogden Matteson died on May 1883 of a stroke at the Galesburg home of her son-in-law, O.O. Comstock. She was buried at Hope Cemetery in Galesburg.

LELA NORRIS GARDNER MCBRIDE - Lela Violet (Norris) Gardner McBride was born November 12, 1905 in Monmouth to Minnie V.I. (Foster) (1882-1970) and Benjamin Franklin Norris (1876-1928). She attended Harding Grade School and Monmouth High School and worked at the Monmouth Telephone Company as a long distance operator for twenty years. She was a lifelong member of the First Christian Church. She lived in Monmouth at 507 South 4th Street and later at 1210 Lincoln Road.

Lela McBride, February 1974

Lela Norris was the third oldest of eight children. Her brothers were Halsey E. (1900-1979), Forrest A. (1910-1961), Franklin D. (1917-1982), and Glenn b. (1925-2001). Her sister were Vada A. (1903-1969), Catherine A. (1908-1993), and Lola F. (1914-1997).

Ralph Meridy Gardner and Lela were married on May 29, 1936. Ralph was the bookkeeper and farm machinery salesman for Merillat Road Supply Company. He died suddenly on February 23, 1949 at the age of forty-two.

They had one child, Joan Louise, born March 25, 1939, who married George W. Jones, Jr. and live in Knoxville, Illinois. Their children are Timothy W. Jones, Anne K. (Jones) Bowman and David D. Jones. Their children are Keegan W., Haley M., and Tessa L. Jones; Kathleen Meridy and Evan A. Bowman; Cody P. and Hannah Louise Jones.

Lela married Frank L. McBride (1906-2001) and at her death on June 20, 1990, they had been married for forty years.

Lela's grandfather, George W. Norris, (1835-1908) was in the 86th Illinois Infantry during the Civil War and survived nine months as a prisoner in the Andersonville prison in Georgia. He came to Monmouth in 1879 and was working at the Weir Plow Company in 1886.

Lela's great-great grandfather, Zebulon Foster, (1775-1846) was a pioneer, coming from New York to Deerfield Township in Fulton County, Illinois in 1830. They descended from Christopher (1603-1687) and Frances (Stevens) Foster who embarked from London, England on June 17, 1635 in the "Abigail" settling in Southampton, Long Island, New York.

FRANK AND TWILA MURDOCK MCCLURE - Frank McClure was born June 1, 1913 in Cameron, Illinois. Twila Murdock was born November 1, 1913 in Barney, North Dakota. They married on February 21, 1934. Frank and Twila farmed in the Cameron, Alexis, and Kirkwood areas before moving to the Abingdon area. They have always farmed. They raised hogs, fed cattle and milked dairy cows. Crops included corn, soybeans, oats, and hay. Twila died April 2, 1963 of cancer. Frank married Frances Standard and they live near Galesburg.

Frank and Twila had 3 children. T. Maxine married Russell Stewart of Monmouth and they had four children. Dale married Ramona Boylen of Kirkwood, Illinois and they had three children. Roger married Marsha Hickerson of Abingdon, Illinois and they had three children. Roger later married Virgina Shoop of Alexis, Illinois and they had one daughter.

Frank's parents were Glenn and Mary (Rhykerd) McClure of Cameron. Both Glenn and Mary were born in Cameron. They had six children: Evelyn, Frank, Isabel, Erma, Glenola, Joan, and Harold. They farmed in the Cameron area. Grandparents were Frank and Clara (Groves) McClure, who originated from Pennsylvania and Ward and Nellie (Squire) Rhykerd of Surrey, near Cameron.

Twila's parents were Hal and Pluma (Dunbar) Murdock of Monmouth. Hal was born in Cameron and Pluma was born in Monmouth, Illinois. They raised 6 children: Harold, Lee, Helen, Twila, Clifford, and Dale. A daughter, Gertrude, died in infancy. Grandparents were John and Effie (Shaw) Dunbar of Monmouth.

JAMES MARTIN MCCLURE - James Martin McClure and Mary Ann Mount McClure were born and married in Shelby, KY. They moved to McDonough Co. IL. then Warren Co. around 1840. Family records show them moving to Barnes City, Iowa in 1855. Their names appear on the 1860 census in Warren Co. IL. Mary Ann McClure died in Warren Co. IL. Jan 30th 1880 according to death certificate dated at Leux by Undertaker Duncan and Korllman of Monmouth, IL. She was buried in the Harper/Boswell Cemetery in Barnes City.

James and Elizabeth McClure

James and Mary had eight children. John Thomas, Nancy Jane, Lucindy C., Minerva, William Atwell, Martha Ellen, Angeline, and James Martin.

The youngest was James Martin born in Warren Co. in 1850, before they moved to Barnes City. His oldest son was Eddie Alfred McClure. He had thirteen children, nine of whom survived to adulthood. They were: Carlyle, Alice, Everett, Bertha, Eva, Glema, Ines, John and Vida.

Vida married Charles Leonard in Barnes City, IA. They had five children: Charles Alfred Jr., Clifford Peter, William A., Lee Holland, and Kendal Dean. They moved to Monmouth about 1948. He was assistant manager for Selbey, with Bob Hamilton. They bought a house at 220 South B. St. in Monmouth and moved to Biggsville in 1951.

In 1950 E.A. McClure was visiting Vida and Charles in Monmouth and while he was there he visited with a relative who he said was a cousin. I have not been able to locate any of the family, although I am sure there must still be some around.

In 1950 Charles and Vida had their fourth son, Lee Leonard, born in Monmouth. (By Bill Leonard)

ALBERT EMMETT MCCOMBS - Albert Emmett McCombs was born in Paigeville, Allen Co., KY, 31 August 1837. His parents, Hugh Doddy and Diadema (Tinsley) Ritchie McCombs, died in 1842 leaving five young children. They tried to place the children with relatives, but had to place Albert and Perlina in an orphanage in Edmonson County, KY. Mr. John Chandler took the children as apprentices from the orphanage, promising to provide them with food, clothes and an education. In the fall of 1852, they moved to Coles County, Illinois, where they lived for four years. During this time Albert bought a horse, which John Chandler sold and kept the money, so Albert left and went to work for himself. The summer of 1856 was very wet in the area where he was living and portions filled up with stagnated water. With very few exceptions, every person had malaria, so later in 1856, at age 19, Albert Went to Warren County, Illinois where he engaged in logging, breaking prairie and driving oxen teams for about five years.

Albert Emmett McCombs and second wife, Elizabeth "Lizzie" (Alley) McCombs

On June 28, 1860, Albert married Sarah Hannah Gordon in Monmouth, Illinois. They resided in Roseville where Sarah's family, George Ross and Elizabeth Finley Baird Gordon lived with their children. Albert and Sarah had a son, William Francis McCombs, on 28 March 1861. On 2 August 1862, Albert enlisted in the Union Army from Roseville.

His company went up the Tennessee River to Fort Henry and Fort Hyman— one on each side of the river. Their company divided into squads, and were stationed at different points on the river for the purpose of keeping the passage open so supplies could be brought to the main army, which was farther back. That country was swampy and very unhealthful and it wasn't long before a large number of the company was ill and had to be taken to Mound City Hospital. After staying there two months and twenty days, Albert was sent home to Roseville. His health didn't improve and the Dr. said he couldn't help him any more and he had better take a sea voyage to California. "You may live to reach there or you may die along the way."

On 7 May 1863, Albert, Sarah, "Frank", Sarah's mother and three of her children started for California. Sarah's father was already in Northern California, having crossed the plains before the family left.

Albert and the family went first to New York and got a boat from there to go to Panama, before the canal was built. They had to walk ten miles on land, then went across Central America by ambulance wagons. They took a boat from San Juan to San Francisco, arriving there 13 July 1863. Albert had still not recovered and claimed he regained his strength back by killing birds and wild game to eat and providing wild game for a resort in Lake County, California. He and Sarah had two more children who died from diptheria as young children. Sarah died in 1877 at age 37. Albert eventually remarried and they lived to celebrate their 50th Wedding Anniversary. He received a small Civil War pension and lived an active life until his death, 6 December 1931, at age 94. He had never returned to Illinois and many of his descendants still live in Northern California.

HARRY AND ELIZABETH MCCONNELL - McConnell, Harry Clifford, the son of George and Agnes McConnell, was born in Sumner Township Warren County on October 22, 1886. He had one brother, William Clarence McConnell and one sister Hadassah McConnell. He married Elizabeth Chloe Gallaugher, daughter of Michael Rankin and Minnie Gallaugher on February 3, 1910.

Harry C. McConnell

They were married in Spring Grove Township. Harry McConnell was a farmer by occupation and Chloe, as called by family and friends, was a homemaker. The McConnells had five children, Hugh Rankin McConnell, Mrs. Elmer (Ruth) Strand, Mrs. W.C. (Mildred) Adair, Mrs. Robert (Vera) Garth, and Mrs. John (Mary) Gibson.

Chloe died on March 17, 1948 in Iowa City, IA. After Chloe's death, Harry got remarried to Vera Strawn on September 3, 1952 and she passed away ten years later on September 22, 1962.

While residing in rural Warren County Harry was a member of the Warren County Farm Bureau, Vice Chairman of the Warren County ASCS office, McGaw Corner School Board member for 33 years, and attended the Cedar Creek Presbyterian Church until it disbanded.

As Harry got older, he would celebrate his birthdays in unique ways including airplane and boat rides.

Harry McConnell died on August 24, 1984 at 97 years of age. One daughter, Ruth, one brother, and one great-grandchild, preceded him in death. At the time of his death he had 12 grandchildren, 26 great-grandchildren, and 1 great-great-grandchild.

HUGH AND EDITH MCCONNELL - McConnell, Hugh Rankin the son of Harry and Chloe McConnell, was born on October 15, 1910 near Monmouth. Hugh had four sisters, Ruth, Mildred, Vera, and Mary. He was reared in the Monmouth area and was graduated from Monmouth High School in 1929.

Hugh R. McConnell

He married Edith Josephine Carlson on January 21, 1936. They were married in Monmouth. He farmed most of his life retiring in 1984 and she worked for the Monmouth Hospital's accounting department and was also a homemaker. They had three children, Nancy Jo, Betty Joan, and Hugh Thomas.

Hugh was a member of the First Lutheran Church in Monmouth, and served on the church board, served on the Warren School Board, was a member of the Warren County ASCS Committee, President of the Warren County Prime Beef Festival in 1974 and a member of the Warren County Farm Bureau.

Hugh died on December 18, 1997 in Mesa, Arizona, where he spent his winters after retirement. Edith died on January 19, 2000 in Monmouth. Their eldest daughter and their parents preceded them both in death. Two sisters preceded him in death as well.

RALPH MCCOY - Rev. Elijah McCoy purchased a 10-acre plot of land in Section 16 of Tompkins Township in 1867. Rev. McCoy was not new to Warren County because he was one of four ministers who organized the Monmouth Presbytery of the Associate Presbyterian Church. The Associate and Associate Reformed Presbyterian Churches united in 1858 to form the United Presbyterian Church. Rev. McCoy had served the Associate Presbyterian Church in Peoria County near Trivoli. Prior to that he served a congregation in Adams County, Ohio. Rev. McCoy apparently served as a supply pastor after coming to Warren County. In 1875, he collapsed and died while serving communion at the Kirkwood United Presbyterian Church.

Ralph McCoy Family, circa 1920. Margaret Emma (Thompson), Margaret Ruth (Sanner), Lulu Marian (Randall), Louise (Stewart), Mildred (Birdsell) and Ralph T. McCoy

Elijah McCoy was born in Ohio County, West Virginia. He married Jane Moore in Belmont County Ohio. Two sons and two daughters grew to adulthood from this marriage, Sarah, Anne, Joseph William, and John Ralph. Anne married Robert Patton in Peoria County. In Warren County, Sarah (Sally) married Mathew Wood and Joseph William (Will) married Margaret Emma (Maggie) Thomson (see Thomson). John Ralph married Mary Ann Wood in Page County, Iowa. All except Joseph William migrated west after their marriage. Sally went to Western Iowa, Anne to Kansas and John Ralph to Nebraska via Western Iowa.

Will McCoy and Maggie Thomson were married in 1875. A son, Ralph, was born in 1876; and, in 1877, Will McCoy died. The land in Section 16 was sold to Maggie's brother, William, who sold it out of the family about 10 years later. Maggie and Ralph lived with Maggie's parents, John and Rachel Thomson in Section 10 of Tompkins Township (see Thomson).

Ralph McCoy married Lulu Randall (see Randall) in 1898. They lived in the same house in which Ralph grew up in Section 10 of Tompkins Township. Living with them was Maggie and her widowed mother, Rachel. In 1898, Maggie McCoy purchased 80 acres from the heirs of her father. Ralph farmed that 80 and raised his family there. Rachel Thomson and Maggie McCoy continued to live with Ralph and his family until they died.

Ralph and Lulu had three daughters Louise, Mildred and Margaret. Louise was born in 1903. That made four generations living in the same house. Louise was sick quite a bit during her first winter apparently because of the cold in the little old house. Thus, a new house was built on the same lot that still stands today. The house and land are owned by Mildred Birdsell. All three daughters graduated from Monmouth College and became teachers. Louise taught mathematics at Monmouth College before she married Carl Stewart (see Stewart). Mildred taught at Orangeville, Illinois before she married Everett Birdsell (see Thomson). Later she taught Latin at Warren School. Margaret married Cliff Sanner (see Brown-Randall et al.) after teaching at the Coonville school and in Michigan.

The Birdsells had a stillborn daughter who is buried in the Kirkwood Cemetery. The presence of her grave in the Center Grove Cemetery makes five generations of McCoy and Thomson descendants in that cemetery.

DAVID NEIL MCCRERY - Neil's ancestors have been residents of Warren County since 1834. His great-great-grandfather, David H. McCrery was born in 1777; his great grandfather John C. McCrery in 1808, and grandfather, David Hawthorn McCrery in 1830. They were all born in Abbeville, South Carolina.

In 1834 they came by wagon with a group and settled with others in Warren County that had come ahead of them known as the Reverend Thomas Clark Settlement. They were all of Presbytery faith. David H. and John C. and their wives are buried in the Ceder Creek Cemetery in Sumner Township. They both purchased ground in Spring Grove Township. John C. was one of the founders of Ceder Creek Church and one of the first elders. He also was one of the first on the board of Monmouth College. His wife was Jane Foster from Abbeville, South Carolina. Their children were David Hawthorn, Samuel F., Joseph, Nancy, Ester, James, Margaret Mary and Araminta.

David Hawthorn McCrery was Neil's grandfather. He married Catherine Struthers in 1884 and they bought a farm in Spring Grove Township. Both are buried in Monmouth Cemetery, Monmouth, Illinois. He died in 1903. Their children were Ida, Sophronia, James, John, Elizabeth, Myrtle, Celia, David, Dwight and Ernest.

David Neil and Dorothy (Lantz) McCrery, taken in 1937

Ernest Allen married Lulu Gilmore November 9, 1903. They moved on to a farm in Spring Grove Township, which Ernest had purchased early in the year. They lived there till September of 1937 and moved to Monmouth.

Neil married Dorothy Mae Lantz and they took over the farming then.

Ernest and Lulu's other children were Gertrude, Orpheus, Myrtle, Dale, Erma and William.

Neil was born on the farm June 4, 1915. He and Dorothy had three sons; David Neil Jr., Dennis Lantz, and John Douglas. They moved to Monmouth in May 1981, when John Douglas got married and took over the farm. Neil died March 1, 1987.

1. David Neil Jr. married Judith Purlee and they have three sons. A.) David Neil III married Katherine Meridith. They have two children; Evelyn and David Neil IV. B.) Robert Michael McCrery married Grace Livingston. They have two children, William and Sarah. C.) Mark Preston never married.

2. Dennis Lantz McCrery married Carol Neal and they have three children. A.) Dennis Lantz Jr. married Amy Larson. They have two children, Cassandra and Derrick. B.) Heidi married Mark Stein. They have one son Zebulon. C.) Molly married Ismael Bitar and they have two sons, Ethan and Tyler.

3. John Douglas married Annette Gawthrop and they have one daughter, Claire that they adopted from China.

The McCrery family have owned the same farm for ninety-nine years and had hogs being raised on it continuously.

Ernest Allen McCrery died May 1, 1947. Lulu May Gilmore died January 8, 1964. Annette Gawthrop McCrery died October 20, 2000. All three are buried in the Warren County Memorial Cemetery, Monmouth, Illinois.

MARK AND VIVIAN MCCULLOCH - Mark F. McCulloch and Vivian I. Bryan were married May 1, 1915, at the bride's home in Princeton, IL, where they graduated from high school. Mark's parents were John McCulloch (b. in Scotland) and Lizzy Stephenson. Vivian's parents were Amos Bryan and Maggie Elliott. Both families farmed in Bureau County.

Mark's family had roots in the Oneida area. Wanting to be closer to Oneida, John McCulloch bought two farms near Monmouth for his two children. John and Lizzie bought a home in

Monmouth at 310 S. Third. Mark and Vivian moved to the farm just south of town in 1918. Mark's sister, Jessie, owned the other farm several miles west of Larchland. She married Bill Watson and settled in Lawrenceberg, TN, never living in Warren Co.

Mark and Vivian McCulloch, about 1940

Mark and Vivian's original house faced a country school known as the Enterprise School. They had two children, Marjorie (1918) and Roger (1923). In the 20's they built a corn crib, a horse barn, and then a brick home on the east side of the road. Mark raised oats and corn. He sold seed oats and later DeKalb seed corn. He raised clover and soybeans for hay. He began harvesting beans when it was a novelty, before their value as an oilseed was well known. He farmed with horses and had a milk cow for milk, cheese and butter. Vivian tended the garden and the chickens, sold eggs and cooked for the hired men.

Marjorie graduated from MHS in 1935. She graduated from Monmouth College in '39 with a double major in chemistry and biology. She attended the Northwestern Univ. Medical Campus in Chicago to study the new field of medical technology. In 1941 she returned to Galesburg where she worked in the labs at Cottage Hospital and Mayo General Army Hospital.

Roger graduated from MHS in 1940, enrolled at Monmouth College, then enlisted in the U.S. Arrny. He served in the Signal Corps in the Philippines with a friend from Wataga, Albert Lundgren. After the war, Roger attended the University of Illinois, graduating with honors in economics and marketing.

Marjorie married Vergil Anderson from Oneida in 1946. They farmed east of Knoxville and had two children, Betsy and Jim. Vergil made trips to Kansas and Texas to buy feeder cattle. He also sold real estate, specializing in farms. He had a fatal coronary in 1956. Marjorie continued to work as a medical technologist until she retired in 1977. She lives on their farm at Knoxville.

Betsy graduated from the University of Illinois. She worked in Kansas City where she met Michael Hamil. They married and had two children and later divorced. Betsy, Joe and Allison Hamil live on the family farm at Monmouth.

Jim graduated from Monmouth College. He married Carolyn Nelson (daughter of Clarence and Olga) of Galesburg. They have two children, Kirk and Megan. Jim's family lives in Danville, IL, where he is Senior Vice President of Old National Bank.

Roger worked for Boise Cascade, designing corrugated packaging. He married Marion Moore in 1962 in Oak Park, IL. They had no children. They lived in LaPorte, IN until he retired early due to Parkinson's Disease. They moved to Wilmington, NC, where he died in 1995.

Mark continued to farm until 1965 when he rented to Eugene Galusha, who continued the farrning operation for 36 years. Vivian passed away in 1973. In the late 70's Marjorie cared for Mark so he could stay in his own home. He passed away in 1981.

KENNETH AND JULIA MCDANELD - Kenneth Henry McDaneld married Julia Anna Bratkovic in Monmouth, Illinois. They have two sons Timothy Kenneth and Joseph Henry, both born in Monmouth, Illinois. Timothy married Jeanette Marie Spangler, and they have two sons, David and Adam. David married Kimberly Mae Lewis and they have a son Konrad Lewis McDaneld. Joseph Henry married Sherri Talbot and they have three children, Joseph Henry, Alexander Coy and Emila Grace.

Kenneth's parents were Henry Osborn and Velma May Taylor McDaneld. They moved to Warren County about 1959 from Marion County, Illinois.

Henry's parents were Coy and Lucy Smith McDaneld and they had four children Henry, Martha, Velma and Dorathy. Lucy came from a family of 17 children.

Coy's parents were John Lewis and Nancy Edith Crose and they raised 13 children in Salem, Illinois. Kenneth's great-great-grandfather Frances Wells McDaneld was drafted in the Civil War in December 1864 and died in Nashville, TN. in February 1865, leaving four children and his wife Nancy Caroline Cockrun. Frances was born in Indiana to Josephus and Catherine Wells McDaneld, they had 9 children. Catherine's father was Frances Wells. Josephus's parents are John and Phebe Richardson McDaneld, they were married in Warren County, Ohio in 1803. John's parents were Daniel and Rhoda McDaneld.

Julia Anna Bratkovic was born and raised in Monmouth her whole life. Her parents were Joseph Mike and Mary Ann Piper and she has one brother James Joseph Bratkovic. Julia's father came to America in 1913 from Austria. He married Mary Piper on July 12, 1933 in Wheaton, Illinois. Joseph's parents were Anthony and Anna Julia Miller Bratkovic.

Mary was born to James Baker Piper and Neva Jane McIntyre Piper. They had four daughters, Mary, Helen, Martha Jane and Dorathy.

Mary's grandparents were born in Schleswig, Holstein, Germany. Henry and Dora Sass Piper were married in Germany and with one small son Fritz and a newborn daughter Sophia they came to America in 1869 on the ship called the Cimbera. They arrived in New York September 24, 1869 and from there they came to Warren County, Illinois.

They lived and raised five more children in Little York, Criss, Mary, John, William and James. Sophia married William Henry Walters, Fritz moved to Oklahoma, Mary died while a small child, John married Delaware Ardent. They had two children, but died very young. William died as a young man.

Mary's maternal grandparents were Alexander and Izora Haines McIntyre. They lived in Sumner Township and raised 13 children.

LETTICE MCGREGOR - Lettice McGregor born 1798 in Pennsylvania was living with her daughter, Mag McGregor Parkinson (Mrs. John) on 1860 Warren County Spring Grove Township Census. Mary, born April 1822 in Pennsylvania and died August 1900 in Denver, Colorado is buried in Spring Grove Cemetery in Warren County, Illinois. Lettice's son, John G., was born in 1820 in Pennsylvania and died in 1899. John G. married Margaret Harsha, born 1833 and died April 16, 1889. Both are buried in Sugar Tree Cemetery, Hale Township, Warren County, Illinois with her parents, George W. Harsha born May 10, 1792 and died December 20, 1882 and Mary Reid Harsha who died February 4, 1876 at age 85 years. George Harsha served in Strait's Company New York in the War of 1812. John McGregor and George Harsha were farmers. John and Margaret McGregor's children: Jennie R.H. born 1864 and died June 14, 1880; Ella born 1866 and died 1921; Ida born 1868 and died 1930, all three never married and are buried by their parents in Sugar Tree Grove Cemetery. Other McGregor children were: Martha McGregor married James Warren Hill; James H. married Lizzie J. Shoemaker March 5, 1861 in Warren County, Illinois; Matthew was a cabinet maker; Joseph was a traveling photographer who homesteaded in Armour, South Dakota, enlisted in Army in 1865 and is buried in Brush, Colorado.

MCINTYRE - DuWayne Eugene "Duke" McIntyre was born February 27, 1945, and Beverly June McIntyre was born September 5, 1947, in Monmouth, Illinois. They married August 8, 1965, at the Christian Church in Monmouth. They have one daughter, Tami Dawn McIntyre, married to Troy Cox on June 14, 1987 at the Roseville Christian Church. Tami and Troy have two sons, Troy Tyler and Joshua Tanner and live in Taylor Mill, Kentucky. They are expecting their third child in September 2002.

DuWayne and Beverly McIntyre, January 2000 in Maui, Hawaii

DuWayne's parents were Russell Howard McIntyre and Marie Elizabeth Cook McIntyre of Roseville, Illinois. His grandparents were William Porter and Rebecca Hanna Reynolds McIntyre and maternally, Charles Albert and Bertha Matilda Bower Cook. His family originates from Ireland and Scotland.

Duke is the 12th of twelve children. His siblings are Ruth, Theodore, Helen, Dorothy, Floyd, Ilene, Charles, Kay, Dean, Donald, and David. Ted, serving in World War II in Germany, upon notification of his birth informed the family that his name was too long and they should just call him "Duke". That nickname has been the name of choice since.

Duke enjoyed motorcycle racing and demolition derby events and has several trophies from those fun days.

Bev is the middle child. Her 11 year older brother, Henry Lee Nevius, died in August, 1988, and James Robert Nevius was born December 24, 1953 and died December 26, 1953. Her parents were Robert Henry Nevius and Beulah

Evelyn Cole of Roseville. Robert's father, John Rowland Nevius, purchased the farm in 1871, where Duke and Bev have lived since 1966 located 2 miles north and 1 mile east of Roseville. John was a veteran of the Civil War serving in the 83rd Infantry Company D from Mercer County. His photo in his Civil War uniform is in the family album. He is mentioned in 1886 Portrait and Biography of Warren County. At that time, his first wife, Elizabeth, had died without children. In 1895, he married Nettie Jane Brady. They had three children, Mary Josephine Nevius; Grace Louise Nevius Elander; and Robert Henry Nevius. Five generations: John Rowland Nevius, Robert, Bev, Tami, and Tyler, all lived on this farm. In 1969, Duke and Bev removed the original farmhouse and built a ranch style home where they reside today. Duke farms the 93 tillable acres and raises White Park cattle. Our photo was taken in Maul, Hawaii, January 2002 far from the fields of Illinois.

Bev's ancestry dates to 1620 when Johannes Nevius arrived in New York from Holland. The Nevius family has been traced to the Roman Empire. *Joannes Nevius and His Descendants A.D 1627-1900* was published in 1900 by author Abraham Van Doren Honeyman.

Duke and Bev are members of the Roseville Christian Church. Duke's working career began with Wells Pet Food Company in Monmouth. He is currently working as a mill man for Monmouth Feed Service. Bev's working career began with the Roseville Independent newspaper. She is currently working at Western Illinois University in Macomb.

JAMES R. AND LORETTA M. MCKEE - James R. McKee was born March 26 1933, in Ormonde, in Warren County. He attended Little York and Monmouth Schools. Loretta M. Benson was born December 7 1932, in Warren County, approximately 4 miles west of Monmouth, on Highway # 34. She attended Monmouth High School, later continuing her education at Carl Sandburg College in Galesburg Illinois, and Montgomery Ward Sales Agency School in Paoli Indiana. They were married April 6, 1952 at the First Presbyterian Church in Monmouth, with Reverend Arthur R. Hall officiating. They have three children, Jacqueline G., James J., and Todd K.

Loretta and James McKee

Jacqueline married Steven Larson, they had two sons, Eric S. and Jason A. Jacqueline and Steve were divorced and later Jacqueline married James Geer on 8/15/1992. Jacqueline and James live in Galesburg, Illinois. Jacqueline attended Warren School, graduating in 1974; later she continued her education at Carl Sandburg College.

James J. graduated from Warren High School in 1978; later he continued his education at Carl Sandburg College. He married Diane Cadwell in 1978 and later they were divorced. James J. married Angela Greenlief 9/23/1984; they have three children, Dustin J, Jessica A., and Alan J.

Todd K. attended Warren High School graduating in 1980, then he attended Southern Illinois University, Carbondale graduating in 1985. He married Freda Caroline Barrett June 8, 1985; they have four children: Alexandria S., Dalton B., Addison E., and Cole B.

James R.'s parents were Wm. Carlton "Jack" McKee, and E. Leota Harvey both of Monmouth. They were married April 5, 1924. His grandparents were Charles B., and Sarah A. (Darrah) McKee. Loretta was the eldest of two daughters of John G. Benson and Stella M. Richardson of Monmouth, Ill. Her grandparents were Elbert D. and Elizabeth A. Richardson.

James R. served in the U.S. Army Feb. 1953 - Jan. 1955, is a member of American Legion Post #136, V.F.W. Post # 2301, a Korean War Veteran, and a member of the First Christian Church of Monmouth. James worked for Admiral, Rockwell Int., Magic Chef, and Maytag Corp. for 45 years, retiring in 1997.

James and Loretta were the owners of Montgomery Ward Catalog Sales Agency in Monmouth from 1974 to 1977. Loretta was employed as Human Resources Manager at Western Stoneware, in Monmouth for 21 years (April 1978-June 1999).

In 1972 -1973 they built a new home, one mile North of Monmouth on Highway # 67. Jim did most of the construction himself.

Loretta served as President of the Warren County Heart Association Board, Vice Chairman of the Warren County American Cancer Society Board for several years. She was a member of the Altrusa Intl. Inc. Club of Monmouth serving as President in 1998-1999, and was chosen Outstanding Woman of the Year in 2000. She was a Monmouth Chamber of Commerce Ambassador for several years, received the "Athena" Award from the Chamber & Bruce Foote Oldsmobile in 1995. She was a member of The First Christian Church, of Monmouth. She served as Treasurer for the Monmouth Kiwanis Club, and as Secretary & Treasurer for the Monmouth Crime Stoppers organization.

ABRAHAM MCKINNEY - Washington County, PA tax records listed Abraham McKinney as a tailor. The year 1826 lists him single, 1827 lists him married. James and Eleanor Brownlee sold Abraham two lots in Taylorstown, near Washington, PA., January 2, 1832 for $50.00—a much lower price than he sold a lot to someone else! Four years later Abraham sells these lots on September 22, 1826, and evidently starts West. On March 6, 1837 he buys 160 acres near Monmouth, Illinois. Half of the land he then sells to William Muncy, his sister Nancy's son. Later, Nancy Muncy, now widowed, marries William Nash, an important pioneer in Warren County history records and a key player in the story of Abraham and Ann Brownlee McKinney.

On May 28, 18-37, Abraham., Ann, and Abraham's sister Jane, join North Henderson Church. Abraham becomes an elder February 11, 1841. When he dies on September 29, 1843, Ann requests the court to have William Nash as executor. Since Abraham had borrowed money from Ann's brother, Elisha, and father-in-law, James Brownlee, to make the trip West, and had been busy clearing land, farming and building a double log cabin for his wife and seven daughters, there had not been time yet to repay the money borrowed. The law demanded that his creditors be satisfied, so everything had to be sold. The farm went on the auction block, and January 30, 1846, was bought by guess who? - James and Eleanor Brownlee.

On March 11, 1846, William Nash became guardian for the younger children. James and Eleanor sell the farm on June 10, 1848. Although no death date has been found for Ann, one would surmise she must have died in late 1845 or early 1846. 'The farm would not have been sold or a guardianship set up if she were alive. Later two sons of William Nash marry McKinney girls, Two others marry Struthers brothers—a familiar name in Washington, PA and Srathaven, Scotland!

Although a week was spent in Washington, PA searching every possible record, nothing surfaced about Abraham's parents. He states in the census records that he was born in Ireland. Sarah Ann's sister, Nancy, in later years, came to Albia, IA to be near Sarah Ann. She married Thomas Bell. Leona McKissick was a small child at the time. Nancy gave her a wooden box she said was made by her father, Abraham, and brought from Ireland. Madorie Tedford Cunningham has this box today.

Abraham McKinney b ca 1800, Ireland; d 29 September 1843, Warren County, IL m ca 1826/27 to Ann/Anna Brownlee b ca 18 10, Washington County, PA daughter of James and Ann Clark (or "Polly" Jolley) Brownlee Jr. She d 1845/46.

Children: 1. Mary Jane m Hugh Nash, 2. Elizabeth Eleanor m James L. Struthers, 3. Sarah Ann m (1) Joseph McKissick (2) Thomas Wilson, 4. Nancy Marie m Thomas Bell, 5. Adaline Clark m James B. Nash, 6. Margaret Almira m John Struthers, 7. Amanda Cordelia m George McCreedy.

JOHN MCKISSICK - John McKissick, Sarah Martin, William and Susanna Martin arrived from Down County, Northern Ireland, landing at Charleston, SC on the ship "Jane" (National Archives Record) on November 21, 1821. John listed on ship record as age 25; Sarah age 20; William 25; Susanna 23. Going to western South Carolina they joined the already established Scottish community at Chester.

October 29, 1824, John bought 100 acres for $245. 00, situated on Rocky Creek, a Scottish settlement, in the 48th year of American independence! John was an elder in the Smyrna Associate Presbyterian congregation. April 2, 1825, court records show he and Sarah declared their intention to become citizens. This was finalized October 22, 1832, a month before he sold his farm, November 25, 1832 for $350.00. Historical records indicate that these Scotsmen opposed slavery and were no longer welcome in the area. Ruth Sloan, granddaughter of William McKissick, said they "lost" one brother in the move West. In the neighboring county of Union there was a slave-owning McKissick who became very wealthy, educated, and well-known in South Carolina.

Coming west they stopped in the Bloomington, IN area. William Martin, William McKissick and John all bought land and started farming. February 27, 1837 John bought 120 acres for $250.00. Sons, William John and James married Martin girls. John served as an elder; first in a country church – a log cabin – and later the congregation built a frame building in Bloomington. Unknown forces were at work to send them, again, westward. William McKissick and William Martin went directly to the Albia, IA area. James, John's son also went to Iowa.

John sold his Indiana farm February 3, 1844 for $325.00 and moved to Warren County, IL, to the farming community in the northern area of the county. He and Sarah joined the Associate Presbyterian Church, the first church in the county, called the Henderson congregation. Sarah, Joseph and John joined by letter on May 21, 1836. Sarah Ann McKinney joined by profession of faith. In December John became the church's 17th elder. No record of land purchase in Illinois. The 1850 census lists his profession as tailor. Abraham McKinney was also a tailor; perhaps he and John worked together. Their children grew to care about each other, Joseph married Sarah on November 2, 1848. Sister Mary married Henry Allen January 27, 1848. October 1, 1849, James Henry McKissick was born to Sarah and Joseph. The following March the McKissick family: John, Sarah, Joseph and Sarah Ann requested their church letters, moving to Albia, IA. William John and Jane followed between 1850 and 1851; Henry and Mary Allen stayed in Monmouth area until after 1855.

In July 1850 Joseph died. The November 1850 Warren County, Illinois census listed Sarah Ann living with sister Mary Jane, and her husband Hugh Nash. February 6, 1852 Sarah Ann married Thomas Wilson, a man 27 years older. In 1871 he died, leaving her with nine children to raise. Records indicate James Henry lived with her before his marriage; it is believed he helped raise the children. Later she lived with James, her first born. She outlived him, dying in 1923 in her ninety-second year.

Arriving in Iowa, John bought 50 acres of homestead land August 5, 1851 for $1.25, situated on land now called the Stanley Bay Farm.

John McKissick married Sarah Martin probably soon after arrival in the United States in 1821. John died 13 March 1859; Sarah died 4 March 1859, Albia, Iowa; both buried in Pleasant Divide cemetery. Next to them are William and Sarah McKissick, together in death as they were in life. Today their stones are white and beautiful, having been restored by their great-great grandchildren – an activity sparked and carried to completion by Charles Swanson. It is believed William and John McKissick were brothers.

RALPH AND LILLIAN MCKISSICK - Ralph and Lillian McKissick came to Kirkwood as a young couple with a baby, and in 1967 they celebrated their 50th wedding anniversary there, before moving back to their home town, Albia, Iowa.

Ralph McKissick, born 3-22-1890 on a farm near Albia, Iowa, was the oldest son in a family of twelve children. His father, James Henry, was born in the Monmouth area in 1849, the only son of Sarah Ann McKinney and Joseph McKissick. Sarah Ann and Joseph's parents, Ann Brownlee and Abraham McKinney and Sarah Martin and John McKissick had come from Pennsylvania and South Carolina by wagon, settling near the North Henderson Church in the early 1830's. The McKissick family moved on to homestead land in Monroe County Iowa in the late 1840's. When Ralph's father became ill, he had to quit school in the 6th grade and go to work to help his mother. When he was a young man, people in the county came to him to break their horses, for he had a way with animals. The story goes that he owned and trained two Clydesdales, and at the county fair they were bought by Busch Brewery, becoming their first show pair.

In Kirkwood, Ralph helped organize the Central Feed and Produce Company, later going into poultry work, and then selling feed to farmers. He loved to help young farmers get started. In exchange for buying feed, he helped them with their feed lots. At the age of 75, still working, he was top salesman in four states. In addition to his farmer families, he loved his church, serving as an elder, teacher and delegate to the General Assembly of the United Presbyterian Church from the Monmouth Presbytery. When I attended the 100th anniversary of the Kirkwood High School Alumni Association in May, 2002, and was recognized as Ralph's daughter, stories about my dad poured forth from so many people. He died in Albia, Iowa November 24, 1968.

Lillian Owen, born 3-10-1895, near Albia, Iowa, was the daughter of a Welsh coal miner immigrant, Hugh Owen, and Blanche Bettis, descendent of a long line of early American pioneers. Hugh and Blanche had 12 children with eight surviving, 7 girls and one boy. Throughout her life, Lillian and her sisters were very close friends and family gatherings were precious times. After graduating from high school, Lillian taught in a country school for 5 years before marrying Ralph McKissick on June 1, 1917 in Albia. They lost one baby, Richard Owen, and later had Martha Jean, born 9-28-27. Lillian participated in many community activities, and for years taught adult Bible classes. She died in Des Moines, Iowa on December 27, 1979.

Martha Jean graduated from Kirkwood High School (1945), Monmouth College (1949), University of Illinois (M.S. 1953). On June 16,1953 in Loveland, Colorado she married James Richard Mattoon, who received his undergraduate degree from the U. Of Illinois (1953) and his Ph.D. in Biochemistry at the U. of Wisconsin (1957). He has taught at the U. of Nebraska, Johns Hopkins Medical School, and the U. of Colorado. Their children are Thomas Edward, and Jean Ellen Mattoon Fassler. There is one grandson, Travis Andrew.

(Submitted by Martha McKissick Mattoon)

MCMULLEN BROTHERS - There was a time, when the tiny communities of Swan Creek and Point Pleasant were the little piece of heaven that anyone could ever want. In the mid-1800's fertile fields, hills that harbored outcrops of coal, and various small businesses made this area a place to call home. It was no different than any other place: trains that ran daily, horse and buggies that tromped through the streets, and people going their own way at a slower pace. All but gone are the numerous stories, some of which included pranksters who put Doc's buggy on top of a building, the outhouses that were toppled, and the things that the kids would do on Halloween. Those years were simpler, slower times, but they could be fun times as well. It was during this time when the McMullen family moved west to Warren County.

About that time, Elmwood and Farmington were places that many McMullen families visited or stayed. My great-grandfather, Jacob E. McMullen, was born about 1852 in Elmwood. Jacob and his father's family later moved to Warren County before 1860 and landed in the area of Swan Township. People of Irish descent were known to work odd jobs, such as miners, bricklayers, and they worked for a time on James Tucker's farm where an 8-sided home still stands today. Jacob then married Mary McKenzie in 1881 in the area, and had Charles Edward (1884), Marie (1890) and Fern (1897).

Charles Edward and Leona (Stevenson) McMullen, 1904

Charles Edward, the only son of Jacob, married Leona Stevenson in Roseville (m 1904). After a honeymoon spent at the World's Fair in St. Louis, they moved to Point Pleasant Township, near where Point Pleasant Cemetery now is located. Charles became an established carpenter, later owning his own contractor business, building or remodeling several structures in the area.

The couple had two sons Marvin Le Moine (b 1908) and Charles Leonard (b 1915). Shortly after Charles Leonard was born, Leona died from cancer, leaving Charles with a seven year old and an infant to raise. His mother, Mary McMullen, helped to raise the boys, until he married Osra Parsons in 1918. Ed passed away in 1943 and Osra later died in 1968. Leonard married Lois Green in 1937. They had three sons, Rex (b 1939), Graham (b 1945), and Larry (b 1947). Marvin married Laura Haffner in 1928 and had two kids: Barbara Leona (b 1933) and Lynn "Bud" (b 1936). Marvin later married Bernadine Clewell in Peoria in 1948, and had two girls, Suzanne Marie (b 1952), and Mary Lou (b 1956). Barbara married Hillion Hines in 1953 and had one son, Randall Mark. Lynn married Patsy Wheeler in 1961 and had Robert (b 1961), Renee (b 1964), and Terry (b 1970). His wife later died in 1990. Suzanne married Art Nolan in 1980. They have no children; but are no longer married. Mary Lou was born with a mental disability and is in a developmental institution.

Leonard and Lois McMullen have many grandchildren and many great-grandchildren, all residing in California. Marvin passed away in 1986, Laura McMullen, his former wife, passed away in Pekin, Illinois in 1994, and Bernadine McMullen passed away in 1996 in Peoria.

Charles and Catherine McMullen - William (b 1823), Samuel (b 1823), Suzanna (b 1827), Charles Jr. (b 1830) James (b 1835), and George W. (b 1939).

Charles Jr. (mother unknown)- Jacob E. Randy and Stacy Brown Hines (m 1980) - Erin (b 1985), Caitlin (b 1987). Robert and Ammie McMullen (m 1995) Kodi - (b 1991), 2 daughters in Washington state. Renee and Ed Hartman (m 1983)- Haley (b 1995), Hanna (b 2000). Terry and Teresa Hagan McMullen (m 1991)- Patrice (b 1992), Kathryn (b 1996)

R. JEREMY AND ALICE (FRANTZ) MCNAMARA - The McNamara family moved to Monmouth in the summer of 1964 from Oxford, Ohio, where R. Jeremy McNamara had been a professor at Miami University. The family included Jeremy and his wife, Alice, who were both natives of Portsmouth, Ohio, and children Maura and Barry.

Jeremy, born Jan. 25, 1932, was the son of Robert J. and Dorothy (Goetz) McNamara, while Alice, born Aug. 24, 1931, was the daughter of Joseph and Nettie Velara (Wheeler) Frantz. They were married Aug. 22, 1953 in Portsmouth.

Starting in 1965, the McNamaras lived at 723 East Archer. Although that home no longer exists, Jeremy and Alice resided in the house through 1991, and Barry and his new family lived there until 1996, when they moved away from Monmouth and sold the house to Monmouth College.

Jeremy came to Monmouth to serve as an English professor, and he taught at Monmouth College for the next 31 years, retiring in 1995. He was one of three MC professors who gave the commencement address in 1996, and his career was noted for his appreciation and encouragement of scholarship. He earned the Sears-Roebuck Foundation Award for Teaching Excellence and Campus Leadership in 1990.

In 1999, he returned to the college to teach for one year, the same year that Barry began a job at MC as associate director of college communications and sports information co-director. That job brought Barry (born July 26, 1963 in Oxford) and his family back to the area from Galva, Ill. The family included children Sean (born April 8, 1990 in Monmouth) and Kelsea (born Oct. 29, 1993 in Monmouth) and his wife, Vicki (Talley), who was one of six children born to Carol (Gregory) and the late Jerry Talley. Both Vicki (born Sept. 10, 1963 in Monmouth), and Barry graduated from Monmouth High School in 1981, and they were married May 27, 1989. Barry worked at the Daily Review Atlas newspaper from 1988-95, serving as editor the last four years, and Vicki worked for 11 years at Community Memorial Hospital.

Alice and Jeremy's other child, Maura, was born May 10, 1960 in East Lansing, Mich., with cerebral palsy, and in her younger years, she benefited greatly from Monmouth's Warren Achievement Center. The family could often be seen taking walks through the east side of town near the college campus, with Jeremy or Alice pushing Maura in her wheelchair. Maura, a 1979 MHS graduate, eventually moved to a residence in the Quad Cities more suited to individuals with cerebral palsy, but her parents, and particularly her father, were still often seen on their walks around town.

At the time of this writing, Jeremy is enjoying his retirement, and he and Alice live at 617 East Archer. Barry and his family live at 1025 East Third. When not working at the college, Barry is an advocate for youth soccer, and Vicki works at the Warren County United Way and aspires to a second career as a Christian speaker.

MEANS - Joseph Means: child of Joseph—John Means, born 1678, Fermanaugh, Tyrone Co. Ireland; died January 20, 1737/38 Makefield Twp. Bucks Co., Pa. Married Mary Spencer, born about 1695, Derry, Ireland; died after 1739, Buckingham Twp, Pa. Married Elizabeth McCord 1693 in Fermanaugh, Tyrone, Ireland. She was born before, 1679; died 1717 in Ireland. John came to colonies 1718, accompanied by 3 children: William, Robert, Nancy.

John's burial – Deep Run Presbyterian Church, Bucks Co., Pa. Robert Means born 1713, Fermanaugh Co., Ireland. Died 1779 Mifflin Co., Pa. Married Nancy Kelly, September 16, 1742, Philadelphia, Pa. Daughter of John Kelly, Mary Spencer. Born 1721, died in Mifflin Co. Pa. Children: John, Margaret, Robert, James, Jane, Joseph, Mary, George, Nancy, William.

S. Oscar Means

Robert George Means, born December 9, 1713, Kentucky; died February 5, 1877 in Roseville, Warren Co. Illinois. He married (1) Mary Buchanon August 27, 1835 in Ripley Co. In. daughter of William Buchanon and Elizabeth. She was born 1814, died March 18, 1841, Jefferson Co. In. (2) Elizabeth Bates April 21, 1842, Jefferson Co. In. daughter of Mr. Bates and Margaret. She was born July 24, 1820 in Indiana, died August 19, 1897 in Swan Creek, Illinois. Children: William, James, George H., Martha, Sarah, Samuel D., Robert born Kentucky, moved to Indiana 1835, to Warren County 1850's. 1870 lived Carthage Township Illinois, was farmer.

Samuel Oscar Means, born October 28, 1849, Elkhart, Indiana, died January 31, 1907 Jonesboro, Arkansas. Married Hannah Jane Lionberger, September 29, 1871, Hancock Co. IL, daughter Emanuel Lionberger and Mary Browning. Hannah born February 19, 1852, Illinois, died September 9, 1899. Both buried Warren County Cemetery. Samuel moved from Indiana to Roseville, Illinois. There 20 years, moved to Monmouth, Illinois. Was carpenter and active in trade union circles, member Monmouth Carpenters Union, President Monmouth Trades Assembly, served board of directors Galesburg Labor News. Member of First Methodist Church. Children: Mary, Sarah, Alvin, Lenna, Oscar S., Ida, George B., David, Fred, Arthur, Lola.

George Browning Means, born February 7, 1885; died November 10, 1946. Married (1) Emma Hunter 1899, died June, 1917. (2) Annie Victoria Moore, 1918. Born May 9, 1887, died January 2, 1969. Were married in Columbus, Georgia. Lived in Monmouth, Illinois in house father built. Both buried Monmouth Cemetery.

George was machinist, setting up road equipment for Merrilet Road Supply. He was member 165th Company Coast Artillery Corps, Independent Order Odd Fellows, Encampment, Mooseheart Lodges. Both members First Christian Church. Children: Helen, Lois, Vivian, Georgene, Grace, Ida, Annie.

Georgene Means, only living survivor, born May 5, 1919, Monmouth. Attended local schools; Harding, Central Junior High, Monmouth Senior High, Lincoln College, Carl Sandburg – studying tax, accounting, computers. Work: Ford Hopkins Drugs, Formfit, Inspector Iowa Army Ordnance Plant. Retired from Wilson Plant 1982. Since 1984 working for self in Health Home Care and Companionship.

Married Donald M. Holeman, Sr. 1939; born October 23, 1913 Roseville, Illinois, died October 1, 1955. Buried Monmouth Cemetery. Children: Donald, Jr., Ronald, Theodore, Jan Wesley, Jeffrey. Been member of Friendship Rebekah Lodge #22 since 1942, Past President Rebekah District #11, Warren Co. Illinois Genealogical Society, First Christian Church. Still in family home of grandfather, 907 South B Street, Monmouth, Illinois.

OLIVER AND DORCAS (MEADOWS) MEEKER - Sunday, February 15, 1920, saw the sun sink on a romance of life whose various chapters were constancy, love, comradeship and devotion. The romance of a man and woman who have cherished the comradeship of the other through all the joys and heartaches, all the sorrows and happiness of almost seventy years of wedded life-as the shadow of life passed over at the home of Mr. and Mrs. Oliver Meeker at the birth of the new Sabbath day and Mr. Meeker with the memories of a loving and devoted helpmate, who that day was called to her great reward, no doubt but looked with wistful eyes to the sinking rays of life wishing that they might not be parted even in death. Perhaps it was such a desire heard by the Great Ruler of all that led to his passing away the following Wednesday just as the sun was dropping, behind the horizon. Thus it was – as he would have had it – he could not let her go alone and side by side they entered the Promised Land.

The life of Mr. and Mrs. Meeker has been a beautiful chapter in the history of our community, living as they have a quiet, simple, sincere life rich in love for each other, their family and their fellowmen – a life of integrity and usefulness – a life which found their keenest pleasures in the gifts of nature – sunshine, a green field, an open road, the eternal mystery of growing things and their children – they won their way into the hearts of all who were honored to know them.

Few have been privileged as they to note the tremendous march of progress which completely, revolutionized the economic structure of the entire world. They have witnessed the kaleidoscopic changes of this nation and the world for ninety years. The revolution of power, the coming of steam and electricity, the change from the ox-cart, the wagon, the buggy, train, automobile, and aeroplane, the marvelous inventions of labor saving machinery on. the farm from the old plows and other machinery. They had helped to change this nation from a rough frontier to a nation without a peer in the world. Theirs was a life of romance whose history would fill a volume for theirs was the romance of world building.

On July 11, 1830, at Crawfordsville, Indiana, occurred the birth of Oliver Meeker. At the age of four (in the fall of 1834) his parents moved to a farm near Henderson Grove. In 1835 they moved to North Henderson township, Mercer County. Oliver was of a family of eleven children, three of whom survive his death, William Meeker and Alex Meeker of Alexis, and Mrs. Celia Starring of Carney, Nebraska.

Mrs. Meeker, whose maiden name was Dorcas Meadows, was born November 6, 1829, in Sullivan County, Indiana. As a little girl she moved with her parents to Rivoli Township,

Mercer County. She was of a family of ten children, all of whom preceded her in death.

On April 7, 1850, Mr. and Mrs. Meeker were married in Rivoli Township by the Reverend David Bruner, of the Methodist Church. Ann Whiteman acted as bridesmaid and James Terry as best man. The bride was very much in style with a white dress and white cap with 7 yards of ribbon around it. The groom was quite correct in a broadcloth pigeon tailed coat and a high stove pipe hat.

After the ceremony was completed, the happy young couple left for the home the bridegroom had prepared for his bride. It was no five thousand dollar bungalow with piano and mahogany furniture – but a log cabin built by Oliver's half brother, John Meeker, and what little furniture there was had been made by the groom. Their first breakfast was cooked over an open brick fireplace. At this time, 1850, there was no town of Alexis, North Henderson, Viola, or Aledo. Galesburg was a little village and Monmouth was only a handful of humble homes. Keithsburg and Rock Island with the advantage of river traffic were the important towns of this section. There were no stores or doctors or post office or any of the present day "necessities" within miles of this little frontier home.

Money was scarce and everyone was poor. As a young man Mr. Meeker dressed hogs, hauled them to Keithsburg and sold them to William Gale, dressed at $2.40 a hundred. He hauled hogs to Galesburg and received $1.98 a hundred. William Garrett bought corn from him as low as 10 cents per bushel and at that time his good wife paid 50 cents a yard for calico and 80 cents a yard for muslin. They knew what hard times were.

Mr. and Mrs. Meeker were blessed with ten children, two of them dying in infancy and eight lived to manhood and womanhood. Of these eight, three preceded their parents in death. Mrs. Louise Susan Wallace passed away thirty-five years ago, Mrs. Amanda Wixson and Mrs. Florence Robinson died twenty-three years ago. The following children survive their parents: Mrs. Sophia Steepleton, North Henderson; Mrs. Anna Thompson of Galesburg, Royal C. of San Diego, California, John of Wichita, Kansas, and Timothy of North Henderson.

For sixty years they lived on the old homestead, five miles north and one mile east of Alexis. They moved into Alexis almost ten years ago. At the time of their death they were the oldest living settlers of Mercer and Warren counties. Their friends were numbered by hundreds and no man can speak ill of them. They had lived honest, straightforward, God-fearing Christian lives and were a credit to the community, state and nation, and their memory will be a beautiful inheritance of coming generations.

At the time of his death, Mr. Meeker was 89 years, 7 months and 7 days of age and Mrs. Meeker was 90 years, 3 months and 9 days of age.

A double funeral was held in the Presbyterian Church Friday afternoon, February 20, at 1:30, and they were laid to rest side by side in the Alexis cemetery.

GUS T. AND BESSIE LINMAN MELBURG

- Gus T. Melburg and Bessie Linman were married on June 16, 1886 at the First Lutheran Church in Monmouth, this being the first marriage ceremony performed in the old church building, which later was occupied by the West Side United Presbyterian Church, and then the Masonic Temple in the 200 block of South E Street. They lived all their married life at 221 South D Street, except for a brief interval living at the Schulz mansion, site of the present Lutheran Church. They celebrated fifty-eight years of marriage. The Melburgs were parents of Arthur Theodore (b. 1887) m. Ethel Mackey, Oquawka; Ernest Clifton Melburg (b. 1890) m. Esther Johnson, Ames, Iowa; Edna Sagred Amalia (b. 1893) m. Hilding Matson, Monmouth; and Leonard Wilfred Melburg (b. 190 1), a Monmouth attorney, m. Myra Arexine Stice, Riverside, California. There were eight grandchildren and one great grandson. Two of the grandchildren, Leonard Leroy Melburg and Robert Theodore Matson were in the U.S. military service for World War 11.

Gus and Bessie Melburg

August Theodore Melburg (Magnusson in Sweden), the eldest of ten children, was born on July 6, 1864 in Reftele, Jonkoping Lan, Smaland, Sweden, to Magnus and Christine (Kristina Svenson) Arvidson. He immigrated in 1882 at the age of eighteen; two brothers and a sister later immigrated: Alfred (b. 1870) Mon-mouth, Joseph (b. 1873) Sterling, and Fina Amalia (b. 1888) New Britain, Connecticut. Siblings remaining in Sweden were Karl Frithiof, Oscar, Manfred, John Albert. Two brothers died in infancy. For sixty-three years, Mr. Melburg had been a tailor in Monmouth, and had his own shop at 115 W. 1st Avenue and 110 1/2 South Main Street, and was one of the oldest men still active in business in Monmouth. He was a deacon and trustee in the Lutheran Church, and secured the Schulz property, along with A.L. Martin, on which the church stands. He was a member of Monmouth Lodge No. 397, B.P.O.E. (Elks Club). Gus Melburg died May 8, 1944 in Monmouth.

Bessie Linman (Bengta Nelson in Sweden) was born on February 19, 1861 in Ljungryda, Jamshog, Blekinge, Sweden, the youngest of ten children. Her parents died before she was five years old, and she lived with an aunt and uncle until age ten, when she came to America with an older brother, Nels Linman (b. 1857). She resided in Roseville with her brother, Swan N. Linman. Bessie moved to Monmouth and attended Willitts School (First Ward). She joined the Fist Lutheran Church in 1883 and had the longest contmuous membership of any person then living. Bessie Melburg died on March 31, 1949.

ORA AND MINNIE MELTON

- Ora Melton was born in Harrison County, Indiana on September 18, 1895. Minnie Bryant was born in the same county on March 2, 1896. They married on February 17, 1916. They moved to Warren County, Illinois with their small son Murl in the spring of 1917.

Orand and Minnie Melton Family, 1942. Front row: Dorothy, Ora, Minnie, Sarah. Back row: Lelia, Jerry, Murl, Herbert (Dutch), and Mary.

Ora worked by the month for Henry Pattison whose farmland was on the north side of the county line in Mercer County. After a couple of years Mr. Pattison rented them 120 acres on the thirds. The Meltons furnished the labor and received one-third of the income. They also had a few cattle and raised hogs. The next year they were able to buy a half inerest in everything so they rented fifty-fifty. During this time two more children were born: Lelia and Herbert (Dutch).

In 1924 they rented a 160-acre farm in Section 9, Sumner Township, one mile south of the Mercer-Warren County Line in the Duck Creek School District. They lived there three years and two more children were born: Mary and Gerald (Jerry).

In 1927 they rented 240 acres of land from three different landlords. They moved onto the Decker 80, located 1/4 mile east of Duck Creek School in Section 4, Sumner Township. After 80 acres of this land was sold, Ora started a general trucking business. They milked cows, raised hogs and chickens and had a big garden. They lived on this farm until 1939. While living there two more children were born: Dorothy and Sarah.

In the spring of 1939 they rented 160 acres in Section 6, Sumner Township from Iva Ranney. In 1940 they were able to rent an additional 190 acres from Mrs. Ranney. Their son Murl and his wife Mabel moved into a house on this land to help with the farming. In 1946 Mrs. Ranney sold all her farmland and Ora and Minnie purchased the 160 acres where they lived.

They moved to Little York in 1983. Ora died August 31, 1985, and Minnie died December 1, 1990. Although they were not native born citizens of Warren County, they lived nearly all their productive years and raised seven children there.

Murl born September 30, 1916, was in the Civilian Conservation Corps from October 1934 until July 1935, and then became a farmer. He married Mabel Logsdon who worked as a hot lunch cook for twenty years. They had four children: Susie, James, Thomas, and Ann.

Lelia born December 12, 1918, was a teacher both before and after her marriage to Fred Olson, a farmer and World War II veteran. They had four children: Peggy, John (deceased), Nancy, and David.

Dutch born December 26, 1922, was a farmer and a rural mail carrier for twenty years. He was a World War 11 veteran. He married Helen Pomeroy. Helen was a substitute mail carrier and a school bus driver. They had eight children: Linda, Lois, Cheryl and Carol (deceased twins), Robert, Jack, Donna, and Jay. Dutch died December 23, 1997.

Mary born July 7, 1924, was a teacher before and after her marriage to Deen Lincoln, a farmer and World War II veteran. They have three daughters: Sarah Jane, Virginia (Ginger), and Marianne.

Jerry born December 19, 1926, is a farmer. He is a World War II veteran. He married Virginia Boock. They have three children: Gary, Mary Susan, and Kathy.

Dorothy born June 29, 1929, was a homemaker. She married Donald Miller, a farmer and miner from Colorado. They have four children: Jean, Dwight, Dwayne, and Judy.

Sarah born December 19, 1931, was a secretary before and after her marriage to Edward Burns, a farmer and auctioneer. They have Burns Trailer Sales business. They have five children: Connie, Charles, Herbert, Sarah (Sally), and Scott.

MELVIN BROTHERS - Melvin brothers, Merle and Lowell, were born a year apart - Merle 19 February 1906 - Lowell 31 July 1907. They were sons of Ralph W. and Dora (Feagans) Melvin and spent their early life in LaHarpe and Sciota areas. Born on a farm east of Blandinsville. Merle attended schools in Raritan and Monmouth. The family moved to Monmouth when he was 10. His marriage to Erma Payne was on 6 February 1928. They had two sons and two daughters - the boys Billy G. of Little York and Robert Dean of Champaign, the daughters Norma Lea (Mettler) of Monmouth and Judith Merle (Owens) of Clinton. Another brother, Vernon and an infant sister died. Lowell married Bonnie (Green) 14 February 1928. They had two sons and a daughter - James A. of Stronghurst a banker, John L. of Cameron, and Barbara married to Donald Howe who passed away and married later to Lowell Gardner living in California. From these are 9 grandchildren for Lowell and 6 for Merle grandchildren

Merle Melvin

Merle was a trucker and like his brother worked for Barnes Bros. Grocery many years. He was a city employee - 8 years as cemetery sexton, water department and landfill supervisor. A former member of Ninth Avenue UP Church, he joined Emmanuel Baptist when it closed.

Lowell, when Ninth Avenue closed, joined Faith UP Church. He enjoyed activities of senior citizens and traveling. He was a WWII veteran, a member of the Army Medical Department. Prior to military service he worked for 16 years at Barnes Bros. grocery delivering groceries - until they closed. Then 14 years driving a bread truck for Strand's Bakery and returned to Barnes Super Valu until he became eligible for Social Security. Lowell was an avid Chicago Cubs fan. Moved from South "A" to Lake Warren where he could fish at will. In a scenic area of Colorado and early one morning, climbed high atop a lookout stand and met his friend Bud Barnes standing there.

Merle passed away at his home 622 South Eighth at 68 on 25 June 1974. He had been in poor health several years. Lowell was 66 when he passed away 1 May 1974, the same year his brother died.

HOLLIS AND EDITH MELVIN - The couple were members of Grace Presbyterian Church.

Hollis was an avid golfer, spending lots of time at the Gibson Woods golf course. He served on the Monmouth Park Board, part of the time as president. He was active at Strom Center, supported the United Way Fund, helped with the Citizens Lake project, and was involved in Kiwanis Club and the Boy Scouts.

Edith, Melissa, Hollis Melvin, Carthage, 1949

Edith was a member of PEO and enjoyed reading and gardening.

Hollis and Edih raised tea roses, and it was not unusual for a friend to receive a "rose bowl" with one of the beautiful blooms.

Melissa married Lester Brent Killey of Monmouth in 1960. They had three children: Barbara Lee (1961), Adam Everett (1962), and Lynne Anne (1965). Melissa and Lester divorced in 1976.

Hollis died in Monmouth October 11, 1979, preceded in death by all of his brothers and sisters. Edith died five years later in Durango, Colorado, on October 4, 1964, leaving a surviving brother, John R. Mayor.

Hollis Chester Melvin was born July 2, 1904, in Raritan, Illinois, to Lewis and Lillie (Atwater) Melvin. He and twin brother Holland were numbers nine and ten of eleven children. Hollis spent his early life in and around Raritan and LaHarpe, Illinois. He graduated from LaHarpe High School and from Culver-Stockton College at Canton, Missouri. He did graduate work at the University of Wisconsin, The University of Illinois, and the University of Iowa.

On June 28, 1934, he married Edith Mayor, daughter of James and Edna (Roberts) Mayor, of LaHarpe. Edith was born Nov. 6, 1904. She attended Western State Teachers College, and taught in the LaHarpe schools at the time of their marriage.

The couple resided in Carthage, Illinois, where Hollis worked as an elementary school principal and for a while as an insurance salesman. Edith taught in the Carthage schools.

In 1948, Hollis, Edith, and their daughter Melissa (born December 19, 1937) moved to Monmouth, Illinois, where Hollis became principal of Willits Elementary School, retiring in 1971. Edith taught first grade at Willitts until her retirement.

CHARLES AND EDITH (JOHNSON) MENELY - The name Menely was foreign to Warren county until 1913 when Charles Thomas Menely came to Monmouth from Rushville, Illinois and married Edith Josephine Johnson the daughter of John Adolph and Hilda Marianna (Anderson) Johnson. Charles (called Chick) took up the tailoring trade and was a tailor in Monmouth for nearly 50 years.

The Charles Menelys in 1929

To this union four children were born, all of whom attended Monmouth Public Schools.

The first born, Robert Charles, attended the University of Illinois until going into the Seabees in 1944. After World War II, he married and settled in California.

Harold Thomas was the second son born to this marriage and he became a dry cleaner in Monmouth, after serving his hitch in the Army during World War II. He and his family settled in Florida.

Finally, a girl, Jane Louise was born to the Menelys. She attended Monmouth College and Moser Business College in Chicago. She married Clarence Wilbert (Bill) Cochran of Kirkwood at the Methodist Church in 1946 after Bill finished his hitch in the Army during World War II. They raised their family in Kirkwood.

The fourth child born to Edith and Chick was William Arthur (Bill). He joined the Navy before he finished high school and after World War II attended Monmouth College and Gem City Business College before marrying Josephine McCoy of Monmouth. They settled in California.

WILLIAM DAVIDSON MILLEN - William Millen was born in Monmouth, Illinois, March 30, 1911, son of Theodore Melville Millen and Martha Weed Millen. There were four boys - Samuel, Theodore, William and James. His father was Warren County Librarian for 32 years, 8 a.m.-9 p.m. six days a week.

The family lived on ten acres at 505 Sunny Lane - With four sons: Sam, Ted, Bill and Jim there was always something happening. One day they found some Civil War caps. They fired one or two for the loud popping noise and smoke; then the old Civil War gun was aimed at several persons, but never fired. Finally it was turned toward the front door and fired from the kitchen; leaving a hole more than a yard in width and length in the dining room wall. The load in the gun had been placed there during the Civil War!

William attended grade school, high school, Monmouth College and Pittsburgh - Xenia Seminary, graduating with a Master's Degree in 1936. In 1947 he was given a Doctor of Divinity degree from Monmouth College.

William and Clara Millen

Ed and Ruth Parsons Miller 1944

He served a total of twenty-five years as pastor of churches in Lisbon and Vernon, Wisconsin; Tulsa, Oklahoma; Philadelphia and Ellwood City, Pennsylvania; and Nampa, Idaho. He became a Field Director of the Board of National Missions of the United Presbyterian Church, USA 1960-1968; Director of the Church Finance Campaign Service in New York 1969-1977. Those were busy, happy years as his wife was able to travel with him. There two children were reared. They traveled all over the mainland U.S., including Hawaii and Puerto Rico.

When he lived in Wisconsin he sang with the all male chorus in Milwaukee, Wisconsin; also sang over WTMJ radio as the Singing Milkman for the Golden Guernsey Company.

He was a charter member of the Sussex, Wisconsin Lion's Club. He was interested in the Boy Scouts of America serving as President of the Ore-Ida Council; President of the Nampa, Idaho Rotary Club; trustee of the College of Idaho in Caldwell, Idaho; and a Paul Harris Fellow.

After retiring to Rio, Illinois he was asked to go to Denver, Colorado for two years to be a Director for the Major Mission Fund of the Presbyterian Church. Upon returning to Rio, he served as Minister of Visitation at South Park Church in Rock Island, Illinois and interims at churches in the area. He was a member of Great Rivers Presbytery and served on committees in Presbytery, Synod and General Assembly.

After retiring again he was asked to take the presidency of the alternatives for Older Adults in Rock Iland County and the surrounding counties.

He married Clara Virtue of Hanover, Illinois in 1936. They have a son, James W. Millen (and Gail), Canton, Michigan; a daughter Mary Cook, Galesburg; four grandchildren and three great-grandchildren.

On his acreage in Rio, he raised vegetables, fruit, flowers and honey.

He and Clara are fully retired and living in an apartment in Galesburg, Illinois. They celebrated their 65th wedding anniversary in June 2001.

CARL/CHARLES EDWIN MILLER - Miller, Carl/Charles Edwin (C.E. or "Ed") was born in Coldbrook Township, Warren County, IL on January 26, 1894. His father, John Gustaf Miller (b. October 29, 1863-d January 21, 1937) first immigrated to Illinois in 1887 then returned to Sweden and later returned to Illinois in 1891, and Hilda Marie Carlson Miller (b July 8, 1866-d October 18, 1937) came to Varna, Illinois and then to Galesburg, Illinois in 1890 from Sweden where she was born. John and Hilda were married on August 20, 189 1. Ed lived in Knox County during his teen years coming to the Swan Creek area later. He married Ruth lone Parsons of Swan Creek on September 21, 1927 in Peoria. She was the daughter of Rollin A. Parsons (b June 9, 1837- d October 29, 1917) and Jemima R. Collins Parsons (b April 17, 1859- d July 14, 1946). She was born in Point Pleasant Township, Warren County, IL and attended schools there. There was one son born to this marriage, William Edwin. They moved to Roseville in 1941 where they continued to reside.

CRAIG AND MAURA MILLER - Craig Lawrence Miller, son of Lawrence and Judith (Glenn) Miller, was born April 16, 1974 in Moline, Illinois. He has one brother Kyle Glenn Miller (Linda Johnson) born in 1969.

Craig and Maura Miller

As a young boy Craig attended Cameron School for his first three grades. Then transferring to Warren School until his graduation from high school in 1992. Craig worked during his high school years at Wareco in Monmouth, Illinois. After high school, Craig went on to study at Carl Sandburg, Community College in Galesburg, Illinois for eighteen months, then following up one semester at Spoon River Community College in Macomb, Illinois. During these years Craig ran the farm (Jewell Farm) as his father was in ill health. He farmed 160 acres with corn and soybeans, and worked with the flock of sheep his parents owned. Upon leaving college Craig gained employment at Alexis Fire Equipment in Alexis, Illinois and worked there in the electrical department for approximately two years until moving on to Stanton's Heating and Air Inc. Craig began employment at Painter Farm Equipment in Monmouth, Illinois in March of 2000. Assembling Kinze planters and troubleshooting with farmers individually is part of what his job entails. Craig now has assumed the Jewell farm and lives there farming and raising sheep.

Maura Erin (Denison) Miller, daughter of Timothy and Joye (Reynolds) Denison, was born March 18, 1975 in Monmouth, Illinois. She has one brother Michael Kenneth Denison (Christina Wiley). Maura began and ended her education at Warren School. She attended Immaculate Conception School in Monmouth, Illinois for grades 1 through 8. She worked several summers detasseling for Pioneer Seed Corn Monmouth, Illinois. Upon graduating in 1993, Maura worked a part time summer job at Save A Lot in Monmouth, Illinois until she left for college in September. She went to Midstate College in Peoria, Illinois for three semesters, meanwhile working for American Family Insurance. Upon returning home she became employed by Giant Foods in Monmouth, Illinois as a cashier. Eventually, she was transferred to the bakery as a cake decorator. Upon leaving Giants she worked at Wareco in Monmouth, Illinois for a short stint, Maura then married February 16, 1995 (divorced late 1996) and had a daughter, Lindsay Rose, October 5, 1995, born at St. Mary's Hospital in Galesburg, Illinois. She began her schooling at Warren School 2001. June 1996 Maura gained employment at Eagle Country Market as a Cake Decorator. August 2001, Maura began Little Wren Pottery, makinggarden gift items and she continues to decorate cakes from home.

September 1997 Maura and Lindsay purchased a home at 1124 S. 6th Street Monmouth, Illinois. Living there until June 2001. May 1, 1999 Craig and Maura were married in a ceremony performed by Father Carl LoPresti at Immaculate Conception Church in Monmouth, Illinois. One year later May 2, 2001 Hanafin "Hana" Jewell Miller was born at St. Mary's Hospital in Galesburg, Illinois. Craig adopted Lindsay June 2001. Our family resides on the Jewell Farm 1182 140th Ave Monmouth, Illinois.

HENRY MILLER - Five generations of farmers Section 15, Lenox Township, Warren County, Illinois.

Eugene and Marcelyn Miller, 50th Wedding Anniversary, June 16, 1996

Henry Miller, wife and family came to Warren County, Illinois in 1856. He was born in Lewis County, West Virginia 9-15-1813, miarried 1831 and died 7-20-1892 in Holdrege, Nebraska. His wife, Mary Catherine Tole was born 3-4-1813, died 4-17-1909 and was buried in Monmouth, Illinois. They raised 10 children, namely; George, Catherine, James, Elizabeth, Hiram, Mary, Henry, John Wesley, Peter, and Martha. He was a carpenter and farmer. They lived 60 rods North of his grandson, J. Alven Miller, and SW of his son, John Wesley Miller, and farmed in Section 15, Lenox Township. Henry and his brother Jacob started the United Brethren Church in Larchland, now known as the United Methodist Fairview Center Church located in the center of Lenox Township.

John Wesley Miller was born 6-10-1848, married 9-12-1875, died 9-29-1916. His wife,

Catharine Radmacher was born 10-29-1855, died 7-31-1931. They are buried in Monmouth, Illinois. Their children were: Cora, Grace, Mary, John Alven, Ethel, Catherine Addie, and Ruby. He, his wife and family were quite active in the church his father started. He was known for his fine horses and offered stud service for a large area. He was a prosperous farmer and left a farm to each of his children.

John Alven Miller was born 6-8-1884, married 2-9-1910, died 10-4-1970. His wife, Lavinia Troxel was born 9-21-1889, died 3-20-1957. They are buried in Monmouth, Illinois. They had six children: Lawrence, Louise, John, William, Dorothy Pauline, and Alven Eugene. They all attended and supported the Fairview Center Church. Lavinia was a member of the Ladies Aid and Missionary Society. She baked for The Pantry for many years and was the first to make and introduce potato chips to the area, making one or two gallons per week. The family raised and sold frying chickens, dressing from 50 to 100 chickens each Friday afternoon. He was an avid hunter and fisherman and raised his sons to do the same. He played the harmonica with a small musical group, Lincoln (banjo), Munson (violin), McEwen (mandolin) and his sister, Ruby, played piano for special occasions. Besides farming he raised hogs, sheep and cows, and did custom work. He was well known and had a large circle of friends.

Alven Eugene Miller was born 1-2-25 and married 6-16-46. His wife, Marcelyn Meyer was born 11-10-1924. They raised two children, Kevin born 2-6-1953 and Kimberly born 1-17-1956. Eugene graduated from Monmouth High School and farmed all his life. He is the present owner of the Miller land in Section 15, Lenox Township. They attend and support the Fairview Center Church, both were Sunday School teachers, and held various offices in the church. He and Kevin raised Purebred Duroc hogs, showing in Local, State and National shows for many years. He adjusted hail losses for twenty-three years and sold Multi-peril and Hail Insurance, retiring in 1995. His family, grandchildren and one great grandchild are his pride and joy. Kimberly graduated from Texas Womens University, Denton, Texas with a degree in Occupational Therapy. She married Steve Cridelich 1-2-1988, and lives in Oregon, Wisconsin. They have two children, Seth and Abigail.

Kevin Eugene Miller is the fifth generation to farm the land. He was born 2-6-1953 and was married 5-16-1981 to Becky (Breen) Dixon who was born 6-29-1954. They have four children, Joe and Ryan Dixon, Erin and Brock Miller. Kevin graduated from Illinois State University with a degree in Business Administration and they live near Biggsville, Illinois, and farm in both Henderson and Warren counties. Kevin was a Union school board member for eight years, and they are active mebers of the Biggsville United Methodist Church.

HOWARD G. MILLER - The first f this family to come to the United States was Charles Peterson Miller. He was born in Kyrkhult Beking, Sweden, on January 3, 1849, and came to America as a young man. In Chicago, Illinois, he married Nellie Gisselson Gibson on February 28, 1880. Nellie had been born on May 22, 1858, in Kyrkhpt, Sweden.

This couple came to Warren County and settled on a farm, four miles south of Monmouth, where they had five children: Blanche, Clara, Royal, Ernest W. and Helma. Nellie died on December 24, 1915, and Charles P. died on February 29, 1929.

Ernest was born August 20, 1886; he married Pearl E. McIntyre on January 1, 1914. They lived on a farm three and a half miles south of Monmouth. They had four children: a stillborn son, Mabel, Mildred and Howard Glenn Miller born July 13, 1919,

Howard went to the Enterprise Grade School before going to Monmouth High School where he graduated in 1937. Upon graduation he engaged in farming with his father. His father, Ernest W. died on March 9, 1961. He lost his mother, Pearl, on September 14, 1973.

On October 10, 1940, Howard married Regena L. Howard. Regena was born March 9, 1922, in Pike County, IL, the daughter of John Wesley and Reta Howard. The Howard family moved to Warren County when Regena was three. She attended Columbia Grade School, and went to Kirkwood High School for two years. She then transferred to Monmouth High School where she graduated in 1940.

After their marriage, Howard and Regena moved to a farm south of Cameron. While living there the first child, Linda Jean, was born on October 8, 1941. In 1943 the family moved to a farm four and a half miles south east of Monmouth. Their son, Gary Howard, was born May 22, 1945.

In 1955 Howard became part-owner of the Allis Chalmer Machinery Dealership, and the family moved to 500 North Sunny Lane in Monmouth.

Howard and Regena bought a home at 315 South First Street in 1958. Their second daughter, Rhonda Kay, was born on October 14, 1966. All three children graduated from Monmouth High School.

Linda Jean graduated from Western Illinois University in Macomb with a major in music. Gary Howard graduated from Purdue University, Lafayette, Indiana as a Civil Engineer. Rhonda Kay graduated from Knox College in Galesburg with a Bachelor of Arts Degree.

After retirement, Howard started repairing and refinishing furniture in his shop at 315 South First Street, where he is still keeping busy in November of 2001.

JACK K. AND REBECCA (DAMEWOOD) MILLER - Rebecca J. Damewood was born 8 February 1928 to Arthur W. and Florence E. (McKee) Damewood. She attended Garfield and Central Jr High schools, graduating from Monmouth High in June 1947. She attended West Side and Heritage U. P. churches. She worked at several restaurants and F.W. Woolworth. She graduated from Morris School of Cosmetology, working for Colwell Beauty Shop several years before starting her own shop. Rebecca married Jack K. Miller 27 November 1949, a locomotive engineer for M&ST L and CN&W railroads. They have two children: J. Kenneth, born 18 December 1952 and Sherrie P., born 11 March 1955 in Monmouth. Both children attended Garfield and Central Jr High, graduating from Monmouth High in 1971 and 1973. Kenneth attended Centerville Jr College and N.E. Missouri State University, and has been Supervisor for several meat-packing plants in the area. He married Teresa Hasse October 15, 1977. Their children: Jacob - July 26, 1980; Joseph - November 8, 1982 and Jesse - March 23, 1986. All three attended Willitts and Central Jr High, graduating from Monmouth High. Jacob graduated from Augustana College in June 2002. Joseph attended South East Jr College and should graduate in 2003. They attended Heritage and Lutheran churches.

Sherrie married Joseph Creighton III - October 10, 1981. Their children: Justin E. - May 22, 1988 and Shane M. - January 17, 1991. Both attended Lincoln and Central Jr High and will go on to Monmouth High. They attend Heritage U.P. Church.

Siblings of Rebecca Damewood: Rocelia Lee, born February 2, 1933, died July 25, 1995; married John Barry. Their children are J. Arthur, Mark and Dalinda.

Elizabeth Ann, born November 20, 1934; married Richard Armstrong August 4, 1954. Their children are Paula, Lucinda and Craig. Richard died April 13, 1995. Charles Edward was stillborn September 28, 1936.

Donald Clair, born April 28, 1939, married Shirlee Patterson. Their children are Jeffrey, Mischelle, Alischa, and Heather.

Rebecca's father was born February 1, 1898, Eagle Rock, Virginia; died

March 24, 1955. He was a local livestock trucker. His parents were John A. and Emma (Martin) Damewood. They married June 31, 1881, in Virginia. They moved to Kirkwood, Illinois and had a total of 15 children. John was born August 25, 1855 - Botetourt Co, Virginia; died January 17, 1944. Kirkwood, Illinois. Emma Martin was born n Craig County, Virginia November 27, 1866; died January 26, 1944, also in Kirkwood.

Rebecca's mother was born October 4, 1906, Monmouth, Illinois; died August 1, 1971. - married Arthur Damewood August 26, 1927. Her parents were Dolly (Miller), born October 8, 1877 - died February 17, 1932; married Clarence McKee October 5, 1904. Clarence was born March 11, 1877; died March 29, 1941. They had three girls: Florence, Mildred and Mary Jane.

LAWRENCE A. MILLER - Miller, Lawrence A., oldest son of J. Alven and Lavinia (Troxel) Miller, was born on February 9, 1911 in Lenox Township, Warren County, on his parents' first wedding anniversary. He attended Monmouth High School, graduating in 1928. While in high school, he was on the football team as well as participating in various other activities. He then attended Monmouth College, where he also played football. Lawrence married his high school sweetheart, Edith Jewell Kyle, on August 12, 1930 in DeWitt, Iowa. They had four children: Lawrence (Larry) A. Jr. (Judith Glenn), a farmer in Warren County who raised grain, hogs and sheep; Linda Jewell (Terry Bristow), an elementary teacher and librarian; Thomas Wesley (Sherry Bryant), a teacher and school administrator; and Stephen Kyle (Mary Merillat), a professor of education at the University of Louisville.

Lawrence farmed as long as his health permitted, but was in poor health, suffering from Multiple Sclerosis, for eighteen years before his death on April 12, 1961. He was a member of the Fairview Center E.U.B. Church and spent his entire life in Warren County. Edith Kyle Miller was born June 12, 1912 in Caldwell, Idaho to Ralph Dean and Edith Merle (Merle) Jewell. She was the oldest of eight children. She moved to Warren County with her family in 1919 where her father took up farming. Edith went to Monmouth High School, graduating in 1930. In high school she was in the Honor Society and participated in many activities. She especially enjoyed being on the debate team and working on the school paper and yearbook staffs. Edith attended Western Illinois University, majoring in Home Economics and later took many library classes. She was an active member of Fairview Center Church. Mrs. Miller worked as a reference librarian at the Warren County Library in Monmouth for many years. She also helped with the Bookmobile and presented a weekly library broadcast on the local radio station.

Lawrence and Edith Miller, 1950

In 1968 she moved to Prescott, Arizona where she cared for her mother and worked at the Prescott Public Library as a reference librarian until her retirement in 1981. She was very active in the communities where she lived. Edith moved to Tacoma, WA in 1989 to be closer to her daughter. She died on October 2, 1990. Both she and Lawrence are buried at Monmouth, Illinois.

LAWRENCE A. JR. AND JUDITH A. MILLER - Lawrence Adelma Miller Jr. was born on March 7, 1935 at the hospital in Monmouth, Illinois. He was the oldest son of Lawrence A. and Edith (Kyle) Miller. He had two brothers, Thomas Wesley and Stephen Kyle and one sister Linda Jewell (Bristow). He was reared and educated in Monmouth where he attended Monmouth public schools and then attended Texas A & I in Brownsville, and then the University of Illinois. He left college to begin farming because of the ill health of his father.

Larry married Judith A. Glenn on June 2, 1958 in Quincy. They resided with his parents for a year while Judy completed her nursing education. In the spring of 1960, Judy and Larry moved to the "Jewell Farm" located in Lenox Township where Larry was a producer of Berkshire hogs and Suffolk Sheep. They had two sons: Kyle Glenn Miller (Linda Johnson) who resides in Florida and Craig Lawrence Miller (Maura Denison) who resides on the same farm that Larry operated for forty years. Craig and Maura have two daughters, Lindsay Rose and Hanafin Jewell.

Larry's interest in livestock remained strong throughout his life. He was president of the Warren County Pork Producers, President of Illinois Lamb and Wool Producers, board member of the National Sheep Producers Council, member of the National Meat Board, and was elected to the Western Illinois Agricultural Hall of Fame. He also was named Warren County's Outstanding Young Farmer in 1971. He spent his entire life in Warren County but traveled extensively to assist with his livestock interests. He judged livestock at many County and State fairs, with a particular interest in educating young people about livestock production. Larry's other interests included his family and many friends for whom he was always "on call" for advice and assistance with livestock or other activities. He was an avid sports fan, coaching Jr. Sheriff Softball and never missing a sports event in which his sons participated. He died July 15, 2001 after declining health for five years.

Judith Ann Glenn was born April 23, 1938 at Monmouth Hospital in Monmouth, Illinois to John H. and D. Lorene Glenn. She has one sister, Barbara J. Bragd who resides in Florida. She graduated from Monmouth High School in 1956 and then attended Galesburg Cottage Hospital School of Nursing, graduating in 1959. She returned to Bradley University, Peoria, Illinois in 1980 and completed her Bachelor of Science degree in 1986. She worked at various clinical and management positions at Monmouth Hospital her entire nursing career. Her nursing experience assisted Larry throughout their life together as they were considered the "people to call" when an emergency occurred. Aside from her nursing career, Judy's interest was primarily her family and friends. Both Judy and Larry were members of the Fairview Center United Methodist Church.

THOMAS AND SHERRY (BRYANT) MILLER - Miller, Thomas Wesley, son of Lawrence and Edith (Kyle) Miller was born on August 4, 1941 in Monmouth, Illinois. He attended Monmouth High School, graduating in 1959. He then attended North Central College in Naperville, Illinois where he majored in mathematics and biology. He graduated in 1963 with a B. S. degree and a secondary teaching certificate.

Upon leaving North Central, Thomas took a job teaching mathematics with Community Unit School District 300 in Carpentersville, Illinois. He served as track and cross country coach for Irving Crown High School until 1975 when he was appointed Athletic Director at the new Harry D. Jacobs High School in Algonquin, Illinois. He received a Master of Arts Degree in mathematics from Bowdoin College in Brunswick Maine in 1974. In 1986 he became Assistant Principal at Jacobs High School and served in the position until his retirement in June 2002. He is a member of the First United Methodist Church in Dundee, Illinois where he spent many years teaching Sunday School and serving in various leadership positions.

On June 20, 1971, Thomas married Sherry Lynn Bryant in Carpentersville Illinois. Sherry is the daughter of Donald M. and Shirley (Weden) Bryant. They have two children; Laura Beth, born on January 30, 1980 in Elgin Illinois, and Brian Wesley, born on October 19, 1983 in Libertyville, Illinois. Thomas, Sherry, Laura, and Brian reside in Dundee, Illinois.

WILLIAM EDWIN MILLER - Miller, William Edwin the only child of C. E. "Ed" Miller and Ruth lone Parsons Miller of Swan Creek, IL, was born in McDonough County, IL on August 20. 1933. He attended Swan Creek and Roseville Elementary Schools and graduated from Roseville High School. His college years at Western Illinois State College were interrupted by military service in the Army. After completing basic training at Fort Leonard Wood in Missouri, he married Janet E. Braun in Roseville, Warren County, IL. He served the rest of his military career in the 18th Engineers in Giessen, Germany (1954-1956). During the last half of his duty in Germany his wife, Janet joined him in Giessen, Germany.

Returning to the US after military service he attended Western Illinois University at Macomb, Illinois and graduated with a B.S. degree in Business. He was employed by Gale Products of Galesburg and later by Alexis Fire Equipment Co. of Alexis. He then became a partner in an insurance firm in Roseville until he opened his own tax and accounting service also in Roseville.

The William Miller family. Back row: Brian, Diane Miller Belluomini and Mary; Larry and Jenna Nevins; Paul and Nancy Miller, Blackburn and Adam and Andrea. Front row: Cathy Miller Nevins, Bill Miller, Ben Nevins, Jill Belluomini, Janet Braun Miller.

His parents were residents of Warren County for many years, his mother, Ruth Parsons was born in Point Pleasant Township in Warren County. Ruth's father, Rollin Parsons, came by Conestoga wagon from Astubula County, OH in the early 1840s eventually settling in Warren County. His father Carl/Charles Edwin –"C.E. or Ed" Miller was born in Coldbrook Township, Warren County of Swedish parents, John and Hilda Miller. They immigrated in 1890 and were married in the First Lutheran Church in Galesburg, IL in 1891.

His family embraces his wife and three daughters. Nancy Sue was born in Frankfurt, Germany (state of Hesse) on August 20, 1956. The second daughter Cathy Ann was born July 24, 1958 and the third daughter, Diane Elaine was born July 10, 1962, both were born in Warren County.

He served as Village Clerk for the village of Roseville for 29 years. He was photographer or timer for the Roseville Schools athletic department for many years.

Janet Braun Miller is the daughter of Laurence Braun and Alberto Slusher Braun. She was born July 18, 1933 in Muscatine County, IA. She had two brothers, Loren and Randal. Her parents divorced in 1939 and her mother later married Ernest C. Bacon and lived in Point Pleasant, Warren County. She attended elementary schools in Muscatine County, Rock Island, Henderson and Warren Counties in Illinois. She graduated from Roseville High School and Western Illinois State College with a B.S. degree in 1955. She married William Miller in the Roseville Methodist Church on November 28, 1953. Upon graduation from college she joined her husband in Giessen, Germany. While in Germany she did substitute teaching in the American Dependent School there. When she returned to Roseville she taught for 21 years, in the Roseville High School, until she retired.

STANLEY BRUCE MILLS - Mills, Stanley Bruce, was born February 24, 1953, at Monmouth Hospital and has lived his entire life in Warren County. His parents are Robert Eugene Mills and Marjorie Jean Gavin. "Bruce" has a younger brother, Rex Eugene (Beth Stall) and a younger sister, Susan Ann (David Icenogle). Bruce attended Little York Elementary, Yorkwood Junior High School in Kirkwood, and graduated from Yorkwood High School in 1971. Along with his father, Bruce has always worked in agriculture, farming in Warren, Henderson and Mercer counties. Bruce has served as Sumner Township Clerk and is currently serving as Township Trustee. Bruce married Susan Kesinger on July 23, 1976, at the First Baptist Church in Monmouth, IL.

S. Bruce and Susan Mills family, January 2002.

Susan Kesinger was born March 19, 1953, at Monmouth Hospital. She was the third of seven children born to Don E. Kesinger and Vivian Mercella (Maberry) Shores. Susan and her two older sisters, Donna and Margaret "Peggy," three younger brothers: David, John and Harvey, and youngest sister, Janet, were all raised at 205 North Sunny Lane in Monmouth. They all attended Willits Elementary, Central Junior High and Susan graduated from Monmouth High School in 1971. She was baptized and became a member of the First Baptist Church in Monmouth in 1976. She serves as Sumner Township election judge and is involved with Presbyterian Church camping programs. Susan is a sales representative for Market Day.

After Bruce and Susan married they moved to the former "Parson Place" located on Highway 135, one mile south of Little York in Sumner Township. There they raised their four children, being actively involved in their lives and constantly "on the go."

Bruce and Susan's oldest son, Anthony Paul, was born in Monmouth on July 11, 1972. He first attended schools in Little York and Kirkwood, then Yorkwood and graduated in 1991. When younger, Tony was active in the Henderson County 4-H, raising and showing pigs and chickens at the fairs. He pitched for the Jr. Sheriffs Softball League summer program in Little York. He participated in football, basketball and track in school and the YMCA. He worked on the farm, was a car salesman in Aledo and Galesburg, and is currently working on rural Monmouth farms.

Jacob Nathaniel was born in Monmouth on November 9, 1977. Jacob attended schools in Monmouth and graduated from Yorkwood in 1996. He participated in basketball when he was younger. He worked in the workshop at Achievement Industries in Monmouth and is currently employed through Monmouth School District #38 as a lunch program worker. Jacob lives at home and is known as "Grandma's helper," assisting with the lawn mowing and other tasks.

Rachel JoAnn was born in Monmouth on February 20, 1980. She was actively involved in many extracurricular activities including cheerleading, basketball and volleyball before she graduated as salutatorian of the 1998 class at Yorkwood. She double majored in Sociology and Spanish at Illinois College in Jacksonville, IL. Rachel has received the Bachelor of Arts degree and graduated with Phi Beta Kappa honors in May 2002. She will continue her graduate studies at Chapel Hill, North Carolina. Rachel is married to William Dudenhausen, III, from Chatham, IL. They reside in North Carolina.

Johnathon Bruce was born on Sept. 1981 at Monmouth. Johnathon has always enjoyed work on the farm and is talented and creative, inventing some unique items and pieces of machinery. John participated in 4-H, F.F.A., track, football and especially enjoyed basketball. He graduated from Yorkwo in 2000. Johnathon is presently living at home and majoring in Agriculture at Carl Sandburg College in Galesburg. This summer he is employed with a wheat harvesting crew, traveling through the Great Plains and Canada.

ROBERT EUGENE MILLS - Mills, Robert Eugene was born October 28, 1923, on a farm near Berwick, Warren County, IL. His father, Harry Benjamin Mills (1888-1976) was born in upper Strausburg, Pennsylvania. Harry's mother died at his birth and his sisters raised him in Horse Valley, Pennsylvania. Harry was working for the railroad when he found himself in Warren County, IL. and decided to settle here. He realized his lifelong dream to farm when he when he began work on the Wiswell Farm south of Cameron, IL. There he met his future bride, as she was employed as a household worker on the farm.

Robert E. & Marjorie Mills family. Jan. 2002

Robert's mother was Hylma Sofia Zalborg Anderson (1895-1983). Hylma's father, Albert William Anderson (1863-1956) was born in Boras, Vestergotland, Sweden and came to America in 1881. Hylma's mother, Hulda Hoglund (1867-1927), immigrated from Yulaelrascarn, Sweden and married Albert in 1890. Both were of Lutheran faith.

Hylma Anderson and Harry Benjamin married and raised their family in Warren County. Robert is third oldest with an older brother and sister, Harry Benjamin, Jr. (Dorothy Boyd, Thelma) and Mildred (Paul Ryder), two younger brothers, Donald (Marian Thompson), and James (Penelope Heston); and youngest sister, "Betty" Elizabeth Ann (Raymond Bruyn). When Robert was about 5, his family moved northeast of Monmouth, acquired and settled on what is known still today as the "family farm," Along with his siblings, Robert attended rural Frymire School (which still stands) northeast of Monmouth and graduated from Monmouth High School. As youngsters, the Mills brothers raised and enjoyed showing steers for 14 years at County and State Fairs. They won numerous awards, including top honors at the Chicago International Fair, which at the time was the largest livestock show in the world. Around 1946 Robert enlisted and served in the National Guard. On January 25, 1952, Robert married Marjorie Jean Gavin at her parents' home in Little York.

Marjorie Jean Gavin, the oldest of three daughters, was born at Monmouth Hospital on February 13, 1928. Her father, Francis Edward Gavin(1901-1981), born in Hale Township to William and Kathryn (Kinney) Gavin, married Mary Jane Brownlee on January 25, 1927. Mary was born August 31, 1903, in rural Little York, to John and May (Armstrong) Brownlee and died May 23, 1965. Marjorie and her sisters, Martha Ann (Carl Krusmark) and Margaret Lucille (William Biddle), were raised on the family farm north of Little York. Marjorie worked on the farm and attended rural Brownlee School north of Little York and Little York High School.

After their marriage, Marge and Bob, as they were known, lived and farmed northeast of Gerlaw, IL. Their first child, Stanley Bruce (Susan Kesinger), was born on February 24, 1953; son, Rex Eugene (Teresa Baynes, Beth Stall) followed on March 11, 1955. In 1956 they moved to the McBride farm north of Little York. On September 3, 1958, their daughter, Susan Ann (David Icenogle) was born. Their children were confirmed in the Lutheran Church and are now married with families.

Bob and Marge have faithfully served their church, schools, community and families well. Bob served on the Little York School Board prior to its reorganization and ultimate merging of the former Little York and Kirkwood Schools (Yorkwood School District). Marge has actively served with the Little York Farmerettes for several years as well as helping with farm work and wherever else needed. Presently, Marge and Bob still reside a mile north of Little York while Bob continues to farm and Marge maintains her reputation as being one of the best cooks in Warren County. They enjoy nine grandchildren, two step-grandchildren, and one step-great grandchild.

MILNE - Christopher McQuiston Wilmoth is included in the 2001 *Who's Who In America*. His mother, Helen Margaret Milne was born and raised in Monmouth, attended Monmouth College, married Clifford Lee Wilmoth whom he met at the College, and who became world renowned as a surgeon in New York, and later in Pittsburgh. Because of respect. for his mother and all she stood for, Mr. Milne changed his last name from Wilmoth to Milne late in life.

Of Scotch-Irish heritage, Mr. Milne traces his roots back to Monmouth, and frequently enjoys pilgrimages to his ancestral surroundings.

For over 100 years, the Milne and McQuiston families have been part of Monmouth, and Warren County, Illinois.

In the 1890's, James Milne, a stonemason, moved to Monmouth from Scotch Grove, Iowa, because of-the college. He had two sons, James Joseph and Hector.

James, after graduating from Monmouth College, married Margaret McQuiston, one of 12 children of William Hugh and Nancy Walker McQuiston.

Milne Mfg. Co.

William McQuiston was the first photographer west of Chicago and many of his 8 X 10 inch glass plate negatives are still intact. His home was where Grier and Cleland Halls at the college stand now.

J.J., as James came to be known, began the manufacturing of stump pulling equipment. The factory was located at the junction of Eighth Avenue and the Burlington Railroad tracks. The sets of pulleys and wire cables which made the clearing of woods easier for farmers ("with this equipment, a farmer can clear any stump with the aid of only one horse") were shipped by rail all over the United States, and even to Russia to clear land for crops.

The buildings built and used by the Milne Manufacturing Company are still standing today, being used as the County Highway garage.

J.J.'s brother, Hector, lived west of town and had the Sunnyside Shetland Pony Farm which became nationally famous through its association with the *Saturday Evening Post*.

As a promotion for the *Saturday Evening Post* magazine, around 1920, the publisher offered prizes to the schoolboy selling the most subscriptions to the weekly. In each city along the East Coast, the winner would receive a Shetland pony. Along with his parents, the fortunate youngsters got free round-trip train tickets to Monmouth. At Monmouth the newsboy could take his pick of the hundreds of ponies on the Milne spread, west of town. Family and pony would be shipped back to the boy's hometown.

J.J. had four children: Hugh, who became a missionary for the United Presbyterian Church, serving in India and Pakistan for 42 years; Halma, who married the publisher of the *South Bend Tribune*, and taught English in high school until her retirement; Helen, who married C. Lee Wilmoth and lived in Pittsburgh until her death in 1963; and James Walker Milne, who became a trial lawyer in Chicago, and taught law at the John Marshall Law School there.

Walker had four children, Phyllis, Margaret, Nancy and Jimmie Joe.

On the McQuiston side of the family, Mel McQuiston owned the McQuiston Book Store which stood until 1970 on the southwest corner of the Square. All twelve of the McQuiston children are buried in the original Monmouth cemetery.

Until Ma Bell took over the Phone Company, Hugh McQuiston was the President and General Manager of the Monmouth Phone Company. His son was employed by ARAMCO and lived in Saudi Arabia most of his adult life.

Of the McQuistons and Milnes, 28 graduated from Monmouth College.

The J.J. Milne residence also still stands at the corner of Eighth St. and Second Avenue. The Hector Milne home stands on the road west of town at the traffic light.

JOSEPH W. MISSAVAGE - Joseph W Missavage was born in Royalton, IL. March 24, 1920 of Polish Lithuanian extraction. His father was a coal miner. He attended Royalton and Zeigler schools. He played football, basketball and baseball. He had a try out with the St. Louis Cardinals in 1936, and was offered minor league contract, but his father wouldn't sign the contract for him.

Joseph W. Missavage, 1976

In 1938 he came to Monmouth College on a football scholarship and part time employment with the Illinios Bankers Life Insurance Company. He played football, and was All Conference his senior year. In December of 1941 he received a letter from the Philadelphia Eagles football management if he was interested in playing pro- ball if they drafted him. The SSS settled that question- he was told that he would be drafted into service soon. In Jan 7, 1942 he enlisted in Air Force to become a pilot. During pre-flight training he was told that he didn't have 20-20 correctible vision. He was put in ground forces of the Air Force. He attended Anti-Aircraft Officer's Candidate school in June 1943, and was commissioned a 2nd Lt. and assigned to the Army post at Ft. Bliss, Texas.

In October 1943 he coached and played halfback for Ft. Bliss Army football team. His star player was Tony Canedeo of the Green Bay Packers.

He attended the Adjutant General's school at the Pentagon and the Ft. Benning Infantry School in 1944. Later in 1944 he was sent to North Africa and then to Southern Italy. He was in 10th Mt. Division, and fought his way up from Naples to Rome, Assisi, Sienna, Florence, and Bologna, and was near the Austrian border when war ended.

After that he was in on a private audience with Pope Pius the XII. The Pope made the sign of the cross on his forehead and thanked God for his safe journey through the war.

In 1945 he was promoted to Captain, and spent time on the French Riviera before being sent to the Orient, via Panama Canal. He landed on Okinawa in October 1945. He spent time in Philippines; then was transferred to Japan to serve in the occupation forces. He spent 9 months in Kyoto, and 3 months in Yokohama area. He was in Nagoya, Hiroshima, Nagasaki and Tokyo. He returned to U.S. and was discharged from service in November 1946.

He married Lucile Lynch during the war in May 1942. He was father of David, Joann, Margaret, John, James, Jane, Mary, Thomas, Paul, and Doug. He has 17 grandchildren and 7 great grandchildren.

He was divorced in 1975 and married Regena Wolf in 1976. He was married to her for 22 years. She died in 1997. He traveled extensively starting in 1977 and was in all 50 states and much of Canada and Europe.

He owned and raced a string of pacing and trotting racehorses for many years. He farmed from 1947-1987, fed prime beef cattle and was one of the top Pioneer seed dealers from 1960-1987.

He was a member of many organizations including Immaculate Conception Catholic Church, K of C, Elks, VFW, American Legion, Phi Kap and ATO fraternities. He was secretary and president of the original Yorkwood School Board for 9 years.

He retired in 1987. He has a home in Kissimmeee, Florida, spends 7 months there and 5 months in Monmouth area.

He has a friend, Dorothy Scott in Maine. He visits there each year in July. He visits his sister Dorothy in Royalton, Ill., brother Richard in Florissant, MO., and 2 brothers Gene and Len. One brother Charles, deceased.

He spends time at the office of Pioneer warehouse owned by his sons Tom and Jim and their wives Teri and Martha. They also farm extensively in the area. He spends time with daughter Jane and Larry Mitchell, who farm extensively in the Cameron area. His son Paul graduated from Eureka College, is a coach and pro basketball player in Luxembourg, and is a talk show host on a local radio station. He formerly coached in Illinois high schools, including his alma mater, Yorkwood. His son John works for the *Houston Chronicle* in Texas. His oldest son David was a Green Beret paratrouper in Vietnam (jumped many times behind enemy lines). His daughter Mary graduated from Iowa Weslyan, and lives in Colorado.

EDNA IRENE MOORE - Moore, Edna Irene lived to the ripe old age of 104. She died on Friday November 12, 1999. She was born November 20, 1896 in Monticello, the daughter of Joseph and Emma (Haldeman) Pierce. She was reared and educated in Aledo, Illinois before she married Ray I. Moore July 16, 1913 in Aledo. He died August 31, 1968.

Edna spent most of her time raising her children and as a housekeeper for the Joseph and William Hayman families. Ray was a farm laborer around Mercer County. When her family grew up she moved to Monmouth, Warren County to be near her only daughter Ruth and son in law Harley Chard. Ray and Edna bought a home on South Main Street just south of the railroad tracks across from the headquarters of Brown-Lynch-Scott, a mail order hardware outlet with many stores in surrounding counties. Ruth worked in the shipping department there. The original Weir Plow Company built the complex, then sold to Monmouth Plow before selling to Brown-Ly nch-Scott. All were major employers in Monmouth.

Edna came to Monmouth at the right time and became part of a team that brought self service meats to western Illinois. She had been sought out by Barnes Super Valu along with Ruth Stull and Opha Hopkins to solve the wrapping in cellophane of fresh meat cuts in this new concept. Each cut had to be priced and labeled and displayed for customer acceptance and convenience. It was agreed that Edna would work until she could become eligible for Social Security.

She had a son, Joe, although accepted for military service during World War II, was handicapped in body and mind. Joe roomed many years at Pinewood Nursing Home in Monmouth to be near his sister and mother. Edna outlived four of her sons - Willis, John, Joe and Wade. The two remaining were Ralph and his wife Mary of Viola and James (Deanna) of Knoxville. In all she and Ray had 15 grandchildren, 30 great grandchildren, 22 great-great grandchildren and one great-great-great grandchild. One special grandchild was Sharon Adams and her husband Duane of Matherville who spent many hours with her grandmother.

Edna was baptized into the Monmouth Christian Church, as was Joe. Ruth and Harley were already immersed as Christ asked.

MORLING - John Albert Morling immigrated to America from Sweden in 1884. He married Clara Amelia Johnson in Woodhull, IL in 1890. They first stayed at the Jenny Lind Chapel in Andover, Illinois until John got a job in Woodhull, Illinois where he worked as a blacksmith. They lived upstairs over a grocery store on the east side of Main Street in Woodhull. While there, their first child was born, Clarence Morling in 1891. In 1893 a daughter was born, Violet Morling. They then moved to a cabin near Cameron, located close to Elephant Rock in Section 27 of Coldbrook Township, where Wallace Morling was born in 1896. John worked at a blacksmith shop in Surry until August of 1896 when he purchased land at what is known as 357 Railroad Street in Cameron, Illinois and built a blacksmith shop of his own. (Picture was taken inside that blacksmith shop). They moved to a house on the north edge of Cameron where Dewey Morling was born in 1898. John and Clara lived in that home until their death. Clara died in 1941. John died in 1952. They celebrated their 50th wedding anniversary in that home, in 1940. Dewey Morling married but never moved away from that home. He died in 1969. Violet Morling worked in Washington D.C. until her retirement. Then she moved back to Cameron and lived in that same home until her death in 1970. Violet never married so a Morling lived in that home for 74 years. During the early years (before the children went to school) the family spoke Swedish at home. From their window they watched the Santa Fe Railroad being built over the C.B. & Q. Dad told about the large tent where the horses mules and men were fed and housed while the construction was being done.

Morling Blacksmith Shop in Cameron, IL

Before World War I Grandpa (John) and Dad (Wallace) did blacksmith work and in the teens they also sold Moline Universal tractor and farm equipment.

Wallace told me of the time he demonstrated a tractor east of Galesburg. He drove the tractor to the farm but when he got to the railroad underpass on County #10 he unbolted all of the lugs from the wheels, drove through the underpass and then rebolted the lugs on the wheels. He failed to sell the tractor so he repeated the process on the way home.

J.A. Morling & Son patented the Morling scoop board December 15, 1915 and they were made in the shop in Cameron.

During World War I both Clarence and Wallace were in the army. Clarence was in the Quartermaster Corp. and never went to Europe but Wallace was on the ship on the way over when the war ended so it returned to America.

In 1923 John and Wallace became Chevrolet dealers and continued that until 1948. In 1929 the wooden blacksmith shop was torn down and the brick shop was built. That building is still owned by Roy and Dale Morling, where Cameron Machine Products owned by Ron Hanson is in business.

During the 1930's and until his death Dewey Morling used part of the shop for his feed grinding and corn shelling business.

Clarence Morling returned from the war and married Hilma Pearson. They had one son Curtis, and started farming near Galesburg (where Henry Hill Prison) is now located. Wallace married Anna Amelia Applequist in 1925. They had 2 sons, Dale and Roy. Wallace continued in the shop until 1948. He had moved from Cameron in 1942 to a farm near Galesburg, where he lived until he moved to Galesburg in 1981. He died in 1999 at 103 years of age. A grandson Keith Morling still lives and farms on that farm. A granddaughter, Valerie Edwards, and her family live 2 miles east of Cameron and have a Cameron address. So a Morling has been in or near Cameron Illinois for a long time.

Submitted by Dale and Lucille Morling

WILLIAM AND FRANKIE (HOLMES) MORRELL - William and Frankie (Holmes) Morrell moved to Little York from Knox County in 1961. William had been a farmer all his life and Frankie a homemaker. Frankie was born and raised in the Oneida, IL community. She attended Western IIL University and taught school in Oneida for two years before she married William. She organized and led one of the first 4-H clubs in Knox County. She led a 4-H club in Victoria for several years and again organized one in Knoxville when she moved there. She was a leader for about 20 years. She taught sewing and did custom work for years, She was a member of "The Good Neighbors Club" and the Knox Co. Home Bureau. She died of cancer on November 4, 1968 while still residing in Little York.

William came from Schuyler County and farmed all his life, working as a farm hand until 1940 when he rented a farm near Maxey Chapel. They then moved to Victoria for several years and then moved just east of Knoxville. They had a farm auction and he retired in 1952. After that he went to work at the Swanson Seed Farm at Wataga. His last steady work was for Dale McWilliams each fall making sorghum. He did day work only, after that. When he was unable to care for himself any more he moved into the Applegate Nursing Home. He transferred to several homes and came back to Applegate where he died on July 6, 1983 at the age of 91.

They had three daughters: Elwilda who married Glenn Osborn in 1952 and resided in Warren County from then until their demise, she in October 2000 and he in April 2002.

Back row: Bill and Frankie Morrell; Josephine, Elwilda, Phyllis

Their second daughter was Josephine who married Robert Perrin in October 1958. Josephine died of cancer October 7, 1993. Robert still resides in Little York.

Their third daughter, Phyllis, is married to Dwaine Geldbrandt and they reside in Harlingen, Texas.

SAMUEL GARISH MORSE - Samuel Garish Morse was born May 23, 1786 in Windham County CT. he was the son of David and Anna (Newman) Morse. Samuel came to Illinois in 1811. He first settled in Vandalia for several years, and then moved to Madison County. The county was so large that it was divided into smaller counties. The part of Madison County that he was living in became Bond County. Samuel was in the Illinois Rangers in the War of 1812, and during the skirmish of 1814 he was appointed Second Lieutenant in the Volunteer Militia. Samuel was Bond County's first sheriff. He was appointed to the Illinois Constitutional Convention of 1818. He married Polly Kirkpatrick in (Madison County) in 1814. They had two daughters; Adeline, born in 1816 and Harriet, born in 1818. Polly must have died shortly after Harriet's birth. Samuel then married Polly White in Madison County in 1820. They had a son, Roswell Newman Morse born in 1821. Polly (White) died shortly after Roswell's birth. Samuel then married Jane M. Kirkpatrick in (Bond) County in 1823 (Cousin to Folly Kirkpatrick). They had eight children. William B.; Samuel M.; David E.; Mary S.; Asenath; Emaline; John Q.; and Margaret Ann.

Samuel moved to Warren County about 1828- 1829. He and Thomas Pearce founded the village of Berwick in 1836. The area was first called "Bowling Green." Samuel raised his family there and was very active in business and politics. There is quite an interesting article in the "Minutes of the sixty-third annual session of the Central Illinois Conference of the Methodist Episcopal Church, Sept 1918." The article was on the life and death of Rev. Roswell Newman Morse, Samuel's first son. To quote a couple of paragraphs on Roswell's father.

"He came of good parentage. His father, Samuel 0. Morse was a man of great natural ability, and had convictions and clear ideas on the great moral questions of his day. He was a member of the first Constitutional Convention of the great state of Illinois and when at the convention the fate of Illinois as a free or slave state trembled in the balance, his voice plead for freedom and finally his vote wheeled the state into line with the free states of the Union.

"The son whose death we mourn, profoundly respected his father's integrity, intellect and piety, and the son formed his own life after the pattern of his honored father's life and soon the questions that agitated church and state R. N. Morse could always be counted on the right side."

Samuel and Jane raised their family in Berwick. Some of the children stayed in the area and married into other pioneer families. Samuel died in 1863 and is buried in the Berwick Cemetery, along with his wife of many years Jane (Kirkpatrick) Morse and several of their children.

KARL AND PEARL MUNSON - Karl Anders Munson was born in Kisa, Sweden. As a young man he worked in a sawmill learning about many types of wood and learning some carpentry skills. At the age of nineteen in 1907, Karl joined the Swedish Navy as a fireman serving on the battleship, King Oscar. He also was an engine oiler and shoved coal into the boilers. In 1908 he was stationed on the Drestighatan, a cadet training ship. Karl was the steam launch engineer. He joined on the pretense that he would be discharged when the boat reached Ellis Island. King Gustav granted a special permit for his release from the Navy because of his good work record. He traveled by train to Galesburg, Illinois in 1909. Upon arrival in Galesburg, Karl began work at the repair yards for the Chicago Burlington and Quincy railroad. He also became a member of the Knights Templars, an organization opposed to the use of alcoholic drinks. One of the reasons he immigrated to the United States was to make a better life since Sweden was in a deep recession.

Karl and Pearl Brown were married June 5th 1915. They had five children: Karl Everett (Virginia Leonard), Ruth B. (Earl Lyons), Mildred B. (Dale Van Riper), Dorothy Kathryn (Lloyd Winbigler) Dora Rose Anna (Kenneth Glenn Reynolds). Pearl was a schoolteacher in a one-room schoolhouse, Brush Run, with children in all eight grades. Karl built them a new home on Elm Street in Galesburg, soon selling it to begin farming near the village of Dahinda. After farming for twelve years, in 1929 he studied with a well-known architect and built another home which they lost in the Great Depression.

After moving to Monmouth in 1932, Karl and Pearl opened the Munson Appliance Company. Everett and Ruth both worked for them. Upon retirement, Karl began repairing violins, violas, cellos, and bass violins. Many of his instruments were often sold and played by outstanding professional musicians. He also rented them out to students for a fee. Pearl served as bookkeeper and secretary throughout all the business years.

LOREN E. MURPHY - Murphy, Loren Edgar, oldest son of James and Ann (Deakin) Murphy, was born in Cuba, Fulton County, Illinois, July 23, 1882. He graduated from Cuba High School and attended the University of Michigan College of Law in Ann Arbor, graduating in 1906.

Upon graduation, he moved to Monmouth where he opened a law practice. In 1908 he formed a partnership with C.M. Huey in an office on the north side of the Square. After practicing law for four years, Mr. Murphy was elected County Judge in 1910 and again in 1914.

Mr. Murphy chose a life of public service. After serving as County Judge until 1918, he was President of the Board of Monmouth Hospital from 1918 to 1923. In 1923 he was elected President of the Board of Education and served in tht position until 1927 when he resigned to run for Mayor of Monmouth, for which he was elected to serve two terms.

The Loren E. Murphy family, circa 1938.

In 1932 Mr. Murphy was appointed Circuit Judge to fill the unexpired term of Judge W. Fred Graham, and was elected to a six-year term in 1933. Also that year Mr. Murphy was appointed to the Fourth District Appellate Court at Mount Vernon, serving until 1939.

Mr. Murphy was elected to the Illinois Supreme Court in 1939 for a nine-year term, during which time he served as Chief Justice in 1942-43 and 1947-48. He's listed in *Who's Who in America* during that time.

In 1948 he was named Vice-President and Chief Counsel of the Bankers Life Assurance Company, retiring in 1956.

On November 26, 1910, Mr. Murphy married Besse Ditto, daughter of Lewis Napoleon and Elizabeth (Wheatley) Ditto at the Ditto home in Bald Bluff, Henderson County, Illinois. Loren and Besse met at the boardinghouse where both lived upon moving to Monmouth. Besse was an elementary schoolteacher at Willits School. The announcement of their marriage on page one of the *Monmouth Daily Review*, November 28, 1910, stated, "Cupid Triumphs Over New Judge."

After residing at 812 West Broadway several years, they moved to their home at 314 South Third Street, where they lived for almost 50 years. They were the parents of eight children: Elizabeth (1912-1957) (Henry Buck); Dorothy (1914-2001) (George Griffith); Margaret (1916-1995) (John Morris); Genevieve (1919-1995) (Gilbert Ralph); Loren E., Jr. (1921-living) (Orpha Swanson); Wayne D. (1924 living) (Ezevel Yankaukas); C. Darrel (1926-living) (Jean Lauver); and Lewis D. (1929-living).

During World War II, Mr. and Mrs. Murphy had three sons and three sons-in-law in the Armed Services. Their fourth son, Lewis, served in the Air Force during the Korean War. Lewis later followed in his father's footsteps, becoming a lawyer and Associate Judge in the Ninth Circuit from 1969 to 1987.

Mr. Murphy maintained his interest in farming from his boyhood, owning two farms. He enjoyed weekends on the farm tending his orchards, livestock and crops.

Mr. Murphy died June 2, 1963, in Monmouth at age 81. Mrs. Murphy died January 18, 1978, in Monmouth at age 93. Both are buried in Warren County Memorial Park Cemetery.

Submitted by Diane (Murphy) Witwood, granddaughter

MARTHA ABBEY MURPHY - Martha Abbey was born on March 20, 1922 in rural Warren County, the daughter of William and Lena (Riggs) Abbey. She had an older brother, Richard. The family moved to the Kirkwood area when Martha was five years old, and she attended Kirkwood Grade School and graduated from Kirkwood Township High School in 1940.

Martha Abbey Murphy

After high school graduation Martha enrolled in the Nursing Program at Burlington Protestant Hospital in September 1940, graduating in 1943. Upon graduation as a Registered Nurse she enlisted in the United States Army Nurse Corps. She served her country for two years. One of these years was in Europe. From England her group landed in LeHarve, France. From there they were sent to Germany where Martha was sent to a front line Evacuation Hospital in Germany and their group followed Patton's army in the north of Germany.

Upon return to the United States in 1946 Martha went to California and worked in the hospitals in Palo Alta and Menlo Park. It was there she met Donald T. Murphy. Martha and Don were married March 29, 1947. Two of their children were born in California: daughter Linda and son John.

In September 1950, as a member of the Naval Reserve, Don was called back into service during the Korean War and served aboard an aircraft carrier that was stationed in Japan. Martha and the two children returned to Kirkwood in 1951 and stayed until Don was released from service in 1952. At this time the Murphys moved to Michigan and in May 1953 their youngest child, daughter Marcy, was born.

The Murphys lived in Michigan until 1955 and at that time they returned to the Kirkwood area. Don farmed until 1969 and worked for Yorkwood School and then for 15 years he worked at Monmouth College retiring in 1984 because of ill health. Don passed away March 1, 1985.

Martha worked at Monmouth Hospital five years and as Yorkwood School Nurse for thirteen years and lastly, as nurse in Dr Arora's office in Monmouth for ten years retiring in 1984.

All three Murphy children attended Yorkwood Schools and graduated from Yorkwood High School. They have moved to different areas and have blessed the Murphy family with four grandchildren and six great-grandchildren.

EVERETTE AND IVA PEARL (GIBB) MYERS - Iva Pearl, oldest daughter of Lawrence Wesley and Maria (Hull) Gibb, was born Feb, 1918 The family lived between Smithshire and Kirkwood near the Maple Grove School. Lawrence's brothers: Shirley (died in his 20's) and Ed; sisters were Hazel, Georgia, Mabel, and Louella (who was a young girl when her mother died.) Lawrence's parents were John and Joanna (Staley) Gibb married 18 March 1891. Second wife was Lulu McLane.

Maria's parents were George and Maria (McMahill) Hull; brothers: Clarence, G. W. Charlie and Oscar; foster sister, Emma. Iva graduated from Maple Grove school where father and grandmother had both graduated. She remembers "fun days" going to Uncle Ed's and sliding down the "perfect hill." Cousin Harold Hull, Uncle Earl and Ed and families all lived near the corner of Maple Grove school in the "good old days" Neighbors were Rays, Gridleys, Fillmans, Oscar Williams and Clarence Hull.

Front row: Shirley, Paul Cleo Gibb. Second row: Isabel Uhlmann, Iris Gibb, Lawrence Gibb. Maria (Hall) Gibb, Anna Mae Gibb, Barbara Joan Myers. Back row: Dale Uhlmann, Lyle Gibb, Cleo Gibb, Iva Myers, Everette Myers 1951

The teacher was Mildred Francis at the time they took the 8th grade test at the courthouse in Monmouth when a neighbor took Iva and cousin Eddie, his son to take the exams and was impressed because they got to "eat out."

The family lost their land in 1933 and moved to Maquon near London Mills, IL. Remembers how sad everyone was to leave their old home. Mother drove car and relatives and friends helped father and Cleo drive the horses and cattle through and someone, about half-way, letting them leave the animals overnight.

Lawrence died 24 July 1955; Maria died 17 Oct 1992. Iva's siblings were: Elouise (who died shortly after birth and is buried in Ellison cemetery); Isabel died 24 Feb 1992; Cleo died Dec 1977; Lyle Dean died 10 Nov 1990; (all buried Oaklawn cemetery); Anna May married Lyle Clay who died suddenly Aug 1988. She lives in Knoxville.

Iva Pearl married Everette Henry Myers 3 Oct 1936 at Minister Virgil Essex home in Knoxville. The Myers family had moved from the neighborhood when the Gibb family in moved in but came back to Community Club and the couple met there.

Children of Everette and Iva Pearl were Barbara Joan born 11 Dec 1937 and Linda Kay born 11 Aug 1951. Everette died 14 Aug 2000 and Barbara Joan died 11 Aug 2001; both are buried in Wiley cemetery.

Iva Pearl Myers now resides in Ellisville, Illinois.

HENRY L. AND MARGARET (BALDWIN) MYERS - Henry (Hank) Myers was born in Sacramento, CA to Frieda M. (Stonie) and (Harold) Flynn Myers April 2, 1936.

Margaret L. Baldwin was born June 19, 1938 to Everett G. and Nannie Belle (Ketchum) Baldwin in Hancock County. She graduated from Monmouth High School in 1956.

Margaret and Hank met in Monmouth on a blind date after he came here with a friend from Ft. Leonard Wood, MO. They were married in Reno, Nevada on March 3, 1957. They lived in California for the first five years. The older children were born in Sacramento: Deborah (Debbie) November 26, 1957; Kary November 29, 1958; Douglas January 12, 1962. After moving to Illinois Lisa was born January 26, 1965.

Hank worked on the farm for a few years, then worked at Admiral on the assembly line. After Margaret went to work at Admiral (now Maytag), Hank went to work at the meat packing house in Monmouth. He continued with the various owners until he retired in 1998. Margaret retired from Maytag in 1998.

They were living in Monmouth. During the time they were raising their family, Hank was Wabelo leader and Scout Master and Margaret was a den mother. They also liked to bowl, bowling in mixed league and regular league for many years. They also took lessons for country line dancing and enjoyed it very much.

They retired in 1998 and decided to sell their home and travel around the country. They still come back to Warren County to visit.

Debbie married Roger Conard August 27, 1977. They have three children: Amanda born July 8, 1978; Nathan April 2, 1980; and Hannah May 25, 1981. Nathan has a daughter Cady born Feb. 16, 2001.

Kary married Judi Robinson December 18, 1982. They have two boys: Zackary born September 22, 1987; and Logan born December 7, 1994.

Douglas married Sandra Frakes, and has two children: Aaron April 26, 1985; Kaylon December 28, 1988. They divorced. He married Helen (Mettler) Norton, and has one son Jared March 6, 1993.

Lisa had twins, Adam and Abbey born December 9, 1985.

Margaret and Hank are now traveling in their motor home.

CARL HENRY AND GERTRUDE (BRANDT) NELSON - In March 1903 when the ice and icebergs had cleared out of the North Sea and it was safe for a sailing vessel to travel from Halmstead, Sweden to New York in the United Sates of America, Carl Henry Nelson, age 15, son of Nils and Anna Bingston, left his home on the coast Of western Sweden to travel alone to the United Sates.

Ahead of him was a long voyage of three to four weeks before he would see the Statue of Liberty on Ellis Island in New York Harbor. The voyage in the small sailing vessel was stormy and rough. He spent as much time as possible on deck in the open air, so he would not become seasick.

On a foggy, dreary day in late April, he was on deck, huddled among the coils of rope, trying to stay dry and out of the weather, when out of the fog … there it was … the Statue of Liberty … America.

After several days, he was cleared at Ellis Island, if he had a job and would become an American citizen. His job was covered by his sponsor, an uncle in North Dakota, whom he had never seen. After several more days on Ellis Island, he was allowed to leave.

With a ticket attached to his jacket, a sack lunch a small satchel and fifty cents in his pocket, he was put on a train to Pittsburgh. Pennsylvania. From there the train would travel to Chicago, Illinois then to Minneapolis, Minnesota, on to Fargo, North Dakota and finally to Oakes, North Dakota.

In early June he arrived in Oakes, a 15-year-old boy, in a large, strange country, a different language and a complete change of lifestyle. From Oakes, he set out on foot, following the railroad tracks eight or ten miles to Clement, North Dakota. It was mid-morning that June day of 1903, when an elevator operator saw him and noticed the tag on his jacket. The man knew that the boy was looking for someone and being Norwegian himself, could understand enough Swedish to learn where the boy wanted to go. The operator showed the young lad the right road to his uncle's farm.

Carl H. and Gertrude Nelson

He walked another six miles to the farm. The door to the farmhouse was standing open. A lady inside was preparing the noon meal. He knocked on the door and in a timid voice asked the lady inside "Moster?" which means aunt in Swedish. The lady turned, saw the lad and said "My God, it is Carl."

The lady was his Aunt Emma Johnson, the wife of his uncle, Swan Johnson. They had several children: Henry, Emard, Chester, Lenard, Stanley, Jennie and Bennie. Carl lived with his aunt and uncle and grew up with his cousins. His aunt and cousins taught him to read and write the English language and he taught himself the basics of arithmetic, He never obtained any further schooling than what he had had in Sweden before arriving in the United Sates.

During the years following 1903, he worked on his uncle's farm and on other farms in the vicinity, helping on the threshing runs during the long harvest seasons. Later, he worked at a lumberyard in Fullerton, North Dakota and resided in a hotel there.

One winter day in January 1908, Carl had some time off and decided to ride by horseback to Oakes. By leaving early in the morning, he would be able to visit everyone, spend some time in town and still return to the hotel in Fullerton after sunset that same day.

About mid-morning, it started to snow, continuing to grow worse and by mid afternoon, it was a North Dakota blizzard. Carl started back to Fullerton, unable to see in the snow. Admitting to himself that he was lost, he decided the best thing was to stay with the horse, give him his head and let him wander wherever he wanted to go. Finally they came to a barn where they spent the night. By morning the storm had ceased somewhat and by following a rope that was tied between the barn and the house, discovered he was at a neighbor's house about eight miles from his uncle's farm. Carl thoroughly believed he owed his life to his horse "Peggy."

In 1913, Carl had a bout with typhoid fever. He had to give up his job at the lumberyard and returned to his uncle's farm at Clement and helped with the fall harvest.

Soon, the wandering fever hit again and the in spring 1915, at age 28, Carl found himself getting off a train in Stronghurst, Illinois, where he had some second cousins. With their help, he found work on the farm of Jake Neff. In January 1917, leaving Stronghurst area, he went to Kirkwood, Illinois, finding temporary work and staying with his uncle, Ben Hendrickson. Here again was another family of relatives, with cousins about the same age. After work, he was more or less involved with the young people of the neighborhood.

In December, 1917, through the efforts of the Hendrickson's girls, he met two Swedish sisters who were housemaids at the Tubbs' and Rickett's home in Kirkwood. Their names were Gertrude and Bertha Brandt from Mjolby, Sweden.

In May 1918 (15 years after arriving in America) when he learned he wouldn't be accepted in the Army of the country he loved, Carl and Gertrude were married on February 1. They lived in a small house on the east edge of Kirkwood until March 1920, then moved to a small farm about 1 1/2 miles south of the community of Reed on the Oquawka road. They called it "The Farm On The Hill' because the house was set back in a hill facing the southeast. There was a spring a short distance from the house and barn which supplied the needed water for the family and livestock. It was at this house that their son Henry Gilbert was born.

In March 1922, they moved to the Carmichael farm southeast of Kirkwood, On August 17th, that year, Lyle Brandt became a member of the Nelson family. Hank and Lyle left their marks around this farm for many years.

The Nelson family was getting fairly well settled on this farm and, after much discussion and cooperation from the landlords, Dr. Frank and Nellie Kyler, they decided to return to North Dakota, finish up some business and show off their family out there. They made the trip in a Model T Ford Touring car with some following highlights:

Early on the rainy morning, August 17, 1925, leaving home in the Model T, loaded with a small kerosene stove, some metal dishes, pots, pans, water, groceries, clothes, towels, etc., extra spare tires, two five-gallon cans of gas, fastened to the running board on the left side of the car, oil and a tent. The tent fastened to the running board on the right side of the car, extending out ten/twelve feet, having flaps on three sides with the car making the fourth side, making a snug place. With an army cot for Carl, Hank, Gertrude and Lyle were fairly comfortable inside the car. The back of the front seat had been cut down on both sides, hinged at the bottom to lay back and make a bed. Side curtains filled in the left-hand side. For protection, Carl kept a ballpeen hammer close-by.

Leaving early in the morning, traveling all day, having two flat tires, they arrived in Ottumwa, Iowa that night. and Omaha, Nebraska the second night. Traveling northwest they entered Black Hills, South Dakota and remember a sign reading "Last chance for gas for 200 miles." Anytime they stopped for gas, flat tires, or just plain relief by the side of the road, Lyle and Hank would jump out of the car, hit the ground running and explore everything. They were on the road probably 10-12 days, depending on flat tires

Arriving at Clement, North Dakota, and the Smestead home of Carl's cousin Jennie, Hank and Lyle found three girl cousins: Lucille and Ruby being regular tomboys, with Esther, the oldest being more reserved. Many happy days were spent playing on the dirt bank down the lane, spending evenings at a 2-acre pond fed by an Artesian well, probably fishing there, but Artesian water tastes salty so maybe fresh-water fish couldn't live there. Returning there in 1970, the pond seemed smaller, but the well was still running, slower but still furnishing water. They returned to Illinois in October 1925.

Gertrude received a letter from Jennie at Christmas 1925, saying Esther had recovered from infantile paralysis but was paralyzed from the waist down, In spring 1926, Jennie and Esther stayed with the family when they went to Children's Hospital, St Louis, where Esther was fitted with back and leg braces. Esther lived to 45 years, working at North Dakota State Capitol Building, living alone and unmarried.

Things went well on the farm, with a good landlord; always making a living, very little money but with a nest-egg in the bank from the sale of the homestead in North Dakota. February 2, 1929, all banks failed, and the nest-egg was gone. That was hard for Carl and Gertrude and it took them many years to recover. They always had something to eat, clothes on their backs. Gertrude raised chickens and went back to work part time for the Rickett's family. They were pleased to have her back and treated her as one of their family.

Depression days were hard and as head of the house, Carl did what lots of other men had to do, having a six-foot frame and strong back, he was more or less happy with what he did. He was handy with a saw and hammer, cement work, butchering, timber work and was a shade-tree mechanic. Any honest job was none too great or small for him.

Lyle remembers, along with his Swedish accent and broken- english, Carl had a hard time carrying a tune, but anytime at school-gatherings or meetings, when 'America the Beautiful' was sung, you could hear him very plain. He got to be an American citizen the hard way, but was very proud of it.

The depression continued with more chickens, hogs, and cows; and with a good landlord, the children grew up in a healthy, rural life. Gertrude continued to work part-time at the Ricketts. A little money was put aside every week.

In August 1940, Carl loaded Gertrude, Ann and a neighbor, Mr. Hickok into a 1939 DeSota and went back to North Dakota in style. But that is another story that must be told by the ones who experienced it.

DOUGLAS AND KRISTEN (FAUSETT) NELSON - Douglas Edward born. May 22, 1955, Monmouth, Ill. son of Vail and Louise (Rask) Nelson. Siblings: Sandra, Judith, Ronald. Married Dec. 20, 1975, Aledo, Ill. to Kristen Diane Fausett bor July 13, 1955 Rock Island, Ill., daughter of Jerry and Joan (Luckenbill) Fausett. Brother; Monte.

Doug attended Kirkwood Grade Schools, Yorkwood Jr./Sr. High School graduating in 1973. Graduated Monmouth College 1977 with B.A. in Physical Education. Member of Alpha Tau Omega Fraternity. Member of College Football team for 4 years. After Graduation began teaching Northwestern School District #175. Taught in this district 8 years. The 1st 3 were in Blandinsville and the next 5 in Sciota at Northwestern Jr. High. Taught Jr. High Science & Physical Education. Coached Jr. High track, basketball and baseball. Then taught at Dallas City Elementary K-8, Physical Education. Also coached baseball and basketball, and served as Athletic Director and Dean of Students. Graduated from Western Illinois University in 1999 with a Master's in Educational Administration. Now principal at Aledo Jr. High School, Aledo, Ill.

Kris attended Aledo Elementary School, Jr. High School & Aledo High School graduating in 1973. Graduated Monmouth College in 1978. Member of Pi Beta Phi Sorority and was a cheerleader. Began teaching Jr. High Science in V.I.T. schools at Table Grove for 2 years, Southern Jr. High 6 years, Dallas City 3 years and Colchester 6 years. Graduated Western Illinois University 1996 with a Masters in Educational Administration. Now principal at Yorkwood Jr./Sr. High school.

*Matthew Vail born June 8, 1976, Galesburg, Ill. Attended Northwestern Elementary and Dallas City Elementary, Dallas City Jr./ Sr. High Schools graduating in 1994 as Valedictorian, was a member of National Honor Society. Attended Illinois State University for a semester transferring to Monmouth College and graduating in 1998, Suma Cum Laude. Member of Alpha Tau Omega Fraternity. Attended University of Illinois Veterinarian Medical School, graduating 2002. Married Faith Nicole Danielson born Sept 3, 1977 Carthage, Ill., daughter of Rick & Robin (Schroeder) Danielson, on June 19, 1999. Faith graduated from Dallas City High School 1995.Graduated Monmouth College 1999 with B. A. in Business. Matt will be practicing in Quincy, Ill. Daughter: Hayley Faith born March 20, 2002, Urbana, Ill.

*Nicole Kristen born Feb. 28, 1980 Macomb, Ill. Attended Northwestern Elementary and Dallas City Elementary & Jr. High School and Yorkwood High School graduating in 1998 as Valedictorian, was a member of National Honor Society. Attending Western Illinois University. Member of Students Assoc. of Nutrition Education.

*Joni Louise born March 4, 1985, Macomb, Ill. Attended Dallas City Elementary & Yorkwood Elementary and Jr./Sr. High School. Member of the National Honor Society and is active in athletics.

Members of Immaculate Conception Church, Monmouth, Ill.

LYLE AND MYRNA NELSON - There are many families who make up Warren County - some known; some unknown - but all contributing to the fabric of the county. Myrna Jean (Stice) and Lyle Brandt Nelson of Cameron have been part of that weave for all of their lives.

Myrna was born at home in Cameron on July 3 0, 1921, in a house a block south of the 4-way stop. Her parents, M. Elta (Anderson) and Bert M. Stice had relatives who ranged from Kentucky to Texas, but Warren County was finally their home. Bert and Elta took up residences in Cameron and Gerlaw before finally settling with their two girls (Myrna and her older sister, Lois M. (Stice) Terpening) in a house on North E. Street in Monmouth.

Myrna graduated from Monmouth High School in 1939 and met the man she was to marry later that summer. She worked at the pottery and was an Operator at the Monmouth Telephone Company before the wedding in 1944.

Lyle Brandt Nelson was born in Kirkwood, Il to Swedish immigrants, Gertrude (Brandt) and Carl Henry Nelson. He was the second of three children born to this couple who passed through Ellis Island, New York, destined for the Midwest. Carl arrived in 1902 on a sailing ship and went to live with family in North Dakota; Gertrude and her sister Bertha arrived in 1910 with train tickets for Monmouth, IL. Carl and Gertrude were married in Kirkwood in 1919 and lived out their lives on a farm near Minor Hill, on old US Rt. 34 between Monmouth and Galesburg.

Lyle and Myrna Nelson

Lyle graduated from Kirkwood High School in 1940, but he had met his true love the previous summer. On December 14, 1944, Myrna Stice and Lyle Nelson were married in a small ceremony. After several other jobs, Lyle began his life as a Warren County farmer, working farms owned by Cowden (past of Monmouth, around Warren School), Flaherty (north of Monmouth) and finally settling on the Frantz place, 1 1/4south of Cameron. The Frantz place was to become "the Nelson place" in the late 1960's, and it was here Lyle and Myrna were to spend 51 of their 57 married years.

The story is not finished yet. Two children were born to Lyle and Myrna: Michael Lee Nelson (February 28, 1948) and Marla Jean Nelson (26 December 1953). Both are married; Mike to Sheila (Bishop) Nelson and Marla to John David Johnson. There are grandchildren in the mix: Jon-Mychel Brandt Nelson (married to Sarah DeBlieck); Julia Christine Nelson; Amelia Johnson and Cassandra Johnson. Myrna, now retired from the Cameron Post Office, is active with her family, loves to dance, refinish antique furniture, sew and quilt with the Christian Church Quilters. Lyle has retired from farming, but still helps John when needed. He also loves to dance and spends many hours designing and building miniature farm implements. Lyle has always been a tinker; he once improvised a fender for a Chevy coupe when parts were hard to come by during WWII. The fender was only used when it was wet and muddy; otherwise it was carried in the trunk.

Isn't it amazing to think that 2 children; 4 grandchildren; 10 1/2college degrees- several farms farmed, bought and sold-, a multitude of students taught and molded and several computer systems pondered would all come about through a meeting at the Warren County Fair in Roseville in 1939.

RONALD & SUE (HAYNES) NELSON - Ronald Vail born June 15, 1950, Galesburg, Ill., son of Vail and Louise (Rask) Nelson. Siblings: Sandra, Judith and Douglas

Ron was married June 11, 1977 at his home north of Kirkwood to Emily Sue Haynes born May 31, 1955, Monmouth, Ill., daughter of James and Marcia Anne (Eckley) Haynes. Siblings: Thatcher George, Mary Anne and Sarah Beth.

Ron attended Roseville Elementary, Kirkwood Elementary, and Yorkwood Jr./Sr. High school graduating in 1968. Graduated Monmouth College with a B. S. Physics. Member of Alpha Tau Omega fraternity. Graduated University of Illinois with a B.S. in Civil Engineering. After graduating, he painted houses and barns. Ron began working for State Bond & Mortgage in 1975. In 1981 he started his own financial planning business. In 1983 he won $10,000 with a hole-in-one shot in the local Jaycee Golf Tournament.

Sue attended Bushnell schools graduating in 1973. Graduated with a B. A. in English and History from Monmouth College in 1977. She has taught English at Central Junior High School in Monmouth since 1978.

* Emily Sue born Oct. 23, 1983, Galesburg, Ill. Attended Yorkwood schools. Member of National Honor Society and active in athletics. She was an Illinois State Scholar. Graduated in the spring of 2002 and plans on attending college. Member of the Presbyterian church in Kirkwood, Ill.

* Abbey Leigh born May 31, 1985, Monmouth, Ill. Attends Yorkwood Jr./Sr. High School. Member of National Honor Society and active in athletics. Member of the Presbyterian Church in Kirkwood, Ill.

VAIL AND LOUISE (RASK) NELSON - Vail Pershing Nelson born Feb. 14, 1919, Altona, Ill., died Jan. 8, 1962, Iowa City, Ia. Graduated, Altona High School in 1936. Married Sept. 20, 1942, Altona, Ill., to Margaret Louise Rask, born Feb. 8, 1924, Kirkwood, Ill., daughter of Mannie and Lillian (Erlandson) Rask.

Vail started farming near St. Augustine, Ill., moved to the Coldbrook area, then Kirkwood, then Roseville and back to Kirkwood in 1950.

Louise attended Tubbs school, Newman school at Knoxville, Ontario elementary and Oneida High School, graduating in 1941. She graduated Western Illinois University in 1966 with a B.A. in Elementary Education. Taught 5th and 6th grades at Yorkwood Elementary then went to Roseville Elementary in 1970 teaching kindergarten and 3rd grades. She retired in 1998.

*Sandra Louise - see James & Sandra (Nelson) Johnson

*Judith Elaine - see Judith (Nelson) Ross

*Ronald Vail - see Ronald & Sue (Haynes) Nelson

*Douglas Edward - see Douglas & Kristen (Fausett) Nelson

WILLIAM HOCKMAN & EDAH (SMITH) NEWMAN - William Hockman Newman, oldest son of Cyrus Travis and Mary Samantha Gasconade (Hockman) Newman, was born March 29,1888 in Camden County, MO. Siblings were: Lola, Sarah, Marguerite, Vernon and Leroy.

William (Willie) attended schools at Climax Springs, MO, a town founded and named by his grandfather, William Washington Hockman. As a young man he drove a horse-drawn buggy for Dr. Koertz and hauled freight by wagon from Climax Springs to Warsaw, MO fording the Osage River. Warsaw is now on the Lake of the Ozarks and also the site of Truman Dam and Lake.

William and Edah Newman

While living in Climax Springs he met Edah Smith who was employed at the hotel there. They were married in Climax Springs November 3, 1912.

Edah Smith was born March 16, 1892 near Edwards MO the daughter of William Hobson and Mary (Arnett) Smith. Siblings: Dora, Rhoda, Lemuel, Adah, Oliver, Mattie and Alvin.

The young couple were farming near Edwards MO when their four daughters were born: Pauline on August 4, 1913; Irene on July 7, 1915: Lola on April 23, 1918 and Lillian on November 10, 1922

In November 1925 the family moved to Windsor MO where Willie was employed at a Hereford cattle farm. The family moved February 1929 to Ponemah, Warren County IL then to Kirkwood. Willie at that time was employed by the Prairie Pipe Line Company. In 1931 he was hired by the Village of Kirkwood as superintendent of water and streets, a job he held for many years. His final years of employment were at Western Stoneware Company in Monmouth, retiring at age 72.

Edah was a homemaker, gardener, quilter and did some home nursing. She was an active member of the Kirkwood Methodist Church, the Kings Daughters Sunday School class and leader of the children's King's Heralds for several years. William was also a member of the Kirkwood Methodist Church, Methodist Men, and Kirkwood Boosters Club. His hobbies were hunting and fishing and listening to the radio especially when the St. Louis Cardinals were playing

The Newmans are buried at Center Grove Cemetery, Kirkwood.

Submitted by Lillian Vice

JAMES NICOL - James Nicol married Susan Giles in March 1810 in Rock Island County. They were the parents of four children. Drennen drowned in the Mississippi when he was a young man. David at the age of 16 was killed in the Civil War. Rachel Jane graduated from Monmouth College in 1868 and was a co-founder of the Pi Beta Phi fraternity there. After graduation she studied medicine and received her M. D. from a medical school in Philadelphia. After practicing medicine at the New England hospital, she entered the University of Zurich, Switzerland to continue her studies in medicine and surgery. While there she caught pneumonia and passed away in 1881. William John was born in 1847 and was about five years old when the family left Edgington and came to Warren County and settled on a farm one mile north and one mile west of Little York.

In 1882 William married Sarah McCracken, daughter of Frederick and Mary Jane Osborn McCracken, in Oquawka. They had two sons: William Ira born in 1884, and George Leonard born in 1889. Sarah died in 1905 and William passed away in 1908. The boys stayed on the family farm. Ira did the farming, and George attended Monmouth College. George went on to study at several music conservatories in the East. He was a well-known pianist in his home community playing in many recitals, weddings and funerals, as well as the the Cedar Creek Church which the young men attended regularly.

George served in World War I and was able to return home, but without his health. He passed away in 1932.

William John and Sara A., two sons: Ira (standing) and George (sitting).

Ira married Mary Lulu Campbell, the daughter of John and Jenny Campbell, in April of 1919. They became the parents of four children: John William, Mary Jean, George Richard, and Florence Rachel.

In 1957 Ira passed away, and Mary died in 1975. They were buried at Cedar Creek Cemetery where the other members of the Nicol family had been interred.
Submitted by Florence Carver

IRA NICOL - William Ira Nicol was born in 1884 near Little York, Illinois, the son of William and Sarah McCracken Nicol. His mother died in 1905, and his father died in 1908. Ira became a farmer on the land where his grandfather, William John Nicol, started farming around 1852.

Ira married Mary Lulu Campbell, daughter of Jenny and John Campbell, in April of 1919. They were the parents of four children: John William was born in 1920 in Clear River, Minnesota; Mary Jean was born at the family home near Little York in 1923, George Richard was born in 1924 a couple of months after the family home had burned to the ground, and Florence Rachel was born at home in 1926.

Bill married Helen Bertelsen in 1941, and they had one son, George Ira, born in 1947. Bill then married Blanche Ramb, and they had two children: Mary Ellen born in 1949 and William Charles born in 1950. Blanche passed away in 1966. In 1970 Bill married Janette Malm. He passed away in Texas in 1995.

His son, George Ira, married Kathy Engles in 1969, and they became the parents of Kimberly Ann. He later married Barbara Kruger and they had a daughter, Kristina. Mary Ellen married Alan Hough in 1970. They live in Austin, Texas, and have three children: Travers, Drenan and Charles Alan. William Charles married Brenda Shotts in 1970, and they adopted Lori in 1980. He later married Kay Lynn Macken.

Mary Jean marrried Charles Tharp from Kentucky in 1947. She worked at the Little York bank for 44 years while Charles helped Richard with the Nicol farm. Charles passed away in 1988 and Mary Jean in 1997. They are buried at Cedar Creek Cemetery.

Richard married Helen Jane Nelson in 1948, and they were the parents of two children: Mary Annette born in 1954 and Richard Gilmore born in 1957, but who passed away in 1961. In 1965 they adopted Sean. In addition to farming Richard owned and operated a farm service store in Little York for several years.

Mary Ann married John McCann in 1976, and they have two daughters. Lindsey is a graduate of Monmouth College, and Corey is presently a student there.

Sean married Patricia Elliot in 1979, and they are the parents of four children. Melissa was born in 1983, Ashley in 1986, Jennifer in 1988, and Eric in 1996.

Florence married Howard Carver in 1947, and they have two sons, Bruce and Jeff. Bruce graduated from Iowa Wesleyan at Mt. Pleasant, Iowa, and is the general manager of the John Deere factory in Horicon, Wisconsin. Bruce married Lynn Foutch in 1976, and they have one daughter, Christy. Christy is a graduate of Stetson University in DeLand Florida. Jeff graduated from Monmouth College in 1991 and farms the Nicol family farm.

BARBARA JEAN BROWNLEE NICHOLS - Nichols, Barbara Jean Brownlee, the daughter of James Samuel and Bessie A. (Ikerd) Brownlee (life-long residents of Warren County), was born at Monmouth Hospital on November 6, 1929. Her sister, Lavonne Kay Brownlee Hawk (deceased in 1989) was born March 1, 1933. The Brownlees farmed at Eleanor in Sumner Township for over 50 years. The Brownlee family tree has been traced back in Scotland to the 1400's. The James Brownlee family were members of the Sugar Tree Grove United Presbyterian Church. James died January 23, 2000, at the age of 92.

Barbara Nichols

Barbara Nichols attended the rural schools of Cedar Hill and Denny, graduated from Little York High School, and went on to Western Illinois University, receiving a BS in Education in 1951. She taught Business Education at Joy, Greenfield, and Virden, Illinois High Schools. She married John F. Nichols of Greenfield, Illinois, in 1954, and they resided in Springfield, Illinois, where son James Lee Nichols was born in 1958. Barbara and son, James, returned to Monmouth in 1962, where she began teaching at Monmouth High School. During this time she continued her education at the University of Illinois and finished a MS in Education at Western Illinois University, Macomb, and went on to teach 23 years at Monmouth,. High School. - Upon retiring from teaching, Mrs. Nichols continued working part time for the Warren County Library, the Warren County Circuit Clerk and Beal, Pratt and Pratt Attorneys.

Barbara Nichols was a member of the Monmouth, Illinois, and National Education Association while teaching, and became a Life Member of Illinois Retired Teachers. She was a Charter Member of Gamma Lambda Chapter of The Delta Kappa Gamma Society for Woman Teachers, an active member of Beta Sigma Phi, and a member of the Galesburg Prairie China Painters Guild. Barbara is- a working volunteer at Community Medical Center, Monmouth. She enjoys traveling; which includes Europe (five times), Canada, The Caribbean Islands, Hawaii, and many other states.

Son James Lee Nichols married Lisa Smith of Elmwood, Illinois, in 1984, and their daughter, Amanda Irene, was born at Monmouth's Community Memorial Hospital April 16, 1989. James, Lisa, and Amanda reside in Monmouth.

ABRAHAM OGDEN - Abraham Ogden was born about 1770 in or near Manchester, England and came to the United States in 1793. He was a merchant in the textile business; he sold out his interest and returned to England for two years. Returning to NY in 1797, he settled in Floyd Township, Oneida County NY and married at Rome NY to Keziah Houghton, born 1788, daughter of Rufus Houghton and Mary Gleason.

Berwick Cemetery Ogden Plot, 17 burials including the oldest in the cemetery (Ann Delucia Ogden, 1840

Abraham Ogden was a gentleman farmer with a 100-acre farm; he was a member of an Oneida County grand jury in 1797, served during the War of 1812 for which his widow received a pension, may have been involved in the building of the Erie Canal and was a representative to the NY State Whig convention in 1834.

Abraham and Keziah Ogden had nine children; two girls, Sarah and Mary, did not survive infancy, and a son Aaron died in NY at the age of 26. They are buried in Wright Settlement Cemetery, in Rome NY. The surviving children were Franklin Ogden b. 1808 married Jane Briggs, Ann Ogden b. 1810 married Elon Matteson, Eliza Ogden b. 1815 married Zephaniah Lewis, Rufus Ogden b. 1818 married Narcissa Wilbur, Harriet Ogden b. 1819 married James Riddle and James Ogden b. 1821, died unmarried.

Abraham's two oldest children were married in NY; in 1839, they and their young families left NY; Abraham, age 69, followed them by Conestoga wagon to Warren County, IL with his wife and remaining children, settling on a farm in Lenox Township. By 1840, Abraham Ogden was a school trustee in Lenox Township, following a lifelong interest in education.

In 1840, Abraham Ogden's granddaughter, Ann Delucia Ogden, age 2, died. She was the first burial at Berwick Cemetery. Later that year, Abraham's youngest son, James, died at age 19. In 1845, Abraham Ogden died at Berwick at age 75, and his widow, Keziah, lived with her daughter Eliza Ogden Lewis for the remainder of her life. She died in 1872 at age 85. The Ogden plot in the Berwick Cemetery consists of a large family stone surrounded by 17 individual graves representing four generations of the Ogden family.

Abraham Ogden's farm remained in the family until 1920. Franklin Ogden passed the family farm to his son Delos and moved to Galesburg; Ann Ogden Matteson was widowed in 1845 in Warren County and moved with her young children to Galesburg where she died in 1883; Rufus Ogden farmed in Cold Brook Township and then moved to Mayville, MO; Zephaniah and Eliza Ogden Lewis farmed in Lenox Township until 1869 and then moved to Galesburg; Harriet Ogden was sent to Indiana to school, married James Riddle there and settled in Mattoon, IL.

Many of Abraham Ogden's grandchildren, great-grandchildren, great-great-grandchildren and at least one great-great-great grandchild attended Knox College in Galesburg. His merchant's gold scales, used before the United States had a settled currency, were donated to the college by his great granddaughter, Adeline Lewis Eagan.

ALBERT BRIGGS OGDEN - Albert Briggs Ogden was born on 15 Jun 1845 at Warren County, IL, son of Franklin Ogden and Jane Briggs. He was the youngest son and one of only two of Franklin Ogden's eight children to survive childhood; he was 12 years younger than his brother Delos.

Albert Briggs Odgen and Harriet Giddings Ogden

Albert attended the University of Chicago but was wild to join the Union army. In 1863 he enlisted in Co. A, 17th IL Volunteer Cavalry as a second bugler but rose the rank of sergeant. In 1865 he was involved in post-war uprisings of soldiers demanding discharges and was charged with mutiny and dishonorably discharged. In 1866 by authority of the War Department the dishonorable discharges were revoked and he was honorably discharged.

In 1867 Bert married Harriet Giddings in Warren County, daughter of Moses Giddings and Sophia Stafford. In 1878 they moved to Ft. Collins, Colorado, just before Leander Giddings moved there. He started a number of short-lived businesses and was elected City Marshall. In 1894 he and Harriet moved to Cripple Creek where he went into the dairy business. Albert and Harriet Ogden had no children.

In 1904 Harriet Giddings Ogden died. Albert moved back to Ft. Collins and in 1905 married Leander Giddings' widow, Addie. She died in 1908, after which he lived at the YMCA until 1911 when he married Delia Smith Giddings, widow of Leander's younger brother George.

Albert Briggs Ogden died in 1917. He had been such a colorful local character that the local newspaper ran a 16-inch obituary. He is buried there in the Grandview Cemetery, between Harriet and Addie.

FRANKLIN OGDEN - Franklin Ogden was born in Floyd Township, Oneida County, NY on 25 July 1808, the son of Abraham Ogden and Keziah Houghton. He was the second of nine children and resided on his father's farm until adulthood. On 11 Oct 1832 he married Jane Briggs, age 18, daughter of Joseph and Charlotte Briggs of Rome, NY.

Franklin Ogden and second wife, Cynthia Richardson Whiting Ogden, circa 1850.

After their marriage Franklin and Jane Ogden moved to Wyoming Township, Genesee County (now Wyoming County) NY. In 1837, seeking good farmland and following the founders of Knox College to western IL, Franklin inspected the territory and selected land in Berwick Township. Franklin Ogden and Ann Matteson and their families traveled overland "emigrant fashion" to settle in Warren County, followed by their parents and younger, unmarried brothers and sisters. Between 1840 and 1863, Franklin owned four farms in Berwick, Lenox and Floyd townships.

First wife of Franklin, Jane (Briggs) Ogden, circa 1849

Franklin and Jane Briggs Ogden had seven children; Franklin Delos Ogden b. 1833 married Harriet Lewis, Eliza Jane Ogden b. 1836, Ann Delucia Ogden b. 1838, Allen Briggs Ogden b. 1840, James Ogden b. 1841, Albert Briggs Ogden b. 1844 and Joseph Briggs Ogden b. 1848. Ann Delucia died in 1840 and was the first burial at Berwick cemetery. In 1848, Jane Briggs Ogden died with her newborn son Joseph. Both are buried at Berwick.

On 21 Sep 1850 the widowed Franklin Ogden married his wife's widowed cousin Cynthia Richardson Whiting. She was born in 1817 in NY and died on 29 Sep 1851, along with her infant son, Bela Whiting Ogden. Both are buried at Berwick.

On 26 May 1853 Franklin married another widow, Sarah Jane ("Jennie") Pollock Baker, age 23. One month later, an epidemic of diphtheria at Berwick took the lives of Eliza Jane Ogden, age 16, Allen Briggs Ogden, age 13, and James Ogden age 12. All were buried at Berwick Cemetery. Franklin Ogden was seriously ill but recovered, his new wife and his sons Delos and Albert Briggs Ogden were spared.

Delos Ogden attended Knox College and then set himself up as a stock farmer, taking over the family farm in 1866 and living in Floyd township for the rest of his life. Albert Ogden attended the University of Chicago and then enlisted in Co. A., 17th Illinois volunteer cavalry. He married Harriet Giddings in 1867 in Warren County where they remained until 1878 when they moved to Cripple Creek, Colorado. After Harriet's death Bert married Addie Giddings in 1905 and after her death married Delia Smith Giddings in 1911 in Ft. Collins CO and died there in 1917.

In 1863, Franklin Ogden moved into Berwick, where he was a merchant, engaged in the pork packing business, and lost all his money. In 1865, Franklin moved to Galesburg, where he was a manufacturer of composition stone. He was a lifelong member of the Baptist Church, a deacon at Berwick. He died 16 Dec 1900 and was buried with his first two wives at Berwick. Jennie Ogden lived with her stepson Delos Ogden and then with her step-granddaughter Mary Ogden Capps until 1920. Jennie is not buried in the Ogden plot at Berwick.

FRANKLIN DELOS OGDEN - Franklin Delos Ogden, called "Delos" or "F.D." to distinguish him from his father, was born on 01 Oct 1833 at Rome, Oneida County, NY, son of Franklin Ogden and Jane Briggs, and came to Warren County, Illinois with his parents in 1840 at age 6. Delos was the oldest of eight children of whom only two survived to adulthood.

Portrait of Ogden family, circa 1890. Charles Lewis Ogden b. 1876, Harriet Lewis Ogden b. 1845, Jeanette (Nettie) Ogden Mann b. 1866, Edwin Briggs Ogden b. 1868, Asa Abraham Ogden b. 1869, Evelyn Ogden b. 1874, Mary Adeline Ogden Capps b. 1878, Ralph Ogden b. 1872, Franklin Delos Ogden b. 1833.

Delos Ogden was a lifelong member of the Baptist Church. In the 1850's he attended Knox College and then went into the stock business.

After 1863) he managed his father's 160-acre farm in sections 20 and 21 of Floyd Township.

On 24 March 1866 Franklin Delos Ogden married his first cousin, Harriet Lewis, daughter of Zephaniah Lewis and Eliza Ogden. and they took over the Ogden family farm one mile South of Cameron. Delos and Harriet Ogden had seven children, Jeanette, Edwin, Asa, Ralph, Evelyn. Charles and Mary Adaline.

Jeanette Ogden b. 1866 married Walter Mann and lived at Alexis, then LaGrange, Edwin b. 1868 married Alice Hogan moved to Denver, Colorado; Asa Abraham b. 1869 unmarried, moved to North Dakota to help his widowed sister Mary and settled with her in Beloit, Wisconsin; Ralph b. 1872 married Elisabeth Rassbach and moved to Colorado where he had a series of jobs eventually settling in Fort Collins, Evelyn b. 1974 unmarried, moved to North Dakota to her widowed sister Mary and settled with her in Beloit, Charles Lewis b. 1876 married Stella Jackson and practiced law in Galesburg, and Mary Adaline b. 1878 married O.A. Capps and lived in Lenox Township until 1920, moving to North Dakota until the death of her husband in 1920 and later settling in Beloit. Wisconsin.

Delos Ogden died at his home on 13 Feb 1912, survived by his wife, seven children and stepmother. His eldest son Edwin maintained the home farm and provided a home for his widowed mother until she died in February 1920, when the farm was sold. Today the only real estate remaining to the Ogden family in Warren County is in the Berwick Cemetery.

RUFUS OGDEN - Rufus Ogden was born in Floyd Township, Oneida County, NY in 1818, the youngest son of Abraham Ogden and Keziah Houghton. In 1836 or 1837 he arrived in Cold Brook Township, Warren County, IL, a youth of 17. He came to Illinois either by himself or with other immigrants from Oneida County, NY, and was followed by the other members of his family and was living in his father's household in 1840. He became a member of Berwick Baptist Church in 1841 and was a member there at least through 1886.

On 25 Apr 1843 Rufus married Narcissa Wilbur, daughter of Baptist minister R. M. Wilbur and Harriet Phelps. The Wilbur family were early settlers of Warren County who later moved to Henry County, IL. Rufus and Narcissa had six children; the three oldest, Aaron, Elon and Arthur, all died in childhood in Warren County. Aaron is burried at Berwick Cemetery. The survivinng children were Harriet b. 1850, Eugene b. 1853 and Eliza b. 1858.

Rufus farmed in Sections 18, 19 and 20 on Cedar Creek in Cold Brook Township. At one time he owned 568 acres. He was a gentleman farmer and general businessman at Cameron, a widely known breeder of county fair and state fair champion Clydesdale horses.

The Ogden children grew to adulthood in Warren County, but the entire family moved away in the 1880s. Harriet Ogden married Orestes A. Spickerman; Eugene Ogden married Ida Belden, daughter of Daniel Belden and Rachel Lockwood, in 1882 at Galesburg and soon after moved to Maryville, Nodaway County, MO; and Eliza Ogden married Frank Goodspeed and moved to Iowa. Eliza attended Knox College.

Narcissa Wilbur Ogden died in 1893 and Rufus died 03 Aug 1896. All three of Rufus Ogden's children were living in Maryville, MO when Rufus died.

DELMAR J. AND JUNE (ROGERS) OHREN - The Ohren family, of German and Swiss extraction, came to America in the 1860's in the, hopes of farming. Delmar Ohren was born in Bond County in 1925; his father, Edw. P. Ohren was a farmer, his mother, Alvina Suess, a homemaker.

Delmar and June Ohren

In 1944 Del joined the Navy V-5 program, receiving training in St. Peter, MN, and was in the pre-flight program at St. Mary's near San Francisco, CA. After the war he entered the University of Illinois where he received his bachelor's degree in Agriculture.

Del became the Assistant Farm Advisor in Christian County, IL where he met June Rogers who was employed in the Home Extension Office there. June was born in Taylorsville, IL on June 1, 1929, the daughter of Bert H. and Helen E. (Hatfield) Rogers. Del and June were married on August 20, 1949, in Taylorville.

In 1951 Del, June, and their nine-month-old daughter Belinda moved to Monmouth, IL where Del became the Assistant Farm Advisor at the Warren County Farm Bureau.

Del served as a city alderman for eight years during the 1960's. June and their daughter Anita owned and operated a women's apparel shop, The Phone Set, at 218 S. Main Street for twenty years. June was a part-time teller at the National Bank of Monmouth for six years.

Belinda Del was born July 27, 1950, in Taylorsville, IL. After graduating from high school, she attended the James Millikin University in Decatur, IL for two years, then transferred to Western Illinois University in Macomb. Belinda married John M. Campbell of Monmouth, and they had two daughters - Jennifer and Elizabeth. Belinda passed away with cancer in 1998.

Anita Fay, the second daughter, was born November 2, 1952, at the Monmouth Hospital. Anita enrolled at Carl Sandburg for two years and transferred to Monmouth College for the last two years. She married Gary Romine, but the marriage ended in divorce eleven years later.

David Edward, the third child, was born in March of 1966. Loving the game of golf, he went to Danville Area Junior College in Danville, IL following high school graduation to learn to be a golf course superintendent. Presently he resides in Wildwood, IL where he is in charge of the 18-hole golf course at the nearby Great Lakes Naval Training Center.

HEIDI ELIZABETH (BARNES) O'KANE - O'Kane, Heidi Elizabeth (Barnes), youngest of the five children of Estelle and Bud Barnes, was born January 28, 1960. Welcoming her were her sister, Jennifer, brothers Mark, Blake, and Lance. Heidi attended Garfield grade school, Central Jr. High, and Monmouth High School, as did her father. She graduated in 1978 from high school, then continued her education at Cornell College, Mt. Vernon, Iowa graduating in 1982. Her brother, Dr. Blake Barnes and his wife Nancy Currie, also graduated from Cornell College. It is unique in curriculum, students pursue only one course at a time. At college she met Tom O'Kane from Skokie near Chicago and they were married in 1983. Heidi's degree was in elementary education, Tom's in business. He had finance positions in oil at Hobbs, New Mexico and returning to the Chicago area before taking the same position for Michael Foods owning "Pappeti Foods" in the egg processing business in Lenox, Iowa. Creston, Iowa, was their choice for living, buying a spacious home with a swimming pool. Daughter Erin was born in New Mexico, son Paul was born when they lived in Glenview, Illinois, and daughter Elizabeth in Mundelein. Heidi has many friends. She has been active in many areas: as a substitute teacher, Methodist church in their Bible school, P.E.0, and most important as a mother following her children's pursuits. Erin is on the golf team as well as making the high school flag team. Paul participates in all sports, especially baseball and Elizabeth enjoys the dance. All are good students.

Tom and Heidi O'Kane

Tom grew up in Skokie, where he attended Catholic Schools before choosing Cornell College, where he lettered as a first baseman on the baseball team. He has a keen sense of humor, yet very serious about his work. He sings in the Methodist choir and is their finance officer. He also coaches boy's baseball teams. Because Tom's parents are first generation immigrants from Ireland and he has relatives there, a wonderful family vacation was arranged to meet his grandparents, who in 1998 were alive and well.

LENORE JEAN (HANSON) AND CHUCK MERRILL ORWIG JR - Lenore was born November 5, 1934 to Henry Hanson and Fay Fisher Hanson. She was born and raised in the same house. Jeanne attended Monmouth schools and graduated from High School in 1952. She worked at Woolworth Dime Store, Bankers Life, and Second National Bank.

Jeanne and Chuck Merrill Orwig were married September 12, 1953 in Biloxi Mississippi. He was in the US Air Force during the Korean Conflict. Chuck was born in Galesburg January 31, 1934 to Charles Merrill "Merle" and Floradel Simpson Orwig. He attended Galesburg schools and graduated in 1951. He played in many Country Western bands including Mid Western Ramblers on WGIL Radio while in high school. The Chuck Orwig's Band was started in 1950, which played for many dance and service clubs. He started "Prime Time Jazz" after moving to Kewanee in 1967 and played mostly for private parties in the Quad City area. He worked for his parent's hardware store, Flesher House of Music, and retired from Griggs Music in Davenport, Iowa. After retirement Chuck's band played in area schools for several years teaching the grade school children about jazz and how to be an audience.

Back row: Cheryl, Chuck III, Rich Thompson, Chris, Caron. Front row: Chuck, Jeanne

Jeanne was Galesburg Girl and Brownie Scout leader including a Neighborhood Director. After moving to Kewanee she was Cub Scout leader, Sunday school teacher. She and Chuck were senior high youth leaders for 9 1/2 years in their Presbyterian Church. Jeanne was employed as accountant for Milnes Car Dealership, Johnston's Chiropractic, was a Tupperware Manager and retired as a caseworker for the Illinois Department of Public Aid. For many years Jeanne has made large and small Raggedy Ann and Andy's and gave them to great nieces and nephews. Upon retirement she dresses as Raggedy Ann and visits nursing homes, gives children's sermons at their church and her nephew's church in Greenview, Illinois. Raggedy was also in the Living Windows at Christmas time. She and Chuck have visited Arcola, Illinois several times where the creator of Raggedy, Johnny Gruelle was born.

They had four children. Caron Martha Walter born December 7, 1954 in Riverside, California, the other 3 children were born in Galesburg. Cheryl Mildred born June 8, 1957, Charles Merrill III born September 2, 1960, Christopher Mark born March 14, 1963. They also had a foster son Richard Lee Thompson born June 4, 1957. They have six grandchildren. Rich had 3 children and 2 grandchildren.

GLENN AND ELWILDA (HOLMES) OSBORN - Glenn Phillip Osborn was born 21 Nov. 1929 near Little York, IL to John Claypool and Julia Eveline (Young) Osborn. He attended grade and High School there, graduating from Little York High. He helped with farming on the homeplace until moving his family to Monmouth in 1972. There he was self-employed delivering oil for Sun Oil Company until he sold out and started working at Keister's in 1980. He retired from there in 1999 but still works there part-time. On 25 June 1952 he married Elwilda Morrell in Galesburg, IL.

Elwilda Holmes Morrell was born 10 July 1929 in Plymouth, IL. to William and Frankie (Holmes) Morrell. She grew up in Knoxville and attended grade and High Schools there, graduating in 1947. She was a housewife and worked as a cook in the cafeteria at Monmouth College, then as a seamstress at Smoler Fashions and later did the office work for Glenn. She has two sisters: Phyllis Geldbrandt and Josephine Perrin (deceased). Her hobbies were sewing, and needlework. Both enjoyed reading and playing scrabble and cards. Both active at Oak Terrace and Strom Center, where she served on the Strom Board of Directors and the newsletter. Both helped with dinners, etc. She loved Genealogy and both are Charter Members of the Warren County Genealogical Society where she has served as President, Corresponding Secretary and on Acquisitions and Early Pioneer Recognition Committees. She has received the "Ageless Achievers Award" She was a member of the Little York United Methodist Church. Elwilda died suddenly 3 Oct 2000. Children of Glenn and Elwilda:

Glenn and Elwilda (Holmes) Osborn

David Phillip was born 30 May 1953 at Galesburg, IL. He attended Little York schools and graduated from High school there. He was in charge of tires at Munson's Transportation and now works as a mechanic for Smiley's Towing in Monmouth, he has 2 children: Kim and Mike.

Michael Robin was born 24 Nov 1955 in Monmouth. He attended Little York schools and graduated from Little York High school. He served 20 years in the Military and earned his Law Degree while there. He now works for a Law firm in Boston, Massachusetts. He has 3 children: Malissa, Matthew and Thomas.

William John was born 19 Nov 1958 in Monmouth. He was head of Maintenance for Munson's Transportation and now works for Deford Auto and Electric in Monmouth. He has 3 children: Daniel, Brian and Craig.

Glenn had two brothers, Lawrence born 1931 (deceased) and John born 1923, also deceased.

JOHN OSBORN - On 23 April 1862, Jeremiah Osborn and Elizabeth Day sailed from England's Downs to Pennsylvania as indentured servants of Griffith Jones, a glover. Landing in Delaware on the ship Amity, (one of William Penn's 23 ships) 3 August 1862. After serving their indentureship, they were married. Their son Jeremiah, born circa 1695-1700, marriage unknown. The next Jeremiah, born 1722-1729, married Mary Newman circa 1755-58, was one of the settlers of the Shenandoah Valley. They lived on the South Branch which flowed into the North Branch to form the Potomac River, just below Cumberland, Maryland. This branch of the Osborns went to North Carolina.

In 1790, Jeremiah's son John (27 Oct. 1770-Nov 1848) married Jane Claypool (18 Feb 1869-8 Oct 1834). Their son, John Claypool Osborn, first married Rebecca Murry and started for Illinois in 1830. She died and he later married Mary Moler Moffett, a young widow with two children, on 18 August 1839. Their children: George P. ; four sisters and one brother who was killed in the Civil War. One sister, Mary Jane was the grandmother of Ira Nicol of Little York, Illinois.

John Claypool Osborn & Julia Young Osborn

John Claypool Osborn (30 March 1804-18 March 1874) and Mry Moler Moffett 5 Oct 1810-15 Feb 1892). Their son George Perry Osborn was born 26 June 1835. There was a log cabin there at the time where in 1838 a new home was built which stood on the old homestead North and West of Little York and still stood until recent years.

After the death of his parents George married Amanda Ann Brownlee Douglass 11 Oct 1892. The marriage lasted only until the May term of Court 1901. They had two children: Georgia Marie, (4 Oct 1894 - 19 Nov 1971) and John Claypool (19 Mar 1896-16 Mar 1955).

George was a very colorful person. He ran a still and grew grapes on the north side of the house. When people came to buy wine and hunt (he had a pack of ca 27 dogs), he would put the lantern behind his back and let the men, full of wine run into the creek. He also kept a parrot in a cage on the front porch that would scream when a stranger came near. He bored 5 holes in the bottom of all the chairs. There were two stories as the reason for this (1) when the women of the house washed on the board and set their tubs on the chairs they were never wiped off and so he sat in the water (2) when the children were small they wet their clothing while standing on the chairs and he sat in it?

George died 27 Aug 1902 having provided for his children and names their guardians. His son John Claypool (19 Mar 1896-16 Mar 1955) married Julia Eveline, Young (5 July 1897-20 Jan 1959) on 21 Feb 1922. They raised three sons on the farm that had been homesteaded in 1832, in the same house where the father and grandfather were raised.

ROLAND HERBERT OSWALD FAMILY - Roland Herbert Oswald (10/28/1910 - 12/05/1988) was the youngest of 3 children of Frank Wilson Oswald (4/26/1871 - 8/16/1942) and Lois Kate Ruse (7/27/1872 -5/13/1920). "Wilson" farmed Oswald's mill land and was part of the Ruse threshing team for hire. "Kate" taught school, before her marriage February 21, 1899.

Roland's grandfather, Peter Oswald (1834 - 1912?) emigrated from Sigmaringen, Germany. He was a miller at Payne's Mill on Cedar Creek, owned it and farmed from 1867 to 1879. He then sold that and purchased 15 acres of land with mill and store further downstream, known as

Olmstead's mill. He was miller there until a flood in 1899 washed away the dam. Peter and wife, Anna Patterson, raised 4 children, Ella, John, Frank and Clara (Mrs. David Kilgore).

Peter Oswald Family circa 1912. L: to R: Back row: Frank Wilson Oswald, Clara Oswald Kilgore, Ann, Lois Kate Ruse Oswald, Ella Oswald. Front row: Peter, Roland, Anna Patterson Oswald

Henry Ruse (2/15/1832 - 10/27/1910), Roland's maternal grandfather, emigrated from Suffolk England in 1852. He married Sarah McCreedy (11/14/1845 - 10/10/1921) on January 30, 1862 in Warren County. Sarah emigrated from Ireland with her mother Nancy Davidson McCreedy in 1850. They farmed and raised 4 children, Lois Kate, Effie, (Mrs. George Ellsworth Earp), Harry, and Carl. Remnants of the Ruse house and buildings still stood, next to Gibson Woods golf course, in June 2001.

L: to R: Back row: Mary Jane Dunn Oswald, Catherine Reeves Walters, Andrea and Roland Oswald. Front Row: Mary Walters Oswald, Alex, Valerie and Bill Oswald, 1986

Roland was only 10 when Kate Oswald died. His older brother Henry (11/2/1900 - 4/25/1986) was almost 20. Sister, Ann (9/3/1904 - 4/1/1986), at 16, became a mother figure for her brother. Having no children of her own, she maintained the role all her life. Anna married Bill Stratton in 1931. They owned a neighborhood grocery, and rented rooms in their home, 406 S. 3rd, now known as the Wyatt Earp birthplace. Her father, brothers and family, lived there from time to time. After Bill died in 1957, Ann became a LPN at Monmouth Nursing home.

Roland, a 1928 graduate of Monmouth High School, lettered in field events. His 1927 javelin throwing record may yet be unbroken. Tall and thin, a resemblance to Ichabod Crane, earned him the nickname he carried the rest of his life and much preferred to Roland. "Ick" loved Mary Jane Dunn, daughter of Simeon and Edna Fritz Dunn.

Times were hard, so they eloped, October 15, 1934, but didn't announce it until May 1936. He worked construction jobs, and continued as a carpenter when he joined the 1303rd Army Engineers in 1943 for the duration of WWII. He built buildings, bridges, and airports in 5 European Theatre of Operations Campaigns: Normandy, Northern France, Ardennes, Rhineland, and Central Europe, also in the Philippines, and in Japan during its occupation. He attained the rank of Sergeant. Mary waited in Rock Island, IL welding bomb bay doors for J. I. Case, and living with her sister Ruth Dunn Sims, a military secretary waiting for her husband Milton to return. On his return, Ick continued to build large jobs, commercial buildings, hospitals, and colleges. He was Union Treasurer, and a Monmouth Building Inspector.

Their first son, William Robert, arrived June 25, 1950. Son Jan was born Oct. 4, 1954. He is handicapped by cerebral palsy, but lives an active life at DuPage County Convalescent Center, Wheaton IL. Ick and Mary lived near Monmouth most of their lives, leaving to join Bill in 1986, when Ick's health failed. He died in Wheaton, IL, Dec. 1988, Mary died in Tulsa OK, Oct. 1998. They are buried in Memorial Park Cemetery.

Bill graduated from MHS in 1968, and NIU in 1972 with a psychology degree. He is Human Resource Information Systems Manager for Occidental Petroleum. In 1970 he married Mary Louise Walters, born 1951 in Monmouth to Ernest and Catherine Walters. A 1969 graduate of MES, she attended NIU in Dekalb, IL and worked as secretary, bookkeeper, and floral designer. They have three children. Andi born 1971, in DeKalb, IL, graduated from St. Charles High School and is employed by HealthNet HMO in Woodland Hills, CA. She married Jonathan Myron, web media designer, in 2001.

Valerie, born 1975, in DeKalb, IL, graduated 1993 from Learning Post High School, Newhall, CA. She is studying Speech Communications and History at University of Washington, Seattle.

Alex, born 1977, graduated 1995 from Learning Post High School in Newhall CA, attended Tulsa Community College. He lives and works near his parents in Broken Arrow, OK.

Henry Oswald and wife Lora Black married in 1934. He worked at Monmouth Post Office, and raised 2 daughters. Beverly, a retired teacher, lives in Galesburg. Barbara, a special education teacher, married Max Biddle, school administrator. Retired now, they live in St. Charles Il, near their sons. Steven married to Karen Monk raised 2 sons. Don, married to Jennifer Leonard has 2 daughters. Daughter Lora, husband Tony Wey, their son & daughter, live in Bloomington, IL.

Submitted by William R. Oswald

PACE - This is the story of our Pace family, some taken from authentic data, some by word of mouth. There may yet be records found that would change some of this story, but as we know it now, the second great line of Virginia Pace's is that which can be traced back to a John Pace in Middlesex County in 1693. John's origin is obscure.

Most present day PACE'S believe they descended from Richard and Isabelle Pace of Pace Paines, but so far no definite connection with this line has been found. John's oldest child Sarah is interred in Christ Church Parish Register as born April 24, 1720, naming all his children except Sarah.

Michael Pace – Cumberland Presbyterian Cemetery, Henderson County, Illinois. Nancy (Richards) Pace – Blue Grass Cemetery, Blue Grass, IA.

Joseph, son of John bought land in Groochland County September 22, 1739. He willed his son John 140 acres of the land which figured in a lawsuit in 1809. Our lineage is through this son John. His son Francis, moved to Pittsylvania County, Virginia 1798. At least four sons of Francis moved to Missouri. They were Francis Jr., Edward, Hartwell and James. In 1843 after the U. S. Government had opened land in the western Missouri, they brought their families and settled in Cedar and St. Clair County.

One brother of the Missouiri Pace's did not go to Missouri with the rest. He settled in Western Illinois and Eastern Iowa. Michael Pace, (son of Francis Pace of Virginia), moved from Virginia in 1819 to Washington County, Kentucky. Residing there until 1830 when they became residents of Warren County, Illinois. While a resident in Warren County he served on Petit Jury in 1833. Securing the farm in 1830, the father engaged in its cultivation until the fall of 1835. At which time Mr. Pace came to Iowa, bringing with him his son Michael Perkins Pace to aid in surveying the land for a claim. They returned for the family in May 1836, when they took up their permanent residence in the northern part of Muscatine County, on section 11 in Sweetland Township. By hard labor the land was cleared, and a comfortable home secured, but in October 16, 1846 the death angel visited the pioneer cabin, taking from it the loving mother Nancy Richards Pace, who is buried in Blue Grass Cemetery, Blue Grass, Iowa in Scott County. Five years passed October 23, 1851 and then Michael Pace too (while living with his son Francis Anderson in Warren County) was called to his final home. He is buried in Oquarwka, Illinois - Henderson County, Greenville Township.

Michael Pace was born July 28, 1786 in Goochland County, Virginia. He married Nancy Richards July 7, 1808 in Pittsylvania County, Virginia. She was born July 7, 1788 in Goochland County, Virginia. To this union seven children were born: Joseph, Francis Anderson, Frances (Fannie), Michael Perkins or M.P., Jane (Winnie), Elizabeth and John R. I am pleased to record this sketch of the noble pioneer and his family.

Submitted by Harlan E. Pace

FRANCIS ANDERSON PACE - In August 03, 1838 transfer of land was made to Francis Anderson Pace of the County Warren and State of Illinois, Section 32 - Rozetta Township.

He is the second child of Michael and Nancy Richards Pace, who secured a farm July 27, 1830 in Henderson County and engaged in its cultivation until the fall of 1835, when he came to Iowa.

Francis Anderson Pace

Francis Anderson Pace died in Hastings - Mills County - Iowa October 19, 1893. He was born in Virginia, September 29, 1810, and was united in marriage to Miss Jane Prunty, March 29, 1838 in Kentucky. She died July 14, 1892 in Hastings, Iowa. The fruits of this union were six children, two sons: - William Cyrus, John B. and four daughters - Mary E., Nancy V., Amanda E., Phebe E.

The family lived in Illinois until 1869, then to Kansas, and then on to Hastings, Mills County, Iowa in 1875.

JOSEPH (PADDACKS) PADDOCKS - Joseph Paddocks was born 15 August 1779 in Pennsylvania during the American Revolution, the son of Jonathan and Keziah (Smith) Paddocks. The family moved to the Kentucky "wilderness" sometime before 1788 settling in Fayette County, Bourbon County, Shelby County and finally Hardin County, Kentucky. Jonathan united with the South Fork Baptist Church in Hardin County where he preached for many years and aided in laying the foundation of some of the early churches in the area.

Joseph Paddocks was married in Hardin County, Kentucky 9 September 1800 to Mary (Polly) Gilliland born 9 May 1781 in Pennsylvania, daughter of Captain Thomas and _?_ Gilliland. Ca 1808 Joseph and Mary moved to Harrison County, Indiana where Joseph was a judge in the first Territorial Election held in that county.

Joseph was commissioned a Lt. Colonel in the 1st Regiment of the Indiana Militia 14 November 1810 by William Henry Harrison, Governor of the Indiana Territory. On 28 June 1812 he was commissioned a Colonel in the 5th Regiment of the Indiana Militia by J.M. Gibson, Acting Governor of the Indiana Territory. In December 1825, 1830-31 and 1831-32, Joseph served as representative from Harrison County, Indiana to the State Legislature.

Ca 1836 he sold his property in Indiana and migrated to Kelly Township, Warren County, Illinois along with several members of his family. From 1843-55 he served as Warren County Surveyor. 10 June 1847, Mary (Gilliland) Paddocks died and Joseph began to liquidate some of his property. Tax lists indicate he owned many acres at one time or another mostly in the southeast portion of Kelly Township. Before 1860, he married (2) Maria Smith, widow of Rezin Smith, Sr. and mother of his son-in-law, onas Smith. They moved to Abingdon, Knox County, Illinois where Joseph died 29 January 1865. Joseph and Mary (Gilliland) Paddocks are buried in the Miles Cemetery, Section 25, Kelly Township. Rezin Smith, Sr. and Maria arealso buried there.

Joseph and Mary (Gilliland) Paddocks were the parents of twelve known children. Namely: Jonathan (1801-1885), married Nancy Watson (1807-1869), daughter of Abraham and Eleanor (Rhodes) Watson; Matilda (1804-1888), married Bazil Watson (1804-1865), son of Abraham and Eleanor Watson; Phebe (1805-1882), married Samuel J. Black (1796-1871) as second wife; Thomas born before 1810, married (1) Penelope French; (2) Marinda Williamson;   Male Child - Listed 1810 Census; Leodica (1811-1889), married James Dunn (1810-1876), son of Richardson Dunn I; Susannah (1813-1879), married William Graham (1814-1887); Harvey born ca 1816, died before 1864; Mary Ann born 1819, died before 1860, Married Joseph Dunn; Felix born ca 1820, died before 1864; Rebecca (1882-1883), married Jonas Smith (1826-1893); Julia Ann (1824-1902), married Josiah Ryner (1820-1902) son of Jacob and Rachel Ryner.

Joseph and his offspring were well-known citizens of Warren County before some of them continued their migration West.

SCHUYLER PALMER - Schuyler Palmer was one of the early pioneers of Warren County. In 1855 at the age of 24, he bought the northeast quarter of Section 1, Spring Grove Township, which later became the site of the Village of Alexis. The land was still untilled prairie. He built a home for his new wife and planted his first crop there. In 1867 he sold his land to Thomas Laughead, who in turn sold it to Col. Robert Holloway and J.E. Alexander who plotted the village of Alexis in 1870.

Phelix Nelson, grandson and Schuyler Palmer

After he sold his land to Laughead in 1867, he bought land in Sections 10 and 15. In 1871 he built a home on the Section 15 property called "Evergreen Lawn." The 1872 plat book shows he owned 260 acres of land on the west side of Section 15 and another 160 acres on Section 10 across the road. History says his home and barns were the most substantial in Spring Grove Township. In addition to farming, he also raised Durham cattle, and was road commissioner in Spring Grove Township for 17 years.

Palmer was born November 24, 1831 in Ontario Canada, the son of Wilkinson and Nancy (Hurd) Palmer. His parents were also born in Canada. The ancestors of his father were from NY; his mother's were from CT, NJ, and later still NY. In 1842 the family moved to Whiteside Co., IL in the vicinity of Prophetstown. In 1845 they moved to Warren County, locating in Hale Township. Wilkinson Palmer rented land until 1851 when he purchased 80 acres. The family built a log home on this property. Later Mr. Palmer built a frame home on the property and acquired more land until he became the owner of 200 acres, a portion of which was located in Henderson County.

Schuyler Palmer married Lucy A. Mills December 25, 1856. She was born in Henderson County and was the daughter of William H. and Lucretia (Morris) Mills. Schuyler and Lucy were the parents of 11 children; Mary Palmer, Alice Palmer Gallagher, Lillian Palmer Gilmore, Effie Palmer Armstrong, Henry Palmer, Myron Palmer, Mattie Palmer Armstrong, Lura Palmer Joesting, Eva Palmer Saddon, Katherine Palmer Nelson and George Palmer. Schuyler Palmer died April 28, 1909. His wife Lucy died March 13, 1922. They are buried in the Alexis cemetery.

Submitted by Brenda Sims Fell

GEORGE AND DOROTHY PAPE - Pape, George W., the youngest child of Ruth Fritz and W. Russell Pape, was born in Monmouth on Oct. 30, 1924. The Pape family name came to Warren County in the person of Conrad Pape, Great-Grandfather of George. Conrad Pape and brother, John came from Germany on the sailing ship, *Alexander Von Humboldt*, entering the Port of New Orleans in 1846. Following a stay in the Quincy area, they established neighboring farms in Hale Township in 1853. Conrad and his wife, Cordelia, both lived into their nineties and resided in Kirkwood following retirement from the farm.

Scott Dedeaux Pape, Georgia Lee Pape Handy, Annalee Pape Handy, Thomas Reid Handy III, John Clayton Pape Dorothy Dedeaux and George Wendell Pape.

Richard, older brother of George, graduated from Kirkwood High School, served in the Navy in World War II, and attended Bradley University until his death from pneumonia in 1946. His death came just two weeks after the birth of a daughter, Connie, with his wife, Juanita Worden Pape, another Warren County native.

George graduated from Kirkwood High School in 1942 and entered the US Navy that year with a subsequent Honorable Discharge in 1946. He received a B.S. and M.S. from Bradley University. At Bradley U. he was one of the Founders of the Alpha Sigma Chapter of the Theta XI, which still flourishes on campus. He was also elected to Sigma Delta Psi, an Athletic Fraternity based on surpassing standards in Swimming, Gymnastics, and Track & Field.

George worked in the field of education beginning his career in 1949 as a teacher and coach at Kirkwood High School where he advanced to Principal/Superintendent in 1954. He was married to Dorothy Dedeaux, a Bradley U. Graduate, in 1952. George accepted an Administrative Position at Arroyo Grande High School in California in 1955. The three children of George and Dorothy were born in California namely: Georgia Lee, John Clayton, and Scott Dedeaux.

George and the family returned to Illinois where he served for eleven years as the Principal of Monmouth High School. (See picture) His service at Monmouth High School was defined by student involvement in learning activities in the World of Work. Monmouth High School at that time numbered over 700 students. George was President of the Monmouth Rotary Club and was active in many community affairs, most recent of which was the War Memorial Statue on the grounds of the Warren County Court House.

George worked for the Department of Defense at Great Lakes as an Educational Specialist heading the Curriculum and Instructional Standards Office at Service School Command. (A Naval Training School of 9000 students).

George is a Life Member of the A. Lincoln Masonic Lodge in Kirkwood, a Life Member of VFW Post #2301 in Monmouth, and a long time member of the Monmouth American Legion.

Dorothy (Dedeaux) Pape was the youngest child born to Caroline (Lichtenstein) and Leon Dedeaux in Gulfport, Mississippi. Older children were: Iris, retired, living in Texas, Leon, B.S., Colorado University, and Louie, B.S. and M.S. Oklahoma State, retired to Pennsacola, Florida. Dorothy was raised in the Panama Canal Zone graduating from Balboa High School in 1949. She graduated from Bradley University in 1952 and spent her adult life teaching and raising a family. She has been an avid participant in Genealogical Research, traveling to Europe in search of her "Roots." One branch of her family tree was traced to a 12th Century Cardinal in the Catholic Church when it was headquartered in Avignon, France.

Dorothy and George became first time grand parents with the birth of Annalee Pape Handy, daughter of Georgia (Pape) Handy and Thomas Reed Handy Jr. Georgia was a long time Manager for Barnes & Noble Book Stores. Son, John Clayton, is a Supervisor in the Boca Raton, Florida Parks and Recreation Department, and Son, Scott Dedeaux, is a Senior Planner for the City of Delray Beach, Florida. All of the children are graduates of Monmouth High School. As of 2001 all family members are living in Palm Beach County, Florida.

JAMES B. PARIS - James Buford Paris was born in Gallitan County, Illinois September 24, 1926, son of Charles Ellis and Oneita Blanche Calvin Paris. He has one sister Hildred Alma. In January 1945 he left school and worked for a time at Republic Aviation across the Wabash River in Evansville, IN where the P47 Thunderbolt was built. He joined the Army in January 1945. Upon completion of basic training he was on the way to Japan with occupation forces with a stop off in Hawaii. While there a broken bone in the leg would not heal so he was sent back to the states where he was a patient at the Mayo General Army Hospital in Galesburg.

Ruby Josephine VanTine was born in Henderson County, Illinois on January 30, 1927, the 11th child of Truman L. and Cora Pearl White VanTine. Her siblings were Eleanore, Edwin, Nellie, twins Leah and Reah, Gerald, Roy, Truman Luther, Robert, Zelda, and Helen. In 1941 she moved with her family to Monmouth and graduated from high school in 1945. While in school she worked part time in the cafeteria at Monmouth College and as an usher at the Rivoli Theater. Her first job after graduation was as bookkeeper at Diffenbaugh Lumber and Coal Company, paying $12.00 for a 45-hour week. In October of '45 they met at a USO party held in the Legion which was then above awcocks. Patients from the Army Hospital were brought by bus on these occasions.

James B. and Josephine Paris, their children, their spouses and the grandchildren. Photo taken.November 1983 at their home at 425 W. Walnut in Kirkwood, Illinois

Married on August 1, 1946 their first home was in Newport News, VA where he was stationed until being discharged a few months later. They returned to the area and he took classes in Galesburg and was awarded a GED diploma. His first job was at the Weir Fruit Farm in Henderson County, $18.50 for a 6-day work week. After moving to Warren County in 1948, he was employed as an auto mechanic at several local businesses. He retired from the Illinois Department of Transportation. In 1954 they purchased their first home in Kirkwood where they are still residents. She was a stay at home mom until the children were all in school, then was the Warren County branch librarian in Kirkwood, retiring in 1998.

Their children are James, John, Jerald, Peggy, Jane and Janet. All were born in Warren County except Jane, who was born in Des Moines, IA. Peggy died in 1953 in Des Moines County, IA. Their 5 children and 5 of their 9 grandchildren were Yorkwood High School graduates.

ROLLIN ARTISMUSWARD PARSONS - Rollin Artismusward Parsons was born in Astabula County, Ohio June 9, 1837 and died October 29, 1917 in Warren County, Illinois. The 8th child of David Hastings Parsons, who was born in 1801 Springfield, Massachusetts, and died in 1899 Knox County, Illinois and Lydia Taylor Warren.

David Hastings was a gr-gr-gr-grandson of Joseph Parsons who came from England in 1634; married Mary Bliss in 1646 in Connecticut. David Hastings came to Knox County, Illinois about 1847.

Rollin A. married Rachel Ann Beaty in 1863, Knox County, Illinois. They had eight children one dying in infancy. Rachel died in 1889. Rollin A. married 2nd Mrs. Jeminia (Collins) Beaty. She had two children, John and Mary. Her husband, a brother of Rachel Ann, had abandoned them.

Rollin A. and Jemima were married December 1894 in McDonough. County. They had Osra Consuella born 1895, Rollin Hobart 1897, Ruth Ione 1899 and Ruby Ann 1900. They were all born in Warren County.

Rollin H. worked on farms around Swan Creek as a young man. In the late 1920's he was working with his brother-in-law, Ed McMullen (Osra's husband) as a carpenter. Winters he picked corn. He married Dorothy Lucille Strickler, October 21, 1932, a descendant of Jacob Strickler, born 1699. He was an early resident of Bucks County, Pennsylvania after arriving in the United States. Dorothy was the oldest child of Harry A. Strickler, born Warren County, Illinois and Inez O. Duncan, born in Schuyler County, Illinois.

Rollin and Dorothy had Harold S., August 17, 1933 and Marie Helen, November 24, 1934, both in Swan Creek. In 1936 they moved near Wataga in Knox County until 1939 when they moved south of Berwick, where Harold and Marie started grade school.

Rollin worked on a farm until January 1944 when he started working at Butler Manufacturing Company in Galesburg, retiring in the early 1960's.

The family moved near Alexis in the spring of 1947, where their children finished schooling at Lone Star School.

Harold graduated from Alexis High School in 1951 and started working at Butler Manufacturing Company in October. He served in the Army from July 17, 1953 to June 6, 1955.

In the summer of 1957, Harold met another country kid, a blue-eyed blonde who lived southwest of Little York, Illinois Mary Lou Davis, born May 3, 1941 in Monmouth, Illinois, the only child of LeRoy W. and Margaret Marie (Roberts) Davis.

Harold S. and Mary Lou were married April 1, 1961 (she picked the date) at her home. They have three children. Harold started working at Admiral's in Galesburg, Illinois, a division of Maytag, in 1968 and retired Jan. 1, 1996.

Harold and Mary Lou are enjoying the outdoors, the Genealogy Library and local history.

ROBERT W. AND PATTY D. PAULSGROVE - Robert W. Paulsgrove was born October 10, 1934 at Abingdon, Illinois. Patty D. (Redding) Paulsgrove was born December 4, 1937. They were married on December 4th 1953 at the parsonage of First Christian Church at Monmouth, Il. Robert Paulsgrove is the son of Lester and Lenora Paulsgrove of Galesburg. His grandparents were Adolphus and Merle Hadley of near Seaton and Oscar and Betty Paulsgrove of Galesburg. Robert's paternal ancestors originated in Germany, his maternal ancestors were from England. Robert attended Galesburg schools as well as rural schools in the Seaton area.

Patty (Redding) Paulsgrove is the daughter of Glen and Gertrude Redding of Monmouth. Her grandparents were George O. and Elizabeth Redding of Aledo and Robert and Edna Wells of Monmouth. Her paternal grandparents were from Mercer County. Her maternal grandparents came to Warren County from Jamestown, Pennsylvania. Her great grandfather Robert Laughlin Wells came to Warren County settling at Roseville in the 1860's. Patty attended Harding Elementary School, Central Junior High, and Monmouth High School, as did her mother before her.

Robert and Patty are the parents of two children, Robert W. Paulsgrove and Nancy D. Paulsgrove both of Monmouth. They also attended Monmouth Public Schools. Robert attended Illinois State University and Nancy attended Illinois College in Jacksonville, returning to Monmouth College to graduate with a degree in elementary education. Robert is employed by Knox County Council for Developmental Disabilities as Associate Director of Manufacturing. Nancy is employed by Monmouth School District 38 and teaches 4th grade at Lincoln Intermediate School.

The Paulsgrove family, 1986. Front row: Robert W., Patty D. Back row: Robert Jr., Nancy D.

Robert and Patty are the grandparents of Erin, Caleb, Sean, and Madyson. They have one great grandchild, Olyvia of Youngstown.

Robert was employed by Outboard Marine Corporation in management for 30 years retiring in 1982. He enjoys many hobbies, woodworking, stamp collecting, traveling, gardening, spending time with his family to name only a few. Patty was employed by Warren Achievement Center, retiring in 1998 after 24 years of service. She enjoys church work, quilting, traveling, gardening, and spending time with her family. The Paulsgroves attend Immanuel Baptist Church. Robert and Patty have lived in Monmouth all their married lives with the exception of a ten-month period right after their marriage when they resided in Galesburg. The Paulsgroves have lived in the same block of Monmouth since 1956, and their children and grandchildren also reside in that same block in Monmouth where the parents have lived for nearly 40 years. Robert and Patty will celebrate their 50th wedding anniversary in 2003.

WILLIAM S. AND ALMIRA N. (HARRISON) PAXTON

- William S. Paxton, (b Dec 22,1811 Rockbridge Co., VA, d May 27,1900, Shelton, Greeley Co., NE) was the son of William and Margaret (Struthers) Paxton, He married ca 1854, Birmingham, Erie Co, OH, Almira N. Harrison (b April 7, 1815 Amsterdam, Montgomery Co., NY, d April 10, 1897 NE.)

William was educated in Xenia, Greene Co., OH and from age 16 to 18 worked in the mills. William moved to Sumner Township, Warren Co., IL in Oct. 1831. William next was in the carpenter trade and worked at this occupation until 1854. After that date he engaged in the wagon making trade.

William was a Private in "Company of Captain Peter Butler" during the Black Hawk Indian War in Northern Illinois. Butler's Company was of the "odd Battalion of Mounted Rangers" under Major Samuel Bogart. In 1834, William was Adjutant of the 1st Warren County Regiment of the Illinois Militia and was associated with them until it was disbanded.

As a carpenter and contractor, he erected the first courthouse in Warren Co., IL and returned to Erie Co., OH in 1854 where he lived for 10 years. During the Civil War he "enlisted in the 3rd Ohio Cavalry, but before muster was disabled by falling off his horse, and consequently saw no service in the war."

He was a Presbyterian, old line Whig, and then a Republican. The 1880 Illinois Census indicated that William was a Wagon Maker and they lived in Monmouth, IL. Their child is Ella.

HAROLD WM. PEDIGO

- In 1860, Wm. Craig Pedigo and his family came from Warren County, Kentucky to Warren County, Illinois. He and his family came by boat down the Barren River, Green River, Ohio River and up the Mississippi River to Burlington, Iowa. The family settled in the "Scotch Town" area northwest of Cameron, Illinois.

George Luther Pedigo was the 6th child of Wm. Craig Pedigo and George Elmer Pedigo was George L. Pedigo's only child.

Ruth M. Yenerich Pedigo and Harold William Pedigo, 1987.

George Elmer Pedigo married Louesa O. Latham in 1909. Their children: Mary E. Armstrong, Gwendolyn L. Walker; George E.T.; Harold W.; Clarence L.; Robert A.; Betty J. Grove; Hollis E.; and Jack A. All six sons and one daughter, Betty J. Grove, served with the armed services during World War II from 1941-1945. When first married, Elmer sang in the old Palace Theater at 112 East First Avenue, Monmouth, Illinois, and Louesa played the piano. The theater fare was "a reel and a song for a nickel." They made "good money" at this and lived in the newly built Robinson Flats at 220 East Broadway, Monmouth, Illinois. (Long since torn down.)

Elmer's family later moved to Burlington, Iowa, where he was a crane operator in the railroad shops and a Burlington, Iowa Street Car Conductor. During World War I, he was a machinist in the Arsenal Shops at Rock Island, Illinois.

Subsequently they moved to the General Store in Larchland, Illinois. In the store was the post office where Dad processed the mail and carried it to the train at the small depot. In the wintertime, the local men loafed around the potbellied stove telling stories, chewing tobacco and spitting in flat boxes filled with ashes. The store also bought sour cream that was picked up periodically by a Monmouth cream buyer.

In 1922 the family moved to Monmouth where Elmer ran the Pedigo Grocery at 316 East Euclid Avenue. The store was sold to the W. MacDill family. Elmer retired from the Monmouth Post Office after many years of service.

Harold Wm. Pedigo was born January 22, 1916 in Burlington, Iowa. He attended Monmouth Public Schools, Monmouth College and Carl Sandburg College. Harold worked in the Monmouth Post Office for forty-two years, retiring in 1982. He married Ruth M. Yenerich, the music teacher of the Monmouth Public Schools, on June 10, 1941. He was drafted into the army March 31, 1942, and served until October 31, 1945, serving in the Pacific Theater of War.

Harold and Ruth had three children: Carol M. Phoenix, Violinist, teacher and Assistant Concertmaster of the Quad City Symphony Orchestra; James D. Pedigo, Industrial Arts teacher at Illinois School for the Deaf in Jacksonville, Illinois; and Dr. Julia Pedigo, Professor of Voice at Appalachian State University, Boone, North Carolina.

Harold enjoys weaving and building and repairing looms. He belongs to the "Tromp as Writ" Weavers Guild, Buchanan Center for the Arts, Monmouth, Illinois.

LAWERENCE PEPPER FAMILY

- Lena Geneva Kepple, a resident of Warren County all of her life, was born February 26, 1927 at the Phelps Hospital in Macomb. She was the daughter of Ghlee Kepple and Dolly Kramer who were married May 14, 1919. Lena had three brothers Frederick William born June 13, 1924 and Donald Lee and Ronald Ghlee born October 8, 1929. The family lived on a farm east of Greenbush. The parents were divorced May 5, 1939.

Lawerence Pepper family

Lena received her education at Holeman School. The teachers during these years were Maude Mitchell, Harriet Johnson, Oscar Duncan, Minnie Hodges and Flossie Hinman. Lena graduated from Avon High School in 1944 and attended Western State Teachers College that fall.

On July 7, 1945, Lena married Lawerence Edward Pepper in Roseville. Lawrence was born April 19, 1924 in Seaton, son of Walter Pepper and Mary Davis Pepper. He had a brother Leonard, born March 20, 1920 and a sister Mary Fullerton born March August 11, 1921.

After Lawrence and Lena's marriage, they farmed the Ben Giddings' farm near Monmouth. The following year they rented the Roy Van Riper farm near Kirkwood. In 1954 they moved to a farm near Greenbush where they still reside. In 1966, they bought the George Willard farm. Lawerence retired from farming in 1996.

The couple had five children all born at the Monmouth Hospital. Edward Alan was born April 16, 1948; Michael LaVerne August 1, 1950, Sharon Marie December 1, 1952; Karen Jean, September 14, 1954 and Marvin Dale February 15, 1961. They all graduated from Avon High School. Alan received an associate degree from Canton College. The rest graduated from Western Illinois University, and Dale also received an engineering degree from University of Illinois and his Masters from Lewis University. Alan and Michael are Vietnam Veterans. The Peppers have been active members of the Avon United Methodist Church. Lena joined the church in 1941 and Lawrence joined at Kirkwood in 1946.

Lawerence, after 35 years of being the assessor, retired in 2001. He first worked in

Greenbush Township, then Berwick was added and finally it consisted of Greenbush, Swan and Point Pleasant townships.

Since retirement, the Peppers have enjoyed traveling and the activities of their ten grandchildren.

DONALD WILBUR PERRIN - He was born on Janaury 24, 1932 on a rural route of Seaton, Illinois, a son of Kenneth Dodson Perrin and Dorothy Margaret Lohse Perrin. He has three brothers Robert Leslie Perrin, Raymond Earl Perrin and Jerry Dean Perrin and two sisters Marilyn Louise Perrin and Barbara Elaine (Donald) Owens.

Don Perrin

He attended four grade schools Duck Creek, Brownlee, Old Number 1 and Bald Bluff. He graduated from the Little York High School with class of 1951.

He moved to Monmouth in 1960 and lived at 505 North Sunny Lane, moved to 225 South 2nd Street in 1968 and moved to 1035 East Detroit Avenue in 1988.

On February 11, 1952 he was employed at The Second National Bank as a bookkeeper, was promoted to Head Bookkeeper and then as a Teller. The bank closed in 1964.

He was employed on September 10, 1964 by the Community National Bank in Monmouth as Head Teller. In March 1972 he was elected as Cashier of the bank and served this office for 25 years until his retirement on March 15, 1997. He is still employed as a part time bookkeeper.

On September 10, 1964 he married Winifred Agnes Roche, she died on July 16, 1978 of malignant brain tumor. On June 3, 1988 he married Karen Yvonne Henson Shook.

He has been a Past President of Monmouth Methodist Men, Past Grand Knight of the Monmouth Knights of Columbus having received all 4 degrees and also served as a member of their Honor Guard. He was President of the Monmouth Kiwanis Club twice. He served as the Lieutenant Governor of the 19th Division of Kiwanis from October 1997 thru September 1998. He received the Hixon Fellow award from the Monmouth Kiwanis Club. He was a charter member of the Warren County Illinois Genealogical Society, and served as the first treasurer, He is a Board member of the Warren County Cancer Society and the Warren County Prime Beef Festival.

JOEL AND JONA (WILLIAMS) PERRIN - Joel Robert Perrin was born on Oct. 5, 1960, the son of Robert and the late Josephine Morrell Perrin. He was educated in the Little York Schools and graduated from Yorkwood High School. He worked at his parents' service station in Little York while growing up. Upon graduation he went to work for Munson Transportation as a dispatcher. He was there until they closed and then went to Nestle's Candy Co. in DeKalb, Il. in the same position.

Joel, Jerid, Joshua and Jona Perrin

He married Jona Gay Williams Lloyd on May 14, 1988 in Monmouth, Il. She had been married to Ray Lloyd and had a son Joshua Howard Lloyd born April 15, 1982. Together Joel and Jona have one son, Jerid Christian Perrin. born May 30, 1989 in Monmouth Hospital.

Joshua has twin sons born to Cassis Coons, they are Clayton Riley Lloyd and John William Lloyd born June 30,1999. Jona also worked in the office for Munson Transportation until they closed and now owns and operates her own day care center at their home in Lindenwood, Il.

Jarid plays baseball and other school sports and also plays in the band. Joel is a runner and has competed in several dicathalons in which he ran 2 miles, bicycled for 12 miles and then ran another 2 miles. He also enters in triathalons in which he swims 1/4 a mile, then bicycles 12 miles and runs 2 miles. He has done this for the past four years. He also plays on the softball team at his church.

He and Jona and the children are all active in the Methodist Church.

JOHN AND PEGGY (CHANDLER) PERRIN - John Wendell Perrin is the son of Robert and the late Josephine Perrin. He was born on March 13,1962. He was raised in Little York, attended school there and graduated from Yorkwood High School.

John, Peg, Bradley and Katie Perrin.

He married Peggy Chandler on Oct. 17, 1992. He worked as a dispatcher for Munson Truck lines from the time he got out high school till they closed. He went to work for Starr Trucking and then for DCM Transportation. He is now with Sharkeys Transportation. Peggy worked in the office at the Applegate Nursing Home for a few years and now owns and operates her own day care center out of their home in Monmouth.

They have two children: Bradley Joseph born Aug.12, 1993 in Monmouth and Katie Marie born Feb. 2, 1995 in Monmouth.

Bradley was chosen to be Little Jack Frost in the Christmas Pageant in 1999 and was one of the Backstreet Boys in a talent show at his school. He enjoys playing baseball in Little League. Katie is involved in tumbling and was in the state tournament in 2000 and 2001. She was entered in the "Little Miss" Pageant in Warren Co.in 2000, and 2001 and received the 3rd. runner up in 2002. She also plays Little League. John has been involved in "tractor pulling." He has a M & M UB tractor and has many trophies he has won over the last four years. Peggy and John and their children are very active in the Christian Church in Monmouth.

KENNETH DODSON AND DOROTHY MARGARET (LOHSE) PERRIN - Kenneth Perrin was born May 16, 1908 in Seaton Illinois, son of Alva Perrin and Lula Dodson Perrin, attended local grade school and graduated from the Keithsburg High School. He has one brother John Wilbur Perrin.

Kenneth and Dorothy Perrin

As a young man he helped with a threshing run owned by Leo Perrin. One day they were working at the farm of Lawrence Burns and a young lady was helping serve the dinner to the workers. Her name was Dorothy Lohse, her sister was Irene Burns.

The workers was teasing Kenneth about the young lady that was helping with the meal and they introduced them.

Dorothy Margaret Lohse was born on July 28, 1907 in Gary Indiana, daughter of John Henry Lohse and Alice Fifield Lohse. Dorothy had one brother, John Henry Lohse and three sisters, Lannah Lohse (she died at the age of 11 years) Irene Lohse (Lawrence) Burns and Louise Lohse (Lester) Howe.

Kenneth Perrin and Dorothy Lohse were married on March 1, 1930 in Gary, Indiana. Kenneth worked for the E J and E railroad for a while. Then they returned to Illinois at the start of the depression and lived with his parents north of Seaton, Illinois.

Kenneth Perrin and Dorothy Perrin had six children: Donald Wilbur Perrin, Robert Leslie Perrin, Marilyn Louise Perrin, Barbara Elaine Perrin, Raymond Earl Perrin, and Jerry Dean Perrin. Kenneth worked with the gutter gang in 1934 in construction of the cement highway from the Nicol residence to the Bald Bluff station. He later worked by the month for Elmer Pattison at Duck Creek, Warren Brownlee north of Little York and George Smith in Fall Creek. He and his brother started farming together in 1947. They farmed the farms owned by Clarence Chamberlain until 1960. The death of Mr. Chamberlain caused the farms to be sold. Wilbur and Kenneth held a farm machinery and livestock closing sale on February 23, 1960.

They purchased a house in Monmouth at 505 North Sunny Lane and the family all moved to town on February 29, 1960. Wilbur Perrin and Marilyn Perrin live in the home as of this writing.

Kenneth worked at Munson Feed and Trucking company in Little York for some time, he also was employed Wayne Brothers elevator and Monmouth Implement Company. He enjoyed growing roses.

Dorothy enjoyed raising baby chickens, doing crafts and playing solitare cards She was famous for her raised doughnuts.

Kenneth and Dorothy celebrated 66 years of marriage on March 1, 1996. Dorothy died on November 22, 1996 and Kenneth died on June 18, 1999. They are buried in the Warren County Memorial Park cemetery.

ROBERT AND JOSEPHINE (MORREL) PERRIN - Robert Leslie Perrin was born on April 1, 1933 in Henderson Co. His parents were Kenneth and Dorothy Perrin. His dad was a farmer and Bob worked on the farm and for neighboring farmers until he graduated from Little York High School. In 1953 He went to work for Goff's Service Station in Little York. In 1973 he purchased the station and renamed it Perrin's Service. On Oct. 5, 1958 he married Josephine Morrell in Little York.

Josephine and Robert Perrin

They have two sons Joel Robert born Oct. 5, 1960, and John Wendell born March 13, 1962. Both boys worked at the service station with their folks (Jo was the bookkeeper) until they both went to work at Munson Transportation. With neither boy wanting to take over the service station, Bob sold it after being there for 33 years. He didn't think his retirement was going to affect him too much. He was quoted as saying "I came into this job with nothing and I still have half of it." After selling the station he went to work for Munson Transportation and was there until their close.

Back in 1962 they had the misfortune of seeing their house burn to the ground. Bob was then one of the instigators in starting a volunteer Fire Department for Little York. He has served as a volunteer since then and has been Assistant Fire Chief for 30 years. He is also President of the Board of Trustees at the Methodist Church and has served in many positions there He is a big promoter for the village of Little York and served on the board for eight years. He is also President of the Cemetery board for Little York.

Josephine was the bookkeeper for the service station and also worked as a cook at the school and as caregiver for several individuals around town. Her last position was as activities director at the Applegate Nursing Home. She passed away Oct. 7, 1993 from cancer.

WINIFRED AGNES ROCHE PERRIN - Born on January 5, 1926 at Raritan Illinois, daughter of Timothy Arthur Roche and Mary Winifred St Ledger Roche. She had three brothers, John Joseph Roche, James Donald Roche, Robert Raymond Roche, and four sisters Mary Catherine (John) Grawey, Monica Rose (David) Mackey, Veronica Louise Roche, and Frances Eileen Roche.

Winifred Perrin

She attended three grade schools: Cox, Industry, and Stanley; and two high schools: Media and graduated from Monmouth High School.

Moved to Monmouth in 1945 and resided at 222 South 5th Street. In 1947 moved to 341 South 8th Street and in 1981 moved to 309 North A Street and in 1968 moved to 225 South 2nd Street.

She was employed at Bankers Life Insurance Company when closed, employed at Second National Bank of Monmouth when closed, employed by Johnson & Brown wallpaper and paint store, and was employed at Bowman Shoe Company until forced to leave employment because of sickness.

On September 14, 1968 she was married to Donald Wilbur Perrin at the Immaculate Conception Catholic Church.

She was a member of Altar and Rosary Society of the church and Past President of the Ladies Auxillary of the Monmouth American Legion.

Her main hobby was bowling, and she served as secretary of the league several times. She had a love for baking breads and cooking for family gatherings. She also loved to travel and see the United States points of interest.

She died on July 16, 1978 of a malignant brain tumor.

GRACE (GAWTHROP) PETERSON - Grace Gawthrop was born in Dysart, Tama County, Iowa, March 2, 1902. Parents – Charles C. Gawthrop (1869-1954) and Josephine Holgate Gawthrop (1872-1955). They moved to LaPlata, Missouri when Gracie was still very young. The family moved to Warren County when she was about four. Gracie's introduction to music came on the family's old pump organ. She could play by ear, remembering how her two older sisters worked the pedals while she played. She attended country school and church in the Fairview Center area.

The family moved to Monmouth, where she attended Garfield Grade School, and Monmouth High School, and took a job playing for silent movies at a theater in Monmouth. She began her formal music education at the Monmouth College Conservatory of Music in 1917. In 1920, still a student, her teacher-mentor, Miss Edna B. Riggs, suggested she start teaching piano. Every Saturday was spent teaching scales and simple melodies to children not much younger than herself.

In 1921, she started teaching at Monmouth College. That relationship spanned three generations. In 1922 she received her degree in piano two years later a degree in voice.

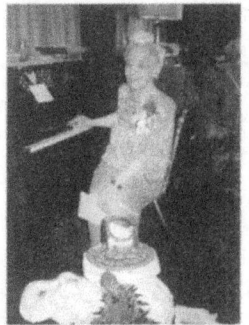

Gracie (Gawthrop Peterson)

Gracie married Harold Peterson, (1896-1962) Monmouth, on December 25, 1925. Soon after their marriage, they started Peterson's Appliance on West First Avenue in Monmouth. During the 1920s, Gracie and her sister, Alice, began performing as the "Gawthrop Sisters," traveling around the Midwest. in the 1940s and 50s, she sponsored the college's Glee Club and organized revues at the Rivoli Theatre in Monmouth. In 1968 she spent 34 days in Europe; the next year Africa, China twice, Australia, New Zealand, Mexico, Hawaii, and countries in South America. She developed travelogues and programs about her favorite musicians; Stephen Foster, Irving Berlin and Victor Herbert. In 1971, she retired from Monmouth College; but the relationship continued as a close one. The front lobby of Wells Theatre bears the title "Gracie Peterson Plaza." She has an archive room of photos and memorabilia that is in Hewes Library at the college. Since 1973 she has been playing piano at Meling's Restaurant, and has played for Monmouth Rotary since 1922.

She is the first woman members of the Rotary. In 1996 she was put in the Guiness Book of Records as the oldest musician still playing professionally. Gracie, now 100 years plus, is still playing at Meling's. She played a concert at the Orphuem Theatre in Galesburg, Illinois to celebrate her 100th birthday; plus she had three other large celebrations, one at Meling's, one at the American Legion, one at the college given by the Crimson Clan. She still lives alone and doesn't know what medicine is; she doesn't take any.

LINDA JOAN PETERSON - Linda Joan Peterson was born on April 10, 1961 to Everett Peterson and Shirley (Hennenfent), at Monmouth Hospital, Monmouth, Illinois, the eldest of two daughters. She grew up in both Henderson and Warren Counties, beginning her education at Biggsville Elementary School for five years and finishing at Warren School, graduating in 1979. She attended Robert Morris College receiving a diploma in secretarial studies in 1980. Becoming more active through the years, she became a Girl Scout at an early age and moved on to chorus ensembles in the 6th through 8th grades and four more years of chorus in high school. Linda was awarded parts in both junior and senior high school plays, served as class secretary for three years and Student Council Secretary for one year. She participated in three years of track and field competition and two years on the pom pom squad. After taking four years of art classes in high school, she maintains an interest in crafting. She has always been very active in the various churches she has attended through the years in various positions and activities.

Linda has one younger sister, Janet Ann Peterson Switzer.

Linda married Stephen Bradley Martin on June 22, 1984 at Heritage United Presbyterian Church in Monmouth, Illinois. Brad is the son of James E. and Sarah J. (Raymond) Martin of Tulsa, Oklahoma. They first lived in Monmouth Township near Cameron, Illinois where their first child Bryan Jordan Martin was born at Community Memorial Hospital in Monmouth, Illinois on 23 August 1986. They made four moves between 1987 and 1995 moving from Illinois to Iowa and back again. Their daughter, Kali Lynn Martin, was born 7 July 1992 at Covenant Medical Center in Waterloo, Iowa. In August of 1998 she and her family made another move to Boca Raton, Florida where they currently reside.

Upon graduating from college, Linda began working as a legal secretary for Hottle & Spears Law Office in June of 1980 where she worked for 11 years. After moving to Clear Lake, Iowa, she became employed by the Ted Enabnit Law Office until May 1992, again as a secretary and as a receptionist at Farm Credit Services in Cedar Falls, Iowa. November 1992 through May 1994. Thereafter, Linda spent about a year and a half as a full time babysitter and is currently a full time mom and volunteer at her daughter's school and her church.

ALEXIS PHELPS - Alexis Phelps was born in Pennsylvania in Palmyra, New York in 1800. He came to Illinois in 1820 settling first near present day Springfield and later at Lewistown.

In 1827 he moved to the Galena area where he became engaged in mining and smelting lead.

He moved to lower Yellowbanks (Oquawka) in 1830 where with his brother Stephen Sumner Phelps they formed the firm of "A & SS Phelps." They engaged in an extensive fur trade with the Sac and Fox Indians and were good friends of Chiefs Tama, Keokuk and Blackhawk. Their brother William established trading stations on the Des Moines River where Farmington and Ottumwa Iowa now stand. William was the husband of Caroline Phelps who wrote a diary of her experiences in the wilderness.

Alexis Phelps married Cornelia Day in 1833 and built this house for their home. It was the first frame house in this part of Illinois. The siding is made from black walnut as were the original shingles.

In 1842 Alexis Phelps contracted to build the Henderson County Courthouse for $1219.00. This courthouse is presently the second oldest courthouse in Illinois still in use.

Stephen A. Douglas presided at the first session of Henderson County Circuit Court in 1841, and returned many times thereafter. While holding court he was often a guest in this home and is reported to have slept in the southeast upstairs bedroom.

Alexis Phelps died December 11, 1846 of a "congestive chill" following a trading trip to the Indians in Iowa. It has been reported that Abraham Lincoln sat with the family at his funeral. Alexis was a member of Oquawka Presbyterian Church and that church's bell was rung for the first time at his funeral. The church and its bell are still in use although it is now the Oquawka Methodist Church.

This house was placed on the National Register of Historic Places in 1982 and has been restored by the Henderson County Historical Society. The house is available for luncheons and receptions by appointment. Please call 768-2403 or 627-2069 for reservations.

DWIGHT R. PIERCE - Pierce, Dwight Randolph, is the oldest child of Dwight Dale Pierce and second son of Marilynn June (Cox) Pierce. Born June 24, 1957, in Peoria, Illinois. Dwight has one stepbrother Richard M. Hidden born 1954, and three brothers: Raymond Dale born 1958, James Russell born 1959, Robert Jason born 1974, and one sister Robyn Marie born 1965. Dwight lived in Peoria until the age of ten going to Peoria elementary schools and then moved to Havana, Illinois, where he attended Havana public schools graduating from the twelfth grade in 1976.

Dwight R. Pierce

After working a few years in construction Dwight began his first day of employment with the Illinois Department of Transportation on January 25, 1979 in Peoria, Illinois. In August of 1990 he transferred to Monmouth, Illinois. Dwight's primary duties with I.D.O.T are sign maintenance, traffic signal repair delineation and reflector maintenance, and mostly operating and maintaining the paint striper. After moving to Monmouth Dwight rented an apartment at 210 North First Street owned by the Palmer's. In 1993 Dwight purchased a home at 705 North "H" Street in Monmouth. While living at the Palmer's apartment Dwight would attend the auctions at Ferrenburg's auction house located behind the apartment and took an interest in collecting, cigarette lighters. Also attending many sales at Simpson Auction House now owned by Jerry and Rose Ballard the collection has grown to several thousands of lighters. Hopefully some day they can be put on public display. Although considered as being taboo or politically incorrect, cigarette lighters are a part of history that has a place in everybody's life good or bad. To end this brief biography I would like to give special thanks to my mother for the many long and hard hours of searching our family history. Thank you Mom.

PITTMAN - In the early 1900's, Albert J. Pittman and three brothers: James, Thomas and Fid came to the Greenbush area to start farming.

Albert (A.J.) Pittman. First residence built late 1800s.

Albert put together an acreage of 318 from what was called wood lots. He grubbed stumps, cleared brush and finally ended with a little over 100 acres of farmland. He raised cattle and hogs and grew crops of oats, corn and various types of hay.

In 1915, he married Bertie Bono from Sheridan, MO. In 1920, they had a son Stephen Albert. His mother died at childbirth and the Frank Beckners raised Stephen until he was school age at which time he returned home to live with his father. Stephen attended the Starr Country School.

In 1940, Stephen married Corene F. Rood. She came from a family of seven daughters. In 1945, their son Larry Leroy was born. Stephen passed away May 23, 1959 at Iowa City Hospital after prostate cancer surgery.

Larry attended Youngstown and Swan Creek Country Schools

In 1961, Corene married Leo M. Koller, and a daughter, Roxann, was born in November.

Larry graduated from Avon High School in 1963. He attended technical school in Quincy. Upon leaving school, he joined the U.S. Air Force and went to Viet Nam. After his return, he was employed by Centel Telephone Co.

In 1970, he married Ruth Ann Herrick of Abingdon, IL. A son, Kent Allen was born July 14, 1974. He is employed as an R.N. at the Methodist Hospital in Peoria, IL.

In the early 1990's, Larry began having health problems which were related to Agent Orange from his service in Viet Nam. His kidneys failed and he was on dialysis for over four years. He lost his battle on November 18, 1999.

DANA L. AND JANICE (JONESON) POOLE - Poole, Dana Lloyd was born Dec. 26, 1960, Monmouth. Dana is the son of David and Lillian Poole of Monmouth.

Dana married Janice Sharon Joneson on Aug. 11, 1984 at the First Lutheran Church in Galesburg.

Dana has two sisters and one brother. DeAnn Cialdella resides in Tinley Park, Il. Nancy Kuhnkey resides in Kansas City, Kansas. David Poole III resides in Garland, Texas.

Janice Poole (March 14, 1962, Galesburg) is the daughter of the late Lloyd Joneson and Ruth Olsen Joneson of Galesburg. Janice has two sisters. Christine Wehrli resides in Peoria, Il. Sandra Neuleib resides in New Windsor, Il.

Dana graduated from Warren High School, 1979. Janice graduated from Galesburg High School, 1980. They both attended Carl Sandburg College. Dana graduated in 1981, and Janice in 1983. Dana was student representative to the Board both years. Janice and Dana were both in *Who's Who Among Students of American Junior Colleges.*

Dana L. Poole family

They have four daughters; Madeline Jane (June 4, 1995), Emma Mae (Nov. 10, 1999), Nicole Christine (Nov. 10, 1999), and Melissa Abigail (Mar. 26, 2001).

Dana and Janice recently purchased 1441 100th St. in Lenox Township from his cousin, Frances Conway. Formerly owned by Frances's grandmother, Dell Ray, who would have been Dana's great, great Aunt. While remodeling their home in Lenox Township they are living at 1625 W. Knox Rd., Galesburg, Il.

Dana is employed by Monmouth College as well as engaged in farming. He is also a partner in Poole's Painting & Decorating.

Dana and Janice attend Fairview Center Church.

DAVID AND LILLIAN POOLE - Poole, David L., born Aug. 25, 1925, Carlinville, Il. is the son of the late David Poole of Carlinville, Il. and Mollie Jackson of Carlinville. After his parents divorced he was raised by Michael and Helen Clifford Seyfrit. He served in the 5th Division, U.S. Marine Corps during World War II, and was at the foot of Mt. Suribachi on Iwo Jima when the U.S. flag was raised there. He married Lillian Mae Parrish (born Dec. 3, 1926, Monmouth) on Oct. 26, 1946. Lillian was the 9th child out of ten born to Willard L. and Abigail Russell Parrish.

David and Lillian Poole

David and Lillian purchased the Russell place from her mother and uncle, Earl J. Russell. Their home is the oldest brick home in Lenox Township. Lillian's great grandfather, Jonathan Russell had the house built by the Rinker brothers after the first frame house burned. Mr. Russell bought brick (formerly in a street) from Galesburg. It was delivered by horse and wagon. The family lived in the loft of the cow barn while the house was being built. It was built in 1874. It was considered very modern because it had a churn run by a gas-powered belt, also a washing machine. The wheels that ran the belts are still in place – no longer used, of course.

David attended Carlinville High School. Lillian graduated from Monmouth High School 1944 and attended Blackburn College when it was junior college. She is now a member of the Blackburn Alumni Board. She met her husband in Carlinville while he was the leader of a dance band, Swing Masters. Her college friend, June Landes Adams, who played in the band, introduced them.

David has played in many bands since moving to Monmouth. He farms, also paints, and adds a little music when time. He's a partner in Poole's Painting & Decorating.

Lillian has served on the Warren County Board of Review (first woman on the board). She also holds a real estate license with Maple City Realty and is a multi-township assessor for Berwick, Floyd, and Lenox townships, the first woman to hold this job in these townships. Years ago her grandfather, Charles Russell was the Lenox Township assessor. She has been very active in United Methodist Women, and the District Methodist Women. Lillian is a member of Holy Hilarity Clown Troupe.

They have three children and raised four, DeAnn Cialdella (Sept. 24, 1955), David Poole III (Mar. 8, 1957), Dana (Dec. 26, 1960) (wife, Janice). They raised Nancy Calson Kuhnkey (husband, Phil) (Dec. 14, 1950) after her mother passed away.

They have 8 grandchildren, Brandon (wife Teresa) Kuhnkey (Jan. 2, 1974), Brian Cialdella (Jan. 27, 1987), Alison Cialdella (May 13, 1989), Nicholas Cialdella (June 26,1992), Madeline Poole (June 4,1995), Emma Poole (Nov. 10, 1999), Nicole Poole (Nov. 10,1999), and Melissa Abigail Poole (March 26, 2001).

David and Lillian are members of Fairview Center Church. David has served as trustee and he and son Dana did the finishing job on all the pews of Fairview Center Church and all the painting of the walls and ceiling.

Lillian teaches her adult Sunday School Class.

THOMAS LIVINGSTON PORTER - Thomas Livingston Porter was born 26 November 1856 on the family farm in Sumner Township to Robert Wray Porter and his second wife, Nancy Robb. Robert Wray Porter's first wife, Annie Matthews (Doyle) Porter had died 27 December 1854, leaving five young children. His brother, Judge John Porter and his wife Mary Ellen (Robb) Porter lived up the road and Mary Ellen's older sister, Nancy was living with them. She had come to Illinois to marry another but the engagement was broken. Nancy stayed with the family to help and she and Robert Wray Porter were married 29 January 1856 back in their old hometown, Alexandria, Huntington County, Pennsylvania. Robert Wray Porter was born in Huntington County on 10 April 1822 to James Porter and Sarah Wray and died in Sumner Township on 15 December 1899. Nancy was born 28 December 1817 in Huntington County and died 7 April 1894.

Nancy and Robert Wray had Thomas Livingston Porter and a daughter Annie Matthews Porter born 1 November 1858.

The family attended the Norwood Church and Robert Wray is buried there with both of his wives.

Fannie Lucie McCutchan also attended the Norwood Church, the daughter of William McCutchan and Rachel McClelland. She was born across the line in Mercer County 23 November 1861. She had a younger brother, Frank, born 15 April 1863. William McCutchan was born in Adams County, Ohio on 21 December 1831 to Robert McCutchan and his wife Mary Glasgow Finley and died 8 April 1907 in Monmouth. Elizabeth Rachel McClelland was born 20 October 1836 in Washington County, Pennsylvania to Richard McClelland and his first wife Susannah Brownlee and died in Monmouth on 12 July 1917. William and Lizzie were married in Mercer County, 14 December 1859.

Thomas Livingston Porter attended Monmouth College and then studied law under his uncle, Judge John Porter. Fannie Lucie McCutchan graduated from Monmouth College in 1886. On 6 June 1888 Tom and Fannie were married at the Norwood Church and moved to Alma, Nebraska. There they raised their family and lived and were buried.

POULSON, SAMUEL - Poulson, Samuel, was the son of Elias and Margaret Wilson Poulson. He was born in Indiana in 1849. He came in a covered wagon to Iowa. He married Louisia LeMasters in 1875. They moved to Illinois in 1906 and he farmed until he retired, moving to Monmouth.

Cornelius Samuel Poulson family, picture taken in 1933. (l. to r.) Seated on grass: Floyd Huffman, George Abel Poulson, Daniel Huffman, Richard Poulson and Theda Thompson Blake. Front row: Minnie Poulson Jones, Irene Poulson Brown, Paul Huffman, Violet Huffman Freed, Anna Poulson Thomas, Florence Poulson Patch, Jewel Poulson Winters, Howard Poulson (holding Jewel's shoulders), Margaret Thompson Fancher and Wanda Huffman White. Middle row: George William Poulson, George William Cornelius Poulson, Beatrice Thompson Scott, Ada Poulson, Lillian Poulson Huffman, Ruth Geneva Poulson Mackey, Minnie A. Roberts Poulson (holding Robert Blackman and Margaret Blackman Reitman), unknown, Ellen Brown Poulson (holding Dorothy Poulson Bohlander) Ethel Poulson Blackman and Ruth Thompson. Back row: Lee Arthur Poulson, Harry Oscar Poulson, Hugh Edward Poulson, Emma Brown Poulson (holding John Poulson), Cornelius Samuel Poulson, Harry Poulson (son of Cornelius), Blanche Poulson Thompson and Ira W. Blackman.

They had eight children, one of which was George W. He was born September 3, 1877 and married Minnie A. Roberts on January 3, 1901. He farmed and lived in Warren County for 50 years. They had six children. Mrs. Grant Mackey, Jr. is still living and resides at rural Monmouth. His oldest child, George W.C. was born October 8, 1901. He married Minnie Ellen Brown in Little York on February 6, 1924. He was a livestock and grain farmer in his later years. He broke horses and trucked in his early years. They had fifteen children, all born in Warren County.

The eldest Minnie and family lived in Warren County for a time, and she now lives in Hannibal, Missouri. She had three children. The second child, Jewel, married Leo Winters a Warren County resident. They had four children, Terry, Mary Beth, Bobby and Paul who all graduated from Monmouth High School. They now reside in Galesburg, Illinois. Irene, the third child, moved to California in 1954. She had three sons, but is now deceased. Anna, the fourth child, married Donald Thomas also a Warren County resident and resided in Monmouth for several years before building a home in rural Warren County. She had four children but is now deceased.

Her husband and two sons, Donald and Ronald, still live in rural Warren County. Her youngest daughter, Kae, lives in Monmouth. George A, the fifth child, was killed in the Korean Conflict. Dorothy, the sixth child, married James Bohlander a Warren County resident. She had two sons and now lives in Galesburg, Illinois. Rose, the seventh child, married Ronald Millard a Warren County resident. After retiring from the military, they built a home in rural Warren County and lived there until Ronald passed away. Rose had two daughters and now lives in Galesburg, Illinois. Phil, the eight child, married Mary Ann Payne and they lived in Monmouth for several years. They had three children. He now resides in Oquawka, Illinois with his second wife Bonnie. He served in the military for three years.

David, the ninth child, was in the Marines for five years. He married his wife, Jean, and they had four children. He lived in Wisconsin for several years and has since moved back to rural Warren County. He is a salesman for Yemm. Marjorie, the tenth child, moved to California many years ago. She had five sons and is now deceased. Sharon, the eleventh child, is married and had four children. She now lives in Abingdon. Becky, the twelfth child, married and lives in California. She had one son. Joy, the thirteenth child, is married and lives in Macomb. She had two children. June, the fourteenth child, still lives in Warren County and had two daughters. Alice, the fifteenth child, has always lived in Warren County. She has one son.

There are many nieces, nephews, cousins, grandchildren and great-grandchildren still living in Warren County.

DR. ROY B. AND GERTRUDE PRICE -
Price, Dr. Roy B. came to Monmouth in 1942 to begin his veterinary practice after graduating from Iowa State College with a Doctor of Veterinary Medicine Degree in 1941. His bride, Gertrude Kingsbury also graduated from Iowa State that year with a BS Degree in Home Economics.

They were married in Davenport, Iowa on 4 April 1942. Roy practiced one year in Seaton, Illinois. Gertrude was teaching high school home economics in Whiting, Iowa. She joined Roy in Monmouth in June of 1942. They resided most of their lives at 1202 North Main Street where they raised their children: James Roy, Susan Jean, and Diana Lynn.

Roy Benjamin Price was born on 10 November 1915 in Effingham County, Illinois. His father was Si Roy Price, son of George William Price and Martha Susan Lewis of Jasper County, Illinois; his mother was Mary Belva Dyson, daughter of Benjamin Franklin Dyson and Dolly Jane Mahaney of Jasper County, Illinois. Roy's father was also a veterinarian who practiced in Effingham, Jasper, and Clay Counties of Illinois.

Dr. Roy B. and Gertrude Price, exact date unknown

Gertrude Flossie Kingsbury was born on 3 September 1918 in Story County, Iowa. Her father was Frank Weldon Kingsbury, son of Horatio William Kingsbury and Sigourney Mabel Taylor of Story County, Iowa; her mother was Birdie Ollie Brooks, daughter of Steven Armine Brooks and Lorena Mabel Clarke of Polk County, Iowa.

Dr. Price had his veterinary office at East Is' Street and later he built a building to the south of his residence on North Main Street where he practiced until he retired December 31, 1976. Dr. Price and his family also were involved in farming and raising popcorn. The Maple City Hybrid Popcorn Company was born in 1954. He owned a farm near Little York where he grew the popcorn. The new office building was also to accommodate the processing of the popcorn. The faily continued with the Maple City Hybrid Popcorn Company until 1970.

Gertrude used her teaching degree as an adult education teacher at Warren High School. Then in 1963 she stepped up to fill the Dean of Women position at Monmouth High School. She continued in this position until her death, on 24 September 1967.

After Roy retired from his veterinary practice he continued to farm northwest of Monmouth where he had built a new home. In 1978 he married June Haley. They lived west of Monmouth until Roy died on 9 January 1982. He died on the farm doing what he loved, caring for his animals.

Roy and Gertrude Price are both buried at the Memorial Park Cemetery in Monmouth.

Presently James is an Episcopalian priest, married to the Rev. Susan Parry Daniel of Dallas, Texas. They live and work in Pittsburg, Texas. James has one son, Samuel R.W. Price, and five stepchildren.

Susan married first, William P. Ryner. They had three children, Mark, Paulla, and Cory Ryner. Susan is presently married to William D. Alexander and living in Muncie, Indiana.

Diana L. is presently living and working in Monmouth.

WALTER EARL PRICE -
Price, Walter Earl, eldest child of Frederick Franklin and Emma Matilda (Strand) Price, was born February 16, 1897, Kelly Township, Warren County, Illinois and died January 8, 1982, at Aledo, Illinois. He was the fourth generation of Prices to live in Kelly Township graduating June 25, 1913, from Starr School and May 30, 1917, from Alexis High School. His great-great-grandfather, Jacob Price (born November 15, 1805, Virginia; died February 19, 1890; buried in Potter Cemetery, Kelly Twp., Warren Co., IL), came from Fayette County, West Virginia, with his wife Rebecca (Walkup) Price (born 1809, Virginia) whom he'd married October 9, 1832. Their sons were Stuart (born January 1836) and Henry (born February 15, 1838; died June 28, 1910, Riverton, Nebraska), and their daughters Lizzie A. (born 1842), Virginia (born 1844), Sarah E. (born 184), and Rebecca (b. 1853). Jacob bought 160 acres in Section 15 of Kelly Township, Warren County, Illinois in 1853 and lived there nearly four decades. On the farm were raised cattle, horses, pigs, wheat, corn, oats, Irish potatoes, hay, butter and molasses. The farm passed to Jacob's son Stuart, to his grandson Frederick and to his great-grandsons Walter, Alvin, and Wilbur. It is currently owned by Alvin's son, Delbert Price, who lives near Alexis, Illinois.

Walter Earl and Laura (Adcock) Price

Walter Earl Price's maternal grandparents, Charles Gustav and Elizabeth Carlson (Johnson) Strand were married January 8, 1876 in Galesburg, Illinois, having immigrated to the United States from Sweden about 1870. Besides Emma Mathilda, they had a daughter Minnie Almedia (Mrs. Robert Smith St. George) and a son Emil Ed Strand.

On February 19, 1924 at Central Church, Galesburg, Illinois, Walter Earl Price married Laura Adcock, born September 8, 1896 (died February 10, 1980, Aledo, Illinois), daughter of Notley Thomas Adcock and Mary Drusilla (Adcock) Adcock. Laura graduated magna cum laude from Knox College, Galesburg, Illinois with the class of 1920. Walter and Laura Price lived on a farm in Coldbrook Township, Warren County, Illinois where Walter farmed a total of 320 acres in Coldbrook and Kelly Townships until his health failed in 1969. Walter was a breeder of Scotch Shorthorn cattle and a director of the Illinois Shorthorn Association. Four children were born to Walter and Laura: Mary Emma (Mrs. Gerald M. Aubertin) (born April 25, 1931), Carbondale, Illinois; Alice Lucille (Mrs. Danny L. Hare) (born October 23, 1933), Viola, Illinois; Charles Francis (born February 14, 1936, died July 15, 2000); Esther Anne (Mrs. Louis W. Patrick) (born January 15, 1938), Joliet, Illinois. The daughters of Walter and Laura continue to manage the farming of the farmland their parents owned. Daughter Mary Emma Aubertin holds an earned doctorate from the University of Illinois in plant cytogenetics. Daughter Alice Hare, a graduate of the University of Illinois in home economics, continues to breed the Shorthorn cattle that her father raised. Son Charles Price graduated from the University of Illinois in agriculture, was a lieutenant colonel in the Army Reserves, a salesman for insurance and agricultural chemicals, and later owned a restaurant at Williamsfield, Illinois. Daughter Esther Patrick attended Bloomington Normal University before her marriage.

Walter and Laura Price can count a total of 15 grandchildren (7 of them holding advanced college degrees): Catherine Alicia (Aubertin) Harris, Mary Anne Aubertin, David Michael Aubertin, Patricia Louise Aubertin, Cynthia Kathleen (Hare) Kermode, Kenneth Daniel Hare, Charles Nathan Hare, Elizabeth Ann (Price) Peters, Deborah Sue (Price) Roberts, Barbara Jean (Price) Simon, Ellen Jane (Price) Connor, Charles Michael Price, Marie Frances (Patrick) Clements, Beverly Lynn (Patrick) Sills, Rollin Keith Patrick (deceased), and 21 greatgrandchildren.

PRESTON PRENTICE PURLEE - Preston Prentice Purlee was born in LeRoy, Kansas 29 August 1869 while his father, Ransom, was homesteading there with Zink and Mitchell relatives. Soon after, his mother, Margaret Monicle Purlee, took Preston and his older brother Lyle back to Washington County, Indiana where they'd started. There four more children were born: Eugene (1872), Leota (1874), Clyde (1876) and Leslie (1881). Preston taught school and learned to fiddle as a young man.

Preston Prentice Purlee

When he was 26, on 15 December 1895, Preston married Essie Louella Morris, the daughter of Caleb and Mary Carr Morris. Preston and Essie had seven children in Indiana: Dare, b. 14 Apr. 1896; Naomi b. 26 Jan. 1898; Bruce b. 10 Jan. 1902 d. 28 May 1930, Chicago; Frank b. 11 May 1904; Robert b. 29 July 1907 and two additional sons who died in infancy. In 1910 Preston explored parts of Missouri, Arkansas, and Illinois by train and horse, searching for a farm to rent. He eventually chose Alexis, Warren County, party so Essie could be near her sister, Josie, Mrs. Jim Sommers, and partly because W.J. Postlewaite was willing to hire him as a shepherding partner and tenant. In 1918 Preston, Essie, and their two "grown" daughters signed Declarations of Loyalty in Spring Grove Township. Dare and Naomi were both educated as elementary teachers at Western Teacher's College in Macomb.

On 8 Dec 1928, Dare married "Woody" Timberlake (b. 29 April 1905, Corydon, IN) and they had two daughters, Mary Alice and Carol. Frank married Jessie Lawless (b. 28 Jan 1908) 31 Jul 1930 and had a long career as a mailcarrier in Alexis. He and Jessie's three children are Bob, Jerry and Faye.

Robert V. Purlee married Evelyn Jellinger (b. 10 July 1914 Mercer Co.) 1 July 1933 and they had six children: Dudley b. 10 April 1935 d. 7 Jan 1999; Judy b. 8 Dec 1938; Marilyn b. 19 Feb. 1943; John b. 26 Oct. 1944; James b. 1 May 1950; and Joe b. 27 June 1951. He and Evelyn bought land in Mercer County in 1939, farming there until his death in 1959.

Preston farmed near Alexis, then near Seaton in Mercer County, where Essie died in 1940. He finally lived with his daughter Naomi at 718 N. Third St., Monmouth, from 1957 until 15 Sept 1965 when he died from old age's complications. His funeral was held at McKnight Memorial Home in Alexis, and he was buried in Belmont Cemetery near Seaton, Mercer Co., IL.

Preston's descendants living in or near present-day Warren County are: Mary Alice Timberlake McKeague, (Mrs. Robert), Alexis; Jim Purlee, farmer and member, Wells Fargo Bank Board, Galesburg; Judy Purlee McCrery, Abingdon, twice a Congressional candidate; Rob Purlee, undergraduate athlete, Monmouth College; Tracey Purlee Winbigler, (Mrs. John), Monmouth; Sam Purlee, Alexis, farmer and Kelly Twp. trustee; Rob McCrery, farmer, grain-elevator operator, and member of Warren School Board; Joe Purlee, Alexis, army veteran and driver for Eby-Brown; and Dave McCrery III, lawyer and lay-missionary to Mexico.

QUINBY - Ivory Quinby I, one of the early settlers of Monmouth, was born in 1817 in Buxton, Maine. He graduated from Waterville College (now Colby College) in 1836. After briefly teaching at Parsonsfield Academy under his Uncle Hosea Quinby and studying law in Saco, Maine, ill health forced him to travel west in 1837. He was not yet twenty years old. After settling i Monmouth and establishing a law partnership in 1839, he married Jane Allen who died in 1847, leaving three children. All three preceded their father in death. After a brief period of the 1840's in the mercantile business in Berwick, he returned to the legal profession. In 1848, he married Mary E. Pearce of Berwick who became mother of their eight children, four of whom reached adulthood. He was elected judge of the Warren County probate court for one term, played a prominent part in building the predecessor of the Chicago, Burlington and Quincy Railroad, twice served as mayor of Monmouth, and established the Warren County Bank in partnership with T.L. McCoy. Ivory was one of the founders of Monmouth College, the Warren County Library and served faithfully on their boards. He died in 1869.

Ivory Quinby III and Elizabeth Goddard Quinby

Ivory Quinby II, the youngest child of Mary and Ivory Quinby I, was born in 1865, just two days after Lincoln's assassination. He was active in the community, as was his father, giving strong support to the YMCA, the Library Association, the college Board of Trustees, the Board of Education, National Bank of Monmouth, and the Methodist Church. In 1891, he was married to Maggie Gibson, who lived only a few months. He married Inez Jewell of Phelps, Warren County in 1895. Two children, Ivory III and Margaret, were born to this union. He was an avid bicyclist and was a familiar figure for many years as he rode about the town. Much of his business activity was associated with insurance, first with S.S. Hallam, then his son, Frank Hallam, and after 1916 as a respected independent insurer. He died in 1926.

Ivory Quinby III was born in Monmouth in 1896. He attended Monmouth College where he majored in chemistry and lettered in four sports. Upon graduation, he attended the University of Illinois Agricultural School in order to manage the family farms. After briefly serving in the Marine Corps during World War I, he worked in New Mexico for two years in mining exploration. In 1925, he returned to Monmouth to marry Elizabeth Goddard. Employed by Victor Chemical Company, the couple lived in Chicago and Minneapolis during their early years of marriage. After the death of his father, he returned to Monmouth to operate the family insurance business. Two daughters, Jane (1926) and Anne (1934) were born to Ivory and Elizabeth. During World War II, Ivory III taught navigation and code at the Naval Flight Preparatory School at Monmouth College. Like his father and grandfather before him, he served on the school board, several Methodist Church boards, 36 years on the college Board of Trustees, many years on the library board, and was president of the Rotary Club. He died in 1967.

Jane and Anne Quinby now live in Colorado. Jane married Irving Lowell in 1948 and they have 5 children and 7 grandchildren. Anne married John Dyni in 1958 and they have 2 children and 3 grandchildren.

RADAR BROTHERS SANDARD SERVICE - The Rader Brothers Standard Service gas station was located six miles south of Monmouth, Illinois on the west side of highway U.S. 67 at Larchland near the corner. The gas station was built in 1926 shortly after the new highway construction was completed. The station was owned by Joseph and Ella (Apsey) Rader, originally from Monmouth, and was operated by their sons George and Frank. The gas station and their home nearby was on forty acres of ground and the farm land was rented to a farmer in the community.

Standing in front of their newly built gas station in the picture above are George Rader on the left and Farnk Rader on the right. It was built in 1926 on the west side of hwy. 67 six miles south of Monmouth, Ill. at the Larchland corner shortly after the highway was constructed

In the beginning, petroleum products, candy and tobacco were sold at the gas station. In later years, pop, ice cream, milk, bread, work gloves and various other sundries were added to the products available for sale. In 1942 a pool table was added to the station to provide recreation for the farmers of the community. Prior to that, only a card table was available.

Frank Rader became stricken with a serious illness around 1930 and was bedfast for several years until his death. At that time Ralph Lee, a local farmer, started working at the gas station and the business name was eventually changed to Rader's Standard Service. Ralph left employment at the station during the late 1930s and several other local farmers worked part time at the station at different intervals until 1945. During this period of time the brand of petroleum products changed from Standard Oil to Mobile for several years and then to Skelly.

In 1945 Wayne Rader, George's oldest son, started working at the gas station. In 1948 George became an independent operator and installed two large underground storage tanks near the station to allow direct delivery of gasoline from the refinery. The business name was changed to Radar Oil Company and bulk delivery of petroleum products to farmers and homes in a broad area surrounding Larchland was made available. Gas was then sold at a discount price at the gas station. Wyane operated the tank wagon farm and home delivery service function in the business operation until 1952. In February of 1952 he was called to active duty with the Illinois National Guard to serve in that capacity until the end of the Korean War. George discontinued the tankwagon bulk delivery service to farms and homes at that time and continued operating the gas station only until his retirement in 1962. During this period his youngest son Larry Rader, a neighbor and Wayne after his release from active duty, worked part time at the gas station as needed.

George Brooks, a local farmer's son, leased the station from early 1962 until late 1965. He sold Shell petroleum products and added new services included oil changes and tire repair. George Crow, a nephew of George Rader, purchased the gas station, home and farmland in 1965. He operated the station for several years before closing it permanently. He eventually sold the station and farmland to William G. Gillen, a local farmer. The gas station and home were demolished and removed from the land in 1991, when the new four-lane highway was built.

CLIFFORD PHILLIP RAMBACK JR. -
Ramback, Clifford Phillip Jr., son of Cifford Phillip Sr., railroad machinist coming to Monmouth to work at the M&St. L roundhouse in the early thirties after serving in the Navy during WWI. His mother, Helen (Banger) of LaPort City, Iowa, a Methodist choir member graduated from nearby Iowa Wesleyan University. Her father was Post Master. They had two sons Frederick "Fred" born 1926 in Monmouth and "Cliff" 5 July 1922. Both were educated in Monmouth. "Cliff", though very intelligent was the type to try anything, including smoking. He joined at 18 the Navy Reserve at Burlington, Iowa, thus was called to active duty before WWII. "Cliff" worked with turbines below deck in the early battles of the Pacific. After the war he graduated an engineer from the University of Illinois. He joined Murray Division of Trance Company in Burlington as troubleshooter, later becoming assistant Division Manager. In July 1952 while located at Brownsville, Texas, met and married Larue Guthrie. Raised her children – four boys, one girl. All born in Houston, Texas.

Clifford Phillip Ramback Jr. and Sr.

Brother "Fred" managed several large companies – lived Las Altos, California, married Joyce (Klang), eventually caring for his mother when she retired working for the State in Havana when she contracted Alzheimer's. Helen's husband divorced her when sent, during the big depression, as WPA officer to Southern Illinois. She declined to go, thus raised her boys alone. The boys later forgave him.

While in Jr. High "Cliff" and neighbor friend "Buddy" Barnes took a rifle and 410 shotgun to Leary's woods. While there decided to build dugouts by throwing limbs and brush on top - one didn't make it and hit the trigger of the shotgun spraying shot in "Cliff's" face. He spent months recovering at Monmouth Hospital, but survived. North "A" was a wonderful place to grow up. He became "Buddy's " best man at his wedding in Stanwood, Iowa, was Godfather of "Buddy's" daughter Jennifer. Both boys entered Monmouth College. Fred was BMOC, joined Phi Kappa Pi fraternity. He and Joyce raised three boys. "Cliff" 51 and "Fred" were heavy smokers both died of emphysema.

GLENN ORLO RANKIN
- Patricia Ann (Rankin) Brown was born on October 31, 1932 in the home built by her grandfather, William Rankin, located south of Biggsville, Illinois in Henderson County, Illinois. She was the third child born to Glenn Orlo and Ruth Winona (Jamison) Rankin. Glenn O. Rankin followed in the family tradition of farming.

In March of 1943 the Rankins moved to the Sickmon farm in Monmouth, Warren County, Illinois. She was in sixth grade at the time and attended Grier School on the East Broadway Road. Her teacher was Eva V. MacIntyre.

Upon graduation from Grier she entered Monmouth High School from which she graduated in 1950. She graduated Western. Illinois Teacher's College and retired from teaching in 1994 from Clarksville, Indiana.

In 1953 she married Robert Norvel Brown, Chicago, Illinois at the Biggsville United Presbyterian Church. They are blessed with two children: Daniel Robert, born in 1956, Clinton, Iowa, and Josie Ann, born 1959, Chicago, Illinois.

Josie has two children, Justin Allen and Anna Ruth Nelson. Josie is married to Joel Larue Nelson of Salem, Indiana.

Her siblings are Glen Dean Rankin, the oldest child in her family, and Rebekah Hollis (Rankin) Sistler, next oldest.

Fond memories held by her are of the large snowman built by her brother-in-law, Peter Owen Sistler, in the front yard of the Sickmon farm, of a nearly fatal horse ride she had on February 2, 1944.

Both Owen and Glen Dean were in WW II. She recalls vividly, meeting their returning trains at the Monmouth CB&Q railroad station. It seemed an eternity for -the arrivals. Baby Margaret Ann (Sistler) Mitchell, Mrs. Dan Mitchell, Galesburg, Illinois was born in 1944. They had readied her to meet her daddy. They had to take her back home as he did not arrive until later that night.

In later years she would be doing a repeat of the same thing with her husband, Bob as he left and returned with the Navy Reserves.

Monmouth and the area hold many joys and tears for her.

THOMAS RANNEY
- Thomas Ranney was first known in the land records of Middletown, CT. He came from Scotland, and grants were transferred to Thomas Ranney dated in 1663. He died June 21, 1713, and is supposed to be the first one buried in what became Ranney Cemetery on Ranney Street in Cromwell, CT.

Mae Ranney Fredrickson, Bertha Ranney Fredrickson, Bernice Ranney Shike, summer 1950

Five generations later a Stephen Ranney was born in Bethlehem, CT on May 24, 1761. He was in the military and became the first Ranney in that line to come west. In 1827 he died in Jackson, MO.

Seven generations after Thomas Ranney, Royal Ranney was born Dec. 10, 1810, in Hartwick, N.Y. Royal married Betsy Gates on Oct. 10, 1839, in Troy, IL. She died Oct. 16, 1901, at Little York, IL and was buried in Belmont Cemetery in Henderson County. Royal had moved with his parents, Jeremiah and Susan Ranney to Cape Girardeau, MO in 1831. In 1848 he moved to Mercer Co., IL and in 1851 to Little York, IL in Warren Co. He died Nov. 20, 1889, and is also buried in Belmont Cemetery.

Their first born, Susan A. born Oct. 4, 1840, married William E. Smith. Their second child, Nathan Cornelius, was born July 4, 1842. Six more children were born, the youngest being Royal Gilbert, born Sept. 1, 1854.

Nathan Cornelius Ranney was born in Jackson, MO. He married Cecelia Whelan, born Oct. 28, 1848, in Brooklyn, N.Y. They were married in Little York, IL on April 7, 1869. He was a farmer, also an army private in Feb. 1864 in Company C, 91st Illinois Cols. He transferred July 1865 to the 28th Illinois Vols. stationed at Brownsville, TX, and witnessed the Battle of Matamoros. He mustered out March 15, 1866, returning to farming in Warren Co. He died there on Sept. 14, 1906. Eight children were born to Nathan and Emily, the 9th generation after Thomas Ranney.

The 9th generation included William Cornelius Ranney, born in Warren Co. on December 12, 1871. A farmer, he married Hilma

Virginia Johnson, born Dec. 23, 1875. Their marriage took place in Warren Co. on Feb. 20, 1895. To this union were born four children, all born on a farm in Henderson Co., and they constitute the 10th generation.

Clyde William, born May 31, 1896, died May 14, 1913. Bertha Clara born April 15, 1914, died June 1, 2000. Bernice Emily born Oct. 7, 1915. Mae Betty born July 21, 1917, died May 22, 2000.

Bertha Clara married Everett Fredrickson on Dec. 12, 1934. They are the parents of La June, Paul William, and Donald Everett. Bernice Emily married C. Merlin Shike on Dec. 29, 1936. They are the parents of Doris Arlene, Charles Merlin, and Gerald William.

Mae Betty married Pete Fredrickson on Dec. 22, 1937. They are the parents of Lawrence Edward, John David, Peter Michael and Darlene Jo., born in Warren Co.

CLEONE (BARNES) RAWSON

Cleone Barnes was born in Abingdon, Illinois August 8, 1918. The daughter of Renalt (Rennie) and Almyra (Bowton) Barnes. Rennie worked in his fathers General Store in Hermon, Illinois until he moved with his family to Monmouth in 1922. Rennie and his brother Verne began their partnership in the grocery business that would last for the next 61 years. Barnes Brothers Groceteria open for business July 1, 1922 at 216 East Broadway, Monmouth, Illinois.

Cleone (Barnes) Rawson

Cleone graduated from Monmouth public schools and continued her education at Christian College in Columbia, Missouri. She received an Associate Degree from Christian College and completed her bachelor's degree at Monmouth College with a major in English and minor in Spanish. While at Monmouth College Cleone joined the Pi Beta Phi sorority, cultivated her love of reading and met her husband Bob Rawson.

Upon graduation from Monmouth College Cleone worked at her father's grocery store while Bob attended Officers Training School at Columbia University in New York City. Cleone and Ensign Robert Rawson were married December 2, 1943. Bob was stationed in New Orleans and Cleone was able to join him. Bob ended his tour of duty in 1946 at a Lieutenant in the Navy and returned to Monmouth to join the Barnes family Grocery Business.

In 1946 a daughter was born to Bob and Cleone, Rebecca Cleone Rawson and in 1950 a second daughter was born, Cynthia Barnes Rawson. While the girls were growing up Cleone became active in the Phi Beta Pi Alumna organization at Monmouth College, the local chapters of PEO, OGM and her love of reading. Cleone began reviewing books for Viking Press and substitute teaching at the area schools for the next nine years.

Cleone began working with Bob in the Grocery business in 1973 until their retirement in 1983.

Upon retirement Cleone and Bob traveled extensiv~ly in the United States, Canada and Europe. Robert Tubbs Rawson died August 1, 1993 and Cleone Rawson died November 16, 2001 after a battle with cancer.

FREDERICK PAYNE RAWSON

Frederick Payne Rawson was born December 29, 1889 at Lewiston, Maine. The son of Charles Henry Rawson and Bertha Louise Hodgman of West Townsend, Mass. The Rawson family moved to Springfield, Illinois in 1895 where Charles operated a music store, was the leader of a municipal band and developed a piano tuning business. Charles and Bertha, their five boys and one girl lived above the music store until June of 1900. Charles made frequent trips to nearby towns for his piano tuning business, however, in early June of 1900 Charles disappeared and was never heard from again. Bertha moved her family back to Lewiston, Maine to live with their Grandfather.

Frederick Payne Rawson

Frederick and his two brothers attended the Good Will School at Hinckley, Maine for worthy but unfortunate boys and girls who had lost one or both parents. Frederick excelled at The Good Will School and returned each summer to help with camp after he graduated. Frederick entered Bowdoin College in 1912, however, his finances began to run low towards the end of 1914 which necessitated him to look for work in order to complete his education. Frederick met with the International Y.M.C.A. Committee in New York City regarding a teaching job at the Continuation School for Apprentices in Honolulu, Hawaii. Frederick was hired and arrived in Honolulu in September to begin his new teaching job. Within two months Frederick had the school turned around and was promoted to principal.

On December 1, 1916 Frederick joined the National Guard of Hawaii and was assigned to the Machine Gun Company. Beginning the first of January 50 young men that were connected with the Y.M.C.A. hired West Point Officers to come in to tutor them in all phases of military subjects. Frederick was not only successful he was recommended for the commission of 1st Lt. of the Infantry. Frederick was promoted rapidly through the ranks of the military due to his hard work and devotion to his job. Frederick met Ruth Tubbs through mutual friends in Honolulu in the fall of 1916 they were married November 7, 1918 Kirkwood, IL.

The war ended and Frederick and Ruth moved to Peoria, Illinois where Robert was born, December 31, 1920. Ruth and Frederick returned to Kirkwood, IL in 1921. Frederick began selling insurance for Northwestern Life and Ruth taught music in the Kirkwood School System for the next twenty-five years.

World War II came in 1941 and Frederick was called back into service as a Capitan of the Infantry. In 1946 Robert was attending Monmouth College and Ruth was teaching so Frederick set sail for the Philippines alone. The following year Frederick was transferred to Yokahoma, Japan where Ruth was able to join him for the next two years. In 1949 Frederick retired from active military duty as a Lieutenant Colonel in the Infantry. They returned to their home in Kirkwood, Illinois and Frederick died in 1952 after an illness of two and a half years.

ROBERT TUBBS RAWSON

Robert Tubbs Rawson was born in Peoria, Illinois December 31, 1920. The son of Frederick Payne and Ruth Tubbs Rawson. Ruth taught music in the Kirkwood School system and Frederick sold insurance for Northwestern Life.

Robert Tubbs Rawson

Bob was educated in the Kirkwood schools and Monmouth College where he was very active in sports receiving the Turnbull Athletic Scholarship. While in college Bob majored in history, joined the Phi Kappa Pi Fraternity. Bob graduated from Monmouth College in 1942 with honors and was immediately sent to Naval Officers Training School at Columbia University. Upon graduation from Officers Training, as an Ensign, Bob married Cleone Barnes, December 2, 1943 in New York City.

Bob returned home following World War II to join the Barnes family grocery business. Bud Barnes and Bob became partners until their retirement in 1983. Bob's business activities included opening three Super Value Stores in Bettendorf, Iowa, Rushville and Mt. Sterling Illinois and an officer of the National Retail Grocers Association. Community activities included President of the Chamber of Commerce, Chairman of the Industrial Development and Expansion for the City of Monmouth, Chairman of the Monmouth Community IMPACT Campaign for a new library and science building at Monmouth College, Member of the Community Memorial Hospital board for 10 years and served as president for two years and elected Man of the Year in 1974.

Bob and Cleone raised two daughters, Rebecca Cleone and Cynthia Barnes. Both girls attend and graduated from Monmouth Public Schools and continued their college education out of state. Rebecca married Barry Troup and lives in Camp Hill Pennsylvania and Cynthia married Bill Gillen and lives south of Monmouth. Bob and Cleone have four grandsons, David and Scott Barr and Patrick and Nicholas Gillen.

Robert Tubbs Rawson died August 1, 1993 at his residence in Monmouth, IL.

RUTH TUBBS RAWSON - Ruth Tubbs Rawson was born in Kirkwood, Illinois, April 17, 1887. The daughter of Willard Clark Tubbs and Emma Smith Tubbs. Willard Clark Tubbs was the President and C.E.O. of the National Bank of Monmouth. Emma Smith Tubbs was a homemaker. Ruth attended Kirkwood Public Schools, graduating from High School in 1906. While attending Monmouth College she studied voice under the direction of Professor Merrill Austin, graduating in 1909. While attending Monmouth College Ruth became active in the Kappa Kappa Gamma Sorority.

Ruth Tubbs Rawson

Following graduation Ruth visited friends and family in Upland, California and was asked to give a program at the Upland Schools. The principal immediately asked Ruth to return the following year to teach and direct the music program in the school system. The next two years of Ruth's life were spent in Upland, California teaching music. In her spare time she directed the choir in the Methodist Church and sang in a quartet.

The following year Ruth continued her education in New York City at the Julliard School of Music where she studied both voice and piano. The summer of 1915 Ruth returned to Illinois before accepting a teaching position in music at a private girls school at the Kawaiahuu Seminary in Honolulu, Hawaii. Ruth was offered the position as soloist in the Congregational Church in downtown Honolulu and preformed many musical recitals. Her two years spent in Hawaii were filled with many wonderful memories and the opportunity to meet her husband Frederick Payne Rawson. Frederick was teaching at the trade school in the Y.M.C.A. in Honolulu.

World War I began and Frederick was assigned to the second Infantry at Ft. Shafter. Ruth returned to the states in 1918 and was married November 7, 1918 in her home in Kirkwood, Illinois. The war ended and Frederick and Ruth moved to Peoria, Illinois where Robert was born, December 31, 1920. Ruth and Frederick returned to Kirkwood, Illinois in 1921. Frederick began selling insurance for Northwestern Life and Ruth taught music in the Kirkwood School System for the next twenty-five years.

World War II came in 1941 and Frederick was called back into service. Robert was attending Monmouth College and Ruth finished the school year before she joined Frederick in Florence, South Carolina. In 1946 Frederick sailed for the Philippines and Ruth returned to Kirkwood. Frederick was promoted to a lieutenant Colonel in the army and was sent to Japan for the Army of Occupation the following year. Ruth and Frederick left for Yokahoma, Japan in October of 1947 for the next two years. In 1949 Frederick and Ruth returned to America and Frederick died in 1952 after an illness of two and a half years.

Ruth spent her remaining years in Kirkwood living next door to her sister Lelah. She continued to travel throughout the world, her love of music, family and friends until she died in January 15, 1985 at the age of 97.

MARSHALL BEDFORD AND NANCY C. (RAY) RAY - Marshall Bedford Ray was one of the large landowners and a successful farmer who resided in section 26, Lenox Twp. and was the son of Garland and Sarah (Lee) Ray, native of Kentucky.

Marshall Bedford Ray and Nancy C. Ray, wife of Marshall B.

His parents came to this county in 1835, and take rank among its pioneer settlers. They first located Roseville Twp, where they resided for about a year, then they moved to Lenox Twp., residing there until death. Sarah Ray died 2-24-1868 and Garland Ray died 4-12-1881. They had 10 children: Amelia A., Harriet E., Henrietta M., James W., Marshall B., Eletha, Clarinda J., Julia A., Susan A. and Nancy Elizabeth.

Marshall Bedford Ray cemetery stone

Marshall Bedford Ray was born in Edmonson Co., Ky., Feb. 6, 1828 and was nine years old when he came with his parents to this county where he, too, lived until his death. He was the owner of over 1200 acres. All but 30 acres of this ground was tillable. 210 of those acres were in Roseville Twp. the rest in Lenox Twp., Warren County, Illinois. His home farm was 500 acres with about 100 head of cattle, 20 head of horses and colts and he fattened about 100 head of hogs annually. He had married Miss Nancy C. Ray on 9-5-1850. Nancy was the daughter of John and Sarah Ray, natives of Kentucky. Marshall and Nancy were blessed with 10 children: Richard H., Emeline, Laura J., Letitia, John L., Theodosia, Mary, Hiram, Hattie, and Martha (deceased). Those who lived in Lenox Twp were Richard, Emeline (Mrs. Tilford Rice), John, Theodosia (Mrs. William Parrish), Mary (Mrs. Theo C. Alexander), Hiram and wife Delia Jane (Eaton) Ray, Hattie (Mrs. Martin Landon) of Berwick Township. Laura (Mrs. John Chapman) and Leititia (Mrs. William Cane) lived in Iowa.

Mr. Ray has held the office of Highway Commissioner and Overseer of Highways. He was a Democrat. He and his wife were early member of the Baptist Church. June 1877, Garland Ray gave the first land in Lenox Twp. for Union Cemetery. In 1898 Garland's son Marshall Bedford Ray deeded the first addition to that Cemetery.

Marshall Bedford's tombstone contains a massive red granite ball 12 feet in circumference and 3'8" feet in diameter. It sets on a base that reads "Ray." It stands about 6'6" tall. The monument was imported from Italy and shipped up the Mississippi to Oquawka.

Marshall and the others went to Oquawka with teams and wagons and brought the ball and base to the Union Cemetery. Marshall saw the stone set before his death. Garland Ray's stone is the tall white stone in background. Small flat stones are used to identify each of Marshall Ray's family members buried in his lot.

Hiram and Delia Ray had one son Walla Edward, born 9-20-1896 who died at age 2 of pneumonia and a daughter Sena Elizabeth born, 2-27-1895 who would later marry David R. Smith. For a continuation of David and Sena Smith family look elsewhere in this book under David and Pearl Smith.

Submitted by Virginia Greiner, Fairfield, IA.

W. DONALD AND HARRIET RAY - Wilbur Donald Ray was born December 6, 1932, in Monmouth, Illinois. Harriet Albin was born November 16, 1938, in Decatur, Illinois. They were married Deceber 23, 1961, at the Illini Congregational Church located near Warrensburg, Illinois. They have three sons and a daughter. Douglas Donald is married to Sue Metz May. They have five children: Sarah, Aaron, Ashley, Megan and Josh. Doug graduated from the University of Illinois and is a farm manager. Mark Allan is engaged to marry Abbie Belshaw Harrison. Mark graduated from Western Illinois University and works for 1st Farm Credit Services. Jeffrey Phillip, the youngest son, graduated from the University of Illinois. Jeff spent two years in Ukraine as a volunteer and working for a joint agriculture venture. He earned his master's degree from Purdue University. Jeff is employed by Prudential. Karen Marie, a beautiful daughter, was born 1972 and died in 1997. She gave the Ray family something very special.

Don's parents are Wilbur Ray and Doris Bullwinkle. The Rays came to Illinois via Kentucky from England. They settled near Berwick. Wilbur's mother was Lillian Taflinger who came to Illinois via Indiana. Doris's father came to Illinois on an orphan train from New York. Her mother was Maggie Albert.

Harriet's parents are Orville Albin and Estella Holderness. The Albins came from Scotland and Ireland in the early 1700s settling in Virginia. Several brothers moved to Ohio. After serving in the Civil War, Orville's grandfather settled near Decatur. He took his family to near Sac City, Iowa, but when the grasshoppers devoured his crops and his wife and child died, he returned to Macon County. His wife (surname Bartch) had come to the United States with her parents and sister from western Germany in 1852. Orville's grandfather remarried (his first wife's sister) and seven more children were born. Orville's mother was Flora Watkins (Watkins came from England early in this country's history). Estella's grandparents, Holderness, came from England. Her mother, Elisa Wagner, came from Germany, at the age of 19.

W. Donald Ray family, March 28, 2002.

Don has three sisters and one brother: Mary Ann, Jane, Joyce and Wayne. Harriet has two sisters and one brother: Betty Norma and Richard.

Don graduated from Monmouth High School in 1951. He attended Ag Short Courses at the University of Illinois. He served in the Army in Germany for a year and a half. When he returned from the Army in 1955, he began his farming career.

Harriet graduated from Warrensburg-Latham High School in 1956 and from the University of Illinois (Business Education) in 1960. Her first teaching position was at Monmouth High School. In 1989, she returned to teaching at Warren School. She took graduate courses at ISU in computer technology and computer applications to keep abreast of rapidly changing technology.

Don and Harriet are members of the Fairview Center United Methodist Church. Don and Harriet have been active in their church and community organizations.

ABIGAIL T. RAYMOND - In the McMahill Graveyard in Greenbush Twp. of Warren County, now located on Little Swan Lake, you will find a lovely old headstone marking a burial in 1871. This is the final resting place of my great-grandmother, Abigail T. (Stone) Alvard Raymond Chase. The inscription reads as follows: Abigail T., wife of S. Raymond, Died Feb. 4, 1871, Aged 70y 7m 9d, "Her toils are past, her work is done. And she is (not legible) She fought the fight the vicory won And entered into rest."

This early pioneer woman was born June 26, 1800, the daughter of Lyman Stone. In Huron County, Ohio, Vol. I O.S., page 128, a marriage certificate filed and recorded Feb. 1825, Nathan B. Johnson, E.F. (not in record) Probate Judge, on 20th February, 1825, solemnized the marriage of Simeon Raymond and Mrs. Abigail S. Alvard, which was also his second marriage.

Simeon was drowned rafting logs in 1847, leaving three children: Thaddeus born ca. 1828 in Ohio (see Census of 1880 for Raisinville Twp, Monroe County, Michigan) Louise (who married a Mr. Rothwell and lived for a time in Muscogan, Illinois), and eleven-year-old Simon Martin Raymond born 23 Sept. 1836, Monroeville, Huron County, Ohio.

Abigail T. Raymond, about 1850s.

Following the death of Simeon Raymond, Abigail married a third time to a Mr. Chase and they had two sons, half-brothers to Simon M.

I have heard the story that Mr. Chase would not allow the name "Raymond" to be spoken in their home. It is unknown when Abigail came to Illinois. In her final years, Simon brought his ailing mother to live with him in Walnut Grove, where she died in McDonough County, Illinois. Her epitaph was Simon's final word!

CHARLES VILASCO RAYMOND - Charles Vilasco Raymond was born 5 Nov 1890 near Walnut Grove, Illinois, eighth child of Simon Martin Raymond (1836-1909) and second wife, Sarah Elizabeth Foresman (1855-1936), married Ruby May Thomson (1894-1978) on 24 December 1919, in Bushnell, IL. Charlie died on 20 Dec 1964, in Macomb McDonough Dist. Hospital and is buried with his wife in the Forest Lawn Memorial Gardens, Masonic Division, Macomb, Illinois.

Charles V. Raymond family, July 27, 1947. Martin, Lyle, Keith, Roland, Reta, Ruby, Charles V. Raymond, Sarah

C.V. Raymond was a "family man". His father, Simon M. Raymond, died when Charlie was 18 years old and he promised him he would always take care of his mother, Sarah E. Raymond, until her death as well as raise his younger three siblings still living at home. He had helped his father in the grain elevator, worked as a farmhand and as a clerk for Tucker's General Store before serving in the US Army.

He served in WWI as Corporal in US Army in Co "B" 54th Ammunition Train. On duty with American Expeditionary Forces in France 1918 to 1919, inducted 2 Apr 1918 and honorably discharged 4 Mar 1919. His three oldest sons also served their country in WWII. Martin and R. Lyle in U.S. Navy and D. Keith in U.S. Army.

He returned from France following WWI and married the local school teacher, Ruby May Thomson. They were parents of six children. Martin Vilasco born 13 Nov 1920, Richard Lyle (Barney) born 27 July 1923, Donald Keith (Ick) born 18 Aug 1925, Reta May born 28 March 1927 (wife of Jack H. Mariner), Roland Curtis (Sol) born 12 May 1929, and Sarah Joan born 8 Sept 1936 (wife of James E. Martin).

They farmed at various locations in McDonough County, Warren County and Fulton County. Charlie farmed in Greenbush Township 1930 to 1940, land owned by Hugh Crawford then William Funcheon, now part of Little Swan Lake and location of the McMahill Graveyard, burial site of Raymond ancestors. Over 30 years Charlie served as president of the cemetery association, finally getting it under Perpetual Care by State of Illinois a year before his death.

In 1943, Charlie rented the Della Bishop Farm in Swan Township, until retirement in 1957 and moving to Bushnell, Illinois. Charlie, a Pioneer Seed Corn salesman for over 20 years, annually earned a Pioneer turkey enjoyed by his family on Christmas as well as trophies now treasured by his family. He has 22 grandchildren, many great-grandchildren and great-great-grandchildren, some living in Warren County in 2002.

He became ill and passed away only 4 days prior to celebration of their 45th Wedding Anniversary, which would have been Christmas Eve of 1964. He attended school at Walnut Grove. He was a member of the Good Hope Masonic Lodge, Modem Woodmen on America, and Bushnell Post of the Veterans of Foreign Wars. The VFW Post conducted military honors at the graveside.

SARAH JOAN RAYMOND - Sarah Joan Raymond, youngest child of six born to Charles V. Raymond, and Ruby May Thomson, on 8 Sept 1936, in Greenbush Twp, Warren Co., Illinois. First grade began at Pittenger School, McDonough County, but spring of 1943 her parents moved to Warren County so she finished first grade at Sisson School in Swan Twp, attended consolidated Youngstown School for seventh and eighth grade, graduated from Roseville High School in 1954. Her father offered to send her to W.I.U. to college if she would promise to attend four years and graduate. But, she was "in love" so Charlie used the profits of her 4-H Corn Project to make down payment on a 1952 Chevy. That allowed her to live at home and drive to Monmouth where she was employed at Gambles Skogmo Warehouse #8 in the accounting department. This set the pattern for her career life, working fifteen of the first thirty years after marriage as a bookkeeper in local businesses, namely full time as Deputy Warren County Clerk, 1966, Bookkeeper at Colonial Nursing Home, Applegate Manor, then accounting office of Husky Bilt Buildings until birth of third son, Charles in 1972. Sarah also was employed part-time for eleven years as an office secretary for John Ockert during Warren County Fair week, and again part-time for Check-R-Board Feed Store in Cameron in 1970's.

She married 3 Sept 1955 in the Roseville Methodist Church. See James Edward Martin biography for additional information regarding her "most important career" of raising their three sons.

Sarah, always seeking spiritual knowledge of relationship with GOD through Jesus Christ, lead her to teach adult Sunday School class at Belmont Church from 1960's to 1970, the years they lived and farmed in Little York area. She had many interests which led to the Monmouth Altrusa Club nomination for Outstanding Young Women of America, being published in the 1968 Edition. Besides homemaking projects, family genealogy, she became Secretary-Treasurer of the "History Group" in Monmouth. With the guidance and cooperation of Don Kirkpatrick and Herman Kington of Roseville, she incorporated the Warren County Historical Society as a Non-Profit Organization and together they established the Warren County Museum located in Roseville.

Sarah Joan (Raymond) Martin, January 1997

Following farming, the family lived near Cameron for seven years and there Sarah learned of the Baptism of the Holy Spirit which changed the course of their lives. Selling their Illinois home and lands, they removed to Broken Arrow, Oklahoma where Jim and Sarah attended Rhema Bible Training Center, graduating in 1979. After a trip to Israel and the Middle East, she volunteered as office secretary for Faith Fellowship Church of B.A. Later, 1986, Sarah also graduated from The School of the Local Church after having been employed by Victory Christian Center in 1980's. Today, Sarah is retired and lives in south Broken Arrow.

SIMON MARTIN RAYMOND - Simon Martin Raymond, born 23 Sept 1836 in Huron Co., Monroeville, Ohio, the third child of Simeon (1794-1847) and Abigail T. (Stone) (1800-1871) Alvard Raymond. Simeon came as far West as the railroad in December 1855 to Farmington, IL. He removed to Prairie City, IL in 1856, where he met and married 1 Dec 1859 Mary G. Livingston (1844-1876). They were parents of three children before her death 23 Apr 1876. (See her biography for details).

In his early days in Illinois, he rode over the country buying livestock, then his drovers would drive the stock on hoof to local markets or the nearest railroad to be shipped to Chicago market.

He served in the Union Army in the Civil War as a private of Captain John B. Johnson's Co. "D" 137th Regiment of Illinois Infantry Volunteers; one of the "One-Hundred Men" mustered in 4 May 1864 at Quincy, IL. At Memphis he was assigned to the 4th Brigade District of Memphis. The regiment was discharged at Springfield, IL, on 24 Sept 1864. His discharge states he was 5 feet 7 inches high, dark complexion, blue eyes and brown hair and by occupation when enrolled, a farmer. His name appears on the Civil War Statue on the lawn of the Warren County Court House in Monmouth. He returned to Walnut Grove where he was a landowner and farmer.

Simon Martin Raymond, about 1877.

Simon remarried 23 July 1877 to Sarah Elizabeth Foresman (1855-1936), (See her biography for data on their eleven children and also FORESMAN ancestors). In 1892, he moved his family into Walnut Grove where he operated a grain elevator and continued to be a livestock buyer. He and his wife were commonly known as "Uncle Simon" and "Aunt Sarah" around the Walnut Grove area—an affectionate tribute to them.

After the death of Simon, 2 Oct 1909, burial in McMahill Graveyard in Greenbush Township of Warren County, Sarah continued to live in the homeplace in Walnut Grove and with help of son Charlie, to rear their three younger children. Simon is the eighth generation of Raymond descendants in America. His immigrant (ancestor, William Rayment (ca. 1637, England - 29 Jan 1709, Mass.), and brother John Rayment came to America with their sister Elizabeth not later than spring of 1651 settling at Beverly, Mass. Soon after arriving in America, the family changed the family name Rayment to Raymond. They were the children of George Rayment of Glastonbury, England, grandchildren of Robert Rayment of Charlton Mackrell, England, and great-grandchildren of William Rayment of Hawkchurch, England. The Parish Records at Charlton Mackrell show baptism of George, son of Robert Rayment per Henry F. Waters AM, Genealogical Gleanings in England, III (1901). The will of George Rayment of Glastonbury, dated 26 June 1651, states that they had already gone to New England and one shilling is left to son John and one pound to son William, if they came to Glastonbury to get it! The Rayment Coat of Arms: "argent three bars, sable, crests depicts a right arm embowed in armour, grasping a battle axe, all proper" has been found at the burial place of William Rayment of Ilchester and Chard. There's a definite connection between the family of William of Hawkchurch and son George and William of Ilchester per Essex Co. Land Records (1651).

Simon's ancestors were also very patriotic, immigrant William (1637-1709), served in King Philip's War 1675, and fifth generation, William (b.1749), as Pvt. in Major Paul Raymond's Militia (See Mass. Men in War of Revolution, 1011 and 1013).

CHARLES ALEXANDER REYNOLDS – "LONESOME CHARLEY" - Charles Alexander Reynolds, a scout for George Armstrong Custer, was likely born in rural Floyd Township on March 20, 1842. His parents, Dr. Joseph Reynolds and Phebe (Bush) Reynolds, came from Kentucky in the 1830s. Although playing an active role at the new Meridian Christian Church near Berwick, the Reynolds returned to the Bluegrass State in November 1844.

"Lonesome" Charley Reynolds

While living in Stephensburg in Hart County, Charley's mother died. Over the next few years, Dr. Reynolds' strong will and love of horses, hunting, and nature helped Charley adjust and grow. During the 1850s, Dr. Reynolds married again to Lydia Burton and the family came back to Illinois and Knox County where Charley attended his cousin's preparatory school at Abingdon College.

Traveling evangelist Pardee Butler convinced Dr. Reynolds to take his family west in 1859 to join the "free soilers" heading for "Bleeding Kansas." While Charley's father took up farming and politics at the village of "Pardee," Charley rejected an agrarian lifestyle and headed to the Colorado gold fields. Turned away by an Indian attack, Charley tried trapping and riding a mail route. After the onset of Civil War, he became part of the 10th Volunteer Infantry.

Serving along the turbulent Missouri-Kansas border, the 10th Kansas fought at the Battle of Prairie Grove, Arkansas in 1862. In 1863, Charley got an assignment escorting horses along the Santa Fe Trail. Finding interest in this territory and business, after his enlistment ended in 1864 Charley made one or more trips down this commercial route.

Working next as a buffalo hunter to the Nebraska railroad companies, he gained the respect of Buffalo Bill Cody. By the 1870s Charley was working at army posts across the Dakota Territory supplying meat to the soldiers. Serving on the Yellowstone River expeditions of 1872 and 1873, he gained the admiration of soldiers, like Custer, for finding and killing scarce game with amazing marksmanship. Therefore, "Lucky Man" was chosen to hunt and scout for Custer's 1874 Black Hills expedition. Custer also gave him the mission of riding secretly to Fort Laramie with news of their discovery of gold.

Despite an infection on his gun hand, Charley helped guide the 1876 Little Bighorn expedition to the famous fight of June 25th. Although warned about the number of warriors by Reynolds and other scouts, Custer feared their arrival had been discovered and ordered the 7th Cavalry to attack. Riding in the assault led by Marcus Reno, Charley fought along the skirmish line in the lower valley before Reno's force was ordered into some nearby timber. After confusing orders from Reno to retreat again, Charley attempted to flee. Albeit putting up a valiant fight, but he failed to escape. His body was identified and buried several days later; yet, his gravesite and remains became a matter of several markings and relocations. Today, a lone gravestone in a farm field south of the Little Bighorn River testifies to his unassuming but significant role as a western legend.

JAMES AND EUNICE REYNOLDS - James Howard Reynolds, Jr. was born in Galesburg, IL

November 27, 1934 to James Howard Reynolds, Sr. and Dorothy A. Mills Reynolds of Cameron, IL. He married Eunice Peterson on February 28, 1953 at the home of her parents Chester H. Peterson and Orpha V. Johnson Peterson near Monmouth, IL. Eunice was born near Alexis, IL on August 12, 1933.

James graduated from Little York High School in 1952 and Eunice graduated from Little York High School in 1951. They are the parents of Jay Reynolds, a rancher in Missouri; Jeff Reynolds, a Vice President of Marketing (children's books) for Scholastic Publishers in Danbury, Ct.

Julie is married to Lt. Col. Scott Buhman currently residing in Wheaton, IL where Scott chairs the R.O.T.C. Dept. at Wheaton College. Jon is married to Rae Moore Bennett and resides in Monmouth, IL. Jon is employed at Machine and Grind in Aledo, IL. Rae is owner operator of Rae's Place in Monmouth, IL.

Grandchildren include Casey and Brady Reynolds, Jaime, Kelly, Carrie Grace and Aaron Buhman, Chuck (and Ali) and Bill (and Julie) Bennett. There are also two great-grandchildren, Noah and Olivia Bennett.

James was the grandson of Samuel and Minnie (Bradbury) Reynolds, a prominent farmer in Floyd Township, near Berwick and Cameron, IL. James Howard, Sr., being the fourth child in this family, whose history is in the Warren County Historical Books circa 1920s. Maternal grandparents were Ralph and Winnie (Robinson) Mills of the Cameron area. James Howard Reynolds, Sr. married Dorothy A. Mills February 20, 1932 in Galesburg, IL. Paternal grandparents of Eunice were August F. Peterson and Hilma Dahl Peterson.

August came to America at the age of 14 from Sweden and landed in New York, working his way to finally arrive at Alexis, IL several weeks later. It is quoted that he spent his last dime to see the Brooklyn Bridge before beginning his trip westward. Maternal grandparents were John E. and Nellie (Nelson) Johnson of the Alexis area. Orpha, their oldest child, graduated from Alexis High School in 1918, receiving her teaching certificate after taking summer classes at Western IL University in Macomb, began teaching rural schools in the Alexis and Lynn Center areas. She married Chester Peterson on February 8, 1922 and they farmed in the Mercer and Warren County areas.

James and Eunice farmed for twenty-five years, with all of their children graduating from Yorkwood High School. James worked for Yorkwood School for 10 years and for Monmouth College 16 1/2 years, retiring in 2000. Eunice has been employed by Dr. Philip Sexton since 1975.

KENNETH AND ROSE REYNOLDS - Kenneth Glenn Reynolds was born July 29, 1919 in Eleanor, Illinois to Arthur Glenn and Dora Anna (Rule). He had twin brothers Willard W. and Wendell W. and one sister Mary Frances who died as an infant. Kenneth attended Monmouth High School and graduated in 1937. After school he was drafted into the Marines during World War II. Stationed at El Toro Marine Base in California where he was an aircraft mechanic. After the war, Kenneth made his life's work farming.

On January 23, 1943 Kenneth married Dora Rose Anna Munson in the First Christian Church in Monmouth, Illinois. They have four children. Karl Glenn (Mary Jo Harris), Joyce Elaine (Timothy Otis Denison), Mary Alice (Richard Craig Cavanaugh), and Lloyd Kenneth (Karen Hester). They have ten grandchildren and eight great-grandchildren as of 2002.

Dora Rose Anna Munson was born October 30, 1924 in Knox County, Illinois to Karl Anders and Pearl (Brown) Munson. She was the fifth of five children. Karl Everett (Virginia Leonard) Ruth B. (Earl Lyons) Mildred B. (Dale Van Riper) and Dorothy Kathryn (Lloyd Winbigler). The Munson's lived in Abingdon until 1932 then moved to Monmouth. Rose graduated from Monmouth High School in 1942. In 1960 Rose was licensed to sell securities and opened an insurance office in 1976 in Alexis Illinois. Later opening offices in other locations.

Kenneth and Rose have been active in Cedar Creek and Little Cedar Presbyterian Churches serving as elders.

MARSHALL AND HARRIETT REYNOLDS - Harriett Ferne Simpson was born September 29, 1922 Monmouth Hospital, Monmouth, Illinois. The daughter of Clifford Hill and Edna Grace (Josephson) Simpson. Harriett married Marshall Lee Reynolds May 15, 1945 at Norwood Presbyterian Church, Mercer County Illinois. Marshall was born November 17, 1925 near Stillwater, Oklahoma Payne County. They met while Marshall was a patient at Mayo General Army Hospital, Galesburg, Illinois, where Harriett was a civil service worker.

Harriett and Marshall Reynolds

Harriett graduated from Alexis High School in 1940 and attended business College in Burlington, Iowa. In September 1941 Harriett received an appointment to work at the U.S. Navy Department in Washington, D.C. In June 1942, Harriett was recruited to transfer to the U.S. Treasury Department which was moving some of its offices to the Merchandise Mart in Chicago. In December 1943, Harriett transferred to the Mayo General Army Hospital in Galesburg, Illinois.

Marshall worked at the Agriculture barn at A & M College in Stillwater, Oklahoma before entering in the service. Besides being a full time farmer for 50 years, he worked as deputy sheriff in Mercer County and as a Driver's License Examiner. Six daughters were born to them: Janice Ferne married Joseph Dean Sharer, Beverlee Marie married Bruce Floyd, Marlene Lois married Roger McCurdy, Marsha Ruth married Jeffrey Blaine Hardacre, Rita Kaye married Karl Aronson and Rosalee May married Kent Peterson.

Marshall owned and operated a farm in Mercer County for 50 Years.

Harriett is a member of Norwood Presbyterian Church since childhood, a member of Warren County NSDAR with James Couples Foster Jr. of South Carolina her Revolutionary ancestor. Both are Elders of the Norwood Church, Charter members of Warren County Genealogical Society. Alexis American Legion and Auxiliary and Aledo VFW and Auxiliary.

CHARLES RHINEHART - Rhinehart, Charles Jenson was born on the family farm in Hale Township, Warren County, Illinois in 1875. His father, David William Rhinehart was born in Ulster Co., New York in 1824 and came to Warren Co in a covered wagon with his bride, Mariah Bruyn in 1854. Mariah was born in Ulster Co New York in 1832. David and Mariah homesteaded in a log cabin. Later they built the farmhouse, which is still standing. They raised 8 children, William, Nathaniel, Lefever, Headley, John, Cornelia, Laura, and Charles. Charles went to Brown's Business College. He met Bessie May Walker at the Kirkwood Presbyterian Church. They were married on Dec 26, 1909. Bessie's father was Denny Walker, who trained horses and owned a grocery store in Kirkwood. He married Martha Lettie Johnson. Her father was Captain James Johnson who served with the 59th infantry in the Civil War. Charles and Bessie loved God, the farm, and their family. They raised crops, cattle, hogs, chickens, horses, & 2 children, Mary Ellen and David Walker. The family enjoyed ball games, operas, and concerts. Charles farmed the family farm with horses, and then purchased a tractor in 1942. He played the harmonica and sang. Bessie played the piano and sang with her lovely alto voice. Bessie was a seamstress. Mary Ellen & David attended country school at Hornbeck. They rode their pony or walked. They went to Kirkwood High School. Ellen graduated from Monmouth College and earned her Masters Degree in Education at Colorado State University. She taught school until she married Ross Edgar Hanna September 4, 1943. They had 2 children, Ross Edgar Hanna Jr. and Sarah Mae, who married Dennis Allaman from McDonough County. They now live on the Rhinehart family farm where they raised 4 sons, Chad Harrison, Craig Charles, Clinton Bruce, and Carlton Ross. Chad and Laura (Whitsitt) have a daughter; Grace Ann. Craig and Heidi (Hollar) have 2 sons Andrew Morrison and Ian James. Edgar and his wife Nancy now live in Rock Island. He does computer work after retiring from being a pilot. Edgar has 3 daughters Becky Zug, Jenni Guidry, and Merry Linnenkemp. Becky & Jay have 3 children, James, Sea Jay, and Michael. Merry & Matt have 2 daughters, Maddelyn and Mattie. David Rhinehart graduated from the University of Illinois, married a nurse from Biggsville, Jane Kilgore. They moved to Havana where David became the manager of Mason County Production Credit Association. They raised 2 sons, Kenneth and Carl. Carl had 2 sons, Steve and Allen. Allen has 2 sons, David and Issac.

ARTHUR AND PATRICIA (VAN RIPER) RICE - Patricia Van Riper was born on Feb 21, 1932 in Monmouth, Illinois. Her parents were Roy Conelius Van Riper and Carol (Brent) Van Riper. Her grandparents were Cornelius and Eldora (Brooks) Van Riper whose family had come to Illinois from New Jersey to engage in farming and the buying and selling of land. Cornelius and Eldora had four children; Glenn, who died at age 2, Gertrude, Edward, and Roy, born on May 23, 1902. They lived on the family farm east of Kirkwood and engaged in farming.

Following high school, Roy attended Iowa Sate College in Ames, Iowa for an agriculture course. On May 24, 1930, he married Carol Louella Brent, daughter of Frank and Louella (Crane) Brent, and they took up residence on the family farm in Kirkwood. To this union were born 3 children, a son who died at birth, Doris Patricia, and Cornelius Brent. Cornelius, known as Neil, died as the result of an automobile accident on May 6, 1961. Carol and Roy were active in the Kirkwood Methodist Church. The original Methodist Church was purchased by the Van Riper family when the new stone church was built. The building was moved to the farm and served as a hay and dairy barn. Patricia remembers many happy hours playing in the hayloft where the choirloft was still intact. When Carol and Roy were retired from active fanning, they pursued their hobby and business of buying and selling antiques. They enjoyed going to antique shows over the country for several years, combining travel and business. Roy passed away in April of 1970.

Patricia (Van Riper) and Arthur Gardner Rice

Patricia, following graduation from Kirkwood High School in 1950, attended Cottey Jr College in Nevada, Missouri for one year. She enrolled at DePauw University in Greencastle, Indiana and graduated in 1954 with a B.A. in Home Economics and Music. She accepted a position with the Michigan State Extension Service as a Home Economist in Centreville, Michigan. Patricia met a local farmer, Arthur Gardner Rice, just returning from the service. They were married in Kirkwood on Feb 26, 1956.They continued in the dairy farming business along with cash crops. Patricia has worked as an elementary music teacher, nutritionist, organist, and choir director. She and her husband have both been active in community affairs as well as the Centreville United Methodist Church where she is currently a lay member of the Annual Conference, lay speaker, organist, choir director and Stephens Minister. Patricia has also been active in the Amos Sturgis DAR chapter. She has also served in leadership roles with the Three Rivers Hospital Auxiliary. Four children were born to this marriage. Karen Stephenson is a project manager for Howe Marketing and is currently working to finish her degree. Marianne Plaunt received a PhD Degree and is working in research. Larry pursued a degree in agriculture at Michigan State University and later received a law degree from the University of Illinois. Barbara Hansberry is working as an English language instructor for non-English speaking children in California. Patricia and Arthur have nine grandchildren they enjoy very much. When not farming, they enjoy traveling.

JASON AND JENNIFER (FERNALD) ROBBINS - In the year 2002, the Jason and Jennifer Robbins family lived in Monmouth, Illinois at 828 East 1st Avenue. Head of the family was Jason, then aged 24, a partner in a pallet recycling business, RBJ Inc, and owner of eight local real estate investments sold on contract. His wife Jenny was 25 years old with a Bachelors degree in English and Communication from Monmouth College, and currently occupied with homemaking. The children were Isabella Justice, two years old, born May 11, 2000; and Abigail Eliza, eight months old, born October 16th, 2001.

Jason Carl Robbins was of German extraction. His father's family had come to America in 1851. Jason was born and raised in Monmouth. His father, Richard Robbins, was also a partner in RBJ Inc. His mother was Kathleen Huebner, employed by RBJ Inc for secretarial work. Kathleen's family had come to America in 1893 to avoid the draft in Germany.

Jennifer Liberty Robbins had married Jason on July 19, 1997 at the Stuart House in Monmouth, IL. Her parents were Gary Fernald and Sherry Stevenson. Born in Monmouth October 2, 1976, she had been reared in Monmouth, and had met Jason at the wedding of Bryon and Kimberly Robbins. Jennifer and Jason Robbins both attended Countryside Bible Church. The truth of the bible was a cornerstone of their lives.

WILLIAM ERNEST ROBINSON - Robinson, William Ernest (Ernie) the son of William E. and Nellie E. Noble Robinson was born (1/18/1919) in Sangamon County near Pleasant Plains, Il. and raised on the family farm. He attended a country one-room school, Pleasant Plains High School, and later graduated from the University of Illinois where he met his future wife, Mary Kathryn Jackson (Mary K.) who was also attending the University. After graduating in 1940, Ernie worked for the Dekalb Hybrid Seed Co. for two and one-half years, until being inducted into the U.S. Army in November 1942. He served in the veterinary service until January 1, 1946.

50th Wedding Anniversary of Mary K. and Ernest Robinson

It was during the war that he and Mary K. were married at her parent's home near Joy, Illinois on May 16, 1943. While Ernie, as a Staff Sergeant, was stationed at Camp Ellis for two years, they lived in Macomb and Mary K. worked at the camp in the Finance Department. After being discharged from the army, Ernie and Mary K. moved on 3/10/1946 to the Frymire farm that her father had purchased, east of Cameron, Ill. where they raised grain and livestock. They had one of the first cattle confinement operations in the area. In 1980 they built a new home across the road from the original family homestead.

Both are active in the community. Ernie has served on different Committees and the council of the First United Methodist church, Finance Committee of the Warren County Board, president of the Farm Bureau Board, president of the Warren School Board, president of the Tri-County Livestock Feeders Association, and a member of the governor's Ag. Advisory Board.

Mary K. Jackson was born at home 12/23/1921 to Chester H. and Della Longley Jackson of Joy, Il. in Mercer County and raised on the family farm. She went to Joy Consolidated School and attended the University of Il. Before marriage she worked in the Aledo National Bank. After moving to Cameron she has been active in church (local, district, conference), Warren School (as volunteer aide), president - Warren County Homemakers, president of the Farm Bureau Women's committee, Hospital Auxiliary (out-patient host and gift shop clerk), and 4-H leader.

Their four children are: Janet Kay, William Chester, Alyce Ann, and Edward Ernest. Janet married William H. Underwood on 10/17/1965. William (Bill) married Karen R. Jenks 8/27/1967. Alyce married J. David Jenks 8/17/1969. Edward married Catherine Sjeklocha on 2/23/1974. All four children and their spouses settled on farms in the immediate area and raised their own families. They are each one active in community affairs.

Ernie and Mary K. have eleven grandchildren: Deborah A. Underwood Ornduff (Greggory), Bradley W. Underwood (Kimberly), Brian W. Robinson (Jennifer), Mark J. Robinson (Jody), Amy K. Robinson Anderson (Robert), Tricia K. Jenks Place (Jeffery), Andrew D. Jenks (Jackie), Thomas A. Jenks (Jill), Aaron E. Robinson (Megan), Kristin M. Robinson, and Adam M. Robinson.

ROBERT AND MARILYN RONEY - Robert D. Roney was born January 10, 1925 in Monmouth, IL. Marilyn J. Roney was born May 31, 1925 in Monmouth, IL. They were married November 8, 1947 in the home of Marilyn's parents, Lee C. and Marie Bradford Thompson. They have two children, Kathleen M. and Karen L. Kathleen is married to Robert G. Thompson and lives in Kirkwood, IL. Karen is married to Gary Craig and lives in Longmont, CO. They have two grandchildren, Jennifer Higbee and Brandon Higbee.

Kathy Thompson, Bob Thompson, Brandon Higbee, Gary Craig, Karen Roney, Robert Roney and Marilyn Roney

Robert's parents were Frank Willard Roney and Ethel Ostrom Roney. His grandparents were Jesse Roney and Fannie Winebright Roney. His great grandparents were Samuel Wilson Roney and Sarah Eaverson Roney. Great, great grandparents, Hamilton Roney and Margaret Mackey Roney were the earliest Warren county residents, settling in Hale Township in 1836. Hamilton built a stone house where he lived and had a blacksmith's shop. Willard Roney was born in this house. Hamilton also farmed 800 acres there, which he had purchased from the government for $1.25 per acre. The Roneys came here from Pennsylvania and Ohio.

Marilyn's grandparents on her father's side were W.I. and Della Shaw Thompson. Great grandparents were Josiah and Elizabeth McCrery Thompson. Josiah was the first family member to come to Warren County. He arrived here in 1854 from Ohio and before that the family lived in Thompsontown, Pennsylvania. They were of Scottish descent. The following year Josiah's parents, William and Margaret Wilson Thompson, arrived and purchased 80 acres of land in Spring Grove Township. William and Margaret Thompson both died two years later and are some of the first to be buried in Monmouth Cemetery.

Robert Roney graduated from Little York High School in 1942. He joined the Navy in 1943, serving in World War II aboard the USS *Cowell* and the USS *Guam*. He was discharged from the service in 1946.

Robert and Marilyn now live on the family farm of 300 acres in Spring Grove Township. Part of the farm includes the original 80 acres which is now 148 years in the same family.

Robert grows corn and beans. He also feeds cattle. For fifty years he has been involved in the Warren County Prime Beef Festival.

Marilyn graduated from Monmouth High School in 1943 and from Monmouth College in 1947. She is a member of Alpha Xi Delta Alumnae, Monmouth College Crimson Clan, CMC Auxillary and Warren County DAR.

They are members of Faith United Presbyterian Church in Monmouth. Robert is currently serving as trustee and Marilyn is a former deacon.

ROBERT AND ILA VENARD ROSEBERRY - Robert R. Roseberry, son of Charles E. and Floy Roseberry of Carthage, Illinois, was born on July 20, 1919 in Low Point, Illinois. The family moved to Carthage, Illinois where he attended schools. After graduating high school he attended Carthage College before enlisting in Armed Forces Air Corps. After discharging from service he became employed by Benner Tea Co. who then sent him to their Food City store in Monmouth, Illinois. This is where he met his future bride-to-be Ila Venard.

They were married on October 23, 1948 at the Methodist Church in Henderson, Illinois by Rev. Carl Just. In 1951 Ila was employed by Illinois Power Co. where she retired at the end of 1990. Robert was later employed by Illinois Power Co. in the Galesburg Meter Dept. He died on September 6, 1991.

ALBERT AND PENSA (BROWN) ROSS - Albert Ross was born 1861 in LaHarpe, Hancock County, Illinois, to Dennison and Elizabeth (Adams) Ross, formerly of Muskingham County, Ohio. Albert married Pensa Brown, daughter of Henry and Julia Brown. He was a farmer and even after retirement to Monmouth, continued going to the farm on a daily basis.

Albert and Pensa had two sons: Ralph, born in 1889 and Beauford born 1892.

Albert died in 1945, Pensa in 1958. Both are buried in Monmouth cemetery.

L: to R: Standing: Merrill, Lloyd, Dean. Seated: Albert, R.K. (Kessler), Ralph and Bill.

Ralph married Nellie Kessler, daughter of Philip and Nora Kessler. They farmed in Tompkins Township. Ralph, like his father, came to the farm almost daily after retirement, from his home in Monmouth. Ralph and Nellie were the parents of four children; Elizabeth, born 1912, married Frank Olson, parents of Conrad, Philip, Kessler, and Steve. She died 1989. Ralph Kessler (R.K.), born 1917, married Donna, parents of Jerry. R.K. later married Pauline (Bush) and died 1983. Merrill, born 1919, married Margaret Holt, parents of Merrillyn, Ralph and Julia. After her death, Merrill married Marie Rosenbaum. Merrill died 1995. Margaret, born 1922, married Richard Abbey, parents of David, Karen and Kirk. Margaret later married Russell Counterman, she died 2001.

Ralph died 1974, Nellie 1972, both buried in Monmouth cemetery.

Beauford Ross, married Mary Riner, daughter of Harry and Solame Riner. Beauford farmed west of Monmouth. They were the parents of three boys:

Dean, born 1916, married Josephine Parrish, were parents of Jim, William Pensa, Albert, Katie, Celia and Samantha. Dean died 1978.

Lloyd, born 1918, married Mahota Gippert, were parents of Richard and Billy Dean.

William, born 1920, married Carolyn (Stoops) Heatherly and were parents of Mary, Patricia, Laura, and Charles in addition to Carolyn's sons Ted and Tim.

Beauford died in 1920. Mary in 1977. Both are buried in Monmouth cemetery.

DEAN R. ROSS - Ross, Dean R. of 1135 East Detroit Avenue was born 29 October 1916 at Monmouth. His mother, Mary (Riner) raised the three boys after his father Beauford B. passed away. They were Dean, Lloyd and Beauford and lived on North 1st Street, last house on the westside in the 400 block. Across the street was plumber Rademacher, who taught the younger brother his trade. Lloyd graduated from college as a sanitary engineer in Texas. Dean received his education graduating from Monmouth College in 1938, during the depression. He worked in the meat department at Barnes Bros., where he received the nickname "Picklejar." He seemed to always have his hand in the big jar holding sweet pickles.

He married Josephine Parish 18 January 1942 in Gary, Indiana and began farming. In fact he continued farming when he returned from four years of service with the U.S. Airforce during WWII, until his health failed. There had been a concern for months about Lieutenant Ross, until finally on 28 August 1944, it was reported he was a prisoner of the Bulgarian government. The word came to his wife through the Red Cross. He has been reported missing in action on 18 May over Albania. He had been serving as a Bombardier with a Liberator squadron of the 15th Army Airforce in Italy and was participating in long-range bombing attacks on the Balkins, Austria, and Northern Italy. Earlier there was a letter that said he was returning from a bombing mission and was reported over Debar on the border between Albania and Yugoslavia. He asked for homing instructions, but it failed to come through to his base, and it was indicated that the whole crew were able to get down safely. He had been decorated for bombing raids made between 18 March and 3 April and by then completed 23 combat missions over enemy held territory.

He and Josephine had three sons: James of Monmouth, Williard of Salt Lake City, Utah, and Albert of Springfield; three daughters, Gary (Penny) Bass of Monmouth, Kathryn A. Ross of Springfield, and Celia Lou Ross at home; a grandson James Dean of Monmouth. An infant daughter died earlier along with a brother Lloyd and his parents.

DENNISON AND ELIZABETH (ADAMS) ROSS - In 1859, 52 year old Dennison Ross, his second wife Elizabeth (Adams) Ross, and their six children left their home in Salem Township, Muskingham County, Ohio to begin the long trek to Illinois. They traveled by raft, floated down the Ohio River to the Mississippi River, and then upriver to Oquawka, Illinois. This was the second time Dennison had resettled westward, having moved with his parents, Lyman and Judith (Frazier) Ross from Westerly, R.I. to Salem Township, Ohio.

Sons of Dennison and Elizabeth (Adams) Ross. L: to R: Front: William, Connie, George D. Rear: Fred, Albert.

Dennison's first marriage was to Cyrene Spencer, daughter of William and Catherine Spencer, in 1831, in Muskingharn County, Ohio. They were the parents of eight children. Cyrene died in 1844.

Dennison married Elizabeth Adams, daughter of George and Christina (Wertz) Adams in 1845. They were the parents of: Susan, born 1846, married Moses Buffington; Christina, born 1848, married B.R. Higgison; George born 1851, married Laura McCarty; Mary, born 1853, married Isaac Garret; Conrad, born 1855, married Ruth; Charles, born 1857, died 1857; Charles "William", born 1858, married Sarah Parkhurst. These children were all born Salem Township, Muskingham County, Ohio.

Dennison first settled near LaHarpe in Hancock County, Illinois, where their son Albert was born in 1861. He married Pensa Brown. Later, resettling in Tompkins township, Warren

County, Illinois, where two more children were born: Frederick, born 1864, married Cora Hinman; Chester, born 1871.

At age 21 each of Dennison's sons was given a team of horses, a wagon, and a plow and told to "Go West." All but the three youngest followed this advice Albert purchased farms in Tompkins Township. Frederick remained on the home place and Chester remained at home, being handicapped as a result of a childhood illness. Fred and his wife had no children.

Dennison died in 1880, Elizabeth in 1902. Both are buried in Ellison Cemetery with their son Chester.

HAROLD WILLIAM ROSS - Once upon a time, Charles Henry Ross immigrated from Scotland to Sussex County Delaware. He struck an iron ore deposit on his property and became a wealthy man. Charles married Priscilla Jones on December 18, 1828. They started a family and then decided to move on. With a stop in Ross County Ohio and Muncie Indiana for a couple of years, they moved on to the Bloomington Illinois area. They finally arrived in Warren County around 1854. The family settled the homestead in Ellison Township, 5 1/2 miles west of Roseville, on the NE corner of the crossroads. Charles and Priscilla ended with a small tribe of 13 children.

Mr. and Mrs. Harold W. Ross

One of those 13 children was Charles Hiram Ross, born in 1844. His wife, Mary Elizabeth Johnson was born in 1853. Of their union in 1872, 13 children were born. Charles passed on in 1908, and Mary in 1942.

William Ross was the 6th child, of Charles and Mary, born in 1881. William grew to be a tall, lanky lad and married Jessie Ray in 1902. Jessie was born in Ellison Township in 1884. The couple raised six children on a farm 4 miles north of Roseville, which they obtained in 1914. William and Jessie passed away in 1964 and 1965, respectively.

Frances Louise Taylor married Harold William Ross, the 5th child, in Kahoka Missouri on August 8, 1940. Both were born in Warren County, Frances Louise in 1920 and Harold in 1916. They reared all of their four children on a farm just South of Kirkwood. In 1966 the couple moved back to the farm Harold grew up on north of Roseville. With the children growing older and moving out, Harold continued to farm until the mid-1970s. Harold passed on in April of 1993, and Louise in August of 2002.

The first child of Harold and Louise was named Elizabeth Ann, born in 1942. She married Albert Rossell. The couple reared a son, Keith, husband to Erin. Keith and Erin have two children, Bailey and Kylie. Liz works at a credit union in Galesburg, and they live in Alexis.

In 1945, Judith Kay was the second child to arrive. She previously was married to Ken Pierson. They had two children, Laura and Michael. Laura was married to Paul Niedernhofer and they have children, Elysia and Tate. After serving in the Marines, Michael is living and working in Karnak, Illinois. Judy works for an orthodontist and lives in Springfield.

Thirdly, Janet Marie arrived in 1947. Janet was previously married to David Rutledge. The couple had two children, Karen and Christine. Karen is married to James Hammerlund, and has a daughter from a previous marriage, Sydney Marn. Chris, divorced, is the mother of two children, Anna Raes and Clinton Rutledge. Janet wed LeRoy Hammond in January of 1999. They all reside in Monmouth. Janet was the Warren County Clerk and Recorder from 1986 to 2002.

Along came the baby brother, James Harold in 1951. Jim and Julie Pierce wed and had two children, Rick and Randi. Rick served in the Air Force and lives in Knoxville Illinois. Randi married Tony Jones and has two children, Ashley and Nathan. Jim had a long career with the Air Force with stations all around the world. He now works for and resides in Monmouth.

Submitted by Karen Hammerlund

JUDITH (NELSON) ROSS - Judith Elaine (Nelson) Ross born Feb. 5, 1947, Galesburg, Ill., daughter of Vail and Louise (Rask) Nelson. Siblings; Sandra, Ronald, Douglas

Judy attended Kirkwood Elementary, Ellison, Roseville Elementary and Yorkwood Jr./Sr. High School, graduating in 1965. In high school was a member of the "Gay '90s" singing group who appeared on the "Ted Mack's Amateur Hour." Attended Augustana College 1965 - 1967 and graduated Monmouth College 1969 with a B. A. in History. While attending Augustana was a member of the Freshman Honor Society. After graduation did secretarial work in Michigan, New Jersey, Pennsylvania and Illinois. Currently teaches History at Yorkwood High School, coaches High School Scholastic Bowl Team and Yearbook advisor.

James Dean born August 13, 1977, Galesburg, Ill. Graduated Yorkwood High School 1995, graduated Augustana College, 1999 with a B. A. in Biology. After graduation did research for the University of Illinois at Chicago. Presented a research paper in Budapest, Hungary, in 2001.Currently a graduate student at the University of Illinois in Chicago.

Robert Nelson born Dec. 8, 1979, Galesburg, Ill. Graduated Yorkwood High School 1998, where he received the All State Scholar Athlete Award and the Peoria Journal Starr all area football team. Graduated Northern Illinois University 2002 Cum Laude with a B.S. in Computer Science. He received the Dean's Award for the top computer science student. He was president of the Student Advisory Board and a Kemper Scholar. In the summer of 2001 he worked in the World Trade Center in New York City.

Both James and Robert performed with the Ecumenical Singers in Washington, D.C., in the summer of 1995.

Judy, James and Robert are members of the First Lutheran Church, Monmouth, Ill.

DANIEL & MARGARET (GUMMERSON) ROTH - Margaret Gummerson, daughter of Albert and Jean (Morrison) Gummerson, was born December 4, 1918 at Monmouth Hospital on E. Euclid Ave., Monmouth. She had one brother who died in 1973. The family lived at 520 N. 6th Street. She attended Garfield school. Her teachers were Jessica Gerry, Eleanor Harrison, Mary Lepper, Daphne Benson, Lou Minton Keff, Estelle Erlandson and Miss Gill.

Margaret and Daniel Roth, November 18, 1946.

Her father was a brickmason and there was more work in Galesburg, so they moved there in 1930. She attended Hitchcock Junior High 7th through 9th grades. She was a Camp Fire girl while living in Galesburg.

The family moved back to Monmouth in 1932. She graduated from Monmouth High School in 1936; graduated from Monmouth College in 1940.

Her maternal grandfather George Webb Morrison was a member of the Monmouth Police Department for 33 years. He served as Police Chief under Mayor Braun; was working as Desk Sergeant in the late 1920s. He was a dear man who taught Margaret to play cribbage and solitaire.

Her paternal grandmother Malena Person Gummerson was married in Sweden to Swan Gummerson. He died in 1894. Her grandmother lived at 902 S. 5th Street, and though the walk from North 6th street to South 5th street was a long one, Margaret enjoyed doing it as she grew up.

She was a member of First United Presbyterian Church (now Heritage church). She sang in the choir under direction of Glenn Shaver during high school and college.

After college graduation she taught high school classes at Monroe Center and Victoria, IL. Margaret then moved to Chicago where she met Daniel Roth. They were married November 18, 1946 at First United Presbyterian Church by Rev. John Eastwood. They have lived in the Chicago area since their marriage. They are the parents of:

Deborah died in 1974.

John lives Placitas, New Mexico, married Dana Patterson 1975 – one son Micah, one daughter Kyndra married Abraham White December 15, 2001.

David, lives upper Manhattan, New York city - three daughters Sara, Grace, Laura; one son Daniel

Mary lives Round Lake Beach, IL.

Daniel and Margaret have lived at 915 Safford Ave., Lake Bluff, IL since 1950. They have been active with the Lake Bluff-Lake Forest Senior group for 20 some years. Daniel is a member of the 2001 International Barbershop Harmony Chorus Champion of Northbrook, IL

Although Margaret has not lived in Monmouth for about 60 years, she still has, strong feelings for the town. She appreciated the small town atmosphere where she could walk to school, to downtown, to visit friends or relatives without the fear of being shot or attacked. She wishes Good Cheers to all for years to come.

JUDSON AND LAURA ELLEN (McREYNOLDS) RUSSELL - Judson Beach Russell was born December 18, 1854 in Clymer, Chataqua County, N.Y. to Jonathan and Lydia (Evans) Russell. Judson and Laura Ellen McReynolds, born March 2, 1853 in Pique, Ohio were married in Roseville, Warren County, IL on December 20, 1877.

Judson and Laura Russell, wedding.

Laura Ellen was a very proper lady. One September she thought she had all her canning for the winter done and Judd came home with five bushels of peaches and tomatoes. She took one look and said "Oh S___t." This was so unlike her that Judd went to the phone and called her daughter Grace and told her that she had better come home right away as something terrible has happened to your mother.

The Russell Sisters

The family lived on a farm east of Roseville and later moved into a large home on the east edge of town. This house is still standing.

At one time J.B. ran a grocery store in Roseville. They had a neighbor who used to borrow coffee from Laura and it was always the best grade. The neighbor returned the cheapest grade, so Laura put it aside and the next time she borrowed coffee, Laura gave her back her own coffee.

Judson and Laura had eight living daughters. Jenny had a doll she called Cabie. It's name was Katie but she couldn't talk plain, When Myra Luella was born, Jenny was brought in to see the new baby and she said "O Cabie." Luella was called Cabe the rest of her life.

Edith died of scarlet fever at the age of 20. Jenny June married Arthur Edwin Winebright 26 February 1903. Luella married George B. Wheeler of Peoria. Josephine married Clifford Lewis of Warren County. Ruth married Viggo H. Johnson of Colorado. Grace married Earl Byram of Knox County. Flora married Emmons Smith of Iowa (my parents). Ferrill married George Lewis of Warren County. Clifford and George Lewis were brothers.

Judson died May 18, 1929 and Laura Ellen died Dec 15, 1924. Both are buried in Roseville cemetery.

Submitted by Rleanoe G. Thomason

MITCHEL AND JULIE (CASTEEL) RUSSELL - Russell, Mitchell Paul, son of David and Camilla (Tochalauski) Russell, was born on October 13, 1975 in Spring Valley, Illinois. Mitch has one brother Matthew Russell who was born in 1977. Mitch attended Henry Elementary School in Henry, Illinois for grades K-5. Then he finished his schooling in the Dunlap School District in Dunlap, Illinois. Mitch graduated from Dunlap High School in 1993. Upon graduating from high school Mitch enrolled at Illinois Central Community College. Mitch attended ICC for one year and lived with his parents while recovering from an ankle surgery he had from a football injury. Mitch then transferred to Monmouth College in Monmouth, Illinois where he played an active role in the Monmouth Fighting Scots Football Program. He served as co-captain of the team for two of his four years at Monmouth. Mitch graduated with a Bachelor of Arts Degree in Physical Education in May of 1998. Upon graduating from Monmouth College in 1998 Mitch served as a local substitute teacher in the Monmouth area. Mitch received his first teaching Job in the Galesburg School District in the fall of 1999. Mitch stayed in the Galesburg District for just one year. In the summer of 2000 Mitch accepted a position with the Avon School District teaching Physical Education and coaching football.

"Mitch," Julie, Chloe

Julie Anne (Casteel) Russell, daughter of Thomas Casteel and Margaret "Peggy" (Gillen) Casteel, was born August 5, 1974 in Monmouth, Illinois. She has two brothers, Jeff Casteel and Jim Casteel. Julie attended kindergarten in the Yorkwood and Warren school districts then attended Immaculate Conception School for grades one through six. She then returned to Warren School for grades seven through twelve. Julie graduated from Warren High School in May 1992. Upon graduating she enrolled at Carl Sandburg Community College in Galesburg, Illinois. She attended CSC one year then transferred to Monmouth College in Monmouth, Illinois where she majored in Elementary and Special Education. In December of 1996 Julie graduated from Monmouth College with a Bachelor of Arts Degree in Elementary and Special Education. Upon graduating from Monmouth College in 1996 Julie served as a local substitute teacher in the Monmouth area. Julie received her first teaching job in the AlWood School District in Woodhull, Illinois in the fall of 1997 teaching special education and coaching volleyball and track.

Mitch and Julie were married on June 20, 1998 at Immaculate Conception Church in Monmouth, Illinois. In November 1999 Mitch and Julie purchased their first home at 133 South 9th Street in Monmouth, Illinois. This is where they currently reside. On March 17, 2000, their first child, Chloe Casteel Russell was born at St. Mary's Hospital in Galesburg, Illinois. Carter William Russell was born June 21, 2002.

JACOB AND RACHEL RYNER - Jacob Ryner born 1793 Montgomery Co. Pa. married there 4 Feb. 1816 to Rachel Spencer, born 20, June 1798, daughter of James and Elizabeth (Smith) Spencer Jr. He was a Revolutionary War soldier. Rachel's granfather was William Spencer, from England. Jacob' father was Nicholas Ryner, his grandfather was William Ryner from Germany.

Jacob Henry Ryner and Anna Emma Cobb (first wife of Jacob Henry Ryner).

Jacob and Rachel moved to New York state 1829, stayed there four years, then to Lorain Co. Ohio. In 1838 they moved to Warren Co. Illinois. Jacob being well to-do, came to Illinois with two teams of horses and two wagons. They drove a small red cow which provided milk for their daily fare of cornmeal mush, arriving in Warren Co. after two months journey, they rented a farm in Monmouth TWP for three years. In 1841 they bought a farm located, section one Monmouth TWP, which became the homestead of 80 improved acres, living there until his death.

Children of Jacob and Rachel: Spencer, married Emily Buttles; Daniel, married Julia A. Fisher; Josiah, married Julia Ann Paddock; Jonathan, married Philena ?; Emaline, married Ethan Cox; James S. married first Mary E. Wallace, then Mary E. Gordon; Henry, wife unknown; Jacob Warren, married Martha Jane Smith; Eliza, married Edward Morrow; Alice, no record.

About 1845 Jacob and Rachel visited Pennsylvania making the entire journey with their team of horses and a lumber wagon starting in August, returning November, same year. Jacob died 11 June 1863; Rachel died 2 June 1886. Both buried Mosher cemetery Warren Co. IL.

Their eighth child Jacob W. born 1836 Lorain Co. Ohio married 6 December 1865, Monmouth, Il to Martha Jane Smith born 15 October 1847 Loraine Co. Ohio, farmed homeplace until his death 5 December 1890. She stayed on farm, with Jacob H. until her death 1931.

Their children all born in Warren Co. Il: Alice, married Charley Black; Joseph Warren, married Mary Stella Stevenson; Edward Everett, married Hattie Mae Smith; Jacob Henry, (third child) born 25 March 1871 married 6 July 1893 to Annie Emma Cobb born 1876 London England. She came to U.S. 1883 (aged 10 years) with her mother Jane Ann Fletcher Cobb and her sisters Celia and Florence and brother Archie Cobb.

Annie's father William Cobb died in Balsar, Bombay, India in 1878 while working as a locomotive engineer. William and Jane Ann married 25 February 1872 Parish Church, Parish of Acton, Middlesex Co. London, England. Jane Ann died 1884 Warren Co. buried Gerlaw Cemetery.

Annie died as the result of a sledding accident 4 April 1894 buried Mosher Cemetery.

Their daughter Alta Leone born 5 February 1894. Jacob then married 15 February 1906 to Bertha Stevenson, born 15 January 1878, daughter of John Thomas and Nancy Ellen Hamilton Stevenson of Cutler, Perry Co. Illinois. They had four children: Lois, Anna Mae, Ruth and Edna.

Jacob Henry died 21 September 1956, Bertha died 18 May 1974, both buried Mosher Cemetery.

Alta Leone Ryner married David Smith 24 December 1914, Monmouth, Illinois.

RICHARD AND GRETA (PETERSON) RYNER

Richard Ryner was born November 1, 1918, Gerlaw, Il., the son of Eugene and Caroline (Peterson) Ryner. On November 1, 1945 he married Greta Lucille Peterson at Fairview Center Church, Warren County. She is the daughter of Emmett and Ruth (Crandall) Peterson and was born July 22, 1926 in Monmouth.

Ryner family. Front Row: Kristy, Benjamin, Robyn, Heather, Rick. Back row: Robert, Richard, Rodney, Greta, Nancy, Heidi.

Richard attended grade school in rural Spring Grove Township, and graduated from Alexis High in 1937. He worked the family farm, worked for F.S., and later was Road Commissioner for Monmouth Township. They both enjoyed camping and square dancing. He also liked to bowl and she loved reading and did needlework.

Richard passed away August 30, 1999.

Greta attended West Prarie elementary school and graduated -from Monmouth High in 1944. She received a license in Cosmetology in Galesburg in 1960, owned her own shop and still works there part-time.

Their three children were all born in Monmouth and attended school there. They are:

Nancy E. born June 11, 1947, married Rodney Stahl in Fresno, CA on July 20, 1967. They are the parents of Heidi Eylene born July 2, 1970 and Heather Christine born January 8, 1972. Both in Boulder City, NV.

Richard Eugene Jr. born March 13, 1949. Has two children: Laura born Oct 28, 1996 and James, born April 6, 1998.

Robert E. born May 2, 1954. Has children: Kristy Anne, born 25 Dec 1978; Benjamin Robert born April 26, 1983 and Robyn R. born October 28, 1984. All born in Monmouth, IL.

Greta still lives in Monmouth.

GLENN EDWARD SANBERG

Sanberg, Glenn Edward, was born June 26, 1914 in Red Oak, Henry County, Illinois. His father was Henry Edward Sandburg (Sanberg) 1882-1961 also born in Andover, son of Augustus Samuel Sandburg, 1891-1925 and Ida Marie (Carlson) Sandburg, 1859-1929. Glenn's mother was Elnora (Vinstrand) Sandburg, 1891-1948, daughter of Nels E. Vinstrand, 1859-1933 and Anna Louise Lilly (Lilja) Vinstrand, 1864-1937.

Glenn attended Edward's Valley one-room grade school in Andover Township and graduated from Woodhull High School in 1932. He farmed with his father in Andover Township. Glenn left for the service in 1941 serving in Iceland, Northern Ireland and the Northern European theater as Staff Sergeant and Section leader in the 5th Infantry Division 3rd Army. He was discharged July 4, 1945 and received the Bronze Star during service.

Glenn married Mildred Easley in 1945. She was born July 9, 1912 in Schuyler County and died in 1975. Her parents were Charles Easley and Alma (Foster) Easley. Mildred attended Industry High School, Western Illinois University and completed graduate work at Iowa State University. She taught at Roodhouse High School, Wataga, Brown Business College and Carl Sandburg College, Galesburg.

Glenn and Mildred met in 1940 in Wataga and married December 30, 1945. They resided in Moline, moving to Kirkwood in 1947. Glenn owned and operated Kirkwood Oil and Gas Company with his brother-in-law Robert Henderson as partner. Glenn and Bob married twin sisters in a double wedding ceremony and operated the station from 1947-1972. Glenn moved to a farm in rural Kirkwood in 1957 and farmed until 1985.

Glenn and Mildred's children are Gary Edward, born December 30, 1947, married Judith Ann Holgren June 4, 1983 and Nancy Ann, born April 4, 1951 died March 8, 1999, married John Francis Kennedy, June 25, 1977. There are four grandchildren, Adam, Benjamin and Caleb Sanberg and Laura Kennedy.

Glenn married Doris (Warner) Holford May 19, 1984.

In researching his ancestors it was interesting to note the different spellings of the family name. Henry's parents were listed as "Sandberg" on his Record of Baptism, yet on the cemetery headstone they are "Sandburg." Glenn's parents were Sanberg which is the spelling used at the present time. How, why and when the spellings were changed remains a mystery.

DAVID C. SANDSTROM

Sandstrom, David C., son of Clarence and Ruth (Themanson) Sandstrom was born in Monmouth on May 26, 1947. He has one brother, Dean. His parents were owners of the Sandstrom Produce, buying cream, eggs and chickens from local farmers. David's grandparents on both sides were Swedish immigrants who settled in Warren County in the late 1800's.

David, Rose, Mark (22), Mike (16) Sandstrom, March 1998

As a boy, David lived in Monmouth going to school at Garfield through the fifth grade. In the summer of 1958, he and his parents moved to a farm east of town. He then attended Warren School, graduating in 1965. After high school David worked on the farm with his father and also was a custodian at Warren School. In August 1966, he was drafted into the U.S. Army. He took his basic training at Ft. Campbell, KY and his A.I.T. at Ft. Huachuca, Arizona. In January 1967, he was sent overseas to Kaiserslautern, Germany to work at a large supply depot. In August 1968, he was honorably discharged.

Upon his return home from the service, David resumed working at Warren School and assisting his father on the farm. At school he met and later married Rose Ann Carlberg who was a physical education instructor at the time. This union took place August 1, 1971, at the Methodist Church in Galva, IL. They lived in Monmouth.

Rose Ann (Carlberg) Sandstrom was born January 17, 1947, at Galesburg, the only child of Arthur and Pearl (Wexell) Carlberg. Her great, great grandmother on her mother's side was an original descendent of the Bishop Hill Colony. She graduated from Cambridge High School in 1965. She received a Bachelor of Science in Physical Education in 1969 from Western Illinois University after which she accepted a teaching position at Warren School. She worked there until 1976.

In 1973, David resigned his custodial position at Warren School and took over his father's farm in Roseville Township. In September 1976 after tearing down the old farmhouse and putting up a new one, the family moved to the 160-acre farm where they still reside today. David also owns half interest in a farm with his brother, Dean, in Sumner Township. Rose owns her family farm in Henry County. In 1985, Rose began working for Monmouth School District #38. She teaches physical education and gifted.

Two children were born from this marriage: Mark David born February 13, 1976, in Galesburg, IL, attended Roseville Schools, graduating in 1994. He graduated from Monmouth College in 1998 with a Bachelor of Arts in Education. He currently is a teacher in the Middle School at Abingdon, IL, Assistant High School Football Coach and Head High School Basketball Coach. He has a home in Abingdon.

Michael Alan was born September 3, 1981, in Galesburg, IL. He attended Roseville Schools, graduating in 1999. He is currently a student at Northern Illinois University in DeKalb, Illinois studying meteorology.

Both Rose and David are active. Rose was a 4-H leader for 13 years and is currently on the Roseville School Board acting as secretary. Both are active in the First Lutheran Church in

Monmouth. They have served on various committees. David has served two terms on the Church Council.

DEAN SANDSTROM FAMILY - Victor and Ida (Swanson) Sandstrom immigrants of Sweden arrived in America in 1869, settling in Reed, Henderson County. C.V. Clarence Sandstrom was born April 24, 1905. In 1916 Victor purchased a farm in Warren County. Clarence attended rural schools and graduated from Monmouth High School in 1924. He went into the Produce business and in 1929 he started a business of his own, Sandstrom Produce.

Sandstrom: Dean, Stephen, Douglas, Carolyn, Sandy and Cathy, January 1996

He married Ruth Themanson on April 14, 1929 at the First Lutheran Church Parsonage. She assisted him in the business. Dean Clarence was born May 31, 1935. His brother David Clarence was born May 26, 1947.

Dean went to Monmouth public schools and graduated in 1953. He worked in the family business from a very early age, learning to test cream and grade eggs. He also ran routes through the country picking up chickens, eggs and cream. He served in the U.S. Army from 1955 - 1957 most of it being in Hawaii, upon returning he purchased the business from his father.

He met Carolyn Swartout, a great-great-granddaughter of Eli Farnham a pioneer of Log City, Galesburg, and married on March 2, 1958 at the First Methodist Church, in Galesburg.

They resided in a rental apartment until May and then moved into their first home at 320 North F. St. Catherine born April 5, 1959 was their first child, Sandy followed on May 24, 1960 and Douglas on Sept 16, 1961. Dean was still in the Produce then but with farmers not raising chickens anymore he gave it up and went to work at the Gamble Skogomo Warehouse and helped his father on the farm in the evenings and weekends. Carolyn baby sat for extra income and found herself expecting again. Stephen was born June 7, 1965. Dean's brother David graduated from Warren High School that June. When Stephen started kindergarten Carolyn went back to work. It took two incomes to raise a family of four kids. Cathy, Sandy, Doug and Steve were all active in Scouting, Y.M.C.A., Rainbow Girls, Band and Track.

After graduation from M.H.S. Catherine entered the Air Force in the fall of 1977, serving 4 1/2 years of active duty. After 1981 she enlisted in the Air Guard while attending Southern Illinois University, in Electrical Engineering. Upon graduation she was employed by G.T.E. Government Industries, moving to California. Later she went to work for Air, Inc. and transferred to the Navy Reserve and retired from there in Jan. 2000 as a Lt. Jr. Grade.

Sandra graduated from M.H.S. in 1978 in the top 10 of her class and enrolled at Augustana College, Rock Island, Illinois that fall. She graduated in 1982 and attended Western Illinois University to get her Masters in Speech and Language Disabilities. She is a Pre-K speech teacher at Enterprise Elementary in Enterprise, Florida.

Douglas joined the Army his senior year and left shortly after graduation in 1979. He is still serving and is currently attending Sergeant-Major school at Ft. Bliss, Texas. In the last 22 years he was stationed 5 times in Europe, Panama, and stateside. After graduating he was stationed at Foil Campbell Kentucky as of Sept. 6, 2002 He became Command Sergeant Major. He also completed a course in AirAssault training with the 101st. Airborne Division. While he and Cathy were both stationed in Germany we visited them and had a wonderful time.

Stephen after graduating from M.H.S. in 1983 joined the Navy and was stationed at MirMar Naval Station in Calif. Upon returning to Monmouth he resides on the grandparents farm east of Monmouth. He is currently employed by Robert Thompson Trucking. He is quite mechanical minded. He has run demo-derby cars several times at the fairs in the county.

Sandra married Todd Dasso, on Dec. 18, 1982 and gave us our first granddaughter Kimberlee born, Jan. 14, 1986 followed by Alyssa born on Feb. 28, 1988 and Jessica born June 23, 1990. Douglas married Sara Tranter on April 28, 1984 and they have two sons Carl born Sept. 2, 1988 in Germany and Patrick born March 23, 1995 in Tampa, Fl. Catherine married David Conry Jan 16, 1996 and they have a daughter Christina born May 31, 1999 and a son Matthew born July 7, 2001.

Dean is a life member of the First Lutheran Church; a member of Monmouth Masonic Lodge; Order of Eastern Star; and Warren County Genealogical Society.

Carolyn joined the First Lutheran Church April 1958. She is a Past Matron of the Order of the Eastern Star and a former member of the D.A.R. She has a pioneer certificate in the Knox County Genealogical Society. She was employed at several places in Monmouth, starting with the Produce Station and then the First National Bank, W.R.A.M. Radio station, Sprugeons, Newsland, Monmouth Airport, and most recent Save-A-Lot Foods.

Dean and Carolyn are both enjoying retirement and are both Charter Members of the Warren County of Illinois Genealogical Society.

HARRY AND RUTH (LUCAS) SCHWEITZER - On March 26, 1892 in Hale Township, Monmouth, IL a son, Harry Luft Schweitzer, was born to Jacob Frederick and Lena Olga (Luft) Schweitzer. Harry, being their only child, was born and raised on the family farm that had been homesteaded by his grandfather. This farm is currently owned by the fifth generation of Schweitzer's. German was spoken only at home thus making school a difficult adjustment. He attended a one-room schoolhouse completing eight grades before graduating from Monmouth High School in 1911. Ruth Gale (Lucas) Schweitzer, Harry's wife, was born at home on October 13, 1894. She was the third child born to Albert B. Lucas and Harriet Emmaline (Bolon) Lucas who lived in the Sugar Tree Grove community. Ruth completed nine grades in a one-room schoolhouse. God gifted her with a beautiful soprano voice that led her to studying at the Monmouth College Conservatory.

Ruth and Harry Schweitzer

Harry and Ruth met at a Sugar Tree Grove Church social. They were joined as one on November 23, 1913 by the Reverend Samuel Brown of their church. A seamstress was brought in a few weeks prior to sew the brides trousseau. They set up housekeeping on the Schweitzer family farm. Two children were born to Harry and Ruth; Dorothy Jean (10/3 1/18) and Robert (3/2/23). In 1929 they moved their small family to a farm in the Monmouth Township which was located directly east of the present day Gibson Woods Golf Course. When Dorothy married Ralph Ault in 1939 they joined the Schweitzer's on the farm. While waiting for a house to be built Harry and Ruth moved to an apartment located on 400 North A, Monmouth around the mid 1940's. The new house on 216 West Euclid was completed in 1947. That was a busy year for the couple as they also built a cabin and a lake known as Schweitzer's Timberlake near their Hale Township farm.

Harry enjoyed photography, being outdoors, and keeping journals. In 1923 he built a radio from a kit which many neighbors came to enjoy this new form of entertainment. Ruth, a 45-year member of the local garden club, had a special green thumb and had arrangements in many flower shows. She gave unselfishly to her family and church. They both took pleasure wintering in Long Beach, California for many years.

Mr. Schweitzer could always be found chewing on a piece of straw until a sliver lodged in his throat when he was 39 years old. An infection set in causing him to have 40 operations on his throat. A serious infection took his life on October 20, 1970 after his appendix burst. After devoting her life to her eight grandchildren and sixteen great-grandchildren, Ruth went to be with the Lord shortly after her 101st birthday in November 1995.

LYLE SEDWICK - This account is to verify that Lyle D. Sedwick and Arlene Davidson Sedwick moved to Alexis, Warren County, in August 1988. They owned and operated the Dairy Barn in Alexis from 1982 until they retired in 1989.

Lyle descends from the Sedwick and Bridger families of Mercer County and was born and raised in the Galesburg, Knox County area. Arlene is from Yates City and later the Galesburg area.

The Sedwicks were married in the First Christian Church Galesburg on 7 June 1953 by Rev. T.W. Jolly. Their church membership today remains with the Christian Church in Gerlaw, Illinois.

Twin daughters were born to this marriage: Elaine Kay Dean now of Monmouth and Ellen Fay Klump of Knoxville Illinois. They boast of having two children, five grand children and three great-grandchildren.

CLIFFORD AND MARGARET (LENZ) SHAFER - Shafer, Clifford E., is the oldest son of Clifton Eugene and Ethel Lucille Shafer. To this union was born six boys and four girls, there were Raymond, Gloria, Meridith, Ada, Helen, Joan, Lyle, Richard, and Robert.

"Cliff", as he was known, grew up in Henderson County, Illinois. He was born at Stronghurst 29 April 1921. The family lived on a farm west of Stronghurst and Cliff, the oldest, started school at Maple Grove, a one-room school with eight grades. They then moved to Kirkwood, where his father farmed for two years before moving to a farm one half mile west of the Biggsville Junction on Route #164, where most of the brothers and sisters went to Hazel Dell school, which was one and a half miles east. As a youth he was presented a 24 Caret award by radio station WLS for saving the life of a lad in the "Old Swimming Hole."

In September 1940 Cliff met Margaret Lenz and on 11 May 1941 in Cahokia, Missouri they were married. They came to Monmouth in Warren County where Cliff got a job at the "Old Vac" factory. He later took a job with "Larson's Furniture Mart" delivering furniture. It was at this time Cliff went out on his own, free lancing – laying inlaids, carpet, and ceramic tile. He was also learning to recover furniture. In 1961 it became his full time occupation – he is still active at 81 years old. When the "Farm King" store built north of town. Margaret became office manager until retiring. She helps Cliff manage the shop now and enjoys reading. For outside entertainment they enjoy the Monmouth travel club and Cliff has organized the Tri-County Scottish Rite Club.

They love their four children; Lee Shafer of Athens, Illinois, Jane Morris of Naperville, Illinois, June Podschweit of Batavia, Illinois, and Larry Shafer of Lampoc, California. The entire family were baptized in the First Christian Church of Monmouth, where Cliff was Sunday School Superintendent several years. They have lived at 508 South "B" Street in Monmouth forty-nine years. Both have been active in "Christian Keenagers" sponsored by the church for the Senior Citizens of Monmouth. They have a great love for friends who need comfort and care.

Cliff's greatest love is in Masonry. He received the honorary 33° from the Moline Consistory when he was inducted in Pittsburg, Pennsylvania – the highest degree in Masonry. He belongs to all Masonic Bodies; Blue Lodge, Chapter, Council, and Commandery. He has also joined the Eastern Star and Low Twelve Club. He was chosen by his friend and Mason Most Worshipful Grand Master John Louden Jr. in 1994-96 to the position of Worshipful Junior then Senior Grand Deacon. His picture adorns the wall of the temple for his outstanding service to Monmouth Lodges. As a fifty-year member he has served as Master of the Lodge at Monmouth (1961 & 62) two terms and in Kirkwood in 1993. He was secretary of the Lodge during its "Centennial" celebration and District Deputy Grand Master of the 4th Western District eighteen years. He has memorized every word of the Blue Lodge as well as every procedure as a certified Lodge Instructor. He has done all this with only an eighth grade education. He has educated himself.

JOHN AND RUTH SHAUMAN - John McNary (Mac) Shauman was born. July 31, 1923 in Monmouth, IL. Ruth Meyer was born January 23, 1920 in her grandparents house at Jack's Mill near Oquawka, IL. They were married September 17, 1944 in the home of Ruth's parents near Rozetta, IL. They have two children, Wendell who married Janet Agan and Judith who married Daniel Fillip. They have four grandchildren: Austin, Janelle (Reeder), and Michael Shauman and Carrie Filip (Bland). They have four great-grandchildren: Sadie, Jefferson, and Alexis Shauman and Jordan Reeder.

Ruth and John (Mac) Shauman

Mac's parents were Hugh McNary and Dorothy Burgland Shauman. Mac had a sister, Marian Hutchisson, and a brother, Gerald. Hugh was born in Monmouth on August 26, 1896. Dorothy was born on October 8, 1896 in a sod house near Enid, OK. She was reared in Dodge City, KS until her mother, Hattie Tarbox Burgland, died. At the age of six, her father, Peter, sent her back to Kirkwood to be raised by an aunt. Ruth's parents were John Carl and Bessie Edith Radmacher Meyer. Ruth had a brother, Glen Melvin Meyer, and a sister, Marcelyn Lois (A. Eugene) Miller.

Mac lived most of his life on the farm in section 11 and 12 in Tompkins Township on which he was reared. The house he was raised in was built for his parents in 1918 when they were married. Mac and Ruth reared their family in the same house. Mac farmed in Warren and Henderson counties buying four farms. He continued a long family history of multi-livestock enterprises. He milked 25-35 Ayrshires for over twenty years. He and his father had a registered herd of Shorthorns for a number of years. He farrowed 100-150 sows per year for many years. Mac's father started him farming on a 17-acre field. In 2002, he planted that field for the 61st time. He served on the Warren County Farm Bureau board, the Stock Land FS board and worked with extension farm advisors. He served on the school board of Coonville School and the Kirkwood elementary school board.

Ruth was involved with home extension and served on the Farm Bureau Women's committee. She was actively involved with her children's school activities and in the Kirkwood Presbyterian Church. She served on Session, taught Sunday School and vacation Bible school, played the piano and organ and was active in the women's association. Ruth worked at the National Bank of Monmouth for 25 years where she was the first woman teller. When drive up banking began, she worked the drive up window. She also was the farm's bookkeeper.

Mac and Ruth traveled through much of the US, especially the western states. In 1993 they traveled to Alaska for their fiftieth anniversary.

WENDELL AND JANET AGAN SHAUMAN - Wendell Lee Shauman was born October 19,1945 and Janet Mae Agan was born February 2, 1945, both in Monmouth, IL. They were married in the Alexis EUB Church on August 20, 1967. Their children are Austin Donald, Janelle Ruth (Reeder), and Michael John. Austin's children are Sadie Lynn, Jefferson Scott, and Alexis Donielle Shauman. Janelle has a daughter Jordan MaeAnn Reeder. Michael is studying aviation at Southern Illinois University and was a certified instrument flight instructor at age 19.

Wendell's parents are John M. and Ruth Meyer Shauman. Wendell has one sister Judith Filip. He was raised in the farm home three miles east of Kirkwood on what has commonly been referred to as "Shauman's corner." Wendell graduated from Yorkwood High School in 1963 and then attended Monmouth College where he majored in chemistry and received his B.A. in 1967.

Janet and Wendell Shauman, December 2000

Janet's parents were Orville and Alice Davis Agan. Janet has two sisters, Judy (Malcolm) and Betty (Beeson) and three brothers, John, James, and Dennis. Janet was raised in Alexis graduating from Alexis High School in 1963. She attended Western Illinois University majoring in mathematics and received her B.S. Ed. in 1967.

Wendell and Janet began their life together in Lincoln, NE. Wendell earned an M.S. in Agronomy and a Ph.D. in Genetics (Corn Breeding). Janet taught math at Waverly Jr.-Sr. High School while earning her M.Ed. They moved to Bloomington, IL 1971 where Wendell was a corn breeder for Funk Seeds doing research from IL to Pennsylvania and north into Canada. While running a corn-breeding nursery in Peru, IN, they discovered distant Shauman relatives and much family history going back six generations. They returned to Kirkwood in 1975 to be fifth generation farmers. They began on Wendell's great-grandfather Hugh Thomson's farm. Janet returned to teaching high school math in 1984 at Monmouth High School.

Both were active in civic organizations. They were 4-H leaders. Both were members of the session and parish council of the Westminster UP church in Kirkwood. Janet taught Sunday School and Bible school and served as clerk of session. She belonged to P.E.O., sang with Monmouth Ecumenical Singers, and was active on committees in the Monmouth schools. Wendell served on extension youth and executive councils and the Warren County Farm Bureau holding all the offices and was chosen for the first class of the IL Agricultural Leadership Program. He served on the Yorkwood school board for nearly twenty years. He served on the state boards of IL Farm Bureau, IL Soybean Association, and IL Corn Marketing board, a unique accomplishment. The U of IL Dean of Agriculture, the director of the IL Department of Agriculture, the Council for Agricultural Research, and the Lt. Governor appointed Wendell to various state committees. He served on a national committee for the American Farm Bureau, was a director of the US Grains Council, and was involved with the US Meat Export Federation and the National Corn Growers Association.

DAVID R. AND PATSEY HALEY SHELTON

- David R. Shelton (1792-1847) and Patsey Haley Shelton (1795-1883), were born in Virginia, and were married in Barren County, Kentucky, in 1813. He was a school teacher there for several years, but eventually returned to farming. Patsey's father was Henry B. Haley and her mother Jane Rivers. David was a veteran of the War of 1812, and he and Patsey received bounty lands and pensions in Illinois after the war.

Shelton tombstone, Silent Home Cemetery. David R. – December 23, 1792 – March 16, 1847, age 54y 2m 23d – died and buried at Hazel Green, Wisconsin. Patsey – June 12, 1795 – November 30, 1883, age 88y 5m 15d – his wife

John Talbor purchased land in Warren County, Illinois, in 1828 and passed the word back about the potential there, so that same year in Whitman, Lucas, Haley and Murphy men came and purchased land. The following year they moved their families from Kentucky.

David and Patsey moved their twelve children in 1837, and in two years had a new home. Their farming expanded as each son and daughter moved to their own land. Years later they owned many acres as an expanded family.

David meanwhile had lead mining interests in Hazelgreen, Wisconsin, and died there of an illness and was buried there in 1847. Patsey died on her farm near Cameron in 1883 and inscriptions of each one are on her tombstone at "Silent Home" Cemetery in Cameron. Many of their children are also buried there.

Samuel T. Shelton, their 3rd son wrote a 24-page biography of his parents and family, and the following is the first two pages of it, published in 1884 by the *Monmouth Review*:

From: Family Record of David and Patsey Shelton, December 23, 1792, to November 30, 1883. By S.T. Shelton. Published 1884. Printed by Monmouth Review Job Print. From a copy in the possession of Mrs. H.T. Zimmerman, Cameron, Ill., (1950).

"I have, in making up the Record, given Grandfather Shelton's Family Record (which I have copies from the old family Bible when there on a visit in 1881) and then father's family record ... I have failed in getting Grandfather Haley's family record.

Grandfather Shelton moved from Virginia to Kentucky in an early day. He settled on a farm on Dix River, near Danville, and built a mill on said river. He served in the Revolutionary War of 1776, for which he and his widow drew a pension. She survived him several years. He was an Elder in the Presbyterian Church of Danville for many. They both died and were buried on the old homeplace where they settled more than one hundred years ago.

I visited their old home in the fall of 1881 for the first time, went into the old stone house and also went to where they were buried nearby and stood by their graves in sad contemplation of the past. Uncle Thomas lived on the old home for many years. He subsequently sold it and moved nearer to Danville where he died in 1871. His children, most of them, still live near the old home. Grandfather's other children moved to other states and the dates of their deaths are known by me.

Grandfather Haley also came from Virginia in an early day to Kentucky, and settled in Barren County near Prewitt's Knob, where he was engaged in farming, selling goods, and peddling during the war of 1776. He and his wife were members of the Baptist Church. They both died and were buried on the old homeplace, near the old brick house that has stood there over a hundred years. I also stood by their graves, and my thoughts were full of the scenes of the by-gone days.

My father and mother were married in that old brick house over seventy years ago. I was born not far from that spot some sixty years ago; hence the surroundings made an impression on my mind not soon to be forgotten.

Father, after living for a few years at two or three places, finally settled on a farm near the old home of my mother. Father being a cripple (a stiff ankle), was educated in Danville College, that he might follow some profession. He, however, only followed teaching for a few years, and then chose farming which he followed the remainder of his life.

All their children except the youngest were born there. Their oldest daughter was also married at their old home, whom we left when our family left there on the 27th day of October, 1837, for Warren County, Illinois, where we arrived on 24th day of November, 1837. The elder daughter and her husband, left behind, came on the next fall.

The outfit for moving was a large Kentucky wagon with a yoke of oxen in the tongue and a span of horses in lead. Had very fine weather till we crossed the Illinois River at Beardstown, after which it rained and snowed, rendering travel almost impossible; which caused stops with the early settlers who also gave us a cordial welcome to their log cabins and feasted on venison and wild turkey, which was no small job when we remember there were twelve of us to feed.

We finally reached our log cabin which had been vacated for us. It was called "catch-'em-all" because so many lived in it. The idea would be considered incredible now of so large a family wintering in such a building. The cabin was about sixteen feet square; built of round logs, cracks filled with black mud, puncheon floor, roof of split boards held on by large poles, chimney wood and mortar, back and jams of dirt beat in solid with a maul. The cooking vessels consisted of skillot, oven, pot, frying pan, and coffee pot, stoves not being heard of at that time. No matches yet; had to go to a neighbor's and "borrow some fire."

We lived in this cabin some two years and then settled on a place in Floyd Township. Sarah, the youngest daughter, was born in that cabin.

Father, with some others, went into the lead mines in Wisconsin in 1845 and spent the summer. He returned there again in 1847 on business and in a short time was taken sick and died on the 16th of March, 1847, and was buried near Hazel Green, Wisconsin. Peter went for him in a carriage but father died before he reached there. In those times there were not railroads or telegraphs; besides the roads or highways were no railroads or telegraphs; besides the roads or highways were little worked owing to the thinly settled condition of the country. It was therefore almost impossible to remove the remains of one any considerable distance in those times.

Mother remained on the old home the remainder of her life. She drew a pension several years for services of father in the War of 1812. Their children, except three, remained in Illinois where they all procured homes. Peter went to Iowa where he died. Henry and Sarah are living in Missouri. Father and mother and all their children, except one, were members of the Christian Church as were a large portion of grand great-grandchildren.

Trusting that each of our large family will continue this record by adding to it that they may hand down to their posterity a family record our children's children will highly appreciate, the thought led me to undertake to work of procuring this record, thinking how much I would like to be able to go back in the past centuries and have a record of our ancestors."

– S.T. Shelton, Cameron Ill., February 28th, 1884. (The foregoing is the Preface to the Family Record published 1884).

Samuel Shelton, born November 3, 1758. Died May 28, 1833. From Louisa County, Virginia. Jane Henderson, born March 19, 1758. Died September 11, 1841. From Hanover County, Virginia. They were married May 22, 1781. Had children:

William H., February 8, 1782. Elizabeth A., March 16, 1784. Peter S., June 15, 1787. Mary H., June 30, 1790. David R., December 23, 1792, March 16, 1847; married Patsey Haley. Nancy H., July 5, 1795. Thomas, October 16, 1797, December 8, 1871. John H., December 5, 1799.

David R. Shelton, as a young man, came to home of Patsey Haley's father for the purpose of interviewing him. David R. was seeking a position as a school-teacher and it was in connection with this that he called at the Haley home. Patsey, seeing him ride in (on horseback), said to herself: "There's *my* man." And so it proved, as in due course they were married. (This from Betty Clayton. It was told to her by Julia Shelton Clayton.)

Samuel T. Shelton also wrote in his biography, "When the day closed, the mantel of the old fireplace was covered with offerings of the little ones, Patsey would sit watching the fire and smoking her pipe of peace."

Henry Haley Shelton was born 1817 in Boyle County, Kentucky and moved with his parents David and Patsey to Barren County, Kentucky, and on to Cameron, Illinois. He married Mary Bourne in 1841, and Jane Vaughn in 1851. Henry, David and Patsey were members of the Cedar Fork Christian Church in Warren County.

Henry and Jane moved to Mercer County, Missouri in 1858 and farmed in Mercer and Grundy Counties. Henry was a member of Company "B", 23rd Missouri Infantry at the Battle of Shilo and was badly injured. They each are buried at "Honey Creek Cemetery" in Grundy

County, Missouri. He died in 1888 and Jane in 1891. Jane was born in 1831.

Submitted by Dale K. Shelton, great-great-grandson of David and Patsey

SHERIDAN FAMILY - Sheridan, Robert Eugene, was born in Monmouth, Illinois, on March 8, 1921, the youngest child of Philip Henry and Mildred Murphy Sheridan. Bob married Pauline Leafgreen (b. 9/4/1920), daughter of William and Estella Leafgreen of Rio, Illinois, on May 5, 1940. The couple remained wedded until Bob's untimely death on December 26, 1990.

Timothy, Bob, Pauline, Mary Lou, William Sheridan

Family records show that James and Rose Sheridan, from Cork and Dublin, Ireland, eloped and traveled to America on their honeymoon around 1846. They became shipwrecked off the coast of New York City and were separated for three days. The couple settled for several years in Erie, Pennsylvania, eventually moving to Cascade, Iowa, by covered wagon. James and Rose raised eight children including John Augusta (b. 12/10/1852).

John Augusta Sheridan moved to Cameron, Illinois. In December 1880, he married Mary Jane Marsh (b. 5/6/1860), the daughter of Andrew and Emmaline Baker Marsh. John and Mary initially farmed land north of Coldbrook and later purchased and farmed land near Cameron. The couple had six children including Philip Henry (b. 1/28/1892) and Laura (b. 5/17/1890).

Philip Sheridan married Mildred Murphy, while Laura wedded Axel Ahlstrand. Philip and Mary had five children. Two sons died at birth, and a daughter, Elsie, succumbed at age 22 months. The deaths of Mildred (d. 7/31/22) and Phil (d. 6/2/25) orphaned their two surviving sons, John Henry and Robert Eugene. Aunt Laura and Uncle Axel Ahlstrand took John and Bob into their home and raised them, along with their daughter, Evelyn.

An active youth, Bob enjoyed duck hunting, fishing, sailing, and school sports. Working for his uncle's construction firm, Bob developed into a knowledgeable and highly skilled carpenter. After graduating from Monmouth High School in 1938, Bob attended Monmouth College where he played football and joined the Alpha Tau Omega fraternity. Meanwhile, he met future spouse Pauline on a blind date arranged through friends.

The couple married in 1940. Their first child, Mary Louise, arrived on January 5, 1941. A son Robert William (Bill) came along on August 15, 1943. The family resided in Monmouth as Bob continued to work for Ahlstrand construction.

Bob volunteered for military duty in June 1944. He entered service at Ft. Sheridan, Illinois, and received basic training at Camp Roberts, California. Pfc. Sheridan served in Company F, 163rd Infantry Regiment, 41st Division, as a Rifleman. He saw duty in New Guinea, Leyte, Mindanao, Mindoro, Philippine Islands, and the Tawi-Tawi group near Borneo. Near Tamboango, Mindanao, Bob took a machine gun bullet in the ankle. Subsequent duty took him to Okinawa and Kure, Japan. Bob received one battle star, an Arrow Head, a Purple Heart, and the Combat Infantryman's badge.

While Bob fought in the Pacific, Pauline, Bill and Mary resided in Galesburg. After being discharged from service, Bob rejoined both his family and uncle's construction company. With assistance from fellow carpenters, Bob built a family home at 1116 East First Avenue, Monmouth. The family assumed residence in 1948. On January 18, 1954, a second son, Timothy Philip, was born.

Committed to service, Bob assumed an active role in community affairs. He held memberships in the American Legion, VFW, and Odd Fellows. He served as a volunteer fireman and held leadership positions with the Red Cross, Prime Beef Festival Committee, Lion's Club, Zoning Board of Appeals, MHS Athletic Booster Club, and First Lutheran Church. For many years, he taught Sunday school and coached summer league softball and baseball.

Bob's work career shifted from carpentry and cabinet making when he became manager of Warfield's Lumber Yard. Bob gained specialized training in kitchen design and used his knowledge and skill in the construction and remodeling of many homes in the region. In the mid 1960s, Bob joined the sales team of Galesburg Glass Company. He remained with that organization for over twenty years. In the late-1980s, son Bill coaxed Bob into joining Sheridan Oil Company in Normal, Illinois. He proudly worked with his son until the time of his death.

Having stayed at home to raise their children, Pauline managed the Phone Set Shop for several years in the 1960s. In 1970, she embarked on a new career, enrolling in the Licensed Practical Nursing program offered through Carl Sandburg College. She completed her degree as a Phi Beta Kappa graduate. For the next eighteen years, Pauline worked full-time at Monmouth's Community Memorial Hospital.

Despite his active involvement in community affairs, Bob Sheridan's greatest source of satisfaction came from his family. He was a devoted son-in-law to Bill and Estella Leafgreen. He demonstrated great love for his wife Pauline and their three children. Bob and brother John retained a special bond through the years. The emergence of grandchildren and great-grandchildren brought extraordinary pleasure to the Sheridans.

Daughter Mary Lou graduated from Monmouth High School in 1958. She attended Monmouth College until marrying Daniel Lindberg (Kirkwood) on June 7, 1959. The couple had three children, Gaye Kathleen (Kathy), David, and Melissa. A career employee for the Kroger Company, Dan recently retired as a store manager. Meanwhile, Mary continues to work in banking in Litchfield, Illinois. Kathy married Scott Gray on August 16, 1980. The couple resides in Beaverton, Oregon, and has three children, Amanda, Kathleen, and Bradley. David (Morton, Illinois) married Janet Mennering on June 23, 1984. They have a daughter, Danielle. Melissa (Portage, Indiana) married Michael Anderson on June 21, 1986. The Anderson's have three children, Jacob, Jessica, and Jeremy.

In 1961, Bill Sheridan graduated from MHS. After attending the University of Illinois and Monmouth College, Bill finished his Bachelor's degree in marketing at the University of Iowa. Bill married the former Jalaine Light of Monmouth on August 14, 1965. A member of the Army ROTC, Bill received commissioning as a 2nd Lieutenant and served in Viet Nam. Bill and Jalaine eventually settled in Normal, Illinois, where they raised their three children, Jeffrey, Stephanie, and Ashley. Jalaine has worked as a nurse and school health educator. She also assists Bill who founded and heads Sheridan Oil Company, along with managing several other business ventures. Daughter Stephanie married Tony Sandre on October 3, 1998. The couple has a son, Jackson Anthony.

Tim Sheridan graduated from MHS in 1972. He matriculated to DePauw University where he received a Bachelor's in political science in 1976. Tim earned a Master's in college student personnel administration at Indiana University in 1979. On August 9, 1980, Tim married Gina Burgan of Anderson, Indiana. Currently, he serves as Director of Student Judicial Programs and as an adjunct professor at Western Illinois University. A former teacher, Gina is an ordained clergy serving as the Associate Pastor for First United Methodist Church in Galesburg, Illinois. The couple has two children, son Corey and daughter Kelly.

Celebrating Christmas as a family brought special joy to Bob and Pauline. Granddaughter Kathy recalled sitting next to Grandpa during a candlelight Christmas Eve service at First Lutheran Church. As the family packed tightly together in the pew singing "Silent Night," the glowing candles enhanced the twinkle in his eye. Grandpa Bob surveyed his family, then leaned over to Kathy and said, "It doesn't get any better than this."

DAVID AND MARY LEE SHUNICK - The Shunick family traces their ancestors back to David Shunick who was born in Killeagh, County Cork, Ireland in 1796, and died August 14, 1879 in Spring Grove Township, Warren County, Illinois. He married Mary Lee in Ireland in 1824. He came to the U.S. in 1851 with his six sons leaving his wife Mary to come at a later date, but she died in Ireland.

The oldest son Edmond (1825-1914) married Hanora Croft (1826-1902). They had 13 children but only 6 were living when their father died in 1914. They were Dave Shunick of Alexis, Ed Shunick of Cameron, Mrs. James Noonan and Mrs. John Noonan of Monmouth, Mrs. Pat Conroy of Bloomington and Mrs. John Welsh of Galesburg.

The second son was Richard Shunick (1826-1907) who was 22 when they came to the U.S. He married Elizabeth O'Neill and had 6 children, 4 sons and 2 daughters: Thomas, M.D., Edward J., David, Mrs. Mary Baldwin and Mrs. Nelle Boozan.

The third son was Morris Shunick (1830-1864), born in County Cork, Ireland, and died in Warren County, IL. He married Bridget Boozan (1836-1918) and had one step-son, Morris.

The fourth son was John Shunick (1830-1898) who married Catherine Lee (1836-1902). They were married in Albany, N. Y. in 1855. Their 14 children were: John W., Mary Mollie, Anastasia, Julia Agnes, Morris J., Frannie, Harriett, Nora, Anna, Kate, Frances, David Henry, Blanche and Theresa.

The fifth son was David (1834-1917), born in Kelleagh, County Cork, and died in Warren County. He married Julia O'Connell (1850-1882). They had 6 children: Mary, Julia, Elizabeth, Ellen, Nora and Thomas.

The sixth son was Thomas (1834-1913), also born in County Cork. He married Ellen Mahoney (1844-1895). They had 12 children, but only 6 survived their father. The surviving children were Thomas Jr., Morris T., William Charles, Madge Fitzgerald and Mrs. Martin Graham.

RICHARD AND ELIZABETH O'NEILL SHUNICK - Richard Shunick (1826-1907), second son of David Shunick (18261907) and Mary Lee, came to the U.S. from Ireland with his father and five brothers in 1851. Richard married Elizabeth O'Neill, and they had six children, 4 sons and 2 daughters: Thomas, Edward J., M.D., Daniel, Mrs. Mary Baldwin, and Mrs. Nelle Boozan.

Thomas (1858-1927) married Mary Stack (1859-1944). They had four children: Edward James, Richard Louis, Elizabeth Clare and Hanora Marie. Edward James married Nell McNamara Cooke and had two sons: Robert who married Mary Jane Blake and had one stepdaughter Regina, and John R. who married Judith A. Dennison. They had 3 children: Jennifer Ann, John R. and Julie Ann.

Elizabeth Clare (Bessie) married John Collins, and they had two daughters, Mary Rose and Elizabeth. Mary Rose married Leonard Durch and had 3 daughters: Denise Ault, Renee Carpenter and Mary Louise. Elizabeth married Tom O'Brien and had a daughter, Lorraine, and a son, Thomas, Jr.

Hanora Marie (Nona) married Edward Conley and had a daughter, Mary Alice.

Richard Loui (9-26-1888) married Sadie Cavanaugh (12-26-1889), and they had 6 children: Lucille, Vera, Rosemary, Ruth, Richard E. and Thomas J.

RICHARD AND SADIE CAVANAUGH SHUNICK - Richard Louis Shunick was born September 26, 1888, the son of Thomas Shunick (1858-1927) and Mary Stack (1859-1944). He married Sadie Cavanaugh who was born December 26, 1889. Their 6 children were Lucille, Vera, Rosemary, Ruth, Richard E. and Thomas J.

Richard L. and Sadie Cavanaugh Shunick family. L: to R: Sister M. Bernadette, O.S.B., Vera Shunick Cofield, Rosemary Shunick, Sister M. Veronica, O.S.B., Richard E. Shunick, Thomas J. Shunick, circa 1985

Lucille (now Sister M. Bernadette) and Ruth (now Sister M. Veronica) entered St. Mary Monastery of the Sisters of St. Benedict at Nauvoo, Illinois. In 2001 the Sisters moved from Nauvoo to a newly constructed monastery in Rock Island, Illinois.

Vera married Earl C. Cofield. Earl was parts manager for the Chevrolet-Cadillac Dealership in Monmouth for 35 years. Vea was the secretary for the Warren County Highway Department. Their 4 children are Gregory, Joseph, Philip and Rosemary. Gregory and his wife Connie have 2 children, Jennifer and Jason. He works for General Motors in Parker, Colorado. Joseph and his wife Julie Freil have 2 sons, Justin and Andrew. Joseph is the Vice-president of the University of Massachusetts and lives in Needham, Massachusetts.

Philip, the president of Junior Achievement for Utah and Wyoming, is located in Sandy, Utah. His 2 daughters are Calla and Megan.

Rosemary married Jeffrey Freel with Meredith Publishing Company in Des Moines, Iowa. She is a guidance counsler at Southeast Polk High School near Altona, IA. They have 2 children, Allison Marie and Jonathan Earl.

Rosemary (1920), the third daughter of Richard and Sadie Shunick, was employed in the office of Wirtz Book Store for a number of years and later was the administrative assistant in the office of the Federal Land Bank Association of Monmouth until her retirement in 1985.

Richard E. Shunick (1924) married Margery Ann Berger and had 5 children, 1 daughter and 4 sons. Julie Ann married Thomas Brown o Dallas, Texas and has 3 chldren: Erin, Richard and Brendan. Their 4 boys – David, Mark, Brian and John – are all located in the Phoenix area. Dick served in World War II and later worked with the Dept of Interior with the Bureau of Reclamation. For a number of yars he was the project manager for theCentral Arizona Project before retiring in Scottsdale, AZ.

Thomas (1927-1997) married Liane Enderlin, and they had 3 children: Richard Lawrence, Michael Thomas and Sheila Ann. Richard is with American Air Lines at O'Hare Airport in Chicago; Michael is an antique dealer in the St. Louis area; and Sheila, a lawyer, lives in Webster Grove, MO. with her husband, Judge Michael Burton. Their 3 children are Thomas, Molly, and Caroline. Tom served in both World War II and the Korean War. He was the Art Director at a Moline television station for many years. Liane taught school for 25 years. Upon their retirement they moved to Lake Warren north of Monmouth.

THOMAS SIENKEWICZ - Sienkewicz, Thomas J., son of Edmund R. and Maria F. (Liguori) Sienkewicz, was born on April 29, 1950 in Hoboken, New Jersey. He was the first of five children. Tom attended St. Peter's Preparatory School in Jersey City, New Jersey, and the College of the Holy Cross in Worcester, Massachusetts, from which he graduated with honors in Classics in 1971. He then obtained a M.A. (1973) and Ph.D. (1975) in Classics at The Johns Hopkins University in Baltimore, Maryland. While at Hopkins he met his future wife Anne Frances Waterman. They were married in Rockport, Maine, in 1972.

Anne Frances Waterman Sienkewicz, daughter of Richard D. and Dorothy (Stump) Waterman, was born on November 14, 1950, in Rockland Maine. She was the oldest of three children. Anne was valedictorian of the last graduating class of Waldoboro High School in 1968 and attended the University of Maine at Orono and Laval University in Quebec. Anne received her B.A. in French with highest distinction from the University of Maine in 1971 and then an M.A. (1974) and Ph.D. (1978) in French at The Johns Hopkins University in Baltimore, Maryland. Anne and Tom studied in Paris, France, during the academic year 1973-1974.

Sienkewicz Family

Tom was a professor of Classics at Howard University from 1975 until 1984. During this period Tom and Anne lived first in Severn, Maryland, and then in Mount Rainier, Maryland. They also lived for four months in Scotland in 1980. Their three children were all born in Washington, D.C.: Marie Kathleen on July 19, 1977, Julia Alice on March 21, 1980, and Richard Oscar on August 13, 1982.

In 1984 the Sienkewicz family moved to Monmouth, Illinois, where Tom became the Minnie Billings Capron Professor of Classics. In 1992-1993 he was the visiting director of the ACM Program in Florence, Italy. Anne has taught French at Monmouth, Knox, and Augustana Colleges. From 1997 to 2000 she was the administrative assistant for the Warren County United Way. In 2000 she became the administrative assistant and bookkeeper for the Western Illinois Chapter of the American Red Cross in Galesburg, Illinois.

Marie, Julia, and Richard graduated in 1996, 1998, and 2000 respectively from Monmouth High School where all were inducted into the National Honor Society and the Academic Hall of Fame. Marie graduated from Bowdoin College in Brunswick, Maine, with a B.A. in Classics, summa cum laude in 1999, and from the University of Illinois in Urbana with an M.L.S. in 2001. She is presently working towards a degree in Veterinary Medicine at the University of Illinois. Julia graduated from Mt. Holyoke College in South Hadley, Massachusetts with a B.A. in Art History with honors in 2001. She is presently working towards a Ph.D. in Art History at the University of Illinois. Richard is a East Asian Studies major at Lawrence University in Appleton, Wisconsin.

The family has lived at 1103 East Second Avenue in Monmouth since 1985 and attend Immaculate Conception Catholic Church.

JOHN AND KATHERINE SIMONSON - Simonson, John E., son of S.V.A. and Bessie (Henry) Simonson, was born in Wolseley, Saskatchewan, Canada on 9 March 1922. He returned, with his parents, to Warren County, Illinois in 1925.

After serving for four years in the United States Navy during World War II, he worked for the Barrows-Addleman garage for several years before becoming an Illinois Patrolman until his retirement in 1981.

Katherine and John Simonson, 1998

He married Katherine Huston, daughter of Frank C. and Margaret (Frank) Huston, on 28 February 1945. Katherine was a teacher at Harding School, Monmouth, and at Roseville Elementary School, retiring in 1976.

They have two children: Janice Simonson Bocke (Joseph) of Quincy, Illinois and Miles K. Simonson (Victoria) of Long Beach, California. Their three granddaughters are Elizabeth Katherine Buck, Denver, Colorado; Amy Kristine Summers, Atlanta, Georgia and Jennifer Simonson, deceased. Their great-grandson is Tyler J. Buck, Denver, Colorado.

John and Katherine reside in Roseville where they are members of the Roseville Methodist Church.

ALEXANDER C. SIMPSON - Emma Green(e) Hill married Alexander Cunningham Simpson March 8, 1888 in Warren County Illinois. Alexander was born 26 May 1863 in Suez Township Mercer County Illinois and died February 5, 1949 in Monmouth, Illinois. He was a farmer and member of the Norwood Presbyterian Church and is buried in the Norwood Cemetery Suez Township Mercer County. They reared their children on the farm. Their children: Rex Kenneth Simpson born 23 Jan 1889 died 26 Nov 1979 married Florence Hennenfent 24 February 1921.

Alexander Cunningham Simpson and wife Emma Hill.

Thomas Moore Simpson born 7 December 1890, died 24 January 1975.in Clinton, Iowa, married Florence Alma Bates 12 May 1921; Clifford Hill Simpson born 15 September 1892, died 5 February 1977 in Galesburg, Illinois, married Edna Grace Josephson 18 February 1914 in Mercer County, Illinois and died May 23, 1989 Monmouth Illinois; Bessie Leona Simpson born 7 August 1895, died Nov 1955, married George Alvin Renard 6 February 1918 in Warren County Illinois; Hugh Lytle Simpson born 12 August 1897 died 17 September 1975 in Bend Oregon, married Gladys Elizabeth Pollock 25 June 1929 in Albany, Oregon; Nellie Kathryn Simpson born 2 December 1902, died 5 November 1980, married Harry Claude Thompson 4 October 1921 in Chicago, Illinois. Alexander's parents, Robert Moore Simpson and Catherine Lang came to Illinois about 1855 from Pennsylvania. Alexander's grandparents Alexander Moore Simpson (1807-1889) and Margaret Cunningham (1810-1890) also came to Illinois about 1855 from Pennsylvania. Alexander's great-grandfather, Robert Simpson, born 1773 in Ireland and died September 1, 1848 in Huntingdon County Pennsylvania. Robert married Nancy Moore April 3, 1798 in Huntingdon County, Pennsylvania to whom at least 4 children were born. Robert married Sarah Jackson August 22, 1822 in Huntingdon County Pennsylvania. Sarah came to Illinois with her step-son, Alexander Moore Simpson. They all were farmers and became members of the Norwood Presbyterian Church.

DANIEL S. SIMS - Daniel S. Sims moved to Little York in 1964. Dan brought with him his wife, the former Jane Van Eaton, and three children. Dan and his father, Frazier Sims, owned a grocery store and locker plant in Seaton prior to the move.

Jane and Dan Sims

Dan began employment at First State Bank of Little York in 1960, as assistant cashier. At that time R.L. Brownlee was president, Ray M. Whiteman cashier and Mary Jean Tharp assistant cashier.

In January 1970, the stockholders voted to build a brick colonial style bank that was opened in May 1971. Dan served as its president until the bank was sold to owners of Monmoth Trust and Savings Bank in 1985. He served on that board one year as Senior Vice President before retiring in 1988. Dan's son, Tom, worked at the bank from 1973 to 1989.

Dan served on the Aledo and Yorkwood Boards of Education for a total of 7 years. During this time the Yorkwood District consisting of Kirkwood and Little York voted to build a high school half way between the two communities. Dan served on the Carl Sandburg College Foundation Board for 3 years.

Other community services include: 16 years as Village Clerk, 3 years on the Warren County YMCA Board, 3 years on the Warren County United Way Board as a charter member, and as a member of the volunteer fire department. Both Dan and Jane served as volunteers in Warren County at Community Memorial Hospital.

Dan is a lifetime member of the Presbyterian Church in Seaton and Little York. He served as elder for many years and as Sunday School Superintendent, and a member of the choir. He was active in the Monmouth Ministry Council for 5 years.

Dan is a Life Member of the Seaton Masonic Lodge and a Past Master. He was a Mohammed Temple Shriner for over 20 years. Dan was also a member of Aledo Shrine Club and Moped Parade Unit.

Much satisfaction came to Dan as an active member of the Lions Club. He was Charter President of the Little York Lions Club and the District Governor of Illinois 1977-78. He was chairman of the fund-raisers for 18 years. The main fund-raiser was selling California roses, and 400-500 dozen each year were sold. Dan and Jane attended 18 International Lions conventions, one of which was in Tokyo.

The Sims lived in Little York for 34 years, then Dan and Jane moved to Maryville, Tennessee to be near their son Tom and his family. Both Dan and Jane work as volunteers at Blount Memorial Hospital. Both are active in their new church. Dan works with the North Maryville Lions Club. Despite busy schedules the Sims make time to visit son Steve in Plantation, Florida and daughter Jody in San Diego, California and the three grandchildren.

After leaving Little York, Dan continues to live his life of service to others. He constantly strives to make this world a better place for his family and future generations.

D. RAYMOND AND HELEN SIMS - D. Raymond Sims and his wife Helen have resided on their farm in Warren County for over 50 years. Their farm is in Kelly Township, on the county line, 4 miles east of Alexis. The 132-acre farm was bought in 1947 from Carl Nelson of Chicago. In the tornado that destroyed Shanghai in 1868, all the buildings on the farm but the house were destroyed.

Helen and D. Raymond Sims

Mr. Sims is the son of William and Grace (Sharp) Sims. Mrs. Sims is the daughter of Harry and Evelyn (Nelson) Carlson. The Sims' have four children; Larry, Gary and Gene Sims of Alexis, and Brenda Fell of Galesburg.

Mr. Sims served on the Kelly Township board, and raised Hereford cattle. Mrs. Sims is active in the Alexis U.P. Church, the Daughters of the American Revolution, and was active in the P.T.O. Both received their education in Alexis. Their children all received their education at the Alexis Schools.

Submitted by Mrs. Raymond Sims

DEANE AND HELEN (NELSON) SLATER - Slater, M. Deane – 1480 60th St. Monmouth, IL, Tompkins Township; wife Helen J. (Nelson) Slater.

Deane's parents: Michael and Blanche (Long) Slater. Helen's parents: Oscar and Maude (Wetander) Nelson.

Deane's grandparents: Daniel and Elizabeth (Kelly) Slater and Ben and Ethel (Miller) Long. Helen's grandparents: John and Anna (Gustafson) Nelson and Charles and Augusta (Kullman) Wetander.

One of the Slater farms has been in the family for over 100 years and the farms are currently being farmed by son, Bill. Deane is a retired farmer and former co-owner of Abingdon Farm Equipment in Abingdon, IL.

Parents of six children: Robert Deane (Pam) Slater; Connie Lea Slater (deceased); William Gene Slater; Bonnie Jane (Robert) Teske; Becky June (Jim) Moore; Betty Louise (John) Frost.

Twelve grandchildren: Jim Slater, Cynthia Glisan, Patty Procino, Brandon Slater, Julie Seitz, Billy Slater, Nicole Jones, Kelli Winbigler, Megan Moore, John Frost, Dustin Frost and Britni Frost. Great-grandparents of fourteen children.

Members of Fairview Center United Methodist Church, and were married there on September 19, 1943.

C. ROY SMALLWOOD - C. Roy Smallwood, 94, of Monmouth, died at 9:10 p.m. Sunday, August 27, 2000, He was born 22 July 1906 in Rush Hill, Missouri, the son of Clarence L. and Fanny Iola (Wycoff) Smallwood. His early life was in Rush Hill. As a boy they moved to Monmouth where he attended public schools and graduated from Monmouth High School.

He married Madeline Estil Smallwood 24 December 1926 in Mexico, Missouri. Early on Roy served a time in the Illinois Militia. While in high school he was employed by the NBC Dairy part time. He later worked for the Illinois Bankers Life in Monmouth, where he managed the printing department. After their closing, Roy worked with his son, Bill, for twelve years at Norris Office Equipment of Monmouth until his retirement. He was a long time member of the First Christian Church of Monmouth, where he served as financial secretary, was a Deacon on the Church Board, When building their new building he helped in roofing the sanctuary. He was a member of the Kiwanis Club. Being an outstanding track man in high school, he loved sports – golf, bowling, and pool. Earlier he enjoyed Church League Softball and was an avid sports fan. He enjoyed motorcycles and rode his until the age of 91. His greatest joy was his family.

Survivors include his wife of 73 years. They had two sons, one John Estil was killed while serving on a U.S. Navy Submarine, the other, Bill and his wife Erma (Norris) of Monmouth, who have three children: Mary Ann and her husband, David Armstrong of Gull Lake, Michigan and their children Elissa, Spencer and his wife Melissa; a grandson, John Armstrong and his wife, Terry, of rural Monmouth, and her children – Jared, Brittany, Hilary and Jacob; and a granddaughter Susan Schilson and her husband, Terry, of St. Petersburg, Florida and his children – Scot, Timothy, Trea and Remi.

ADAM SMITH - Adam Smith was born to Samuel and Dora (Gaddis) Smith on May 23, 1840. Adam came to Warren County when he was eighteen years old from County Down, Ireland. He found work by the month as a farmhand. One such farm he found work on was that of James C. and Margaret (Brown) Nash who were among the early settlers of Warren County. The Nash's came to Warren County in 1835. While working on their farm he met and married their daughter, Elsie C. Nash who had been born in Warren County on September 23, 1836.

In 1883 Adam bought 80 acres in Section 21., Hale Township from Joseph Brown. Adam and Elsie (Nash) Smith had two sons, Robert James and Fred Brown. Adam died on May 6, 1898. At that time Elsie traveled to Stetler, Canada spending 4 years before she returned to the United States. Upon arrival back to Monmouth Elsie spent a year in town before returning to the farm. She died on March 5, 1919.

CLEO CLYDE AND GERALDINE ALICE GALBREATH SMITH - Cleo Clyde Smith, son of Alvia and Maggie Gearheart Smith, was born April 7, 1915 at Raritan, Illinois. When Cleo was a small child the family lived at Raritan and moved to Kirkwood in 1927 where he attended school and graduated from Kirkwood High School with the class of 1935. He had one brother, Harold Smith, who resides in Roseville. For several years after graduation Cleo worked for his Uncle Fred Smith at Smith's Grocery and in 1938 purchased the store from his uncle and then operated Smith's Grocery for forty-seven years before retiring. During this period Cleo was called into service in the Army and served in the Occupational Force in Japan for 4 years. Cleo Passed away in 1999 and is buried in Center Grove Cemetery at Kirkwood.

Cleo and Geraldine Smith

Geraldine Galbreath was born July 26, 1914 in Monmouth Hospital, daughter of Ivan Earl Galbreath and Mabel Jones Galbreath. She attended rural schools near Kirkwood and is a graduate of Kirkwood High School. After high school Geraldine helped her parents on their farm. In 1936 Cleo Smith and Geraldine were married and together they owned and operated Smith's Grocery. Geraldine also worked at the Yorkwood High School as secretary for 16 years retiring from that position in 1980. Geraldine has one sister, Mary Galbreath Easum of Monmouth.

Cleo and Geraldine had one daughter, Sandra and she and her husband Jerry Perrin live in Eldridge, Iowa. The Perrins have two sons, Rod and Cory and have five grandchildren all of Eldridge, Iowa.

Cleo served as Mayor of Kirkwood two terms, was active in the United Methodist Church serving as Lay Leader a number of years and held many other offices in the church. He was a member of the former Kirkwood Lions Club, Methodist Men, Booster Club, American Legion and Kirkwood Senior Citizens. Geraldine, also an active member of the United Methodist Church, taught Sunday School, is a member of the Kings' Daughters Sunday School Class, United Methodist Women, Kirkwood Senior Citizens and Chapter T, PEO.

DAVID AND ALTA RYNER SMITH - Alta Leone Ryner born 5 February 1894 Warren Co. Il. daughter of Jacob Henry and Annie Emma (Cobb) Ryner, Married 24 December 1914 Monmouth Il to David Smith, born 22 May 1887, Cutler, Perry Co. Il to Francis William an Sarah Margaret (Stevenson) Smith who married 31 December 1874, Perry Co. Il. Alta Leone died 18 August 1967, Monmouth, Il. David died 4 April 1984 David and Alta lived and farmed near Aledo, in Mercer Co. Il and near Little York in Henderson Co also Warren Co. Il.

David Smith family. Anna Margaret, Mary Louise, Donald David, Myra Leone, David (Dad), Betty Joan, Alta Leone (Mom), about 1941-42.

To this union were born; Donald David born 24 October 1915 married on 19 December 1945 to Dorothy Kell, daughter of Roy and Slyvia Kell. Mary Louise, born 7 Janauary 1917 married Roger Loveridge, son of Thomas and Pearl Loveridge. Mary died July 6,1984. Anna Margaret, born 25 January 1919, married on 7 January 1942 to Jack Snell son of Herb and Abby Snell, Jack is a WWII Veteran. Myra Leone born 19 January 1921, married on 9 August 1942 to Fred Brown son of Walter and Sadie Brown, Fred died 1 January 1994. Betty Joan born 19 February 1934, married on 3 July 1952 to Wayne Lee Kinkaid son of Frank "Dutch" and Rita Kinkaid.

DAVID AND PEARL SMITH - David Ralph Smith and Pearl Mae Yung were married Galesburg Il, 3-29-1967. David's parents were David "Clete" Smith (farmer) and Alice "Gertrude" Smith, (bank secretary) of rural Monmouth. Pearl's parents were Lawrence Yung (grain/livestock farmer and breeder of draft horses) and Marjorie (Campbell) Yung (teacher) of Alexis. Pearl has a brother Frank and wife Mary Yung of Alexis who had 3 sons and a daughter, and a sister Bernice (Mrs. Greg Errion) of' Collierville, Tn. who had two sons. David has been a grain/livestock farmer and conservationist in Warren County all his life. Pearl is a registered nurse and helps in their farm operation.

Pearl and David Smith

In 1853 David's (great-great-great-grandfather) William B. Smith age 60 along with his married son (GG Grandfather) David R. Smith age 41 and wife Elizabeth (Keller) Smith and their family including David's (G Grandfather) Charles J. Smith age 5 left from Rockingham County, Virginia to settle in the Illinois prairies. They stowed away their belongings in a wagon and started overland for Wheeling, W.Va. where they took passage on a boat and traveled by water to Oquawka. From there they again started overland, following one of the trails leading from the river town toward the east and finally came to a stopping place, now known as Lenox Twp. Warren Co. Il. where they established their farming. They were members of the Berwick Baptist Church, and were active in building the present Berwick Baptist church in 1859. In 1856 William B. Smith was found frozen to death on a day the temperature was 24 degree below zero. Charles J. Smith married Sarah Rounds 10-1-1875 and had five children Eva, Georgia (Mrs. Van Tassel), Myrtle, David R. and wife Sena (Ray) Smith, and Harold and wife Viola (Hartman) Smith. Charles raised and fed livestock and was a grain farmer.

David R. and Sena Smith were David's grandparents. They were grain/livestock farmers in Lenox Township and experienced the depression years. Their three children:

Frances (Mrs. Lyle Conway) had two sons: James and wife Barb, and Gary and wife Lynn of Berwick whose children are Brad, David and Katherine.

Ray E. and wife Phyllis Hayes who had three children: Marjorie (Mrs. Lanny Ford) who had three sons: Jeff, James and Jerry; Marilyn (Mrs. Allie Hasse) with son Tony and daughter Vickie; Terry and 1st wife Judy of New Braunsfels, Texas had two children Travis and Tracey. Terry's second wife is Connie.

David "Clete" and wife Gertrude (Tierney) Smith whose five children were Virginia (Mrs. Don Greiner- Fairfield, IA) Irene (Mrs. Dick Johnson- Winfield, IA) David R. (wife Pearl- Monmouth, IL) and Earl L. (wife Phillis- Kirkwood, IL) and a son Allen Clete who died in infancy. David's other Great-great-grandfather, Marshall Bedford Ray and Marshall's father Garland Ray gave the ground for Union Cemetery, Lenox Township, Warren Co. Also see Tierney and Ray elsewhere in this book.

EARL AND PHILLIS SMITH - Earl and Phillis (Cantwell) Smith were married 2-23-2002 and live in Kirkwood, Il. Earl has lived his lifetime in Warren County. He is the son of the late Clete and Gertrude (Tierney) Smith.

Earl and Phillis Smith

Earl grew up a farmer. He was the barn man for The Monmouth Sale Barn for many years, a dispatcher for Munson Truck Line and is now a welder for L & M Manufacturing. He raises quarter horses.

Phillis is the daughter of Roy and Bernice Cantwell of Bradford, Illinois. Phillis is employed as a production manager at Maple City Steel.

Earl has three daughters; Gina (Mrs. Rick Schulz) with sons, Dallas and Brayden. Brandy with a son Nathan, and Autumn in college. Phillis has three sons, Jerimi Jackson, and Roy "Joe" and wife Amanda Jackson, and Andrew Hickman. Her daughter Rene (Mrs. David Stick) has a son Brandon and a daughter Katlynn Garner.

FRED BROWN SMITH FAMILY - Fred B. Smith was born in Hale Township, October 27, 1881, the son of Adam and Elsie C. (Nash) Smith who were natives of County Down, Ireland and Hale Township, respectively. He attended public schools and the Monmouth Business College. After the death of his father in 1898, Fred B. lived for a time with his mother, before traveling to Alberta, Canada, with his older brother, Robert James Smith, to homestead land. In doing so Fred and Robert loaded a train with all of their livestock, equipment, etc. While there they built a farmhouse. Fred B. sold his shares to his brother and returned to Warren County around 1911. He then purchased Robert's interest in the old homestead of eighty acres in Section 21, Hale Township and became one of the enterprising farmers of Warren County raising Duroc-Jersey hogs. Fred B. built the exact same farmhouse on the Hale Township property as they had built in Alberta, Canada.

On September 2, 1912 Mr. Smith was married to Mrs. Emma J. (Drake) Harris. Emma was born in Iowa to Whitman and Amanda (Hodges) Drake and was the widow of Lewis Morris Harris. Mr. and Mrs. Smith had two children: Elsie Mae, born January 28, 1914 married Kenneth Jenks; and Mary Faye, born October 9, 1916 married John Brownlee. The United Presbyterian Church of Henderson, later known as Sugar Tree Grove Presbyterian Church, held the membership of Mr. and Mrs. Smith until their deaths of March 4, 1958 and March 11, 1960 respectively.

Fred B. Smith was a Republican and served as township assessor for two years, road commissioner for one year, and in the spring of 1921 was elected supervisor of Hale Township. Fraternally he belonged to Monmouth Lodge No. 577, I.O.O.F. and was popular for being a man who makes and retains his friends.

LESTER LLOYD SMITH - Lester Lloyd Smith, a member of one of Warren County's earliest pioneer families, served as the county's superintendent of highways for 10 years before failing health forced his retirement on Oct. 1, 1963.

John Smith, his great-great grandfather, left Pilot Knob, Ky., in 1800, and came to Warren County with his wife, the former Ursala Hendricks, in 1831, settling on a farm near Berwick.

The early date of their arrival in the place they chose as their home can be put in perspective only by considering the fact that it was only six years after Warren County was created by an act of the Illinois Legislature on Jan. 13, 1825.

John Smith built his cabin near Berwick in the same year that the county's first court house was built on N. Main St. at Archer Ave. in Monmouth. He served as a member of the first Warren County Grand Jury, empaneled on June 14, 1832.

The Smiths, also were active in business and religious affairs. It was in their home that a small group of friends met in July 1833, to form the Cedar Fork Baptist Church, which later became the Berwick Baptist Church.

Lester L. Smith

Although some of their neighbors migrated further west in fear of the threatened re-crossing of the Mississippi River by Chief Black Hawk in 1832, the Smith family, including eight children, remained. Mr. Smith died in 1839.

James Andrew Jackson Smith, a son of John and Ursala Smith, was only one year old when his parents arrived in Warren County. He had a creative mind and the "air ship" he built to display at the 1901 Pan American Exposition in Buffalo, N.Y., attracted a lot of attention, but unfortunately not enough financial backers to enable Mr. Smith to pursue his dream of flying, the way Wilbur and Orville Wright did a few years later.

He died on March 8, 1905, in Fontanelle, Iowa, but a son, Marquis Lafayette Smith, born on Feb. 14, 1866, near Berwick, spent his entire life in Warren County, first at Avon and later in Monmouth, where he had a cement contracting business.

He and his wife, the former Carrie L. Chatterton, were married in 1889 and resided in Avon for 20 years before moving to Monmouth and building a home at 1042 E. Detroit Ave. They were the parents of a daughter and five sons, one of whom was Lester L. Smith, who became his partner in the cement business. That experience was valuable to him during his career with the county highway department at a time when numerous highway bridges, many still in use, were constructed.

Lester Smith was born on Oct. 6, 1899 and was married to Eunice VanTine of Monmouth April 9,1921.

Upon the death of his father on July 4, 1926, Mr. Smith continued operating the construction business until 1933, when he accepted a position with the Warren County Highway Department, later becoming its chief engineer.

Mr. Smith became assistant highway superintendent under the late Donald Walker, upon whose death in Jan. 1953, he was appointed by the Warren County Board to be highway superintendent, serving in that capacity until his retirement more than 10 years later.

Mr. Smith died on Feb. 29, 1964, survived by his widow, two daughters, Martha Hallam and Shirley Fullerton, both of Monmouth and Robert Smith of Bushnell.

SMITH-MULLEN - "As I only knew one grandparent, the other three died before I was born. Therefore, my family history will center on my grandmother Adelia D. Smith Mullen and her parents and family." She was born to Phineas Pierce and Mary Ellen McCormick Smith on April 24, 1857 in Swan Township, Warren County. She married James Lawrence Mullen January 4, 1883, in Fulton County. He was born December 25, 1852, near Cincinnati, Ohio. His parents were from Ireland. Her husband died August 15,1893, leaving two children and one deceased son. Their daughter, Edna Fay, was born April 8, 1888 in Fulton County, and first married C. Vincent Grimsley May 16, 1911. After he died she married his brother, Guy E. Grimsley, July 12, 1919. Edna died November 10, 1983. William P., born November 18, 1891, in Fulton County. He married Alta Ione Rose June 20, 1917, and he died January 6, 1981.

Grandma Adelia, William and Edna Mullins, 1908

After the death of her husband, Adelia was a live-in housekeeper. Her son lived with her up until the time he lived with the David Link family near Avon. Edna lived with her Aunt and Uncle in Warren County.

On December 25, 1907, Adelia married Francis "Frank" Van Velser, in Fulton County. He had served in the Civil War. After his death Adelia lived with her daughter and family six months of the year and her son's home the other six months. She died in Monmouth on June 18, 1941.

Her parents became residents of Illinois in 1819, only one year after the territory achieved statehood. After leaving Scott County in 1850 they moved to Hancock County for one year before moving to Warren County in 1851. Phineas was born, 1817 in Bradford County, Pa. and Mary Ellen, born 1817 in Knox County, Tn. They were married in Scott County September 17, 1840. Phineas died in Fulton County July 18, 1898 and Mary Ellen March 18, 1908, at the home of her son Phineas, Jr., in Chariton, Lucas County, Iowa.

The first four Smith children were born in Scott County, the fifth in Hancock County, next four in Warren County. Mariette – June 28, 1841, she married James Calvary Morris; Lucy P. – July 17, 1843, married George Hoisington; Charles R. – May 30, 1845, single; Jedadiah- December 17, 1847, single; Phineas P., Jr,. – April 4, 1851, first married Mary F. Kimmons. After her death he married Anna Elizabeth Beasley; Nancy Ann – August 27, 1853, married George W. Ray; Adelia D. – April 24, 1857; Mary E. "Fannie" – August 24, 1859, married George Powers; one child died in infancy.

"I never had the privilege of knowing any of my grandmother's family as they were all deceased before I was born, except for one sister who died when I was one year and three months old and her youngest sister died six months before my grandmother, but she lived in Centralia, Washington and never returned to Illinois after she moved west."

ROBERT AND HELEN (CUMMINGS) SMITH

- Helen Smith's great-great grandfather was James Kerr Cummings, who was born July 4, 1813, in Scotland. The Cummings family came to the United States in 1828, and in 1837, James K. Cummings moved to Fulton County, Illinois. He moved again in 1856, this time to Kirkwood, Illinois, where he engaged in the grocery business for 12 years, the hardware business for 5 years, retiring in 1878. In addition to his businesses, he also farmed the 162 acres he owned, which was the northwest quarter of Section 4, Tompkins Township. He was married to Mary (Eveleth), and they had four children: Susan Jane, James H., Melissa, and Eunice. (Melissa and Eunice died before reaching adulthood.) James K.'s first wife, Mary, died in 1878 and he married Eliza Bowen in 1879. James died September 3, 1894, but Eliza survived him until October 23, 1946. All three – James K., Mary, and Eliza – are buried in Center Grove Cemetery in Kirkwood, Illinois.

Helen and Robert Smith, 40th anniversary, 1980

James K.'s son, James H. Cummings, married Cordelia (Holcomb). One of their sons, Fred Kerr Cummings, was born in 1881 on the family farm, and later married Pearl (Stewart) on September 18, 1912. Pearl had moved to Kirkwood in her teens from Abingdon, Virginia. Helen Viola Cummings was born to Fred and Pearl April 9, 1915, in the same family home as her father, Fred. She was an only child, although twin brothers were born and died at birth. Helen graduated from Rock Island Business College, and later worked at Block and Kuhl and Yaeger-Jacquin School Supplies in Peoria, Illinois. There she met her future husband, Robert William Smith, and later they also both worked at Hyster Company. Helen also worked for Caterpillar Company for 15 months before moving back to Kirkwood.

Robert (Bob) William Smith was born July 19, 1916, in Springfield, Illinois to Walter David and Nellie (Crompton) Smith. He was educated in Springfield Public Schools and attended Feitshans High School, Springfield. He first worked at Yaeger-Jacquin School Supply, where he and Helen met, and later became a welder for Hysters Heavy Equipment in Peoria, Illinois. He was also employed for a time by Montgomery Elevator Company, and he later installed the elevator in the Warren County Courthouse. Robert also worked for R.G. LaTourneau Company.

Bob belonged to a motorcycle club, and he and Helen both enjoyed riding. They married March 24, 1940, in Peoria, and lived there until 1950. Both of their children were born there: Carolyn Sue was born January 9, 1941, and Nancy Jo was born January 4, 1944. Carolyn Sue (Hawk) has three children – Curtis, David, and Lisa – and she now lives in Monmouth, Illinois. Nancy Jo (Roseberry) has two children-Mark and Jessica and she lives in Louisville, Kentucky.

After Helen's father, Fred Cummings, died as a result of an automobile accident in October 1944, she and Bob and their children returned in 1951 to the family farm where she was born, and Bob took up farming. Although the original farmhouse had burned on March 17, 1947, a new home was built there in 1950, where Helen still resides. While farming, Bob also worked for a number of years as a receiving clerk at Gamble-Skogmo Warehouse in Monmouth. He was also a blacksmith, a rural mail carrier, and a part-time carpenter. Helen worked in the office at Gamble-Skogmo for a time, but later took a job as Postal Clerk in Kirkwood, where she retired after 24 years there. Helen's hobby was collecting stamps. Robert collected coins, enjoyed bowling and golf, and was a member of the Monmouth Masonic Lodge #37 AF&FM. Before joining the Monmouth chapter, he was very active in the Kirkwood Masonic Lodge. They were also members of the Immanuel Baptist Church, Monmouth, where Helen taught Sunday School and held several church offices, and Robert was a deacon and a trustee.

Robert died March 23, 1992, and is buried in Center Grove Cemetery in Kirkwood.

RICHARD AND BEVERLY SPANGLER

- Richard Dean Spangler was born to parents Truman (Tim) Allen and Mary Elizabeth Galbraith Spangler in Burlington, Iowa. His paternal grandparents were Charles Allen and Dora Elizabeth Mills Spangler. Great-grandparents were Joseph Allen and Gertrude Delila McOlgan Spangler. Great-great-grandparents were Jacob Aaron and Lucy Rozetta Gray Spangler. Jacob Aaron came to Warren County from Gettysburg, Pa in 1850, married Lucy on 19 January 1851 in Monmouth. They settled in Oquawka, Illinois and had 7 children. Great-great-great-grandparents Samuel and Barbara Slagle Spangler. Great-great-great-great-grandparents Jacob and Eve Catherine Spangler of Gettysburg, Pa. Jacob's grandfather fought in the Revolutionary War with Washington according to the history written in The Mercer and Henderson County history book of 1882.

His maternal grandparents were George Franklin and Maggie Sage Galbraith. George's parents were Franklin and Parradine Fort Galbraith. Franklin came to Henderson County when it was a part of Warren County. Franklin's parents were Thomas and Margaret White Galbraith. Richard's grandparents on the Sage side were David C. Sage and Mary Osborn Sage, and his parents were Gidion and Mary Clark Sage.

Richard grew up in Henderson County and married Beverly Jean Shaner and they have four children, Jeanette Marie, Linda Sue, Cindy Lou and Clint Eugene. Jeanette married Timothy Kenneth McDaneld and they have two sons, David and Adam. David married Kimberly Lewis and they have one son, Konrad Lewis McDaneld.

Linda married Robert Calvillo, Cindy married John Dean and Clint married Rhonda Woolsey.

Beverly Jean Spangler grew up outside of Rozetta, Illinois. Her parents were Harold

Whitmore and Margaret Ida Themanson. Margaret's parents were John Arthur and Elsie Kleinkoff Themanson, John's parents came from Sweeden in 1869 and were married in Knox County and settled in Monmouth and raised their children. They were John and Ida Charlotta Themanson.

Harold's parents were Charles William and Mertie Francis Whitmore Shaner. Charles's parents were Robert and Mattie Jennings Shaner. The Shaner's came from Roanoke, Virginia about 1901. Lived in Macomb and Little York, Illinois, raised 13 children. Their names are Harold Whitmore, Evelyn, Roy, Ralph Frances, Ivan J., Katherine, Margaret (died infant), Davis O., Charles Jr., Caralee, Betty, James and Erma.

Beverly attended the Lutheran Church in Monmouth while she was growing up. Her siblings are LeRoy Harold, who died in 1957, and Marilyn Jo and Susan Marie.

Richard and Beverly Spangler own and operated Bev's Flowers Are Us at 123 South First Street in Monmouth.

JAN AND DICK SPEER FAMILY - The Speers were Scotch-Irish, coming to Pennsylvania from North Ireland in 1832. James Rogers Speer moved to northwest Illinois in 1833 and had one of the first farms in what was to become Elizabeth Township in Jo Davies County in 1838. The county history called him "Poor in purse but possessed of great courage and endurance." He bought his farm from the government at the Dixon land auction in 1847, paying $337.50 for 270 acres. Later, he and his sons bought a tract of 945 acres on the north edge of Hanover for $21000. Quoting history, "They paid for it, to the astonishment of their neighbors."

Jan and Dick Speer family

His grandson, Thomas Roscoe Speer, married Hazel Lanphere and moved to part of her father's farms in Tompkins Township, Warren County. They had a daughter, Marian, born December 15, 1923 and a son, Richard, born August 16, 1926. Hazel Lanphere was a granddaughter of Washington Lanphere who came to Warren County from upstate New York in 1844. Lanpheres had lived in New England from colonial times. His youngest son, Sloan Lanphere, inherited the home place and added to it. Richard Speer and his son David now own the home place, about four miles southwest of Monmouth.

The Peasleys were Welch-English and came to Massachusettes in the middle sixteen hundreds. One Peasley woman had the distinction of being hanged as a witch. They had proof. She had walked from Amesbury to Newbury afoot over a muddy road without "fouling her clothing." They moved to Connecticut, then to New Hampshire, then to Quebec, then to Montreal and then to what was to become Henderson County in 1836.

Jan (Jane Ann) Peasley's great-grandfather, John S. Peasley, was a farmer and a millwright, building the first mill at Hopper. Decorah was built on his farm when the Santa Fe went through. James Francis (Frank) Peasley was her grandfather and George Frederick (Fred) Peasley her father. She grew up on his farm west of LaHarpe. She was born May 31, 1929 in LaHarpe. She married Richard July 3, 1954 and they have always lived on the home farm east of Kirkwood. Jan taught Home Economics before marriage and was a substitute teacher and Girl Scout worker. She was also a leader in United Presbyterian Women.

Richard farmed and is now retired. He has been active in Freemasonry, holding district and state offices. They have three children. Deborah was born April 12, 1955. She married Larry Lawson who is FmHA manager in Princeton. They have five children. David was born April 4, 1956. He works as a computer consultant in Melbourne, FL. His wife's name is Ann. Daniel was born March 2, 1965. He makes Irish harps and dulcimers in Hendrixville, IN. He is married to Deb and has three children.

WILLIAM SHERMAN SPENCE - William Sherman Spence was born December 2, 1868 in Perryton Township, Mercer County, Illinois, the son of David and Elizabeth Braucht Spence. He was a carpenter by trade. He married Ella Huldah Henry, September 18,1895 in Aledo, Illinois at her Uncle's house. She was born March 19, 1875 in Fort Madison, Iowa, the daughter of Luther and Roseanna Gbenk Henry. Ella died in 1964 and William died Feb. 28, 1960. They are both buried in Little York, Illinois.

Their children were, Ethel, Ernest, born February 27, 1901, near Seaton, Illinois, Lewis, Geneva, William David, and Milo.

Ernest Spence was a farmer who married Gertrude Johnson, October 5, 1922 in Monmouth, Illinois, the daughter of John Emil and Nellie Nelson Johnson. John Johnson was a farmer and a coal hauler. Nellie was the daughter of Nels Fredich and Sarah Hallengren Nelson. Gertrude was born November 7, 1903 in Alexis, Illinois, and died January 17, 1987. Ernest died October 21, 1955. They are buried in Alexis, Illinois.

Their children are Robert, Chester, Dorothy Jean, John (Jack), born April 4, 1933 and Betty. John, (Jack) is a farmer in Henderson County, Illinois. He married Dorothy Ann Thieme, March 1, 1952 at Fall Creek Church. She was born December 17, 1934 to William and Lucy Fair Thieme.

Their children are Gary, born August 14, 1952 in Monmouth, Illinois, who married Renee Corinne Faudree, July 17, 1971 at Fall Creek Church. Renee was born December 14, 1951 in Fort Madison, Iowa to Wendell and Violet Gilbert Faudree. Gary and Renee farm in Warren and Henderson County. They have lived in Rozetta Township, Henderson, County for 23 years. Their daughter is Tracy, born March 19, 1973 in Monmouth, Illinois who married Alexander (Andy) Engstrom October 15, 1993 in Minot, North Dakota where Andy was stationed in the Air Force.

Bryan William, their son, was born June 17, 1975 in Monmouth, Illinois. Both Tracy and Bryan graduated from Union High School in Biggsville, Illinois. Bryan married Jaclyn Johnson on July 28, 2001, in Monmouth, Illinois.

Russell Spence born June 14, 1955 married Rhonda VanTine, October 10, 1976. Their daughter, Ashley was born May 11, 1981.

Cindy, born December 3, 1957, has two daughters, Lucinda and Katie Hennenfent.

Danny, born August 5, 1959, married Vicki Morey, April 27, 1980. They are the parents of Holly, Jackie and Brad.

William (Bill), born March 6,1962, married Paula Reimolds, September 20,1981. Their children are Heath and Travis.

A.W. SPICER FAMILY - Alexander W. (1822-1911) and Flora Elliot (1825-1913) Spicer came to Monmouth from New Concord, Ohio in 1857. He made a 42-day journey by covered wagon bringing their possessions. She traveled by train bringing their 4 children ages 9, 8, 6 and 2. Their destination was a farm just north of Monmouth. The following year the family purchased land near Burgess in Mercer County where the family grew to nine children. They attended the United Presbyterian Church south of the North Henderson creek.

1224 N. Main St., Monmouth, 1919

In 1881 Alexander moved the family back Monmouth, settling on a farm one mile north of the city. Two of his sons attended Monmouth College. In 1889, retiring from farming, he built the house at 202 W. Boston and moved into town, where they were founding members of the First United Presbyterian Church. Five of his children survived him, Wylie E. Spicer of San Diego, CA; Thomas W. Spicer of Monmouth; John R. Spicer of Beatrice, NE; Oliver A. Spicer of Monmouth; and Mrs. Bell Johnson of Alexis.

202 W. Boston, Monmouth, 1890.

Thomas (1848-1946) farmed north of Monmouth. His son, Zenas (1884-1980) joined his father in farming. Zenas attended Monmouth College and was a published composer of organ music.

Oliver Alexander Spicer (1865-1942) attended Monmouth College, class of 1887, where he met his wife Mary Frances Graham (1864-

1905). They had four children. Two years after the death of Mary Frances, Oliver married Margaret Woolridge, and in 1918 built the house at 1224 North Main. The house originally had a large front porch. Oliver was a farmer and stockman, and a member of the board of directors of the Monmouth Trust and Savings Bank. He was a devoted member of the First United Presbyterian Church where he was clerk of the sessions for 23 years. Of his four children, one remained in Monmouth, L. Ray Spicer.

One mile north of Monmouth.

L. Ray Spicer (1900-1977) was born at the Spicer farm just north of Monmouth. He married Frances Marie McKelvie (1904) from Alexis in 1924. She was in nurses training at Monmouth Hospital. Ray was a lifelong farmer in the Monmouth area and lived in the brick house where he was born from 1942 until his death in 1977. They were lifetime members of the First United Presbyterian Church, where Ray served as an elder and chairman of the trustees. They had two sons, Leland (Lee) Ray Spicer Jr. and Donald Wylie Spicer.

Leland (Lee) R. Spicer (1925) was also born at the Spicer Farm. In 1950 he married Geraldine F. McCoy (1930). In 1990, after a long career in Chicago, Lee retired and moved back to his birthplace, the fourth generation to occupy the brick house and farm first acquired by A.W. Spicer 120 years earlier. Lee and Gerry attend Faith United Presbyterian Church and are members of the Warren County Saddle Club. They have four children and four grandchildren.

ORRIN AND LEONA (PETERSON) SPROUT - Sprout, Orrin Eugene, son of Vincent Everett and Marian Fern (Parsons) Sprout was born in Warren County, September 26, 1915. He attended 8 years at the Means school in Floyd Township. He helped on his father's farm. Orrin was one of five children, Burnill, (Florence Parrish) deceased, Marian (Max) Peterson, deceased, Donna Dell Bogert, of Monmouth, and Florence (Robert) Baker of Virginia. On November 23, 1935, he married Leona Mae Peterson, daughter of Emmett and Ruth (Crandall) Peterson. They were married at the Fairview Center Parsonage, by the Rev. Will Arbogast. They still attend Fairview Center regularly. He is the oldest living male member of the church. They will celebrate 69 years of marriage this year. Leona is one of ten children; Kathryn (David) Edwards, deceased; twins: Ray (Martha) Peterson, deceased; Faye (Emerson) Dafly, deceased; Lee (Helen)Peterson, twins: Max (Marilyn) Peterson, Maxine (William) Martin, Lois (Edward) Appleby, Helen (John) Bruyn, Greta (Richard) Ryner.

Orrin and Leona Sprout

They have farmed in Floyd Township all their married life, still living in the farm home he was raised in. His father built the house in 1911. It was a Sears Roebuck home. He moved into it at the age of four.

They are the parents of four children; Beverly (Gerald) Clark, Rural Kirkwood; Ronald (Joan), of Monmouth; Karen (Roger) Mansfield, of Larkspur, Colorado, Maurice of Normal, Ill. Eleven grandchildren, sixteen great-grandchiddren.

After retiring from the farm, gardening became his hobby, raising many fruits, vegetables and flowers, giving many away to family and friends, canning and freezing the rest.

Orrin's two grandsons, Brad and Brian Clark, now farm his land.

Orrin, for many years played ball on the Fairview Center church team, coached Junior Sheriff teams in the 50's. He served as church treasurer for many years.

Leona has crocheted afghans for all her children, grandchildren and great-grandchildren. Always has homemade cookies for all who come to visit, especially her grandchildren.

Orrin's grandfather on his maternal side was Horace Parsons, Great-grandfather, Henry Charles Parsons, an early pioneer to Warren County arriving in 1849. Orrin's fraternal grandfather was Ira Jacob Spout, Great-grandfather, William Sprout, who arrived in Warren County in 1851.

Leona's grandfather on her maternal side was Archibald Crandall, Great-grandfather Emery Hill Crandall, who fought in the Civil War. Her paternal grandfather was Charles Peterson, coming to the United States from Sweden in 1875, at the age of 22.

ROBERT AND SYLVIA (PARSONS) STACK - Sylvia Lou Renee (Parsons) Stack, born July 25, 1963 in Monmouth. The eldest of 3 children born to Harold S. and Mary Lou (Davis) Parsons. Attended Yorkwood and Alexis Elementary Schools. Alexis Jr. High School and Alexis High School. During high school, was very active in FHA serving as historian, secretary and president. Also, was a member of the Who's Who in American High School Students.

In 1988, graduated from Robert Morris College, Carthage, Illinois, as a Medical Assistant. Acquiring certification status soon after graduating she found employment with Dr. M.I. Rajput in Aledo, Illinois. There she worked for 8 years before moving to Ohio in 1996.

March 29, 1997, she married Robert Wayne Stack, Summit County, Barberton, Ohio. He was born April 25, 1942, Summit County, Akron, Ohio, the only child of Vern Howard and Gladys Eva (Burchfield) Stack. His mother's family is of Quaker descent which founded Richmond, Ohio. Bob is a Vietnam Veteran, serving in the Air Force with an elite special ops group.

Sylvia (Parsons) and Robert Stack

Sylvia has worked for Dr. Chris D. Marquart, MD, for 5 years and in 1999 they moved to Cuyahoga Falls, Ohio to be closer to her job.

RICHARD WALKER STALEY - Staley, Richard Walker was born at Smithshire, IL on July 26, 1924. His parents were Earle D. Staley and Ester (Walker) Staley. Dick attended Hornbeck grade school and Oquawka and Kirkwood High Schools. Dick was drafted into the Army Air Corp in March 1943. He served at Roswell, New Mexico. He was discharged as a Corporal at McClellan Field, Sacramento, California on February 4, 1946.

After returning from the service Dick has resided in Warren County. He worked at the Iowa Ordinance Plant, the Farmall Plant in Rock Island, and Alton Box in Galesburg where he retired in 1986. Now Dick resides at Oak Terrace in Monmouth.

Dick is a member of the Kirkwood Presbyterian Church, where he served as an elder and on the session committee.

TED AND VIRGINIA STANSELL - Virginia Winning and Ted Stansell met in Chicago shortly after World War II in which Ted served with the 90th Infantry Division in Counter intelligence, landing on Normandy Beach on D + I, receiving a Bronze Star and a battlefield commission as 2nd Lieutenant. In 1950 they married and moved to Monmouth, Ted to practice law with Henry Smith, a law classmate at Northwestern University and a Monmouth native. They have three children, Martha, Barbara and James who after college, law and graduate schools now live in Arlington, Virginia, Houston, Texas and Lansing, Michigan where they are an attorney with the Justice Department, PhD psychologist, and consulting economist with the Michigan Legislature respectively. Following the death of Henry Smith in 1960, Ted has practiced law with Kenneth Critser, Richard Whitman and Greg Baber until retiring in 2002.

Virginia, a native of Rossville, Illinois and a graduate of Illinois Wesleyan University has been active in The League of Women Voters, Y.M.C.A. (Board President), United Way Board, Right-to-Read Board, and a number of other organizations; Ted, likewise, was active in the community as board member of School District 38, Monmouth College Senate, Security Savings and Loan Association (Chairman), Warren County Bar Association, Y.M.C.A. (President), Kiwanis (President) and other local organizations. Both have been Board members, teachers and active

Virginia and Ted Stansell

in the United Methodist Church in Monmouth. They are proud grandparents of six grandchildren.

MIKE AND JENNIFER (BARNES) STAUTH - Stauth, Jennifer (Barnes) said, "I grew up in a typical midwestern town, where my father owned a third generation grocery store. He always came home for lunch, and we were always a very close family.

Jennifer and Mike Stauth

As the oldest of five kids, I got very patient in a hurry. It seemed like there was always a baby in the house, and I enjoyed that care taking aspect of my childhood. Then, when I went to school, I decided the minute I walked into my first grade room and saw my teacher that was what I wanted to be.

If I had my druthers and a million dollars, I'd go to school forever. I couldn't think of anywhere I'd rather be, so the next logical thing was to be a teacher."

For years before moving to Jackson in August of 1976, Jennifer and her husband, Mike, packed up their gear every summer and camped out in Jackson Hole.

In the summer of 1973, they decided to build their "retirement home." She said, "We bought a little lot with a tiny little house on it on Kelley Street for about $8,000, and we lived in the little house while we started working on building a new one. Those were wonderful summers. We didn't have any idea how to build a house, but we would just read books and save our money all winter, and come out and work on the house during summer. We did everything but dig a hole. I mixed the mortar myself in a big barrel, and shoveled it up to Mike and our brothers, who came out one summer to help. They didn't know what they were doing, so they went up to the Americana and watched them lay concrete, and then came back and did it on our house. Eventually, we all got faster."

Her brother slept in a tent and Mike's brother slept in his car every night with an electric blanket plugged in from out our window.

We didn't have TV," she said, "so we walked down to Jackson Drug every night to get an ice cream and read magazines." Each fall we would go back to our teaching jobs. Our relatives thought we were crazy building a summer home at 25. Jennifer was pregnant when they finally finished the house. She was due in a month and knew she wouldn't be teaching for a while, so decided to stay. They took leaves of absence and thought they would try it for a year.

Their first son, Jason, was born that September, and Sean was born in 1978. Both boys have now graduated from Harvard with engineering degrees. The parents still live in their "retirement home," and are active in community affairs. Both find time to fish, hunt, camp, and enjoy archery. She wishes her boys to have a zest for life and learning, have good friends and good times.

VERNON THANE STAUTH - Stauth, Vernon Thane, the oldest child of Vernon Griffith "Griff" Stauth and Mary Immel was born in Dodge City, Kansas on February 24, 1915. Four brothers and two sisters were subsequently added to the family. He attended school in Ensign, Kansas and graduated from high school there. After high school, there was no work in the "Dust Bowl" Kansas, so he headed out to Colorado and scraped out a meager living in Westcliff in the high Rockies. Then his brother got him a job working the wheat harvest from Texas up the mountain front to Canada. He enlisted in 1940 in the Army Air Force and qualified to be an airplane mechanic. He trained around the United States, until late 1943 when his outfit went over through North Africa, Sicily, and invaded Italy at Anzio. He was a crew chief, flight chief, and line chief at his base in Italy until 1945. He returned to Dodge City, Kansas and met Lorraine Pickens, who worked there for the Santa Fe Railroad. Lorraine grew up on a farm in Jasper County, Illinois, in a large family of eight. After high school graduation, she worked in many jobs in many places including Chicago, San Francisco, Florida, and Whitehorse, Canada in the Yukon, before coming back to work for the Santa Fe Railroad.

Stauth Family. Back: Mike, Cam, Dave. Front: Lorraine and Vernon.

Vernon and Lorraine were married in June, 1946 in Dodge City. Their first son Michael was born there in 1947. Vernon took a job with Martin Mayrath, an old neighbor of his just down the road from the Stauth homestead. Martin had invented and patented the grain auger. Business interests caused a move to Gering, Nebraska, where two more boys, Cameron and David, were born. Mayrath opened an auger plant in Monmouth, Illinois, which brought Vernon, his brother Sam, and their families to be residents of Monmouth. Vernon worked several different jobs before retiring from Ralph Wells in 1981 and moving to Oregon. Lorraine worked at many jobs in Monmouth including WRAM radio, Monmouth Review Atlas, and Monmouth correspondent for Galesburg Register Mail.

All three boys graduated from Monmouth High School. Mike graduated from Monmouth College, along with his wife Jennifer Barnes, and they both taught school in Monmouth for six years before moving to Jackson Hole, Wyoming. Cam graduated from the University of Illinois in journalism and is a successful writer living in Oregon with his family. Dave graduated from Northern Illinois University in journalism and is now a public relations journalist for the science department at Oregon State University.

Jennifer and Mike had two sons; one Jason Thane born 15 September 1976, the other Sean Alexander born 28 August 1978. Both were superior students and received large scholarships - Jason to Colby College in Maine and Sean to Dartmouth College in New Hampshire. Jason graduated Phi Beta Kappa, took a special program in electrical engineering at Dartmouth, graduated and was immediately hired by Allegro Micro Systems in nearby Concord. Sean graduated, entered Engineering School, graduated, and decided he needed a business degree to be more hirable.

PAUL K. STEVENS - Paul K. Stevens, the oldest son of David and Mary Boling Stevens, was born in Bristol, Tennessee on May 14, 1914 but came to Illinois in his teens and settled in Warren County. He worked for farmers near Kirkwood and Little York before enlisting in the Civilian Conservation Corp and working in Ludington, Michigan helping build roads and doing conservation work. He married a local schoolteacher, Audrey Bass, on November 27, 1937. Paul farmed at several locations near Little York but later changed his occupation from farming to sales. The family lived in several locations before moving to Roseville in January, 1962. Paul managed the Martin and Clark store there and won an all expense paid trip to the World's Fair in New York City for winning a selling contest. His last job was as a car salesman at Russ Motors in Monmouth.

40th Wedding Anniversary, November 27, 1977. David, John, Mary, Charles, Stan, Audrey and Paul

He earned the nickname "Mr. Jeep" for his outstanding job of selling cars and Jeeps. He was forced into early retirement because of failing health. His wife also retired from teaching and from managing their antique shop "The Copper Kettle." Paul died on October 10, 1995. He and his wife had raised five children: David, Mary,

Stan, Charles and John. The three older children attended grade school at Little York and graduated from high school there. David enlisted in the air force and after his term in that service married Mary Berthold and worked at Haben's Locker Plant in Little York before moving to Boulder Hill near Montgomery, Illinois. He has three sons: David, Doug and John Robert. Mary attended Western Illinois University then worked as a bookkeeper for Martin and Clark. Later she married Kenneth West of Victoria, Illinois. They raised three children: Teresa, Jay and Todd. They farm near Victoria. Stan married Kay Armstrong and farmed near Little York. There were two children, Michael and Chrystal. After their divorce Stan married Renee Anderson and they have a son Kyle. Stan farmed for several years but later became a welder at the John Deere Plant in Moline. Charles and John both started grade school at Little York but graduated from high school at Roseville. Both boys served their country in Viet Nam. Charles was in the army and John was a Marine. Charles married Laurie Walters and they have a son Sean. They were divorced shortly after his return from Viet Nam. Later he married Karen Johnston and they lived in Iowa and Texas before settling in Florida. They have a daughter Andrea. Charles has always been in sales and at present is managing housing parks in Kissimmee and Emerald Lake i Florida. John enlisted in the marines after graduation from high school. After serving in Viet Nam he got a college education and has worked in Iowa and Minnesota. He married Mary Quigley of Bethesda, Maryland and they have a son Patrick and a daughter Alexis. At the present time John has a marketing and communications business named "Renaissance" in Marshalltown, Iowa.

JOSEPH STEVENSON - Joseph Stevenson (1827-1914) was born near Decatur, Ohio, the son of Robert and Sarah Beard Stevenson. He wed Mary J. Patton in Ohio. The couple moved to Monmouth Township, Warren County, IL, around 1851, and settled on land along the east side of (now) route 67 about 2 miles north of the city of Monmouth. They had 3 children – Robert McC., John P., and Martha Louise (Mrs. W.O. Miller). Mary Patton Stevenson died when the children were small, and Joseph married Belle Crawford Green in 1864. She had been born in the east, but is said to have come to live with an uncle in Warren County after her parents died in an accident. Belle and Joseph had two sons – Wm. G. and George J. Wm. G. was born in 1865. The family moved into Monmouth by 1870, and lived at 120 North C Street until 1906 when Joseph, Belle, John P., and George moved to Tarklo, MO, where Joseph died in 1914. Belle died in Tarkio in 1924. Robert M. had married Nina Bruner in 1874 and was working in the bank in Alexis. Martha Louise, one of the six founders of Kappa Kappa Gamma, had attended Monmouth College and had wed Wm. O. Miller in 1874.

As a young man, Wm. G. attended Monmouth College and then became associated with Wm. S. Wier in the Monmouth Plow company. In July of 1887 he and Mr. Weir, together with R.M. Stevenson, organized the Bank of Alexis. Mr. Weir became President, R.M. was named Vice President, and W.G. was Cashier. The bank was founded as a privately owned institution. It later became a stockholder concern under State & Federal regulations. Wm. G. married Ella Kobler, daughter of George Jacob & Anna Marie Stenz Kobler of Monmouth in October of 1887. The couple had three children – Ricka (Mrs. John H. Rogers), AnnaBelle (Mrs. Benjamin V. McClanahan), and Joseph K. The family lived in Alexis until 1917, when they returned to live in Monmouth at 318 W. Broadway. Ella died in 1934, and in 1936 W.G. wed Emma Eckhart of Monmouth. W.G. was a member of the Alexis U.P. Church and Monmouth Elks lodge and was Vice President of the Alexis bank at the time of his death in 1940.

Joseph Stevenson, his son William G. Stevenson, his son Joseph K. Stevenson

Joseph K. grew up in Alexis and received his schooling there and at Northwestern Military Academy in Lake Geneva. In June of 1924, he married Virginia Hixson in Evanston, IL, and became associated with his father in the bank in July of the same year. The couple lived their entire married life in Alexis. They had a daughter, Betty (Johnston/Cody) adopted in 1929, and a son Wm. H, born in 1931. Joe was associated with the bank for 42 years and was a leader in his church and community. He was President of the bank at the time of his death. During his 42 years the bank moved first from the west side of Main Street to the east side, then to a new building on East Broadway in 1964.

William H. Stevenson and Joseph K. Stevenson

Wm. H. (Bill) attended Alexis schools, Augustana College, and WIU before enlisting in the Air Force during the Korean conflict in 1950, serving most of his 3 years in England. Upon his return home he wed Dorothy Benson of Orion in August, 1954, and followed family tradition by becoming associated with his father in the bank that same month. The couple became the parents of 3 children – Patricia (Mrs. Gene Sims), Linda (Mrs. Robb Tollefson), and Wm. B., born in 1959, 1961, and 1963 respectively. Bill was with the bank for 29 years, and was President at the time of his death in January of 1983.

When Mary Weir Huff died some months later, the bank was sold, the business association between the Weirs and Stevensons had lasted through three generations. The Stevenson children are all in financial businesses – Patty serving with Farmers State Bank of Western IL (formerly Bank of Alexis) as a loan officer, Linda associated with Bank One in Green Bay, Wisconsin, and Bill as a CPA with Equitable Insurance Company's property division in Chicago.

JOHN CECIL STEWART - John Cecil (J.C.) Stewart and Louisa Schultz were married in Henderson County in 1891. After farming briefly in Point Pleasant and Spring Grove Townships, they settled in Lenox Township about 1895. They, along with Louisa's mother and aunts, purchased land in Section 2 that is currently owned by their descendant Russell Stewart. They built the farmstead that included the house, two large barns, a crib and various other buildings. They raised two boys, Carl and Frank, and one daughter, Madge.

Carl Stewart showing "Dale," a purebred Percheron Stallion, 1940.

J.C. was the son of Samuel and Elizabeth (Rankin) Stewart and Louisa was the daughter of Johann Carl (C.J.) and Maria (Wiegand) Schultz, all of Henderson County.

J.C. and his son, Carl, raised purebred livestock, horses, cattle, hogs and chickens. In particular, they were breeders of Percheron horses. They raised and sold colts that were "broken" for farm work. After J.C.'s death in 1931, Carl continued to farm with horses and raising and selling colts well into the 1940's. He designed special "bigteam" hitches to allow an additional horse in teams that pulled discs and moldboard plows. The additional horse was added because of the heavy (large clay content) soils on the farm. In 1910, the Monmouth Review reported that J.C. Stewart made a "clean sweep" of prizes with his Percherons at the Mercer County Fair. Carl was featured in a Successful Farming article titled "Hard Against the Collar" in which his farming of 385 acres with horses was described. Crops raised in rotations were corn, oats, leguminous forages, wheat and soybeans.

Carl married Louise McCoy (see McCoy; Thomson). They raised two sons, Russell and Cecil. Russell carried on farming the land purchased by his ancestors and expanded the operation with the use of modern machinery and technology. Cropping systems changed to primarily corn and soybeans. Russell's livestock operation consisted of feeding cattle and raising hogs. The Stewart land is now farmed by Russell and two of his sons, Dean and Kenneth. Russell and his wife Maxine (McClure) of rural Kirkwood have two additional children, Ron and Wendy. Wendy is married to Richard Brokaw. Brokaws live in Henderson County. Ron lives in Monmouth.

All three of J.C. and Louisa Stewart's children graduated from Monmouth College and from the University of Illinois. Frank married Leota Adams from Peoria County where they were pioneers in the Hybrid Seed Corn Industry from their farm near Princeville. Madge married Paul Sanmann who died at a young age. After spending over two decades in Champaign and Chicago, Madge Sanmann returned to Monmouth in 1950 and taught Sociology at Monmouth College for the remainder of her career.

After graduation from Monmouth High School, Carl and Louise's son, Cecil, attended the University of Illinois then completed a career on the faculty of Iowa State University.

Russell and Maxine's children, Dean, Ron, Wendy and Kenneth represent the fifth generation of Stewarts in the Warren and Henderson County area. Four of those generations have been on the same farm in Lenox Township.

MARGARET AGNES STEWART - Stewart, Margaret Agnes, was born December 5, 1913 and raised in Monmouth, Warren County, Illinois. Her father, Henry Wylie Stewart, owned a bus company and was a tenor soloist who studied under Enrique Caruso. He loved to sing and perform with Dr. Glen Shaver of the Monmouth College Conservatory of music. Her mother, Bess (Butler) Stewart, was active in her church and community. Margaret was close to her younger sisters Betty (Beatty) and Mary Lou (Martindale).

Margaret started her college days at Indiana University where she joined Kappa Kappa Gamma Fraternity. She went back to Monmouth College to get her degree before moving to Chicago to work. She met and married James Harris Bone in 1941. When Jim got out of the Army after World War II, they moved to San Diego where he became clinic manager at Rees-Staley Medical Clinic. They bought one of the first houses built on the hill above Ocean Beach.

Margaret and Jim's son, James Stewart Bone, now lives in Mission Viejo. Their daughter, Mary Elizabeth "Betsy," now lives in Indianapolis with her husband Dave Bikoff. Margaret was very involved with her children' activities. During that same time, she began her memberships in numerous womens' organizations that she maintained throughout her life. They included P.E.O., Athenanuem, San Diego Womens' Club, Kappa Kappa Gamma Alumni, and Panhellanic Association. She was also a founding member of the Childrens' Hospital Auxillary. If that wasn't enough, Margaret also became a Bookstore Manager at Cal Western (now Pt. Loma Nazarene University) and even opened up her home to P.E.O. travellers with "Margaret's Bed & Breakfast."

Perhaps most important, Margaret was a good friend to many. She was a member of the Point Loma Community Presbyterian Church on Chatsworth Blvd., where she met the Evers sisters, Doris Dusch and Bethany Engel, who both attended Monmouth College and live close by on Point Loma Hill above Ocean Beach.

She passed away at 88 years March 19, 2002 at her home. Survivors include her daughter "Betsy" of Indianapolis, son Jim of Mission Viejo and sister Mary Lou Martindale. She also leaves three grandchildren and three Great-grandchildren.

RUSSELL AND MAXINE (MCCLURE) STEWART - Russell Stewart was born February 25, 1935 in Monmouth, Illinois. Maxine McClure was born November 19, 1934 in Monmouth, Illinois. She married Russell on July 31, 1955 at the Kirkwood United Methodist Church at Kirkwood, Illinois. In 1955 they moved into a house on the Cameron Road, east of Monmouth, where they still reside. Russell and Maxine have farmed all their married life. Their farm consisted of prime farmland in Lenox Township. They raised corn, soybeans, wheat, oats, and hay. They had a cow herd, raised hogs, and fed feeder cattle for numerous years. By the mid-1980s, they were raising only corn and soybeans.

Russell Stewart Family

They have 4 children. R. Dean Stewart married Linda Hill of Monmouth and they had 3 children: Michael, Barry and Jena. Dean then married Julie Zbikowski of Detroit, Michigan and they had 2 daughters, Makayla and Sidney. Dean farms. Rondell never married and has worked for the Warren County Highway Department. Wendy married Richard Brokaw of Stronghurst. They have 2 sons, Matthew and Nicholas. Wendy works for the Warren County Soil and Water Conservation District and farms with her husband. Kenneth has one son, Kyle. Ken works for the BNSF Railroad and farms.

Russell and Maxine are members of Fairview Center United Methodist Church, rural Monmouth. Their strong community involvement included Russell's 22 years and Maxine's 16 years as 4-H leaders.

Maxine's parents were Frank and Twila (Murdock) McClure. They also had 3 children: Maxine, Dale and Roger. Frank was born in Cameron, Illinois. Twila was born in Barney, North Dakota. Grandparents were Glenn and Mary (Rykerd) McClure of Cameron, Illinois and Hal and Pluma (Dunbar) Murdock of Monmouth. Hal was born in Oklahoma and Pluma was born in Monmouth, Illinois. Great-grandparents were Frank and Clara (Paulsgrove) McClure, who originated from Pennsylvania.

Russell's parents were Carl and Louise (McCoy) Stewart. They had two sons: Russell and Cecil. Carl was born in Pleasant Township, Warren County, Illinois and Louise was born in Kirkwood, Illinois. Grandparents were John (J.C.) and Louisa (Schultz) Stewart of near Monmouth and Ralph and Lulu (Randall) McCoy of Kirkwood.

JOHN AND MARY ELIZABETH STIVERS - John Max Stivers was born in Alexis Ill November 30th 1909 to Frank and Minnie Metzner Stivers. In 1933 he married Mary Elizabeth Lingafelter in Keithsburg Illinois. Mary was the daughter of Bessie and Harvey Lingafelter. John and Mary had eleven children. The last child died at birth. The first three years of this union John worked with the WPA in Chicago. In 1937 the couple moved to Monmouth where John worked for the Western Stoneware Company and Mary worked at the Hamilton Egg Company. At this time the couple purchased a home at 840 North D St. All of the children attended Willitts School, Central Jr. High and Monmouth High School. In the following years John ventured out and established his own business. First in the cement block business and later forming Stivers and Sons Construction Company. The construction company was established in the mid-forties. Mary also continued to contribute to the family finances by working at the Formfit Company and later as a Licensed Practical Nurse. She was employed by both Monmouth Hospital and the Warren County Home in an LPN capacity. The Stivers and Sons Company is located on West 6th Avenue and Mary and John moved to a home next to the company location in the sixties. John retired from the business passing it on to his oldest son Jack. Upon Jacks death in 2001, the business was passed on to his sons who continue to carry on the Stivers and Sons tradition .

Mary Elizabeth and John Stivers

Mary passed away in 1991 and John passed away in 2001. Five of the children have been life long members of the Monmouth Community. They are John (Jack), Beverly Ballard, Wendell, Pamela Lybarger and Debra Dycus. The remaining children are: Jim residing in Mundelein Ill., Sharon Horvath residing in East Moline, Ill., Diana Madrid, Micheal and David all residing in New Mexico.

Submitted by Sharon Stivers Horvath and Beverly Stivers Ballard

ROLLAND AND MARJORIE HILL STONE - Rolland Clyde Stone was born December 9, 1922 in Knox County, Delong, Illinois at home. His parents were Earl Smith and Lucille Jeanne (Callahan) Stone. Except for two short periods, he has always lived in Warren County, Illinois. His father was a farmer and his mother a homemaker. He attended "Star," "Shanghai" and "Indian Grove" country grade schools, all in Warren County. He graduated from Alexis Community High School, Alexis, Illinois in the spring of 1940. He farmed before marriage to Marjorie Ann Hill of the Norwood, Illinois Area on May 24, 1946 in the Norwood Presbyterian Church, Norwood, Illinois.

His wife was the youngest child born to Harry Morton and Constance Gail (Miller) Hill. She was born October 1, 1926, Monmouth, Illinois. Her brothers and sisters are Robert Morton born February 12, 1919, Norwood, Mercer County, Illinois; Donald Russell born May 8, 1921, Monmouth, Illinois and Irene Elizabeth born December 4, 1923 Alexis, Warren County, Illinois. Their father was a farmer and carpenter and their mother was a homemaker. Marjorie attended country grade schools, "Robb," "Legal Corners" and "Center" all in Mercer County, Illinois. She graduated from Alexis Community High School, Alexis, Illinois. She attended Bradley University, Peoria, Illinois for one year and taught at "Center" Grade School for one year before being married. They moved to a farm just south of the "Science Hall Grade School," Gerlaw, Illinois and continued farming.

Rolland and Marjorie Stone

To this union were born four children: Patricia Ann, September 30, 1947; Allen Richard, September 15, 1950; Shirley Jane, May 20, 1953 and David Eugene, February 25, 1956.

They left the farm in the spring of 1969 and moved west of Monmouth, Illinois. Rolland worked at QMC-Gale Products until he was laid off in 1983 as the plant was closing down. Marjorie worked at the Iowa Army Ammunition Plant, Middletown, Iowa until September 1975 and later at Admirals, Galesburg, Illinois until 1986.

They moved to 316 South "C" Street, Monmouth in January 1975 which they had purchased and where they still live.

Their daughter, Patricia Ann, passed away on April 10, 1956 in Delavan, Wisconsin. Their son, David Eugene, who was in the Air Force and stationed at Scott Air Force Base, Illinois with the rank of Chief Master Sergeant, passed away on April 3, 1996 at the Air Base. Both are buried in the family plot in Warren County Memorial Park Cemetery, Monmouth, Illinois. Allen Richard is employed at Illinois Cement, LaSalle, Illinois. Shirley Jane graduated from Illinois Wesleyan University, Bloomington, Illinois and the University of Illinois Medical School, Chicago, Illinois. She has been in practice since 1985 in Dixon, Illinois. Her specialty is O.B. and GYN.

They have 5 grandsons, 4 granddaughters as well as 2 great-grandsons and 1 step great-granddaughter.

They are members of the First Christian Church, Monmouth, Illinois.

RUSSELL K. AND LORETTA (SWARD) STRONG - Russell K. Strong was born 19 Feb 1915, Media, Il. He married Mayme Loretta Sward, 1 Oct 1950 in Kirkwood, Il. Russell's parents were Cleve and Edith (McMein) Strong. Reared and educated in Monmouth, he worked several years at Young's Grocery, worked as barber since 1950, operating his own barber shop here many years. He was a Staff Sergeant in the army during WWII in Phillipines, New Guinea, and Japan; member J.W. Clendenin Post 2301, both members of Westminster U.P. Church, Kirkwood. Russell died 5 June 1996 in Monmouth, buried Center Grove cemetery, Kirkwood.

Loretta was born 14 April 1922 in Kirkwood to Charles John and Mary Jane (Dughman) Sward. Charles was born 3 June 1885 in Jonkoping, Sweden to John A. and Amanda (Johnson) Sward. The family came to the U.S. when Charles was a small child, first to Burlington, Ia, then Fall Creek area, settling in Kirkwood area. Charles and Jane were married 2 March 1910 at Kirkwood, where he farmed until 1940, then worked in the shipping room at Western Stoneware for 10 years. Was member of Kirkwood Odd Fellows, both were members of the Kirkwood Westminister U.P. Church. Jane was born 12 Feb 1888 in Ellott, Ia and was reared and educated there. Was a member of Kirkwood Rebecca Lodge. Charles died 7 Feb 1964 and Jane died 28 July 1964, both buried Center Grove cemetery, Kirkwood.

Loretta and Russell Strong, October 1990

Loretta's sister Lucille Jeanette was born 25 Sept 1911 near Kirkwood, attended Center Grove and Kirkwood grade schools, graduating Kirkwood High in 1929. She did housework in various homes, worked Woolworth's during WWII and was married 4 April 1942 to James R. Dugan, born 21 Nov 1902, Bald Bluff Township, Henderson Co. to James and Mae (Young) Dugan. They lived in Little York community, farming and operated Standard Service Station, Little York 16 years she helped with bookkeeping. Both were members Little York Methodist Church. He served in Air Force during WWII. Member American Legion and B.P. 0. E. # 397. He died 4 June 1975, buried Center Grove, Kirkwood. Lucille later lived Oak Terrace and now in Lamoine Nursing Home, Roseville. She loved dancing, reading, and knitting. They had no children.

Loretta attended Center Grove, Cedar Ridge(Henderson Co.) grade schools graduating Kirkwood High 1940. She worked collection department Il. Banker's Life; bookkeeping at Gamble's Store and Central Feed and Produce, Kirkwood 12 years where she helped with other things including delivering feed occasionally. (She remembers the lid coming off of a can of paint she was shaking up in the paint mixing machine); was office manager Dee Harrison Ford Dealership until retiring. Loretta's hobbies: reading, knitting, sewing, flower gardening, attends YMCA 2-3 times a week. She is a member Warren Co. Chapter DAR, Oquawka Rebecca Lodge and lives Monmouth. Their son Gary Eugene was born 7 Aug 1952 is an Airline Pilot and lives Raleigh, N.C. and has sons Eric and Kevin.

STRUTHERS FAMILY - My great, great grandfather, William S. Struthers Jr. was born May 13, 1789 in Glasgow, Scotland. He came to the United States around 1790 with his parents, William and Janet (Lindsay) Struthers and siblings. They settled in Rockbridge County, Virginia. He married Martha Eleanor Saville on September 27, 1816 in Rockbridge County, Virginia. The Struthers' family decided to move west settling in Greene County, Ohio. William Jr. and Martha were the parents of eight children. His wife died after the birth of the eighth child. He later married Elisabeth Alexander. William S. Struthers' parents had died and again he had the urge to go west. He moved his family to Monmouth, Warren County, Illinois along with his sister Jennet who was born in Scotland in 1788 and died November 11, 1862 in Monmouth. William S. Struthers Jr. died March 31, 1861 and is buried in the Monmouth cemetery.

William Saville Struthers. Civil War picture of Illinois soldier. LeAve in 1861-1865.

His son, William Saville Struthers, born May 3, 1825 at Rockbridge County, Virginia fought in the Civil War with the Army of Illinois.

His first wife was Julia Ann Dean who was born 1829 Greene County, Ohio and were married there in 1849. They were the parents of four children: Clark Warren born 1850, infant son born and died 1851, Louisa Belle born 1853 and Alonzo Harvey born June 19, 1856.

Julia Ann passed away October 11, 1863 and is buried in the Monmouth cemetery.

William Saville married Julia's cousin, Mary Jane Parry in 1865 and they had six children.

In 1874 William Saville decided to go west and his entire family settled in Sedgwick County, Kansas near the town of Clearwater. He is buried in the Ruby cemetery along with his wife. He passing away July 7, 1887 and his wife in 1896.

His son, Alonzo Harvey Struthers born June 19, 1856, Warren County, Illinois could not find a Kansas girl that pleased him so he returned to Monmouth and married his sweetheart Lucinda Elizabeth McBroom on September 22, 1878 at Monmouth. She was born February 12, 1856 in Zanesville, Ohio. Lucinda's mother was a Hickman and the Hickman and McBroom families became permanent residents of Warren County, Illinois. Alonzo and Lucinda lived in Monmouth where they became the parents of three children: Julia Corena born June 19, 1879; Thomas Dean born August 2, 1881 and Ruth Elizabeth born September 1, 1883. Alonzo returned to Sedgwick County, Kansas. It has been said that his wife was afraid to go West as she feared the Indians. They had three more children: Harvey Lee born October 17, 1886, Sarah Amy Jessie born July 26, 1890 and my mother, Jennie Belle who was born November 17, 1893. Jennie Belle married James Franklin Williamson on February 16, 1921 at Wichita, Sedgwick County, Kansas. My father was born May 29, 1891 in Mercer County, Kentucky. He passed away January 16, 1966 and my mother lived to be 100 years old passing away February 6, 1994. They are buried in the Clearwater Cemetery just as Jennie's parents are. To this union six children were born: Doris, Edith, James and Ruth who were triplets. Hugh and myself, Judy born August 22, 1931. I married Donald S. Huntrods, November 22, 1950 in Clearwater, Kansas. We live at St. Charles, Iowa and have three children.

WILLIAM STRUTHERS - William Struthers (b May 13, 1789 in Scotland, d March 31, 1861 near Monmouth, Warren Co., IL) was the son of William and Jane (Lindsay) Struthers. He married (1) Sept. 27, 1816, Rockbridge Co., VA, Martha Eleanor Saville (b Aug. 14, 1796 near Lexington, Rockbridge Co., VA, d Oct. 2, 1830 in Greene Co., OH) Martha was the daughter of M/M Robert and Deborah Saville. He married (2) Elizabeth L. Alexander (b April 21, 1799 in Ohio, d Oct 21, 1856, Warren Co., IL)

William came to the USA with his parents in 1795, landing at Norfolk, VA. He was a soldier in the War of 1812 and was a Private in Captain John McMillin's Company of Light Infantry detached from the 8th Regiment Rockbridge County, VA and attached to the 4th (Boyd's) Regiment VA Militia. They most likely lived in the Effinger, Rockbridge Co., VA area.

In 1830 they left Virginia and moved to the Xenia, Green Co., OH area. William's wife Martha is buried in Old Massies Creek (Stevenson) Cemetery near Xenia, Greene Co., OH. The children of William and Martha Struthers are: James, Marry, Debora, Martha, Elizabeth, William, Margaret, and unnamed male child.

William and 2nd wife Elizabeth came to Monmouth, IL in 1854 and settled on a farm just north of the town. Elizabeth was originally buried at Cedar Creek Cemetery near Little York, IL. Later her body was moved to the Monmouth Cemetery, Monmouth, IL and it is believed that her body was the first one to be buried in that cemetery. William is buried next to Elizabeth in the Monmouth Cemetery, Monmouth, IL. The children of William and Elizabeth are John, Unnamed Daughter, and William.

JOHN AND ARIZONA (CREGER) SWARTS - John Isaac Swarts born 14 June 1860 Abingdon, VA to John and Mary (Mouls) Swartz married 26 January 1885 Greendale, VA Arizona 'Zona' Hinda Creger, born 6 December 1864 to Michael and Surphina (Williams) Creger. They farmed near Abingdon; children all born there. In 1912 they moved to Warren County, IL with the younger children. John worked as farmhand until poor health prevented, then bought a home in Kirkwood. John died 30 August 1920, Monmouth. Family continued to live there. Arizona lived with daughters Mary Ketchum and Martha Vestal during last year, dying 31 July 1949, Smithshire.

Children:

Mary Margaret Surphina born 12 February 1887, died 12 September 1969, Monmouth. Married 4 March 1908 Abingdon, VA Frank Martin Ketchum; 10 children (biography this book).

Virginia A. born 24 October 1888, died 19 January 1890 Abingdon, VA.

Martha Nora born 23 October 1890, died 26 December 1973, Monmouth; married 22 December 1909, Abingdon, VA Charles H. Vestal, 8 children.

John Isaac and Arizona (Creger) Swarts, 1920s.

William Robert born 4 January 1893, died 21 October 1918, Camp Sheridan, Alabama.

Nannie Manuel born 22 December 1896, died 1 October 1956, Galesburg; married 18 July 1914 Monmouth William Omar Myler, 5 children.

Maude Frances born 10 January 1895, died 20 September 1915, Kirkwood.

Claude Denton; born 3 June 1902, died 23 August 1972, Long Beach, CA; married 15 June 1927 Monmouth, Eva Elizabeth Johnson; divorced.

Nina Ernestine born 15 February 1909, died 1 May 1911, Abingdon, VA.

Families of Mary and Frank Ketchum and Martha and Charles Vestal came together to Warren County in 1919. Frank farmed and Charles farmed and worked lumberyard.

William did farm work; entered service 31 May 1918, stationed Ft. Thomas, KY; transferred to Ft. Sheridan. AL then Hot Springs, NC where he served as guard at German Prison Camp. Returned Camp Sheridan August 1918. In Quartermaster's Corps at time of death. Was first soldier from Kirkwood area to succumb to Spanish Influenza. His body arrived Kirkwood, taken directly to Center Grove cemetery due to sickness at home. Flags flown at half-mast in Kirkwood in his honor.

Nannie and Will Myler lived many years in Iowa; in Illinois Kirkwood, Media and Galesburg. He did some farming, then carpenter by trade.

Maude Swarts died age 20, buried Center Grove Cemetery.

Claude worked for highway department several years; farmed after marriage in Monmouth, Alexis and Roseville areas. He later was a construction worker on several big dams in the country, including Boulder/Hoover Dam. Settled in California he was a pipefitter and boilermaker on large construction jobs. Died 23 August 1972, California; buried Center Grove cemetery, Warren County, IL.

Being a history buff, Lori (Trego) Robinson knew these ancestors only from proven facts and family stories she enjoys, but appreciates the contributions they made to the history of Warren County, IL.

Submitted by Great-great-granddaughter Lori (Trego) Robinson

MARY ANNE AND IVAN SWENSON - Mary Anne Phillips was born January 21, 1928 in Warren County, the second daughter of Orilla Jane Ross and Winnie Everett Phillips whose wedding date was May 22, 1924.

Orilla was born on March 25, 1907 in Warren County, IL; the daughter of Charles Edward (Bud) Ross and Sophronia Irene Waldron who had married on January 21, 1904. Winnie Everett was born in Rushville, IL on August 2, 1899.

Mary Anne attended elementary school at Jackson Corners for two years. After moving to Alexis she attended Union School. She is a 1946 graduate of Alexis High School.

On December 15, 1946 she married Ivan Carl Swenson at the Monmouth Lutheran Church.

Ivan was born December 14, 1920 in Vena, Sweden, the son of Carl Erik Svensson and Elsie GUNHILD Svensson. Carl was born on August 4, 1885 in Murlunda, Sweden. Elsie was born on July 12, 1897 in Vena, Sweden.

David, Carl, Mary Anne, Ivan, Dwain, Gayle, Sherri, November 1965

In 1922 they came to America arriving at Ellis Island in April and went immediately to Galesburg, IL. At first they lived near Rio, IL, then moved to Missouri, returning to Macomb, IL before finally settling in Warren County along Route 67 in Spring Grove Township.

Ivan attended Foster Grade School and Alexis High School where he met Mary Anne, his future wife.

In 1945 he moved with his mother and brother Harold to Seaton, IL in Mercer County.

After their marriage Ivan and Mary Anne lived in Seaton for twenty-five years. Their five children: Carl, David, Dwain, Gayle, and Sherri were born during those years.

They bought the Gorley Farm in Sumner Township on November 23, 1963; the day after President Kennedy was assassinated. The Gorley Springs on that farm has a flow of sixty gallons a minute.

In November 1971 they moved to Little York where they now reside.

Ivan's hobbies include hunting, fishing, and searching for Indian relics. Mary Anne has always enjoyed working with children and has been a Sunday School teacher, a room mother, Cub Scouts, Youth Advisor, and Girl Scout leader. She is a homemaker who enjoys her family, her yard, and her garden.

JOHN C. SZALTIS - Szaltis, John C., eldest son of Leonard and Dorothy Szaltis, came to Monmouth in 1973 to attend Monmouth College. While there, he participated in many sports, most notably wrestling. Also while attending college, he met his future wife, Bea Zavorski. John graduated from Monmouth College in 1975 with a Bachelor of Arts Degree. He found numerous opportunities of employment in the area including a teaching and coaching job at Costa Catholic School in Galesburg, Illinois in 1976. In, 1981 he decided to switch professions and go into law enforcement. He became a police officer with the Monmouth Police Department. His employment there lasted until 1986. After that, in 1986, he was employed at the newly opened Hill Correctional Center in Galesburg, Illinois where he has been employed ever since.

Bea M. Szaltis, middle child of Joseph and Ethel Zavorski (who later resided in Monmouth), came to Monmouth to attend college as well. Without ever having laid eyes on the campus, she came to Monmouth aboard the train and got off at the E Street station. Ironically, this is the street where she would later reside. After graduating from Monmouth College in 1974 with teaching certificates in Special Education, she gained employment through Warren Achievement School in Monmouth. She worked there for eighteen years until the school closed in 1994. Currently, she is employed by West Central Illinois Special Education Coop. She attended Fairview Center United Methodist Church in rural Monmouth.

Leonard Szaltis was born December 21, 1981 at St. Mary's Hospital in Galesburg, Illinois. He was later baptized at St. Patrick's Catholic Church in Galesburg. For his education, he attended Willits Elementary School, Central Junior High School, and graduated from Monmouth High School in June of 2000. He was an active member of Boy Scout Troop 355 in Monmouth and received his Eagle Scout Award on January 21, 1999. Leonard is also a member of the Warren County Genealogical Society. He attended the Church of the Immaculate Conception in Monmouth.

Joseph Szaltis was born at St. Mary's Hospital on July 29, 1985. He was baptized at the Church of the Immaculate Conception. Joseph attended Willits Elementary School, graduated from Immaculate Conception School, and is now attending Monmouth High School. He, too, was an active member with Boy Scout Troop 355 at the First Methodist Church in Monmouth.

Sarah Szaltis was born June 29, 1987 at St. Marys Church and then baptized August 1, 1987 at the Church of the Immaculate Conception. She attended the Monmouth public schools including Willits and Central Junior High and is currently attending Monmouth High School. She was an avid sports athlete and had played in many organizations including the Shooting Stars of Monmouth. Sarah attended the First Christian Church in Monmouth.

CHUCK AND LINDA TALLEY - Charles Francis Talley was born 19 May 1941 in Monmouth, Illinois. Chuck's father was Ira James Talley, born 14 June 1908, died 29 December 1979. Ira's father was Andrew Talley, born 1 March 1869, died 17 May 1943. Ira's mother was Mary Susan Edwards Talley, born 27 September 1874, died 21 September 1927. Chuck's mother was Helen Louise Parrish Talley, born 16 July 1916, died 18 June 1951. Helen's father was Clarence Ernest Parrish, born 22 July 1881, died 24 August 1960. Helen's mother was Alfarietta Alice Earp Parrish, born 18 April 1886, died 27 December 1965. Chuck is a first cousin three times removed from Wyatt Earp.

Chuck married Linda Lee Staff 8 July 1962 at the First Christian Church in Galesburg, Illinois. Linda was born 11 April 1944 in Rushville, Illinois. Linda's father was Alfred Edson Staff, born 23 January 1915, died 3 July 1978. Alfred's father was Cadmus Adonis Romulus Staff – called Romie – born 24 October 1884, died 14 December 1966. Alfred's mother was Opal Irene Heaton Staff, born 28 June 1890, died 21 December 1943. Linda's mother was Martha Jane Worrall Staff, born 4 January 1914, died 5 January 1979.

Martha's father was Edmund Burke Worrall, born 23 September 1881, died 4 August 1941. Martha's mother was Susie Mae Burkhalter Worrall, born 23 May 1888, died 13 December 1972.

Chuck and Linda Talley May 19, 1999

Chuck and Linda have two children. Debra Lynn Talley was born 5 January 1964 in Monmouth, Illinois. Debi is a teacher in South Bend, Indiana. Jeffrey Charles Talley was born 1 January 1967 in Monmouth, Illinois. Jeff worked for Intergrated Ag. (The Red Tractor) in Galesburg, Illinois. Jeff has a daughter, Kameryn Darlene Talley, born 20 May 1996 in Galesburg, Illinois. The Talleys are members of the First Christian Church in Monmouth, Illinois.

Chuck went to Harding Grade School, Central Junior High School and graduated from Monmouth High School in Monmouth, Illinois. Linda went to L.T. Stone Grade School, George Churchill Junior High School and graduated from Galesburg Senior High School in Galesburg, Illinois. Both have taken some college courses.

As a young teen, Chuck worked at the White House Dairy, Country Kitchen, A&W Root Beer Stand, detasseled corn and unloaded boxcars for Monmouth Fruit Company. Linda did some babysitting. She was a CNA and became Activity Director at Monmouth Nursing Home. Chuck worked for Doster Oil Company, Kroger Grocery Store, Joe Danforth Plumbing, Heating and Cooling and was a firefighter for the City of Monmouth. He retired from firefighting in 1991. Chuck works for the City of Monmouth, Illinois as Building Official, Plat Officer, Plumbing Inspector, County Zoning Administrator and Cemetery Supervisor.

Linda is a member of the Warren Chapter (formerly Puritan and Cavalier) DAR and volunteers for the American Red Cross. Chuck is a member and Past Master of the Monmouth Masonic Lodge #37 A.F. & A.M., is Past President of the Kiwanis Club and is Captain of the Monmouth, Warren County Auxiliary Police. They belong to the Warren County, Illinois Genealogical Society.

JAMES MELVIN TALLEY - James Melvin Talley and Serena Zell Jennings were united in marriage June 25, 1884, in Warren County, Illinois, the origin of their nativity.

Serena was born October 3, 1866 in Swan Township to Edmund and Emily Cline Jennings, the fourth of five children born to this union. Her father and mother migrated to Warren County from the states of Indiana and Ohio, respectively. She and her husband lived in the Swan Creek area during their married life where James was engaged in farming. An active member of the Youngstown Christian Church, Serena was baptized there January 11, 1908.

James and Serena Talley, wedding June 25, 1884

James was born January 9, 1859 in Roseville to William Jr. and Pernecia Perkins Talley, the third of eight children. His father migrated from the state of Kentucky and his mother was of Illinois birth.

To this union the following children were born: Hazel Viola, born December 21, 1884; married Charles Alden Howe. Harry Brown, born March 27, 1887; married Minnie Eugenia Booton. Goldie Elma, born May 26, 1889; married Joseph Frederick Seckman.

After James passed away June 7, 1905, Serena eventually moved to Roseville where she resided until her death, November 26, 1957. Both she and James were laid to rest in Bond Cemetery, Greenbush Township.

FRANK THEMANSON - Themanson, Frank, age 74, of 610 North D Street was born 6 April 1902 in Monmouth, Illinois. He was the tenth child of John and Ida (Carlson) Themanson. He was reared and educated in Monmouth and graduated from Monmouth High School. He served in the Coast Guard during World War II. After the death of her husband, Dean Dalton, Frank married his wife, Vada, 3 March 1963 in Monmouth. They resided in Berwyn, Illinois. He retired in 1966 and they returned to Monmouth to make their home. She died 20 January 1969. He immediately left their apartment and never returned, leaving breakfast dishes on the table, food, and all his belongings.

Frank and Vada Themanson, March 29, 1964

Frank was a grocer in his early years working for the Scott Brothers "Pioneer" grocery, the Vogt grocery, and Barnes Bros. Grocery and Meats located at 200 East Broadway. He was an excellent clerk, very dependable, respected by his customers. He was not one to banter with other clerks, but tended to business. After the war he worked for Western Electric Company in Cicero until he retired.

He was a member of the Lutheran Church, a fifty-year member of Monmouth Lodge #37 AF

& AM and also belonged to the American Legion Post 136.

Survivors include two brothers and a sister, George Themanson and Mrs. Clarence (Ruth) Sandstrom, and Fred Themanson of Galesburg. He was preceded in death by his wife, parents, and eight brother and sisters. He died of a heart attack and left his memorial money to the Heart Association.

THIEME - Henry C. Thieme was born in 1839 in Germany. He married Magdalena (Lena) Jacob who was born December 27, 1844 in Dettwillwer, Germany. She came to America in 1871. She Joined the Gerlaw Presbyterian Church on June 15, 1890, having been a former member of the Little York, Illinois Presbyterian Church.

Henry died November 11, 1891 at the age of 52. Lena died September 1, 1895. They are buried in Gerlaw, Illinois Cemetery next to the grave of their baby son, Harry, born June 1881, died January 1882. At the time of Lena's death, she had two sisters and two brothers living in America and two sisters and one brother still living in Germany.

Their children were Charles J. Thieme born November 20, 1872 in Monmouth Illinois, George B. Thieme and Edward Thieme.

Charles married Anna Gallaugher November 28, 1894 in Gerlaw, Illinois. She was born January 11, 1868 in Mercer County, the daughter of William and Margaret Muir Gallaugher. Charles and Anna farmed south west of Little York, Illinois. This family farm is now farmed by Gary Spence, a great-grandson. Charles died February 13, 1923 and Anna died July 25, 1957 at the Morefeld and Newell Nursing Home in Monmouth, Illinois. She was the last surviving member of a family of ten children. They are buried in Little York, Illinois. Their children were William (Bill) Henry Thieme and George Edward Thieme.

Bill was born July 22,1901 in Warren County, Illinois. He married Lucy Fair October 20, 1925, in Aledo, Illinois. Witnesses to the marriage were his brother, George and Mary Martin. Bill farmed and also sold insurance through the Thieme Insurance Agency in Little York, Illinois. He died October 5, 1970. Lucy died January 16, 1996 at the Monmouth Nursing Home. They are buried in Little York, Illinois close to his parents.

Children of Bill and Lucy are Marjorie, born October 24, 1927, Dorothy Ann, born December 17, 1934 and Charles(Chuck), born January 27, 1947. Marjorie married Edward Smith. Their children are Kathy, Kerry and John. Dorothy Ann married John (Jack) Spence. Their children are Gary, Rusty, Cindy, Danny and Bill. Chuck married Delores Davis. Their children are JoAnne, James, Angela, and Bill.

George Edward Thieme was born in 1904. He married Mary Martin. George was also in the insurance business. They had two daughters, Phyllis and Janet. Phyllis married Dean Goldnetz. Janet married Robert Zenner. George died November 7, 1960. Funeral services were held at the Gerard Funeral Home in Canton, Illinois.

FRANCIS JOSEPH "FRANK" THOMPSON - Francis Joseph "Frank" Thompson was born May 8, 1952, the son of Robert C. and Elizabeth Mills Thompson. Frank, is the fourth of nine children: Ann Thompson Ringoen, Reynolds; Steve Thompson, Roseville; Bob and Frank Thompson, Kirkwood; William "Bill" Thompson, Avon; Ed and Roy Thompson, Roseville; Rose Thompson Boaz, Roseville; and Joe Thompson, Berwick.

Frank went to a one-room school, Barr School, six miles west of Monmouth, the first and second grades. From third though ninth grades he went to Yorkwood, except fifth grade when he went to Roseville. The last three years of high school he went to Roseville.

Frank and Robert C. Thompson

Frank worked at Stock Land FS, Monmouth; Huskee Built, Monmouth; Sprout Farms and Amoco Fertilizer, Roseville; Thompson Trucking, Kirkwood; Robert C. Thompson Feed Store and self employed painting contractor and fire extinguisher sales.

On June 25, 1976 Frank married Anita Kaye Sparrow, born Jan. 1,1957, at St. Patrick's Catholic Church, Raritan, Illinois. On June 21 1972 Mitchell Lee Thompson was born. May 6, 1979 Jamie Kay Thompson was born. Mitch and Jamie both graduated from Yorkwood high. Mitch graduated from WIU in law enforcement. Jamie married Justin Bert Raymond on April 21, 1999. On May 1, 2000 Jamie gave birth to Nolan Bert Raymond.

Frank loves his family very much and is very proud of all of them. He says, "Don't be afraid to let your family and friends know you care about them because it sounds corny or soppy. We all need to know we are loved, there is nothing more important that we can do for our family."

The Thompson family has had two special pets over the years. Shelia, a yellow Lab that died in the fall of 2000 and Bear, a three legged, stub tailed, longhaired cat still alive and in charge of the house.

From 1985 to 1990 Frank put together two books of ideas to help the American farmer; the books are called *The American Farmer Book I and II*. The books were full of ideas from farmers and others on how to get fair prices for farmers and show the importance of farmers to our country and world. The books generated two to four million dollars worth of positive press about the American farmer. The books were written about in newspapers including *The New York Times*, *Peoria Journal Star*, and *Des Moines Register*.

On Jan. 31, 2000 Frank started a campaign called *Change the World*, gathering ideas to help slow down murder and suicide throughout our country and world. The *Change the World* concept promotes love for fellowman and letting each other know we are loved.

On April 27, 2001 Frank and his dad, Robert C. Thompson, accepted Jesus as their personal savior. On July 10, 2001 Robert died, thank God he was ready.

Change the World is ongoing; through press coverage it has reached one to two million people. Frank has talked to over ten thousand one on one and in groups. Frank speaks to groups of all types. His phone number is 309-768-2458, address P.O. Box 254 Kirkwood, Illinois 61447, Web site www.geocity.com/changetheworld00 . We all need to do what we can to make the world a better, safer, happier place. Love is the answer.
Submitted by Frank Thompson

THOMSON - "Uncle Hugh and Uncle James came out here after they were released from the Civil War," was the way Margaret McCoy Sanner described the arrival of the Thomsons in Warren County. Hugh's and James's parents, John and Rachel (Francis) Thomson purchased land in Section 10 of Tompkins Township in 1868. They came from Smithfield Township, Jefferson County, Ohio where they were prominent in the community. In Ohio, they had participated in the formation of the Piney Forks United Presbyterian Church and donated the land on which the church was built. Including Hugh and James, John and Rachel had nine children. Two daughters had married and remained in Ohio.

Four generations living in the same household, 1908

Margaret Emma (Maggie) Thomson was the eighth of the nine children. She married Joseph William (Will) McCoy in 1875 (see McCoy). A year later, a son, Ralph, was born and another year later, Will died. Maggie and Ralph moved into the house on the Thomson land in Section 10 with her parents. John Thomson died in 1887. The land was farmed by James Thomson who lived the next house east. Maggie McCoy purchased 80 acres of the land from the other heirs of her father in 1898. Ralph attended Monmouth Business College but gave up business opportunities to do the farming.

Also in 1898, Ralph McCoy married Lulu Randall (see Brown, Randall, et al.). Ralph farmed the 80 acres in Section 10 and raised his family there. Rachel Thomson and Maggie McCoy continued to live with Ralph and Lulu the rest of their lives. Ralph and Lulu had three daughters Louise, Mildred and Margaret. Louise was born in 1903. That made four generations living in the same house until Rachel died in 1910. Louise was sick quite a bit during her first winter apparently because of the cold in the little old house. Thus, a new house was built on the same lot. It still stands today. The house and land are currently owned by Mildred Birdsell.

Mildred McCoy married Everett Birdsell of Kirkwod. They purchased the Shellane propane gas franchise from Brown Lynch Scott. Everett delivered bottled gas to rural customers and when rural electrification came about, he wired many rural homes for electricity. Milly and Everett expanded their business to include appliances. They owned and operated Birdsell's Appliance in Kirkwood for many years. Milly also taught Latin in Warren School. She and Everett had two daughters and a son. Amy Lu Birdsell married Rodney Wolf of rural Kirkwood. Both Rod and Amy graduated from Bradley University. They live in Washington, IL. Amy retired as the librarian for Caterpillar and Rod is a retired self-employed contractor. Bruce Birdsell graduated from Monmouth College and married Serena Foote. They live in Maryland where Bruce works for the elevator company that purchased Montgomery Elevator. The Birdsell's other daughter was stillborn and is buried in the Kirkwood Cemetery. The presence of her grave in Center Grove Cemetery makes five generations of McCoy and Thomson descendants in that cemetery.

RUBY MAY THOMSON - Ruby May Thomson, daughter of William Matthew Thomson and Ida Caroline Wilson, born 20 July 1894, McDonough County, and died 10 Feb 1978 in Macomb, Ill, and is buried by her husband in Forest Lawn Memorial Gardens near Macomb. She married Charles V. Raymond on 24 Dec 1919 in Bushnell, Illinois. She is the mother of six children, See Charles Vilasco Raymond for more details.

Ruby May (Thomson) Raymond July 20, 1976 – 82nd birthday

Ruby was born into a family not wealthy in worldly goods, but rich in family heritage as well as Christian values. William and Ida Thomson raised seven children, namely: Melvin Ray (1890-1964), Olen Clayton (1892-1956), Ruby May (1894-1978), Nellie Chrystal (1897-1975), Charles Scott (1899-1973), William Virgil (1901-1966) and Ida Fern (1906-1996).

Ruby earned a four year scholarship and graduated 24 July 1914 from the Academy of the Western Illinois State Normal School (Now Western Illinois University) at Macomb, Ill. She taught three years at Lickskillet School near Adair, one year at Walnut Grove West School 1917-1918, and later four months in Warren County at the Crawford School District. She was a wonderful mother and "teacher" for her six children.

Always wanting to be a writer, Ruby began writing short stories of her eventful life in rural Illinois having seen this country evolve from transportation by horse and buggy to Man walking on the Moon on her 72nd birthday! Following her death, her daughter Reta May Mariner completed the 172 page book, *Wheels of Life 1894-1978* by Ruby May Raymond, printed by Carlberg Publishing Co, Roseville, Ill, 1978.

It is a record of her stories, a genealogy of her ancestors and those of husband Charlie, their families and life together over 45 years, biographies of children and grandchildren, service records of family, Revolutionary to Viet Nam.

Ruby enjoyed people and made many friends as she was an active member of Lucille Chapter of the Order of Eastern Star, the Daughters of the American Revolution, the Royal Neighbors Lodge, the Rebekah Lodge, the Carnegie Mutual Club, the Center Household Science Club, the Macomb Veterans of Foreign Wars Auxiliary and the United Methodist Church of Bushnell.

Ruby joined the Royal Neighbors of America in 1918, serving the Walnut Grove Camp 1935 to 1950 as Recorder, then Bushnell Camp twelve years as Recorder and camp's Oracle 1959-1960. She received her 50-year membership pin on July 7, 1973.

Ruby extensively researched her Thomson Family Tree basing her D.A.R. membership on her ancestor, John Thomson, Soldier of the American Revolution from Virginia. He was a brother of statesman, Charles Thomson, Secretary of the First and Second Continental Congress of the United States of America and designer of The Great Seal.

Ruby was a gifted writer, her essay, "Famous Illinois Women" won I.W.F.C. Contest's First Place Certificate of Merit and Points for the Carnegie-Mutual Club in 1966, also a First Place Citation in State of Illinois Contest of Federated Illinois Women's Clubs.

JAMES AND JOSEPHINE TIERNEY - Ireland was experiencing the Potato Famine 1845-1849 when the first of our Tierney ancestors came to America – James and Mary (Clark) Tierney of Cavan Co Ireland.

Tierney family L: to R: Francis, "Joie" Josephine Irene, Gertrude, James and Josephine

James and Mary were the parents of 7 children: Margaret, James, Owen, Mary, Catherine, Bernard "Barney," and Patrick. Margaret, Mrs. McKeney stayed in Kingsport and Belfast areas of Ireland. Margaret had 3 children. James lived in England and Ireland. Mary died at age 20. Catherine, Owen, Barney and Patrick came to America with their parents. Owen and Barney remained single. Catherine married James Colgan and Patrick married Alice (Kelly) Lynch, Tierney, Logan. They settled in the Good Hope, then Raritan area. Patrick and Alice Tierney had two children, Alice who died in infancy and James Patrick who would later marry Josephine "Joie" Irene Collins. Mrs. Alice Tierney was a widow three times before her death.

It was James b.1871 and Josephine Tierney b. 1877 who first moved to Warren County in 1926. Their 3 children were Francis born 1906, Mary "Josephine" born 1911 and Alice "Gertrude" born 1914. Francis married Loretta Boozan and lived on farms in Warren County Rural Kirkwood, Il. Their daughter Pat married Kenny Arnold, Media, Il. Arnold's had three children Brad, Brian and Kim. Francis son, Mike, married Karen Cassiday and they live in Kirkwood and farm in that area. They have two children Nancy (Mrs. Patrick McGrail) Tennessee and John who is married to Amelia Fillman and lives rural Kirkwood.

2. Josephine married Bill Flaherty and lived Alexis, Joy and Viola, Il. They had five children; James-Florida, Bill-deceased, Barb (Mrs. Dave Jensen)Wisconsin, John-California, and Leo-deceased.

3. Gertrude married Clete Smith and they farmed most of their life in Warren Co. (exception Henderson Co 1940-1942, Texas 1951).Their five children Virginia (Mrs. Don Greiner) Fairfield, Ia, six children Mark, Cindy, Jeff, Sally, Phil deceased and Chris; Irene (Mrs. Dick Johnson) Winfield, Ia, three children, Rick, Mike and Jackie Jo.; David married Pearl Yung and they have farmed all their married life in the Monmouth area; Earl married Terry Thompson of Monmouth had three daughters Gina, Brandy and Autumn. Earl is now married to Phillis Cantwell and they live in Kirkwood, Il. Phillis has four children, Jeremi, Joe, Rene and Andie. Clete and Gertrude's fifth child, Allen Clete, died in infancy. (Also see "Ray" and "David and Pearl Smith")

ROY AND GERALDINE (RENNER) TINKHAM - Roy D. Tinkham was born August 4, 1913 on a farm near Kirkwood, IL. E. Geraldine Renner was born November 18, 1919 on a farm near Delavan, IL. They were married December 19, 1943 at her mother's home in Morton, IL. They are the parents of six children.

L: to R: Seated: Linda Tinkham, Geraldine Tinkham and Mary Tinkham. Standing: Ronald Tinkham, Patricia Mac Intosh, Tom Tinkham and George Tinkham.

Ronald married Katie Boone. They are the parents of Becky and Mike. They have a Motorcycle Shop and Christmas Tree Farm south of Kirkwood.

George married Linda Gillock. They have two sons, Brent and Colin. They live in Springfield, IL. where George is an attorney with the IL. Department of Transportation.

Linda teaches school in Portland, OR.

Patricia married Mike Mac Intosh. They have two daughters, Katie and Megan and a son, Nickolas. They live in Wheaton, IL. Pat is a P.E. teacher.

Thomas married Linda Patterson. They have three daughters, Sarah, Jennifer and Amanda. They live in Colleyville, TX. Tom owns an Electrical Contracting firm.

Mary is married to Robert Kean. They are the parents of Rachel and Matthew. They live in Minneapolis, MN. Mary has her Ph.D. in chemistry and works for 3M. Robert has his Ph.D and works for Cargill Corporation.

Roy's parents were Forrest and Orpha (Becktel) Tinkham. Forrest farmed and was road commissioner in Tompkins Township for several years. Orpha attended Media-Weaver Academy and taught in country schools in Illinois and Iowa before her marriage.

Geraldine's parents were Warren and Maude (Duncanson) Renner. After their marriage they homesteaded in Wyoming. After living on the land for 3 years, the US Government gave them the deed for 320 acres. Maude attended Green Valley school and Normal Teacher's School. She taught in country schools in Illinois and Wyoming Warren was a farmer and ran the grain elevator at Winkel, Illinois.

After high school Roy helped his father farm and in the winter he was a chef at the Blackhawk and other hotels in the Quad-Cities. He worked with the Boy Scouts for many years. He was a licensed pilot and gave several people their first airplane ride. Roy passed away in June 1975.

Geraldine attended Green Valley Schools and graduated from the University of Illinois. She taught Home Economics, General Science and Girl's PE at Kirkwood High School. before their children were born. She was a Den Mother, Girl Scout Leader and Sunday School Teacher. She taught at Biggsville Grade School 1967-1970. She continues to live on Catalpa Grove Farm.

JOHN C. TOAL - John C. Toal, Sr., born November 4, 1939 in Monmouth and Mary Alice McLoskey born June 8, 1941 in Monmouth, were married December 26, 1964 at the Immaculate Conception Church, Monmouth. They have one daughter Kathleen married to Bruce Lee and a son John C. Jr (Jack), married to Amy Howe.

John's parents were Carroll Paul Toal and Bernice Shunick Toal of Monmouth. His grandparents were Joseph Dominic Toal and Nellie Gallagher Toal of Monmouth and his great grandparents were Edward Toal and Ann McPharland (also spelled McFarland) of Ireland.

Edward 1820-1880 and Ann 1833-1927 were married October 18, 1852 in County Armagh, Ireland. They came to America that same year on the sailboat *Olympia*, sailing from Liverpool and landing in New Orleans. They went to Cincinnati and came by boat to Burlington and then by rail to Monmouth in 1856 Edward was a laborer and well digger. He planted the trees in Coburn Square, now called West Park. Ann attended the first mass celebrated in Monmouth held in the West Ward School which then stood on the site of the present High School. They were the parents of four children.

Joseph Dominic 1870-1963 and Nellie Gallagher 1876-1932 were married November 7, 1900 in Monmouth. They were the parents of 4 children. J.D. spent more than fifty years on the railroads. Forty-eight were spent with the C.B.&Q and forty of these were in serving Monmouth as engineer of the switch engine.

Carroll Paul 1901-1994 and Bernice Shunick 1904-2001 were married October 3, 1939 in Monmouth. They had five children. He worked as a telegraph operator for the Burlinton Railroad and had a lifetime career at the National Bank of Monmouth.

Mary Alice Toal was the third child of Robert T. McLoskey and Elizabeth Dickson McLoskey of Monmouth. Her grandparents were John Anthony (Jack) McLoskey and Lillian Shawler of Monmouth. Her great grandparents were Robert H. McLoskey and Nancy Ann Lafferty. Great-great grandparents were Anthony A. McLoskey and Elizabeth Pollock.

Anthony, born in 1819, was a cabinet maker and kept at North Henderson the first Post office between Monmouth and Rock Island. He married Elizabeth in 1845. She was born in Columbus, Ohio. They had four children.

Robert H. was born in 1848 in Davenport. He was a veteran of the Civil War and had been Commander of McClanahan Post No. 330, Grand Army of the Republic. He was detailed to keep telegaph lines between Donaldson, Tenn. and Paducah Ky. His original outfit from Iowa was cited for its service by President Abraham Lincoln. Robert was a painter by profession. He married Nancy Ann Lafferty who was born at her father's home in Norwood in 1849. They had five children.

John Anthony (Jack) 1885-1950 served on the board of supervisors for at least twelve years and served as treasurer of the Illinois Township Officers Association. Jack married Lillian Frances Shawler 1888-1970 in 1906. They had two sons, Robert T. and Leo. Leo was a Captain in the U.S. Marine Corps in WWII and was killed in the invasion of Pelileu.

Robert (Bob) 1907-1990 married Elizabeth Dickson 1904-1981 and they had four children. Elizabeth was from Carrollton and they married in 1929. Bob was a funeral director and embalmer. He served as Director of Field Activities Illinois Department of Public Health., served as Township Supervisor, was a representative in Illinois where he was minority whip, and was a member of the 88th U.S. Congress. He was a farm operator and manager.

John and Mary Alice have always lived in Monmouth. John worked at Wirtz Book Store, The Model Clothing, Co. and for the Warren County Housing Authority. He is a Fourth Degree Knight and a member of the Immaculate Conception Church. He attended Monmouth College. Mary Alice also attended Monmouth College. She taught P.E. and Spanish and was a substitute teacher. Their daughter Kathleen and Bruce Lee are the parents of Brandon, Breayn, Kelsey and Kathryn. Their son Jack and Amy Howe are the parents of Jessicah, Alec, and Jared.

CARROLL VANCE TREGO - Carroll Vance Trego born 7 October 1941 Monmouth, Il to Gerald and Ethel (Ketchum) Trego. Siblings: Kaylene and Claude (Butch). Carroll Married 22 January 1961 to Helen Keller in Minot ND. Divorced 1965. Children: Linda Lee born 12 December 1961, Minot, ND. Troy Duane born 24 October 1963, Monmouth, Il.

M2 Jerilyne Sue Stephenson 13 November 1965, Espanola NM.

Children: Sherry Dawn born 6 May 1967 Monmouth Il. Lori Lynn born 2 September 1970, Denver CO.

Grandchildren: Jessica Ann Robinson born 7 February 2000 to Richard and Lori (Trego) Robinson, Plano, TX. Alexis Jayde LeFils born 6 December 2000 to James and Sherry (Trego) LeFils, Dallas, TX

Attended schools in Monmouth and graduated Monmouth High School in 1959. Air Force from August 1959 to September 1968. Served in Minot ND; Tin City AK, Clovis NM; and Bien Hoa; South Vietnam. Served as heavy equipment

Carroll, Lori, Sue, Sherry, James

repairman. Moved to Northglenn CO. and worked as mechanic on over the road trucks until moving to Sanger, TX in 1974. Ran auto and truck repair shop as Trego's Mechanic Service from 1974 to 1987. Worked as service manager for Chevrolet dealership in Sanger until opening The Car Care Center of Sanger in 1996. Carroll is an ASE Master Certified Technician in both Automobile and Heavy Trucks. He has served as Chapter Vice President, President and Sec/Treas of the Denton Tx Chapter of the Association of Automotive service Providers of Texas.

CLAUDE "BUTCH" AND TERESA "TESSA" (COX) TREGO - Claude Allen "Butch" Trego was born on August 12, 1957 in Monmouth, Illinois to Gerald F. and Ethel (Ketchum) Trego. His siblings are Carroll Vance, Sanger, Texas and Kaylene L. (Trego) Blanchard, Houma, Louisiana.

Tessa and Butch Trego

Butch attended Willits Grade School, Central Junior High School and graduated from Monmouth High School in 1975. During his childhood he was a member of Boy Scout Troop 355 under the direction of troop leader Richard Wolfe where he earned Order of the Arrow and Eagle Scout honors and also played Lions League Baseball under coach Jerry McBride.

After high school he attended Western Illinois University and Carl Sandberg Junior College pursuing a degree in Biology. While attending these universities he worked for Pizza Hut as a cook then as an Assistant Manager for the Mt. Pleasant, Iowa, Dixon, Illinois and Monmouth, Illinois stores. In 1981 Butch left Pizza Hut to pursue a degree in Respiratory Therapy at Blackhawk College in Moline, Illinois and in June 1983 he graduated with an Associate Degree in Respiratory Therapy.

After graduation Butch worked as a staff therapist and evening shift supervisor for Illini Hospital in Silvis, Illinois. In 1987 he was recruited to Dallas, Texas to work for Dallas Institute for Rehabilitation as a pm supervisor and in

1990 he accepted the position of Director for Respiratory Care for Baylor Institute for Rehabilitation. While working for the Baylor Health Care System Butch met Carolyn Ann Crisp and they were married on October 10, 1992. Also entering into the marriage was Carolyn's son Joshua Crisp. The couple divorced in August 1997.

In 1997 Butch also accepted the position of Corporate Director Clinical services for SCCI Corporation (a long term care hospital organization). In June 1998 while working for SCCI he completed a BS degree in Business Management at LeTourneau University in Dallas. Soon afterwards he left SCCI and began working as a cost containment consultant for numerous hospital corporations. In 2000 Butch left consulting to return to work as a therapist and attended the University of Texas at Dallas and in June 2001 completed a masters degree in Business Administration in Change Management.

Teresa "Tessa" Masterson was born April 12, 1959 in Amarillo, Texas where she attended elementary and intermediate schools and graduated from Tascossa High School in 1977. Tessa married Rhett Cox in 1979. On March 14, 1986 Tessa gave birth to Nichol Rhett Cox. In May 1991 Tessa graduated from Brookhaven College with an Associates degree in Nursing. She since went on to become certified in critical care and emergency nursing. Tessa and Rhett divorced in 1998.

In 1999 Butch met Tessa while working at Zale Lipshy University Hospital. After a two-year relationship they married in Princeville Kauai, Hawaii on September 12, 2001. Also joining the marriage was Tessa's son Nichol Cox. In 2002 Butch accepted a position at VersaMed, a ventilator corporation, as the company Clinical Applications Specialist. Butch, Tessa and Nichol continue to live in Carrollton, Texas.

CLYDE E. TREGO, SR.

Clyde Eugene Trego Sr. was born September 9, 1927 in Larchland, Illinois. He is the 7th child of Ralph W. and Ida (Johnson) Trego and the grandchild of Kerlin Filmore and Margaret (Hood) Trego and Carl and Beatrice (Edman) Johnson. In 1936 Clyde's fam-

Marsha Simpson, Sandra Gray, Tim, Doug and Rodger Trego. Sitting: Clyde Jr., Clyde Sr., Anna

ily moved from the farm to Kirkwood, Illinois. When Clyde was 15 years old he went to work for the Burlington Railroad. He worked there until 1944, when at the age of 17, he joined the United Sates Navy. He served as Fireman First Class on the USS *Ajax* and the USS *Calido* and was stationed in the Pacific outside of Japan during WWII. He received an honorable discharge in 1946 and returned to Illinois. In 1947 Clyde married Marjorie Darlene Grammont of Monmouth, Illinois. They moved to Wichita, Kansas in 1948 where he went to work for The Zogleman Motor Company. In 1949 their first daughter, Marsha Ann, was born and in 1951 their second daughter, Sandra Kay, was born. Clyde and Darlene divorced in 1952.

In 1954, Clyde married Anna Lucille Cooper. They had four sons, Clyde Eugene Jr., Douglas Allan, Rodger Dwayne, and Timothy Neal. They also had one daughter, Anna Christina, who died shortly after birth. Clyde and Ann will celebrate their 50th wedding anniversary in August of 2004 and, along with all of their children, plan to take an Alaskan cruise.

In 1964, Clyde went to work for a relatively new aircraft company in Wichita – "Lear Jet." He worked as a lead-man in maintenance until his retirement in 1992 at the age of 65.

Clyde has always enjoyed taking something old and broken, which most people would think beyond repair, and making it like new again. He is always in the market for old, broken and unusual clocks to repair. He has built two grandfather clocks and a clock that he has made all of the gears out of wood. He enjoys woodworking and has made several pieces of furniture. In 1987, while still working full time at Lear Jet, he along with wife, Anna, and two of his son's, Clyde Jr. and Tim, built the home they presently live in.

Today, Clyde and Anna enjoy retirement. They keep busy with family and church and they hunt for broken clocks at garage sales, estate sales and auctions. They have eight grandchildren and two great-grandchildren. All of the grandchildren at one time or another has, with the help of grandpa, built something in "Dad's" woodworking shop. Even as the children and grandchildren have gotten older they still go to Dad's or Grandpa's (Clyde) for repair and advice.

DALE EDMAN AND DIANA KAY (PESTLE) TREGO

Dale Edman, second child of Ralph Woodburn and Ida Christine (Johnson) Trego, was born October 28, 1918 in Monmouth, Il. He has four brothers, Gerald Fillmore and Robert Leroy, both deceased; Clyde Eugene of Wichita, Kansas and Herbert Conard of Monmouth, Il. He has three sisters, Virgie Pauline Farrar of South Chicago Heights, Dorothy Mae Lober of Blandinsville, Il and Margaret Catherine, deceased. Dale's parents lived in Monmouth until the spring of 1921, when they moved to a farm near Kirkwood. Dale attended first and second grades at Moore School. The family moved to Ponemah in 1927 for about a year, then to Little York area where Date attended Duck Creek School. From there they moved to Stronghurst for a short time, then moved back to Kirkwood where he attended sixth, seventh and eighth grades at Moore School. He attended ninth grade at Kirkwood High School. After attending the first year of High School, Dale enrolled in the Civilian Conservation Corps and was there from 1936-1939. In 1941 Dale was drafted into the Army and served in the Aleutian Islands and the Pacific Theater. He was released from the Army in 1945.

Dale married Mildred Botkins of Biggsville on June 24, 1941 and lived in Monmouth. Mildred worked at Boeing Aircraft, Wichita, Kansas during the time Dale was in service. After he was discharged they returned to Monmouth and Wilfred Dale was born to them on November 6, 1946. They later moved to Wichita, Kansas and their daughter, Norma Jean was born there on July 8, 1953 They lived in Wichita for about twenty years, before returning to Monmouth. Dale was a mechanic all his life. Dale and Mildred were divorced on April 9, 1974.

Dale and Diana Trego, June 15, 2002.

Dale later married Mildred (Martin) Carr. She lived in Avon, Il. Mildred was first married to Edwin Carr. He died in a farm accident on June 2, 1972. Dale and Mildred were married April 12, 1974 in Avon, Il. They lived on a farm south of Avon where Dale worked as a mechanic and worked on clocks. Mildred died February 23, 1999. Dale moved to Bushnell and on August 30, 2001 married Diana Kay Pestle in Bushnell. Diana was born October 19, 1965 in Macomb, Il. Her parents were Ralph Lee and Betty Lou (Clayton) Pestle.

GERALD & ETHEL (KETCHUM) TREGO

- Gerald Fillmore "Jerry" Trego born 22 May 1916 Monmouth, IL to Ralph and Ida (Johnson) Trego. Siblings: Dale, Virgie, Margaret, Dorothy, Robert, Clyde, Herbert. Married 15 July 1939 Kahoka, MO - Ethel Lorraine Ketchum born 27 July 1918 Bristol, VA to Frank and Mary (Swarts) Ketchum. Moved to IL 1919. Siblings: Clarence, Lucille, Roy, Hazel, Nannie Belle, Robert, Dorothy, Grace, William.

Gerald and Ethel Trego, 1994

Gerald attended schools in Warren and Henderson Counties, Graduating from Kirkwood High 1934. 1935-36 worked CCC camp Savanna, IL helping build Mississippi Palisades State Park. Did day and mechanic work several years. They moved to Wichita, Kansas 1942 where he worked in heat treat department Beech Aircraft until 1945. Returning to Monmouth, was fireman on M&STL, then Gaskill Motors, Elmer's Service, E &A Motors as mechanic and body repairman. Retired 1980.

Ethel attended Center Grove school, graduated Kirkwood High 1935. Did housework starting at twenty-five cents per day, then $5.00 per week! Seamstress at Formfit 1948-1970; Smoler's 1970-1979 (cutting room last 5 years)

Girl Scout leader three years; Cub Scout Den Mother seven years; Den Mother Coach two years. Charter member Warren County, Illinois Genealogical Society; Recording Secretary; Research Chairman since 1983; Certificate chairman; acquisitions 8 years; helped walk and catalog cemeteries; prints publications and copies records; board member.

Charter members Aledo Moose Lodge: Jerry as Trustee, Ethel as Senior Regent, received Academy of Friendship and College of Regents degrees. Both enjoyed league bowling many years.

Gerald died 30 August 1998, Galesburg, IL.

Children all born and attended grade and high school Monmouth.

Carroll Vance born 7 October 1941, graduated 1959, entered Air Force 1959, served Ft. Belvoir, VA, Minot, ND; Tin City, AK; Clovis, NM; Vietnam. Discharged 1968, lived Denver, CO worked Cummins Engines and International Harvester on heavy equipment; moved to Sanger, TX 1974 mechanic at several garages, shop manager Chevrolet; since 1986 owns Car Care Center, Sanger. Married Helen Keller January 1961, Minot, ND, divorced. Children: Linda Lee born 9 Dec 1961, Minot, ND; Troy Duane born 24 October 1963, Monmouth, IL.

M2 Jerrilynne Sue Stephenson 13 November 1965, Espaniola, NM. Children: Sherry Dawn born 6 May 1967, Monmouth, IL; Lori Lynn born 2 September 1970, Denver, CO.

Kaylene Louise born 7 January 1946; graduated 1963, attended AIC, Davenport, IA; ICA Beauty School and graduated 1998 Southeastern College, Burlington, IA. Worked Gamble-Skogmo, Monmouth; Inspector IAAP, Burlington; lived Wichita, KS; Danville, IA; Houma, LA. M1 William John 25 Feb 1967, divorced. Adopted Jennifer Lynn 1989, Burlington. M2 Kenneth Michael Blanchard 15 July 2000. Now office manager Lewis Infant Center, Houma, LA.

Claude Allen 'Butch' born 12 August 1957, graduated 1975. Attended Western Illinois University; Carl Sandburg; Blackhawk College; North Texas University, graduated Master's degree Business Administration May 2001. Respiratory Therapist 20 years at Illini Hospital, Moline; Baylor and Heartland Hospitals, Dallas, TX. M1 Carolyn Crisp, divorced. M2 Theresa 'Tessa' Cox 12 September 2001, Hawaii. Gerald and Ethel both members First Christian Church, Monmouth.

RALPH AND IDA (JOHNSON) TREGO - Early 1880's, Kerlin Filmore Trego born 1 April 1856, Cumberland County, PA to Jacob and Elizabeth (Woodburn) Trego, came to Warren County, IL. There he married Margaret Hood, born 9 March 1858 to Walter and Sarah (Gettemy) Hood, who owned and farmed W1/2 SE 1/4, Section 22 Hale Township.

Kerlin's son Ralph Woodburn Trego born 22 August 1884 Monmouth, IL married on January 1, 1916 Monmouth, IL. Ida Christine Johnson born 11 May 1891 Torup, Sweden to Karl and Beatrice (Emanuelsdotter) Johnson.

Karl Johnson immigrated from Guttenberg, Sweden to Sciota, IL 13 May 1902 on "Saltic" ship, entering at Ellis Island. Later that year Beatrice followed with children Ida, Bertha and Jennie. They lived on farms in McDonough county. Three children were born there: Elsie, Hilding, Eldin. They attended public schools there.

Ralph and Ida Trego, circa 1956.

Kerlin was carpenter, auctioneer and contractor, laying tile for Monmouth Country Club; built all but one of houses 100 block North 'D' street with help of son.

Ralph worked Pattee Plow Company; carpenter and farmer in Warren and Henderson counties; later at Monmouth Pottery. Retired to Kirkwood. Ida did housework for Dr. Ebersole; later Mrs. Ricketts, Kirkwood; Nora Tubbs, Monmouth. Ralph died 20 November 1961, Monmouth. Ida died 6 March 1984, Monmouth. Children:

Gerald Fillmore born 22 May 1916 Monmouth; died 30 August 1998, Galesburg, IL. Married 15 July 1939 Kahoka, MO Ethel Lorraine Ketchum; three children. He was auto mechanic and body repairman.

Dale Edman born 28 October 1918 Monmouth. M1 Mildred Elizabeth Botkin 23 May 1941 Memphis, MO; 2 children. M2 Mildred May (Martin) Carr 12 April 1974, Avon, IL. M3 Diana Pestle 30 August 2001 Bushnell, IL. He was auto mechanic, served WWII Aleution Islands, Japan.

Virgie Pauline born 1 December 1921 Kirkwood IL married George Farrer 21 December 1940 Chicago; five children. Lived Chicago; he worked fertilizer plant.

Margaret Catherine born 18 April 1923 Kirkwood, IL; died 2 May 1925 Kirkwood, IL.

Dorothy Mae born 24 May 1924 Kirkwood, IL married 18 January 1953 Blandinsville, IL Max Edward Lober.

She attended Sunny Ridge school near Raritan, graduated Media High. After marriage they farmed Blandinsville area, McDonough County. She worked Raritan State Bank; Grate's Service, Blandinsville; Treasurer Northwestern School, Sciota.

Robert Leroy born 24 August 1925 Kirkwood, IL; died 16 February 1998, Peoria, IL MI Betty J. Stewart 7 November 1945 Kirkwood; 4 children. M2 Barbara (Richey)/Ryner 24 November 1971 Oquawka, IL. Auto mechanic; mechanic Knuckles Farm Equipment, Abingdon, IL.

Clyde Eugene born 6 September 1927 Larchland, IL. M1 Madorie Darlene Grammont 26 July 1947, Monmouth; 2 children. M2 Anna Lucille Cooper 25 August 1954 Wichita, KS; 5 children. US Navy, Pacific Theater, WWII; Maintenance Lear Jet, where she works heat treat department.

Herbert Conard born 28 October 1928 Stronghurst, IL. Married Agnes (Griffin) Sage/Chick 15 April 1965 Monmouth; 2 adopted and 2 stepchildren. Section hand CB&Q Railroad; served Korean war.

Submitted by daughter Dorothy Lober

ROBERT AND BETTY (STEWART) TREGO - Robert Leroy Trego born August 24, 1925 in Kirkwood, Warren Co., IL. Son of Ralph Woodburn and Ida (Johnson) Trego. Attended Warren Co. public schools including Moore and Tubbs and Kirkwood High School. Working as a mechanic most of his life, he worked and lived in Chicago, Aledo, Peoria, Monmouth and, Abingdon, IL. Working for 21 years at Abingdon Farm Equip. for Bob Knuckles and Bob Slater. Bob Trego was a craftsman as a mechanic and woodworker.

Betty and Bob Trego and Mabel Stewart

Betty Jean Stewart born June 30, 1928 in Monmouth, Warren Co, IL. Daughter of Archie and Mabel (Blunt) Stewart. Attended Monmouth public schools and Monmouth High School. Working at many different jobs to help supplement the household income. Betty Trego enjoyed needlework when she had time.

Bob and Betty were married on November 7, 1945 in Kirkwood, Warren Co., IL. They lived in Chicago, IL for several years. They moved to Aledo in 1954 and to Abingdon in 1958. There they lived until their divorce in 1971. They had four children together:

Larry Dean, May 13, 1946 (Susan D. Westover). Working at Gates Rubber Co. of Galesburg, IL. Children: Ronald Dean, Roger Douglas, Robert Daniel (Chuck), Randy David, Tony Duane, Troy Dustin.

Robert Leroy Jr., January 9, 1948 (Barbara J. Buck). Working at Farmland Foods of Monmouth, IL. Children: Angela Lynn, Eugene Buck, Brandy Lee, Beauman Scott.

Jacqueline Marie, March 14, 1950 (William L. Davis). Homemaker. Children: Cathy Lynn Martin (Foster Daughter), Susan Domever (Foster Daughter) (Kevin Sickles).

Richard Dale, June 14, 1951 (Carol Hendricks). Working at Maytag Products of Galesburg, IL. Child: Nikki Michelle.

Bob later married Barbara (Ritchey) Ryner from Monmouth. Bob and Barb Sr. had a food wagon they took to baseball games. Bob enjoyed his grandchildren very much. He enjoyed remodeling his home and building additions on. He made clocks for all his children among other hand-crafted projects. He made many items for his wife and sisters.

Betty later married Marion Hopkins from Abington and they had one son together on February 12, 1974, James Edward Hopkins. Betty enjoyed learning to quilt and made all her children and grandchildren quilts. She enjoyed family and we had many family gatherings, which usually included Bob and Barb Sr.

WILLIAM URBAN - William Urban grew up in Kansas and Oklahoma, and attended the University of Texas in Austin, where he met his wife, Jacquelynn. After he taught a year at the University of Kansas, Bill and Jackie Urban moved to

Monmouth in 1966 to join the history department at Monmouth College. Monmouth was completely new to them. Bill's grandfather had, however, visited Monmouth in 1906 while working his way through medical school selling stereopticons; he sent his future wife a postcard picturing the fountain on Monmouth square. Mary Crow and Doug Spitz persuaded them that Monmouth College was an excellent place to teach and that Monmouth was a good community for rearing children.

Jackie and Bill Urban, early 1990s

In 1970 they bought the house at 1062 E. 2nd (at Olson Corners) originally built by Barzillai Beckwith in 1864-65 and considerably remodeled over the years. There they reared their three children -Ilsabe, Elke and Karl. They also had as guests for a year of high school Susann Betyna from Germany and Zulfy Morris from Puerto Rico, and for shorter periods and summers several Japanese students. They are Quakers and attend meeting for worship in Galesburg.

Bill has written a dozen books on medieval history, was editor of the *Journal of Baltic Studies*, and was named the Lee L. Morgan professor of history and international studies. He has been a regular contributor of essays to local and regional newspapers and a speaker at service clubs and churches. He directed the Associated Colleges of the Midwest programs in Florence, Italy, Zagreb, Yugoslavia, and Olomouc, Czech Republic; and he spent several Sabbaticals in Germany. He was awarded a Fulbright senior research grant for a year in Germany in 1975-1976 and has received numerous smaller grants. Since he often took his family for these long stays, the children attended local schools and learned German. Ilsabe later spent her junior year abroad in Munich, and Elke took a summer program in Trier.

Back when Bill first began coaching the college soccer team (1968-1981), he sent his players to help Marc Waggener start the first youth soccer program at the YMCA, and for many years Bill's players and former players were very active in keeping the program alive.

Jackie had been a Russian and German major, and she and Bill were married in Hamburg, Germany, in 1965. Beginning in 1978 she taught German at Monmouth College, and occasionally Spanish and English as well. A student of Bernice Fox, she later taught Latin at Monmouth High School. Early risers can see her walking the dogs at dawn.

Over the years Bill has assigned history majors topics on local and college history. His 1978 *History of Monmouth College* (with Mary Crow and Charles Speel) and the pageant *Founders' Days* projected for the college's sesquicentennial celebration in August 2002 reflect this strongly, as have his publications concerning Wyatt Earp's highly interesting father, Nicholas.

JAMES AND SARAH (BROKAW) VAN ARSDALE

In the spring of 1872, James Bergan and Sarah (Sally) Brokaw Van Arsdale moved to 80 acres they had purchased for $59/acre in Section 7 of Point Pleasant Township. James, born October 30, 1844, was the son of William and Johanna Bergan Van Arsdale who came from Somerset County, New Jersey to Illinois in the spring of 1850. They first homesteaded on a farm near Fairview, Ill. And later in 1865 moved to land they purchased 1 1/2 miles south of Raritan, Ill. in Henderson County. William represented the 6th generation of Van Arsdales in American, the first being Symon Janse Van Arsdalen, who emigrated from the Netherlands to New Amsterdam in 1653.

Sarah, Paul, James Bergen and Nellie Van Arsdale

Sally Brokaw Van Arsdale was born November 3, 1848 to Henry and Mary Baird Brokaw, who moved from Somerset County, NJ to Raritan, Ill. in the late 1950s. Henry represents the 7th generation of Brokaws in America, descending from Bourgon Broucard (Brokaw) and Catherine Lefever, who came to America sometime between 1672 and 1675. The Broucards were French Huguenots who moved from France because of religious persecution to Germany and later to the Netherlands, from where they emigrated to New Amsterdam. Sally Van Arsdale's father, Henry, enlisted in the Union Army in 1864 and later died because of disease in Natchez, Miss. where he is buried.

James and Sally Van Arsdale raised two children on their Homestead in Point Pleasant Township, Nellie born in 1876 and Paul born in 1879. The Van Arsdales enlarged their farm in 1891 by purchasing 61 acres for $70/acre in section 18 across the road from the Homestead. In 1906 they added 22 more acres in section 18 for $150/acre. Sally died in 1908 and James in 1909.

Nellie Van Arsdale married Andrew (Drew) Kershaw in 1903 at the Van Arsdale Homestead. Drew managed a store in Raritan for a time but later worked for the *Stronghurst Graphic* in Stronghurst, Ill. Nellie and Drew attempted to homestead land near Wheatland, Wyoming in 1909, but lasted only one growing season. Upon their return, they purchased a half interest in the *Stronghurst Graphic*. In 1912 they became sole owners of the paper, which they managed until 1926.

Members of the Van Arsdale family have been major landowners in Point Pleasant Township from 1872 until the present time. They trace their ancestry from the Netherlands to New Amsterdam in 1653, to New Jersey in the early 1700s, to Fairview, Ill., in 1850, to Henderson County in 1856, and finally to Warren County in 1872.

PAUL AND LETTIE (PERRINE) VAN ARSDALE

James and Sarh (Sally) Brokaw Van Arsdale raised two children on their homestead in Point Pleasant Township, Nellie born in 1876 and Paul born in 1879.

Pauline Rankin, James Van Arsdale, Clyde Van Arsdale, Dorothy Nollen, Lettie and Paul Van Arsdale, about 1944

Paul Van Arsdale married Lettie Perrine in January of 1904 and started married life on a farm in Section 7 of Point Pleasant Township. In 1906 they moved to a place near Stronghurst in Henderson County, but were back at the Van Arsdale farm in Point Pleasant Township in 1908. When Paul's father died in 1909, Paul and Lettie were the sole managers of the farm first established in 1872.

Paul and Lettie raised a family of four children on the Van Arsdale Homestead. The oldest child, Pauline, was born in 1905 and married Elmer Rankin in 1927. They moved to the Rankin farm 1 1/2miles north of Raritan, where they lived until their deaths in 1947 and 1986 respectively. Dorothy, the second child, was born in 1907. She married Rev. Marion Nollen of Pella, Iowa and together they served churches in Lafayette, Ind. and Cambria, Wis. Marion died in 1958 and shortly after that Dorothy moved to Pella, Iowa. She lived there in her own home until 2001, when she moved to the Pella Regional Health Care Center. The third child and first son of Paul and Lettie Van Arsdale, was James Bergen Van Arsdale born in 1910. James first married Martha Carmer in 1934. She was the daughter of Fred and Mary Carmer who farmed in Section 10 of Point Pleasant Township. Martha died a year after their marriage, after which James married Helen Randolph in 1937. James and Helen Van Arsdale moved to a farm 1 1/2 miles south of Raritan, but James continued to help his father farm land in Section 7. The fourth child and second son of Lettie and Paul Van Arsdale was Clyde Perrine Van Arsdale born in 1917. He married Bernice Hartgrove in 1945 and farmed in Point Pleasant Township both at the home place and on land in Section 18. Bernice died in 1998 and Clyde in 2001.

Paul and Lettie Van Arsdale continued to add to their original Van Arsdale Homestead by buying further land in Sections 7 and 18. When Paul died in 1958, the land was divided among his three children, with monetary compensation to the children of Pauline Rankin, since she had died in 1947. This land is still farmed by the sons of James and Clyde Van Arsdale. Paul Ray Van Arsdale, son of James and Helen Van Arsdale, manages the original Van Arsdale Homestead in Section 7. Paul and his wife Connie live south of Raritan. Jan J. Van Arsdale, son of Clyde and Bernice Van Arsdale farms land in sections 6, 7, and 18. Jan and his wife Susan live in Roseville.

CHARLES FRANKLIN AND JOSEPHINE (MONHART) VAN TINE

"Charel Fonteyn, a Frenchman, and wife" booked passage in 1658 on *The Gilded Beaver* from The Netherlands to the New World, (also bringing along their cow.) Some 200 years and 8 generations later, Charles Franklin Van Tine was born in New Brunswick, New Jersey on June 9, 1847, the youngest of a family of 13, 9 of them boys. At the age of 17, he came to this area, following several older brothers. Settling first at Raritan, he soon came to Warren County, and was a lifelong resident there. (Due to the strong Dutch influence in "New Amsterdam." the name Fonteyn had become Van Tine.) At age 18, he served in the Civil War, the Illinois Cavalry Unit, enlisting on March 9, 1865 and receiving his discharge at Memphis, Tennessee on September 30, 1865.

Charles Franklin and Josephine (Monhart) Van Tine

Charles and Josephine Monhart, also of French descent, were married in Monmouth on September 5, 1871. Josephine had lived in Oquawka with her mother and sister, her father having left his family during the Gold Rush days and was never again heard from. Nine children were born to Charles and Josephine: Howard, Pearl, Alice, Elizabeth, Eleanor, Hiram, Truman, Frank (deceased at age 14 from ruptured appendix), and Elmer. All the children lived in and around Monmouth until early adulthood. Hiram was an adventurous young man and traveled to Alaska in his early 20s. For many months his family did not hear from him and did not know his whereabouts. He then returned, settling in Kansas City, Missouri where he worked many years for Ford Motor Company. He and his wife, Anna Barth, had one adoptive son, Ivan, who died at age 17. Howard married Henrietta Gray of Kirkwood, and their children were: Hazel, Clifford, Percy, Homer, Ruth, Eunice, Jeanette, and Marcella. Howard and family lived for a time in Michigan, returned to Monmouth where their children attended Monmouth schools. Pearl married John Welch; their children were Gladys, Mildred, Charles, Ralph, and Harvey. Alice married Will Kniss; they had two sons, Arlo and Delbar. Elizabeth married Henry Conn and had one daughter, Pauline. Eleanor married Jess Meek; they had no children. Truman married Pearl White, their children were Eleanore, Edwin, Nellie, Reah and Leah, Gerald, Roy, Luther, Robert, Zelda, Josephine and Helen. Elmer married Carrie Cook, one son born to them, Wayne. Alice Kniss and family were lifelong residents of Monmouth as were Howard and Truman, except for Howard's time in Michigan and 25 years Truman spent in Henderson County. Charles followed the occupation of painter and decorator as did several of his sons and grandsons. Following Josephine's death or. January 7, 1913, he spent one year in the Soldiers' and Sailors' home in Quincy, then returned to Monmouth and made his home with his children. He died in Monmouth on December 14, 1917 suffering from exposure, frostbite and infection brought about by a fall he took while out hunting. He is buried in Monmouth Cemetery as are Josephine, Frank, Elizabeth, Alice, and his brother Peter. Howard and Truman and their wives are buried in Warren County Memorial Park Cemetery. Several of Charles and Josephine's descendants living in and around Monmouth presently are Shirley Neill-Fullerton, Martha Hallam, Robert Smith, Larry and Wayne Rader, Susan Onion, Edwina Thomas, Rhonda Spence, Roy, Gerald, Robert and Helen Van Tine, and Josephine Paris.

TRUMAN AND PEARL VAN TINE

Truman and Pearl Van Tine were natives of Warren County and spent their entire lives here except for a 25 year stay in Henderson County between World Wars I and II. Truman, son of Charles and Josephine Van Tine, was born at Kirkwood on August 14, 1886 and shortly thereafter moved with his family to Monmouth. Pearl, third child and third daughter of James and "Addie" (Blair) White, was born near Swan Creek on September 10, 1889. She moved to Monmouth with her family from there while still in elementary school. She and Truman met in Monmouth through mutual friends and were married on March 18, 1907 by Dr. J.F. Jamieson at his residence at 921 East Second Avenue. The ceremony was performed early Wednesday evening before Dr. Jamieson was due at Ninth Avenue Church prayer meeting. Following the ceremony, the bridal party went around the corner to the home of Pearl's parents on South 9th Street for a wedding supper, at which a dish featuring sliced bananas, a rare treat, was served! They settled in Monmouth with Truman working at Weed Fruit Farm on North 14th Street, after which he followed his family's trade of painting and decorating, and became a member of Painters, Decorators and Paperhangers of American Local Union #708, members totaling 19. In spring 1916 they moved with their family of five children to rural Biggsville where Truman worked at farming.

Truman and Pearl Van Tine and family

The next 25 years were hard ones – the Depression years, the loss of a daughter in childbirth, a serious vehicle accident involving three of their sons and a neighbor boy, leaving their son, Robert, with life-changing injuries, spending many weeks in Burlington Hospital, and the serious illness of another son, Luther, calling for many weeks in Monmouth Hospital, then weeks of recuperation. Spring 1942 found them living at Weir Fruit Farm where Truman was foreman, United States was at war and two sons, Luther and Gerald had gone to serve their country, leaving the family without transportation since Truman did not drive.

With the help of Truman's brother, Howard, who with his family ran a fruit and flower farm at 915 South 11th Street, Truman and Pearl bought a property at 520 South 11th Street – thus they were back in Monmouth! The front room of the house was a small grocery store and they continued it. (Neighborhood groceries flourished at that time – 14 in town in addition to downtown and Main Street's larger stores.) So successful was the business that an addition was built doubling the size of the store. Truman suffered a massive heart attack on November 15, 1954, passed away 3 days later. Pearl continued the business for several years until with the advent of "supermarkets" it was no longer profitable, the property was sold. Pearl passed away March 1, 1974 at her home on West Broadway at age 84 and is buried in Warren County Memorial Park Cemetery as is Truman.

Their family totaled 12 children, 10 of them growing to adulthood. In March 1914 twin girls were born at their home. Premature by several months, these tiny babies were not expected to survive, prompting a loving neighbor, Mrs. Landuyt, a devout Catholic, to baptize them. But around-the-clock care was given by family and friends, who created an incubator in a dresser drawer lined with blankets and kept warm with fruit jars of warm water.

Survive they did – a miracle of love which astounded even the doctor, Dr. C.O. Burgess. Sadly, twin Leah contracted Pneumonia at the age of 10 months and died. Twin Reah died in childbirth in 1936 and son Luther died in the service of his country on December 18, 1944 in the Battle of the Bulge. Their descendants and their families now number 167 with five of their children and grandchildren living in this area.

RICK AND CAROLYN VARNER

Ricky Reed Varner, son of Charles and Donna (Morgan) Varner, was born August 6, 1955 in Galesburg, Ill. He has two brothers, Charles L. "Lucky" Varner, Jr., born October 14, 1953 and Burl E. Varner, born December 7, 1957. Rick attended R.O.V.A. schools and graduated in 1973. Rick worked as a janitor while attending school. After graduation he started working at Admiral's in Galesburg. After putting in over 20 years he left and started working for a telemarketing company out of Peoria, Ill. He spent 5 years on the road collecting payments for them.

Back row: Matt Gilson, Jim Willenbrink. Middle row: Julie Varner, Deidra Varner Gilson, Angie Varner Willenbrink. Front row: Carolyn Varner, Madison Willenbrink and Lani Varner.

Carolyn May Dowell, daughter of George and Margaret (Lyon) Dowell, was born September 21, 1951 in Galesburg, Ill. She has two brothers, Kenneth E. Dowell, born January 30, 1950, and James E. Dowell, born May 27, 1953, and one sister, Judith Ann Dowell, born December 11, 1957. Carolyn attended school in Knoxville, graduating in 1969. While attending high school she worked at the Knox Co. Nursing Home in Knoxville serving the evening meal. She then attended Carl Sandburg College, graduating in 1971 with a degree in Computer Programming. She was called by Butler Mfg. Co. in Galesburg, Ill., asking her to work part-time keypunching for them the summer of 1971. She then was called to work full time in April 1972. She worked for them three years before becoming pregnant with her first daughter, Angela Marie, born December 13, 1974.

On May 24, 1975, Rick and Carolyn were married in the Knoxville United Methodist Church. They lived outside Dahinda, Ill., for a short time until a fire destroyed their home. They moved in with her parents until they found a house in Berwick and moved into it March of 1976. On October 15, 1976 they welcomed their second daughter, Julie Ann, into their home. On March 18, 1979 they had another daughter, Deidra Jean, and one short year later had their last daughter, Lani Sue, born February 29, 1980. All 4 daughters attended school in Roseville with the last one graduating in 1998. In the fall their oldest daughter Angie was married to James R. Willenbrink at the Naval Chapel in Norfolk, Va. They had a daughter, Madison Ione, born May 18, 1999.

On December 15, 1999, Rick had a heart attack and died. He is buried in the Wataga Cemetery. On April 29, 2000, their daughter Deidra married Matthew Gilson of Galesburg in the First Assembly of God Church in Abingdon, Ill. They now reside in Knoxville, Ill. During the Labor Day weekend in 2000, their daughter, Lani, moved to Virginia Beach to live with the oldest sister Angie and her family. On August 3, 2001, their daughter Julie gave birth to a son, Scott Joseph. They reside in Galesburg, Ill.

DEBRA KAY VEST - Debra Kay Vest was born in Monmouth, Illinois on January 26, 1952. For more family information on Debra's childhood years, please see the biographical information on Neill and Glendora Vest, her parents, and Nancy and Mitchell Vest, her sister and brother.

Debra Vest holds a doctorate in English and founded the Vest Conservatory for Writing. She is a published poet and fiction writer. Debra, also a prolific gardener, and an exceptionally strong swimmer – delighting in braving long distances, choppy waves and all kinds of water temperatures, no matter where she finds herself.

In 1975, Debra married Timothy Roy Holte and moved to Milwaukee, Wisconsin, where they still reside today with their big white dog Oliver – an important part of the family. Tim is a manager at U.S. Filter and a semi-professional fine arts photographer. His award winning images have been honored at the John Michael Kohler Arts Center in the *Milwaukee Journal*.

Debbie has commented that some of her best family memories are from the time she spent in Monmouth, Illinois, and Warren County, even though she moved from there when she was only 10 years old. She frequently draws on those memories in her writing.

JOHN ELI AND AMANDA JANE (MITCHELL) VEST - John Eli was born near Carthage, IL in 1873 and married Amanda Jane Mitchell in 1902. They were married in Galesburg, IL, moved and lived in Monmouth most of their lives. The couple had seven children: Gerald M., born 1902; Wayne W., born 1906; Doren D., born 1911; Sarah S., born 1914; John E., born 1917; Richard L., born 1921; and Neill G., born 1924.

Doren, John, Neill, Amanda Jane, John Eli, Wayne, Sarah and Dick Vest, January 1946.

Each of the children was educated in the Monmouth school system until they graduated from high school. Five of the children graduated from college, two children, Gerald and John, graduated from Monmouth College.

Gerald, after completion of college, moved to Washington DC. He worked with the U.S. War Department in Washington. He was first married to Lottie Richardson from Monmouth but then later married Eddie May Kay, known as Kay. Gerald remained with the U.S. Government his entire career and Kay was Manager of the International Chamber of Commerce of the United States.

Wilfred Wayne who went by the name Wayne, married his childhood sweetheart, Jeanette Lamp of Rock island, IL. They had a daughter and two sons and worked in Monmouth and Galesburg most of their lives, living close to John Eli and Amanda Jane. Everyone appreciated the special care they took of Amanda Jane after the death of their father.

Doren Dale moved to Washington, DC. after high school and worked for Government Services, Inc. He graduated from college and continued to work at Government Services until he retired and became the Dean of Benjamin Franklin University. Doren was married twice – first to Marion, the mother of his two children, and later to Willamena (Willie). They spent the balance of their lives in Florida.

Sarah, after finishing college, married Joseph Earl Dixson from Stronghurst, IL. They had twin sons and a daughter and lived in Minneapolis, MN. Joe died at age 39, an untimely death. They were so young ... Sarah worked diligently to raise her children and remained in Minneapolis until her death in 1996.

John was popular throughout his school years and lived in Monmouth until his graduation from Monmouth College. He served as an officer in the U.S. Army during WW II and worked as a Manpower Specialist for the Army for 22 years in Washington, DC. He married Mary Frances Dolan (Foo) in 1941 and had two children. John and Foo are happily retired in Florida.

Richard finished his school years in Monmouth and then was employed at the Burlington, IA Munitions Plant until he was accepted by the Army Artillery Division. He served in WW II in Europe where he participated and was wounded in a number of major battles. "Dick" returned and married Helen Jane Miller. Even though Dick and Jane didn't stay married, they had four fine children including a daughter and three sons.

Neill, the youngest of the family, ("My mother would always tell me that I was the most expensive child she gave birth to. My delivery cost $15.00.") received his education in Monmouth until he attended college in Washington DC. As a boy he attended Maude Alma Maine School in Monmouth that taught music, dance and other performing arts. His brother Richard also attended this school. They were a team.

Neill was in the Army a short time during WW II and then worked and attended college in Washington, DC. He married Glendora Grapes in 1945 and they moved to Monmouth in 1948 to begin their family. Debra, Nancy, and Mitchell were born at Monmouth Hospital and delivered by Dr. Wendell Roller. They moved to Kansas City with Gambles in 1961 and then were transferred to Minneapolis in 1967.

Glendora died in 1977 after a courageous fight with cancer. It was a very difficult illness and her passing was a terrible loss for the family. Later, in 1980, Neill married Phyllis Kopesky who had been widowed and also had three children. All the offspring live in Minnesota, Iowa, and Wisconsin.

MITCHELL GRAY VEST - Mitchell Gray Vest was born in Monmouth Illinois on January 28, 1957. He is pictured here on Father's Day, 2002 with his dad, Neill Gray Vest. To learn more about his family and upbringing, please read the John Eli Vest, Neill Vest, and Nancy and Debra Vest biographical information.

Mitchell Gray and Neill Gray Vest, Father's Day at Nancy's, 2002

Mitch graduated from Eden Prairie High School, and then took some specialized vocational training before deciding to became an entrepreneur and run a successful small business in partnership with his sister Nancy. Later he became an accomplished carpenter, building custom homes with Terry Eggan, Nancy's husband, often in the extremely bitter Minnesota cold. For the last five years, Mitch has worked for United Airlines at the Minneapolis-St. Paul International Airport.

As of this writing Mitch is divorced and living in Bloomington, MN. He loves motorcycles and has driven in several motorcycle races, including on ice! He likes jamming on his guitars and listening to good music, especially the blues.

The Vests have stayed a close family. Mitch talks to his sisters regularly. He visits his dad, Neill Vest, and his step mom, Phyllis, often, and makes himself available to help them with a variety of chores around their Bloomington home.

NANCY JO VEST - Growing up in the small town of Monmouth, Illinois back in the 1950's and early 60's was an experience that is hard to imagine today. A young child was safe on the small town streets and most everyone seemed to know each other and each other's kids. There was plenty of freedom to roam. Although Nancy and her siblings, Debra Kay Vest, and Mitchell Gray Vest, moved from Monmouth after only living there a few short years, Monmouth would always hold singular memories of wonderful times and cherished connections with special people.

Terry Eggan and Wife Nancy Vest

Nancy was born in Monmouth, Illinois on May 12,1954. As a young married couple, her parents, Neill Gray Vest and Glendora Margaret Vest, moved to the small town of Monmouth from Washington D.C. to have their family. Neill was born in Monmouth, and he had family and friends there, it was the obvious choice.

Neill's mother, Amanda Jane Vest was widowed by then, but was able to live in the family homestead in Monmouth which was just a couple doors down from her son Wayne W. Vest and his wife Jeannette (Lamp) Vest. Everyone loved Grandma Vest. She spent a lot of time in the kitchen cooking and singing old-time songs, and oddly enough was a great fan of wrestling that she watched on TV. Her home had a secret stairway for hiding and made-up games, and a worn piano that Nancy loved to play on with her dad. Neill taught Debbie and Nancy some simple duets (Mitch was still too little), which were repeated loudly and often, and with typical Vest flourish.

When the kids got restless at Grandma's they could run across the yard to visit their Aunt Jeannette and Uncle Wayne. The door was always open, and usually there were homemade treats waiting- like sweet and tart cherry pie, or dense brownies with dark runny frosting. There was even a rope swing that could be jumped on right from the back porch, and lots of trees and flowers to admire.

The Vest family developed many lasting friendships in Monmouth. Nancy loved visiting her "adopted grandma" Mrs. Drayson, who always invited her into her home for some gumdrops and a peek at her fancy doll on the bed upstairs. There were also visits to Verna and Daryl Davies' house, and the Jackson's, wonderful family friends. Nancy also had many grand adventures with her favorite playmate Patty Bolon.

Nancy remembers helping her mother sell poppies on Veteran's Day, hunting spicy scented green walnuts in Monmouth Park, and the thrill of dressing up as a cowgirl to march down the street with her brother and sister in the annual Halloween parade.

Occasionally Nancy and Debbie were given 25 cents each to walk the several blocks to town by themselves. There they split an assortment of pastel colored coconut bon-bons, a cherry Coke and each had money left over for a toy at the dime store. Even at eight years old, Debbie knew how to add and divide exceptionally well, so the girls often pooled their money (Fifty cents!) for maximum buying power. They were independent ladies with their own money – rich and free.

In 1961 Neill's work with Gambles caused him to be transferred to Kansas City. Moving from Monmouth was tough for Nancy and her family, they loved it there, and it was hard to leave friends and family behind.

Neill was transferred again to Eden Prairie, MN, in 1967. Nancy, Debbie, and eventually Mitch, each attended the Eden Prairie schools, where Nancy first met a boy named Terry Eggan. She was not quite thirteen then; he was fourteen. Soon, they were her high-school sweethearts and enjoyed swimming in the lakes, riding the Eggan horses and plenty of school activities in what was then a small rural town.

Nancy and Terry married in 1975. Although her mother was very ill with cancer, the whole family attended. Mitch was Best Man and Debbie the Maid-of-Honor. Both her mother and her father walked her down the isle. Nancy graduated from college, worked in social services for a while, and eventually started a successful small business with her brother Mitch. They really enjoyed working together.

In 1977, not long after her marriage, Nancy's mother's died from ovarian cancer. It was a terrible loss for Nancy as well as her family. She had loved her mother very, very much and she had died at only 54 years old.

Today, Nancy and Terry live in a new home in Eden Prairie, which is now a busy suburb of Minneapolis. Terry designed the house himself and also built it along with the help of his father Will, and several other members of his family. Terry even built a large pond and rocked waterfall on the lot by first drawing it out using flour to mark the shape of the pond- just to see how it would look. Terry is a Realtor and Nancy is a publicist and marketing consultant. As of this writing Nancy and Terry have been happily married for 27 years.

Although every life has its highs and lows, Nancy feels blessed to have a wonderful husband, the pleasure of loving and lasting relationships with her father and the rest of her family, good friends, and among many other things – some lovely memories of a few sweet years growing up in Monmouth, Illinois.

NEILL AND GLENDORA VEST - Neill Vest was born in 1924 and educated in the Monmouth school system. Mitchell Sporting Goods and C. W. Woods employed him before entering the Army in WW II. He was discharged in late 1943 from the Army Finance Corp because of medical reasons.

In January 1944 Neill moved to Washington, DC. And was employed by Government Services, Inc. At the same time he entered Benjamin Franklin University (now known as George Washington University). He also met Glendora M. Grapes from Augusta, WV while in Washington and they married on September 1, 1945. (In Neill's words, "Glendora and I didn't date a terribly long time before I knew she was the one I wanted.") Neill and Glendora were both employed by United Nations Relief and Rehabilitation Administration. They both completed their college education before leaving Washington.

Neill Vest family. Neill, Glendora, Debbi, Nancy and Mitch, July 1961.

Glendora had rheumatic fever as a child and it left her with a heart condition. Doctors in Washington advised the couple to move from Washington and obtain a slower pace to help Glendora's condition. They agreed since they also wanted to start a family, and felt that a small town environment would be best for raising their children. Monmouth was the ideal choice. They moved from Washington to Monmouth in late 1948 and lived with Neill's mother until they were settled and Glendora became more familiar with the town. Neill's father had passed away in 1947.

The couple became active in church, service clubs, etc., and consequently met Harold and Gracie Peterson. The Peterson's had completed two apartments above Peterson Electrical and Appliance Store in downtown Monmouth, and Gracie had encouraged them to move into the apartment next to her and "Pete" above the store. Glendora and Neill lived there until they bought a home at 319 S. 5th in late 1952. Neill worked at Peterson's Electric until he joined Gamble-Skogma, Inc. in January of 1955.

Neill and Glendora had three children. Debra born in 1952, Nancy born in 1954, and Mitchell born in 1957. All were born at Monmouth Hospital with Dr. Wendall Roller attending. The Vest family had a very pleasant life in Monmouth and later moved to Kansas City and then to Minneapolis with Gambles. ("Our decision to have children was the best one we ever made," said Neill. And after discussing the choices he and " Glen" had made in life he said, "If I were to do it over again, I wouldn't change a thing.")

Glendora continued to have rheumatic heart problems in 1960. The Vests moved to Eden Prairie, MN in 1967. It was then discovered that Glendora had Ovarian Cancer in 1974 and she died after a courageous battle with the disease in November 1977. Her passing was a terrible loss for her family and friends.

Debbie, Nancy, and Mitch finished high school in Eden Prairie, MN. The girls both graduated from college and married prior to their mother's death. Glendora was so thankful that she was able to participate in their weddings. As of this writing, Debbie, a professor, private writing coach and author, lives in Milwaukee, WI, and Nancy, a marketing and public relations consultant, lives in Eden Prairie, MN. Mitch presently lives close to his father in Bloomington, MN and is employed by United Airlines. There are no grandchildren. The three children remain close to friends in Monmouth, and enjoy their visits there.

Neill remarried in 1980 to Phyllis Kopesky. Phyllis's husband had been killed in an auto accident some years previously and they had three children. Phyllis and her children share the grandchildren with Neill. Neill and Phyllis spend much of their time in Florida and always stop in Monmouth coming and going to Florida. Monmouth has always been home.

SARAH SHIRLEY VEST - Sarah Shirley Vest was born at home in Monmouth on April 29, 1914. Her parents were John Eli Vest (1873-1947) and Amanda Jane Mitchell Vest (1880-1972). John Eli was born near Carthage, IL, and Amanda Jane Mitchell was born near Biggsville, IL. They were married on November 26, 1902. Sarah was the fourth of 7 children; Gerald Mitchell, Wilfred Wayne, Doren Dale, Sarah Shirley (Dixson), John Edward, Richard LeRoy, and Neill Gray Vest. John Eli (Jack) worked as a railroad car repairman in Monmouth until he was injured in June of 1915. He then homesteaded in Circle, Montana near Paris from 1916-1919. Jack and 9 year-old Wayne went first, to build the home for the family. Then Amanda brought children Gerald, Doren, Sarah and baby John Jr. by train in 1917 to join John Sr. and Wayne. They all returned to Monmouth in 1919 and lived with Amanda's parents, (William Ritchie and Sarah Mitchell) until they got a home of their own. They lived for many years at 1003 East 5th Avenue, Monmouth, IL.

Sarah Shirley Vest and Joseph Earl Dixson, June 3, 1940.

They were members of the Ninth Avenue Presbyterian Church for many years. At the time of his death he had been the night engineer at the Monmouth City Water works for 16 years. Sarah graduated from Monmouth High School in 1932, and went on to graduate from Western Illinois University at Macomb, IL with a degree in Physical Education. After graduation she taught swimming at the Monmouth YWCA until she married Joseph Earl Dixson of Stronghurst on June 3, 1940. They had 3 children, twin sons Joseph Eugene and John David, and a daughter Cynthia Jane, After World War II they moved to Minneapolis, Minnesota where Joseph Earl worked for an insurance company, he died June 12, 1953. Sarah reared the children alone, and after they were older she worked for the Minneapolis YWCA.

She died March 7, 1996 and they are buried in Stronghurst cemetery. Joseph Eugene married Peggy Dale on June 3,1970, they have 3 children. A daughter Mary Margaret 2nd twin sons Joseph and John David.

Mary Margaret is married to Scott Snow and they have a daughter Amanda Latricia. John David is married to Melissa Husnick and they have a daughter Heavynlee.

WAYNE AND JEANETTE VEST - "Wilfred Wayne Vest was born at home in Monmouth on Sept 18, 1906. His parents were John Eli (1873-1946) and Amanda Jane Mitchell Vest (1880-1972). John Eli was born near Carthage, IL, and Amanda Jane Mitchell was born near Biggsville, IL. Wayne was the second-born of 7 children, Gerald Mitchell, Wilfred Wayne, Doren Dale, Sarah Shirley (Dixson), John Edward, Richard LeRoy, and Neill Gray Vest.

Barton W. Vest, Jeanette (Lamp) Vest, Wilfred Wayne Vest, Elaine L. (Vest) Cassiday Schultz and Wayne Wilfred Vest.

John Eli (Jack) worked as a railroad car repairman in Monmouth until he was injured on 6/11/1915. He then homesteaded in Circle, Montana near Paris from 1916-1919. Jack and 9-year-old Wayne went first, to build the home for the family. Then Amanda brought children Gerald, Doren, Sarah and baby John Jr. by train in 1917 to join John Sr. and Wayne. They all returned to Monmouth in 1919 and lived with Amanda's parents, (William and Sarah Mitchell) until they got a home of their own. They lived many years at 1003 East 5th Avenue, Monmouth, IL.

Wayne graduated from Monmouth High School in 1925. He worked for Kroger Grocery Store in both Monmouth and Rock Island, IL. He also worked for Vern Arnold Grocery Store (in the building that now houses the Monmouth Fire Dept.), and the Railroad. In 1942, he started working for Rowe Manufacturing Co. in Galesburg, as Traffic Manager. During the Depression, he married Jeanette Louise Lamp on March 18, 1930 in Ottumwa, Iowa. He repaired shoes in the basement, and worked for the Railroad and the Pottery. They had 3 children, Wayne Wilfred Jr., Barton William, and Elaine Louise. In 1941 they bought a home at 621 South 9th Street, where they planted an orchard of fruit trees, raised chickens and sold eggs. They lived there until the summer of 1997, when they moved in with their daughter (Elaine) and son-in-law (Bill) in Mt. Prosect, IL. Wayne passed away March 25th, 1997 when he was 91-1/2 years old, and is now buried in Monmouth Cemetery. Jeanette will turn 95 years old on April 24, 2002.

Jeanette was born in Rock Island, IL to Arthur William and Hollis Edith (Culton) Lamp. Jeanette was the first-born of 3 children, Jeanette Louise, Loretta Marguerite and Henrietta Latha. Arthur worked for his fathers business, delivering ice and artesian well water in Rock Island. He met and married Hollie in Stark County when he was working for the Rock Island Railroad. They homesteaded in 1908 in Witten, South Dakota, and moved back to Rock Island in 1911, when he returned to his job at the Railroad. Arthur later moved his family to Monmouth and moved next door to John Eli and Amanda Vest, where the children all became friends. Wayne gave Jeanette rides to school on his bike.

Wilfred Wayne and Jeanette's son, Wayne Jr. married Beverly Warnecke, and had 3 children. Pamela Mae married Larry Border and had a daughter, Amanda Jane. Kurt Wayne has not married. Victoria Virginia married Christiaan Cook, and had two sons, Ian Christiaan, and Sean Cullen.

Wayne and Jeanette's son Barton William married Phyllis Jean (Gehr) and had no children together.

Wayne and Jeanette's daughter Elaine Louise married Carl Calvin Cassiday, and had 3 children, Holly Sue married Paul Smith, David Roy has not married, and Janet Lyn married Craig Thomsen. Elaine remarried William Schultz, Jr. on Sept. 10, 1977.

CHARLES H. & MARTHA (SWARTS) VESTAL - Charles Henry Vestal was born 1 April 1884 in Abingdon, Va., the 2nd son of Samuel H. & Laura (Seamore) Vestal, both natives of North Carolina. Siblings were (all born Abingdon, Va): Maller L.; Robert A.; Hagy; (twins) Cohn & Minnie; Client; Ida; Liza; and Alice.

Charles and Martha Vestal

Martha Nora Swarts was born 23 October 1890, Abingdon, Va. to John Isaac and Arizona Hinda (Creger) Swarts, natives of Abingdon, Va. Siblings (all born Abingdon, Va); Mary Margaret; Virginia A.; William E. ; Maude F.; Nanme M.; Claude Denton and Nina M.

Charles and Martha were married in Abingdon 22 December 1909. They lived in that area until 1919 when they moved to Warren County, IL.

Charles worked in lumberyards in Kirkwood and also on farms in the area. The family moved quite often over the years as he would buy homes, do improvements on them and sell them at a profit. By doing this he was finally able to purchase a 200-acre farm with a two-story twelve-room house where they lived the rest of their lives. This was located with 160 acres in Ellison township, NW 1/4 Section 30 and 40 acres in Media township NE 1/4 Section 25. Charles died 1 December 1957. Martha died 26 December 1973.

Their children were: Maurice C. born 23 December 1910 married 4 December 1959 Marie Colley Cavins. No children. Maurice entered the service 30 June 1942 Scott Field, IL, overseas for 31 months with Military Police in Australia, New Guinea, Phillipines, and Japan, discharged 22 December 1945, Jefferson Barracks, Missouri. Farmed homeplace retired to Roseville and Monmouth. Died 13 December 1992.

William James born 7 February 1913 married 4 December 1945 Mildred Sloss, two children: William inducted 1942 Scott Field, IL. Overseas January 1944, served England, Belgium, France and Germany, wounded in action in France, back to States at Fort Riley, Kansas, discharged 5 October 1945. Lives on own farm northwest of Monmouth.

Herman, born 11 March 1915, married 8 September 1937 to Lucille Hawk. 5 children. He died 6 April 1996. Farmer and cemetery sexton.

Egbert Edward, born 1 September 1917, married Catherine Coogan July 1943. She died October 1943. Married 6 October 1947 Ruby Smith. Inducted 5 March 1941 Camp Forrest, Tennessee, cook until May 1945 overseas February 1944 served Ireland, England, France, Germany, Austria, Scotland, Wales, Belgium. Discharged 9 November 1945 Camp McCoy, Wisconsin. Died 24 April 1957.

Helen Arizona born 2 November 1919, married 18 February 1942 Howard Hardin. 2 children. She died 22 July 1985. Gilmer, born 17 April 1922. (Separate biography)

Laura Virginia, born 12 September 1924, married 3 July 1950 LaVerne McFate, 1 son. Died 21 November 1985. Katherine Lee, born 30 July 1927, married 22 October 1949 Don Waterson. 2 children. Died 27 February 1994. Last 5 children born Warren County, IL.

GILMER AND MARY (FRAZEE) VESTAL - Gilmer Vestal was born 17 April 1922, Warren County, IL. to Charles Henry and Martha Nora (Swarts) Vestal, natives of Abingdon, Virginia, He attended grade schools in the area, did not attend High School because with one brother married and three more in the service, he was needed at home to help with farming. Remembers when he was about 11 years old, living on the Loudon farm on the north edge of Kirkwood, there were 10- 12 cows to milk. His mother paid him 5 cents a day to wash the cream separator before going to school … 35 cents a week ! He had to run to school before the last bell. His teacher, Mima McClymonds, asked his father why Gilmer was always late starting for school. When she learned he had chores to do she said she would never mark him tardy.

Later Gilmer hunted wild asparagus and walnuts, in season, to sell; groundhog scalps brought 16 cents each. Most of his money went to buy books and school clothes … blue denim shirts – 45 cents; overalls – 98 cents; work shoes – $1.00 a pair. "I really felt like a well-dressed dude." He kept a few nickels for a plug of chewing tobacco – 5 cents each!

Gilmer enlisted in Army 12 July 1944 at Ft Sheridan, IL Served in New Guinea, Philippines and Japan in Army of Occupation. Back to states. Discharged and re-enlisted, serving in Military Police at Ft. Jackson, South Carolina; later as driver for Colonel Paget. Promoted to Staff Sargeant, discharged November 1946, Ft. Dix, New Jersey.

Gilmer was married 16 November 1945 at Rushville, IL, to Mary Catherine Frazee, daughter of Thomas and Mary Ellen (Hamm) Frazee. She was born Roseville, IL. attended schools at Roseville and Little York.

Gilmer, age 21 and Mary (Frazee) Vestal, age 22.

Gilmer and Mary worked on farm for Robeson of Monmouth; rented house in Kirkwood and did carpenter work with Fred Gordon 4 years; worked for Leonard Ockert, Roseville, feeding cattle; rented the farm and worked for John Ockert 37 years. Retired to Monmouth.

Children were: Gilmer Eugene, born 30 December 1946, has son Roy Allen; worked Gates Rubber 30 years. Sharon Kay, born 1 January 1948, no children; IBM Specialist in North Rockford, Florida, Martha Ellen, born 2 September 1949, no children, worked Super 8 Motel; has Motel cleaning service. Sandra Lynne, born 22 June 1952, single, no children, Motel work. Mary Ann, born 20 June 1958, 2 children: Trisha and Clayton, Lives Florida. Cynthia Lee, born 24 December 1959, has daughter Tara, lives Roseville, works Home Management Service. Gary Lee, born 1 June 1961, single, no children, lives Crystal Springs, Florida, working orchards in winter.

Gilmer proudly received his High School Diploma on 9 April 2002 in Roseville where he now resides.

BENJAMIN FRANKLIN AND BESSIE (YATES) VICE - Benjamin Franklin Vice, second son of Jimmerson and Sarah Ann (Doore) Vice was born December 12, 1875 in Clark County MO. He had 6 brothers and 3 sisters. Ben was a farmer.

Bessie Gertrude Yates was born May 12, 1888 in Clark County MO the 7th of 8 children born to James McKenny and Catherine Jane (Toops) Yates.

Benjamin and Bessie were married June 16, 1909 in Monmouth. Bessie was a homemaker and Benjamin farmed. They were the parents of 3 sons: Harry Leroy born November 18, 1912 (adopted); Paul Eugene born October 6, 1921; and Wayne Franklin born September 2, 1925 died October 16, 1926.

The family lived in the Roseville community and there reared their family. Both sons graduated from Roseville High School. Harry married Mildred Hudson on March 30, 1944. They had four daughters, Joyce, Judy and twin girls Bonnie Lou and Connie Lee. Paul married Lillian Newman June 8, 1946. They are the parents of Mary Suzanne, David Paul and Edah Lee.

Bessie died March 8, 1944 and Benjamin died April 29, 1956. Both are buried in the Roseville Cemetery next to their son Wayne Franklin.

Submitted by Paul Vice

PAUL EUGENE AND LILLIAN (NEWMAN) VICE - Paul Eugene Vice was born October 6, 1921 near Roseville IL son of Benjamin Franklin Vice and Bessie Gertrude (Yates) Vice. The family farmed near Roseville moving into Roseville in 1935. Siblings: Harry Leroy and Wayne Franklin Vice.

Paul attended McCurdy Grade School, Roseville Grade School and graduated from Roseville High School in 1940. He worked at Skelly Gas Station until inducted into the Army in June 1942. He had basic training in Camp Lee, Virginia, graduated from Ordnance School at Sumter, SC; served in Texas and departed overseas from California August 1943 on the Bosche Fontaine. He served as motor mechanic, 263d Ordnance Co. for 2 1/2 years in New Guinea, New Britain and the Philippine Islands. He returned stateside in December 1945, was discharged from service at Jefferson Barracks MO arriving home Christmas Day 1945.

Lillian and Paul Vice, 50th Anniversary, June 8, 1996

Paul started working for the US Postal Service April 1946 as Railway Mail Clerk 4 years as substitute and 7 years as clerk on the Chicago, Fort Madison and Kansas City run. February 1957 he was assigned as a foreman at the Galesburg Depot Transfer Office and was there 5 years. In 1962 he was assigned to the Galesburg Post Office retiring as Night Supervisor of Mails on April 20, 1979.

Lillian Newman was born November 10, 1922 near Edwards, Benton County MO to William Hockman Newman and Edah (Smith) Newman. The family moved from rural Windsor MO in 1929 to Ponemah in Warren County and later to Kirkwood. Siblings were: Pauline, Irene and Lola. Lillian attended Crews School in MO, Liberty School, Ponemah, Kirkwood Grade School, graduated from Kirkwood High School in 1940 and Peoria Institute of Business in 1941. For 5 years she was a secretary at Illinois Bankers Life Assurance Company, Monmouth.

Paul and Lillian were married June 8, 1946 at Kirkwood Methodist Church by Rev. Alvin Jones. They lived in Monmouth 3 years then purchased a home in Kirkwood and moved December 1949. In 1952 they purchased a home at 405 W. Walnut where they still reside.

Children: Mary Suzanne b. July 24, 1949 m. Wesley Edward Scroggins Aug. 30 1969. David Paul b. July 6, 1952. Edah Lee b. January 3, 1956 m. Thomas Alan Hefley August 6, 1983.

All three children are Yorkwood High School graduates. Mary Suzanne attended Illinois College, Jacksonville; David, Carl Sandburg College, Edah Lee graduated from Western Illinois University, Macomb.

Grandchildren: Alison, Daniel and Patrick Scroggins.

Lillian returned to work as Kirkwood Branch Librarian 1962-1965, Warren County Library 1965-1974 and Western Illinois Library System 1974 – retiring in 1984.

Paul and Lillian are active members of the Kirkwood Senior Citizens, Kirkwood United Methodist Church and Sunday School, having been teachers, youth leaders and choir member. Lillian also sang in the ladies Wesleyette quartet for a number of years. Paul is a life member of the National Association of Retired Federal Employees and life member of American Legion, Post #765, Stronghurst. He is an Associate member of the American Postal Workers Union. Lillian is a member of Kirkwood Community Club, United Methodist Women and Tompkins Sunshine Unit of Home Extension.

Submitted by Lillian Vice

CLARENCE AND MARIETTA VICKROY - Clarence Vickroy was born in Moline, Illinois on August 10, 1926. His mother was Swedish and his father English and Irish. Marietta Van Opdorp was born in Adkinson, Illinois on May 30, 1926. Her mother was Belgian, and her father was from Holland. On February 4, 1950, they were married and established their home in Geneseo, Illinois where Clarence worked at the Klavohn Furniture Store.

The Vickroy family

It was in Geneseo that their first three children were born: Debbie on November 30, 1951; Randy on May 20, 1954; and Rick on September 3, 1955.

In February of 1956 the family moved to Monmouth to establish Vickroy's Furniture Store. Four years later Dawn was born on April 16, 1960, followed by their last child, Rod, on May 8, 1964.

Debbie, the first-born, married Tony Fritzel of Galesburg on June 30, 1973. Debbie was a second grade teacher at Costa in Galesburg and retired in 2001. Tony is a comptroller for Dick Blick Art Materials. They have two children. Jason, who was born November 14, 1975, married Sara Medhurst of Galesburg on May 26, 2001, and they live in St. Paul, MN. He is a graduate of Illinois State University and is the branch manager of Catholic Charities Drop In Center in Minneapolis while his wife is an X-ray technician. Mandy was born on January 25, 1979. She is a graduate of Drake and works in Chicago as a junior director of merchandising for Dick Blick.

Randy, their second child, graduated from Monmouth College in 1976 and got his masters' degree from Denver University. He lives in Denver, Colorado and is a financial consultant.

Rick married Julie Kinney on May 8, 1999, and they have two children. Tess was born on October 27, 1999, and Cullen was born January 27, 2002. This family lives in Monmouth where Rick works for Vickroy's Furniture in sales, managing deliveries, and planning floor displays.

Julie teaches kindergarten in Abingdon.

Dawn married Steve Schisler on June 2, 1979, and they have three children. She works for Vickroy's in sales, buying, and merchandiising while Steve is a Claims Training Specialist for Country Insurance. Melissa, born June 19, 1980, is a graduate of Loras College in Dubuque, Iowa, with a degree in Media/Communications/Television and is employed at KWWL at Waterloo, Iowa. Jacob is a junior at Yorkwood High School, and Jordan is in eighth grade at Yorkwood. They have a rural Monmouth address.

Rod married Kim Shelbourn in Chicago on June 17, 1995. Rod is an interior architect with RTKL Worldwide in Chicago. Kim is with Jones, Lang, LaSalle Real Estate as a strategic occupancy planner. They have two sons: Jack, born October 9, 2000; and Julian Charles, born May 3, 2002. This family resides in Barrington Hills, Illinois.

ABNER WALKER - Abner Walker was born August 10, 1796 in Lexington, Rockbridge County Virginia. Abner was a descendant of John Walker of Wigton Scotland who settled in Chester County, PA between 1726/28. Jane Damron was born January 21,1809 Adair County in the State of Kentucky. Record of their marriage is October 20,1829 in Columbia, Adair County Kentucky. The Walker Family moved to McDonough County in 1830. Their family began in Illinois with the following children: Walker, George Alexander; born September 26,1830. Walker, Cyrus Allen; died May 1833. Walker, Mary Elizabeth; born September 25, 1834. Walker, Lawson N.; born August 21, 1836. Walker, Abigail; born, December 16,1839. Walker, Cornila born 1840, died 1840. Walker, Joseph Gilmer born, August 6,1842. Walker, John Kelso born, January 24,1845. Walker, Mildred born, March 18,1848 [Documents list her name as Wellen Mildred Walker]. Walker, Chloe born April 15,1851.

Mildred Walker Fouke – 51, Grace N. Fouke – 27, Forrest City, Missouri, 1899

George A. Walker was born in Morgan Co, Chloe Walker, was born in Warren Co, the rest were born in McDonough County, Illinois.

Abner Walker was a natural mechanic; built Grist mills for grinding grain; also built and operated several sawmills in McDonough County. Abner was a contractor and built many houses, two of which are still standing in the year 2002. The one built for his brother, Judge Cyrus Walker on Randolph Street, Macomb in 1836. This home was considered at the time, it was built, to be one of the finest in Macomb. The other home still standing today was built for his brother Allen H. Walker, it too is an outstanding home and occupied by Alan W. Walker, the Great-grandson of Allen H. Walker.

The first suction pump used in this section was of Abner's manufacture and nothing better succeeded it until after the turn of the century.

The Walkers resided in McDonough County until they moved to Greenbush, in October 1849.

The census conducted in Warren County, Illinois on September 23,1850-listed Abner Walker and Jane as innkeepers in the town of Greenbush, Warren County. The hotel was located on the north side of the square, in the village of Greenbush.

The Abner and Jane Walker were living in Greenbush and had a very nice family until the fateful day of Sunday June 15,1851. *The Atlas* newspaper of Monmouth, Illinois reported the following: Thursday Evening, June 19,1851 under 'Deaths,' "We learn that a son of Abner Walker, who resides at Greenbush, about 16 years of age, died suddenly on Sunday last of a disease resembling cholera."

The Atlas Newspaper, Monmouth, Friday June 27,1851 reported, "Deaths from Cholera: We published last week (June 24,1851) a notice of the death of Mr. A. Walker, living at Greenbush, supposed to have been from Cholera. It now becomes our painful duty to record the sudden death of several other persons in that town and vicinity: Mr. Abner Walker and daughter Abigail - the latter, some 12 years of age." *The Atlas* continues to list several other citizens stricken with Cholera, with a PS: "Since putting the news in type, we have been told that a number of deaths in the vicinity of Greenbush will number at least 14 or 15."

The headstones in the Greenbush Cemetery, Illinois cemetery in Warren County record the following: Walker, Lawson H. August 21, 1836 – June 15, 1851, son of A. and J. Walker. Walker, Chloe died September 23, 1852 age 1y5m8d, daughter of A. and J. Walker. Walker, Abigail; December 16, 1839 – June 24, 1851, daughter of A. and J. Walker. Walker, Abner; August 10, 1796 – June 24, 1851. Walker, Jane; died January 24, 1855 age 45y3d, wife of A. Walker. Walker, George Alexander; died October 4, 1872; aged 41 years.

With the deaths of Abner and Jane and three of their children, the remaining minor children were appointed a guardian. Squire Jenkins Buzan and Mary Elizabeth Walker had married on August 3, 1854. Squire J. Buzan was appointed legal guardian for Joseph Gilmer Walker, John Kelso Walker and Mildred Walker.

DOROTHY FLORENCE (PINNEY) WALKER - Dorothy Florence (Pinney) Walker, born May 30, 1910 and died May 23, 1992. Married Herman Lee Walker, December 1, 1928. All through her life she enjoyed working in a large flower and vegetable garden and planting trees and shrubs. She enjoyed genealogy, and they took trips out east to search for family history. Dorothy was the second daughter of six children, three brothers are still living. Wendel, Merlyn, and Donald, born to Earle Raldsmond Pinney born October 5, 1886 and died March 9, 1966 and Eyra Watson born December 14, 1885, and died July 14,1989, at the age of 103. She sewed her own clothes, enjoyed gardening and her family. She belonged to the Colfax Club, and Home Extension, and lived alone her last 23 years on the farm. Earle's father Charles O. Pinney, born September 13, 1846 and died April 5, 1931 was married December 11, 1873 to Florence Eldridge born November 24, 1854 and died July 22, 1932.

She was the daughter of Norman Eldridge, he was the brother of Truman Eldridge, the founder of Roseville, Illinois. Norman Eldridge married Nancy Janette Cole born March 19, 1817 and died January 12, 1879. Earle was the youngest child with three older sisters. Earle soon won the respect from his sisters and a lot of other people. He served on many township and county committees. He worked hard and required those who worked with him to do the same. People sought his advice for many things. He worked at the A.S.C.S. office and also advised as a farm manager. He took courses from Western University to do wood working and had a well equipped shop and made some beautiful wooden tables out of native wood. The end of Earle's life came quickly as he was killed one and a half mile north of his home in Point Pleasant township in a car-truck accident, and he and Eyra are buried in Point Pleasant cemetery, Warren County. Eyra was the daughter of John Watson. He was born January 26, 1854 and died August 9, 1932, His mother Eva Smith, was born August 15, 1858 and died February 5, 1932. Eva was the daughter of Addison Sidney Smith born December 29, 1823 and died December 22, 1906. Addison's father, John M. Smith, was a native of Pennsylvania and connected 5 years with the Commissary department of the regular army, during the period of the second war with Great Britain or the War of 1812. He was stationed at Rock Island, and while there, became well acquainted with Black Hawk, the famous Indian Chief. Addison served on township offices such as supervisor, town clerk, assessor, justice of the peace and held the office of School treasure for thirty six years. Addison read medicine and studied law, He was a citizen of extra ordinary intelligence and education. While John and Eva raised their family of six, they always had a flock of chickens, milk cows, a large garden and many flowers, Eva was a home made artist and painted many pictures. When they moved to the south edge of Roseville they enjoyed the open countryside on three sides. They are buried in the Roseville Mausoleum, Warren County.

HERMAN LEE WALKER - Herman Lee Walker, born November 4, 1906 and died August 29, 1976. He was a farmer. He enjoyed going fishing on the Mississippi River, bowling and playing cards. He was the son of Presley Walker born October 7, 1880 in Waterford County, Kentucky.

Dorothy and Herman Walker

Presley was the fifth child of eight, born to Joseph born December 17, 1847 and died May 10, 1921 and Josephine (Guthrie) born May 7, 1849 and died January 15, 1895, they were married May 5, 1864, and were farmers. As the siblings reached maturity they went out on their own to make a living, and as a result Presley had a brother and sister that also came to Illinois and lived and raised their families here and in neighboring counties. Maude was born May 15, 1878 and died August 4, 1958, the fifth child of fourteen. Her father Stephen Stanley born October 13, 1838 and was killed March 2, 1907 at his home near Mulvane, Kansas, while clearing timber land, a limb broke from a tree, swayed back and threw a limb in his direction and struck him in the head. He was knocked down by the blow. When his companions reached him he was unconscious and remained that way until death the same day. Maude's Mother Demarious (McDermit) born September 19, 1854 and died January 29, 1900 along with five infant children are buried on the east side of the Raritan Cemetery, Henderson County. Stephen also lived near Raritan part of the time. When Presley and Maude were approaching marriage her dad moved the family back to Kansas, but Presley sent money for Maude to return and they married November 5, 1902. Presley and Maude would seek bachelor farmers, and Presley would work by the month for the farmer and Maude would do his housework, garden, cook, clean, and laundry. They did this until Presley saved enough money to buy a farm in Point Pleasant Township, Warren County. Presley hand picked his corn and dried his own seed corn for the following year and shelled it by hand, they had two living children Beatrice Walker (Rosen) and Herman Lee Walker. Herman and Dorothy had two children Patricia Ann born August 29, 1930 and Richard Lee born December 31, 1932.

MILDRED WALKER - Mildred Walker was the 9h child of Abner and Jane Walker of Greenbush, Warren County. Mildred was born in Macomb, McDonough County, Illinois, March 18, 1847. She moved with her family to Greenbush October 1849. She was only 4 years old when Cholera struck their family in June 1851, taking her father, one brother and one sister the same week.

Mildred Walker Fouke, 80; Grace Fouke Zimmershcied, 57 and Ida Zimmerschied, 17. Photo was taken at Broken Bow, Nebraska, 1928

Then in 1852, her younger sister Chloe also died in Greenbush. Within 3 years her mother Jane died, (some say she died of a broken heart), leaving three minor children, Joseph, John and Mildred.

August 3, 1854 oldest sister Mary Elizabeth Walker married Squire Jenkins Buzan, a friend of the Walker family. Squire engaged as a salesman for the N.P. Tinsley store in Macomb, until October 1849, when he came to Greenbush and commenced business for himself, running a general store. With the death of Jane Walker in 1855, Squire Buzan was appointed Legal Guardian for Joseph Gilmer Walker, John Kelso Walker and Mildred Walker in 1857, until they reached the age of 14 years.

Squire and Mary Buzan continued to operate the General Store in Greenbush until 1866. They purchased a farm in Berwick Township about 1857.

In 1861, Mildred's brother Joseph G. Walker enlisted in Company E, 33rd Illinois Infantry and taken prisoner in the fall of 1861 at Pilot Knob, Missouri. He was exchanged. Taken sick with brain fever at Helena, Arkansas. Joseph Walker was placed on a boat and sent North. August 1862, the family was notified and sent his brother George Alexander Walker to St. Louis to meet him. But, he learned that his brother was dead.

July 26, 1862, brother John Kelso Walker enlisted in Company H, 83rd Illinois Infantry and served 3 years, upon discharge he returned to Warren County and married Ann Jewell January 30, 1867, (6 children).

Squire and Mary Buzan, decided to move west and were living in Iowa in September 1866. They lived in Doniphan County, Kansas in October 1870, settled in Forrest City, Holt County, Missouri, by October 1873. Mildred Walker departed from the Buzan Family while they were living in Kansas. Mildred Walker married Richard Reynolds Fouke, a Civil War Veteran, on December 24, 1870 in Hiawatha, Brown County, Kansas; she was now 21 years of age. The newly weds made their home in Brown and Washington County, Kansas. To this union three children were born: Fouke, Roscoe 1871 - died young. Fouke, Nellie Grace October 26,1872 Washington County, Kansas, married Peter J. Zimmerschied 9/23/1907; 3 Children, Paul J. Zimmerschied 7/31/1909, Ida Mac Ziminerschied 5/26/1911, Joseph Fouke Zimmerschied 6/1913. Fouke, Paul Richard July 31, 1875, Nebraska, married Ida E. McKnight, June 1907, no children.

Richard R. Fouke was working for the railroad as a butcher and about 1879, Mildred Walker Fouke had had her fill of the prairie homestead life and left for Forrest City, Missouri to live with the Buzan Family. Mildred, Nellie Grace and Paul Richard Fouke lived in Forrest City and worked for Squire Buzan, until his death in 1893.

Nellie Grace Fouke and Paul Richard Fouke headed west to Hot Springs, South Dakota, taking Mildred with them. Nellie Grace Fouke established millinery shop in Spearfish, South Dakota. She married Peter Joseph Zimmerschied, a young cattle rancher from Carlile, WY, September 23, 1907, in Sundance, WY. Paul R. Fouke married Ida Elizabeth McKnight in the June 1907, they married in Hiawatha, Brown County, Kansas, made their home with Mildred Walker Fouke in Hot Springs, South Dakota.

Mildred Walker Fouke never remarried, split her residence between her two children; she died in Vona, Colorado on February 21, 1938 at age 90. Mildred's daughter, Nellie Grace is buried next to her, she died October 21, 1970, 4 days short of 98 years of age. Mildred's son Paul Richard Fouke, died August 30,1955 in Long Beach, CA., age 80.

RICHARD LEE WALKER - Richard Lee Walker, born December 31, 1932, son of Herman and Dorothy (Pinney) Walker. After High School graduation went to Bradley University one year. Then was drafted in the Army during the Korean

War. When he came home on furlough from Fort Sill, Oklahoma he married Marie Corzatt, June 16, 1953. He had orders to go to Korea, and was gone for seventeen months, he became a Sergeant Chief of the Survey Section. After he returned home he found a farm to rent in Point Pleasant Township and farmed there 43 years. They now live two and one-half mile South of Roseville, His parents bought land and built a house in the 1960's. Only after they bought the ground did they learn from the abstract that it had belonged to Dorothy's great-great-grandfather Joseph Watson. Richard's hobbies are bowling and fixing things. He has bowled in a league for 41 years. He always held offices in churches he has been in, and other civil organizations. Marie helped Richard with the farming, while his father was living they farmed together. Marie had a garden and canned and froze fruits and vegetables, and raised chickens for eggs and to eat and raised hogs and beef cattle. Richard and Marie have a daughter Tina born December 2, 1955, she went to Special Education classes all through her school years. After graduation she started working at Achievement Industries. She lives in a group home in Monmouth and has worked at the work shop for 28 years. She attends the First Christian Church. Son Roger Lee, born September 14, 1962. After he graduated from High school he went to Southeastern Jr. College where he took classes in carpentry and He has put that education to use many times in their home.

Front row: Matthew and Sarah Walker. Second row: Tina, Marie and Susan. Third row: Dick, Stephen and Roger. Back row: Patrick, Matthew, David and Alyssa.

He has four children. Matthew Lee, born July 23, 1983, Sarah Ann born January 28, 1985, Stephen Micheal born September 23, 1986 and David Joseph born February 3, 1989. He is now married to Susan Snyder, and he has three step children, Alyssa born September 8, 1987, Matthew and Patrick born September 1, 1988 The Children are all in school. Roger and Susan live near Atlanta Georgia where they both work as Telecommunication Analysts.

BELLIS – WALLER - On November 4, 1936, a daughter, Christa Marie, was born to Ernie and Dorothy (Bertram) Bellis. Seven months later, June 28, 1937, a son William Gene was born to Norman and Evelyn (Perry) Waller, both in the old Monmouth Hospital (now Pinewood Health Care Center). (Christa's grandparents, Chris and Mary Bertram owned and operated the Maple City Dairy for many years.)

Who could have known then that these two babies would end up together years later! Christa's parents divorced and both remarried. Her dad married Julia Worrell and her mom married Charles Elliott. They are all deceased now, as are Bill's parents. She has two sisters and three brothers and he had three brothers. Frank is deceased.

Bill and Christa Waller. August 5, 1999

They both graduated from Monmouth High School and Christa went on to Monmouth College for two years. Bill was in the Army from 1957-1959, spending a year in Germany where his dad had fought in World War II, and was a POW of the Germans for some time. They were married on November 28, 1959, in the first Lutheran Church of Monmouth, by Reverand Raymond Swanson, and have always been members of that church.

They became the parents of a son, Kristen William Waller, who was born on December 25, 1967, and their lives became more enriched after that. When he began school, Christa became a "professional" volunteer in the school system. She was a room mother, Cub Scout den mother, art presenter, PTC secretary and president, tutor and a District #38 School Board member for 10 1/2 years. Bill was very actively involved also. He was a charter member of the Carl Sandburg College Board, an auxiliary policeman, on the Zoning Board of Appeals for the city, United Way Board, charter member of Crime Stoppers and served eight years as an alderman on the City Council.

Kristen graduated form Monmouth High School and also went on to Hamilton Technical College. He married Diane Musser and they live in Galesburg, Illinois.

Bill worked for Harry Foust, Gosney Construction, Wilson Foods in the maintenance department for 19 1/2 years and then at the National Guard Armory for over 13 years. He is now medically retired. Christa was a teacher's aide at Head Start, substituted at both M.E.L.C. and Teddy Bear Day Care before she started doing child care in their home. She has worked at Econo Foods now for over seven years.

They are both actively involved with the American Legion Post. He has been commander of the Sal's for the past three years and she is historian and national security chairman for the Ladies Auxiliary. She is now on the Habitat for Humanity Committee and is chairman for the Monmouth Patriotic Fund to get flags back up on the city square. He has been a member of the Lion's Club for 32 years, serving as president twice and has league bowled for over 35 years. "We have always lived in Monmouth and always will" they say!

ERNEST WARREN WALTERS - Ernest Warren Walters, born 08/27/1905 on Will Walters farm near Little York, Illinois, was son of William Henry Walters and Sophia Marguerite Piper who married in Warren County 2/29/1888. Will left Pennsylvania in 1882, at age 16, to come "West." Sophie emigrated from Germany in 1869 with parents Henry and Dora Sass Piper.

Ernest Warren Walters family. Ernest and Catherin Reeves Walters, Raymond, Mary and John Walters, 1955

Ernie had 2 brothers, Henry, 15 years older, Harold, 4 years younger, and a large networking family who pooled equipment and labor. He grew up with an avid interest in mechanical vehicles, spending all time possible in Henry's Ford garage. After graduation from Aledo High School in 1925, he specialized in auto repair, and helped Will maintain the farm. From horses and teams, through threshers and steam, he adapted his skills to rapidly modernizing vehicles, often making his own tools. Ernest worked for several local garages, L. T. Hall, E&A Motors, Thompson Ford Garage, and was employed by Monmouth City Garage, when he died, in 1972. He was buried in Old Cedar Creek Church Cemetery with 7 generations of family. An outdoorsman, Ernie loved to hunt, fish, and walk the timbers he grew up in. He belonged to the Odd Fellows, Masons, and Methodist Church.

Catherine, his wife, born 6/15/1913 in Brookport, IL to Rev. Raymond and Ruby Armstrong Reeves, was first of 4 daughters. She and Ernest met at Little York Methodist Church where her father was new pastor. He married them in 1933, and she moved to the farm. In 1946, they bought the house on 2nd Avenue, where Catherine lived for 50 years and raised 3 children. Widowed early, she did custom sewing and elder care. She was actively involved in Methodist Church and community activities, until moving to her daughter's Oklahoma home in 1999.

Raymond, born 02/21/1935, on the Walters farm, graduated from Monmouth High School in 1953. After service in the Army, he earned a psychology degree from Cornell College, IA, in 1959. He met Neola Kubicek, daughter of Hubert Kubicek and Martha Kvidera, at Cornell, where she studied to be a guidance counselor. They married in 1966. Raymond spent most of his career as a psychologist at Illinois State Mental Hospital, Elgin, retiring in 1997. He and Neola live in Hoffman Estates, IL. Daughter, Amy, born June 1970, is a community psychologist. She, husband George Mueller and daughter Kaitlyn, live in Bloomington IL.

Mary was born 04/13/1951. A 1969 graduate of MHS, she attended NIU in Dekalb, IL and worked as secretary, bookkeeper, and floral designer. In 1970, she married Bill Oswald, son of Roland and Mary Dunn Oswald. He graduated from MHS in 1968, NIU in 1972, and is HRIS Manager for Occidental Petroleum. They have three children. Andi, born in 1971, is employed by HealthNet H.M.O. She lives in Woodland Hills, CA with husband Jonathan Myron. Valerie, born 1975, is studying Speech Communications and History at University of Washington, Seattle. Alex, born 1977, graduated from High School in Newhall CA, attended Tulsa Community College. He works and lives near his parents in Broken Arrow, OK.

John, born 12/09/1952, is a 1971 MHS graduate, and served as an Army MP. He earned a Horticulture Degree from SIU in 1976 and has won awards for landscape design. He works for Arthur Clesen, Inc. Jane Steis and John married in 1974. She is the daughter of Parker and Joan Steis of Monmouth. Jane, also a graduate of MHS and SIU, is a pharmacy assistant. They live in Hanover Park, IL, and have 2 children.

Beth, born 1980, is studying graphic arts at College of DuPage. She has a son, Cole Gear. Nathan, born 1982, attends Columbia College of the Arts in Chicago, IL (See William Henry Walters Family and Roland Herbert Oswald Family).

Submitted by Mrs. Catherine I. Walters

WILLIAM HENRY WALTERS - William Henry Walter, born 03/06/1866, in Silver Springs Township, Cumberland County, PA, to Joseph Henry and Mary Hoenshell Walter, was 3rd of 12 children and at least 6th generation Pennsylvanian. In 1862, at age 16, he began working his way West as a laborer. Passing through Warren County, he worked for Henry Piper. Captivated by Piper's daughter, Sophia, Will traveled on to Kansas, then returned to marry her. Two sisters came later to raise families in the Monmouth area, Catherine Elizabeth (Mrs. Isaac Fink), and Anna (Mrs. Harvey Zimmerman). Will and two brothers added an "S" to their last name.

William Henry Walters and Sophia Piper Walters with sons Joseph Henry, Ernest Warren and Harold Dell Walters at their farm near Little York, Illinois.

Sophia Marguerite Piper came to Warren County from Germany in 1869, age 3 mos., with her parents Henry and Dora Sass Piper, and brother Fritz, age 2. Of five siblings born later, only descendants of James and Neva McIntire Piper's 3 daughters remain in Warren County. Fritz joined the Oklahoma land rush. Settling near Muskogee, he married Mary, a Cherokee woman, and had 1 daughter in 1901.

Will and Sophie, married 02/29/1888, in Sumner Twp. They farmed near Little York, tenants at first, then bought their own farm. Will owned threshing equipment, moveable sawmill, and stone crusher, frequently contracting out his own varied services, and those of his sons, linking them with the extended family. Will retired to Monmouth in 1941 and died 05/16/1944. Sophia died 10/16/1953. They were active in the early Cedar Creek Church and are buried in Cedar Creek Cemetery, near the site of the original church, along with 5 of their 6 children and members of 7 generations of Walters, Sass, & Piper family. Only Harold and Ernest lived to raise family.

The eldest son, Joseph Henry, born in 1890, owned a Ford garage in Little York, and was a photographer. He married Edna Howe in June 1918, and joined the War Effort. He died at Fort McHenry, MD, April 1919, of influenza. Many turn-of-the-century photos taken by Henry of family, schools, churches and community, survive.

Harold Walters, born 09/30/1909, graduated from Little York High School, and Illinois Wesleyan College in 1935. He remained in Bloomington, IL, owned an insurance agency and was very active in the community. An ordained minister, he played Christ in Bloomington's "American Passion Play" for 24 seasons. In 1932, he married Thelma Kniss, a teacher. They raised 2 children, Joanne and Thomas, then divorced in 1962. He and 2'd wife Margaret Hallstein had been married 21 years, when he died 10/21/1987. Ann, born 11/30/1933, is a retired High School teacher. She and her writer/drama professor husband, Sam Smiley, live in Tucson, Arizona. They have three sons. Mark, and wife Cathy Taylor Smiley live in Virginia. They have a son and daughter. Steven married Sally Smith. They, their son and daughter, live in New Jersey. Sean and his wife Lana Nonweiler are raising 3 children, in Hanover Park, IL. Tom was born in 02/05/1937. He came home after military assignment in Germany, was killed in a Colorado auto accident in 1970. He and wife Donita Simpson had a daughter, Diane, and son, Whitney. Whitney and wife Marcie have a son, Tom.

Ernest, an excellent auto mechanic, remained in Monmouth married to Catherine Reeves and had 3 children, Raymond, Mary and John. (See Ernest Walters Family).

Submitted by Mary Oswald

D. EDGAR AND BLANCHE WARNER - Daniel Edgar Warner was born on November 22, 1876 at Anderson, IL. He was known as Edgar. His early life was spent in Gladstone, IL before moving to Kirkwood, IL in 1912 with his wife and two sons.

Edgar's father, Asa Harve Warner, was born in 1823, and died in 1910. His mother, Anna Jane Waddell was born in 1840 and died December 10, 1927 in Gladstone, IL. Anna Jane's father was Martin L. Waddell; her mother was an Indian, Katie Davis Waddell. Edgar had four brothers: Mert, George Martin, James Edward, and Asa Harvey, and a sister Alice.

Edgar was a veteran of the Spanish-American War and served three years in the Phillipine Islands.

He worked for 25 years as a section foreman for the C.B.&Q. Railroad. After a long bout with cancer, he died on March 31, 1931.

Blanche May Tweed married Edgar on March 30, 1910. Their first home was in Gladstone where two of their five children were born.

Blanche was born in Carns, Nebraska, on December 15, 1887 and died January 16, 1978. Her father, John W. Tweed, a retired section foreman for the C.B.&Q., was born November 2, 1862 in Gladstone and died March 13, 1949. John was the son of Hiram and Lucy (Sage) Tweed. Blanche's grandmother Lucy was the daughter of Gideon Sage who founded Sagetown on a part of his land. Later Sagetown became Gladstone. Her mother, Hattie J. (Billings) Tweed was born on May 25, 1869 at Sutton Corner, Pennsylvania and died August 17, 1949.

Blanche was a homemaker. Edgar and Blanche had five children: Chester Lee Warner, Sr. (Feb. 11, 1911 -Nov. 24, 19 71), Roy Dale Warner (Sept. 24, 1912-Feb. 19, 1961), Mildred Darlene Warner (Aug. 18, 1926), Doris Mae Warner (Holford) Sanberg (Jan. 2, 1929), Juanita Fern Warner (June 12, 1931 -June 18, 1931)

DORIS MAE WARNER - Doris Mae Warner was a daughter of D. Edgar and Blanche Tweed Warner. She was born and raised in Kirkwood, Illinois. Attended the Kirkwood schools and graduated from Kirkwood High School. She worked for Formfit, Kirkwood Branch Library, Birdsell's Appliance and Western Illinois Library System. She attends the Kirkwood United Methodist Church and belongs to the United Methodist Women, Kirkwood Senior Citizens, Oquawka Rebekah Lodge and Tompkins Sunshine Unit. She married David Martin Holford on November 3, 1950. He died on May 11, 1969.

They have three children – Steven Gale born on October 4, 1951, Janet Kay born on October 2, 1953 and Martin Paul born on September 24, 1959. One daughter Rhonda Lynn is deceased.

Steven was married to Karen Egger and they had three children. Steven Kenneth, Kristal Kay and Jennifer Lynn. Kristal has a son Carson Weir Huff.

Janet married James Lee Cook, son of Ben and Flora Cook. They have two sons, Jason Buchanan and David James. Jason married Lori Lee Hart. They have two children – Riley Christine and Maxwell Buchanan.

Doris later married Glenn Sanberg on May 19, 1984. Together they deliver means from the Village Center to the home bounds.

Warner family. Chester, Blanche, Dale, Mildred, father Edgar - 1916 (superimposed) and Doris.

MILDRED DARLENE WARNER - Mildred Darlene Warner, a daughter of D. Edgar and Blanche Tweed Warner was born and raised in Kirkwood, Illinois. She attended the Kirkwood schools and graduated from Kirkwood High School. She and her sister Doris with Patricia VanRiper and Doris Gunter Young sang as a quartet called the Candy Stripers. She attends the Kirkwood United Methodist Church where she sang in the choir and also taught Sunday School for over twenty years. She belongs to the United Methodist Women, Tompkins Sunshine Unit of the Warren County Home and Community Association.

She joined the Kirkwood Rebekah Lodge on December 15, 1944 and is currently a member of the Oquawka Rebekah Lodge. A member of the Kirkwood Senior Citizens, volunteers at the Village Center serving meals, sometimes delivering them. A substitute for Carol Barron when she was unable to work. She was has one son Douglas Ray Warner who was born December 1, 1960. He attended Kirkwood Grade School, then Yorkwood where he graduated in 1978. He enlisted in the United States Air Force and served twenty years. He was stationed in Minot, North Dakota; Abilene, Texas; and Wichita, Kansas. He has been to Guam, Turkey, Panama, Egypt, Philippines and England. He spent over one year in South Korea retiring as a Master Sergeant. He resides in Bel Aire, Kansas where he works for Raytheon Aircraft Company of Wichita, Kansas.

ROBERT AND DONNA (KESINGER) WARREN - Donna Elaine Kesinger was born 11 August 1949 in Champaign/Urbana, Illinois to Don Edward and Vivian Marcella (Shores) Kesinger. They moved to Monmouth, Warren County, Illinois in 1950 when her father was assigned as Unit Conservationist there. Donna attended local grade schools and graduated from Monmouth High School in 1957. Donna graduated from Drake University in Des Moines, Iowa and moved to Minneapolis, MN. She married Robert (Bob) Warren of Davenport, Iowa in 1970.

Donna and Bob have two children: Paul Robert (1972) and Kathryn Meredith (Katie) (1974) who became brother and sister to Laura Ashley (1953) in later years.

Bob, who was vice president at Campbell-Mithun Advertising and Donna, a corporate administrator and writer, lived in Minnetonka, MN. Bob originated the "Reach Out and Touch Someone" ad for AT&T and Bozell Advertising.

Grandchildren are: Jonah Verner (1996), Haley Verner (1999) and Rain Kelly-Warren (1996) all of Minneapolis, MN.

Donna's brothers and sisters are: Margaret (Peggy); Bank Salazar (1951) of Monmouth; Susan Eloise Mills (1953) of Little York; David Mark (1954) of Warrensburg, MO; John Daniel (1957), Harvey Earl (1959) and Janet Elisa Cohn (1960) all of Monmouth.

Each year the Kesinger family gathers in Monmouth on Christmas Eve to attend Christmas Eve church services, remember the dad they knew as Santa Claus for many community events and recite their father's lyric "Ump-pa-ha." Whether the lyric was originally written by Don or someone else is unknown but the tale it tells of a family who enters into a day of folly on a sleigh ride, is full of laughs, typical of the kind of day they both wanted of every day for those they loved – days filled with a passion for life, fun and lots of laughter.

JOHN W. AND CINDY L. (VESTAL) WATSON - Cindy L. Vestal born December 24, 1959 is the daughter of Gilmer and Mary C. (Frazee) Vestal.

There were seven children in the family: Gilmer Eugene - born December 30, 1944, Sharon Kay - born January 1, 1948, Martha Ellen - born September 2, 1949, Sandra Lynn - born June 22, 1952, Mary Ann - born June 20, 1958, Cynthia (Cindy) Lou - born December 24, 1959, and Gary Lee - born June 3, 1961.

Cindy was born one mile North of Roseville and attended Roseville schools, graduating from Roseville High School.

Cindy and Tara Watson on Easter, March 31, 2002

When a teen Cindy, with her brothers and sisters and her Dad, walked the bean fields for Ockert Farms. When it was time to go home for lunch the kids would ride in the back of John Ockert's truck and be treated to a soda pop at Farmer's Grain before going home and let Dad, (Gilmer Vestal) go home by himself.

Cindy married John W. Watson on December 29, 1996. They have one daughter, Tara L. - Cindy works as an Addus Home Care Aid for the elderly.

LARRY ALAN WATSON - Larry Alan Watson, son of LeMoine Earl Watson and Norma Elizabeth (Suter) was born May 7, 1937, Monmouth Hospital, Monmouth, IL. His father was born February 24, 1905 near Roseville, IL. LeMoine was a farmer until the mid 1940's when he took a job at Dale Watson Seed Co. in Roseville, IL, then Gamble Warehouse in early 1950's and retired in 1971. He died July 23 1976 in Monmouth, IL. Norma was born March 18, 1910 near Greenbush, Illinois. Norma retired from Formfit and Smoler Bros after 25 years.

Larry's first home was in Roseville, IL. His parents then moved to Berwick and later to Cameron, IL, where he attended a one-room school at Coldbrook School through part of the fifth grade. They moved to Greenbush in the spring of 1948 where Larry finished fifth and sixth grade. Continuing his education he attended seventh through 10th grade at Avon, IL, his class being the first freshmen in the new high school. In spring of 1953 they moved to Smithshire, IL, and Larry attended Roseville High School for eleventh and twelfth grade were he was on the track team and set a few records in the 220 yard dash and the 440 yard dash. He graduated Roseville High School in 1955.

Larry enlisted into the Army September 1955; he went to basic training at Fort Riley, KS. After boot camp he was trained as Fire Control Instrument Repairman in Aberdeen, MD. He was sent to Korea March 1956, were he served as Artillery Office Clerk, Unit Supply Clerk, Company Clerk and Tech Supply Clerk. July 4, 1957, he was sent to Fort Polk, Louisiana as instrument repairman, Unit Supply Clerk, Company Clerk, Post Ordnance Clerk. He received an Honorable Discharged in September of 1958.

Larry worked for Dekalb Seed Corn Co., Monmouth, IL then CB&Q Railroad, Galesburg, IL. On December 27, 1959 he moved to Monmouth, IL, and married Betty Myers of Monmouth, IL. Betty was the daughter of Helen Gertrude Myers and Charles Lawrence Myers of Monmouth, IL. Betty was born on June 10, 1944, in Monmouth, IL.

Larry worked for the Department of Agriculture in 1960 and 1961. He then worked for International Harvester, East Moline, IL, March 1961 as a Sub Assembler and retired March of 1993, as an Inspector/Repairman. 1966 through 1968 he attended Carl Sandburg College, Galesburg, IL on a GI bill and studied Business Administration. Betty and Larry began selling Miracle Maid Cookware in 1968 and in 1972 they were promoted to unit manager and required to move to the Quad City, IL, area. They moved to East Moline, IL. In 1974 they were promoted to Area Managers and moved to Bettendorf, IA, were they reside today. They won two trips to the Bahamas Islands in 1972 and in 1974. In 1979 they quit selling cookware. After retirement (1998) Larry took a job at K-Mart in Sporting Goods.

Larry loves hunting, fishing and stock car racing. Each year he spends three weeks in the Colorado Rockies hunting deer and elk with his brother-in-laws and friends who lived in Denver, Colorado. He owned a stock car from 1989-2000 and raced at Blue Grass, IA; Aledo, IL; East Moline, IL; and Wappello, IA.

Grandchildren: Curtis Wayne Sturms, August 13, 1980; Cindy Lou Charboneau, May 26, 1983; Misty Kay Watson, November 29, 1980; Randall Torrington Ramsey, 11 September 4, 1988; Jason Torrington Ramsey, November 12, 1990; Cara Lynn Maere, August 21, 1996; Deseara Briza Watson, May 27, 1985; Paul David Watson, June 4, 1987; Audria Ann Martinez, August 9, 1989; Breanna Danielle Martinez, April 20 1994; Carrissa Sarree Watson, February 2, 2002;

Great-grandchildren: Austin Wayne Charboneau-Fillman, August 19, 2000; Nathan Hulbert Kimbrough III, August 31, 1997; Navia Kay Patricia Terrell, August 30, 2000.

NORMA ELIZABETH (SUTER) WATSON - Norma Elizabeth (Suter) Watson, daughter of Joseph Andrew and Millie Ann (Smith) Suter, was born March 18, 1910, near Greenbush, Illinois. Her father was born July 15, 1880 near Greenbush. He was a farmer in the Greenbush and Youngstown communities. He died on March 12, 1963 in Avon, Il. Her mother was born November 16, 1888 near Alexis. She died June 26, 1981 in Macomb. They were the parents of Nellie Naomi, Norma Elizabeth (Watson), George Andrew, Doris Vivian (Ragon), Roberta Katherine (Sammons), and Richard Dean.

LeMoine and Norma Watson, 1967

Norma received her education in the Crawford and Hoisington grade schools in Swan

Township. She then attended Youngstown High School 2 years and graduated from Roseville High School in 1928. She stayed in Roseville during the week and rode the train back to Youngstown on the weekends. Then she attended Business College in Macomb. During the depression work was hard to find so she did housekeeping for families until on August 18, 1931 she married LeMoine Earl Watson in Streator, Il. He was the son of Harlan H. and Pearl Boyd (Woodward) Watson. He was born February 24, 1905, near Roseville. He attended Roseville High School and Gem City Business College in Quincy. He was a farmer and later was employed at Dale Watson Seen Co. and Gamble Skogmo Co. LeMoine died July 23, 1976 in Monmouth. They were the parents of Clarice Juanita Watson (Hendel), born July 17, 1932 and Larry Alan Watson born May 7, 1937.

In 1961 they moved to Monmouth where Norma continues to live. She was employed at Formfit and Smoler Bros. for 25 years. Then she worked part time for Paralee Apparel and Newsland until she retired at 79 1/2 years in 1989.

She enjoys her family and has made numerous quilts for them. She likes to read and take care of her yard and flowers. She is a member of the Roseville Methodist Church.

WILLIAM JASPER WATSON - William Jasper Watson was born in Kelly Township, Warren County, Illinois 9 October 1837, the 5th child of Bazil and Matilda (Paddocks) Watson. Bazil and Matilda, both born in Kentucky, were married 28 September 1826 in Harrison County, Indiana and migrated to Section 11, Kelly Township, Warren County, Illinois circa 1836-37. Bazil was the son of Abraham and Eleanor (Rhodes) Watson and Matilda was the daughter of Joseph and Mary (Gilliland) Paddocks, all early Kentucky residents.

William Jasper Watson

William Jasper Watson enlisted in the 1st Iowa Battery, Iowa Volunteers 17 August 1861 and fought in the Union Army of the Civil War. He participated in the Battle of Pea Ridge (Ark.), the Battle of Vicksburg, the Battle of Shiloh, the Battle of Lookout Mountain and the Atlanta Campaign. He was discharged 10 August 1864 at Davenport, Iowa.

He was married at Monmouth, Illinois 12 April 1866 to Christiann Brittingham, who had been born in Peoria County, Illinois 19 February 1847, the daughter of George Riley and Sarah Ann (Butler) Brittingham. Later in 1866 William and his bride, along with several members of her family, went to Kansas to homestead.

William was a farmer, but served four years as Deputy Sheriff of Linn County, Kansas. He was well-known for his lengthy beard. Here is a quote from a Linn, Co., Kansas newspaper of the time, "Mr. Watson has probably the longest whiskers of any man in Kansas. They measure exactly 3 feet 9 1/2 inches and are light golden in color. After repeated entreaty, Mr. Watson combed out his whiskers and they hung below his knees."

In the late 1890s William and Christiann moved back to Kelly Township, Warren County, Illinois where he died 7 June 1909. Christiann died at Abingdon, Knox County, Illinois 14 July 1923. Both are buried in the Abingdon Cemetery, Abingdon, Illinois.

William and Christiann were the parents of thirteen children. Namely: Alise Linetti (1867-1939). Married (1) George W. White; married (2) Jacob Hoppaugh. Five children. Jennie Frances (1868-1945). Married Charles Townsend. Two children. Fred Ulysses (1869-1948). Married (1) Perlina Bruce; married (2) Pearl _?_. Three children. Bazil Riley (1871-1951). Married Stella Hobson. Three children. Albert Edwin (1872-1951). Never married. Della Edith (1874-1948). Married Clinton Bryan. Two children. Edna Mabell (1876-1952). Married Frank G. Miles. Six children. Laura Maude (1878-1943). Married Edward T. (Bob) Gillen. Three children. Katie Weaver (1880-1941). Married John Lee Ralph. Fifteen children. William Taylor (1883-1971). Married Edith Glass. Four children. Tillie Blanche (1884-1973). Married (1) William Croy; married (2) J. C. Cross. Three children. Biddle Valentine (1886-1945). Married (1) Maude Kingsley; married (2) Rhea Mills. Three children. Anna Letitia (1892-1922). Married Frank Yarde. Two children. Several of these children also returned to Warren County, Illinois with their parents and lived out their lives in the area.

ELIZABETH AND IVAN WAUGH - Ivan Rexford Waugh was born in rural Henderson County, October 5, 1908, to Orville K. and Lula Moore Waugh of Larchland. He was one of ten children.

Ivan and Elizabeth Waugh

Elizabeth Smith was the first child of Leo G. and Pearl Hottle Smith. Leo was the son of Nathan N. and Ella Jones Smith and was born in Henderson County, IL. Nathan's father had been born near London, England, and came to the U.S. as a young man. Pearl, the daughter of James E. and Nelia Watson Hottle, was born in Mauchport, Indiana, and came with her parents to Illinois in 1892. Leo and Pearl were married in 1916. Their second daughter was Mary followed by a son William. They lived on the farm where Leo was born. Leo died in 1972 in a house fire. Pearl died in 1980.

Ivan attended grade school in Henderson County and started to high school at Seaton. Transferring to Aledo High School, he graduated in 1928. Then he had several jobs: farming, ushering at Paramount Theater in Peoria, the Bald Bluff filling station, and the Little and Guilinger Garage in Little York. Later he worked for the Illinois Department of Transportation until he became a self-employed decorator – painting and wallpapering for over 40 years.

Elizabeth attended Bald Bluff Grade School and graduated from Seaton High School as valedictorian in 1935. After two years at Western Illinois University, she began her teaching career at Maple Grove near Keithsburg then taught at Robb, Cedar Creek and Little York Grade School. At Little York she taught the upper grades for 27 years, part-time a teaching-principal and grade school basketball coach during World War II at L.Y. She also taught one year at Law School. She taught art at Yorkwood K- 10 for four years before retiring after thirty-seven years in the classroom. Later she subbed for 19 years. She graduated from Western in 1959.

Elizabeth and Ivan were married on June 1, 1941. In the summers Elizabeth and Ivan traveled widely. In the United States they went from the East Coast to the West Coast, to Hawaii and Alaska. They also visited Mexico, Nova Scotia, England, and Eastern Europe. Ivan became afflicted with Parkinson's Disease and passed away on July 22, 1996.

Mary, Elizabeth's sister, graduated from Seaton High School in 1937, later moving to Sioux City, IA. She married George Grimesey, a Purple Heart veteran of World War II. Their two children are Leo and Jane. Bill, her brother, was a graduate of Little York High School in 1939. He served in the Medical Corp in World War 11 at Braintree, England.

A farmer, he married Ruby Richardson of Rio, Illinois. Their children were Bonnie, Karen and Larry. Bonnie Skripps is the Acting Dean of Education at Western, Karen Lufkin works for children's services in Galesburg. Larry died at 19 of a cerebral hemorrhage. They have one granddaughter, Kirsten Bruns. In 1994 Bill and Ruby moved to Monmouth where Bill died on May 8, 2001, following a stroke.

JAMES MARTIN AND SUSANNAH SALLING WEBB - Webb, Rev. James Martin and his wife Susannah nee Salling came to Warren County from Edmonson County, Kentucky before 1850. He was a traveling Baptist preacher and preached at the New Lenox Baptist Church. He and Susannah had 40 acres in Roseville township, Warren county, bought from Mr. Pleasant Ray in 1851.

They came with a large family: 1. James Shadrack Singleton b. 1 January 1834 d. 10 March 1851, 2. Alexander Warren b. 1 June 1835 m. Margaret Guess 6 September 1859 in Kentucky, m. Elizabeth Guess 9 Mar. 1860 in Kentucky, m. Arabell Logan 3 February 1869 also in Kentucky returning to Warren County, 3. Nancy Elizabeth b. 2 September 1836 d. 11 September 1860 m. George W. Gunter 16 November 1854, 4. Jeptha Grigory Jones b. 11 April 1835 d. 1925 m. Ruth Ann Bullock 26 July 1863, 5. Margaret Maria Jane b. 25 November 1840, 6. Missouri Anne Blair b. 26 November 1842 m. George W. Gunter 5 February 1862. Their family included William b. 1867 and Susan J. b. 1869 (Nancy's children), Nancy E. b. 1863, Robert b. 1866, Porozoda b. 1867, and Mary b. April 1870, 7. Mary Adair b. 20 February 1844 d. June 1931, 8. James Willis b. 07 January, 1846, 9. William Henry Harrison b. 17 January, 1848 d. 24 November, 1850, 10. Richard Edwin b. 19 February, 1850 d. November, 1929, 11. Sarah Angeline Webb b. 05 March 1852, 12. Joshua Mortimore Webb b. 31 March 1853 d. 26 October 1952 m. Esther Marriete Corp 12 August 1880 in Missouri (she died 12 July 1889), m. name unknown, m. name unknown, and m. Elizabeth Gertrude Bailey 27 March 1860. 13. and 14. twins who died in infancy, names unknown.

James and Susannah (Susan) saw two sons, William H. H. and John S. S., and one daughter Nancy and one grandson, John W. Gunter buried in the Lenox Union Cemetery. Five years later Susannah was buried in the same cemetery.

Rev. James traveled to Kentucky and married widow Mary P. Saltzman 20 October 1867. They returned to Warren county, Illinois where he died before 1870. Mary P. Saltzman Webb later married Wilson Gunter.

After Rev. James Webb died, the youngest child, Joshua Mortimer, lived with his brother, Jeptha, in Missouri where he later met and married Esther Mariette Corp. They had 3 daughters, Martha Carrie Susanna Elizabeth b. 22 August 1883, Laura Grace Cleveland b. 13 July 1885, and Bertha Frances Irene b. 7 August 1887. Esther died 12 July 1889 in Nebraska. Joshua allowed other families to care for his two older daughters to adulthood and Thaddeus and Cecilia Adams to adopt Bertha Frances. Joshua stayed in contact with all three all of his life. In later years he owned a newspaper stand in San Diego, California where he died at 99 years old.

Webb, Saling, and Gunter families came to Warren County from Edmonson County, Kentucky. Some members remained in Illinois; others moved to settle in Missouri, Nebraska and California.

Submitted by Virginia Robertson Alyea

DR. AND MRS. J. STAFFORD WEEKS - Stafford and Winifred Weeks and their daughters Pamela, Cynthia and Wendy moved to Monmouth where Dr. Weeks assumed a position with Monmouth College in 1959. At various times he served as Professor of Religious Studies, Chaplain of the College, and Dean of the Faculty. He is a Presbyterian Minister. He served the College until 1986 at which time he served as Visitation Pastor for the United Methodist Church, resigning in 1994. Over the years he served as a supply or interim pastor for many churches, including Second United Presbyterian, Sugar Tree Grove, and Biggsville United Presbyterian Churches. He also served three terms on the Monmouth School Board. His activities include the Monmouth Rotary Club, the Monmouth Municipal Band and the Maple City Dixieland Band.

Mrs. Weeks was active on the committee that started Jamieson Center and was Secretary of the Board of the Warren Achievement School, She worked with Girl Scouts, with organizations at Faith United Presbyterian Church, including Bible School, Icebreakers, and Wednesday Night Live. She is a longtime member of PEO.

Pamela, now Mrs. James Braun, lives in Ballwin, MO where she teaches children with handicaps. She has two sons, Benjamin and Joel. Cynthia, now Mrs. Kim Fraser, lives in Champaign, IL. She works at Carte Clinic, where she counsels and works with a group on improving health delivery programs. She has a son Matthew. Wendy, Mrs. Wendy Feldner, lives in Kewanee, IL and works as a counselor at Blackhawk East Community College. She has two children, Seth and Hannah.

Stafford and Winifred Weeks have lived at 114 South Tenth Street since 1960, They came to Monmouth from Huron, SD where Dr. Weeks taught at Huron College for six years. Prior to going to South Dakota they had lived in Chicago while he finished his graduate work at the University of Chicago.

FRED AND MARILYN WELCH - Welch, Fredrick J., the youngest child of Archibald Welch and Alma Fredricka (Riley) Welch, was born in Little York, Illinois on January 19, 1924. He had one brother, John W. Welch, who was seven years older.

Debbie, Fred Jr., Cindy, Fred Sr. & Marilyn 1971

He attended Little York Grade School until 1938 when he and his family moved to Indianapolis, Indiana. He graduated from the 8th grade in Indianapolis and then returned to Little York in 1940. He graduated from Little York High School in 1942. In the fall of 1942 he entered Western Illinois University in Macomb as a freshman. He enlisted in the United States Navy in early 1943 and was discharged in January of 1946 As RM 2/c serving the majority of time in the South Pacific.

He married Marilyn Lois Jones on September 18, 1946 and then farmed with Howell Brownlee on the Brownlee farm 2 miles North of Little York. In 1957 he opened the J & W Hardware Appliance and LP Gas Business in Little York with Senius Jensen, Marilyn's step-father. When Natural Gas moved into the area after a few years, he sold the LP Gas Business to Great Plains Gas and went into management with National Propane.

In 1977 he and his wife, Marilyn, moved to the U.S. Virgin Islands. They lived on both St. Thomas and St Croix where he served as Vice-President and General Manager of Carib Gas Corporation. They returned to Little York in 1986 and he remained with National Propane until his retirement in 1988.

Born to Fred and Marilyn were the following children: Deborah Lynn, 7/27/1947; Fredrick Howell, 10/30/1950; Cynthia Ann 10/24/1953.

He and his wife purchased their home in Little York from Charlys and Helen Hines in 1957. The home was built in 1836 by the first postmaster in Little York and served as a stage coach inn on the M.A.M. Trail. He and his wife still live in this house and enjoy being a part of their family and traveling.

ROBERTA "BOBBY" (MCVEY) WELLS - Roberta "Bobby" (Mcvey) Wells, daughter of Robert and Vera McVey came to live in Monmouth, Illinois, when her father and his twin brother, Richard McVey came to Monmouth from Carthage, Illinois. They were honored to take part in the travels of "The Great Nicola" as he and his brother traveled around the world with his magical act. One can visualize how a magician could take advantage of twins in his act. Bobby tells us, "Daddy and Dick were to go on a world tour with the magician from Monmouth, The Great Nicola, but Daddy and Vera Stephens (Mom) wanted to get married! Dick, Daddy's twin, kidnapped him so he could not get married! But their father, George McVey, a local pig and grain farmer just east of Monmouth, located daddy tied up in his basement and released him. Mom and Dad married the next day and Uncle Dick didn't get to go on the world's tour!" It was on this tour that the magician lost his entire props, when his ship sunk off the coast of Singapore in the Indian Ocean. The McVey brothers were both early aviation enthusiasts and purchased the Hudson automobile dealership and built their display room and garage on the northeast side of the 400 block on North Main Street to be near to their first love flying airplanes. Bob was the master mechanic while Dick sold cars.

Roberta McVey Wells

It was the boys sister, Margaret Deschwanden, that invited Bobby, when ten or eleven years old, to spend fifth grade, the school year of 1933-34, with her on Kauii Island in Hawaii. She was living in Carthage at the time. Her Uncle Fred was in management with the Alexander & Baldwin Company, now the California and Hawaiian (C&H) sugar and pineapple company. The "Headline" news story in San Francisco Examiner said, "Girl, 11, Makes Long Voyage" - The Oakland Chronicle made national news when it reported she had to return after five months on the death of Mary Lou, her seven year old sister. The Golden Gate Bridge hadn't even been built yet! Her Aunt Margaret graduated from Monmouth College and after one year of teaching in Illinois traveled to Hawaii and married Fred Deschwanden. She taught many years at the Oriental School in Hawaii.

On the 4th of July holiday in 1940, the year Bobby graduated from high school, her father's airplane crashed and he was killed. The whole town was saddened. Bobby and her mother remained in Monmouth. They were living in an apartment just north of the Colwell Annex, then used as a bowling alley.

She said, "Bill and I started dating in High School - our lockers were next to each other. Our first date was 28 April 1938. We went to a Scout dance. We had to walk to the dance because Bill was not old enough to drive - he being just 15." In High School in 1940 she became a member of the girls secret sorority, one of the girls that together purchased a Model T Ford touring car, painted it white with the name Jezebel printed on its sides. Since secret societies were banned from Monmouth High School as well as dancing, it was they that organized dances, where the girls wore formal and the boys tuxedos. Big bands were contracted for under $50. On weekends several couples joined in attending the cowboy movies at the Bijou Theater. After a snack at Hawcock's Cafe or Martin's Diner, it was a ride with "Bud Grier driving to Monmouth Park literally often making his own roadway."

After high school she went to Monmouth College, where she joined Kappa Kappa Gamma still dating Bill a year behind her in school. In December of 1941 war was declared and many college boys joined up. Bill followed her to college and graduated in 1945. When he was called into service they were married. He was commissioned a Navigator-Bombadier and was sent overseas to fly combat in a B-17 - 22 missions. During the war Bobby and her mother moved to Galesburg, where son Billy was born. Her husband was notified and he celebrated with an old friend Bud Barnes in his apartment in London. While on leave in London, Bill had the privilege of using the apartment, since Bud had his room in the 150th Station Hospital nearby.

After the war Bill accepted a position with his father, Ralph Wells. Bobby and her mother, who was so helpful in helping her raise their baby boy, rented the upstairs of a house rented from her mother. Bill bought an old second hand pickup truck painted green. They felt fortunate to be one of the few who had transportation. Vera had remarried to "Pop" Schaffenberg and she babysat several of the children of Bobby and Bill's friends. They had moved and purchased the mansion in the 200 block on East Franklin Avenue.

WILLIS "BILL" WELLS - Willis "Bill" Wells was the twin son of Ralph and Winifred Wells, ex-mayor of Monmouth. Ralph, after graduating from the University of Illinois in the school of agriculture was sent to Warren County as the Farm Advisor. He had a limp caused when as a teenager he carried newspapers for extra money. His leg became infected from rubbing against the news bag. The Doctor had to operate and left the cast on too long and his leg didn't grow like the other one - thus the limp. It caused him much pain, but he didn't let that stop him. He first roomed at the YMCA and played pool at the Grand many evenings. He was instrumental in forming The Land Bank to help farmers in borrowing money and also introduced them to raising soybeans as a second money crop. He was considered a pioneer in this and purchased his own processing plant in Albert Lea, Minnesota. After leaving the Farm Bureau he and a partner joined in buying an elevator, tore it down and built Well's elevator that dominated Monmouth's skyline. His partner absconded with the company funds, but not giving up, bought the local dog food manufacturing factory to process corn. When his three younger boys returned from service, they each joined him in this endeavor to make it very successful. Older brother Ralph Jr. chose California to live, where he developed better sound systems and recorders for movie studios. Bill was the first to return and joined his father in management. Louise Levine, company secretary, told "Mister" Wells, his father, not realizing it, that he had to pay Bill for his work, whence a wage was negotiated. Bill always called his father, Mister Wells.

Bill's twin Norman, who graduated from the University of Illinois and had lived in the ATO fraternity house returned to establish a Chapter at Monmouth College. His expertise was selling. Younger brother, Adrian, also graduated as an engineer from the University and was a "Sea Bee" in the Navy. He was ideal to run the plant, making many cost-saving adjustments. There was a younger sister, Dorothy, whose husband is a professor at the University of Missouri.

Bill Wells on kitchen patio, 1990.

Bill married Roberta "Bobby" McVey shortly after he was drafted into military service and they had their first son of four. Bill Jr. went into school administration after a year or two of teaching. He became Principal of the Murray, Kentucky, High School. He was "Rotarian of the Year" in 2002. Rob, the second son was a graduate engineer, and worked for AT&T laying the Atlantic cable. He lived on ship board months at a time. Randy, the third son was a broker on the Chicago Board of Trade. All boys were married except Dyke, "J.D.", whose music involvement took him to New York City for several years. He now lives near his mother in Rio Verde, Arizona and works for Walgreen Drugs.

After the boys were settled in school, Bobby returned to Monmouth College to graduate with son #1 (Bill jr.) and receive her teaching certificate. She taught until retirement the 6th grade at Willitts Grade school in Monmouth.

Eventually the Dog Food Business, still called Wells, was sold to National Can Company, after expanding into plants in Tennessee and Wisconsin. Bill stayed on as an executive with the buyers, National Can Co., and traveled each week to Chicago. He became a golf enthusiast and moved from the mansion on East 2nd Avenue to a new home adjoining Monmouth Country Club. They bought a retirement home in a new Golfing Development, called Rio Verde, and have remained there. Bill passed away and was placed in the lot they had previously purchased next to their church in Rio Verde.

ALAN WELTY - Alan Welty, son of Allen Melvin Welty and Betty Jean (Lusk) Welty, was born May 13, 1949 in Monmouth Hospital at 515 East Euclid Ave. Monmouth, Il. Alan had one sister, Jennifer Jean (Welty) Clark. As a young boy, Alan first attended Muddy Corners, a one-room school two miles North of Berwick, Illinois, on the West side of curve. Alan went through first grade at Muddy Comers and then attended Alexis schools through 8th grade. He then attended Monmouth High School where he graduated in 1968. His trade was Tool and Die and his profession was Illinois Correctional Officer. Alan's hobby was archery, trap and skeet shooting.

Alan's grandparents were Melvin Allen Welty and Mildred Carlette (Carstensen) Welty and Wilson Thomas Lusk and Ada Erma (Loptien) Lusk.

Alan Welty family, 1983

Alan's great-grandparents were John Jacob Welty and Ida Bella (Allen) Welty and Carl Carstensen and Amalia Matilda (Lepper) Carstensen and Harvey Wilson Lusk and Mary Evaline (Estell) Lusk and Edward Charles Loptien and Nellie Threasa (Fetterley) Loptien.

Susan Elizabeth (Becker) Welty, daughter of Harry Samuel Becker and Mary Josephine (Goranson) Becker, was born January 8, 1951 in Monmouth Hospital at 515 East Euclid Ave. Monmouth, Il. She had three brothers, John Dorn Becker, Mark Darren Becker, Harry Kevin Becker, and two sisters, Alice Agneta Becker and Idalu Josephine (Becker) Tumquist. Susan began her education in Dumas, Texas and went through the 10th grade there. She went to Monmouth High School her junior year and her senior year at Yorkwood High School where she graduated in 1969. After high school Susan studied at Carl Sandburg Community College in Galesburg, Il, and graduated in 1973 as a Registered Nurse. She first found employment at the Community Medical Center 1000 West Harlem Ave. Monmouth, Il, and then to OSF St. Mary Medical Center at 3333 North Seminary St. Galesburg, Il. Susan's hobbies were needlework, gardening and reading.

Susan's grandparents were Samuel Dorn Becker and Matilda Josephine (Sundin) Becker and Johan Gotthild Goranson and Ida Elda (Hull) Goranson.

Susan's great grandparents were Jacob Becker and Mary (Doran) Becker and Gustav Sundin and Anna Matilda (Seaburg) Sundin and John Peter Goranson and Agneta Josephine (Carlsdotter) Goranson and Alvey Pierce Hull and Susan Elizabeth (Roop) Hull.

Alan and Susan were married September 12, 1970 at the First Christian Church 201 East Second Ave. Monmouth, Il. Their first daughter, Malinda Marie Welty, was born January 21, 1971 at Cottage Hospital, 695 North Kellogg St. Galesburg, Il. Eight years later, their second daughter, Tristen Sue Welty was born on February 24, 1979 at OSF St. Mary Medical Center at 3333 North Seminary St. Galesburg, Il.

Mindy married Keith Myers on November 6, 1994. They had three children; Devon Elizabeth Myers, Kyle William Myers, and Connor Samuel Meyers. Tristen had one daughter Lauren Josephine Welty.

ROY FRANKLINN WERTZ - Wertz, Roy Franklin, the oldest child of John (of Wertzville, PA) and Martha (Lackey) Wertz (of Hale Township) was born in Hale Township, Warren County on November 8, 1902. He had one sister, Anna, and four brothers, George, Claire, John and James. During his childhood the family moved to a home on South 11th Street in Monmouth, where Roy lived while attending school. Prior to 1920 the family left Warren County and relocated to Mercer County. On July 3, 1926 Roy married Violette Ralston. They established housekeeping in rural New Windsor, Mercer County, Illinois, where Roy worked many jobs, including working for the rail road, coal mining and farming. One daughter, Shirley, was born of this marriage.

Shirley attended school in rural Mercer County and graduated from New Windsor High School. On January 11, 1949, Shirley married Dale Dunlap, also of New Windsor. Their first home was in Viola, Mercer County, Illinois. They were engaged in farming and resided there until February of 1958. Many years after the Wertz family had left Warren County, this extension of the family returned. Dale, Shirley and their three children, Judi Larry and Jill settled on a farm in rural Warren County south of Little York, where Dale continued to farm and in later years worked for Munson Transportation and Shirley worked as a custodial engineer. The continue to reside in this home south of Little York.

Their first daughter, Judi attended grades 1 through 6 at Pleasant Green School and graduated from Yorkwood Jr. Sr. High School. After graduation she married Rick Anderson of rural Little York and they made their home in Monmouth where they are still residents with their daughter Erin, who is a senior at Monmouth High School. Judi is employed in the admissions office of Monmouth College and Rick is an independent contractor.

Their son, Larry, also attended Pleasant Green School for grades 1 through 6 and graduated from Yorkwood Jr. Sr. High School. After graduation Larry married Karen Wotherspoon of Normal, Illinois. They currently reside in Jamestown, North Carolina and have two sons, Justin, who is a senior at North Carolina State University and Mark is attending the Universal Training Institute in Houston, Texas. Larry is employed at the corporate office of Syngenta Company in Greensboro, NC and Karen is a computer programmer for Raintree, Inc.

Their youngest daughter, Jill, attended Little York Grade School and graduated from Yorkwood High School also. She married Terry Morris of Monmouth and they reside in Monmouth, with their daughter, Megan, a junior at Monmouth High School. Jill is the Warren County Circuit Clerk and Terry is employed as a groundskeeper for Monmouth College.

HOWARD WESTERFIELD - Howard Westerfield was born in Monmouth, Warren County, Illinois, March 21, 1917, to William Franklin, "Frank" and Ethel June (Thomas) Westerfield. They were married in Monmouth on August 27, 912. Howard attended Willits, Garfield, Central Junior High and Monmouth High School.

He was employed at Johnson Bros. Cigar Store before being called into service. June 25, 1941 he was sent to Camp Callan, near San Diego, Ca., for preliminary training. October 20, 1941, he was sent to the Aleutian Islands to join Battery C, 206th C.A. (A.A.), as an anti-aircraft gunner. On January 30, 1944 he was headed home on furlough, six cars of the train he was on, derailed at Great Falls, Montana. After his furlough, he was sent to Fort Bliss, Texas. July 16, 1945 he witnessed the test of the atomic bomb, but didn't know what it was until after Japan was hit. October 6, 1945, he was honorably discharged from the army.

Howard Westerfield

August 18, 1946 Howard and Mabel (Grimsley) Westerfield were married in Monmouth. They lived here until September 1956, when they moved to Henderson County, Il., and returned to Monmouth, August, 1965. They were the parents of two children. Janis born December 1, 1949, Steven, November 19, 1950, both born in Monmouth. They attended grade school and part of high school in Henderson County, but graduated from Monmouth High School. 1971, Janis graduated from Augustana College, Rock Island, Illinois. She married Craig Erickson, August 28, 1971, in Monmouth. They moved to LaCrosse, Wi. where Janis was employed as a Medical Technologist. In 1974 they moved to Chaseburg, Wi.

Steve graduated in 1971 from Southern Illinois University, Carbondale, Il. He became a pilot based at San Juan, Puerto Rico. Later decided to attend John Marshall Law School, where he graduated and passed the Illinois Bar July 7, 1978. As flying was his passion, in 1981, he moved to Houston, Texas to fly for Continental Airlines, where he continues to fly. He never married.

Howard retired from International Harvester Co., East Moline, Il., on December 1975. He died in Monmouth, on November 25, 1986. He was the grandfather of two, Bryan Erickson, born, December 3, 1977, and Erin Erickson, born February 22, 1982, both at LaCrosse.

Howard's grandparents, George and Elizabeth (Mulligan) Westerfield married in Monmouth on January 9, 1879. George was born January 27, 1851, in Canton, 11. At the age of one, he came with his parents to Monmouth. July 28, 1883 he filled out Homestead Entry papers, but didn't move to the 160-acre land at Knox County, Verdigre, Nebraska until February 15, 1884. Three of their children were born in Monmouth; Mary, Frank, and Frederick, two more in Nebraska. The first born in Nebraska lived two years and the last born was Cora. Their mother died in Nebraska in 1893, she was born in New York City, 1853. After her death George sold their land and the family moved back to Monmouth in 1894. George died in Monmouth on November 25, 1930.

Howard's father was the second child of George and Elizabeth. Frank, born September 26, 1881, and died January 21, 1969. June was born, June 1, 1890, died September 15, 1973. Their children were Richard, Virginia, Howard, Byron and Barbara, all born in Monmouth. J. Lillian Thomas was a stepdaughter of Frank's.

MABEL (GRIMSLEY) WESTERFIELD - Mabel (Grimsley) Westerfield was born November 26, 1920, McLeansboro, Hamilton County, Il. to Guy and Edna (Mullen) Grimsley. The family lived here until moving to Ponemah, Warren County about, 1924. Their father bought an acreage with house and grocery store, which included a post office. Their father also worked for Fletcher Smith, as a grain elevator operator. It took a lot of jobs to make a living. He served in France during World War I, from October 5, 1918, until honorably discharged at Camp Grant, June 3, 1919. He had left for France eleven days before his brother, Vincent, died at Monmouth Hospital, during the flu epidemic. His widow was left with two children, Charles Norman and V. Dale. Avis was born two and a half months after his death. Guy married his brother's widow and raised two of his brother's children and four of their own. Charles was adopted by the father's Uncle Norman and Aunt Anna, and changed Charles' name to Norman Ethan Pinney.

Mabel (Grimsley) Westerfield

Guy and Edna were married in Monmouth, July 12, 1919. Their children were Mabel; Alta born June 16, 1922, McLeansboro; Charles born, November 14, 1925, Ponemah; Robert, May 16, 1927, Ponemah.

In Ponemah, most of the men were either employed as farmers or worked for the oil pumping station. When ever other station was closed, Ponemah was one to go. Families were either transferred, or out on their own. Their family moved to Monmouth in September 1933. During World War II, Dale served in the Army, Charles in the Marine's, and Robert in the Navy.

Guy, born to Charles Lewis and Effie (Pinney) Grimsley, January 29, 1889 in Warren County, and died in Galesburg, Illinois May 21, 1967. Edna, born April 8, 1888, Fulton County, Illinois, and died in Monmouth, November 10, 1983.

Mabel attended her first seven years of school at Liberty School, east of Ponemah. Eighth grade at Central Junior High and Monmouth High School. She was then employed as clerk at Kimble's Store until J.C. Penny Dept. Store opened their new store in Monmouth. She was hired as a clerk, then in two months became cashier and bookkeeper for seven years. She gave three months notice before leaving the company in February 1949. She married Howard Westerfield in Monmouth, August 18, 1946. Their first child, Janis was born December 1, 1949 and Steven born, November 19, 1950, both in Monmouth. The family moved to Henderson County, Illinois in 1956. When Steve became interested in flying, we moved back to Monmouth in 1965 to be near their airport for his flight training.

In late 1961, Mabel went back to work, and was hired as a bookkeeper at the Daily Review Atlas. Agar Packing came to Monmouth in 1966 and she was hired as office clerk. Agar was sold to Wilson Packing in 1968. Here she worked as billing and invoicing clerk, until retiring in 1983.

Howard, born March 21, 1917, died November 25, 1986 in Monmouth.

JOEL AND ELIZABETH WHITE - Joel V. White, born in Virginia in 1834, came to Warren County from near Firfield, Iowa in the 1870s with his children, Arabella, 10; James, 6; Carrie, 2; his wife, Mary Elizabeth Hall of Fulton County, Illinois, having passed away in summer 1869 at age 32. Shortly thereafter, Joel moved to the Swan Creek area. James stayed with his father and the girls were taken in by family friends to raise. Arabella married Oris Hoyt and they became the parents of two sons, Lee and Guy. Lee attended medical school in Chicago, became a physician, and practiced many years in Roseville. He and Bessie Jones Hoyt's two sons, John and Robert, also became a physician, and practiced many years in Roseville. Guy Hoyt and his wife, Gladys, settled in the Los Angeles, California area where Guy had a career in education administration. They had one daughter, Helen, who became an accomplished musician.

James and Addie White and family

James married Susan Adeline ("Addie") Blair, also of Swan Creek, on October 8, 1884 at the home of Willia N. Whitaker, who performed the ceremony. They settled in Swan Creek area where James farmed, making frequent trips to Kansas to visit Addie's parents, Alex and Melissa Blair, who had moved there. Two of Jim and Addie's children, Zoa and Joel, were born near Walton, Kansas during their visits. In the late 1890s, they moved to Monmouth where their last two children, Lee and Clarence were born, Jim working at a variety of jobs – clay miner (east of 11th Street), a milk deliveryman, the pottery. 1922 found them living at 826 South A Street where Addie succumbed to cancer on November 29 at age 57. She is buried in Monmouth Cemetery as is James who passed away on June 22, 1954 in Ft. Madison, Iowa where he had lived since his remarriage to Mary Elizabeth ("Lizzie") Means Blair, the widow of Addie's brother, Oscar. Jim and Addie's children were Zoa (George), Jessie (Witt) Pearl (Van Tine), Joel, Ira, Ruby (Coburn-Zimmerman), Lee and Clarence. All lived in Monouth until early adulthood. Of Jim and Addie's 28 grandchildren, 13 survive at this writing, 8 of whom live in this area: Roy and Gerald Van Tine, rural Gladsone, Robert Van Tine, Stronghurst, Helen Van Tine, Monmouth, Josephine Paris, Kirkwood, Dorothy Patton, Galesburg, and Guy and Glenn White, Quad-Cities. Other are in Naperville, Arizona, Texas and Michigan.

Joel V. White remarried on November 15, 1874 to Laura Lieurance, daughter of a neighboring Swan Creek family and 19 years his junior, and they had four children, Bruce and Cecil living to adulthood. Joel died at his home in rural Roseville in 1897 at 63. His widow subsequently married Joseph Kidd, had a family and remained in touch with Jim and Addie's family, to whom she was affectionately known as "Aunt Laurie."

RALPH AND MARTHA WILLIAMS MCCLINTOCK WHITEMAN - Once upon a time in Monmouth, IL. a farmer's daughter, Martha (Williams) McClintock and a banker's son, Ralph Whiteman, were maried on September 7, 1986 at Faith United Presbyterian Church. On their first anniversary one year later they were the parents of nine children! To be historically correct, they already had nine kids when they were married from previous marriages; Martha had 5 sons and Ralph had 3 daughters and 1 son. From that group by 2002, there had come 13 grandchildren including one set of twins.

Ralph and Martha Whiteman

Martha Jean was born in Swan Creek, IL. on February 25, 1929 to George and Ruth (Raymond) Williams. George was a tenant farmer in western IL. Ralph Edwin was born on February 12, 1928 in Monmouth to Wendell and Gladys Lucille (Zimmerman) Whiteman. Wendell was president of Monmouth Homestead and Loan for 25 years. Martha had 2 brothers, Leo and Gail, as did Ralph, Donald and Richard.

Martha's major career achievement, other than birthing a basketball team, was owner of McClintock Realty for a number of years. One of her interests, golf, resulted in a city championship. She worked both as a nurse's aid and for the county government in her early life. She served on the board of the Monmouth Country Club, Chamber of Commerce and Warren Achievement Center and was president of Today's Woman Investment Club as well as being both elder and deacon of Faith Church. She was an accomplished and dedicated quilter and participated in many quilt shows.

Ralph succeeded his father as president of the Monmouth Homestead and Loan. During his 35 years with the firm it grew from 5 million in assets to 110 million and became Security Savings Bank. He also served 42 years in the U.S. Navy and Naval Reserve, rising in rank from Seaman Recruit to Captain. He headed or served on the board of directors of many community activities such as the Y.M.C.A., Buchanan Center, Chamber of Commerce, Monmouth Country Club, Monmouth College Senate, Faith United Presbyterian Church, the Library and the Economic Development committee. Desireing to pay back the community in which he was raised, he served as a public school tutor and art presenter for many years and founded the Halls of Achievement for the Monmouth public schools and Monmouth College. He participated in organized athletics into his 70's including college sports and national Senior Olympics competition. His undergraduate work was at Monmouth College and his graduate work at Indiana University. The youngest person ever to work at the Monmouth Post Office, he started at the age of fourteen during WWII.

Their children chose careers such as judge, business owner, mechanical engineer, college professor, teacher of disabled students, railroad conductor, health advocate and automotive services.

Although they traveled extensively through business and military responsibilities as well as recreationally, they both always eagerly returned to the area of their lifetime roots.

RICHARD AND PATRICIA WHITEMAN - Richard L. Whitman was born January 11, 1947, in Peoria Illinois, and Patricia E. Thackrey was born September 5, 1949, in Newton Illinois. Richard graduated in 1965 from Canton High School; Patricia graduated in 1967 from North Clay Community High School, in Louisville, Illinois. They met at Eastern Illinois University, where Richard graduated as valedictorian 1969. Patricia graduated in 1970. They initially lived in Chicago, Illinois, where Richard was a student at the Northwestern University School of Law, from which he graduated 1972 Cum Laude; Patricia worked as a statistician in the Investment Research Department of Harris Trust and Savings Bank.

After a brief stay in Louisville, Illinois, they moved in November 1973, to Monmouth where Richard joined the firm of Kritzer, Stansell, and Critser. In 1978, Richard became a partner in the firm which is now known has Stansell, Whitman & Baber. He practices in a general practice which includes personal injury, general litigation, probate, estates and trust, divorce and family law, bankruptcy, representation of banks, collections, and real estate. In addition to practice of law, Richard has also authored a chapter on "Actions in Accounting" in the Illinois Institute of Continuing Legal Educations book known as *Chancery and Special Remedies*, as well as articles on warranties granted in the sale of a new home, which appeared in 1979 in the Illinois Trial Lawyers Journal, an article in the Monmouth Review Atlas, in May 1994, entitled, "Talk that is Crude will Get you Sued." Patricia has taught mathematics at the Central Jr. High school and currently works as secretary and receptionist, in the office of Stansell, Whitman & Baber.

The Whitmans have two children. Richard Whitman, Jr. who was born January 12, 1979, graduated in 1997 from Monmouth High School, and in the spring of 2002, from Western Illinois University, where he majored in Business Finance.

The Whitman's second son, Alexander C. Whitman, was born May 15, 1984, and graduated from Monmouth High School, in the Class of 2002. He plans to attend Illinois State University and major in Psychology.

Since December of 1980, the Whitmans have made their home in the house at 324 North 2nd Street, which was built in 1877 by the Buck family. Both Richard and Patricia, are founding members of the Couples of Monmouth Investment Club, where Richard has served as president, and Patricia as secretary. Both of the Whitmans and their sons are regular and active members of the First Christian Church, of Monmouth, Illinois.

WILLIS AND MARY WILEY - Reuben Wiley married Martha Brown in Warren County on February 11, 1875. They had a son and two daughters. Their son Thomas Willis Wiley (1/8/1878) married Mary Francina Ramsey (11/26/1886), daughter of Catherine Ramsey; Willis and Mary lived on the family farm near Little York, Illinois. Willis and Mary had five daughters, Nelle, Bird, Martha, Ruth, and Catherine. Nelle was killed in an automobile accident the summer following her graduation from Iowa State University at Ames. Bird married Albert McCutchan, who farmed in Mercer County; they had three sons, Maurice, Stephen, and Tom. Martha married William Davey of Pittsburg; where the couple lived with their children, Ruth, Rick, and Tom. Ruth Wiley and Jack Woodward, of Monmouth, married and later moved to California. They had no children. Catherine married Max Hamilton of Avon, Illinois and had seven children, Martha Kai, Mary Chris, Catherine Marie, Constance Sue, William Wiley, Corrine Bird, and John Butler. The Hamilton family resided in Warren County.

Catherine Hamilton is the only surviving child of Willis and Mary Wiley. She is currently working as House Director for a sorority at the U of Illinois and lives at 302 East Armory, Champaign, Illinois 61820.

ABRAHAM ALLEN WILLET - Abraham Allen Willet was born on June 20, 1825 in Alabama and first moved to Mercer County, Illinois in 1841. His two uncles and father, Andrew, came form England in 1818. Andrew lived in Alabama, Tennessee and Texas. Andrew died of an illness while serving in Sam Houston's Army on June 28, 1836. Abraham's mother, Julia, and seven children stayed in Texas till she remarried and they moved to Arkansas. Julia had six more children and they were forced from their home during a Civil War battle in 1862. Julia moved to her sons home in Illinois that year and remained till 1865 when she moved to Kansas.

Top row: Andrew Willett, Ulysses Grant Willett, James Clifford Willett, Daniel Perry Willett, Schuyler Sylvester Willett. Bottom row: Catherine Matilda Willett, Katherine Matilda 'Green' Willett (mother), Lucy Gertrude Willett

Abraham married Martha Sprague in 1849 and they had six children before Martha died in 1864. Abraham's second marriage was to Katherine or Catherine Green and they had eight children. Abraham died in New Windsor on December 31, 1899 and Katherine died in New Windsor July 26, 1919. Both are buried in a cemetery southwest of New Windsor along with Abraham's two brothers and one sister.

Abraham's twelfth child was Andrew Willett born January 12, 1875 in Mercer County. Andrew was a farmer and later a trucker. At one time delivered coal to the power plants in Alexis. Andrew married Maude Stickle in 1897 and they had ten children. Maude's father was in the cavalry for four years during the Civil War and is buried in Henderson Cemetery. Andrew and Maude are both buried in Rio. He died June 16, 1958 and she passed away February 20, 1966.

Floyd Webster Willett was the second child of Andrew and Maude. Floyd was born March 22, 1900 in Mercer County and died November 19, 1973. His wife Ellen Anna Amanda Johnson was born April 16, 1902 Mercer County and died January 25, 1987. During the first winters after he married, Floyd worked in the coal mine outside of Alexis. He was a life long farmer and rented a farm one mile from a Mister Anderson and they raised three sons there. Floyd purchased a farm seven miles south of Alexis in 1957 and farmed there the rest of his career. On retiring they moved to Alexis onto property formerly owned by Ellen's parents John Johnson. A couple years later they moved to a house six blocks awa and lived there till their death. Ellen was born at home and never had a birth certificate.

Floyd Webster Willett's first son, Floyd LeDale Willett was born October 21, 1921 and went into the Army during World War II. He sereved in Europe with the 101st Airborne. He farmed for a few years and then moved to Monmouth in 1956 and worked as a driver for Standard Oil and Monmouth Fruit Company. He married Ruby E. Anderson of Alexis in 1942. Their four children Gerald 1946, Larry 1947, Anna 1951 and Anita 1952, were raised in Monmouth.

Floyd Webster Willetts' second son, Lyle Duane Willett was born August 1927. Lyle started out farming in the Galesburg area. He retired from Moormans feed mill and lives in Alpha. He and Betty Lundquist had four children.

Floyd Webster's third son was Donald, born October 1931. Donald farmed, worked in a Galesburg factory and raised four children with Mary Miller. He is retired and lives south of Monmouth near Roseville. Donald served in the Korean War.

Gerald Willett lived and worked in Monmouth till his death in 1975. His four sons live in the Monmouth area.

Larry Willett went into the army in 1966 then returned in 1972. Larry graduated from Western Illinois University and returned to the Army in 1980. He is still on active duty and will retire about 2004. While in Monmouth Larry had a paper route, worked at a drive-in and for Krogers in high school and also 1972 to 1976. Larry is a helicopter pilot and maintenance test pilot. Larry was in Vietnam, Japan, three tours in Korea, six locations in the United States, and deployed to Bosnia. Four of his children live in Galesburg and Monmouth, one child lives in Denver, Colorado.

Anna Willett is a long time nurse in Galesburg and presently lives on a farm with her husband Larry Doubet outside North Henderson. Anna had three children by her first marriage and two of them live in Galesburg.

Anita Willett married a career army man, Paul Creek from Alexis. Anita left Monmouth after her marriage and returned more than 20 years later to Alexis. Anita and Paul then moved to Alaska and Paul works at Fort Waignright. Anita is a long time nurse and they had five children.

PAUL AND JOAN (HINTON) WILLIAMS - Paul Emerson Williams was born Feb. 20, 1931 in hospital at Canton, IL to Gilford & Alma (Kemper) Williams. They lived at Fairview, IL at the time. He graduated 1949 from VIT HS, Table Grove, IL. He went into the Army and served in Germany three years. His parents had moved to Kirkwood, IL in 1950 and ran the Williams' Service Station. He came to Kirkwood after he was discharged in 1954 were he ran the garage until 1967. He then worked as a Mechanic at IAAP at Middletown, IA until he retired in 1995. The last several years he has been Campground Host at Keithsburg, IL. Paul is a Third Degree Mason in the A Lincoln Lodge, NO. 518 in Kirkwood, IL. He has been Sec., and is a Past Master.

Williams family. Paul, Dan, Julie, Rick, Mitzi, Jeff, Brandon, Andy, Leta, Roger, Megan Brooke, Sharee, Alice Hinton, Joan and Tracey.

He married Alice Joan Hinton June 12, 1955 at Kirkwood, IL. She was born Jan. 20,1936 in rural Canton, MO to Curtis Aldwin & Alice Deara (Risk) Hinton. They came to Kirkwood in Nov of 1945. Joan is the eldest of 9 sisters and brothers. Joan graduated from Kirkwood HS 1954. Joan taught Sunday School for a number of years. She was Den Mother, Cub Master and Committee member for the Cub Scouts. She was also a Girl Scout Leader. She went to work at Glastex Co., in Monmouth, IL in 1972. Went to work at Admiral's in Galesburg, IL 1974 until retiring in 1998.

They are members of the Westminster Presbyterian Church. They are the parents of five children.

1. Roger Lee born March 20,1956. He graduated from Yorkwood H.S. in 1978. He did odd jobs and he worked for the Kirkwood Park Distract and served on the board. He served on the Warren Co. Fire Protection Dept. He served as assistant and Chief. He joined the A. Lincoln Masonic Lodge #518. Served all post and is Past Master. He married April 6, 1997 in Peoria, IL to Leta Patricia Hearne born Dec. 19,1959 to Patrick and Mary (Wagner) Hearne. They live in Peoria, IL.

2. Glen Andrew born Sept. 23,1957. He graduated 1976 from Yorkwood H.S. He lived 20 years in Fl. Returned to Kirkwood in 1997 doing odd jobs.

3. Richard Paul born April 9, 1962 married March 22, 1997 in Monmouth, IL to Tracey Ann Skees born March 17, 1971, 3 children.

4. Mitzi Jo born June 2, 1967 married Nov. 23, 1985 in Kirkwood, IL to Jeffery Martin Sharer born March 20, 1966 They farm in the Bald Buff area. They are very active in the school. Mitzi is on the school board at Yorkwood. They have Megan, 1988; Brooke, 1990 and Brandon, 1994.

5. Daniel James was born May 19, 1969. Married July 6,1996 in Monmouth, IL to Julia Sueann Fillman. Julia was born June 17, 1973 to Don and Kathy (Stacker) Fillman. Dan is a Policeman in Galesburg, IL. Julia is an elementary teacher in Monmouth, IL. They have Jacob, 1998; Makenzie, 1999 and new one in 2002.

RICHARD AND TRACEY WILLIAMS - Rich Paul Williams was born April 9, 1962 at Monmouth Hospital Monmouth, IL to Paul and Joan Williams living in Kirkwood, IL. He graduated from Yorkwood H.S. 1980. He had been on the wrestling team. He and two other friends went to Denver, Col. and worked for a few months. He returned home to enter the US Coast Guard. Feb. 1982 he had his training in Alamoda, Cal. His last ship was Coast Guard Cutter Chase 718. He was discharged 1986 from Boston, Mass.

Rick, Tracey, Zach, Nate and Rachel Williams

He went to work for Preferred Cable Co. And worked in several states. In Aug. 1990 he entered school at Hamilton Tech in Davenport, IA and working for Cox Cable Co. He graduated from there Dec. 1991. He got a job working for Motorola in Mt. Pleasant, IA. In 2000 Motorola sold Mt. Pleasant division to Celestrica. He got a job with them. He drives from Monmouth every day.

He met Tracey Skees at the wedding of his cousin Matt Hinton and Jenny Garner. Jenny and Tracey went all though school together. Rick and Tracey Skees were married March 22, 1997 at the Heritage United Presbyterian Church in Monmouth, IL.

Tracey Anne Skees was born March 17, 1971 to Bruce and Penny (Morris) Skees. Penny was married several times and Tracey wanted t live with Grandparents, Dick and Pauline (Smith) Morris in her later four years. She graduated 1989 from onmouth H.S., Monmouth, IL. She graduated from WIU in Macomb, 1993. She started teaching English in Monmouth H.S. Aug. 1993. She was also the Cheerleading Coach for five years. She got her tenure 1995.

They brought the house at the corner of 229 South 9th St. and Second Ave. in Monmouth, IL in Oct. 1997.

They have twin sons and a daughter. 1. Nathan Paul born Nov. 12, 1998 at Cottage Hospital, Galesburg, IL. 2. Zachary Eric born Nov. 12, 1998 at Cottage Hospital, Galesburg, IL. 3. Rachel Anne born Feb. 8, 2001 at Cottage Hospital, Galesburg, IL.

GEORGE H. WILLARD (1877-1965) - On April 27, 1877, George H. Willard was born in Greenbush Township to William Willard and Elizabeth (McClurg) Willard.

He received his education at the Starr School in the southeast corner of Warren County. He was an active member, as well as President and Secretary of the Starr Literary Society organized around November 1893. This is clearly documented by two original secretarial books of the society now in my possession.

My childhood memories are filled with stories he would tell of the building of the covered bridge, south of the Village of Greenbush, township of Warren County. I also remember stories of his days as an assistant in the sorghum mill.

George lived with his father and mother until he married Bertha May Matthews of Roseville, IL in October 1916. Except for two years when he operated a meat market in Ellisville, IL, he was a farmer by trade. The first farm he rented was the Whistler farm just north of now Swan Lake. Following that he moved to the George Loftis farm in Swan Township; from there he rented a farm now owned by Phillip Kramer, north from where the Starr School stood. In 1924, he migrated back to the homeplace where he was born in Greenbush Township.

George and Bertha May Willard had 3 children: William Gerald Willard born 1917, Greenbush Township (Warren County). Married Dorothy White, reside in Avon and have two children, Beryl and Kathleen.

Mary Alice Willard (Smith) born 1920, Swan Township (Warren County). Married Paul Smith, reside in Galesburg and have three children, Ronald, Deborah and Gregory.

Martha Elizabeth Willard (Wolf) born 1922, Greenbush Township (Warren County). Married Leland Wolf, reside in Good Hope and have five children, Marsha, Ralph, Carol, Marilyn and Willard.

George H. Willared died July 14, 1965 and is buried at Avon Cemetery in Avon, IL. His wife Bertha died March 9, 1976, and is also buried at Avon Cemetery in Avon, IL.

Submitted by Gerald Willard

ISAAC NEWTON WILLIS - Willis, Isaac Newton, the son of Edward and Margaret (Taggart) Willis was born in McDonough County, Ill. February 9, 1874. He married Cora Eldora Dennis, daughter of Nathan and Martha (Ash) Dennis on March 19,1903 in Monmouth in the Baldwin Hotel. Cora E. Dennis was born February 16, 1876 in McDonough County as one of 12 children who lived around Good Hope, Ill.

Isaac and Cora purchased a farm two miles northeast of Monmouth in approximately 1903. They built a new home on that site in 1940-41, which is located north of the Monmouth Airport at 810 210th Ave, Monmouth, Ill.

Isaac and Cora had three children, twin daughters Faye and Fern, born December 11, 1907 who both died in childhood, and one son, Everett Dennis born December 12, 1910 all in Monmouth, Ill. Isaac died January 14, 1941 from a heart attack while building the current house on the aforementioned farm. He served as road commissioner and also acted as chairman of the Good Roads committee of the Monmouth Chamber of Commerce. Isaac was also elected chairman of the Warren County Republican Central committee, a position he held for four years. He also campaigned for Illinois State Representative of the 32nd District in 1916, but was defeated in the primary election.

Cora E. Willis died October 17, 1959 at the age of 83 at her home, where she lived with her son Everett and his wife Ila Mae (Powell) Willis.

Everett D. Willis was reared and educated in Monmouth and farmed in the Monmouth area. He married Ila Mae Powell on April 25, 1941 in Monmouth. Ila Powell was the daughter of William H. and Hilda E. (Carlson) Powell of Alexis, Ill. Everett sold John Deere machinery in Stronghurst until the death of his father Isaac when he returned to manage the farming operation in January 1941.

Everett and Ila had two children: Kent Everett born December 31, 1944 and Karen Jean born June 7, 1947. Kent E. Willis married Kathryn Jean Winbigler daughter of Lloyd and Pauline (Lantz) Winbigler on June 16, 1967 in Gerlaw, Il. Kathryn was born September 24, 1947 as the second child to Dorothy Kathryn (Munson) Winbigler, first wife of Lloyd Winbigler, who later died due to complications from childbirth.

Karen Jean married Lou Fideli in 1968. They had two children: Andrea born October 26, 1974 and Mark born June 29, 1976. Karen and Andrea live in Schererville, IN. Mark resides in Knoxville, TN. Karen has been employed since 1985 as an English teacher in the Lake Central School Corporation, St. John, IN.

Kent and Kathryn had four sons: Craig Evertt born March 9, 1970; Chad Ryan born December 2, 1972; Cameron Lloyd born May 8, 1975; and Kent Christopher (K.C.) born October 11, 1979, all in Monmouth, Ill. Craig married Jill Schultz August 20, 1994. They have two sons: Reid Everett born October 12, 1997 and Jay Craig born May 26, 2000. Chad married Jolene Graham August 3, 1996 and Cameron married Stacey Young June 16, 2001.

JOHN SOUTHERLAND AND MARY WINBIGLER - Elias Winbigler (born 1815 Frederick, Maryland) married Amanda Gordon (born 1815 Springboro, OH) and came to Warren County in 1859 from Sullivan County, IN, settling on a farm in sections 28 & 29 of Spring Grove Township. Elias and Amanda had 7 children: John Sutherland, the only child to have children, illuminated below; Chalmers Baldridge, born 10 October 1843 died 20 March 1927, a

John Sutherland Winbigler and Mary Winbigler family. (l. to r.) Front row: Mary, Jessie, Dr. Edward Sutherland. Middle row: Guy Gordon, Dr. Bryce Rex, Roy, Frank Max. Top row: Hugh Draper, Harry Lloyd.

farmer; Gordon Orlando, born 26 March 1847, served through the Civil War in the Union Army and then died August 1868 at the hands of Indians on the Republic River in Kansas; Julia Emazetta, born 10 March 1849 died 20 June 1922; Dr. Clarence Willard, born 13 September 1851 died 26 June 1939; Anna Jane, born 13 February 1854 died 6 October 1875; and Alice, born 1 March 1857 died 27 May 1941, who held the chair of Math and Astronomy at Monmouth College for several years. Elias died in 1864; Amanda followed in 1874.

Their son John Sutherland Winbigler, born Sullivan County IN 3 November 1841, left Monmouth College his sophomore year and enlisted in Company 1, Fiftieth Illinois Volunteer Infantry. He fought at Forts Henry and Donaldson with Grant's Army and participated in the battles of Shiloh and Corinth. He re-enlisted in 1864 and served in General Sherman's Atlanta campaign and the March to the Sea. John enlisted as a private, was promoted corporal 25 November 1862; made fourth sergeant 21 October 1864; and was finally a first lieutenant 14 June 1865.

On 20 February 1867, John married Mary Louise Small born 11 July 1847 Washington County NY. John and Mary had 9 children: Dr. Edward Sutherland born 24 November 1867 died 12 February 1934 Alexis; Guy Gordon born 27 June 1869 died 1 December 1938, a farmer who lost his arm in a threshing machine in 1909; Hugh Draper born 2 November 1870 died 11 July 1956 Bayfield WI; Roy born 6 January 1873 died 20 April 1938, a farmer in Sumner Township; John Carl born 1 February 1876 died 4 March 188 1; Dr. Bryce Rex born 19 January 1878 died 20 November 1929 Aledo, Mercer Co., IL; Frank Max born 5 August 1880 died 22 May 1963, fanner, teacher and Warren County School Superintendent 1919-1943; Jessie born 22 April 1883 died 11 February 1963 and Harry Lloyd born 21 May 1889 died 16 August 1963.

John Sutherland Winbigler died 30 December 1897; his wife Mary died 1942.

Harry Lloyd, their ninth child, married Bertie Mabel Bates (born Bond County IL 3 October 1892) 4 October 1917. They had 5 children: Helen Louise, a nurse, born 11 September 1918; Lloyd Franklin, a farmer, born 7 December 1919; Martha F., a nurse, born 7 December 1921; Hugh Willard, a fanner, born 2 September 1924; and Marion Jean, born 12 November 1926.

Harry died 1963; his wife Bertie and their daughter Martha were killed in a car accident while traveling in Mexico in 1956.

Lloyd and Hugh bought the family farm in 1964.

LLOYD FRANKLIN WINBIGLER AND ORA (PAULINE) WINBIGLER - Lloyd Winbigler was born 9 December 1919 in Monmouth, IL, the son of Harry Lloyd Winbigler, born in Warren County, IL and Bertie Mabel Bates, born in Bond County, IL. Pauline (Boots) was born 27 September 1926, in Maquon, IL, the daughter of Earl Warren Lantz, born in Warren County, IL and Mazzie Lillian Black, born in Henderson County, IL.

Lloyd married Dorothy Kathryn Munson, on June 5, 1942 at the First Christian Church in Monmouth. They had two children: Carol June LeGate (Ronnie), born August 23, 1943 and Kathryn Jean Willis (Kent), born September 24, 1947. Dorothy Kathryn passed away September 26, 1947. She was born November 17, 1924.

Pauline married Donald Roberts on May 12, 1946 in Washington D.C., where Pauline was serving in the U.S. Navy during WWII. They had one son, Ronald (Ron) Greg Roberts (Carol Hayes), born April 3, 1948 in Monmouth, IL. They were divorced in 1950. Lloyd adopted Ron in 1958.

Lloyd Winbigler family. Front row: Roy, Randy. Middle row: Kathryn, Pauline, Lloyd, Donna. Back row: Ron, Regina, Carol, Rick.

Lloyd and Pauline were married July 28, 1951 at the Warren County Farm in Lenox Township, where Pauline's father was the superintendent. They had 5 children: Regina Kay Settlemeyer (Tom) of Charlotte NC, born April 4,1952; Richard Alan (Donna Morrison), born August 29, 1954; Donna Ann Ramsey (Bill), born August 15, 1956; Randall Kent (Janice Eckdahl), born August 19, 1959; and Roy Charles (Laura Lindsay), born August 23, 1961. The last child was born on the first child's birthday.

The family all attended Gerlaw Christian Church at Gerlaw, IL. Lloyd was an Elder, a Deacon, Chairman of the Board, and Treasurer. Pauline taught Sunday school, was a Deaconess, helped with Ladies Aid and Christian Women's Fellowship. All eight children were baptized at the church.

Lloyd has farmed his entire life with his brother, Hugh, on the farm, founded by his Great-grandfather, Elias, in 1857. He took on the responsibility of running the farm at the age of 16 when his father became ill. The farm is located 7 miles north of Monmouth on US Highway 67 in Sections 28 & 29 of Spring Grove Township. Pauline was a homemaker.

Lloyd and Pauline graduated from Monmouth High School and all the children graduated from Warren High School, 2 miles east of Monmouth.

Lloyd & Pauline have traveled extensively. They have been to all the states of the US, plus New Zealand, Australia, Panama Canal, Fuji Islands, Aruba, Barbados, Canada, and Mexico.

Both Lloyd and Pauline served their community extensively by serving on many boards and committees, being involved in numerous organizations throughout their lives.

RICHARD (RICK) AND DONNA WINBIGLER - Richard Winbigler was born 29 August 1954 in Monmouth, IL, the son of Lloyd Franklin Winbigler, born in Monmouth, IL, and Ora Pauline Lantz, born in Maquon, IL. Donna Morrison Winbigler was born 22 September 1956, in Moberly, MO, the daughter of Billy Vernon Morrison, born in Canton, MO, and Erma Leta Winget, born in Shelbina, MO.

Rick and Donna were married 21 July 1978 at the First Baptist Church in Monmouth. They have three children: Joel Morrison, born 22 March 1983, number one in his graduating class at Monmouth High School, a National Merit Scholar inducted into the Monmouth High School Academic Hall of Fame currently attending Iowa State University on a full four-year scholarship; Kyle Alan, born 15 December 1986, a sophomore at Monmouth High School who plays football and is working towards being an Eagle Scout; and Jenni Kristine, born Leap day, 29 February 1992, currently a fifth grader at Lincoln School in Monmouth.

Rick is the fifth of eight children. His brothers and sisters are Carol June LeGate (Ronnie); Kathryn Jean Willis (Kent); Ronald Greg (Carol Hayes); Regina Kay Settlemeyer (Tom); Donna Ann Ramsey (Bill); Randall Kent (Jan Eckdahl); and Roy Charles (Laura Lindsay).

Donna has one older sister, Debra Sue Hoff (Dave).

Back: Rick, Joel, Kyle. Front: Jenni, Donna.

Rick attended Warren School all 12 grades graduating in 1972. He attended Carl Sandburg College in Galesburg, IL, and graduated from Western Illinois University in Macomb, IL in 1979 with a BS in Ag Science. From 1974-1976, he worked at Smoler's Manufacturing in Monmouth. Rick has worked for Pioneer Hybrid from 1980-1985, Americana Seeds from 1985-1987, Farm Service Agency in 1988, and Warren County Soil and Water Conservation District from February, 1989 to the present as the Resource Conservationist.

Donna attended Monmouth schools, starting at Garfield Elementary and continuing at Central Jr. High. She graduated from Monmouth High School in the top 10 of her class in 1974; then with honors from Illinois State University, Normal, IL, in 1978 with a BS in Elementary Education. She taught 6th grade at Warren School from 1978 until 2002, at which time she started teaching middle school math there.

Rick and Donna attend the Gerlaw Christian Church which Rick has attended all his life, having been a Deacon, an Elder, Board Chairman, Board Vice Chairman, and currently serving as Church Secretary. Donna has been a Sunday School teacher, Church Organist, and Deaconess. Rick was baptized on April 10, 1966. Donna was baptized at the First Baptist Church in Monmouth on April 10, 1966. That is not a misprint! Their three children were all baptized at the Gerlaw Christian Church: Joel, 22 May 1994; Kyle 24 November 1996; and Jenni, 14 November 1999.

They have resided at 509 East 1st Avenue in Monmouth since November 1982.

WOOLLEY AND BUCK - Patty was born on March 17, 1919 to Lessie and Wilbur Woolley in Aurora, Illinois. She met John Haben in the grocery store in Little York where he was working for his mother, Nellie, and her husband, Ed Stotts. Patty would go to the store with her grandparents, Murray and Ada Buck. On a dare John asked Patty for a date one New Year's Eve. They took in a movie at the Rivoli Theater in Monmouth. Then they went to Hawcock's, a famous eating place then.

Wilbur and Lessie Buck were married on January 31, 1917 on her parents' farm west of Iveydor School which is on Route 135 south of Little York. (Now it has been made into a home.) Then they lived on a farm about a mile southeast of Oswego, IL that belonged to Wilbur's folks. They moved to Aurora and sold it to Wilbur and Lessie.

Wilbur Mitchem Woolley had been born on the Oswego farm on July 28, 1894 to Sarah Delphine (Delia) and Lewis (Doc) Woolley. Wilbur was the youngest of eight children. He died April 28, 1967 in Aurora, IL.

Lessie Louise had been born on the farm west of Iveydor school on December 29, 1896 to Ada and Murray Buck. She had two younger sisters. Lessie attended Iveydor School for eight years. Since they had only three years of high school at Little York, she went to a girls' school in Aurora, Illinois. Her roommate was a cousin of Wilbur's. She would go home on weekends with her, and it was there that they met. Lessie died November 19, 1973 in Aurora.

Her father, Murray Ellis Buck, was born July 17, 1866 to Julia Ann and, Cyrus Buck. Murray had a brother, Clarence Buck of Monmouth. Clarence became an Illinois State Senator. Clarence's son-in-law was Dr. Glenn Ebersole who practiced medicine in Monmouth. Murray died in January 1940.

Lessie's mother, Ada Gertrude, was born on June 20, 1869 in Monmouth to Catherine and Jacob Morningstar. She graduated from high school and attended Monmouth College. On November 3, 1892 she married Murray Buck. They lived on the farm west of the Iveydor School until they retired. Ada died December 28, 1945.

Murray's parents, Cyrus Leach Buck and Julia Ann Bake, were married in 1862. They lived on another farm southwest of Little York whose farmhouse was back in a lane that was lined with trees. Cyrus was born December 24, 1829 and died August 22, 1907 in Monmouth. Julia Ann Bake was born in 1833 in Oxford, Ohio. She died in 1902 in Monmouth.

Lessie's father, Jacob Morningstar, was born April 14, 1837 in Ohio. When he came to Monmouth he worked in a pottery plant on the northeast edge of Monmouth, not the one that exists today.

Lessie's mother, Catherine Strahorn, was born in Monmouth on November 27, 1842. Jacob and Catherine were married December 11, 1866. Jacob died in 1914, but Catherine lived to be 105 years old, dying on August 15, 1947 in Monmouth.

GEORGE K. YOUNG - George K. Young was born near London Mills to Lance and Helen Baumann Young on January 2, 1922. After his parents were divorced, he lived with his mother and brother, Donald L. Young, at their grandparents, Jake and Lillie Baumann, near Youngstown, IL. After his mother married George C. Anderson they lived in the Smithshire and Roseville areas. His half brother, Harold Lee Anderson, was 11 years younger than George. He attended Roseville High School, but came to his aunts home, Cleo, Iva and Barbara Shields, to finish at Monmouth High School in 1941. Always liking to work with his hands, George built the miniature House of seven Gables that was in Miss Anderson's class room for many years. After graduating he worked with Mr. Shields in the construction business.

George K and Helen L. Young, 1974

In 1942 he was drafted into the Army, and left for Ft. Lewis, WA. There he met up with his long time future friend, Paul Glenn of Plymouth. They served in Hawaii, the Pacific Theater and Japan, before being discharged in December 1945. After military service he returned to Monmouth and worked with Mr. Shields. He later completed 20 years of military service in the Reserves.

On October 26, 1947 George married Helen Geltmacher, the daughter of Orville G. and Mabel Beal Geltmacher of Good Hope. They made their home in Monmouth. They both loved to skate and spent many hours at the Rainbow Roller Rink, as long as his health permitted. George continued in the construction business until he was employed at the U.S. Post Office as a letter carrier. During his lifetime he was plagued with many illnesses, but was known as a diligent worker who just kept going.

George and Helen adopted Debra and Rodney in May 1955. George's theory was that anyone that needed a home or help in times of trouble would be taken into their home. It was a haven for many people over the years, including foster children.

George was involved in many volunteer projects, such as Auxiliary Police, American Legion, Child Welfare programs, First United Methodist Church, where his family started a project for the senior citizens. This group of as many as 45, met at their home or at the church monthly for food, fun and fellowship. They were taken on sight seeing trips, on the highway and water, and was a "looked to entertainment" for many years. All members of the family worked on this project and was greatly missed by Rodney when he went to the Army. To this day, Debra and Rodney are very good with older folks.

This quiet man was known for getting things done, and one who could always be depended on, no matter how sick he was.

In June 1975 he was forced to retire from the Postal Service due to many years of illness. He passed away on October 7, 1975, and was buried at the Good Hope Cemetery.

GEORGE WASHINGTON YOUNG - George Washington Young (10 May 1849- 19 Feb 1926) came to Illinois at age 16 with some Civil War soldiers, settling near Seaton. He later married Lucinda Crabtree, whose father was 1st Lt. in the Co. of which Abraham Lincoln was Captain during the Black Hawk War. George lived near Sunbeam several years and farmed near Little York, moving there about 1900. He carried mail from the post office to the depot about 20 years, receiving $14.00 per month and furnished his own horse and buggy. He was caretaker of the cemetery during summers for $10.00. His hobbies were hunting, fishing and playing horseshoes. They were parents of six children. His second son, Edward Lewis married Elvira Lightner. Their daughter, Julia, married John C. Osborn, of Warren County.

Quoting from an article in the *Monmouth Review* of 1920: "George Young, veteran mail carrier and sexton of Little York cemetery, is the only man in Little York who ever saw Abraham Lincoln and probably saw the great President oftener than any man in this part of Illinois. Mr. Young was in his teens during the Civil War, living in Washington, D.C., working in the Navy Yard making shells. The President often visited the yards and shop where he worked, accompanied by cabinet members and ladies of the official circles. On several occasions he brought one of his sons with him. During these visits the President talked with the workmen and watched the operation of the machines. Another frequent visitor was Admiral Dahlgreen, who was in charge of the fleets.

"When Mr. Lincoln visited the shop he wore the customary tall hat and long black coat, not exceptionally neat but gave the appearance of being well-dressed. He usually wore a sad expression as though something weighed on his mind, yet his voice was very pleasant when he spoke. When Lincoln came to the Navy Yard the customary salute of 23 guns were fired, but work went on as usual in the shops. He would talk to any of the men and appeared to be just as common as when he was a poor boy in Illinois. Mr. Young recalls the night Lincoln was killed, all Washington was in an uproar, everyone was out, on horseback, in carriages and on foot, seeking for the murderer. George lived near the bridge that Booth crossed making his escape. He was in the Navy Yard when Booth's body was brought back – some did not think it was Booth's body."

A later article states: when the Navy Yard was remodeled, plans called for the closing of the door Lincoln used when he visited, but so much opposition was raised that it was left as it is.

HAROLD AND DORIS YOUNG - Harold Parker Young was born August 17, 1930, in Monmouth Township, Illinois. His parents were Asa W. Young and Luverne Parker Young. Harold has spent his entire life in Warren County. He attended Frymire School where Mrs. Edna

Harold and Doris Young

287

Malley was his teacher for all eight years. He graduated from Monmouth High School and attended Monmouth College before going into farming with his father.

Harold lives on the farm located in Section twelve, Monmouth Township, where he grew up. Part of this farm has been in his family since 1832. He has been a member of Coldbrook Christian Church all his life, as have many generations of his family before him. His great-great-great-grandparents were two of the forty-three members who started the Coldbrook Church in 1839, known in the beginning as Talbot Creek Church.

Besides farming, Harold and his wife operated Young's Hiway Marine for twenty years, Young's Limousines for seven years, and as a retirement business, Young's Used Cars. His hobbies have been flying, boating, family and county history, and visiting with people.

In 1951, he married Doris Gunter, daughter of Bert and Myra Rezner Gunter of Kirkwood. Doris was born and raised in Kirkwood, graduated from Kirkwood High School and attended Western Illinois Teachers College, now known as Western Illinois University. She taught at Barr School and Kirkwood Elementary School. Her main interest besides her family has been music. She taught piano to many area children, directed choirs, and for many years was a member of Sweet Adelines, a ladies organization for singing barbershop style music. She directed the local chapter in Monmouth and later was assistant director of the Heart of Illinois Chorus in Peoria. Harold and Doris have built two calliopes which Doris has played in parades and festivals all over the area. They have three children; Marcee and her husband Jim Hudson who, along with their two children, Emily and Andy, live in rural Monmouth; John, who lives in Atlantic City, New Jersey; and Patty, her husband Mark Hasenstein and his son Joe, who lives in Peoria.

JOHN YOUNG - John Young was born October 15, 1810 in Koenigsbach, Durlach, Grand Duche, Baden, Germany. He was reared in the Protestant Lutheran faith. He received a fair education, but often missed school to work as a shepherd to help support the family. At age 19 he came to New York City on June 20, 1830, arriving with just five cents in his pocket and a knife hidden in his boot. He was a hard worker, and worked at everything from grinding razors to mowing with a scythe. On December 26, 1834, he became a member of the Independent Order of Odd Fellows, and was an active member throughout his lifetime. On June 20, 1835 he married Catherine Ehrhardt, a recent immigrant from Alsace, at that time a part of Germany; his friend, Francis Staat had married her sister.

John Young

In August of 1836 John Young and Francis Staat came west in search of a new home. They chose Illinois, went back to New York City for their wives, and settled five miles east of Roseville. In the spring of 1837 John bought 50 acres of land for $1.62 per acre. By hard work clearing trees and plowing the prairie sod, he earned enough to buy more land; the farm would contain 320 acres by the time he retired.

Their family had many disappointments. Two of their seven children died in infancy. Three of their four daughters had no children; the fourth daughter had three children, but none of these had children. Their only son, John F., did not like farming. In 1864 at 22 years of age, John F. married Caroline Simmons, they moved to Iowa where he unsuccessfully tried to make a living mining coal and later by running a tavern. Before the birth of their fourth child they returned to his father's farm. At that time, 1872, John and Catherine retired from farming, and moved to a comfortable home in Bushnell where they spent the remainder of their lives. That same year they gave their farm to John F.; each of their four daughters received $3000. In 1876 John F.'s wife, Caroline, died leaving four children from four to twelve years old. John F.'s sister, who lived on an adjoining farm, reared his four-year-old daughter; he hired an 18-year-old to keep house for him and rear his three boys. She was Emma Drake; they were married the next year and in time had six more children.

John Young's farm has always been owned by members of the Young family. At the present time there are thirteen direct descendants living in Warren County. Some Youngs live in other part of Illinois, but most have settled in Iowa, Minnesota, California, Arizona, Ohio, Tennessee, Georgia or Florida, with a few in several other states.

JOHN PETER YOUNG - John Peter Young (Johan Petter Samuelsson) the oldest son of Samuel Pettersson, a shoemaker, and Lena Cathrina Hansdotter, was born June 9, 1835 in Nybo, Stora Gluggebo, Svinhult Sweden where he lived until he was 17. John Peter emigrated to America in 1852 from Larstop, Ingatorp, Sweden. Due to his youthful age on the voyage to America, he was nicknamed "Young," a name he assumed for the remainder of his life. John Peter first settled in a Swedish settlement at New Windsor, where he secured employment in a store.

He remained in New Windsor until 1868 when he relocated to Monmouth, which was his place of residence during the remainder of his life. John Peter opened a grocery store and restaurant, which he operated for many years, twice being burned out. Later in life he abandoned the business and began the intensive cultivation of his gardens on East First Avenue, and for a time engaged in fur trade, buying many raw furs from amateur trappers in the surrounding county.

Many beautiful shade trees which grace the streets in the east part of Monmouth stand as monuments to Mr. Young's forethought and civic pride, as many years ago he often went into the timber near Monmouth, and selecting particularly promising specimens, brought them into the city and planted them, watching over them until the reached a stage in their growth where they were able to withstand the elements.

Mr. Young was twice married, the first wife being Helen C. Samuelson of Berlin, Mercer County, who died (1862) at the birth of her son Arnold Webster Young, later of Richland, MO. Mr. Young was again married after taking up residence in Monmouth, the second wife being Caroline E. Anderson, whom he claimed as his bride September 8, 1863 in Burlington. Four children were born to this union. Those included Mrs. Helen Steinbarger and Frank of Monmouth, John of Chicago and Charles of Boston.

John Peter died May 2, 1917, at his home, 1032 E. First Avenue, Monmouth. He gained a wide circle of friends who remembered him as a companionable sort of man who had many acquaintances and made few enemies. At the time of his death, two sisters, Mrs. Anna G. Fitts of San Francisco and Mrs. Helen Nelson of Wichita, and two brothers, Simon F. of Pasadena, CA and Edward G. of Riverside, CA. and two grandchildren Keith Young of Monmouth and Barbara Louise Young of Boston, survived.

Following the death of his father Samuel Pettersson, (1854) in Sweden, John Peter's mother, Lena Cathrina Hansdotter, and six siblings, Gustaf Adolf, Emelia Charlotta, Helena Sophia, Stina Greta, Simon Fredrik, and Anna Albertina, emigrated to America and Illinois during the period 1858-1868. Two other sisters remained in Sweden, Augusta and Mathilda Catharina. John Peter's mother remained in Monmouth, and died January 9, 1884 (Helen C. Young).

Index

A

Abbey 217, 242
Abbott 126
Aber 143
Acheson 44, 64
Ackerman 188
Adair 22, 128, 129, 203
Adams 63, 88, 216, 232, 242, 259, 280
Adamson 135
Adcock 88, 233
Addleman 16, 22
Adkins 186
Adkisson 20, 89, 170
Agan 89, 126, 247
Agee 31
Agnew 176
Ahlstrand 249
Aids 40
Akin 23
Albert 56, 237
Alcock 116
Aldridge 89, 134
Alexander 89, 91, 106, 183, 226, 233, 237, 260, 261
Algren 84
Alhstrand 159
All 143
Allaman 64, 90, 105, 109, 159, 193, 240
Allegro 103
Allen 9, 15, 21, 63, 90, 91, 107, 124, 148, 149, 150, 161, 164, 177, 180, 181, 207, 234, 281
Allison 91
Almaguer 85
Alstine 156
Altenbern 155
Alumbaugh 63, 91, 92
Alvard 238, 239
Alvin 162
Alyea 280
Ambrose 92, 96, 114
Andersdotter 201
Anderson 9, 15, 21, 22, 61, 63, 92, 100, 109, 121, 131, 132, 134, 137, 164, 165, 181, 184, 190, 193, 199, 205, 211, 214, 219, 241, 249, 258, 282, 284, 287, 288
Andrews 99, 118
Anjon 200
Appellate 38
Appleby 256
Applegate 44, 85
Applequist 216
Apsey 235
Arbogast 29, 256
Archer 64
Armatus 149
Armes 187
Armsby 11
Armstrong 93, 106, 128, 137, 147, 175, 185, 212, 214, 226, 228, 252, 258, 276
Armstrongs 129
Arnett 220
Arnold 145, 264
Arntzen 95
Aronson 240
Arora 61, 217
Arrant 161
Arthurs 22
Arvidson 209
Ash 285
Atchison 20
Aten 31
Ater 197
Atkins 161
Atwell 131
Atwood 11
Aubertin 233
Aulgur 124
Ault 16, 93, 101, 152, 171, 246
Aupperle 55, 94
Ayers 84
Azdell 15

B

Babcock 16, 94, 166
Baber 43, 256, 283
Bacon 20, 94, 213
Bagge 169
Bagley 21, 143
Bailey 18, 95, 280
Baird 45, 203, 268
Bake 287
Baker 95, 105, 115, 148, 222, 249, 256
Balasic 135
Balcon 36
Baldwin 95, 159, 180, 191, 218, 250
Ballard 38, 231, 259
Ballew 39
Banger 235
Bank 179
Banta 141
Bar 22
Barannan 62
Barber 183
Barclift 199
Barger 112
Barker 192
Barnes 15, 63, 68, 74, 90, 95, 96, 97, 99, 100, 102, 121, 137, 143, 151, 164, 173, 183, 184, 192, 210, 223, 235, 236, 257, 281
Barnett 9, 154
Barnum 36, 145
Barr 237
Barrett 206
Barron 151, 278
Barrows 16
Barry 62, 121, 142, 212
Barta 64
Bartch 238
Barth 269
Bartlett 146, 164
Barton 43, 106, 179
Bass 242, 257
Bastian 116
Bateman 54
Bates 208, 251, 286
Baughman 182
Baumann 118, 287
Baxendale 138
Baxter 60, 64
Baynes 214
Beach 191
Beachler 169
Beal 22, 38, 39, 97, 98, 151, 287
Beam 98
Beard 143, 258
Beardsley 64
Beasley 173, 254
Beaty 201, 227
Beck 32, 36
Becker 98, 128, 197, 281
Beckert 115
Beckner 194
Beckners 231
Becktel 265
Beckwith 268
Bedford 23
Beeman 31
Beeson 89, 247
Behrens 99
Belden 223
Bell 42, 44, 90, 159, 173, 206
Bellis 99, 276
Belt 103
Bengtson 201
Benn 137
Benner 15
Bennett 99, 100, 116, 120, 135, 240
Benson 153, 206, 243, 258
Berg 26
Bergan 268
Bergen 191
Berger 250
Berlin 230
Berner 134
Berry 31, 167
Berryman 149
Bersted 16
Bertelsen 221
Bertelson 22
Berthold 258
Bertram 276
Best 100, 116
Bethel 195
Bethell 69
Betson 103
Bettis 207
Betyna 268
Beuhl 197
Bickett 198
Biddle 22, 147, 214, 225
Biebers 168
Bikoff 259
Biles 164
Billings 277
Bingston 218
Bird 150
Birdsell 9, 125, 204, 263, 264
Bishop 64, 155, 220, 238
Bisluk 156
Bitar 204
Bixler 97
Bjorenson 140
Black 188, 225, 226, 245, 286
Blackburn 81, 172
Blair 43, 269, 283
Blake 91, 96, 250
Blakewell 190
Blanchard 134, 135, 265, 267
Bland 247
Blankenship 112
Blaylock 136
Blevins 20, 149
Bliss 227
Block 179
Blodgett 165
Bloomfield 151
Blossom 202
Blough 62
Blucker 166
Blunt 193, 267
Boaz 263
Bobb 62
Bocke 251
Bodeen 42
Bodenbender 178
Boeding 123
Bogard 122
Bogart 64, 228
Bogert 256
Boggs 168, 196
Bohlander 233
Bohn 62
Bolender 143
Boling 257
Bolon 246, 271
Bonawitz 159
Bond 10, 66, 93, 170
Bone 259
Bonior 154
Bono 231
Boock 69, 187, 210
Boone 100, 101, 264
Boostrom 101, 112
Booth 287
Booton 262
Boots 286
Booz 57
Boozan 101, 250, 264
Boozel 168
Border 272
Borstel 173
Bost 115
Bostic 92
Bosworth 64
Botkin 267
Botkins 266
Boulton 117
Bourne 110
Bowden 77
Bowen 254
Bower 205
Bowers 176
Bowles 184
Bowlyou 41
Bowman 14, 15, 46, 98, 102, 202
Bowton 236
Boyd 20, 90, 214, 261
Boydstun 179
Boyer 145, 159
Boylen 186, 202
Bracewell 39
Bradbury 240
Bradford 95, 241
Bradley 63, 168
Brady 62, 206
Bragd 102, 103, 213
Brainard 159
Brainer 20
Brakeman 9
Brand 119
Brandt 218, 219, 220
Brandy 111
Brankin 178
Brannon 62
Braselton 23, 44
Bratkovic 205
Braucht 255
Braun 213, 280
Bray 21, 62
Brazelton 153
Breen 212
Brent 9, 61, 66, 103, 181, 182, 193, 240, 241
Brewer 63, 169
Bride 120, 146
Bridwell 45
Briggs 103, 221, 222
Bright 43
Brink 39
Brinton 89, 103, 118, 140, 189
Bristow 103, 212, 213
Britt 11, 46
Brittingham 279
Brodsky 103
Brokaw 122, 258, 259, 268
Brooks 20, 21, 43, 54, 63, 104, 110, 121, 148, 152, 172, 186, 187, 233, 235, 240
Brotton 196
Broucard 268
Broughman 126
Brown 9, 11, 15, 22, 38, 104, 105, 111, 134, 140, 141, 151, 153, 154, 170, 171, 174, 176, 184, 187, 189, 193, 217, 232, 235, 240, 242, 246, 250, 252, 263, 284
Browning 173, 208
Brownlee 22, 56, 91, 106, 114, 115, 147, 157, 158, 160, 184, 185, 186, 206, 207, 214, 221, 224, 229, 232, 251, 253, 280
Bruce 90, 107, 148, 150, 279
Bruening 15
Bruington 8, 160
Brummer 175
Bruner 31, 145, 209, 258
Bruns 279
Bruyn 171, 214, 240, 256
Bryan 112, 204, 279
Bryant 14, 24, 209, 212, 213
Buchanan 49, 107, 108, 187, 188
Buchanon 208
Buchholz 81
Buck 167, 189, 217, 251, 267, 286, 287
Buckingham 130
Buckley 20, 59
Buckmaster 160
Budd 136
Buffington 242
Buffum 22
Buhman 240
Bulen 63
Bullock 141, 279
Bullwinkle 237
Bunker 152
Burbridge 145
Burchfield 256
Burford 178
Burgan 250
Burgess 269
Burgland 59, 167, 247
Burke 55, 113

Burkhalter 262
Burkhart 140
Burkholder 143
Burkitt 108
Burlingame 141
Burns 62, 108, 147, 210, 229
Burrell 77, 148, 154
Burt 98, 120
Burtiss 156
Burton 239, 250
Bush 239, 242
Bushnell 168
Bushong 69
Bussinger 33
Bute 24, 63
Butler 31, 40, 63, 109, 179, 192, 194, 228, 239, 259, 279
Buttles 244
Buzan 31, 109, 275
Bybee 22
Bycroft 20
Byerly 192
Byers 60
Byram 244
Byrne 59

C

Cadena 146
Cadwell 206
Cain 199
Caldwell 44, 90, 107, 156, 159
Callahan 259
Callow 62
Calvillo 254
Calvin 227
Cameron 8
Campbell 44, 112, 131, 140, 158, 221, 223, 252
Canada 124
Cane 31, 237
Canedeo 215
Cannon 109, 145
Cantwell 253, 264
Capps 110, 111, 172, 223
Carlberg 245
Carlisle 132
Carlsdotter 98, 281
Carlson 111, 173, 189, 202, 204, 211, 245, 251, 262, 285
Carlstedt 131
Carmer 268
Carmical 144
Carnes 148
Carothers 116, 178
Carpenter 183
Carr 111, 191, 234, 266, 267
Carson 18, 34, 112, 155
Carstensen 281
Carter 64, 157
Carver 221
Carwile 99
Case 80
Cassiday 9, 264, 272
Casteel 3, 112, 113, 116, 166, 180, 244
Cater 119
Catlin 61
Cavanaugh 62, 70, 72, 113, 142, 186, 190, 193, 240, 250
Cavins 272
Celin 159
Cesna 156
Cessna 156
Chamberlain 230
Chamberlin 92, 113, 114
Chandler 114, 115, 124, 129, 138, 203, 229
Chapin 99, 123
Chaplin 191
Chapman 55, 115, 116, 141, 237
Charboneau 278
Charboneau-Fillman 278
Chard 215
Charlotta 255
Chase 85, 238
Chatterton 253
Cheesman 100
Cheney 191
Chewning 133
Chick 151, 267
Chilton 129
Chrisman 113, 116, 156
Christian 39
Church 39
Churchill 46, 134
Chy 198
Cialdella 231
Clarion 96
Clark 8, 13, 20, 26, 90, 106, 107, 115, 116, 117, 121, 137, 184, 189, 197, 254, 256, 264, 281
Clarke 63, 233
Clay 218
Claycomb 8, 111, 191
Claypool 224
Clayton 62, 63, 84, 99, 118, 119, 248, 266
Cleave 155
Clements 46, 234
Clemmensen 128
Clendenen 136
Clendenin 160
Clesen 277
Clewell 207
Clifford 137
Cline 262
Clore 192
Clute 119
Cobb 245, 252
Coburn-Zimmerman 283
Cochran 20, 120, 168, 211
Cockrun 205
Cody 239, 258
Coffey 39
Coffman 154
Cofield 186, 250
Cohen 63
Cohn 179, 278
Cokel 62, 108
Colclasure 120, 187
Cole 100, 172, 189, 206, 275
Coleman 9, 179
Colfax 20
Colgan 264
Collins 62, 63, 120, 121, 122, 123, 134, 211, 227, 250, 264
Colwell 15, 75, 94
Combs 201
Comstock 202
Conant 134, 155
Conard 184, 197, 218
Concannon 155
Condreay 64
Conlee 197
Conley 250
Conlon 21
Conn 269
Conner 121
Connor 234
Conrad 32
Conroy 250
Conry 246
Conway 26, 60, 121, 253
Coogan 171, 273
Cook 21, 121, 137, 145, 168, 198, 205, 269, 272, 277
Cooke 43, 250
Cooksey 136
Coon 191
Coons 229
Coop 183
Cooper 44, 85, 122, 197, 198, 266, 267
Cordell 69
Corley 31
Corman 21, 63
Cornell 63
Cornwallis 154
Corp 280
Corsepius 141
Corzatt 9, 21, 122, 169, 186, 276
Costello 62, 121, 122, 123
Cotton 128
Coulter 28
Counterman 242
Coursey 89, 124
Courtney 61, 116
Cover 149
Cowden 156, 220
Cowick 77
Cox 9, 43, 64, 110, 124, 125, 189, 191, 205, 231, 244, 265, 266, 267
Cozadd 28
Crabtree 287
Craig 146, 241
Craine 177
Cramer 152
Crandall 181, 197, 245, 256
Crane 39, 110, 122, 170, 225, 241
Crawford 158, 238
Creek 284
Creger 161, 180, 261, 272
Creighton 212
Creswell 23, 198
Crisp 266, 267
Cristine 193
Critser 125, 256, 283
Croft 250
Crompton 254
Cromwell 149
Crookham 9
Crose 205
Crosier 150
Cross 279
Crow 75, 121, 235, 268
Crowe 132
Croy 279
Crozier 9
Crummer 168
Culton 272
Culver 39
Cummings 188, 254
Cunningham 69, 153, 164, 206, 251
Currie 149, 223
Curtis 126, 158, 170
Custer 239
Cyrene 116

D

Dafly 256
Daggett 149
Daily 120
Dakin 46
Dale 41, 272
Dalton 262
Damewood 89, 126, 127, 152, 174, 180, 212
Damron 109, 274
Danforth 127, 130
Daniel 233
Danielson 219
Dannaken 63
Darnell 151
Darrah 64, 122, 201, 206
Dasso 246
Daugherty 114
Dauma 64
Davenport 57
Daves 162
Davey 284
Davidge 150
Davidson 9, 12, 31, 45, 64, 106, 179, 246
Davies 271
Davis 9, 11, 16, 20, 22, 61, 63, 78, 127, 128, 134, 140, 175, 187, 194, 227, 228, 256, 263, 267, 277
Davisson 143
Dawson 64, 127
Day 123, 176, 224, 231
Deakin 217
Dean 102, 128, 141, 163, 235, 246, 254, 260
Deator 9
DeBlieck 220
Decker 168
DeCosta 190
DeCounter 128
Dedeaux 226, 227
Defenbaugh 128, 129, 130
DeHague 9
DeJanes 56
DeKeyrel 179, 187
Dell 55
Delphine 287
Demoss 23
Denison 62, 64, 130, 131, 171, 173, 211, 213, 240
Dennis 131, 285
Dennison 250
Dernlan 133
Deschene 112
Deschwanden 280
DeScregges 177
Detmer 132
Deuger 132
Devlin 64, 184
Dew 68
Dewey 9
DeWitt 124
Deyarmon 162
Dick 63
Dicks 64
Dickson 22, 265
Diffenbaugh 86
Dilkes 163
Dilts 132, 133, 134
Disney 116
Disseler 95
Distin 173
Ditch 21
Ditmars 197
Ditto 217
Diven 166
Dixon 13, 20, 62, 128, 176, 187, 212
Dixson 11, 270, 272
Dobey 60
Dobkins 159
Dodd 152
Dodson 41
Dolan 270
Doll 109, 187
Dollinger 8
Domever 267
Donaldson 119
Donegan 182
Doore 273
Doran 281
Doty 15, 132, 133, 191
Doubet 284
Douglas 68, 231
Douglass 74, 224
Dowell 154, 270
Downer 112
Downes 132, 133, 139, 167, 174, 180
Downey 55
Downs 115
Doyle 72, 190, 232
Drake 170, 171, 253, 288
Drayson 271
Drexel 168
Driffill 134
Driscoll 62, 134
Drummy 35
Dudenhausen 214
Duffner 164
Duffy 35
Dufva 132
Dugan 75, 260
Dughman 260
Duke 77, 125
Dulin 62
Dunbar 75, 85, 203, 259
Duncan 39, 105, 227, 228
Duncanson 265
Dungan 134, 135
Dunker 39
Dunkle 63
Dunlap 13, 282
Dunn 62, 165, 225, 226, 276
Durch 250
Dutton 44, 135
Duvall 190
Dycus 259
Dyer 153
Dyni 235
Dyson 233

E

Eagan 222
Early 135, 187
Earp 18, 19, 135, 136, 144, 187, 202, 225, 262, 268
Easley 245
Eastwood 243
Easum 136, 252
Eaton 110, 121, 136, 179, 237
Eaverson 241
Eberhart 150
Ebersole 18, 267, 287
Eby 187
Eckard 118
Eckdahl 286
Eckhart 258
Eckley 19, 41, 137, 220
Edgerton 63
Edgington 116
Edman 266
Edmison 64
Edmond 92
Edwards 42, 64, 72, 123, 184, 216, 256, 262
Edwin 63

Efaw 29
Egan 62, 191
Eggan 270, 271
Egger 277
Ehrhardt 170, 288
Einfeldt 93
Ekerberg 32
Ekwall 186
Elander 206
Elder 188
Eldridge 20, 39, 69, 153, 162, 177, 274
Elkipton 121
Elliot 150, 221, 255
Elliott 39, 63, 137, 204, 276
Ellsworth 18
Elmore 43
Elting 176
Emans 20, 21
Emanuelsdotter 267
Emerick 114, 115, 137
Emery 139
Enderlin 35, 62, 138, 148, 250
Endicott 167
Engdahl 113, 150
Engel 96
Engles 221
Engstrom 141, 255
Enlow 10
Epley 138
Epperson 31
Ericksdotter 159
Erickson 58, 102, 138, 139, 282
Ericson 18
Erlandson 139, 174, 199, 220, 243
Errett 31
Errion 252
Erwin 59
Erzinger 156
Espy 30, 81
Esquibel 135
Essex 218
Estell 197, 281
Estil 252
Evans 38, 43, 85, 197, 244
Eveleth 254
Everet 60
Everly 181
Evers 97, 259
Ewalt 5, 140
Ewbank 33
Ewing 18, 28, 177
Ezell 136

F

Fahlund 140, 189, 202
Failor 134
Fair 63, 122, 140, 255, 263
Fairbanks 132
Fairfield 152
Fall 36
Farm 167
Farnham 246
Farrar 266
Farrenkopf 20
Fassler 207
Faudree 141, 255
Fausett 219, 220
Fayette 62
Feagans 210
Fee 160
Feehan 115
Feichtner 132
Feighner 132
Feldner 280

Fell 134, 167, 226, 251
Fellow 143
Felt 41
Feltmeyer 198
Fendler 145
Fergueson 132
Ferguson 31
Fernald 28, 141, 241
Ferris 141
Fetterley 197, 281
Fideli 285
Fifield 229
Filbert 142
Filip 247
Fillip 247
Fillman 156, 182, 264, 285
Fillmans 218
Filmore 267
Finch 46, 63
Findley 44, 150
Fink 38, 277
Finley 173, 232
Firoved 76, 77
Firth 59
Fisher 42, 57, 141, 145, 159, 184, 185, 244
Fitch 192
Fitts 288
Fitzgerald 116, 156, 250
Fitzpatrick 62
Flack 140
Flaherty 220, 264
Flanagan 113, 142, 164, 166, 186
Flannigan 62
Flatley 155
Fleet 193
Fleharty 151
Fleming 13, 127, 142
Fletcher 59, 160, 161, 245
Floren 32
Florence 105
Florey 110
Floyd 240
Fogarty 113
Fogelburg 139
Foley 55, 123, 190
Follmer 143
Fonteyn 269
Foote 16, 69, 264
Forbes 55, 145
Ford 253
Foreman 119, 143
Foresman 142, 238, 239
Forrester 168
Fort 154, 254
Foster 11, 21, 88, 107, 143, 144, 201, 202, 230, 240, 245
Foster-McGaw 55
Fouke 275
Foust 44, 113, 276
Foutch 221
Fowler 164
Fox 22, 97, 268
Foy 149
Frailey 20
Frakes 150, 218
Francis 218, 263
Frank 60, 219, 251
Franks 92
Frantz 78, 208, 220
Fraser 62, 68, 280
Frazee 273, 278
Frazier 242
Freand 107
Freburg 143, 199
Fredrickson 144, 145, 173, 174, 236

Freed 53
Freel 250
Freeman 153
Freil 250
French 131, 226
Frieden 197
Friedstrom 32
Fritz 226
Fritzel 274
Frost 252
Frymire 145
Fuess 101
Fugate 187
Fullerton 167, 253
Funcheon 238
Futhey 22

G

Gabby 138
Gabrielson 189
Gaddis 252
Galbraith 254
Galbreath 9, 60, 103, 136, 252
Gale 146, 209
Gallaghan 126
Gallagher 226, 265
Gallaugher 140, 146, 149, 203, 263
Galloway 125, 149
Galusha 55
Garafola 90
Gardner 8, 11, 112, 150, 172, 177, 202, 210
Garfield 54
Garland 122, 146
Garner 285
Garret 242
Garrett 64, 137, 209
Garth 44, 203
Garza 184
Gaskill 16, 84, 146
Gaston 31
Gates 235
Gavin 62, 78, 107, 113, 134, 138, 142, 146, 147, 150, 185, 186, 214
Gawthrop 204, 230
Gayer 78
Gbenk 255
Gear 277
Gebauere 117
Gebrig 129
Geer 39, 147, 206
Geers 21, 199
Gehr 272
Geiger 173
Geisz 55
Geldbrandt 216, 224
Geltmacher 151, 287
Gerlaw 21, 55
Gerry 243
Gettemey 99
Gettemy 187, 267
Ghrist 130
Gibb 9, 148, 176, 217
Gibbler 31
Gibson 23, 44, 53, 90, 91, 93, 148, 149, 150, 177, 178, 203, 212, 226, 234
Giddings 10, 44, 63, 152, 222, 228
Giese 53
Gilbert 116, 141
Giles 144, 220
Gilfillan 115
Gill 243
Gillander 143

Gillen 11, 62, 113, 126, 147, 149, 150, 235, 236, 237, 244, 279
Gillette 150
Gilliam 41
Gilliland 226, 279
Gillis 39
Gillman 129
Gillock 264
Gilmore 21, 93, 149, 150, 166, 204, 226
Gilson 270
Gippert 242
Gitterman 39
Givens 31
Gladfelter 78
Glass 151, 279
Gleasman 55
Gleason 111, 221
Glenn 151, 172, 173, 211, 212, 213, 287
Glisan 252
Globe 96
Goddard 192, 234
Godfrey 115, 120, 168, 169
Goettsch 121
Goetz 208
Goff 186
Goforth 132
Goldfield 96
Goldnetz 263
Goode 151
Goodspeed 223
Goodwin 85
Goranson 98, 281
Goransson 111
Gordon 21, 62, 116, 203, 244, 273, 285
Gossett 20, 64, 152
Gottler 62
Goyer 145
Grabowski 64, 152
Grace 94
Graham 44, 62, 107, 121, 144, 168, 217, 226, 250, 255, 285
Grammont 267
Granger 197
Grant 20
Grapes 270, 271
Graves 146
Grawey 230
Gray 21, 249, 254, 269
Green 20, 21, 64, 116, 193, 207, 210, 258, 284
Greenleaf 18
Greenlee 176
Greenley 95
Greenlief 206
Gregg 66
Gregory 63
Greifenberg 117
Greiner 152, 174, 237, 253, 264
Grier 53, 281
Griffin 40, 267
Griffith 152, 217
Grim 180
Grimesey 279
Grimm 180
Grimsley 17, 18, 58, 153, 170, 254, 282
Griswold 170
Groninger 114
Grove 228
Groves 203
Grupy 68
Guanzon 113

Guerrero 61
Guess 279
Guidry 159, 240
Guiher 64
Guldbeck 132
Gulick 124
Gullberg 24, 153, 154
Gummerson 193, 243
Gunhild 261
Gunter 279, 288
Gunther 170
Gustafson 154, 252
Gustav 217
Guthrie 235, 275
Guttermuth 21

H

Haben 155, 286
Hadley 227
Haffner 207
Hagan 207
Hagar 140
Hageman 94
Hagemann 55
Hahn 63
Haines 120, 205
Haldeman 155, 215
Hale 63
Haley 8, 45, 132, 233, 248
Halford 63
Hall 15, 16, 20, 31, 41, 44, 60, 64, 74, 115, 135, 155, 156, 206, 276, 283
Hallam 77, 93, 102, 156, 157, 182, 234, 253, 269
Hallbick 85
Hallengren 255
Hallstein 277
Halpin 35
Hamberg 84, 155
Hamil 205
Hamilton 15, 64, 76, 157, 158, 160, 203, 245, 284
Hamm 273
Hammerlund 243
Hammock 158
Hammon 63
Hammond 84, 139, 175, 243
Hamsher 44
Hanafin 131
Hanan 9
Hancock 60
Hand 185, 194
Handy 227
Hanen 22
Hanes 38, 39
Haney 102, 116, 182
Hanley 19, 66, 158
Hanlin 121
Hanna 6, 21, 23, 90, 158, 175, 240
Hannaman 202
Hanon 26
Hansberry 241
Hansdotter 288
Hanson 55, 109, 159, 216, 223
Hansson 159
Haptonstall 85
Hardacre 240
Hardesty 69
Hardin 59, 72, 78, 159, 160, 171, 273
Harding 6, 43, 78
Hare 233
Harkins 115
Harlan 116

291

Harmon 16
Harmony 152
Harper 146
Harrington 57, 116
Harris 26, 105, 192, 234, 240, 253
Harrison 111, 172, 226, 228, 237, 243, 279
Harsha 205
Hart 84, 161, 168, 199, 277
Hartgrove 268
Hartley 124, 140
Hartman 207, 253
Hartsook 114
Hartzell 44
Harvey 140, 206
Hasenstein 288
Hass 179
Hasse 212, 253
Hasselquist 32
Hasten 155
Hatchitt 31
Hatfield 223
Hawcock 62, 68, 161
Hawk 21, 221, 254, 273
Hawkins 125, 161, 186
Hawthorne 106
Hayden 153
Hayes 20, 23, 41, 85, 141, 190, 253, 286
Haynes 64, 112, 137, 162, 220
Hays 38
Haywood 53
Hazen 61
Healy 62
Heap 39, 152
Hearne 284
Heasley 38
Heatherly 242
Heaton 78, 262
Hebbard 20
Heck 155
Hector 196
Hedberg 181, 182
Hedges 20, 145
Hedrick 19
Heffernan 147, 186
Hefley 273
Heflin 63
Heitzman 198
Helgerson 111
Helm 199
Helms 119
Helvestine 137
Hemm 126
Hempt 111
Hendel 128, 162, 163, 194, 279
Henderson 18, 90, 121, 146, 172, 245, 248
Hendricks 267
Hendrix 124
Henley 196
Hennefent 9
Hennenfent 119, 138, 146, 147, 150, 201, 230, 251, 255
Henrichs 163, 164
Henry 64, 207, 251, 255
Henshaw 202
Hensieigh 75
Hensley 178
Henson 64, 229
Herbert 109, 230
Herkelman 161
Herman 146
Hernandez 103
Herrick 231
Herron 164

Hester 240
Heston 55, 214
Hewitt 82
Hibbard 63
Hickerson 203
Hickman 18, 63, 253, 260
Hicks 154
Hidden 231
Hiett 173
Higbee 135, 156
Higgins 36, 60
Higgison 242
Higgs 90
Hill 20, 85, 95, 144, 164, 205, 251, 259
Hillen 143, 172
Hillis 119
Hillmans 22
Hillyer 128
Hilten 9
Hindman 122, 195
Hines 186, 193, 207, 280
Hinman 228, 243
Hinton 164, 165, 284, 285
Hippen 113
Hirsch 15
Hixson 258
Hobson 279
Hockman 220
Hodge 165
Hodges 10, 228, 253
Hodgman 236
Hoenshell 277
Hoff 191, 286
Hoffman 113, 165
Hoffmann 116
Hofstetter 60
Hogan 223
Hogg 148, 150, 178
Hogue 15, 91, 146, 150, 178
Hoisington 254
Hoke 145
Holcomb 254
Holden 137
Holder 39
Holderness 237, 238
Holeman 208
Holford 245, 277
Holgate 230
Holgates 29
Holgren 245
Hollar 90, 240
Hollenberg 21, 187
Holler 14
Holliday 63, 74, 77, 136, 172
Hollis 41
Holloway 21, 166, 226
Holm 32
Holmberg 85, 114
Holmes 216, 224
Holt 166, 242
Holte 270
Holter 151
Holtkamp 124
Holverson 64
Homey 23
Homrich 190
Honeyman 206
Hooblers 129
Hood 194, 266, 267
Hook 18, 22
Hooks 64
Hoon 177
Hoots 146
Hoover 74
Hope 88

Hopkins 267
Hoppaugh 279
Hopper 9
Hopping 63
Horn 62
Horner 86
Horney 127
Horschler 162
Horton 119, 147
Horvath 259
Hoteling 180
Hotelling 177
Hottle 101, 279
Hough 221
Houghton 191, 202, 221, 222, 223
Houlihan 64
House 63, 140, 166, 167
Houseman 41
Housh 146
Howard 11, 72, 98, 212, 240
Howe 210, 229, 262, 265, 277
Howell 150
Howells 168
Howes 98
Howse 33
Hoyt 283
Huber 132
Huddlesons 195
Hudson 273, 288
Huebner 241
Huey 61, 217
Huff 258, 277
Hughes 8, 20, 31, 52, 127, 134, 167
Hull 98, 167, 173, 217, 281
Hultz 130
Hume 152, 195
Hummell 133, 134, 167
Humphrey 95
Humphreys 21
Hunt 196
Hunter 41, 167, 208
Huntrods 261
Hurd 11, 226
Hurka 55
Hurley 40
Huseman 53
Husnick 272
Huss 154, 173
Husted 135
Huston 21, 46, 62, 94, 116, 121, 168, 251
Hutchins 39, 168, 169, 189, 190
Hutchinson 160
Hutchison 18
Hutchisson 247
Hynek 170

I

Icenogle 195, 214
Ickes 177
Ikerd 221
Imbody 157
Immel 257
Ingersoll 11, 168
Ingram 110
Inman 64
Irey 195
Irish 114
Irwin 61, 143
Isaacson 146
Ischer 63
Ishmael 64
Ives 20, 63

J

Jack 9
Jackson 22, 39, 97, 168, 177, 188, 223, 232, 241, 251, 253, 271
Jacob 146, 263
Jacobs 146
Jacobson 32, 170, 171
Jacoby 143
Jaggers 39
James 107, 142, 171, 280
Jamieson 30, 269
Jamison 235
Janssen 139
Jared 63
Jarvis 9
Jeanes 196
Jebb 113, 197
Jellinger 234
Jenkins 186
Jenks 80, 93, 110, 131, 141, 171, 193, 241, 253
Jennings 255, 262
Jensen 9, 61, 112, 168, 171, 172, 198, 264, 280
Jewell 11, 110, 172, 173, 188, 212, 234, 275
Jobusch 85
Joesting 226
Johannesson 102
John 185, 267
Johnson 20, 21, 24, 26, 32, 39, 61, 64, 68, 75, 77, 90, 93, 110, 111, 112, 115, 120, 122, 127, 134, 137, 139, 140, 141, 145, 152, 169, 170, 173, 174, 189, 190, 194, 195, 197, 201, 209, 211, 213, 216, 218, 220, 228, 233, 236, 238, 240, 243, 244, 253, 255, 260, 261, 264, 266, 267, 284
Johnsson 159
Johnston 116, 135, 141, 175, 258
Jolley 106, 111
Jolly 246
Jonas 175, 176
Jones 39, 40, 41, 55, 78, 92, 115, 128, 134, 135, 143, 164, 174, 176, 178, 202, 224, 243, 252, 273, 279, 280, 283
Joneson 231
Jonsdotter 159
Jordan 110
Joseph 166
Josephson 240, 251
Joss 11
Joyslin 183
Jung 187
Junkin 44
Jury 156
Just 242
Justus 84, 132

K

Kahler 77
Kaiser 165
Kalb 152
Kalina 170
Kampen 198
Kane 9, 123, 131, 143, 176
Karns 148
Kaska 175
Kaster 109
Kattell 141

Kavanaugh 113
Kay 270
Kean 265
Keating 91
Keech 196
Keff 243
Keister 21
Kell 252
Keller 137, 253, 265, 267
Kellogg 13, 198
Kelly 11, 20, 35, 41, 64, 85, 111, 176, 177, 208, 252, 264
Kelly-Warren 278
Kelsey 31
Kemp 154
Kemper 284
Kemplin 131
Kempt 45
Kenan 119, 177
Kendal 23
Kendall 22, 44, 150, 176, 178
Kennedy 245
Kenneth 96
Kennon 198
Kepple 178, 179, 187, 228
Kermode 234
Kern 33
Kersey 88, 156
Kershaw 268
Kesinger 18, 179, 214, 278
Kessler 242
Ketchum 95, 100, 112, 113, 116, 126, 127, 132, 133, 152, 166, 174, 179, 180, 218, 261, 265, 266, 267
Kett 4
Kettenring 181
Kettering 55
Kidd 31, 283
Kidder 22
Kiddler 57
Kilgore 189, 225, 240
Killey 66, 105, 111, 156, 181, 182, 183, 193, 210
Kimble 183, 187
Kimbrough 278
Kimmons 254
King 183, 184
Kingsbury 191, 233
Kingsley 279
Kington 21, 23, 170, 239
Kinkaid 64, 88, 184, 252
Kinnan 191
Kinney 3, 62, 64, 107, 113, 142, 145, 147, 150, 184, 185, 186, 214, 274
Kinvig 181, 182
Kirby 20, 21
Kirk 156, 194
Kirkpatrick 20, 21, 52, 216, 217, 239
Kirkwood 249
Kishline 119
Kitchin 84
Kitzmiller 38
Klang 235
Klein 64
Kleinkoff 255
Kline 131, 168
Klump 246
Knarr 183
Kneen 122, 136, 186, 187
Kneer 166
Knickerbocker 148
Knight 43
Kniss 55, 269, 277

Knotts 20, 45
Knox 134
Knuckles 267
Kobler 102, 161, 258
Koch 26
Koehn 64
Koertz 220
Koke 75
Koller 231
Koltveit 129
Kopesky 270, 272
Kramer 178, 179, 187, 228, 285
Kremer 108
Krieger 93
Kritzer 20, 125, 283
Kroger 15
Kruger 221
Kruideneir 187, 188
Krull 110
Krummel 44
Kruse 118
Krusmark 22, 147, 214
Kubicek 276
Kuhlman 168
Kuhnkey 231, 232
Kulczewski 42
Kullman 252
Kuns 129
Kvidera 276
Kyle 172, 188, 212, 213
Kyler 219

L

Lackey 281
Ladwig 173
Lafary 9
Lafferty 134, 265
Lafrey 197
LaGrange 31
LaGrow 189
Lair 55
Lakis 69
Lamp 270, 271, 272
Landis 110
Landon 119, 237
Landuyt 62, 269
Lange 85
Lankford 39
Lanphere 63, 181, 188, 255
Lant 154
Lantz 167, 188, 204, 285, 286
Larkin 21, 84, 127
Larkins 143
Larson 15, 22, 140, 189, 199, 201, 202, 204, 206
Latham 228
Lathrop 21
Laughead 226
Laughlin 62
Lauver 24, 217
Law 59, 107, 148, 150, 159
Lawhorn 39, 168, 169, 189
Lawless 88, 234
Lawrence 229
Lawson 100, 255
Lawton 138
Leafgreen 249
Leake 195
Leary 20, 22, 62
Leaverton 168
Leck 40
Ledger 62
Lee 20, 39, 55, 62, 110, 113, 150, 159, 167, 172, 190, 201, 202, 212, 235, 237, 250, 265

LeFebvre 151
Lefever 268
LeFils 180, 265
Lefler 135
LeFort 197
LeGate 28, 286
Lehmann 137
Leighty 21, 194
Leininger 157
Leins 62
LeMasters 232
Lemkau 39
Lemmerman 78
Lemmon 180
Lenahan 113, 147, 185
Lenehan 147
Lenihan 142, 186
Lenz 117, 130, 154, 247
Leonard 31, 39, 129, 146, 203, 217, 225, 240
Leonilda 140
Lepper 243, 281
Lester 63, 229
Letchfield 62
Levengood 63
Levine 281
Levis 89
Lewallen 169, 189
Lewis 60, 97, 110, 115, 179, 190, 191, 192, 205, 221, 222, 223, 233, 244, 254
Lichtenstein 227
Liebenthal 121
Liedman 197
Lieurance 283
Liggett 56, 131, 153, 188
Light 249
Lightner 287
Liguori 250
Lilja 245
Lincoln 40, 61, 63, 191, 192, 210, 212, 231, 265, 287
Lind 167
Lindberg 249
Lindbergh 18
Linde 132
Lindsay 260, 261, 286
Lingafelter 259
Link 254
Linman 192, 201, 209
Linn 178
Linnenkemp 159, 240
Lionberger 208
Lipes 193
Lipp 193
Little 140
Litton 112
Livermore 20, 21, 125
Livingston 18, 104, 105, 182, 193, 194, 204, 239
Livington 56
Lloyd 229
Lo Preste 62
Lober 266, 267
Lock 194
Lockridge 153
Lockwood 11, 20, 26, 223
Loduca 190
Lodwick 197
Lofftus 9, 20, 122, 195
Loftus 81
Logan 8, 26, 120, 264, 279
Lohse 229
Longley 241
Looney 126, 170

Loper 197
LoPresti 212
Loptien 197, 281
Lorimer 32
Lorraine 100
Loso 157
Lotz 187
Louck 140
Louden 247
Louquet 120
Lovdahl 195
Lovell 60, 134
Loveridge 196, 252
Low 39
Lowe 91
Lowell 234
Lox 135
Loya 196
Lozier 64, 91, 113, 197
Lubben 91
Luby 35
Lucas 12, 66, 132, 196, 246, 248
Luckenbill 219
Luecke 187
Lufkin 279
Luft 246
Lugg 74
Lukens 197
Lundquist 284
Lundy 129
Lupton 55
Lusk 12, 117, 143, 144, 197, 281
Lutz 95
Lybarger 21, 72, 259
Lynch 15, 62, 77, 197, 215, 264
Lyon 270
Lyons 55, 62, 217, 240

M

Maberry 214
MacDill 228
MacDonald 145
MacIntosh 264
MacIntyre 235
Mack 35
Macken 221
Mackey 186, 209, 230, 232, 242
MacMaster 110
MacMurray 88
Madigan 174
Madrid 259
Maere 278
Maginn 181
Magnusson 201, 209
Mahaney 233
Mahoney 250
Main 131
Malcolm 89, 247
Maleys 44
Maliskis 187
Malley 55, 288
Malm 221
Malone 101, 151
Manlove 125
Mann 39, 223
Mannon 121
Mansfield 256
Manuel 21, 103, 113
Marcase 164
Mariner 238, 264
Markham 63, 176
Markleys 168
Marks 179
Marlow 33
Marquart 256

Marrah 21
Marschall 116
Marsden 154
Marsh 249
Marshall 63, 192, 198
Marston 134
Martin 16, 22, 24, 32, 41, 120, 123, 126, 127, 158, 189, 190, 198, 199, 200, 201, 206, 207, 209, 212, 231, 238, 256, 263, 266, 267
Martindale 259
Martinez 278
Mason 20, 62, 129
Massey 121
Massingill 26
Masters 196
Masterson 266
Mathews 63
Mathias 2
Matlock 31
Matson 140, 189, 201, 202, 209
Matteson 202, 221, 222
Matthews 177, 285
Mattison 201
Mattoon 64, 207
Mattson 141
Mauk 21
Maxwell 149
May 237
Mayberry 179
Mayfield 197
Mayfred 15
Mayor 210
Mayrath 257
McAnally 120
McBride 30, 92, 141, 202, 265
McBroom 260
McCamy 20
McCann 62, 221
McCartney 63
McCarty 242
McCaw 22, 101
McClanahan 190, 258
McCleary 20, 62, 113, 190
McClelland 232
McClellen 148
McClenahan 44
McClery 62
McClintock 84, 188, 283
McClung 39, 143
McClure 202, 203, 258, 259
McClurg 285
McClymonds 273
McCombs 203
McConnaughay 168
McConnell 55, 138, 149, 157, 203
McCord 208
McCormick 39, 115, 131, 254
McCoy 38, 104, 105, 162, 190, 191, 197, 204, 211, 234, 256, 258, 259, 263
McCracken 220, 221
McCreedy 206, 225
McCrery 22, 106, 144, 175, 188, 194, 204, 234, 242
McCulloch 204
McCullough 102
McCurdy 91, 173, 240
McCutchan 232, 284
McDaneld 205, 254
McDaniel 107
McDermit 275
McDill 144
McDonald 23, 39
McDorman 63

McEwen 212
McFarland 120, 121, 123, 265
McFate 171
McGaughey 141, 184
McGinnis 111
McGivney 62
McGrail 264
McGraw 198
McGrew 153, 194
McGuire 74
McHale 161
McHenry 126
McIntire 277
McIntosh 60, 76
McIntyre 119, 177, 205, 212
McKeague 234
McKee 149, 206, 212
McKelvey 150
McKelvie 21, 131, 132, 256
McKeney 264
McKenion 134
McKenna 135
McKenzie 151, 207
McKeown 111, 181, 198
McKinney 106, 206
McKissick 90, 206, 207
McKnight 275
McLane 218
McLaughlin 9, 60, 62, 69, 110
McLean 37
McLoskey 177, 265
McMahill 218
McMaster 187, 189
McMein 260
McMichael 53, 196
McMillan 124, 158
McMillin 261
McMullen 207, 227
McMurtry 88
McNair 178
McNamara 208
McNary 247
McNeil 12, 63, 132
McOlgan 254
McPharland 265
McPherron 18
McQuiston 107, 214, 215
McReynolds 244
McVey 33, 98, 182, 193, 280, 281
McWhorter 162, 168
McWilliams 216
Meacham 9, 122
Meachum 26
Mead 194
Meadows 192, 208, 209
Meals 95
Means 208, 283
Medhurst 274
Meek 269
Meeker 103, 208, 209
Mehl 38, 39
Melburg 201, 209
Meleney 190
Melin 64
Meling 19, 28
Meloan 8, 31
Melton 190, 192, 209
Melvin 89, 182, 210
Menely 82, 120, 211
Mennering 249
Meridith 204
Merillat 212
Merion 59
Merle 212
Merrell 111
Merrick 14

293

Merrifield 178
Merry 13
Messenger 134
Messer 175
Mettler 210, 218
Metzner 259
Meusborn 187
Meyer 212, 247
Michael 44
Michaels 195
Mickle 181
Mikita 16
Miles 11, 63, 279
Millard 143, 233
Millen 211
Miller 29, 31, 84, 85, 103, 111, 131, 160, 172, 173, 181, 188, 205, 210, 211, 212, 213, 247, 252, 258, 259, 270, 284
Milligan 168
Mills 113, 132, 142, 147, 150, 151, 156, 168, 170, 171, 179, 190, 191, 214, 226, 240, 254, 263, 278, 279
Millward 8
Milne 214, 215
Milton 156, 157
Minor 39
Missavage 183, 215
Mitchell 21, 23, 39, 63, 64, 104, 144, 177, 215, 228, 235, 270, 272
Mitten 82
Modrena 159
Moffet 4, 86
Moffett 224
Mohr 122
Monhart 269
Monk 225
Monroe 20, 120
Monticue 195
Moody 131
Moon 110, 186
Moore 9, 14, 20, 44, 69, 72, 115, 122, 168, 169, 176, 181, 183, 204, 205, 208, 215, 251, 252, 279
Moorhead 138
Moran 62
Morehead 190
Morey 151, 152, 179, 255
Morford 20, 191
Morgan 61, 196, 268, 269
Morling 8, 216
Morningstar 287
Morrell 116, 216, 224, 229
Morris 62, 84, 153, 158, 217, 226, 234, 247, 254, 268, 282, 285
Morrison 37, 59, 168, 176, 243, 286
Morrow 90, 144, 244
Morse 8, 36, 216, 217
Mortlands 129
Mott 19
Moulden 173
Mouls 261
Mounce 64
Mount 203
Mowen 69, 181, 183
Mowery 20
Moyer 28, 32
Muck 28
Mudd 140

Mueller 130, 276
Muir 132, 146, 263
Mulberry 170
Mulder 117
Mulhatten 159
Mullen 153, 254, 282
Mulligan 282
Mulnix 144
Mumey 103
Mumma 171
Muncy 206
Munson 14, 131, 212, 217, 240, 285, 286
Murdock 15, 202, 203, 259
Murphy 8, 35, 45, 60, 62, 63, 131, 156, 217, 248, 249
Murrell 195
Murry 224
Musgrove 14
Musser 276
Myers 30, 63, 95, 96, 197, 217, 218, 278, 281
Myler 261
Myron 225, 277

N

Nagel 131
Nash 206, 207, 252, 253
Neal 204
Neals 22
Need 63
Neff 126, 219
Neill-Fullerton 269
Neilsen 189
Nellie 155
Nelson 14, 32, 69, 105, 108, 113, 137, 146, 174, 189, 201, 205, 209, 219, 226, 235, 243, 251, 255, 288
Neuleib 231
Nevius 205
Newberry 149, 159
Newkirk 195
Newman 43, 216, 220, 224, 273
Nichol 15, 18
Nicholas 136
Nichols 85, 104, 221
Nicklin 198
Nicol 220, 221, 224
Niedernhofer 243
Niles 180, 184
Nilsdotter 111
Nilsson 201
Nimrick 167
Nipper 63
Noble 241
Noel 62, 85
Nolan 207
Nolen 200
Nollen 268
Nonweiler 277
Noonan 138, 150, 250
Nordstrom 39
Norman 174, 197
Norris 116, 129, 202, 252
Northam 146
Norton 218
Norville 127
Norvilles 168
Nostrand 190, 191
Nott 63
Nuckles 139
Nussle 85
Nye 66

O

Oaks 122
Objartel 172
O'Brien 14, 62, 113, 120, 142, 146, 150, 190, 250
Ochert 103
Ockert 57, 238, 273, 278
O'Connell 250
O'Connor 62, 150
O'Daniel 64, 76
O'Donnell 62
O'Dowd 62
O'Farrell 35
Ogden 11, 110, 111, 191, 202, 221, 222, 223
Ohlemeyer 14
Ohren 223
O'Kane 223
Olin 124, 150
Oliphant 146
Oliver 9, 21, 40
Olsen 231
Olson 9, 32, 93, 114, 115, 138, 140, 154, 164, 165, 167, 187, 210, 242
Omie 201
O'Neill 142, 250
Onion 269
O'Riordan 192
Orndoff 150
Ornduff 241
Orobia 102
Orr 158
Ortery 119
Orwig 159, 223
Osborn 64, 216, 224, 254, 287
Ostdiek 124
Ostrom 167, 241
Oswald 224, 276, 277
Overmyer 177
Overstreet 145
Owen 207
Owens 10, 35, 62, 103, 210, 229

P

Pace 225
Paddacks 226
Paddock 36, 244
Paddocks 226, 279
Padella 72
Page 112
Paine 22
Painter 101
Palmburg 175, 192
Palmer 13, 63, 146, 151, 152, 197, 226
Palmquist 45
Palocz 199
Pape 13, 188, 226, 227
Paris 60, 227, 283
Parish 115, 116, 242
Park 111
Parker 61, 117, 189, 190, 197, 287
Parkhurst 242
Parkinson 205
Parks 148, 150
Parrinello 110
Parrish 64, 103, 173, 178, 179, 232, 237, 242, 262
Parry 260
Parsons 128, 207, 211, 213, 227, 256
Paschal 153

Passage 9
Patch 42
Paternoster 165
Patrick 234
Patterson 55, 62, 88, 177, 186, 212, 225, 243, 264
Pattison 209, 229
Patton 116, 159, 204, 258, 283
Paul 20, 196
Paulsgrove 227, 228, 259
Paulson 123
Paxton 11, 228
Payne 95, 210, 233
Peacock 80
Pearce 9, 216, 234
Pearl 218, 283
Pearrson 111
Pearsall 63
Pearson 15, 56, 69, 216
Pease 95
Peasley 255
Peck 178
Pedigo 228
Peel 129
Peirce 192
Pempek 132
Pence 188
Pendarvis 20
Penn 139
Penney 15
Pepper 179, 228
Periogy 39
Perkins 22, 63, 262
Perrin 61, 64, 115, 122, 186, 193, 194, 216, 224, 229, 230, 252
Perrine 21, 110, 139, 268
Perry 276
Persdotter 111
Person 140
Pestle 266, 267
Peters 198, 234
Peterson 5, 16, 32, 43, 89, 115, 117, 131, 140, 146, 175, 189, 190, 200, 230, 240, 245, 256, 271
Petrick 64
Pettersson 288
Pettett 95
Pfuehler 154
Phebus 181
Pheiffer 95
Phelps 6, 11, 12, 55, 100, 101, 191, 223, 231
Phiffer 111
Phillipi 29
Phillips 261
Piatt 143
Piccolo 135
Pichaske 181, 183
Pickerall 129
Pierce 20, 64, 75, 175, 176, 215, 231, 243
Pierpoint 63
Pierson 243
Pine 64
Pingrey 77
Pinkerton 172, 173
Pinney 20, 125, 153, 170, 274, 275, 282
Pipe 196
Piper 117, 195, 205, 276, 277
Pirtle 156
Pittard 190
Pittman 57, 231
Pius 215

Place 241
Plaunt 241
Plotz 193
Poblanz 97
Podlashes 35
Podschweit 247
Polich 198
Poling 33, 60
Polk 168
Pollock 144, 222, 251, 265
Polly 156, 196
Pomeroy 210
Poole 41, 231
Porter 21, 37, 55, 64, 162, 232
Postlewaite 234
Potter 11, 59
Poulson 232
Powell 135, 193, 285
Powers 134, 254
Pratt 26, 39, 98
Prendergast 35
Pressley 15, 48
Price 43, 122, 233, 234
Prince 16
Procino 252
Prouty 20, 57
Provost 194
Prunty 114, 226
Pullen 189
Purcell 9
Purlee 204, 234
Purn 32

Q

Quigley 23, 258
Quinby 6, 234
Quinn 23

R

Rademacher 242
Rader 11, 235, 269
Radmacher 212, 247
Radmacker 64
Ragland 8, 45
Ragon 63, 278
Rahn 8
Rajput 256
Rakoczy 127
Ralph 217, 279
Ralston 55, 282
Ramb 221
Ramback 97, 235
Ramer 163, 168
Rampy 136
Ramsdell 36
Ramsey 278, 284, 286
Randall 40, 104, 193, 204, 259, 263
Randolph 174, 268
Randy 207
Rankin 4, 18, 46, 91, 121, 235, 258, 268
Ranney 144, 145, 190, 198, 210, 235
Rapp 39
Rask 174, 219, 220, 243
Rassbach 223
Rast 40
Rauch 103
Rawson 68, 96, 97, 121, 236, 237
Ray 11, 23, 44, 68, 85, 110, 113, 119, 121, 127, 152, 172, 179, 232, 237, 243, 253, 254, 279
Rayment 239

Raymond 22, 142, 151, 194, 198, 199, 200, 231, 238, 239, 263, 264, 283
Rays 218
Rea 176
Read 62
Reagan 18
Reardon 143
Red 199
Redding 227
Redington 190
Reed 21, 134, 168
Reeder 247
Reedy 62
Reese 139
Reeves 39, 134, 146, 276
Reid 205
Reimolds 85, 255
Reinhold 152
Reitman 154
Remmington 129
Renard 251
Renner 39, 264
Renwick 167
Repp 174
Reyburn 167
Reynolds 9, 40, 64, 131, 205, 211, 217, 239, 240
Rezner 288
Rhinehart 60, 90, 159, 240
Rhodes 226, 279
Rhykerd 203
Rice 63, 111, 121, 237, 241
Richard 168
Richards 225
Richardson 205, 206, 270, 279
Richey 22, 267
Richeys 44
Ricketts 267
Rickwood 92
Riddle 221, 222
Riggs 11, 172, 217, 230
Riley 38, 280
Riner 242
Ringdahl 32
Ringoen 263
Rinker 232
Riper 217, 240
Ripple 95
Risk 164, 165, 284
Ritchey 267
Ritchie 11, 37, 203
Rivers 248
Robb 156, 232
Robbins 69, 141, 241
Roberts 22, 36, 115, 128, 144, 189, 210, 227, 232, 234, 286
Robertson 178
Robeson 44, 273
Robinson 4, 9, 95, 107, 209, 218, 240, 241, 261, 265
Robison 11, 111
Robson 152
Roche 62, 229, 230
Rockwell 22
Rockwood 191
Rodgers 90
Rogers 4, 33, 55, 132, 135, 154, 190, 223, 258
Rogoway 185
Roller 64, 72, 183, 270, 271
Romano 19
Romine 168, 223
Roney 241, 242
Roob 124
Rood 231

Roop 98, 281
Root 85
Rorabaugh 152
Rosander 192
Rose 131, 254
Roseberry 242, 254
Rosen 275
Rosenbaum 242
Rosenberger 33
Ross 20, 31, 41, 90, 115, 127, 138, 168, 195, 202, 220, 242, 243, 261
Rossell 243
Rossman 159
Roth 33, 243
Rothwell 238
Rounds 253
Roundtree 140
Rowe 176
Rowland 134
Rowley 60, 113, 190
Rule 131, 240
Rupp 126
Ruse 224
Russ 16
Russell 38, 39, 113, 140, 191, 232, 244
Ruthe 192
Rutledge 13, 243
Ryan 131
Ryder 214
Rykerd 259
Rylander 192
Ryner 28, 78, 112, 167, 174, 184, 226, 233, 244, 245, 252, 256, 267

S

Saddler 149
Saddon 226
Saettler 62
Sage 100, 254, 267, 277
Sailer 163
Salazar 179
Saling 280
Salisbury 9
Salling 279
Saloway 103
Salter 24
Salts 134
Saltzman 280
Sammons 278
Samuelson 288
Samuelsson 288
Sanberg 60, 245, 277
Sanchez 182
Sandberg 178, 196
Sandburg 93, 166, 245
Sanders 179, 193
Sandre 250
Sands 23
Sandstrom 15, 64, 245, 246, 263
Sanford 64
Sanmann 259
Sanner 104, 186, 204, 263
Sass 205, 276, 277
Savage 182, 200
Saville 260, 261
Sawvell 9
Sawyer 18, 77
Schafer 33
Schaffenberg 281
Scharf 91
Schaumbacher 39
Schaumleffel 63

Schilson 252
Schisler 62, 127, 141, 168, 274
Schlaf 201
Schlobohm 63
Schmalshof 64
Schmit 113
Schnitker 124
Schoendeider 187
Schofield 172
Schoonover 168
Schreck 62
Schreiber 62
Schroder 197
Schroeder 219
Schuchman 38
Schultz 258, 259, 272, 285
Schulz 253
Schwartz 137
Schwass 85
Schweigert 16
Schweitzer 44, 93, 246
Scotland 274
Scott 15, 20, 22, 37, 68, 77, 99, 115, 116, 134, 215
Scovill 161
Scripture 63
Scroggins 273
Scymanski 135
Seaburg 281
Seamore 272
Searcy 43
Sears 41
Seaton 63, 201
Seckman 262
Sederwall 81
Sedwick 140, 200, 246
Seigler 187
Seitz 252
Selby 54
Seldon 44
Selken 138
Sells 140
Serrano 180
Settlemeyer 286
Severs 147
Seward 55, 192
Sexton 9, 61, 240
Seyfrit 232
Shafer 63, 173, 247
Shafman 187
Shambaugh 154
Shaner 254, 255
Sharer 164, 240, 285
Sharp 251
Sharpe 85
Shauman 89, 247
Shaver 102, 243, 259
Shaw 28, 44, 68, 168, 203, 242
Shawler 265
Shea 113, 190
Sheare 150
Sheese 64, 85
Shelbourn 274
Sheller 96
Shelton 132, 248, 249
Sheridan 249
Sherman 173
Sherwin 11
Shields 287
Shike 168, 190, 236
Shimmin 22, 122, 169
Shinkel 192
Shirley 137
Shoemaker 63, 205
Shoemate 139

Sholes 33
Shook 229
Shoop 203
Shores 179, 214, 278
Short 146
Shotts 221
Showalter 100
Shrode 137
Shunick 56, 62, 138, 142, 190, 250, 265
Sias 42
Sickles 267
Sickmon 162
Siemens 61
Sienkewicz 250
Sills 234
Siltman 20
Simmons 10, 22, 64, 104, 153, 170, 172, 288
Simon 234
Simonson 251
Simpson 119, 164, 193, 240, 251, 277
Sims 46, 225, 251, 258
Sincox 181
Singleton 170, 279
Sistler 235
Siverly 61
Sjeklocha 241
Skees 285
Skinner 13, 33, 62
Skripps 279
Skubic 154
Slagle 254
Slas 9
Slater 62, 251, 267
Sloan 63
Sloss 171, 273
Slusher 213
Slusser 62
Small 97, 286
Smallwood 252
Smeed 141
Smiley 43, 277
Smilth 264
Smith 8, 9, 21, 26, 33, 39, 41, 60, 62, 63, 69, 85, 89, 90, 97, 100, 121, 136, 138, 139, 140, 143, 151, 152, 153, 154, 156, 157, 162, 171, 173, 174, 184, 194, 197, 205, 220, 221, 226, 229, 235, 237, 244, 252, 253, 254, 256, 263, 269, 272, 273, 275, 277, 278, 279, 282, 285
Snavely 112
Snell 135, 252
Snider 195
Snodgrass 60, 158
Snow 272
Snyder 31, 117, 156
Solokowski 183
Sommers 234
Sonesdotter 159
Soule 128
Souther 64
Spalding 35, 63
Spangler 145, 205, 254
Sparks 33
Sparrow 75, 263
Speel 268
Speer 60, 63, 187, 188, 255
Spence 140, 141, 255, 263, 269
Spencer 14, 208, 242, 244
Spicer 151, 153, 255

Spickerman 223
Spiegel 62
Spiker 63, 78
Spisak 146
Spitz 268
Spooner 109
Spout 256
Sprague 284
Spray 147
Sprout 111, 115, 117, 256
Squire 196, 203
St. George 233
St. Ledger 85, 230
Staat 20, 199, 288
Stacey 196
Stack 250, 256
Stacker 285
Staff 262
Stafford 114, 222
Staggs 63
Stahl 245
Staley 218, 256
Stall 214
Stamp 131, 151
Standard 113, 202
Stanfield 63
Stanley 63, 184, 275
Stansell 125, 256, 283
Stanton 111
Stark 102
Starr 123
Starring 208
Stauffer 42
Stauth 257
Stearns 31
Steel 197
Steele 115, 178, 184
Steepleton 103, 209
Stegall 196
Stein 204
Steinbarger 288
Steinberg 200
Steis 277
Stemp 131
Stenz 258
Stephenson 64, 107, 204, 241, 265, 267
Stevens 33, 76, 116, 122, 126, 170, 172, 202, 257
Stevenson 28, 31, 64, 106, 141, 158, 181, 183, 193, 207, 241, 245, 252, 258
Stewart 63, 68, 143, 152, 167, 168, 190, 202, 204, 254, 258, 259, 267
Stice 20, 209, 219
Stick 253
Stickle 284
Stine 53
Stinemates 46
Stitt 111
Stivers 101, 259
Stodolkiewicz 125
Stokes 64, 135, 186, 192
Stombaugh 113
Stone 41, 152, 156, 238, 239, 259
Stonie 218
Stoops 242
Storm 136
Stott 22
Stotts 114, 155, 287
Stough 116
Strahorn 287
Strand 21, 203, 233
Stratton 225
Straus 134

295

Strauss 132
Strawn 203
Stremmel 103
Strickler 3, 20, 163, 166, 227
Strietmatter 140
Striffler 150
Stringfellow 153
Stripe 146
Stromire 119
Strong 20, 64, 89, 172, 173, 260
Struthers 106, 144, 158, 204, 206, 228, 260, 261
Stuart 158
Stubblefield 90
Stump 251
Sturms 278
Suess 223
Suits 114
Sullivan 60, 62, 113, 142, 150, 190
Summers 251
Sundin 98, 281
Surphina 261
Suter 162, 278
Sutes 158
Sutherland 136
Sutton 191
Svenson 209
Svensson 102, 140, 261
Swain 86
Swan 148, 159
Swanson 20, 32, 102, 140, 173, 189, 207, 217, 246
Sward 260
Swartout 246
Swarts 113, 126, 127, 133, 179, 180, 261, 266, 272, 273
Swartz 36, 119
Sweeney 178, 193
Swenson 261
Swiger 95
Switzer 159, 197, 231
Szaltis 261, 262

T

Tabb 178
Tabernacle 33
Tabone 62
Tafflinger 20
Taflinger 237
Taggart 285
Talbor 248
Talbot 11, 205
Talbott 76, 82, 184
Taliaferro 20, 63
Talley 28, 64, 111, 208, 262
Tatman 167
Taylor 20, 39, 89, 110, 116, 189, 197, 205, 233, 243, 277
Teare 77
Teel 41
Tenhaaf 115
Tenold 113
Tepen 123
Terpening 11, 165, 219
Terrell 278
Terry 42, 115, 156, 170, 209
Teske 252
Thabit 79
Thackrey 283
Tharp 221, 251
Themanson 245, 246, 255, 262, 263
Thieme 38, 122, 140, 146, 255, 263

Thiesen 161
Thomas 9, 69, 88, 104, 140, 233, 269, 282
Thomason 244
Thompson 2, 9, 16, 20, 21, 41, 43, 63, 64, 113, 124, 134, 146, 147, 159, 176, 191, 198, 209, 214, 224, 242, 251, 263, 264, 276
Thomsen 272
Thomson 143, 186, 198, 199, 204, 238, 258, 264
Thorpe 135
Thurman 164
Tierney 121, 152, 174, 253, 264
Timberlake 234
Tinder 182
Tinker 36
Tinkham 63, 69, 264
Tinsley 109, 203
Tinsman 169
Tipton 9
Toal 62, 265
Tochalauski 244
Todd 13, 64, 131, 167, 195
Tole 212
Tollefson 258
Tomlin 143
Tompkins 9
Tonnemaker 168
Tonsman 9
Toops 119, 273
Toothe 63
Torrance 76, 122, 195
Towney 62
Townsend 172, 173, 196, 279
Tracy 54, 194
Tranter 246
Trego 3, 64, 100, 180, 261, 265, 266, 267
Tribble 168
Trigg 112
Trimble 41, 63
Triplett 20
Trone 166
Trostle 38
Trotter 41
Troxel 212
Truman 13
Trummel 170
Tubbs 20, 78, 236, 237, 267
Tucker 20, 39, 138, 207
Tumquist 281
Turnbull 11, 12, 18, 21, 44, 72, 81, 159
Turner 2, 68, 97
Tweed 277
Twomey 9, 11, 13, 120, 190

U

Underwood 189, 241
Upton 92
Urban 267
Utescher 168

V

Vail 33, 198
Van Arsdale 268
Van Cleave 156
Van Eaton 251
Van Opdorp 274
Van Riper 217, 228, 240, 241
Van Tassel 253

Van Tine 269, 283
Van Velser 254
Vance 131, 141, 161
Vanderwall 119
VandeVoort 64
VanFleet 182
VanRiper 182, 277
Vanskike 186
VanTine 227, 255
Vantine 157
Varner 132, 269
Vaughn 82
Venard 111, 242
Verkler 183
Verner 278
Vernoy 174
Vertrees 9
Vest 270, 272
Vestal 261, 272, 273, 278
Vice 220, 273, 274
Vickroy 83, 185, 274
Vincent 109, 201
Vinstrand 245
Virtue 211
Vogt 99
VonKannon 62
Voorhees 156, 186, 191
Vorys 156
Vosburg 131
Vugteveen 85

W

Waddell 103, 277
Waddill 196
Waggener 268
Wagner 238, 284
Wagy 176
Wainman 21
Waldron 261
Walker 18, 28, 33, 38, 75, 90, 109, 122, 160, 192, 228, 240, 253, 256, 274, 275
Walkup 233
Wallace 8, 11, 21, 30, 31, 40, 44, 53, 64, 102, 151, 209, 244
Waller 59, 276
Walsch 39
Walsh 43
Walter 277
Walters 38, 112, 131, 193, 205, 225, 258, 276
Walton 24
Waltz 114
Warden 62
Warfield 16, 159
Waring 194
Warnecke 272
Warner 60, 111, 245, 277, 278
Warren 6, 8, 168, 179, 227, 278, 279
Washington 66, 90, 154
Waterman 251
Waters 239
Waterson 171, 273
Watkins 33, 238
Watson 9, 20, 21, 42, 54, 57, 122, 128, 153, 162, 163, 205, 226, 274, 275, 276, 278, 279
Watterman 141
Waugh 12, 122, 279
Wayne 37
Webb 63, 150, 279, 280

Webber 150
Webster 63, 66, 71
Weddelin 32
Weden 213
Weeks 61, 280
Wehrli 231
Weir 11, 64, 117, 187
Weiskopf 92
Weklenbauger 62
Welch 9, 190, 269, 280
Weldon 35
Wells 33, 85, 134, 135, 188, 227, 257, 280, 281
Welsh 140, 250
Welty 15, 98, 117, 197, 281
Wenstrom 118
Wentworth 61
Wertz 242, 281, 282
West 33, 133, 168, 258
Westerfield 58, 64, 138, 139, 282
Westfal 154
Westfall 10
Weston 64, 181
Westover 267
Wetander 251
Wexell 245
Wey 225
Wheatley 217
Wheeler 139, 143, 207, 208, 244
Whelan 235
Whisler 64
Whitaker 283
White 15, 16, 68, 74, 89, 159, 194, 216, 227, 243, 254, 269, 279, 283, 285
Whiteleather 15
Whiteman 13, 80, 209, 251, 283
Whitenack 191
Whiting 222
Whitman 45, 125, 132, 248, 256
Whitmore 255
Whitsitt 240
Widener 134, 135
Wiegand 258
Wier 258
Wignall 198
Wilbur 110, 191, 221, 223
Wilcox 37
Wiley 65, 78, 131, 211, 284
Wilkins 21
Willard 228, 285, 286
Willenbrink 270
Willet 284
Willey 175
William 100
Williams 18, 104, 140, 143, 148, 158, 159, 161, 190, 218, 229, 261, 283, 284, 285
Williamson 168, 226, 260
Willis 28, 285, 286
Willits 54
Wilmoth 214, 215
Wilsey 63
Wilson 30, 33, 149, 154, 196, 206, 207, 242, 264
Wimmer 158
Wimp 62
Wimpress 53
Winbigler 13, 20, 138, 189, 217, 234, 240, 252, 285, 286
Winebright 9, 181, 182, 193, 241, 244
Wingate 93

Winget 286
Wingo 198
Winkler 82
Winning 256
Winston 77
Winters 62, 77, 176, 233
Wirtz 15, 143
Wise 23, 201
Witt 175
Witte 134, 139
Witwood 217
Wixson 209
Woerly 127, 151
Wolf 215, 264, 285
Wolfe 265
Wolford 166
Wolter 140
Wood 21, 39, 133, 204
Woodburn 267
Woods 15, 16, 76, 77, 142, 146, 192
Woodward 21, 279, 284
Woodworth 132
Woolley 155, 286, 287
Woolridge 256
Woolsey 254
Woolworth 15
Worden 226
Work 60
Worley 197
Worrall 262
Worrell 276
Worth 152
Worthington 28, 168
Wotherspoon 282
Wray 232
Wright 12, 31, 42, 69, 165, 253
Wycoff 252
Wykoff 141

Y

Yankaukas 217
Yard 8
Yarde 55, 196, 279
Yates 273
Yeoman 36
Yocum 69
Yocums 168
Yoho 20, 42
Yokel 20
Young 3, 20, 24, 59, 63, 121, 123, 151, 170, 224, 260, 277, 285, 287, 288
Younger 140
Youngquist 32
Younquist 10
Yung 252, 264

Z

Zavorski 261, 262
Zbikowski 259
Zellmer 151
Zenner 263
Zimmer 75, 78, 85
Zimmerman 248, 277, 283
Zimmerschied 275
Zivanov 149
Zug 159, 240
Zuker 64

Warren County, Illinois

Public Square, Monmouth, Illinois 1800s.

Karl Gullberg's cousin (Carlson) repairing tire – Kirkwood/Smithshire area.

www.ingramcontent.com/pod-product-compliance
Lightning Source LLC
Chambersburg PA
CBHW080836230426
43665CB00021B/2855